ENVIRONMENTAL PSYCHOLOGY

ENVIRONMENTAL PSYCHOLOGY

FOURTH EDITION

PAUL A. BELL
Colorado State University

THOMAS C. GREENE
St. Lawrence University

JEFFREY D. FISHER
University of Connecticut

ANDREW BAUM
University of Pittsburgh

HARCOURT BRACE COLLEGE PUBLISHERS

Fort Worth   Philadelphia   San Diego   New York   Orlando   Austin   San Antonio
Toronto   Montreal   London   Sydney   Tokyo

Publisher	TED BUCHHOLZ
Editor in Chief	CHRISTOPHER P. KLEIN
Assistant Editor	LINDA WILEY
Project Editor	LOUISE SLOMINSKY
Production Manager	DEBRA A. JENKIN
Art Director	BURL DEAN SLOAN
Photo Researcher	MARTIN A. LEVICK

1000718451

Cover Photo: Aurora Borealis © J. Warden / West Stock

Illustration credits begin on page 615 and constitute a continuation of this copyright page.

Address for Editorial Correspondence:
Harcourt Brace College Publishers
301 Commerce Street, Suite 3700
Fort Worth, TX 76102

Address for Orders:
Harcourt Brace & Company
6277 Sea Harbor Drive
Orlando, FL 32887-6777
1-800-782-4479, or 1-800-433-0001 (in Florida)

Library of Congress Catalog Card Number: 95-80945

ISBN 0-15-501496-X

Printed in the United States of America

5 6 7 8 9 0 1 2 3 4 039 9 8 7 6 5 4 3 2 1

PREFACE

Environmental psychology continues to be one of the most exciting fields of study we have known. We constantly interact with the environment; it influences us and we modify it in everything we do. We respond to the environment and to how we perceive it. If it stimulates us in ways we do not like we do something about it. We can manipulate the environment to construct a home, a golf course, or a factory. When we do so, we modify the way we perform everyday activities, but we also may have a long-term impact on the environment. What can we do to promote harmony between our actions and the environment we construct? What can we do to make sure our long-term impact on the environment is beneficial, or at least not harmful? The field of environmental psychology has developed around these questions.

Environmental psychology, then, deals with the reciprocal relationships between humans and the built and natural environment. Sometimes these relationships have strong biological roots, and other times they are the product of experience and of culture. Our subject matter deals with everyday behavior. We study the problems and opportunities people encounter as we interact with the environment; we also study ways we can develop more compatible relationships with the environment.

With this fourth edition of our book, we have retained many of the features of the earlier editions. We have maintained scientific rigor while emphasizing clarity of key points and challenges of the future. While updating all the material, we have also included more historical perspectives on issues such as the way humans have viewed nature across the centuries and the ways we have designed cities and college campuses. We have also included a much more international flavor to reflect the current status of the field. Because environmental psychology deals with so many diverse topics that at some level have common theoretical roots—from perception and cognition to disasters and crowding and design of residential and institutional environments—we have elaborated considerably more on the eclectic theoretical model that we introduced in the first edition. After the theory chapter in which we first describe the model, we include it in every subsequent chapter as a way of pulling the diverse elements of the field together.

The introductory chapter defines the history and scope of the field and describes the advantages and disadvantages of the methods used to derive our scientific knowledge of environment and behavior relationships. Chapter 2 juxtaposes innate versus learned ways of dealing with the environment; we describe historical changes in the ways humans view nature, how natural scenes benefit us psychologically and physiologically, how we assess built and natural environments, and how we form attitudes toward them. Chapter 3 describes perception of the environment and cognitions about it—input, storage, and retrieval of environmental information, including cognitive mapping and wayfinding. Chapter 4 describes some of the major theories—arousal, adaptation level, overload, stress, ecological psychology—that environmental psychologists employ, and also introduces the framework for the eclectic model of environment–behavior relationships that we use in the rest of the book.

Chapter 5 begins our discussion of "disturbed environments," examining noise, ways we adapt to noise, and what we can do to minimize this stressor. Chapter 6 examines weather, climate, and behavior. Chapter 7 explores large-scale disturbances in the environment—natural disasters, technological catastrophes, toxic exposure, and air pollution. Chapter 8 begins our discussion of how humans use space—personal space and territoriality—followed by Chapter 9 on crowding and high population density. Chapter 10 integrates much of the material in Chapters 4 through 9 in terms of how it all comes together in cities; we explore the advantages and disadvantages of living in urban areas and what we can do environmentally to make cities more habitable. Chapter 11 examines how we can use design principles to create more livable environments, and Chapters 12 and 13 extend these principles to specific environments—residential and institutional environments in Chapter 12, and work, learning, and leisure environments in Chapter 13. Finally, Chapter 14 discusses intervention strategies for modifying environmentally destructive behaviors and improving our relationship with the environment.

We conceived this and earlier editions of *Environmental Psychology* as a primary text for environment and behavior courses (environmental psychology, social ecology, architectural psychology, ecological psychology, environmental design and the like). It can also be used as a supplement to courses using more specialized materials.

We continue to be excited about this developing field, and hope you share our excitement. As always we invite your feedback on our product, especially on ways to improve it.

ACKNOWLEDGMENTS

It was 20 years ago, when we were completing our graduate studies, that two of us (Paul Bell and Jeffrey Fisher) discussed writing a text in environmental psychology. Following through on that discussion, we published the first edition of this text in 1978. The product of our efforts is now in the fourth edition. Many things have changed over 20 years. We have progressed from being young assistant professors in their mid-twenties to being middle-aged full professors. The first edition was composed entirely on typewriters, the third and fourth entirely on computers. Our publisher has changed ownership three times since we began. We have added two coauthors with great talents and reputations over the editions. Much of the original material from the first edition has changed so much it is now unrecognizable. For the fourth edition we would like to emphasize that Tom Greene took the lead on revising a disproportionate amount of the text, and should be considered a "co-first author."

Our efforts have not been isolated, and we have had much support. For this edition we especially thank the editorial and production staff at Harcourt Brace, Christopher P. Klein, Editor in Chief; Linda Wiley, Assistant Editor; Louise Slominsky, Project Editor; Debra A. Jenkin, Production Manager; and Burl Dean Sloan, Art Director.

We are also grateful for the ideas and suggestions of our reviewers, Gary Evans, Cornell University; Lee A. Jackson, University of North Carolina at Wilmington; James Rotton, Florida International University; Lloyd K. Stires, Indiana University of Pennsylvania; and George I. Whitehead, Salisbury State University.

We again thank Ross Loomis for the use of his material from the first edition.

Some of the individuals who helped with photocopying, library work, mailing, proofreading, and other crucial tasks include David Abraham, Lynda Christensen, Andrew Jay Fisher, Traci Fleming, Mary Francis Hatch, Michele Hayward, Stan Jurgens, Andrea Leclerc, Lori Oakes, Keri Pankonin, Laura Shanon, and Elizabeth Van Engel.

Many of these tasks were again accomplished with the assistance of our wives, Patty, Mela, Allison, and Carrie. Their encouragement and tolerance of our persistence was most reassuring. As with our other editions, we thank our family and friends for their patience when we sacrificed time with them to work on "the manuscript."

CONTENTS

Preface   v

Chapter 1   The Why, What, and How of Environmental Psychology   1

Why Study Environmental Psychology?   2
What Is Environmental Psychology?   6
Definitions of Environmental Psychology   6
Characteristics of Environmental Psychology   7

How Is Research in Environmental Psychology Done?   10
Research Methods in Environmental Psychology   11
Data Collection Methods   15
Ethical Considerations in Environmental Research   22

Preview of the Content Areas of Environmental Psychology   24
Chapter Summary   25
Suggested Projects   25

Chapter 2   Nature and Human Nature   27

Introduction   28
Human Nature   30
Experience: Attitudes and Ethics   31
Where Do Attitudes and Ethics Come From?   31
Do Environmental Attitudes Predict
    Environmental Behavior?   31
The Changing Meaning of Nature in North America   33
Contemporary World Views: The Role of Humans in Nature   36

Biological Influences: Biophobia and Biophilia   39
Biophobia   39
Biophilia   39

Environmental Assessment   42
Quality Assessments   42

The Scenic Environment: Landscape Aesthetics and Preference   45
The Descriptive Approach: Using Experience and Artistic Judgment   46
Physical-Perceptual Approaches to Scenic Evaluation   48
Psychological Variables in Landscape Assessment   49
Conclusions From Studies of Landscape Aesthetics   57

Natural Landscapes as Places   57
Chapter Summary   59
Suggested Projects   60

Chapter 3   Environmental Perception and Cognition   61

Introduction   63
Characterizing Environmental Perception   64
Perspectives on Environmental Perception   67
Nativism Versus Learning   70
Habituation and the Perception of Change   76

Environmental Cognition   77
An Informal Model of Spatial Cognition   78
Cognitive Maps   80
History of Cognitive Mapping   80
Current Perspectives   83
Methods of Studying Cognitive Maps   84
Errors in Cognitive Maps   88
Acquisition of Cognitive Maps   93
Memory and Cognitive Maps   96

Wayfinding   100
Action Plans and Wayfinding   100
Setting Characteristics That Facilitate Wayfinding   102
Maps   103
Movies, Slides, and Models: Facilitating Spatial Learning   104

Chapter Summary   106
Suggested Projects   107

Chapter 4 Theories of Environment–Behavior Relationships 108

Introduction 111
The Nature and Function of Theory in Environmental Psychology 112
   Hypotheses, Laws, and Theories 113
   Functions of Theories 114

Environment–Behavior Theories: Energizing a Growing Field 115
   The Arousal Approach 116
   The Environmental Load Approach 118
   The Understimulation Approach 121
   Adaptation Level Theory: Optimal Stimulation 122
   The Behavior Constraint Approach 126
   The Environmental Stress Approach 131
   Barker's Ecological Psychology 139

Integration and Summary of Theoretical Perspectives 146
Chapter Summary 148
   Suggested Projects 149

Chapter 5 Noise 150

Introduction 151
What Is Noise? 153
   Perceiving Noise 154
   Annoyance 158
   Sources of Noise 159

Effects of Noise 160
   Health Effects of Noise 161
   Noise and Mental Health 166
   Effects of Noise on Performance 167
   Effects of Noise in Office and Industrial Settings 172
   Noise and Social Behavior 176

Reducing Noise: Does Anyone Notice? 181
Chapter Summary 182
   Suggested Projects 182

Chapter 6 Weather, Climate, and Behavior 184

Introduction 186
Geographical and Climatological Determinism 189
   Early Beliefs About Climate and Behavior 192

Later Climatological Determinism   192
Current Views and Distinctions   194
Biological Adaptations to Climate   195

Heat and Behavior   195
Perception of and Physiological Reactions to Heat   196
Heat and Performance   199
Heat and Social Behavior   201

Cold Temperatures and Behavior   207
Perception of and Physiological Reactions to Cold   207
Cold Temperatures and Health   209
Cold Extremes and Performance   210
Cold Extremes and Social Behavior   210
Summary of Temperature Effects on Behavior   211

Wind and Behavior   211
Perception of Wind   212
Behavioral Effects of Wind   213

Barometric Pressure and Altitude   215
Physiological Effects   216
Acclimatization to High Altitudes   216
Behavioral Effects of High Altitudes   217
High Air-Pressure Effects   217
Medical, Emotional, and Behavioral Effects of Air-Pressure Changes   217
Summary of Air-Pressure Effects   221

Integrating Weather and Pollution Effects: A Final Note   222
Chapter Summary   223
Suggested Projects   223

Chapter 7   Disasters, Toxic Hazards, and Pollution   224

Introduction   225
Natural Disasters   226
Characteristics of Natural Disasters   229
Perception of Natural Hazards   231
Effects of Natural Disasters   234
Children and Disasters   240
Age and Disaster Response   241
Environmental Theories and Disasters   242
Summary   243

Technological Catastrophe   244
   Characteristics of Technological Catastrophe   245
   Effects of Technological Disasters   248
   Summary   253

Effects of Toxic Exposure   254
   Occupational Exposure   255
   Nonoccupational Hazards   259

Air Pollution and Behavior   261
   Perception of Air Pollution   262
   Air Pollution and Health   264
   Air Pollution and Performance   267
   Air Pollution and Social Behavior   269
   Summary of Air Pollution Effects on Behavior   269

Chapter Summary   270
   Suggested Projects   271

Chapter 8   Personal Space and Territoriality   272

Introduction   274
Personal Space   275
   Functions of Personal Space   275
   Methods of Studying Personal Space   279
   Situational Determinants of Personal Space: Research Evidence   280
   Individual Difference Determinants of Personal Space:
     Research Evidence   282
   Physical Determinants of Personal Space   286
   Interpersonal Positioning Effects   287
   Spatial Zones That Facilitate Goal Fulfillment   287
   Consequences of Too Much or Too Little Personal Space   290
   Consequences of Personal Space Invasions   295
   Summary of Personal Space   303

Territorial Behavior   303
   The Origins of Territorial Functioning   305
   Functions of Territoriality   306
   Methods of Studying Territoriality in Humans   308
   Research Evidence of Territorial Behavior   308
   Territory and Aggression   312
   Territory as a Security Blanket: Home Sweet Home   315
   Some Design Implications   316

Chapter Summary   320

Suggested Projects   321

Chapter 9   High Density and Crowding   323

Introduction   325

Effects of Population Density on Animals   326

Physiological Consequences of High Density for Animals   327

Behavioral Consequences of High Density for Animals   328

Conceptual Perspectives: Attempts to Understand High-Density
Effects in Animals   331

Summary   333

Effects of High Density on Humans   333

Methodologies Used to Study High Density in Humans   334

Feeling the Effects of Density: Its Consequences for Affect,
Arousal, and Illness   336

Effects of Density on Social Behavior   339

Effects of High Density on Task Performance   344

Putting the Pieces Together: Conceptualizations of Density
Effects on Humans   346

Eliminating the Causes and Effects of Crowding   355

Chapter Summary   365

Suggested Projects   365

Chapter 10   The City   368

Introduction   370

Effects of Urban Life on the City Dweller: Conceptual Efforts   372

Overload Notions   373

Adaptation Level   373

Environmental Stress   373

Behavior Constraint   374

The City as a Behavior Setting   375

Integrating the Various Formulations   376

Effects of Urban Life on the City Dweller: Research Evidence   376

Stress   377

Affiliative Behavior   379

Prosocial Behavior   380

The Familiar Stranger   381

Crime   382

Health   384

Homelessness
Summary   387

Environmental Soluti
A Little Piece of Natu
Designing Urban Play
Revitalizing Entire Urb
Revitalizing Residential
Revitalizing Commercial

Escaping to the Suburbs
Chapter Summary   408
Suggested Projects   409

✔**Chapter 11   Architecture, I**
for Human Bel

Introduction   411
History, Culture, and Design Pr
The Physical Environment: Exte   influence   415
Architectural Determinism   416
Environmental Possibilism   416
Environmental Probabilism   416

The Designer's Perspective   417
The Process of Design: Fostering Communication   419
The Gaps   421
Fostering Participation   422

Substantive Contributions   423
Privacy   424
Materials and Color   425
Illumination   427
Windows   428
Furnishings   428
Architectural Aesthetics   429

Selecting Alternatives: The Design Cycle   431
Stages in the Design Process   431

American College Campuses: An Example of Design Dynamics   432
Planning for the Future   434

Human Factors: Engineering for Human Design   435
Communicating With Machines   438

442   443

Contents

Chapter Summary
Suggested Projects

Chapter 12   Design i
Envir

Introduction
The Resid
Att

xvi

n Residential and Institutional
onments   444

445

ential Setting   447
chment to Place   448
Homes   449
Neighborhood and Community Environments   458
Summary of Residential Environments   461

Institutional Environments   462
Hospital Settings   463
Prison Design and Behavior   468
Designing for the Elderly   469

Chapter Summary   477
Suggested Projects   478

Chapter 13   Work, Learning, and Leisure
Environments   479

Introduction   481
Work Environments   482
A Brief History of Workplace Design   483
Ambient Work Environments   484
Furniture and Layout   488
Territoriality and Status in the Work Environment   488
Efficiency and Workflow   489
The Electronic Office   489
Designing the Office Landscape   491
Job Satisfaction and the Work Environment   493
Summary of Design in the Work Environment   493

Learning Environments   494
Classroom Environments   495
Libraries   498
Visitor Behavior in Museum Environments   500

Pedestrian Environments: Shopping Malls, Plazas, Crosswalks   504
Management of Natural Lands for Leisure   507
Whose View?   507
Multiple Demands   509

Focusing on Needs and Outcomes   512

Congruence Between User and Setting   514

Prelude to Preservation   515

Summary: Leisure and Recreation Environments   515

Chapter Summary   516

Suggested Projects   517

**Chapter 14   Changing Behavior to Save
the Environment**   518

Introduction   520

Environmental Psychology and Saving the Environment   521

The Commons Dilemma as an Environment–Behavior Problem   525

Encouraging Environmentally Responsible Behavior   533

Conserving Energy and Water   534

Conserving Energy   534

Conserving Water   543

Source Reduction and Recycling   544

Antecedent Interventions   546

Contingent Strategies   548

Littering   549

Antecedent Interventions   549

Consequent Strategies   551

Vandalism   552

**Encouraging Environmentally Responsible Behavior:
An Assessment of the Present and the Future**   555

Chapter Summary   556

Suggested Projects   556

Glossary   557

References   567

Credits   615

Author Index   619

Subject Index   636

ENVIRONMENTAL PSYCHOLOGY

The Why, What, and How of Environmental Psychology

WHY STUDY ENVIRONMENTAL PSYCHOLOGY?

WHAT IS ENVIRONMENTAL PSYCHOLOGY?

Definitions of Environmental Psychology

Characteristics of Environmental Psychology

HOW IS RESEARCH IN ENVIRONMENTAL PSYCHOLOGY DONE?

Research Methods in Environmental Psychology

Experimental Research

Correlational Research

Descriptive Research

Data Collection Methods

Self-Report Measures

Observational Techniques

Task Performance

Trace Measures

Choosing Measures

Ethical Considerations in Environmental Research

Informed Consent

Invasion of Privacy

PREVIEW OF THE CONTENT AREAS OF ENVIRONMENTAL PSYCHOLOGY

CHAPTER SUMMARY

Suggested Projects

KEY TERMS

accretion measures
affordances
archival data
behavior mapping
behavior settings
confounds
correlational research
dependent variable
descriptive research
environment
environmental psychology
erosion measures
experiential realism
experimental method

external validity
hodometer
independent variable
informed consent
internal validity
invasion of privacy
observation
random assignment
reliable
self-report measures
simulation methods
unobtrusive measures
valid

WHY STUDY ENVIRONMENTAL PSYCHOLOGY?

In a play, the stage and scenery provide the context of what is going on: the kind of room the characters are in, the way it is decorated, and the amount and nature of its furnishings help us to interpret what is happening. They provide meaning for the actors' and actresses' actions and determine where they can walk, lean, or otherwise interact with props. For the play, the stage and scenery are the **environment** in which the story unfolds. The meaning of behavior on the stage and what can and cannot be done are determined by this environment. The theater would be far less entertaining or educational without the context provided by its environment.

In real life, our behavior also occurs in the context of an environment, one that is constantly changing and rich in information. Unlike the setting on a stage, however, it provides more than meaning. Our environment also provides us with basic needs for life, including food, water, and air to breathe. It is also modified by our actions, and is irrevocably altered whenever one of us changes it. Our environment includes all of

our natural and built surroundings, and is a delicately balanced system that can easily be bruised or damaged. Whenever we change some part of it, other parts also change, and these other changes may be unintended or even dangerous. Concerns about what we were doing to our environment reached unprecedented prominence in the 1960s and have continued to be an issue of serious concern as consequences of years of neglect have become apparent. The depletion of the ozone layer of the atmosphere, reports of hospital waste washing up on beaches, discussions of the greenhouse effect and changing climatic conditions, and problems storing radioactive or toxic chemical waste reflect these problems. In truth, we have done much to remedy the damage we have done to the environment and have taken steps to prevent some new problems. Yet, the pollution of our air and water, increasing energy use, crowding, noise, toxic accidents, and other environmental problems continue (see Figures 1–1 through 1–5). What more can be done to deal with the situation?

Figure 1-1 Humans are animals who have a remarkable ability to manipulate their environment. When humans alter their environment, they often remove habitat for other species, but sometimes can live in harmony with nature. In altering the environment, we often establish territorial defenses. Elk are so plentiful in the community depicted in this photo that residents use wire fencing to protect trees from the hungry herd.

Figure 1-2 The design of some dormitories and housing projects has been associated with withdrawal in social relationships and may encourage some forms of maladjustment. Other designs, however, seem to foster healthier forms of human interaction, perhaps by allowing more control over privacy and crowding.

Figure 1-3 In March 1979, an accident struck the Three Mile Island nuclear power plant, causing 400,000 gallons of radioactive water to collect in the containment building. More than a year later, unhealthy psychological reactions attributable to the accident were still apparent in some residents of the area. In some ways, these reactions resemble the response victims have to natural disasters, but in other ways they do not.

Figure 1–4 Cities are typically associated with high rates of crime, pollution, and social decay. They also are associated with cultural opportunities such as professional theater and sports, great art and science museums, and specialized medical services not available in smaller communities. Research suggests that viewing natural scenery has restorative, calming effects on people who are under stress. Some designers and planners believe that adding "natural" expanses of greenery and water to urban areas can remove some of the harshness of city life.

Figure 1–5 A substantial amount of petroleum use in the United States is for transportation. Of that, a large portion is consumed by automobiles. Although behavioral techniques can be used to increase ridership on mass transit, both private automobile and mass transit forms of commuting are associated with various types of stress reactions.

In a sense, environmental psychology deals with "environment" at two different levels. On the one hand, environmental psychology is concerned with environments as the *context* of behavior: our moods and behaviors are meaningful only if they can be understood in terms of their context. The environment also determines which behaviors are possible, how difficult or successful they may be, and so on. You cannot sit unless there is a chair, and cannot walk where there is a wall: these environmental features make some actions possible and others difficult or impossible. These **affordances** are possibilities allowed or provided by an environment and are strong determinants of behavior. In the classic *Gestalt* insight studies by Kohler (1970), the solution to the ape's dilemma was provided by the environment: the ape found himself in a cage, with bananas hanging overhead and out of reach, and few if any resources available. The environment did not provide any way to jump high enough to get them, but provided tools (e.g., pieces of sticks that could be put to-

gether and used to knock the bananas down). The insight of which Kohler wrote was the recognition of a solution to the problem (how to get the bananas) that was afforded by the environment. Similar affordances are reflected in the building materials for homes (usually what is plentiful in the area, such as brick or wood) or in the pathways worn across lawns where people choose to walk.

Environmental psychology, then, is very concerned with the environment as a determinant or influence on behavior and mood. As we will discuss later in this chapter, environmental influences on mood and behavior are pervasive and important. In this way, our field of study is similar to social psychology or developmental psychology. The environment provides meaning and affects behavior just as do social settings or age or developmental stages. One can act silly in certain settings (at home in your room) or at specific ages without fear of embarrassment, but there are combinations of developmental, social, and environmental conditions (such as during an oral examination or at a funeral or wedding) in which silliness is inappropriate or out of place.

Environmental psychology is also concerned with the *consequences* of behavior on the environment, and more broadly, with larger scale environmental problems such as pollution, recycling, and ecosystem issues. This is a very different focus, though it follows from the basic premise that behavior and the environment mutually affect one another. So how does behavior affect the environment?

Environmental psychology has evolved in part to provide some answers to this question. Some environmental problems are almost always human-made. Air pollution, a common problem in large cities, is one of these problems, and because human behavior causes it, it seems plausible that modification of behavior will offer one of the best ways to curb or eliminate it. Principles of learning, motivation, perception, attitude formation, and social interaction help explain why we ever engaged in and accepted polluting behavior in the first place. Principles of developmental psychology, social psychology, abnormal psychology, and physiological psychology help explain the deleterious effects of pollution on humans. Furthermore, research on attitude change, behavior modification, social behavior, and personality can suggest some steps that will be necessary to change behavior in order to reduce pollution.

Environmental psychologists also study how specific environments affect people. The design of buildings, once primarily concerned with how they looked, now includes considerations of how they affect people who use them. Principles of crowding, privacy, personal space, and environmental perception, as well as noise, temperature, air circulation, and cost may all be factors in how a building is designed and how well it serves its intended function. College dormitories may now be designed to accommodate the social needs of students as well as more traditional concerns such as cheap housing for large numbers of residents and control of

their noise. Housing projects, racked by major failures years ago, may now include a range of behavioral criteria in design and construction.

In the process of suggesting possible solutions for environmental problems, psychologists are gaining considerable practical knowledge about relationships between behavior and environment as well as gaining invaluable information about conceptual or theoretical models of human behavior. For this reason, environmental psychology not only is practical but also provides a meaningful focus of traditional psychological disciplines. The tendency to picture environmental psychology as an applied field is due, in part, to the fact that many of the things environmental psychologists study are chosen because they are problems or opportunities to improve some aspects of our management of our surroundings.

However, research in a number of areas, as well as the development of theories to describe behavior across different situations (see Chapter 4), reflects the fact that environmental psychology is also concerned with building basic knowledge of human behavior and how it interacts with the environment.

In this chapter, we will talk about many aspects of environmental psychology. First, we must define our field and consider its characteristic approach and basic assumptions. Environmental psychology is distinctive in many ways, and these factors shape the methods that can be used to study environment–behavior relationships. Hence, we will also discuss methodological issues: How does one go about studying the processes and problems encompassed by environmental psychology? Many obstacles to reliable study of these phenomena are difficult to overcome, and designing and adapting procedures and measures to do so is one of the field's most challenging aspects. Finally, we will discuss some ethical issues associated with the field and preview the content areas to be discussed in the rest of the book.

WHAT IS ENVIRONMENTAL PSYCHOLOGY?

DEFINITIONS OF ENVIRONMENTAL PSYCHOLOGY

The preceding discussion of environmental psychology should convince you that the field offers present-day relevance for the discipline of psychology as well as the exciting possibility of a unique perspective on environmental problems. Yet, this does not really *define* "environmental psychology." Like most areas of psychology, it is easier to list what environmental psychologists do than to define the field.

Early definitions of environmental psychology emphasized the relationship between behavior and the physical environment, as in Heimstra and McFarling's (1978) definition of the field as the discipline concerned with relationships between behavior and the physical environment or Proshansky's (1976b) characterization of the field as "the attempt to establish empirical and theoretical relationships between the behavior and experience of the person and his built environment" (p. 303). More recent definitions, though somewhat more inclusive, are essentially the same. In the *Handbook of Environmental Psychology*, Stokols and Altman (1987) define the field as "the study of human behavior and well-being in relation to the sociophysical environment" (p. 1). Similarly, Russell and Snodgrass (1987) define environmental psychology as the "branch of psychology concerned with providing a systematic account of the relationship between a person and the environment" (p. 245).

These definitions provide us with a general idea of what environmental psychology is, but are so general that they could conceivably include many other areas of psychology. For example, conceptualizing the field as the study of the relationships between environment and behavior suggests

that learning, perception, and sensation (to name but a few possibilities) are a focal part of the field. To be sure, these areas of psychology describe relationships between environmental and behavioral variables. They are not, however, central to what we mean by environmental psychology. In addition, such definitions do not emphasize the bidirectional nature of environment–behavior relationships: Environments affect behavior and behavior affects environments. Limiting definitions to the relationships between behavior and the *built* environment is also unsatisfactory because it omits the nonbuilt environment (e.g., the natural landscape).

Our definitional dilemma should be clear by now: How do we define environmental psychology narrowly enough so that we do not include areas that environmental psychologists would agree are not part of the field, yet broadly enough to include all the topics that environmental psychologists would insist are part of it? One option alluded to above is to define the field operationally: Environmental psychology is what environmental psychologists do (Proshansky, Ittelson, & Rivlin, 1970). We could then proceed to describe the areas studied by environmental psychologists and the research methods they apply (which we will do in a moment). However, if forced into a corner at pencil-point by students demanding to know what answer to give to the test question, "Define environmental psychology in 25 words or less," we would hazard the following definition, with all its potential shortcomings: **Environmental psychology** is the study of the molar relationships between behavior and experience and the built and natural environments. We will now describe certain characteristics of environmental psychology that make the field unique and further delimit its scope.

CHARACTERISTICS OF ENVIRONMENTAL PSYCHOLOGY

The two primary distinctions between environmental psychology and other fields of psychology are (1) the perspective it takes in studying its subject matter and (2) the kinds of problems or settings that are selected for study. The perspective that environmental psychology takes is that since environmental effects on behavior are important, much of our research should involve naturalistic studies of behavior in the built and natural environments. That means the settings chosen for study are likely to be outside the laboratory (though not always), and the problems studied are likely to be how we do or do not adjust to the normal and disturbed features of those settings. We shall describe some characteristics of this perspective, drawing on several sources (e.g., Altman, 1976a; Ittelson et al., 1974; Proshansky, 1976b; Wohlwill, 1970). Our list of characteristics of environmental psychology is by no means exhaustive but simply reflects the unique perspective of the field.

First and foremost among these characteristics is an emphasis on studying environment–behavior relationships as a unit, rather than separating them into supposedly distinct and self-contained components. Traditional approaches to the study of sensation and perception assume that environmental stimuli are distinct from each other and that the perception (or response to) the stimulus, being distinct from the stimulus itself, can be studied somewhat independently of it. Environmental psychology looks upon the stimulus and its perception as a unit that contains more than just a stimulus and a response. The stimulus-response perceptual relationship between an urban landscape and an urban inhabitant, for example, depends not just on the individual stimuli in the landscape. It also depends on the patterning, complexity, novelty, and movement of the contents of the landscape and on the past experience of the perceiver (e.g., whether he or she is a long-time resident or a newcomer), his or her ability to impose structure on the landscape, his or her auditory (perceived through the ear) and olfactory (perceived through the nose) associations with the landscape, and his or her personality characteristics. In environmental psychology, all these things make up one holistic environmental-perceptual behavior unit. Like Gestalt psychology, which influenced American psychology during the mid-twentieth century, the whole is greater than the simple sum of its parts. This is what "molar" refers to in our definition of the field and helps to draw boundaries between environmental psychology and sensory or other areas of psychology.

To use another example, to the environmental psychologist an overcrowded dining hall consists not just of separate episodes of people getting in each other's way, but of a physical setting containing a high density of people who interact with each other and with the physical setting in very predictable ways, and who experience certain pleasant and unpleasant consequences of these conditions (Figure 1–6). Thus, the environmental setting constrains (limits, influences, and even determines) the behavior that occurs in it. Furthermore, as the occupants of this setting move about, they change some aspects of the environment and of their experience of crowding. If the behavior is studied in isolation, separate from these particular environmental conditions, the conclusions derived from the studying process will inevitably be limited. The environment cannot be studied separately from the behavior, and the behavior cannot be studied separately from the environment, without losing valuable information. This does not mean that environmental psychologists never take a close look at a particular environment–behavior

Figure 1–6 To the environmental psychologist, this crowded dining area consists not just of separate episodes of people getting in each other's way. It is a physical setting containing a high density of people who interact with each other and with the environment in very predictable ways, who experience certain pleasant and unpleasant emotional states, and who anticipate consequences of these conditions.

relationship in a laboratory setting, but it does mean they assume from the beginning that such dissection of an integral unit cannot tell the whole story.

Another assumption underlying environmental psychology is that environment–behavior relationships are really *inter*relationships: The environment influences and constrains behavior, but behavior also leads to changes in the environment. Consider the issue of energy resources and pollution. The availability of certain energy sources in the environment determines whether certain types of energy-consuming behavior will occur, but that behavior in turn determines the type of pollution that will result. Oil shortages may increase conservation and affect many aspects of one's lifestyle, which in turn may lead to a reliance on other forms of energy, to new forms of pollution, and so on. With continued consumption, energy resources are differentially affected, and this in turn can shift consumption patterns. Note that this example also demonstrates that environment–behavior relationships need to be studied as units in order to see the whole picture.

A third characteristic is that environmental psychology is less likely to draw sharp distinctions between applied and basic research than are other areas in psychology. Other fields of psychology engage in theoretical or basic research as the primary means of understanding behavior. The major goal of such research is to gain knowledge about the subject matter through discovering cause-effect relationships and building theories. If such research also leads to the solution of a practical problem—which it often does—that is well and good, but a practical application is not necessarily a goal of that research. Applied research, on the other hand, is intended from the start to solve a practical problem, and it is valued not for its theoretical relevance but for its specific utility. Theory building may result from applied research, but is not its primary focus.

In contrast, environmental psychology usually undertakes a given piece of research for both applied and theoretical purposes at the same time. That is, almost all research in environmental psychology is *problem-oriented* or intended to be relevant to the solution of some practical issue, and thus the cause-effect relationships and theoretical material evolve from this focus. Research areas, such as the effects of pollution on behavior, changing environmentally destructive behavior, and the design of environments for efficient human use, are concerned with applications and practical matters, yet much of the factual content and theoretical underpinnings of environmental psychology derive directly from this type of research. Once again, this does not mean that environmental psychologists cannot take a practical problem into the laboratory for controlled study, but it does mean that the laboratory research of an environmental psychologist is oriented toward solving real-world problems (Figure 1–7). Environmental psychology is the study of molar relationships among environment, mood, and behavior and is characterized by a focus on behavior *in* the environment, the assumption that environment and behavior mutually affect one another, and an interest in environmental problems. How does this translate into research and theory? An example here may help. If one is interested in the effects of crowded living conditions, options of ways to proceed may be limited. Because residential crowding is a *chronic* condition lasting for months or years, it is unrealistic to assume that one could reproduce it in the laboratory with human subjects. Use of animals could help here, though relationships between environment and behavior are likely to differ across species. More importantly, the fact that it occurs where people live makes it different from crowding in any other setting. As a result, a study of crowded housing would of necessity be of a residential environment, and researchers have studied a variety of them, ranging from crowded prisons to college dormitories, public housing, and apartment buildings. The belief that behavior and environment mutually affect one another could lead to including measures of what residents do to reduce crowding (such as personalizing their space, altering their space design) and how it affects experience. The problem-focused nature of environmental psychology could lead to development of an intervention to reduce crowding or distress. In Chapter 9, we discuss the development of research on crowding, consistent with the previously mentioned assumptions of environmental psychology.

Environmental psychology is part of an interdisciplinary field of study of environment and behavior. Environmental perception, with its emphasis on the perception of a whole scene, is relevant to the work of landscape architects, urban planners, builders, and others in related fields. The study of the effects of the physical environment (noise, heat, and space) on behavior is relevant to the interests of industrialists, lawyers, architects, and prison, hospital, and school of-

Figure 1–7 The laboratory research of environmental psychologists is oriented toward solving real-world problems. In this photograph, a researcher is using a computer exercise to understand how people value public goods, such as clean air and wilderness areas, as described in Peterson et al. (1995).

ficials. The design of environments is of concern not only to architects and designers but also to anthropologists, museum curators, traffic controllers, and office managers, to name but a few. Moreover, changing environmentally destructive behavior is of concern to everyone who is aware of the dangers of pollution, urban blight, and limited natural resources. Perhaps the need for this type of interdisciplinary perspective is reflected in the growth of related fields, such as urban sociology, sociobiology, behavioral geography, urban anthropology, and recreation and leisure planning. Throughout this textbook we will draw on these and other disciplines in order to explain environmental-psychological phenomena.

In summary, environmental psychology is characterized by the following: (1) study of environment–behavior relationships as a unit; (2) study of the interrelationships of environment and behavior; (3) a relative lack of distinction between applied and theoretical research; (4) an interdisciplinary appeal; and (5), as we will see, an eclectic methodology (i.e., a rich mixture of methods). Let us turn now to a description of the methodology of environmental psychology.

WHERE DID ENVIRONMENTAL PSYCHOLOGY COME FROM?

The scientific study of the relationships between environment and behavior can be traced back to studies in the dawning years of this century (e.g., Gulliver, 1908; Trowbridge, 1913). Nineteenth-century psychologists had begun to study human perception of environmental stimuli such as light, sound, weight, pressure, and so on, and emphasis on learning and the advent of behaviorism led to intensive study of such environmental events as reinforcement schedules and early childhood experience. By the 1940s, a modest amount of research on environment–behavior links had been reported, including early work in behavioral geography, the psychology of cognitive maps of environments, and urban sociology (Moore, 1987). However, these studies did not systematically approach the interaction of environment and behavior in its fullest sense. The studies of how design factors affect the development of social relationships among students reported by Festinger, Schachter, and Back (1950) represent a turning point in the development of systematic study of environment and behavior.

During the 1950s, work in this area slowly increased. Lewin (1951) had conceptualized the environment as a key determinant of behavior, and even though his emphasis was primarily on the social environment, the importance of his theory for environmental psychology is often discussed. Barker and his colleagues compiled extensive systematic research on environment and behavior relationships during this period, examining effects of environments on the behavior of children, comparing behavior in small towns and in schools (Barker & Gump, 1964; Barker & Wright, 1951, 1955). Research on spatial behavior, psychiatric ward design, and other aspects of environment–behavior relationships also developed during this period (e.g., Hall, 1959; Osmond, 1957). Architects and behavioral scientists began what has become a long-standing collaboration in an effort to achieve another objective: designing buildings to facilitate behavioral functions.

HOW IS RESEARCH IN ENVIRONMENTAL PSYCHOLOGY DONE?

Are environmental psychologists and other psychologists similar or different in the way they view research? As mentioned earlier, two unique qualities of environmental psychology are that it studies environment–behavior relationships as whole units and that it takes a more applied focus than other areas of psychology. These qualities affect environmental psychologists' approaches to research in several ways. Most important is the fact that they tend to conduct research in the actual setting that concerns them and thereby preserve the integrity of that setting (Patterson, 1977; Proshansky, 1972; Winkel, 1987). Thus, they are more inclined to use techniques that take them to field settings

Other lines of work have also fed into the present field of environmental psychology. Already noted work by Barker on ecological psychology (see box on page 16) emphasized the ways in which the entire environment influences the types of behavior that will occur within it, and work by E. T. Hall (1959, 1966) in *proxemics*, or how we use space, as well as the work of researchers interested in the effects of crowding (Calhoun, 1962, 1964) have stimulated volumes of research on these areas of human−environment interaction. Research in environmental psychology in the United States, Canada, Europe, and Japan began to flourish, and other work in perception and cognition played a significant role in environmental psychology as well. With the advent of concerns over energy use and preservation of the natural environment, more and more researchers are looking into ways of changing our wasteful and destructive practices of interacting with the environment.

By the mid-1970s, these developments led a few psychology departments to offer formal programs of study in environmental psychology, and many more departments began to offer courses with that title. Textbooks on the subject emerged, journals devoted to the field (such as *Environment and Behavior* and the *Journal of Environmental Psychology*) were started, and organizations such as the Environmental Design Research Association were formed. The American Psychological Association has officially recognized environmental psychology (in conjunction with population psychology) as one of its divisions, and international societies, such as the International Association for the Study of People and Their Surroundings, have become active. While the growth of the field has leveled off in recent years, its activities and concerns remain important and exciting.

rather than to abstract important aspects of reality for study in the laboratory, as is typical of many research psychologists.

RESEARCH METHODS IN ENVIRONMENTAL PSYCHOLOGY

Basically, environmental psychologists have the same "arsenal" of research methods as other psychologists; they just use it somewhat differently. It includes experimental methods, correlational methods, and descriptive methods. We will describe each of these techniques, first noting general strengths and weaknesses and then evaluating their appropriateness for research in environmental psychology. It will become apparent that, because of the different research values held by environmental psychologists, their choice of methods frequently differs from that of other psychologists. The description of their methods is brief and introductory and should give you enough background to understand the methodological issues in the rest of the text.

Experimental Research

Only one methodology allows researchers to identify with certainty the variable that is causing the effects they observe in an experiment. It is called the **experimental method**, in which the researcher systematically varies an **independent variable** (e.g., heat) and measures the effect on a **dependent variable** (e.g., performance). Usually two or more levels of an independent variable are used (e.g., 70, 90, or 100 °F for levels of heat) and often multiple dependent measures are used (e.g., measures of mood and performance). Two forms of control are necessary in experimental research. First, only the independent variable is allowed to differ between experimental conditions, so that all other aspects of the situation are the same for all experimental conditions. When variables other than the ones being studied also vary across different conditions, they are considered **confounds**. Second, subjects are randomly assigned to experimental treatments. This **random assignment** makes it improbable (with a sufficient number of subjects) that differences between treatment conditions are caused by factors other than the independent manipulation (e.g., different personality types); in other words, experiments should be high in **internal validity:** they should be conducted in such a way that the effect on the dependent variable is due to differences in the independent variable and not due to any other factors. Experimental methodologies may be used in both laboratory and field settings, although it is clearly more difficult to manipulate variables and establish controls in the field.

While experimental methodologies have [dom]inated in most areas of psychology, [h]ave not dominated research in envi[ronme]ntal psychology to the same extent.

Although the fact that they permit causal inference is an advantage, for environmental psychologists the liabilities of experimental methods frequently outweigh their benefits. One problem is that the degree of control required often creates an artificial situation, which destroys the integrity of the setting. This makes findings from these studies less generalizable to the real world; that is, it reduces **external validity**. Further, it frequently is possible to maintain the control necessary for an experiment only over a brief period, which makes most experimental studies short-term. Since many environmentally caused effects do not manifest themselves over a short term, this is a problem.

However, experimental studies in the laboratory can be useful for studying environmental issues. For example, as we will see in Chapter 5, Glass and Singer (1972) used artificial laboratory conditions to specify some of the psychological aspects of exposure to noise and were able to discover relationships that would have been difficult if not impossible to find in field studies or nonexperimental investigations. In these studies, subjects in a laboratory were exposed to predictable and unpredictable noise, and some were provided with a sense of control over the noise by virtue of having a way to shut off the noise if they wished. Predictable noise had few negative effects on subjects, while unpredictable noise had several effects. More important, the sense of control attenuated the negative consequences of unpredictable noise. The nature of this phenomenon and the need to isolate individual causes made laboratory experimental study the only feasible way to study these relationships.

An alternate approach to experimental laboratory techniques is to conduct field experiments. By transferring many aspects of experimental science to a field setting, we can increase realism and generalizability and still have enough control over the variables we are studying to be able to derive causal relationships. Subjects are still randomly assigned to conditions, as the independent variables are manipulated by the experimenter. Field experiments, however, are difficult to set up and often appear a little artificial, as conditions must be manipulated in order to study whatever is of interest. Artificiality reduces **experiential realism**, or the extent to which the research experience resembles that of the real world, and impacts the subject as intended.

An example of the value of field experimentation is provided by a study of territoriality conducted by Edney (1975). In general, research on territoriality has been difficult to carry out in the laboratory, because it requires the experimenter to induce feelings of ownership in subjects. Since territoriality already exists in one's home environment, Edney decided to run a field experiment using students' dormitory rooms as the laboratory. He randomly assigned half the subjects to their own room (the "resident" condition) and half to the rooms of other students as "visitors." Subjects performed a variety of tasks within this context. The results, reviewed in more detail in Chapter 8, showed that people experience more control when on their home ground than when visiting the territory of another, and perceive their own territory as more pleasant and private. More important for our present purposes is that Edney successfully used a naturalistic setting to observe an environmental phenomenon and to study its effects in a systematic, causal manner. Because subjects were randomly assigned (i.e., to resident and visitor conditions), a degree of control was established over extraneous variables. Experiential realism and external validity were enhanced by the field setting, so this study represents the best of both experimental and field research.

For a variety of reasons, researchers are often unable to do research in the field. The appropriate settings may not be available, the logistics of doing a field study may be too great, or sufficient control may not be attainable. Some researchers have responded by using **simulation methods**, by introducing components of a real environment into an artificial setting. By simulating the essential elements of a naturalistic setting in a laboratory, experiential realism and external validity are increased, and some experimental rigor is retained.

Simulation techniques are useful for studying aspects of human–environment behavior other than crowding. One area of environmental psychology, discussed in Chapters 2 and 3, is concerned with how people perceive their environment and what factors affect their preference for various settings. Clearly, it would be impractical to study these phenomena by driving subjects around to a variety of places and having them make ratings; yet, at the Berkeley Environmental Simulation Laboratory, people could be "driven through" suburban neighborhoods or urban blocks by means of a large-scale environmental simulation (McKechnie, 1977). One of the elements in the lab was a scale replica of the environment placed on a large platform. Suspended overhead was a gantry on which a camera could move in any direction and give the viewer an "eye-level" perspective while moving around the model. With the increased sophistication of computers and computer-aided design systems, sophistacated simulations using computer graphic representations of various environments for research purposes should not be far in the future.

A more traditional means to view the natural environment experimentally is by showing subjects photographic slides of a wide range of settings. In such a simulation, researchers might vary the complexity of urban and rural slides (Herzog & Smith, 1988; R. Kaplan, 1987; Wohlwill, 1976b) that subjects are asked to rate. This would provide information about how complexity affects preference in urban and rural contexts. Overall, slides offer several advantages as a simulation of the real environment: they are easy to present to a small or large group, they are inexpensive to produce and obtain, and they allow a wide variety of scenes to be shown at one time.

Correlational Research

In **correlational research** the experimenter does not or cannot manipulate aspects of the situation and cannot randomly assign subjects to various conditions. In this method, the relationship between *naturally occurring* situational variations and some other variable can be assessed through careful observation of both. Assume that a researcher wants to compare responses to high and low density in a department store (Figure 1–8). By observing the naturally occurring variations in density and shopping behavior, he or she can make a statement about whether changes in one are related to changes in the other. However, density is not under the experimenter's control but is instead manipulated by time or other factors, subjects are not randomly assigned to time, and the type of control characteristic of experimental studies is not exercised. As a result, a causal inference cannot be made. By not being able to randomly assign people to shop at times when density is high or low, one cannot rule out the possibility that the observed relationship between density and shopping behavior may be caused by a third variable; for example, different types of persons may prefer to shop either during busy or slack hours. Further, without an experiment, we know nothing about the *direction* of a relationship between two variables, because we are unsure which variable is the antecedent and which is the consequent. Thus, correlational methods are relatively low in internal validity.

Although correlational methods are clearly inferior to experimental methods in terms of ability to explain the "why" of a reaction to environmental conditions, they offer certain important advantages for the environmental psychologist. First, it is impossible or unethical to manipulate many environmental conditions that are studied, making experimental research out of the question. When this is the case, such as in studies of disasters, correlational methods permit the experimenter to use the natural, everyday environment as a laboratory. In such research, artificiality is not a problem, and generalizability—or external validity—is greater. What types of correlational research are done by environmental psychologists?

Figure 1–8A & 8B   If we use the correlational method to study the relationship between density of shoppers and shopping behavior, we cannot be certain that density causes differences in behavior. To infer cause and effect, we need to use the experimental method.

Two groups of studies can be identified. One group determines the association between naturally occurring environmental change (e.g., natural disasters) and the behavior of those in the setting. Another group assesses relationships between environmental conditions and archival data (e.g., the relationship between housing density and crime rate). **Archival data** means data that can be found in historical records such as police reports or meteorological records.

Descriptive Research

Experimental studies provide causal information, and correlational research tells us if relationships exist between variables. **Descriptive research** reports reactions that occur in a particular situation. Since such research is not constrained by a need to infer causality or association and often need not generalize to other settings, it can be quite flexible. The main requirement is that measurements be **valid** (i.e., they should measure what they profess to measure) and **reliable** (i.e., they should occur again if repeated). Under these conditions, we can assume the results are an accurate representation of reality.

In general, descriptive techniques are used more frequently in environmental psychology than in other areas of psychology. Their use is prompted to a large extent by the young age of the field and partly by the phenomena being studied. As Proshansky (1972) has stated, the environmental psychologist "must be [concerned at this point] with searching out the dimensions and more specific properties of phenomena involving human behavior in relation to physical settings" (p. 455). Thus, we must often answer such basic questions as "What are the patterns of space utilization?" before using more sophisticated methodologies to test for underlying causes. In other words, descriptive research may be needed to identify behaviors that occur in a particular setting, so that

they can then be studied in other ways. Descriptive research done by environmental psychologists includes studies of people's movements in physical settings, studies of the ways people perceive cities, and studies of how people spend their time in various settings. (For an example of this type of descriptive study, see the box on page 16.) Two types of descriptive research that are becoming increasingly important are environmental quality assessment and user satisfaction studies, in which environments are evaluated in terms of satisfaction or other characteristics by people who use them. For the most part, these studies rely on asking people about their needs, quality of life, and satisfaction. However, quite a number of different measurement techniques are used in research employing experimental, correlational, and descriptive methods.

DATA COLLECTION METHODS

Many of the ways in which environmental psychologists measure variables that they are studying are common in all areas of psychology. Other methods are more eclectic, borrowing from several fields, and a few measurement strategies are more or less specific to environmental psychology. The important thing to keep in mind when evaluating and choosing different data collection methods is that the assessment of behavior, mood, or response to environmental conditions should be as unobtrusive as possible. Measuring response to a situation should not change the way the setting is perceived. Ideally, subjects should not be aware of what you are measuring or when you are measuring it. This is not always possible and many measurement strategies have evolved.

Self-Report Measures

The most obvious way to measure moods, thoughts, attitudes, and behavior is to ask subjects how they feel, what they are thinking,

BARKER'S BEHAVIOR SETTINGS:
One Example of Descriptive Research

Probably the most extensive program of descriptive research ever done by an environmental psychologist was performed by Roger Barker. Barker's research centers around the concept of **behavior settings**, which he describes as public places (e.g., churches) or occasions (e.g., auctions) that evoke their own typical patterns of behavior. Barker feels the behavior setting is the basic "environmental unit" and that research which describes behavior settings in detail "identifies discriminable phenomena external to any individual's behavior" (Barker, 1968, p. 13) that have an important bearing on it.

Fourteen years of such descriptive research were summarized in the book *The Qualities of Community Life* (Barker & Schoggen, 1973). Here, the behavior settings of two towns, "Midwest" (located in the midwestern United States, with a population of 830), and "Yoredale" (located in England with the population of 1,310), were detailed. The descriptions are based on the reports of trained observers. Some of their findings are quite interesting and certainly tell us something about the character of the two towns. For example, Midwest had twice as many behavior settings involving public expression of emotions, and the structure of the settings provided children in Midwest with 14 times as much public attention as Yoredale children. Religious behavior settings also were more prominent in Midwest than in Yoredale, as were educational-government settings. However, in Yoredale, more time was spent in behavior settings related to physical health and art. We will describe Barker's behavior setting approach in more detail in Chapter 4.

---

or what they do or have done; we call this approach the use of **self-report measures**. By interviewing subjects, having them answer questionnaires, and using projective techniques, a great deal of important information can be obtained. Thus, if you are interested in the effects of noise on mood, you might ask subjects living in noisy and quiet areas how they feel during noisy periods, all of the time, or in whatever frame of reference you are investigating. The directness of measurement inherent in this technique is a clear advantage, but several problems characterize self-report as well.

First, self-report measures require that what you are assessing is something of which subjects are aware. These measures are also influenced by subjects' interpretations, and therefore a number of sources of bias have to be taken into account. In the event that you are studying controversial issues, such as the impact of building high-level nuclear waste depositories near communities, self-reports may reflect more than just how people feel or what they think. If you ask people if construction of such a depository would cause them to feel anxious or stressed, their stated preferences for construction might not be their true preferences. People who are opposed to the project might believe that if they say they would feel very anxious and stressed, the construction might not occur. Conversely, people in favor of the project could minimize negative mood to bolster the likelihood of construction. For such a case, the responses collected might not reflect mood as much as people's "votes" for or against the project.

Another problem is that people may not interpret questions or response options in the same ways. The ways in which concepts are understood or defined may vary, resulting in misleading answers to questions that the researcher thinks are clear. In crowding studies, for instance, researchers frequently ask subjects if they feel crowded or to rate how crowded they feel. The value of doing this is dependent on all people having similar definitions of crowding. However, Mandel, Baron, and Fisher (1980) found that this is not the case, and that men and women differ in their notions of crowding. When given a choice between two definitions of crowding, one dealing with there being too many people in a setting and the other dealing with there not being enough space, men chose evenly, while women were more likely to choose the definition emphasizing numbers of people. Thus, subjects responding to self-report measures may have different ideas from the experimenter about what questions and answers mean, and may differ from one another in these interpretations as well.

Regardless of these problems, self-report measures are often the only way to collect certain types of data, and as a result, effort has been directed toward minimizing these and other sources of bias. One way to do this is to develop measures that are standardized, or for which norms are available. Standardization of questionnaires or surveys is done by testing them on several different samples to estimate how people respond to them; these norms or estimates of "normal" responding can then be used for comparison to unique samples to which these instruments are administered. Thus, symptom checklists such as the Symptom Checklist 90 (SCL-90; Derogatis, 1977) were given to several different samples and norms developed so that

responses of subjects in a specific study can be compared to how people in different types of groups typically respond. Finding that symptom reports of people living in crowded urban areas approximate those of psychiatric inpatients, while those of uncrowded subjects are more like "normal" nonpatient responses, tells us more than just that crowded people report more symptoms than do people who are not crowded. It also gives us an idea of how intense their discomfort may be and whether it is enough of a problem to require some action.

The most common ways of collecting self-report data are by constructing and administering questionnaires and by interviewing people. Questionnaires are easy to administer and relatively inexpensive to produce and distribute, require little skill to administer, can be given to large numbers of subjects at a time, and can accommodate people's desire for anonymity by not requiring subjects to give their names. However, it requires a great deal of experience and many validation studies to construct a good questionnaire, so many researchers opt to use questionnaires constructed by others. One advantage to this is obvious: The questionnaire has already been used in other studies so we have an idea of how good it is. However, scales such as the Perceived Stress Scale (Cohen, Kamarck, & Mermelstein, 1983) or Moos and Gerst's (1974) University Residence Environment Scale will only be useful if they measure concepts that you are also trying to study.

Interviews are not used as often as are questionnaires, partly because they are more costly and time consuming. Ordinarily, it will take longer for subjects to participate in interviews than to complete questionnaires, and only one subject can be interviewed at a time. As with questionnaires, skill and experience are needed to construct questions and code responses in interviews. However, when using interviews, subjects can be asked to explain inconsistencies in responses or expand on their answers. People may also be more likely to voice honest opinions than when asked to write them down.

Another form of self-report measure is cognitive mapping, which is used to create "maps of the mind." Through a variety of procedures, described in Chapter 3, such images are transposed to paper. Cognitive maps are extremely valuable to researchers as a means of understanding how people code spatial information about their everyday environment. In addition to examining the mapping of city environments, studies have looked at how college campuses, local neighborhoods, and even nations are perceived. Through the use of these techniques, perceptions of various demographic groups can be measured and compared, and factors that afford qualitatively different perceptions can be identified.

Observational Techniques

A major measurement technique in environmental psychology, probably second in use only to questionnaires, is direct **observation**. In this method, people watch others and report their behavior and interactions in a given setting. These techniques can take many forms, ranging from informal observation of an environment, to a recorded narrative of what is seen, or to structured observation in which areas of the setting are preselected and particular behaviors are recorded on special coding forms (see Lofland, 1973). The advantage of observational methods over other techniques is the opportunity to gain first-hand knowledge of the way people behave in natural settings, as described in the box on page 20.

Unlike self-report measures, which assume subjects are able to express themselves, observational methods measure actions people may not even be aware they are performing. Since they can also be used without the subject's knowledge (i.e., can be **unobtru-**

sive), they minimize responses that are the result of people knowing they are being watched.

Observational methods have a number of disadvantages as well. One is that human error may be made in coding behavior. Examples include misidentifying one behavior for another, or being unable to code all the activity because it is occurring too quickly. The researcher using observational methods must also interpret the behaviors that are seen, and his or her interpretation may not be the same as the purpose of the behavior for the people being observed. Observational methods are also time-dependent, which means that the investigator must be present when the behavior under study is taking place. This can often be inconvenient and time consuming, especially for behaviors that are infrequent. Some of these problems can be alleviated through the use of instrumentation (e.g., photographic equipment), but errors in coding and inferences based on them pose problems. However, use of these methods can yield valuable information as seen in the box on page 20.

If you are interested in how people react when the distance between them and the other is small, you could ask people how they would react or how much space they would want. A better way to study this is to observe people under varying conditions in which they are close to others, recording whether they move away, how much they look at, talk with, or touch other people, and how far they stand or sit from others (e.g., Caudill & Aiello, 1979; Fagan & Aiello, 1982; Greenbaum & Rosenfeld, 1978). While it is possible that subjects could estimate how far away they might sit or whether they would leave, it is less likely that they could report how much eye contact or touching they might exhibit. Since these behaviors are important aspects of how people use space, an observational study is probably better in this case.

There are times when human observation is not the most productive, economical, or feasible way to collect data. Behavioral events may be sporadic, taxing the attention of the observer and wasting time in long waits with little opportunity to collect data (Lozar, 1974). The area being observed may be too large for one or even several individuals to cover. In these cases, the researcher must either create a device that will do the job or choose from available instruments.

One type of instrumentation that functions quite well as a surrogate observer is photographic equipment. With increasing availability of photographic supplies at reasonable cost, photographs and videotapes are being widely used by researchers. These media preserve records of the environment and events in it for future reference. They may be viewed repeatedly, even for different purposes and different studies.

Davis and Ayers (1975) listed a number of uses for photographs. They may be used to inventory the physical environment, as when Hansen and Altman (1976) used photographic records of dormitory room walls to code the types of posters and the extent to which the walls were covered. Photographic techniques also offer the investigator a means of counting the number of occurrences of a behavior of the people in a given setting. In one study, Preiser (1973) videotaped a large suburban shopping center and later coded the tape to determine the number of persons in particular areas. Photography can be used to identify and investigate selected details of activity, as was done in a study by Baxter and Deanovich (1970) who recorded personal space between subjects. Davis and Ayers (1975) investigated pedestrian flow on an airport escalator and were able to record visual searching by those coming off the escalator, progression into the movement system, and other multiple-behavior sequences.

One interesting type of instrumentation is the **hodometer**, which contains pressure-

Figure 1–9A & 9B   An example of instrumentation. This mat and bench have switches hidden within them (the cover has been removed from the right side of the mat to reveal the switches that are activated by wires within the mat). The distance between two people on the mat or bench can be detected on the readout panels to the right of each. The readout can be located in an adjacent room so that the device is unobtrusive. Described in Barnard & Bell, 1982; Kline & Bell, 1983.

sensitive pads covering the entire floor of a room. Every time someone walks on a pad, a hidden counter increases by one, such that higher numbers indicate greater traffic around that pad. This device can be used to map the movement patterns of museum visitors (Bechtel, 1970). Similarly, mats or benches with switches hidden underneath them can be used to detect distances people maintain from each other under a variety of environmental conditions (Barnard & Bell, 1982; Kline & Bell, 1983; see Figure 1–9).

Finally, engineers, architects, and designers have developed techniques to measure the full range of ambient conditions, such as

BEHAVIOR MAPPING:
Observing People in Places

Few techniques are available to observe and record information about a large number of people in a given area. From such a mass of activity, an interpretable measure of behavior must be constructed. One specialized means of accomplishing this task is **behavior mapping**, which is concerned with accurately recording people's actions in a particular space at specific times. In this technique, observers record the behaviors occurring in one or more settings with the use of a preconstructed coding form developed through a series of steps (Ittelson, Rivlin, & Proshansky, 1976). First, the area to be investigated is defined. It may be a large hospital ward, a series of classrooms, or even a single room. The observers initially make narrative observations of the behavior occurring in the setting, either by taking notes or by tape-recording their impressions. From this information, categories of behavior and interactions are organized and listed on a coding form. Using such forms, the observers code actions that occur in each area of the setting during the period of research.

Behavior mapping can serve a variety of purposes (Ittelson et al., 1976). It may be used to describe behaviors in the setting. In this context, schemes can be developed to code interactions among specified individuals and also to index the type of interaction and where it is taking place. Mapping may also be used to compare behaviors occurring in different situations and settings or behaviors in the same setting at different times of day. It is also a means of learning about the utilization of equipment and facilities (e.g., whether areas are used as intended). Finally, behavior mapping can be employed to predict the use of new facilities.

the amount of light, noise, temperature, humidity, and air motion (see Rubin & Elder, 1980, for a description of these measures). Some of the methods are inexpensive and easy to learn to use. Since environmental psychologists study the physical setting as well as the behavior occurring within it, ambient conditions are critical measures in studies that must either control for these factors or systematically manipulate them. As an example, Weinstein (1980) measured noise levels on the street of a heavily trafficked urban neighborhood as a means of selecting subjects who lived close enough to the noise to be affected by it.

Task Performance

In some studies the effects of environmental conditions on subjects' abilities to perform is of interest. Some occupational settings may be characterized by high-volume intermittent noise, confinement in isolation, high levels of density, and thermal extremes; it is important to determine how these conditions affect performance. Tasks used to assess environmental effects on performance may deal with manual dexterity and eye-hand coordination, performance on cognitive tasks, or with virtually any other aspects of performance. We will discuss here only one task used in environmental research, although a brief search through the literature would reveal many others.

One of the most important aspects of using task performance as a measure of some environmental condition or change is to select a task that requires the kind of skills or effort you want to study. For instance, if you are interested in how some independent variable affects tolerance for frustration, you might want to measure persistence on difficult tasks. This has often been done by using a frustration tolerance task developed by Feather (1961). In this measure, which is also discussed in relation to Glass and Singer's (1972) noise research in Chapter 5, four line drawings are presented on separate pieces of paper. Subjects are given each type of drawing and are told to trace each line without going over any line twice and without lifting the pencil from the sheet. If they make an error, they are to start on a new form. Subjects are also told that if they complete a particular form or give up on it, they should go on to the others. Unknown to them, however, two puzzles are not solvable, and constitute the measure for frustration tolerance. All the experimenter has to do to measure persistence is to count the number of discarded forms, the amount of time spent on the unsolvable cards, or both.

Trace Measures

Physical traces, that is, evidence of specific activities (e.g., cigarette butts in an ashtray as a means of measuring cigarette smoking or wear patterns on a lawn as a measure of traffic patterns), can be used to assess the effects of different settings as well. These *trace measures* are called **erosion measures** if they signify something taken away or worn down (e.g., wear patterns on carpet) or **accretion measures** if they signify something left behind (e.g., fingerprints on a display case).

For example, littering may be seen as an indication of the perceived quality of a setting and of the perceived degree of personal responsibility for it. A study by Geller, Witmer, and Orebaugh (1976) varied the anti-litter message on the bottom of handbills that were given to shoppers in a grocery. By counting the number of handbills deposited in the proper receptacles they were able to show that when shoppers were given the location of trash cans, they were more apt to dispose of the paper properly. Patterson (1978), while studying the issue of fear of crime in the elderly, counted the number of visible markers (signs such as "No Trespassing," barriers such as fences, viewing devices in the doors, and personalized items such as welcome mats) as indications of territoriality. His findings indicated that greater territoriality was related to less expressed fear of crime.

Choosing Measures

With this array of possible measurement strategies, how does one go about selecting the measures for a particular study? Obviously, many factors are involved, including cost, whether we have certain types of instruments, and so on. The most important determinant is the question you are asking: If you are interested in arousal, physiological measures might be used with self-reported mood measures and, perhaps, performance measures. If behavior is the key variable, observation and self-report might be used. There are, however, some issues that are relevant in all studies of environment–behavior relationships.

Many measures are obtrusive—their use means that subjects are *aware* they are being studied. Obtrusive measures are easier to use, but when people are aware of being measured (as well as of *what* is being measured), their responses may be different than they would have been if the measures had been disguised. With unobtrusive measures, the observer is not in sight and people are not told about being watched, though this may give rise to ethical concerns. Similarly, use of instruments such as the hodometer can be unobtrusive. Many of these measures, however, have been created for specific study purposes. For example, Bickman and his colleagues (1973) dropped stamped, addressed envelopes in high- and low-density college dormitories and studied helping behavior as a function of density by comparing rates at which letters were found and mailed. Subjects were not aware of being in a study when they found and mailed the letter. Similarly, Cialdini (1977) used littering to predict votes in the 1976 United States presidential election. To do this, he observed whether people discarded or kept a Ford or Carter communication that had been positioned on their automobile windshield, and predicted that people would vote for the candidate whose communication they kept. Similarly, Webb et al. (1981) proposed assessing the popularity of various environmental settings in museums by measuring the number of nose and hand prints on the display case. For an extensive discussion of other clever and useful unobtrusive measures see Webb et al. (1981).

The bottom line in doing research in environmental psychology is to apply measurement techniques that address the questions you are asking, that disturb the setting as little as possible, and that allow you to study real people in real environments. Field studies combining self-report, observation, and task performance, such as a study reported by Fleming, Baum, and Weiss (1987), are one way to achieve this. By observing people's behavior in their neighborhoods, gathering extensive self-report data as well as physiological data bearing on arousal, and by measuring tolerance for frustration on a challenging task, it was possible to document several aspects of living in crowded urban neighborhoods. Integrated studies of laboratory, field, and archival data are also useful in developing a comprehensive picture of the problem under investigation.

ETHICAL CONSIDERATIONS IN ENVIRONMENTAL RESEARCH

Before continuing our discussion of what environmental psychologists study and how they do so, we should describe some of the ethical problems and considerations that arise in all environmental research. As you may have noticed, many design and measurement techniques require that the subject be unaware that an investigation is taking place. This frequently improves the validity of research in a number of important ways. Unfortunately, however, it also raises a number of ethical questions.

In 1953, the American Psychological Association (APA) issued a statement on ethics in research, which has been revised since then. Many general texts on social research have devoted entire chapters to ethics (e.g., Cozby, 1993; Solso & Johnson, 1994), and environmental psychology also addresses this concern. In addition, federal government directives have been issued concerning protection of human subjects when environmental research is being performed under a government grant or contract. Most colleges and universities have review boards to advise the investigator on difficult and ethical issues in research design.

Many ethical considerations appear relevant to environmental research. Especially important are lack of full and **informed consent** by the subject and **invasion of privacy**. We will limit our discussion to these topics, but the interested reader is encouraged to seek out other sources.

Informed Consent

Whenever possible, subjects should be informed of all aspects of a research project, so they can decide whether or not they wish to participate. The assumption is that a lack of such information restricts freedom of choice. However, careful consideration suggests that informed consent is not always possible or desirable. For example, the researcher working with the developmentally disabled may find it impossible to fully explain a highly technical study. Further, many field studies must be performed unobtrusively, or subjects' knowledge would bias the results to the extent that they are misleading. In considering these problems, Patterson (1974) writes that before unobtrusive field research is undertaken, an assessment has to be made concerning the extent to which human welfare and dignity are in jeopardy, and these concerns must be weighed against the value of the experiment. In effect, the researcher should assure himself or herself that the major issues to be illuminated by the study justify the slight discomfort to subjects who are not offered an opportunity to give consent.

Another issue related to informed consent concerns whether subjects who participate in experiments without their knowledge (such as observations of pedestrians at a crosswalk) should be told about the study later. Is it better to leave subjects unaware, so that they will not be upset by the realization of having been in an experiment? Or is it the right of all subjects to receive a full explanation of the purpose and intent of the study? Informing subjects after the experiment has taken place may oversensitize them to the possibility of future research or observation taking place in everyday settings. For some people, the fear of being unwitting participants in research at other times might be quite distressing. On the other hand, there are strong ethical concerns (e.g., the subject's right to know) which the researcher must weigh before withholding such information.

Invasion of Privacy

What is the rationale for assuming it is permissible under some conditions to observe people without their knowledge? Obviously,

an invasion of privacy is involved in such situations. Since people in public settings realize they are under informal observation by others, most researchers believe formal observation should be no more threatening. However, Davis and Ayers (1975) suggest that if experimental subjects in a public setting become aware of being observed and choose not to participate, the experiment should provide them with an alternative route or area that is not being monitored. While potentially this leads to selection bias in subjects involved in the study, it may importantly protect people's right to privacy.

The assumption that under some conditions researchers have the "right" to observe people requires us to judge when behavior falls in the public domain and when it should be considered private. A comment by Koocher (1977) concerning a study in which people's personal space was invaded in a restroom highlights this issue (see Chapter 8). Middlemist and his co-workers (1976) assessed the physiological effects of personal space invasion in a men's lavatory by measuring duration and persistence of urination. This was accomplished by stationing an observer with a periscope and a stopwatch out of the sight of the restroom users. Among other things, Koocher commented that the experiment invaded the subjects' privacy, even though it was in a public place, because of the nature of the observation. He also felt there was potential harm for subjects who might have discovered accidentally that they were being observed. In response, Middlemist et al. (1977) stated that the information obtained was available to anyone and that the subjects were involved in an everyday public occurrence. Further, they mentioned that in a pilot study, half of the subjects were later informed that they had been watched and had no objection to the procedure. Obviously, both Koocher and Middlemist et al. may have valid points, and we should realize that sometimes there cannot be absolute ethical guidelines. It is the responsibility of every researcher to consider ethical questions as well as experimental design in conducting behavioral studies.

PREVIEW OF THE CONTENT AREAS OF ENVIRONMENTAL PSYCHOLOGY

Thus far we have described the characteristics of environmental psychology and reviewed briefly the methodological perspectives of its practitioners. The remainder of this textbook is devoted to an examination of the contents of the field, including empirical findings and theoretical perspectives. As indicated in Figure 1–10, we will begin with a discussion of nature and human nature; humans are biological creatures who manipulate their environment. Our interactions with the built and natural environments have bio-logical underpinnings, but are heavily influenced by experience—experience that leads us to form attitudes about environments and to assess those environments. Next we will discuss environmental perception and cognition, examining the ways in which environments are perceived, how these perceptions are retained and altered by situational factors, and how we negotiate our way through environments. We will then look at ways in which the environment influences behavior, beginning with theoretical perspectives

Figure 1–10   Organization of the book.

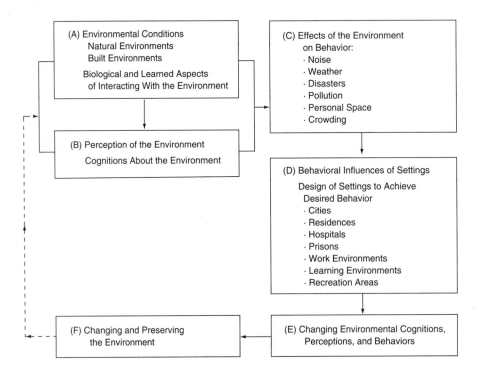

on environment–behavior relationships. We will also see how stress and other reactions to the environment are influenced by such factors as noise, temperature, disasters, air pollution, personal space, and crowding. Then we will examine the behavioral relationships involved in defined settings such as cities, residential settings, hospitals, prisons, work environments, learning environments, and recreation areas. In doing so, we will see how knowledge of these environment–behavior relationships can be used in designing environments for maximum human utility. Finally, we will conclude with intervention strategies for modifying environmentally destructive behavior and improving our relationship with the environment.

CHAPTER SUMMARY

Environmental psychology is concerned with studying environmental issues by drawing on the knowledge and techniques of many areas within psychology, and as such it serves as a meaningful focus for these areas. It is easier to describe environmental psychology than to define it, but one reasonable definition lists it as the study of the interrelationship between behavior and the built and natural environments. The distinguishing characteristics of environmental psychology include the following: (1) environment–behavior relationships are integral units; (2) environment–behavior relationships are reciprocal or two-way; (3) the contents and theory of the field are derived primarily from applied research; (4) the field is interdisciplinary in nature; and (5) environmental psychology employs an eclectic methodology.

Methods employed by environmental psychologists include experimentation, from which cause and effect can be inferred; correlation, which is suitable for certain field settings but ambiguous in inferring cause and effect; and description, which is often a necessary first step in new areas of research. Specific research techniques are either obtrusive, in which individuals know they are being studied, or unobtrusive, in which they do not know they are part of research.

The field of environmental psychology is complex, partly because of the phenomena it studies. Characteristics of its approach are, in a sense, contradictory. Its insistence on the integrity of the person–environment unit means that generalization from study to study is difficult, and that suitable methods must be chosen to account for behavior without disturbing or changing it. Its focus on problems means that the phenomena of interest will be derived from the real-world expressions of these problems, posing additional challenges. By innovative use of the laboratories, procedures, and measures of other areas of psychology and through development of new approaches to research, environmental psychologists have worked to overcome these and other obstacles.

SUGGESTED PROJECTS

1. How would you define environmental psychology? Would you define it at all? Is there value in defining it? Compare your answers with your classmates'. What do your definitions (or reasons for nondefinitions) have in common? At the end of this course, see if you change your mind about your answers to this question.

2. Try an experiment that involves the importance of context. Tape-record a passage from a play or movie, and play it back for people after describing either the actual setting for the scene or a completely different setting. Do people tell you the same things about the two settings?

3. Look up an environmental psychology research article listed in the references. What methodology was used? How could the research be done using a different methodology?

4. Make a list of environmental problems you would like to see psychology try to solve. As this course progresses, annotate your list to include the psychological principles and research you think would be applicable to solving the problems you named.

Nature and Human Nature

INTRODUCTION

HUMAN NATURE

EXPERIENCE: ATTITUDES AND ETHICS

Where Do Attitudes and Ethics Come From?

Do Environmental Attitudes Predict Environmental Behavior?

Attitude Specificity
Normative Influences
Attitude Accessibility

The Changing Meaning of Nature in North America

Contemporary World Views: The Role of Humans in Nature

BIOLOGICAL INFLUENCES: BIOPHOBIA AND BIOPHILIA

Biophobia

Biophilia

ENVIRONMENTAL ASSESSMENT

Quality Assessments

Indices of Environmental Quality
Affective Appraisals

THE SCENIC ENVIRONMENT: LANDSCAPE AESTHETICS AND PREFERENCE

The Descriptive Approach: Using Experience and Artistic Judgment

Physical-Perceptual Approaches to Scenic Evaluation

Psychological Variables in Landscape Assessment

Berlyne's Aesthetics: Formalizing Beauty
The Kaplan and Kaplan Preference Model
Individual Differences in Preference
Evaluation of the Psychological Approach

Conclusions From Studies of Landscape Aesthetics

NATURAL LANDSCAPES AS PLACES

CHAPTER SUMMARY

Suggested Projects

KEY TERMS

adaptation level (AL)
affect
affective appraisals
anthropocentric, anthropocentrism
attitude
biophilia
biophobia
coherence
collative stimulus properties
complexity
deep ecology
descriptive approach
diversive exploration
ecocentrism
empiricism
environmental assessment
Environmental Emotional Reaction
Index (EERI)

Environmental Quality Index (EQI)
ethic
homocentric, homocentrism
land ethic
legibility
mystery
nativism
perceived control
Perceived Environmental Quality Index (PEQI)
physical-perceptual approach
place attachment
preservationism
psychological approach
resourcism
restorative environment
specific exploration

INTRODUCTION

Road trip! School is out, and before summer jobs begin, Danna and Andrea are setting out on a two-week vacation in the California Sierra Nevada; a sojourn to a land of calendar pictures—snow-capped peaks, dramatic glacial valleys, and roaring streams.

DANNA: "This is going to be so much fun it makes me smile just to think about it!"

ANDREA: "You bet, hanging out in the mountains with my best friend. What could be better?"

DANNA: "Yep, back to nature with Andi; I'm psyched!"

Upon their return two weeks later, much had changed. It began with their first night in the mountains. Andrea wanted to stay in an old lodge with a great view of the lake and a continental breakfast. Danna had planned on a "leisurely" six-mile hike to a remote location as far as possible from any signs of human activity. Their compromise was to stay in an established U.S. Forest Service campground with a fire grate, picnic table, and a nearby shower facility. At breakfast Andrea leafed through advertisements for alpine slides and golf courses, while Danna tried to map out ways to avoid contact with "civilization." Later, in Yosemite National Park, Andrea was awestruck with the beauty of the glacial valley. Danna, on the other hand, could not recover from her disgust with the intrusions of humanity and human constructions into the landscape that was so dear to the wilderness advocate John Muir.

A sad ending would be the dissolution of their friendship, but this is not a sad story. What was clear was how different they were in their *expectations for the trip and in their definitions of nature and the natural. Friends they remain, but as Andrea said early in the trip, "I guess we'll just have to agree to disagree about nature."*

A few years ago Stephen and Rachel Kaplan wrote a book with the intriguing title *Humanscape: Environments for People* (Kaplan & Kaplan, 1978). The book, an edited volume of readings from the 1970s, still has much to offer for those with interests in environmental psychology, but our present interest is primarily in its title. Consider it again: *Humanscape*. Ponder the word . . . , allow yourself to daydream a bit. If you were skilled enough to paint a picture of such an imaginary place, what would it look like? Perhaps the title implies a *humane* place, a place where humans live and prosper. Would it be a wilderness landscape like the nature images depicted on calendars gracing office walls? If so, (somewhat ironically) a humanscape would seem to be a place that is nearly unmodified by human activity. On the other hand, history convinces us that, at least in contemporary Europe and North America, wild landscapes are almost immediately modified when humans arrive. Perhaps the humanscape of your imagination is a place that reflects all sorts of human activity, like a farm, or even a city. Where *do* we belong? Our attitudes toward built, modified, or natural environments seem to reflect conflicts between positive and negative characteristics of each (see Figure 2–1). The city is a source of stimulation and opportunity, but also a place of noise, crime, and pollution. Wilderness may provide an escape from urban ills, but the price is often a loss of convenience and comfort, and a different set of dangers. Even pastoral landscapes of cultivated fields and small villages are difficult to distinguish reliably from suburbia—a place that is increasingly regarded with ambiguity (e.g., Altman & Chemers, 1980).

Many authorities report that natural land-

Figure 2–1 Attitudes toward environments reflect conflicts between positive and negative features.

scapes are preferred over urban scenes (e.g., Kaplan & Kaplan, 1982; Ulrich, 1986). But what is the definition of naturalness? Is nature found only in a true wilderness? As Wohlwill (1983) remarked, nature is at once a common intuitive category, and one that is very difficult to operationally define. He concluded that natural environments are defined more by what they are not than by what they are; that is, natural environments show few overt signs of human-caused processes. Actually, research in forest environments (Daniel & Boster, 1976; Herzog, 1984) suggests that aesthetic evaluations are sometimes higher in *managed* (i.e., human-manipulated) forests that are thinned to encourage larger diameter trees and that have less downed wood. Landscapes categorized as "natural" encompass many obviously manipulated environments such as golf courses and parks (Ulrich, 1986).

Why do we find nature attractive? It may be that natural scenes are fundamentally simpler than cityscapes and represent relief from the frenzy of city life. Perhaps natural scenes tend to create an optimal level of comfort, and this comfort may differ depending on our individual experience with either urban or rural locations. It may be that people desire contact with the organic world because it exhibits growth and change, or because wilderness or other natural areas act as symbols of our individual value systems or culture (Wohlwill, 1983). In this chapter we will examine several perspectives on our views of nature. This will include a look at whether our views are in part inborn or are largely influenced by experience. We will see how we form attitudes toward natural and built environments, how we assess environments, and how landscape elements influence our preferences for natural and built scenes.

HUMAN NATURE

Before we investigate *humans in nature*, we might be wise to consider *human nature*. One issue is whether humans are part of nature, or somehow are separate from it. Consider this question: What are the characteristics of a wilderness? Many North Americans would agree with the view, codified by wilderness legislation, that wilderness exists only in places that show the absence of human activity. Is a city as wild as a campground? Is a campground with fire grates and privys as wild as a remote site with little evidence that it has ever been visited by humans? Perhaps we are left with a dichotomy of human versus wild that inevitably leads us to conclude that what is human is not wild. If so, how can we be part of nature, and if not part of nature, are we above it? The conclusion that we *are* above nature seems to have been the dominant perspective of European and North American politics since the Industrial Revolution. Perhaps it has gotten us into trouble (see Figure 2–2).

Even if humans are part of nature, what are the characteristics of our species? Even so-called primitive societies use fire, make clothing, and build shelter. It seems to be our nature to modify our surroundings. Even confirmed backpackers rely on tents, well-made boots, and other forms of technology. Again, it may be our nature that has gotten us into trouble, particularly in this century as our numbers have multiplied and our ability to use (or misuse) technology has grown. Thus we almost seem destined to an ambivalent relationship with wild areas. Perhaps they are nice places to visit, but few of us live there without making significant modifications.

One of the oldest controversies in psychology is whether human behavior comes to us fairly automatically (**nativism**) versus the view that it is highly dependent on either cognitive processes or learning (**empiricism**). The controversy extends to explanations for our feelings for natural places. Are our reactions to nature automatic and common to nearly all humans, or are they the result of our individual learning and our culture?

Figure 2–2   Modern North American life seems to separate us from nature.

EXPERIENCE: ATTITUDES AND ETHICS

What is your attitude toward air pollution, wilderness landscapes, or litter? If you found our question easy to answer, you must have an intuitive understanding of the term "attitude," yet a formal definition has sometimes been elusive. Attitudes cannot be directly observed, but must be inferred from behavior, including self-reflections and reports. Most theorists would agree that **attitudes** represent a tendency to *evaluate* an entity such as an object or an idea in a positive or negative way (Eagly & Chaiken, 1993). The term "attitude" is typically used when our focus rests on the affective (emotional) reactions of an individual or class of individuals, particularly those we believe to be based on their beliefs and learning histories.

An ethic or ethical system is an even broader construct than attitude. An **ethic** represents a system of morals or standards held by a person, culture, or religion. Informally we might think of an ethic as based on a collection of related attitudes underlain by some abstract principle that gives the ethic both a generality and a moral tone that is not necessarily part of a mere collection of attitudes. As we proceed, we will discuss the changing attitudes of Americans toward nature and consider how these have led to several different value systems—or ethics—that underlie contemporary environmentalism. We will see how our attitudes and value systems change and color our relationships with the natural world.

WHERE DO ATTITUDES AND ETHICS COME FROM?

For many years social psychologists have studied and theorized about the factors involved in attitude formation. For a much more thorough discussion of the area than we can give here, we refer you to any basic textbook in social psychology or to one of several current reviews (e.g., Eagly & Chaiken, 1993; McGuire, 1985). Although evidence indicates that some attitudes may arise at least partly from genetic sources (e.g., Arvey et al., 1989; Keller et al., 1992) or may be triggered directly by sensory input (e.g., Zajonc, 1984), most theorists believe that attitudes are primarily learned (Baron & Byrne, 1994). Thus, attitude formation probably involves many of the principles of classical conditioning, instrumental conditioning, and social learning familiar to introductory psychology students. One important finding is that attitudes formed through direct experience are stronger than attitudes formed from observing or listening to others (Fazio et al., 1982). In environmental education, for example, direct experience would seem to be more useful than lectures, commercials, and written appeals in encouraging environmentally responsible behavior.

Of course, culture shapes our learning history, and thus, our attitudes. Culture is at least as important in influencing our broader ethical positions. American and Western European cultures are dominated by a Judeo-Christian religious heritage, enthusiasm for science, and a governmental tradition of economic capitalism. A sophisticated evaluation of these and other influences is generally beyond the scope of this text. On the other hand, the applied activities of environmental psychologists in natural environments require, at the very least, a sensitivity to the ethical differences that underlie our perceptions of natural environments and our actions toward them.

DO ENVIRONMENTAL ATTITUDES PREDICT ENVIRONMENTAL BEHAVIOR?

We assume attitudes at least influence behavior. For example, if someone thinks that wilderness landscapes are inviting, that person is more likely to engage in activities in wild landscapes. But how strong is the attitude-behavior link? For years, social psychologists were frustrated by findings that on the surface, at least, attitudes were not consistent with behaviors. With additional research, psychologists have begun to understand the attitude-behavior link, and (with some relief) can demonstrate that attitudes do predict a variety of social behaviors (Baron & Byrne, 1994). Perhaps an example will serve our examination of some of the complexities in linking attitudes and behavior. What do you suppose would be the result if you were to ask 50 of your friends whether unspoiled nature is (1) beautiful and (2) important? We will predict that most say that nature is both. Why then, is so much litter removed from almost every North American recreation area (Figure 2–3)?

Figure 2–3 Parks and natural areas are, unfortunately, often despoiled by litter.

Attitude Specificity

One answer is that specific attitudes are much better predictors of behavior than general ones. A more predictive question might have asked whether litter removal in public areas is best left to paid clean-up crews. Similarly, generally positive attitudes toward the environment may not ensure that a particular individual will consistently recycle, backpack, *and* avoid the overuse of garden chemicals.

Normative Influences

According to Fishbein and his colleagues (Fishbein & Ajzen, 1975), expressed attitudes are also influenced by social norms. These norms, together with attitudes, determine behavioral intentions, which in turn predict overt behaviors. For example, it is normative today to express concern over environmental problems, although actual feelings about wildlands or pollution may not be as strong as the social norm. As a result of our attitude we may say that we intend to be environmentally conscious, and presumably, this makes us more likely to behave in environmentally sound ways. Initially, Fishbein and Ajzen (1975) expected that behavior and behavioral intentions would be nearly perfectly correlated. It is now clear that a number of variables affect our behavior directly without operating on behavioral intentions (Chaiken & Stangor, 1987). For example, Ajzen (e.g., Ajzen & Madden, 1986) adds a dimension of **perceived control** reflecting the degree to which an individual perceives obstacles that would limit his or her intended actions, or perceives that he or she has a degree of individual control over the situation (more on perceived control in Chapter 4). According to Fishbein and Ajzen (1975), a general attitude may not predict a specific behavior. Nevertheless, a multiple-item scale measuring components of an attitude can help predict a class of behaviors. A pro-environmentalist may not keep the thermostat at 65 °F in the winter, but someone who adheres to several pro-environmental concepts probably does engage in more pro-environmental behaviors (recycling, carpooling, water conservation) than someone who is not concerned with the environment.

Attitude Accessibility

Another research approach assumes that some sort of attitude activation is necessary before an attitude can direct behavior in a particular situation (Fazio, 1990; Fazio & Zanna, 1981; Fazio et al., 1986). According to this view, the strength of the association between an attitude and a particular attitude object or situation will determine the degree to which that attitude is activated and, thus, exert influence on behavior. This strength will vary depending upon such factors as direct experience with the attitude object and the number of times the attitude has been expressed (Baron & Byrne, 1994; Chaiken & Stangor, 1987). At the extreme, an attitude might be inaccessible or unformed in memory. It could even be that an otherwise dedicated environmentalist has never even considered the idea that trash left in an arena after a hockey game is a form of litter.

Finally, several researchers believe that attitudes actually *follow* behavior (Bem, 1971; Festinger, 1957). That is, it may be that if we first change behaviors, attitudes consistent with those behaviors will develop in order to maintain consistency between our behavior and our attitudes as we perceive them or wish them to be perceived by others. Although evidence indicates that attitudes do sometimes become more similar to actual behavior, this observation does not always hold true. Just because we are paying for pollution control devices on our cars does not mean that our attitudes toward air pollution are changing (O'Riordan, 1976). It

could be, of course, that attitudes both precede behaviors and follow from them.

The nature (if any) and strength of the relationships between environmental attitudes, ethics, and environmental behaviors are obviously very complex issues. It seems that attitudes are imperfect predictors of behavior, and that they sometimes precede behaviors and sometimes follow them. In the meantime, is it really worth the effort to try to change environmental attitudes in the direction of greater environmental consciousness? Given the consequences of continued environmentally destructive ways, we think the answer is obviously "Yes!" In Chapter 14 we will suggest some of the directions these efforts should take to reduce our use and misuse of resources.

THE CHANGING MEANING OF NATURE IN NORTH AMERICA

In seeking to understand modern North American feelings toward nature in general, perhaps we should begin by examining the historic attitudes toward the wilderness held by Europeans (see Nash, 1982; Oelschlaeger, 1991; White, 1967, for reviews). Do the terms "gorgeous," "inspiring," "relaxing," or "refreshing," sound reasonable when describing the Alps? If so, you may be surprised to learn that in medieval Europe "terrible," "horrible," or even "disgusting" would be much more likely descriptors. In fact, Europeans so abhorred the wilderness that travelers sometimes insisted on being blindfolded so that they would not be confronted with the terror of untamed mountains and forests! Furthermore, European Christians inherited a biblical prejudice: The Garden of Eden was a paradise from which humanity was ejected, and the desert wilderness was the land of hardship to which humans were banished (see Nash, 1982). St. Francis of Assisi was a notable exception who believed that wild creatures had souls and preached to them as equals. However, a rigid church government branded his views as heretical, perpetuating the dominant view of wilderness as profane (Nash, 1982).

During the period of Enlightenment, European attitudes moderated. Fueled partly by scientific discoveries, natural phenomena were seen by some as complex and marvelous manifestations of God's will. By the end of the 1600s European intellectuals were increasingly fascinated, rather than repulsed, by nature. Nevertheless, this attitude was primarily a luxury enjoyed by privileged city dwellers rather than those who were forced to contend more intimately with the dangers of untamed wild lands.

Eventually, some Europeans sailed for America seeking a land they had been told was a paradise; it was a land where Native Americans held strong spiritual values associated with nature—values usually emphasizing harmony with nature and with the spiritual power therein (e.g., McLuhan, 1971; Tuan, 1974). Most Europeans found anything but the "easy life." Eastern North America was, of course, a wild forest before European settlers began clearing it for farming. Whatever their original attitude, early European settlers in North America found that the necessities of food, shelter, and safety depended on overcoming the new American wilderness.

> The pioneer, in short, lived too close to the wilderness for appreciation. Understandably his attitude was hostile and his dominant criterion utilitarian. The *conquest* of wilderness was his major concern.
>
> *(Nash, 1982, p. 24)*

Nash compared the environmental values of the Puritan settlers of New England with those held by the colonialists of the Mid-Atlantic and southern states. The Puri-

tans found themselves in a threatening environment of harsh winters and poor soil. The combination of this harsh environment and their conservative religious tradition led the Puritans to view the wilderness around them as a hostile, threatening landscape inhabited by servants of the devil (one of their unfortunate views of Native Americans). Thus, the Puritans saw themselves as envoys from God whose mission was to pacify the wilderness and break the power of evil. As their already poor farm land was exhausted by ill-advised farming practices, the descendants (both genetic and intellectual) of the Puritans moved westward, clearing forests and fencing prairies in an effort to conquer the vast American wilderness.

Although their principal attitude toward nature was also utilitarian, the settlers of the Middle Atlantic colonies benefited from a more hospitable environment and expressed somewhat different attitudes (Nash, 1982). Many were of the Anglican faith, and most were better educated, wealthier, and more likely to study and appreciate natural phenomena than were the Puritans of New England. Virginian Thomas Jefferson may have epitomized the attitudes of the late eighteenth-century gentleman-naturalist (Figure 2–4). He believed that nature could be better managed through understanding rather than conquest (Altman & Chemers, 1980). Under this premise, President Thomas Jefferson charged the Lewis and Clark expedition of 1803 with providing detailed reports of natural phenomena. In spite of his more benign attitude toward nature, the gentleman-naturalist still most appreciated pastoral vistas and rural landscapes of farms and country lanes, not the true wilderness. Yet in Jefferson, and those like him, we can see the beginnings of an attitude of conservation and curiosity rather than exploitation and loathing for nature and wild things.

It may have taken the development of Romanticism in Europe in the eighteenth,

Figure 2–4 Thomas Jefferson's landscape at Monticello.

and early nineteenth centuries to persuade Americans to look at the true wilderness with pleasure rather than disdain. The Romantic tradition grew largely from an urban literary elite who found themselves attracted to the contrasting rugged vastness of wilderness. Wilderness was the inspiration for the evolving concept of the sublime: a sense of awe and reverence, sometimes mixed with elements of fear (e.g., Burke, 1757; Kant, 1790). America did not have the cultural traditions, material wealth, or power of the Europeans, but size and diversity of wilderness lands was one domain in which the New World could compare favorably with the older cultures (Nash, 1982). In the decades following the American Revolution, the wilderness became a source of national pride with at least a grow-

ing minority of Americans. Soon American writers like James Fenimore Cooper and painters like Thomas Cole and Albert Bierstadt (see Figure 2–5) began to celebrate and romanticize the vistas of the great untamed lands of North America. Those who celebrated wild lands were still a small minority compared with those who viewed them with hostility, but we can see, at least for some, the establishment of the wilderness as a place of beauty.

Clearly, North American attitudes toward wilderness landscapes have changed since the colonial period (Merchant, 1992; Nash, 1982; Oelschlaeger, 1991; White, 1967). Still, for Americans near the end of the twentieth century, reactions to the wilderness often remain ambivalent. We are

Figure 2–5   Albert Bierstadt's *Looking Up the Yosemite Valley.*

increasingly urban (see Chapter 10 for a discussion of some of the psychological implications of city life). We are also disproportionate users of technology and heavy consumers of natural resources and energy. Indeed, in Chapter 11 we will highlight various attempts to use architecture and design to modify environments for the benefit of humans. On the other hand there is a literary, artistic, and philosophical tradition that associates the wilderness with beauty and even religious experiences. An appreciation of wild lands is one legacy of leaders like Thomas Jefferson and artists like Thomas Cole. Late nineteenth-century writers like Henry David Thoreau and John Muir established a literary and philosophical tradition more recently articulated by modern environmentalists like Edward Abbey, Annie Dillard, Wendall Berry, Aldo Leopold, and Wallace Stegner. These North American authors are by no means the first to appreciate

nature, of course. Although their influences on North American attitudes are less apparent, the importance of both nature and culture are at least as well demonstrated by Chinese and Japanese painters who preceded Western artists in celebrating wilderness landscapes by more than a thousand years (Nash, 1982). Certainly the petroglyphs, totem poles, and oral history of Native American peoples are testimony to their appreciation of nature long before Europeans arrived in North America.

CONTEMPORARY WORLD VIEWS: THE ROLE OF HUMANS IN NATURE

Perhaps wild lands will always inspire both fear and appreciation. Even restricting ourselves to twentieth-century European and North American history, it seems clear that the appreciation of nature is heavily influenced by culture and fashion (e.g., Duncan,

1973; Hecht, 1975). If attitudes are so transitory, is there any reason to make the ethical leap to suggest that any particular relationship with nature is "best"? Although many psychologists might prefer to avoid such value-laden questions, the applied nature of environmental psychology makes it difficult for us to maintain such reserve. Briefly, one reason (which we will elaborate shortly) is because there is biological evidence that contact with certain natural landscapes can have restorative effects on modern humans. More in line with our present discussion, however, is the conviction that our planet is facing a global ecological crisis and that our survival depends on our ability to change human behavior NOW! Much of Chapter 14 is devoted to examining ways in which psychology can promote environmentally sensitive changes in individual behaviors and attitudes. For our present discussion we will take a more global approach. We wish to better understand differing ethical views of our relationship with nature and the wilderness.

We might begin at the end of the nineteenth century with a convergence between the appreciation of nature sparked by Romanticism and the new realization that humans were part of an interconnected web of life, a view fostered by Darwin's *Origin of Species* (1859). Americans began to realize that the supply of natural resources was finite. Under President Theodore Roosevelt's leadership, the federal government began efforts to manage natural resources to *conserve* them for human use. According to Oelschlaeger (1991), this became entrenched as **resourcism** (resource conservation), which remains the dominant American perspective on natural lands. Notice the **homocentric** or **anthropocentric** assumption (see Figure 2–6) of this view that natural landscapes are stockpiles of raw material to be transformed into the wants and needs of *humans*

Figure 2–6 Can natural landscapes be "managed" as measurable (economic) commodities?

(Merchant, 1992; Oelschlaeger, 1991). A resource manager's job is to use rational means such as scientific discoveries to maximize the output of natural resources for human use.

Preservationism is a less common, but still influential view that differs from resource conservation in emphasizing a holistic view of nature that assumes that an intact ecosystem is greater than the sum of its parts. An ecosystem has evolved into a complex system of interdependent parts, and changes to any one of these may have devastating effects on any of the others. Thus, preservationists value programs that maintain intact ecosystems such as wilderness areas. According to Oelschlaeger, preservationism rejects a strictly economic approach to valuing nature in favor of species diversity, rarity, or beauty. Nevertheless, critics charge that preservationists retain an essentially anthropocentric world view in their advocacy of preservation of intact ecosystems. For example, you may have heard the argument that we should preserve tropical rainforests in order to avoid unwittingly destroying some plant or animal with as yet undiscovered uses, such as a cure for cancer. Without belittling the goal, we must point out that this argument still assumes the anthropocentric goal of managing nature for the benefit of humans.

Finally, **ecocentrism** maintains that natural ecosystems possess value in their own right, independent of their value to humans. Humans have no special standing, and ethical human actions will be those that promote all life on earth. Aldo Leopold's (1949) **land ethic** is the best known example of an ecocentric world view.

> In short, a land ethic changes the role of *Homo sapiens* from conqueror of the land community to plain member and citizen of it.
>
> *(Leopold, 1949, p. 204)*

Leopold's land ethic is remarkable in its simplicity. Unlike the sometimes piecemeal aggregation of specific attitudes that may or may not result in consistently pro-environmental behaviors, adoption of a land ethic (if successful) could result in a complete restructuring of a person's or a culture's values in an ecocentric direction.

You may also have heard of the increasingly popular term **deep ecology** which is a form of ecocentrism that emphasizes a critique of modern technology, science, and political structures. Many deep ecologists would assert that we have arrived at a global crisis because our culture is dominated by a mechanistic world view that is perpetuated by science and adapted to serve the domination of capitalism (e.g., Merchant, 1992). If they are correct, humankind endangers the natural world, so we must promote sociocultural change.

A recent movement which attempts to rectify damage humans have caused to natural environments is termed *green justice* or *environmental justice*. Adherents of this movement seek a balance of the interests of nature and ecology over mere anthropocentric interests. The interested reader is referred to the Fall 1994 *Journal of Social Issues*, which is devoted entirely to the topic.

We have moved quite far from the traditional posture of psychology to at least attempt to remain objective and "value free," yet we maintain that a familiarity with contemporary environmental thought is both instructive and necessary for an understanding of our culture's view of nature. We are left with a question: Is the appreciation of wilderness (and nature in general) *entirely* culturally determined? Many would say "yes" or "nearly so." Yet recent evidence from biology and biological psychology suggests that natural environments may affect us in a more direct way that is less filtered by culture and learning.

BIOLOGICAL INFLUENCES: BIOPHOBIA AND BIOPHILIA

In 1984, Edward O. Wilson used the term **biophilia** to describe what he believed to be a human need for contact with nature. According to Wilson, this need is a modern manifestation of a genetic predisposition to be attracted to other living organisms. Steeped in evolutionary theory, this view emphasizes that human history did not begin in the relatively short period of the last ten thousand years for which we have evidence of settlements and agriculture. If the history of our species is short, the history of civilization is much shorter still— perhaps only the most recent 1 percent of human history (Altman & Chemers, 1980; Wilson, 1993). Thus, Wilson asserts that humans are a species whose bodies, and especially whose brains, evolved in an environment dominated by the need to survive in nature. It would be surprising if the influence of these earlier environments has already vanished in the short time since the advent of urban environments. Psychologically, humans may behave in accordance with functional-evolutionary principles (e.g., Kaplan & Kaplan, 1982; Ulrich, 1979, 1981, 1983, 1993); that is, the function of much of human behavior is to further our chances of survival and is guided by inherited behavioral tendencies acquired by our species through evolution. What causes us to behave in a functional manner? Such behaviors in humans, like in other animals, are presumably based not on some rational evaluation of a situation, but instead, on a predisposition to *like* environments in which we are prepared to function well.

BIOPHOBIA

One of the strongest arguments for biophilia is presented by its converse, **biophobia** (Ulrich, 1993). Biophobia might be understood as an example of prepared learning (Seligman, 1970). Prepared learning refers to a propensity to learn quickly and to retain aversions to certain objects and situations that have threatened humans throughout evolution. Although modern technology has minimized the dangers of encounters with spiders or snakes, a propensity to quickly learn or to retain learned fears might persist in the gene pool. Research generally supports this proposition for humans and other primates (Cook & Mineka, 1989, 1990; Kendler et al., 1992; McNally, 1987; Ulrich, 1993), especially the proposal that learned fears of certain biophobic objects or situations will be resistant to extinction.

Not all humans fear spiders or snakes, and relatively few of the individuals who do have themselves been bitten. According to Ulrich (1993), whether particular individuals develop these fears will depend on their own experiences or on those of people around them. Fear may never be learned if the object is never encountered. On the other hand, there is ample evidence that humans can learn vicariously; that is, by observing the reactions of others. Thus, one of the important functions of human culture and communication may be to allow individuals to learn of natural dangers without themselves being endangered.

BIOPHILIA

The positive effects of biophilia are not as well documented as their phobic converses, and research on these effects most commonly targets reactions to natural physical environments rather than to animals (Ulrich, 1993). The general argument for biophilia is similar to its phobic counterpart: Because our species evolved in a natural environment, we may have a biologically prepared readiness to learn and to retain positive responses to certain aspects of nature. Ulrich proposes three potential responses to biophilic nature: attention/approach/liking; physical and psychological restoration; and enhanced cognitive performance. Evidence for the final category remains limited, and we will delay our examination of positive or liking responses for our general discussion of landscape aesthetics.

Some of the most direct support for biophilia comes from studies showing that contacts with certain types of nature create what are called *restorative responses;* settings which foster these responses are termed **restorative environments** (see Figure 2–7). Perhaps life has included high levels of stress in all eras of human existence. Whether the source is a dangerous predator or the pressure of a deadline, humans always seem to pay a price for their stressful existence (see Chapter 4). Countering this stress, restorative responses may include reduced physiological stress, reduced aggression, and a

Figure 2–7 Perhaps natural environments can help to restore physical and psychological health.

restoration of energy and health. According to the functional-evolutionary perspective, humans should have a biologically prepared affiliation for certain restorative natural settings, but no such prepared response to urban environments since these have generally affected only a few generations of human experience.

Whatever the reason for our affinity to natural elements, evidence shows that natural scenes may possess restorative powers. For example, Ulrich (1979) demonstrated that viewing a series of nature scenes could lessen the effects of the stress induced by a college course examination. A subsequent study (Ulrich, 1984) compared the postsurgical recovery rates for hospitalized patients whose rooms overlooked either a small stand of trees or a brown brick wall. Those with the more natural view had fewer postsurgical complications, faster recovery times, and required fewer painkillers. Other studies suggest that exposure to natural scenes can reduce presurgical tension and anxiety (Ulrich, 1986). One recent study is particularly instructive (Ulrich et al., 1991). The study investigated the effects of viewing videotapes of natural or urban scenes during a short recovery period following a stressful video. The stress-inducing video, a 10-minute black and white film which was originally intended to reduce industrial accidents, depicted simulated blood and mutilation. After viewing the film, participants watched one of six 10-minute color videos of everyday nature or urban scenes. Viewing scenes of water or a parklike setting not only resulted in more positive feelings, but was also associated with lower levels of several measures of stressful arousal (including blood pressure, skin conductance, and muscle tension; see Figure 2–8). Unlike nature-dominated videos, urban scenes failed to show stress recovery effects. Perhaps most interestingly, both the stress-inducing movie and the nature video

Figure 2–8 Scenes of water or parklike settings are associated with lower levels of stressful arousal.

were associated with cardiac deceleration (a response that is characteristic of heightened attention), whereas the urban scenes were not. According to Ulrich, the results are consistent with the hypothesis that attention-holding properties of scenes can work two ways. As a component of dangerous encounters with nature, attention may be paired with stress, whereas attention to other natural environments may result in calmative, restorative physiological effects.

We have highlighted two extreme viewpoints regarding the role of nature in the lives of modern humans. Even our limited excursion into Western European and American attitudes has provided ample evidence that nature plays a unique role in different societies, demonstrating the importance of learning and culture. On the other hand, the biological view emphasizes commonalities across cultures based on our shared biological heritage as *Homo sapiens*. Of course, it seems likely that human reactions to nature involve both biology and learning. No matter what the underlying source, the research on physiological reactions to natural scenes makes it clear that the effects of natural environments are anything but trivial. Of course the term "natural" might be used to refer to anything from the deepest wilderness to an isolated tree in the middle of a brick plaza. In Chapter 10 we present a limited examination of natural elements such as parks and playgrounds in urban environments, and in Chapter 13 we will consider management of public lands to facilitate outdoor recreation. For the balance of this chapter, however, we will review some of the contributions of environmental psychology to the assessment of the quality and attractiveness of natural and constructed landscapes.

ENVIRONMENTAL ASSESSMENT

QUALITY ASSESSMENTS

Environmental assessment broadly encompasses efforts to describe environments or their components (Craik & Feimer, 1987). In the United States, for example, the National Environmental Policy Act of 1969 (NEPA) has been one factor stimulating the development of programs to assess environmental dimensions such as air and water quality. Monitoring these and other characteristics of environments can assist in documenting the effects of historic environmental changes and in predicting the future impacts of proposed projects.

Indices of Environmental Quality

Using modern technology, we can assess pollution levels, noise levels, property deterioration, and other directly measurable aspects of the environment. Such measures can be incorporated into an objective indicator or **Environmental Quality Index (EQI)**. Although these indices themselves are presumably objective physical measures, the term "quality" implies a subjective evaluation. For example, the concentration of a known chemical toxin considered acceptable by one person or organization may be quite different from that acceptable to another. These differences of opinion reflect contrasting attitudes based on the beliefs or feelings that reflect our individual learning and background.

In some instances the goal of assessment is not to determine the presence or level of some physical constituent of environmental quality but rather the perceived environmental quality as estimated by a human observer. This assessment method may not require sophisticated technology, although it does require careful attention to psychological measurement techniques. Typically, some sort of self-report scale asking for subjective assessment of the environmental quality is employed, and results in a **Perceived Environmental Quality Index (PEQI)** (Craik & Zube, 1976). The PEQI (pronounced PEE-kwee) is designed to serve a number of assessment purposes. As a measure of average responses of an affected population it may be one component of environmental impact statements or provide baseline data for evaluating environmental intervention programs. It also facilitates comparison of trends in the same environment over time, comparison of different environments at the same time, and detection of aspects of the environment that observers use in assessing quality. A somewhat different analysis may demonstrate individual or group differences in environmental perception. Currently, PEQIs exist for assessing air, water, and noise pollution, residential quality, landscapes, scenic resources, outdoor recreation facilities, transportation systems, and institutional or work environments (Craik & Feimer, 1987; Craik & Zube, 1976).

PEQIs provide an estimate of the perceived presence of environmental qualities, but not our feelings or emotional reactions to them (Craik & Feimer, 1987; Ward & Russell, 1981). Instead, **Environmental Emotional Reaction Indices (EERIs)** assess emotional responses such as annoyance or pleasure (e.g., Russell & Lanius, 1984; Russell & Pratt, 1980; Russell, Ward, & Pratt, 1981). Thus, the absolute measured level of sound might be reflected in an EQI, the human perception of this sound in the environment would result in a PEQI, and the emotional reactions engendered by these perceptions would be best characterized by an EERI. These indices may yield very different results. For example, a moderate level of sound might prompt an extremely negative

AN EXAMPLE OF ENVIRONMENTAL ASSESSMENT:
Visibility and the Perception of Air Pollution

As we will see in Chapter 7, air pollution has a number of negative effects on human health. One additional concern that has received increased attention is the need to protect visual air quality (e.g., Stewart, 1987; Stewart et al., 1983). In the United States, the National Park Service, the U.S. Forest Service, and others are concerned about the impact of air pollution on the scenic vistas in parks and wilderness areas (Figure 2–9). As part of the amended Clean Air Act of 1977, the United States Congress sought to protect and even enhance the visual air quality (defined as the absence of discoloration or human-caused haze) of many pristine areas. The federal land manager is charged with the complex problem of determining whether a given change in visual air quality will have an impact on visitor enjoyment. Since visual air quality is based on human perceptions and emotional reactions, measures of this phenomenon must be based on or validated against human responses (Craik, 1983; Stewart et al., 1983). Two critical issues parallel the distinction we have drawn between PEQIs and EERIs. First it is necessary to determine how much of an increase in haze is required to cause a perceptible change in the environment. In addition to the concentration and composition of pollution, the detectability of haze is dependent on factors such as color, whether it is layered in a band (layered haze does not occur naturally), and the angle of the sun. However, according to the Clean Air Act legislation, demonstrating that haze is detectable is not enough. The second critical issue is to determine whether haze, even if it is detectable, significantly changes a visitor's experience. As you might expect, different individuals and different organizations disagree on the definition of "significant."

Figure 2–9 Impact of air pollution on scenic vistas

emotional reaction if the respondent wished quiet for study, but high levels might enliven a party (the box on this page discusses some of the issues in assessing air quality, just one example of the distinction between different types of environmental assessment).

Affective Appraisals

Just what are the emotional reactions to environments? Russell and Snodgrass (1987) observe that definitions of emotions (often referred to by psychologists as **affect**) are ambiguous. Emotional reactions may be relatively long-term tendencies to feel love toward some individual, or short-term affective states. In the present discussion, we will focus on **affective appraisals**, which are emotions directed toward something in the environment. How many terms could be used to create an EEQI describing the affective quality of a place? We can think of

dozens, perhaps hundreds, but Russell and his colleagues (e.g., Russell & Lanius, 1984) have developed a circular ordering of 40 descriptors of places (see Figure 2–10) that include many commonly used emotional terms. Notice that these adjectives can be represented as a circular array in a space defined by two underlying bipolar dimensions. The horizontal axis ranges from un-

Figure 2–10   According to the Russell and Lanius model of the affective quality of places, emotional reactions to environments can be described by their relative position on unpleasant-pleasant and arousing-not arousing continua. Note that we have few words for emotional neutrality.

Adapted from Russell, J. A., and Lanius, U. F., 1984. Adaptation level and the affective appraisal of environments. Journal of Environmental Psychology, 4, 119–135.

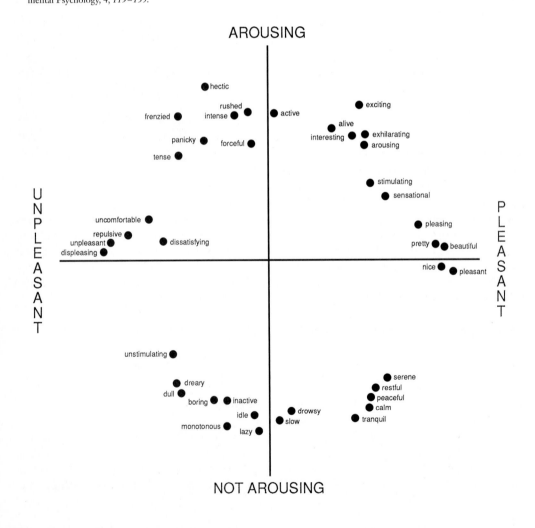

pleasant to pleasant, and the vertical axis ranges from sleepy to arousing. To pick two examples, the model implies that a serene environment should be pleasant, but somewhat unarousing, whereas a frenzied environment is both arousing and unpleasant.

How might we account for the fact that in using the same psychological dimensions for evaluating identical environments, individuals often differ in their preferences? One answer lies in the concept of **adaptation level** (Helson, 1964; Wohlwill, 1974). We will describe the concept of adaptation level in more detail in Chapter 4, but for now we can think of *adaptation* as "getting used to" a component of an environment and *adaptation level* as our preferred level of stimulation from that component. Individuals may have different levels of preference for complexity, causing the objectively measurable level of complexity in one scene to be too low for one individual, but too high for another. In other words, experience may lead different individuals to prefer different levels of complexity. Wohlwill refers to an individual's optimum level on any one dimension as his or

her adaptation level, and deviations from that optimum lead us to change things (e.g., through arousal reduction or sensation seeking). Russell and Lanius (1984) provide an interesting example of the effects of adaptation on emotional appraisals of landscape scenes. Recall the model of affective appraisal of environments presented earlier in which emotional reactions could be described by a model composed of two independent dimensions, pleasure and arousal (Russell & Snodgrass, 1987). Russell and Lanius (1984) found that exposure to a slide of known emotional appraisal (say, gloomy and unarousing) would be associated with a tendency to evaluate a subsequent target scene in a direction emotionally away from the first stimulus (in our example, toward exciting and less gloomy). Stated simply, adaptation to one landscape is likely to bias affective evaluations of subsequent scenes in a predictable fashion. In Chapter 4 we will see how adaptation level can be used to explain not only individual differences in environmental evaluation but also individual differences in responses to environmental stimulation.

THE SCENIC ENVIRONMENT: LANDSCAPE AESTHETICS AND PREFERENCE

Picture what you consider to be a beautiful landscape. Is your imaginary scene one of snow-capped peaks? A rocky seashore? Perhaps a pastoral scene of rolling hills, covered wooden bridges, and rustic fences? Do you think the scene you are imagining is much like that imagined by people the world over when responding to the same question, or are there differences between individuals and cultures? What can we learn about humans as a species from their landscape preferences? Theoretical questions like these have attracted the attention of a number of environmental psychologists and other be-

havioral scientists (see Daniel & Vining, 1983; Kaplan, 1987, 1989; Kaplan & Kaplan, 1989; Ulrich, 1986; Zube, Sell, & Taylor, 1982, for reviews).

A primary impetus for investigations of landscape aesthetics was provided by governmental legislation of the 1960s and 1970s that required the inventory and preservation of scenic resources (Zube et al., 1982). As an example, suppose we are building a new road to a remote forest recreation area. We want the new roadway to provide access and attractive vistas; but we do not want it to become an unpleasant intrusion for either the motorists or for hikers and campers in the recreation area. How do we provide access and maintain scenic quality?

THE DESCRIPTIVE APPROACH: USING EXPERIENCE AND ARTISTIC JUDGMENT

Not surprisingly, many of the most widely applied principles for landscape assessment and management evolved from the design tradition of landscape architecture. This approach, which we call the **descriptive approach**, emphasizes design principles derived from experience and artistic judgment. In particular, vast areas of public lands such as national parks, national forests, and national wilderness areas have been assessed using descriptive landscape inventory, an ap-

proach derived from the writings of Burton Litton (1972). The basic elements of perception are said to be line, form, color, and texture. Patterns of these dominance elements and contrasts created by these patterns are thought to be organized by the viewer's perceptual system, causing a focus of attention on a particular component of a landscape vista. For example, two nearly parallel lines form an axial landscape which focuses one's attention at the distant point where the lines seem to converge (see Figure 2–11). Similarly, contrasts in lines, forms, colors or textures are likely to draw attention (Figure 2–12). This description is not inconsistent with the more empirically derived perceptual data. In Chapter 3 we will see that the human visual processing system is specialized for the detection of contrasts

Figure 2–11 In an axial landscape such as this photograph of the Mall in Washington, D.C., attention is drawn by converging lines on a focal point, in this instance, the Washington Monument.

Figure 2-12   Contrasts in lines, forms, colors, and textures are likely to draw attention.

and is particularly "hard-wired" to detect certain simple lines or shapes (e.g., Goldstein, 1989; Heft, 1983; Hubel & Wiesel, 1979) and to seek a focal point or other source of organization (Ulrich, 1979).

Given that these principles help to determine what will receive attention, what determines whether the scene is evaluated as pleasant or unpleasant? In general, experts surmise that natural landscape components are preferred to those that are the result of human activity. For example, natural scenes in which contrast is high often receive positive evaluations. The contrast of snow-capped mountain peaks with the green valleys at their feet probably heightens their visual appeal. Similarly, many of the scenic areas of the American Southwest are particularly striking because they showcase the brilliant hues of desert sandstone. On the other hand, one would probably wish to minimize contrasts that draw attention to utility lines, mines, and commercial establishments. Again, we have introduced empirical data

supporting the importance of nature in human responses to landscapes (e.g., Heerwagen & Orians, 1993; Kaplan & Kaplan, 1989; Ulrich, 1993).

It seems safe to assume that landscape architects and other natural resource specialists are among the most sensitive and knowledgeable observers of landscapes, but their design training may have also led them to perceive landscapes in ways that differ from the general public's (Kaplan & Kaplan, 1989). In relying on the artistic tradition, the descriptive approach may also be deficient in terms of formal demonstrations of reliability and validity (Daniel & Vining, 1983; Kaplan & Kaplan, 1989; Ulrich, 1986). For the past two decades, interest has increasingly focused on supplementing expert opinions with preference models based on the responses of recreationists and other users (Ulrich, 1986). Enter psychologists and other behavioral scientists. In the United States, for instance, some of the most consistent support for behavioral research has been provided by the U.S. Department of Agriculture's Forest Service (Kaplan & Kaplan, 1989; Ulrich, 1993). How might behavioral scientists differ from design professionals addressing issues of landscape aesthetics? The term "scientist" suggests that method is the source of one difference. Although we have made it clear that environmental psychologists are quite eclectic in their methodology, most would gravitate to an *empirical* approach emphasizing objective observations of individual users rather than design professionals. In addition, we can assume that psychologists are likely to be most interested in investigating psychological variables: behaviors or mental events that reveal the environment as it is filtered and focused by perception (see Chapter 3). As you might have predicted, psychologists have contributed both

methods and psychologically-based variables to the literature of landscape assessment.

PHYSICAL-PERCEPTUAL APPROACHES TO SCENIC EVALUATION

One of the most direct extensions of psychological methodology is represented by what we will call the **physical-perceptual approach**. These strategies emphasize characteristics of the physical environment that can be related statistically to judgments of preference or landscape quality. Naturalness and the presence of water or vegetation are examples of physical landscape characteristics that might be used to predict negative or positive evaluations of scenic quality (see Figure 2–13). In an early study, Shafer, Hamilton, and Schmidt (1969) assessed the

Figure 2–13   Physical landscape characteristics may predict evaluation of scenic quality.

preferences of individuals for landscapes in the Adirondack Mountains of New York State and found that preferences were associated with such factors as the area of immediate vegetation multiplied by the area of distant vegetation, vegetation multiplied by the area of water, and so on. In another study, Zube, Pitt, and Anderson (1974) studied scenes of the Connecticut River Valley and found that scenic quality was related to such components as land-use compatibility, absolute relative relief (i.e., differences in height, such as from valley to mountain top or canyon rim to the valley floor), height contrast, and density of edges of bodies of water. Other features that have been found to be important include debris in stream beds, width and height of a stream valley, and stream velocity (Pitt, 1976), as well as natural water area, ruggedness, naturalism (Palmer & Zube, 1976), and forest management practices (Daniel & Boster, 1976).

Vining, Daniel, and Schroeder (1984) have extended the same basic model to forested residential landscapes. Presumably, identification of manageable characteristics that are likely to be perceived as unsightly (as may be the case in our example of building a new roadway) may help to avoid conflicts in areas of high visibility or quality. Similarly, Im (1984) applied the physical-perceptual approach to study the relationship between landscape characteristics and visual preferences in the enclosed environment of a college campus. In this instance, visual preferences were most positively affected by the slope of the ground and tree canopy or vegetation coverage, whereas the height ratio (described as the height of the landscaped "walls" in the scene) was negatively related to preference.

The physical-perceptual approach is empirically based, and more in keeping with the traditions of behavioral science than art or professional practice. This approach has probably received the most extensive evalua-tion (Daniel & Vining, 1983), partly because these researchers are quite unambiguous in specifying measurable characteristics of the physical landscape as predictors of scenic quality. Overall, their statistical models do a very respectable job of predicting assessments of scenes (Daniel & Schroeder, 1979; Daniel & Vining, 1983; Pitt & Zube, 1979) and have been frequently applied by resource managers, though rarely by designers (Im, 1984).

A shortcoming of the physical-perceptual approach is that the predictors it generates do not always make intuitive or theoretical sense (S. Kaplan, 1975; Ulrich, 1986.) This criticism is not terminal (who says reality has to be easily understood?), but the predictive equations developed in one setting may only be appropriate for a specific type of landscape. Although the model is attractive because it emphasizes objective characteristics of the environment, psychologists are also intrigued by the possibility that more purely psychological variables might arrive at constructs that are more easily applied to human experience.

PSYCHOLOGICAL VARIABLES IN LANDSCAPE ASSESSMENT

Our emphasis will now move from quantification of physical features of the environment to an examination of psychological or cognitive processes that underlie aesthetic judgments. In this **psychological approach**, predictors such as complexity and coherence are typical, and these variables are primarily located in human perception and cognition rather than the objective landscape. Physical measures of complexity or similar psychological predictors in a scene are difficult to obtain, so measures of these factors must usually be obtained from subjective judgments. In a typical procedure, a panel of judges evaluates scenes on dimensions such as complexity, ambiguity, spaciousness, or uniqueness, and then the same or another panel judges the quality or beauty of the scene.

Berlyne's Aesthetics: Formalizing Beauty

Berlyne (1960, 1974) was among the very first modern psychologists to develop a general model of aesthetics—a model that has more recently been applied to questions of environmental aesthetics (e.g., Mehrabian & Russell, 1974; Wohlwill, 1976a). Two concepts central to Berlyne's notions of aesthetics are *collative stimulus properties* and the dynamics of *specific exploration* versus *diversive exploration*. **Collative stimulus properties** elicit comparative or investigatory responses. That is, they involve some sort of perceptual conflict that causes us to compare the collative stimulus with other present or past stimuli in order to resolve the conflict. Included among Berlyne's collative properties are complexity, or the extent to which a variety of components make up an environment; novelty, or the extent to which an environment contains new or previously unnoticed characteristics; incongruity, or the extent to which there is a mismatch between our environmental factor and its context; and surprisingness, defined as the extent to which our expectations about an environment are disconfirmed.

Berlyne also distinguishes between two types of exploration. **Diversive exploration** occurs when one is understimulated and seeks arousing stimuli in the environment, as when one is "trying to find something to do." **Specific exploration** occurs when one is aroused by a particular stimulus and investigates it to reduce the uncertainty or to satisfy the curiosity associated with the arousal. Originally, Berlyne formulated his notions of collative properties as adjuncts to his notions of exploration, and showed through considerable research that exploration of a stimulus was a function of its complexity, novelty, incongruity, and surprisingness.

Later work by Berlyne (1974) suggested that aesthetic judgments are related to collative properties and exploration along two dimensions. The first dimension is called *uncertainty-arousal*. Research suggests that as uncertainty or conflict increases, arousal associated with specific exploration increases. The second factor is called *hedonic tone*. This factor is related in a curvilinear (inverted-U) fashion to uncertainty. As uncertainty increases, hedonic tone (degree of pleasantness) first increases, then decreases. The latter dimension is closely related to diversive exploration. Apparently, we are happiest with intermediate levels of stimulation or uncertainty and do not care for excessive stimulation or excessive arousal. Berlyne contended that aesthetic judgments are related to a combination of these two factors: uncertainty-arousal and hedonic tone. Consequently, those environments that are intermediate on the scale of collative properties and thus intermediate in terms of uncertainty, conflict, or arousal should be the environments judged most beautiful. Likewise, environments that are intermediate in complexity and novelty and surprisingness should be judged as the most beautiful, whereas environments that are extremely high or low in terms of these collative properties should be judged as less beautiful or even ugly.

Although Berlyne's suggestion of a curvilinear relationship between uncertainty and beauty is supported somewhat by research on nonenvironmental stimuli (e.g., paintings, music), Wohlwill (1976a) pointed out that data on environmental aesthetics are mixed with respect to corroboration of Berlyne's ideas. The property of complexity appears to offer the strongest support for the validity of Berlyne's position as applied to environmental aesthetics. Schwartz and Werbik (1971), for example, made films of simulated trips along a scale-model street in which complexity was varied by manipulating the distance of houses from the street and the angle of houses to the street. Aesthetic judgments were highest at intermediate levels of complexity. Wohlwill (1976a) reported similar results by exposing subjects to slides of human-built environments that varied in terms of complexity: Scenes with intermediate complexity were the most liked. Interestingly, it is difficult to test this hypothesis with natural scenes because they do not have as high a level of complexity as scenes of human-built environments (Kaplan, Kaplan, & Wendt, 1972; Wohlwill, 1976a).

With respect to novelty, incongruity, and surprisingness, Wohlwill (1976a) reported that a curvilinear relationship between aesthetic judgments and these collative properties in environments is difficult to find. Indeed, current research suggests that a rectilinear (direct or straight line) relationship is more correct: The greater the novelty and surprisingness and the less the incongruity, the more liked the environment. Incongruity in this respect has implications for site location of human-built structures in natural environments. Generally, a mix of human-built and natural elements is seen as incongruous, but if there is a predominance of natural elements, such a scene can still be viewed as aesthetically pleasing. For example, a number of buildings dotting a hillside tends to be less pleasing aesthetically than a single dwelling on the hillside. A final note on Berlyne's aesthetics: Just as we stated that extreme complexity cannot be found in natural environments, current research has not found aesthetic judgments curvilinearly related to the collative properties of novelty, incongruity, and surprisingness, possibly because it has not employed high enough levels of these properties in the environmental scenes that were used.

The Kaplan and Kaplan Preference Model

Berlyne assumed that identifiable properties in an objective array of stimuli (complexity, for instance) allow predictable judgments of beauty or ugliness. On the other hand, there are considerable individual differences in perceptions of environments, and people react quite differently to scenes based on their content. For example, it seems plausible to generate two scenes, one urban and one depicting wilderness, that are about the same on all of Berlyne's collative properties. Yet we know that there is a large research literature attesting to the importance—perhaps based on our genetic history—of nature. Culture and experience probably affect other preferences. Some people, if given a choice, would live in upstate New York, others in tropical Florida, and others in the desert of Arizona.

Steven Kaplan (1975, 1987) and Rachel Kaplan (1975) describe the procedures they used in constructing their model of environmental preference. These researchers collected a large number of photographs of various landscapes and asked respondents to classify them according to certain schemes, similar-dissimilar, like-dislike, and so on. Next, the researchers statistically identified the elements in the scenes that led to this classification and evaluation. In this way, they derived two general dimensions that account for preferences for various types of *environmental content* and *spatial configuration* (Kaplan & Kaplan, 1989). Apparently, one of the most striking aspects of content is the presence of nature. For instance, in groups of photographs depicting natural scenes, those with any sign of human activity are usually singled out in the classification process. In scenes of urban environments, those with even modest natural elements are identified. The second major dimension is spatial configuration, characterized by the bipolar qualities of openness versus closeness and defined versus undefined space. We seem to prefer scenes that facilitate travel by being neither too open and without definition nor by being so closed in that they obstruct our vision and travel.

The Kaplans postulate that humans will like or prefer those landscapes in which the traits of our particular species are most useful. That is, we will be attracted to environments that are—or were during most of

IS ONE PERSON'S MYSTERY ANOTHER PERSON'S BUG-EYED MONSTER?

According to the Kaplans' (Kaplan & Kaplan, 1982; S. Kaplan, 1987) model of landscape preference, mystery is an element that increases interest and involvement in a scene by providing the promise of further comprehensive information. Typical examples of scenes with high mystery are those featuring paths curving out of sight or in which part of the environment is obscured or shadowed (Gimblett et al., 1985; Kaplan, 1987; Kaplan & Kaplan, 1982). But perhaps you are wondering whether high mystery is always a positive predictor of preference. Ulrich (1977) provides an example for thought: Imagine yourself walking alone at night past a dark, curving alley (see Figure 2–14A). Would the scene possess mystery? Would the dark, unknown quality of the scene enhance your preference?

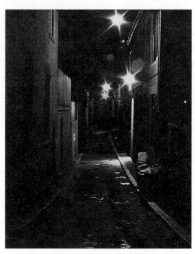

Figure 2–14A   Although mystery is heightened by hidden information, dangerous scenes are not preferred.

You may not be surprised to learn that Herzog (1987) found that deep, narrow canyons and, especially, urban alleys are exceptions to the general pattern of positive association between preference and mystery. There are several ways to deal with this ambiguity. For example, Kaplan and Kaplan (1982) essentially refine their definition of mystery. They suggest that the term is properly applied in instances in which new information is not forced upon the perceiver, but is only suggested or implied (see Figure 2–14B). They emphasize that the viewer must have

human evolution—survivable. Certainly humans, like other animals, have a pressing need for food, water, and shelter. What are our other characteristics? We are neither the strongest nor fastest animal. We have a poor sense of smell. We are awkward swimmers, and (without technology) fly very poorly. Are we particularly good at anything? Perhaps you have already answered our question and are thinking that humans seem to place a higher emphasis on thought and learning than at least most of the animal kingdom. If so, then perhaps you agree that humans are good at, and even like, processing information. Although some students question the proposal that they find processing information pleasant, the popularity of games of knowledge and skill indicates otherwise. This information-processing focus is a cognitive perspective about which we will learn more in Chapter 3. Indeed, humans do seem to be good at processing and remembering information about the content of a setting and making opportunistic use of this information. What type of scene would be most consistent with our skills?

the ability to control the incoming information by choosing whether or not to move physically into a scene. Having control should reduce or eliminate fear (see Chapters 4 and 5 for a more complete discussion of the importance of perceived control in a variety of environmental situations).

Figure 2–14B In this instance, the rock formations may intrigue the viewer, inviting him or her to move into the landscape to acquire more information.

Ulrich (1977) took an alternate perspective when he suggested that mystery will be positively related to preference in situations with little risk, but inversely related in threatening situations. A recent study of the relationship between mystery and danger by Herzog and Smith (1988) concluded that danger undermines preference for scenes and mystery enhances it, but that the two variables act independently of each other. In sum, they conclude that the effect of mystery is nearly always positive, but that in some instances danger may be a more salient cue which overwhelms any positive effect of mystery. Finally, Bernaldez et al. (1987) report some interesting differences in the way mysterious elements are evaluated by people of different ages. According to these researchers, whether a scene exhibiting darkness and shadows is perceived primarily as mysterious or risky and dangerous differs with age. It appears that a childhood fear of darkness and the unknown shifts, until by young adulthood such environments take on a stimulating or artistic quality.

In this context our primary conclusion might be that humans have a fondness for environments that provide generous amounts of comprehensive information. On the other hand, humans are not particularly fast or strong without the aid of technology so we may need a fairly safe place to retreat. Scenes that exhibit both information and safety are said to provide *prospect* and *refuge*. (Appleton, 1975; Greenbie, 1982). Prospect is the ability to gain an open, unobstructed view of the environment, whereas refuge is provided by safe, sheltered places where a person might hide. Prospect and refuge are simultaneously high in parklike scenes that show open but bounded space. Some researchers (e.g., Balling & Falk, 1982; Heerwagen & Orians, 1993) note the resemblance between these landscapes and the African savanna where many believe our species evolved. Perhaps our parks, cemeteries, and campuses are constructed approximations of the ancient environment that shaped the evolution of our species.

So, if the Kaplans and others are correct, people will be attracted to scenes in which human abilities to process information are stimulated and in which this processing will be successful. In more psychological or information-based terms, people will like scenes which are understandable and make sense. In addition, however, people will also prefer scenes that are not too simple or dull. We like scenes that are engaging and involving—scenes that contain some mystery, for example (see the box on pages 52–53).

The Kaplans have organized these information contents of landscapes into a preference matrix with four main components:

1. **Coherence**, or the degree to which a scene "hangs together" or has organization—the more coherence, the greater the preference for the scene. (Figure 2–15A)
2. **Legibility**, or the degree of distinctiveness that enables the viewer to understand or categorize the con-

tents of a scene—the greater the legibility, the greater the preference. (Figure 2–15B)
3. **Complexity**, or the number and variety of elements in a scene—the greater the complexity (at least for natural scenes), the greater the preference. (Figure 2–16A)
4. **Mystery**, or the degree to which a scene contains hidden information so that one is drawn into the scene to try to find this information (e.g., a roadway bending out of sight on the horizon)—the more mystery, the greater the preference. (Figure 2–16B)

At least two of these content categories, complexity and coherence, are very similar to Berlyne's collative properties. A distinction between the Kaplan and Kaplan model and the Berlyne perspective, however, is that

Figure 2–15A   Coherence

Figure 2–15B Legibility

the Kaplans emphasize the informational content of a scene in a functional or ecological sense as one basis of preference judgments. For example, coherence and legibility relate to understanding or "making sense" out of the environment. Complexity and mystery can be considered aspects of "involvement" with the environment, or the degree to which one is stimulated or motivated to explore and comprehend it. Table 2–1 represents the tension between the need to understand and the need to explore in the Kaplan and Kaplan model (S. Kaplan, 1987). We might also think about these components in terms of the degree of effort required to process environmental information or the immediacy of information presented by the landscape. That is, coherence and complexity are thought to require less inference or analysis, whereas legibility and mystery seem to require more cognitive processing. Although the relative importance of each ele-

ment is not clear, we may need only moderate levels of coherence and complexity in order to facilitate information processing, whereas the more legibility and mystery in a scene, the better in terms of preference judgments.

Individual Differences in Preference

Even the most biologically oriented researchers do not suppose that we all have identical landscape preferences. For example, there may be age-related variation in landscape preferences (Balling & Falk, 1982; Bernaldez et al., 1987; Lyons, 1983; Zube et al., 1983). Balling and Falk (1982) report that children prefer savanna-like environments, but that these preferences can be modified and become less and less powerful over a lifetime. Perhaps eventually, familiarity with other types of environments, especially those of "home," supersedes childhood preferences for savanna. In her critique of Balling and Falk, Lyons (1983) agrees that landscape

Figure 2–16A   Complexity

Figure 2–16B   Mystery

preferences diverge with age as well as sex and place of residence, but suggests that the functional-evolutionary perspective underestimates the importance of culture in determining preferences.

Kaplan and Kaplan also emphasize the role of familiarity in assessing scenic value. In general, the familiar, especially the "old

and genuine" aspects of a scene make it more desirable. Furthermore, those who are more familiar with a landscape may include locals as opposed to tourists, and, in a different sense, experts as opposed to laypersons. Ultimately, we await a theory of landscape aesthetics that successfully accounts for both culture and biology.

Evaluation of the Psychological Approach

The Berlyne conceptualization of aesthetics and the Kaplan and Kaplan preference model are but two specific examples of what we have termed the psychological approach to assessment. Daniel and Vining (1983), Heerwagen and Orians (1993), Ulrich (1986), and Zube et al. (1982) review other psychological models. It is encouraging to note that in most

Table 2 – 1   Organization of the Kaplan and Kaplan Model of Environmental Preference*

Characteristics of Information	Understanding	Exploration
Immediate	Coherence	Complexity
Inferred or Predicted	Legibility	Mystery

*Adapted from S. Kaplan, 1987.

cases dimensions such as complexity, coherence, ambiguity, mystery, and especially naturalness are found to predict scenic value by researchers using different methodologies. Unfortunately, there is as yet insufficient agreement on how many of these dimensions we need to assess a scene adequately, and the way we combine the dimensions in judging one scene is not always universal. That is, complexity may best predict quality in one scene and mystery may best predict quality in another.

Although the Kaplan and Kaplan model hypothesizes that content and spatial organization have their underlying roots in human evolution, another criticism of their theory comes from Ulrich's research on biophilia discussed earlier in this chapter. Like the Kaplans, Ulrich (1991, 1993) emphasizes the importance of nature as a content in landscape judgments. For Ulrich, however, these judgments seem to be more purely based on biology and classically conditioned learned associations. Affective reactions would occur almost instantaneously, without the need for the more cognitive processing implied by dimensions such as legibility or mystery.

CONCLUSIONS FROM STUDIES OF LANDSCAPE AESTHETICS

Both the physical-perceptual and psychological approaches are consistent with the scientific tradition of which most of psychology is a part. We have devoted more time to the psychological approach because it provides a richer set of ideas or constructs than the physical-perceptual research, not because it has been shown to be more theoretically correct. In fact, by demonstrating direct relationships between objective characteristics of the physical environment and judgments of scenic beauty, the physical-perceptual approach may be easier to apply to problems of landscape management.

Although there are clearly differences between the descriptive, physical-perceptual, and psychological approaches to landscape assessment, some commonalities are remarkable. The similarity of landscape evaluations by people from different cultures has been demonstrated in a number of studies (e.g., Hull & Revell, 1989). Some landscape features—water for instance—are consistently tied to positive evaluations (Coss & Moore, 1990; Herzog, 1985). There is a general and consistent finding that people from a variety of cultures value *natural* landscapes (e.g., Ulrich, 1993). Sensibly, naturalness—the absence of obvious signs of human intervention—is also a predictive component common to all three of the approaches to landscape evaluation (e.g., Daniel & Vining, 1983; Kaplan & Kaplan, 1989; Ulrich, 1986, 1993; Wohlwill, 1983). To return to our discussion of nature versus nurture, there may be some perceptual similarities common to all humans that underlie scenic beauty evaluations. On the other hand, there is also ample evidence that individuals and cultures differ in the meaning they assign to *particular* landscapes or places, and these differences probably modify those landscape responses that might otherwise be generic to humans.

NATURAL LANDSCAPES AS PLACES

Sometimes affective evaluations are attached to specific geographic locations or settings which have acquired special meaning (e.g., Steele, 1981; Stokols, 1990; Tognoli, 1987; Tuan, 1974). The term **place attachment** refers to the sense of rootedness people feel toward certain places. To illustrate, consider the difference between "house" and "home." Place-centered attitudes are personal, highly valued, and may even be perceived as spiritual or religious (Mazumdar & Mazumdar, 1993; Roberts, 1995). Many researchers emphasize that these components of place are complex, with dynamic interrelationships that defy simplification into cause-effect relationships between discrete, deterministic components (e.g., Low & Altman, 1992; Steele, 1981). The experience of place is likely to be private and different from one person to the next. Many examinations of place are *phenomenological*, that is, based on a person's subjective description of their experiences, and thus, at odds with the empiricism that dominates behavioral science. Of course, important phenomena are not only

those that are conveniently studied. It would be hard to deny the importance of home (see Chapter 12), the effects of forced relocation of the poor or elderly, or the special relationship some people feel for a particular landscape.

What do we know about natural places? They are permeated by affect, partly because of their aesthetic character but also because of their association in memory with events, persons or feelings. Think of a place that has special meaning for you; a place, perhaps, where you would like to take your closest friend. Is part of what makes the place special its aesthetic appeal? Is part of your affection based on the accumulated memories that you associate with it? As you see in Figure 2–17, the meaning of a place results from the accumulated interactions between an in-

Figure 2–17   Meaning of a place involves interactions between life history, the physical and cultural setting, and managerial actions.

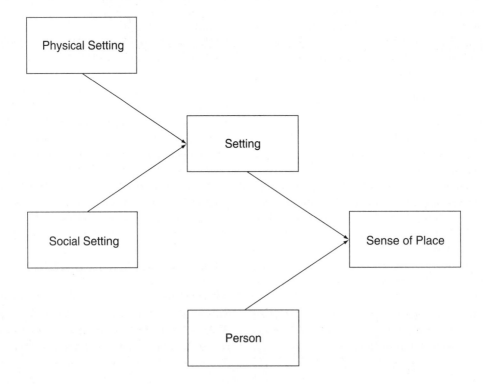

dividual's life history and a setting (Steele, 1981). Place experiences often include some feeling of ownership. Ownership in this case is a psychological phenomenon that does not require legal title to a piece of land or a building, but rather, a sense that the person has some uncommon, special relationship with that particular setting. This quality of psychological ownership has taken many names. It may be termed "territory" (Altman & Chemers, 1980), "kinship" (Mitchell et al., 1991), or drawn as a distinction between the landscapes of "insiders" or "outsiders" (Relph, 1976; Riley, 1992). Although much of what characterizes a place may be very personal, groups and even entire communities can develop place attachments. In fact, an attachment to place is often based more on the history of social interactions at a particular location than on its distinctive landscape or architectural character. Furthermore, the importance of place may vary from individual to individual. Whether or not a person

develops a deep affective relationship with a particular place is based partly on the whims of history, but some individuals seem more likely to develop place attachments. As research continues, it may be that we will identify "place people" as a personality type (e.g., Mitchell et al., 1991; Steele, 1981; Williams & Roggenbuck, 1984). In one investigation of forest landscapes that we will revisit in Chapter 13, Mitchell et al. distinguished between use-oriented visitors and attachment-oriented users. Whereas use orientation resulted in a focus on activities and activity-based experiences, attachment indicated an emotional bond with the setting.

What seems clear is that places are both the *objects* of people's interest, and the *causes* of moods, feelings, etc. Thus, places might best be understood in terms of systems involving physical settings and people acting in them. In the last third of the book, our focus will be on specific places such as residences, institutions, and leisure environments.

CHAPTER SUMMARY

We have covered much ground in our examination of the relationship between humans and nature. For each of us this relationship may be based on both learning and biological predisposition. Much of the learned component may be understood in terms of the affect and beliefs that comprise attitudes. Although the link between attitude and behavior is imperfect, we believe that specific attitudes predict behavior. We also briefly reviewed several contemporary attitudes or ethical positions with regard to the relationship between humans and nature. Increasingly, there is evidence for a fairly direct effect of certain forms of nature on our physiological function, and a companion biological influence on landscape preferences.

In addition to these theoretical issues,

we reviewed contributions from environmental psychology to the assessment of natural environments. Appraisals may include the assessment of physical qualities (EQIs), perceived qualities (PEQIs), or emotional reactions prompted by a particular setting (EERIs). In particular, we examined contemporary approaches to the assessment of visual quality and landscape preferences. The descriptive approach emphasizes artistic elements. The physical-perceptual approach emphasizes quantifying elements such as water and amount of wood. The psychological approach emphasizes dimensions such as coherence, legibility, complexity, and mystery that are more "in the mind" than in the physical components of the scene itself. Finally, we introduced a discussion of place.

The concept of place attempts to integrate the character of a setting with the personal, often powerful, emotions and memories an individual associates with it.

SUGGESTED PROJECTS

1. Ask a few friends to provide adjectives to describe several campus environments. Can you place each of the adjectives generated by your friends into the bipolar model of affective reactions suggested by Russell and his colleagues (refer to Figure 2–10)? Is there any difference between the assessments of friends from uptempo city environments and those from more rural homes?

2. Ask several friends to describe a "special place." To what degree are their descriptions based on physical characteristics of the setting? Do they also report personal experiences and emotional associations?

3. Review the discussion of resourcism, preservationism, and ecocentrism. Which of these three ethics is closest to your own view? Hypothetically, how would your experience of nature and your behavior change if you were to adopt one of the other ethical perspectives?

Environmental Perception and Cognition

INTRODUCTION

CHARACTERIZING ENVIRONMENTAL PERCEPTION

Perspectives on Environmental Perception

Traditional Approaches to the Perception of Size, Depth, and Distance

Holistic Analysis

Gestalt Psychology

Nativism Versus Learning

Brunswik's Probabilism

Ecological Perception of the Environment

Perception of Affordances

Some Implications for Environmental Perception

Habituation and the Perception of Change

Habituation or Adaptation

Perception of Change

ENVIRONMENTAL COGNITION

AN INFORMAL MODEL OF SPATIAL COGNITION

COGNITIVE MAPS

History of Cognitive Mapping

An Image of the City: Kevin Lynch

Elements of Cognitive Maps

Additional Early Observations

Current Perspectives

Methods of Studying Cognitive Maps
Sketch Maps
Mapping Reactions to Remembered Environments
Recognition Tasks
Distance Estimates and Statistical Map Building

Errors in Cognitive Maps
Types of Errors
Familiarity and Socioeconomic Class
Gender Differences

Acquisition of Cognitive Maps

Memory and Cognitive Maps
The Form of the Representation
Distance
Structure

WAYFINDING

Action Plans and Wayfinding

Setting Characteristics That Facilitate Wayfinding

Maps
You-Are-Here Maps
    Structure Matching
    Orientation

Movies, Slides, and Models: Facilitating Spatial Learning

CHAPTER SUMMARY

Suggested Projects

KEY TERMS

adaptation
affordances
analog representation
augmentation
cognitive map
complexity of spatial layout
cue utilization
degree of visual access
differentiation
distortions
districts
ecological niche
ecological perception
ecological validity
edges
empiricism
environmental cognition
forward-up equivalence
functionalism
Gestalt principles
habituation
landmarks
legibility
lens model

linear perspective
multidimensional scaling
nativism
nodes
paths
perception
phenomenology
policy capturing
propositional storage
recognition task
reference point
semantic networks
sensation
sequential maps
sketch map
spatial maps
structure matching
survey knowledge
transactional approach
transition
wayfinding
Weber-Fechner function
you-are-here maps

INTRODUCTION

Consider for a moment the conversation that might occur if Craig, an imaginary individual from the metropolitan area of Atlanta, Georgia, were to visit his old friend Cheryl at her home in Fishtail, Montana on a sunny morning in May. The temperature is in the low 60s, and Craig thinks it is a little chilly compared to his warmer and more humid Atlanta home. Cheryl doesn't find it cool at all. She is thrilled to bask in the warm sun after a long winter in the foothills of Montana's mountains. Craig appreciates Fishtail's clean, crisp air, but he is unnerved by the remoteness of the little hamlet. Cheryl doesn't even think about the air. Clean air and distant vistas have always been part of this, her long-time home.

The sunny day in Fishtail is an ideal occasion for Cheryl and Craig to hike in the nearby Bearstooth Mountains. Good company and good conversation—the day flies by. Presently, Craig becomes concerned that they are hiking deeper and deeper into the wilderness and farther and farther from dinner and a comfortable bed. Just as he is about to voice his fears, they break out of the trees and into the trailhead parking lot where their car remains just as they left it. "How could I have been so turned around?" Craig mutters to himself.

Perception presents us with a "picture" or best guess as to the present state of the environment around us. Of course, the specific form of the perceptual input varies. It may be the visual image of a landscape vista, the smells and sounds of a city street, or even the text of this book. Often this information seems to be stored and recalled as images or maps. The physiological processes that allow sensation are grounded in observable biological processes and events. However, the world as we "see" it also includes elements retrieved from experience and memory. One of the hottest debates in psychology concerns whether or not the subjective experience of "seeing" a mental image or map corresponds in any way to the actual mental representation or storage system. In the present chapter we will also try to understand how this information is stored, retrieved, and referenced in our daily interactions with the world around us. Humans are not "stuck" in the environment of the present or even conventional reality. Think of the room in which you are reading right now. Can you imagine how it would look if you were somehow able to view it from a window in the ceiling? Even when we are not actively viewing, hearing, or smelling an environment, we can experience it mentally. We acquire facts and opinions about the world around us, and remember emotional reactions to environments from experience. Presumably, we can use this mental representation of the physical environment to make plans, to understand the terrain around us, or to solve problems involving an environmental context— finding a dry cleaning establishment, for example. In general, researchers refer to this ability to imagine and think about the spatial world as **environmental cognition**.

CHARACTERIZING ENVIRONMENTAL PERCEPTION

Perhaps when you opened this book, you expected to read about ways of using psychology to address environmental problems such as pollution, crowding, noise, or extreme temperatures. Perhaps you expected to learn about psychology applied to the human-dominated processes of designing buildings and cities. You may even have expected to read about psychology applied to environments such as wilderness areas in which humans are dwarfed by their surroundings and our intrusion is minimized. We consider all of these content domains or topics to be within the scope of this book. Across the variety of issues and environments a common principle applies: Humans change the environment in both intentional and unintentional ways, and are, in turn, changed by the places they inhabit. In almost every case, our actions are informed by clues about the state of this interaction—clues gathered from the world by our senses and reconciled with information from our prior experiences. Although we will focus on vision, the modality through which most humans acquire most of their knowledge about the environment, we should recognize that other senses may exert powerful influences. For example, some research suggests that olfaction (the sense of smell) exerts particularly powerful influences on emotions (Porteous, 1985), and memory (Engen, 1982).

Historically, psychologists have made a distinction between two processes that gather and interpret environmental stimulation. The term **sensation** has been applied to the relatively straightforward activity of human sensory systems in reacting to simple stimuli such as an individual sound or a flash of light (e.g., Goldstein, 1989). Of course your awareness and evaluation of striking architecture, sublime landscapes, or distasteful dumps is probably founded on the sensations created by an array of photons of light stimulating individual receptor cells in your eyes. Our focus, however, will be on **perception**, a term that is applied to the more complicated processing of complex, often meaningful stimuli like those we encounter in everyday life (see Figure 3–1).

Differing views of the process of perception underlie some of the most enduring theoretical debates in all of science and philosophy. As we emphasized in Chapter 1, the most important distinction between environmental psychology and other fields is not the particular setting for behavior, nor even the content such as crowding, personal space, or perception, but rather, the perspective the field takes on studying its subject matter. In this chapter we will use the processes of perception to illustrate the distinctive approach of environmental psychology to some of these enduring theoretical issues.

Perceptual processes were among the earliest topics for nineteenth-century psychol-

Figure 3–1   Perception: Processing the sensory information encountered in everyday life

ogists as they tried to establish their infant field. Initially, many researchers attempted to understand how individuals differed in sensing lights, colors, or other phenomena. These researchers hoped that carefully trained subjects could learn to accurately report their sensory experiences. For example, a researcher might ask "In looking at this orange, is the sensation of color more or less important than the sensation of shape?" Soon, however, psychologists began to doubt the veracity of such introspective reports. Can a person really inspect and accurately report his or her own sensory experiences? Researchers began to insist that psychology was a science, and that science could only investigate observable (physical, behavioral) phenomena, not unobservable mental events. Another way of saying this is that psychology was moving away from subjective reports of personal experiences (known as **phenomenology**) toward a preoccupation with externally observable events as the only legitimate source of data (a position known as **empiricism**). New studies focused on biological events that led to sensations. The structures of the eyes or ears, for example, were seen as the neurological basis for the simple sensations generated by points of light or sound. Using this approach, scientists believe that they have now demonstrated that at least part of what we perceive is based on a simple, mechanical transmission of a sensory message from one part of the nervous system to another. For example, a point of light striking a small area on the eye's retina apparently begins a neural signal that moves through individual cells in several layers of the retina, to the thalamus (a structure located deep in the brain), and eventually, to the occipital lobe at the back of the brain. Two researchers (Hubel & Wiesel, 1968) eventually won a Nobel prize for their demonstration that certain small and identifiable areas of the brain become electrically stimulated by very specific patterns of light. For instance, one group of cells is stimulated when a horizontal line of light falls across an area of the retina, a different group of cells becomes stimulated when the line is vertical, and other cells seem to respond to movement going only in a certain direction. From this so-called primary visual receiving area in the back of the brain's cortex, messages spread to other adjacent parts of the parietal and temporal lobes of the brain. So we think your "mind's eye," as you read the words on this page, is partly in the very back of your head, but spread out over as much as 40 percent of your cerebral cortex (Goldstein, 1989).

Try to think of some place that is very special to you. Perhaps this is a place where you would like to take a close friend if he or she has not seen it. Perhaps this is a place known only to yourself, or perhaps the location is famous. It may be wild or urban, but what is most important is that it is special to you. Now that you have pondered for a few moments, consider a question. Do you think the methods of science and empiricism can capture all of the perceptual experiences that make the place meaningful? Even if they could adequately describe all of the physical characteristics, would they be able to understand the influence of this place on you? We think that you may be convinced that understanding environmental perception is quite a complex task, and one that may require a variety of modes of inquiry.

Ittelson and his colleagues (e.g., 1970, 1973, 1976, 1978) were among the first to focus on environmental perception. Ittelson (1978) notes that environmental perception includes cognitive (thinking), affective (emotional), interpretive, and evaluative components, all operating at the same time across several sensory modalities. As we perceive an environment, the cognitive processes involved might include what we can do in an environment, as well as visual, auditory, and other imagery of the scene. Moreover, we might expect to compare this environment with other places we have experienced or read

about in the past. When we say that perception involves reliance on experience and memory, we imply that cognitive processes are involved in perception (e.g., Neisser, 1976). Later in this chapter we will examine our memory for environments, especially as a basis for finding our way. In addition to cognitive processes, our feelings about the environment influence our perception of it, and our perceptions influence our feelings. To pick an extreme example, one person viewing a machine-cut swath in a forest might view it as an ugly scar, whereas another might see it as an attractive sign of jobs and prosperity. Thus, environmental perception includes both an assessment of what is in a scene, and an evaluation of the good and bad elements. These affective or evaluative components (some of which we reviewed in Chapter 2) and the beliefs that underlie them are the roots of the attitudes we hold toward an environment. In this chapter we will focus on perception as a process for gathering information about the world and as a source of affective responses and associations.

Environments are rich in stimuli; in fact, the environment contains more information than we can comprehend at once, so we must selectively process it. Right now, make a conscious effort to process all of the stimulation coming from the environment around you. You may hear the sounds of others, a cough, the turning of pages, or someone shifting positions. Can you feel the pressure of your chair, the temperature of the room, perhaps a draft from a nearby door? You may detect the odor of someone's perfume or the printer's ink on the pages of this book, and you may find yourself distracted by activity outside a window. On reflection, it is quite an accomplishment to make sense out of all of this confusion! Again, we foresee an important role for cognitive processes, specifically, *information processing*. As we will see in Chapter 4, an inability to process important information because of an information overload is one explanation for some of the detrimental effects environments have on us. On the other hand, we actually seek certain levels of comprehensible information. Perhaps you agree that this inclination may underlie our attraction to such apparently different environments as exciting amusement parks and informative museums.

Finally, the perceptual process involves actions by us. We bring expectations, experiences, values, and goals to an environment; it provides us with information; and we perceive it through activity. One part of this activity is simple exploration to orient ourselves in an environment (discussed in more detail in the second half of this chapter); another part is designed to find strategies for using the environment to meet needs and goals; and a third part is related to establishing confidence and feelings of security within the environment. Since social and cultural factors, such as sex roles, socioeconomic status, and exposure to modern architecture influence what one learns or what one has the opportunity to experience, it stands to reason that factors such as culture also influence perception.

PERSPECTIVES ON ENVIRONMENTAL PERCEPTION

Traditional Approaches to the Perception of Size, Depth, and Distance

Traditional laboratory investigations have focused on *object perception*—that is, the patterns of sensation that allow us to scan our memories and to recognize distinct objects with which we have had some prior experience (Ittelson, 1970, 1973, 1978; Kaplan & Kaplan, 1982). But the day-to-day challenges of life in the complex environments of the real world are not so simple. We must not only recognize objects, but also locate them in the context of three-dimensional space, to know how far away they are, how fast they are moving, and the importance of these ob-

jects to us (Kaplan, 1982). Thus, although environmental psychologists recognize that laboratory studies of simple stimuli offer a useful—and in fact necessary—foundation, they find their special challenge in the almost overwhelming complexity that characterizes real-world stimuli such as landscapes, buildings, and cities. Nevertheless, much of what we know of environmental perception rests on straightforward extensions of conventional perceptual theory. Consider the interacting experiences of size, distance, and depth. Among the most powerful cues (at least for those of us raised in North America or Europe) is **linear perspective**. It was not until the 1400s that artists discovered the depth-producing convention that lines that are parallel in a landscape will converge as they grow farther away. Receding railroad tracks are perhaps the most familiar example (Figure 3–2).

Forced perspective is an interesting three-dimensional application of the same principle. Figure 3–3 shows two buildings of

Figure 3–2 This railroad track is a powerful demonstration of linear perspective as a distance cue.

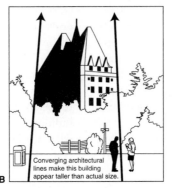

Figure 3–3   The Chateaux Laurier Hotel in Ottawa, Ontario (A). Methods for creating forced perspective (B). Disney's re-creation at Disney World (C).

similar architectural style. In fact, the building on the left (the Chateaux Laurier Hotel in Ottawa, Ontario) was the model for the building on the right (the Canadian building at Disney's Epcot Center). The center drawing shows how the designers used forced perspective to make this and other relatively small Disney buildings appear to be as tall as their grander inspirations. Of course there are a number of other examples of the use of linear perspective and other cues to create architectural effects. Occasionally, visual illusions or other sources of misinterpretation lead to less happy, even life-threatening consequences. Chapter 13 provides examples of such misinterpretations in aviation and other workplaces.

Holistic Analysis

One traditional goal of experimental psychology (and science in general) is to carefully control all possible causes of a phenomenon in an effort to simplify understanding. Much of what we know about human perception is based on laboratory investigations that control the variety and complexity of stimuli in order to more easily determine their cause. These procedures maximize what we called *internal validity* (see Chapter 1). For example, science has learned much from inspection of individual neurons in the human visual system. Perhaps some day we will fully

understand the steps of sensation as a cascade of simple, interacting, almost mechanical events. But is some of the richness of behavior lost in our attempts to simplify it? As we said in Chapter 1, a most important characteristic of environmental psychology is a desire to study environment-behavior relationships as *holistic units* rather than separating them into smaller component stimuli and responses. Consider a study of landscape perception like those discussed in Chapter 2 as an example. A fairly simple study might ask participants to rate the attractiveness of slide photographs; we might think of attractiveness as a dependent measure. But what are the independent or predictor variables? Colors in the photographs (there might be thousands)? Objects like trees, waterfalls, or animals? Weather conditions? Should we include the topographic relief created by mountains, plateaus, and river canyons as well as human intrusions like litter or pollution's haze? Add other modalities like smell and sound, and traditional experimental control over the individual stimuli seems absurd. But our desire to know about human reactions to the environment in which we participate does not seem absurd at all. We would really like to know what makes one landscape in all of its richness and complexity more attractive than another. Some more molar (larger) analysis seems necessary.

Whereas conventional approaches to perception often discuss how a sensory mechanism detects a single aspect of an object in the environment, in environmental perception we are concerned with a more holistic, encompassing process. The systems approach is one perspective that emphasizes this complex interaction of environmental stimuli and the personality of the perceiver which ultimately forms the experienced environmental unit. Although the patterns of mutual influence are complex, presumably the total system is a construction of these interacting but still separable parts (Altman & Rogoff, 1987). A **transactional approach** goes one step further and proposes that the system cannot be divided into separate elements or discrete relationships without losing information. Rather, the experienced environment is an event in time whose components are so intermeshed that no part is understandable without the simultaneous inclusion of other aspects of the instant. In Chapter 4 we will examine one of the best examples of a transactional approach, the ecological psychology of the late Roger Barker and his colleagues (Barker, 1968, 1979, 1987, 1990).

Gestalt Psychology

You may recognize that this emphasis on holistic, global responses is similar to the position taken in the first half of this century by the founders of the Gestalt school of perception. As you may know, the Gestalt psychologists rejected the notion that an understanding of human perceptual processes could be furthered by reducing these processes into smaller and smaller basic units. Instead, the founders of Gestalt psychology, Max Wertheimer, Wolfgang Kohler, and Kurt Koffka, concluded that the whole is different from just a simple sum of its component parts. Some of the earliest demonstrations of their **Gestalt principles** involved the apparent movement effect. Although both a child's flip book and motion pictures

are made up of dozens of stationary scenes, flashing pictures one after another creates perceived movement (Goldstein, 1989; Rock & Palmer, 1990). The animated sequence may be built of discrete scenes, but its impact can best be understood as a moving whole. Just as a melody is different from a collection of its component notes and a dance is different from its steps, a landscape is more than just an array of light particles. Shape and melody are examples of what Gestalt psychologists called *emergent properties*.

Gestalt psychologists attempted to specify rules by which we organize small parts into cohesive wholes and why some of these objects become the focus (*figures*) of our attention, and others the *ground*. These so-called "laws" of organization outlined by the Gestalt psychologists are discussed in most introductory psychology texts and in courses devoted to sensation and perception (see Figure 3–4). One overriding principle of organization the Gestalt psychologists called *Prägnanz*. Basically, this principle states that when there is some ambiguity in the visual

Figure 3–4 Examples of Gestalt Psychology's laws of organization. (A) Proximity: Do you see six lines or three pairs of lines? (B) Closure: Do you see a circle and square even though the figures are not complete? (C) Similarity: Do you see 25 letters or a pattern of X's and O's?

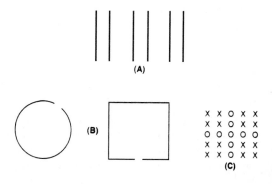

Figure 3–5 In this photograph several different buildings are unified by a common theme or style in their facades.

array, the viewer will perceive the simplest shape consistent with the information available (see Figure 3–5). Beyond a wealth of striking examples and illusions, however, the place of Gestalt theory in modern psychology's understanding of perception is unclear (Goldstein, 1989; Lang, 1987), but see Rock and Palmer (1990) for a readable, positive update. In general, the Gestalt principles of grouping have withstood the test of time, although the original explanations for them have not. One thing is more certain. Gestalt psychology has had a disproportionate influence on architects and other design professionals. In fact, Gestalt psychology is probably the most influential theory of perception on designers in this century (Lang, 1987). This prominence reveals a good deal about the needs of architects, and about the relationship between psychology and the design professions (see Chapter 11). An architect needs to understand the visual effect of his or her design. What elements of a building's shape will be perceived as dominant? Can a new building facade be harmoniously joined to an old one? Gestalt psychology recognizes the importance of holistic analy-

sis, and offers workable answers to some of these pragmatic questions.

NATIVISM VERSUS LEARNING

In Chapter 2 we introduced one of the oldest controversies in psychology. It concerns the degree to which human perception comes to us fairly automatically (**nativism**) versus the view that perception is highly dependent on learning through direct observation (another manifestation of empiricism). In psychology this controversy often focuses on nature (e.g., unchanging genetic influences) and nurture (learning) in human behavior. Perception of depth, and the sometimes attendant fear of heights, might illustrate both sides of the issue. We have already observed that the depth and size cues received from linear perspective appear to be at least partially constructed from our processing of learned cues. On the other hand, the Gestalt psychologists believed that perception was quite automatic, requiring little learning. As we will see, more recent theorists (e.g., Gibson, 1979) also propose that many aspects of perception, particularly the elements of depth perception called *texture gradients*, are unlearned and automatic to all humans with normally functioning visual systems.

Brunswik's Probabilism

One theory that seems particularly applicable to environmental perception is the probabilistic model of Egon Brunswik (1956, 1959). Brunswik's position would be on the learning side of our nativism–learning continuum. His approach, also known as the **lens model** (see Figure 3–6), envisions the perceptual process as analogous to a lens wherein stimuli from the environment become focused and perceived through our perceptual efforts. Brunswik differentiated between *distal* stimulus variables which are the source of incoming sensory patterns (a distant mountain, for instance) and *proximal* stimuli (the actual pattern of light on the retina of an observer's eye). The proximal stimulus includes a great deal of complexity. Embedded in this complexity is both redundant information and ambiguity about the

nature of the sensory world. Consider the world that lies behind this page as you read. Some things are completely covered by the book and are unknowable except in memory. Other objects may be partly occluded (perhaps part of your own hand if you are holding the edge of the book) and provide incomplete information. In noncontrived situations, your knowledge of the sensory word is almost always incomplete. The actual lens in Brunswik's model represents the mental processes that search for relevant cues and weight those that experience has demonstrated to be most important in drawing perceptual conclusions.

Perhaps an example will illustrate the fundamentals of Brunswik's model. Suppose that, like our fictional Cheryl and Craig, you and a friend are hiking a mountain trail in the wilderness of Montana. Suddenly you notice movement in the bushes to your right! Your perceptual processes become focused on gathering information from the environment so that you can identify the stimulus and decide on the appropriate behavior. In

Figure 3–6 Brunswik's Lens model. Environmental stimuli become focused through our perceptual efforts. Distal cues are based on objective features of the environment and are of different importance in accurate perception (ecological validity). These cues are, in turn, weighted and processed differently by individuals (cue utilization) in making perceptual judgments.

Adapted from Brunswik, E. (1965). Perception and the representative design of psychological experiments. Berkeley: University of California Press.

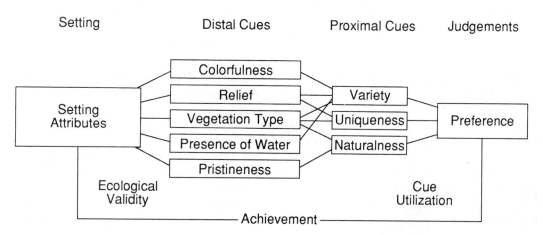

BRUNSWIK'S LENS MODEL

little more than an instant you decide to carefully back off from what you perceive to be a foraging grizzly. Seconds later your companion laughs, and points to a very small, albeit very loud, chipmunk. How did you make such a mistake? We know that not all stimuli presented by the environment are equally useful in accurate perception. Some of the information presented by the environment may be insufficient, superfluous, or even misleading. The noises coming from the bushes beside the trail provided useful, but not sufficient, information to make an accurate perceptual decision. Noise is one characteristic of animal movements, whether by a chipmunk or a grizzly bear, so it is one useful cue, but perhaps not as useful in this instance as knowing the animal's size. Each of the stimuli emanating from the environment might be assigned a weight probability based on its usefulness in supporting accurate perception. In Brunswik's terms, these stimuli vary in their ecological validity.

However, two observers might differ in their interpretation of the situation, even when each receives the very same stimulus array. You and your companion might weight the environmental information differently in making a best guess or probabilistic judgment. Perhaps you were just thinking of reports of grizzly bear attacks in nearby Glacier National Park, or perhaps your friend was daydreaming and did not even hear the noises. Thus, not only do certain environmental stimuli differ in their objective usefulness (**ecological validity**), but individuals may weight them more or less appropriately (**cue utilization**) because of past experiences, personality, or other differences. Rather than simply determining the judgments of the average observer, Brunswik's model fosters **policy capturing**, a procedure that determines the idiosyncratic patterns of weights assigned by individual judges (Craik & Appleyard, 1980). Subsequent analysis may reveal that certain individuals (perhaps possessing common background or personality

traits) share similar weighting profiles or policies, a valuable insight that might have been overlooked by traditional averaging techniques.

A concrete example of Brunswik's approach is provided by Stewart's (1987) attempt to develop an observer-based assessment of the visual air quality in Denver, Colorado. Referring once more to Figure 3–6, the environment of interest is a particular scene being viewed and rated by an observer. Certain attributes of this environment can be determined using objective physical measures. Objective attributes might include the concentration of particulates and other pollution in the air, the angle of the sun, sky conditions, or humidity. Presumably, these objective characteristics of the environment form the basis for ratings of subjective attributes such as the color of the air or the clarity of distant objects, and, in turn, these subjective attributes are weighted by individual observers in reaching their overall judgments of air quality. The researcher could investigate a variety of questions, including the contribution of various objective physical attributes to judgments of visual air quality, the importance of subjective attributes in making quality judgments, and individual differences in weighting these attributes.

Ecological Perception of the Environment

The perceptual experience consists of many "significances," or meaningful stimuli or events that reach our awareness. That is, we are most likely to notice those things of significance to us as members of the human species, perhaps because they help us to survive. A name for this perspective from the traditional study of perception is **functionalism**. According to this view (e.g., Kaplan & Kaplan, 1982), our perceptions are molded by the necessity to "get along" with the environment. For example, we compare present sensations with past ones in order to see if the present stimuli signal danger or serve as cues for food or shelter. Often theorists suggest that these functional processes have evolved biologically as part of our species' adaptation to environmental demands. Of course evolution implies change, but by emphasizing the importance of biological or genetic influences, these functional theories are quite nativistic with respect to the perceptions of an individual human.

Our discussion of perception of the environment (particularly from the functional perspective), would not be complete without considering J. J. Gibson's **ecological perception**. Gibson was critical of standard perceptual theory's emphasis on the processing of individual cues in static, "snapshot" visual images. According to Gibson (1950, 1966, 1979), rather than perceiving individual features or cues that we organize into recognizable patterns, we respond to (detect or tune in) meaning that already exists in an ecologically structured environment. We may overlook some of this embedded meaning, but it is readily available to an appropriately attuned organism mobile enough to experience it (see also Heft, 1981, 1989).

Let us reexamine Gibson's proposal. For Gibson, we are organisms wandering a surface between our medium (air for humans) and the substance of the earth. Figure 3–7 presents a fairly simple surface (with the irregularities of hills and most objects removed). Imagine yourself moving forward, right, or left through the illustration. The *texture gradient* of the surface provides *invariant information* that remains constant.

Figure 3–7 A landscape according to Gibson

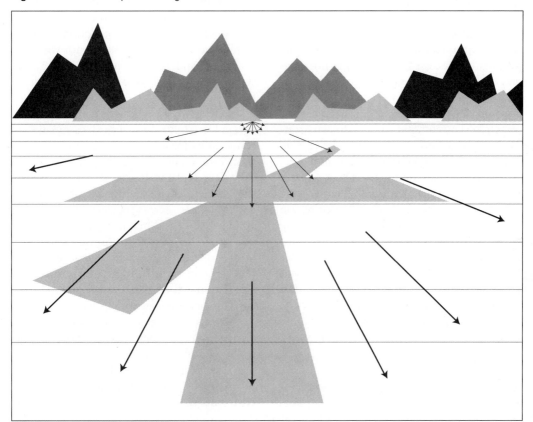

According to Gibson, invariant information remains part of the scene irrespective of the movement, or even the existence of an observer. For instance, the illustrated scene would be the same if you returned exactly to your starting vantage point, and even as you run forward, the texture gradient continues to stretch ahead of you. But unlike a snapshot, our visual world is constantly moving as we turn our heads, walk, run, or observe some other moving object. The changes in the optic array as we move through the environment stream by, providing powerful information about location, depth, the orientation of surfaces, and, of course, movement. One early application of his theory was to pilot training in the Second World War.

We have noted that the conventional approach to perception considers perception of the external environment as a function of a variety of interpretive psychological processes; that is, a stimulus activates a specific nervous system receptor, and the pattern of receptor stimulation is interpreted with the memory of past experiences to get information about the environment. From the conventional perspective, we have to interpret disconnected stimuli in order to construct something meaningful about the environment. Gibson considered these to be special, rather artificial circumstances. For him, perception of the environment is more direct and less interpretive than this. That is, perceptual patterns convey much information quite directly—without elaborate processing by higher brain centers. Furthermore, Gibson believed that perception is much more holistic, so that properties of the environment are perceived not as distinct points but rather as meaningful entities. Let us develop the Gibsonian approach to perception a bit further by exploring the concept of affordances.

Perception of Affordances

According to Gibson, we receive much valuable information directly through our perception of the environment. Gibson viewed organisms as actively exploring their environment, encountering objects in a variety of ways. Through this process, we experience the surface of an object, its texture, and angles from different perspectives. This allows us to perceive an object's invariant functional properties, in other words, "useful" properties of an object that do not change, such as "hardness." The *invariant functional properties* of objects as they are encountered in the course of an organism's active exploration are termed **affordances**. The notion of affordances will become clearer as we look at a few examples. If an object is solid rather than liquid or gaseous, if it is inclined toward the ground at an angle other than 90 degrees, and if at least part of it is higher than the organism, then that object affords shelter. If an object is solid and rigid, if it is raised off the ground, if its top surface is fairly horizontal to the ground, then the object affords sitting or "sittability." If an object is malleable, can be placed in the mouth whole or in pieces, and is of such biochemical substance as to provide nourishment, then it affords "eatability."

Obviously, what affords shelter, sittability, and eatability for a fish does not necessarily do so for a human; what affords these things for a human does not necessarily do so for an elephant. In this sense, affordances are species-specific (although there is, of course, overlap across species). Furthermore, an object affords different things to different species. Whereas a tree affords shelter to a bird and food to certain insects, it affords fuel (among other things) to humans. For this reason, affordances must be viewed from an ecological perspective.

From this perspective, we can see that affordances involve perceptions of the ecologically relevant functions of the environment. To perceive affordances of the environment is to perceive how one can interact with the environment. It is through perception of affordances that an organism can find its niche in the environment. An **ecological niche**, according to Gibson, is simply a set of affordances that are utilized. In this regard, humans possess a remarkable talent: We can alter an environment so that it affords almost anything we want—for example, more expensive shelters, more beautiful scenery, and so on. In doing so, we may change the affordances of that environment with respect to other humans and other organisms. When we dam a river to create a lake, which affords us water and recreation, we may also change the immediate environment so that it affords life support for fish and waterfowl but does not afford life support for groundhogs, bats, or for the farmer who lost his or her home and cropland to the lake. Perception of this changed environment, then, depends on the gain and loss of affordances for each organism. Certainly, many of the changes we humans have imposed upon our environment for our short-term benefit have had severe long-term consequences for both our species and others. Our skill in manipulating the affordances of our environments is both wonderful and dangerous.

Some Implications for Environmental Perception

In one sense, Brunswik's and Gibson's theories could have hardly been more different. Brunswik emphasized perception as a process of probabilistic calculations influenced by individual differences whereas Gibson insisted that perceptual "truth" lies in the environment and can be perceived directly with little or no complex interpretation. What they shared, however, was a belief that perception can best be understood by examining the complexities and challenges of perceivers in the real world. Like the Gestalt theorists, their emphasis on holistic, molar analysis anticipated the approach to perception that is most characteristic of modern environmental psychology.

A classic example of cultural differences in perception is based on the fact that certain cultures emphasize rectangular construction, and others employ curvilinear construction, or at least less rigor in erecting vertical and rectilinear walls (Allport, 1955; Allport & Pettigrew, 1957; Segall, Campbell, & Herskovits, 1966). As a result, members of cultures with "carpentered" environments see lines on two-dimensional surfaces in a different way than do members of cultures with less carpentered environments. Take the Müller-Lyer illusion depicted in Figure 3–8 as an example. To most of us, the horizontal line at the top appears longer than the one on the bottom, even though both lines actually are the same length. Apparently, because we live in an environment in which construction is rectangular, we infer three-dimensional space. The horizontal line at the bottom, however, appears to be closer than the diagonal lines and thus, appears to span less space than the line at the top. Members of African cultures that use rounded construction and pay less attention to rectilinear (straight line) corners tend not to be deceived by this illusion: Their culture and ecology do not require them to perceive intersecting diagonal lines as implying depth (see also Bartley, 1958).

Figure 3–8 The Müller-Lyer illusion. Which of the horizontal lines appears longer?

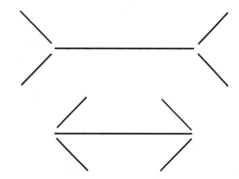

HABITUATION AND THE PERCEPTION OF CHANGE

It is apparent that environmental perception is a very complex and involving process. Because all we know of our world is filtered through perception, perceptual processes underlie much of the balance of this text. In this chapter we will select just a few topics that elaborate on this process and reveal something of the scope of the field. First, let us briefly examine habituation and the perception of change.

Thus far we have talked about perception without regard to time. That is, we have noted some of the principles and properties of environmental perception as if perception is constant from one moment to the next. Once we consider time as a variable in environmental perception, at least two important phenomena emerge: habituation (adaptation), and perception of change.

Habituation or Adaptation

What happens if a perceivable stimulus does not change across time? The answer involves what is known as **habituation** or **adaptation**: If a stimulus is constant, the response to it typically becomes weaker over time. Many who live near freeways, for example, at first find it difficult to sleep, but after a few nights they become habituated to the noise and have little trouble sleeping. Should they have guests overnight, however, the guests are likely to be bothered by the noise.

Explanations for adaptation or habituation tend to be either cognitive or physiological (Evans et al., 1982; Glass & Singer, 1972). Sometimes the distinction is made that "habituation" refers to a physiological process and "adaptation" to a cognitive process. Often, however, the two terms are used interchangeably.

Physiological explanations of habituation emphasize the notion that the receptors themselves fire less frequently upon repeated presentation of a stimulus. Cognitive explanations of the phenomenon propose a cognitive reappraisal of the stimulus as less deserving of attention after repeated presentation. The first time you hear a loud noise, you allocate considerable attention to it to find out what it is and to determine whether it is a potential source of threat. Once you know that it is a train, a trash truck, or your neighbor's car, however, you probably evaluate it as nonthreatening to your well-being and thus attend to it less. However, from a cognitive perspective, our example may reflect more of a response bias than a perceptual shift. That is, rather than actually perceiving the noise as less noxious, nearby residents may simply learn to respond to it less intensely or less frequently (e.g., Evans et al., 1982).

Adaptation is not always successful in eliminating unpleasant environmental stimuli, of course. If the stimulus is too unpleasant, it may well continue to be perceived as annoying (e.g., Loo & Ong, 1984). Furthermore, as we will discuss in more detail in Chapters 4 and 5, even adaptation that appears successful may require the mobilization of the body's physical or cognitive resources and eventually contribute to a general breakdown that may be manifested in stress disorders.

An important factor in adaptation, also discussed in Chapters 4 and 5, is the predictability or regularity of the stimulus. We are more likely to adapt to a constant hum in the background than to the irregular noise of a jackhammer. Bursts of noise that come at regular or predictable intervals are easier to adapt to than unpredictable stimuli, but more difficult to adapt to than constant stimuli. Once we adapt to a stimulus and the stimulus ceases, as in the interval between bursts of noise, our adaptation to the stimulus also dissipates somewhat. When the stimulus recurs, we must adapt again. Furthermore, unpredictable stimuli require that more attention be allocated for evaluation of the stimuli as threatening or nonthreatening. Thus, predictability is an important variable in the adaptation process.

Perception of Change

If we readily adapt to environmental stimulation, will we perceive change in such things as air pollution and urban blight? If we live in an area where air pollution is high, and we adapt to it, how can we perceive changes in the level of pollution? Sommer (1972) suggests that the answer lies in the **Weber-Fechner function** of psychophysics. This function, derived from the research of the late nineteenth century, is based on the amount of incremental increase or decrease in intensity of a stimulus that is required before a difference is detected between the new and old intensities. Stated simply, this law says that the intensity of a new stimulus required for it to be perceived as different from the present stimulus is proportionate to the present stimulus. To use an economic example, there seems to be more of a difference between one and two dollars than between 1,000,001 and 1,000,002 dollars. It takes only a small increment to detect a difference in very low-intensity stimuli but a much larger increment is needed for high-intensity stimuli. This function (though not as mathematically accurate as more modern psychophysical functions) generally applies to all forms of stimulation, including light, sound, pressure, and smell. Sommer suggests that the law applies not just to individual stimuli in a laboratory but to urban pollution as well. That is, a community with little pollution might become alarmed when clouds of brown smog suddenly appear, but large urban areas with heavy smog should require extremely high levels of additional pollution before becoming alarmed. Similarly, we might expect strip-zoning in small communities where careful neighborhood planning exists to be noticeable enough to spur the community to action against such blight. Larger communities where strip zoning is commonplace, however, would probably not care as much when one more fast-food chain appears on the strip.

Sommer proposes that we take advantage of the Weber-Fechner phenomenon in changing detrimental environmental behaviors. Any time we are asked to change our lifestyles to preserve the environment, there is resistance. But what if the change in lifestyle is so small as to go unnoticed? We might be able to make subtle changes that have a great impact on the environment. Requiring that beverages be sold in returnable containers, for example, is not as drastic a measure as banning beverages in all containers. Requiring that recyclable containers be separated from other trash is even a smaller step than banning nonreturnable containers, and so on. In other words, if the perceivable change is small, we will be less resistant to it than if it is large.

Furthermore, change that is rapid (such as walking or burning) is more easily detected than change that is slow (such as growth). There is ecological survival value in knowing that one's environment is changing rapidly. Imagine, for example, the importance of prompt reaction if a forest fire endangers your home. Unfortunately, comparable damage that occurs slowly (as when pollution from cities kills trees), is less noticeable.

◼ ENVIRONMENTAL COGNITION

The rich perceptions that result from our constant encounters with stimuli from the environment shape our experiences, but perception without cognition would leave us fixed in the present instant of time. Although perceptual theorists differ in the importance they place on memories and cognitions, almost all would agree that perceptions are both shaped by our experiences and expectations from the past and are a primary source of our thoughts in the future. Perhaps it is surprising that psychologists have historically shied away from discussing such "cognitive" matters as memory and mental images. Their reluctance may reflect the objection of behaviorists and others to the study of the "unobservable and unmeasurable" events that occur as we process mental information. Relatively recently, some psychologists have "rediscovered" these complex operations of memory, thinking, problem solving, and imagery (see Evans, 1980; Gärling & Evans, 1991; Golledge, 1987; Kitchin, 1994; McDonald & Pellegrino, 1993; Neisser, 1976). Directly observable or not, information from memory gives us important clues to those aspects of the environment that are most salient or important to us. Have you ever been lost? Particularly in remote regions, people report that being lost is a threat to survival, and a profoundly troubling challenge to our self-confidence. When applied to large-scale environments, memorable features may be useful for finding our way from one place to another and back again. Easily remembered environments are easier to travel through, and the opportunities they provide are more apparent. Although the most direct example of a practical reason for cognitive maps is to avoid being lost, researchers believe an understanding of these cognitive structures can also offer powerful insights into a variety of other questions, both practical and theoretical. An understanding of the characteristics of environments that make them more memorable may be important to the success of designers and planners in achieving their design goals (see Chapter 11). For instance, simply being more comprehensible may make environments more aesthetically pleasing (see Chapter 2). Mapping techniques may also offer managers valuable clues about the geographical distribution of areas that are pleasant or unpleasant, familiar or unfamiliar, or dangerous versus safe (e.g., Brantingham & Brantingham, 1993). Canter and Larkin (1993) have even used knowledge of cognitive maps to help British police predict the hiding places of criminals! Finally, inspection of environmental memories may offer a way to "get inside our heads" for insights into the way humans store, process, and retrieve information. Many find this to be one of the most fundamental, fascinating, and controversial areas in all of psychology.

AN INFORMAL MODEL OF SPATIAL COGNITION

The ability to capitalize on a rich and varied environment is at least partially dependent on the human propensity to store geographical information. Humans have long sought to represent this information physically as maps. The oldest known map dates from 2500 B.C. (Beck & Wood, 1976). Useful as maps and charts may be, however, people more typically travel through a familiar environment without these aids. How is this accomplished? Many psychologists suggest that all humans carry with them an organized mental representation of their environment, commonly referred to as a *cognitive map*. Simply stated, a **cognitive map** is a mental framework that holds some representation for the spatial arrangement of the physical environment. However, the term "cognitive map" may be an unfortunate coinage (e.g., Kitchin, 1994; Kuipers, 1982). Is the cognitive map something a research participant draws to represent his or her spatial memory? Is it a stored image that roughly corresponds to the actual spatial environment? Is it simply a metaphor: a mental structure that is used as if it were a physical map? Is it simply an unfortunate, but convenient fiction (Kitchin, 1994)? We will cautiously adopt the term "cognitive map," but we caution you to think of it as an inexact, perhaps even inaccurate description of the spatial environment.

No matter what the status of these "maps," it does seem clear that they are not the same as a cartographer's in either physical form or in content. They are sketchy, incomplete, distorted, simplified, and idiosyncratic. We might think of them as composed of three elements: places, the spatial relations between places, and travel plans (Gärling, Böök, & Lindberg, 1984). In this instance, *place* refers to the basic spatial unit to which we attach information like name and function, and perceptual characteristics such as affective quality or affordances (see Chapters 2, 12, and 13 for a somewhat more complex understanding of place). Depending on the scale of the particular cognitive map we are consulting, a place may be a

room, a building, a town, a nation, or a planet. In addition, cognitive maps reflect *spatial relations*, such as the distance and direction between places and the inclusion of one place within another, as your room is inside a building which is itself within the boundaries of a town, and so on. Finally, Gärling et al. (1984) propose the concept of *travel plans* as an important bridge between the mental world of cognitive maps and the navigation and other behaviors that they support.

Whether maps are stored in the mind or on paper, we might ask, "What do maps do for us?" We have already suggested that a primary use is to facilitate *wayfinding*. **Wayfinding** is the adaptive function that allows us to move through an environment efficiently to locate valuable items like food, shelter, or meeting places within the environment (E.g., Downs & Stea, 1977; Evans, 1980; Kaplan & Kaplan, 1982). This leads us to propose an informal model (see Figure 3–9) which emphasizes travel from one place to another as a primary goal of spatial

Figure 3–9 An informal model of spatial cognition. Instructions from other humans, printed maps, and memories of past travels help an individual form an action plan for a proposed journey. The success or failure of this plan as it is carried out becomes stored in memory and leads to place associations, future travel plans, and an evolving cognitive map for future reference.

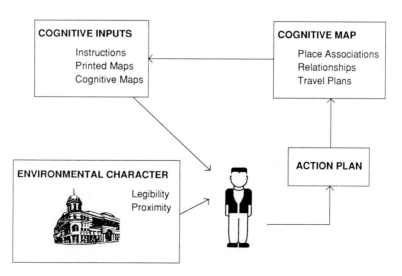

cognition. Before we begin a journey, we construct an action plan, that is, a strategy or itinerary for our movements (Gärling et al., 1986; Russell & Ward, 1982). Our plan will need to include some sort of information about the relative locations of places. Without this information we would have to search haphazardly, hitting or missing desired locations in a very inefficient way. In a new environment we may need to depend on a physical reference such as an atlas or a friendly passerby in order to formulate our travel plan (of course, we may later use our own cognitive maps to communicate locations to others and to understand others' communications about location to us). Being able to "visualize" the directions someone gives us, and associating the directions with familiar landmarks and paths enhances our wayfinding ability. In the absence of such physical aids or in well-known environ-ments, we consult the spatial representation in our memory, our cognitive map.

Which comes first: the cognitive map or the first wayfinding event? Notice that although our figure recognizes a cognitive map as a source of information for the first construction of plans, acquisition of the map is itself the result of previous experience in the environment. Somewhat arbitrarily we begin our discussion with the stored information residing in cognitive maps. We will first review several early studies that helped to establish an interest in spatial cognition and some of the methods employed by modern researchers. Then we will examine the way distortions in our memories and the process of acquisition offer clues to the underlying structure of spatial information. Finally, we will investigate the application of these cognitive representations to the process of wayfinding.

COGNITIVE MAPS

The topic of cognitive mapping has fascinated not only environmental and cognitive psychologists, but also researchers in geography, anthropology, and environmental planning and design. Cognitive maps are a very personal representation of the familiar environment that we all experience. Take a few moments to think about the layout of your campus. Try to imagine several vistas and the paths you most frequently take. Now on a clean sheet of paper try to draw a sketch map of the campus showing important features so that a stranger could use your sketch to find his or her way around. This is, of course, your personal cognitive map. You will probably want to refer to it often as you continue reading this chapter.

HISTORY OF COGNITIVE MAPPING

Cognitive maps have attracted the attention of researchers for many decades (e.g., Trow-bridge, 1913). Modern study of these maps has its most direct roots in the work of E. C. Tolman (1948) who described the way in which rats learn to "map" the environment of an experimental maze. Tolman's basic strategy over a number of experiments was to first train rats to take a particular path in a maze in order to reach a food reward. When the path was later blocked, the rats seemed able to switch to another previously unused path that led toward the goal. Some rats would choose a path never before used and pass up one that had been reinforced if the new path was a more direct route to the goal box (Tolman, 1948; Tolman, Ritchie, & Kalish, 1946). Thus, the rats seemed to have learned not just a series of turns or responses, but also a general idea of the location of the reward relative to the starting position. In order to describe this place information that his rats had apparently learned, Tolman coined the term "cognitive map."

An Image of the City: Kevin Lynch

At first few investigators were interested in pursuing the study of cognitive maps. Although it would be an exaggeration to say that Tolman's work was forgotten, it was not until the publication of *The Image of the City* by the urban planner Kevin Lynch (1960) that there was widespread interest in understanding the formation and use of humans' cognitive maps.

As a planner, Lynch was among the first in his field to try to understand such subjective concerns as people's feelings about the quality of their environment and how their perceptions could be used in environmental design. *The Image of the City* remains a classic reference in cognitive mapping (Langdon, 1984). In it, Lynch simultaneously established a field of inquiry, a methodological approach to data collection, and a vocabulary for describing features of cognitive maps—a vocabulary that is still widely used. For both historical and pragmatic reasons then, Lynch's approach seems to merit a detailed discussion.

Lynch based his intial ideas about cognitive maps on data gathered in Boston, Jersey City, and Los Angeles. Lynch asked participants in his studies to draw sketch maps of their city, to give detailed descriptions of certain routes such as the path from home to work, and to list the most distinctive and vivid elements of their respective cities. Upon comparing these data, he identified different elements that seemed common across the three different cities (see Figure 3–10).

Elements of Cognitive Maps

Return to your sketch map of campus. Are there obvious streets and buildings designated on it? Are there broad areas you could designate as "fraternity row" or "dormitory area" or "athletic complex"? Lynch found that five categories of features could be used to describe and analyze cognitive maps: paths, edges, districts, nodes, and landmarks. **Paths** are shared travel corridors such as streets, walkways, or riverways. **Edges** are limiting or enclosing features that tend to be linear but are not functioning as paths, such as a seashore or wall. Notice that in some instances one person's path (the rail line of a commuter train) may be another person's edge (if the rail line divides a town). **Districts** are larger spaces of the cognitive maps that have some common character such as "Fraternity Row," or the "Chinatown" found in many cities. **Nodes** are major points where behavior is focused, typically associated with the intersections of major paths or places where paths are terminated or broken, such as a downtown square, a traffic circle, or the interchange of two freeways. Finally, **landmarks** are distinctive features that people use for reference points. Usually, landmarks are visible from some distance, as in the case of the Washington Monument or a tall building in a city. Can you identify examples of these five categories on your campus map?

Additional Early Observations

The basic elements (paths, landmarks, nodes, edges, districts) outlined by Lynch seem well established (Aragones & Arredondo, 1985; Evans, 1980), although some have suggested that these elements are most applicable to environments on the scale of cities (for which Lynch developed them) rather than smaller or larger units of analysis. Lynch was part of the team that helped to maintain the delightful pedestrian corridor stretching from Boston's Commonwealth Avenue, through the Public Garden and Boston Common, and (with minor breaks) all the way to a revitalized Boston Harbor. Central in the plan is the Quincy Market (see Figure 3–11), a successful downtown redevelopment that attracts both tourists and residents. Other early researchers who were inspired by Lynch noticed stylistic differences in people's cognitive

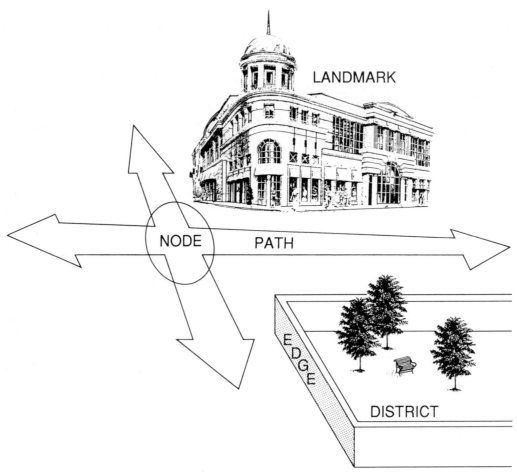

Figure 3–10   A diagram illustrating all five of the major elements in a cognitive map.
After Lynch, K. (1960). The image of the city. *Cambridge, MA: M.I.T. Press.*

maps. Lynch's associate Donald Appleyard (1970), for example, used sketch maps to evaluate the images of residents in a city in eastern Venezuela. These maps seemed to fit into one of two categories: those predominantly made up of elements that one might encounter sequentially in traveling from one place to another, such as paths (**sequential maps**), or those that instead emphasize spatial organization (a common term for this type of bird's-eye view is **survey knowledge**) such as landmarks or districts (Appleyard called these **spatial maps**; see Figure 3–12).

At least for these city dwellers, Appleyard reported that most maps were sequential, that is, rich in paths and nodes. As we will see, this interest in the acquisition of cognitive spatial knowledge and the distinction between sequential and survey knowledge remains very current. The qualitative differences between sequential or route maps or survey maps may be indicators of shifts in the underlying knowledge structure that occur as children move through different stages of thought or as adults acquire more detailed knowledge of a new environment.

Figure 3–11 Quincy Market in Boston, MA. A successful marketplace that profited from Lynch's application of cognitive mapping research

CURRENT PERSPECTIVES

More and more researchers began to discover cognitive mapping in the following decades, leading to the present variety of research goals and methods all described loosely by the terms "cognitive map" or "spatial cognition." As we said, cognitive mapping has evolved from several disciplines, especially psychology, planning, and geography. This reflects the excitement of interdisciplinary research so characteristic of environmental psychology (see Gärling & Golledge, 1993). At least partly because of differences between these disciplines, however, the general topic of cognitive mapping is a loosely organized literature based on a variety of methods and research goals (Kitchin, 1994).

One might think of an individual's finished cognitive map as representing a personal understanding of his or her environment. Certainly some features of the physical environment possess characteristics that are likely to cause them to be perceived as more important or distinctive, and thus, more likely to be stored in memory. Planners have been especially concerned with these physical characteristics (Gärling & Evans, 1991; Kaplan & Kaplan, 1978, 1982, 1989; Kitchin, 1994; Wohlwill, 1973, 1976a). Often the features of concern to these researchers are those that make an environment legible (see Figure 3–13). **Legibility**, another term popularized by Kevin Lynch, reflects the degree to which an environment is easily learned and remembered. Legibility may be

Figure 3–12 Idealized examples of sequential (left) versus spatial cognitive maps.
After Appleyard, D. (1972). Styles and methods of structuring a city. Environment and Behavior, 2, *100–118.*

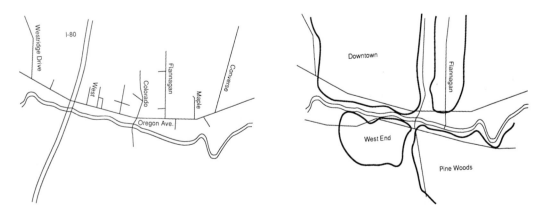

Figure 3-13   Scenes that allow aerial or long-range perspective are often rated as highly legible.

so important that it affects our emotional reactions to the environment. Indeed, in Chapter 2 we discussed legibility as one important predictor of landscape preference.

In addition to the physical characteristics of a city or rural environment itself, you might expect that different individuals will place varying weights on certain environmental features. For example, you are likely to know more about the area of a college campus nearest your dorm or along your most frequent path to class. We might expect your map to be somewhat different from a person's living in a different location or from that belonging to a faculty member. Almost all researchers agree on the importance of these individual differences in experience, but this has been a particularly important topic for psychologists.

METHODS OF STUDYING COGNITIVE MAPS

Given the variety of disciplines and specialties that have found interest in the general topic of cognitive mapping, you may not be surprised to learn that there are almost as many methodological techniques for gathering and analyzing cognitive maps as there are researchers. This diversity is exciting,

but often the source of serious difficulties because data gathered using one method cannot easily be compared with data produced by another. In fact, these methodological problems may be among the most serious faced by researchers in the area (Evans, 1980; McDonald & Pellegrino, 1993). As we will see, Evans was correct in asserting that methodological studies are sorely needed to compare different procedures for accuracy and utility. These remarkable differences prevent the slow accretion of the data base that should form the foundation of future research; certainly these differences will make our review of the field more difficult. Let us begin by describing some of the most common methodological approaches.

Sketch Maps

As you recall, Kevin Lynch (1960) employed several methods in his early investigations of people's responses to the spatial environments of Los Angeles, Jersey City, and Boston. His primary method, however, was to ask subjects to draw a **sketch map** of their city—a map drawn on paper representing their view of the city layout (Figure 3-14). This approach has remained among the most popular, and was responsible for establishing the vocabulary of cognitive mapping terms

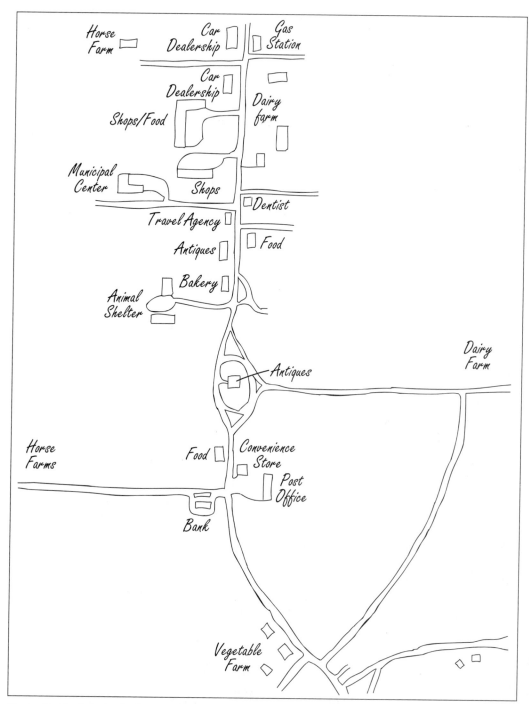

Figure 3–14 A student's sketch map of her hometown

such as paths, landmarks, districts, nodes, and edges. Sketch maps provide a rich source of data. They have several liabilities, however, and these seem to become more and more serious as researchers become more sophisticated in their research questions.

Sketch maps are flawed if observed differences in them are not primarily the result of differences in the mental maps that they are meant to measure. We have already observed that sketch maps require participants to take a perspective that places them in the air above the terrain being mapped—a perspective they are unlikely to have experienced. It is quite possible that drawing ability (Blaut & Stea, 1974), or experience with maps (Beck & Wood, 1976; Dart & Pradham, 1967), contaminates the maps produced by subjects. If so, those with sophisticated drawing skills will be more able to express their knowledge on paper.

Sketch maps may be as difficult to interpret as they are to draw. Consider the task of a researcher faced with the job of analyzing your sketch map along with those drawn by others in your area. Should the analysis include a list of named buildings or other landmarks and paths? Probably, but can the researcher correctly identify unlabeled (but drawn) buildings and streets? What if they appear on a map but in the wrong place? The researcher may notice **distortions**: streets that intersect at the wrong angle, for instance, or missing curves in rivers; but how can these distortions be quantified? In spite of these liabilities, sketch maps are still common. They generate extremely rich data in a manner that usually seems to be ecologically valid (realistic and reasonable). In fact, sketch maps are probably about as valid and reliable as other methods of assessing spatial knowledge (Blades, 1990; Newcombe, 1985).

Mapping Reactions to Remembered Environments

Geographers like Peter Gould and Rodney White (1982) present a different approach

to mental maps. Whereas the primary focus of the methods presented so far is to reproduce the person's mentally stored image of an environment, Gould's approach recovers not a person's cognitive map, but rather characteristics or qualities assigned to places within a person's environment. These are compiled and subsequently represented graphically on a map. Various statistical approaches have been employed, but all depend on asking subjects to rate or rank a number of different points according to some evaluative dimension, such as preference as a place of residence. The final results can be superimposed as shaded regions (these may correspond loosely to Lynch's districts) on an accurate basemap. These shaded regions represent the collective assessments of subjective qualities such as attractiveness (Gould & White, 1982; Lloyd & Steinke, 1986), or familiarity (e.g., Gale et al., 1990), and can be on virtually any scale. For example, Figure 3–15 shows Gould and White's desirability ratings for areas of the United States based on data collected from California residents. Notice the areas of high preference include the West Coast, Colorado, and New England. On the other hand, the Deep South and South Dakota receive lower ratings. How would residents of a different location, say the Deep South, respond? As you can learn from Figure 3–15, people tend to like their own regions, even if others in the nation are less favorably impressed. This seems reasonable, if for no other reason than self-selection.

Although the results of these geographical studies of preferences provide visually interesting summaries of people's evaluations of regions, some (e.g., Golldege, 1993) conclude that they are less successful as predictive or explanatory devices. Nevertheless, you might like to turn briefly to Chapter 11 to inspect Figure 11–13 where we demonstrate the use of a similar geograhical mapping technique as part of the planning process on a small college campus.

Figure 3–15 A preference map of the United States as reported by California residents.

Recognition Tasks

In his early investigations of residents' images of Boston, Kevin Lynch also asked participants to report whether they recognized photos of landmarks which were interspersed in a collection of pictures of unfamiliar locations. Lynch seems to have included this **recognition task** as a reliability check for his more familiar sketch map procedure. Stanley Milgram and his associate (Milgram & Jodelet, 1976) revived this approach because it avoids many of the problems inherent in having people with varying abilities draw sketch maps. Unfortunately, the procedure limits our ability to compare the orientations and geographical distances between spatial elements that are often evident both in various mapping techniques and in direct distance estimates as discussed below. In addition, this technique emphasizes *recognition* (the ability to recognize a place you have seen before) over *recall*, which asks you to remember and reproduce as much as you can with-

out the assistance of photos to jog your memory. To illustrate, would you typically draw and label the location of your favorite dry cleaner on a sketch map of your hometown? We predict that you usually would not. Would you recognize the same dry cleaning establishment from a picture of it? Probably. An emphasis on recognition and recall is not necessarily a liability. Some researchers (e.g., Passini, 1984) believe that recognition tasks more closely approximate the way most of us deal with movement within familiar environments (we will return to this issue in our discussion of wayfinding later in this chapter). Still, it should be clear that these recognition tasks are quite different from the standard sketch-map technique, and thus, not directly comparable.

Distance Estimates and Statistical Map Building

A number of researchers have also employed an approach that avoids sketch mapping by asking people to simply estimate the distances between locations in a large-scale environment. Of course these distances probably represent some of the information included in a person's sketch map, and being able to estimate distance is an important need for someone wanting to travel in his or her environment. One well-known statistical approach is **multidimensional scaling**, a statistical procedure in which participants estimate the distances between a number of buildings or other locations in the environment. Given the distance estimate between each point and each of a number of other points, a computer can generate something resembling a map by optimally placing each location on a two-dimensional grid so as to most closely account for each component distance estimate. You might be able to imagine one informal form of this scaling without knowledge of the underlying mathematics. If you were to ask a group of your friends to estimate the distance between each pairing of 20 buildings, you could calculate the mean estimated distance between each pair of locations. Now, cut a piece of yarn to a scaled length representing each distance, and stretch out all of the yarns so that they connect to tacks (representing the buildings). If all of your friends were absolutely accurate for each distance estimate, the procedure should generate an accurate map. Of course, consistent distortions would be interesting too. For instance, your friends might consistently exaggerate the distance of unpleasant or uncommon travel paths.

Although multidimensional scaling eliminates some of the problems of other methods (e.g., differences in drawing skills), it too has problems. Later in this chapter we will encounter one of the most serious: Increasing evidence indicates that a person's estimate of the distance from point A to point B is not necessarily the same as his or her estimate of the distance from point B to point A!

Our description might have prompted you to consider other problems. Unlike an unbounded sketch map, the procedure we have described focused not on *what* paths or landmarks a person remembers but on the estimated distances between locations presented by the researcher. In general, distance estimates may be more easily quantified than sketch maps, but they also lack some of the intuitive ecological or face validities.

ERRORS IN COGNITIVE MAPS

Types of Errors

Cognitive maps are rough approximations rather than perfect representations of the physical environment. In fact, we can identify several sources of error that frequently occur in them. First, cognitive maps tend to be incomplete. We often leave out minor paths and details, but sometimes we even omit districts and landmarks. Second, we often distort our representation of the environment by placing things too close together, too far apart, or aligning them improperly. In a manner quite similar to the Gestalt principles of good form, people seem to simplify patterns of paths and space to make them as comprehensible as possible (de Jonge, 1962). For example, circles, lines, and right angles are more easily used and remembered than quarter-circles and complex curves. Other investigators have at least partially confirmed de Jonge's hypothesis. We tend to represent nonparallel paths as being parallel, nonperpendicular paths as being perpendicular, and curved paths as being straight (Appleyard, 1969, 1970; Byrne, 1979; Evans, 1980; Lynch, 1960; Milgram & Jodelet, 1976). Most errors in cognitive maps of cities occur at street intersections where people have a tendency to misestimate the size of intersection angles. Acute intersection angles are often overestimated and obtuse angles are underestimated. Figure 3–16 shows an intersection in a small town. As you might expect from our discussion, the intersection is

Figure 3–16 A nonperpendicular intersection in a small town that is remembered as perpendicular by even long-time residents.

incorrectly depicted as a right angle in almost all cognitive maps of the area. Perhaps the error was compounded in this example by the designers of two of the buildings adjacent to the intersection. The building on the left (a bowling alley) actually matches the acute angle of its side of the intersection, whereas the building on the right matches the obtuse angle of its street boundaries. The irregularities of the buildings come as a complete surprise to even long-time residents of the village.

People also have a tendency to overestimate the size of familiar areas in their cognitive maps (see Figure 3–17). For example, Milgram and Jodelet (1976) found that Parisians seem to increase the size of their home neighborhood out of proportion with the rest of Paris.

A third type of error involves **augmentation,** or the addition of nonexistent features to a map. Appleyard (1970) provides a

classic example of these augmentations. A European engineer visiting Guyana included a nonexistent railroad line in his sketch map because experience led him to predict a rail connection between a steel mill and a mining port. In this instance, the engineer's experience led him to infer a logical, but nonexistent, map component. Notice that this same phenomenon (sometimes referred to as *inferential structuring*) may often lead subjects to make correct assumptions, but these may properly be called augmentations if the person's cognitive map represents features that have never actually been experienced. In these instances, the experimenter is unlikely to recognize the augmentation, and will miscode an interesting error as an accurate response.

Altogether, then, our cognitive maps are clearly not always very accurate representations of the physical environment. Understanding the sources of these errors may well

Figure 3-17   People tend to overestimate the size of familiar areas. Here is a humorous example of the way our cognitive maps can be affected by where we live.

give us insights into the effect of individual differences in such factors as experience, age, skill, or personality. Furthermore, some researchers are using insights gained from either the errors people make in spatial cognition tasks, or differences in the speeds at which features can be recalled, to learn more about the basic processes underlying human memory.

Familiarity and Socioeconomic Class

The types of errors in our maps, as well as the degree of detail in them, vary according to several factors. As you might expect, a number of studies have shown that the more familiar you are with an environment, the more accurate and detailed are your cognitive maps of it (e.g., Appleyard, 1970, 1976; Evans, 1980; Gärling, Böök, & Ergezen, 1982; Hart & Moore, 1973). In general, long-term residents draw richer and more accurate maps (Beck & Wood, 1976). For

example, Holahan (1978) found that students drew more complete and detailed maps of the parts of campus they use more frequently. Interestingly, however, Beck found that three- to seven-year residents drew better maps than did natives (those living in the mapped area for more than 15 years) or newcomers (those in residence for fewer than three years). Apparently, natives have a wider exposure to the city, and thus, draw their maps from several points of reference using several coding schemes. Beck hypothesized that this complexity and richness may make a native's map unadaptively rigid. Even familiarity with a particular type of environment can be helpful when you encounter a new situation that has at least some familiar characteristics. For example, Kaplan (1976) found that prior experience with a natural environment increased accuracy in locating such features as distinct pine trees and hills.

Several authors report that familiarity

probably explains the frequent observation that people from higher socioeconomic status groups draw more thorough maps than the poor (e.g., Appleyard, 1976; Orleans, 1973). That is, upper- and middle-class individuals probably have more experience with broader areas of a city than lower-class individuals whose mobility is restricted, primarily by the lack of easy access to transportation. In the classic study, Donald Appleyard reported that motorists (generally from the upper class) had the most sophisticated maps of a Venezuelan town, whereas those forced to walk produced less sophisticated sketches. Public transportation users fall somewhere in between (Beck, 1971). In sum, those with more travel experience make better sketch maps (Beck & Wood, 1976). Even more important than just being mobile, those who must attend to the passing environment (drivers, for instance) are more likely to process street names, directions, addresses, and distances. Thus, public transportation users who may well travel great distances but attend only to the passing sequence of stops do not produce the richness or accuracy of the cognitive maps of drivers. In sum, the longer we have experience with an area and the more movable we are within it, the more thorough our cognitive maps.

Perhaps it is only "common sense" that the quantity of information stored in memory increases with exposure, and that the opportunity to experience an environment differs by socioeconomic class, age, and perhaps, gender. It is important not to underestimate the value of these observations, however, nor their usefulness for planners and geographers. Nevertheless, perhaps a more interesting area for psychological research centers not just on the importance of familiarity and experience in adding to the quantity of stored information, but also on the qualitative changes in cognitive maps (and the memory storage and retrieval processes underlying them). Some early suggestions of such qualitative changes can be found in Appleyard's (1970) study in Venezuela. You will recall that Appleyard distinguished between *sequential* sketch maps emphasizing paths and nodes and *spatial* maps featuring a high proportion of landmarks and districts. Appleyard noted that maps were more spatial for long-term residents than for newcomers, and that spatial elements were more prominent in familiar areas of the city. More recent research has systematically investigated this phenomenon. Evans, Marerro, and Butler (1981) and Gärling et al. (1981) report that the basic path and node structure appears to be learned first, and then, as an individual spends more time in the environment, he or she fills in other details such as landmarks. Thus, as an individual becomes more familiar with an environment, his or her cognitive map of it becomes more spatial. Devlin (1976) also supports the primacy effect for path structure in learning new environments, again suggesting that familiarity can lead to more spatially oriented maps.

On the other hand, Heft (1979a) reported that adults rely more on landmarks to learn a route through a novel path network the first time they traverse it as compared with later occasions. This would seem to be the reverse of the path-primacy effect. Perhaps elements such as landmarks are used for wayfinding, but are not always represented in sketch maps. In support of this view are several comparisons between adults and children that suggest that one important difference between the maps drawn by people of different ages is that adults are more likely to attend to landmarks that lie at critical points on a route, such as the point at which one has to make a turn, than are children.

Gender Differences

Do males and females differ in their cognitive mapping abilities? Several researchers (e.g., Maccoby & Jacklin, 1974) have reported that males may possess superior visual and spatial skills, at least on paper-and-pencil tasks. If this generalization is true, one might expect males to be superior in their ability to draw complete and accurate cognitive maps. There is also some evidence (Bryant, 1982) that having "a good sense of direction" is more important to the self-esteem of males than it is for females. If so, one might expect males to be superior to females for motivational reasons, even if they possess no native superiority.

Some researchers have found evidence for gender differences in the final product of cognitive mapping exercises, although they conclude that these sex differences are most likely due to differences in familiarity with an area (e.g., Evans, 1980). Appleyard (1976), for example, found men's maps to be slightly more accurate and extensive than women's, but attributed this difference to the higher exposure of men to the city. Some researchers have given subjects both cognitive mapping and paper-and-pencil tasks, and have found sex differences on the paper-and-pencil tasks, but not for spatial memory (McNamara, 1986).

More theoretically interesting than simple measures of overall competence in drawing cognitive maps are a limited number of studies suggesting that the cognitive maps of men and women are about equally accurate, but stylistically different. Again, some hint of differences between the maps of males and females appeared in Appleyard's early investigations; females seemed to be somewhat more spatially oriented than males. Other researchers have concluded that females are as accurate overall as males in their maps, but that women emphasize districts and landmarks, whereas males are more likely to emphasize the path structure (McGuinness & Sparks, 1979; Pearce, 1977). In a pair of related experiments, McGuinness and Sparks (1979) found that women included fewer paths between landmarks, included more landmarks, were less accurate in

placing buildings with respect to the underlying spatial terrain, but were more accurate than males in the placement of buildings with respect to their distance from one another. Interestingly, the second experiment of the pair demonstrated that females actually did know the locations of many roads and paths that they had not voluntarily included in sketch maps. It seems that women often remember the location of these features, but do not always include them in their maps unless specifically asked to do so. McGuinness and Sparks conclude that whereas females seem to approach the organization of topographical space by grouping landmarks and establishing their distance from one another, males are more likely to begin with a network of roads and paths, which may provide a somewhat more accurate framework. In a more recent study, Holding (1992) again examined the prediction that buildings in the same hierarchical cluster are closer together than equidistant buildings belonging to different clusters. For this task, distance estimates of females were more affected by cluster membership than were those of males. In general, males may begin by setting up an organizational framework of paths and nodes for their sketch maps and then superimpose features such as landmarks and districts on this established framework. On the other hand, women may be more likely to try to establish individual relationships between landscape elements or clusters of elements without this organizing framework provided by path networks.

Some other differences have apparently been uncovered. Orleans and Schmidt (1972) found that whereas men typically used base-map coordinates when they were provided, women generally ignored these coordinates and used their home as a reference point. In addition, Ward, Newcombe, and Overton (1986) have reported that males are more likely to voluntarily give compass directions or distance estimates phrased in measurements such as mileage than are females when asked to give directions based on a map. Nevertheless, when instructed to phrase their directions using these dimensions, females were as successful as males. Thus, females may be as capable of using cardinal directions and mileage estimates as men, but have a stylistic preference not to do so.

In conclusion, females probably are as capable as males in mapping their surroundings, but some stylistic differences await further investigation. Even if these differences are valid, the source of these differences is unclear. They may be explained by differences in experience, familiarity, or the socialization process, but a biological component cannot yet be entirely eliminated.

ACQUISITION OF COGNITIVE MAPS

We have noted several instances in which spatial cognition does not match cartographic maps. In general, cognitive maps be-

come more similar to cartographic maps as an environment becomes more familiar (e.g., Evans et al., 1981). Many researchers are interested in the distinction between route and survey knowledge, a distinction described years ago by both Tolman (1948) and Appleyard (1970). Imagine taking a guided tour through a sequence of landmarks in an unfamiliar environment (see Figure 3–18). As you see from Figure 3–18, your route in this hypothetical case spans five landmarks labeled "A" through "E." Now suppose that someone asks you to take another journey, this time from A to D. Would you be able to retrace your steps again to find the location you visited on the tour? If you can you have demonstrated some form of spatial learning. Perhaps an even more interesting question is whether you retrace the sequence of landmarks or decision points from your original tour, or are able to take the "shortcut" directly from A to D following the dashed

Figure 3–18 The solid line indicates the routes a person has traveled between five landmarks. If he or she has developed a survey map, it will also be possible to take a previously untraveled shortcut indicated by the dashed line.

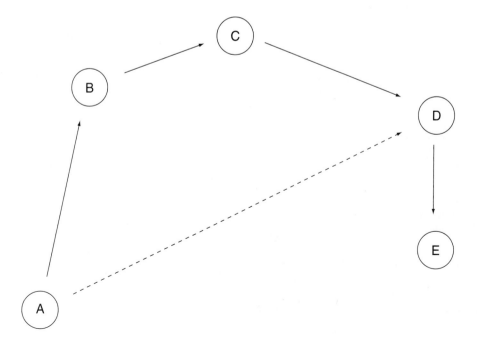

line. Such shortcuts are generally regarded as evidence that a person has moved from sequential or route understanding to survey knowledge. The two most common situations in which to investigate this process are with children (for whom many environments will be unfamiliar) and with adult newcomers.

Much of the interest among developmental psychologists and others investigating children's spatial cognition is based on the implication that the changes that occur in these maps reflect not only a change in the amount of information in memory, but also a change in the type of information and the way it is used (see Heft & Wohlwill, 1987). For example, differences between children and adults may reflect not just less experience, but that children employ a very different approach to problem solving than adults.

The most influential theory of cognitive development as applied to spatial cognition is the one proposed by Jean Piaget and his colleagues (Piaget & Inhelder, 1967). In one classic study, Piaget asked children to sit in a chair and to view a table on which were placed three model mountains (see Figure 3–19). Three other chairs were placed around the table, upon one of which was seated a doll. From a set of drawings, the

Figure 3–19   Piaget's three mountain problem

child was asked to select a view of the scene as it would appear to the doll. Children younger than seven or eight typically chose not the view from the doll's perspective, but the view they themselves saw. Piaget termed this *egocentrism*.

According to Piaget, during the egocentric phase, the child's frame of reference is centered on his or her own activities. Environmental features in the child's spatial image are disconnected and the environment is fragmented. Later, the child's map is oriented around fixed places in the environment that the child has explored, but not necessarily the place he or she now occupies. These known areas are, however, disjointed. Finally, the child's frame of reference assumes the characteristics of a spatial survey map with a more objective representation of the environment.

Ironically, Piaget's conclusions may have initially reduced interest in children's spatial abilities because his research led to the conclusion that children could not understand and use maps until about the age of seven. Although several studies have provided some support for the idea that qualitative changes in cognition occur during childhood (e.g., Acredolo, 1976, 1977), more recent research leads us to temper Piaget's conclusions. For example, although some changes in children's ability to interpret aerial photographs occur between kindergarten and grade two (Blades & Spencer, 1987; Stea & Blaut, 1973), children seem better able to make use of aerial photographs (Blaut & Stea, 1974) and maps (Blades & Spencer, 1987; Rutland, Custance, & Campbell, 1993) than Piaget would have predicted. Evidence shows that even three-year-olds have at least some ability to perform in ways that indicate the beginnings of what we have called survey or spatial representations (DeLoache, 1987), although this ability improves significantly with age (Rutland et al., 1993).

Many studies support Piaget's observation of spatial egocentrism. Somewhat more controversy surrounds the argument whether these findings reflect a truly different way of thinking, as Piaget would imply, or a slow increase in the quantity of environmental information and cognitive skills. Much of the research on children's cognitive maps is based on studies which have employed models to simulate environments. It may be that the relatively poor mapping abilities demonstrated by children participating in studies which employ this method have resulted as much from the artificial methodology of the research as actual mapping deficits (e.g., Cornell & Hay, 1984; Evans, 1980). Research in large-scale environments has found children to be more capable at younger ages than was suggested by the studies employing models or sketch maps (e.g., Cousins, Siegel, & Maxwell 1983).

A related topic under investigation is the accuracy and complexity of cognitive maps. Siegel and White (1975) suggest that children's representations of the spatial environment progress through four sequential developmental stages. First, landmarks are noticed and remembered; second, paths between landmarks are constructed; at the third stage, landmarks and paths are organized into clusters; and finally, these clusters and other features are correctly coordinated into an overall framework. Notice that whereas many believe that children first focus on landmarks and then move on to route (path) information as they mature, this trend may not parallel the evolution of adults' cognitive maps.

Although Piaget believed that children's strategies for spatial problem solving differed from those of adults, many researchers conclude that the cognitive maps of adults in new environments also develop from route to survey knowledge in a manner much like the age-related changes observed in children (Golledge et al., 1985; McDonald & Pellegrino, 1993). Individuals knit together a cognitive map from the accumulation of information acquired by traveling different routes in a new environment, eventually allowing them to take "shortcuts" like the one demonstrated in Figure 3–18. McDonald and Pellegrino conclude that the processes may generally follow a sequence from landmarks to routes to survey knowledge. The process seems complex. Many of these routes do not overlap, or share only a few common locations, and our discussion of distance estimation concluded that estimates of the distance from one location to a second are not necessarily the same as those for the same route traveled in the other direction (e.g., Golledge et al., 1993).

Adults are likely to have at least one advantage over children; they are more likely to understand and have access to published cartographic maps. Of course, the whole purpose of most maps is to provide an accessible and permanent record of spatial information, so maps should be valuable aids for spatial learning. Is information learned from a map different from that acquired from experience? People may learn from maps quite differently than from actually moving through an environment (Thorndyke & Hayes-Roth, 1982). Map learners are privy to a bird's-eye view of the environment, and thus, may acquire survey knowledge because a map provides direct access to global relationships of distance and location. On the other hand, although spatial learning based on actual navigation in the environment may be more difficult to obtain, it benefits from the advantages of ecological context and perhaps, more accurate representation of the travel distances for each leg of a journey.

In their review, McDonald and Pellegrino (1993) differentiate between primary and secondary spatial learning. Primary learning involves direct experience moving through the environment, whereas secondary learning comes from studying maps or other environmental descriptions. Over time, the spatial representations acquired through actual navigation become more like that of survey knowledge. In instances in which the environment is relatively simple with streets laid out in rectangular grids, navigation may quickly lead to more accurate survey knowledge than that gained from maps (Thorndyke & Hayes-Roth, 1982). Most maps present an aerial view, and this perspective presumably facilitates the development of survey knowledge. Despite these advantages, learning about an environment from maps sometimes results in certain distortions that seem to appear in maps generated from primary experiences. For instance, the orientation of a cartographic map you use to learn a new environment may affect the orientation of your subsequent memory (MacEachren, 1992; Warren, 1994; Warren & Scott, 1993). If you study a map that is drawn and labeled according to the convention that north is "up," you may always assume that locations east of the center of the map are "right" and those west are "left." This presents no problem as long as you travel northward, but perhaps you have experienced the common confusion of reorienting your mental map when you travel in a southerly direction. Cognitive maps constructed from actual experience seem not to suffer from this orientation specificity. In our discussion of wayfinding at the close of this chapter we will revisit orientation problems as we consider "you-are-here" maps in places like airports and shopping centers.

MEMORY AND COGNITIVE MAPS

We have seen some characteristics of sketch maps and other physical representations of human cognition. Notice, however, that cognitive maps themselves have no external physical existence; they reside only in our minds. Let us turn now to a very fundamental question: Exactly how is a cognitive map represented in memory? Psychologists have differing opinions on the matter (Evans,

1980; Searleman & Hermann, 1994), and investigations of this representational question have sparked sophisticated studies by both environmental and cognitive psychologists. Some of the most interesting questions concern the exact form of the mental representation and the organization and structure of a memory or retrieval process (McNamara, 1986).

The Form of the Representation

One of the most fundamental issues is the form of the mental representation of spatial knowledge. One view is that we have an image or mental "picture" of the environment in our memory. This view, termed the *analogical* or **analog representation** (meaning the mental map is an analogy of the real world), says that the cognitive map roughly corresponds point for point to the physical environment, almost as if we have a file of slide photographs of the environment stored in the brain (e.g., Cornodoli & McDaniel, 1991; Glicksohn, 1994; Kosslyn, 1975).

Another view, the *propositional approach*, advocates more of a meaning-based or **propositional storage** of material. The environment is represented as a number of concepts or ideas, each of which is connected to other concepts by testable associations such as color, name, sounds, and height. When we call on this propositional map, we search our memory for various associations, and these are reconstructed and represented as a mental "image" or as a sketch we draw (Anderson & Bower, 1973; Pylyshyn, 1973, 1981).

Current thinking combines these two approaches, concluding that cognitive maps contain both propositional and analogical elements (e.g., Evans, 1980; Gärling et al., 1984; Kosslyn, 1980, 1983; Searleman & Hermann, 1994; Tye, 1991). For example, most information about the environment may be stored in memory through propositions, but we can use this propositional network to very quickly mentally construct an analogical image that has many of the qualities of a photograph. We may then use this image, rather than the propositional network some researchers suppose to underlie it, to solve spatial cognition problems.

Distance

Some understanding of the distances between locations is necessary if we are to use a cognitive map for wayfinding. If maps are analogs of the real world, distance may also be represented in the stored memory itself. For example, when people are asked to judge whether a pair of states (e.g., Georgia and Mississippi) are closer together than another pair (e.g., Michigan and Iowa), the more similar the distances within the two pairs, the longer it takes to make a decision (Evans & Pezdek, 1980). Moreover, recall of distance between two points is longer the greater the distance on a map (Kosslyn, Ball, & Reiser, 1978). From such evidence some have concluded that cognitive representations of the environment require scanning for judgments to be made about them. The more information we must scan, the longer it takes to make judgments about spatial relationships (e.g., Kosslyn, 1983). This provides some support for the analog model.

An analogical storage of spatial information is not the only explanation for many of the observed distance effects, however. Perhaps a longer pathway also provides more opportunities to acquire the bits of knowledge that make up propositions. For example, judgment of traversed distance, that is, the distance we have traveled over a given period of time, is in part dependent upon the number of turns we make as we travel. In one study, students walking a path designated by a line of tape placed on a floor judged a path to be longer the more right angle turns it contained (Sadalla & Magel, 1980). In addition, the more intersections a path crosses, the longer the path is judged to be (Sadalla & Staplin, 1980b).

Sadalla and Staplin (1980a) report a third study involving paths marked with tape. One path had intersections marked with proper names that occur frequently in the English language (e.g., "Lewis"), and another path had intersections marked with relatively unfamiliar names (e.g., "Talbot"). These researchers found that you are likely to judge the familiar-named path as being longer, presumably because you have more information about it stored from associations with the familiar names. Generally, the more information we must scan in our memory while making a "mental journey" through an environment, the farther the distance we assume we have traversed. As you may remember from our brief discussion of multidimensional scaling, however, recent findings indicate that the estimated distance between point A and point B on a cognitive map is not necessarily the same as the distance from point B to point A (Cadwallader, 1979; Foley & Cohen, 1984; Lee, 1970; Sadalla & Staplin, 1980b). This irreversibility casts doubt on the regularity assumed by so-called *Euclidean* models, but has sparked a growing interest in other models of cognitive structure.

Structure

One line of reasoning begins with the assumption that humans are limited in their ability to process incoming information (e.g., Miller, 1956). Too much information may tax our perceptual and cognitive abilities, resulting in cognitive overload (see Chapter 4 for an additional discussion of environmental load as a theoretical explanation for a variety of behaviors). Perhaps you have read elsewhere that humans seem to benefit from strategies that organize the complex information they wish to remember (lists of letters or numbers, for instance) into a smaller number of meaningful "chunks." People seem to divide spatial information in a manner similar to chunking (Allen, 1981; Allen & Kirasic, 1985). Although the criteria for inclusion in a chunk or cluster may differ, good candidates are landmarks that are both near to each other and similar in architecture and use. Perhaps this amounts to a "rediscovery" of what Lynch termed "districts." Let us resurrect our discussion of cognitive distance. A considerable line of evidence indicates that landmarks within the same cluster are judged to be closer to each other than to a third, equidistant point outside of their cluster or region (Hirtle & Jonides, 1985; Holding, 1992; McNamara, Hardey, & Hirtle 1989). Moreover, each cluster may itself be represented by a **reference point**, a sort of "best example" that symbolizes all of the locations within the cluster (Couclelis et al., 1987; Sadalla, Burroughs, & Staplin, 1980). As illustrated in Figure 3–20, we might imagine the world as a sea containing islands of known regions (or districts) within which distance estimates are fairly accurate, but between which knowledge is less precise. Within each island one particularly important reference point, often a landmark, may serve as the cognitive anchor for the entire region.

Perhaps clusters or regions are organized in some orderly fashion in memory.

Figure 3–20 Relationships between clusters and reference points may affect distance estimates and knowledge of even well-known areas.

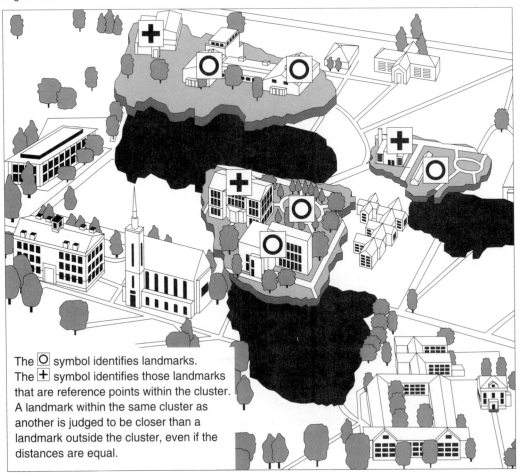

The ⬚ symbol identifies landmarks.
The ⊞ symbol identifies those landmarks that are reference points within the cluster. A landmark within the same cluster as another is judged to be closer than a landmark outside the cluster, even if the distances are equal.

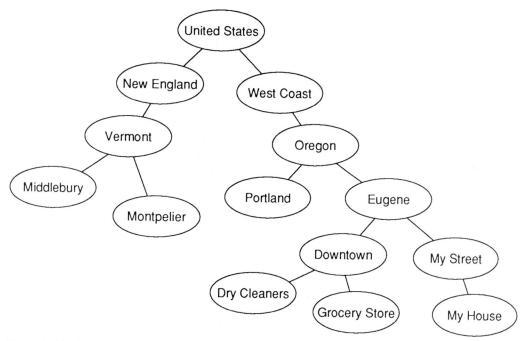

Figure 3–21 An example of a semantic network as it might underlie a person's cognitive map.

Some time ago, Collins and Quillian (1969) demonstrated that the retrieval of information from semantic memory (memory for concepts) sometimes acts as if it is based on a hierarchical memory network. That is, information may be stored according to some organizational system that is based on ordered categories. This is typically presented as a tree diagram illustrating the relationships between concepts as branches like those in Figure 3–21. Presumably, some sort of sequential search of levels in these categories occurs when one is asked to determine relationships between concepts. The exact form of these **semantic networks** is controversial and the subject of a great deal of research in cognitive psychology (see Best, 1986; McDonald & Pellegrino, 1993).

For our present purposes, what is most interesting is the idea that some form of a network might also describe the way in which spatial information is represented in memory. Some evidence shows that, for spatial memory at least, there may be an upper limit to how much a person can remember (Byrne, 1979; Tversky, 1981). A networked storage process would be a rather economical system in the memory space it requires because information common to all members of a spatial cluster or category (perhaps symbolized by the reference point) could be stored only once. All points in Montana are west of all points in South Dakota, for example; so, you do not have to remember separately that Billings is west of Spearfish, that Bozeman is west of Rapid City, and Great Falls is west of Sioux City. Although theoretically efficient, this storage system might be subject to certain types of errors which would make some memories more difficult or time-consuming to retrieve than others. A study reported by Stevens and Coupe (1978) provides an opportunity to experiment with an interesting example. First draw a map of the United States. Now indicate the locations of San Diego, California, and Reno, Nevada. Do not read further until you have done so. Finished? Except for those living near the West Coast, most people place San Diego west of Reno apparently because they think of California, the larger category to which San Diego belongs, as being west of Nevada. As you will see upon consulting a United States map, San Diego is actually east of Reno! As is often the case, things probably are not so simple. A simple tree diagram or *hierarchical network* cannot explain all of the phenomena we have observed in cognitive maps. At the present time, however, versions of the network model (e.g., Gärling et al., 1984; Kaplan & Kaplan, 1982) remain popular within the cognitive mapping literature. Perhaps McNamara's (1986) "partially hierarchical" structure represents the data as well as any. This means that memories may be stored according to hierarchical principles, but that there remain some interconnections between areas that cut across this hierarchical structure. However the exact process occurs, most studies, whether they are lab studies (Allen, Siegel, & Rosinski, 1978; Lindberg & Gärling, 1983) or field studies (e.g., Beck & Wood, 1976; Byrne, 1979), indicate that spatial information is acquired quickly and that forgetting is minimal.

WAYFINDING

Most of the research we have presented to this point has focused on a rather static, plain-view map of the environment residing in memory (for now, we will lay aside the argument concerning the specific form of this representation). Other authors (e.g., Byrne, 1979; Cornell & Hay, 1984; Gärling et al., 1986; Passini, 1984) are interested in wayfinding, the process by which people actually navigate in their environments.

One of the most profoundly troubling experiences we can face is being lost. In such an instance, our human capabilities of information processing and storage have deserted us, and because most of us are dependent upon others and technology, our very survival may be threatened. Being truly lost may be a relatively rare phenomenon, but newcomers commonly experience the stress and anxiety that accompany disorientation in both buildings and natural environments (e.g., Cohen et al., 1986; Hunt, 1984). For some groups, this stress may be particularly serious, even life-threatening (Hunt, 1984).

ACTION PLANS AND WAYFINDING

Gärling et al. (1986) propose one model of wayfinding which may prove useful in organizing our discussion (see Figure 3–22). We will provide a hypothetical example to illustrate the different steps of the model. Imagine that a friend has asked you to drop off some clothes at a drycleaning establishment. First, we determine a destination. Should you take your friend's dry cleaning to your favorite establishment, or to one closer to your friend's home for his or her convenience? Assuming that you decided to choose a dry cleaner near your friend's home, the second step requires the new target destination to be localized; that is, you must determine the general location of the target environment. If you are unfamiliar with your friend's neighborhood you may need to use a telephone book or some other source to pinpoint the target. Third, a route is chosen between your present location and the dry cleaner, again requiring you to ask directions

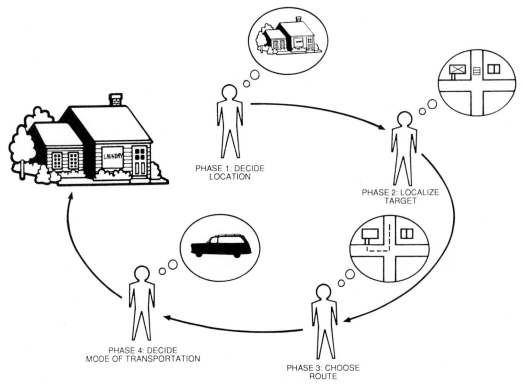

PHASE 1: DECIDE
LOCATION

PHASE 2: LOCALIZE
TARGET

PHASE 3: CHOOSE
ROUTE

PHASE 4: DECIDE
MODE OF TRANSPORTATION

Figure 3–22 Wayfinding: A hypothetical example of a trip to retrieve one's laundry

or to refer to a map if you are unfamiliar with the neighborhood. Finally, you must make a choice of travel mode, depending on factors such as the distance to the destination and the availability of transportation.

Notice that the model emphasizes an internal psychological process that lets us anticipate or rehearse what will eventually be our actual behavior in moving through the environment. Thus, Gärling et al. have adopted the concept of action plans (Russell & Ward, 1982) as links between stored environmental information and wayfinding behavior.

A good cognitive map would be one excellent wayfinding aid, but some authorities doubt whether a person actually needs a detailed map, either mental or on paper, to find

a travel goal. For example, Passini (1984) suggests that wayfinding might best be viewed as a sequence of problem-solving tasks that require a certain amount of stored environmental information. This may be an easier task than drawing your route on a sketch map for at least two reasons. First, assuming you have at least some experience in the environment in question, you are facing a task of recognition. Instead of recalling a cognitive map, you may only need to recognize a particular environmental feature such as a landmark as you encounter it, and to make a correct decision, such as to turn left, when in its presence. Second, wayfinding is in some way self-correcting. If you find yourself suddenly moving into unfamiliar terrain, you may retrace your steps to the point where you erred and try again. Thus, errors in wayfinding need not be cumulative. You may have misjudged the distance or direction from one building to another slightly. Once you do manage to find your way to this key decision point, minor errors earlier in the journey are no longer of any consequence. Traditional cognitive maps are less forgiving. You may recall that intersections between roads are typically remembered as right angles, even when the actual angle varies from 60 to 90 degrees. Byrne (1979) suggests that precise information concerning the shape of intersections may be missing from memory entirely. Perhaps, for wayfinding purposes at least, it is sufficient to have a network map which preserves only the connections between steps along a route, but which requires neither knowledge of the distances between choice points nor the precise angle at which routes join. On the other hand, it may be that although one can travel successfully along a predetermined route by recognizing a succession of choice points, a more sophisticated navigation system would allow a person to arrive at the same location via a number of different (perhaps shorter) routes and to find a new location based on its location with reference to some known landmarks. This more sophisticated type of wayfinding may require the richer spatial understanding characteristic of cognitive maps.

SETTING CHARACTERISTICS THAT FACILITATE WAYFINDING

Earlier in this chapter, we noted Kevin Lynch's (1960) emphasis on legibility, which largely determines the degree to which an environment facilitates cognitive mapping. Gärling, Böök, and Lindberg (1986) expand on this concept and describe three characteristics of physical settings that are likely to affect wayfinding: the degree of differentia-

tion, the degree of visual access, and the complexity of the spatial layout. **Differentiation** refers to the degree to which parts of the environment look the same or are distinctive. In general, buildings that are distinctive in shape, easily visible, well maintained, and free-standing are better remembered (Appleyard, 1969; Evans et al., 1982). In the context of interior environments, for example, Evans et al. (1980) demonstrated the effectiveness of color coding in improving wayfinding in a building's interior. Evans et al. (1982) report a variable they label "context," which seems closely related to the distinctiveness created by contrasts in line, form, color, or texture as discussed in descriptive landscape systems (see Chapter 2). In addition to differentiation, the ability to learn a new environment may depend on the **degree of visual access**. This is the extent to which different parts of the setting can be seen from other vantage points. Of course, Lynch (1960) recognized the importance of visual access in what he termed landmarks. More recently, Evans et al. (1982) speak of **transition**, or direct access from a building to the street. Finally, **complexity of the spatial layout** refers to the amount and difficulty of information that must be processed in order to move around in an environment. Too much complexity undermines both navigation and learning. For example, Weisman (1981) found that simple floor plans facilitated wayfinding in campus buildings. Simplicity was even more important than familiarity with the setting in predicting wayfinding difficulties. Taken to an extreme, no amount of familiarity may be able to compensate for extreme architectural complexity (Moeser, 1988). We hasten to distinguish between the complexity of a route or route network, as the term is used here, and the complexity of a particular facade, which should contribute to differentiation as discussed above.

MAPS

Thankfully, humans often acquire a variety of printed maps and atlases for use as they journey into unfamiliar terrain. We have already briefly discussed the role of cartographic maps in the acquisition of spatial data, and concluded that people may learn somewhat differently from them than from actually moving through an environment. In complex environments with many nonperpendicular paths, maps may remain the most efficient method of route learning (Moeser, 1988). What can we do to improve them?

You-Are-Here Maps

One problem with maps is that people sometimes have difficulty translating maps into usable navigation tools (Levine, 1982; Thorndyke & Hayes-Roth, 1982). For example, have you ever consulted a **you-are-here map** in a shopping center, museum, or subway terminal? Was the map easy to read and understand, or did you find yourself nearly as confused after reading the map as when you began? Marvin Levine and his associates (Levine, 1982; Levine, Marchon, & Hanley, 1984) have explored the design and placement of these "you-are-here" maps, and have outlined several simple principles that dramatically improve the usefulness of these orientation aides.

Structure Matching

The first problem faced by a you-are-here map user is **structure matching**, that is, the need to pair known points in the environment with their corresponding map coordinates. If a person reading the map is unable to accomplish this task, even an accurately drawn map will not be very useful. Technically, Levine argues, two known points on both the map and in the terrain provide the minimum amount of information necessary for a person to relate any object in the environment with its map symbol. A viewer must know not only where he or she is, as would a person viewing Figure 3–23, but also the location of a second pair of points. For example, the figure shows buildings that can be easily identified both on the map and in the environment visible to the visitor. Although in the future this is accomplished by attaching a sign to building L, we note that the same end might be achieved by using a caricature map symbol that resembles the building as it would be seen from the position of the person reading the map (rather than an aerial or blueprint perspective).

A second way of providing two-point correspondence is to carefully place the map near an asymmetrical feature. This allows the visitor to pinpoint his or her location and that of nearby features. In addition, Levine encourages the use of a bipart you-are-here symbol (also in Figure 3–23). Here both the map the viewer is reading and the position of the visitor are indicated, technically fulfilling the need for two points and allowing the viewer to correctly bring the map and the environment into correspondence.

Orientation

As former Boy or Girl Scouts may know, a map is most easily used if it is placed parallel to the ground and turned so that it is oriented with the terrain. Thus, a goal that is ahead of you on the map is ahead in the terrain, and something to the right on the map is to your right in the environment. In some instances, you-are-here maps in a building can be displayed horizontally so that the map is properly oriented. In most cases, however, practical reasons require the map to be hung vertically on the wall. Although it may not be obvious, correct alignment of these maps may be critical to ensuring that they are easily understood and used by visitors. Levine, Marchon, and Hanley (1984) propose that wayfinding maps are best when

Figure 3–23 Structure matching in you-are-here maps. In this map, labels and caricature map symbols allow the user to match the map with the surrounding terrain.
Adapted from Levine, M. (1982). You-are-here maps: Psychological considerations. Environment and Behavior, 14, *221–237.*

what is forward on the ground is up on the map (Figure 3–24). This **forward-up equivalence** also ensures that what is to the right in the terrain is to the right on the map and so forth. Levine et al.'s (1984) experimental data show that misalignment of you-are-here maps by 90 degrees or more seriously misleads people, even those who have been alerted to the misalignment!

Unfortunately, the Levine et al. (1984) study also showed that this principle is regularly violated in airports, offices, and other buildings. The severity of the violation may range from being a small inconvenience to shoppers, to potentially life-threatening danger in the case of fire-evacuation maps in an office complex.

MOVIES, SLIDES, AND MODELS: FACILITATING SPATIAL LEARNING

Although some have expressed concern that even carefully prepared photographic simulations of routes may be inferior to actual walks as wayfinding training aids (Cornell & Hay, 1984), other studies have successfully employed slide photographs as environmental simulations (e.g., Cohen et al., 1986; Hunt, 1984). In fact, casually acquired familiarity may never match the level of spatial understanding achieved by subjects given planned instruction (Moeser, 1988). It also follows that if some method could be found to accelerate spatial familiarity, some of the distress associated with relocation could be

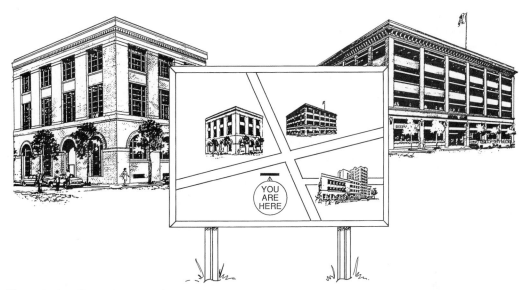

Figure 3–24 Forward-up equivalence aids in orienting you-are-here maps.
Adapted from Levine, M. (1982). You-are-here maps: Psychological considerations. Environment and Behavior, 14, 221–237.

reduced. Some researchers have focused on the need to assist children in adjusting to new spatial environments. For example, Cohen and his associates (Cohen et al., 1986) investigated the effect of two spatial familiarization experiences on the attitudes of five- and six-year-old kindergarten boys. Two weeks before the start of school some of the boys were given either an on-site tour or a simulated tour accompanied by a scale model of their school. Boys who received either familiarization treatment felt more secure and comfortable several weeks after the start of school than a control group which received no training.

In another study with a quite different population, Hunt (1984) investigated procedures for improving the wayfinding abilities of senior citizen volunteers in an unfamiliar nursing home. One group of subjects was given a site visit in which they individually received a guided tour through the experimental building. Members of the second experimental group were individually shown photographs of the building ordered in the same sequence as experienced by those on the guided tour. As they viewed the slide photographs, this group could also inspect three-dimensional models of the building's floor plan and exterior. Participants in both treatment conditions were generally superior to a control group on a variety of on-site wayfinding tasks. This result was not surprising; it confirms the usefulness of some prior exposure to an environment, whether simulated or in the form of a tour. More interesting, however, are the differences between the simulation and site visit groups. The groups were similar in their ability to find their way to places along a previously learned route, but members of the simulation group were superior in their ability to find new locations, their ability to identify photographs of building landmarks, and in their understanding of the exterior shape and the spatial configuration of the building. In sum, both groups could learn sequential routes, but the simulation group apparently had a richer and more flexible mental image (presumably because of their exposure to the bird's-eye views provided by the scale models).

Of course much of the wayfinding information we acquire comes directly from other people—our friends, acquaintances, or a helpful stranger. Information may include oral instructions, simple sketch maps, or more complex drawings. Interestingly, verbatim instructions (either written or oral) seem superior to more complex or graphic maps that emphasize the overall geography or survey knowledge (Kovach, Surrette, & Aamodt, 1988). Just as not everyone is equally successful in wayfinding, not everyone is equally skilled in giving spatial information. Vanetti and Allen (1988) suggest that the ability to give useful route instructions depends on both spatial skills and verbal ability. Unless a person knows a spatial layout, he or she is not likely to give useful instructions. On the other hand, if that person is unable to express those instructions clearly, pure spatial knowledge will not be of much use. To examine these ideas, Vanetti and Allen divided subjects into high and low spatial ability and high and low verbal ability groups. Interestingly, there was little difference between the groups in the ability to follow route instructions, but those with high spatial ability were more likely to suggest a more efficient route to others.

We might conclude our discussion of wayfinding by noting that people are generally more successful at wayfinding than in cognitive mapping. This observation may be most clearly seen at the extremes of the age spectrum. In spite of the data we reviewed regarding possible deficiencies in children's cognitive maps, particularly their tendency for environmental egocentrism, children beyond kindergarten age seem quite competent at wayfinding. We have already characterized wayfinding as primarily a recognition task and distinguished it from sketch maps that emphasize recall. In addition, many measures of cognitive mapping ability such as sketch maps depend on skills such as drawing ability that are not so clearly or so often demanded as wayfinding skills in the real world. Finally, perhaps some individuals, particularly children, are intimidated or overwhelmed by the complexity of the task requested by many cognitive map studies, but perform well when faced with an ecologically valid situation.

CHAPTER SUMMARY

Whereas the conventional approach to perception examines the way the brain interprets messages from the sensory organs about specific elements in the environment, environmental perception views the perceptual experience as more encompassing, including cognitive, affective, interpretive, and evaluative responses. Moreover, environmental perception is likely to consider the person-environment relationship from a holistic-systems or transactional perspective. Environmental perception involves activity on our part, especially in terms of exploring the environment to determine what needs it meets. In addition, exposure to a particular environment may result in adaptation or habituation—the weakening of a response following repeated exposure to a stimulus.

The line between perception and cognition is a hazy one. Cognition integrates memory and experience with a judgment of the present derived from perception to help us in thinking about, recognizing, and organizing the layout of an environment. Cognitive maps are our mental representations of this layout and can be analyzed through a variety of methods. The best known approach to cognitive mapping is that of Kevin Lynch, who emphasized the major elements: paths, landmarks, nodes, edges, and districts.

Cognitive maps are not perfectly accurate representations of the environment; they contain distortions, omissions, and other errors. These errors often reflect the importance of familiarity with an environment. Current thinking suggests that cognitive maps may be stored as images, as propositions, or both. Propositions, in particular, are often thought of as organized into networks, but the specific form of storage remains controversial.

Action plans serve as the bridge between stored mental images or facts and actual behavior in the environment. The process of using stored spatial information along with maps and other aids is called wayfinding. It seems that wayfinding may involve both recognition of landmarks and other features at choice points, and the recall of a more sophisticated survey or spatial map. Architectural features which make an environment more distinctive or simpler to understand may improve wayfinding. Other attempts to convey spatial information, such as signs and training programs, are likely to improve wayfinding abilities and to reduce the stress of disorientation.

SUGGESTED PROJECTS

1. Show a group of friends a picture of a place on campus and ask them to describe the place. Take another group of friends to the same actual place and ask them to describe it. How do the two groups differ in their descriptions? What do your findings suggest about environmental perception?

2. Ask several friends to draw cognitive maps of your campus. Are the major components similar to each other and to the map we asked you to draw while reading this chapter? Do the maps differ by academic major or year in school? Are there any instances of distortions which are consistent with our examination of cognitive maps?

3. Re-read the section on multidimensional scaling. Now create a chart showing each combination of pairs for 20 campus locations. Pick one pair that is intermediate in distance and likely to be very familiar to everyone who spends time on campus. Use this as your measurement standard (because many people do not "think" in feet, yards, or meters). Ask your class or a few friends to estimate the distance between each location and every other location in terms of the unit of measurement you constructed, and calculate means for each pairing. Finally, cut yarn or string in lengths proportional to the mean distance estimates between buildings and connect these to tacks (representing the buildings themselves). With a little stretching here and there you should find that your procedure has captured a fairly accurate map of campus.

4. Inventory the you-are-here maps in your town or campus. Do any of these maps violate any of the principles outlined by Levine (1982)? What could be done to improve these maps as wayfinding aids?

5. Make up a short questionnaire to administer to your friends. Ask them to indicate the direction they would travel to get from one to the other ten pairs of cities. We suggest that you include in your list Reno, Nevada, to San Diego, California; from Oklahoma City, Oklahoma, to Lexington, Kentucky; from Windsor, Ontario, to Albany, New York; from the Atlantic entrance of the Panama Canal to the Pacific entrance; and from London, England, to Minneapolis, Minnesota. Inspect an atlas and construct your own answer key. What kinds of errors did your friends make? Were the pairs of cities we chose particularly difficult? Did you find support for the Stevens and Coupe (1978) position that errors reflect the organizational hierarchy of cognitive maps? Why or why not?

Theories of Environment–Behavior Relationships

INTRODUCTION

THE NATURE AND FUNCTION OF THEORY IN ENVIRONMENTAL PSYCHOLOGY

Hypotheses, Laws, and Theories

Functions of Theories

ENVIRONMENT–BEHAVIOR THEORIES: ENERGIZING A GROWING FIELD

The Arousal Approach

The Environmental Load Approach

The Understimulation Approach

Adaptation Level Theory: Optimal Stimulation

Categories and Dimensions of Stimulation

Optimizing Stimulation

Adaptation Versus Adjustment

Evaluation of the Optimal Stimulation Approach: Breadth Versus Specificity

The Behavior Constraint Approach

Types of Control

Aspects of Helplessness

Value and Limitations of the Behavior Constraint Approach

The Environmental Stress Approach

Characteristics of Stressors

  Cataclysmic Events

  Personal Stressors

  Background Stressors

Appraisal

  Types of Appraisal

  Factors Affecting Appraisal

Characteristics of the Stress Response

  Physiological Response

  Coping Strategies

  Adaptation

  Aftereffects

Assessing the Stress Model

Barker's Ecological Psychology

The Nature of the Behavior Setting

Staffing the Setting: How Many Peas Fill a Pod?

INTEGRATION AND SUMMARY OF THEORETICAL PERSPECTIVES

CHAPTER SUMMARY

Suggested Projects

KEY TERMS

adaptation
adaptation level (AL)
adequately staffed
adjustment
adrenal
aftereffects
alarm reaction
ambient stressors
applicants
appraisal
arousal
background stressors
behavior constraint
behavior setting
behavioral control
bivariate theory
capacity
cataclysmic events
catecholamines
challenge appraisal
cognitive control
control models
coping
corticosteroids
curvilinear relationship
daily hassles
decisional control
denial
determinism
directed attention fatigue (DAF)
ecological psychology
empirical
empirical laws
en masse behavior pattern
environmental competence
environmental load
environmental press
environmental stress model
epinephrine
equilibrium
extra-individual behavior pattern
galvanic skin response (GSR)

general adaptation syndrome (GAS)
generalizability
harm or loss appraisal
heuristics
homeostatic
hypothesis
intervening construct
learned helplessness
maintenance minimum
mediating variable
model
nonperformers
norepinephrine
overload
overstaffed
overstimulation
palliative
palmar sweat index
perceived control
performers
personal stressors
physical milieu
primary appraisal
primary control
psychological reactance
psychological stress
reactance
refractory period
repression-sensitization
REST
reticular formation
restorative environments
restrospective control
screening
secondary appraisal
secondary control
sensory deprivation
social comparison
social support
staffing theory
stage of exhaustion
stage of resistance

standing patterns of behavior
stress
synomorphic
systemic stress
theory

threat appraisal
transactional approach
understaffed
understimulation
Yerkes-Dodson Law

INTRODUCTION

You awake one morning anticipating an important job interview with a lab on campus. Unfortunately, your roommate had different ideas about when the alarm should be set, and a blaring radio awakens you an hour earlier than anticipated. But with your adrenalin pumping, you cannot filter out the noise of the morning and thus cannot go back to sleep. Grudgingly, you shower and get dressed and prepare for breakfast. But another roommate used the last of the coffee to stay up studying the night before, and you are now in a grumpy mood. Heading to your early-morning class, you encounter a construction project that requires a five-minute delay; but the delay seems like half an hour, as irritable as you have become. So concerned about getting to class on time, you don't see a stop sign, and the ever-present local law enforcement issues you a ticket. As you finally arrive for class, the only seats available are in the front row where you are under intense scrutiny from the instructor or in the back where it is difficult to see. You take a seat in the back and discover that the first part of the hour is devoted to a half-hour film you have seen in three other classes. Your mind wanders. Then the instructor announces that the final exam must be changed to a day when you are already scheduled to be on a trip with your family; you had been planning to visit your uncle on that trip, who had recently been forced out of his home because a nearby waste dump had been discovered leaching toxic chemicals into the neighborhood. You feel as if you are

losing control of the events in your life. You retreat to a nearby scenic park where you can collect your thoughts. It is a refreshing experience, at last, and you feel restored. Unfortunately (the same term used when your day began), the time passes quickly and before you realize it, you have missed the job interview. Rushing to the lab, you discover that the manager has had so few applications, your lack of promptness is forgiven and you receive an interview anyway. You retreat to the comforts of your room and receive a call from a friend you have not seen for several months. Sharing the experiences of the day seems to help. Eventually, you fall asleep exhausted.

Although it is unlikely that all of the above events would happen to you in one day, they are typical of the things we encounter in a life's journey as we interact with our physical and social environments. Although the events and the reaction to them seem disjointed, environmental psychologists are interested in developing unified theories that would explain such disparate person–environment interactions. In this chapter we will examine the use and development of some of the relevant theories that are employed in environmental psychology today. We will begin with a general discussion of the concept and function of theory, then examine some specific psychological theories that have evolved to explain the nature of environment–behavior relationships, and conclude with our own synthesis of these various orientations.

THE NATURE AND FUNCTION OF THEORY IN ENVIRONMENTAL PSYCHOLOGY

The scientific method is really little more than a specific way of gaining knowledge. Scientists, whether devotees of environmental psychology or any other field, assume there is a great deal of order in the universe that can be discovered with appropriate methodology. Before the application of scientific inquiry, however, this universal order is perceived more as chaos or uncertainty than as something systematic. Science (or more specifically the scientific method) is simply a set of procedures for reducing the uncertainty, thereby gaining knowledge of the universal order. It is to these procedures that we owe our progress thus far in environmental psychology. Other approaches to gaining knowledge do exist, of course, such as the methods of religion. In religion, the basis of reducing uncertainty is tradition, faith, revelation, and in many cases, experience. The basis of reducing uncertainty in the scientific approach, on the other hand, is a mathematical prediction of observable events. Once we can predict with a degree of certainty what will happen to phenomenon "A" (e.g., crime or violence) when a change occurs in phenomenon "B" (e.g., population density), we have taken a giant step toward a scientific understanding of these phenomena.

Suppose, for example, that we want to apply scientific methods to discover the principles involved in getting people to reduce air pollution. We assume that such principles exist (e.g., appealing to conscience, implementing government regulations, administering punishment), and that through scientific inquiry we can not only discover them, but we can also predict how much air pollution will be reduced by applying the principles in varying amounts and combinations. Moreover, the principles should also predict the positive and negative conse-

quences of their application (e.g., cleaner air, better health, potentially reduced profits and productivity of an industry, higher utility bills). Such predictions, however, are rarely perfect. To the extent that our predictions of the phenomena are not perfect, uncertainty remains about the portion of the ordered universe under study, but we continue our quest for knowledge to reduce this uncertainty further.

Thus, scientists assume that events in the universe are related to other events in the universe, and that through scientific inquiry these relationships can be discovered and their consequences predicted. Using scientific methods, environmental psychologists observe fluctuations in some phenomena (e.g., climate changes, inadequate space in an office) and predict their subsequent impacts (e.g., violence, reduced productivity, efforts to change interior design of space). Research in psychology, then, is the search for the antecedents of our various behaviors, including environmental factors, biological influences, and intrapsychic (cognitively or emotionally generated) events (cf. Franck, 1984).

We should note that the assumption of causation in science involves a philosophical notion of **determinism**. In an absolute sense, a deterministic system implies the opposite of "free will." In a softer interpretation, we can study many interrelated determinants of an outcome, including personal choice (cf. James, 1979; Rotton, 1986). Environmental psychologists are often more concerned with analyzing patterns or shapes of relationships than with a narrower focus on antecedent–consequent dependencies in an environment–behavior system. Altman and Rogoff (1987), for example, note the value of a **transactional approach**, which concentrates on the patterns of relationships rather than on specific causes, although R. Kaplan (1987) cautions that there can be problems of inference in some research that takes a transactional perspective. We should point out that from the perspective of a purist, once we decide that a phenomenon, psychological or otherwise, is indeterminate or is unpredictable, we are really saying that this phenomenon is not within the realm of scientific inquiry, and that we cannot gain knowledge about it through scientific methods.

HYPOTHESES, LAWS, AND THEORIES

How do we proceed with scientific research in environmental psychology? Most likely, we start with simple observations. We might observe, for example, that as the concentration of inmates in prisons increases, violence goes up. We have observed two phenomena, prison population density and violence, and we have noted a relationship between the two: As one increases, the other increases (i.e., they are *positively correlated*). We might then hypothesize, or formulate a hunch, that high population density in prisons leads to increased aggression and violence. (We should caution that actual studies show the effects of prison crowding to be complex, as we discuss in Chapter 9.) The next step in scientific methodology is critical—testing the hypothesis. A **hypothesis** is a proposition; in science it is empirically testable. All methods of gaining knowledge generate hypotheses. What makes science unique is the method of verifying the hypotheses. Whereas religion may rely on faith, tradition, or individual experience to verify hypotheses, science insists that hypotheses be verified by publicly observable (**empirical**) data. Recall that we described in Chapter 1 several means of acquiring such data. When these observable data do not support the hypothesis, the scientist must either modify the hypothesis or generate an entirely new hypothesis and test it again. If we took the

question into the laboratory and found, for example, that putting several individuals into a small room did not increase their level of aggressiveness, we would have to reject the idea that crowding causes aggression and come up with a more complicated hypothesis. For example, maybe it is only under conditions of deprivation, such as boredom, that crowding leads to increased aggression. This is a testable proposition. Indeed, as we shall discover in Chapter 9, several investigators have looked at the combined effects of crowding and other variables, such as poverty, on aggression.

Once we have gathered a number of empirical facts, we can proceed to a more abstract and theoretical level to explain these facts. A word on the distinction between empirical laws, theories, and models may be helpful here. **Empirical laws** are statements of simple observable relationships between phenomena (often expressed in mathematical terms) that can be demonstrated time and time again. Such things as the law of gravity, the law that magnetic opposites attract, and the law of effect in psychology (i.e., behaviors that lead to pleasurable consequences are likely to be repeated) are easy to demonstrate at an empirical level. Theories usually involve more abstract concepts and relationships than empirical laws and consequently are broader in scope. Theories are not as a rule demonstrable in one empirical setting but are inferred from many empirical relationships. Examples include the theory of evolution, the theory of relativity, and equity theory in psychology (dissatisfaction in a relationship occurs if outcomes are not proportionate to inputs). Finally, a **model** is usually more abstract than an empirical law but is not as complex as a theory. Models are usually based on analogies or metaphors. For example, as was observed in Chapter 3, investigators have assumed that mental maps resemble the ones drawn by cartographers. To take another example, more than one theorist (e.g., Knowles, 1980a) has drawn an analogy between magnetic or gravitational force fields and the distance that strangers maintain between themselves and others. A model is often an intermediate step between the demonstration of an empirical law and the formulation of a theory. The distinction can be made that a model is the application of a previously accepted theoretical notion to a new area, but in practice the terms "model" and "theory" are often used interchangeably.

It may be helpful to think of theory as existing at several levels. **Heuristics** are simple principles that facilitate decision making. For example, the representativeness heuristic says that we decide whether an item fits a category (e.g., whether a sound is meaningless or whether it signals something) based on how representative it is of other items in that category (e.g., whether it resembles other known signals). A model is more elaborate and is based on analogies. A **bivariate theory** simply relates two variables, such as temperature and violence. Well-articulated theories are often quite elaborate and relate multiple concepts to each other.

Basically, a **theory** consists of a set of concepts plus a set of statements relating the concepts to each other. At the theoretical level, we might say that the undesirable effects of high population density in prisons are mediated by the stress associated with high density. That is, high population density leads to stress, and stress in turn may lead to a variety of undesirable consequences, such as increased violence or mental illness. The concept of stress in this example is relatively abstract, in that it is not directly observable but rather is inferred from events that are observable. Such inferred phenomena are often termed **intervening constructs** or **mediating variables** (see also Baron & Kenny, 1986). Empirically, we might infer stress from autonomic arousal (e.g., increased blood pressure, heart rate, or skin temperature), from verbal and nonverbal signs of anxiety, or from a disintegrated quality of behavior.

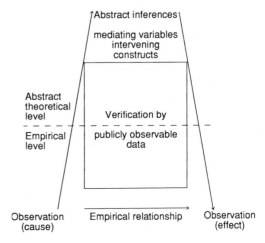

Figure 4–1 Theories usually involve abstract inferences about mediators of empirically observed cause and effect relationships.

The distinction between direct observation and abstract inference is one of the main differences between the empirical and theoretical levels of scientific inquiry (Figure 4–1).

FUNCTIONS OF THEORIES

We can identify at least three basic functions of theories. First, theories help us to predict relationships between variables, which implies that we can control what happens to one variable by regulating another variable. For example, if we know that certain conditions of prison crowding lead to violence (i.e., cause violence), we can control the violence to some extent by changing the crowded conditions. If our crowding theory says that stress mediates a relationship between crowding and violence, we might also control violence by controlling stress.

A second function of theories is to summarize large amounts of data. Instead of having to know thousands of pieces of data about the levels of stress and violence under thousands of levels of crowding, if we have a good theory we can summarize all this information in a few theoretical statements. Such summaries in turn help us predict events that we may not yet have observed at the empirical level. A third function of theories is the generalization of concepts and relationships to many phenomena, which helps to summarize the knowledge in a particular area. For example, if our theory states that high levels of stress lead to increased levels of violence, this implies that we can generalize the theoretical notion to *any* factor that increases stress, including crowding, noise, poverty, and marital discord. Furthermore, if we can establish that a particular environmental event, such as wild fluctuations in temperature, is stressful, then we can infer from our stress theory that this environmental event will lead to more violence. If empirical evidence does not suggest that a theory generalizes very well, the theory should be modified or rejected in favor of theories that do offer good **generalizability**. In one sense, the issue of generalizability is troubling for environmental psychologists, since we like to study environment–behavior relationships in the context where they naturally occur. This proclivity may mean that many relationships observed may well not exist in any other context. This is just one reason elaborate theories are difficult to generate in environmental psychology (cf. Altman & Rogoff, 1987; R. Kaplan, 1987; Winkel, 1987). Nevertheless, most scientists, including environmental psychologists, would agree that a good theory is high in generalizability.

In addition to these three basic functions, theories are useful in other ways. For one thing, they help to generate additional research by suggesting new relationships between variables. Many scientists assert that the best research is that generated by theories. Another use for theories is in the application of research to practical problems. Solutions to problems are often needed quickly, with little time available for basic research. If theories already exist, they can suggest solutions. In a broader sense, theories can help guide policy decisions. Nuclear theory, for example, gives us an idea of the feasibility of using nuclear power to generate electricity as well as an idea of the environmental hazards involved, and thus is useful in establishing public policies on nuclear power (cf. van der Pligt, 1985).

Theories in environmental psychology, as in any scientific field, must be constantly evaluated, just as hypotheses must be verified. The basic functions of theories suggest the criteria by which theories should be evaluated. First, a theory is valuable to the extent that it predicts. Given two theories about the same environment–behavior relationship, the one that predicts most accurately most of the time is considered more valuable. Second, good theories do a superior job of summarizing many empirical relationships. Third, a valid theory must be very generalizable. Given two theories about the effects of noise on performance, the one that applies to more situations is the more valuable. Fourth, the most useful theories suggest new hypotheses to be tested empirically. In most scientific endeavors, much of the significant research is generated from theories rather than used to construct new theories. Since this research is crucial to our understanding of the phenomena under study, theories that suggest new areas of investigation are highly valued. Let us turn now to some of the theories in common use in environmental psychology.

ENVIRONMENT–BEHAVIOR THEORIES: ENERGIZING A GROWING FIELD

One of the difficulties facing environmental psychology is the lack of a unifying direction in the research of the field. Since one of the functions of good theories is to provide a focus for research, a number of environmental psychologists have made efforts to build models and theories about environment–behavior relationships. These relatively young theories tend not to be very complex and tend to be restricted to a somewhat limited predictive domain (cf. Proshansky, 1973; Stokols, 1983). Theories or models restricted to environmental perception or cognition (e.g., the lens model) have been covered in Chapter 3. In this chapter, we will present a set of theories whose predictive domains are largely restricted to the effects of environmental conditions on behavior. The empirical data to which these theories are most applicable will be described in subsequent chapters on such topics as noise, weather, air pollution, personal space, crowding, and urban environments. Specifically, we will examine for now the following six theoretical perspectives, which are probably the most dominant ones in environmental psychology: (1) the arousal approach; (2) the stimulus load approach (overload and underload); (3) the adaptation level (AL) approach; (4) the behavior constraint approach; (5) the stress approach; and (6) the ecological psychology approach. We will then see how these various formulations can be integrated into an eclectic model that we will use repeatedly in the remainder of the book. In general, these theoretical approaches suggest that the environment impinges on us and we react to it; how and why this happens varies from theory to theory. All of these approaches, however, imply that we adapt to the stimulation; that is, we change our reaction to it over time, which we describe as *adaptive* or *maladaptive* depending on the consequences.

Before elaborating on these various approaches, it will be helpful to keep several points in mind. First, theoretical concepts are not always easy to grasp, and the reader may feel overwhelmed with just one reading of this chapter. Full development and application of the material will become clearer in subsequent chapters. Second, we often rely on more than one theory to explain a given phenomenon. As we will see in the discussion of stress, mediators of these various conceptual approaches often occur together, and it is sometimes useful to appeal to more than one approach to explain the data. Finally, different theories are useful at different levels of analysis. For example, ecological psychology is especially applicable to group behavior, whereas the other approaches are often more useful at the individual level of analysis.

THE AROUSAL APPROACH

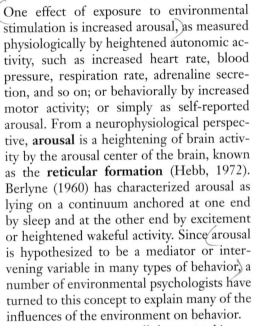

One effect of exposure to environmental stimulation is increased arousal, as measured physiologically by heightened autonomic activity, such as increased heart rate, blood pressure, respiration rate, adrenaline secretion, and so on; or behaviorally by increased motor activity; or simply as self-reported arousal. From a neurophysiological perspective, **arousal** is a heightening of brain activity by the arousal center of the brain, known as the **reticular formation** (Hebb, 1972). Berlyne (1960) has characterized arousal as lying on a continuum anchored at one end by sleep and at the other end by excitement or heightened wakeful activity. Since arousal is hypothesized to be a mediator or intervening variable in many types of behavior, a number of environmental psychologists have turned to this concept to explain many of the influences of the environment on behavior.

In fact, you may recall that arousal is one of the dimensions along which any environment can be evaluated (Russell & Snodgrass, 1987). The arousal model makes distinct predictions about the effects on behavior of *lowered* arousal (i.e., toward the "sleep" end of the continuum) as well as *heightened* arousal, and is quite useful in explaining some behavioral effects of such environmental factors as temperature (Bell, 1981), crowding (Evans, 1978; Seta, Paulus, & Schkade, 1976), and noise (Broadbent, 1971; Klein & Beith, 1985).

We should emphasize that pleasant as well as unpleasant stimuli heighten arousal. An exciting date or a thrilling ride at an amusement park can be just as arousing as noxious noise or a crowded elevator.

What happens to behavior when the arousal level of the organism moves from one end of the continuum to the other? As you might expect, several things occur. For one, arousal leads people to seek information about their internal states. That is, we try to interpret the nature of the arousal and the reasons for it. Is the arousal pleasant or unpleasant? Is it due to people around us, to perceived threat, or to some physical aspect of the environment? In part, we interpret the arousal according to the emotions displayed by others around us (Reisenzein, 1983; Schachter & Singer, 1962; Scheier, Carver, & Gibbons, 1979). In addition, the causes to which we attribute the arousal have significant consequences for our behavior. For example, if we attribute the arousal to our own anger, even though it may be due to a factor in the environment, we may become more hostile and aggressive toward others (e.g., Zillmann, 1979). However, attributing the arousal to anger may not be the only reason for increased aggression. According to several theories of aggression (Berkowitz, 1970; Zillmann, 1983), if aggression is the response most likely to occur in a particular situation, then heightened arousal will facilitate aggression. We find, for example, that when noise increases arousal, it may also increase aggression (Geen & McCown, 1984; Geen & O'Neal, 1969; see also Chapter 5).

Another reaction we have when we become aroused is to seek the opinion of others. We in part compare our actions to those of others to see if we are acting appropriately and to see if we are better off or worse off than others (Festinger, 1954; Wills, 1981). This process is known as **social comparison**. We can feel better about our own circumstances if we compare our standing with others who are faring more poorly. Victims of natural disasters, for example, become very aroused by the circumstances and seek to compare their fate with the fate of others (Hansson, Noulles, & Bellovich, 1982).

Arousal also has important consequences for performance, especially as formulated through the **Yerkes-Dodson Law**. According to this law, performance is maximal at intermediate levels of arousal and gets progressively worse as arousal either falls below or rises above this optimum point. Moreover, the inverted-U relationship between arousal and performance varies as a function of task complexity. For complex tasks, the optimum level of arousal occurs at a slightly lower level of arousal than for simple tasks, as depicted in Figure 4–2. This **curvilinear relationship** appears consistent with other findings (see page 122) that humans seek an intermediate level of stimulation—too much or too little is undesirable (Berlyne, 1960, 1974). From an environment–behavior perspective, we would expect that as environmental stimulation from crowding, noise, air pollution, or any other source increases arousal, performance will either improve or deteriorate, depending on whether the affected person's response is below, at, or above the optimum arousal level for a particular task (see also Broadbent, 1971; Hebb, 1972; Kahneman, 1973). Apparently, low arousal is not conducive to maximum performance, and extremely high arousal prevents us from concentrating on the task at hand.

The arousal approach fares reasonably well as a theoretical base in environmental psychology, although it does have shortcomings. Performance and aggression can be predicted from the effects of the environment on arousal, and the arousal notion does generalize to several environmental factors, most notably noise, heat, and crowding. Unfortunately, arousal can be difficult to measure with a high degree of confidence and generalizability. Some measures used in research

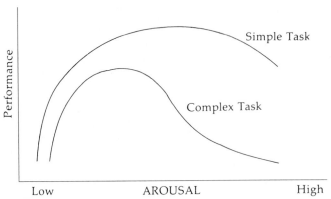

Figure 4–2   The Yerkes-Dodson Law predicts an optimal level of performance for simple and complex tasks, with arousal below or above the optimum resulting in performance decrements.

include heart rate, blood pressure, respiration rate, blood vessel constriction, **galvanic skin response** (or **GSR,** meaning electrical conductance of skin due to sweating), **palmar sweat index** (reaction of palm sweat with a chemical), urine secretion, brain wave activity, physical activity level, muscle tension, skin temperature, and self-report scales. Physiological indices of arousal are not always consistent with each other and are often not consistent with self-reports, such as paper-and-pencil measures of arousal (cf. Cacioppo & Petty, 1983; Dienstbier, 1989). Whereas one measure may indicate increases in arousal in a given situation, other measures may show decreased or unchanged arousal. Which measure to choose in predicting behavior thus becomes a serious problem. Nevertheless, the arousal notion is a useful one and will probably continue to be incorporated into those environment–behavior relationships to which it is applicable.

THE ENVIRONMENTAL LOAD APPROACH

Imagine you are trying to study for three exams you have the following day but your roommate wants to watch television, there is a loud party next door, and two friends come by to entice you to go out for pizza. How can you possibly study for your exams with all this going on? This situation is similar to the circumstances under which the **environmental load** or **overstimulation** approach explains environment–behavior relationships. Especially useful when describing reactions to novel or unwanted environmental stimuli, the model derives from work on attention and information processing, and can be described in four parts (Broadbent, 1958, 1963; Cohen, 1978; Easterbrook, 1959; Milgram, 1970):

1. Humans have a limited capacity to process incoming stimuli and can invest only a limited effort in attending to inputs at any one time.
2. When the amount of information from the environment exceeds the individual's capacity to process all that is relevant, information **overload** occurs. The normal reaction to overload is a type of "tunnel vision" in which we ignore those inputs that are less relevant to the task at hand and devote more attention to those that are relevant. We often take ac-

tive steps to prevent less relevant or distracting stimuli from occurring. For example, Ahrentzen and Evans (1984) noted how teachers modify the classroom environment to minimize distractions.

3. When a stimulus occurs that may require some sort of adaptive response (or when an individual thinks such a stimulus will occur), the significance of the stimulus is evaluated by a monitoring process, and a decision is made about which coping response, if any, to employ. Thus, the more intense or unpredictable or uncontrollable an input, the greater its adaptive significance and the more attention paid to it. Furthermore, the more uncertainty generated by an input about the need for an adaptive response, the more attentional capacity allocated to it.

4. The amount of attention available to a person is not constant and may be temporarily depleted after prolonged demands. After attending to prolonged demands, the total capacity for attention may suffer from an overload. For example, after studying hard for several hours, it is difficult to do anything that demands much attention.

What happens to behavior when an overload occurs? The answer depends on which stimuli are given adequate attention and which are ignored. Generally, stimuli most important to the task at hand are allocated as much attention as needed, and less important stimuli are ignored. If these less important stimuli tend to interfere with the central task, ignoring them will enhance performance. If, however, a task requires a wide range of attention, as when we must do two things at once, performance on less important tasks will deteriorate. In an interest-

ing demonstration of this process, Brown and Poulton (1961) required subjects driving a car either in a residential area (relatively small number of important inputs) or in the parking lot of a crowded shopping center (relatively large number of important inputs) to listen to a series of taped numbers and determine which numbers changed from one sequence to the next. More errors were made on this secondary numbers task when subjects drove in the shopping center, presumably because in the shopping center more attention had to be allocated to important stimuli connected with driving, to the detriment of the less important stimuli of the numbers task.

According to the overload model, once capacity for attention has been depleted owing to prolonged demands, even small demands for attention may cause overloading. Interestingly, once exposure to unpleasant or excessive stimulation has ceased, behavioral aftereffects, such as decreased tolerance for frustration, errors in mental functioning, and less frequent altruistic behavior, may occur (see Chapters 5 and 6 and the box on page 120 for research examples). The overload model attributes these aftereffects to a reduced capacity to attend to relevant cues.

Georg Simmel, a sociologist writing about a century ago, attributed behavioral pathologies in large urban areas to a type of overload (e.g., Simmel, 1957 translation). Milgram (1970) also suggested that the deterioration of social life in large urban areas is caused by the ignoring of peripheral social cues and a reduced capacity to attend to them because of the increased demands of everyday functioning. Thus, urban ills, such as bystanders ignoring others in distress, may be due in part to an environmental overload in which the hustle and bustle of everyday life in the city requires so much attention that there is very little left over for "peripheral" social concerns. Some city dwellers may be forced to develop an aloof attitude toward

THE AFTERMATH OF OVERLOAD

We have noted that we tend to narrow attention and ignore noncentral information when our processing capacity becomes overloaded, so that performance may deteriorate. Interestingly, for some time *after* the overload has apparently stopped, we may suffer from the cost of recovering from the overload. Cohen and Spacapan (1978) reported two studies demonstrating this aftereffect of overload.

First, 80 research subjects viewed a panel of 12 lights, with each light one of three different colors. When a light came on, the subject had to press one of three keys corresponding to the matching color. In a *low-load* condition, the time between consecutive illuminations was 0.8 second. In the *high-load* condition, the time between lights was 0.4 second. Thus, in the high-load condition subjects had to process more information in a given interval of time. Once they had finished the task, subjects were asked to work on some paper-and-pencil puzzles which were actually impossible to solve. Those who had been in the high-load condition spent almost two minutes less than those in the low-load condition before giving up on the puzzles. Apparently, the higher load reduced tolerance for the frustration of working on the puzzles.

In a second study, 40 students individually walked through a shopping mall and listed and priced various items in the stores according to a prearranged set of instructions for 26 tasks. All subjects had 30 minutes to complete the sequence of pricing tasks. High-load subjects were given twice as many items as low-load subjects to list for each task. In addition, half the subjects conducted their mall survey on weekday afternoons (low shopper density) and half on weekend afternoons (high shopper density). The very last pricing task occurred in an isolated hallway. As the subject finished it, an experimenter's assistant (unknown to the subject) standing nearby pretended to lose a contact lens. As the environmental load model would predict, fewer subjects helped look for the lens in the high-load than low-load condition (17 percent versus 57 percent), and fewer helped in the high- than low-density condition (also 17 percent versus 57 percent). Thus, even after an apparent overload, there is a negative impact on task performance and social behavior. Cohen and Spacapan also interpreted their results in terms of aftereffects within the context of the environmental stress model, which we discuss beginning on page 131.

others in order to allocate enough time to everyday functioning (see Chapter 10).

You have probably experienced overload by the end of finals week. What do you do about it? You probably do something to "get away from it all." The notion of overload is particularly germane to the study of leisure environments and other settings which are termed restorative environments in which we have *restorative experiences* that we described in Chapter 2. Kaplan and Kaplan (1989) suggest that prolonged concentration on a task leads to **directed attention fatigue (DAF)**, which is a state of mental exhaustion similar to overload. Their research suggests that recovery from DAF is most likely in a restorative environment, defined as having four characteristics: (1) *being away*, or something other than your normal environment; (2) *extent*, or providing an experience that is extended in time and space; (3) *fascination*, or being interesting and engaging; and (4) *compatibility*, or the ability of the environment to support what you intend to do. A wilderness experience, for example (Hartig, Mang, & Evans, 1991), or a museum visit (Kaplan, Bardwell, & Slakter, 1993) may meet the requirements of a restorative environment for some people. Those who engage in activity in a restorative environment typically report increased interest and acuity in dealing with the task that led to DAF (e.g., Kaplan et al., 1993). Natural environments are believed by many to be most effective in this regard (Parsons, 1991). We will see more about these benefits of natural environments in Chapter 13.

The environmental load model stands up to theoretical scrutiny about as well as the arousal model. It does predict some of the behavioral consequences of excessive environmental stimulation. However, there are many difficult-to-determine 'if's' incorporated into the model, including whether or not in a given situation an overload occurs, whether a specific task is important, whether ignoring less important stimuli facilitates or impairs performance on a particular task, and whether demand has been sufficiently prolonged to deplete attentional capacity. In terms of generality, the model applies to mental and motor performance and to at least some social behaviors. As far as generating research is concerned, the environmental load model does suggest many possibilities, including evaluating whether or not a given environment is likely to produce an overload, and assessing the extent to which attentional depletion contributes to social and environmental problems.

THE UNDERSTIMULATION APPROACH

The environmental overload approach suggests that many environment-behavior relationships, especially those leading to undesirable behavioral and affective (emotional) consequences, are a function of too much stimulation from too many sources. A number of theorists have suggested, however, that many environment–behavior problems result from **understimulation**, or *too little* stimulation. **Sensory deprivation** studies (e.g., Zubek, 1969) suggest that depriving individuals of all sensory stimulation can lead to severe anxiety and other psychological anomalies, although some of these effects may be due to suggestibility from laboratory procedures such as the prominent display of a "panic button" and signing liability release forms mentioning the possibility of serious damage (cf. Barabasz & Barabasz, 1985). In a study of students sharing a ten-person living facility, Brown (1992) discovered that solitude was a common experience but could often be felt as aversive. On the other hand, there may well be benefits of reduced stimulation (see box on page 123). For example, floating in an isolated tank of water may increase creativity and decrease anxiety, hostility, and depression (Forgays & Forgays, 1992; Forgays et al., 1991). Nevertheless, other research has documented the deleterious effects of understimulation on such processes as the maturational development of the young (e.g., Schultz, 1965). Drawing on these sources, some theorists suggest that the environment should sometimes be made more complex and stimulating in order to restore excitement and a sense of belonging to individuals' perceptions of their environment.

Even limited sensory deprivation can have predictable effects on us. For example, Antarctic isolation has been shown to modify performance on a task (Barabasz & Barabasz, 1986). Moreover, the isolation of solitary sailing or from being an aircrash survivor in a remote region can generate a "sensed presence" of another individual even when no such person exists (Suedfeld & Mocellin, 1987).

Although cities may have an overstimulating social environment, they may subject inhabitants to an understimulating physical environment. Urbanologist A. E. Parr (1966) has contended that fields, forests, and mountains contain an unending variety of changing patterns of visual stimulation, but that urban areas contain the same patterns repeated on every street. In many tract housing developments in particular, the structures all resemble each other. According to Parr, the giant skyscrapers lining city streets and the interiors of modern windowless structures instill a sense of enclosure rather than a sense of being drawn to the next horizon. Parr and others assert that this lack of stimulation leads to boredom and is in some way responsible for such urban ills as juvenile delinquency and vandalism and poor education (cf. Heft, 1979b).

To study some of these problems of understimulation, Wohlwill (1966) advocated scaling environments along a number of dimensions of stimulation, including intensity, novelty, complexity, temporal change or variation, surprisingness, and incongruity. As we will see in Chapter 10, the desire for these types of stimulation may explain why people leave cities in great numbers to live in more "natural" environments.

As a theoretical approach by itself, the understimulation angle does help predict some environment–behavior relationships, but it stands in marked contrast to arousal and overload theories that examine the same environments and find too much stimulation. Moreover, some researchers claim that benefits can be derived from deprivation of sensory stimulation (e.g., Suedfeld, 1975). We will reserve further judgment on the understimulation theory until we have examined a theoretical approach that attempts to consolidate the understimulation and overstimulation approaches.

ADAPTATION LEVEL THEORY: OPTIMAL STIMULATION

If the research evidence supporting the arousal and overload theories suggests that too much environmental stimulation has deleterious effects on behavior and emotions, and if the evidence supporting the understimulation approach suggests that too little stimulation similarly has undesirable effects, it stands to reason that some intermediate level of stimulation would be ideal. This is the approach taken by Wohlwill (1974) in his **adaptation level (AL)** theory of environmental stimulation. Borrowing from Helson's (1964) adaptation level theory of sensation and perception, Wohlwill began with the assumption, for example, that humans dislike crowds, at least on certain occasions, as when trying to make last-minute Christmas purchases or trying to leave a packed football stadium at the end of the game. On the other hand, most of us do not like total social isolation all day, either. Along these lines, Altman (1975) describes environmental mechanisms by which we regulate privacy to achieve the desired level. Wohlwill believed that the same applies for all types of stimulation, including temperature, noise, and even the complexity of roadway scenery. What we usually prefer is an optimal level of stimulation (see also Zuckerman, 1979).

Categories and Dimensions of Stimulation

At least three categories of environment–behavior relationships should conform to this optimal level hypothesis, according to Wohlwill. These categories are sensory stimulation, social stimulation, and movement. Too much or too little sensory stimulation is undesirable, too much or too little social contact is undesirable, and too much or too

REST:
The Benefits of Sensory Deprivation

We have noted that reduced stimulation can have deleterious effects on people. In contrast to such findings, many studies suggest that there are actually benefits to boredom. A procedure called **REST**, or Restricted Environmental Stimulation Technique, or Restricted Environmental Stimulation Therapy (Suedfeld, 1980; Suedfeld et al., 1990) involves placing a person in a soundproof, darkened room or into a darkened water tank (Figure 4–3).

The potential benefits of REST seem to cover many areas (Barabasz & Barabasz, 1993). For example, reduced stimulation seems to have favorable outcomes for hyperactive and autistic children (Suedfeld, Schwartz, & Arnold, 1980). Biofeedback seems to have more positive effects when combined with REST (Lloyd & Shurley, 1976; Plotkin, 1978). Hypertension (high blood pressure) can be reduced with REST (Fine & Turner, 1982; Kristeller, Schwartz, & Black, 1982; Suedfeld, Roy, & Landon, 1982), and REST can help some individuals stop smoking (Suedfeld & Baker-Brown, 1986).

Figure 4–3   An example of a REST chamber. The participant lies on a fluid-filled mattress in the chamber, and the doors are closed, reducing the noise to minimal levels.

How does REST achieve these results? No one knows for sure, but one proposed avenue is that with reduced extraneous stimulation, subjects can better recognize internal states, such as high blood pressure, and thus take more effective self-regulatory steps. Another possibility is that REST disorganizes established mechanisms for maintaining chronic maladaptive patterns, and thus permits new, more adaptive mechanisms to occur. More complex cognitive and physiological avenues have also been explored (Suedfeld et al., 1990).

However it works, REST has become commercially popular. That is, businesses provide REST-type tanks or beds for clients to purchase or rent on a short-term basis. We suspect such ventures will spur more investigations into the value of REST procedures.

little movement is undesirable. (Do you see the similarity between this notion and the Yerkes-Dodson Law described under arousal theory?) These categories in turn vary along at least three dimensions that have optimal levels. The first dimension is *intensity*. As

we have noted, too many or too few people around us can be psychologically disturbing. Too little or too much auditory stimulation has the same unwanted effect. We have all experienced the irritation of neighbors making distracting noise while we were trying to listen to a lecture or concert, of loud stereos playing when we are trying to study, and of children screaming when adults are trying to carry on a conversation. On the other hand, if you have ever been in a soundproof chamber for very long, you know that the absence of external sound becomes very unnerving after only five or ten minutes.

Another dimension of environmental stimulation is *diversity*, both across time and at any given moment. Too little diversity in our surroundings produces boredom and the desire to seek arousal and excitement. Too much diversity—as in the typical "strip" of fast-food franchises, gas stations, and glaring neon signs common in many towns and cities—is considered an eyesore. As we saw in Chapter 2, considerable research (see Wohlwill, 1974) indicates that the perceived attractiveness and the degree of pleasant feelings associated with a human-built scene are maximized at an intermediate level of diversity.

The third dimension of stimulation is *patterning*, or the degree to which a perception contains both structure and uncertainty. The total absence of structure that can be coded by information-processing mechanisms, such as diffuse light of a constant intensity or a single tone at a constant volume, is disturbing. By the same token, a very complex pattern that contains no predictable structure is also disturbing. To the extent that a modern built environment is so diverse and complex that we have difficulty imposing a perceptual structure on it, we probably experience that environment as stressful. Urban street patterns are a good example of this dimension. Parallel streets in intersecting grid patterns can be monotonous. On the other hand, complex layouts with no predictable numbering or no easy access to major arteries can cause confusion. An intermediate level of patterning, with gently winding streets and cul-de-sacs, is usually comfortable, yet pleasantly stimulating.

Optimizing Stimulation

After assuming the general rule that there are optimal levels of environmental stimulation, Wohlwill introduced a modifier to this rule by further assuming that each person has an optimal level of stimulation, which is based on past experience. Thus, Tibetan people live comfortably at altitudes with so little oxygen that most of us would have difficulty maintaining consciousness; they have adapted to a level of oxygen concentration quite different from what most of us would consider ideal. Similarly, those of us who live in cities probably have a higher level of tolerance for crowds and less tolerance for isolation than do most residents of rural areas. After a person raised in a rural area has lived in a city for a few months or years, he or she probably acquires a greater tolerance for crowds than the rural resident who never moves to a city. Wohlwill referred to this shift in optimal stimulation level as **adaptation**, defined as a shift in our judgmental or affective responses to a stimulus following continued exposure to it.

Adaptation levels not only differ from person to person as a function of experience, but also change with time following exposure to a different level of stimulation. For example, Bih (1992) described how Chinese students moving to New York City adapted over time, Yamamoto et al. (1992) studied how Japanese adapt to the workplace following university graduation, and Laska (1990) observed how people make long-term adaptations to repeated flooding of their homes. Thus, how one evaluates and reacts to a given environment along a particular dimension is in part determined by how much that environment deviates from one's adaptation level on that dimension. The more an environment deviates from the adaptation level, the more intense the reaction to that environment should be. As you may recall from Chapter 2, variation in individual perceptions of what constitutes a "beautiful" or "desirable" environment is considerable. Adaptation level theory suggests the reason for this variation involves individual differences in adaptation level along several relevant dimensions. For example, Mocellin et al. (1991) found that anxiety levels did not increase among groups stationed in harsh, isolated Arctic and Antarctic environments; quite likely, adaptation levels were already suitable for these circumstances (cf. Harrison, Clearwater, & McKay, 1991). Why do people differ so much in their assessment of environmental risk, such as perceived danger of toxins? Differences in adaptation level may be the explanation (Vaughan, 1993; see Figure 4–4).

Adaptation Versus Adjustment

Adaptation level theory postulates an interesting environment–behavior relationship in

Figure 4–4 Differences in adaptation level may explain why some people pay heightened attention to environmental risk and others minimize the same risk. Grieshop and Stiles (1989) found that over 25 percent of their household respondents reported suffering illness from pesticide exposure, yet there was high risk-taking in pesticide use even among those who perceived higher danger. Perhaps adaptation level of perceived risk explains such findings.

the distinction between adaptation and what Sonnenfeld (1966) calls **adjustment**. Adaptation refers to changing the response to the stimulus, whereas adjustment refers to changing the stimulus itself. Adjustment in this case does not refer to the adjustment–maladjustment continuum conceptualized in clinical psychology (i.e., an internal, psychological state), but rather to a mechanism by which we change the environment. For example, adaptation to hot temperatures would involve gradually getting used to the heat so that we sweat more efficiently on exposure to it. Adjustment would involve either wearing lighter clothes or installing an air-conditioning system so that the temperature stimulus striking our skin is much cooler. For most organisms and for early human societies, adaptation was probably a more realistic option than adjustment. For modern societies with advanced technology, however, adjustment is so clearly a realistic option that we prefer it over adaptation. Witness, for example, one response to the need to adjust thermostats so that heating the indoor environment will use less energy. Rather than adapt to temperatures that are only slightly below what we perceive as optimal, we often resort to highly polluting wood-burning stoves or fireplace inserts that will let us maintain the old adaptation level. In general, adaptation level theory suggests that when given a choice between adapting and adjusting, people will take the course that causes the least discomfort.

Evaluation of the Optimal Stimulation Approach: Breadth Versus Specificity

It should be obvious that adaptation level theory incorporates some of the best features of arousal, overload, and understimulation theories. As such, it has rather broad generality; it is applicable to physical and social environments as well as to all forms of sensation and perception. AL theory also suggests that future research might well concentrate on the adaptation process in order to solve many environmental problems. One difficulty that arises with this theory, however, is that since it allows for so much individual variation in adaptation level, it becomes very difficult to make more general predictions about environmental preference and environment–behavior relationships. This problem typically arises in behavioral science theories. The more specific the elements from which predictions are made, the less general the predictions; the more general the predictors, the less precise the predictions.

Another problem with AL theory is that it is often difficult to identify an "optimal" level of stimulation before we make a prediction. We mentioned that in environmental aesthetics it has been proposed that an intermediate level of complexity leads to optimal judgments of beauty. This prediction often proves incorrect, in part because we have difficulty defining what we mean by an intermediate level of complexity. In order for AL theory to work, we would need to see what conditions maximize judgments of beauty, then define that level of complexity as intermediate. What is really needed is more research that quantifies levels of environmental stimulation. Only then can we know how well AL theory predicts environment–behavior relationships.

THE BEHAVIOR CONSTRAINT APPROACH

According to the theoretical perspectives we have examined thus far, excessive or undesirable environmental stimulation leads to arousal or a strain on our information-processing capacity. Another potential consequence of such stimulation is loss of **perceived control** over the situation. Have you ever been caught in a severe winter storm or summer heat wave and felt there was nothing you could do about it? Or have you ever been forced to live or work in extremely crowded conditions and felt the situation was so out of hand there was nothing you could do to overcome it? This loss of perceived control over the situation is the first step in what is known as the **behavior constraint** model of environmental stimulation (Proshansky, Ittleson, & Rivlin, 1970; Rodin & Baum, 1978; Stokols, 1978, 1979; Zlutnick & Altman, 1972). So important is the feeling of perceived control that some would classify the behavior constraint model as a subunit of a "**control model**" that is more global. Whatever classification one might prefer, the concepts in the model are extremely important to environmental psychologists.

The term "constraint" here means that something about the environment is limiting or interfering with things we wish to do. According to the behavior constraint model, the constraint can be an actual impairment from the environment or simply our belief that the environment is placing a constraint on us. What is most important is the cognitive interpretation of the situation as being beyond our control.

Once you perceive that you are losing control over the environment, what happens next? When you perceive that environmental events are constraining or restricting your behavior, you first experience discomfort or negative affect (i.e., have unpleasant feelings). You also probably try to reassert your control over the situation. This phenomenon is known as **psychological reactance**, or simply **reactance** (Brehm, 1966; Brehm & Brehm, 1981; Wortman & Brehm, 1975). Any time we feel that our freedom of action is being constrained, psychological reactance leads us to try to regain that freedom (cf. Strube & Werner, 1984). If crowding is a threat to our freedom, we react by erecting physical or social behaviors to "shut others out." If the weather restricts our freedom, we might stay indoors or else use technological devices (e.g., snow plows, air-conditioned cars) to regain control. According to the behavior constraint model, we do not actually have to experience loss of control for reactance to set in; all we need do is *anticipate* that some environmental factor is about to restrict our freedom. Mere anticipation of crowding, for example, is enough to make us start erecting physical or psychological barriers against others.

What happens if our efforts to reassert control are unsuccessful in regaining freedom of action? The ultimate consequence of loss of control, according to the behavior constraint model, is **learned helplessness** (Garber & Seligman, 1981; Seligman, 1975). That is, if repeated efforts at regaining control result in failure, we might begin to think that our actions have no effect on the situation, so we stop trying to gain control even when, from an objective point of view, our control has been restored. In other words, we "learn" that we are helpless. Students who try to change a class schedule but are rebuffed by the registration office numerous times soon "learn" that they are helpless against bureaucracy. Similarly, if efforts to overcome crowding are unsuccessful, we may abandon our attempts to gain privacy and change our lifestyles accordingly. During a very severe winter we sometimes hear reports of individuals "giving up" trying to keep warm when their fuel supplies become depleted, and some people die as a result. While less severe than death, learned helplessness often leads to depression.

The behavior constraint model, then, posits three basic steps: perceived loss of control, reactance, and learned helplessness. The use of this model thus far in environmental psychology has been relatively limited, although components are often discussed within the context of the stress or load models. Whether treated within the behavior constraint model or within some other model, it is clear that perceived loss of control has unfortunate consequences for behavior, and that restoring control enhances performance and mental outlook. For example, Glass and Singer (1972) found that telling subjects they could reduce the amount of noxious noise in an experiment by pressing a button reduced or eliminated many of the negative effects of noise, even though subjects did not actually press the button. That is, simply perceiving that they could control the noise reduced the adaptive costs of that stress. Perceived control over noise has also been found to reduce its negative effects on aggression (Donnerstein & Wilson, 1976) and helping behavior (Sherrod & Downs, 1974). Moreover, perceived loss of control over air pollution seems to reduce efforts to do anything about the problem (Evans & Jacobs, 1981). Similarly, perceived control over crowding reduces its unpleasant effects (e.g., Langer & Saegert, 1977; Rodin, 1976), and perceived control over crime may motivate us to employ more prevention measures (Miransky & Langer, 1978; Tyler, 1981). Moser and Levy-Leboyer (1985) showed that loss of perceived control over a malfunctioning phone led to acts of aggression, but the availability of information designed to restore control improved the situation. Similarly, Rochford and Blocker (1991) observed that perceived control over the threat of flooding was associated with greater activism to do something about it.

Perceived control also has implications for institutional environments. Langer and Rodin (1976), for example, manipulated the amount of control residents of a nursing home had over their daily affairs. For instance, one group was told the staff would take care of them while another group was told they were responsible for themselves. One group was given plants to raise themselves, while the other group was given plants to be cared for by the staff. After three weeks, residents in the high-control group showed greater well-being and enhanced mood and more activity than those in the low-control

ENVIRONMENTS AND THE ELDERLY:
Environmental Press and Competence

Adaptation level theory posits that each person has an optimal level of stimulation along several dimensions. A special application of this idea is a model of **environmental press** developed by M. Powell Lawton and Lucille Nahemow to describe environments for the elderly (Lawton, 1975; Lawton & Nahemow, 1973; Nahemow & Lawton, 1973). This model posits that the demands (i.e., press) an environment places on its occupants as well as the competence of the occupants determine the consequences of interacting with the environment. If the impact of the press is within the **environmental competence** of the individual to handle it (i.e., within the adaptation level), positive feelings about the environment occur and the behavior is adaptive. If the press is considerably weaker or stronger than the competence of the individual (i.e., outside the adaptation level), negative feelings and maladaptive behavior occur. Thus, an understimulating nursing home environment or a fast-paced, crime-ridden neighborhood may both be outside the desired adaptation level for press and competence. We will see in Chapter 12 how environments for the elderly can be designed to suit their needs.

condition. Even 18 months later the high-control group had more positive outcomes (Rodin & Langer, 1977; see also Lemke & Moos, 1986; Rothbaum, Weisz, & Snyder, 1982). Schulz (1976) has also documented positive effects of a perceived-control intervention for the institutionalized elderly. After the intervention was terminated, however, those in the high-control condition showed an especially rapid decline (Schulz & Hanusa, 1978), perhaps because a lessened sense of control produced learned helplessness and depression. Schutte et al. (1992) have developed a scale to measure perceived control in the institutional setting and have found that it is an efficient indicator of whether or not interventions do indeed increase perceived control.

Types of Control

Several attempts have been made to elaborate on the types of control we can have over our environment. Averill (1973), for example,

distinguishes between categories of: (1) **behavioral control**, in which we have available a behavioral response which can change the threatening environmental event (e.g., turning off a loud noise); (2) **cognitive control**, in which we process information about the threat in such a way that we appraise it as less threatening or we understand it better (e.g., deciding that a contaminant in our water is not toxic); and (3) **decisional control** in which we have a choice among several options (e.g., choosing to live in a quiet rather than a noisy neighborhood). Behavioral control can be manifested either through regulated administration, in which there is control over who administers the threatening event and when they do it, or stimulus modification, in which the threat can be avoided, terminated, or otherwise modified. Cognitive control can be manifested either through appraisal of the event as less threatening or through information gain about such factors as predictability or

PERCEIVED CONTROL AND RESEARCH ETHICS: *A Dilemma*

We have noted that perceived control over unpleasant environmental stimulation, such as noise, reduces the negative consequences of exposure to the stimuli. An interesting problem in this regard has arisen in the area of laboratory research on environmental stressors. Gardner (1978) notes that for years it was possible to demonstrate such effects as reduced proofreading speed and accuracy when laboratory subjects were exposed to uncontrollable noise. Subsequent research, however, has failed to find these detrimental effects. What went wrong? Gardner provides evidence that the "culprit" is a set of research ethics guidelines established by the federal government and implemented by universities and other research institutions. Among these guidelines is a requirement that subjects be informed of potential risks when participating in experiments, even though the risks are minimal. Moreover, subjects must be told that they are free to terminate the experiment at any time and must sign an "informed consent" statement disclosing the risks and the termination provision. Gardner provides evidence that such informed consent procedures amount to giving subjects perceived control over the stressor, and thus stress effects are reduced! The situation is then an ethical dilemma: How can one ethically do experimental research on stressful environmental conditions if the ethical procedures in effect eliminate the negative reactions to these conditions? Gardner proposes that where risks are minimal, the need to know about these effects justifies modification of the informed-consent procedures. Such a decision would rest with an Institutional Review Board to ensure the safety of subjects. Alternatively, more emphasis may have to be placed on field research involving observance of naturally occurring instances of the stressor. Ultimately, we suspect the ethical dilemma can never be fully resolved (see also Dill et al., 1982).

consequences. Thompson (1981) has noted that there are some questions about this type of categorization, and adds a category of **retrospective control**, in which we perceive present control over a past aversive event. Weisz, Rothbaum, and Blackburn (1984) distinguish between **primary control**, meaning overt control over existing conditions, and **secondary control**, meaning accommodating to existing realities and becoming satisfied with things the way they are (see also Thompson, 1981). These authors note that there may be cultural differences in the emphasis placed on primary versus secondary

control (cf. Azuma, 1984; Kojima, 1984). Apparently, the amount of control we have is important: Being able to control both onset and termination of a noise results in better adaptation than control over just onset or just termination of the noise (Sherrod et al., 1977). We may also have more control over some areas of our lives (e.g., our bedroom) than over others (e.g., our community; see Paulhus, 1983).

It would be an oversimplification to state that the greater the control we perceive over our environment, the better we are able to adapt to it successfully. In fact, there are some circumstances under which control can lead to increased threat, anxiety, and maladaptive behavior (e.g., Averill, 1973; Folkman, 1984; Thompson, 1981). For example, knowing that you can control a potential flood by building a larger levee may make you worry about the expense and time commitment of the intervention. Or, if your dwelling is built near a toxic waste dump, perceived control through the option of moving away may heighten concern about losing close neighbors and forsaking the emotional attachment to your dwelling. Interestingly, sometimes we actually prefer less control. Certain evidence even suggests that some elderly people prefer less personal control over health-related decisions and wish that others would make these decisions for them (see Rodin, 1986; Woodward & Wallston, 1987).

Aspects of Helplessness

Just as research has progressed on the perceived-control component of the behavior constraint model, so has research on the reactance and learned-helplessness components. For our present discussion, the work on learned helplessness seems especially important. For example, Hiroto (1974) found that when subjects were given a chance to terminate an aversive noise, those who had previously been able to control it learned to terminate it. Those who had previously been unable to control the noise, however, responded as if they were helpless, and failed to learn the termination procedure. Similarly, a field study with school children found that those who attended noisy schools near Los Angeles International Airport showed more signs of learned helplessness than those from quieter schools (Cohen et al., 1980, 1981).

Learned helplessness effects have been interpreted in terms of attribution theory (e.g., Abramson, Seligman, & Teasdale, 1978; Miller & Norman, 1979; Peterson & Seligman, 1984; Sweeney, Anderson, & Bailey,

1986; Tennen & Eller, 1977). Attributions are inferences about causes of events or about characteristics of people or events. Although the details of the attribution interpretations of learned helplessness are too extensive for in-depth coverage here, we can make a few broad statements. In general, helplessness effects are more likely to occur if we attribute our lack of control over the environment to: (1) stable rather than unstable factors (e.g., to our physical or mental inability to do anything about it rather than to our temporary lack of time to act on it); (2) general rather than specific factors (e.g., attributing pollution to all industry rather than to a specific factory); and, (3) internal rather than external locus of control (e.g., attributing our discomfort in a crowd to our own preference for open spaces rather than to the behavior of others in the crowd). In a confirmation of this attributional approach, researchers found that those who attributed negative outcomes to global (general) factors showed helplessness deficits in settings both similar and dissimilar to the setting where an initial negative outcome occurred. Those who attributed the initial negative outcome to specific factors, however, showed helplessness effects only in settings similar to the initial one (Alloy et al., 1984).

Value and Limitations of the Behavior Constraint Approach

Research on reactance, perceived loss of control, and learned helplessness is certain to continue, whether interpreted from the perspective of the behavior constraint model or from some other perspective. The model itself has considerable, though limited, utility. In instances of perceived loss of control, the model is quite useful in predicting some of the consequences. In cases in which there is no reason to infer perceived loss of control, however, other mediators, such as stress, arousal, and overload, are probably necessary to explain environment–behavior relationships. Moreover, the behavior constraint approach places much emphasis on individual reactions, and can minimize the need to look at the entire setting (e.g., Stokols, 1979).

THE ENVIRONMENTAL STRESS APPROACH

Another theoretical approach, which is widely used in environmental psychology, is to view many elements of the environment, such as noise and crowding, as stressors. Stressors—including job pressures, marital discord, natural disasters, the turmoil of moving to a new location—are considered to be aversive circumstances that threaten the well-being of the person. **Stress** is an intervening or mediating variable, defined as the reaction to these circumstances. This "reaction" is assumed to include emotional, behavioral, and physiological components. The physiological component was intitially proposed by Selye (1956), and is often called **systemic stress**. The behavioral and emotional components were proposed by Lazarus (1966), and are often called **psychological stress**. Since physiological and psychological stress reactions are interrelated and do not occur alone, environmental psychologists usually combine all the components into one theory, or the **environmental stress model** (e.g., Baum, Singer, & Baum, 1981; Evans & Cohen, 1987; Lazarus & Folkman, 1984).

Sometimes the term "stress" is restricted to environmental events, and an additional term, "strain," is used to describe the consequence within the organism. However, we will use "stress" to refer to the entire stimulus-response situation, "stressor" to refer to the environmental component alone, and "stress response" to refer to the reaction caused by the environmental component.

As we will see, some components of the arousal, environmental load, adaptation level, and behavior constraint approaches fit very well into an environmental-stress frame-

work. Overload, for example, can be viewed as one consequence of coping with stress, and heightened arousal is certainly a component of stress. Similarly, an optimal level of stimulation (i.e., stimulation at the adaptation level) should result in little evidence of a stress reaction, but multiple constraints on behavior might be expected to lead to considerable signs of stress.

We will organize our discussion of stress into three basic parts. First, we will consider the *characteristics of stressors*, such as how long they last or how often they occur. Since the degree to which these events actually cause stress is dependent upon how they are interpreted (i.e., whether people notice them and decide that they might be harmful or aversive), we will also discuss the *appraisal of stressors*. Finally, the kinds of *stress responses* that occur (physiological reactions, cognitive factors, coping strategies, aftereffects) will be considered.

Characteristics of Stressors

There are a number of ways we might classify stressors. Lazarus and Cohen (1977) have described three general categories of environmental stressors: cataclysmic events, personal stressors, and background stressors. These vary according to *severity of impact* as well as other dimensions such as the ease of the **coping** or adaptation process in response to them.

Cataclysmic Events

Natural disasters, war, nuclear accident, or fire (Proulx, 1993) are unpredictable and powerful threats that generally affect all of those touched by them. Such **cataclysmic events** are overwhelming stressors that have several basic characteristics. They are usually sudden, giving little or no warning of their occurrence. They have a powerful impact, elicit a more or less universal response, and usually require a great deal of effort for effective coping. The accidents at Three

Mile Island and Chernobyl, the Mount Saint Helens eruption (Adams & Adams, 1984), as well as the more common tornadoes, hurricanes, and other natural disasters (Baker & Chapman, 1962; Baum et al., 1980; Baum, Fleming, & Davidson, 1983; Hartsough & Savitsky, 1984; Pennebaker & Newtson, 1983; Sims & Baumann, 1972) can all be considered in this category of stressors.

The powerful onset of sudden cataclysmic events may initially evoke a freezing or dazed response by victims (e.g., Moore, 1958). Coping is difficult and may bring no immediate relief. However, the severely threatening period of such an event usually (but not always) ends quickly, and recovery begins. A tornado may strike for only a brief time, and other cataclysmic events may be over in a few days (Baum, Fleming, & Davidson, 1983). When the process is allowed to proceed without a return of the stressor, rebuilding progresses and more or less complete recovery is generally achieved. In the case of Three Mile Island or Love Canal, where rebuilding is not what is needed (nothing was actually destroyed), and the damage already done is less important than the damage that may yet come, recovery may be more difficult.

One important feature of cataclysmic events, which is in some ways beneficial for the coping process, is that they impact on a large number of people. Affiliation with others and comparing feelings and opinions with them have been identified as important styles of coping with such threats (e.g., McGrath, 1970; Schachter, 1959), since **social support** can moderate the effects of stressful conditions (e.g., Cobb, 1976). Because people are able to share their distress with others undergoing the same difficulties, some studies have suggested that cohesion results among these individuals (Quarantelli, 1978). Of course, this does not always happen, and residents cannot "band together" to fight a stressor indefinitely. When a stressor persists in an apparently unresolvable manner, problems of a different kind can arise—including learned helplessness.

Personal Stressors

A second group of stressors may be termed **personal stressors**. These include such events as illness, death of a loved one (e.g., Greene, 1966; Hackett & Weisman, 1964; Lehman, Wortman, & Williams, 1987; Parkes, 1972), or loss of one's job (Dooley, Rook, & Catalano, 1987; Kasl & Cobb, 1970; Kessler, House, & Turner, 1987)—events that are powerful enough to challenge adaptive abilities in the same way as cataclysmic events. Personal stressors generally affect fewer people at any one time than do cataclysmic events, and may or may not be expected. Frequently, with personal stressors the point of severest impact occurs early and coping can progress once the worst is over, although this is not always the case. Often the magnitude, duration, and point of severest impact of cataclysmic events and personal stressors, such as death and loss of a job, are similar. However, the relatively smaller number of people who experience a particular personal stressor at any one time may be significant, because there are fewer others to serve as sources of social support. Also, a cataclysmic event such as a flood can result in the loss of a loved one or loss of a job or other personal stressor.

Background Stressors

Less powerful, more gradual but more chronic and almost routine stressors are termed **background stressors**. Rotton (1990) prefers to divide background stressors into two types. **Daily hassles** (or micro-stressors) are stable, low-intensity problems encountered as part of one's routine (Lazarus et al., 1985; Zika & Chamberlain, 1987), such as we described in the opening paragraph of this chapter. **Ambient stressors** are "chronic, global conditions of the environment—pollution, noise, residential crowding, traffic congestion—which, in a general sense, represent noxious stimulation, and which, as stressors, place demands upon us to adapt or cope" (Campbell, 1983, p. 360).

Whereas daily hassles (losing things, home maintenance) are unique each day and affect a specific individual, ambient stressors such as pollution impact a larger number of people, are chronic and nonurgent, and are difficult to remove through the efforts of one individual. While many background stressors are mundane and of relatively low intensity, some may not even be noticeable, like certain instances of air pollution (e.g., Evans & Jacobs, 1981). Any one or two background stressors may not be sufficient to cause great adaptive difficulty, but when a number occur together they can exact a cost over time and may be as serious as cataclysmic events or personal stressors. Regular and prolonged exposure to certain low-level background stressors may even require more adaptive responses in the long run than more intense stressors. For example, long-term exposure to noise (Cohen, Glass, & Singer, 1973), neighborhood problems (Harburg et al., 1973; White et al., 1987), and long-term commuting stress (Singer, Lundberg, & Frankenhaeuser, 1978) can be quite problematic.

With background stressors, it is often difficult to identify a point at which "the worst is over," and it may not be at all clear that things will get better. In fact, things may go from bad to worse. In addition, the benefits for coping of having others who "share in the experience" may not be as great as for other types of stressors. This may be because the intensity of background stressors is frequently so low as to never raise the need for affiliation; or, alternatively, social support may not be appropriate in these situations (cf. Campbell, 1983).

Appraisal

A given environmental event may or may not be a stressor in all circumstances, and in the same circumstance it may be a stressor to some individuals and not to others. The probability of an event becoming stressful is determined by a number of factors (Evans & Cohen, 1987), including the characteristics of the event and the way individuals appraise it. Thus, in order for the stress process to begin, there must be cognitive **appraisal** of a stimulus as threatening. To use an environmental example, 90°F (32°C) to a native southerner is not likely to be very stressful in midsummer. To someone living in Barrow, Alaska, however, the mere thought of experiencing 90°F for a few hours a day may well be evaluated as threatening. In other words, the same stimulus that may not be stressful in one situation may be stressful in another—the stimulus has not changed, but the individual's appraisal of it as threatening or nonthreatening has changed. Moreover, cognitive appraisal that an aversive event, such as crowding, is pending is often sufficient to elicit a stress response, even though the physical event itself does not happen (e.g., Baum & Greenberg, 1975).

Lazarus (1966) suggested that this cognitive appraisal is a function of individual psychological factors (intellectual resources, knowledge of past experience, and motivation) and cognitive aspects of the specific stimulus situation (control over the stimulus, predictability of the stimulus, and immediacy or "time until impact" of the stimulus). The more knowledge one has about the beneficial aspects of a source of noise, or the more control one has over the noise (in terms of terminating or avoiding it), the less one is likely to evaluate that stimulus as threatening, and the less threatening the situation is likely to be.

Types of Appraisal

Cognitive appraisal of a situation is more complex than merely assessing its potential threat (see Baum et al., 1982, for a review). Several different types of appraisal are possible. **Harm or loss appraisals** focus on damage that has already been done (Lazarus &

Launier, 1978). For example, victims of a natural or technological disaster could be expected to make harm/loss evaluations. In general, rapid loss of resources is associated with traumatic stress (Hobfoll, 1991). In contrast, **threat appraisals** are concerned with future dangers. Environmental toxins such as pesticides may evoke perceived threat to one's health, and threat appraisals may precede exposure to them. Perceived threat from and stress reaction to a chronic toxic hazard is likely to be worse than that associated with a quick-hitting flood (Baum et al., 1992; Baum & Fleming, 1993). The ability to anticipate potential difficulties allows us to prevent their occurrence, but may cause us to experience anticipatory stress. It is hard to say which is worse—seeing one's home destroyed in a hurricane (harm/loss) or not knowing how one will be sheltered from the elements until one can build a new home (threat). As this example suggests, threat and harm/loss appraisals usually go hand-in-hand (Lazarus & Folkman, 1984). **Challenge appraisals** are different from others because they focus not on the harm or potential harm of an event, but on the possibility of overcoming the stressor. Some stressors may be beyond our coping ability, but we all have a range of events for which we are confident of our ability to cope successfully. Stressors that are evaluated as challenges fall within this hypothetical range (Dienstbier, 1989; Lazarus & Launier, 1978).

Factors Affecting Appraisal

A number of factors have been identified that affect our appraisals of environmental stressors. These include the characteristics of the condition in question (e.g., how loud a particular noise is), situational conditions (e.g., whether what we are doing is compatible with or inhibited by the potential stressor), individual differences, and environmental, social, and psychological variables. To cite but one example, the upper-middle-class resident of a large city may be less likely to

experience difficulty as a result of urban conditions than a poorer resident of the same city. Or, he or she may be better able to avoid the seamy side of the city, and thus less likely to be exposed to aversive urban conditions. Attitudes toward the source of stress will also mediate responses; if we believe that a condition will cause no permanent harm, our response will probably be less extreme than if it carries the threat of lasting harm. If our attitudes are strongly in favor of something that may also harm us, we may reappraise threats and make them seem less dangerous.

We described the influence of perceived control when discussing the behavior constraint approach. Perceived control is also an important mediator of stress, providing a sense of being able to cope effectively, to predict events, and to determine what will happen. Giving subjects information about a stressor prior to their exposure to it helps them to plan and predict what will happen. Such information increases perceived control and reduces the threat appraisal made when the stressor is experienced. For example, the stress associated with surgery or aversive medical procedures can be reduced by providing patients with accurate expectations of what they will feel (e.g., Johnson, 1973; Johnson & Leventhal, 1974). Other studies have found that accurate expectations about high levels of density reduce crowding stress (Baum, Fisher, & Solomon, 1981; Langer & Saegert, 1977).

Coping styles or behavior patterns also appear to affect the ways in which events are appraised, as well as which types of coping are invoked. Work on a number of these dimensions, such as **repression-sensitization** (the degree to which people think about a stressor), **screening** (a person's ability to ignore extraneous stimuli or to prioritize demands), and **denial** (the degree to which people ignore or suppress awareness of problems), has indicated that people differing along these dimensions may interpret situations differently (e.g., Bell & Byrne, 1978; Collins, Baum, & Singer, 1983; Janis, 1958; Mehrabian, 1976–77). A study by Baum et al. (1982), for example, suggests that individuals who cope with overload by screening and prioritizing demands are less susceptible to the effects of crowding than people who do not cope in this way.

Another moderator of stress appraisals may be social support—the feeling that one is cared about and valued by other people, and that he or she belongs to a group (Cobb, 1976). Many have long believed that interpersonal relationships can somehow protect us from many ills (e.g., Cohen & Wills, 1985; Jung, 1984). However, the effects of having or not having social and emotional support have not always been clearly demonstrated (cf. Ganellen & Blaney, 1984; Hendrick, Wells, & Faletti, 1982). One possible reason is that those from crowded homes or other backgrounds of social distress may respond to others through withdrawal rather than attachment (Evans & Lepore, 1993).

Characteristics of the Stress Response

A distinction is often made between **primary appraisal**, which involves assessment of threat, and **secondary appraisal**, which involves assessment of coping strategies. Appraisals of stressors help determine responses to them. If an appraisal is "negative" and an event is seen as being dangerous, responses that prepare us to cope will ensue. These stress responses involve the whole body. Physiological changes are part of this response, most reflecting increased arousal. At the same time, emotional, psychological, and behavioral changes may also occur as part of the stress response.

Physiological Response

Part of the response to an aversive or stressful stimulus is automatic. Selye's (1956) **general adaptation syndrome (GAS)** consists of three stages: (1) the alarm reaction, (2) the stage of resistance, and (3) the stage of ex-

haustion. Initially, an **alarm reaction** to a stressor causes autonomic processes (heart rate, adrenaline secretion, and so on) to speed up. The second stage in the stress process, the **stage of resistance**, also begins with some automatic mechanism for coping with the stressor. If heat is the stressor, sweating occurs; if extreme cold is the stressor, shivering may occur. When these homeostatic mechanisms do not restore **equilibrium**, signs of exhaustion or depleted reserves will be observed as an organism enters the last of Selye's three stages, the **stage of exhaustion**. The primary indicants of this stage are ulcers, adrenal enlargement, and shrinkage of lymph and other glands that confer resistance to disease.

Some responses to environmental stress are virtually indistinguishable from those evoked by direct assault on body tissue by pathogens. Recalling Selye's three-stage process, it appears that stress results in heightened secretion of **corticosteroids** during the alarm reaction, followed by a decline in reactivity (as measured by this secretion) through resistance and exhaustion. Subsequent work has also identified the **catecholamines—epinephrine** and **norepinephrine**—as active in stress. Research has associated emotional distress with these same patterns of arousal (e.g., Konzett, 1975; Schachter & Singer, 1962). Further, challenge, loss of control or predictability, and psychosocial stressors have been linked to increased **adrenal** activity (Frankenhaeuser, 1978; Glass, 1976; Konzett et al., 1971).

Increased catecholamine and corticosteroid secretion is associated with a wide range of other physiological responses, such as changes in heart rate, blood pressure, breathing, muscle potential, inflammation, and other functions. Catecholamines also appear to affect cognitive and emotional functioning, and elevated levels of epinephrine or norepinephrine in the blood may affect our mood and behavior (Baum, Grunberg, & Singer, 1982).

These findings may also be viewed as consistent with pioneering work by Cannon (1929, 1931), who suggested that epinephrine has a positive effect on adaptation. Epinephrine provides a biological advantage by arousing the organism, thus enabling it to respond more rapidly to danger. When extremely frightened or enraged, we experience an arousal that may be uncomfortable, but which readies us to act against the thing that scares or angers us. Thus, stress-related increases in catecholamines may facilitate adaptive behavior.

Some studies have shown superior performance on certain tasks following epinephrine infusion (Frankenhaeuser, Jarpe, & Mattell, 1961) and among people with higher catecholamine output in the face of challenge (e.g., Frankenhaeuser, 1971). On the other hand, arousal has been associated with impaired performance on complex tasks (cf. Evans, 1978). Decreases in problem-solving abilities, increases in general negativity, impatience, irritability, feelings of worthlessness, and emotionality may all accompany a stress response, and emotional disturbances such as anxiety or depression may occur.

Coping Strategies

In the stage of resistance many coping processes are also cognitive, so that the individual must decide on a behavioral coping strategy. According to Lazarus (1966), the coping strategy is a function of individual and situational factors, and may consist of flight, physical or verbal attack, or some sort of compromise. Lack of success in the coping process may increase the tendency to evaluate the situation as threatening. For example, Faupel and Styles (1993) found that victims of hurricane Hugo reported more stress if they had engaged in activities to prepare for the disaster; perhaps the experienced devastation in spite of preparation increased perceived threat. Associated with this cognitive coping process are any number of emotions, including anger and fear. To use another example, the stress reaction to a large crowd in a city might consist of evaluation of the crowd as threatening, physiological arousal, fear, and flight to a less crowded area (Figure 4–5).

Many ways of categorizing coping strategies have been developed (see Aldwin & Revenson, 1987). Two useful distinctions employed by Lazarus and his colleagues are (1) *direct action* or *problem-focused*, such as information seeking, flight, or attempts to remove or stop the stressor; or (2) **palliative** or *emotion-focused*, such as employing psychological defense mechanisms (denial, intellectualization, etc.), using drugs, meditating, or reassessing the situation as nonthreatening (see also Roth & Cohen, 1986). To the extent that direct action is not available or practical, palliative strategies become more likely. For example, for residents near the Three Mile Island nuclear disaster, direct action was limited in effectiveness, so palliative measures would be more probable (Baum et al., 1980; Houts et al., 1980). Interestingly, a sense of humor helps cope with most if not all types of stress (Martin & Lefcourt, 1983).

Adaptation

As previously noted, if the coping responses are not adequate for dealing with the stressor, and all coping energies have been expended, the organism will enter the third stage of the GAS, the stage of exhaustion. Fortunately, something else usually happens before exhaustion occurs. In most situations, when an aversive stimulus is presented many times, the stress reaction to it becomes weaker and weaker. Psychologically, this process is called *adaptation*. Adaptation to a stressor may occur because neurophysiological sensitivity to the stimulus becomes weaker, because uncertainty about the stressor is reduced, or because the stressor is cognitively appraised as less and less threatening. Visitors to a polluted city, for example, initially

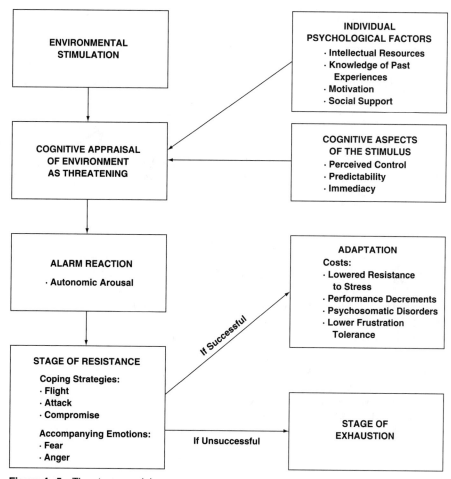

Figure 4–5   The stress model

may suffer overt physiological symptoms, such as shortness of breath, and may express a great deal of fear about the potential health consequences of exposure to atmospheric pollutants. On successive days in the city, however, these visitors, realizing that they have not died yet, may "lose" the fear of breathing the air (see Chapter 7). As another example, consider the stress that might build as one moves to a new office; all of the old emotional attachments, productive work habits, and spatial organization could be threatened. But even small improvements in the new office, such as increased lighting

or more privacy, may reduce the threat and stress associated with the move (Spreckelmeyer, 1993).

Adaptation to stress is both beneficial and costly. Almost all events in life, from birth to attending school to driving on freeways at rush hour, involve some degree of stress. Obviously, the individual who has been exposed to stress and has learned to handle it is better able to deal with the next stressful event in life. In this sense, the "teaching" function of stress is beneficial to the organism as long as the stress can be handled—the experience boosts self-confidence and provides skill development (e.g., Aldwin & Stokols, 1988; Martin et al., 1987). We have seen that environmental stress sometimes improves performance, probably because the arousal associated with stress (if it is not too severe) facilitates performance. Exposure and adaptation to stressful events may also be costly, however. If the total of all stresses at any one time exceeds the capacity of the individual to cope with them, some sort of breakdown, physical or mental, is almost inevitable. Psychosomatic disorders, performance decrements, and lowering of resistance to other stressors are often the costs of adapting to prolonged or excessive stress. Still another cost, one that we have treated previously as a separate theoretical approach, is the resulting cognitive overload: Our information-processing capacity becomes so overloaded by the stressor that additional processing is difficult and more prone to error. Some costs of adaptation may occur during exposure to the stressor, including performance decrements and physiological wear and tear. Other costs may occur after the stressor is no longer around. For example, as we will see in Chapter 5, even after an aversive noise has stopped, tolerance for frustration, accuracy of mental functioning, and even altruistic behavior (see box on page 120) may continue to be impaired (see also Cohen, 1980).

Cognitive deficits associated with stress may be caused by behavioral strategies that are used for coping with stress—"tuning out" or narrowing one's field of attention (e.g., Cohen, 1978). When under stress, we may be unable to concentrate or unwilling to put effort into a task (e.g., Glass & Singer, 1972). In other ways, our coping response may be specific to the stressor being experienced, reflecting the specific causes of our discomfort. People may respond to crowding that is due to too many people by withdrawing and avoiding social contact, whereas their response to crowding that is due to limited space might be aggression (e.g., Baum & Koman, 1976). A person might respond to job loss actively if the loss was caused by a lack of effort rather than ability, or may become helpless under certain conditions.

Aftereffects

Following adaptation to stress, there may be long-term consequences—or **aftereffects**—after the stressor has terminated. These are not specific to certain stressors, but appear to reflect more general effects (Cohen, 1980) and fit in with Selye's (1956) notion of limited adaptive energy. As exposure to stress increases, adaptive reserves are depleted, causing aftereffects and reductions of subsequent coping ability. Evidence for the existence of poststressor effects comes from a number of sources, including research on the effects of noise (e.g., Glass & Singer, 1972; Rotton et al., 1978; Sherrod & Downs, 1974; Sherrod et al., 1977), crowding (Evans 1979a), and electrical shock (Glass et al., 1973).

Psychological effects that linger or persist may also reflect consequences of adaptation. Calhoun (1967, 1970) has referred to **refractory periods**, which are periods of time during which an organism recovers from a bout with a stressor. If the refractory period is interrupted by another encounter, increased stress-relevant problems are likely. Recovery from stress, as with recovery from overload, is likely to be facilitated by experiences with natural environments (Ulrich et al., 1991).

Some long-term aftereffects may be physiological. The cascade of neurochemical events in the stress response is thought to have an impact on the immune system. That is, exposure to environmental stressors could lead to impaired functioning of the immune system, and thus in the long run to decreased resistance to infectious diseases and, via immune malfunctioning and other pathways, increased risk of some diseases such as cancer and heart disease (Maier, Watkins, & Fleshner, 1994). Prolonged or sudden elevation of circulating catecholamines may damage body tissue, and is suggested as a cause of the development of hardening of the arteries and other diseases of the blood vessels (Schneiderman, 1982). Indeed, the relationship between stress and health is one that is of ever increasing interest in modern times (e.g., Bernard & Krupat, 1994).

Assessing the Stress Model

When we evaluate the effectiveness of using stress as a mediator for a theoretical approach in environmental psychology, we find that it does an admirable job with the data in its predictive domain. The stress approach does help predict many of the consequences of environmental deterioration as well as the presence or absence of observable effects of such specific stressors as crowding and extremes of heat and cold. In this respect, the stress approach has a great deal of generality: It applies to many situations and accounts for the combined effects of many environmental and social stressors that are presented at the same time (e.g., Levine, 1988). Perhaps for this reason the stress approach suggests many directions for new research. If we treat a given environmental event as a stressor, then we should be able to predict its effects, with or without the presence of other stressors, from our knowledge of the effects of other stressors. Furthermore, we should be able to use present knowledge about coping with stress to help control reactions to unwanted environmental stressors. On the other hand, one problem with using only the stress approach as a theoretical inroad in environmental psychology is that the identification of stressors is somewhat ambiguous (e.g., Lazarus et al., 1985). For example, suppose we expose individuals to a particular stimulus and get no stress reaction. Should that stimulus be regarded as something other than a stressor, or did those particular individuals just not evaluate it

as threatening under the experimental circumstances? In addition, stress models have some difficulty predicting exactly when individuals will cope with a stressor in different ways; that is, we do not easily predict when someone will use palliative versus direct action strategies—we know that people use these different strategies, but describing the chosen path after the fact is easier than predicting it ahead of time.

BARKER'S ECOLOGICAL PSYCHOLOGY

The theoretical perspectives reviewed up to this point have been concerned primarily with the specific effects of the environment on behavior; but, with the exception of the behavior constraint model, they have not been concerned much with the effects of behavior on the environment. Yet, as we have noted many times, behavior inevitably influences the environment. The **ecological psychology** approach views environment–behavior relationships as two-way streets or, in other words, as ecological interdependencies.

Barker (1968, 1979, 1987, 1990) and his colleagues have been the principal advocates of the ecological approach. The focus of Barker's model is the influence of the **behavior setting** on the behavior of large numbers of people, which is termed the **extra-individual behavior pattern**. The unique aspect of Barker's approach is that the behavior setting is an entity in itself. It is not an arbitrarily defined social-scientific concept but actually exists and has a physical structure, although it does change over time (Wicker, 1987). In order to understand just how this behavior setting functions, we will first look at some characteristics of the behavior setting, then see how the setting fits into Barker's theory of staffing. For additional reading, you might wish to consult the July 1990 issue of *Environment and Behavior*, which was written by Barker and his students and colleagues and is devoted entirely to a commemoration of the functioning of the Midwest Psychological Field Station, which was the setting of much of Barker's early work.

The Nature of the Behavior Setting

A number of behaviors can occur inside a structure with four walls, a ceiling, and a floor; but if we know that the cultural purpose of this structure is to be a classroom, then we know that the behavior of the people in the structure will be quite different than if its purpose is to be a church, a factory, or a hockey arena. The fact that this behavior setting is in a built environment also tells us that the extra-individual behavior will be different from that in the natural environment of a forested wilderness or a desert. This cultural purpose exists because the behavior setting consists of the interdependency between **standing patterns of behavior** and a **physical milieu**. Standing patterns of behavior represent the collective behaviors of the group, rather than just individual behaviors.

These behaviors are not unique to the individuals present, but they may be unique to the setting. If the behavior setting is a classroom in a lecture-oriented course, then the standing patterns of behavior would include lecturing, listening, observing, sitting, taking notes, raising hands, and exchanging questions and answers. Since this **en masse behavior pattern** occurs only in an educational behavior setting, ecological psychologists would infer that knowing about the setting helps us predict the behavior that will occur in it. The physical milieu of this behavior setting would include a room, a lectern, chairs, and perhaps a chalkboard and microphone. Once the individuals leave the classroom, the physical milieu still remains, so the standing behavior patterns are independent of the milieu. Yet they are similar in structure **(synomorphic)** and together create the behavior setting (Figure 4–6). A change in either the standing behavior patterns (as when a club holds a meeting in the classroom) or the physical milieu (such as

Figure 4–6 According to Barker's ecological psychology, knowing about the physical setting tells us much about the behaviors that occur there. In the setting shown, what behaviors can you always expect to see?

when the class is held outdoors on the first warm day of spring) changes the behavior setting.

How can we use the behavior setting conceptualization to understand environment–behavior relationships? Perhaps a few examples can best illustrate the utility of this approach (see also Wicker & Kirmeyer, 1976). One very famous application of ecological psychology was described in Chapter 1. In this study, Barker and his colleagues (Barker & Schoggen, 1973; Barker & Wright, 1955) compared a small town in Kansas with one in England. They found, for example, that in England behavior settings under the control of businesses were more common, and the behavior in them lasted longer. In settings involving voluntary participation, however, Americans spent more time and held more positions of responsibility than did the Britons. (The significance of such findings will be more apparent later on in the discussion of staffing.) Wicker (1979, 1987) notes that ecological psychology methods are very useful for such diverse goals as documenting community life, assessing the social impact of change, and analyzing the structure of organizations for such factors as efficiency of operation, handling of responsibility, and indications of status. In addition, as Bechtel (1977) noted, ecological psychology can be useful in assessing environmental design. By carefully examining the behavior setting, one can analyze such design features as pathways, or links between settings, and focal points, or places where behavior tends to concentrate. In the lobby of a building, for example, it is important to separate pathways to various elevators, offices, and shops in order to avoid congestion and confusion. An information center in the lobby, though, would be most useful if placed at a focal point. As another example, open-plan (i.e., no internal walls) designs in schools and offices, although having advantages, often lead to inadequate boundaries between behavior settings, thereby causing interference with the intended functions (e.g., Oldham & Brass, 1979). We will discuss more of these kinds of design implications in Chapters 11, 12, and 13.

Staffing the Setting: How Many Peas Fill a Pod?

What happens if a behavior setting such as a classroom or theater has too few or too many inhabitants for maximum functioning efficiency? Do students at small schools, for example, take on more roles of responsibility than students at larger schools? Studies of these questions from the ecological psychology perspective have led to what is called **staffing theory** (Barker, 1960; Barker & Gump, 1964; Wicker & Kirmeyer, 1976; Wicker, McGrath, & Armstrong, 1972). Historically, this concept was termed the *theory of manning*, but today it is known by the gender-neutral phrase *theory of staffing*.

In order to understand the theory, let us first define some terms proposed by Wicker and his colleagues that are related to the concept of staffing. The minimum number of inhabitants needed to maintain a behavior setting is defined as the **maintenance minimum**. The maximum number of inhabitants the setting can hold is the **capacity**. The people who meet the membership requirements of the setting and who are trying to become part of it are called **applicants**. **Performers** in a setting carry out the primary tasks, such as the teacher in a classroom, the workers in a factory, or the cast and supporting staff in a play. **Nonperformers**, such as the pupils in a classroom or the audience in a theater, are involved in secondary roles. Maintenance minimum, capacity, and the applicants are different entities for performers and nonperformers. For example, maintenance minimum for performers in a classroom would be the smallest staff

AN ECOLOGICAL PSYCHOLOGY APPROACH TO MANAGING SMOKING IN PUBLIC

With today's increased consciousness about the dangers of secondary cigarette smoke, battles commonly erupt between smokers' and nonsmokers' rights. Why, nonsmokers ask, can't smokers obey nonsmoking signs? Is it because smokers are merely disrespectful? Gibson and Werner (1994) suggest that the answer may rest more in environmental layout and cues than in individual personalities. Although ecological psychology principles have typically been applied to settings where occupants are relatively permanent, Gibson and Werner used an innovative approach to demonstrate that the principles apply to airport concourse waiting areas where occupancy is short-term. In doing so, they illustrated how ecological psychology principles can be used to help manage the conflict between smokers and nonsmokers.

One aspect of Barker's conceptualization involves the circuitry of the setting—those elements by which it is regulated. For example, the setting program defines what is supposed to happen in the setting, and the deviation-countering circuit restores order to violations of the program. Gibson and Werner view smoking in a nonsmoking area as a violation of the program. The problem, they suggest, is that the program is not always obvious. Recall from Chapter 3 that legibility is an important aspect of defining the ease of cognitive mapping in a city. Lack of legibility may also be a factor in smokers lighting up in nonsmoking areas. In one study, Gibson and Werner found that smoking was much more likely in ambiguous areas than in clearly marked nonsmoking areas. In another study, they created a distinct boundary between smoking and nonsmoking areas, or they kept the boundary ambiguous by having a row of chairs cross between the two areas. In addition, ambiguity was created by sometimes having ashtrays in nonsmoking areas—all of this despite the clear presence of "No Smoking" signs. Again, they found that the more ambiguity, the more smoking in nonsmoking areas, i.e., the more violation of the setting program. In fact, when boundaries were distinct and ashtrays not present, no one ever smoked in a nonsmoking area. In a third study, these researchers found that nonsmokers' responses to an intruding smoker could be predicted by location and legibility of the setting. Nonsmokers were more likely to reprimand a smoker in a nonsmoking area (i.e., counter the deviation or defend the territory) if the violation occurred in the center of the area versus the edge of the designated nonsmoking area; deviation-countering was also more likely to occur if the program of the nonsmoking area was highly legible, i.e., if the boundary was distinct and no ashtrays were present.

Thus, it seems that legibility is important in getting people to conform to a setting's program. Furthermore, increasing legibility may help manage conflicts.

(teachers, custodians, secretaries, deans) required to carry out the program. For nonperformers, maintenance minimum would be the smallest number of pupils required to keep the class going. Capacity for performers in a classroom might be determined by social factors (e.g., how many teachers are most effective in one setting) and by physical factors, such as the size of the room, number of lecterns, and so on. For nonperformers, room size would be the primary determinant of capacity. Whether your class contains 10 or 1,000 students depends in most cases as much on classroom size as on educational policy. For performers, applicants are the individuals who meet the requirements of the performer role and who seek to perform, as in the number of teachers available to teach a given class. Applicants for nonperformers are those who seek secondary roles, as in the number of students trying to get into the class. If students are available but do not seek to get into the class, or if teachers do not want to teach a given class, then they are not considered applicants.

If the number of applicants to a setting (either performers or nonperformers) falls below maintenance minimum, then some or all of the inhabitants must take on more than their share of roles if the behavior setting is to be maintained. This condition is termed **understaffed**. If the number of applicants exceeds the capacity, the setting is **overstaffed**, and if the number of applicants is between maintenance minimum and capacity, the setting is **adequately staffed**. Wicker (1973) has labeled an adequately staffed setting with a low number of participants as *poorly staffed*, and an adequately staffed setting with a high number of participants as *richly staffed*. Thus, we can consider a continuum of participation levels from understaffed to poorly staffed, adequately staffed, richly staffed, and overstaffed.

When conditions of understaffing exist, the consequences for the inhabitants of the setting are many. As stated earlier, inhabitants must take on more specific tasks and roles than would otherwise be the case. As a result, inhabitants have to work harder and at more difficult tasks than they would otherwise, and peak performance on any task is not as great as in an adequately staffed setting. Furthermore, admissions standards to understaffed settings may have to be lowered, and superficial differences among inhabitants may be largely ignored, whereas in adequately staffed settings these differences are highlighted to fit each person into his or her appropriate role. Each inhabitant in an understaffed setting is more valued, has more responsibility, and interacts more meaningfully with the setting. Since understaffed settings have more opportunities for the experience of failure as well as success (owing to the increase in number of experiences per inhabitant), these settings are likely to result in more feelings of insecurity than are adequately staffed settings. The consequences of understaffing are summarized in Table 4–1.

Overstaffing, on the other hand, results in adaptive mechanisms being brought into play to deal with the huge number of applicants. One obvious solution would be to increase the capacity, probably through enlarging the present physical milieu or moving to a larger one. Another adaptive mechanism would be to control the entrance of clients into the setting, either through stricter entrance requirements or through some sort of funneling process (Figure 4–7). For example, Wicker (1979) describes how ecological psychologists implemented and evaluated a queuing (waiting line) arrangement at Yosemite National Park to alleviate overcrowding and associated disruptive behavior at bus stops. Still another regulatory mechanism would be to limit the amount of time inhabitants can spend in the setting. These three mechanisms are elaborated in Table 4–1.

Table 4–1   Consequences of Understaffing and Mechanisms for Regulating
the Population of a Behavior Setting*

Consequences of Understaffing

Setting occupants typically:
1. Increase effort and/or spend more time to support the setting.
2. Participate in a greater variety of tasks and roles.
3. Participate in more difficult and important tasks.
4. Assume more responsibility in the setting.
5. Perceive themselves and others in terms of task-related characteristics.
6. Become more important to the functioning of the setting.
7. Pay less attention to personality and other non-task related differences between individuals.
8. Lower admissions standards for applicants.
9. Accept lower levels of performance for themselves and others.
10. Feel insecure regarding the success of the setting.
11. Experience success and failure frequently.

Mechanisms for Regulating the Population of a Behavior Setting

1. Regulating access of applicants into the setting:
   by scheduling appointments for entrance;
   by increasing or decreasing recruiting;
   by raising or lowering admissions standards;
   by asking applicants to wait in holding areas;
   by preventing unauthorized entrances.
2. Regulating the setting's capacity:
   by changing the arrangements or contents of the physical milieu;
   by changing the duration (hours open) of the setting;
   by increasing or decreasing staff (performers) to handle applicants;
   by assigning staff (performers) to different tasks as demands of applicants increase or decrease.
3. Regulating the time applicants or inhabitants can occupy the setting:
   by admitting applicants at different rates;
   by changing the limits on how long people can stay;
   by using a fee structure based on length of stay;
   by establishing priorities for dealing with different classes of applicants;
   by changing the standing patterns of behavior to facilitate the flow of applicants.

Adapted from Wicker, A. W., & Kirmeyer, S. (1976). From church to laboratory to national park. In S. Wapner, B. Kaplan, & S. Cohen (Eds.), Experiencing the Environment. Used by permission of Plenum Publishing.

In general, predictions for staffing theory have been supported by research. For example, in a laboratory study involving too many, too few, or an intermediate number of participants to run a complex racing game, those in understaffed conditions reported feelings of involvement in the group and having an important role within the group (e.g., Wicker et al., 1976). Studies of large versus small high schools (Baird, 1969; Barker & Gump, 1964) suggest that students in small schools (which are less likely to be overstaffed) are indeed involved in a wider range of activities than students from large schools, and are more likely to report feelings of satisfaction and of being challenged. Similar results have been reported for colleges as well (Baird, 1969; Berk & Goebel, 1987). Even student groups within college conform to the principles of staffing: As group size declines, groups become more open to prospective and new members (Cini, Moreland, & Levine, 1993). Studies of large versus small churches (e.g., Wicker, 1969; Wicker & Kauma, 1974; Wicker, McGrath, & Armstrong, 1972; Wicker & Mehler, 1971) also

Figure 4–7   Funneling is one way to regulate entrance into a potentially overstaffed behavior setting.

indicate that members of small churches are likely to be involved in more behavior settings within the church (e.g., choir, committees) and to be involved in more leadership positions; such predictions are based on the assumption that smaller churches are more likely to be understaffed and larger churches overstaffed. Norris-Baker and Scheidt (1990) have shown that staffing theory is useful in evaluating the effects of population decline in a small rural community. Altogether, then, these and other studies suggest that staffing theory is very useful in assessing involvement and satisfaction within a number of environments, from businesses (e.g., Greenberg, 1979; Oxley & Barrera, 1984) to mental institutions (e.g., Srivastava, 1974) to schools and churches, and to "home, sweet home" (Jones, Nesselroade, & Birkel, 1991).

Barker's approach has its advantages and disadvantages. It necessitates using a field observation methodology (described in Chap-

ter 1) that gives the theory the advantage of using real-world behavior. It certainly insists on preserving the integrity of the person–environment interrelationship. However, it includes the disadvantage of not being able to study many detailed cause-and-effect relationships in the laboratory, though certainly some laboratory research on ecological psychology principles has been and will continue to be conducted (e.g, Wicker, 1987; Wicker & Kirmeyer, 1976). Studies of real-world behavior in context lead to difficulties of interpretation without scientific control of variables. For example, the observed effects of large versus small schools or churches could be due to differential group influence such as staffing demands, or to individual differences in the types of people who choose to affiliate with large versus small institutions. Here we have a theory that is so broad in its scope that specific predictions about one person's behavior become difficult to

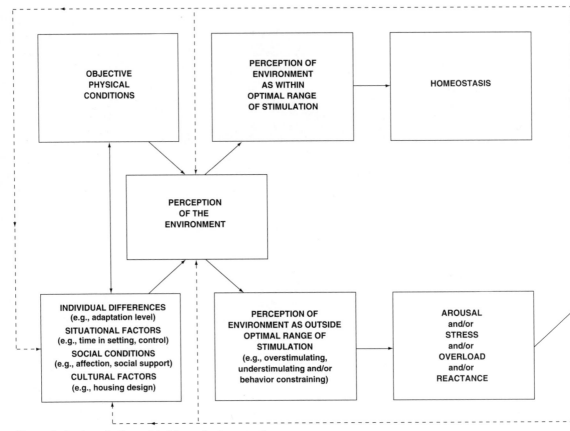

Figure 4–8 An eclectic model of theoretical perspectives

make and troublesome to confirm. Since this approach is designed to study group behavior, it does a respectable job of handling group data in the context of a given setting, but it does not handle individual behavior as well as other theories. To its credit, ecological theory does generate many valuable research questions, such as what common properties of certain behavior settings result in the same group behavior, what happens when the structure of a behavior setting changes, and what effects one behavior setting has on behavior in another setting. Finally, the ecological approach is applicable to a large variety of settings and circumstances (Sommer & Wicker, 1991).

INTEGRATION AND SUMMARY OF THEORETICAL PERSPECTIVES

It is worth repeating the caution that our earlier discussion has by no means covered all theories employed by environmental psychologists. Rather, they are simply the most common approaches presently in use, and they are not at all mutually exclusive. Each theory selects one or two mediators inferred from empirical data and attempts to explain

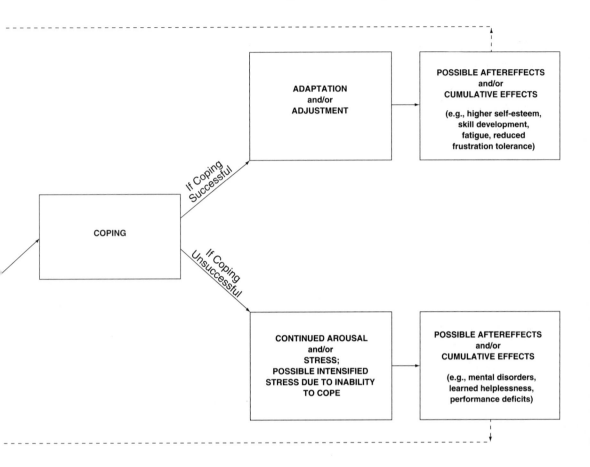

a large portion of the data using the mediator. Just because one mediator explains a particular set of data, however, does not mean that other mediators do not operate in the same set of data. It is entirely conceivable, for example, that loud noise produces information overload, stress, arousal, and psychological reactance all at the same time in the same individual. Overstaffing can lead to loss of perceived control, and loss of control, alone, usually increases arousal (Wright, 1984). Futhermore, regardless of which of these mediators is involved (either alone or in combination), any number of coping responses are likely to result, such as flight, erecting barriers or other protective devices, ignoring other humans in need, and directly

attempting to stop or reduce the stimulus input at the source. Although one particular mediator may best predict or explain which coping responses will occur in a given situation, other mediators are not necessarily excluded from that or similar situations. It is our position that all of the mediating processes discussed thus far probably occur at some time, given all the possible situations in which environmental stimulation influences behavior. Therefore, we now present an eclectic scheme of environment–behavior relationships as a summary and integration of the theoretical concepts we have discussed in this chapter.

This scheme of theoretical concepts is presented in the flow chart in Figure 4–8.

Objective environmental conditions, such as population density, temperature, noise levels, and pollution levels, exist independent of the individual, although individuals can act to change these objective conditions. The scheme includes such individual difference factors as adaptation level, length of exposure, perceived control, personality, privacy preference, and competence to deal with the elements of the environment, as well as such social factors as liking or hostility for others in the situation. Perception of the objective physical conditions depends on the objective conditions themselves, as well as on the individual difference factors and the attitudinal, perceptual, and cognitive processes discussed in Chapters 2 and 3. If this subjective perception determines that the environment is within an optimal range of stimulation, the result is **homeostatic**, the adjective form of homeostasis, or an equalization of desired and actual input. On the other hand, if the environment is experienced as outside the optimal range of stimulation, (e.g., understimulation, overstimulation, or stimulating in a behavior-constraining manner—including being overstaffed or understaffed), then one or more of the following psychological states results: arousal, stress, information overload, or reactance. The presence of one or more of these states leads to coping strategies. If the attempted coping strategies are successful, adaptation or adjustment occurs, possibly followed by such aftereffects as lowered frustration tolerance, fatigue, and reduced ability to cope with the next immediate stressor. Cumulative aftereffects might include any of these, but would also include increased self-confidence and a degree of learning about coping with future occurrences of undesirable environmental stimulation. Should the coping strategies not be successful, however, arousal and stress will continue, possibly heightened by the individual's awareness that the strategies are failing. Potential aftereffects of such inability to cope include exhaustion, learned helplessness, severe performance decrements, and mental disorders. Finally, as indicated by the feedback loops, experiences with the environment influence perception of the environment for future encounters and also contribute to individual differences for future experiences.

We present this model not as a completely developed environmental theory but merely as an attempt to integrate the various mediating concepts that have been applied to environment–behavior relationships. Undoubtedly, some data exist that do not support one aspect or another of this integration. However, we think this eclectic approach will help explain many of the environment–behavior relationships to be covered in the remainder of the textbook. We will continue to see this model in following chapters, where we will discuss how the physical environment (noise, air pollution, weather), personal space and crowding, cities, and built and natural environments influence specific behaviors. When appropriate, we will point out how the various theoretical notions in this chapter help explain those specific influences.

CHAPTER SUMMARY

Environmental psychology, as a science, seeks to understand cause-and-effect relationships through prediction, and uses publicly observable data to verify these predictions. Once enough predictions are verified, theories are constructed, which consist of a set of concepts and a set of statements relating the concepts to each other. Usually, theories infer that a more or less abstract variable mediates the relationship between one observable variable and another. Good environmental theories should predict and summarize empirical data, should offer generalizability to many situations, and should suggest ideas for research.

The arousal approach to environment–behavior relationships suggests that environmental stimulation leads to increased arousal. According to the Yerkes-Dodson Law, this increased arousal will improve or impair performance, depending on whether the individual's arousal is below or above an optimal level. Other behaviors, such as aggression, also tend to follow this curvilinear relationship with arousal.

The information overload model proposes that our capacity to process information is limited and that when excessive stimulation occurs, peripheral inputs are ignored in order to give adequate attention to primary tasks. As a result, responses to these peripheral nonsocial or social stimuli are minimal or nonexistent. The understimulation approach notes that monotonous environmental stimulation leads to boredom and thus to behavioral deficiencies. Wohlwill's approach posits an individual difference variable, or adaptation level (AL), such that stimulation levels above or below this AL will bring discomfort and efforts to reduce or increase the stimulation. The behavior constraint model proposes that perceived loss of control over the environment leads to reactance or efforts to regain freedom of action. If these efforts at reassertion are unsuccessful, learned helplessness may be the result.

The stress model of environment–behavior relationships posits that once stimuli have been evaluated as threatening, coping strategies are brought into play. These strategies can be beneficial, as when their use results in learning more efficient ways of coping with stress. However, prolonged exposure to stress can lead to serious aftereffects, including mental disorders, performance decrements, and lowered resistance to stress.

Barker's ecological psychology model examines environment–behavior interdependencies and focuses on the behavior setting as the unit of study. If the number of applicants to a setting falls below maintenance minimum, performers and nonperformers in the understaffed setting must take on additional roles in order to maintain the setting.

Finally, there is no reason to assume that only one mediator operates in any given environment–behavior situation. An eclectic model is offered that attempts to integrate a number of different theoretical concepts.

SUGGESTED PROJECTS

1. Observe a behavior setting for a week. What behavior patterns are always present? Is the setting understaffed, overstaffed, or adequately staffed?
2. Keep a diary for a week or more of all the events that constrain your behavior. Do you respond with reactance, learned helplessness, or some other behavior?
3. Keep a log of your performance levels in classroom, study, and leisure situations, noting your arousal level and amount of environmental stimulation. Does your performance vary as a function of arousal level, overload, or underload?
4. Construct your own model of environment–behavior relationships. How well can you integrate the various theoretical perspectives discussed in this chapter and the previous one?

Noise

INTRODUCTION

WHAT IS NOISE?

  Perceiving Noise

  Annoyance

  Sources of Noise

    Transportation Noise

    Occupational Noise

EFFECTS OF NOISE

  Health Effects of Noise

  Noise and Mental Health

  Effects of Noise on Performance

    Effects During Exposure

    Aftereffects

    Noise and Children's Performance

    How Do These Effects Occur?

  Effects of Noise in Office and Industrial Settings

  Noise and Social Behavior

    Noise and Attraction

    Noise and Human Aggression

    Noise and Helping

REDUCING NOISE: DOES ANYONE NOTICE?

CHAPTER SUMMARY

  Suggested Projects

KEY TERMS

aftereffects
amplitude
annoyance
decibels (dB)
frequency
hearing loss
hertz (Hz)
hypertension
loudness
masking
narrow band

noise
noise-induced permanent threshold shift (NIPTS)
perceived control
pitch
sound
temporary threshold shifts (TTS)
timbre
tonal quality
white noise
wide band

INTRODUCTION

It was competition for the loudest sound system in the high school parking lot. Reeves had just installed 8 new 14-inch woofers in his Corolla and wanted to blast away Harrison. It seems Harrison had what most conceded was the clear winner for the last three months. Mr. Martinez, the science teacher, had loaned the guys a sound-level meter from time to time, and no one's amplifier had yet exceeded the 142 decibels achieved by Harrison. To top it off, the morning cruise around the school with sound systems blaring consistently yielded more neighborhood complaint calls to the principal when Harrison entered the parade.

Reeves' older brother had suggested that before he try to beat out Harrison, he might want to get his hearing checked. In a college psychology class the brother had observed class members as they tested each other on an audiometer; those with loud sound systems in their cars showed a distinct hearing deficit that they had not been aware of before seeing the audiometer's printed output. Reeves wondered about the advice from his brother, but for the moment, beating Harrison seemed more important. The audiometer could wait a few years.

Distinctions among types of stressors are useful in several ways. With some stressors, like disasters (see Chapter 7), we study cataclysmic events, the most powerful kinds of stressors that humans experience. These events severely tax our ability to cope, and it is difficult to believe that anyone exposed to an earthquake, tornado, or nuclear accident would not be very aware of what was happening. Another kind of stressor, which may actually be more harmful for mood, behavior, and health, is recurrent or continuous lower intensity stressors that are "normal" and routine. They are part of the "background" in that they are always (or frequently) there. Noise is one such stressor. In many cases, noise is not readily noticeable by longtime residents of noisy areas. Noise is common and widespread and often occurs regularly or all of the time. Because it is less intense than are more dramatic stressors, noise may cause few or no acute effects. However, ambient stressors that persist may be more likely to cause long-term reactions, allowing for the possibility of effects on health and well-being.

Of the many environmental stressors, noise is one of the most thoroughly studied. And no wonder; noise is one of the most frequently mentioned stressors in surveys of what people like and do not like in their neighborhood or community. In part, this may be due to its pervasiveness in our society. Consider some of its many sources: traffic, aircraft, construction, sirens, trains, equipment at work, machinery, and, of course, other people. Everywhere we go there is noise, particularly if we live in cities (Figure 5–1). Sometimes we can adapt to noise, and may not even be aware of it as we get used to it at a certain level. However, research suggests that noise can harm us in many different ways, and studies have sought to define these consequences, identify factors that make the effects of noise more or less severe, and reduce noise levels or noise-related health problems. Regulations governing noise exposure have been put into effect, reflecting recognition of this important problem.

But how does noise affect us? Why is it that under some circumstances we can adapt to noise and under others we cannot? Why would trains that noisily pass our home every three hours be easier to get used to than an occasional aircraft passing overhead? How can it be that people talking softly but audibly during a movie can be more annoying than the loud sounds of rock music? In this chapter, we will discuss these issues and the kinds of problems that have been associated with noise exposure. Keep in mind as we go through this research that noise is considerably less powerful or overwhelming than are events such as disasters, but that it may be possible that noise can cause more severe and/or long-lasting consequences. How can this be? Could the repetitive or constant nature of noise be responsible for these effects, suggesting that cumulative effects over time can exceed those of very severe, acute events?

In this chapter we will briefly discuss the nature of sound and noise—how we perceive them, how they are measured, and where they

Figure 5–1A   Noise is one of the most frequently mentioned stressors in surveys of what people like and do not like in their neighborhood or community.

Figure 5–1B   In many cases, air pollution and noise are not readily noticible by long-time residents in the areas where they routinely occur. Both of these types of ambient stressors may have long-term consequences for health and well-being.

come from. The effects of noise on a range of physiological, psychological, and behavioral variables are considered as well, and research on occupational exposure to noise is summarized. As we will see, noise effects on task performance and social behavior have received a great deal of attention. We also discuss some attempts to apply what we know and to evaluate the effects of noise abatement programs. In Figure 5–2 we show how these noise effects can be conceptualized within the eclectic environment–behavior model we presented in the previous chapter; that is, noise outside the desired level requires adaptive efforts that may or may not be successful. In the process of adapting to noise, we may experience arousal, overload, loss of perceived control, and a range of physiological and psychological concurrent effects and aftereffects.

WHAT IS NOISE?

The simplest and most common definition of **noise** is "unwanted sound." You may enjoy listening to your favorite rock group on your stereo, but if the music disturbs your roommate's studying or sleep, then as far as your roommate is concerned the rousing sound of the talented musicians is noise. The sound of a garbage truck making pickups early in the morning may be necessary in order to maintain healthy sanitation, and for the early riser this sound may provide a wake-up cue signaling a bright new day. But if you do not

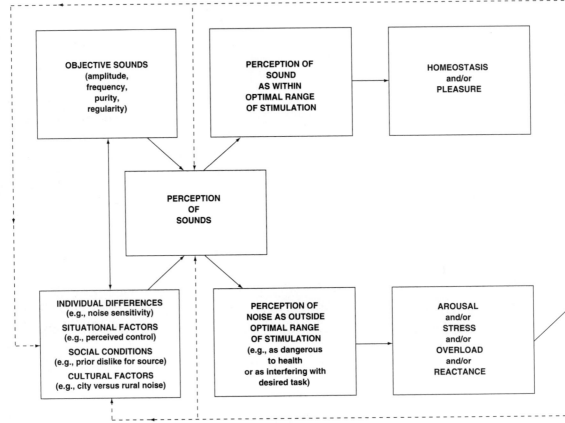

Figure 5–2   An eclectic model of theoretical perspectives as applied to noise

wish to be awakened so early in the morning, then the motorized contraption is making noise. Loud industrial machinery, jet aircraft, computer line printers, and pneumatic hammers also generate noise, but only if someone finds the sound undesirable. Of course, some sounds are more likely to be unwanted, either because they interfere with activities or because of their tone, loudness, or quality. However, few if any sounds are always or never unwanted and nearly any sound can be experienced as noise under the right conditions. The physical condition, sound, is necessary but not sufficient to produce noise. Thus, the concept of noise implies both a significant psychological component ("un-wanted") as well as a physical component (it must be perceived by the ear and higher brain).

PERCEIVING NOISE

The measurement of sound is based primarily on its physical components, although the brain's interpretation of the sound is also crucial to the structure of the measuring scale. Physically, **sound** is created by rapidly changing air pressure at the eardrum. As air molecules are forced together, positive pressure is created, and when they are pulled apart, negative pressure results. This alternating pressure can be represented graphically by waves,

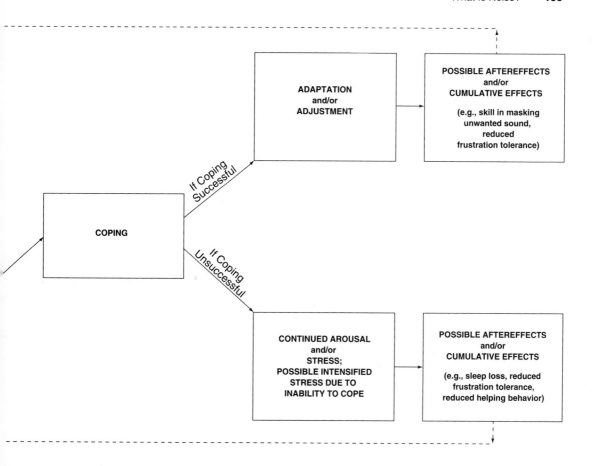

the peaks of the waves representing positive pressure and the valleys reflecting negative pressure (Figure 5–3). These alternating pressures cause the eardrum to vibrate. The eardrum then transmits these vibrations through the structures of the middle and inner ear to the basilar membrane in the cochlea (Figure 5–4A & 4B). Tiny hair cells in this membrane, which are activated by the noise vibrations, pass along the noise stimulation through the auditory nerve to the temporal lobe of the brain. Auditory *sensation* is initiated by activation of the nervous system by the sound stimulus. *Perception* begins somewhere between the basilar membrane and the temporal lobe of the brain, where

a code we have yet to unravel completely—although it probably involves the pattern of neuron firing (i.e., nerve cells transmitting messages) and the rate at which neurons fire—allows the organism to interpret the sound stimulus.

Examine the waves depicted in Figure 5–3 once again. Physically, the more times per second the wave motion completes a cycle (from peak to valley), the greater the **frequency** of the sound. Psychologically, frequency is perceived as **pitch**, i.e., highness or lowness. The normal human ear can hear frequencies between 20 and 20,000 cycles per second, or **hertz (Hz)**. However, most sounds we hear are not a single frequency but

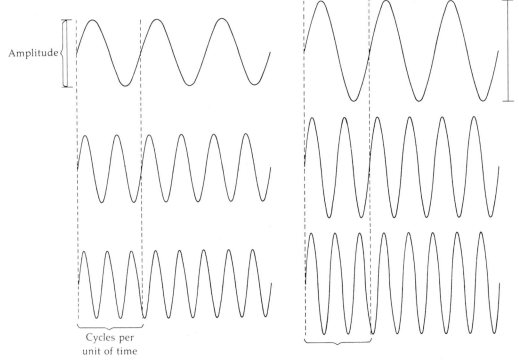

Amplitude

Cycles per
unit of time

Figure 5–3   Examples of sound waves. Frequency increases from top to bottom; amplitude increases from left to right.

a mixture of frequencies. Psychologically, purity of frequency is known as **timbre** or **tonal quality**. Sound stimuli that consist of few frequencies are often called **narrow band** sound, whereas stimuli with a wide range of frequencies are called **wide band**. Extremely wide-range unpatterned frequencies are called **white noise**.

Sound waves also vary in height or **amplitude**, experienced psychologically as **loudness**. The greater the amplitude of a wave, the greater the energy or pressure in the sound wave and the louder the sound. The smallest pressure or threshold that a young adult can detect is about 0.0002 microbars, or dynes per square centimeter, where a dyne is a measure of pressure. At 1,000 microbars, the pressure is experienced more as pain than as sound. Measures of loudness must cover an enormous range of pressures, and to help

Figure 5–4A   Schematic diagram of human ear, showing important structures associated with perception of sound
From Gardner, E., 1975. Fundamentals of neurology, *6th ed. Philadelphia: Saunders.*

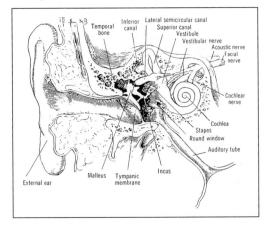

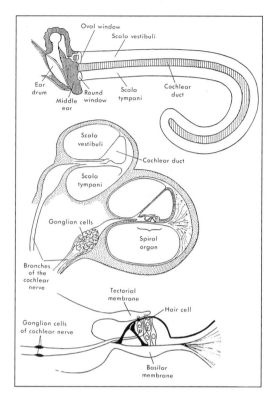

Figure 5–4B Internal structure of human auditory system
From Gardner, 1975.

Table 5–1 Decibel Equivalents of Microbars

Sound Pressure in Microbars	Equivalent Decibels
0.0002	0
0.002	20
0.02	40
0.2	60
2.0	80
20.0	100
200.0	120
2000.0	140

has 10 times more pressure than another, but it does not necessarily mean that the more intense sound will be perceived as 10 times louder. The human ear is differentially sensitive to sounds at different frequencies, and more intense pressure has different effects at varying frequencies. For this reason, sound intensity is sometimes measured in quantities called phons or sones; we will use the more common decibel scale when discussing noise in this text, but you may want to

us understand and study noise, a more workable scale of sound pressure has been developed that uses **decibels (dB)** as the basic units of sound (decibels are a logarithmic function of microbars). Table 5–1 gives the corresponding decibel equivalents of audible ranges of pressure. Note that an increase of 20 decibels represents a tenfold increase in pressure: A sound of 80 dB is not twice as intense as one of 40 dB, it is 10 times 10, or 100 times, as intense. Figure 5–5 lists some common sounds associated with various points on the decibel scale.

The decibel scale measures the physical component of sound or noise amplitude. However, this scale does not accurately reflect the perception of loudness. That is, a difference of 20 dB means that one sound

Figure 5–5 Some common sounds associated with the decibel scale

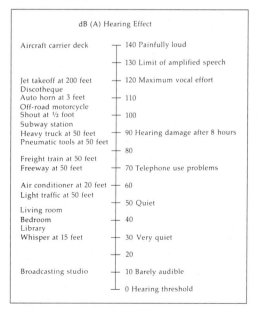

consult a sensation and perception text or psychophysics text for a discussion of phons and sones.

ANNOYANCE

Some kinds of noise are more annoying than others. As you might guess, loud noises are often more annoying than quieter noises. However, there is usually more to it than that. Noise is a disturbing environmental phenomenon because disturbing is, by definition, unwanted. It is this irritating and distracting psychological component that causes noise to be a problem. Kryter (1970) and Glass and Singer (1972) point out that some types of noise are more annoying than others. Three major dimensions influencing the **annoyance** (i.e., irritating) characteristics of noise are: (1) volume; (2) predictability; and (3) perceived control. Thus, all other things considered, loud noise, unpredictable noise, and low perceived control should increase annoyance or negative reactions to noise.

How are we affected by noise at different volumes? Above 90 dB, which is the level of noise produced by a heavy truck 50 feet away, noise becomes psychologically disturbing and after repeated periods of exposure for eight hours or more, physiologically damaging to hearing. Moreover, the louder the noise, the more likely it will interfere with verbal communication, and the greater the arousal and stress associated with it, the more attention one allocates to it.

Unpredictable, irregular noise is generally more annoying than is predictable or constant noise. A constant unbroken noise (especially if it is not loud) is not disturbing. Once it is broken up into periodic "bursts," however, the noise becomes more disturbing; if we then make the bursts of noise aperiodic (i.e., coming at unpredictable or irregular intervals), the disturbing quality becomes even more pronounced (e.g., Glass & Singer,

1972). The more unpredictable the noise, the more arousing it is, and the more likely it is to lead to stress (unpredictable noises may be evaluated as more novel or threatening than predictable ones). In addition, more unpredictable noises require greater attention to understand and evaluate them, leaving less total attention available for other activities (e.g., Easterbrook, 1959). Finally, it is easier to adapt to a predictable noise, since the same stimulus is presented over and over again; with unpredictable noise, adaptation is more difficult.

Noise over which we have no **perceived control** is also more disturbing than noise we can control readily. If you have the means to stop or muffle a noise, you are less annoyed by it than if you cannot control it. For example, if you are using a noisy power saw, you can control the noise by stopping the saw. If your neighbor uses the saw next door, however, you have less immediate control over the noise, and so it is more disturbing. If you can close your window and reduce the intrusiveness of the sound, it may not bother you as much, even if you do not actually close the window. Of course, you could close it and find out the noise is still loud and disturbing. It may not always be good to test our perceived control!

From the theoretical perspectives discussed previously, we know or can propose that uncontrollable noise is more arousing and stressful, requires more attention allocation, and is more difficult to adapt to than controllable noise. Lack of control over noise can lead to psychological reactance and attempts to regain freedom of action by trying to assert control. If such efforts are unsuccessful, learned helplessness can result (see Chapter 4), in which a person simply accepts the noise and never tries to control it, even though control may become possible at a later time.

These three noise variables can, of course, occur in any combination. That is, we can have loud, predictable, uncontrollable noise, or quiet, unpredictable, uncontrollable noise, and so on. As we will see later in this chapter, loud, unpredictable, uncontrollable noise has the most deleterious effects on behavior. Although these three factors are probably the most important in determining the effects of noise on behavior, research (Borsky, 1969) suggests that other factors also influence how annoying noise is. Annoyance increases if: (1) one perceives the noise as unnecessary; (2) those who generate the noise are perceived as unconcerned about the welfare of those who are exposed to it; (3) the person hearing the noise believes it is hazardous to health; (4) the person hearing the noise associates it with fear; and (5) the person hearing the noise is dissatisfied with other aspects of his or her environment.

SOURCES OF NOISE

As you might guess, noise can theoretically come from almost anywhere. Because it has a subjective component (it must be judged as unwanted), noise can come from anything that makes a sound. And, as you would also expect, the same sound may be unwanted at some times but not unwanted at other times. A dripping faucet passes as a faint whisper against the background sounds of a busy afternoon, but at night, when we are trying to sleep, it can be noisy and very disruptive! In contexts where sound is either so loud that it is considered to be a noise, or is softer but more irregular or disruptive, most people will complain about noise. We will briefly discuss two of the common settings where noise can be a problem.

Transportation Noise

Noise caused by cars, trucks, trains, planes, and other modes of transportation is of great interest for a number of reasons. First, it is very widespread. Surveys have indicated that automobile noise is the most often

mentioned source of urban noise, and that opening of new highways is associated with increases in annoyance among nearby residents (Lawson & Walters, 1974). Reports estimate that 11 million or more Americans are exposed to vehicular noise at or above levels that risk hearing loss (Bolt, Beranek, & Newman, 1982; Galloway et al., 1974). Increases in air traffic have increased noise levels around airports, and studies have shown that half to two-thirds of those people living near airports where aircraft noise is a problem report annoyance and unhappiness about the noise (e.g., Burrows & Zamarin, 1972; McLean & Tarnopolsky, 1977). Some evidence suggests that airport noise or noise from airplanes overhead is associated with higher blood pressure and ear symptoms as well as annoyance (Ising et al., 1990). We will deal with this research in more detail later in this chapter. Rail traffic also continues to be a problem. Estimates in New York City alone suggest that a half million residents are exposed to loud (85 to 100 dB) noise from rapid transit trains (Raloff, 1982). Thus, the pervasiveness of noise generated by transportation systems makes it important to study. Several studies indicate that the more exposure to transportation noise one receives, the greater the annoyance among community residents (Fidell, Barber, & Schultz, 1991).

A second characteristic of transportation noise is that it is usually loud. This is clear from the sound levels noted above, as well as from estimates of sound levels near airports (ranging from 75 to 95 dB). A quick glance at Figure 5–5 also provides evidence of this, as do EPA measurements of noise levels in third-floor apartments next to freeways in Los Angeles (90 dB; see Raloff, 1982). Annoyance, however, does not appear to be related to loudness itself; acoustic (volume) and non-acoustic (e.g., predictability) factors in ratings of annoyance jointly determine the mood effects of noise (Green &

Fidell, 1991). For example, a study of annoyance due to airport noise near Hartsfield International Airport in Atlanta indicated that annoyance was not reduced by insulation that reduced sound in some people's homes (Fidell & Silvati, 1991).

Occupational Noise

Noise exposure in the workplace is a second major problem and has also received a great deal of research interest as well. One characteristic of occupational noise, particularly office noise, is that it is very wide-band noise, being made up of many sounds of differing frequencies. If extreme, this may result in a white noise that actually masks ("covers up") noise and results in a tolerable situation. However, if not that broad, the resulting noise may be resistant to adaptation and more likely to cause annoyance and distress (Loewen & Suedfeld, 1992). As a result, examination of effects of office noise, as well as possible ways to reduce these effects, should consider the frequency as well as loudness of the noise in influencing psychological reactions to it.

Occupational noise is also very pervasive, and sound levels in many occupational settings are loud. More than half of United States production workers are exposed to regular noise levels above the point at which hearing loss is likely, and more than 5 million are exposed to levels above the legally permissible ceiling of 90 dB (OSHA, 1981). Construction workers may be exposed to equipment noises of 100 dB, aircraft mechanics to levels ranging from 88 to 120 dB, and coal miners to continuous levels between 95 and 105 dB (Raloff, 1982). For reasons noted above, these exposures are sufficient to cause concern and underscore the need for continued research on noise and its effects.

Regardless of the source of noise, it can have unpleasant and/or unhealthy effects on us. Sources of noise and annoyance are not limited to the major ones described in the preceding section (transportation and workplace noise). An interesting study of residential noise makes this point well. Observing that noise produced by air conditioners is often substantial, Bradley (1992) surveyed 550 people, roughly equal numbers of whom lived in noisy or quieter areas and owned or did not own an air conditioner. Noise measurements were made as well. The physical level of noise (loudness) was related to annoyance and to reports of hearing neighbors' air conditioners, and the amount by which air conditioners' noise exceeded ambient noise levels was also related to annoyance. Negative reactions to the air conditioner noise were common and tended to occur most frequently in quieter neighborhoods where the air conditioner noise exceeded background levels (Bradley, 1992). As we might have expected, owning an air conditioner resulted in less annoyance from air conditioner noise, presumably because some of the noise was being generated for the person's comfort.

EFFECTS OF NOISE

The most logical or expected effects of exposure to noise is hearing loss, and this consequence of noise is an important concern for employers and regulators as well. Although very loud sounds (e.g., 150 dB) can rupture the eardrum or destroy other parts of the ear, damage to hearing from excessive noise usually occurs at lower noise levels (90 to 120 dB) because of temporary or permanent damage to the tiny hair cells in the cochlea of the inner ear (Figure 5–4). Such **hearing loss** is measured in terms of a baseline of "normal" amplitude thresholds at given frequencies. When a hearing loss occurs at a given frequency, it requires more than the normal amplitude (in dB) for a person to hear that frequency, i.e., the amplitude threshold is greater. The usual index of hearing loss for a given frequency, then, is the number of decibels above the normal threshold required to reach the new threshold. Such hearing losses are generally identified as one of two types: (1) **temporary threshold shifts (TTS)**, in which the normal threshold returns within 16 hours after exposure to the damaging noise; and (2) **noise-induced permanent threshold shifts (NIPTS)**, which are typically measured a month or more after the cessation of exposure to the damaging noise (Kryter, 1970).

Hearing loss, which affects millions of people, is a serious problem in this country. A 1972 Environmental Protection Agency (EPA) survey estimated that close to 3 million Americans suffer noise-induced hearing loss. A report by Rosen et al. (1962) compared the extent of the problem in the United States with a much quieter Sudanese culture, and found that 70-year-old Sudanese tribesmen had hearing abilities comparable to those of 20-year-old Americans! To avoid serious hearing loss among industrial workers, the Occupational Safety and Health Administration (OSHA) has established guidelines that allow only limited exposure to noise, (e.g., eight hours for 90 dB, four hours for 95 dB, two hours for 100 dB, and so on). However, some trucks can, at some distances, emit noise of 95 dB. Thus, individuals living near heavy traffic routes are undoubtedly exposed to noise levels for at least brief periods of time exceeding government industrial standards. Some of the potential consequences of such exposure are reflected in the box on pages 162–163.

As was the case with annoyance, absolute levels of noise alone do not determine hearing loss. Recent research, for example, suggests that certain drugs may increase the damaging effects of noise (Miller, 1982). Studies with animals have indicated that administration of an antibiotic in conjunction with exposure to noise can increase the effects of the noise and cause greater hearing loss than would the drug or noise levels alone (Raloff, 1982). Other drugs, including aspirin, may also interact with noise and increase effects on hearing, but evidence remains mixed. At this point it appears that a few drugs can, in combination with noise, cause increased hearing loss, but the magnitude of effect of most is small.

College students and teenagers are frequently exposed to another damaging source of noise—loud rock music. Several studies (e.g., Lebo & Oliphant, 1968) found that rock groups playing in discotheques are exposed to music from 110 to 120 dB for nonstop periods of up to one and one-half hours. Serious hearing loss can result (the federal industrial limit for 110 dB sound is 30 minutes a day). Other research (EPA, 1972) has studied hearing loss across samples of several age groups, and found frequencies to be 3.8 percent of sixth graders, 10 percent of ninth and tenth graders, and a whopping 61 percent of the 1969 college freshman class! More current rock music, as different as it is from '60s acid rock, is still loud enough to cause hearing loss.

HEALTH EFFECTS OF NOISE

High levels of noise can also lead to increases in arousal and stress (e.g., Cohen et al., 1986; Glass & Singer, 1972). We might expect, then, that the incidence of diseases related to stress—**hypertension** (high blood pressure), ulcers, etc.—would increase as one is exposed to higher levels of more unpredictable and/or uncontrollable noise.

BEYOND THE LABORATORY:
Costs in the Classroom

Cohen, Glass, and Singer (1973) theorized that urban noise may impair the educational development of children if it is severe enough. Studying a large high-rise apartment complex situated over a noisy highway in New York City (see Figure 5–6), the investigators found that noise exposure on the lower floors of the complex was more severe than on the upper floors. While carefully controlling for such factors as social class and air pollution, which might also vary with the floors of the building, the researchers found that children on the noisier lower floors had poorer hearing discrimination than children on the upper floors.

Moreover, the hearing problems of children on the lower floors may have influenced their reading ability, for it was found that they had poorer reading performance than children on the upper floors.

Figure 5–6 This is the high-rise apartment building used in the study described here. Note the traffic passing underneath.

Research evidence on this relationship is not conclusive but suggests that noise can harm health. Earlier studies done in this area provided only weak evidence for noise as a pathogenic agent (Cohen, Glass, & Phillips, 1977). On the other hand, noise has been linked to spontaneous outbreaks of illness related to stress (e.g., Colligan & Murphy, 1982) and to incidence of neurological and gastrointestinal problems (National Academy of Sciences, 1981).

More recent research has provided more evidence of noise–health linkages. Studies suggest that noise affects immune system function in humans and animals that could render us more susceptible to infection (e.g., McCarthy, Ouimet, & Dunn, 1992; Sieber et al., 1992; Weisse et al., 1990). Ulcers in particular appear more likely among workers exposed to a lot of occupational noise. Doring, Hauf, and Seiberling (1980) have suggested that sound can affect intestinal tissue directly, so it does not even have to be heard to predispose a worker to digestive problems. Sustained noise exposure is associated with constriction of peripheral blood vessels in animals (Millar & Steels, 1990). At least one study (Ando & Hattori, 1973) has found an association between exposure of expectant mothers to aircraft noise and infant mortality. Finally, survey or correlational studies have found that frequent exposure to

In another study, Bronzaft and McCarthy (1975) compared the reading skills of children from two sides of a school building. One side of the building was adjacent to elevated railroad tracks, but the other side was much quieter. It was found that 11 percent of teaching time was lost in classrooms facing the noisy tracks. Not surprisingly, the reading skills of children on the quieter side of the building were superior to those of children on the noisy side (see also Crook & Langdon, 1974).

Research also suggests that aircraft noise has effects on children's performance. Cohen et al. (1986) studied children attending school near the Los Angeles International Airport. Some were in schools in which aircraft noise was very loud (up to 95 dB), while others were in schools where there was considerably less noise. After controlling for the effects of socioeconomic variables and accounting for differences in hearing loss, results of a multimeasure assessment indicated that children attending noisier schools had more difficulty solving complex problems. In addition, Damon (1977) found that children living in housing where traffic noise was high were more likely to miss school.

Can such problems be prevented? A report by Ward and Suedfeld (1973) suggests that they can. In response to a plan for routing a major highway next to a classroom building, the researchers played tape recordings of traffic at noise levels that simulated those of a real highway. Interference with learning was discovered before construction began, suggesting that we can plan ahead to avoid problems of this kind.

noise is associated with reports of acute and chronic illness (Cameron, Robertson, & Zaks, 1972) and with increased consumption of sleeping pills and the need to see a physician (Grandjean et al., 1973). The latter studies, however, are not definitive because they do not control for related factors such as housing conditions, income, or education.

It has also been demonstrated that exposure to loud or frequent noise (e.g., living near an airport, working in a noisy setting) leads to heightened electrodermal activity, constriction of peripheral blood vessels, higher diastolic and systolic blood pressure, and increased catecholamine secretion (e.g., Cohen et al., 1986; Evans & Cohen, 1987; Evans & Lepore, 1993; Glass & Singer, 1972). Data from school children attending schools near the Los Angeles International Airport have indicated that exposure to noisy conditions at school is associated with elevated blood pressure relative to that observed among children attending quieter schools (Cohen et al., 1986). In addition, workers exhibit lower blood pressure and lower levels of epinephrine in their urine when they wear hearing protectors that reduce the intensity of noise (Ising & Melchert, 1980). The physiological changes accompanying exposure to noise are also associated with stress reactions and cardiovascular disorders, but few controlled experimental studies have been conducted that indicate a direct link between noise and heart disease.

One study has provided a good deal of information about how noise may facilitate the development of hypertension. Subjects who were already diagnosed as having moderately high blood pressure were exposed to 105-dB noise for 30 minutes, and blood pressure measurements were made during quiet and noisy periods (Eggertsen et al., 1987). During the noise there was a significant increase in systolic and diastolic blood pressure, marked primarily by an increase in peripheral vascular resistance as the force of the heart contractions actually decreased. Thus, stress due to noise exposure was associated with constriction of blood vessels (consistent with animal studies showing vasoconstriction during chronic noise exposure). This suggests a mechanism by which noise may contribute to hypertension. Research indicates that the constriction of blood vessels that is associated with noise exposure does not habituate very well when noise is loud or unexpected (Jansen, 1973). This means that, over time, very loud or unexpected noise continues to affect blood vessels long after subjects have "gotten used to the noise" and other physiological responses have diminished. Responses such as heart rate or skin conductance tend to be modest and to decrease with repeated exposure (Borg, 1981; Glass & Singer, 1972).

Most of these studies suggest that noise can cause a variety of physiological changes that may contribute to disease. The links to disease, however, are less well established—all of which is to say that despite reported increases of several stress indicators or measures of cardiovascular function when people are exposed to noise, these studies do not show a relationship between noise and cardiovascular disease or infectious illness.

One argument against the hypothesis that noise can affect health is that studies using hearing loss as an indicator of noise exposure have shown few if any relationships between noise and cardiovascular function or disease among Air Force aircrews (e.g., Kent et al., 1986). However, these correlational studies rely on a strong relationship between hearing loss and noise exposure and cannot address other causes of hearing loss or aspects of noise other than those linked to hearing loss. It is also possible that the self-selection biases in aircrew members might have affected the results. Other studies have examined health problems among industrial workers as a function of exposure to noise, and these studies (e.g., Cohen, 1973; Jansen, 1973) typically find modest relationships between exposure to high noise levels and cardiovascular disorders, allergies, sore throats, and digestive disorders.

Interestingly, younger and less experienced workers appear to suffer more from noise exposure, suggesting that more experienced workers have adapted to the noise. Unfortunately, industrial studies rarely control for other factors that may account for adverse health effects, such as factory conditions, exposure to pollutants, and stressful work activity. As a consequence, conclusions about effects of noise on health must be guarded. Futhermore, some studies (e.g., Finckle & Poppen, 1948; Glorig, 1971) report no association between industrial noise exposure and many of the disorders we have noted.

Another way of studying the health-impairing effects of noise is to examine how it interacts with other stressors or behaviors. For example, we know that noise increases people's blood pressure and other signs of arousal, as does cigarette smoking. How do the two affect us if we smoke while exposed to noise? Given that smoking is described by many who smoke as an effective coping strategy that calms them down, will it cancel the arousing effects of noise or add to them? A study by Woodson et al. (1986) looked at this question in a sample of women. Forty-eight women who smoked and 12 who did not smoke participated in the study and were exposed to noise. The smokers were assigned to a smoking group or a sham-smoking group (puffing on unlit cigarettes) in which they did not actually smoke any cigarettes. The nonsmokers were assigned to a sham-smoking control group. Subjective distress reported by subjects increased during the session, but did not increase for those allowed to smoke. The arousing affects of smoking did attenuate some noise-related arousal. Smoking appears to reduce some of the physiological responses to noise, particularly noise-induced increases in heart rate and vasoconstriction. This may have been partially due to the periodic nature of the noise exposure (noise was not continuous), since studies of continuous stressor exposure and smoking find the opposite effect or no effect at all (e.g., MacDougall et al., 1983; Suter et al., 1983).

It is also possible that noise can affect health by changing behaviors that are related to health. If people drink more coffee or alcohol, smoke more cigarettes, or fail to exercise because of noise exposure, then relationships between noise and health might be mediated by these behaviors. A study by Cherek (1985) provides some evidence of this by showing that increasing loudness of noise was associated with increased cigarette smoking. As can be seen in Figure 5–7, higher dB levels of noise were associated with higher levels of smoking during an experimental laboratory session as well as with how people smoked. The louder the noise, the more puffs they took when they smoked and the longer the average duration of each puff.

Overall, it is difficult to relate noise *directly* to adverse effects on physical health. More likely, adverse effects of noise exposure on health occur primarily in conjunction with other stressors (such as industrial pollutants, on-the-job tensions, economic pressures, and so on), or are limited to those who

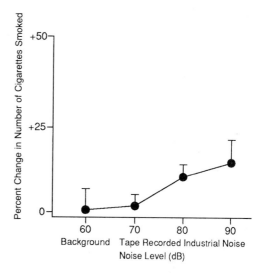

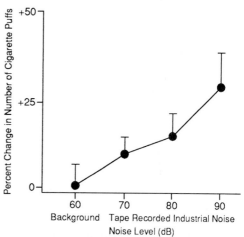

Figure 5–7 The top graph indicates the percent change in the number of cigarettes smoked per session for all subjects at industrial noise levels of 60, 70, 80, or 90 decibels. The bottom graph shows the percent change in the number of cigarette puffs per session. Data points represent the mean percent change values for all subjects, with the mean at the baseline (60 dB) condition set at zero. The vertical lines on each data point represent the standard error of the mean.
Adapted from Cherek, 1985.

are particularly susceptible to certain physiological disorders (Cohen, Glass, & Phillips, 1977). For example, in one study, noise effects on blood pressure were seen only in people with family histories of hypertension (Theorell, 1990). However, the relationship suggested by these data is strong enough to warrant more attention.

NOISE AND MENTAL HEALTH

We have noted that exposure to high levels of noise leads to the heightened physiological activity typical of stress and suggested that physical health may be affected as well. Some have assumed that stress is the link between noise and health problems. Since stress is a causal factor in mental illness as well, we might expect noise exposure to be associated with mental health problems (for a review, see Cohen, Glass, & Phillips, 1977; Kryter, 1970). Industrial surveys typically report that exposure to high-intensity noise is associated with headaches, nausea, instability, irritability, anxiety, sexual impotence, and changes in affect or mood (Cohen et al., 1977; Miller, 1974; Strakhov, 1966). As with surveys of physical health and noise exposure, the results of these studies must be interpreted with caution, since other stressors related to home and work were usually not fully considered or controlled. In a relevant experimental study, Ward and Suedfeld (1973) found that exposure to "piped-in" traffic noise caused people to experience more tension and uncertainty and led people to talk faster than people in a group exposed to normal sound conditions. However, a study of 2,398 men in the United Kingdom showed that traffic noise was related to annoyance but not to psychological disorders (Stansfield et al., 1993).

An interesting but controversial series of studies examined the relationship between airport noise and mental health near London's Heathrow Airport. In one study (Abey-Wickrama et al., 1969), researchers compared psychiatric admission rates for high and low noise areas around the airport and found higher rates of admission in the noisier area. Chowns (1970) challenged these results suggesting that differences in who lived in the two areas may have varied in important ways, but Herridge (1974) found similar though weaker results with improved survey techniques (see Figure 5–8). Jenkins et al. (1979) found some evidence of increased psychiatric admissions as a function of noise exposure, but subsequently found more convincing evidence of non-noise factors affecting admissions (Jenkins et al., 1981). However, Kryter (1990) has argued that these data actually reflect a positive relationship between noise and psychiatric admissions, which are determined by other factors as well as by noise.

Evidence that noise can make people more emotionally reactive and "upsettable" is derived from studies linking noise with hormones associated with emotionality. In one study, uncontrollable noise exposure caused increases in oxytocin secretion among women considered highly emotional, suggesting an association between noise and emotionality (Sanders, Freilicher, & Lightman, 1990). However, assessment of psychological or emotional disturbances in noisy and quiet areas has provided no reliable evidence of noise contributing to the development of psychopathology (Stansfield, 1992). As with physical health, we should explore the possibility that noise contributes to mental illness primarily in combination with other factors that precipitate or permit mental disorders to develop. For example, in addition to influencing stress, noise exposure may lead to loss of perceived control and learned helplessness (see Chapter 4), which in turn increases susceptibility to psychological disorders. Cohen et al. (1977) noted that residents of high-noise areas tend to "give up" and not complain about the noise because they believe their voices will carry little weight with authorities. Together with the social and economic burdens typical of high-noise areas of cities, a sense of hopelessness and helpless-

Figure 5–8 Some research has tried to associate airport noise with mental health problems of residents in the area. Although the findings are controversial, there is limited evidence that psychiatric hospital admissions are unusually heavy for areas surrounding airports.

ness may develop, which can make psychological disorders more likely.

EFFECTS OF NOISE ON PERFORMANCE

Effects During Exposure

People often report that they make more errors in noisy than in quiet settings, but their beliefs about noise do not always match their performance (Smith & Jones, 1992; Smith & Stansfield, 1986). Laboratory research on the influence of noise on performance has shown mixed results. For detailed reviews, the reader is referred to Cohen et al. (1986) and to Stansfield (1992). Briefly, whether noise affects performance adversely, favorably, or not at all depends on the same properties of noise discussed earlier (i.e., intensity, predictability, controllability), the type of task performed, and stress tolerance and other personality characteristics of the

individual (e.g., Baker & Holding, 1993; Cohen & Weinstein, 1982; Koelega & Brinkman, 1986). Very loud noise (more than 100 dB) appears to affect performance in some ways. However, in general, data from laboratory research suggest that regular noise in the range of 90 to 100 dB does not adversely affect performance of simple motor or mental tasks. However, noises in this amplitude range that are unpredictable (intermittent at irregular intervals) will interfere with performance on vigilance tasks, memory tasks, and complex tasks in which an individual must perform two activities simultaneously. On the other hand, Glass and Singer (1972) found that even these performance problems were minimal and/or overcome by individuals who perceived that they had control over the noise (i.e., could stop it if they wished). Other research (Broadbent, 1954) suggests that sudden, loud, unpredictable noise may momentarily distract an individual from a task and

NOISE SENSITIVITY

As you might expect, people vary in how they react to noise. Even with rather loud noises, not everyone exposed will be annoyed or upset by noise, even though at relatively low noise levels, some other people will report annoyance and distress. To capture these differences and try to systematize them, researchers have employed the concept of *noise sensitivity* in an attempt to better explain general reactions to noise. "High sensitive" or "vulnerable" means that they are very sensitive to noise and their threshold for distress is relatively low—even low or moderate noise may disturb them. "Low sensitives," on the other hand, show greater resistance to the effects of noise and ordinarily do not report annoyance at low, moderate, or even some higher levels of noise. Because annoyance is negative and suggests distress, highly sensitive people are generally regarded as being more vulnerable to the effects of noise.

Consistent with this, research has shown that noise sensitivity is related to annoyance at varying levels of noise and is associated with psychological disorders and mental health (e.g., Bullen et al., 1986; Iwata, 1984; Job, 1988; Stansfield, 1992). A study of road traffic noise found that sensitivity to noise, measured on a noise sensitivity scale (see Table 5–2), was an important variable in determining response to the noise (Stansfield et al., 1993). Noise exposure was related to annoyance, but men who were more noise sensitive complained more and were more annoyed. Noise exposure was not related to psychiatric diagnoses in this sample, but noise sensitivity was related to prevalence of psychological disorders and trait anxiety (Stansfield et al., 1993).

Table 5–2 Items on the Noise-Sensitivity Scale

1. I wouldn't mind living on a noisy street if the apartment I had was nice.
2. I am more aware of noise than I used to be.[a]
3. No one should mind much if someone turns up his stereo full blast once in a while.
4. At movies, whispering and crinkling candy wrappers disturb me.[a]
5. I am easily awakened by noise.[a]
6. If it's noisy where I'm studying, I try to close the door or window or move someplace else.[a]
7. I get annoyed when my neighbors are noisy.[a]
8. I get used to most noises without much difficulty.
9. How much would it matter to you if an apartment you were interested in renting was located across from a fire station?[a]
10. Sometimes noises get on my nerves and get me irritated.[a]
11. Even music I normally like will bother me if I'm trying to concentrate.[a]
12. It wouldn't bother me to hear the sounds of everyday living from neighbors (footsteps, running water, etc).
13. When I want to be alone, it disturbs me to hear outside noises.[a]
14. I'm good at concentrating no matter what is going on around me.
15. In a library, I don't mind if people carry on a conversation if they do it quietly.
16. There are often times when I want complete silence.[a]
17. Motorcycles ought to be required to have bigger mufflers.[a]
18. I find it hard to relax in a place that's noisy.[a]
19. I get mad at people who make noise that keeps me from falling asleep or getting work done.[a]
20. I wouldn't mind living in an apartment with thin walls.
21. I am sensitive to noise.[a]

Note. *Most items are presented on a 6-point scale ranging from agree strongly (1) to disagree strongly (6).*
[a] *Item scored in opposite direction before responses are summed.*
Taken from Weinstein, 1978.

thereby cause errors if the task requires much vigilance or concentration. Woodhead (1964) noted that recorded sonic booms caused momentary errors in a task requiring intense concentration.

To some extent the kind of effects that noise has on task performance may be a matter of personality or differential sensitivity to noise (see box above). Research has indicated that noise effects on performance may depend in part on personality, as in Auble and Britton's (1958) finding that only subjects who are high in anxiety are adversely affected by noise on certain types of tasks. Other individual differences may be important as well (Vallet, 1987). Extroverts are generally under-aroused relative to introverts, suggesting that extroverts should show better performance when working in noisy conditions. Indeed, this has been observed (e.g., Campbell, 1992; Dornic & Ekehammar, 1990), and some evidence suggests that extroverts prefer working in noisier settings (Blake, 1971; Davies & Hockey, 1966; Geen 1984). Age, sex, and other characteristics could also be influential. Children do not experience as much disturbed sleep, and younger subjects have been shown to have smaller physiological changes when exposed to noise than do older subjects (Vallet, 1987). Comparison of noise effects on task performance among adults or children age 6 or 9 years showed effects at all ages (von Wright & Nuimi, 1979). All showed slower performance, but children's performance improved under some conditions. However, among younger people, sex differences appear to exist in response to noise, with females exhibiting more sleep disturbance than males (Lukas, 1975). Research on sex differences in adults is inconsistent: Some studies indicate that women are more adversely affected than are men (e.g., Gulian & Thomas, 1986) while others have found no differences (Edmonds & Smith, 1985). Finally, limited re-

search (e.g., Corcoran, 1962) suggests that the arousal properties of noise may actually facilitate performance for individuals who have been deprived of sleep for a day or more.

Exposure to loud, uncontrollable noise appears to bias retrieval of information from memory, causing more attention or greater recall of negative mood-laden items or memories (Willner & Neiva, 1986). This is not unlike observations of depressed people, who suffer from negative memory biases and seem better able to retrieve unpleasant memories (e.g., Fogarty & Hemsley, 1983). Since exposure to uncontrollable stressors has been shown to lead to symptoms of learned helplessness, and helplessness may be associated with depression, all of this seems to fit together. Or does it? Failure on a computer game task, which should also contribute to learned helplessness, did not affect retrieval of negative memories (Isen et al., 1978). Though the effects of noise in distorting memory observed by Willner and Neiva (1986) were found only when the noise was uncontrollable, it may be that some characteristic of noise is also important in this relationship (cf. Bell et al., 1984). The effects of stressors on this sort of memory distortion and bias toward negative recollections represent an important area for future research.

Aftereffects

Noise has more than just immediate effects on performance. Glass, Singer, and Friedman (1969) had subjects perform tasks after a 25-minute exposure to 108-dB noise. One task involved attempts to solve puzzles that were actually unsolvable (Figure 5–9). The number of attempts to solve such puzzles served as an index of tolerance for frustration, or persistence. The second task involved proofreading a manuscript, which required considerable vigilance and concentration. Compared to a no-noise control group and groups exposed before the task

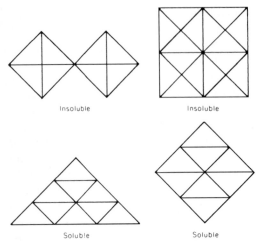

Figure 5-9 Examples of puzzles used by Glass and Singer (1972). Figures must be drawn without crossing a line or lifting the pencil.
Adapted by Glass and Singer from Feather, 1961.

to either predictable *or* controllable noise, subjects exposed before the task to 108 dB of unpredictable *and* uncontrollable noise showed one-half to one-third as much tolerance of frustration and also made considerably more proofreading errors. Apparently, the **aftereffects** of noise can be as severe as the effects during perception of the noise. In a similar experiment, it was found that aftereffects depend on the amount of perceived control (Sherrod et al., 1977). These researchers gave some subjects control over starting the noise, and still others control over both starting and stopping it. Another group had no control over the noise. Results showed that the greater the perceived control, the more persistent subjects were in working unsolvable puzzles once the noise had stopped.

Such aftereffects can also be explained by the theoretical approaches discussed previously. For example, arousal remains elevated for a time after an arousing stimulus (such as noise) has ceased. Thus, this "carried-over" arousal can account for some after-

effects. The environmental load approach also suggests that once an attention-getting noise has stopped, a fatigue effect ensues, and it takes time to reallocate enough attention to perform a mental task. If the noise is presented with perceived control, less attention is allocated to it to begin with, so recovery time is less, and the potential for learned helplessness is decreased.

Noise and Children's Performance

Cognitive impairment by noise among children also has been observed, though it appears that these effects are not universal. For example, Hambrick-Dixon (1986) studied children who attended day-care centers close to noisy elevated subways and others far from the subways. Psychomotor task performance was impaired by experimentally imposed noise in a laboratory setting, but the nature of performance during noise was determined by the noisiness of their day-care center. Children from the noisier centers performed *better* when exposed to noise than when not, while children from quieter centers showed the opposite pattern.

In a series of studies examining the effects of chronic exposure to loud aircraft noise at school, Cohen et al. (1986) compared problem-solving performance of children from noisy and quiet schools near Los Angeles International Airport. Subjects were given either a solvable or an unsolvable task before performance was assessed, and in one of the samples, subjects were allowed to choose a game to play if they wished. Results showed that children attending noisy schools were less likely to solve the solvable task than were students from quieter schools. Regardless of whether they were pretreated with success or failure on the first puzzle, they were less able to solve the second task, and were more likely to give up. These data suggested that students from noisy schools were simply less able to solve cognitive tasks.

To some extent this was due to the tendency of children from the noisier schools to give up more quickly. Of those children given a choice during the experimental sessions, children from noisier schools were less likely to make the choice than were children from quieter environments.

These studies also examined school achievement and distractibility among the young students. Over time, the effects of chronic exposure to aircraft noise did not dissipate; that is, the effects did not decrease or go away with time. Instead, students seemed to be more distractible the longer they attended school under noisy conditions. School achievement was not affected by noise levels in schools, but was affected by noise levels at home.

A more recent study of chronic exposure to airport noise was done near the Munich International Airport in Germany (Evans, Hygge, & Bullinger, 1993). A group of 135 third- and fourth-grade students living near the airport or in quieter, urban neighborhoods was studied in air-conditioned, sound-proof trailers parked near the students' schools. A range of measures was collected, including blood pressure, levels of stress hormones, and several indices of various cognitive abilities and task performance. The children living near the airport showed clear evidence of stress when compared to the quieter neighborhood students, showing higher levels of epinephrine and norepinephrine in their urine, higher diastolic blood pressure, and greater blood pressure reactivity during a cognitive task (Evans et al., 1993). Chronic noise exposure did not affect performance on some tasks, as no differences were found for reaction time and embedded figures tasks, but memory and reading task performance was better among children from quieter neighborhood settings. Students living in noisier areas (near the airport) were less motivated,

showed less tolerance for frustration, and were more annoyed (Evans et al., 1993).

These field studies provide strong support for those who argue that chronic exposure to noise is associated with chronic stress and impairment of cognitive performance. Other explanations for these effects, such as actual auditory damage or loss of hearing were ruled out in this study, and results were consistent with other studies of airport and traffic noise exposure and classroom noise (Hygge, 1993). Issues such as how long these effects of noise exposure last once subjects are no longer exposed to the noise (they move or the airport is closed) are under study, and more research is needed to better understand the scope and extent of stress and cognitive deficits associated with noise.

How Do These Effects Occur?

One theory of how noise affects task performance is that it "masks" internal speech, or makes it more difficult to "hear ourselves think" (Poulton, 1977). When inner speech is blocked or cannot be used, noise has more negative effects on task performance (Wilding & Mohindra, 1980). Other studies have found some evidence that noise masks internal speech and that this leads to poorer performance, but evidence does not indicate that this is the only way noise affects our work (Jones et al., 1979; Smith, 1988). Other theories posit comprehension as the primary "victim" of noise, and studies also provide some support for this idea. Noise appears to reduce comprehension of reading material (Hockey, 1979; Smith & Stansfield, 1986). Broadbent (1971) argued that noise can affect task performance by increasing the likelihood that dominant or readily available information will be used in making decisions. In other words, noise causes people to use less of the information available and to sample or recall primarily dramatic, well-learned, or easily produced responses.

Several studies have provided evidence of this narrowing of attention phenomenon, including poorer recall of irrelevant or peripheral information available during a task, or poorer ability to access uncommon or rarely used information (e.g., Hockey & Hamilton, 1970; Houston & Jones, 1967; Smith, 1982).

All of these models of noise effects on performance have weaknesses or parts for which the data do not provide support. Given that these and other models of noise impact do not satisfactorily account for what we have learned about noise and task performance, how can we explain why noise affects performance only in certain circumstances?

One way to answer this question is to turn to the theoretical approaches discussed in Chapter 4. It might also be useful to examine once again Figure 5-2 showing our eclectic model applied to noise. For example, adaptation level theory predicts variations in performance for different levels of skill, experience, and stimulation for each individual. Furthermore, the Yerkes-Dodson Law and arousal theory suggest that noise that is arousing will facilitate performance on simple tasks, up to a point. However, high levels of arousal interfere with performance on complex tasks, and extremely high levels of arousal interfere with performance on simple tasks. Data from research on noise and performance are consistent with this explanation and suggest that arousal characteristic of stress can interfere with memory, reading, and problem-solving abilities.

Environmental load can also be used to explain many findings bearing on the relationship between noise and performance. Researchers have argued that unpredictable noise requires greater allocation of attention than does predictable noise, and it would therefore interfere more with performance. For complex tasks, even more attention is required for optimal performance, and any stimulus that distracts us or calls attention away from the task will hurt performance. Behavior constraint models can also explain some aspects of noise exposure, such as why lack of perceived control over noise hurts performance: When control is apparently lost, more effort may be given to restoring control than to attending to the task at hand, resulting in poorer task performance.

One of the ways in which noise may contribute to physical and mental health problems as well as mood and performance deficits is by disturbing sleep. Noise wakes us up, and makes it harder to fall asleep. We all know that from personal experience, and studies have confirmed that noise, even in hospital-like settings, can lead to stress and poor sleep (Topf, 1992a, 1992b). In another study, objective measures of noise exposure (e.g., loudness) were not related to sleep or to reported health, but subjective measures of noise exposure (e.g., annoyance) were related to sleep (Nivison & Endresen, 1993). Most likely, people learn to ignore noise that occurs continuously or regularly and adapt to such noise without losing much sleep; however, the effort required and one's sensitivity to the noise may affect sleep and health.

EFFECTS OF NOISE IN OFFICE AND INDUSTRIAL SETTINGS

How many of these effects of noise show up in real-world settings such as an office? One study, a survey of 2,391 employees in offices before and after office renovation, found that more than half reported that noise bothered them at work (Sundstrom et al., 1994). Irritation due to noise was also associated with dissatisfaction, and when renovated offices were noisier than they had been before renovation, job satisfaction declined (Sundstrom et al., 1994). As can be seen in Figure 5-10, changes in office design that resulted in less noise increased satisfaction with the new set-

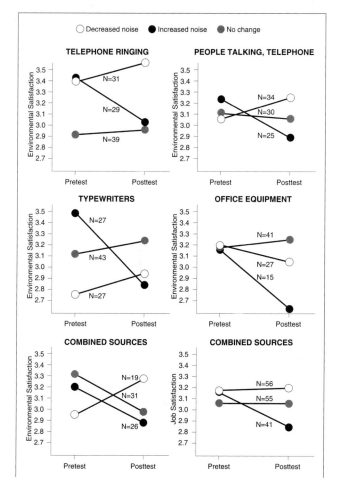

Figure 5–10 Changes in environmental and job satisfaction concurrent with increased, decreased, or unchanged disturbance by noise from specific and combined sources
From Sundstrom et al., 1994.

ting, while changes that led to more noise also decreased satisfaction.

One of the most serious problems of background noise in commercial and industrial settings is its interference with communication (MacKenzie, 1975; Nemecek & Grandjean, 1973). When a number of distinct auditory signals are presented simultaneously, it is often difficult for the human ear to distinguish or discriminate among them. This phenomenon is known as **masking** and it accounts for our difficulty in hearing others talk in the presence of loud background

noise. The background noise in the Glass and Singer (1972) research was created by combining simultaneously the sounds of a mimeograph machine (a type of copier), a calculator, a typewriter, two people speaking Spanish, and another person speaking Armenian, with the final effect being little discriminability among the various sounds due to masking. Interestingly, it has been found that loud background conversation interferes with performance more than noise that is not distinguishable as conversation (Olszewski, Rotton, & Soler, 1976). Apparently, we try to hear background conversation as communication, so we pay a lot of attention to it. Nonconversational noise, however, requires less attention but does interfere with efforts to communicate.

Difficulty in hearing a communication varies not only according to amplitude and frequency of background noise (the more similar the frequency of the noise and of the communication, the worse the interference), but also according to the distance between communicator and listener. Figure 5–11 demonstrates the combined effects of ambient noise amplitude and interpersonal distance on communiciation. These "acceptable" levels of background noise are sometimes referred to as *speech interference levels* or SILs (Beranek, 1957). Limited research (e.g., Acton, 1970) indicates that some communicative adaptation to background noise does occur, so that we can learn to communicate effectively in the presence of many types of background noises. Thus, industrial workers accustomed to a noisy environment were found to be more effective in communicating against a loud background noise than were university employees accustomed to a quieter environment. Beranek (1956, 1957) examined self-reports of employees in offices and factories to determine what noise levels they considered acceptable in their work environments. Results correlated quite well with what might be predicted from SIL data, suggesting that 55 to 70 dB is acceptable for executive offices. Many designers and builders use these standards today (MacKenzie, 1975).

Research on the effect of noise on productivity in industrial settings generally finds no direct effect of noise on nonauditory performance (Kryter, 1970). However, several studies have purported to show that noise reduction can boost productivity. Broadbent and Little (1960) found that in a film-producing factory, reduction of ambient noise from 99 dB to 89 dB resulted in fewer

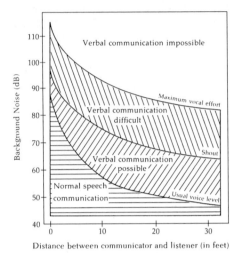

Figure 5–11 Relationship between communication effort, noise level, and interpersonal distance *Adapted from Miller, 1974.*

errors by workers. Kovrigin and Mikheyev (1965) reported that increasing background noise from 78–90 dB to either 85, 90, or 95 dB reduced the number of letters sorted per hour by postal employees. Kryter (1970) suggests that because such studies are conducted in field settings not subject to strict laboratory control of extraneous variables, the results are inconclusive at best. Reduction of noise, for instance, may boost employee morale, which in turn boosts productivity. In other words, mediating variables, such as morale, fatigue, or communication difficulty, may be more significant than direct effects of noise on performance. Nevertheless, if noise influences productivity even indirectly, industry would certainly want to take such influences into account by designing equipment and working space with noise levels in mind.

Concern over productivity, morale, and detrimental health effects of noise has led many industry and government officials to emphasize noise abatement factors in office and industrial settings (see also MacKenzie, 1975). Among the more common abatement

THE SST:
Why So Loud?

One of the marvels of space-age technology is supersonic flight and the arrival of the supersonic transport (SST) for commercial passengers. The American version of the SST was scuttled for economic and environmental reasons. The British-French Concorde, however, went into production and has been controversial ever since. Among its problems is noise. Engines on an SST must be slim and trim for better flight. As engine diameter decreases and speed increases, the exhaust noise becomes greater. Typical concorde noise on a runway is 100 to 120 dB, depending on one's distance from the jet. This is 10 to 20 dB greater than subsonic jets. Research suggests that a single flight of an aircraft 10 dB louder than another produces the same annoyance level as 10 flights of the less noisy aircraft.

Another noise problem with the SST is sonic booms. These thunderclap sounds are produced by any supersonic aircraft. Sound travels at a speed of 334 meters per second (747 miles per hour). The SST moves faster than the noise it produces (since passengers are ahead of the sound, they do not hear it as someone on the ground does). Consequently, the sound waves crowd together, increasing their pressure and causing a sonic boom. The tail of the aircraft leaves a partial vacuum, lowering the pressure as it passes. The result is an increase in pressure followed by a decrease. These pressure changes

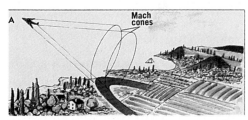

Figure 5–12 Cones representing increased and decreased pressure in a sonic boom. The area where the cones intersect the ground (shaded gray) experiences the sonic boom.
From Turk, A., Turk, J., Wittes, J.T., and Wittes, R., 1974. Environmental Science. *Philadelphia: Saunders.*

move away from the jet in the pattern of cones (Figure 5–12), so that anyone on the ground between the two cones hears the boom. If the aircraft is long enough, the positive and negative pressure changes may be heard as two distinct sounds. The boom itself continues from the time the aircraft breaks the sound barrier until it resumes subsonic speeds, but a person on the ground hears it only 0.1 to 0.5 second. Thus, the entire area over which the SST flies at supersonic speeds will experience the sonic boom. For this reason, the SST has been forbidden to fly over the United States at supersonic speeds (Turk et al., 1974).

procedures are use of thick carpeting, suspended and acoustical tile ceilings, sound-absorbing wall materials, heavy draperies, and even plants. Other approaches involve making machines quieter in the first place, such as putting a layer of felt between typewriters and desks, enclosing computer printout equipment with felt or foam-lined covers, and producing equipment with less noisy components. Still another approach is to mask noise with constantly humming ventilating equipment or piped-in music. Whatever the technique, we suspect that an increasing emphasis by labor and management will be placed on reducing noise in work environments.

NOISE AND SOCIAL BEHAVIOR

If noise has stressful, arousing, attention-narrowing, or behavior-constraining properties, exposure to it will be likely to influence interpersonal relationships. We will now look at three specific social relationships—attraction, altruism, and aggression—to determine just what noise can do to social interaction.

Noise and Attraction

One might expect loud, disturbing noise to have a deleterious effect on feelings of liking toward others. That is, noxious stimuli associated with others may lead to less pleasant evaluation of those others. One way to measure attraction, as suggested by research on personal space, is to examine physical distances between ourselves and others; we stand or sit closer to those people we like than to those we dislike. Thus, if interpersonal distance is an indicator of attraction and if noise decreases attraction, we would expect noise to increase interpersonal distancing. In support of this hypothesis, Mathews, Canon, and Alexander (1974) found that even a noise of 80 dB increased the distance at which individuals felt comfortable with each other. Also, in a correlational study, Appleyard and Lintell (1972) found less informal interaction among neighbors when traffic noise was greater. While this could suggest that noise lowers attraction toward others, additional interpretations are possible.

Other researchers (Bull et al., 1972) have found equivocal results on the relationship between noise and attraction. These researchers found that although exposure to 84 dB of background noise led to less liking in most cases, females actually reported more liking for similar others when exposed to noise. Research by Bell and Barnard (1977) suggests a partial explanation for this unexpected finding. Apparently, males exposed to noxious environmental stimulation momentarily prefer more distant, less affiliative social interaction. Females, on the other hand, may well prefer closer, affiliative social interaction in order to share their uneasiness with others who are experiencing discomfort. Thus, in some circumstances noise may decrease attraction, and in other cases it may increase attraction. Kenrick and Johnson (1979), for example, have shown that among females, exposure to aversive noise may increase attraction toward one who shares the aversive experience with the subject, but decreases attraction toward someone not actually experiencing the noise.

One explanation for some effects of noise on attraction is that noise affects the amount of information that people gather about another person. Theories that suggest that noise causes people to narrow their attention and focus on a smaller part of their environment also suggests that noise causes people to pay attention to fewer characteristics of other people. Thus, noise could cause a distortion in perceptions of other people. Research by Siegel and Steele (1980) suggests that this may be the case; these researchers found that noise led to more extreme and premature judgments about other people but did not cause these judgments to be more negative.

Noise and Human Aggression

Research on the effects of noise on aggression has been much more conclusive than research on noise and attraction. Several theories of aggression (Bandura, 1973; Berkowitz, 1970) predict that under circumstances in which aggression is a dominant response in the behavior hierarchy, increasing an individual's arousal level will also increase the intensity of aggressive behavior. Thus, to the extent that noise increases arousal, it should also increase aggression in individuals already predisposed to aggress (e.g., Zillmann, 1979).

Geen and O'Neal (1969) sought to test this hypothesis by first showing subjects either a nonviolent sports film or a more violent prize-fight film, with the expectation that the violent film would predispose subjects to aggress. Next, subjects were provided with an opportunity to aggress against a confederate "victim" by ostensibly delivering electric shocks to that person. In many studies of aggression, subjects are given the chance to shock a confederate or stooge victim, and the shock level (intensity, duration, or number) they choose is the index of aggression. No shocks are actually administered, although the subject, until the end of the experiment, is led to believe that he or she is actually delivering shocks. During the shock phase of the experiment, Geen and O'Neal exposed half the subjects to the normal noise level of the laboratory and the other half to a two-minute burst of continuous 60-dB white noise (i.e., a broad band of frequencies). It was predicted that the 60-dB noise would increase the level of aggression of subjects exposed to the violent film. Results, as depicted in Figure 5–13, suggested that both the violent film and the added noise increased the number of shocks delivered to the victim. Furthermore, the greatest aggression occurred under the condition that combined the violent film with the arousing noise, as originally predicted.

Additional laboratory research on noise and aggression has been conducted by Donnerstein and Wilson (1976). Recall that Glass and Singer (1972) found unpredictable noise to be more aversive than predictable noise. One would thus expect unpredictable noise to

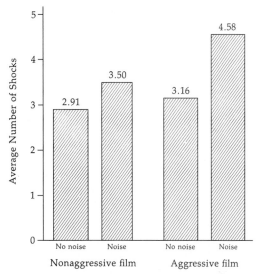

Figure 5–13 Average number of shocks delivered to the victim as a function of noise level and type of film

Adapted from Geen and O'Neal, 1969. Copyright 1969 by the American Psychological Association. Reprinted by permission of the author and publisher.

be highly arousing and consequently to lead to heightened aggression, in accordance with the dominant response hypothesis noted above. Donnerstein and Wilson exposed subjects to either 55 dB or 95 dB of unpredictable, one-second noise bursts while they were ostensibly administering electric shocks to a confederate of the experimenter. In addition, half the subjects previously had been either angered or not angered by this victim. As expected, angered subjects delivered more intense shocks than nonangered ones. Furthermore, the 95-dB unpredictable noise increased aggression relative to the 55-dB unpredictable noise only for angered subjects. Apparently, noise made no difference in the intensity of shocks delivered by nonangry subjects.

Following Glass and Singer's findings that controllable noise is less aversive and arousing than uncontrollable noise, we would expect that if subjects were given perceived control over noise, the noise would be less aversive and less likely to facilitate aggression. Donnerstein and Wilson tested this hypothesis by conducting a second experiment to determine the effects of additional noise variables on aggression. As subjects worked on a set of math problems, they were exposed either to no artificial noise, to 95 dB of unpredictable and uncontrollable noise, or to 95 dB of unpredictable noise that they believed they could terminate at any time (i.e., over which they perceived they had control). All noise was terminated when subjects began the shock phase of the experiment, so that only the aftereffects of noise could influence aggression. As in the previous experiment, subjects were either angered or not angered by the victim, in this case immediately after the math task. The results, depicted in Figure 5–14, suggest that more intense shocks were delivered by angry than nonangry subjects, and that unpredictable and uncontrollable noise increased aggression for angry subjects. The 95-dB noise had no effect on aggression, however, when subjects perceived they had control over it.

The finding that noise increased aggressiveness only when people were angry suggests again that the noise served to facilitate aggression caused by anger rather than creating or causing the aggression directly. Konecni et al. (1975) also found this to be the case—noise increased aggressiveness only when subjects had been provoked and made angry.

These experiments suggest, then, that under circumstances in which noise would be expected to increase arousal or when there is a predisposition to aggress (i.e., when subjects were already angry), aggression is increased. However, when the noise does not appreciably increase arousal (as when an individual has control over it) or when the individual is not already predisposed to aggress, noise appears to have little, if any, effect on aggression. Cohen and Spacapan (1984) have argued that noise strengthens or

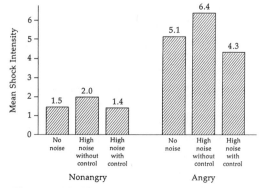

Figure 5–14 Mean intensity of shock delivered by subjects as a function of noise condition and anger arousal

Adapted from Donnerstein and Wilson, 1976. Copyright 1976 by the American Psychological Association. Reprinted by permission of the author and publisher.

increases aggression but does not provoke it. In order for noise to affect aggressive behavior, the behavior must be present for other reasons.

Noise and Helping

Research suggests that noise influences at least one more social phenomenon— whether or not people help each other. It seems reasonable to assume that aversive noise that makes us irritable or uncomfortable will make us less likely to offer assistance to someone who needs help. Research in social psychology has indicated that people are more likely to help others when they are in a good mood than when they are more negative (e.g., Isen, 1970), and since noise can result in the latter condition, it is likely that helping would also be affected. Another reason for this expected decrease in help is offered by the environmental load approach discussed in Chapter 4. Since noise reduces the attention paid to less important stimuli, if social cues that someone needs help are less important than cues associated with a more important task, then noise should make us less aware of signs of distress. Cohen and Lezak (1977) demonstrated that the content of slides depicting social situations was less well remembered under noisy than under quiet conditions when subjects were asked to concentrate initially on material other than the slides. Under such conditions, social cues in the slides were relatively unimportant, so noise interfered with attending to those cues.

Consistent with this, two experiments, one conducted in the laboratory and the other in the field, suggest that noise does indeed decrease frequency of helping (Mathews & Canon, 1975). In the laboratory experiment, subjects were exposed to 48 dB of normal noise, to 65 dB of white noise piped into the laboratory through a hidden speaker, or to 85 dB of white noise from the same speaker. As subjects arrived for the experiment, they were asked in turn to wait in the laboratory for a few minutes with another individual (actually a confederate of the experimenter), who was seated and reading a journal. On the confederate's lap were additional journals, books, and papers. After a few minutes, the experimenter called for the confederate who, upon getting up, "accidentally" dropped the materials right in front of the subject. The dependent measure of helping was whether or not the subject helped the confederate to pick up the spilled materials. Results suggested a definite decrement in helping in the loud-noise conditions: 72 percent of the subjects helped in the normal noise condition, 67 percent in the 65-dB condition, and only 37 percent in the 85-dB condition.

The Mathews and Canon field experiment revealed even more interesting results. In this study, a confederate dropped a box of books while getting out of a car. To emphasize his apparent need for aid he wore a cast on his arm in half of the experimental situations. Noise was varied by having another confederate operate a lawnmower nearby. In the low-noise condition, the lawnmower was not running, and background noise from normal sources was measured at 50 dB. In the high-noise condition, the lawnmower was running without a muffler, putting out an 87-dB din. Once again, the dependent measure of helping was how many passing subjects stopped to assist the confederate pick up the dropped books. As can be seen in Figure 5–15, noise had little effect on helping when the confederate was not wearing a cast. But when the confederate wore a cast (high-need condition), the loud noise reduced the frequency of helping from 80 percent to 15 percent! Apparently, noise led subjects to attend less to cues (i.e., the cast) that indicated that the person needed help.

A series of studies by Page (1977) also provide evidence that noise can reduce the likelihood that people will help each other. In one study, subjects encountered a confederate who, with an armful of books, had

Figure 5–15 Percentages of subjects offering help as a function of noise level and need of victim
Adapted from Mathews and Canon, 1975. Copyright 1975 by the American Psychological Association. Reprinted by permission of the author and publisher.

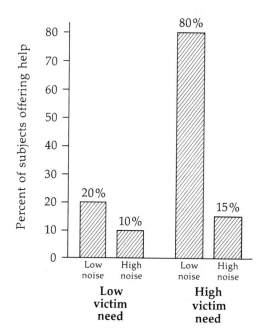

dropped a pack of index cards. They were exposed to one of three levels of noise (100 dB, 80 dB, or 50 dB) at the time they saw the confederate drop the cards. Results of this study suggested that people helped most under low levels of noise. However, these results were not strong (see also Bell & Doyle, 1983).

A second study reported by Page (1977) found stronger results. In this one, subjects saw a confederate drop a package while walking past a construction site. When the jackhammers were being used on the site, noise levels were 92 dB; when they were not being used, levels were 72 dB. Thus, depending on the jackhammers, subjects saw a confederate drop a package during one or another level of noise. People were less likely to help the confederate when noise levels reached 92 dB than they were when it was a less noisy 72 dB.

These results suggest that people who experience noise simply may not notice that someone needs help. Page (1977) conducted one more study in which people were approached and directly asked whether or not they could provide change for a quarter. In this context, "narrowing of attention" could not explain any negative effects of noise on helping. However, noise once again decreased the likelihood that people would respond to the request.

The reasons for the suppressing effects of noise on helping behavior are not yet known for sure, but the most likely explanations still appear to be the "narrowing of attention" notion and the "mood" explanation. Nevertheless, each of these has been disconfirmed by at least one study. A study that argues against the idea that noise reduces helping by putting people in bad or irritable moods was reported by Yinon and Bizman (1980). They exposed subjects to one of two noise levels (high or low) while they worked on a task, and then gave them

positive or negative feedback on their performance. After this, subjects encountered someone who asked them for help. One might expect the combination of the negative feedback and loud noise to dampen subjects' moods and cause them to refuse to help. This is not, however, what was found. Under the high-noise condition, no differences in helping between the positive and negative feedback groups were found. Only under low noise did the feedback make a difference. Apparently, the loud noise distracted people from focusing on the feedback or provided a reason for the negative feedback. Although it is still possible that mood states were involved, their role in this study does not appear to be crucial.

We have seen thus far that perceived control over noxious noise reduces its impairment of performance and its facilitation of aggression. A study by Sherrod and Downs (1974) similarly demonstrated that perceived control reduces the negative influence of noise on helping behavior. In that study, subjects participated in a proofreading task while simultaneously monitoring a series of random numbers presented on audio tape. Three conditions were established: (1) a control condition in which the numbers were superimposed on the pleasing sounds of a seashore (e.g., waves striking the beach); (2) a complex-noise condition in which the numbers were superimposed over a round of Dixieland jazz and another voice reading prose; and (3) a perceived-control condition using the same tape as the complex-noise condition but with the subjects told they could terminate the distracting noise if they so desired. After 20 minutes in one of these situations, subjects left the laboratory and were approached by an individual asking their assistance in filling out forms for another study. The most help was volunteered by subjects in the seashore sound condition, for whom noise was least noxious. Subjects

2. Make a tape recording of an ambiguous sound—one that could be almost anything, or at least could be from one or two or three different sources. Tell some people each of the possible causes. For example, a high, whining sound could be interpreted as radio static or a dentist's drill. Do the labels you attach to the sound make it more unpleasant or annoying?

3. Observe the way furniture is laid out in various places around campus and see if there are effects of noise on the ways in which people use these places and furniture arrangements. What happens in places where furniture is set up to encourage people to talk if there is loud noise coming from nearby? Explore other settings as well. What patterns do you see?

Weather, Climate, and Behavior

INTRODUCTION

GEOGRAPHICAL AND CLIMATOLOGICAL DETERMINISM

Early Beliefs About Climate and Behavior
Later Climatological Determinism
Current Views and Distinctions
Biological Adaptations to Climate

HEAT AND BEHAVIOR

Perception of and Physiological Reactions to Heat

Complicating Factors

Heat and Performance

Laboratory Settings
Industrial Settings
Classroom Settings
Military Settings
Interpreting the Data

Heat and Social Behavior

Heat and Attraction
Heat and Aggression
Heat and Helping Behavior

COLD TEMPERATURES AND BEHAVIOR

Perception of and Physiological Reactions to Cold
Cold Temperatures and Health
Cold Extremes and Performance
Cold Extremes and Social Behavior
Summary of Temperature Effects on Behavior

WIND AND BEHAVIOR

  Perception of Wind

  Behavioral Effects of Wind

BAROMETRIC PRESSURE AND ALTITUDE

  Physiological Effects

  Acclimatization to High Altitudes

  Behavioral Effects of High Altitudes

  High Air-Pressure Effects

  Medical, Emotional, and Behavioral Effects
  of Air-Pressure Changes

  Summary of Air-Pressure Effects

**INTEGRATING WEATHER AND POLLUTION EFFECTS:
A FINAL NOTE**

CHAPTER SUMMARY

  Suggested Projects

KEY TERMS

acclimation
acclimatization
air ionization
alveolar walls
ambient temperature
barometric pressure
Beaufort Scale
chill factor
climate
core temperature
curvilinear relationship
decompression sickness
deep body temperature
determinism
effective temperature
ELF-EMF
frostbite
Gaia Hypothesis
greenhouse effect
heat asthenia
heat exhaustion
heat stroke
humidity
hypothalamus

hypothermia
hypoxia
linear relationship
long, hot summer effect
negative affect-escape model
negative ions
one atmosphere
ozone
ozone hole
peripheral vasoconstriction
peripheral vasodilation
piloerection
positive ions
possibilism
probabilism
Seasonal Affective Disorder (SAD)
tactile discrimination
Temperature–Humidity Index (THI)
terraforming
thermoreceptors
weather
wind chill
wind speed
wind turbulence

INTRODUCTION

It is the year 32,825 and the great city of Seltisar has changed considerably over the past 30,000 years. A geologic uplift combined with shifts in upper-atmospheric air currents has cooled the city 20 degrees below its average 25,000 years ago. Snow occurs 300 days per year and the surrounding plants are very different from those of the Great Millenium of Heat that was recorded between 5125 and 6231. The museum shows that clothes during those times were much thinner than the layers and layers now typical. Citizens cannot imagine that track meets and soccer games were actually held outdoors back then. A popular exhibit describes the Dordellian War of 5172–5178.

Humans had finally achieved a degree of world peace for 2,000 years before this one erupted. Historians disagree about its causes; some say it was aggravated by the high temperatures, others that it was fought over declining crop yields and water rights associated with the reduced flow of upland rivers. With all of the snow today, it is hard to imagine that people could have gone to war over water. What they do agree about is that the dramatic decline of the population helped end the war.

Strange as it may seem, this imaginary tale taps some of the relationships between weather, climate, and behavior that scientists study today. Just how do temperature, humidity, wind, and air pressure affect behavior? We are all familiar with certain consequences of exposure to these factors. When it gets cold outdoors, we behave in ways that minimize discomfort, such as putting on heavy coats. When the wind blows down the street at 50 miles per hour (80 km/h), we behave in ways that will minimize our discomfort from wind exposure, such as not riding a bicycle and walking at an angle to the ground to maintain our balance. When we travel from a cool community to a very hot one, we may restrict our outdoor activity.

Research in the past decade has told us much more about what behavior to expect when people are exposed to abnormal levels of heat, cold, and wind. Such research lets us answer rather detailed questions about specific environment–behavior problems. For example, *how* do high outdoor temperatures affect the level of aggressive and violent behavior in society, as suggested by the popular notion of the **long, hot summer effect**? Or *how* do weather changes affect mental health and interpersonal relationships? Such questions about the influence of the physical environment on personal and interpersonal behavior are becoming more and more important for at least two reasons. First, humans are constantly exposed to natural changes in the physical environment. Parts of the United States typically undergo temperature changes from −20 °F to 100 °F (−29 °C to 38 °C) in different seasons. Some cultures exist in hot tropical climates, whereas others thrive in arctic conditions. Do such temperature differences influence behavior? What if climatological changes, which according to many climatologists are becoming more and more extreme, should result in exaggerated cold or hot temperatures? If a long, hot summer effect really does exist, and if climatological changes result in average daily summer temperatures of 110 °F in urban centers, are we likely to see disastrous rioting and violence? Whatever the case, it becomes important for us to know the behavioral influence of extreme or even very mild natural changes in the physical environment.

The second major reason why we need to know more about the effects of the physical environment on behavior is that we ourselves are making drastic changes in the natural environment, changes that we may be able to correct if they can be shown to have deleterious effects on behavior. For example, if high winds have negative effects on mental health, physical well-being, and behavior, we might want to reevaluate building designs that actually increase wind speeds in pedestrian areas. Another example is the case of modern technology actually heating up our cities. Waste heat from the compressors of air conditioners, heat-absorbing concrete, and air pollutants from burning fossil fuels that trap heat close to the surface (the greenhouse effect—see box on pages 190–191) are actually heating up cities to levels of 10 °F (6 °C) or more above the temperature of the surrounding countryside. In 1991, retreating Iraqi military forces set fire to more than 700 Kuwaiti oil wells, sparking concern that regional or global weather change could result; fortunately, substantial associated weather change did not seem to occur (Hoffman, 1991). But could we possibly be adding to a long, hot summer effect by the way our daily living habits alter the physical environment?

Whether the source of environmental stimulation is derived from natural or human causes, the concern of environmental psychologists is the same: What differences in behavior can be expected under different conditions in the physical environment? In previous chapters we have seen how we perceive and process information about the general environment, how we can view environment–behavior relationships from several theoretical perspectives, and how environmental components—e.g., noise and air pollution—influence us. In the present chapter we will examine in detail weather and climate as important types of physical environmental factors, how they affect us, and how these effects can be explained from various theoretical perspectives. Specifically, we will look at the

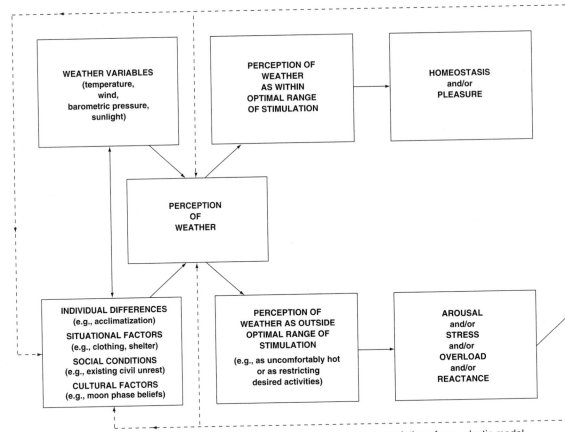

Figure 6–1 The effects of weather variables on people can be interpreted by a variation of our eclectic model of environment-behavior relationships.

behavioral effects of weather variables—heat, cold, wind, and barometric pressure—as well as at the effects of climate. As we do so, perhaps it would be helpful to keep Figure 6–1 in mind as an overall framework; you will recognize this as a variation of our eclectic model from Chapter 4. The objective physical environment (e.g., heat, altitude), individual factors such as how accustomed we are to the climate, and our perception of the weather as outside an optimal range all lead to mediational states (e.g., arousal) and to coping strategies such as escape or sweating; in the process, health, performance, and social behavior may be affected.

We should mention one caveat before proceeding: Although we will primarily discuss

each of the meteorological factors separately (e.g., cold, wind, and low air pressure), in actuality they often occur together with each other as well as with air pollution (as discussed in Chapter 7), so that it is often difficult to attribute a given behavior change to any one of the factors. We will shortly have more to say on combinations of factors when we discuss climate, here as well as at the end of the chapter. In addition, and closely related to the last point, we should briefly note a distinction between weather and climate. Essentially, **weather** refers to relatively rapidly changing or momentary conditions, such as a cold front or a heat wave. **Climate**, on the other hand, refers to average weather conditions or prevailing weather over a long period of time. The distinction is important

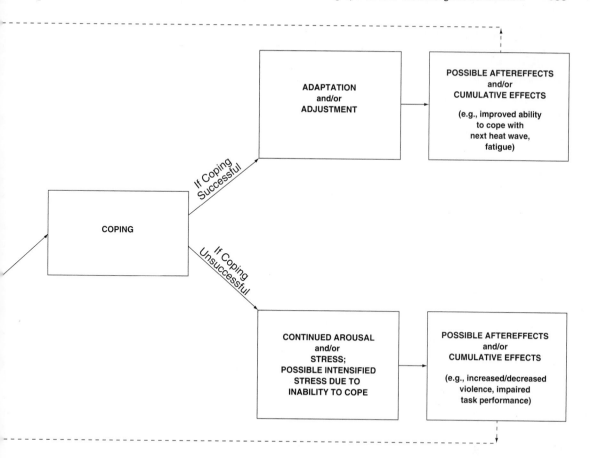

for environmental psychologists because the measured effects of climate on behavior are often not the same as the measured effects of weather on behavior. For example, climatological precipitation has definite behavioral correlates, but weather measures of precipitation do not predict behavior very well. Also, we can rarely study these variables alone but rather must control for effects of cultural and social factors that also affect behavior, and it is easier to control for these factors when studying climate than weather. All of these distinctions will become clearer as we first look at formulations about climate and behavior, and then examine how individual weather variables impact behavior.

GEOGRAPHICAL AND CLIMATOLOGICAL DETERMINISM

Much of the literature on the influence of climate on behavior is quite speculative, and not based on sound empirical data. Very early writings on the topic, in fact, are based on nonsystematic observation, and many of the later writings are based on flawed observations. More recent investigations, however, include careful biological measurements that

REALLY HEATING IT UP:
The Greenhouse Effect, the Ozone Hole, and Terraforming

A growing concern that you have probably heard about is the so-called atmospheric greenhouse effect. In a horticultural greenhouse, glass panes help trap heat from the sun: What enters the greenhouse does not easily escape back into the atmosphere. Much of the sun's heat that strikes our planet is transmitted back out from the planet surface into the atmosphere and on into space. Atmospheric conditions regulate the rate at which this heat is lost. Clouds, for example, may prevent some sunlight from hitting the ground, but also tend to trap more heat that would otherwise escape from the ground into the atmosphere. Pollutants and natural emissions, such as carbon dioxide, also tend to trap heat. As we add more carbon dioxide to the atmosphere, we trap more heat. This is the atmospheric **greenhouse effect**: Emissions are thought to warm the planet up. Several factors may moderate the effect, such as the ability of oceans to absorb the heat, the ability of forests to absorb carbon dioxide, or even an atmospheric-cooling effect of some human-produced aerosols (Charlson et al., 1992). The **Gaia Hypothesis** even says the process is self-regulating by the Earth (e.g., Lovelock, 1988). That is, the heating and cooling fluctuates as vegetation, animal life, oceans, and the atmosphere absorb or release heat and emissions. The great fear is that we have overdone things: cut forests, increased domestic animal herds and rice paddies (which release large volumes of methane gas), and increased fossil fuel emissions so much that the Earth may become permanently overheated. Over the last century, the Earth's surface may have warmed approximately 1 °C, which is equivalent to 1 to 3 °F (e.g., Kerr, 1988a). Over the next 50 to 100 years, we could warm up another 2 to 5 °C. What will this do? Melting of even part of the polar ice cap will cause coastlines to move many miles inland. Animal habitats will shift by hundreds of miles, and many species will become extinct (e.g., Roberts, 1988). Tropical diseases would become more prevalent in parts of the world that are not tropical today, increasing deaths by hundreds of thousands (Stone, 1995), and deaths due to heat waves could increase by hundreds in any given city (Kalkstein & Smoyer, 1993).

The **ozone hole** is a related problem to worry about (e.g., Kerr, 1992a). Atmospheric ozone absorbs harmful ultraviolet sunlight, among other things (see box

show at least some physiological adaptations associated with climate. Altogether, it is instructive to examine the evidence from both the early and recent literature. In doing so, it is helpful to keep in mind three perspectives which we will cover again in the chapters on architectural influence. Briefly, these perspectives are **determinism, possibilism,** and **probabilism** (cf. Rotton, 1986). In terms of climate, *determinism* suggests that climate forcefully causes a range of behaviors, such as heat waves causing crimes. As noted in Chapter 4, environmental psychologists take a broad view of determinism, which means that many interrelated variables contribute to predicting our behavior. Some of the clion page 220). It apparently is becoming rapidly depleted over Antarctica and the Arctic in a pattern called the ozone hole. Human use of chlorofluorocarbons is thought to be a major cause of ozone depletion. The ozone-destroying process occurs heavily in stratospheric ice clouds. The greenhouse effect warms planet Earth but cools the stratosphere, causing more ice clouds to form and destroying more ozone. Although natural events such as the eruption of Mt. Pinatubo in 1991 seem to decrease atmospheric ozone (Kerr, 1993), and although some serious scientists and some commentators such as Rush Limbaugh have charged that the ozone threat is nothing short of a hoax, most scientists believe it is cause for serious concern (Taubes, 1993).

Can anything be done? Reducing harmful emissions is one solution (Rubin et al., 1992), and in Chapter 14 we will discuss the techniques environmental psychologists advocate for getting us to change our environmentally destructive behavior. Another solution is to use nature. Burning fossil fuels releases 5 billion tons of carbon per year. Some 7 million square kilometers of trees (about the size of Australia) would absorb that much carbon and turn it into wood (e.g., Marland, cited in Booth, 1988). Because of deforestation of areas such as Brazil and Southeast Asia, we would need to plant still more trees, but the idea, considered far-fetched by some, does have its advocates.

Speaking of the far-fetched, another planet might actually benefit from the greenhouse effect, if you consider invasion by humans beneficial. **Terraforming** refers to changing an uninhabitable planet into a habitable one. One proposal to terraform Mars is to add chlorofluorocarbons to its atmosphere. Mars needs to be heated up to be habitable by humans. Since its atmosphere has no ozone, chlorofluorocarbons would not deplete ozone, but rather would trap solar heat in a greenhouse effect. Ice caps would partially melt, releasing water for plant life, which would cycle enough carbon dioxide and oxygen (over hundreds of years) into the atmosphere to make Mars habitable (McKay, as cited in Davis, 1989)!

matological determinists we discuss in this section, however, proposed a more specific determinism of single-factor explanations. *Possibilism* proposes that climate sets physical limits within which behavior may vary, such as modest winds permitting sailing but high winds restricting bicycle riding. *Probabilism* falls somewhat in between these two posi-

tions, implying that climate does not absolutely cause specific behaviors, but does influence the chances that some behaviors will occur and others will not. For example, snow decreases the probability that people will drive and increases the probability that people will engage in winter sports. Determinism, possibilism, and probabilism are not necessarily mutually exclusive; they may be differentially applicable to different domains of behavior. For example, climate may influence what type of farming one practices by determining which crops cannot be grown in an area, but making it possible (but not inevitable) that other crops can be grown in the same area (cf. Gärling & Golledge, 1993). Similarly, high population density seems to be associated with high average snowfall, perhaps because the higher density increases the collective ability to cope with the disruptive effects of snow (Guterbock, 1990).

It is also appropriate to note that geographical and climatological determinism are closely linked. Indeed, most of the time the two are simply called "geographical determinism." It is often difficult to separate geographic influence from weather influence, since geography plays a major role in weather. Mountains, for example, are usually associated with high altitudes, cooler conditions than surrounding lowlands, wet weather on the side of the mountains facing prevailing atmospheric movements, and dry weather on the side away from oncoming storms. Since the geography and the climate are so closely linked, it is not easy to say whether the weather or the geography is primarily responsible for associated behavior (Figure 6–2).

EARLY BELIEFS ABOUT CLIMATE AND BEHAVIOR

Suspicion that climate determines behavior has been around practically since the beginning of civilization. Sommers and Moos (1976) provide a much more thorough review of early writings than can possibly be covered here. The ancient Greeks, including Hippocrates and Aristotle, believed that weather and climate influenced bodily fluids, which in turn influenced individual disposition. The Roman Vitruvius and the Arab Ibn Khaldun, along with Aristotle, believed that

geography and climate made some people more industrious than others, some more spirited, and so on. Not surprisingly, each writer indicated that the prevailing climate in his own region led to superior civilizations! For example, Khaldun believed that moderate climates fostered superior cultures. How, then, could his own civilization on the hot, dry, Arabian peninsula be at an advantage? His answer was that cooling waters of the sea moderated the Arabian climate sufficiently to produce overall favorability (Sommers & Moos, 1976).

LATER CLIMATOLOGICAL DETERMINISM

Sommers and Moos (1976) review the writings of numerous more recent authors, most of whom make equally presumptuous and self-serving observations about climatological influences (see also Glacken, 1967). Some later geographical determinists include such theorists as Carl Ritter, Frederic LePlay, Edmond Demolins, Henry Buckle, and Ellsworth Huntington. Three of these are particularly interesting for the details of their beliefs. Buckle, for one, was the son of a wealthy London merchant and was widely traveled. In *The History of Civilization in England* (1857–1861), he posited that labor conditions and climate were closely intertwined: Cold climates inhibited work and hot climates led to lethargy; temperate climates, however, were thought to be invigorating. With fertile soil available, then, temperate climates would lead to heavy production. Moreover, Buckle believed that the advancement of a culture was tied to the creation of a leisure class, which was possible only if some other class produced more than was needed. Thus, temperate climates in regions with fertile soil permitted the necessary overproduction, which permitted the rise of the leisure class, which theoretically, at least, enabled the entire civilization's advancement.

Figure 6–2A & 2B Some examples of the connection between geography and climate. (A) The high altitude of the mountain range pulls enough moisture out of the atmosphere to provide extensive forests on the slopes. This moisture does not fall on the relatively dry plains, which require irrigation for any farming. A similar pattern accounts for desert areas of many parts of the globe, including the western United States. (B) Cities, with their concrete canyons and industrial and transportation pollution, create "heat islands" such that they are several degrees warmer than the surrounding countryside.

The "proof" of Buckle's theory came from his "observations" of conditions in such diverse regions as Central America, Ireland, Egypt, and India. So inviting was the theory that it was intellectually popular for some time after its writing (Timasheff, 1967). It is also worth summarizing the beliefs of theorist Ellsworth Huntington (1915, 1945), who held that climatic factors other than temperate conditions were necessary for the growth of major civilizations. The major ingredient was hypothesized to be seasonal change and moving storms. The change could not be too severe, but regular changes should require adaptation, and as "necessity is the mother of invention," the adaptations encouraged creative solutions, which invigorated the civilization. Huntington did indeed collect sociological data on such things as productivity, suicides, and library circulation to support his point of view that geographic bands producing these changing climate conditions were associated with advancing civilizations (Sommers & Moos, 1976). It should be noted that Huntington believed that many factors besides favorable climate influence the growth of civilizations. Similar to Huntington's ideas about climate adaptation, Markham (1947) suggested that the most important climatic factor for the development of a civilization was living in a cool enough region that technology became necessary in order to keep warm. He noted, for example, that the Romans developed a central heating system, using pipes to distribute warmth through buildings. How important is this factor? Markham noted that this heating system deteriorated shortly before the decline of Roman civilization.

While appealing in some respects, these geographical and climatological deterministic beliefs have only tenuous empirical evidence, at best, to support them. Climatological experiments on a culture are not practical, so we are left with correlational data—and there are many factors, such as war, natural resources, and technological innovation, which are difficult to measure and assess as possible explanatory variables in climatological studies. In this light, few scientists today would endorse very strong statements of climatological determinism. It is overstepping the cause-and-effect boundaries of methodology to assume that just because a civilization occurs in a given climate, the climate is a prerequisite for that civilization. Of course, long-term climatological change can have substantial influences—on a civilization and even on evolution. About 55 million years ago, a dramatic global warming brought crocodiles to northern Canada; it also led to the appearance of modern mammals such as rodents, primates, and split-hoofed animals. Then, about 34 million years ago, a dramatic global cooling led to the extinction of about 60 percent of European mammals (Kerr, 1992b). In terms of human civilization, Henry (1994), for example, describes how climatological change was associated with shifting elevations of winter and summer camps for prehistoric humans over tens of thousands of years. Similarly, climatological change and associated resource depletion probably account for the disappearance of the Anasazi—the ancestors of Navajo, Hopi, and other tribes—in the southwestern United States about 800 years ago (e.g., Frazier, 1986). In contrast, most of the remainder of this chapter will examine shorter-term weather variables and behavior.

CURRENT VIEWS AND DISTINCTIONS

Along with the above caveat on overstating causal relationships, several additional methodological cautions are warranted. Recall that weather refers to short-term variations and climate to average weather over a longer period. Thus, on a given day, a city in the northern United States might have a higher temperature than a city in the southern part of the country, but on the average, temperatures in the south are higher. Now consider that more violent crimes occur in the south than elsewhere. Can we conclude that heat has a causal role in these crimes? The problem is that many variables, such as food preferences and ethnic mix, differ between the two regions. Contemplating correlations between so many climatological and sociodemographic variables, we must be very cautious about conclusions (cf. Anderson, 1987; DeFronzo, 1984; Rotton, Barry, & Kimble, 1985). In addition, there are seasonal differences in behavior (e.g., automobile buying, television programs, gift purchases) that probably have nothing to do with weather—although the weather certainly varies with these activities. It is the case that more assaults and homicides occur in the United States in summer than winter, but the peak time for homicides is December. Thus, we should not conclude that meteorological variables are responsible for seasonal differences in behavior.

It is also worth noting that biometeorologists in Europe (e.g., Muecher & Ungeheuer, 1961; Tromp, 1980) have focused on the possible effects of "weather phases," or correlated patterns of changes in meteorological conditions (e.g., a storm front). North American researchers, on the other hand, look more at specific variables, such as temperature, precipitation, or barometric pressure. We have organized this chapter primarily around the latter approach for ease of presentation, but we must keep in mind that weather variables such as wind, humidity, and barometric pressure are themselves correlated.

BIOLOGICAL ADAPTATIONS TO CLIMATE

An area of study with more convincing evidence of climatological influence is that of measuring physiological or other biological factors within a culture that is exposed to extremes of climate. For example, Frisancho (1979) reviews many lines of evidence that people living at high altitudes, such as in Tibet or Peru, in the hot climates of Africa, or in the cold environment of Lapland, may have developed special physiological capabilities for coping with these extremes. Such adaptations may even be genetic, such that ancestors with these adaptive characteristics were more likely to survive the extremes and pass their hereditary characteristics along to the next generation. For example, hearts may be larger and their walls thicker among high-altitude cultures, since hearts need to circulate more oxygen-rich blood at altitudes where oxygen is in relatively lower atmospheric concentration. Some such adaptations may well be acquired (i.e., accruing during one's lifetime) rather than genetic. We will have some more to say about these adaptations as we cover individual weather variables in the remainder of this chapter.

HEAT AND BEHAVIOR

Ambient temperature is a term used to describe the surrounding or atmospheric temperature conditions. In the natural environment, humans experience a range from arctic cold to debilitating tropical heat. As stated previously, temperature is one factor in the physical environment that humans are changing through urbanization and industrialization. Hurt (1975) noted that 20 years ago air conditioners in the downtown area of Houston put out enough waste heat (i.e., heat blown out the window off the "hot" end of the compressor) in eight hours to boil ten kettles of water the size of the Astrodome! Unfortunately for those who must go outdoors, this heat and heat from additional sources stays in the general area of the city, so that urban centers are typically 10 to

20 °F (6 to 12 °C) hotter than surrounding agricultural areas. As will be seen in this section and the next, extremes of heat and cold, regardless of the source, can have dramatic effects on people.

PERCEPTION OF AND PHYSIOLOGICAL REACTIONS TO HEAT

Perception of temperature involves physical as well as psychological components. The primary *physical* component is simply the amount of heat in the surrounding environment, typically measured on the Fahrenheit or Celsius scale. One *psychological* component of temperature perception is centered on the internal temperature of the body, known as **core temperature** or **deep body temperature.** Another psychological component involves receptors in the skin **(thermoreceptors)**; although some receptors seem to be sensitive to lower temperatures and others to higher temperatures, both types respond to change in temperature more than to absolute temperature (cf. Craig & Bushnell, 1994). This is why you may perceive even mildly warm water as very hot when your hands are extremely cold from being exposed to winter air.

Since perception of ambient temperature is largely dependent on differences between body and ambient temperatures, the mechanisms controlling body temperature have much to do with the perception of ambient temperature. Body temperature is regulated by the need to keep core temperature close to 98.6 °F (37 °C). Since death occurs when core temperature rises above 113 °F (45 °C) or drops below 77 °F (25 °C), maintaining it at a normal level is mandatory for survival. Without a defensive or adaptive mechanism, the body would overheat when exposed to high ambient temperatures and would "freeze" when exposed to cold ambient temperatures. Fortunately, a number of such adaptive mechanisms under the general control of a brain center known as the **hypo-thalamus**, are available for use whenever core temperature is threatened by adversely hot or cold ambient conditions. When core temperature becomes too hot, the body responds by activating mechanisms designed to lose heat, such as sweating, panting, and **peripheral vasodilation**. The latter process refers to dilation of blood vessels in the extremities, especially those near the surface of the skin, which allows more blood to flow from core areas to surface regions. This blood carries with it the excess core heat, which is removed through air convection or sweating (note that peripheral vasodilation allows more sweat to reach the surface of the skin). In "heat wave" emergencies, the body may increase the supply of water available for evaporation by suppressing urine formation and extracting water from body tissues. Such dehydration causes us to become thirsty and to replenish our body's supply of water, which is another process mediated by the hypothalamus. When these adaptive mechanisms fail, a number of physiological disorders can result, including heat exhaustion, heat stroke, heat asthenia, and heart attack (see box on page 197). Interestingly, blood pressure may increase upon initial sensation of ambient heat, owing to a "startle" response or alarm reaction (see page 197). Once vasodilation begins, blood pressure drops. With heat stroke, blood pressure may rise again, then fall off as coma and death approach. Clearly, measuring blood pressure only once during heat exposure is not a good indication of the overall picture.

Prolonged exposure to moderately high ambient temperatures need not have disastrous consequences. Individuals who move from cool climates into very warm climates can adapt to the hot environment without too much difficulty. This adaptation process is known as **acclimatization**, and it primarily involves changes in physiological adaptive mechanisms. For instance, the body may "learn" to start sweating much sooner after the onset of high ambient temperatures (Lee,

PHYSIOLOGICAL DISORDERS ASSOCIATED WITH PROLONGED HEAT STRESS

When the body's adaptive mechanisms to heat stress fail to keep core body temperatures close to 98.6 °F (37 °C), a number of physiological disorders can occur. Among the more common are:

1. **Heat exhaustion**, characterized by faintness and nausea, vomiting, headache, and restlessness. This disorder results from excessive demands on the circulatory system for blood. Water needed for sweating, blood needed near the skin surface for heat loss through convection, and blood needed for normal or increased metabolic functioning place too much strain on the body's capacity to supply blood. Continued loss of salt and water through sweating compounds the problem. Replacement of lost water and salt, together with rest, will both prevent and cure heat exhaustion.

2. **Heat stroke**, characterized by confusion, staggering, headache, delirium, coma, and death. This disorder results from the complete breakdown of the sweating mechanism. Because body heat cannot be lost, the brain overheats. Survival or prevention of brain damage depends on quick action—the most effective being immersion in ice water. When a victim collapses from heat, the continuation of sweating implies heat exhaustion; the absence of sweating implies heat stroke.

3. **Heat asthenia**, characterized by fatigue, headache, mental and physical impairment, irritability, restlessness, insomnia, loss of appetite, and lethargy. Its specific causes are unknown, although one theory implicates the clogging of sweat glands by excessive perspiration. The cure for heat asthenia includes intake of water and change of climate.

4. Heart attack, resulting from excessive demands on the cardiovascular system due to increased need for blood by the body's cooling mechanisms. During urban heat wave conditions, most deaths beyond what would normally be expected are caused by heart attacks.

For more information on heat and cold disorders, the reader is referred to Kalkstein and Davis (1989).

1964). How long does it take to acclimatize when moving from a warm to a cold environment, and vice-versa? Tromp (1980) suggests that the answer is no more than 3 to 14 days, depending on an individual's cardiovascular fitness.

Sometimes the distinction is made between acclimatization, meaning adaptation

to multiple stresses in an environment (e.g., temperature, wind, humidity) and **acclimation**, meaning adaptation to one specific stressor in an experimental context (see Frisancho, 1979). In our discussion, we will use the term acclimatization, since in most environments we must adapt to more than one element. Frisancho (1979) indicates that

Figure 6–3 Acclimatization may occur through genetic changes, developmental changes, physiological changes, or behavioral changes. This desert is normally very hot and dry, but can be cool and wet at times. What would you do to acclimatize to this environment?

acclimatization may occur through developmental changes, through genetic adaptation, or through physiological and behavioral changes following prolonged exposure to heat. The Saharan Touareg, for example, have tall, slender bodies that maximize surface cooling area in proportion to the amount of body tissue that produces heat. Behaviorally, the Touareg avoid heavy exercise during the highest temperatures of the day and wear loose, porous clothing (Beighton, 1971; Frisancho, 1979; Sloan, 1979). Keep in mind, though, that non-native visitors to hot regions can usually acclimatize in a few days. Leithead and Lind (1964) suggest that maximum efficiency in acclimatization occurs with exposure of 100 minutes per day (Figure 6–3).

Complicating Factors

Since perception of ambient temperature depends to some extent on the functioning of the body's thermoregulatory adaptive mechanisms, any environmental factor that interferes with these mechanisms will influence perception of ambient temperature. The primary environmental factors in this regard are humidity and wind. The higher the **humidity** in a hot environment (i.e., the more saturated the air with water vapor), the lower the capacity of the air to absorb water vapor from sweat. This is the reason, for example, that conditions of 100 °F (38 °C) and 60 percent humidity are perceived as more uncomfortable than those of 100 °F and 15 percent humidity. Thus, perception of ambient temperature is not a function of temperature alone. Psychologically, the problem of perceptual measurement can be partially solved by taking into account a comfort level that is influenced by both temperature and humidity, thus creating a new ambient environment index. One such index is known as **effective temperature**. A chart showing some effective temperatures is presented in Table 6–1. Other similar indexes exist, such as the **Temperature–Humidity Index**, or **THI** (see Tromp, 1980 for a summary).

Since the amount of air flowing over the skin determines how much sweat is evaporated as well as how much body heat is carried off by convection, **wind speed** must also be taken into account in perceiving ambient temperature. On a hot day, a breeze helps carry heat off the body and thus has a cooling effect. As we will see shortly, wind on a cold day further chills the skin and thus amplifies that temperature effect, as well.

HEAT AND PERFORMANCE

Laboratory Settings

Laboratory studies of the influence of high ambient temperatures on performance have examined such varied behaviors as reaction time, tracking, and vigilance, as well as memory and mathematical calculations (Bell, Provins, & Hiorns, 1964; Griffiths & Boyce, 1971; Pepler, 1963; Poulton & Kerslake, 1965; Provins, 1966; Provins & Bell, 1970; Wilkinson et al., 1964). In general, temperatures above 90 °F (32 °C) will impair mental performance after two hours of exposure for unacclimatized subjects. Above this same temperature, moderate physical work will suffer after one hour of exposure. As temperatures increase, shorter exposure times are necessary to show performance decrements (e.g., Poulton, 1970). Interestingly enough, some researchers find that heat has no influence on performance, others find that heat is detrimental to performance, and still others find that heat improves performance. Moreover, some studies suggest that as temperatures rise, performance first improves and then deteriorates, whereas other studies show this pattern for one task but the reverse pattern (i.e., initial decrements followed by improvements) for other tasks (see Bell, 1981; Hygge, 1992; and Sundstrom, 1986b, for reviews). Hancock (1986) notes that performance on vigilance tasks is impaired when thermal homeostasis is disturbed, but improved when a new equilibrium state is reached. In general, heat impairs complex mental tasks after prolonged exposure, impairs motor tasks after fairly brief exposure, and may impair or enhance vigilance. Before examining possible explanations

Table 6–1 Effective Temperature (°F) at 0 Percent Humidity as a Function of Actual Temperature and Humidity

Relative Humidity (%)	Thermometer Reading (°F)					
	41°	50°	59°	68°	77°	86°
	Effective Temperature					
00	41	50	59	68	77	86
20	41	50	60	70	81	91
40	40	51	61	72	83	96
60	40	51	62	73	86	102
80	39	52	63	75	90	111
100	39	52	64	79	96	120

for these complex findings, let us first examine heat research from applied settings.

Industrial Settings

Industrialists, such as steel manufacturers, are naturally concerned about the effects of blast furnaces and other hot industrial environments on workers who are in these surroundings for eight or more hours a day. Generally, exposure to such industrial heat can cause dehydration, loss of salt, and muscle fatigue, which taken together can reduce endurance and hence impair performance. For example, one study found that productivity of women apparel workers declined as temperatures increased (Link & Pepler, 1970). In order to overcome or avoid such problems, care is generally taken to ensure that workers have an adequate intake of water and salt, are not exposed to intolerably hot conditions for long periods of time, wear protective clothing, and, when new on the job, have adequate time to adapt to working conditions (see Crockford, 1967; Hill, 1967; Sundstrom, 1986).

Classroom Settings

Temperature appears to have some effects on classroom performance. Pepler (1972) studied climate-controlled (air-conditioned) and nonclimate-controlled schools near Portland, Oregon. In nonclimate-controlled schools, academic performance showed more variance (i.e., wider distribution of test scores) as temperatures rose. However, at climate-controlled schools, such variability did not occur on the warmest days. Apparently, some students suffer more than others when heat waves hit the classroom! Support for this finding has been reported by Benson and Zieman (1981), who found that heat hurt the classroom performance of some children but actually helped the performance of others (see also Griffiths, 1975; Figure 6–4).

Figure 6–4 Research suggests that weather variables, including heat and barometric pressure, may influence disruptive behavior and academic performance of children in the classroom. Interestingly, for some children heat has beneficial effects, whereas for others it has detrimental effects. In this classroom, there is no air conditioning and the only window cannot be opened. What adaptive responses would you expect when the weather gets hot?

Military Settings

If ambient heat has any deleterious effect on performance, the consequences of moving unacclimatized troops into a tropical area (e.g., from North America or Europe to the Persian Gulf) could be disastrous. Adam (1967) has reviewed a number of British military studies that generally found that 20 to 25 percent of troops flown into tropical regions from more moderate climates suffered serious deterioration in combat effectiveness within three days and became in effect "heat casualties." Solutions to this problem include allowing several days for acclimatization or expanding the number of troops available to allow for heat casualties.

Interpreting the Data

How can we account for the complexity of the above research findings? Why does heat sometimes hurt performance and sometimes help it? Sundstrom (1986b) notes that body temperature, metabolic cost of physical activity, acclimatization, skill level, motivation, and stress (including threat appraisal) are all factors that make a difference in the impact of heat on performance. Bell (1981, 1982) offers several other suggestions, which require an integration of several theoretical perspectives presented in Chapter 4 (see also Figure 6–1). First, arousal explains some heat effects. Initially, exposure to heat may cause a brief "startle" response that heightens arousal and hence improves performance (e.g., Poulton, 1976; Poulton & Kerslake, 1965; Provins, 1966). Moreover, Provins (1966) suggests that heat may eventually lead to overarousal, causing performance decrements (cf. Bell, Loomis, & Cervone, 1982), as would be predicted by the Yerkes-Dodson Law (see Chapter 4). Eventually, high temperatures would result in physical exhaustion (see box on page 197) as the body can no longer keep core temperature at a safely functioning level, so performance

would completely deteriorate. A second mediator of performance, then, is core temperature (see Provins, 1966). A third mediator of performance is attention, as examined in the overload interpretation of environmental stress. As heat stress increases, attention is narrowed toward stimuli central to the task at hand, so that performance on noncentral activities deteriorates (e.g., Bursill, 1958; Pepler, 1963). Bell (1978), for example, found that as heat increased, performance on a secondary task suffered, but performance on a primary task did not. A fourth mediator of heat effects is probably perceived control, as advocated by the behavior constraint model. According to this interpretation, as heat stress increases, individuals feel less and less in control of the environment, and thus performance deteriorates. Greene and Bell (1980), for example, found that subjects in a 95 °F (35 °C) environment felt more dominated by it than did subjects in more comfortable temperatures. Finally, each individual almost certainly has an adaptation level or maximum level of tolerance for heat. Wyndham (1970), for example, has reported considerable variation in acclimatization to heat, with individuals having lower body temperatures being most tolerant of high ambient temperatures (see also Greene & Bell, 1986; Rohles, 1974; Wilkinson, 1974). In sum, arousal, core temperature, attention, perceived control, and adaptation level all probably operate as explanatory mechanisms in understanding the effects of heat stress on task performance.

HEAT AND SOCIAL BEHAVIOR

Heat and Attraction

Most individuals exposed to high ambient temperatures will report subjectively that they feel uncomfortable and perhaps irritable. Ruback and Pandey (1992), for example, found that rickshaw passengers in

India reported more negative feelings as the temperature became uncomfortably hot; interestingly, they found that telling people about the effects of heat gave them a greater sense of perceived control. We might expect that unpleasant feelings associated with heat or other factors would also give us an unpleasant disposition toward others. According to one model of attraction (Byrne, 1971), we should expect a decrease in interpersonal attraction when we are experiencing the unpleasant effects of either debilitating heat or cold. Griffitt (1970) demonstrated precisely this effect by asking subjects to evaluate anonymous strangers who seemed to agree with subjects on either 25 percent or 75 percent of a set of attitudes. Subjects performed this evaluation task under an effective temperature of either 67.5 °F (20 °C) or 90.6 °F (32 °C). The results indicated that high ambient temperatures decreased attraction, regardless of the degree of attitude similarity. Griffitt and Veitch (1971) reported comparable results.

However, research by Bell and Baron (1974, 1976) suggests that heat may have a relatively minor influence on attraction under other circumstances. In two experiments, these researchers found that heat did not influence attraction toward another person in the room if that person had recently complimented or insulted a subject. In this situation, the compliment or insult appears to be so overwhelming as to "wipe out" any possible influence of heat (see also Bell, Garnand, & Heath, 1984). Rotton (1983) notes that in the Griffitt studies, subjects were rating hypothetical strangers who were not actually present, whereas in the Bell and Baron studies, subjects rated a real stranger who was actually present in the same room. Perhaps when the stress is not shared with someone actually present, attraction decreases; but when someone is there to share the distress, the decrease may not occur (Figure 6–5).

Heat and Aggression

During the urban and campus riots of the 1960s, a popular belief arose that riotous acts of violence were in some way precipitated by the unrelenting heat of the summer months. Indeed, this supposed influence of heat on

Figure 6–5 As in the hypothetical graph on the left, heat may decrease attraction when people share the discomfort of the heat. However, as in the diagram on the right, heat may not affect attraction when the target does not share the discomfort with the subject.

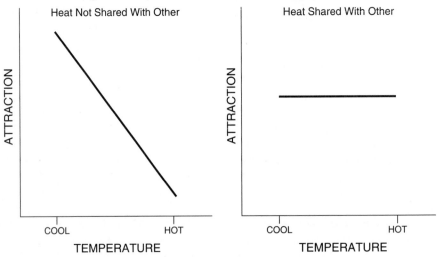

aggression was popularly known as "the long, hot summer effect." It became common for television commentators and newspaper editorial writers to mention fears that "It's going to be another long, hot summer!" High ambient temperatures became even more suspect when the United States Riot Commission (1968) noted that, of the riots in 1967 on which records were available, all but one began on days when the temperature was at least in the 80s (above 27 °C). A more formal study by Goranson and King (1970) strongly suggested, as evidenced in the graph in Figure 6–6, that heat-wave or near-heat-wave conditions were associated with the outbreak of the riots. So strong has the belief in the relationship between climate and violence become that even the *Uniform Crime Reports* of the Federal Bureau of Investigation (FBI) has listed climate as a variable of importance in explaining the incidence of crimes (FBI, 1981). Even major league baseball seems susceptible to the heat-aggression phenomenon: More batters are hit by "wild" pitches as the temperature increases (Reifman, Larrick, & Fein, 1991)!

Actually, systematic study of temperature and violence goes back a century or so. Anderson (1989) notes three types of studies

that have examined this relationship over the years. *Geographic region* studies compare crime rates across different regions of a country or continent. For example, you might divide your native country into the warmest, temperate (intermediate), and coolest thirds and then see if violence is most prevalent in the hottest region and least common in the coolest region. Indeed, studies often find just such results, although sometimes the outcome is equivocal, especially when you take into account other variables such as socioeconomic status that may vary by region (e.g., DeFronzo, 1984; Rotton, 1986). *Time period* studies make it somewhat easier to control for these extraneous variables. In a time period study you measure violence across intervals of time such as days or months. You then see if the number of crimes in a day or month correlate with the average (or high or low) temperature for each time interval. Again, these studies often show that violence increases with time (e.g., Anderson, 1987; Anderson & Anderson, 1984; Cotton, 1986; Harries & Stadler, 1988; Rotton & Frey, 1985). Even violent sex crimes seem to increase with temperature (Cohn, 1993; Perry & Simpson, 1987; Rotton, 1993a). However, in time period studies we do not know the temperature at the time a given act of violence occurred; two violent crimes on the same day may have occurred at different times when the temperature was very cool or very warm, and we would not know that temperature had anything to do with either crime. A more accurate strategy would be to employ a *concomitant* temperature study, in which the temperature is known at the actual time of the violence. Once again, these concomitant studies often find that aggression goes up with heat. For example, Baron (1976) found that automobile drivers honked their horns (which can serve as a measure of irritation or hostility) more when temperatures were above 85 °F (29 °C) than when they were below. For

Figure 6–6 Average daily mean temperatures before, during, and after riot outbreak.

From Goranson & King, 1970. Reproduced with permission.

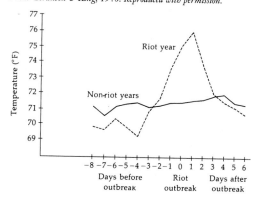

drivers in air-conditioned cars, however, heat did not increase horn-honking.

However, one series of laboratory concomitant studies has found a rather unexpected pattern to the temperature–aggression relationship. For example, Baron and Bell (1975) arranged for laboratory subjects to be either provoked or complimented by a confederate before being given an opportunity to aggress against this individual by means of ostensible electric shock. It was found, as might be anticipated, that subjects in comfortable ambient temperature conditions (73 to 74 °F; 23 °C) were more aggressive toward an anger-provoking confederate than toward a complimentary confederate. However, subjects in uncomfortably hot conditions (92 to 95 °F; 35 °C) showed just the opposite behavior: These individuals showed reduced aggression toward the insulting confederate but increased their level of attack against the friendlier one. Several other studies by the same research team found the same pattern: Provoked subjects in a hot lab showed a relatively low level of violence

(Baron, 1972; Baron & Bell, 1976a; Bell & Baron, 1976). How can we explain this unexpected pattern?

There are many potential explanations for this and other patterns observed in the data (see Anderson, 1989). Due to space limitations, we will concentrate on the explanation that has provoked the most attention and the most debate. Specifically, Baron and Bell invoked what is now termed the **negative affect-escape model** to account for these results. According to this explanation, negative affective feelings may be a mediator in the relationship between heat and aggression. This relationship takes the curvilinear form of an inverted U. Up to a critical point, negative affect increases aggressive behavior, but beyond this point, stronger negative feelings actually reduce aggression, since flight behavior or other attempts to minimize discomfort become more important to the individual than does aggressive activity (see Figure 6–7). Laboratory tests of the proposition of a **curvilinear relationship** between negative affect and aggression, using heat as

Figure 6–7   The negative affect-escape model predicts that up to a point, the discomfort of heat increases aggression; however, extreme discomfort tends to decrease aggression because people would rather escape the situation than fight.

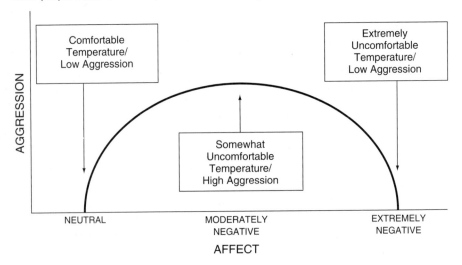

one factor influencing affect, have been generally affirmative. What these findings suggest with regard to the relationship between high ambient temperatures and aggression is that there is a critical range of uncomfortably high ambient temperatures at which aggression may well be facilitated. On the other hand, extremely high ambient temperatures, especially when combined with other sources of irritation or discomfort, may become so debilitating that aggression is no longer facilitated and may well be reduced when individuals prefer to concentrate on escaping the heat.

Other research supports various aspects of the model. For example, the escape tendency is illustrated by Rotton, Shats, and Standers's (1990) finding that on hot days Miami pedestrians walked faster to get to their air-conditioned cars than they did to shop on the streets (see also Palamarek & Rule, 1979). Similarly, Kenrick and MacFarlane (1986) studied horn-honking in both moderate and very hot temperatures (well above 100 °F, or 38 °C) in Phoenix, Arizona. Honking increased with temperature, and this effect was strongest for those with their automobile windows rolled down. Such results should not be surprising, since the honking was always at a car that did not move when a traffic light turned from red to green. Thus, honking was perceived as instrumental in obtaining relief from the discomfort of the heat, especially for drivers with their windows down (and presumably with no air conditioning): If the stalled car would only move, drivers could get some relief from the heat, and honking might be a way of prompting the driver of the stalled car to get on with it. In addition, some research on unpleasant odors (Rotton et al., 1979) and on cold temperatures (Bell & Baron, 1977) also supports an inverted-U relationship between negative affect and aggression.

But the failure of most geographic region and time period studies to show any inverted-U (curvilinear) relationship between temperature and aggression has sparked a heated debate about whether extremely uncomfortable temperatures actually do decrease aggressive tendencies (Anderson, 1989; Anderson & DeNeve, 1992; Bell, 1992). Although at least one field study supports the curvilinear relationship (Schwartz, 1968), it may be that the lab studies showing the inverted-U do so because of a methodological artifact; for example, subjects may attribute extreme discomfort to factors other than anger toward the potential victim, which in turn could lead them to decrease their aggression (see also Anderson, 1989; box page 129). However, since carefully controlled laboratory experiments usually (but not necessarily) have more internal validity than do correlational studies, perhaps the explanation lies elsewhere. Bell (1992) and Anderson (1989), for example, note that geographic region studies, in averaging the temperature across long periods of time, probably mask the effects of very high temperatures. That is, the really high temperatures are averaged in with more moderate temperatures and high rates of crime are averaged in with lower rates of crime, such that the averages do not show the extremes necessary to detect a potential decline in violence at very high temperatures. A similar problem occurs with time period studies (e.g., Rotton & Frey, 1985). The time interval studied may simply not have enough very hot days to detect a decline in violence associated with escape motives. Other variables may also be operating in time period studies that are controlled in laboratory studies. However, controlling for humidity, wind, air pollution, and other atmospheric variables in a time period study still results in a **linear relationship** between temperature and violence (Rotton & Frey, 1985). Perhaps other explanations for the inconsistencies are needed. Bell and Fusco (1986, 1989), for example, suggest that on very hot days, the spread of violence widens: Some days show high violence and some low violence, whereas at cooler temperatures the spread from day to day is not as great. In essence, both linear and curvilinear trends may be in the data, but the curvilinear trend is masked by the increasing variation in violence as temperatures rise (see Figure 6–8). Thus, escape and aggressive tendencies may both be operating under high temperatures, but other variables such as alcohol consumption, availability of escape, or attributions about the source of discomfort may determine whether escape or aggression become manifest. Depending on which of the other variables are operating, extremely high temperatures could be associated with either increased or decreased aggression. Moreover, the many types of studies conducted so far use very different measures of violence. The influence of temperature on willingness to deliver electric shock in the laboratory may be somewhat different from the influence of temperature on willingness to commit murder or rape; field studies sometimes find a temperature relationship with one type of crime but not another (e.g., Anderson, 1987; Perry & Simpson, 1987). Whatever the explanation, the debate over the temperature–aggression relationship is sure to continue (see also Anderson & DeNeve, 1992; Boyanowsky et al., 1981–82; Cohn, 1990; Rotton, 1993a; Simpson & Perry, 1990).

Heat and Helping Behavior

A third type of social behavior that may be affected by high ambient temperatures is that of offering assistance to someone in need of help. Some social psychological research has indicated that when people feel unpleasant, they are not inclined to help others, whereas other research suggests that when people feel bad they do indeed help others in order to feel better (e.g., Cialdini & Kenrick, 1976; Weyant, 1978). Since heat obviously produces discomfort, what might it do to helping behavior?

One study found that after leaving an uncomfortably hot experimental room, subjects were less likely to volunteer their assistance in another experiment than subjects who had been in a more comfortable environment (Page, 1978). Another study (Cunningham, 1979) similarly found that when subjects were asked to help in an interview, willingness to help declined as temperatures rose in summer months, but willingness to help increased when temperatures rose during winter months. Other research, however,

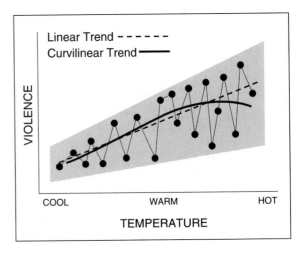

Figure 6–8 Laboratory studies tend to confirm the curvilinear relationship between heat and aggression posited by the negative affect-escape model. However, archival studies of violent crimes tend to show a linear increase in crime as temperatures increase. As the shaded cone shows, the variance or difference in violent crime from day to day tends to widen as the temperature increases. Bell and Fusco (1986, 1989) suggest there is room for both the curvilinear and linear outcomes within this cone, depending on such factors as alcohol consumption and the availability of escape from the heat.

has failed to find a relationship between heat and helping. For example, outdoor temperature was found to have no effect on the amount of tips left at an indoor restaurant (Cunningham, 1979). Moreover, neither high nor low temperatures reduced helping when a person: (1) using crutches dropped a book; (2) lost a contact lens; (3) dropped a sack of groceries; or (4) asked for help in a survey (Schneider, Lesko, & Garrett, 1980). Data from Bell and Doyle (1983) also failed to show that heat had any effect on helping, either during or after exposure to high temperatures. With so little data available, it is difficult (and unwise) to draw firm conclusions about the relationship of heat to helping behavior. It is possible, though, that discomfort increases helping in some cases and decreases it in others, so that these two tendencies may "cancel out" each other in many instances (e.g., Cunningham, Steinberg, & Grev, 1980). In addition, many factors, including the expressions on our face, may be related to signals that the brain interprets in terms of temperature fluctuations, so feeling good or bad from exposure to temperature changes—and resulting behavior patterns—may be mediated by a much more complex set of events than a simple model would imply (Zajonc, Murphy, & Inglehart, 1989).

COLD TEMPERATURES AND BEHAVIOR

PERCEPTION OF AND PHYSIOLOGICAL REACTIONS TO COLD

The physiological reaction to cold ambient temperatures (i.e., below 68 °F, or 20 °C) is in many ways the opposite of the reaction to heat. In contrast to overheating, when core temperature becomes too cold (as detected in part by the hypothalamus), the body reacts by activating mechanisms that generate and retain heat, resulting in increased metabolism, shivering, peripheral vasoconstriction, and piloerection. **Peripheral vasoconstriction** serves just the opposite function of peripheral vasodilation: It keeps core heat inside the body and away from the surface where it is easily lost through convection. This constriction process also makes more blood available to internal organs, which are generating more heat through increased metabolism. **Piloerection** refers to the stiffening of hairs on the skin, usually accompanied by "goose bumps." This skin reaction increases the thickness of a thin layer of insulating air close to the skin, which again helps to minimize heat loss by convection. As with perception of heat, humidity and wind influence perception of cold. High humidity speeds heat loss, as does wind, so both amplify the perception of cold. The **chill factor** or **windchill** index shows how much colder wind makes an already cold temperature feel. For example, an ambient temperature of 23 °F with a wind speed of 15 mph has the same psychological effect as an ambient temperature of –1 °F with no wind. Table 6–2 depicts the broad range of the chill factor index. In very cold temperatures,

Table 6–2 Wind-Chill Index*

Actual Temperature (°F) at 0 mph	5 mph	Wind Speed 15 mph	25 mph	35 mph
		Equivalent Temperature (°F)		
32	29	13	3	–1
23	20	–1	–10	–15
14	10	–13	–24	–29
5	1	–25	–38	–43
–4	–9	–37	–50	–52

*Equivalent temperatures (°F) at 0 mph as a function of actual temperature and wind speed.

PHYSIOLOGICAL DISORDERS ASSOCIATED WITH PROLONGED COLD STRESS

If cold exposure persists for long periods of time, two serious consequences can result. One danger is **frostbite**, characterized by the formation of ice crystals in the skin cells. Since the initial reaction of the body to cold stress is constriction of surface blood vessels, freezing of the skin is not uncommon. Another danger of cold exposure arises when the adaptive mechanisms fail to maintain core body temperature. A decline in core temperature is known as **hypothermia**. In the initial stages of hypothermia, cardiovascular activity, including heart rate and blood pressure, is dramatically increased. As core temperature falls between 86 °F and 77 °F (30 to 25 °C), cardiovascular activity falls off and becomes irregular. Below a core temperature of 77 °F, death due to heart attack is likely to result. At an intermediate stage of hypothermia, clouding of consciousness and coma may well occur. If the victim has not found shelter by this time, the loss of mental functioning may preclude an effort to seek warmth or assistance. Since inadequate clothing in extremes of cold is most likely to precipitate hypothermia, it is those individuals caught unprepared for cold stress, such as mountain climbers faced with sudden cold winds or shipwreck victims in Arctic waters, who are most likely to suffer the disorder. Removal of wet clothing and provision of warmth are necessary to save the lives of hypothermia victims.

it becomes extremely important for thermoregulatory survival to take windchill into account. Just how critical this factor can be is illustrated by the fact that exposed human skin will freeze in less than one minute at −40 °F with a 6 mph (10 km/h) wind, at −20 °F with a 20 mph (32 km/h) wind, and at 0 °F with a 30 mph (48 km/h) wind!

Acclimatization to cold environments may take several forms (see also Bell & Greene, 1982). For example, the Alacaluf Indians of Tierra Del Fuego have an elevated metabolism that seems to keep body temperature elevated in the cold environment (Hammel et al., 1960, as cited in LeBlanc, 1975). Bushmen of the Kalahari Desert and Australian aborigines have another adaptive mechanism for tolerating very low nighttime temperatures. In these populations, shivering does not occur as it would in unacclima-

tized individuals, but rather core temperature actually drops at night (LeBlanc, 1975). Moreover, LeBlanc (1956) reported reduced shivering in a group of Canadian soldiers who had been moved to a cold climate, and Budd (1973) found a similar pattern for Australians of European heritage on an Antarctic expedition. Exposure to cold increases circulation in the hands for Eskimos (LeBlanc, 1975) and for fishermen on the Gaspé Peninsula of Quebec (LeBlanc, 1962). In sum, several mechanisms are available for acclimatization to cold environments.

At least two other factors besides acclimatization modify the effects of cold temperatures. First, humans rarely have to work or interact in unprotected cold climates. We usually wear protective clothing in uncomfortably cold situations. If we do not, disease or death is not unlikely. Because of the cloth-

AMBIENT TEMPERATURE AND DRIVING: Can Temperature Cause Accidents?

In a review article, Provins (1958) noted that efficiency of driving an automobile may well be affected by ambient temperature. Obviously, cold temperatures that contribute to icy road conditions in turn contribute to accidents. But cold or hot temperatures may also directly affect driving performance in at least four ways:

1. Temperatures below 50 °F (10 °C) or above 90 °F (32 °C) reduce grip strength and impair muscle dexterity, which could diminish control over steering, braking, and shifting gears.
2. Temperatures below 50 °F (10 °C) or above 90 °F (32 °C) also reduce **tactile discrimination** (sensitivity of touch), which could reduce a driver's "feel" for the road.
3. Temperatures below 55 °F (13 °C) or above 90 °F (32 °C) impair vigilance and tracking performance, possibly making a driver less cognizant of potential hazards and traffic directional or signaling devices.
4. If high or low temperatures produce irritation, drivers may become more aggressive and take more dangerous risks.

When high wind speeds (such as would be experienced by drivers of convertibles or motorcycles) are added, these temperature effects probably become more severe. Perhaps still more frightening is the possibility that increased levels of carbon monoxide and oxidants in the blood of drivers further reduce mental responsiveness (cf. Ury, Perkins, & Goldsmith, 1972). Data are scarce and somewhat inconclusive on the influence of these environmental variables on driving efficiency, but we should think about the possible consequences when behind the wheel in cold temperatures.

ing factor, performance outcomes in studies of cold environments are somewhat difficult to interpret. If workers on the Alaskan pipeline wore heavy clothing, their efficiency was not dramatically affected. This does not, however, mean that cold temperatures do not affect performance. A second factor complicating the relationship between cold and behavior is that some parts of the body may be cold, while others are not. Whether only the hands are cold, or whether the core temperature is lowered, may make a difference. In addition, in the section on heat we noted that increases of only 10 to 15 °F (6 to 9 °C) above comfort levels (i.e., above about 70 °F,

or 21 °C) often affect performance and other behavior. Comparable temperatures below comfort levels (i.e., 55 to 65 °F, or 13 to 18 °C) are rarely studied. Instead, research on cold tends to concentrate on behavioral effects of temperatures below 55 °F (13 °C). With these facts in mind, let us now examine some of the research on cold temperatures and behavior.

COLD TEMPERATURES AND HEALTH

We have already mentioned that prolonged exposure to cold can lead to hypothermia and frostbite. Do people living for long periods of time in cold climates experience health effects due to the cold temperatures? The answer appears to be "probably not directly." Eskimos in North America and Lapps in northern Scandinavia do not seem to suffer prolonged disorders associated with cold temperatures. Any noticeable differences from other societies are probably the result of culture. If adequate clothing and shelter are available, cold temperatures are not all that hazardous to health. (For a review of design considerations for adequate shelter in cold climates, see Matus, 1988.)

Mental health also appears not to be directly related to cold temperatures. A study on health at Antarctic stations (Gunderson, 1968) found that although residents experience insomnia, anxiety, depression, and irritability, these effects appear more attributable to isolation and work requirements than to climate. To the extent that climate is a factor, concern about it and perceived threat from it are probably more important than temperature itself.

COLD EXTREMES AND PERFORMANCE

Humans on Arctic expeditions, military maneuvers, and in underwater diving occupations often experience extremes of cold. Research on cold stress and performance (see Fox, 1967; Poulton, 1970; Provins & Clarke, 1960, for reviews) suggests that even temperatures of 55 °F (13 °C) can reduce efficiency in reaction time, tracking proficiency, muscular dexterity, and tactile discrimination. As temperatures fall below this level, performance usually deteriorates further. Some evidence (cf. Fox, 1967) suggests that this deterioration is at least partly due to overload and heightened arousal. That is, the body's mechanisms are heavily allocated to maintaining adequate core temperature, so there is not enough energy or attention left for optimum performance on manual and mental tasks. If the hands are exposed, loss of tactile discrimination and stiffening

reduce manual dexterity. If the hands do not become cold, lowered core temperature may still hurt performance, though probably not as much. Interestingly, if the hands are kept warm, considerable cooling of the rest of the body can be tolerated without severe performance decrements (e.g., Gaydos, 1958; Gaydos & Dusek, 1958).

Whether less chilling temperatures (55 to 65 °F, or 13 to 18 °C) actually enhance performance cannot be stated with confidence. However, we might speculate that if the physiological reactions to slightly cooler temperatures increase arousal without overburdening the body's adaptive mechanisms, performance might be slightly enhanced (e.g., Clark & Flaherty, 1963).

Walking speed tends to increase in cold temperatures, presumably to increase body temperature and/or to hasten the escape from the cold (Rotton, Shats, & Standers, 1990). Some people appear to be more bothered by cold than others, and performance is less severely affected by cold for some individuals (cf. Fox, 1967). Furthermore, practice on tasks in cold temperatures can improve performance, so some adaptive mechanisms seem to be at work. Adaptation level to cold almost certainly plays a role in these temperature–performance relationships.

COLD EXTREMES AND SOCIAL BEHAVIOR

Surprisingly little research has been done on the effects of cold ambient temperatures and social behavior. One interesting bit of laboratory evidence does suggest that "low" temperatures around 62 °F (16 °C) make subjects feel more affectively negative (Bell & Baron, 1977). Consequently, one might expect low ambient temperatures to influence aggression in the same curvilinear fashion as high ambient temperatures in the lab. Bell and Baron (1977) found exactly this result: Moderately negative feelings associated with cold temperatures tended to increase aggression, but more extreme negative feelings associated with cold actually decreased aggression. Moreover, Rotton (1993b) found that fewer sex crimes were reported on cold days. Although such results are far from conclusive, they are supported by other research (Bennett et al., 1983) and do suggest that more studies would be valuable in this area (see also Boyanowsky et al., 1981–82). All of these results do bring to mind "cabin fever," the idea that people forced indoors for prolonged periods during cold weather become agitated and hostile. However, Christensen (1982, 1984) found the idea to be no more than folklore, and Rotton and Frey (1985), studying temperatures as low as 5 °F (–16 °C), found no increase in family and household disorder associated with cold conditions.

As cited above for heat effects, Cunningham (1979) reported a slight decrease in helping with an interview as temperatures declined in the winter, although Schneider et al. (1980) found no effects of cold temperatures on helping. Informal observation has shown that cold, harsh winters tend to increase helping behavior and to reduce crime rates. Bennett et al. (1983) reported supportive evidence for these observations and suggested a cold weather helping norm as one explanation. Others have noted that the

severe winter of 1977 resulted in many acts of kindness, such as people rescuing others and sharing food and shelter. In addition, criminal activity during that winter was relatively mild. Attributing such behavior to temperature is speculative, and, as is the case for evidence on heat and helping, there is too little research available to draw any firm conclusions on the relationship of cold temperatures to helping behavior.

SUMMARY OF TEMPERATURE EFFECTS ON BEHAVIOR

The body reacts to high and low ambient temperatures by respectively losing or preserving body heat. Associated physiological activity tends to increase arousal, leading to improved performance at low levels of arousal and deteriorated performance at higher levels. Attention, perceived control, and adaptation level also play a role in the relationship of temperature to behavior. Heat has been shown to affect attraction, aggression, and helping behavior in complex ways, depending on other factors. Cold ambient temperatures appear to influence aggression in much the same way as hot temperatures and may increase helping behavior under some circumstances.

WIND AND BEHAVIOR

Anyone familiar with the "Windy City" of Chicago knows how discomforting wind can be when all you want to do is walk along a sidewalk. Few areas of the world can escape this natural phenomenon, although winds tend to be more severe in certain regions. Winds formed in tornadoes and hurricanes can easily reach speeds in excess of 80 mph (129 km/h). Parts of the Rocky Mountain states, especially those regions where the mountains meet the plains, experience wind speeds of over 100 mph several times a year. Fortunately, because of the altitude and cli-

mate, such Chinook winds are so thin and dry they do little physical damage, but they do cause discomfort and inconvenience (try riding a bicycle in one!). On the other hand, in 1988, storms in Chicago blew out 200 windows in the 110-story Sears Tower, moved a refrigerator across a room, and blew furniture, briefcases, and papers onto the streets below (Johnson & Richards, 1988). Such natural winds are not all that humans are exposed to. As indicated in more detail in Chapter 13, tall buildings create uncomfortable and even dangerous winds in the hearts of our major cities (see box on page 505). Because of the influence of buildings on natural wind patterns, these human-made (or human-altered) winds can far exceed natural winds in both speed and **wind turbulence** (gustiness, shifting directions). Some people attribute the Sears Tower winds to wind tunnel effects of nearby skyscrapers. As urban structures are built taller, we can expect even more exposure to these unnatural winds. Thus, we suspect that potential effects of wind on behavior will become a more important topic for future research within environmental psychology. Of course, there is a beneficial side to wind; it blows away pollution from large cities (to the misfortune of some of those downwind), and it is useful as a power source. We may be able to harness the wind to provide as much as 20 percent of the electricity demand of the United States (Abelson, 1993). On the other hand, wind can have immediate unpleasant effects on us, as we discuss below.

PERCEPTION OF WIND

Although the body has specialized receptors for detecting light, sound, odors, and so forth, there are no receptors designed specifically for wind detection. Thus, to detect wind we have to rely on several perceptual systems. If you are actually in a wind, pressure receptors in the skin probably tell you the most about its presence: The stronger the wind, the more pressure on exposed skin. If the wind is particularly cold or hot, moist or dry, then temperature receptors in the skin also signal its presence. Muscular effort in resisting the wind is still another clue you can use to detect the force of a wind. The sight of others being blown over or of flags whipping tells you about the force of the wind even if you happen to be in a shelter. Finally, wind makes noise as it brushes past the ears or moves around obstacles, and the intensity and frequency of these sounds gives you a clue to the wind's presence and force. One of the earliest and most widely known indexes for evaluating wind is a scale developed by Admiral Sir Francis Beaufort in 1806. The **Beaufort Scale**, depicted in Table 6–3, was orginally devised for activities at sea, but it has been adapted to land use over the years. As can be seen from this scale, wind effects range from problems of keeping hair combed to having difficulty walking and even to being knocked off one's feet by gusts of 45 mph (72 km/h) or more. Cases have actually been

Table 6–3 Beaufort Wind Scale and Related Effects*

Beaufort Number	Wind Speed (mph)	Atmospheric and Behaviorial Effects
0,1	0–3	Calm, no noticeable wind.
2	4–7	Wind felt on face.
3	8–12	Wind extends light flag; hair is disturbed; clothing flaps.
4	13–18	Dust, dry soil, loose paper raised; hair disarranged.
5	19–24	Force of wind felt on body; drifting snow becomes airborne; limit of agreeable wind on land.
6	25–31	Umbrellas used with difficulty, hair blown straight; walking becomes unsteady; wind noise on ears unpleasant; windborne snow above head height (blizzard).
7	32–38	Inconvenience felt when walking.
8	39–46	Generally impedes progress; great difficulty with balance in gusts.
9	47–54	People blown over by gusts.

The Beaufort Wind Scale contains three additional levels that involve damage to property.   Courtesy of A. D. Penwarden.

reported of individuals (especially elderly persons whose agility is less than ideal) being killed by winds that blew them over.

More scientific and precise scales of wind effects on humans have been proposed by Penwarden (1973). Some of these proposed indexes include force of wind on the body (which takes body surface area into account), angle at which one can lean into a wind, and body heat loss due to various types of winds. This body heat loss index would of course be influenced by moisture content and temperature of the wind, as indicated in the previous discussion of windchill.

BEHAVIORAL EFFECTS OF WIND

Very little systematic research has been conducted to date on the specific behavioral effects of wind. A very intriguing series of wind studies, however, has been reported by Poulton et al. (1975). These researchers exposed female subjects to winds of either 9 mph or 20 mph (14.5 or 32.2 km/h), with varying degrees of turbulence, in a wind tunnel. Basically, these wind conditions were intended either to be just strong enough to be noticeable and cause slight discomfort or to be extremely uncomfortable and detrimental to performance. Air temperature varied between 65 °F and 70 °F (18 °C and 20 °C), with humidity at 70 to 85 percent. Among the findings were that high wind and gustiness (1) significantly deflected subjects from walking a straight path; (2) increased the time required to put on a rain coat from 20 to 26 seconds; (3) increased the time required to tie a headscarf by 30 percent; (4) increased subjects' blinking to 12 to 18 blinks per minute; (5) increased the time required to pick selected words from a list and to find a circled word in a newspaper; (6) caused more water to be spilled when poured into a wine glass; and (7) increased feelings of discomfort and perceived windiness (see also Cohen, Moss, & Zube, 1979). Taken alto-gether, these results generally suggest that winds influence affective feelings and at least some types of performance. Since some of these effects can be quite disturbing subjectively, we anticipate that many cities will adopt codes to regulate the extent to which new buildings will be allowed to produce annoying winds.

Correlational research has examined interesting behavior patterns associated with winds around the world, such as the Föhn, Bora, Mistral, and Scirocco in Europe, the Sharav and Chamsin in the Near East, the Chinook in Colorado and Wyoming and Santa Ana in California, and the Pomponio in Argentina (Sommers & Moos, 1976). The Föhn and Chinook are warm, dry winds that descend from mountains. It is not uncommon for residents in these regions to attribute depression, nervousness, pain, irritation, and traffic accidents to wind (Sommers & Moos, 1976). In the Middle East, some governments even forgive criminal acts that are committed during the periods of disturbing winds. In an empirical study, two researchers (Muecher & Ungeheuer, 1961) measured performance on several tasks. As expected, performance was worse on days of Föhn-like weather than on less stormy days. In addition, they and other researchers (e.g., Moos, 1964) have reported that accident rates increase just before or during the approach of the winds. Rim (1975) examined performance of individuals on psychological tests during hot, desert wind (Sharav) periods in Israel, and compared their scores with subjects taking the tests on less turbulent days. The windy days led to higher scores on neuroticism and extraversion, and to lower scores on IQ tests and other measures. Although results are often inconsistent, research in the United States has shown some relationship between windy days and poor classroom behavior (e.g., Dexter, 1904) and between wind speed and mortality rates, felonies, and delinquency (Banzinger & Owens, 1978; for a

AIR IONIZATION AND ELECTROMAGNETIC FIELDS:
Mediators of Weather–Behavior Relationships?

Lightning and other factors may ionize the air. In **air ionization** the molecules in the air partially "split" into positively and negatively charged particles. Moreover, extremely low frequency electromagnetic fields (**ELF-EMF**) are associated with some low altitude weather disturbances. Could it be that these factors play a role in the influence of the weather on behavior? Some researchers think so, at least to some extent. For example, there is evidence that the **negative ions** slow brain waves (Assael, Pfeifer, & Sulman, 1974), speed up reaction time (Hawkins & Barker, 1978; Slote, 1961; Wofford, 1966), facilitate other performance tasks (e.g., Baron, 1987a), enhance positive moods (DeSanctis, Halcomb, & Fedoravicius, 1981), moderate aggression (Baron, Russell, & Arms, 1985), and intensify interpersonal attraction (Baron 1987b). Under some circumstances, however, these effects can be opposite to what others have found (cf. Baron, Russell, & Arms, 1985). **Positive ions** are associated with worsening performance and mental outlook, although some people are more sensitive to ion effects than others (Charry & Hawkinshire, 1981). Interestingly, one interpretation of the disruptive effects of the Sharav wind in Israel (see p. 213) is that this wind generates an excess of positive ions (Sulman et al., 1970).

Research on low-frequency electromagnetic fields suggests that such fields may slow reaction time, impair estimation of time (constricting time), and lead to complaints of headaches and lethargy (for reviews, see Beal, 1974; Persinger, Ludwig, & Ossenkopf, 1973). Recent controversial research suggests that when EMFs are generate by high-power electrical lines they may be associated with increased frequencies of diseases such as leukemia and cancer (e.g., Savitz & Calle, 1987;

review of these studies, see Campbell & Beets, 1981). Whether these effects are directly attributable to wind, to air pressure changes, or even to atmospheric ion changes, is subject to debate (see box on this page). Also, temperature and other weather changes usually accompany winds, so more than one factor may account for wind effects. For example, Cunningham (1979) found that wind was associated with increased helping in summer months and decreased helping in winter months, which suggests that the effects of wind are mediated by what they do to perception of temperature (i.e., chilling effect in winter, cooling effect in summer).

However, Cohn (1993) found that even controlling for other weather variables, wind was correlated with domestic violence; interestingly, with all the statistical controls in place, domestic violence was slightly less likely to occur as wind speed increased. Quite probably, weather conditions increase the stress one experiences, and the heightened stress leads to many of the psychological effects discussed in Chapter 4. Moreover, attention, arousal, and loss of perceived control are likely to mediate many wind effects. Further discussion along these lines is presented in the following section on altitude and barometric pressure.

Savitz et al., 1988). The potential dangers of EMFs are hotly debated. Findings do not always replicate, and often results of one study are in the opposite direction of the results of another study. The magnetic field of a power line is hundreds of times weaker than Earth's natural magnetic field, and is weaker than the pull of the moon on our bodies. Riding a bicycle through Earth's magnetic field creates at least as much electric field within the body as does walking under a power line. Moreover, the more carefully extraneous, potentially confounding variables are controlled for, the weaker the effects reported. Furthermore, it is difficult to find a dose–response relationship; that is, the longer one is exposed to EMFs the greater the risk should be, but studies sometimes find that a lower dose leads to higher risk. New studies do appear which suggest cause for concern, however, so we can only feel confident that the debate over EMF dangers will continue (Bennett, 1994; Florig, 1992; Oak Ridge Asscociated Universities Panel, 1992, 1993; Stone, 1992). Interestingly, Holden (1995) cites two studies suggesting that EMFs may increase growth in plants.

Whether or not ions and ELF-EMF account for the effects of weather on behavior is unknown. The effects of ions noted above are primarily from laboratory conditions with higher levels of negative ions than would be found in natural settings (Culver, Rotton, & Kelly, 1988; Kroling, 1985; Reiter, 1985; Rotton, 1987a). As with all individual weather variables, more than one factor is operating at a time, so it is difficult to conclude that any one mechanism "causes" the observed behavior or feeling state. It is intriguing to consider the possibility, however, and we are sure that experimentation and speculation will continue in the area.

BAROMETRIC PRESSURE AND ALTITUDE

Many people live at rather high altitudes, such as in the Rocky Mountain region of the United States, the Tibetan Plateau of southern China, the Andes, and the high plains of Ethiopia. Others of us travel to these high places. Still others experience high altitudes in aircraft or experience below sea-level conditions during underwater dives. At high altitudes we are exposed to a variety of stresses, most notably **hypoxia** or reduced oxygen intake resulting from low air pressure. Other high altitude stresses include increased solar radiation, cold temperatures, humidity, high velocity winds, reduced nutrition, and strain from negotiating rough terrain (Frisancho, 1979). In underwater environments we also experience problems from high pressures, cold temperatures, and physical exertion. Thus, it is appropriate to examine the physiological and behavioral changes associated with altitude and air pressure differences. (For more detailed reviews, see Frisancho, 1979; Heath & Williams, 1977; Miles, 1967; Pawson & Jest, 1978; and Walder, 1967).

PHYSIOLOGICAL EFFECTS

Normal atmospheric or **barometric pressure** at sea level is 14.7 pounds per square inch (psi) (1.022 kg/cm²). Lower than normal pressures occur as one rises higher and higher above sea level. Under normal air pressure conditions, oxygen is taken into the body through the **alveolar walls** of the lungs, with the pressure difference between the atmosphere and sides of the walls being just enough to "force" oxygen into the body. In low pressure environments, however, it becomes more difficult for oxygen to pass through the alveolar walls, resulting in reduced oxygen available, or the hypoxia noted above (see also Ernsting, 1963, 1967). Hypoxia has a number of physiological and behavioral consequences; and, it should be mentioned, hypoxia is not limited to high altitude environments, but is also a major problem in carbon monoxide pollution, as discussed in Chapter 7. Most habitable environments are located below 15,000 feet (4,572 m), though at much higher altitudes, two special air pressure problems occur. First, above 30,000 feet (9,144 m), the pressures on the interior (body) side of the lung walls becomes so much greater than the pressure on the atmospheric side that oxygen actually passes from the blood into the atmosphere. Second, above 63,000 feet (19,203 m), air pressure is so low that water in the body at a core temperature of 98.6 °F (37 °C) will actually vaporize.

As stated above, the hypoxia at high altitudes has a number of physiological ramifications. Frisancho (1979) provides some interesting details. Visitors to high-altitude areas are likely to experience deeper, and perhaps more rapid, breathing to help compensate for hypoxia. As a result, more carbon dioxide is removed from the lungs, leading to increased alkalinity of the blood. In addition, resting heart rate increases, though maximum heart rate during exercise decreases. Consequently, total cardiac output is reduced, and enlargement of the heart may occur. Red blood cell count increases, hemoglobin concentration increases, but plasma volume decreases, so total blood volume is largely unaffected. Moreover, retinal blood vessel diameter increases and light sensitivity of the retina decreases. Also, an increased desire for sugar will likely be experienced, although hunger is suppressed and weight loss likely. Hormone production is also affected by high altitudes: Adrenal activity increases and thyroid activity decreases. Testosterone production and sperm production decrease, and menstrual complaints may increase. In sum, initial exposure to high altitudes leads to many physiological changes.

ACCLIMATIZATION TO HIGH ALTITUDES

Fortunately, most of the physiological changes noted above are short-term responses to high altitudes, and, as Frisancho (1979) elaborates, acclimatization to the environment at these elevations does occur. For example, hemoglobin concentration levels off after six months and testosterone production returns to normal after a week of high altitude exposure. Acclimatization is not without long-term consequences, however. Populations native to high altitude areas do show physiological differences from lowland natives, probably as a result of developmental adaptations. For example, high-altitude natives show larger lung capacity, higher blood pressure in the pulmonary (leading to the lungs) arteries, lower weight at birth, slower growth rates, and slower sexual maturation (Frisancho, 1979). Although some of these differences may be attributable to nutrition, genetics, and culture, many of them are almost certainly tied to the hypoxic environment of high elevations.

BEHAVIORAL EFFECTS OF HIGH ALTITUDES

Obviously, extreme hypoxia will lead to loss of consciousness and death. Performance impairment, however, occurs well before this extreme stage. To the extent the body can compensate for hypoxia, high altitudes will not show substantial performance decrements. During strenuous work, however, the capacity of the body to compensate for hypoxia is taxed, and performance decrements are likely to be observed. Task performance can be impaired by altitudes as low as 8,000 feet (2,438 m). Learning of a new task can be impaired by rapid decompression to altitudes as low as 5,000 feet (1,524 m). In general, learning of new things is more affected by high altitudes than is recall of previously learned material (Cahoon, 1972; Denison, Ledwith, & Poulton, 1966; McFarland, 1972). We should note that such learning impairments are generally of small magnitude, and people living at high altitudes are certainly capable of learning. Also, we should note that the challenge of high-altitude mountaineering is exhilarating for some adventurous individuals; the exhilaration may even be in part a consequence of knowing that one has successfully faced the dangers of hypoxic effects. Ewert (1994) documents how exhilaration, excitement, and accomplishment motivate those who climb in Denali National Park, Alaska.

HIGH AIR-PRESSURE EFFECTS

Extremely high pressure is experienced primarily under the sea. For each 33 feet (10 m) of depth, the pressure increases by 14.7 pounds per square inch (psi) or by **one atmosphere** (1.033 kg/cm²). Thus, at 33 feet (10 m), the pressure is 29.4 psi (two atmospheres), at 99 feet (30 m) the pressure is 58.8 psi (four atmospheres), and so on. Hazards encountered at such pressure extremes (see also Miles, 1967; Walder, 1967) include:

1. Increased breathing difficulty caused by reduction of maximum breathing capacity (reduced by 50 percent at a depth of 100 feet (30 m);
2. Oxygen poisoning caused by breathing excess oxygen or oxygen under pressure;
3. Nitrogen poisoning caused by the narcotic effects of breathing nitrogen under extreme pressure. Symptoms include light-headedness and mental instability.
4. **Decompression sickness** caused by nitrogen bubbles forming in body tissues (especially in the circulatory system) when one rapidly changes from a high-pressure to a lower-pressure environment. The "bends" is one relatively acute form of decompression sickness. Permanent damage to the bones may also result from rapid decompression.

Most of these high pressure problems can be corrected or prevented by breathing the proper mixture of air for the diving depth and by surfacing slowly to permit the gradual release of nitrogen from tissues.

MEDICAL, EMOTIONAL, AND BEHAVIORAL EFFECTS OF AIR-PRESSURE CHANGES

Low and high barometric or atmospheric pressures are not only associated with altitude. All of us, in fact, are subjected to often dramatic swings in barometric pressure associated with weather changes. Hurricanes, cyclones, and other "tropical storms," for example, are special types of low-pressure weather systems. Clear, sunny skies on the other hand, are generally associated with high pressure. Do these changes in

A RECYCLED CYCLE:
Moon Phases and Behavior

Folklore and commonly held beliefs maintain that many aspects of our behavior are related to phases of the moon. Sexual prowess, menstrual cycles, birth rates, death rates, suicide rates, homicide rates, and hospital admission rates are among the phenomena various people claim are affected by the moon. Often, it is maintained that a full moon increases strange behavior. Surveys of undergraduates indicate that half of them believe people behave strangely when the moon is full (Rotton & Kelly, 1985b). Other beliefs are that the tidal pulls of full and new moons influence human physiology or psychic functioning, or that the moon's perigee (closest distance to the earth) and apogee (farthest distance from the earth) influence us in strange ways. Indeed, the word *lunacy* is derived from a belief in a relationship between the moon and mental illness.

From time to time, research appears that actually gives credence to such beliefs. For example, Blackman and Catalina (1973) found that full moons were associated with an increase in the number of patients visiting a psychiatric emergency room. In another study, Lieber and Sherin (1972) reported a relationship between moon phase and homicide. Rape, robbery, and assault; burglary, larceny, and theft; and auto theft, drunkenness, disorderly conduct, and attacks on family and children have also been linked to a full moon (Tasso & Miller, 1976). At first glance, then, it would appear that science has confirmed the folklore of the ancients (see also Garzino, 1982).

Not so fast! Closer examination of the data indicates that the mysticism of the lunar cycle may be more myth than reality. Campbell and Beets (1978), Campbell (1982), Frey, Rotton, and Barry (1979), Kelly, Rotton, and Culver (1985–86), and Rotton and Kelly (1985a, 1987), reviewed the available research on the topic

barometric pressure affect our feelings and behavior?

According to a number of researchers, the answer is "yes," although the picture is a bit cloudy (pun intended) in that: (1) the data are not always consistent from study to study; and (2) humidity, temperature, and wind variations accompanying pressure changes may account for the observed psychological changes (see also Campbell & Beets, 1977; Moos, 1976).

In general, researchers have observed three types of effects that air pressure changes have on people: increased medical com-

plaints, increased suicide rates, and increased disruptive behavior. With respect to medical complaints, many arthritis victims claim that their condition worsens with changes in weather. Indeed, Hollander and Yeostros (1963) have reported scientific evidence of both increased complaints and medical indications of increased arthritic impairment associated with rising humidity. Moreover, Muecher and Ungeheuer (1961) report an association between general medical complaints and changing weather, especially low pressure or stormy weather.

A number of studies have been con-

and concluded that no firm relationship exists between any lunar variable and human behavior, although lunar tides do affect some marine organisms (see also Atlas, 1984; Byrnes & Kelly, 1992; Jorgenson, 1981; Laverty et al., 1992; Lester, 1979; Lester, Brockopp, & Priebe, 1969). For example, studies conducted over a period of three to five years may report a relationship between the full moon and suicide or homicide for only one of the years studied. Researchers who conclude that such a relationship exists are ignoring the fact that it does not exist for the other years, or that these behaviors are actually lower during full moons for another year. Moreover, it is consistently found that crimes increase on weekends. For some periods of the year, lunar phases may coincide with weekends. Data based on only these periods will obviously show a relationship between the moon and crime, but data based on other periods will show the opposite relationship or no relationship at all. In addition, a self-fulfilling prophecy may operate: If police believe crime increases during a full moon, they may become more vigilant at these times and thus arrest more people. Altogether, the evidence reviewed by Campbell and Beets (1978) and by Frey, Rotton, and Barry (1979) suggests that positive links between moon phases and behavior are spurious and are attributable to mere chance probabilities in the data or to variables not considered by individual investigators. Why do these mistaken beliefs persist? Reasons include misconceptions about physical processes (Culver, Rotton, & Kelly, 1988), attitudes acquired from one's peers (Rotton, Kelly, & Elortegui, 1986), and cognitive biases, such as basing conclusions on only a few occurrences. Given the tenacity of beliefs in moon phases causing disruptive behavior, we suspect the lunacy of it all will continue for some time!

ducted over the years to examine the relationship of mental hospital admissions and suicide rates to weather changes. Both of these clinical occurrences show fluctuations with seasons, with the highest rates coinciding with the increased temperatures and daylight hours of spring and summer months (see Campbell & Beets, 1977; Sommers & Moos, 1976). Although early studies seemed to uncover a reliable relation between changes in barometric pressure and suicide, these relations have not been observed in more recent studies that have subjected larger sets of data to more appropriate and intensive statistical analyses. It is entirely likely that weather associations with mental hospital admissions and suicide rates reflect seasonal variations, and that the social contact that goes along with seasonal variations accounts for the behavioral pathologies (e.g., Kevan, 1980; Sanborn, Casey, & Niswander, 1970).

Finally, several studies have shown that disruptive school behavior and police dispatch calls fluctuate with weather, especially air pressure changes. As early as the turn of the century, one researcher found that low barometric pressure and wind and humidity

SUNLIGHT:
Its Many Effects

One weather variable that has significant impact on humans is sunlight. As indicated by Frisancho (1979), thermonuclear reactions within the sun convert millions of tons of hydrogen into millions of tons of helium every second, releasing radiant energy in the process. Approximately eight minutes after it leaves the sun, some of this energy reaches the earth in various wavelengths. Ranging from short to long wavelengths, the energy takes the form of x-rays, ultraviolet rays, visible light, infrared rays, and radio waves. The wavelengths shorter than visible light are hazardous to life. Fortunately, most of these wavelengths are either absorbed by ozone, blocked by ozone, or "consumed" in the process of making ozone high in the atmosphere. **Ozone** is a form of oxygen in which three atoms are molecularly combined (O_3). As you are probably aware, there has been concern in recent years that several human-generated substances, most notably chlorofluorocarbons in aerosol propellants, destroy the layer of ozone that protects us from harmful solar radiation. When it hits certain atmospheric pollutants, sunlight leads to photochemical smog (see page 265). The solar energy that does reach the surface of the earth can also harm us through sunburn and as a factor in skin cancer. To protect us from some of this danger, the skin produces melanin and other dark pigments to act as a partial shield, a process we know as *tanning* (see Frisancho, 1979). Exposure to excessive midday sun has been implicated in cataracts (Taylor et al., 1988).

Sunlight is not just potentially harmful, of course, but provides us with light, heat, and through photosynthesis, food. Moreover, sunlight induces the skin to produce Vitamin D.

fluctuations were associated with poor behavior in the classroom (Dexter, 1904). Similar findings have been reported more recently (e.g., Auliciems, 1972; Brown, 1964; Russell & Bernal, 1977). Also, it has been found that complaints to police and investigative activity increase with low pressure and high temperature, and that accident reports and related investigations increase with stormy weather (Sells & Will, 1971; Will & Sells, 1969).

What do the above findings mean? Are our mental health and behavior helpless victims of barometric and other weather changes? Fortunately, the answer seems to be "probably not." First, the effects of weather changes on most psychological and behavioral indices are small relative to the influence of other factors, such as social conflict. Second, to the extent that weather does affect behavior, it probably does so indirectly, as an added stressor, similar to "the straw that broke the camel's back." For example, increased suicide rates associated with pleasant weather probably reflect increased time available to interact in stressful social situations, and increased opportunities to worry about these social stresses (see Sommers & Moos, 1976). Similarly, weather changes may simply provide something else to worry about and cope with, adding to the strain on adaptation capacity that has been built up by other stressors. Nevertheless, the additional

Behaviorally, increased hours of sunlight have been associated with increased suicide rates and crime rates (see Sommers & Moos, 1976). These effects most probably are not due directly to sunlight, but rather to increased opportunities to encounter social stress, which may lead to depression and suicide, and increased opportunities to engage in criminal activity. There are seasonal trends in suicide rates, with a peak in spring to early summer. Noting seasonal trends, Kevan (1980) concluded from a review of over 80 studies that suicide is not related to meteorological factors.

Interestingly, two experiments by Cunningham (1979) suggest that sunlight not only leads to good moods in people, but is also associated with increased altruistic behavior! In one of these experiments, people in Minneapolis were greeted by an experimenter as they walked outdoors, and were asked to answer a few brief questions. Subjects were more willing to answer the questions the more sunshine was present, regardless of any other weather conditions in both summer and winter. In the second experiment, waitresses in a restaurant were found to receive more tips with increased sunlight. This relationship was found even though customers were indoors and were not experiencing direct sunlight at the time of leaving the tip. Moreover, the more sunlight, the more positive the mood of the waitresses. Cunningham interpreted these results in terms of mood: The more pleasant we feel, the more willing we are to be kind to and to help others (cf. Cialdini & Kenrick, 1976; Weyant, 1978). Apparently, sunlight really does have prosocial benefits!

stresses brought about by the weather must be dealt with, and may have important consequences, especially under times of other duress. (For another viewpoint, see the box on page 222.)

SUMMARY OF AIR-PRESSURE EFFECTS

Low air pressure is associated with high altitudes and stormy weather conditions. High pressure is found in underwater environments and in fair weather circumstances. At high altitudes, the major stress is hypoxia, or low oxygen intake. Adaptation to hypoxia may have short-term and long-term consequences, including respiratory, cardiovascular, and hormonal changes, as well as performance impairment. High pressure in underwater environments may lead to breathing difficulty, oxygen poisoning, nitrogen poisoning, and decompression sickness, although steps may be taken to avoid these problems. Low pressure associated with weather changes may coincide with increased medical complaints, high suicide rates, and increased disruptive behavior. These observations associated with weather may be due to weather variables other than air pressure, and are likely attributable to additional stress to go along with social stresses and other sources of duress.

FEELING DOWN IN THE WINTER:
Seasonal Affective Disorder

We have noted that many human activities, including crime rates and suicide rates, vary with the seasons. For millenia, physicians have observed that depression and mania (a hyperactive state opposite of depression) often come and go with the seasons in some individuals—so much so that at one time depression was thought to be caused by cold and mania by heat (Jackson, 1986). Psychiatrists have recently given the name **Seasonal Affective Disorder**, or **SAD**, to a depressive cycle that varies with the seasons (Rosenthal et al., 1984). SAD usually occurs in women, begins in early adulthood, and the depressive episode typically shows excessive sleep (hypersomnia), fatigue, craving for carbohydrates, and weight gain. Since the most studied pattern is for depression to occur in the winter and a brighter mood (hypomania) to occur in summer, and since the hypersomnia is reminiscent of hibernating animals, the shortening and lengthening of daylight that goes with the seasons has been thought to be a potential causal factor. Indeed, the depression episodes often respond well to intense artificial light (e.g., Rosenthal et al., 1984; Wehr et al., 1986; Figure 6–9). This pattern has been tied to a substance called *melatonin*, which is involved in hibernation and which declines in concentration in animals exposed to bright light. However, melatonin does not seem to decrease with light therapy in humans (Wehr et al., 1986), and some people have a "reverse" cycle with the depressive episodes occurring in summer months (Wehr, Sack, & Rosenthal, 1987), so the connection of SAD to melatonin and number of daylight hours

Figure 6–9 Exposure to intense artificial light seems to relieve symptoms of SAD.

seems questionable. Another possibility is that a brain chemical called *serotonin*—which is related to some forms of depression—may play a role in SAD. Although the reasons behind SAD are unclear, it has generated much clinical and research interest, and will certainly continue to do so for years to come (see also Nowak, 1994; Rosenthal, 1993). A newsletter can be obtained by writing the National Organization for Seasonal Affective Disorder (NOSAD), P.O. Box 40133, Washington, DC 20016.

INTEGRATING WEATHER AND POLLUTION EFFECTS: A FINAL NOTE

For the most part, we have treated individual weather variables as if their effects on health, mental outlook, and behavior are separate from other factors. We wish to conclude by noting that such singular effects rarely occur in our lives. That is, as noted previously, hot days are often associated with high barometric pressure and calm winds. Stormy days usually involve changes in temperature, wind, humidity, and air pressure. High altitudes not only result in reduced oxygen supply, but in increased exposure to solar radiation. As Suedfeld (1991) notes, individuals stationed in Antarctica face not only cold temperatures, but high altitudes, high winds, unusual light–dark cycles of the sun, and social isolation as well (details provided in the November 1991 issue of *Environment and Behavior* on polar psychology). Moreover, low winds and temperature inversions increase the concentration of air pollutants, and high humidity can intensify the effects of photochemical smog (see Chapter 7). Thus, weather and air pollution variables are interrelated, and one can rarely conclude with certainty that a given behavior or health effect is attributable to any one of these factors (cf. Rotton & Frey, 1985).

CHAPTER SUMMARY

Weather (short-term changes in temperature, storms, and the like) as well as climate (longer-term changes) have measurable impacts on human behavior. Climatological determinism suggests that these effects are profound, but current research suggests that the effects are quite complex. Exposure to heat or cold results in a number of physiological adaptive steps aimed at maintaining a stable core body temperature. Heat impairs performance only when it is extremely uncomfortable, and heat may actually facilitate performance if it is only moderately uncomfortable. Uncomfortable heat tends to reduce interpersonal attraction. Moderately uncomfortable heat increases aggression. Controversy exists over whether even more uncomfortable heat increases or decreases aggression. Extremes of cold impair performance and may also influence aggression in the same manner as extremes of heat. Winds can be quite disturbing and interfere with many types of performance. Health complaints and accident rates also appear to be associated with high-wind conditions. Low barometric pressure at high altitudes leads to hypoxia and other forms of physiological distress, but we can adapt to low- and high-pressure environments. Changes in air pressure associated with weather patterns can have deleterious effects on us. In general, weather effects occur in combination with each other and with pollution effects.

SUGGESTED PROJECTS

1. Keep a daily record of temperature and humidity readings. Obtain crime reports from the local newspaper or from the police department. Is there a relationship between weather and crime?

2. Keep daily records of temperature, humidity, and wind conditions. Using a stopwatch, check walking and bicycle riding speeds of students as they make their way across campus. Do these speeds vary with weather conditions?

3. Using a sound-level meter, check the noise levels of winds on a breezy day. Is the noise level higher around buildings?

4. Time the length of lectures in your various classes. Are weather conditions related to length of lectures?

Disasters, Toxic Hazards, and Pollution

INTRODUCTION

NATURAL DISASTERS

    Characteristics of Natural Disasters

    Perception of Natural Hazards

    Effects of Natural Disasters

    Children and Disasters

    Age and Disaster Response

    Environmental Theories and Disasters

    Summary

TECHNOLOGICAL CATASTROPHE

    Characteristics of Technological Catastrophe

    Effects of Technological Disasters

        The Buffalo Creek Flood

        The Three Mile Island Accident

    Summary

EFFECTS OF TOXIC EXPOSURE

    Occupational Exposure

        Sick Building Syndrome

    Nonoccupational Hazards

AIR POLLUTION AND BEHAVIOR

    Perception of Air Pollution

        Perception of Air Pollution Through Smell

        Perception of Air Pollution Through Vision

        Other Means of Detection

        Other Factors Affecting Perception of Pollution

    Air Pollution and Health

    Air Pollution and Performance

    Air Pollution and Social Behavior

    Summary of Air Pollution Effects on Behavior

CHAPTER SUMMARY

    Suggested Projects

KEY TERMS

air pollution syndrome (APS)

carbon monoxide (CO)

cataclysmic events

conservation of resources (COR) theory

crisis effect

daily hassles

disaster events

disruption

event duration

levee effect

low point

natural disaster

olfactory membrane

oxides of nitrogen and sulfur

particulates

passive smoking

personal stressors

photochemical smog

post-disaster groups

Post-Traumatic Stress Disorder (PTSD)

radon

social support

technological catastrophe

INTRODUCTION

Most of us know what natural disasters are. When hurricanes or tornadoes strike, it is difficult not to notice them. Winds of 100 mph or more, flooding, falling trees, damaged buildings, and, in some cases, death, may occur, and even if the storms are not particularly destructive, they take over the headlines in areas about to be hit or already hit. Earthquakes and other natural disasters are similar; their presence is hard to deny, the threats they pose are intense, and they can kill or maim.

Toxic hazards and air pollution on the other hand, are not always obvious. Sometimes they make us cough or cause our eyes to water or our drinking water to taste bad, but for much of the time we are not very aware of it. Yet, toxic chemicals can cause or contribute to cancer and can damage our heart and lungs and affect our behavior. Silent, constant exposure to toxic hazards may be more harmful in the long run than are more "memorable" disasters. Their dramatic nature aside, disasters are not necessarily more lethal than less obvious stressors.

Some disasters are also toxic and involve "silent" exposure to toxic substances. We accept pollution as an inevitable consequence of

civilization and technological expansion. Where would we be without our cars, one of the great polluting inventions? However, we are not as charitable about other forms of toxic agents in the environment. Accidents such as at Three Mile Island (TMI), Bhopal, Chernobyl, and Love Canal have sharpened our awareness of the vast possibility for toxic exposure in our world, and we do not like it. However, this form of exposure to potentially harmful agents is also a by-product of technology, and one could ask, as we did about autos, where would we be without plastics or nuclear power? The issues surrounding toxic exposure will also be considered in this chapter.

In discussing stress, we noted that Lazarus and Cohen (1977) distinguished between three types of events that cause stress. One type, **daily hassles**, referred to small-magnitude events that occur repeatedly—commuting to work, going to class, and so on. Another kind of stressor, termed **personal stressors**, referred to more powerful threats or losses that occur on an individual level, including loss of a loved one, loss of a job, and other personal problems. Still another type of stressor was called **cataclysmic events** to capture the intensity of these events and their potential for widespread devastation and destruction. These sudden, powerful events typically require a great deal of adaptation in order for people to cope, and large numbers of people are affected. They include war, imprisonment, relocation, and natural disaster (Lazarus & Cohen, 1977). As major events with the potential to kill, maim, disrupt, and wipe out communities, disasters are important environmental stressors. However, there are many different kinds of disasters and although some of the characteristics of cataclysmic events are shared by most disasters, other cases are different. In this chapter, we will consider the distinction between natural disasters—caused by natural forces—and human-made catastrophes which are due in some way to our actions or modification of the environment. We will consider natural events in the first sections of this chapter. As we do so, keep in mind that many natural disasters—wind storms and droughts, for example—are closely related to the weather phenomena we described in the previous chapter. Finally, we will discuss toxic hazards and air pollution, increasingly common and important environmental phenomena that have a number of implications for mood, behavior, and health.

Some naturally occurring phenomena may contribute to air pollution and/or intensify its effects, but, the majority of air pollution effects or influences on human behavior are human-made. However, human-made does not necessarily mean modern. Air pollution is not just a recent problem caused by industrialization or by automobiles. Recent evidence uncovered by researchers suggests that hundreds of years ago humans may have suffered medical effects of air pollution. *The Rocky Mountain News* reported in 1977 that the body of an Eskimo woman who apparently died in an earthquake or landslide some 1600 years ago was discovered on Saint Lawrence Island in the Bering Sea in 1972. Because the body appeared to have been frozen shortly after death, medical specialists were able to perform a detailed autopsy; they found that the woman had black lung disease, a condition that apparently resulted from breathing some form of highly polluted air. Experts speculated that years of inhaling fumes from lamps that burned seal oil or whale blubber could cause black lung, a disease frequently found in coal miners. Human beings have long been capable of modifying their environments, and air pollution caused by people changing the environment around them may have a long history.

NATURAL DISASTERS

Natural disasters are relatively infrequent events, but their dramatic qualities make them memorable and seem more frequent. Few of us will directly experience more than one or a few such events in our lives, and then only if we live in areas where they are likely. Earthquakes in California, hurricanes along the Gulf Coast and the Atlantic seaboard, tornadoes in the southeast and midwest, tsunamis in Hawaii—these are all instances of powerful natural events that tend to occur in certain areas of our country. Defining these events is an important place to begin our discussion of natural disasters. The massive flooding in the midwest in 1993, the onslaught of Hurricane Andrew in 1992, and the earthquakes in California in 1989 and 1993 are vivid examples of events that we label "disasters." Examining what they have in common may help us to better understand what makes a disaster a "disaster" (Figure 7–1).

Figure 7–1   Natural disasters often leave vast destruction in their wake, as in this Florida community following Hurricane Andrew's visit in 1992.

Natural disasters have been difficult to define, not because we do not know what they are, but because specific criteria are hard to establish. The "natural" part is easy: Natural disasters are caused by natural forces and are not under human control. They are uncontrollable, the product of the physical forces that govern the earth and atmosphere, and people must learn to deal with them when they strike. Defining what constitutes a disaster, on the other hand, is a little trickier. Since it is obvious that not all storms are disasters, what distinguishes disasters from less serious events or series of events? We could simply list all of the events associated with disaster, such as hurricanes, tornadoes, earthquakes, or tsunamis, but this may not be satisfactory because these storms or events

do not always cause damage. Typically, one of these **disaster events** must cause damage or death before it is considered a disaster. How should we define or quantify damage? Should it be viewed on the individual level, as death, injury, or loss? Is there a cutoff, a certain amount of damage above which an event is a disaster and below which it is not? Or, should responses by victims (for example, if they panic) be used to index disasters? Definitional issues have posed problems for researchers interested in disaster and extreme stress.

In our society, the emphasis on what makes a disaster "disastrous" seems to be on effects. The Federal Emergency Management Agency (FEMA), the governmental unit responsible for helping disaster victims, offered the following definition:

> A major disaster is defined. . . as any hurricane, tornado, storm, flood high water, wind-driven water, tidal wave, tsunami, earthquake, volcanic eruption, landslide, mudslide, snowstorm, drought, fire, explosion, or other catastrophe . . . which, in the determination of the President, causes damage of sufficient severity and magnitude to warrant major disaster assistance.
>
> *(1984, p. 1)*

Thus, the nature of the event (is it one of these disaster events?) and the extent of damage are used to officially designate disasters. We must keep in mind, however, that this definition is used to determine whether and if emergency aid and relief are to be given. As a result, it focuses on issues related to taking such action. It shares the same biases as most of us. Disasters are destructive. A tornado in a desolate desert where no one lives and no one may even be around to see it is not a disaster, but the same tornado loose in downtown Birmingham is.

Quarantelli (1985) has argued that physical indices of damage and destruction are not sufficient to define disasters. The magnitude of impact of a disaster event may be better viewed in terms of **disruption**, the degree to which individual, group, and organizational functioning is disturbed and can no longer function as it used to. It is possible for natural events like earthquakes to be destructive but not disruptive, though the two are frequently related. An earthquake could cause the kind of damage depicted in Figure 7–2, which is sure to cause considerable disruption, or it could strike a more remote area in which similar damage inconvenienced only a few people. More importantly, it is possible to have little visible destruction with great disruption. Thus, storms that cause great disruption by the threats they pose might be considered to be disasters even if they end up doing little damage. The advantage of using this kind of definition is that

disruption can be measured and provides an important outcome estimate by telling us how much disorganization or interruption of normal life occurs. Again, earthquakes in desolate areas can cause destruction but may cause little disruption among the few people living there. Conversely, disasters such as major snowstorms may cause little physical disfigurement but a great deal of disruption as cars are abandoned, accidents increase, and people experience great difficulty getting from place to place. This approach suggests that disaster events—those occurrences that can cause disasters—must disrupt victimized communities in order to be considered a disaster. This makes disasters a little easier to measure and allows a number of events, such as blizzards and droughts, to be included as disasters.

Measuring disruption is fine, but the

Figure 7–2   Earthquake damage like this near Northridge, California, can cause disruption for weeks or months after the quake.

same problems of how much must occur or where the cutoff for distinguishing between disasters and nondisasters may be, arises as soon as we try to apply this definition. Consequently, most definitions are vague about how much disruption is needed to distinguish between a disaster and just a "bad scene." We can define **natural disasters** as events caused by natural forces that disrupt the communities that they strike (see Figure 7–1). We can probably also assume that this disruption must be substantial. There are a number of characteristics of these events that distinguish some natural disasters from others, but for now, we will settle on this as a definition.

Our definition of natural disasters thus includes extreme weather of any kind (heat, cold, hurricanes, tornadoes, blizzards, ice storms, wind storms, monsoons, etc.). Earthquakes and volcanic eruptions, mudslides, and avalanches are also natural disasters, but may be affected by human alteration of the earth. Underground bomb testing, for example, could cause some of these events under certain conditions. We also include floods in our definition, even though these are often caused by a combination of natural events (e.g., rain) and actions taken by people (e.g., improper use of riverbanks). Some floods are almost entirely caused by humans, as in the case of dam failure. These would be more appropriately considered as **technological catastrophes** or mishaps. Other cataclysmic events that are human-made, including mine disasters, air crashes, nuclear accidents, toxic waste contamination, among others, may also be considered technological mishaps.

Research on natural disasters is difficult to conduct for a number of reasons. To start with, these events are almost always studied *after they have already occurred.* As a result, we cannot get information about people before they were exposed to the disaster and, therefore, cannot demonstrate changes in mood and behavior. Even if we compare a group of disaster victims to a control group of people who were not exposed to the disaster we cannot be sure that differences we observe were not present before the disaster. A second problem is the choice of an appropriate control group. With whom shall we compare our findings about victims of a storm or earthquake? Finally, choosing measures is difficult, because research must often be conducted in recently devastated, often chaotic conditions far from the researcher's laboratory. Obtaining samples of subjects is also problematic, because recruitment for a study often must be done quickly. Many times, one cannot sample randomly and must resort to quasi-random or non-random sampling (e.g., selecting every third person on a given street). This may cause the sample to be nonrepresentative of the entire area affected by the mishap and can limit the degree to which we can make general statements about our findings. Despite these methodological problems, research has identified several important characteristics of disasters and has begun to document effects of these events on victims.

CHARACTERISTICS OF NATURAL DISASTERS

Partly because of these measurement problems, our understanding of natural disasters is not complete. However, a great many studies of these events have been done, and we have learned a great deal about them. We are now familiar with the basic properties of cataclysmic events such as natural disasters. In addition to being *sudden*, they are usually *unpredictable*. We may have some warning. Living near a fault tells you that there may be an earthquake there—but it does not tell you when it will occur. Living in a "tornado alley" may mean that tornadoes are likely but does not pinpoint the time or place of an individual twister. Weather alerts often provide warning of imminent tornadoes, but do not specify exactly where the funnel will touch down. These reports can provide adequate warning of some storms and floods, but often do not. Natural disasters are typically viewed as *uncontrollable* and not as predictable as we would like.

The destructive power of natural disasters is sometimes enormous and usually substantial. In other words, they usually do damage and sometimes wreak havoc. The sheer magnitude of some disasters makes them unique among stressors. Anyone who has ever lived through an earthquake, a fierce coastal hurricane, or a tornado can attest to this. Natural disasters are usually *acute*, as they often last only seconds or minutes and rarely persist for more than a few days. Heat waves, droughts, and cold spells may persist longer, but most storms, quakes, and other mishaps are over quickly. Once the crisis has passed, coping can proceed, and rebuilding and recovery can be achieved. Usually, this coping requires a great deal of effort.

Of these and other characteristics of disasters, which are most important in determining how people will react? There is no easy way to answer this question, particularly because not all disasters share all of these features. Some may be sudden, some more drawn out. Some may cause destruction, others may not. Is it possible to identify characteristics that will allow us to predict whether a disaster will have major effects? **Event duration**—how long the disaster event affects people or how long it is physically present—is one important variable (e.g., Bolin, 1985; Davidson & Baum, 1986). The longer a disaster event lasts, the more likely victims will be exposed to threat or harm, and so longer events may have bigger effects. Consider the possible effects of varying speeds with which disasters strike and subside: Some, like tornadoes, strike quickly and disappear almost as quickly as they appeared. Others are slower to develop and take longer to recede, as in the case of

many floods. Which is worse? The answer to this clearly depends on several other factors such as how strong the storm was or how much destruction was done. However, the length of time a disaster lasts should affect how people caught in it react.

Related to event duration is the presence of a **low point** in a disaster, the point when things are as bad as they are going to be and will now only improve over time (Baum, Fleming, & Davidson, 1983). Once past, recovery may unfold as the threat posed by the disaster recedes and attention will next focus on secondary stressors and rebuilding. Some disasters have very clearly defined low points. When a tornado strikes, it does its damage and leaves. From this point on, the trend is toward improvement of conditions as recovery efforts restore community services, rescue victims, rebuild homes, and so on. However, other disasters have less clearly discernible low points that are not easily seen or predicted and that increase the duration of the disaster. Earthquakes may be followed by tremors and aftershocks that may obscure the fact that the major damage has already occurred. Each aftershock is accompanied by fear, distress, and apprehensiveness about harm yet to come. Similarly, long-lasting disasters, such as the crippling droughts of 1987 and 1988, or floods in 1993, may never seem to "hit bottom," as things just keep getting worse. The impact of multiple events associated with disaster (e.g., a cluster of tornadoes, several earthquakes, or strong aftershocks) could in part be explained as the effect of a new threat when the previous one was over and victims thought the threat was gone. Clearly, the duration and intensity of disasters are important, and the low point may provide a way of looking at them that taps into several aspects of these stressors.

Another characteristic of a disaster situation that appears to affect whether it has severe consequences is whether people have adequate *warning* of the storm, quake, or other disturbance. Fritz and Marks (1954) suggested that a lack of warning can increase the consequences of a disaster. However, being warned of a disaster does not ensure minimization of consequences, as the effectiveness of the warning system, the preparedness of a community, and other factors affect usefulness of alerting news. This was shown in a study of response to warnings of a flash flood (Drabek & Stephenson, 1971). The effectiveness of repeated warnings in getting people to evacuate was undermined by several factors. First, when families were separated at the time of the warning, they showed more concern about finding each other than with evacuation. Unless a direct order to evacuate was given, people first sought confirmation of the danger and the need to leave. Further, though the news media actually notified the most people, it was the least effective in producing appropriate responses.

One can easily think of instances in which warnings and evacuations cause problems all by themselves. Say, you are living in a coastal area and a hurricane warning is issued. All people living in a particular area are advised to leave their homes and move to higher ground for the storm. Clearly, some people will ignore these warnings, but many will heed them. Without adequate planning, roads may become jammed and people may not know where to go. Some people may panic as they are stuck in traffic, others may become belligerent because evacuation is taking so long, and still others may worry about their unprotected homes. Even if the hurricane turns and heads back out to sea, sparing the community, it has caused a great deal of disruption because people responded to warnings but the plans for evacuation were not clearly drawn.

Other disaster characteristics are listed in Table 7–1. Clearly, disasters can involve a number of factors—they can cause injuries or death, massive property losses, and considerable disruption. They occur in a context as

Table 7–1   Characteristics of Disasters That May Affect Response by Victims

- Life threat
- Injury
- Witnessing injury or death
- Death or injury of relative or friend
- Preparedness of community
- Social cohesion of community
- Financial loss
- Property/possession loss
- Separation from family

well, and the extent to which communities are prepared for the disaster, conduct orderly pre- and post-disaster procedures (e.g., evacuation), and are able to pull together and rebuild quickly also affect the impact of a disaster on individual victims. When people are exposed to extreme life threat, as is the case in a number of disasters, one would expect reactions to be more extreme. Similarly, when one is injured and/or witnesses others' injury or death, when one is bereaved either before or because of the disaster, and/or when losses are substantial, we would expect stronger, longer-lasting reactions and, perhaps, some negative consequences.

Natural disasters, then, have a number of important characteristics. They are sudden, powerful, and uncontrollable, cause destruction and/or disruption, are usually relatively brief in duration, have low points, and sometimes may be predicted. How perception of these characteristic features contributes to the ways in which disasters affect people is the topic of the next sections (Figure 7–3).

PERCEPTION OF NATURAL HAZARDS

At the beginning of this chapter we discussed the fact that people might not be able to discern accurately how much risk is posed by various hazards. To some extent this is due to the dramatic nature of some hazards.

Figure 7–3 Earthquakes and other disasters can cause great destruction and disruption, but how affected people are depends on whether they work or live near or in the most heavily affected areas.

Natural disasters are more dramatic than other hazards such as air pollution, and this may lead some people to assume they are riskier and more hazardous.

Which factors influence whether individuals are aware of the potential consequences of becoming hazard victims? We will discuss several factors that researchers have found to be important in hazard perception (for more detailed reviews of factors involved in the perception of hazards, see Burton & Kates, 1964; Burton, Kates, & White, 1968; Kates, 1976; Saarinen, 1969). Among these factors are the crisis effect, the levee effect, and adaptation.

The **crisis effect** refers to the fact that awareness of or attention to a disaster is greatest during and immediately following its occurrence, but greatly dissipates between

disasters. Flood warnings, for example, may be largely ignored until there is a flood. Once the flood occurs, there may be a rush to study the problem, together with the implementation of some public works program. Efforts to prevent the next disaster, however, frequently disappear after this initial rush of activity. The same principle holds for droughts: We tend to take strong water conservation measures only when the drought arrives. We do not practice stringent measures between droughts, and we do not limit population in areas that are drought-prone so that there is more water available in time of drought.

While this may operate at a societal level, the consequences of the crisis effect are also important for the individual. A good example of this is how we responded to the oil shortages of the 1970s. After waiting in long lines for gasoline, people became very conservation-minded, bought small economy cars, and so on. Now, years later, we have an oil glut, and though at a societal level some conservation efforts persist (e.g., more mileage-conscious drivers in smaller, more fuel-efficient cars), as individuals we have largely forgotten about the problem. The next round of shortages may change that.

The **levee effect** pertains to the fact that once measures are taken to prevent a disaster, people tend to settle in and around the protective mechanisms. Levees are built to keep floodwaters where they belong and out of populated areas. After a levee is built, however, houses and factories are constructed on what was once considered to be a dangerous floodplain. Unfortunately, levees are built with projected figures for floodwaters in mind, and projections often go wrong. Many communities along the Mississippi River are testimony to this fact. The levee effect also applies to such preventive measures as breakwaters along coasts and reservoirs in drought-prone areas: Once they are built, people flock to settle nearby.

A third factor involved in hazard perception is *adaptation.* Just as we adapt or habituate to a noise or odor, so, too, do we adapt to threats of disaster. Apparently, we can hear so much about a hazard that it no longer frightens us. Large populations in earthquake-prone regions of the world such as California, Iran, Japan, and parts of China attest to this adaptation phenomenon. Floods, mine disasters, and hurricanes follow the same principle: People in the area "learn to live with it." In learning to live with it, they generally discount the possibility that they themselves might become victims (e.g., Kates, 1976).

Several variables appear to influence adaptation to potential hazards. For one thing, when the hazard is closely related to the well-being or resource use of a community, the inhabitants are more aware of the danger. Individuals whose businesses depend on coastal tourist industries, for example, may take more precautions against hurricane damage than residents whose well-being does not depend on the tourist industry. Farmers are much more aware of the drought hazards than are nonfarmers in the area. Ski resort operators are probably also more likely to be aware of drought hazards, and people with lung diseases are more sensitive to air pollution than those with healthy lungs. Thus, if one's well-being is closely related to the resource that poses a hazard, one is less likely to adapt in perceiving the hazard.

Personality variables may also affect how we perceive hazards, or at least what we do once they are perceived. Sims and Baumann (1972) noted that although the heaviest concentration of tornadoes is in the Midwest, most tornado-related deaths occur in the South. After eliminating natural explanations for this phenomenon, such as stronger storms or higher concentrations of population in the South, the researchers suggested that there might be regional differences in subjective perception of danger, and thus less preparation for disaster by Southerners. The researchers found that such differences related to the personality dimension of internal–external locus of control. "Internals" believe they are in control of their own fate, whereas "externals" believe outside sources, such as powerful persons, government, God, or fate control their destinies (Rotter, 1966). In interviewing residents of Illinois and Alabama, Sims and Baumann found that the Illinois residents felt luck had far less to do with their fate than Alabama residents did. Furthermore, Illinois residents appeared to take more precautions when storms approached, such as listening for weather bulletins and warning neighbors, whereas Alabama residents paid less attention to the need to listen to radio or television bulletins. Apparently then, personality plays some major role in determining humans' perceptions of their control over hazards.

In another study of flood victims in Carman, Manitoba, Canada, it was found that another personality characteristic was associated with efforts to minimize flood damage, such as through elevating houses, installing sump pumps, and purchasing insurance (Simpson-Housley et al., 1982). Individuals of this personality type are known as "repressors" and tend to deal with threat by denying the existence of the threat and not verbalizing uneasy feelings about a potential danger. Although intuitively it seems odd that such individuals would be the ones to take more precautions against disaster, perhaps by doing so they feel they are in a better position to deny or avoid disaster if damage does occur in an area. Whatever the case, it does appear that personality plays a role in determining humans' perception of their control over hazards (see also Hanson, Vitek, & Hanson, 1979; Jackson, 1981; Shippee, Burroughs, & Wakefield, 1980).

EFFECTS OF NATURAL DISASTERS

Research has produced varying findings about how disasters affect behavior and mental health. Some studies suggest that disasters result in profound disturbance and stress that may lead to continuing emotional problems, whereas other studies suggest that psychological effects are acute and dissipate rapidly after the danger has passed (Rubonis & Bickman, 1991). Although conclusions based on studies of disasters are limited by many methodological problems, one can generally conclude (1) that disasters appear to cause substantial distress and mental health problems immediately after their impact; (2) that most of this distress is short-lived and by a year or two after disasters, most victims have adjusted; and, (3) that severe chronic stress or psychiatric impairment due to natural disasters is unusual and may be limited to those victims experiencing frequent intrusive thoughts about the disaster or those with prior histories of psychological problems (e.g., Baum, Cohen, & Hall, 1993; Kardiner et al., 1945). During the actual precipitating event (i.e., the storm or earthquake that causes the disaster) behavior may be dramatically affected, and people may be frightened. The negative effects that many of us expect to appear once the danger has passed are common but they dissipate more rapidly than many people think. In fact, some studies have found that overall effects of disaster may be positive, because of increased social cohesiveness as victims band together in local groups and help others cope.

Obviously, the rational response to an oncoming disaster is to run and hide—to take shelter and other precautions to adequately protect life and property. However, we do not always have enough warning to do that, and even when warnings are issued, protective behaviors are not always the first thing we implement. Some people do not take warnings seriously, particularly if the area they live in has had several "false-alarms" or predicted storms or earthquakes that did not materialize. Some want to be spectators. Along the east coast of the United States, when hurricanes are approaching, some people go out to "watch" them arrive. Hurricane parties are not uncommon in areas where these storms strike. However, not everyone wants to watch the raw power of nature at its most destructive, and response to natural disasters ranges from well-planned emergency behavior to random, nonproductive activity (Figure 7–4 A & 4B).

One thing people do not do very often is panic in the face of a natural disaster (e.g., Quarantelli & Dynes, 1972). The immediate response by some is withdrawal, and many people at first appear to be stunned after a disaster has struck. Menninger (1952) reported that these responses included apathy, disbelief, grief, and a desire to talk about the

Figure 7–4A & 4B   Constructive responses to disaster include efforts to minimize damage and disruption, but other behaviors can increase disruption. In Figure 7-4A (top), volunteers are building sandbag levees to hold back flood waters near St. Louis in 1993. Some people may be more fearful and this can make recovery more difficult (Figure 7-4B).

SOCIAL SUPPORT AND DISASTER

To some extent, positive social effects of disasters may be related to effects of the disaster on social support and one's sense of where he or she fits into a social network. **Social support** is usually defined as a person being valued and esteemed by other people and being able to get help, emotional support, or other aid if it is needed (e.g., Cobb, 1976; Cohen & Wills, 1985). Traditionally, it has been viewed as independent of stress; that is, we have a given level of social support, and while it may help us cope with stress, it is more stable and lasting and is not "used up" by stress. Having social support is a good thing. People with more social support usually fare better in dealing with stress, and appear to have fewer adjustment problems after disasters (e.g., Fleming et al., 1982; Norris & Murrell, 1984; Thoits, 1982). However, some stressful situations obviously change how much social support we have. Loss of a spouse, close friend, or other confidant by divorce, death, graduation or relocation alters one's base of support, in turn contributing to problems associated with stress (Eckenrode & Gore, 1981; Rook & Dooley, 1985).

Kaniasty and Norris (1993) addressed the possibility that disasters can "deplete" available social support, rendering it less effective in buffering stress. We know that people experiencing stress usually receive support if it is available, and that stress seems to increase need for support (Cohen & Hoberman, 1983; Kaniasty & Norris, 1991). One can reasonably expect that disasters will increase people's needs for support, particularly if they are injured, homeless, or otherwise affected by the disaster. Victims of disasters should have greater need for support after a disaster than before it.

At the same time, disasters appear to decrease the amount of social support that is available. This is true for several reasons. First, the number of people in

experience with others. Perception of time may be affected; some people may report everything speeding up while others report that everything seemed to be happening in slow motion. Episodes in which the victim feels like a spectator, passively watching him- or herself and the carnage around him or her may also be experienced. Some antisocial behavior has been noted. For example, after the earthquake that destroyed large parts of Managua, Nicaragua, in 1972, looting was widespread, even while some survivors made efforts to rescue others, put out fires, and so on (Kates et al., 1973). Studies

have also found evidence of more positive response to disaster. For example, Bowman (1964) observed the behavior of mental patients after a massive earthquake near Anchorage, Alaska, on Good Friday, 1964. The patients' initial response was positive—they wanted to help with problems that arose. Bowman observed "a stimulation of all personnel, a feeling of unity, a desire to be helpful, and a degree of cooperation which I only wish it were possible to have at all times" (p. 314). However, positive effects of disasters appear to be limited to specific situations and settings (see box on pages 236–237).

a social group who need support at the same time is likely to be greater than normal. If a group of 12 friends usually serves as a social support source for its members, the usual scenario is probably one in which a few members need support and the other 9 or 10 are there to provide it. However, after disasters, most of these people probably will need help because they have all been affected by the same major stressor. Can people who need support also provide it effectively? If they cannot, available support will decrease. At the same time, those who are available to provide support after a disaster are facing dramatically increased demand for support and it is possible that they burn out or otherwise cannot keep up with the need around them. Together, these social processes may lead to greatly reduced available support at a time when need for support has increased dramatically (Kaniasty & Norris, 1993).

Evidence of this deterioration of social support following natural disasters has been reported. In a study of severe flooding in Kentucky in 1981 (Kaniasty, Norris & Murrell, 1990), perceptions of social support decreased as a result of the flooding. In a longitudinal analysis of these disaster victims, evidence of decreases in social embeddedness and social support was found (Kaniasty & Norris, 1993). Perceived availability of support also declined and this was related to losses from the flood. However, there appeared to be broad decreases in the extent of and need for social support as well as increased estrangement from one's social networks. The situation was one in which need for support exceeded the amount available and this contributed directly to stress and adjustment difficulties after the disaster (Kaniasty & Norris, 1993).

Disasters disrupt organizations and communities as well as families and individuals (e.g., Wright et al., 1990). The functions once performed by larger groups may be done by small groups of victims. One of the most serious problems in disasters is coordination of various relief efforts. Despite the need for coordination in successful disaster management, large organizations are often hesitant to assume responsibility. This reluctance can promote the emergence of cohesive local groups who must assume responsibility for things not being done by formal organizations. A lapse of authority also contributes to the development of these groups. Positive social response during or immediately after a disaster event also appears to be influenced by the needs of the community. When destruction is so vast that rescue teams and official relief efforts cannot cover all needs, locally based groups may fill the void (Figure 7–5).

As noted earlier, natural disasters do appear to cause stress, anxiety, depression, and a range of other mood or perceptual disturbances. The duration of these effects is not well established nor are the reasons why some people have difficulty adapting to life after

Figure 7–5   Disasters frequently require rescue and recovery, which may be done by trained professionals, volunteers, or spontaneous neighborhood groups.

a disaster. The extreme life threat associated with most major disasters, combined with other factors that could intensify fear and terror during or after the storm, should be expected to induce mood changes and cause at least transient mental health problems. Indeed, research suggests that disaster victims are more likely to exhibit symptoms of stress and emotional problems after a disaster (e.g., Canino et al., 1990; Lima et al., 1991; Shore, Tatum, & Vollmer, 1986). For example, a study of survivors of severe mudslides and flash floods in Puerto Rico in 1985 found increased reporting of medically unexplained bodily symptoms (e.g., pain, nausea) as a result of exposure to the disaster (Canino et al., 1990). Other studies, this time of the 1989 Loma Prieta earthquake in California, found that survivors of the earthquake reported more depression if they experienced difficulties during the earthquake (Nolen-Hoeksma & Morrow, 1991). They also reported about twice as many nightmares as did control subjects at the University of Arizona who did not live near the earthquake (Wood et al., 1992).

Most of the effects of disaster that we have considered so far are more or less immediate reactions—how people feel and what they do as a disaster strikes and just after it has passed. It is not surprising that disasters have strong effects on mood and behavior as they occur or shortly afterwards. Threat to one's life, the possibility of injury or loss of property or loved ones, and often severe disruption of "normal" life all can cause these psychological problems, and all can cause stress. However, as the events associated with a disaster recede, the mental health and stress-related effects we have seen should decrease as well. Some researchers have been interested in whether these are lasting effects of disaster beyond the impact and recovery periods. Most studies of these effects of disasters have used psychiatric interviews of selected groups of survivors. As a result, many findings are expressed as frequency of certain psychiatric problems. More recent research has broadened the base of measurement and elaborated on these earlier findings.

For the most part, these studies find that

intrusive thoughts, anxiety, depression, and other stress-related emotional disturbances have been found among victims of floods, tornadoes, hurricanes, and other natural disasters (Logue, Hanson, & Struening, 1979; Milne, 1977; Moore, 1958; Penick, Powell, & Sieck, 1976; Taylor & Quarantelli, 1976). These effects have been found to last as long as a year, but often do not last that long. Further, they are not nearly as widespread among victims as one might expect. Studies rarely show more than 25 to 30 percent of victims suffering psychological effects months after a disaster, and it appears that people who lost most or were otherwise affected more by the disaster are those who continue to suffer (e.g., Parker, 1977). In other words, it may be more accurate to conclude that the loss of a home or a loved one in a disaster leads to psychological problems than to say that natural disasters cause lasting problems.

A profound form of enduring effect of disasters is **Post-Traumatic Stress Disorder (PTSD)**, an anxiety disorder characterized by having experienced a traumatic event (like a disaster), as well as frequent, unwanted, and uncontrollable thoughts about the event, heightened motivation to avoid reminders of the event, sleep disturbances, social withdrawal, and heightened arousal. This disorder can be thought of as an extreme outcome, as it can be debilitating and difficult to treat. Research on veterans of combat, disaster victims, rape victims, and victims of other crimes and severe stressors has contributed to a growing literature on PTSD. Among disaster victims, PTSD appears to be associated with intrusive thoughts and episodes of reexperiencing the disaster (Solomon & Canino, 1990). Research also indicates that diagnosable PTSD and acute stress have been found among many victims up to four months after tornado and flood disasters (Steinglass & Gerrity, 1990). While some victims continued to experience distress, this study found substantial reductions in stress

and PTSD over the year following these four-month assessments (Steinglass & Gerrity, 1990).

A recent review of studies of the mental health problems that follow disasters suggests that there is a small but significant association between them (Rubonis & Bickman, 1991). Depression was observed in about one-quarter of subjects in 10 studies that measured depression, while nearly 40 percent of subjects in 15 disaster studies exhibited symptoms of anxiety and 32 percent exhibited phobias. However, not all studies provided measures of these and other stress symptoms, and the timing of measures was not considered in this meta-analysis. As a result, the intensity or frequency of general effects can be estimated but the duration of effects cannot be separately assessed. One can conclude, cautiously, that disasters have "small but consistent" effects on mood and well-being and that they can cause stress and a range of psychological problems (Rubonis & Bickman, 1991).

Despite these findings, one can list a number of reasons why acute disaster events could give rise to long-term distress. This is important not only for explaining those long-term effects of natural disasters that have been found but also in understanding the effects of toxic or human-made disasters discussed in the next sections. One theory suggests that intrusive thoughts about the disaster keep the event "alive" in that victims "re-live" the disaster each time they think about it. Thoughts about frightening or threatening experiences, even if they occurred months or years before, can elicit distress and responses like those associated with the actual event (e.g., Hall & Baum, 1995). Disaster victims reporting fewer intrusive thoughts tend to exhibit fewer symptoms of chronic stress, and more ruminative styles have been associated with distress following the Loma Prieta earthquake (Baum et al., 1993; Nolen-Hoeksema & Morrow, 1991). Alternatively, prolonged stress following a disaster could be due to the occurrence of secondary stressors or stressful events that are secondary to (caused by) the disaster and that can cause problems for days, weeks, or months. Data support the idea that these secondary stressors occur as people run into problems with stores and shops being closed, phone and/or power outages, financial aspects of loss (or loss of one's job if your place of business is damaged), or other stressful results of the disaster. Life change is clearly greater after a disaster than would be expected if there had been no disaster (Janney, Minoru, & Holmes, 1977; Melick, 1978; Robbins et al., 1986; see Table 7–2).

A recent study of the effects of Hurricane Hugo examined the relative impact of secondary stressors or chronic stress on post-disaster distress more than a year after the hurricane (Norris & Kaniasty, 1992). Secondary stressors, measured as chronic problems related to financial, marital, parental, filial, and occupational aspects of their lives were strongly associated with distress. Ecological stress (stress derived from aspects of their neighborhood, such as fear of crime) and stress due to continuing consequences of injury were also related to overall mood and distress. Effects of acute stressors associated with the disaster itself, such as loss or life threat as the hurricane came ashore, were largely explained by secondary financial, marital, filial, and physical stress. Long-term distress associated with loss, injury, terror, or other aspects of the disaster may be caused

Table 7–2   Consequences of Disaster That Increase Distress

- Injury (being injured oneself)
- Witnessing injury or death of others (horror)
- Life threat (terror)
- Financial loss/damage
- Separation/relocation
- Disruption of the environment
- Bereavement

by secondary stressors that persist long beyond the disaster itself (Norris & Uhl, 1993).

This conclusion is consistent with research by Erikson (1976) who suggested that many of the symptoms of disaster survivors arise from the destruction of the community and loss of a sense of community and belonging. Disorientation and "lack of connection" are common symptoms among disaster survivors when the community has been torn. Older people may emphasize the loss of items that symbolize their lifetimes—a tree or a garden, for example. Children sometimes take their cues from their parents (Crawshaw, 1963) and respond to their parents' fear or lack of it. When they are exposed directly to environmental disruption, they react strongly to senses of death and mutilation (Newman, 1976). They may also regress to earlier stages of behavior.

CHILDREN AND DISASTERS

As you might imagine, the difficulties in studying disasters are multiplied several fold when trying to study children. In addition to problems of locating and sampling from among dislocated victims and of dealing with possible preexisting personality or mental health conditions, and the like, only a few standardized questionnaires or inventories for use with traumatized children are available, and frequent reliance on parents or other adults to report children's feelings and reactions can lead to error as well (Earls et al., 1988; Green & Fidell, 1991; McFarlane, 1987). In spite of these problems, and because of the importance of understanding how children respond to disasters, some research has been done.

In general, this research suggests that children respond to disasters much the same way as do adults (Garmezy & Rutter, 1985), although in some cases they appear to recover more rapidly (e.g., Green et al., 1994). A study of victims of a wildfire in California indicated that children who lived in homes that were burned (and either destroyed or seriously damaged) reported more evidence of PTSD, including more thoughts and dreams about the fire and more attempts to avoid reminders of the fire (Jones, Ribbe, & Cunningham, 1994). This is consistent with other studies (Aptekar & Boore, 1990; Maida et al., 1989; Shannon et al., 1994; Vogel & Vernberg, 1993). Specific fears related to the nature of the disaster (e.g., high winds if the child was exposed to a tornado), depression, anxiety, and PTSD have been found in child victims of several disasters (Vogel & Vernberg, 1993). However, evidence across several studies suggests that effects on children tend to be mild and may not last very long (Belter et al., 1991; Bromet, Hough, & Connell, 1984; Handford et al., 1986; McFarlane et al., 1987; Sullivan et al., 1991). Denial, projection, and other coping were associated with less distress among children within two months of a fatal lightning strike that they witnessed (Dollinger & Cramer, 1990).

Trait measures of anxiety and emotional reactivity during a severe hurricane were more strongly related to distress three months after the storm (Lonigan et al., 1994). In some cases more severe or longer lasting consequences have been seen but these usually occur after particularly savage disasters (e.g., Yule & Williams, 1990). For example, Terr (1979, 1983) studied child victims of a mass kidnapping in Chowchilla, California, in 1976. Twenty-six children, ages 5 to 14, were kidnapped in their school bus and were held for 27 hours; some of this time was spent in a buried truck trailer. During the year after the kidnapping, nearly all of the children were interviewed and all of them were found to be experiencing some symptoms of stress. Most also experienced intrusive thoughts and dreams, and some evidence of perceptual distortions, fantasies, and anxiety was found (Terr, 1979). A follow-up two to five years after the kidnapping showed that many symptoms were still experienced and that most continued to show signs of distress (Terr, 1983).

AGE AND DISASTER RESPONSE

The fact that kids suffer from disasters is not really surprising, but is of interest nonetheless. More surprisingly, age of children does not seem to have much effect on responses to disasters. While some symptoms may be more likely among younger and older victims, the effect of age on severity of distress depends on the symptom or situation being sampled (Vogel & Vernberg, 1993). At older ages, research has been similarly difficult to interpret. A number of studies indicate that older people are likely to suffer distress after disasters, and in some cases have suggested that worries and concerns may differ from those of younger victims (e.g., Ollendick & Hoffman, 1982). However, comparisons of older and younger victims generally show comparable severity of distress or that older victims are *less* upset and stressed (e.g., Bell, Kara, & Batterson, 1978; Bolin & Klenow, 1982; Huerta & Horton, 1978). Failure to find reliable differences in distress, coupled with findings suggesting that older and younger victims use similar types of coping, suggests that distress following disasters is similar among most or all age groups (e.g., Craig et al., 1992). However, some studies divide victims into three rather than two groups (young/middle/older age, rather than just younger and older) and have found that middle-age flood victims are more likely to exhibit distress than the younger or the older groups (e.g., Gleser et al., 1981). Other studies have found the same curvilinear effect, with middle-age victims showing the most severe effects of disasters (Price, 1978; Shore et al., 1986).

A recent analysis and study by Thompson, Norris, and Hanacek (1993) may help explain these effects. There are several ways to look at the differences in how people of different ages might respond to disasters. For example, Thompson and her colleagues suggest that older victims are likely to receive the greatest *exposure* to disasters or their effects; they are more likely to be injured, less likely to evacuate, and so on (e.g., Bolin & Klenow, 1982). Alternatively, one could argue that older victims have *fewer resources* with which to cope. Either would lead one to predict that older people would show more distress. A third way to think of this, however, would favor the hypothesis that younger people are more adversely affected: If coping *efficacy* and scope of one's coping increases with age, older victims should be able to cope more efficiently, negating and reversing any advantage associated with resources. Finally, if one considers burden, or the extent to which people are in caregiving or provider roles (and assuming that burden makes them more vulnerable to disasters and disruption), our predictions would be more in line with findings suggesting that middle-age people (who are taking care of kids and possibly, their parents) would be most affected.

These four kinds of predictions were systematically evaluated in a study of 831 adults from four areas affected by Hurricane Hugo but varying in severity of storm impact (Thompson et al., 1993; see Figure 7–6). The effect of age on distress was studied 12, 18, and 24 months after the storm. Findings of the study indicated that a number of exposure variables (variables that increased or decreased how much people were affected) were related to post-disaster distress. Injury, life threat, financial loss, personal loss, and scope of exposure all had effects on distress, and age interacted with these variables, indicating that the effects of exposure were greatest among middle-age victims. These findings led the investigators to conclude that, regardless of age, the disaster had a substantial impact on mood and mental health. How-

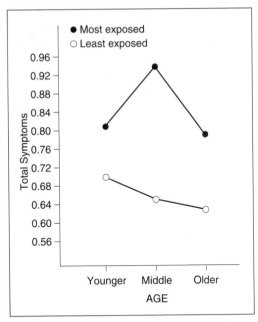

Figure 7–6 Overall symptom levels exhibited by younger, middle-aged, and older adults for those least and most exposed to impact of Hurricane Hugo

ever, the burden hypothesis, positing a more profound impact of disaster on middle-age caregivers, was supported by the finding that the stressor effects of each exposure variable were greatest among this middle-age group (Thompson et al., 1993).

ENVIRONMENTAL THEORIES AND DISASTERS

As we noted earlier, stress formulations as well as other theories or approaches to the study of environmental events can be used to understand the phenomena described in this chapter. Destruction of a community can involve *behavioral constraint*, as options for activity are reduced and behavioral freedom is limited. People may be forced to leave their homes and move to large shelters where behavior must conform to emergency rules. Water and power service may be disrupted, further limiting what people can do, and plans are unavoidably changed by the sudden impact of the event. When our behavior is constrained, we may react negatively to the loss of freedom, feel bad, and act in ways to reestablish our freedom. Continuous constraints on our behavior that cannot be removed may eventually cause us to experience helplessness. Fortunately, once the emergency is past, constraints are reduced and gradually disappear. People return to their homes and normal services are restored. However, for those who are made homeless or that have lost a family member or close friend, constraints and their negative effects may continue. Rebuilding or relocating is necessitated, and choices of activities are further limited by losses and the need to cope with them.

In communities that have lost many people in a disaster, *ecological* perspectives may help to explain the effects of the event. You will recall that *staffing* refers to the number of people in a setting relative to the roles that need to be played. Over- and understaffing, in which too many or too few people are present in the setting, are viewed as negative states that cause problems. Communities are settings, and there are roles that must be played in them. When a large number of the members of the community suddenly die, the community may become understaffed, and those remaining are forced to assume multiple roles. This can cause strain and, coupled with problems caused directly by specific losses, can help to explain the effects of disaster. However, understaffing can also increase cohesiveness among those left, and thus produce positive effects.

A relatively new approach to disaster impact is based on the theory of **conservation of resources (COR)** that was proposed by Hobfoll (1989). The COR proposes that the extent to which people lose important resources (social and psychological resources as well as material resources) or are able to minimize this loss will determine how much stress is experienced. Resources are anything that can help people achieve important goals, and include tangible or material resources, such as money, and social (family roles, work roles) as well as personal (optimism, coping skills) resources (Freedy et al., 1992). Loss or threatened loss of resources should exacerbate stress, while maintaining stable resource bases should minimize stress. Similarly, reestablishing resources after they have been lost should reduce stress, and significant loss in any of these may cause problems. A study of the effects of Hurricane Hugo suggested that resource loss in these domains was associated with distress following the disaster (Freedy et al., 1992). Two to three months after the hurricane, resource loss was strongly related to distress and was the strongest predictor of post-disaster outcomes. The experience of intense resource loss was linked to clinically significant episodes of distress (Freedy et al., 1992). This theory is also applicable to a number of other natural disasters and may prove to be an excellent model for predicting and understanding distress following natural disasters. Figure 7–7 shows how all of these theories can fit the eclectic environment–behavior model we introduced earlier.

SUMMARY

Natural disasters can affect people in a number of ways. They are clearly stressful, limit freedom and behavioral options, deplete resources, and may cause a shortage of people, leading to the breakdown or disruption of a community. People seem capable of coping with disasters, and serious long-term effects of disasters are not extensive. In many ways, these events are similar to disasters caused by human-made parts of the environment. Disasters involving failure of the things we have built, such as dams, bridges, power plants, and mines, also appear to be stressful.

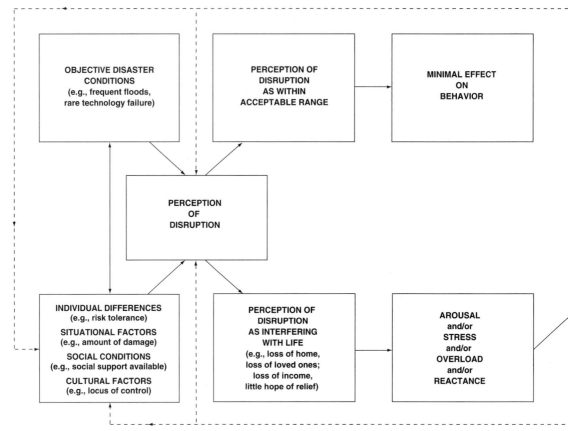

Figure 7–7   Our eclectic model of theoretical perspectives applied to disasters

TECHNOLOGICAL CATASTROPHE

To a large extent our dominance of the natural environment and our adaption to its hazards has been achieved through advances in technology. When we come upon a problem or a threat to continued survival and well-being, we build machines or otherwise fabricate the tools to solve the problem. Improvements in the quality of life, prolongation of life, mastery over disease, and the like are based on a broad technological network we have created. These machines, structures, and other human-created additions to our environment share unparalleled responsibility for supporting our way of life. For the

most part, they accomplish this goal and work well under human control. However, this network occasionally fails, and something goes wrong. As a result, we have blackouts of major cities, transportation accidents, leakage of toxic chemicals from waste dumps, dam failures, and bridge collapses.

Research on human-made disasters shares the same problems as does work on natural disasters. However, many of the characteristics of these catastrophes appear to differ from those of natural disasters, and the effects of being in one may differ as well. We will first consider the characteristics of

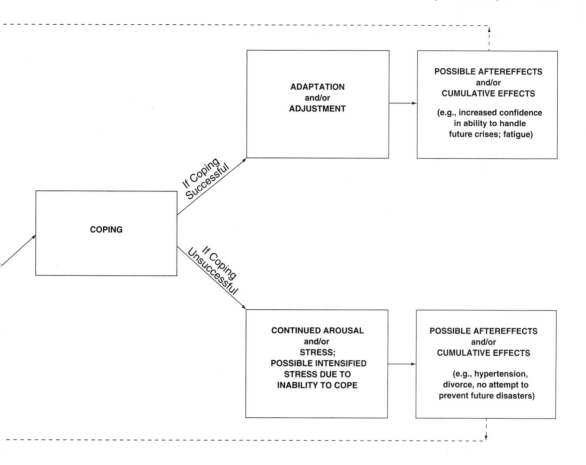

technological catastrophes, comparing them to natural events, and then discuss their effects.

CHARACTERISTICS OF TECHNOLOGICAL CATASTROPHE

What are the differences between these catastrophes and the natural disasters we have already discussed? For one thing, they are *human-made*. They are not the product of natural forces, but rather are caused either by human error or miscalculation, as some part of our extensive technological net fails. The *duration* of technological accidents *is*

variable. They may be acute and very sudden, as in the case of a dam failure or blackout. When a dam fails, the resulting wave of water assumes most of the characteristics of a natural disaster, striking swiftly and continuing on its way. Major power failures can plunge entire cities into darkness in a matter of minutes, but are usually quickly fixed. These technological mishaps are usually brief, and the worst is soon over. However, other technological catastrophes are more chronic and *may not have clear low points.* The discovery of contamination at Love Canal began a chronic period of distress for area residents, as did the nuclear accident at Three Mile Island. In both of these cases, sources of threat (toxic contamination and radioactivity) remained in the area for many years, and required long-term coping with the threats that were posed. For people affected by these events, the worst was not over quickly, nor was it easy to identify the point at which things began to improve. A great deal of uncertainty can accompany such events.

Interestingly, technological catastrophes may be more likely to threaten our feelings of control than are natural disasters. This is somewhat paradoxical, since natural disasters are inherently uncontrollable and we never really expect to be able to control their occurrence. Technological catastrophes, on the other hand, represent the consequences of occasional loss of control over something we normally control quite well. If this loss of control is intermittent, temporary, and not indicative of an entire collapse, why is it so disquieting?

It is possible that because technological catastrophes are *losses* of control we are supposed to have, they shake our confidence in our ability to control events in the future. These events are never *supposed* to happen—technological devices are designed never to fail unpredictably, and to warn us when they are worn out. Thus, nuclear power plants are not supposed to have accidents *ever* and toxic waste dumps are not supposed to leak. But these things do happen, and often appear to occur at random. Instead of saying, "No accidents will happen," we may often find ourselves wondering, "Where will the next explosion occur?" "Which plane will crash?" "Which waste dump will leak?" and so on. While the above analysis is somewhat speculative, it provides some feel for the complexities of people's responses to technological catastrophes. By reducing our sense of control over technology usually taken for granted, these disasters may reduce expectations of control in other areas of our lives. These kinds of events can reduce general

perceptions of control and lead to stress (Davidson, Baum, & Collins, 1982).

While natural disasters often cause a great deal of destruction, human-made catastrophes are often characterized by a *lack of visible destruction*. Natural disasters are more familiar to us, occurring at fairly regular rates around the world in almost predictable ways. The chances are that during some seasons in some regions, tornadoes are likely and that at other times, in other areas, hurricanes are likely. Natural disasters also begin very quickly and, to some extent, can be forecast. They are powerful, among the most threatening stressors we know about, and pass very quickly. Once they pass, rebuilding and recovery can begin, and once these are complete, a sense of closure may be gained.

Technological disasters are less familiar to us, seem to occur less often, but are potentially more widespread. Natural disasters are selective in where they occur; hurricanes tend to be coastal, affecting the eastern and southeastern United States more than the Great Plains, while the converse is true of tornadoes. Technological accidents are not predictable at all: One cannot forecast the breakdown of something that is never supposed to break down in the same way as one can forecast a storm. The onset of technological catastrophes is usually sudden, with little warning. The speed with which these events unfolds often makes them difficult to avoid. As was the case at Buffalo Creek, those in the path of a flood following a dam break have little time to get to safety (see page 249).

Some technological mishaps, such as factory explosions, train accidents, and mine accidents, have a well-defined low point. In these cases, coping with the disaster may be similar to that of natural disaster recovery. However, it appears that some of the most powerful technological disasters may also be those without a clear low point. For example, situations in which individuals believe that they have been exposed to toxic chemicals or

Figure 7–8   Like other technological mishaps, the accident of Three Mile Island has had long-lasting effects.

radiation (e.g., Love Canal and TMI) involve long-term consequences connected with the development of disease many years after exposure. There may be considerable uncertainty about this, and for some technological disasters there is no clear low point from which things will gradually get better. The worst may be over, or it may yet surface. Thus it could be difficult for some persons to return to normal lives after the accident has ended (Figure 7–8).

Another possible difference between natural and human-made disasters is the nature of the post-disaster community response. As we have noted, several studies have found that positive as well as negative effects of disasters are apparent, and that social cohesiveness or feelings of social bonds may be stronger afterwards (e.g., Barton, 1969; Cuthbertson & Nigg, 1987). Following natural disasters, these social changes may provide a crucial resource in aiding recovery from loss and disruption. While these developments do not occur in all areas affected by natural disasters, they are noted often enough

to be considered a possible outcome of a natural disaster. But what about human-made disasters? Are the same changes likely after a human-made accident or hazard has occurred? Anecdotal evidence suggests that controversy and conflict among neighbors may be more likely, leading one to question the post-impact similarities between natural and technological catastrophes.

Cuthbertson and Nigg (1987) studied two human-made disasters to determine whether socially supportive **post-disaster groups** developed in their wake. One involved asbestos contamination at a trailer park, the other spraying of pesticides near residential areas. In both cases, victims included those who were worried about having been exposed to toxic substances (the asbestos and pesticide) and those who thought the exposures were nothing to worry about. Their differences of opinion, common following events involving questionable toxic exposures with long-term, uncertain effects, was the basis for conflict and disagreement among neighbors. Just as at

Three Mile Island, where some are strongly opposed to nuclear energy including the TMI plant while others are strongly in favor, those who were worried and those who were not were in conflict. Cuthbertson and Nigg (1987) found evidence of anger, frustration, resentment, helplessness, defensiveness, and a polarization of attitudes about the hazards, and did not find any evidence of the development of supportive, cohesive groups.

While similar in many ways, technological and natural disasters do appear to be different. These differences may be partially responsible for the greater preponderance of chronic distress among victims of technological accidents that are discussed in the next section.

EFFECTS OF TECHNOLOGICAL DISASTERS

The immediate effects of human-made disasters are often similar to those of natural disasters. This is particularly true when technological catastrophes are like natural ones in duration, suddenness, and so on. Thus, when Fritz and Marks (1954) studied several human-made accidents, including an air disaster in which a plane plunged into a crowd of air show spectators, they found the same types of responses that have been found in studies of natural disasters. Panic did not often occur, and when it did, it was usually seen as an attempt to escape immediate threat. Less than 10 percent of victims interviewed reported that they felt they were "out of control" during the disaster, and while many were confused and disoriented, others behaved in constructive, "rational" ways.

Fewer similarities in response to natural and technological mishaps have been observed when the impact of the technological stressor is longer lasting. When people are told that they have been exposed to toxic chemicals or believe that they have been irradiated, the perceived threat to life and limb may be no less than when a plane is about to crash into a crowd. Clearly, it is less intense, partly because it is longer lasting and usually slower to unfold. Unlike an air crash, where one might have a minute or two at most to decide what to do, people exposed to toxic hazards may have months or years to think about what is happening. Weil and Dunsworth (1958) observed the reactions of townspeople to a coal mine cave-in at Springhill, Nova Scotia. While rescue efforts were in progress, the panic, grief, and anxiety was punctuated by mood swings to euphoria when some miners were rescued, but after rescue efforts had ceased, response appeared to be more suppressed. Long-term response to technological catastrophes has not been studied as much as has acute response to either type of disaster, and more research is needed.

It has been argued that the consequences of technological catastrophes are more complex, and/or longer-lasting than those caused by natural disasters (Baum, 1987; Baum, Fleming, & Davidson, 1983; Gleser, Green, & Winget, 1981). Adler (1943) reported on the effects of a human-caused fire at the Coconut Grove nightclub in Boston. The fire killed 491 patrons of the club and was characterized by great terror. More than half of the survivors developed psychiatric symptoms such as anxiety, guilt, nightmares, and fear a year after the fires. Interestingly, of those who *did not* develop psychiatric problems, 75 percent had lost consciousness during the fire, most remaining unconscious for more than an hour. Of those who *did* exhibit psychological difficulties, only half lost consciousness, mostly for less than an hour. Remaining conscious through the fire appeared to contribute to emotional distress. Unconsciousness, and therefore less exposure to the terror and horror during the fire, was associated with more positive mental health outcomes.

A number of different human-made disasters have been studied, though in many cases there were so few survivors that sample sizes were very small. Leopold and Dillon (1963) reported on a four-year study of victims of a collision between two ships. They found evidence of fairly severe work-related problems and persistent psychiatric distress in more than three-quarters of the survivors. Panic did not occur, but mood disturbances increased over time, and psychosomatic disorders were reported. Henderson and Bostock (1977) interviewed all seven survivors of a shipwreck one or two years afterwards, finding that 5 of the 7 experienced psychological disturbances. Ploeger (1972), in a ten-year study of miners surviving a cave-in, also noted long-term distress. Studies of flooding caused by a dam break at Buffalo Creek have also revealed long-term psychological distress among victims.

One clear consequence of disasters is an increase in the experience of intrusive thoughts and memories. Several studies have linked intrusive thoughts and PTSD with human-made disasters (e.g., Smith et al., 1990), including a recent study of survivors of a ship disaster in which nearly 4 in 10 passengers died (Thompson, Chung, & Rosser, 1994). Intrusive thoughts and neuroticism were elevated among survivors, relative to norms. Many of the emotional effects of disasters are associated with PTSD, and recent research suggests that acute PTSD constitutes or co-occurs with the majority of psychiatric disorders following disaster or trauma (North, Smith, & Spitznagel, 1994). In other words, PTSD was the most frequently seen disorder and when other disorders, such as depression, were present, PTSD was likely to be diagnosed as well. This may suggest that the symptoms and sources of distress in PTSD are fundamental in initial response and coping after disasters and that continued or prolonged PTSD could facilitate the development of depression or other disorders.

Intrusive thoughts or memories may prove to be one of the more "lethal" aspects of disasters for stress and stress-related consequences. Not only do they appear to contribute to chronic stress following disasters (Baum et al., 1993), but they also may affect the likelihood that someone who has been exposed to very stressful events will seek treatment and/or counseling. A study of people who witnessed the murder of a child and wounding of six other students at a suburban elementary school suggests just that (Schwartz & Kowalski, 1992). These witnesses were screened for mental health problems six months after the shooting, and scheduled for a 12-month screening as well. However, almost half did not show up for the second screening, and these people had exhibited more recall of life threat, PTSD symptoms, and depression than those who attended both screening sessions. It is possible that some or all of those not attending the second session were avoiding cues for unwanted memories; similarly, they may avoid use of mental health services because such activity will force them to retrieve unpleasant memories (Schwartz & Kowalski, 1992).

Though the number of studies of human-made disasters has increased and we have learned more and more about them, the Buffalo Creek Flood and the Three Mile Island nuclear accident remain vivid and well-studied examples of these catastrophes. Considering them in some detail will help us understand how these disasters differ from natural ones and how they affect mood and behavior.

The Buffalo Creek Flood

Perhaps the most intensively studied disaster with a human cause is the dam break and flood at Buffalo Creek in West Virginia. On February 26, 1972, a dam constructed by a mining company, which had been dumping coal slag in the creek, gave way and unleashed a wave of millions of gallons of water. The flood washed away houses, automobiles, and everything else in its path, careening off the walls of the valley and killing 125 people. When the wave finally spent its rage and drained into a river at the foot of the valley, it left behind a scene of death and devastation. Five thousand were left homeless, and the valley was disfigured and permanently altered.

The Buffalo Creek flood was clearly due to failure of a human-made device—the dam holding back the creek. As with other technological mishaps, the flood was never supposed to happen. As a result, it was even less predictable than the storms that had swollen the creek behind the dam. And, as we have suggested, this disaster, partly because of its human origins, appears to have had more chronic effects on the victims than ordinary floods or natural disasters. While many of the specific effects are similar to those observed in studies of natural disasters, they seem to have had more lasting consequences.

Research at Buffalo Creek has identified a number of problems occurring as late as two years after the flood. These problems included:

1. *Anxiety*. Fears about the disaster and about the changes in lifestyle that came in its aftermath were common (Gleser, Green, & Winget, 1981; Lifton & Olson, 1976; Titchener & Kapp, 1976).
2. *Withdrawal or numbness*. Almost all researchers at Buffalo Creek noted apathy and blunted emotion after the flood (Erikson, 1976; Lifton & Olson, 1976; Rangell, 1976).
3. *Depression*. Many survivors lost everything they had worked a lifetime for and became sad and subdued (Kilijanek & Drabek, 1979; Titchener & Kapp, 1976).
4. *Stress-related physical symptoms*. Almost all somatic or bodily symptoms, including gastrointestinal distress,

aches and pains, and so on, were increased (Titchener & Kapp, 1976).
5. *Unfocused anger*. Survivors found themselves angry and upset. When disasters are human-made, the rage tends to be worse. This is due, in part, to the fact that although there was a culpable agent, identification of a specific person to blame was difficult (Gleser, Green, & Winget, 1981; Hargreaves, 1980; Lifton & Olson, 1976).
6. *Regression*. Children often regressed to earlier stages of behavior (Newman, 1976; Titchener & Kapp, 1976).
7. *Nightmares*. Dreams about dying in the disaster and about dead relatives occurred frequently. Sleep disturbances were common as well (Gleser, Green, & Winget, 1981; Newman, 1976).

Titchener and Kapp (1976) noted that traumatic neurosis was evident in more than 80 percent of the sample they studied. Anxiety, depression, character and lifestyle changes, and maladjustments and developmental problems in children occurred in more than 90 percent of the cases. Anxiety, grief, despair, sleep disturbances, disorganization, problems with temper control, obsessions and phobias about survival guilt, a sense of loss, and rage were some of the symptoms. Lifton and Olson (1976) listed several characteristics of the flood at Buffalo Creek that intensified the reactions to it: the suddenness, the human-cause factor, the isolation of the area, and the destruction of the community. Survivors were aware of the symptoms. They were surprised at how long they had survived and afraid that recovery was impossible (Lifton & Olson, 1976).

There are many reasons why the Buffalo Creek flood appears to have caused more extensive, longer-lasting psychological distress than do most floods. In fact, follow-up research showed that symptoms of anxiety and depression were still elevated among flood survivors 14 years later (Green et al., 1990a, 1990b). The human cause is but one of these potential reasons, focusing anger on the mining company and affecting the ways in which the disaster was experienced. In addition, the flood was unusually severe, washing away an entire community and causing immense destruction. Recovery was inhibited by delays in removing debris, and it was weeks before homeless survivors were provided with a temporary home. Trailers, brought in to house victims, were not assigned so as to allow friends and family to live together, further disrupting the sense of community that had characterized the valley. All of these factors are likely contributors to the enduring effects of the disaster.

The Three Mile Island Accident

Research at Three Mile Island (TMI) illustrates the kinds of effects that can occur over a long period of time following a technological catastrophe. In March 1979, an accident occurred in Unit 2 at the TMI nuclear power station. Through a number of equipment failures and human errors (see Chapter 11), the core of the reactor was exposed, generating tremendous temperatures. The fuel and equipment inside the reactor was damaged, and by the time the reactor was brought back under control, some 400,000 gallons of radioactive water had collected on the floor of the reactor building. In addition, radioactive gases were released and remained trapped in the concrete containment surrounding the reactor. During the crisis, which lasted several days, there were a number of scares. Some people feared a nuclear explosion, others a meltdown, and still others feared massive radiation releases. Information intended to reduce fears often increased them because it was contradictory or inconsistent with other information that had been released.

Figure 7–9 The presence of toxic chemicals or radiation may lead to evacuation of affected areas. While this response minimizes additional exposure, it also confirms people's fears about how serious the situation is.

An evacuation was advised and this probably contributed to the chaos and fear of the moment (Figure 7–9).

Without a doubt, the accident at TMI had caused stress. During the crisis period there was a good probability that threat appraisal would occur; research suggests that most people living near the plant were threatened and concerned about it (Flynn, 1979; Houts et al., 1980). Immediately after the accident, studies found greater psychological and emotional distress among nearby residents than among people living elsewhere (Bromet, 1980; Dohrenwend et al., 1979; Flynn, 1979; Houts et al., 1980).

Despite the fact that the severe threats associated with the accident disappeared relatively quickly, it does not appear that the kind of recovery that characterizes the aftermath of many disasters followed at TMI. The potential danger of radiation release remained long after the reactor was brought under control. The radioactive gas remained trapped in the containment building for more than a year after the accident. For some area residents the potential for exposure from this source remained a threat, due to occasional leaks of small amounts of the gas. Approximately 15 months after the accident, the gas was released in controlled bursts into the atmosphere around the plant. The radioactive water remained in the reactor building and decontamination of the reactor required many years.

Research on the chronic effects of living near TMI suggests that stress persisted among some area residents up to six years after the accident. Bromet (1980), for example, has reported evidence of emotional distress among young mothers living near TMI a year after the accident and found evidence of more persistent distress among these TMI-area residents as well (Dew et al., 1987). A series of studies has also identified stress effects among some TMI area residents from 15 months after the accident (Baum, Fleming, & Davidson, 1983; Baum et al., 1993; Gatchel, Schaeffer, & Baum, 1985) to more than six years later (e.g., Davidson & Baum, 1986; McKinnon et al., 1989). More recent studies suggest a persistence of symptoms, of sleep-related difficulties, and of arousal related to stress (Davidson & Baum, 1986; Davidson, Fleming, & Baum, 1987). People living near the damaged TMI reactor reported more bothersome symptoms, were more easily awakened at night, and took longer to fall back to sleep than did control subjects (see Table 7–3). Interestingly, urinary norepinephrine levels were higher both while subjects were awake and asleep among TMI area residents, and while

controls showed normal differences between sleeping and waking levels, TMI area subjects did not (Davidson, Fleming, & Baum, 1987). Some differences in immune response were also found, with TMI area residents showing some evidence of fewer numbers of some immune cells and less effective control of latent viruses (McKinnon et al., 1989). Though the intensity of this chronic stress appears to be moderate, the fact that it has persisted for so long is unusual.

These studies were conducted with relatively few subjects, but they examined behavioral and physiological aspects of stress as well as self-report measures (how subjects felt, what they had done recently, etc.). Symptom reporting, task performance, and physiological arousal were measured, the latter by obtaining urine samples from subjects. In general, these studies found that some residents of an area within five miles of the TMI plant reported more emotional and psychological distress, more somatic distress, showed greater stress-related task performance problems, and exhibited higher levels of physiological arousal than did control subjects. Though levels of these variables did not indicate severe stress, they did suggest chronic, moderate-magnitude difficulties. Control subjects lived near an undamaged nuclear plant, a coal power plant, or near no plant at all, and all of them lived more than 80 miles from TMI.

These studies also reported effects of several variables that we have considered as influencing stress. Not all TMI residents seemed to be stressed. Fleming et al. (1982)

Table 7–3   Persistence of Stress at Three Mile Island Three Years After the Accident

Group	Total number of symptoms reported	Being awakened at night (1–7 scale)	Time to fall back asleep (minutes)	Urinary Norepinephrine (mg/ml) Awake	Asleep
TMI	32	3.7	18.0	31.3	35.9
Control	17	2.5	16.3	18.5	13.8

found that TMI area residents who reported having lower amounts of social support exhibited greater evidence of stress than did those who had a great deal of support. Differences along coping style dimensions were also found, as TMI area residents who were more concerned with palliative coping (managing their emotional response) showed fewer stress symptoms than did TMI subjects who were more concerned with taking direct action and manipulating the problem (Collins, Baum, & Singer, 1983). Finally, the continued uncertainty at TMI appears to have suppressed feelings of personal control among TMI area residents, and those who reported the least confidence in their ability to control their surroundings exhibited more symptoms of stress than did residents who were more confident (Davidson, Baum, & Collins, 1982).

The accident at the nuclear power plant at Chernobyl, in the Ukraine in 1986, was considerably larger and more hazardous than the TMI accident. It is generally considered the worst nuclear accident in history and undoubtedly involved much more radiation release and exposure than did TMI. It also affected a larger number of people and appeared to last longer as well. However, research has suggested similarities in acute and more sustained distress around the Chernobyl plant 3, 6, 12, and 20 months after the accident. The MMPI (an instrument containing scales of clinical symptoms) was administered to the Chernobyl workers and a control group of workers from another nuclear power plant (Koscheyev et al., 1993). Workers at the Chernobyl plant showed more symptoms of distress than control subjects and the percentage of workers in the Chernobyl group with at least one elevated clinical scale increased over time, from 18 percent to 33 percent, while the control group had about 10 percent showing at least one elevated clinical scale (Koscheyev et al., 1993).

Clearly, not all technological catastrophes are like these. For a number of reasons, each accident or failure has unique aspects to it. These studies illustrate the potential for acute and chronic consequences from technological catastrophes. In many cases (e.g., power blackouts) the problems are far less serious and consequences more transient.

One more factor probably contributes to the problem at TMI, which has not yet been formally discussed. The accident at TMI involved a toxic substance, radiation, and it is likely that toxic hazards or accidents pose serious threat to perceived health and well-being. Since many modern-day technological mishaps involve toxic substances, it is difficult to know how much this factor contributes to the development of chronic stress. However, the widespread occurrence of toxic hazards and the suggestion that such accidents cause serious problems for victims is cause to consider these hazards in the next section.

SUMMARY

In addition to causing distress, technological catastrophes also involve processes related to the other theoretical orientations discussed in Chapter 4. With few exceptions, technological mishaps lead to behavioral constraint, loss of control, and the problems associated with these states. Evacuation, whether temporary or more permanent, disrupts and limits what we can do. People may find it more difficult to sell their homes if they live near a damaged reactor or hazardous waste site and thus may be limited in their freedom to move. At Buffalo Creek, the destruction of almost everything in the valley also severely limited what people could do, and required almost complete attention to a circumscribed set of recovery options. People could, for example, rebuild their homes and places of business, move to a "safer" nearby area, or

SCAPEGOATS AND DISASTERS

Rumors during and after disasters can develop around who or what was to blame. One pattern is to project blame for disasters onto targets that are not really responsible, rather than to blame those directly involved (Drabek & Quarantelli, 1967). For example, there is a tendency to generalize blame to "big shots" who are in charge of large organizations or who are known to be wealthy and influential. A construction failure in a city is more likely to be blamed on City Hall than on the inspector who worked on that particular project. There is also reluctance to blame the dead following a disaster. A race car driver who lost control of his car and died along with several spectators is later regarded as a hero for keeping his car from colliding with other cars on the track.

Drabek and Quarantelli report that one counterproductive outcome of scapegoating is to focus attention on personalities rather than causes. Another is to delay or completely halt changes in municipal codes, disaster planning, and other direct actions designed to prevent or at least control future disasters.

"call it quits" and leave altogether. Very few realistic options may be available following such an event.

Staffing levels may become important when a community loses many members, but for some technological catastrophes this is not the case. At TMI, the number of people living in the community has not been drastically reduced, while in the Buffalo Creek flood, many people died. Staffing theory will provide useful predictions primarily when losses have occurred.

EFFECTS OF TOXIC EXPOSURE

We know that toxic substances such as radiation, dioxin, and chemical wastes can cause physical health problems, but we are not as well informed about how people respond to known exposure. How do people feel when they believe that they have been exposed to toxic substances and what do they do? Can psychological reactions be understood in terms of beliefs about the toxicity of the substance? What is it about these substances that evokes strong reactions in most of us? Why does exposure to toxic substances as a result of accidents or leaks seem to arouse greater response than toxic exposure that results from air or water pollution?

Consider the case of radiation. Experts argue about what levels of exposure are dangerous. Of course, at very high levels of exposure people die, but the consequences of long-term, low-level exposure are debated. The possibility of being exposed to radiation evokes strong emotional responses in many of us, and we tend to view nuclear power plants as more risky than do experts (Brown, 1992; Slovic, 1987; Slovic, Fischhoff, & Lichtenstein, 1981). In part this is due to the dramatic nature of the nuclear accidents that have occurred. The invisible threat posed by radiation and the possibility of being exposed to it without even knowing it add to the threat. Finally, the effects of radiation may take many years before they can be detected. Cancers and birth defects, two possible consequences of exposure to radiation and to many toxic chemicals, take years to develop or become evident. Long after TMI, Chernobyl, or Love Canal, concerns about possible future exposure may by compounded by worry and fear about effects that have already been set in motion (refer to Figure 7–8, Figure 7–9).

The belief that one has been exposed to toxic substances, regardless of whether one has actually been exposed, seems to be sufficient to cause a stress reaction. In many cases, the extent of real exposure is unclear, but is generally thought to be low. However, some area residents believe that they were exposed to dangerous levels of radiation, and this may have contributed to chronic stress. The lack of early warning signs of toxicants' effects on health, of clear information about whether one was actually exposed to dangerous levels of the toxic substance, and the severity of the long-term consequences of exposure may contribute to uncertainty and distress. The very belief that one has been exposed to toxic substances may cause long-term uncertainty and stress as well as pose a threat to one's health (Baum, 1987). Like many environmental stressors, however, the extent to which this occurs is determined by a number of situational and psychological factors.

Research has considered two different types of toxic exposure, distinguished by where the exposure occurs. Occupational exposure, as the name suggests, occurs at work. Other types of toxic exposure occur at home or in one's neighborhood. Whether the effects of toxic exposure vary as a function of where it occurs is not known. However,

it is clear that exposure to toxic substances in any setting can have substantial effects (Figure 7–10).

OCCUPATIONAL EXPOSURE

One of the sources of toxic exposure that occurs at the worksite is asbestos. Used because of its durability and resistance to heat, asbestos was common in many industries, and it has been estimated that in the past 50 years more than 13 million workers have been exposed to asbestos (Lebovits, Byrne, & Strain, 1986). Some asbestos contamination may be found in schools and old buildings, but for the most part, exposure occurs in occupational settings. When inhaled, asbestos fibers lodge in the lungs where they may be coated by bodily defenses and left there. These particles can then cause damage to the lungs and cause pulmonary diseases, including lung cancer. Asbestos is a particularly risky toxicant to people who also smoke cigarettes. Regardless, the diseases and damage caused by asbestos require long periods of time to develop, so that much harm can be done before an individual recognizes that there is anything wrong.

A study of asbestos workers who were first exposed to asbestos at least 20 years earlier provides some insight into reactions to being exposed to this hazard (Lebovits, Byrne, & Strain, 1986). Most had not been aware of the dangers of asbestos when they started working with it, though they had learned of the risks many years earlier than a control group of people who did not work with asbestos. Asbestos workers were also very aware of the consequences of asbestos: Nearly 80 percent of them had known four or more co-workers who had developed asbestos-related illnesses (less than 10 percent of the control subjects knew anyone with such disease). Consequently, asbestos workers reported greater perceived risk of developing cancer and heart disease than did

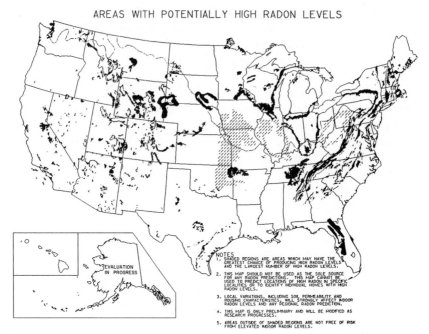

Figure 7–10 Radon, particularly in homes, has emerged as a widespread and serious problem. Occurring naturally, radon is radioactive and thus shares characteristics of many types of hazards.

control subjects (Lebovits, Byrne, & Strain, 1986).

Interestingly, the sample of asbestos workers did not exhibit any more depression, anxiety, or other mental health problems than did control subjects, used mental health services infrequently, and reported comparable perceptions of perceived control as did control group subjects. The asbestos workers also reported that they had not taken preventive precautions, such as wearing masks, visiting their doctor, and so on. A third of them continued to smoke even though they were aware of the special risks of doing so. Apparently denying the risks associated with their occupation and behavior, these workers showed little evidence of distress (Lebovits, Byrne, & Strain, 1986).

Another type of poisoning that often occurs on the job comes from lead exposure. Low-level lead exposure affects the central

nervous system and has been associated with anxiety, neuropsychological deficits, and nervous system disorders (e.g., Browder, Joselow, & Louria, 1973; Grandjean, Arnvig, & Beckmann, 1978; Spivey et al., 1979). A more recent study by Bromet, Ryan, and Parkinson (1986) found few differences in neuropsychological test scores between a sample of lead-exposed workers and a group of nonexposed control subjects, though they did find that exposed workers were more likely to report conflict in interpersonal relationships. This latter finding is consistent with other findings suggesting that lead poisoning may increase aggression and hostility (Spivey et al., 1979).

Sick Building Syndrome

A number of developments in several different fields are also relevant here. For example, studies of "sick building syndrome" suggest complex interactions of toxic and behavioral variables that can cause a variety of problems. Actually, there are two distinct syndromes to consider: *building-related illness*, which involves diagnosable illnesses linked to toxic exposure or some other aspect of an indoor environment, and *sick building syndrome*, which involves symptoms and discomfort but no clear disease (Woods, 1988). In the latter case, several characteristics of the syndrome are evident and suggest psychological or exposure-based origins. For example, symptom distress often diminishes over weekends or after work, and symptoms could be the result of environmental conditions (e.g., headache, eye and nose irritation), stress (lethargy and fatigue), or both (Burge et al., 1987). These reactions can be widespread (up to 80 percent of building occupants have been shown to experience sick building symptoms; Burge et al., 1987) and can be debilitating for those affected.

Causes of these syndromes vary, but are often related to ventilation systems, heating systems, and building design. The prevalence of sick building syndrome is higher in air-conditioned office buildings than in naturally ventilated buildings (Mendell & Smith, 1990) and symptoms are often attributed to poor air quality (Hedge, 1984). However, these explanations frequently fail to explain symptoms. Investigations of many "sick" buildings have not found that indoor air pollutants or air quality cause these symptoms (Hedge, Mitchell, & McCarthy, 1993). Others have proposed psychological causes and discussed mass hysteria or mass psychogenic illness explanations for these symptoms (e.g., Colligan & Murphy, 1979). Studies have suggested that these syndromes reflect preexisting or underlying psychological disturbances, stress, behavioral contagion, or problems at work (Brodsky, 1983; Colligan & Murphy, 1979; Stahl & Lebedun, 1974). However, other studies have not found predicted relationships between personality and

susceptibility to behavioral contagion or between distress and complaints associated with sick building syndrome (e.g., Bauer et al., 1992; Eysenck, 1975). Evidence points to the conclusion that many, if not most, cases of building-related illness or sick building syndrome are caused by real exposure to environmental contaminants (Hodgson & Morey, 1989; Lyles et al., 1991). Smoking, stress, and other behavioral factors appear to play a role in the intensity of symptoms and reporting of discomfort, but the likelihood that these are purely psychological in nature seems small.

Researchers have compiled an impressive list of symptoms of general malaise that have been linked to "sick" buildings. These include eye, nose, and throat irritation (dryness, pain, hoarseness); skin irritation (itching, dry skin; pain); somatic symptoms (headache, nausea, sleepiness, fatigue); nonspecific allergic reactions (runny eyes, nasal congestion, asthma-like symptoms); and complaints about sensory changes (bad odors, bad taste; see Hedge, Erickson, & Rubin, 1994). Correlational studies of office workers in many office buildings suggest that gender, job stress, and use of video display terminals (VDTs) were associated with sick building syndrome complaints (Burge et al., 1987). Other studies have found relationships between symptoms and factors such as air temperature (hotter was associated with more symptoms), allergy history, hours worked each day or week, photocopying, and job satisfaction (less satisfaction was associated with more symptoms; see Hedge, Mitchell, & McCarthy, 1993). While some studies do not find these relationships, others have suggested that job stress or use of VDTs alone is enough to cause some of the symptoms reported as sick building syndrome (e.g., Frese, 1985; Knave et al., 1985; Smith, Cohen, & Stammerjohn, 1981).

Consistencies in findings from studies of sick building syndrome have led to an

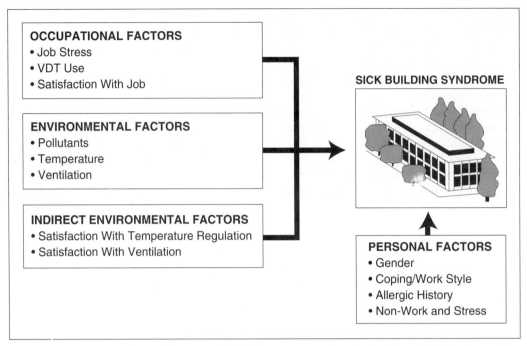

Figure 7–11   A model of factors that cause sick building symptoms; these factors interact to determine workers' experiences and distress.
After Hedge et al., 1989.

eclectic model based on several interacting factors (see Figure 7–11). A recent study of 18 office buildings (Hedge, Mitchell, & McCarthy, 1993) as well as a study of 46 office buildings in the United Kingdom (Hedge et al., 1989) provide support for multifactorial causes of symptoms and suggest that job stress, perceived comfort in the environment, perception of environmental conditions, VDT use, and job satisfaction jointly predict sick building syndrome symptoms.

The development of research in behavioral toxicology is also important in understanding the impact of toxic exposure. Studies of the effects of chemicals on development of organisms (teratology) and examination of behavioral effects of chemical exposure (behavioral toxicology) have identified a number of symptoms and syndromes associated with chemical exposure. For example, Spyker

(1975) suggested 11 assessment categories for studying the effects of chemical exposure *in vitro* or after birth (see Table 7–4). In other words, there are at least 11 different kinds of problems that can occur and a variety of symptoms and ages at which they appear. To evaluate the presence and/or extent of the effects of prenatal chemical exposure (e.g., while pregnant, the mother drank alcohol or took drugs that can cause birth defects), one must consider a complex array of physical and behavioral problems.

In addition to these major effects of chemical or toxic exposure, a number of more subtle behavioral effects are associated with intelligence, developmental processes, and maturation. For instance, several studies have indicated that lead "poisoning" or substantial exposure to lead during childhood is associated with poorer school performance

Table 7-4 Assessment Categories in the Evaluation of Teratogenic Effects*

Assessment Category	Illustration	Age of Testing
1. Morphological characteristics	Limb or facial anomalies	Birth to maturity
2. Physical characteristics	Discoloration of the skin; facial swelling	Birth to maturity
3. Maturational landmarks	Preterm birth (neuromuscular and physical immaturity)	Birth
4. Growth	Small birth size; depressed postnatal growth	Birth to maturity
5. Reflexes	Poorly organized sucking; depressed reactions	Birth to maturity
6. Activity levels	Hypo- and hyperactivity; clinical assessment of apathy	Birth to maturity
7. Neuromuscular and sensory motor capacities	Poor hand–eye coordination (swimming in mice)	Postbirth to maturity
8. Sensory and attentional functions	Deficits in visual, auditory, or olfactory functions; numbness	Birth to maturity
9. Learning ability	Alternation and reversal learning deficits in monkeys; low IQ	Postbirth to maturity
10. Autonomic regulation	Depressed response to stress; emotional lability; tremulousness in infants	Birth to maturity
11. Sexual development	Reproductive failure; menstrual irregularities	Maturity

Adapted from Spyker (1975), Fein et al., 1983.

and lower IQ scores (e.g., Byers & Lord, 1943; Needleman et al., 1979; Needleman, Leviton, & Bellinger, 1982). Exposure to chemicals at doses that do not produce symptoms of "poisoning" can still cause problems, and asymptomatic mothers exposed to lead, mercury, or other toxic substances are more likely to deliver infants who experience symptoms of the mother's exposure (Harada, 1977). Further, consequences of maternal exposure may not show up immediately in infants and may appear later in development (Fein et al., 1983).

Research in these newer areas of behavioral investigation in environmental science will produce new and important information about human susceptibility to toxic exposures. The possibility of discovering effects of low-level exposures to toxic substances, even at levels thought to be safe, underscores the importance of this kind of work. As the number and frequency of toxic compounds and sources of contamination increase and change, we must systematically

evaluate the effects of these exposures on both behavioral and biological processes.

NONOCCUPATIONAL HAZARDS

As with studies of workers exposed to hazardous materials, at least partially with their knowledge and "consent," research on toxic exposure in the home and other places suggests that there are a number of consequences of such hazards. The nature of nonoccupational exposure is varied and the dangers many. In addition, people exposed to toxic substances in their homes or neighborhoods appear to show more effects of exposure than do people exposed to hazards at work. For example, Brown and Nixon (1979) studied farmers exposed to polybrominated biphenyls (PBBs) by contaminated feed, and found increased guilt, depressive symptoms, anxiety, and withdrawal. Living near Love Canal and being exposed (or thinking one was exposed) to the toxic waste there appears to have generated fears about developing illnesses while reducing trust in officials responsible for the situation (Gibbs, 1982; Levine, 1982). And, in two studies of two toxic accidents, one involving pesticide exposure and the other toxic smoke from an explosion in a toxic waste facility (Markowitz & Gutterman, 1986), perceived threat to health was associated with psychological distress.

Several studies have zeroed in on the reactions to living near hazardous toxic waste sites. Love Canal is clearly the most infamous, and studies of people affected by the situation there suggest some evidence of long-term distress (Levine, 1982). Problems began when a chemical company dumped thousands of tons of toxic waste in the canal. The same land was later sold, and an elementary school was built on the site. A neighborhood of several thousand people grew up around the canal area. About 20 years later, it was discovered that hazardous waste was leaking from the canal, and in 1978 area residents were alerted by state officials (Levine & Stone, 1986). Toxic vapors were detected in some homes, increased miscarriage rates were discovered, and offers to move some of the affected residents were announced. The resolution of problems dragged on for years, and the extent of consequences of Love Canal remains to be assessed.

We do know that the Love Canal hazards were stressful for area residents. Of those interviewed in a study reported by Levine and Stone (1986), nearly 90 percent viewed the situation as a problem, and the nature of the problems posed ranged from uncertainty and threat to health, to financial and practical concerns. Residents felt that their health had worsened as a result of living near the canal and reported feelings of lost control and helplessness. Though some positive changes were reported, most evidence suggested a long-term state of distress and worry (Levine & Stone, 1986).

This is consistent with studies of other, less well-known toxic waste hazards. Fleming (1985) reported evidence of chronic stress among a group of people living near a toxic waste site rated as one of the ten most hazardous in the country. Symptoms of trauma were also found among the residents, and the data suggested that the uncertainties surrounding exposure to toxic chemicals were causing people to experience stress (Davidson, Fleming, & Baum, 1986). In another study of people who were using water that had been contaminated by a toxic landfill, chronic stress was once more suggested (Gibbs, 1986). Again, worries and uncertainty about health were prominent, and victims reported high levels of depression, anger, and mistrust. Other studies report worry and concern, anxiety, upset, and other symptoms of lasting distress (e.g., Eyles et al., 1993; Gatchel & Newberry, 1991).

A relatively "new" hazard that may have severe consequences is **radon**, a colorless, odorless gas that comes from uranium deposits in the ground. It is a naturally occurring gas, and small exposures are both normal and of little apparent consequence. However, some people's homes have been found to have radon levels far in excess of safe or normal levels, and the health problems that can result from this kind of exposure are extreme. Apparently, radon problems are more widespread than was previously believed, and it has been recommended that everyone test his or her home for radon levels.

Not unexpectedly, people appear to overestimate the risk of radon problems when they do not have dangerous levels in their homes, though when radon is found, risk is underestimated (Sandman, Weinstein, & Klotz, 1987). As with many sources of danger, people's estimates of risk do not correspond to those made by experts nor are they based on readily apparent criteria (Bostrom, Fischhoff, & Morgan, 1992). Weinstein's study involved 650 randomly sampled people living in an area in eastern Pennsylvania where some of the highest levels of radon have been measured, called the Reading Prong. Another 140 subjects were sampled in areas of New Jersey where radon had also been found in substantial amounts. Of those surveyed, most knew what radon was but made errors in reporting of health consequences. Most important, the study showed that people experienced uncertainty about their risk for health problems. Some denied the threats posed, using characteristics of radon to excuse not having their homes tested; since radon does not infiltrate all homes on a given street, it is likely that some homes will have high readings while others will not.

The invisible nature of radon compares to radiation hazards and toxic chemical contamination. Radon does no damage to buildings and can exist for many years without being detected. However, unlike these other hazards, radon is not human-made but rather is a naturally occurring phenomenon. Thus, it is a natural hazard rather than a techno-logical one, though human factors such as siting and insulation of homes can exacerbate problems (in well-insulated homes, radon may get trapped, and levels may increase due to lack of ventilation).

Radon and other toxins that are natural or a by-product of our technology can occur as "silent" hazards for many years. Often, the only way one can detect them is when one starts to experience the symptoms of disease caused by the toxins. However, once people become aware of the possibility of exposure to toxic waste, radiation, radon, and the like, they appear to experience uncertainty, anger, and stress. In many cases, this stress motivates people to take action, either by moving away from the hazard or working to contain it and reduce the threats involved. However, we all live daily with exposure to toxic substances in the air we breathe, and most of us are aware of this fact. Air pollution affords the most widespread possibility of toxic exposure that we know, yet we do not seem to respond to it in the same way as we do to more dramatic toxic hazards.

AIR POLLUTION AND BEHAVIOR

Our discussion of toxic exposure in this chapter and of noise in Chapter 5 should make it clear that toxics and noise can have consequences for mood, behavior, and health whether we are aware of them or not. Because these stressors are present in so many settings so much of the time, they can be considered ambient stressors. The same is true of air pollution: While it may get worse or better with changes in the weather or season, it is always there and affects us whether we are aware of it or not.

Toxic exposure occurs in many contexts and is not always part of newsworthy events such as a Love Canal. Air pollution has become one of the primary environmental problems of the past few decades. Acid rain is a major issue, as is depletion of the ozone layer of the atmosphere—both threats to our health and well-being produced by pollution. We know that we are walking around in air that is filled with toxic particles generated by exhaust gases from automobiles, aerosol spray emissions, and factory discharges, as well as gaseous and solid airborne particles from industrial wastes. Even the smoke from cigarettes, forest fires, and cozy fireplaces in the home can have seriously adverse effects on health. Among the most common pollutants are carbon monoxide, sulfur dioxide, nitrogen dioxide, particulate matter, hydrocarbons, and photochemical pollutants formed from the reaction of other pollutants with light and heat. Fortunately, with increased environmental awareness and responsibility and passage of legislation such as the Clean Air Act, we are well on our way to reducing many types of air pollution. Nevertheless, the air is still being contaminated and will continue to be for many years to come. In this section we will examine some of the available research on air pollution and then examine the health effects, performance effects, and social effects of air pollution.

PERCEPTION OF AIR POLLUTION

Perception of air pollution depends on a number of physical and psychological factors. What do you think of when you hear the term "air pollution"? Probably, you think of two bad things—bad odors and smoglike conditions. Unfortunately, we depend primarily on our sense of smell and on atmospheric visibility to perceive air pollution. We say *unfortunately* because many of the most harmful types of air pollution are not detectable in these ways. Carbon monoxide, for example, is both odorless and colorless. Moreover, airtight homes designed to restrict heat loss may be two or three times more polluted than outside air (e.g., Guenther, 1982).

Perception of air pollution is also likely to be affected by factors such as annoyance. Attitudes toward the source of pollution or the attractiveness of this source may, for example, affect our perception of pollution or how we report it when asked. Winneke and Kastka (1987) found that pollution from a chocolate factory produced less annoyance among nearby residents than did emissions from a brewery, a tar oil refinery, or an insulation plant. It is possible that exposure to odor was perceived as less intense near the chocolate factory. Other studies suggest that perception of pollution or annoyance caused by it do not always correspond to physical levels of pollution. This means that physical levels of pollutants provide only rough estimates of actual exposure or consequences that are "indirect, behavioral impacts of air pollution" (Evans & Jacobs, 1982, p. 117). The problem of separating one's awareness of a pollutant and one's affective and cognitive reactions to it will be discussed again later in this chapter.

To detect particulate pollution, we may, of course, observe dust on our belongings; for some pollutants, eye and respiratory irritation are cues (cf. Barker, 1976). For our purposes, however, we will first examine perception of air pollution through smell and vision, and then look at an alternative means of perception.

Perception of Air Pollution Through Smell

When pollution is detectable through smell, how do we perceive the smell? The answer appears to be chemically, through the **olfactory membrane**. The *olfactory membrane* lies at the top of the nasal passage, just behind the nose. This membrane, which is similar to the basilar membrane in the cochlea, is lined with hair cells. Gaseous chemicals stimulate these cells as they pass by, sending signals to the brain, which interprets the signals as various odors. Several factors determine whether the olfactory membrane detects a specific odor. For one thing, the chemical stimulating the membrane usually has to be heavier than air. Also, sufficient quantities of the chemical have to be present. This is one reason "sniffing" the air helps you detect odors. To the extent that pollutants are capable of stimulating the olfactory membrane, humans can detect air pollution through smell (for reviews of odor detection, see Berglund, Berglund, & Lindvall, 1976; Turk, Johnston, & Moulton, 1974).

Perception of Air Pollution Through Vision

In addition to noticing smells, most of us infer air pollution from smoglike conditions. That is, we use visual perception to determine the presence or absence of pollution. If a scene looks hazy, especially if the haze is brown, we perceive that pollution is considerable. At least two research studies have suggested that visibility is the primary cue that average citizens use to detect air pollution (Crowe, 1968; Hummel, Levitt, & Loomis, 1973). These researchers asked the open-ended question, "What do you think of when you hear the term 'air pollution'?" There was a strong tendency for respondents to specify effects of pollution, such as smoke or smog, rather than to specify causes, such as factories or automobiles (see Table 7–5).

Other Means of Detection

As stated at the beginning of this section, really harmful pollution is often not detectable by its smell or visibility. What, then, can be used to perceive the presence of pollution? Although sophisticated chemical detection equipment is one possibility, much simpler means are available to everyone. We might turn to pollution experts to find out what to use. According to Hummel, Loomis, and Hebert (1975), experts use automobile concentration as the primary cue in detecting pollution. Since automobiles account for about 50 percent of urban pollution, this certainly makes sense. Hummel and colleagues (1975) found that experts base their judgments of pollution far more on the concentration of automobiles than do nonexperts, and nonexperts tend to use visibility as a cue more than experts do. Other cues useful in detecting air pollution include the absence of rain (rain cleanses the air), the presence of tall buildings (which block winds), and the presence of stop-and-go traffic as opposed to freeway traffic (idling and accelerating automobiles produce more pollution than automobiles moving at a constant speed; see Figure 7–12). Why not instruct the public in the use of such cues as a means of detecting pollution that otherwise would go unnoticed? Hummel (1977) presents evidence that such instruction is indeed possible.

Other Factors Affecting Perception of Pollution

In concluding our discussion of perception of air pollution, we should note that our

Table 7–5 Classification of Typical Definitions of Air Pollution*

Component of Definition	Percentage of Respondents Using Each Component	
	Urban Sample	Student Sample
Specific manifestation (smoke, haze)	43	14
Causative source (cars, industry)	22	43
Effects (health or property damage)	18	9
Combination (two or more of the above)	17	34

Note that causes are specified less than half the time.
From Hummel, Levitt, & Loomis, 1973.

Figure 7–12 People's perceptions of air pollution depend on many cues, particularly when the pollution is not visible. How many cues or contributors to the image of pollution can you find in this picture?

perceptual awareness of pollution may change with our exposure to it and may also depend on other factors (see also Evans & Jacobs, 1981). For example, lower-socioeconomic status individuals tend to be less aware of air pollution than other groups (Swan, 1970). Moreover, time of day and the particular season also make a difference (Barker, 1976). Interestingly, we tend to think "the other guy" has more pollution than we do. That is, we think our own immediate geographic area is less polluted than adjacent areas (DeGroot, 1967; Rankin, 1969).

Stressful life events, or having experienced a good deal of recent stress, appears to be related to perceptions of pollution as well (Jacobs et al., 1984). In addition, anxiety appears to be related to how we perceive air pollution (Navarro, Simpson-Housley, & DeMan, 1987). Because anxiety is characterized by perception of the environment as more threatening or harmful, it should not be surprising that anxiety is linked to perception of pollution; but this anxiety can also lead people to take more positive action to reduce pollution (Navarro et al., 1987). Whether or not one changes his or her behavior to protect him- or herself from the effects of pollution appears to depend on beliefs about nature and dangers of air pollution and other health beliefs (Skow et al., 1991).

Does prior exposure to air pollution decrease or increase our awareness of it? Unfortunately, the evidence is mixed on this question. For example, Wohlwill (1974) compared two groups of people in one location: those who had moved there from a highly polluted region, and those who had moved there from a relatively unpolluted area. The current location was considered more polluted by those from the unpolluted area than by those from the highly polluted area; this suggests that the two groups were using different adaptation levels in making their assessments. In essence, these findings

suggest that the more people were familiar with pollution, the less they were bothered by it (see also Evans, Jacobs, & Frager, 1979). Data from Lipsey (1977) and Medalia (1964) support the opposite position: The more people encounter pollution, the more concerned they become about it. For example, Medalia (1964) found that the longer people had lived near a malodorous paper mill, the more aware they were of its pollution. Whether we actually adapt perceptually to the presence of air pollution or become more sensitive to it with exposure, then, is unclear. As we will discuss in the next two sections, however, there is some evidence that we adapt physiologically and behaviorally to air pollution.

AIR POLLUTION AND HEALTH

The hazardous effects of air pollution on health are becoming well known (see Table 7–6). From time to time, very high concentrations of pollutants have been known to increase the death rate for urban areas, as in the December 1952 disaster in London, in which 3,500 deaths were attributed to excessive levels of sulfur dioxide (Goldsmith, 1968). Such disasters, however, are rare. More worrisome are adverse health effects of high concentrations of pollutants that occur more frequently (Bullinger, 1989; Coffin & Stokinger, 1977; Evans & Jacobs, 1982; Goldsmith & Friberg, 1977; National Academy of Sciences, 1977; Rose & Rose, 1971). As early as the 1970s in the United States, for example, 140,000 deaths were attributable to pollution each year (Mendelsohn & Orcutt, 1979) and the annual cost of air pollution in the United States was estimated at $16.1 billion in 1973 already, when the dollar had comparatively more purchasing power (Lave & Seskin, 1973).

Carbon monoxide (CO), the most common pollutant, prevents body tissues (including those of the brain and heart)

Table 7–6   What You Can't See in the Air Can Hurt You: The Major Components of Air Pollution Have a Variety of Health Effects*

Respiratory symptoms: *Ozone,* formed in sunlight when nitrogen oxides and hydrocarbons combine, aggravates respiratory problems by damaging epithelial cells in the trachea.

Skin problems: *Arsenic,* produced by furnaces, can cause skin cancer. Depletion of the ozone layer of the atmosphere may also contribute to skin cancer.

Nervous system diseases: *Arsenic* and *lead* can disrupt development in children or cause central nervous system problems.

Liver: *Lead* can cause liver disease.

Reproductive difficulties: *Cadmium* can retard development of the fetus.

Eyes: *Hydrogen chloride* causes irritation; *carbon monoxide* and *ozone* affect eye–hand coordination.

Heart: *Carbon monoxide* can reduce blood's ability to carry oxygen and cause symptoms of heart disease.

Lungs: Almost all *particulates* and metals accumulate in lungs and can contribute to cancer.

Based on Newsweek, *29 August 1988, p. 47.*

from receiving adequate oxygen, a condition known as *hypoxia*. Its primary sources include motor vehicles, coal and oil furnaces, and steel mills. Prolonged exposure to heavy concentrations of CO can lead to very serious health problems, including visual and hearing impairment, epilepsy, headache, symptoms of heart disease, fatigue, memory disturbance and even retardation and psychotic symptoms. **Particulates**, such as those containing mercury, lead, or asbestos from industrial sources, leaded gasoline, and so on, can cause respiratory problems, cancer, anemia, and neural problems, among other things. **Photochemical smog** can cause eye irritation, respiratory problems, cardiovascular distress, and possibly cancer. **Oxides of nitrogen and sulfur**, also produced by cars, trucks, and furnaces, impair respiratory function and may lower resistance to disease. Finally, furnaces, smelters, wood stoves, dry-cleaning plants, and petroleum refineries produce arsenic, benzene, cadmium, and hydrocarbons, all of which can cause irritation or illness. For most pollutants, the elderly and the ill are the most likely victims. Physicians have identified an **air pollution syndrome (APS)** caused by combinations of pollutants and characterized by headache, fatigue, insomnia, irritability, depres-

sion, burning of the eyes, back pain, impaired judgment, and gastrointestinal problems (cf. Hart, 1970; LaVerne, 1970). Indeed, the list of ailments aggravated, if not caused, by air pollution seems endless. Some experts believe the majority of human cancer is related to some form of pollution—including air and water pollution and food contamination—and environmental exposure to carcinogens remains a key component of theories of cancer development.

Some research has considered behavioral and mental health consequences of air pollution (e.g., Shusterman, 1992). Data suggest, for example, that people are less likely to engage in outdoor recreational activities when air quality is poor, but these effects are not as clear as one would expect, partly because subgroups of people were not considered. Evans, Jacobs, and Frager (1982) reported that people who exhibited more internal locus of control and who were newly arrived from low-pollution areas more clearly reduced outdoor activities during periods when air quality was poor. Data suggest that air pollution can increase hostility and aggression and reduce the likelihood that people will help each other (Cunningham, 1979; Jones & Bogat, 1978). Finally, there is some evidence that psychological disturbance can follow exposure to air pollution. Symptoms of depression, irritation, and anxiety have been observed after indoor air pollution exposure (e.g., Weiss, 1983), and epidemiological studies have revealed correlations between air pollution levels and psychiatric hospital admissions (Briere, Downes, & Spensley, 1983; Strahilevitz, Strahilevitz, & Miller, 1979; see Figure 7–13). Perceptions of smog were related to symptoms of depression in a survey of randomly sampled residents of Los Angeles (Jacobs et al., 1984). Rotton and Frey (1984) found evidence of increased emergency calls for psychiatric problems when air pollution levels were high, and Evans et al. (1987) found that poor air quality increased the likelihood of distress following major life stressors.

Recall that having experienced stressful life events was related to perceptions of pollution. The more "stressed" people are, the more likely they are to be irritated by pollution. Of concern, then, is whether stress affects how people are affected by air pollution. Are people who have experienced other stressful events (like moving, starting school, or separation from home and family), more likely to show negative effects of air pollution? A study of 500 Los Angeles residents over a three-year period found that having experienced stressful life events was related to more symptoms of emotional distress and mental health problems, and interacted with perceived pollution levels to predict distress (Evans et al., 1987). As can be seen in Figure 7–14, the highest levels of distress were observed among people experiencing stressful life events at medium levels of pollution. These findings suggest that air pollution has similar effects as other stressors when experienced in combination with other problems, and that people who are experiencing stress are more vulnerable to effects of air pollution.

Figure 7–13 Exposure to air pollutants, such as carbon monoxide, oxides of nitrogen, oxides of sulfur, particulates, and photochemical smog, can lead to many adverse health effects including cardiovascular problems, visual and hearing impairment, epilepsy, memory disturbances, and even retardation and psychotic symptoms. Pollution also affects performance and social behavior.

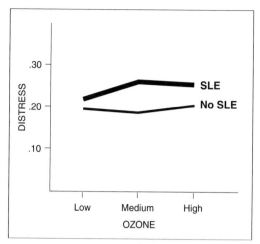

Figure 7–14 Distress under different levels of ozone exposure for those experiencing other stressful life events (SLE) and those not experiencing other stressful life events (No SLE)

Interestingly, there is some evidence that we can adapt physiologically to some pollutants, including photochemical smog (Hackney et al., 1977) and sulfur dioxide (Dubos, 1965). However, the extent of such reduced physiological reactivity is unknown (see also Evans & Jacobs, 1982), and there are certainly limits to the extent to which any organism can adapt to changes in the chemical environment.

AIR POLLUTION AND PERFORMANCE

Most available research on pollution and performance involves studies of carbon monoxide (CO), which results from the incomplete burning of substances containing carbon (see Evans & Jacobs, 1981; National Academy of Sciences, 1977, for reviews). Though some studies suggest that CO exposure has relatively mild effects on performance, others have found that concentrations of CO at 25 to 125 parts per million (ppm) are typical on freeways at rush hour. In one study, Beard and Wertheim (1967) exposed volunteers to concentrations of CO ranging from 50 ppm

to 250 ppm for various periods of time and asked them to make discrimination judgments about time intervals. It was found that 90 minutes of exposure to CO at 50 ppm significantly impaired performance on the time judgment task. As CO concentration increased, shorter periods of exposure were required for similar levels of impairment. Using rats, these researchers also found that 11 minutes of exposure to 100 ppm adversely affected learning in an operant conditioning situation.

Breisacher (1971) has reviewed research indicating that air pollutants, including CO, also adversely affect human reaction time, manual dexterity, and attention (see also Beard & Grandstaff, 1970; Gliner et al., 1975; O'Donnell et al., 1971; Putz, 1979; Ramsey, 1970; Rummo & Sarlanis, 1974). Such research suggests that air pollution on major traffic arteries may impair driving ability enough to increase the frequency of automobile accidents. This possibility is supported by results of a study by Lewis et al. (1970), in which subjects were exposed to "clean" air or to air drawn 15 inches (38 cm) above ground at a traffic site handling 830 vehicles per hour. Performance decrements occurred in three out of four information-processing tasks for subjects breathing the polluted air (see also Horvath, Dahms, & O'Hanlon, 1971). In sum, carbon monoxide appears to be quite deleterious to performance.

Interestingly, there is at least some evidence that we adapt to air pollution behaviorally. That is, after prolonged exposure, our behavior differs from that of those who have experienced only brief exposure. Evans, Jacobs, and Frager (1979), for example, found that long-term residents of the Los Angeles area tended to deny the threat of pollution, felt they were less vulnerable to its effects, and felt they knew more than they actually did about pollution hazards. Those who were newcomers to the area, however, felt more

DOES CIGARETTE SMOKING POLLUTE THE AIR?

For a number of years we have known that tars and nicotine can have major effects on the health of smokers. There is now some evidence that nonsmokers breathing the air in a room where others are smoking may also suffer ill effects. For example, cigarette smoke has been shown to contain significant quantities of carbon monoxide and probably some degree of DDT and formaldehyde as well. A nonsmoker inhaling the air around a person who is smoking may experience an increase in heart rate, blood pressure, and breathing rate (Luquette, Landiss, & Merki, 1970; Russell, Cole, & Brown, 1973). Further, the 1986 Surgeon General's report on involuntary smoking concludes that **passive smoking** can cause disease, that children of smokers have more respiratory infections than do children of nonsmokers, and that we must act as a society to minimize exposure of children and nonsmoking adults to others' tobacco smoke (Koop, 1986).

Opposition to smoking in public places has been growing for many years, and a number of states have adopted laws prohibiting or restricting smoking in elevators, stores, and some restaurants. A number of antismoking groups, including ASH (Action on Smoking and Health), GASP (Group Against Smokers' Pollution), and SHAME! (Society to Humiliate, Aggravate, Mortify, and Embarrass Smokers) have adopted tactics ranging from mildly to overtly hostile in efforts to discourage smokers from "lighting up" in front of them. THANK YOU FOR NOT SMOKING signs are common, as are such signs as YES, I MIND IF YOU SMOKE, SMOKERS STINK, and KISSING A SMOKER IS LIKE LICKING A DIRTY ASHTRAY. Hostile tactics include plucking cigarettes from smokers' mouths and dunking one's hand in a smoker's water glass with the explanation, "You don't pollute my air, I won't pollute your water!" We need not comment on the behavior that is likely to follow such action except to say that it is likely to be consistent with theories of aggression.

Increasing evidence suggests that so-called passive smoking is bad for our health. Research has certainly confirmed that nonsmokers are disturbed by cigarette smoke. In one study (Bleda & Sandman, 1977), smokers were evaluated negatively by nonsmokers if they smoked in the presence of the nonsmokers. Other research indicates that nonsmokers have increased feelings of irritation, fatigue, and anxiety when exposed to cigarette smoke (Jones, 1978). In another study (Bleda & Bleda, 1978), it was found that persons sitting on a bench in a shopping mall fled faster if a stranger next to them smoked than if he or she refrained from smoking. Interestingly, smoke-induced irritation in nonsmokers may occur primarily when individuals are less involved in tasks at hand, rather than when they are intensely motivated by their activities (Stone, Breidenbach, & Heimstra, 1979). Finally, cigarette smoke may not just lead to feelings of irritation and dislike, but to overt hostility as well. Both feelings of aggression (Jones & Bogat, 1978) and hostile behavior increase in the presence of others' cigarette smoke.

positively about the value of mass transit to reduce pollution and more readily looked for information about pollution. Moreover, those newcomers who were internal in locus of control (i.e., felt they controlled their own destiny) were more likely to avoid outdoor activity on high-smog days. Feeling that one is in control of the situation has also been shown to reduce the effects of malodorous pollution on frustration (Rotton, 1983). In sum, pollution affects performance negatively, but we may develop ways of coping with some of these negative effects.

AIR POLLUTION AND SOCIAL BEHAVIOR

Research has shown that malodorous air pollution influences at least three types of social behavior. First, recreation behavior in particular, and outdoor activity in general, are restricted by pollution (Chapko & Solomon, 1976; Peterson, 1975). Second, Rotton et al. (1978) examined the effects of ammonium sulfide and butyric acid on interpersonal attraction. In one experiment, it was found that ammonium sulfide increased attraction for similar others with whom subjects thought they were interacting. That is, when subjects were exposed to an unpleasant odor, attraction toward others who were also exposed to the odor increased. In a second experiment, however, the same researchers found that subjects who did not expect to interact with others evaluated those others less favorably if exposed to ammonium sulfide or butyric acid than if not exposed. It seems that the unpleasant affective states associated with pollution led to decreased attraction if not shared with others, but to increased attraction when odor exposure was the same for all parties. Malodorous air pollution affects more than just attraction to people. Interestingly, foul odors also reduce liking for paintings and photography (Rotton, 1983).

In another experiment, Rotton et al. (1979) investigated the effects of exposure to ethyl mercaptan and ammonium sulfide on aggression. Using the shock methodology common in aggression research (see page 177), the researchers ostensibly allowed subjects to shock a confederate. In accordance with the research on heat and aggression, it was anticipated that exposure to an extremely unpleasant odor (ethyl mercaptan) would increase aggression, but that exposure to a moderately unpleasant odor (ammonium sulfide) would decrease aggression. Consistent with these predictions, it was found that relative to a no-odor control group, the moderate odor increased aggression. In addition, there was suggestive evidence (though not statistically reliable) that the stronger odor decreased aggression.

Two other studies show that air pollution affects our social behavior and the way we feel about other people. Rotton and Frey (1985) found that complaints about household disturbances, including child abuse, were elevated when ozone levels were high compared to when they were low. Pollution may contribute to such behavior by making us more hostile or depressed, a possibility suggested by a study showing that a combination of high life stress and high air pollution predicts how hostile or depressed people feel (Evans et al., 1987). Regardless of how these effects occur, the research on pollution, malodor, and the sick building syndrome, which was described earlier, suggests complex determination of annoyance and distress (Rotton & White, 1995).

SUMMARY OF AIR POLLUTION EFFECTS ON BEHAVIOR

Air pollution consists mainly of carbon monoxide, photochemical smog, particulates, and oxides of nitrogen and sulfur. We primarily detect pollution through reduced horizon visibility, smell, and eye and respiratory irritation. Unfortunately, some deadly forms of pollution cannot be detected readily using these means. Respiratory and cardiovascular problems are the most notable effects of various pollutants, although a number of other adverse health effects are associated with air pollution. Performance deteriorates upon exposure to pollutants in sufficient quantities, especially carbon monoxide. In addition, malodorous pollutants may either decrease or increase attraction and aggression. Physiological and psychological stress, arousal, perceived control, and adaptation level all seem to have some mediational influence in pollution effects.

CHAPTER SUMMARY

Stressors may be categorized as cataclysmic events, personal stressors, or daily hassles and background stressors. This categorization is based on both the power of the event and the number of people affected. At one extreme, cataclysmic events are potent events that demand a great deal of effort from people trying to cope with them. However, they often pass quickly. Disasters are a primary example of such events. At the other extreme are hassles: minor, transient stressors that by themselves demand little effort to cope with them. However, they are repetitive or constant, and over time may exact a substantial cost. Air pollution is one of these background stressors.

Natural disasters are powerful, destructive events that require a great deal of adaptation. They involve threat to life or loss of property, but are usually brief in duration. Most disaster events last for less than a day, some for only a few minutes. Once the disaster has passed, various means of coping may be directed at recovery and a number of effects may occur. Beneficial effects due to the formation of cohesive groups in the face of adversity have been found when these groups stay together long after the disaster. Though there is some concern for long-range effects of these events, research evidence of this is equivocal and most research suggests only short-lived stress reactions.

Technological catastrophes are similar to natural disasters, but are also different in several ways. They are caused by human actions rather than by natural forces, are not necessarily as destructive, are less predictable, and lack a clear low point, after which recovery may begin. These accidents and disasters seem to have few, if any, positive effects and have longer lasting negative consequences, including stress, negative mood, and uncertainty. One reason for this is that the events are human-caused, providing a better focus for blame than in natural disasters. Another is that technological disasters occur when control is lost over something previously under control (natural disasters are never controllable). A final possibility is that technological catastrophes often also involve toxic substances, and we have seen that the possibility of exposure to toxic substances can cause many long-term problems.

We have also discussed a very prevalent but often ignored source of toxic exposure, air pollution. Air pollutants cause or aggravate a variety of ailments, most notably respiratory and cardiovascular problems. Carbon monoxide in sufficient quantities impairs performance. Malodorous pollutants can increase or decrease aggression and attraction, depending on other factors. However, for the most part, we seem readily able to adapt to the threats and irritations that air pollution poses. In part, this may be due to the fact that air pollution effects occur in combination with other variables, such as weather, temperature, and behavioral goals.

SUGGESTED PROJECTS

1. Interview some people who have lived through severe storms, tornadoes, floods, or earthquakes. Ask them how they felt during and just after the event, how they coped, and what they worried about. Now interview some people who experienced some kind of technological accident. Are there differences in their reports?

2. Talk with homeowners in your area. Have they ever heard of radon? How much do they know about it? How concerned are they about it, and how likely are they to test for it? Is knowledge about radon related to fear of it and likelihood of remedial action?

3. Keep a log for two weeks in which you enter your local air pollution and pollen indexes each day. Also, write down your observation about your and others' apparent mood, behavior, and level of activity. Is pollution related to any of these measures of mood and behavior? If so, are people aware of it? Make sure you do not look at the pollen and pollution measures until just before you go to bed each night, so the knowledge of what these levels are do not affect your mood or how you observe others throughout the day. Could you guess about the pollution or pollen levels from your observations of people's behavior?

Personal Space and Territoriality

INTRODUCTION

PERSONAL SPACE

Functions of Personal Space

Size of Personal Space

Methods of Studying Personal Space

Situational Determinants of Personal Space: Research Evidence

Attraction and Interpersonal Distance

Effect of Other Types of Similarity on Interpersonal Distance

Type of Interaction and Interpersonal Distance

Individual Difference Determinants of Personal Space: Research Evidence

Cultural and Racial Determinants of Personal Space

Gender Differences in Personal Space

Age Differences in Personal Space

Personality Determinants of Spatial Behavior

Physical Determinants of Personal Space

Interpersonal Positioning Effects

Spatial Zones That Facilitate Goal Fulfillment

Optimal Spacing in Learning Environments

Optimal Spacing in Professional Interactions

Optimal Spacing to Facilitate Group Processes

Consequences of Too Much or Too Little Personal Space

Predicting the Effects of Inappropriate Distances

The Consequences of Inappropriate Spacing

Consequences of Personal Space Invasions
The Effects of Being Invaded on Flight Behavior
The Effects of Being Invaded on Arousal
Other Effects of Being Invaded
The Effects of Invading Another's Personal Space

Summary of Personal Space

TERRITORIAL BEHAVIOR

The Origins of Territorial Functioning

Functions of Territoriality

Methods of Studying Territoriality in Humans

Research Evidence of Territorial Behavior
Territorial Behavior Between Groups
Territorial Behavior Within Groups
Territorial Behavior When Alone
Signals of Territoriality: Communicating Territorial Claims
Personalizing Territories

Territory and Aggression

Territory as a Security Blanket: Home Sweet Home

Some Design Implications

CHAPTER SUMMARY

Suggested Projects

KEY TERMS

arousal

behavior constraint

compensatory behaviors

equilibrium

ethological models

field methods

individual difference variables

individual personality traits

internality–externality

interpersonal distance

laboratory methods

overload

personal space

privacy

privacy regulation model

reciprocal response

simulation methods

situational conditions

sociofugal

sociopetal

stress

symbolic barriers

territoriality

territories

INTRODUCTION

To help you get a "feel" for the content of this chapter, imagine you are suddenly whisked off to a faraway land. A land full of seemingly normal people with a strange disregard for the need to maintain a personal space "buffer" around their bodies. In this land, it is not uncommon for a complete stranger to sit down right next to you on an empty bus; to stand right in front of you, knees touching yours, and ask you for directions; or to stand an inch away from you in a swimming pool even though there is nobody else around. If you go to the checkout counter in a department store, rather than spreading out and using the space, people in line pack together tightly, so that you can barely fumble for your checkbook. When you go to the beach, you find that people choose to put their towels right next to yours, restricting your movement and comfort, while the entire beach remains vacant (Figure 8–1).

Before long, you discover another peculiarity about these people. You realize that they have no concept of territoriality or territorial behavior. People move randomly from one dwelling to another and have no place they call

"home." They wander into your home without knocking, and proceed to eat your food, use your toothbrush, and sleep in your bed, before walking out and taking some of your things with them. You go out to a fancy restaurant for a romantic evening, and a complete stranger pulls up a chair and begins sampling your food and conversing with your date. The inhabitants of this land seem not to mind that they have nowhere to call their own, or that at any moment a complete stranger might walk in on whatever they are doing.

What would life be like in such a place? How would you feel, and what would you be able to accomplish in life, if you had to live there? While this "fantasy" may seem extreme, it should make you aware of your need to maintain a portable personal space "bubble" between yourself and others, and of the importance of territorial functioning. In this chapter we will discuss personal space and territoriality, two ways in which people create different types of boundaries to regulate their interactions with others in their environment (cf. Altman, 1975). The importance of such boundaries is probably

*quite evident to you from our description
what life would be like without personal sp.
and territoriality.*

Thus far in this book we have examined h
we perceive the environment and how vari
aspects of it impact on us. As we move tow
an examination of the "built" environment in
later chapters of this book, this chapter and
next mark a transition in which we descr
spatial relationships between humans and th
environment. As we will see, these spatial re
tionships have behavioral implications, des
implications, as well as commonalities with
environment–behavior relationships we h
examined thus far.

    Personal space is defined as a portab.u,
invisible boundary surrounding us, into which
others may not trespass. It regulates how
closely we interact with others, moves with us,
and expands and contracts according to the
situation in which we find ourselves. In contrast, **territories** are relatively stationary areas
often with visible boundaries, that regulate
who will interact. The person is always at the
center of his or her personal space—it is always with them. On the other hand, territories,
which often center around the home, can be
left behind. While territoriality is more of a
group-based process, personal space is more
of an individual-level process. We will provide a

between ourselves and others stipul
it is necessary to avoid overstim
cording to this notion (Scott, 1
a proximity to others caus
barded with too many so
uli (e.g., facial detai
alternative formul
tation, assumes
space to avo
with too
arousa
pers

Figure 8–1 In addition to constant spacing between various groups, members of individual groups
maintain relatively constant personal space from
each other.

more comprehensive discussion of personal
space and territorial behavior in this chapter,
and will elaborate on the role each plays in our
lives. For now, it is only important to note some
of the similarities and differences between personal space and territoriality which we have described above.

PERSONAL SPACE

FUNCTIONS OF PERSONAL SPACE

The term "personal space" was coined by
Katz (1937). The concept is not unique to
psychology, and also has roots in biology
(Hediger, 1950), anthropology (Hall, 1968),
and architecture (Sommer, 1959). Both popular and scientific interest in personal space
have intensified greatly during the last two

decades. In fact, over 850 published experiments have been done in this area since 1959.

    What is the function of the personal
space bubble we maintain around ourselves?
A number of conceptual explanations have
been suggested, some of which correspond
to the theoretical formulations we reviewed
in Chapter 4. Briefly, an **overload** interpretation of why we maintain personal space

...ates that
...lation. Ac-
...993), too close
...es us to be bom-
...cial or physical stim-
...s, olfactory cues). An
...tion, the **stress** interpre-
...that we maintain personal
...d various stressors associated
...close a proximity. Further, the
...conceptualization suggests that when
...onal space is inadequate, people experi-
...ce arousal. When this occurs, we attempt
to understand why we are aroused (e.g., is it
because someone we love is close to us, or because someone we fear is close?), and the type
of explanation we come up with determines
how we respond to inadequate personal space.
A fourth conceptual perspective, the **behavior constraint** approach, suggests that personal space is maintained to prevent our
behavioral freedom from being taken away
because others are too close to us.

In addition to these theoretical approaches, which we have discussed in detail
earlier in this book, other explanations have
been suggested for why we maintain personal space. One, proposed by anthropologist E. T. Hall (1963, 1966), conceptualizes
personal space as a form of *nonverbal communication*. According to Hall, the distance between individuals determines the quality and
quantity of stimulation that is exchanged
(e.g., tactile communication occurs only at
close proximity). Distance also communicates
information about the type of relationship
between individuals (e.g., whether it is intimate or nonintimate), and about the type of
activities that can be engaged in (e.g., love-
making cannot occur between individuals
who are far apart).

Another theory, proposed by Altman
(1975), views personal space (and territoriality as well) as a boundary regulation mechanism to achieve desired levels of personal and
group **privacy**. Privacy is an interpersonal
boundary process by which people regulate

interactions with others. Through variations
in the extent of their personal space, individuals ensure that their desired and achieved
levels of privacy are consistent. When it is
impossible to regulate these boundaries so
that privacy is within desired levels, negative
effects and coping will occur.

Related in some ways are the intimacy–
equilibrium model proposed by Argyle and
Dean (1965) and the comfort model formulated by Aiello (1987). According to these approaches, in any interaction (or relationship)
people have an optimal level of intimacy
they want to maintain (Gibson, Harris, &
Werner, 1993). Lovers aspire to more intimate relations than friends, and so on. Intimacy is a function of personal space *and*
other factors such as eye contact, facial gestures, and the intimacy of the topic under
discussion. If the level of intimacy in an interaction becomes too great (e.g., the people
are interacting about too intimate a topic and
too much eye contact is being maintained),
equilibrium will be restored through **compensatory behaviors** in some other modality (e.g., moving physically farther away). If
the level of intimacy is too small, equilibrium will be restored as well (e.g., by moving closer or maintaining more eye contact).
While nonoptimal levels of intimacy will
typically prompt compensatory behaviors,
Aiello (1987) suggests that these may not result from small deviations from an optimal
level of intimacy, and that really large deviations may cause people to completely lose
interest in the interaction.

A final perspective on personal space is
provided by **ethological models** (cf. Evans
& Howard, 1973). These assume that personal space functions at a cognitive level and
has been selected out by an evolutionary
process to control intraspecies aggression, to
protect against threats to autonomy, and
thereby to reduce stress. We should note,
however, that in contrast to the assumption
of ethological models that personal space
evolved naturally, most researchers (e.g., Alt-

IS PERSONAL SPACE REALLY A BUBBLE?

Researchers, including the authors of this text, have a tendency to liken personal space to a bubble of sorts that surrounds us and fulfills a number of functions. While the bubble analogy gives us a concrete image to visualize and may thereby aid our understanding, if taken too literally, it has some drawbacks that may lead to misunderstanding. First, it has been suggested that the notion of a personal space "bubble" emphasizes the protective function of personal space more than the communicative function (Aiello, 1987). Second, one might begin to think that if personal space is analogous to a bubble, it is the same size for all individuals and in all situations, and this is *not* the case. As we will see in this chapter, people have varying spatial zones, and the amount of space we desire between ourselves and others expands and contracts depending on the situation. Personal space is really an *interpersonal distance continuum.*

In addition to the bubble analogy, there are also problems with the term "personal space." One could easily get the idea that since it is "personal," personal space is somehow attached to an individual in all situations. This is also not true; personal space has meaning only with respect to another individual, and does not apply to distance between people and desks, for instance. Also, the label "personal space" may emphasize the idea of *space* and thus suggest that researchers are concerned only with distance. As we will see in this chapter, those studying personal space must also focus on other behaviors, such as body orientation and eye contact, in order to get a complete understanding of spatial behavior (Aiello, 1987; Knowles, 1978). The latter behaviors are interpersonal rather than personal. Overall, the personal, as well as the space, components of the term "personal space" may be misleading.

Due to these possibly misleading aspects of the term "personal space," should we consider replacing it with something else? Some researchers, such as Aiello (1987), have suggested that a term such as **interpersonal distance** might be better to use than personal space. Such a term implies that distance is a continuous dimension in which a variety of behaviors can occur. However, even Aiello admits that the concept is probably too well engraved in our minds—and in the literature— to be readily abandoned!

man, 1975; Cappella & Greene, 1982) would probably argue that it is more a product of learning. However, after it is learned, our spatial behavior seems to be governed unconsciously (i.e., we do not have to "think" about how to position ourselves in different situations).

If all of the conceptual perspectives we have discussed are integrated, personal space may be seen as an interpersonal boundary regulation mechanism which has two primary sets of purposes. First, it has a *protective* function and serves as a buffer against potential emotional and physical threats (e.g., too much stimulation, overarousal leading to stress, insufficient privacy, too much or too little intimacy, physical attacks by others). The second function we have discussed involves *communication* (cf. Hall, 1963, 1968). The distance we maintain from others determines which sensory communication channels (e.g., smell, touch, visual input, verbal input) will be most salient in our interaction. To the extent that we choose distances that transmit intimate or nonintimate sensory cues and that suggest a high or low concern with self-protection, we are communicating information about the quality of our relationship with other persons (i.e., the level of intimacy we desire to have with them).

Size of Personal Space

What determines the size of the personal space we want to maintain between ourselves and others? The distance we maintain must be appropriate to fulfill the two functions of personal space—protection and communication. One determinant of the amount of space necessary to accomplish these functions is the situation (i.e., whom we are with and what we are doing). Certain relationships and activities demand more distance than others for appropriate communication and adequate protection. Situational conditions are not the only determinants of the size of our personal space, however. Some individuals always preserve minimal personal space zones, while others maintain relatively large personal space zones. Individual differences in spatial behavior probably reflect different learning experiences concerning the amount of space necessary to fulfill the protective and communicative functions (cf. Montagu, 1971). Individual differences that affect spatial behavior include gender, race, culture, and personality.

One of the first observational studies of the effect of **situational conditions** and **individual difference variables** on spatial behavior was conducted by E. T. Hall. Hall (1963, 1966) suggested that depending on situational conditions, Americans use one of four personal space zones in their interactions with others. The particular zone that we use depends on situational conditions such as our relationship with the others and the activity we are engaged in. The four zones (which are labeled *intimate distance*, *personal distance*, *social distance*, and *public distance*) vary in terms of the quality and quantity of stimulation that is exchanged (see Table 8–1). Hall's assertions were corroborated in an extensive review of the personal space literature by Altman and Vinsel (1977).

With respect to the effect of individual differences on spatial behavior, Hall observed in cross-cultural investigations that cultures vary widely in terms of spatial behavior, an observation which has been corroborated (Aiello & Thompson, 1980b). Cultural differences were attributed by Hall to different norms regarding the sensory modalities seen as appropriate for communication between people who are interacting. A quotation from Hall (1968) nicely summarizes this finding and suggests how cultural differences in spatial behavior may be the source of considerable miscommunication:

> Americans overseas were confronted with a variety of difficulties because of cultural differences in the handling of space. People stood "too close" during conversations, and when the Americans backed away to a comfortable conversational distance, this was taken to mean that Americans were cold, aloof, withdrawn, and disinterested in the people of the country. It was quite obvious that these apparently inconsequential differences in spatial behavior resulted in significant misunderstanding and intensified culture shock . . . for some Americans overseas (p. 84).

Table 8-1　Types of Interpersonal Relationships, Activities, and Sensory Qualities
Characteristic of Hall's Spatial Zones*

	Appropriate Relationships and Activities	*Sensory Qualities*
Intimate distance (0 to 1½ feet)	Intimate contacts (e.g., making love, comforting) and physical sports (e.g., wrestling)	Intense awareness of sensory inputs (e.g., smell, radiant heat) from other person; touch overtakes vocalization as primary mode of communication.
Personal Distance (1½ to 4 feet)	Contacts between close friends, as well as everyday interactions with acquaintances	Less awareness of sensory inputs than intimate distance; vision is normal and provides detailed feedback; verbal channels account for more communication than touch.
Social distance (4 to 12 feet)	Impersonal and businesslike contacts	Sensory inputs minimal; information provided by visual channels less detailed than in personal distance; normal voice level (audible at 20 feet) maintained; touch not possible.
Public distance (more than 12 feet)	Formal contacts between an individual (e.g., actor, politician) and the public	No sensory inputs; no detailed visual input; exaggerated nonverbal behaviors employed to supplement verbal communication, since subtle shades of meaning are lost at this distance.

*Based on Hall, 1963.

METHODS OF STUDYING PERSONAL SPACE

While Hall's studies were primarily observational and qualitative in nature, many *experimentally based* investigations have considered the effect of situational and individual difference variables on personal space. In this research, several different methodologies have been employed. Many of the experimental studies exploring factors that affect personal space have used **laboratory methods**. Some of this work involves real interaction between people. Here, the personal space between subjects is measured as a function of experimental conditions (e.g., degree of mutual attraction). Other laboratory methods include **simulation methods**—techniques in which subjects manipulate the personal space between dolls or symbolic figures, or approach an inanimate object under various experimental conditions. Another set of stud-

ies has used **field methods**. These involve observing and experimenting with interpersonal positioning in naturally occurring situations, as a function of individual difference or situational variables.

Fortunately, many of the important relationships between situational and individual difference variables and the size of personal space have been corroborated using different experimental approaches. While this has occurred with some regularity (Duke & Nowicki, 1972; Knowles, 1980b), in other cases (e.g., Wann & Weaver, 1993) there have been dissimilar findings for studies that used different methods to assess the same spatial relationship. Knowles and Johnson (1974) suggested that although there is sometimes a general association between the various methods used to measure personal space (i.e., they can be considered to be indicators of the same dimension), the level of convergence is only moderate. Others (e.g., Aiello,

1987; Hayduk, 1983, 1985) have suggested that the different measures of personal space are not measuring the same thing. In general, since it appears that laboratory and field methods that involve actual interaction between subjects are better measures of our spatial behavior than simulation techniques (Aiello, 1987; Hayduk, 1983; Love & Aiello, 1980), they should receive preference from investigators both when planning research and in interpreting discrepant results.

Having discussed the methodologies used to study interpersonal distancing behavior, we now shift our focus to some of the findings that have emerged in this research. Our review will deal first with the relationships observed between situational conditions and personal space. Next, we will discuss findings on the effects of individual difference variables on spatial behavior.

SITUATIONAL DETERMINANTS OF PERSONAL SPACE: RESEARCH EVIDENCE

Experimentally based studies have explored the effects of attraction between individuals, of interpersonal similarity on various dimensions (e.g., age, race), and of the context of the interaction (e.g., positive versus negative) on spatial behavior between individuals. Such studies have identified a number of consistent relationships.

Attraction and Interpersonal Distance

How does attraction between people who are interacting affect the size of the interpersonal distance between them? Love songs often lament one lover's longing for physical closeness with a distant other and suggest that the greater the attraction between individuals, the more physically close they wish to be. There is some truth to this popular notion, but the relationship between affection and personal space is somewhat more complex and depends on the gender of the interactants.

Studies (Allgeier & Byrne, 1973; Byrne, Ervin, & Lamberth, 1970; Edwards, 1972) indicate that when males and females interact, increased attraction is associated with closer physical distance. In one study, Byrne and his colleagues (1970) manipulated attraction by sending male–female pairs, who were similar or dissimilar on a variety of personality traits, on a brief date. From research in social psychology, we know that similar individuals tend to be more attracted to each other than dissimilar individuals (Byrne, 1971). When the "matched" or "mismatched" couples returned from the date, the experimenter measured their degree of mutual liking, as well as the distance between them as they stood in front of his or her desk. The "matched" couples liked each other more and stood closer together than the "mismatched" couples. Additional studies have examined whether the attraction–proximity relationship for opposite-sex dyads occurs because the male moves closer to the female, because the female moves closer to the male, or because both the male and the female move closer to each other. These studies (e.g., Edwards, 1972) suggested that the smaller distances between close friends of the opposite sex were primarily attributable to females moving closer to males they were attracted to (i.e., females respond more to attraction by their spatial positioning than do males).

If the spatial behavior of females is primarily responsible for the attraction–proximity relationship, then the distance between female–female pairs should be determined by their degree of mutual attraction, while the distance between male–male pairs should not. In line with this assumption, it has been shown that while female–female pairs position themselves closer together with increased liking, positioning does not vary with liking for male–male pairs. In one experiment (Heshka & Nelson, 1972), pairs of adults were unobtrusively photographed by researchers as they walked down the street. The use of a standard in each of the pictures permitted a fairly accurate estimate of the distance between interactants. After taking the photograph, the experimenter approached the unknowing "subjects" and asked them what type of relationship they had. It was observed that female–female pairs interacted at closer distances as their relationship became closer, while distance between male–male pairs did not change as a function of friendship.

Why is it that the attraction–proximity relationship holds for females but not males? One explanation derives from socialization differences between the sexes, which could be reflected in spatial behavior with liked others. For males, who may be socialized to be fearful of homosexual involvement and to be independent and self-reliant overall (Maccoby, 1966), and who have less experience with intimate forms of nonverbal communication (Jourard & Rubin, 1968), spatially immediate situations with liked males or females are ambivalent. Close distances with liked males may trigger concerns about homosexuality, close distances with liked females may evoke concerns about dependency, and for males physical closeness and its attendant high degree of sensory stimulation is generally somewhat foreign. On the other hand, females may be socialized to be more dependent, to be less afraid of intimacy with others of the same sex, and generally to be more comfortable in affiliative situations (Maccoby, 1966). They also have more experience as senders and receivers of intimate nonverbal messages (Jourard & Rubin, 1968). Thus, it is not surprising that they have less difficulty responding spatially to liked others (see also Bell, Kline, & Barnard, 1988).

The research demonstrating that in some cases people in dyads interact at closer distances with increasing friendship (cf. Bell et al., 1988; Holmes, 1992) suggests that closer personal space is an outcome of increased attraction. Do individuals viewing people interacting at close range infer higher degrees of attraction? Research evidence suggests that closer distances do serve as indicators of attraction to observers. Mehrabian (1968) found that photographs of people interacting at a distance of four feet were judged to show a more positive interpersonal relationship than photographs of individuals seated 12 feet apart. Other studies (Haase & Pepper, 1972; Wellens & Goldberg, 1978) have reported similar findings.

Effect of Other Types of Similarity on Interpersonal Distance

We mentioned earlier that one type of similarity (personality similarity) leads to attraction, which elicits closer interpersonal positioning (Byrne et al., 1970). Since other types of similarity have been shown to affect attraction (Byrne, 1971), similarity on these other dimensions should also lead to closer interpersonal positioning. This has been found to be true in a number of studies. Closer distances are maintained between individuals of similar rather than dissimilar age (Latta, 1978; Willis, 1966), race or subculture (Aiello, 1987; Willis, 1966), religion (Balogun, 1991), sexual preference (e.g., heterosexual versus bisexual; Barrios et al., 1976), and status (Lott & Sommer, 1967). One setting where status is highly salient is in the military. When initiating an interaction with a superior, the greater the similarity between the initiator and the other in terms of rank, the smaller the interpersonal distance maintained (Dean, Willis, & Hewitt, 1975). Finally, it is at once interesting and unfortunate that those *without* disabilities or stigmatizing diseases prefer to interact at closer interpersonal distances with similar others than with people who have disabilities or stigmatizing diseases like AIDS (Mooney, Cohn, & Swift, 1992; Rumsey, Bull, & Gahagan, 1982).

Why should similarity and attraction lead to closer interpersonal distances than dissimilarity and dislike? People generally anticipate more favorable interactions with similar (liked) than with dissimilar (disliked) others (Byrne, 1971). Since one of the functions of personal space is protection against perceived threats, we *should* be willing to interact at closer distances with similar than dissimilar others because we anticipate fewer threats (cf. Skorjanc, 1991) from them. Maintaining close interpersonal distances with liked others is also a means of fulfilling the communicative function of personal space. By choosing closer distances, we convey information to liked others that we are attracted to them and that we expect to communicate intimate sensory cues to them.

Type of Interaction and Interpersonal Distance

If qualities such as degree of friendship and similarity create expectations of pleasant interactions which in turn affect interpersonal positioning, then situational qualities (e.g., type of interaction, discussion topics) which can be placed on a pleasant–unpleasant dimension should also affect the size of our personal space. This line of reasoning is supported by studies that have varied the affective quality of the interaction situation and observed that negatively toned situations precipitate larger spatial zones (Albas & Albas, 1989; Mandal & Maitra, 1985). In one study, Karabenick and Meisels (1972) found that subjects who were given negative feedback about their performance from a confederate stayed farther away from the confederate than subjects who were given positive feedback. In another, subjects in a stressful interaction maintained more distance than those in a low stress condition (Ugwuegbu & Anusiem, 1982). An analysis of the literature further suggests that women, as opposed to men, are especially apt to react to threatening situations by expanding their personal space (Aiello, 1987; Figure 8–2A–2D).

While it seems that affectively negative

situations generally lead to more distant interactions, there is a special case in which contrasting results are sometimes found. When subjects are angered as a result of personal insults, they may show closer interaction distances than nonangered subjects (Meisels & Dosey, 1971). This may be interpreted as a retaliatory stance that facilitates communication of anger. However, some studies (O'Neal et al., 1979; O'Neal et al., 1980) suggest that anger, like the other negative affects, may also produce farther distances. Additional situational conditions probably determine when anger leads to closer distances (for retaliation), or to farther distances (for protection).

INDIVIDUAL DIFFERENCE DETERMINANTS OF PERSONAL SPACE: RESEARCH EVIDENCE

In addition to situational conditions, differences between individuals or groups that reflect diverse learning experiences also determine the size of personal space (Aiello, 1987). For example, cultural or subcultural norms may affect whether individuals believe it is appropriate to communicate by means of particular sensory modalities or touch, and thus govern the distance chosen to fulfill the *communicative function* of personal space. In terms of the *protective function*, individual differences in learned values relevant to the amount of space needed for protection against perceived threats affect spatial behavior. Although we will find that there *are* consistent relations between individual difference variables and personal space preferences, some findings are inconsistent. This may be due, in part, to the use of different methods in different studies (e.g., simulation versus other techniques). Generally, we have tried to "weight" results from studies using simulation techniques less in arriving at our conclusions.

Figure 8–2A–2D Interpersonal distance and such nonverbal behaviors as eye contact, body angle, and facial expression vary with the affective tone of the interaction context. Can you suggest the affective tone of the interaction situation and relate it to personal space and nonverbal behavior in each of these pictures?

Cultural and Racial Determinants of Personal Space

Assuming that individuals raised in different cultures and subcultures have different learning experiences (Edwards, 1972, 1973), we might expect cross-cultural differences in interpersonal distancing as well as dissimilarities among subcultural groups within a single culture.

There is evidence relating to *cross-cultural* variations in spatial behavior, although the patterns revealed in the research are sometimes inconsistent (Aiello, 1987; Hayduk, 1983; Remland, Jones, & Brinkman, 1991). Hall (1966) proposed that in highly sensory "contact" cultures (e.g., the Mediterranean, Arabic, and Hispanic cultures), where individuals use smell and touch as well as other sensory modalities more, people should interact at closer distances. In contrast, more reserved "noncontact" cultures (e.g., northern European and Caucasian American cultures) should exhibit larger interaction distances. This hypothesis has received support (cf. Aiello, 1987). Hispanics, French, Greeks, and Arabs maintain smaller interaction distances than Americans (Hall, 1966; Little, 1968; Watson & Graves, 1966). Further, Sommer (1969) and Little (1968) reported that the English, Swedish, and Swiss are similar to Americans in the size of their spatial zones. Thus, although the research is not entirely consistent and many cultures have yet to be studied (Aiello & Thompson, 1980b), various cultural groups may need different distances to fulfill the protective and communicative functions of personal space.

The research on *subcultural differences* in spatial behavior within our culture is more confusing (Hayduk, 1983). As we said earlier, subcultural groups tend to interact at closer distances with members of their own subculture than with nonmembers (Aiello, 1987; Willis, 1966). Also, it seems as if Hispanic-Americans interact more closely than Anglo-Americans (e.g., Aiello, 1987; Ford & Graves, 1977). Unfortunately, findings for other subcultural differences (e.g., differences between African-Americans and Caucasians) have often been inconsistent. It has been suggested (Hayduk, 1978; Patterson, 1974) that socioeconomic status may be a better predictor than subculture of learning experiences related to spatial behavior (cf. Scherer, 1974). Although members of a particular subculture may vary greatly in their living conditions, those in a particular socioeconomic group tend to live under relatively similar conditions. However, support for the view that socioeconomic status should have consistent effects on spatial behavior has also been mixed (Aiello, 1987).

Gender Differences in Personal Space

We mentioned earlier that males and females display different spatial behavior with *liked* than *disliked* others. Females interact at closer distances with liked others, while males do not differentiate spatially as a function of attraction. Another interesting question centers around the relative distances at which females and males interact with others, regardless of degree of attraction. Do females generally maintain closer interpersonal distances than males when interacting with people, or is the reverse true?

In terms of interpersonal distance from same-sex others, female–female pairs maintain closer distances than male–male pairs (Aiello, 1987; Barnard & Bell, 1982). Again, these findings may reflect a stronger female

socialization to be affiliative, more experience by females with intimate nonverbal modalities (Jourard & Rubin, 1968), and a greater male concern about not being intimate with others of the same sex (Maccoby, 1966). The tendency for women to interact more closely than men does not hold for all situations. While it occurs in affiliative situations, in contexts that imply threat, women interact at greater distances than men (Aiello, 1987).

How do *mixed-sex* dyads compare spatially with male–male or female–female pairs? When dyads are of mixed sex, distancing depends on the relationship of the people who are interacting. Acquaintances maintain an intermediate distance (between that used by female–female and male–male pairs), while mixed-sex dyads who are in a close relationship maintain less personal space than either male–male or female–female pairs (Aiello, 1987). Interestingly, some research suggests that a woman's point in the menstrual cycle affects the personal space she maintains with opposite-sex others. Females' personal space zones tend to be larger during the menstrual flow than during the middle of the cycle (Gallant et al., 1991). This has been interpreted as reflecting the midcycle peak in sexual desire (e.g., Benedak, 1952). In effect, hormonally determined sexual receptivity may affect personal space in opposite-sex interactions.

Age Differences in Personal Space

Research focusing on personal space from a developmental perspective has been directed at answering two questions: the age at which personal space is first established, and the extent to which children's spatial behavior changes as they become older. Many estimates have been derived from studies concerning when children begin to exhibit personal space. Duke and Wilson (1973) and Eberts and Lepper (1975) found behavioral evidence of personal space in children between 45 and 63 months of age, but other studies (e.g., Meisels & Guardo, 1969) have

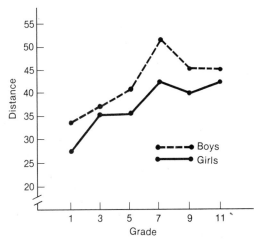

Figure 8–3 Mean interaction distances of male and female dyads at six grade levels

From Aiello, J. R., and Aiello, T., 1974. The development of personal space: Proxemic behavior of children 6 through 16. Human Ecology, *2, 177–189. Reprinted by permission.*

found that personal space behavior begins at a later age. Unfortunately, none of this research sheds much light on how the learning from which spacing mechanisms evolve, takes place.

The second question concerns whether personal space changes with age. It has been found that: (a) children less than five years old show inconsistent spatial patterns, and (b) after age six (grade 1 in Figure 8–3), the older the child (until adulthood), the greater the preferred interpersonal distance (Aiello, 1987; Hayduk, 1983). This pattern holds across cultures (e.g., Lerner, Iwawaki, & Chihara, 1976; Lomranz et al., 1975). Adult-like spatial norms are first exhibited around the time of puberty (Aiello, 1987). In addition to personal space becoming larger with age, the distance adults maintain from children becomes greater as the child's age increases (Larson & Lowe, 1990; Sigelman & Adams, 1990).

Personality Determinants of Spatial Behavior

A major attempt has been made by researchers to identify **individual personality**

traits associated with different personal space behavior. Since personality represents one's way of looking at the world and reflects learning and experience, it seems reasonable that personality orientations should be reflected in spatial behavior.

One personality variable that has been explored in terms of its implications for interpersonal distancing is **internality–externality.** Duke and Nowicki (1972) demonstrated differences in personal space between internals and externals, and suggested how spatial behavior may reflect learning experiences. The theory of internality–externality views an individual's orientation (internal or external) as a reflection of past learning about internal or external causation of events. *Internals* view reinforcements as under the control of the self; *externals* view reinforcements as controlled by external sources. Consistent with this theoretical framework (and with the assumption that learning is reflected in spatial behavior), Duke and Nowicki found that externals desired more distance from strangers than internals. It seems that if past learning leads to the belief that one is in control of a situation, he or she feels more secure at close distances with strangers than if past learning leads to the belief that events are controlled externally.

Several other studies have found that spatial behavior differs as a function of personality. Some researchers (Horowitz, Duff, & Stratton, 1964; Srivastava & Mandal, 1990) compared the spatial needs of schizophrenics and "normals" and found that schizophrenics require more space. It has also been found that anxious individuals maintain more personal space than nonanxious people (Karabenick & Meisels, 1972; Patterson, 1977), that introverts maintain more space than extroverts (Cook, 1970; Patterson & Holmes, 1966), and that those who work in relative isolation (e.g., at computer terminals) require more personal space, even outside of the work setting, than those who do not work in isolation (Gifford & Sacilotto,

1993). Finally, those with high self-esteem maintain smaller personal space than those with low self-esteem (Frankel & Barrett, 1971), people high in need for affiliation prefer closer distances than those low in need for affiliation (Mehrabian & Diamond, 1971a), and field dependent persons maintain closer distances than field independent ones (Kline, Bell, & Babcock, 1984).

The above research notwithstanding, many of the studies that have attempted to relate individual personality traits to spatial behavior have not been terribly enlightening and have resulted in conflicting findings (cf. Aiello, 1987; Hayduk, 1983). Patterson (1974, 1978) has proposed a procedure that may be more fruitful than the individual personality trait approach. Rather than studying single personality traits and their relationship to spatial behavior, Patterson conceptualized personality dimensions in more general terms. He looked at *clusters* of personality variables related to a general approach tendency for social situations (e.g., need for affiliation, extroversion), and related these to personal space preferences. His research demonstrated that such a strategy may yield better, more stable predictors of interpersonal distancing than focusing on individual traits. Another way to maximize the possibility of observing relationships between personality variables and personal space was suggested by Karabenick and Meisels (1972). Specifically, it may be necessary to study such relationships in situations in which the personality trait in question is salient (e.g., studying the relationship between aggressiveness and personal space in an anger-provoking situation), as opposed to the neutral contexts generally employed.

PHYSICAL DETERMINANTS OF PERSONAL SPACE

Although we have focused primarily on situational and individual difference determinants of personal space (as has past research), studies also suggest some interesting *physical* determinants of interpersonal spacing. First, a number of architectural features affect personal space. For example, Savinar (1975) found that males had more need for space when ceiling height was low than when it was high. White (1975) reported that personal space increased with reductions in room size and decreased with increases in room size, and Daves and Swaffer (1971) found that individuals desire more space in a narrow than a square room. Also, Baum, Reiss, and O'Hara (1974) suggested that installing partitions in a room can reduce feelings of spatial invasion. Do we maintain closer distances with others when "in the dark," than when there is light? Gergen, Gergen, and Barton (1973) report that we are more likely to touch others (the ultimate in closeness), which may make many people uncomfortable, when it is dark than under more typical lighting conditions. Perhaps because touching is more apt to occur in the dark, maintaining a close personal space in a place which is dark causes more discomfort than being close when there is full illumination (Adams & Zuckerman, 1991).

In addition to architectural features, people's position in a room, whether they are sitting or standing, and whether they are indoors or outdoors, also affects personal space. Concerning position in a room, several studies (cf. Dabbs, Fuller, & Carr, 1973; Tennis & Dabbs, 1975) found that over a variety of subject populations, people exhibit greater personal space when in the corner of a room than when in the center. Also, it seems that we maintain closer distances when standing than while seated (Altman & Vinsel, 1977). With respect to spatial differences as a function of being indoors or outdoors, Little (1965) and Pempus, Sawaya, and Cooper (1975) found that subjects kept more distance between themselves and others when indoors than when outdoors. Similarly, we prefer greater distances in crowded than in uncrowded conditions (Jain, 1993). The "corner–center," "sitting–standing," "crowded–uncrowded," and "indoor–outdoor" effects may reflect differences in availability of escape; when we know we can get away, we are content with less space.

INTERPERSONAL POSITIONING EFFECTS

Do the same variables that determine the *size* of our personal space affect other aspects of spatial positioning? Studies have shown that besides determining the distance between interactants, individual difference and situational variables affect the body orientation that we maintain between ourselves and others.

One individual difference variable that has been found to affect spatial positioning is gender. While males prefer to interact with liked others in an across (i.e., face-to-face) orientation, females prefer to have liked others adjacent to them. In two related studies, Byrne, Baskett, and Hodges (1971) manipulated the attraction between a subject and two confederates so that the subject liked one of the confederates but disliked the other. The subject was then asked to join the confederates in another room where his or her choice of seats with respect to the liked and disliked confederates was recorded. In the first experiment, which involved side-by-side seating, females sat closer to the liked confederate than to the disliked one, while males showed no preference. In the second experiment, which involved face-to-face seating, males sat closer to the liked confederate, while females showed no preference.

The cooperativeness or competitiveness of the interaction situation also affects spatial positioning. In an initial study, Sommer (1965) observed the spatial arrangement of individuals who were cooperating or competing and found that cooperating pairs sat side-by-side, while competing pairs sat across from each other. A second study found corroborative results. Subjects anticipated either a cooperative or a competitive interaction and sat opposite a decoy in competitive conditions and adjacent to him or her in cooperative conditions.

SPATIAL ZONES THAT FACILITATE GOAL FULFILLMENT

What distances lead to the best results in a dyadic learning situation? What seating position in a classroom will promote the most teacher–student interaction? And where should a therapist position him- or herself to elicit the most self-disclosure on the part of a client, or a doctor sit when giving a patient important health recommendations? These are obviously important questions, and show the applied significance as well as the design implications of research on personal space. Unfortunately, at present we have no completely satisfactory answers, though some research makes an attempt to provide at least preliminary ones.

Optimal Spacing in Learning Environments

We know that the distance between a teacher and a student may affect learning, at least when the two are in a dyadic interaction. Although the results are slightly contradictory, they suggest, in general, that interactions at Hall's personal distance zone (Skeen, 1976), and even at his intimate zone (Miller, 1978), may lead to better performance by the student than the other spatial zones. For example, in the study by Skeen (1976), a subject performed a serial learning task either six inches (intimate distance) or three-and-one-half feet (personal distance) from the experimenter. For tasks of varying levels of difficulty, the learner's performance was better at the personal distance than at the intimate one. In the study by Miller (1978), subjects received instruction at a distance from the instructor corresponding to one of Hall's four zones. Here, the students did better when taught at the intimate distance than at the other three. While the results of these studies are somewhat inconsistent, taken together they suggest that Hall's closer zones, rather than his farther ones, may lead to the best learning by students in teacher–student dyads.

What about typical classroom situations, where there are many students present? Although there is currently no research which definitively identifies how far from the instructor you should sit in order to get the best grade, a study by Kinarthy (1975) may at least provide a hint. In this experiment, trained observers recorded the amount of communication between the students and the instructor. It was reported that seating position does affect communication in the college classroom, even after statistical procedures were used to control for the fact that in many cases students chose their own seats. (Without such controls, it could be the type of person who chose a particular position, rather than the position itself, which caused the effects.) Where is the best place to sit? It seems as if the middle, front section of the classroom is a relatively high communication zone. Sitting there promotes verbalization (except for those who are very low verbalizers) and facilitates attention (Koneya, 1976; Schwebel & Cherlin, 1972; see Figure 8–4). It has been found that people who choose middle-front seats have the highest self-esteem (Hillman, Brooks, & O'Brien, 1991), and also get the best grades in the class (Becker et al., 1973; Sommer, 1972). While the relationship between seating position and grades is just correlational, there

Figure 8–4   Where you sit in a large lecture hall can make a big difference.

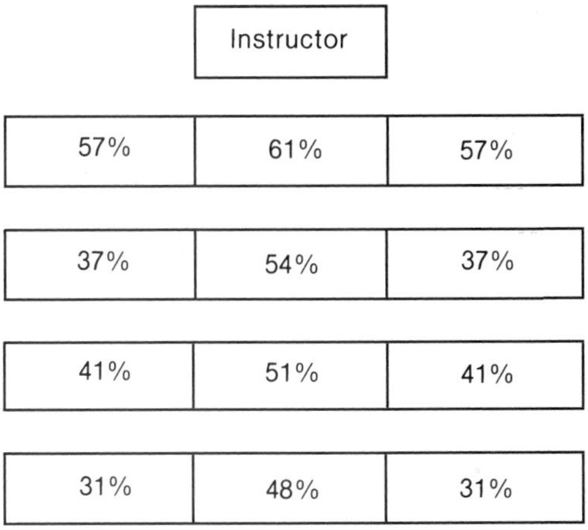

	Instructor	

57%	61%	57%

37%	54%	37%

41%	51%	41%

31%	48%	31%

Figure 8–5 Students' participation in class activities as a function of seating positions
From Sommer, R., 1967. Classroom ecology. Journal of Applied Behavioral Science, 3, 500. *Copyright 1967 by NTL Institute Publications.*

is also some *experimental* evidence that partially supports it (Stires, 1980; Figure 8–5).

Optimal Spacing in Professional Interactions

An interesting question concerns the distance at which people feel most comfortable disclosing personal information about themselves to clinical psychologists. Again, this topic has not been thoroughly researched, although there are preliminary data. Generally, an intermediate distance is preferred for a counseling situation (Brokemann & Moller, 1973), and psychiatric patients talk most about their fears and anxieties at that distance (Lassen, 1973). This pattern of effects also holds for college students. When Stone and Morden (1976) had students discuss personal topics with a therapist at a distance of two feet, five feet, and nine feet, they found that students volunteered the most personal information at the five-foot distance. Since this distance is culturally appropriate for such communications and is expected for them (Brokemann & Moller, 1973), these data support Hall's (1968) prediction that deviation from the appropriate distance elicits negative effects. It should be noted, however, that these data do not generalize to self-disclosures between two strangers in nonclinical interactions (cf. Skotko & Langmeyer, 1977).

How far should a physician position him- or herself from a patient so that the patient's compliance with medical regimen will be highest? According to available evidence, the answer depends on whether the doctor is delivering basically "accepting" or "neutral" evaluative feedback for the patient's self-disclosures. In a study by Greene (1977), close physical proximity strengthened adherence to dieting recommendations when "accepting" feedback was offered, but lowered compliance when "neutral" feedback was given. It may be that the feedback suggested to the patient the type of relationship she had with the practitioner. When feedback was accepting, the closer distance was appropriate and led to more positive effects than the less appropriate, farther distance. On the other hand, when feedback was neutral, a farther distance was viewed as appropriate and led to more positive effects than a close distance. Another way of saying this is that when the intimacy of both the verbal and environmental "channels" was consistent, more positive effects occurred than when there were inconsistencies.

Optimal Spacing to Facilitate Group Processes

Can the spacing between people be manipulated to affect group processes in order to accomplish some desired end? A number of studies suggest that the answer is "yes." Suppose that an environmental psychologist wants to promote interaction within a group. This calls for **sociopetal** spacing (spacing that brings people together, such as the conversational groupings found in most homes), rather than **sociofugal** spacing (spacing that separates people, like the straight rows of chairs found in airports or bus terminals; Osmond, 1957). In an early study, Sommer and Ross (1958) were called in to examine conditions at a Saskatchewan hospital, where a newly opened ward with a lovely, cheerful decor seemed to be having a depressing and isolating effect on patients. They observed that chairs were lined up against the walls, side-by-side. All the chairs were facing the same way, and rather than seeing each other, people just gazed off into the distance. When Sommer and Ross rearranged the chairs into small, circular groups, the frequency of interactions among patients almost doubled. Other studies have similarly found that arranging space so that people face each other more directly results in greater interaction between group members (Mehrabian & Diamond, 1971b). A nonfacing orientation may elicit longer pauses, more self-manipulative behaviors and postural adjustments, and perhaps even more negative ratings of group interaction (Patterson et al., 1979).

How could one manipulate his or her spatial positioning in a group in order to become its leader? It seems that in small group settings, people direct most of their conversation to the person sitting across from them (i.e., the one who is the most highly visible; Michelini, Passalacqua, & Cusimano, 1976). Also, people who occupy a central position in a group initiate the most communications (Michelini et al., 1976). This suggests that one could become highly influential merely by choosing a central spatial orientation where others eye them directly. This assumption has received some support. Those who choose the end of a rectangular table are more likely to be elected foreman in simulated jury studies (Strodtbeck & Hook, 1961) or to otherwise dominate group interaction. Of course, this could be due to the fact that dominant individuals *choose* to sit at the "head" of the table, or it could be a reciprocal relationship. Experimental work still

needs to be done to identify the cause of this effect.

CONSEQUENCES OF TOO MUCH OR TOO LITTLE PERSONAL SPACE

We have seen that situational, individual difference, and physical-environmental variables determine our preferred personal space zone. And we have also seen that some spaces facilitate goal fulfillment more than others. At this point, it is interesting to consider what happens when we are forced to interact with another person under conditions of "inappropriate" (i.e., too much or too little) personal space. For example, imagine an interaction with a door-to-door salesperson who insists on extolling the virtues of his or her product at an inappropriately close distance (e.g., three inches) or an inappropriately far distance (e.g., 10 feet). Would you be likely to buy anything from this person? Since personal space serves some important functions, we can assume that inappropriate distancing often has negative consequences for the interactants.

Predicting the Effects of Inappropriate Distances

The effects of inappropriate positioning can be described in the context of the eclectic environment behavior model introduced in Chapter 4 and presented in Figure 8–6. Before we discuss the model, however, recall that we have observed throughout our coverage of research on personal space that situational conditions and individual differences determine optimal interpersonal distances. It is evident in Phase I of the model that whether we perceive our personal space as optimal or nonoptimal at a particular objective distance from another person depends on situational conditions (e.g., attraction) and individual differences (e.g., personality). If we perceive our personal space as within an optimal range, homeostasis is maintained. If we perceive it as outside this range, a variety of responses may occur.

What is the nature of our response to nonoptimal personal space? The same conceptual formulations used earlier to explain why we maintain personal space (e.g., overload, arousal, and behavior constraint) predict the effects of inappropriate interpersonal distancing. For example, *overload* notions predict that stimulus overload occasioned by an inappropriate personal space should cause performance decrements and elicit coping responses to lower stimulation to a more reasonable level. In terms of the *stress* approach, inappropriate positioning leads to a stress reaction, which may have emotional, behavioral, and physiological components. Coping responses are directed at reducing stress to a more acceptable level.

The *arousal* conceptualization assumes that being too close leads to overarousal and to attributions, and suggests coping mechanisms designed to lower arousal. According to *equilibrium* and *"comfort"* models, distances which are too close or too far will lead to compensatory reactions in other modalities (e.g., changes in body orientation or eye gaze) and, when these are impossible, to a loss of interest in continuing the interaction. Altman's (1975) **privacy regulation model** implies that inadequate personal space will elicit attempts to "shore up" boundary control mechanisms and thus ensure privacy. Finally, the *behavior constraint* approach suggests that inadequate personal space frequently leads to an aversive feeling state and to coping responses that attempt to reassert freedom.

We noted earlier that Hall (1966) proposed a model based on *communication properties* to explain personal space and that ethological models have also been applied (cf. Evans & Howard, 1973). In terms of Hall's formulation, it might be predicted that inappropriate distance constitutes a negative communication and leads to negative attributions and inferences. The *ethological approach* makes still another set of predictions. It assumes that when personal space is inadequate, fear and discomfort are experienced due to feelings of aggression or threat (cf. Evans, 1978).

How can we integrate all these formulations? Although each of the approaches proposes a somewhat different reaction to inappropriate positioning, we should not view them as competing with each other. Rather, it is probable that inappropriate personal space may at times lead to each of the responses we have described. Further, the predictions of all of the conceptual schemes may be integrated into the sequence of events shown in Phase II of Figure 8–6. When personal space is perceived to be inadequate, which may be due to a combination of objective physical distance, and situational and social conditions (Zakay, Hayduk, & Tsal, 1992) various types of coping responses are employed, which may or may not be successful. When coping is successful, it leads to adaptation or habituation, and aftereffects are less likely. If coping is unsuccessful, inappropriate positioning can lead to aftereffects such as dislike for the other, poor performance, and so on.

The Consequences of Inappropriate Spacing

What type of research evidence exists to support the assertions of our model concerning the consequences of inadequate personal space? Which of the above conceptual approaches have received support? Several studies have shown that when an environmental setting forces two people to interact in an inappropriate spatial zone, unfavorable feelings and inferences are elicited. In an experiment on the effects of distance between a subject and a communicator on

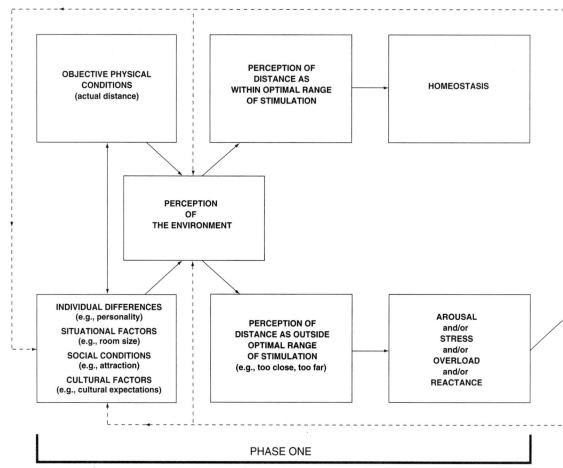

Figure 8–6   Eclectic environment-behavior model adapted to conceptualizing reactions to inappropriate personal space

persuasion, Albert and Dabbs (1970) hypothesized that negative feelings and attributions would be elicited if a communicator and a subject were positioned more or less than five feet apart, an appropriate distance for such interpersonal contacts. Accordingly, the communicator (actually an experimenter) and the subject were constrained to interact at the "appropriate" distance of five feet (1.5 m), or at one of two inappropriate distances (i.e., 2 feet or 15 feet; 0.6 m or 4.6 m). Several effects were measured, and the findings basically supported the prediction. Subjects paid more attention to the commu-

nicator and rated him or her as more of an "expert" at the five-foot distance than at either of the other distances.

Boucher (1972) found parallel results using schizophrenics as subjects. First, interviewers sat down with patients at a distance that was inappropriately close, appropriate, or inappropriately distant. The distance manipulation was accomplished by fastening both chairs to the floor at one of the three ranges so that people in "inappropriate" positions could not adjust their proximity to a more comfortable zone. Following a ten-minute interview under these conditions, the

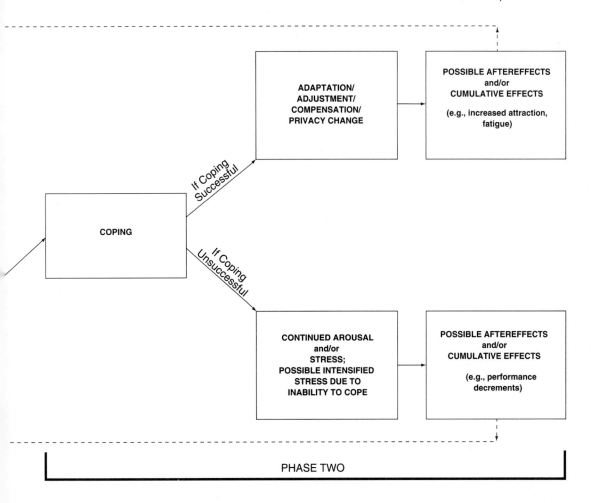

subject's attraction to the interviewer was assessed. It was found that more attraction was expressed for the interviewer at the appropriate distance than at distances that were inappropriately close or far.

Several studies suggest that maintaining inappropriate interpersonal distance is associated with considerable stress. For example, Dabbs (1971) found that a persuasive communicator who was positioned too close caused subjects to feel more pressured, unfriendly, and irritated than they did when a more appropriate distance was maintained. And when Aiello and Thompson (1980a)

had subjects converse at either a comfortable distance or an uncomfortably far one, subjects who sat too far apart not only felt ill at ease, but blamed the other for their discomfort, even though the other was clearly not responsible!

Patterson and Sechrest (1970) reported that subjects evidenced more positive feelings when interacting with a confederate at a moderate distance (4 feet; 1.2 m) than at either a closer distance (2 feet; 0.6 m) or a far distance (8 feet; 2.4 m). Similarly, Bergman (1971) found that subjects in discussion groups with chairs separated by two inches

COMPENSATION VERSUS RECIPROCATION:
Too Close Is Not Always Too Bad

Up until now, we have suggested that inappropriate interpersonal distancing leads primarily to negative consequences (e.g., dislike) and to compensatory reactions (e.g., indirect body orientation). However, we have also noted some conflicting evidence. One conceptual formulation (Patterson, 1976, 1978) suggests a way of integrating both sets of data. Patterson hypothesizes that when two individuals are interacting, a sufficient change in the intimacy of one of them (e.g., moving too close) produces a changed state of arousal in the other. Depending on cognitions about the situation (e.g., attributions), this arousal may be labeled as either a positive or a negative emotional state by the other person. If the arousal is negatively labeled, a compensatory response, such as moving farther away, will occur. On the other hand, if the arousal is positively labeled, a **reciprocal response** (moving still closer to the other) will occur. This model makes an important point: The situation should determine whether the effects of interacting at a very close range will be negative (i.e., eliciting compensatory reactions and dislike) or positive (i.e., eliciting reciprocal reactions and liking). For example, reciprocity may occur when two people like each other, while compensation may occur when they are unsure about their relationship or dislike one another (Ickes et al., 1982).

A study by Storms and Thomas (1977) supports the notion that the situation determines whether interacting at close range is positive or negative. In this study subjects interacted with another who was either friendly or similar, or unfriendly or dissimilar at a very close or normal distance. The other was liked more when he or she sat close than at a "normal" distance in the friendly or similar conditions. In effect, when the situation is positive, closeness may facilitate a desire for reciprocal intimacy. On the other hand, the subject was liked less when sitting close than farther away in the unfriendly or dissimilar conditions. Closeness in this situation promoted disliking and a desire for a compensatory response.

While Patterson's model received some support from research, it has been criticized on theoretical grounds (Ellsworth, 1977; Hayduk, 1983). Hayduk has suggested that it is often difficult to make predictions with the model since it does not specify what causes a positive or negative evaluation of a change in intimacy. Ellsworth believes that the degree of cognitive self-focusing it implies is overstated. Attempts to modify the model (Anderson & Anderson, 1984) have met with some success.

(5 cm) on each side showed more palmar sweat (a measure of arousal) than subjects in discussion groups with chairs separated by three feet (.91 m). All of the above studies on the effects of having to interact under conditions of inappropriate spacing have design implications.

In another study, Hayduk (1981) found a linear relationship between the *degree* to which a spatial arrangement was inappropriate and the amount of people's discomfort. Also, he observed that subjects with smaller personal space zones responded more positively to an inappropriately close distance than subjects with larger zones. Interestingly, a study by Fisher (1974) suggests that inappropriate distances with a similar (liked) other lead to less negative reactions than the same distances with a dissimilar other.

In addition to lowering attraction and persuasibility and causing negative affect, what other effects can inappropriate spatial positioning have? According to Argyle and Dean (1965), nonverbal compensatory coping reactions should occur to restore a comfortable "equilibrium" when the physical distance between two individuals is too close or too far. Although all the implications of this proposition have yet to be tested, a number of studies have provided support for Argyle and Dean's formulation. In one study (Albas, 1991), when an interviewer moved uncomfortably far from a subject during an interview, the subject reestablished equilibrium by coming closer. In another study (Patterson, 1974), subjects interacted with an interviewer at both an appropriate and an inappropriate distance, and changes in eye contact and body orientation were recorded. In this study and others (e.g., Rosenfeld et al., 1984), the results of the distance manipulations on eye contact and body orientation were in line with the equilibrium hypothesis. It was found that with too much proximity, body orientation became less direct and percentage of eye contact decreased.

Other studies consistent with the equilibrium hypothesis have shown that decreased directness of body orientation leads to greater proximity among individuals in the situation (e.g., Felipe & Sommer, 1966). In addition, the longer subjects interact under inappropriate conditions the greater the degree of compensation which is observed (Sundstrom & Sundstrom, 1977). However, research has not always supported

the predictions of the equilibrium notion (cf. Altman, 1973), and some studies find opposite results (i.e., closeness begets closeness). One way of resolving this apparent conflict is indicated in the box. Others have suggested modified equilibrium theories (i.e., the "comfort" model reviewed earlier), which better correspond to certain experimental findings (e.g., Aiello, 1977; Aiello & Thompson, 1980b).

CONSEQUENCES OF PERSONAL SPACE INVASIONS

Research on the consequences of too much or too little personal space suggests that when *ongoing interactions* take place at inappropriate distances, they may lead to lower attraction, negative inferences, and compensatory behaviors. However, what happens when a person is sitting alone minding his or her own business, with no intention of interacting with anyone, and a stranger sits down at an uncomfortably close proximity?

The Effects of Being Invaded on Flight Behavior

An early study of the effects of personal space invasions was conducted by Felipe and Sommer (1966). At a 1,500-bed mental institution where patients spent a great deal of time outdoors, a stranger (actually an experimental confederate) approached lone patients at a distance of six inches (15 cm). If the subject attempted to move away, the confederate moved so as to maintain a close positioning. The flight behaviors of the "invaded" group were compared with those of patients who were not invaded but who were watched from a distance. As can be seen in Figure 8–7, after one minute 20 percent of the experimental subjects and none of the control subjects had fled. After 20 minutes, 65 percent of the experimental subjects had left their places, and only 35 percent of the control subjects displayed such a reaction.

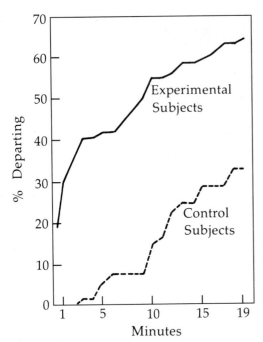

Figure 8–7 Cumulative percentage of patients departing at various intervals
Based on data from Felipe & Sommer, 1966.

Similar results for flight behavior after personal space invasion were reported by Konecni et al. (1975). In this study (see Table 8–2), it was observed that both male and female pedestrians crossed the street more quickly as personal space invasions became more severe. Smith and Knowles (1979) reported the same thing, and also observed that invaded pedestrians formed more negative impressions of the invader, and experienced more negative moods, than those

Table 8–2 Time in Seconds Taken to Cross the Street by Experimental Condition*

	Experimenters' Lateral Distance From Subjects (in feet)			
Sex of Subjects	*1*	*2*	*5*	*10*
Male	7.65	8.45	9.09	9.08
Female	8.94	8.95	9.41	9.79

*Based on data from Konecni et al., 1975.

in control conditions. In another setting, Patterson, Mullens, and Romano (1971) reported that "invaded" subjects turned away, avoided eye contact, erected barriers, fidgeted, mumbled, and displayed other compensatory and coping reactions more than "noninvaded" control subjects. Such reactions are especially common in individuals who choose not to escape altogether, or who do not have the option of escape. In a study by Terry and Lower (1979), it was found that in the latter group the more severe the invasion, the more intense the attempts at perceptual withdrawal. Finally, in research with children, it was found that personal space invasions caused behavior to become more primitive, and to be characterized by increasing movements (e.g., fidgeting; Bonio, Fonzi, & Saglione, 1978).

The Effects of Being Invaded on Arousal

If "invasions" are uncomfortable experiences for the target, invasion victims might be expected to evidence higher levels of physiological arousal than noninvaded controls. Only a few studies (e.g., Evans & Howard, 1972; McBride, King, & James, 1965) have systematically considered the effects of invasion on physiological arousal. A very ingenious study by Middlemist, Knowles, and Matter (1976) bears directly on this question. The setting for the study was, of all places, a three-urinal men's lavatory! The unknowing subjects were lavatory users who were "invaded" by a confederate at either a close or a moderate distance. In the control condition, the confederate was not present. How was arousal measured under these three levels of personal space invasion? Since research indicates that stress delays the onset of urination and shortens its duration, it was reasoned that if closer invasions cause stress, greater delay of onset and shorter duration of urination should result. Accordingly, an experimenter stationed in a nearby toilet stall with a periscope and two stopwatches

Figure 8–8A & 8B Observation apparatus that was used to study the effects of arousal from personal space invasions in a men's room. As you can see, the periscope is quite unobtrusive when hidden by the stall.

recorded the delay of onset and persistence of urination. As can be seen in Figures 8–8A and 8B, and 8–9, results confirmed the assumption that personal space invasions are stressful. Close interpersonal distances increased the delay and decreased the persistence of urination. Perhaps installing

Figure 8–9 Mean persistence and delay of onset for urination at three levels of personal space invasion

From Middlemist, R. D., Knowles, E. S., and Matter, C. F., 1976. Copyright © 1976 by The American Psychological Association. Reprinted by permission of the author and publisher.

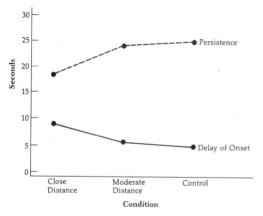

partitions could add to people's comfort in lavatories.

One implication of the arousal elicited by personal space invasions is its effect on task performance. In line with the Yerkes-Dodson Law (page 117), available evidence suggests that the consequences of invasion-induced arousal for performance depend on the complexity of the task. With simple tasks, performance does not seem to be negatively affected by having another too close. With more complex tasks, invasions take a toll. For example, Evans and Howard (1972) and Barefoot and Kleck (1970) found decrements in performance on information-processing tasks as a function of personal space invasion. Thus, it may be that if somebody invades your space when you are in the library studying, the quality of your work will suffer.

Other Effects of Being Invaded

If personal space invasions are aversive for the target, they should elicit a host of additional behavioral reactions. In some situations, it would not be unreasonable to expect

TOO CLOSE FOR COMFORT:
Gender Differences in Response to Invasions of Personal Space

A study by Fisher and Byrne (1975) found gender differences in victims' responses to personal space invasions and demonstrated that invasions affect victims on a broad array of dimensions.

As you recall from earlier in the chapter, it has been found that males prefer to position themselves across from liked others, while females prefer to position themselves adjacent to liked others (Byrne, Baskett, & Hodges, 1971). On the basis of these findings, Fisher and Byrne reasoned that for each sex the spatial position most favored for "liked" others should be the one least favored for an invading stranger. Specifically, it was hypothesized that females should respond more negatively than males to side-by-side invasions of personal space, while males should respond more negatively than females to face-to-face invasions.

The subjects were males and females who were sitting alone at tables in a university library. As they attended to their business, they were "invaded" by a male or female "invader" from either a face-to-face or an adjacent position. After five minutes, the invader appeared to have concluded his or her work and left the area. Three minutes later, an experimenter arrived, claiming to be a student who was conducting a study of people's impressions of various stimuli for an introductory psychology class. The experimenter also claimed to have noticed that someone had been sitting at the subject's table and wondered if the subject could indicate his or her impressions of that person as well as impressions of the library environment on questionnaires. The questionnaires specifically tapped the subject's affective state, attraction toward the invader, perception of the aesthetic quality and crowdedness of the environment, and the positiveness of motivation attributed to the invader.

How did invasion victims respond to the questionnaires? Regardless of the invader's sex, males responded negatively on all measures when the invader sat across from them but were not affected by an adjacent invasion. Females responded negatively when the invader sat adjacent to them but were not affected by one who sat across from them. It is as if special significance is associated with

that personal space invasions could lead to aggression (Ryden, Bossenmaier, & McLachlan, 1991). In fact, sometimes (e.g., during demonstrations in which both pro- and anti-abortion protestors are present) it is necessary to keep people from the two factions apart to prevent personal space invasions from occurring, which helps to avoid aggression (Hern, 1991).

If your personal space were invaded by someone, would you be less likely to help him or her, if given the opportunity? Two sets of studies have looked at the effect of personal space invasions on helping and have reached conflicting conclusions. In one group of studies (Konecni et al., 1975; Smith & Knowles, 1979), a confederate first violated the subject's personal space and then

"face-to-face" positioning for males and adjacent positioning for females, and invading these "special" zones leads to particularly negative reactions.

The results of the study led Fisher and Byrne to make a simple prediction that, if confirmed, would lend additional support to their findings. It was assumed that if males dislike "face-to-face" invasions, they should place their books and personal effects between themselves and facing seats in a library, and if females dislike adjacent invasions, they should place their possessions between themselves and adjacent seats. To test these hypotheses, an observer was sent into the library to record where males and females placed their possessions. The hypotheses were confirmed: Males erect barriers primarily between themselves and facing positions, while females erect barriers between themselves and adjacent positions.

Why is it that the sexes seem to attribute special significance to different spatial positioning arrangements? One possible explanation lies in the socialization process, with males taught to be relatively competitive and hence more sensitive to competitive cues, and females taught to be relatively affiliative and more sensitive to affiliative cues (Maccoby, 1966). Adjacent seating (which occurs in affiliative situations) may signal affiliative demands to females. Females like to have someone they "feel safe with" in this relatively intimate affiliative position and react negatively when it is occupied by a stranger. On the other hand, facing seats (which occur in competitive situations) may signal competitive demands to males. Males like to have a trusted (and nonthreatening) friend in this competitive position.

It is rather humorous, but the gender differences observed in the Fisher and Byrne research may be the source of considerable miscommunication between the sexes. A female who wants to befriend an unknown male may be surprised to find that a nonthreatening (to her) eyeball-to-eyeball approach causes consternation and alarm. In the same way, a male who attempts to ingratiate himself with an unknown female by sitting adjacent to her in a nonthreatening (to him) position may be surprised to find he elicits a "Miss Muffet" reaction.

dropped one of several objects. It was found that when the personal space violation was severe, victims failed to retrieve even objects that seemed to be important. In addition to failing to help the *invader*, Smith and Knowles (1979) reported that the reluctance to help on the part of those who had experienced "severe" invasions also generalized to an unwillingness to assist others in need of aid. A second set of studies (e.g., Baron & Bell, 1976b) found just the opposite: Personal space invasions facilitated helping. However, in these studies confederates asked the subject for help when at either an "invaded" or an appropriate distance. These conflicting findings can be readily resolved. In the first set of studies, the victim may have attributed the invasion to negative intent, dismissed the invader as a "nasty" person, and refused to help him or her. In the second, the invader's violation may have been attributed to the importance of the request rather than to negative personal qualities and therefore resulted in greater helping.

Thus far, we have seen that personal space invasions can cause physiological arousal and cognitive and behavioral responses. Although we can explore many possible ways to view the relation between these, Smith and Knowles (1979) suggest an interesting possibility, which supports Patterson's theory of compensation versus reciprocation (see the box on page 294). Based on some studies they did, Smith and Knowles imply that our initial response to a personal space invasion involves *arousal*. As we know, arousal can have many behavioral consequences, in and of itself. However, they argue that arousal is also followed by a secondary, cognitive response (e.g., attributions). In effect, our arousal response draws our attention to the invader and causes us to try to understand why we are aroused, and why the invader behaved as he or she did. Characteristics of the invader and the situation affect the explanations at which we arrive. These, in turn, determine our attributions to the invader, our liking for him or her, whether we will aggress against the invader, help the invader if he or she is in need, and so forth. While Smith and Knowles' proposed interrelation between the various responses to personal space invasions has received some support, further research is needed.

After exploring the effects of personal space invasion on a wide array of behaviors, an interesting question remains: Do all personal space invaders elicit the same reactions in their victims, or is it more aversive to be "victimized" by some people than others? The model proposed by Smith and Knowles (1979) would suggest the latter. The more negative our attribution for why someone invaded our space, the more uncomfortable

the invasion will make us. While relatively few studies have looked at this question, there are some suggestive findings. First, it appears that people flee more slowly after having their personal space violated by an attractive rather than an unattractive confederate (Kmiecik, Mausar, & Banziger, 1979). Second, some evidence indicates that it may be more upsetting to be invaded by a male than a female. Specifically, Murphy-Berman and Berman (1978) and Bleda and Bleda (1978) observed that male intruders were evaluated more negatively and elicited more movement in their victims than female intruders. Perhaps this is because we attribute more negative motives to male than female invaders. Other research suggests that more negative reactions to male invaders may be limited to *ambiguous* settings (Aiello, 1987). In less ambiguous settings, such as on the beach or in a bar, a male's invasion of a female's personal space may elicit a favorable response (Skolnick, Frasier, & Hadar, 1977). Additional studies suggest that the degree of choice invaders have in their action affects how negatively they are evaluated (Murphy-Berman & Berman, 1978) and it seems that invaders who smoke elicit more flight reactions in their victims than those who do not (Bleda & Bleda, 1978).

What about the effect of invaders of different ages? Fry and Willis (1971) had children who were 5, 8, and 10 years old stand six inches (15 cm) behind adults in theater lines. Five-year-olds were given a positive response, 8-year-olds were ignored, and 10-year-olds were given a cold reaction. Thus, as children get older, they are treated more like adult invaders. Finally, in a study that examined whether the status of the invader affects reactions to him or her, Barash (1973) varied the clothing confederate invaders wore and found that those who wore "faculty-like" attire evoked faster flight than those who wore casual clothing.

How could one ameliorate some of the

negative effects on the victim, if forced to invade someone's personal space? Research by Quick and Crano (1973) found that just saying "Hello" lowered the number of victims who fled, while Sundstrom and Sundstrom (1977) suggest that asking permission can make a difference. Schavio (1975) reported that invaders who were reading newspapers elicited more favorable responses in victims than a "no newspaper" control condition. But perhaps the best way to avoid torturing those you invade comes from research by Smith and Knowles (1979, p. 449), who suggest that "negative reactions occur only when there is no immediately apparent and appropriate reason for the invader to be standing close." So, as long as you behave so that your victim believes you have a good reason for your invasion, you may be able to avoid inflicting pain on others.

Are there gender differences in reaction to personal space invasions? It is interesting to note that males generally react more negatively to invaders than females (Patterson, Mullens, & Romano, 1971), although there are exceptions (Bell, Kline, & Barnard, 1988). On airplanes men use the common armrest three times as much as women, and are more apt to get annoyed if their neighbor uses it. In part, the larger spaces taken up by men and their more negative reactions to invasions may be responsible for the fact that women are typically approached more closely than are men (Long, Selby, & Calhoun, 1980). Overall, women have more tolerance for distances that are inappropriately close than men (Aiello, 1987).

The Effects of Invading Another's Personal Space

We have spoken about how it feels to be the *victim* of a personal space invasion, but have said nothing about how it feels to be the invader. Studies have looked at what happens when people are placed in dilemmas that require them to become personal space "invaders." Several studies have found that people do not even like to *approach* the personal space of others. In one study (Barefoot, Hoople, & McClay, 1972), a lone confederate was stationed 1, 5, or 10 feet (0.3, 1.5, or 3.0 m) from a water fountain. Fewer passersby approached the fountain when doing so would violate the confederate's personal space (i.e., at the 1-foot distance) than when it would not (i.e., at the 5- or 10-foot distances). While people will avoid a water fountain when the setting is uncrowded, it becomes easier to invade someone's personal space (and take a drink) under crowded conditions (Thalhofer, 1980). Surrounded by a crowd we become "overloaded" and are less attentive to social cues (e.g., that we may cause another person discomfort). Another study demonstrated that it may be aversive to approach the personal space of a group, as well as a lone individual. Knowles and Bassett (1976) positioned groups of varying sizes on a hallway bench and observed "deflection" in the walking patterns of passersby as they walked past the seated confederates. As the number of confederates on the bench increased, passersby were "deflected" farther away. Thus, it appears that approaching the personal space of either lone individuals or groups is a threatening experience, to be avoided if possible. Design features that allow people to avoid invading others' personal space would probably be appreciated by many of us.

Several other experiments have looked at the invader's reactions to physically penetrating, rather than merely approaching, the personal space of interacting dyads. One study suggests that for females it is easier to invade the personal space of someone who is smiling than of someone displaying a neutral face, while for males the reverse is true (e.g., Hughes & Goldman, 1978; Lockhard, McVittie, & Isaac, 1977). And, at least for males, it may be still easier to violate the space of one who has his or her back toward

HOW DO GROUPS RESPOND TO PERSONAL SPACE INVASIONS?

In general, we have restricted our attention to the effects of personal space invasions on lone individuals. In a very interesting study, Knowles (1972) extended this line of research to an exploration of how *groups* of people respond to personal space invasions. His findings suggest that groups, like individuals, engage in compensatory responses when their space is invaded, constituting evidence for a group analog to personal space.

What did Knowles do to establish that groups, like individuals, engage in compensatory responses when invaded? On a city street he had a confederate approach a pair of pedestrians (subjects) walking in the opposite direction. The invader walked so it appeared that he or she intended to walk right between the two pedestrians. Over half the pairs moved together to avoid an intrusion and some reprimanded the invader; this suggests that groups try to maintain their personal space—even in the face of invasion. Further, group-level avoidance of intrusion was more frequent when the pedestrians consisted of a male and a female rather than individuals of the same sex. In a later study, Knowles and Brickner (1981) found that the more cohesive the dyad, the more it resisted the intrusion, i.e., protected its "group space."

the invader (Hughes & Goldman, 1978). Efran and Cheyne (1974) found that passersby are less likely to "invade" if the individuals in the dyad are conversing, if they are occupying Hall's personal space zone rather than social distance, and if they are of the opposite sex. Similar results were reported by other studies (e.g., Bouska & Beatty, 1978), which also found that an "invasion" was less likely if the interactants appeared to be of high status (e.g., a businessman, a priest). When it is necessary to invade, the status of the victims also determines how the invader treats them. High-status individuals receive "positive deferential" behaviors (e.g., signals of appreciation), while those with low status receive signs of negative deference (e.g., derogation) from the invaders (Fortenberry et al., 1978). Finally, dyads comprised of individuals who are African American are more likely to be invaded than Caucasian or mixed-race dyads (Brown, 1981).

Even though it is easier to invade some people's personal space than others, it is generally aversive to violate the personal space of others. In a finding that shows just how taxing it is to invade interacting dyads, it was observed that subjects forced to invade tended to look at the floor rather than ahead and to close their eyes (Cheyne & Efran, 1972; Efran & Cheyne, 1974). Further, Efran and Cheyne (1974) reported that the act of invading interacting dyads has affective consequences: Subjects in "invasion" conditions displayed more negative moods and more hostile facial responses than noninvading control subjects. How does the invader react to penetrating a group larger than a dyad? Knowles (1973) created "targets," groups of two or four persons who were interacting in a hallway so that passersby had two choices:

to violate the group space or to go around the interactants. Fewer people penetrated the four- than the two-person group, and low-status individuals were invaded more often than high-status individuals. Thus, not only individuals and dyads but larger groups appear to be aversive to invade. For the invaders, the permeability of interacting targets depends on such factors as status, group size, and sexual composition. Further, it is apparent that groups, like individuals, are recognized as having a sort of personal space. (Note that the study reviewed in the box on page 302, in which groups responded as a unit to a confederate invader, also supports the idea of personal space at the group level.)

SUMMARY OF PERSONAL SPACE

Personal space is an invisible, portable boundary which regulates how closely we interact with others. Many conceptual perspectives may be applied to suggest different functions of personal space. A combination of these approaches implies that personal space serves two major functions: protection and communication.

Personal space expands and contracts depending on situational conditions, and as a function of individual differences. People interact more closely with similar than with dissimilar others, and in pleasant than in unpleasant interaction situations. Individual differences that affect personal space preferences include gender, certain cross- and subcultural differences, age, and personality factors (e.g., internality–externality, anxiety, introversion–extroversion). Physical factors (e.g., ceiling height, position in room) also affect personal space preferences.

Some of the same factors, such as gender and interpersonal attraction, which impact on the amount of personal space we prefer to maintain also affect our interpersonal positioning. In addition, the appropriateness of spacing (e.g., too close versus too far) affects goal fulfillment. Inappropriate spacing also leads to negative affect and to compensatory responses.

Similarly, personal space invasions elicit negative affect, arousal, negative inferences and compensatory reactions. The intensity of negative reactions varies as a function of situational conditions and individual differences. Finally, being placed in the role of personal space invader is aversive, and is avoided if possible. With this capsule summary of personal space in mind, we move on to a discussion of territorial behavior.

TERRITORIAL BEHAVIOR

We mentioned at the beginning of this chapter that both personal space and territoriality are interpersonal boundary regulation mechanisms with certain differentiating characteristics. *Personal space* tends to be invisible, movable, person centered, and regulates how closely individuals will interact. *Territory* is visible, relatively stationary, visibly bounded, and tends to be home centered, regulating who will interact (Sommer, 1969). Also, territories are generally much larger than personal space; and whether or not we are on our own territory, we still maintain a personal space zone.

One way of viewing *territories* is as places that are owned or controlled by one or more individuals. Anyone who has ever been on the sending or receiving end of a statement like "Don't you ever set foot on my property again," has confronted the concept of *territoriality* head on. In addition to the notion of demarcation and defense of space, territories

Figure 8–10 Fences and signs are among the many ways people demarcate and defend their territories.

also play a role in organizing interactions between individuals and groups, can serve as vehicles for displaying one's identity, and can be associated with feelings, valuation, or attachment regarding space (Figure 8–10).

Although most of us have an instinctive feeling of what territoriality is, it is difficult to define, and there is considerable controversy among researchers about what constitutes the best definition. Our definition of territoriality in humans is representative of "mainstream" views in the field (for commentaries on the definitions used by diverse groups of researchers, see Altman & Chemers, 1980; Brown, 1987; Taylor, 1988; Taylor & Brooks, 1980). For us, *human* **territoriality** *can be viewed as a set of behaviors and cognitions a person or group exhibits, based on perceived ownership of physical space.* Perceived ownership as used here may refer either to actual ownership (e.g., as with your home) or to control over space (e.g., you may control but not own your office, if it is part of a building owned by another). Territorial be-

haviors serve important motives and needs for the organism and include occupying an area, establishing control over it, personalizing it, thoughts, beliefs, or feelings about it, and in some cases defending it (Brown, 1987; Taylor, 1988). Note that the concepts of "territory" and "territoriality" illustrate the interdependent nature of human–environment transactions. Without a territory there would be no territoriality, and vice versa (Carpenter, 1958).

According to Altman and his colleagues (Altman, 1975; Altman & Chemers, 1980), three types of territories are used by humans, and this distinction has been supported in research by others (Taylor & Stough, 1978). These differ in their importance to the individual's or group's life—*primary* territories are most important, followed by *secondary* and *public* territories. They also differ in the duration of occupancy, the cognitions they foster in the occupant and others (e.g., the extent of perceived ownership), the amount of personalization, and the likelihood of de-

Table 8–3 Territorial Behaviors Associated With Pri...

	Extent to Which Territory Is Occupied... of Perceived Ownership by Self and...
Primary Territory (e.g., home, office)	*High.* Perceived to be owned... relatively permanent manne... occupant and others.
Secondary Territory (e.g., classroom)	*Moderate.* Not owned; occupa... perceived by others as one... number of qualified users.
Public Territory (e.g., area of beach)	*Low.* Not owned; control is ver... difficult to assert, and occup... is perceived by others as on... a large number of possible u...

Based on Altman (1975).

fense if violated (these differences are highlighted in Table 8–3). As we will discuss later, different types of territories provide different benefits for individuals (e.g., primary territories such as a bedroom promote privacy and control and allow for the expression of one's identity, functions not promoted in a public territory). Therefore, based on the type of activity we want to engage in and the needs it poses, we choose a particular type of territory (Taylor, 1988; Taylor & Ferguson, 1978).

THE ORIGINS OF TERRITORIAL FUNCTIONING

Territorial behavior is practiced by humans and animals. Some researchers consider human territoriality to be *instinctive*, some consider it to be *learned*, and some consider it an *interaction* of the two (cf. Brown, 1987; Taylor, 1988). According to the instinct view, territorial behavior in humans and animals is instinctively determined: There is a drive to claim and defend territory (e.g., humans and animals mark off their turf to keep others out and respond with vocal warnings and bodily threats to invaders; Ardrey, 1966; Lorenz, 1966). Since Earth has a limited

amount of space, and we are all driven to make and defend territorial claims, conflict is inevitable. Needless to say, this set of beliefs makes some fairly pessimistic predictions regarding the future of humankind. However, few investigators hold that territorial behavior is entirely instinctive.

The position that territoriality is *learned* suggests that in humans it results from past experience and from culture. For example, people learn through socialization that certain places are associated with particular roles. And the patterns of learning that occur depend on culture (e.g., some cultures are nomadic and relatively aterritorial, while others are highly territorial). Some proponents of learned territorial behavior assume that such learning is limited to humans; in animals territoriality is instinctively driven. For them, even when humans and animals exhibit similar behaviors, such as aggression against an intruder, the same mechanisms may not be responsible.

Finally, from another perspective, human and perhaps even animal territorial behavior may result from an *interaction of instinct and learning*. This view holds that both processes contribute to territorial actions. The exact way in which this may occur

n & Chemers,
e possible that we
territorial behaviors
t that learning deter-
ty and form of our territo-
ernatively, it has been proposed
guides some types of elementary
al behaviors, while learning is respon-
or more complex ones (Esser, 1976).

It should be noted that while instinct theories have historically been invoked more to explain animal territorial behavior and learning and interactive perspectives have been used more to explain human territoriality, some research suggests replacing the instinct perspective on animal territoriality with a more complex conceptualization. Based on this work, the notion of a territorial instinct in animals which is "unresponsive to learning and driven to expression" is becoming less accepted (Brown, 1987, p. 508). Instead, animal territoriality is viewed more as an adaptive mechanism which is responsive to ecological considerations (e.g., resource availability) and which is flexible across time and different types of settings (Brown, 1987). Given that the conceptualization of animal territoriality has become less biological, the argument that human territoriality is strictly biologically based has come to hold even less weight than before.

FUNCTIONS OF TERRITORIALITY

Just as there may be differences between humans and animals in the mechanisms responsible for territorial behavior, there are differences in the functions territorial behavior plays for each. While it should not be forgotten that there are variations between the species (e.g., Carpenter, 1958), animals maintain territory for such important functions as mating, dispersing the population more evenly, food gathering and protecting food supplies, shelter, rearing of young, and minimizing intraspecies aggression. Thus, territories are often quite essential to their survival. Also, animals tend to defend territories vigorously when violations occur (Edney, 1976), though this depends on resource distribution and competition.

Humans are more flexible with respect to the use of territories for functions such as those mentioned above. For us, many of the purposes territories serve are not as closely related to survival, and they may be seen primarily as "organizers" on a variety of dimensions (e.g., they promote predictability, order, and stability in life; e.g., Edney, 1975). For example, territories allow us to "map" the types of behavior we can anticipate in particular places, whom we will encounter there, what someone's status is, and so forth. In this way they help us plan and order our daily lives. Territories also contribute to order due to their relationship to social roles (e.g., the boss controls his or her office, the company lounge, the lunchroom, etc.). Precisely *how* territories function to "organize things" depends on the particular space in question (for some examples, see Table 8–4). In addition to their organizing function, territories may lead to feelings of distinctiveness, privacy, and a sense of personal identity. People may experience a higher self-concept due to the territories they possess, and the ways they have personalized them. They may even proudly refer to themselves as "the person who lives in the red house on Oak Street." In sum, social, cultural, and cognitive elements are more characteristic of human than animal territoriality. While animal territoriality is rooted in survival needs, human territoriality is also associated with "higher-order" needs (e.g., self-image, recognition; Gold, 1982).

How do humans and animals differ with regard to territorial defense? In general, humans very rarely resort to aggressively defending their turf. When they must deal with territorial invasions, their defense is typically based on laws that defend territorial rights,

Table 8–4 The Organizing Functions of Human Territories in Some Everyday Settings*

For People in . . .	*Organizing Function of Territory*
Public places (e.g., a library, the beach)	Organizes space; provides an interpersonal distancing mechanism.
Primary territories (e.g., a bedroom)	Organizes space by providing a place that promotes solitude; allows intimacy; expresses personal identity.
Small face-to-face groups (e.g., the family)	Clarifies the social ecology of the group and facilitates group functioning; may provide home court advantage.
Neighborhoods and communities	Promotes an "in-group" who "belongs" and can be trusted; differentiates it from an "out-group" who doesn't belong and can't be trusted. In some urban areas, territorial control makes a space safe to use.

After Taylor, 1978.

rather than brute force (Brown, 1987). This is not to suggest that relatively dramatic forms of territorial defense never occur in humans. Indeed, many international problems, as well as interpersonal difficulties (e.g., fights with a roommate over use of the VCR) involve territorial issues and associated aggression. However, one reason for the typically lower degree of territorial defense in humans than animals is that people generally recognize and avoid each other's territory. This varies, of course, with the type of territory (as depicted in Table 8–3 on page 305). In addition, humans routinely entertain others on their turf without aggression. When human territorial aggression does occur, it often takes a different form from that of animals. While human territory-related fighting tends to occur more often at the group level (e.g., one nation versus another), animal fighting is more frequently at the individual level, though it occurs at the group level as well. Unfortunately, humans now have the capacity to destroy one another's territory without physically invading, through the use of long-range weapons (Edney, 1976).

A broad concept of the functions of territory for humans may be achieved through an analysis in terms of the envi-

ronment–behavior theoretical formulations (e.g., arousal, overload) discussed in detail in Chapter 4, and earlier in this chapter in the context of personal space. For example, in terms of the *overload* approach, clearly defined territories reduce environmental load by lending a sense of order that lowers the amount and complexity of incoming stimulation and makes life easier to cope with. In effect, they afford role organization (e.g., the host has one role and the visitor another); allow us to assume continuity in the future (e.g., we will always be able to sleep in our house); and afford us control over inputs from the outside world (e.g., "No Trespassing" signs keep out extraneous inputs). *Stress* formulations view territories as functioning to reduce stress by controlling the amount of stressful stimuli with which we must contend. According to Altman's (1975) *privacy regulation model*, territories are used to maintain a consistency between desired and achieved levels of privacy. From the *arousal* perspective, territories hold down arousal (e.g., by moderating the amount of stimulation we are exposed to). In the context of the *ethological* conceptualization, territories may be seen as preventing aggression and affording identity. Finally, in line with the predictions of *control* models, the fact that territories facilitate unhindered performance of chosen behaviors should be quite beneficial. Territories should also have favorable effects because the "owner" of a territory controls access to it and what goes on there.

METHODS OF STUDYING TERRITORIALITY IN HUMANS

Past research on territorial behavior has focused mostly on animal populations; a relatively smaller amount of work has dealt with territoriality in humans. Those studies which have been done with humans have looked at territorial behavior in both groups and individuals, employing methodologies that range from controlled laboratory and field experimentation to naturalistic observation. In some cases these methodological approaches have inherent problems when applied to human territorial behavior, which may account for the overall lack of research.

Laboratory experiments are difficult to perform with humans because territoriality implies a strong attachment between an individual and a place (see Chapter 12), which is not easy to create under artificial laboratory conditions. Introducing experimental manipulations (e.g., territorial invasions) into real-world settings (e.g., dormitories) where people do perceive a degree of territorial "ownership" avoids this problem, and has provided some rich data. In addition, many researchers have relied on nonmanipulative (and nonexperimental) field observation of behavior in naturally occurring territories.

Unfortunately, nonmanipulative observation is often fraught with interpretive problems. For example, Vinsel et al. (1980) reported an interesting relationship between the way in which students personalized their dorm room (or primary territory) with decorations, and whether or not they dropped out of college during the following year. Students whose decorations showed diversity

and commitment to the university setting were more likely to survive the rigors of college than those whose decorations did not. However, what these data mean is very unclear. It could be that the way nondropouts personalized their territory led to feelings of security, which promoted success in school. On the other hand, personalizing one's dorm room may reflect commitment to it, and lack of personalization may reflect a sense of alienation from that setting that one would expect in someone planning to drop out of school. Other studies employing nonmanipulative observation of territorial behaviors are similarly difficult to interpret.

RESEARCH EVIDENCE OF TERRITORIAL BEHAVIOR

Territorial behavior occurs between groups, within groups, and when alone. It is manifested in many ways, and it will become clear that it has some important consequences.

Territorial Behavior Between Groups

Suttles (1968) observed the territorial actions between various ethnic groups on Chicago's South Side (public territory). Each group claimed and defended a separate territory, and there were some "shared territories" in which certain community resources were used separately by each ethnic group in a prescribed fashion. Different groups would use them, but never at the same time. Another interesting example of group territoriality stems from an analysis of street gang behavior in Philadelphia (Ley & Cybriwsky, 1974a). It was found that street gangs are highly territorial, often taking their names from a street intersection at the center of their territory. Each gang demarcates its territory, and territorial domains are recognized by gang and nongang youth. Outsiders usually avoided the in-group's turf, and were greeted with hostility when they entered.

What functions does territoriality between groups serve? Such actions tend to facilitate trust *within* the group. Sharing a territory can lead to feelings of group identity and security, perhaps because people in the same territory share common experiences (Taylor, 1978). And the security afforded by a territory is important: In some areas of a city having territorial control of a space makes it safe to use (Taylor, 1988). However, the in-group cohesion resulting from territories can have negative effects (e.g., the formation of gangs). It may also cause "outsiders" to be viewed with suspicion. Both of these consequences could elicit aggression.

Territorial Behavior Within Groups

Group members often adopt certain areas as "theirs." In primary territories, families have territorial rules that facilitate the functioning of the household (Ahrentzen, Levine, & Michelson, 1989; Sebba & Churchman, 1983). These support the social organization of the family by allowing certain behaviors by some members, in particular areas (e.g., the parents can engage in intimacy in the bedroom undisturbed; Taylor & Stough, 1978). In one study of territoriality in family life, it was found that people who share bedrooms display territorial behavior, as do individuals at the dining table (e.g., through seating patterns). Territorial divisions in the home depend on the particular activities of family members, as well as whether or not the mother works outside the home (Ahrentzen et al., 1989). Family members generally respect each other's territorial markers, such as closed doors (Altman, Nelson, & Lett, 1972), and a violation of territorial rules often leads to punishment of the one at fault (Scheflen, 1976).

Territorial behavior within groups is not limited to primary territories. Lipman (1967) found that residents of a retirement home made almost exclusive claims to certain chairs in the day rooms. They defended their "ter-

ritory" despite considerable psychological costs and physical inconvenience. Even students stumbling into their 8:00 A.M. class display territorial behavior. Haber (1980) found that in formal style (e.g., traditional lecture) classes, about 75 percent of the students claimed a particular seat, and occupied it more than half the time. In informally run classes, this occurred for only 30 percent of the students. Also, of those students who claimed a seat to be their territory, 83 percent chose the one that they occupied during the first, second, or third class period. In addition to choosing a seat as their territory, many students used markers to delineate their turf. "Marking" (e.g., placing books and possessions to defend one's turf) is also frequent in libraries and cafeterias, among other places (e.g., Fisher & Byrne, 1975; Taylor & Brooks, 1980).

A number of researchers have investigated whether some members of intact groups are more territorial than others. One line of research has searched for gender differences, and it is reliably found that males are more territorial—have larger territories—than females (Mercer & Benjamin, 1980). In addition, some studies with animals show a strong relationship between dominance within a group and territoriality, generally finding that more dominant animals are more territorial. This finding, however, depends on resource scarcity and competition. Although research with humans has sometimes demonstrated mild support for the dominance–territoriality relationship found in animals, in some studies opposite results have been observed. Whether this inconsistency is the result of methodological difficulties (e.g., problems in defining dominance and territoriality operationally; use of unusual subject populations) or the absence of reliable relationships between dominance and territoriality in humans, is at present somewhat uncertain (cf. Edney, 1975). In any event, it seems that the relationship between dominance and territoriality is quite complex (Brown, 1987; Taylor, 1988).

One attempt to interpret these conflicting findings is an analysis made by Sundstrom (1976), who suggested that whether more dominant individuals will display higher or lower territorial behavior depends on the situational context. He posited that in environments offering only a few desirable places (e.g., private rooms in a home for delinquent boys), dominant individuals should end up with them and hence appear to be highly territorial. In contrast, when a setting has no areas that are more desirable than others, dominant individuals should roam over large amounts of space and appear to be very low in territoriality. This hypothesis has been supported, at least in a suggestive sense, by a series of studies. In the stark and rather uniform confines of a mental hospital, Esser et al. (1965) obtained suggestive evidence of an inverse relationship between dominance and territoriality (i.e., more dominant individuals displayed less territoriality). In a home for juvenile delinquents, which presumably had more environmental variation, a direct relationship was found between dominance and territoriality. In addition to its dependence on the level of environmental variation in a setting, the dominance–territoriality relationship also depends on group composition and social organization. It has been shown that adding and removing group members or changing the social organization of the group can significantly affect the nature of dominance–territoriality relationships (DeLong, 1973; Sundstrom & Altman, 1976).

Researchers (e.g., Taylor, 1978) suggest that where a dominance–territoriality relationship does exist, it should facilitate group functioning. This has yet to be tested experimentally—but why do *you* feel this represents a viable hypothesis? Investigators propose that if those with high dominance are recognized as having access to the best

space, this helps clarify the ecology of the group and thus reduces conflicts within it (e.g., Taylor, 1978).

Territorial Behavior When Alone

Territoriality also exists for individuals who are alone. In fact, research suggests that people may feel a stronger ownership of a setting when alone than when part of a group (Edney & Uhlig, 1977). Thus, members of a family or roommates may feel lower responsibility to maintain their turf, and may individually exert less surveillance over it, than single occupants. This also implies that there may be more vandalism, theft, and other similar acts in group than in individual residences.

Signals of Territoriality: Communicating Territorial Claims

What do a backyard fence, a chair with a coat on its back, a nameplate on an office door, and a blanket at the beach have in common? All are ways of communicating territorial ownership to others as well as, perhaps, reassuring oneself regarding ownership or propriety over something (Barber, 1990). We engage in these types of behaviors in primary, secondary, and in public territories. How effective are our various defense strategies in warding off territorial invaders? While it might be speculated that they would be increasingly effective as one moves from public to primary territories, this has yet to be demonstrated. In certain public territories (e.g., an airport, bus station), rather than providing protection from invasion, valuable territorial markers (e.g., a suitcase, a fur coat) are apt to be stolen (Brown, 1987)! In general, research has focused on assessing the relative effectiveness of different types of territorial signals in a particular setting (Figures 8–10 and 8–11).

Sommer (1969) conducted studies that looked at the relative effectiveness of various strategies for warding off territorial invaders

Figure 8–11 Note the various forms of territorial defenses that people employ.

in libraries. At low levels of overall density, people were less likely to sit down at tables with any kind of marker (e.g., a sandwich, a sweater, books) than at tables without such personal effects. However, under conditions of high density, it appears that potential invaders take an attributional approach to interpreting whether or not particular markers really represent someone who intends to return. To the extent that markers are personal and valuable (a coat, a notebook with a name on it), territorial "ownership" tends to be respected. However, when attributions of intent are not clear, as when the marker is a library book or a newspaper, the resulting uncertainty coupled with the fact that only a few seats are available tends to lead to invasions. Are markers belonging to men and women equally effective at defending territories? Research indicates that "male" markers are much more effective at territorial defense than "female" markers, and that ter-

ritories belonging to males (e.g., a man's versus a woman's desk) are less apt to be invaded (Haber, 1980; Shaffer & Sadowski, 1975). It should be noted that although we and others (e.g., Taylor, 1978) consider such markers as books and coats to be territorial indicators, there is debate as to whether they function mainly as territorial markers or as interpersonal distance maintainers (cf. Becker & Mayo, 1971). Resolution of this subtle point is left to future researchers.

Ley and Cybriwsky (1974a) suggested another interesting means of indicating turf ownership. They found that in Philadelphia, wall graffiti offer an accurate indication of gang territorial ownership. As a general rule, gang graffiti (i.e., graffiti that includes a gang's name) become denser with increasing proximity to the core of the gang's territory. These graffiti are readily accepted by neighborhood youth as an accurate portrayal of each gang's area of control. It was also found that often, when street gangs invaded each other's territory, they spray-painted their name in the rival gang's turf. The "invaded" gang generally responded by adding an obscene word after the rival gang's name! Gangs that were not respected (or feared) generally had turf covered with a large amount of graffiti put there by neighboring gangs.

Finally, in addition to traditional (e.g., books, coats) and nontraditional markers, such as graffiti, it has been suggested that *nonverbal* markers may be used to communicate territorial claims. Studies have found that restaurant patrons touch their plates when they have reason to assert a territorial claim (Truscott, Parmelee, & Werner, 1977), and in a video arcade, Werner, Brown, and Damron (1981) found that standing close to or touching a video game protected it from violation by others. In addition, people were more apt to touch their video game to assert ownership when others were approaching.

Personalizing Territories

In addition to staking territorial claims, people tend to *personalize* their territory. Some means of personalizing territory (e.g., working on one's lawn or garden, making improvements to one's property) may provide opportunities for neighbors to get to know each other better, to become more cohesive (Brown & Werner, 1985), and thus enable residents to better distinguish between residents and strangers. This may lead to more surveillance and fewer problems with outsiders (Taylor, Gottfredson, & Brower, 1981). Personalization may also elicit greater feelings of attachment to a place and instill the feeling that it is "comfortable" and "homelike" (Becker & Coniglio, 1975). In addition, personalizations often reflect the self-identity of the owner. For example, artifacts in people's living rooms reflect their social status (Laumann & House, 1972), and decorative complexity of housing interiors

correlates with materialistic values (Weisner & Weibel, 1981). Further, observers form impressions of others' idealized self-images (Sadalla, Burroughs, & Quaid, 1980), of their degree of sociability (Werner, Peterson-Lewis, & Brown, 1989) or of their ethnic identities (Arreola, 1981) from their personalizations. Are there gender differences in the extent to which people personalize and feel attached to territories? The literature suggests that women engage more in personalization and have greater feelings of attachment to their homes than men (Sebba & Churchman, 1983; Tognoli, 1980). Nevertheless, these feelings of person–place attachment are important for both genders, and are one of the many losses experienced by the growing members of homeless people (Rivlin, 1990). For more on homelessness, see Chapter 10 on cities.

TERRITORY AND AGGRESSION

One of the most interesting aspects of territoriality is the relationship between territory and aggression. Although it is not always realized, territory may serve either as an instigator to aggression or as a stabilizer to prevent aggression. The function it serves depends on a number of situational conditions. One factor that affects the relationship between territoriality and aggression is the status of a particular territory (i.e., whether it is unestablished, disputed, or well established). When territory is unestablished or disputed, aggression is more common. Observational evidence to this effect is provided by Ley and Cybriwsky (1974a), who found that street gangs engaged in more intergang violence when territorial boundaries were ambiguous or unsettled than when they were well established. Parallel evidence is available for animals: It has been found that animals fight more when territories are being established or are under dispute than after territorial boundaries have been well drawn (Eibl-Eibesfeldt, 1970; Lorenz, 1966). Apparently, under the former conditions, resource competition becomes more intense.

While unestablished or disputed territory promotes aggression, established territorial boundaries often lend stability and lead to reduced hostility in humans as well as in animals (O'Neal & McDonald, 1976). For example, Altman, Nelson, and Lett (1972) observed that confined groups that established territories early in their confinement evidenced smoother interpersonal relationships and were more stable socially than groups that failed to establish territories early. O'Neill and Paluck (1973) reported a drop in the level of aggression in groups of retarded boys after the introduction of identifiable territories. What are the dynamics of the process by which territorial boundaries decrease aggression? We mentioned earlier that territorial behavior serves an organizing function, indicating what is "ours" and what is "theirs." Thus, well-established territories should be less subject to intrusion, which tends to elicit aggression. In line with this analysis, several investigators (e.g., Mack, 1954; Marine, 1966) have found that the separation of neighborhood ethnic groups by clearly defined boundaries led to decreased territorial intrusion, and less intergroup conflict.

When territorial invasions do occur, what are the consequences? Predicting reactions to territorial invasions is complex because our responses appear to depend on situational conditions. For example, Altman (1975) proposed that the attributions we make for a violation will determine our response, and that we will only consider aggression when we feel the other's behavior was malicious. And generally, we try other verbal adjustive responses (e.g., warning the individual to leave, threatening him or her), as well as physical ones (e.g., putting up a fence, or a "No Trespassing" sign) first, resorting to aggression only when these are unavailable or unheeded. In addition, Edney (1974) suggested that for humans many forms of "appropriate" territorial invasion exist (e.g., when guests are present) that do not elicit aggression.

One additional factor that may determine whether invasion leads to aggression in humans is the location of the territory "under siege" along a primary territory–public territory dimension (Brown, 1987). Invaders of primary territories are likely to elicit the most intense aggression (see Table 8–3). By definition, primary territories are more central to the owner's life, symbolize his or her identity, and are associated with more legitimate feelings of control than public territories. Invasions of primary territories (e.g., homes) are also more apt to be intentional and to involve a deliberate crossing of boundaries or markers than invasions of secondary or public territories. Thus, invaders of primary territories are seen as more threatening and hence are dealt with more harshly. The intensity of the territorial invasion–aggression relationship for primary territories is reflected in the ambiguity of many local laws dealing with the prosecution of a homeowner accused of killing an intruder (Geen & O'Neal, 1976). One means some homeowners use to prevent invasion of primary territories is to erect markers of territorial defense (e.g., "No Trespassing" signs). Edney (1972) compared homeowners who displayed such markers with those who did not. He found that individuals who erected forms of territorial defense had lived in their houses longer and intended to stay longer than people without territorial markers. Further, residents who displayed markers answered their doorbells faster, which may be interpreted as a sign of defensive vigilance.

In contrast to the defensive posture assumed by holders of primary territory, a study by O'Neal, Caldwell, and Gallup (1975) found weaker evidence for territorial defense in public territory. Often, because people have minimal "rights" to public territories, they simply respond to territorial invasions by retreating (Brown, 1987) or do nothing at all. One study was conducted with children who were exposed to a manipulation designed to induce possessiveness toward a carpeted play area. Children were led to another room, where they could press a button to electrically shock a clown who was advancing toward their turf. Invasions under these conditions did not lead to a convincing demonstration of aggression. However, other research (e.g., Haggard & Werner, 1990) indicates that even in public territories, people may exhibit defensive behaviors toward intruders. Haggard and Werner (1990) suggested that under certain conditions people will ask intruders to leave a public territory. Such reactions are most likely to occur if information cues (e.g., signs telling others to keep out) and environmental cues support privacy regulation. In such situations, individuals are likely to cite aspects of the situation (e.g., the signs), or to give other "excuses" (e.g., the difficulty of performing their task with the territorial invader present) as their reason for asking the invader to leave. Attempts to regain public territory are generally preceded by expressions of surprise or intimidation (Taylor & Brooks, 1980). Also, research by Taylor and Brooks (1980) indicates that as the *value* of the invaded public territory increases (e.g., a library carrel versus a seat at a table), the likelihood of its defense rises. Even under some of the conditions which maximize the likelihood of defense of public territories, several studies (e.g., Becker, 1973; Becker & Mayo, 1971) suggest a strong reluctance on the part of subjects to defend them. It seems that flight is the most frequent reaction to invasions of public turf (Brown, 1987).

One means of defending a public territory about to be invaded would be simply *not* to yield to the apparent demands of the territorial invader. In a study by Ruback and Snow (1993), the behavior of individuals who were drinking at a public water fountain whose territory was about to be invaded by another thirsty person, was studied. The results of the study showed evidence of nonconscious racism. It was found that white subjects left the drinking fountain faster when they were intruded by a white territorial invader than in a control condition. In contrast, African-Americans stayed at the fountain *longer* when they were invaded by a white confederate than in a control condition. In a second study, it was found that racially dissimilar, "would-be" territorial invaders waited longer to invade the water fountain than did same-race invaders, and that water fountain drinkers stayed longer (i.e., defended their territory longer) following cross-race territorial invasions than following same-race invasions. Other studies have also shown that under certain conditions, people will refuse to yield public territory. Ruback, Pape, and Doriot (1989) reported that individuals using public telephones spent more time on the phone (i.e., defended their territory more) when threatened by a territorial invasion (another who was encroaching on them and who wanted to use the phone), than in a control condition. Similar observations have been made by Werner, Brown, and Damron (1981).

Finally, it has been found that whether a territory is perceived as temporary or permanent affects our likelihood of aggression in defending it. Schmidt (1976) reported that occupants of permanent territories challenged invaders more quickly and gave them more hostile treatment than occupants of temporary territories. For example, they were more punitive to invaders, and also more aggressive to strangers following an invasion, than those in temporary territories. So, invasions of permanent territories may promote more aggression toward the instigator, as well as more generalized aggression, than violations of temporary territories.

TERRITORY AS A SECURITY BLANKET: HOME SWEET HOME

If individuals are willing to defend territories from invasion by resorting to aggression, it would seem that such areas must be associated with a number of important benefits. The assertion that territories have beneficial aspects is supported by the conceptual analysis we put forward earlier, which suggested that many properties of territories are associated with positive effects. The truth of the saying "Home Sweet Home" has been assessed in a number of experiments. In a study which also supported the assumptions of Altman's (1975) conceptual distinction between primary, secondary, and public territory, Taylor and Stough (1978) found that subjects reported the greatest feelings of control in primary territories (e.g., dormitory rooms), followed by secondary territories (e.g., a fraternity house) and public territories (e.g., a bar). In a great deal of research, feelings of control are related to a sense of well-being, as well as other positive effects (e.g., beneficial implications for health). And a study by Edney (1975) using Yale undergraduates highlights additional benefits of being on one's turf. The experiment took place in the dormitory room (primary territory) of one member of the pair, where the other member was a "visitor." Subjects who were in their own territory were rated by visitors as more relaxed than residents rated visitors, and residents rated the rooms as more pleasant and private than visitors did. Residents also expressed greater feelings of passive control. In a related study, Edney and Uhlig (1977) reported that subjects induced to think of a room as their territory felt less aroused, and found the setting

to be more pleasant than others in the control group.

While being on one's own turf is typically associated with enhanced perceived and actual control, in offices at least, this may depend in part on status. Katovich (1986) had subjects role-play a conversation between an employer and an employee which took place either in the boss's or the employee's office. It was found that the office holder always initiated the handshake at the start of the interaction, but that the power to invite the "visitor" to enter depended on status. While the boss invited the employee to enter when the meeting occurred in his office, he sat down *without* waiting for an invitation when it was in the employee's office! Thus, in certain places, one's territorial "rights" depend on one's status.

An additional advantage of being "at home" is that under conditions that do not promote liking (e.g., competition, disagreement, or unequal roles), the resident has a "home court" advantage that allows him or her to dominate the visitor. Martindale (1971) reported that dormitory residents were more successful at a competitive negotiation task on "their own turf" than were visitors. Similarly, Conroy and Sundstrom (1977) found that when resident–visitor dyads held dissimilar opinions (conditions that cause disliking), residents talked more and exerted more dominance over the conversation than visitors. When the two had similar opinions (conditions that promote liking), visitors talked more and dominated the conversation. The authors interpreted residents' allowing this as a sort of "hospitality effect." In addition, Taylor and Lanni (1981) have shown that residents have an advantage under conditions that do not facilitate liking in triads as well as dyads, and for both low- and high-dominance individuals. The effect is even true of larger groups and in settings other than primary territory. In a comparison of the "home" and "away"

AN ANALYSIS OF THE "HOME-COURT ADVANTAGE"

Just how pervasive is the "home-court advantage" in professional and college sports? A study by Schwartz and Barsky (1977) looked at the outcomes of 1,880 major league baseball games, 182 professional football games, 542 professional hockey games, and 1,485 college basketball games which took place in one year. They assumed that in the absence of a home-court advantage, about half of a team's total wins for the season should occur at home and half "on the road." What did they find? The results are shown in Table 8–5. For all sports, there is a decisive home-court advantage. This varies somewhat according to the sport in question, ranging from professional baseball, where 53 percent of the total wins occur at home, to professional hockey, where 64 percent of the wins during the season occurred at home. The analysis of basketball records, which employs slightly different techniques and which is therefore not incorporated into the table, suggests that still a higher proportion of college basketball contests are won on the home court. This implies that the advantage of the home team becomes more pronounced for indoor than for outdoor sports.

Table 8–5   Percentage of Games Won by Home Team in Baseball, Football, and Hockey in a Given Year.*

Home Team Outcome	Sport			
	Professional Baseball	Professional Football	College Football	Professional Hockey
Win	53	58	60	64
Lose	47	42	40	36
Total	100	100	100	100

*Ties are excluded. After Schwartz & Barsky, 1977.

records of the University of Utah football team over a three-year period, Altman (1975) found that the team won two-thirds of its home games and only one-fourth of its away games (see box on pages 316–317).

SOME DESIGN IMPLICATIONS

Given that territories may be quite beneficial, it is unfortunate that the design of many settings, especially institutions, does not foster these benefits. Most mental hospitals, homes for the elderly, residential rehabilitation settings, prisons, and other institutions do not contain architectural features or permit behavior (e.g., bringing personal possessions, personalizing an area) that promote feelings of personal territory. The contention that these would benefit patients has been demonstrated in research (Barton, 1966). When areas were redesigned to increase territoriality, or residents were allowed to personalize the environment, the social atmosphere of the ward improved and

Other studies suggest that the "home-field advantage" may be greater for better teams. While even mediocre teams benefit, the better the team, the greater the benefit (James, 1984). However, when pressure to succeed is very high, being at home may be a disadvantage. While being on home turf is beneficial to teams in the first few games of the world series, when the series goes to a "sudden-death" seventh game, home teams win less than 40 percent of the time (Baumeister, 1985)! The fact that the home-turf advantage is lowered when the pressure is on is supported by other studies. Often, teams play better at home during the regular season than during the championships or playoffs (Baumeister & Steinhilber, 1984; Heaton & Sigall, 1989).

When being at home *is* advantageous, what types of differences in team play occur? Schwartz and Barsky found that while the underlying factor in the home-court advantage was that superior offensive play occurs at home compared to "on the road," there were no differences for defensive play. How strongly should the home-court advantage be "weighed," compared with factors like team quality? Strikingly, analyses of the data suggested that the advantage from just being on one's own turf can actually be as significant in determining the outcome of a game as the quality of the team!

Are the same factors (e.g., control) responsible here as were responsible for the dominance of the individual who was on "home turf" in the dormitory studies described earlier? While these factors undoubtedly play a role, there is one additional element—home audience support. And Schwartz and Barsky (1977) feel that this factor—the applause for the home team and jeers for the visitors—is an important determinant in the home-court advantage in sports. This may also be why the home-court advantage is greater for indoor sports, where sounds do not get lost in the air. Also, distance between noisy fans and players is greater outdoors than indoors.

more positive feelings toward the environment were observed (Holahan, 1976; Holahan & Saegert, 1973).

Designing space so that it appears to look like someone's turf has other advantages as well. When spaces have clear boundaries that signal they "belong" to somebody, there is evidence that less crime and vandalism occur. In a study of low-cost urban housing developments, Newman (1972) found that public areas having no clear symbols of ownership were more likely to be vandalized than those with well-marked boundaries. (Expanded coverage of this relationship and the factors that may account for it is provided in Chapter 10.) Although Newman's findings have been subjected to methodological criticism (cf. Adams, 1973), supportive evidence is provided in a study that observed the locations where cars were vandalized in inner-city Philadelphia (Ley & Cybriwsky, 1974b). It was suggested that more vandalism took place near "public" places such as factories, schools, and vacant lots than in areas that

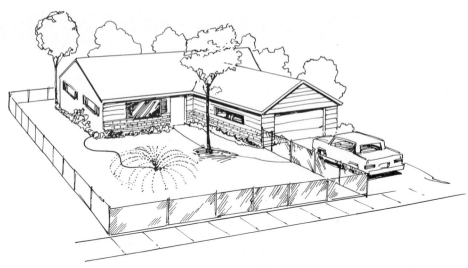

Figure 8–12A   A nonburglarized house on a nonburglarized block
From Brown, 1979; reprinted by permission

signaled territorial ownership, such as private dwellings and small businesses. While the nature of the research precludes a definitive statement, it seems that people tend to respect properties that can be identified as someone's territory more than properties that cannot be easily identified.

An interesting study by Brown (1979) identified a number of specific characteristics of residential areas in general, and homes in particular, that are associated with burglary. Before we tell you what she found, take a look at the houses in Figure 8–12. Which do you think you would rob if you were a burglar? Brown found that signs of defensibility, occupancy, and territorial concern were different in a sample of homes that were not burglarized, than in a corre-

Figure 8–12B   A burglarized house
From Brown, 1979; reprinted by permission.

TERRITORIAL BEHAVIOR AND FEAR OF CRIME IN THE ELDERLY

We have seen that when symbols of ownership are present, less crime and vandalism may occur. Are people who display more territorial markers (e.g., "No Trespassing" signs, fences, external surveillance devices) less fearful of being victims of crime than people who do not display such markers? In an interesting study, Patterson (1978) explored this problem with an elderly population in central Pennsylvania. Since fear of crime is a major source of anxiety for older citizens (some studies have shown it to be greater than fear of illness), determining the effectiveness of territorial markers in ameliorating such fears is important from both an applied and a conceptual perspective. Patterson had interviewers approach the homes of elderly citizens to record unobtrusively any territorial markers.

After gathering these data, the interviewer approached the homeowner and conducted an interview. The interview consisted of several sets of questions, including fear of property loss (e.g., "When I am away, I worry about my property") and

fear of personal assault (e.g., "There are times during the night when I am afraid to go outside"). What were the results of the study? It was found that displaying territorial markers was associated with less fear of both property loss and assault, especially for males (see Figure 8–13).

What do these data mean? It is clear that there is an important relationship between reduced fear of crime in the elderly and territorial behavior. However, since this study is correlational, the mechanism by which territoriality is associated with reduced fear is not clear. One possibility is that erecting territorial markers gives one perceived and perhaps actual control and thus leads to feelings of safety. A study by Pollack and Patterson

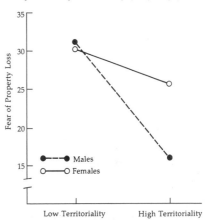

Figure 8–13   Fear of property loss by males and females high and low in territoriality
From Patterson, A. H., 1978. Territorial behavior and fear of crime in the elderly. Environmental Psychology and Nonverbal Behavior, 3, *131–144.*

(1980) as well as research by Normoyle and Lavrakas (1984) tentatively supports this interpretation. If this is the case, there is a clear design implication: Encourage people to display territorial markers to enhance their feelings of security. However, another explanation cannot entirely be ruled out: Those elderly homeowners who feel sufficient mastery of the environment to erect territorial boundaries are also those who would feel secure from victimization in any event. If this is the case, the implications of the research are less clear.

sponding sample which were. Specifically, burglarized homes differed in that the **symbolic barriers** they possessed were public, as opposed to private. For example, burglarized homes had fewer assertions of the owner's private identity (e.g., name and address signs), more signs of public use (e.g., public street signs in front of them), and fewer attempts at property demarcation from the street (e.g., hedges, rock borders). They also had fewer *actual barriers* (e.g., fewer locks or fences to communicate a desire for privacy, and deter public access). Also, on streets where burglaries occurred, there were fewer *traces* (e.g., signs of occupancy) that showed the presence of local residents. Burglarized houses had fewer parked cars and fewer sprinklers operating, and residents were less apt to be seen in their yards by the researchers. In this regard a garage was significant, since it often made it ambiguous whether or not people were home (e.g., a garage without windows can disguise the absence of the car). More burglaries occurred in homes without garages, perhaps because for these homes the absence of cars made it likely that the house was empty. In houses where burglaries occurred, *detectability* (the potential for exercising surveillance) was also lower, and neighboring houses were less visually accessible (see also Brown & Bent-

ley, 1993; MacDonald & Gifford, 1989). While these findings are *consistent* with defensible space theory (Newman, 1972), other findings are not as supportive. In *contrast* to defensible space theory, MacDonald and Gifford (1989) found that a sample of individuals who had actually burglarized homes would *not* avoid houses that looked especially "cared for" (e.g., that had signs of the owner's identity, hedges, or sprinklers). Instead, they seemed to assume that such houses might have valuables inside which would make them an especially *good* target. Additional findings from this study challenged some of the other findings by Brown (1979; e.g., that traces of occupancy, and actual barriers necessarily deter burglary).

Designers should consider the above findings. Too often spaces do not communicate the types of territorial messages they should, or are ambiguous with regard to their territorial status, due to designed-in characteristics. In addition, some territories do not promote the sorts of activities for which people use them (e.g., the value of a primary territory may be hampered due to a lack of adequate soundproofing, or too much visual access). This often leads to lack of use, to use by the wrong parties, or to various types of misuse. Care during the design process could prevent this. ✦

CHAPTER SUMMARY

Personal space is invisible, mobile, and body-centered, regulating how closely individuals interact. It has two purposes: protection and communication. The size of the spatial zone necessary to fulfill the protective and communicative functions changes according to situational variables (e.g., attraction, activity being engaged in) and individual difference variables (i.e., race, personality). Individuals

find it aversive (1) when they are constrained to interact with another person under conditions of inappropriate (too much or too little) personal space; and (2) when their personal space is "invaded" by others. Interacting at inappropriate distances leads to negative affect and negative inferences; personal space invasions precipitate withdrawal and compensatory reactions.

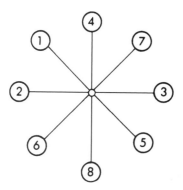

Figure 8–14 Diagramming the shape of personal space

From Duke, M. P., and Nowicki, S. Diagramming the shape of personal space: A new measure and social learning model for interpersonal distance. Journal of Experimental Research in Personality, *1972, 6, 119–132.*

Territory is visible, stationary, and home-centered, regulating who will interact. It serves somewhat different functions in humans and animals; in humans it serves a variety of organizational functions. Human individuals and groups exhibit territorial behavior and have adopted a variety of territorial defense strategies that vary in effectiveness. Territorial invasion by others may or may not lead to aggressive responses by the target, depending on the situation. Further, being on one's own turf has been shown to have a number of advantages and elicits feelings of security and improved performance. Finally, areas that appear to be someone's territory are less likely to be vandalized.

SUGGESTED PROJECTS

1. A scale called the C.I.D.S., or Comfortable Interpersonal Distance Scale (Duke & Nowicki, 1972), permits us to diagram the shape of our personal space without even getting out of our seat! It works like this. Imagine that Figure 8–14 represents an imaginary round room, for which each radius is associated with an entrance. You are

positioned at dead center, facing position number 8. For each of the 8 radii, respond to an imaginary person approaching you by putting a mark on the radius indicating where you would prefer the stimulus person to halt (i.e., the point at which you think you would begin to feel uncomfortable by the individual's closeness). After you have marked all 8 radii, connect the points you have marked and you will know the shape of your personal space.

The C.I.D.S. may also permit you to verify some of the relationships that we have described between situational and individual difference conditions and personal space without leaving your chair. For example, imagine that the approaching individual is a friend and mark the radius; then do the same imagining that he or she is a stranger. Does your experiment confirm the results of the experiments we reviewed which found that people maintain smaller personal space zones for friends than for strangers? Do the same for an approaching individual who is racially similar or dissimilar to yourself or for any of the other relationships we have discussed. You will see how the C.I.D.S. is a useful means of assessing the effects of many factors on spatial behavior. But before you begin, we have one note of caution. Be sure to remember that because the various measures of personal space are not perfectly related (see discussion on page 279), failure to replicate studies with the C.I.D.S., which originally used different methods, does not necessarily mean that the original measures are invalid. Thus, while a replication with the C.I.D.S. of earlier findings that employed other methods is valuable supportive evidence, failure to replicate should not be seen as terribly damaging.

2. Your nearby library offers an opportunity for you to study the fine art of territorial defense. Before you go, make some hypotheses about the relative effectiveness of various types of territorial markers for repelling potential invaders. Consider the possible effects of a wide range of markers, including some you expect to be highly effective and some you expect to be less effective. Collect the necessary materials and report to the library for your experiment.

When you arrive at the library, make mental note of the overall level of population density, and place each of the artifacts you brought at a separate empty table trying not to use too many of the study tables in any one room for your experiment. After you have distributed them all, "make the rounds" of all your experimental tables at 15-minute intervals, noting which markers are more effective and which are less so in preventing territorial invasion. Repeat the procedure using different levels of population density.

3. Position yourself and a same-sex other on either side of a busy doorway through which many people must pass. Face each other and engage in a lively conversation for 15 minutes. Watch the reactions of the passersby, whom you have placed in the role of personal space "invaders." What do they do? Do they force their way through, wait for you to invite them to pass, or look for an alternative exit? Next, remain in your positions but stop conversing for 15 minutes and note whether the reactions of passersby change. Is your personal space more or less difficult to invade when you are talking? Finally, follow the same procedures with an opposite-sex other positioned across the arch from you. Do you find that passersby find it more difficult to violate the personal space of same- or opposite-sex dyads?

High Density and Crowding

INTRODUCTION

EFFECTS OF POPULATION DENSITY ON ANIMALS

Physiological Consequences of High
Density for Animals

Behavioral Consequences of High Density for Animals

Conceptual Perspectives: Attempts to Understand
High-Density Effects in Animals

Summary

EFFECTS OF HIGH DENSITY ON HUMANS

Methodologies Used to Study High Density in Humans

Feeling the Effects of Density: Its Consequences
for Affect, Arousal, and Illness

Affect

Physiological Arousal

Illness

Summary

Effects of Density on Social Behavior

Attraction

Withdrawal

Prosocial Behavior

Aggression

Summary

Effects of High Density on Task Performance

Putting the Pieces Together: Conceptualizations of Density Effects on Humans

Basic Models

The Control Perspective

A Summary Perspective on High-Density Effects

Eliminating the Causes and Effects of Crowding

Predictions From Our General Environment–Behavior Model Applied to High Density

Architectural Mediators of Crowding

Interventions in High-Density Settings

Preventing Crowding From Occurring

Treating the Consequences of Crowding

CHAPTER SUMMARY

Suggested Projects

KEY TERMS

anticipated crowding
behavioral interference
behavioral sink
control
correlational research
crowding
density–intensity
field experiments

high density
inside density
learned helplessness
outside density
privacy regulation model
quasi-experimentation
social density
spatial density

INTRODUCTION

Suppose you are put in charge of a large experimental device called a "mouse universe." You begin with eight mice, four males and four females, in the apparatus and are told female mice can bear a litter of four to eight pups once a month. You are instructed that your job as keeper of the mice is to create a veritable mouse paradise for them, in which they can live, bear young, and do whatever mice like to do, protected from their natural enemies. As an incentive for you to do your job well, your employer offers you a large bonus if the population of the "mouse universe" increases dramatically while you are in charge. To ensure that you get the bonus, you decide to do whatever can be done to provide a utopian setting for the mice. You supply them with unlimited food, water, and nest-building materials. Furthermore, although you do not enjoy it, you clean the mouse droppings that accumulate on the floor of the "universe" frequently to minimize disease.

After creating your "ideal" environment, you sit back and watch, thinking of how you will spend your new riches. At first, things run smoothly; the males are establishing territories and mating with the females in their areas. The females are constructing nests, bearing young (very quickly, to your satisfaction), and successfully raising them to weaning. However, when

the population begins to get larger, you observe that the mice start behaving quite differently from before. Their odd behavior increases as the population increases. Although some animals still maintain their normal lifestyle, most males no longer function well as territorial defenders and procreators (two of their major roles in life), and most females no longer function well as bearers and rearers of young. The birthrate declines rapidly. In addition, the mortality rate of the young becomes extremely high, and some animals become hyperactive and cannibalistic. You envision your bonus disappearing and wonder why these ungrateful creatures are doing this to you. You gave them everything they could possibly need—or did you?

Although the strange behavior of the mice as the population increased may seem bizarre, it is not. Experiments have shown that if animal populations are allowed to multiply unchecked, high-density conditions lead to disease and behavior disorders, even when other aspects of the environment (food, water) are ideal (Calhoun, 1962; Dyson & Passmore, 1992; Judge & deWaal, 1993; Pearce & Patterson, 1993). In fact, our chapter opening description of high-density behavior in mice is based on the results of actual experiments. This research, as well as other, similar, work with animals provided a strong reason for studying the effects of high density on humans, which is the focus of this chapter.

Another initial impetus to research on how high density affects humans was the environmental movement (e.g., the writings of Barry Commoner, 1963; Paul Ehrlich, 1968) and the awareness of upcoming global overpopulation that these writers generated. Concern about global overpopulation continues today. We are going to live in a world characterized by higher and higher population densities, which makes the importance of studying the effects of high density on humans paramount. For example, the present population of the world is about 5.6 billion, and it is increasing by approximately 90,000,000 annually (*Population Today, 1994*). In about eleven years, the world's population will increase by 1 billion—which equals the present population of Europe and North America combined (Lutz, 1994). If current growth patterns continue for the next 42 years, world population will approximately double and in 84 years, the population will quadruple, which will greatly intensify the crowding caused by an expanding population (Figure 9–1).

Will the expected **high density** in humans lead to negative behavior as it did with the mice in our imaginary mouse universe? A final reason for studies on human crowding was early correlational work by sociologists, which examined the relationships between human population density and behavior and health abnormalities. As you may remember from Chapter 1, correlational research does *not* allow us to draw strong conclusions concerning causes

Figure 9–1 Crowding refers to the way we feel when there are too many people and/or not enough space.

and effects. However, some of the initial studies of this type strongly suggested that increases in human population density may be associated with pathology.

In this chapter, we will discuss research and theory on the effects of high density. Our discussion will start with a brief overview of experimental and theoretical work on the reactions of animals to high density. We will then move to the primary focus of the chapter—the effects of high density on humans. After a review of this area, some theories that try to explain human responses to high density will be discussed. The last section of the chapter will focus on several ways to alleviate the causes and effects of high density.

EFFECTS OF POPULATION DENSITY ON ANIMALS

Two major types of research methods have been used to study the effects of density. These include naturalistic observation, which tends to be descriptive, and laboratory methods, which tend to be experimental. In laboratory research methods with animals *and* humans, density is manipulated in one of two ways. **Social density** manipulations vary group size while keeping area constant. A manipulation of social density might entail putting 15 rats (or people) in a given area in the low-density condition and putting 75 rats (or people) in the same area in the high-density condition. Or, it might entail starting out with 15 rats in a constant sized space and observing behavior change as they reproduce, and as population density increases. In contrast, **spatial density** manipulations vary area while keeping group size constant. To manipulate spatial density you might place 15 rats (or people) in a relatively large area in the low-density condition, and 15 rats (or people) in a relatively small area in the high-density condition.

As we will see later in this chapter, there is quite a bit more than what we have said so far to the distinction between social and spatial density. They are not *simply* ways of manipulating density, and are not interchangeable. Rather, they reflect different conditions with different problems and consequences. Under high social density the primary problem is too many other individuals with whom one must interact; under high spatial density the primary problem is too little space. Is it better to manipulate social density than spatial density, or vice versa? The answer is "it depends on what you are studying." Both manipulations are somewhat imperfect. Social-density variations include the confounding of group size and space supply (e.g., group size and space per individual are changed at the same time). In contrast, spatial-density manipulations confound room (or experimental apparatus) size and space per individual (i.e., room size and space per occupant are changed at the same time). One thing we will find in our literature review is that the way in which density is manipulated sometimes affects the results obtained (i.e., social- and spatial-density manipulations do not always yield the same results).

In contrast to laboratory methods in which social or spatial density are typically manipulated by the experimenter, studies employing naturalistic observation assess how naturally occurring density variations affect behavior in "real world" settings. An example of naturalistic observation is provided by the work of Dubos (1965), who found that when Norwegian lemmings become overpopulated, they migrate to the sea where many drown. He attributed this to density-induced malfunctions of the brain. In this study, as in others using naturalistic observation, changes in density occur "on their own"—the researcher does *not* manipulate them.

Given these brief examples of how research with animals is done, let us turn to what has been found in this research. Our discussion will first highlight some of the more consistent physiological and behavioral effects which occur when animals are "densely packed," and will then describe some conceptual perspectives we can use to understand these effects.

PHYSIOLOGICAL CONSEQUENCES OF HIGH DENSITY FOR ANIMALS

Past research demonstrates that when animals interact under high population density, they experience negative physiological consequences. Many of these effects parallel the reactions in Selye's General Adaptation Syndrome, discussed in Chapter 4. For example, high density is associated with changes in a number of body organs, such as the kidneys, liver, and brain (e.g., Myers et al., 1971). Such changes are not indicative of good health! Another consistent finding is that high social and spatial density lead to abnormalities in endocrine functioning, which is an indicator of stress (e.g., Chaouloff & Zamfir, 1993; Christian, 1955).

One important effect of high density on endocrine functioning is that it leads to decreased fertility in both males and females (e.g., Christian, 1955; Ostfeld, Canham, & Pugh, 1993; Snyder, 1966). For example, it has been found that male rats living under high density produce fewer sperm than those under low density (e.g., Snyder, 1966). With females, estrus cycles of "high-density" animals begin at a later age, occur less frequently, and are shorter than those of "low-density" animals (e.g., Ostfeld, Canham, & Pugh, 1993). Given such differences, it is not surprising to find both smaller litter sizes and less frequent births in crowded populations (e.g., Snyder, 1966).

BEHAVIORAL CONSEQUENCES OF HIGH DENSITY FOR ANIMALS

Some interesting studies have found that high-density manipulations can significantly disturb normal social organization in animals (Calhoun, 1962; Dyson & Passmore, 1992; Judge & deWaal, 1993; Pearce & Patterson, 1993). The pioneering work of John B. Calhoun in this area serves as an excellent example of how high density affects animals. Calhoun studied both rats and mice, but his most startling study employed rats. He placed a small number of male and female rats in the apparatus pictured in Figure 9–2 and allowed them to bear young and eventually overpopulate (just like in our chapter opening introduction). The "apparatus," which can comfortably handle 48 animals, consists of a 10 feet by 14 feet (300 by 420 cm) platform divided into four cells, each with a capacity of 12 animals. One of its important

Figure 9–2 The "universe" used by Calhoun (1962) to study the effects of high density on rodent behavior. There are no ramps between pens 1 and 4, which means that they are essentially "end" pens. This eventually precipitates a behavioral sink in pens 2 and 3.
From "Population Density and Social Pathology" by John B. Calhoun. Copyright © 1962 by Scientific American, Inc. All rights reserved.

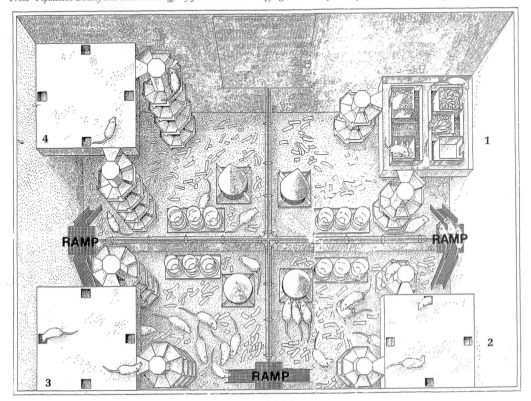

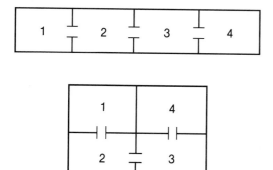

Figure 9–3 If the arrangement of pens 1, 2, 3, and 4 is changed from the one in the top diagram to the one depicted below it, pens 1 and 4 remain "end" pens with only one entrance/exit.

features is that ramps connect all the pens except the two "end" pens, which eventually causes many animals to crowd into the two central pens. Pens labeled "1" and "4" take on the role of end pens, while the other two are more central (see Figure 9–3).

Before they become extremely crowded, "average" male rats busy themselves accumulating a harem, mating with members of the harem, and defending their territory. They do not fight much, and do not mate with females in other harems. Females occupy themselves with building nests and raising their young. They do not fight, and resist advances from males outside their harem. How do rats behave under high density? Calhoun observed that under high density the normal social order disintegrated, and a new one emerged.

Allowing the animals to overpopulate had negative effects on the social behavior of all the occupants of the apparatus, and these effects were particularly negative in pens 2 and 3, where high density was acute. (Calhoun calls this extremely crowded area, which is described in the box on page 330, a **behavioral sink**.) In pens 1 and 4, males and females still attempted to enact their normal social roles. Females engaged in nurturant behaviors and dominant males guarded the

sole entrance and maintained a semblance of territorial behavior. But in the behavioral sink (pens 2 and 3), neither males nor females carried out their roles effectively. Although females in the less crowded pens tried to nurse their young, to build nests for them, and to transfer them in the event of harm, none of these behaviors was effectively engaged in by mothers in the behavioral sink. This accounts, at least in part, for the fact that the infant mortality rate in the behavioral sink was extremely high, with 80 to 96 percent of all pups dying before being weaned. In contrast (but nothing to be pleased about) only about 50 percent of the pups in the less crowded "end" pens suffered this fate. While dominant males protected estrous females in the less crowded pens, packs of socially deviant males in the crowded inner pens relentlessly pursued estrous females, who were unable to resist their advances. This led to a high rate of mortality from diseases in pregnancy (almost half of the females in these pens died by the 16th month of the study), which was not experienced by female residents in the less crowded pens.

Within the bizarre setting of Calhoun's "universe," several social classes emerged, varying in the extent and type of their pathological behavior. There were four groups of males. First, there was a group of dominant males that generally lived in the less crowded pens. These were the most "normal" animals in Calhoun's "universe." They were also the most secure, since the majority of the other animals were victims of almost continuous aggressive attacks. The second group consisted of pansexual males. These animals made advances to females who were not in estrus as well as to males. The third class of males was completely passive and ignored other rats of both sexes. The fourth and most unusual group of males Calhoun termed "probers." These animals lived in the behavioral sink and were hyperactive, hypersexual, homosexual, and cannibalistic. Classifying the

WHAT IS A BEHAVIORAL SINK?

At this point, you probably have the general (and correct) impression that a "behavioral sink," such as existed in pens 2 and 3, is an area in which the negative effects of high density are intensified. However, up to now we have not discussed the dynamics by which behavioral sinks are formed. According to Calhoun (1967), a behavioral sink develops when a population that is uniformly distributed becomes nonuniformly distributed in groups far exceeding optimal size. Two processes are involved in "behavioral sink" formation. First, some aspect of the environment or the behavior of the animals makes population density greater in some places than in others (the absence of ramps connecting pens 1 and 4 did this in Calhoun's study). Second, animals come to associate the presence of others with some originally unrelated activity. For example, in Calhoun's studies, animals came to associate food (a reinforcer) with the presence of others, which caused them to be attracted to areas where there were many animals. As we have seen, the intense crowding and the need to make accommodations to so many others was highly detrimental to the social order. Can you think of any areas in the human environment that would qualify as "behavioral sinks"?

Given an understanding of the dynamics of the behavioral sink, how can this condition and its associated pathology be remedied? One approach taken by Calhoun was to substitute granular food (which can be eaten very quickly) for the hard food pellets (which were very time-consuming to eat) used in his earlier studies. Consequently, it took much less time for animals to eat, decreasing the probability that two or more animals would be eating simultaneously and that the conditioning process described previously would occur. In these studies, behavioral sinks failed to develop, and the pathological behavior associated with high density was less intense, although by no means low. Can you think of a similar means of eliminating the human behavioral sinks you thought of?

---

female rats was relatively simple. One group (which lived in the behavioral sink) was completely abnormal, could fulfill no sexual and maternal functions, and "huddled" with the male rats. The second group (which lived in the less crowded pens) behaved much more like "normal" rats.

While Calhoun's work is clearly important, it is not without criticism. Because of the design of his apparatus, some have claimed that in addition to studying high density,

Calhoun was also manipulating territoriality. Due to design features, some rats became territorial, while others were kept from having territories. The fact that rats in the high-density pens were also less territorial suggests that both high density and lack of territoriality may be responsible for the negative effects. Others have criticized Calhoun's work for having low ecological validity. In the wild, rats are not penned in as in Calhoun's apparatus and tend to emigrate when density becomes too high (Archer, 1970). The latter critics suggest that the way the apparatus was designed, "behavioral sinks" were inevitable. They imply that while the research provides a look at how things could be in the worst of all possible worlds, it may not portray a completely accurate picture of rats' behavior under high density.

Nevertheless, Calhoun's work has been central to the study of the behavioral effects of high density in animals, and some of his results find parallels with other animal populations. For example, Southwick (1967) reported increases in aggression with increasing density in a group of monkeys. Dyson and Passmore (1992) found similiar results for aggression in frogs. Other studies (e.g., Anderson et al., 1977) have found density-related increases in withdrawal rather than aggression among monkeys. In addition, Pearce and Patterson (1993) have found that high density results in withdrawal rather than aggression in pigs. Still other researchers have found, like Calhoun, that crowding affects the sexual behavior of rats in high-density settings (e.g., Dahlof, Hard, & Larsson, 1977; Williams, McGinnis, & Lumia, 1992).

Having discussed the effects of high density on animals' social behavior and physiological responses, one might ask what other consequences high density has for animals. While a complete discussion is beyond our scope, a final effect worthy of mention is that high density is associated with decrements in learning and task performance. Goeckner, Greenough, and Maier (1974) raised rats in groups of 1, 4, and 32, and found that animals raised in the most crowded conditions showed poorer performance on complex tasks, though no performance deficits were found for simple tasks. Further, Bell et al. (1971) reported decreased maze exploration and activity levels under high social density. Pearce and Patterson (1993) similarly found decreased levels of exploratory behavior among crowded pigs.

CONCEPTUAL PERSPECTIVES: ATTEMPTS TO UNDERSTAND HIGH-DENSITY EFFECTS IN ANIMALS

Given that animals respond negatively to high density, what is responsible for these reactions? Several attempts have been made to explain the negative effects of high density on animals. In a sense, these perspectives view the negative responses of animals to high density as *adaptive* mechanisms that act to prevent extinction due to overpopulation. Although none of these conceptual schemes have received unqualified scientific support, they are useful in adding to our understanding of the effects of high density on animals. At this point, we should consider the various viewpoints as "possibilities" and expect the eventual explanation to be an integration of these approaches.

One conceptualization of the effects of high density on animals was proposed by Calhoun (1971). This formulation can be used to explain both the extremely negative consequences that occurred in the behavioral sink and the relatively less severe negative effects that occurred elsewhere. Calhoun assumes that species of mammals are predisposed by evolution to interact with a particular number of others. This is termed their "optimal group size." It leads to a tolerable number of contacts with others each day, some of which are gratifying and some of which are frustrating. Calhoun suggests that as the group increases beyond the optimal size, the ratio of frustrating to gratifying interactions becomes more unfavorable. Further, interruptions in necessary periods of solitude increase, and these are experienced as aversive. This state of affairs becomes extremely debilitating when the number in the group approaches twice the optimal number, and a sustained period under such conditions produces the sort of effects observed in Calhoun's "rat universe" (Figure 9–4).

Figure 9–4 Calhoun suggests that animals are evolutionarily predisposed to interact with a particular number of others. When more than the "optimal group size" are present, interactions become aversive, and at twice the optimal size conditions may become debilitating.

Another conceptualization of the negative effects of high density on animals is social stress theory (Christian, 1955). From this perspective, it is assumed that the social consequences of high density (e.g., increased social competition, effects on social hierarchies) are stressful, and that stress produces an increase in the activity of the adrenal glands as part of a stresslike syndrome. (Recall the evidence described earlier that high density is associated with changes in endocrine functioning.) It is believed that increased adrenal activity is responsible for many of the negative physiological and behavioral effects associated with high density. Interestingly, social stress theory predicts that glandular activity may also moderate a population *increase* when populations are very small. Since its social consequences are not stressful, low density does not elicit negative physiological and behavioral effects, and thus facilitates higher birthrate, longer life span, and so on. Social stress theory involves an endocrine feedback system that keeps density at an acceptable level.

An explanatory framework based on territorial behavior has been proposed in the work of Ardrey (1966) and Lorenz (1966). It assumes that the negative effects of density on animals are caused primarily by aggression induced by territorial invasions. These writers suggest that as population density increases beyond an optimal level, violations of territorial "rights" increase, precipitating high levels of aggression. (The relationship between territorial invasions and aggression in animals was discussed in Chapter 8.) Such aggression results in the negative physiological and behavioral effects described earlier as associated with high density. Under conditions of low density, territories are not violated, aggression is low, and the population can increase toward the optimal level. This formulation, however, cannot explain the effects of density on species of animals that are relatively nonterritorial.

A way to integrate these conceptualizations, as well as others (cf. Frank, 1957; Krebs, 1972; Pearson, 1966, 1971; Pitelka, 1957), has been proposed by Wilson (1975). He assumes that there is a tendency for populations to return to an optimal level of density. How does this occur? It is accomplished by "density-dependent controls" (e.g., by varying levels of aggression, stress, fertility, emigration, predation and disease). According to Wilson, such controls operate through natural selection. For example, at high density, selection may favor an aggressive organism, which will bring the population into decline. At low density, aggressive organisms would be at a disadvantage, and the gene frequencies would change to favor more gentle behavior, permitting the population to expand. Such a process would protect the species from extinction caused by under- or overpopulation.

SUMMARY

Animals experience severe, negative physiological and behavioral reactions to high density. These include changes in body organs, glandular malfunctions, and extreme disruption of social and maternal behavior. Calhoun's research with rodents powerfully demonstrates many of these effects and shows that they are intensified when behavioral sinks develop. Although the findings we discussed in this section are quite consistent, it is important to note here that there are variations among species in the reactions that occur. Finally, several different conceptual schemes have been proposed to explain animal reactions to high density.

EFFECTS OF HIGH DENSITY ON HUMANS

After reviewing studies on the physiological and behavioral effects of high density on animals, as well as some conceptual frameworks in which to view them, it is tempting to speculate about whether this pattern of effects can generalize to humans (Figures 9–5 and 9–6). Scientists and philosophers have puzzled over the differences between humans and animals for centuries, and endless arguments have emerged (see the box on page 335 for a discussion of what we can assume about humans from our study of the literature on animal behavior).

Differences between humans and animals notwithstanding, most early research on human crowding assumed that for us, like animals, high density would lead to uniformly negative effects. To the surprise of everyone, this was not the case. While for animals high density is generally aversive, for humans it depends more on the situation. For the most part, the effects of high densities on people are neither severe nor uniform (Baum & Paulus, 1987). Our discussion of human response to high density will first highlight representative research

findings and then integrate them in terms of the general environment–behavior model presented in Chapter 4. Before proceeding,

Figure 9–5 While it is generally the case that animals respond negatively to high density, for some it constitutes "standard operating conditions" and does not lead to negative consequences. Optimal population densities for some species may appear quite crowded to us.

Figure 9–6 In general, humans evidence more variable reactions to high density than animals do. Sometimes we like it; sometimes we do not.

however, we will pause to consider the methodologies used to study human reactions to high density.

METHODOLOGIES USED TO STUDY HIGH DENSITY IN HUMANS

The method most often used to study high density in humans is laboratory experimentation. As discussed in Chapter 1, laboratory experiments have a number of advantages over other techniques. For exploring high density in humans, however, they have two disadvantages worthy of mention. First, creating high-density conditions in the laboratory is somewhat artificial, which may affect generalizability to the "real world." Second, laboratory experiments can explore only very

short-term high-density effects, which is a serious problem. In attempts to remedy these deficiencies, researchers have increasingly turned to field research techniques (i.e., **field experiments** and field studies). These offer greater realism than laboratory experiments and permit us to study longer-term high-density effects. However, while field experiments permit us to make causal inferences, field studies do not. **Quasi-experimentation**, a field study technique that permits one to more closely approximate a causal inference through the use of certain types of research designs, allows both the realism of field settings (e.g., prisons, dormitories) and some ability to infer causality.

A final research technique for studying high density in humans is **correlational research**. This is used primarily by sociologists and involves correlating different measures of population density with the frequency of various abnormal behaviors. These studies have generally looked at correlations between pathology and two types of density: **inside density** (e.g., number of persons per residence or per room) or **outside density** (e.g., number of persons, dwellings, or structures per acre). Unfortunately, early correlational research failed to control for a number of variables that may vary along with density (e.g., income, education), and the results are of questionable value. A "second generation" of studies has statistically controlled for these confounding variables.

Although these later studies represent an improvement over earlier correlational research, several important weaknesses remain. First, so many different indices of inside and outside density are used that meaningful comparison among studies is difficult. Second, it appears that the most fruitful of the studies have focused on relating smaller scale indices (e.g., persons per room) rather than larger scale indices (e.g., persons per acre) to pathology (Gove & Hughes, 1983). Third, while they can tell us whether various disor-

WHAT DOES ANIMAL RESEARCH TELL US ABOUT HUMANS?

As a rule, it is difficult to assume that the effects of high density on animals will generalize to humans (although in reading this chapter you will find that both species sometimes do respond similarly). Why should we not expect that findings that hold for animals will necessarily occur for humans?

First, animal behavior appears to be determined largely by biological factors, whereas humans depend much more on learning and cultural inputs (Swanson, 1973). Unlike other animals, thought processes and learning play an important role in determining the extent of human stress reactions (Baum & Paulus, 1987). Also, humans have many more means at their disposal to adapt to high density. For example, when the number of interactions between people gets too great, humans have many ways of moderating them (Baum & Paulus, 1987). In addition, while naturalistic high density for animals is almost always accompanied by lack of food, humans are able to live under such conditions and feed themselves adequately. Finally, the fact that most animal data are based on organisms that exist only in high-density settings limits their generalizability to humans, who often have at least brief opportunities to escape (Evans, 1978a, 1978b). Are there situations in which animal responses to high density may be especially likely to generalize to humans? Interestingly, the similarities between human and animal responses to high density may be greatest for human populations whose ability to cope with stressors has broken down and become ineffective (Baum & Paulus, 1987).

If generalizing from animal research to humans can create difficulties, what value does animal research have? We should view animal studies as important in their own right for what they say about the impact of density on animals and as a rich source of hypotheses concerning how humans may respond to high density. For example, the notion of unwanted interaction and social regulation that forms the basis of Baum and Valins' (1977) studies of college dormitories (page 340) was directly derived from Calhoun's notion of balancing frustrating and gratifying interactions. As with animal populations, Baum and Valins and others have found that in humans, exposure to large numbers of others has negative effects, as does a lack of social structure. The value of animal work as a source of hypotheses—and sometimes generalizable data—about human reactions to high density is enhanced by several methodological strengths of animal research over human research:

1. There are ethical problems in studying long-term high density in humans. These make it difficult to do the type of well-controlled studies commonly done with animals.
2. Since animals bear young more quickly than humans, it is possible to observe the cycle in which they reproduce and overpopulate in a much shorter period of time.
3. It is easier to study physiological and behavioral responses of animals without disturbing the process being monitored than it is with humans.

ders are associated with density, correlational studies can give us very little information about the specific cause of the pathology. We will review some of the research employing a correlational approach in the present chapter, but since much of it focuses on the relationship between levels of urban density and urban pathology, this work will be considered more fully in Chapter 10.

Having reviewed the methodologies used in human research on high density, we now turn to the research itself. Our discussion will be organized into conceptually related areas: how density makes us feel (e.g., its consequences for affect, arousal, and illness), how density affects our social behavior (i.e., its effects on interpersonal attraction, aggression, and prosocial behavior), and how density affects task performance. While we will discuss the effects of density on each of these areas separately, it is important to keep in mind that density may have simultaneous effects in several of these areas, and that these effects may be interrelated.

FEELING THE EFFECTS OF DENSITY: ITS CONSEQUENCES FOR AFFECT, AROUSAL, AND ILLNESS

Affect

One of the most common assumptions that people make about crowding is that it makes people "feel bad." Not suprisingly, several studies have reported that high social density may cause negative affective states (Evans, 1979a; Sundstrom, 1975). One field study (Saegert, MacIntosh, & West, 1975) had subjects perform a series of tasks in either crowded or uncrowded settings. It was found that subjects reported more anxiety in the dense than in the nondense conditions, although this probably does not surprise anyone who has ever had to perform a task with hordes of others "breathing down their neck." A study by Baum and Greenberg (1975) found that even the mere anticipation of being in

high-social-density conditions causes a negative mood.

Before concluding that crowding invariably leads to negative moods, however, we should consider some evidence suggesting that the negative feelings caused by high spatial density may be stronger in males than in females. Several studies (e.g., Freedman et al., 1972) found that while males experience more negative moods in high- than in low-spatial-density conditions, the reverse is true for females (Figure 9–7). One way to explain these effects is the finding in the personal space literature (see Chapter 8) that males have greater personal space needs than do females. Alternatively, these findings may reflect the female socialization to be more affiliative (and therefore to have more of an affinity for others at close range), and the male socialization to be more competitive (and thus to view others at close proximity as sources of threat; Maccoby, 1966). Research indicates that women may approach high-density settings in more cooperative ways than do men (Karlin, Epstein, & Aiello, 1978; Taylor, 1978).

It is important to note that the studies that have found uniformly negative moods

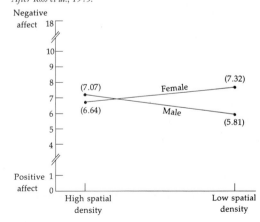

Figure 9–7 Ratings of affective states for males and females in high and low spatial density conditions. Higher scores = more negative affect. *After Ross et al., 1973.*

in response to high density are primarily studies of high *social density*. In contrast, those that reported gender differences in affective response are studies of high *spatial density*. Recall that we said earlier that social and spatial density refer to more than just methodological differences—they reflect very different kinds of problems. It is possible that high social density is equally aversive to men and women, but that high spatial density is bothersome only for males.

Physiological Arousal

If high density affects our feelings, can it also lead to physiological effects, such as increased heart rate? In one experiment, Evans (1979a) had mixed-sex groups of five males and five females participate in a three and one-half hour study in either a large or a small room. Participants' heart rate and blood pressure were recorded both before the experiment began and after three hours. Results indicated that in high-density conditions, subjects showed higher pulse rate and blood pressure readings than in more spacious conditions. Similarly, research by D'Atri et al. (1981) found that increasing levels of population density in prisons were associated with higher levels of blood pressure. When prisoners were transferred back to lower density accommodations, these effects were reversed.

Several other physiological measures of arousal are affected by high density (cf. Baum & Paulus, 1987). Skin conductance (a measure of arousal) has been found to increase significantly over time for subjects in high- but not low-spatial-density conditions (Aiello, Epstein, & Karlin, 1975a), and Saegert (1974) found that exposure to a large number of others leads to arousal as measured by palmar sweat. Finally, Heshka and Pylypuk (1975) compared cortisol levels (indicative of stress) of students who spent the day in a crowded shopping area and those who stayed on a relatively uncrowded college campus. When compared with the control group,

males who had been in the high-density shopping conditions had elevated cortisol levels indicative of higher stress, but females did not.

Field studies in Sweden have also investigated stress-related arousal in high-density settings (e.g., Lundberg, 1976; Singer, Lundberg, & Frankenhaeuser, 1978). Lundberg (1976) studied male passengers on a commuter train, comparing their response to trips made under high- and low-density conditions. Despite the fact that even under the most crowded conditions there were seats available for everyone, negative physiological reactions increased as more people rode the train. Lundberg collected urine samples from the subjects and found higher levels of epinephrine after high-density trips than after low-density ones (epinephrine is an endocrinological marker of stress-related arousal).

Other results, however, qualified the nature of these findings. Regardless of how densely packed the train was, riders who boarded at the first stop experienced less negative reactions and had lower levels of epinephrine in their urine than passengers boarding halfway to the city. Despite the fact that their ride was considerably longer (72 minutes versus 38 minutes), those boarding at the first stop entered an empty train and were able to choose where to sit and with whom they traveled. For example, groups of commuters who were friends could be assured of finding seats together. In this way, they could buffer themselves from the high density that would occur by structuring the setting before it became crowded. Apparently, the **control** afforded initial passengers reduced the effects of high density, while the lack of control associated with boarding an already crowded train resulted in increased arousal (Lundberg, 1976; Singer et al., 1978).

Illness

It would seem reasonable that if high density leads to negative feeling states and to physiological overarousal, living under such conditions would have negative health consequences. High density can contribute to illness due to stress, but can also be associated with poor health because disease can "spread" more quickly in high- than low-density settings (Paulus, 1988). There is evidence in prison settings to support the assertion that high density is associated with decrements in health. McCain, Cox, and Paulus (1976), report that in a prison setting inmates who lived in conditions of low spatial and social density were sick less than those who lived in high densities. Requests for medical attention by inmates were also related to absolute levels of density (Wener & Keys, 1988). Studies also indicated that high density was related to blood pressure increases in inmates and even to increased death rates (Cox, Paulus, & McCain, 1984; Wooldredge & Winfree, 1992; see Figure 9–8).

Further evidence of the health effects of high density is provided in studies done with college dormitory residents. For example, Stokols and Ohlig (1975) observed an association between reports of high density and visits to the student health center, and Baron et al. (1976) found evidence of more visits to the student infirmary by residents in high- than low-social-density dormitories. Finally, Dean, Pugh, and Gunderson (1975, 1978) have reported associations between high density and illness complaints aboard naval vessels.

The relationship between high density and illness has also been assessed by correlational studies. Although several individual studies in this literature support a link between density and pathology, as a whole it is characterized by methodological inadequacies and inconsistent findings. When all of this research is taken as a whole, it does *not* suggest that high density is an important factor in medical pathology (Fuller et al., 1993; Kirmeyer, 1978; Ruback & Pandey, 1991). The reason for the inconsistency between

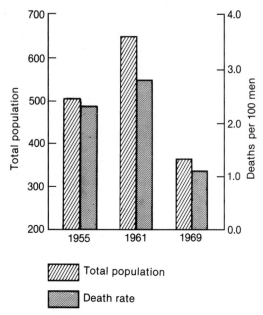

Figure 9–8 As population size increased in prison settings, the death rate in the prison also increased. Decreased population size was associated with lower mortality. These findings controlled for a number of factors, including violent deaths. The correlation between death rates and population size was .81.
Based on data in Paulus, McCain, & Cox, 1978.

correlational work and the research reviewed above is unclear.

Summary

Having considered the effects of high density on affect, arousal, and illness, we can draw several tentative conclusions. First, it appears that high density leads to more negative affective states (especially in males) and to higher levels of physiological arousal, as measured on a wide variety of indices. Further, there is evidence (although somewhat inconsistent) that high density is associated with illness. With this capsule summary in mind, we now turn our focus to the effects of high density on social behaviors such as interpersonal attraction, withdrawal, prosocial behavior, and aggression.

EFFECTS OF DENSITY ON SOCIAL BEHAVIOR

Attraction

Will we tend to like a stranger more if we meet him or her in a crowded subway car or in a more spacious setting? Generally, it seems as though high density leads to decrements in attraction whether we are merely anticipating confinement, are confined for a relatively short period, or are confined for a long time. For example, Baum and Greenberg (1975) found that merely expecting to experience high social density elicited dislike; students who were told ten people would eventually occupy a room liked those they waited with for the experiment to begin less than subjects who were told only four others would be present. In a study of short-term high-density confinement, groups of eight males who were together for an hour attributed more friendliness to other group members under low than high spatial density (Worchel & Teddlie, 1976). Looking at long-term density effects, Baron and his colleagues (1976) reported that dormitory residents living in "triples" (three students in a room built for two) were less satisfied with their roommates and perceived them to be less cooperative than students living in "doubles" (Table 9–1). We discuss other studies on "tripling," and elaborate on the above findings, later in this chapter.

Although it appears that high density leads to lower attraction, there is evidence (as noted earlier for affective state) that for high spatial density, this response is more characteristic of males than females (cf. Epstein & Karlin, 1975; Stokols et al., 1973). For example, in an experiment by Epstein and Karlin (1975), male and female subjects participated in same-sex groups of six. Consistent findings on a variety of measures indicated that while males responded more negatively to group members in high- than low-spatial-density conditions, females liked

Table 9–1 Satisfaction With Roommate Under Crowded and Uncrowded Conditions*

	Uncrowded	Crowded
Satisfaction with roommate	4.9	3.7
Perceived cooperativeness of roommate	4.7	3.9

*Higher numbers indicate more positive responses. (Based on data from Baron et al., 1976.)

group members more under high-density conditions (Table 9–2). We speculated earlier that gender differences in response to high spatial density may be due to different size personal space zones or to the more cooperative socialization of females and the more competitive socialization of males.

Epstein and Karlin (1975) suggest another possibility. They state that while both males and females experience arousal from high spatial density, social norms permit females to share their distress at being "packed like sardines" with others in their group, which leads to greater liking and cohesion. The same norms prohibit males from sharing distress, which causes a more negative response. In a follow-up experiment (Karlin et al., 1976), it was found that when females were not permitted to interact with each other, their positive reactions to high spatial density were attenuated. Support for this interpretation has been limited, however (cf. Keating & Snowball, 1977).

Table 9–2 Ratings of Perceived Similarity Under Crowded and Uncrowded Conditions*

Sex	Crowded	Uncrowded
Male	5.7	4.4
Female	4.2	5.7

*Lower numbers indicate greater perceived similarity. (Based on data from Epstein & Karlin, 1975.)

HIGH DENSITY IN THE DORM:
Where Would You Like to Live Next Year?

One of the most often studied residential environments is the college dormitory. Some important effects of high residential density in this setting were reported by Baum and Valins (1977). These investigators performed studies comparing the responses to high density of students assigned to *suite-style* dormitories and students assigned to *corridor-style* dormitories. Corridor residents shared a bathroom and a lounge with 34 residents on the floor; suite residents shared a bathroom and a lounge with only four to six others (see Figure 9–9A and 9B). All students shared a bedroom with one other student. While the suite and corridor designs were identical in terms of space per person and number of residents per floor, as you might guess, they led to dramatic differences in the number of others that residents encountered constantly.

What were the behavioral effects of the greater number of interpersonal contacts in corridor-style dormitories? Corridor residents responded differently from suite residents in a number of ways. They perceived their floors to be more crowded, felt they were more often forced

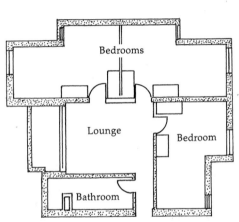

Figure 9–9A & 9B Floor plan of corridor-style dormitory (above) and suite-style dormitory (below). *From Baum & Valins, 1977. Published with permission of Lawrence Erlbaum Associates.*

into inconvenient and unwanted interactions with others, and indicated a greater desire to avoid others. Corridor residents were also far less sociable, perceived

Withdrawal

In support of Baum and Valins' observation that withdrawal may be associated with high levels of social contact (see the box on this page) studies have reported that withdrawal may function as an anticipatory response to high density, as a means of coping with ongoing high density, and as an after-

effect. The mere expectation of high social density elicits withdrawal responses, including lower levels of eye contact, head movements away from others (Baum & Greenberg, 1975; Baum & Koman, 1976), and maintenance of greater interpersonal distances (Baum & Greenberg, 1975). Withdrawal also occurs during ongoing high-density interactions: Subjects are more willing to discuss

less attitude similarity between themselves and their neighbors, and were less sure of what their neighbors thought of them. Not surprisingly, a significantly lower number of corridor residents reported that the majority of their friends lived on the same floor.

It was also found that living in a suite or a corridor-style dormitory led to different behaviors in other places and with other people. For example, Baum and Valins reported that corridor residents looked less at confederates and sat farther away from them while waiting for an experiment. Corridor residents also performed significantly worse than suite residents on tasks under cooperative conditions, although they performed better under conditions that inhibited personal involvement with an opponent. In another study, Reichner (1979) found that when ignored in a discussion, residents of corridor-style dorms felt less badly than those living in suite-style dorms.

What do these data mean? It may be that corridor residents find themselves "overloaded" by their high level of interaction with others, or that they experience frequent *unwanted interactions,* and their withdrawal responses may be interpreted as coping strategies that prevent such involvement. Baum and Valins suggest that high-density living in suites and corridors may be considered as a type of social conditioning process. Obviously, this process results in a more positive orientation to others in suite- than in corridor-style dormitories. Subsequent studies have linked this social conditioning process to later differences in prosocial behavior, to differences in interpersonal bargaining strategies, and to differences in response to violations of social norms (e.g., Davis, 1977; Reichner, 1979; Sell, 1976).

Is there any way to make life in corridor-style dormitories more tolerable? Baum and Valins found that membership in small local groups, when it occurred, tended to reduce many of the negative effects of corridor-style dormitory living. And Baum and Davis (1980) found that an architectural intervention—dividing the long corridor into two shorter ones by adding a door in the middle—reduced overload and eliminated many negative outcomes. How does your own experience as a dormitory resident correspond to these observations?

intimate topics under low-density conditions (Sundstrom, 1975), and both children (e.g., Loo, 1972) and psychiatric patients (Ittelson, Proshansky, & Rivlin, 1972) interact less frequently as room density increases.

Withdrawal due to high density may have a very important consequence: It may disrupt the very social support networks which we rely on to cope with negative life events (Evans et al., 1989; Lepore, Evans, & Schneider, 1991). This may leave people who live under high-density conditions with fewer resources with which to deal with stressors. In addition, Evans and Lepore (1993) have found that individuals from crowded homes were less likely to seek social support from a confederate when they needed it, and rated the confederate to be less supportive, than individuals from less crowded homes. Individuals from crowded homes were also less apt to offer social support to another in need. Evans et al. (1989) and Lepore et al. (1991) found that negative effects of residential crowding were due, in part, to this breakdown in individuals' social support systems. Finally, it appears that withdrawal can constitute an aftereffect of exposure to density. Studies have found that males were less likely to volunteer for another experimental session after experiencing high social density (Dooley, 1974), and groups of males preferred larger personal space and recalled fewer names after exposure to high density (Joy & Lehmann, 1975). Further evidence for withdrawal in high-density environments is reviewed in Chapter 10, which considers the effects of city life.

Prosocial Behavior

If high density leads to lower attraction and to withdrawal responses, how might it affect helping? For example, suppose you lost something of value. Where would you be most confident of finding someone who would help you look for it: in a higher or a lower density building? In a cafeteria which is full, or one that is empty? Interestingly, most research on how density affects prosocial behavior has been done in field settings like these.

In studies that explored how helping is affected by building density, it was found that greater density leads to less helping. For example, Bickman et al. (1973) compared prosocial acts in high-, medium-, and low-density dormitories. Envelopes, which were stamped and addressed, were dropped in the dormitories, and helpfulness was measured by the number that were picked up and placed in the mail. The results showed that 58 percent were mailed in the high-density condition, 79 percent in the medium-density condition, and 88 percent in the low-density condition. In an interesting study, Jorgenson and Dukes (1976) observed

the effect of social density on compliance with a prosocial request (printed on signs) for cafeteria users to return their trays to designated areas. It was found that fewer users complied during high-density periods. A final set of studies which address the effects of high density on helping has compared prosocial behavior in urban and rural areas. These studies are reviewed in Chapter 10.

Aggression

If high density can make us less likely to help others, does it also make us more apt to hurt them? One approach to this question has explored the effects of density on aggressiveness of children's play. This strategy has led to inconsistent results. Some studies (e.g., Aiello et al., 1979; Ginsburg et al., 1977) have found that increased density leads to more aggression; others have found the reverse (e.g., Loo, 1972) and still others (e.g., Price, 1971) have reported no effect. In an attempt to resolve this controversy, Loo suggested that density may affect children's aggression in a curvilinear fashion. This was supported by a study that observed that moderately high density led to increased aggression in males, while very low and very high density led to decreased aggressiveness (Loo, 1978). Subsequent research, however, has shown increases in aggression under conditions of very high social density among boys (Loo & Kennelly, 1979). In another attempt to resolve this controversy, Rohe and Patterson (1974) suggested that competition over scarce resources is a major determinant of children's aggression in high-density situations. If there are more kids than toys and each child wants a toy, aggression is more likely than if there are enough toys to go around. Rohe and Patterson hypothesized and found that increases in spatial density led to more aggression only if resources were limited. This relationship was also reported by Smith and Connolly (1977), who found that increased aggression occurred during play if playground equipment was made more scarce.

Other research has suggested that children's responses to high density change with continuing development (Aiello et al., 1979; Loo & Smetana, 1978). Since children are presumably less restrained and more outwardly aggressive than adults, it may be that high density has more subtle effects on adult aggressiveness. Several studies have addressed the aggression-enhancing effects of high density among adults. Often, it appears that increased density leads to aggression in adult males but not in females, a familiar pattern in high-density research. For example, Stokols and his associates (1973) studied same-sex groups under high and low spatial density and found that males rated themselves as more aggressive in the small room, while the reverse was true for females. Freedman et al. (1972) also found that increasing spatial density was associated with increasingly aggressive behavior among men but not women. When Schettino and Borden (1976) used the ratio of people in a classroom to the total number of seats as an index of density, they found that density was significantly correlated with self-reported aggressiveness for males but not females.

Baum and Koman (1976) found gender differences in aggressive response to **anticipated crowding** as well, but *only* when spatial density increased. Men in small rooms who expected to be crowded behaved more aggressively than did women in the same situation. Further, men were more aggressive in a smaller room than when a larger room was used. However, increases in *social* density did not produce increased aggression. In fact, under conditions where subjects expected large numbers of people rather than limited space, they tended to withdraw rather than act aggressively.

From the studies reviewed thus far, it appears that the aggression-enhancing effects of density may be related more to spatial and resource-related problems than to issues created by the presence of too many people. It also seems that the magnitude of the effect of density on human aggressiveness is less than overwhelming (Baum & Paulus, 1987). The studies that have found increases in aggressiveness during high density have reported them primarily among men, and the effects have been mild at worst. However, it is important to keep in mind that the measures of aggression employed in this research (e.g., subjects sentencing a hypothetical criminal to a longer prison term) have been artificial. They are *not* the sort of aggression one finds in "real-world" crowded environments. One reason for this artificiality is the settings in which the research has been done. Most investigations of adult aggression during high density have been conducted in the laboratory, where subjects are confined only briefly, and where the measures one can use to assess aggression are limited. Overall, the weaknesses of these research methods pose serious limitations to our understanding of the density–aggression relationship.

These problems are only partly resolved by the correlational research that has been attempted. This research involves finding the association between long-term high-density confinement, and "real-world" measures of aggression (e.g., crime). Unfortunately, this body of research contains methodological flaws, and shows a tenuous relationship between high density and various indicators of crime (e.g., Bagley, 1989; Galle, Gove, & McPherson, 1972). However, the more "fine grained" the measure of density used in the study (room density as opposed to people per acre), the higher the correlation with aggression (e.g., Palmstierna, Huitfeldt, & Wistedt, 1991). In addition, there is evidence that high density is even more strongly associated with fear of crime than with actual victimization (Gifford & Peacock, 1979).

An exception to some of the above criticisms of research on the density–aggression link is research that has been done in prisons. Here, people are confined for long periods of time under high density, "real-life" aggression does take place, and there are accurate records of both population density and aggressive behaviors (Pontell & Welsh, 1994). In this context, Paulus, McCain, and Cox (1981) observed that increases in disciplinary infractions were associated with increased population density, and studies by Cox, Paulus, and McCain (1984) found extremely high correlations between prison density and inmate aggression. In one prison, a 30 percent decrease in the census resulted in a 60 percent decrease in assaults. When a 20 percent increase in the census occurred, it was followed by a 36 percent increase in assaults! Similar results are reported by Ruback and Carr (1984). It should be noted, however, that some prison studies have been less conclusive (Bonta, 1986). In addition, the extent to which this body of research could be expected to generalize to other populations living under high density is unclear. Obviously, prison inmates are different from the "person in the street," and prisons are not a typical high-density setting. While this research points to the possibility of stronger relations between density and aggression in the general population than occurred in the more artificial laboratory studies, the extent of its generalizability is uncertain.

Summary

Our discussion of the effects of density on social behavior (i.e., attraction, withdrawal, helping, and aggression) allows us to draw several tentative conclusions. First, it appears that high density leads to less liking of both people and places, and that this relationship is stronger for males than for females. High density also causes withdrawal and less helping behavior in a variety of situations. Concerning aggressive behavior, the findings are somewhat inconsistent, but for certain populations there seems to be a relationship between high density and aggression. The differences between social and spatial density also appear to be important. With these ideas in mind, we turn our focus to the effects of high density on a final and extremely important dimension—task performance.

EFFECTS OF HIGH DENSITY ON TASK PERFORMANCE

One of the most critical questions that can be asked about high density is whether it affects task performance. The answer has important implications for the design of all types of living and working spaces (e.g., schools, workplaces). Most early studies used tasks that were relatively simple to perform and were consistent in finding no performance decrements under high social or spatial density (Bergman, 1971; Rawls et al., 1972). For example, Freedman and his associates (1971) reported that density variations did not affect performance of any of a series of tasks.

Later work, generally using more complex tasks, supports a somewhat different conclusion (Dooley, 1974; Saegert, 1974; Saegert, MacIntosh, & West, 1975). As shown in Table 9–3, Paulus et al. (1976) found that both high social and spatial density led to decrements in complex maze task performance, but these decrements were more pronounced under conditions of high social density. In a field setting, Aiello, Epstein, and Karlin (1975b) observed decrements in complex task performance over time in residents

Table 9–3 Errors in Maze Performance as a Function of Spatial Density and Social Density*

Low spatial density	34.20
High spatial density	37.44
Low social density	32.13
High social density	39.50

*Based on data from Paulus et al., 1976.

of overcrowded dormitory rooms (three persons in a room built for two), as compared with less crowded rooms (two persons in a room built for two). Evans (1979b) also found poorer complex task performance under high-density conditions but no impairment in simple task performance, and Klein and Harris (1979) reported poorer complex task performance in individuals who were anticipating crowding. Finally, Knowles (1983) reported decrements in maze learning under conditions of high social density when all the individuals in the room were watching the subject perform, but *increased* retention of the task, once learned.

How can we reconcile our findings of high-density decrements on some tasks but not on others? One explanation centers around the fact that high density leads to arousal (cf. Evans, 1979a; Worchel & Brown, 1984). The Yerkes-Dodson Law (see Chapter 4), a formulation that relates arousal to task performance, states that arousal *should* interfere only with complex task performance. In terms of this law, our observation that high density causes decrements only in complex task performance would be expected, rather than discrepant. Since the Yerkes-Dodson Law has been supported in numerous research contexts in the psychological literature, it seems quite tenable as an explanation here. In addition, Paulus (1977) offers other suggestions for why density has not consistently affected task performance. He concludes that such factors as the psychological salience of the others present, the feelings of being evaluated, and the number of tasks subjects must perform may be important as well.

An alternative explanation for the past inconsistent findings has been offered by Heller, Groff, and Solomon (1977). They propose that many studies of high density have focused only on the physical aspects of a setting at the expense of the kinds of interactions that are typical of high-density situations. For example, some studies occupy

subjects with tasks so that interaction is minimized. Heller et al. suggest that this kind of procedure reduces the likelihood of finding effects of high density on task performance. In support of this, they showed that decrements in task performance occurred only under conditions characterized by high density *and* interaction among subjects. High-density settings in which subjects did not interact very much did not produce task performance decrements (see Figure 9–10).

Another potential explanation is provided by a study reported by Schkade (1977). She manipulated spatial density and expectancy (how well subjects thought they would do on the task). Results showed that the poorest task performance occurred when density was high and expectations were low—that is, subjects did not expect to do well on the task. Problems with task performance under high-density conditions may be evident primarily when negative outcomes are anticipated.

A final and very important question is whether high density can cause *aftereffects*, as well as immediate effects, on performance. As you will recall, noise has been linked to consequences for performance, occurring *after* exposure, and some studies suggest that

Figure 9–10 Interaction is necessary for density-related task performance deficits to occur.
Adapted from Heller, Groff, & Solomon, 1977.

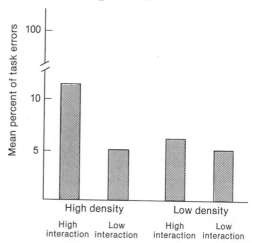

crowding has lingering effects as well. For example, it was found that subjects exposed to high density later showed less persistence at working on unsolvable puzzles than those exposed to low density (Evans, 1979a; Sherrod, 1974). In an attempt to determine whether perceived control would lessen aftereffects, Sherrod (1974) gave some subjects the option of leaving a crowded room to complete the study in a spacious setting (i.e., perceived control). Although no one took advantage of the option, this group showed fewer aftereffects than a group that was not offered an opportunity to leave. The similarity of these findings to those observed by Glass and Singer with noise (reviewed in Chapter 5) further suggests that noise and high density may affect people in similar ways.

PUTTING THE PIECES TOGETHER: CONCEPTUALIZATIONS OF DENSITY EFFECTS ON HUMANS

Up to this point, we have explored a number of density–behavior relationships, finding that high density may lead to various negative effects. As suggested in the general environment–behavior model from Chapter 4, we have seen that high density, like other potential stressors, may lead to (1) immediate effects such as physiological arousal and negative affect; (2) coping responses (e.g., withdrawal); and (3) aftereffects and cumulative effects (e.g., illness). However, high density does not always have negative consequences. For example, it affects task performance in some situations but not in others. Overall, the most appropriate conclusion might be that density negatively affects some of the people some of the time in some ways.

Basic Models

What is it about high density that causes those negative effects which do occur? Sto-

kols (1976) identified three conceptual perspectives—overload, behavior constraint, and ecological approaches—used by different researchers to answer this question. All the approaches have been covered in detail in Chapter 4. Briefly, the *overload* concept posits that high density can be aversive because it may cause us to become overwhelmed by sensory inputs. When the amount and rate of stimulation occasioned by high density exceeds our ability to deal with it, negative consequences occur. In contrast to the overload approach, the *behavior constraint* approach views high density as aversive because it may lead to reduced behavioral freedom (e.g., fewer behavioral choices, more interference). Thus, whether or not we will experience negative effects depends on what we want to do and whether high density constrains us. Finally, the *ecological model* assumes that high density can have negative consequences since it may result in insufficient resources for people in the setting. Resources are broadly defined and include anything from materials to roles. When density causes resources to become insufficient, negative effects occur.

Not surprisingly, additional explanations have been offered to account for how density affects us. *Arousal theory* (Evans, 1978b; Paulus & Matthews, 1980) suggests that high density may increase arousal. As we noted in Chapter 4, arousal has effects on performance in and of itself. Also, arousal may be attributed by the person in an arousing situation to various factors, depending on situational and cognitive cues. For example, Worchel and Teddlie (1976) argue that personal space violations associated with high-density settings cause arousal, which results in a negative experiential state attributed to others being too close. If arousal is misattributed (e.g., is attributed to something *other than* others being too close), the likelihood of a negative emotional state being linked to high density is lessened (Aiello et al., 1983).

Baum and Valins (1977) build upon an

overload framework and propose that the negative consequences of high density are caused by *unwanted interaction*. While too many contacts (overload) may be distressing, this is not always the case—sometimes a large number of social interactions may be bearable or even fun. However, when these interactions are unwanted, problems are more likely. Thus, difficulties in regulating when, where, and with whom one may interact can lead to too many unwanted interactions, and eventually, to stress. In support of this notion, Baum and Valins (1977) consistently found that "tripled" dormitory residents complained about unwanted contacts with neighbors.

Another explanation, the **behavioral interference** formulation (e.g., Schopler & Stockdale, 1977), asserts that when inadequate space or large numbers of people interfere with goal-directed behavior, negative effects are experienced. This explanation is loosely derived from the behavior constraint model discussed earlier, and is supported by studies showing that interference increases the negative effects of high density (Heller, Groff, & Solomon, 1977; Sundstrom, 1975). Unwanted interaction can be subsumed by this model, since it, too, can disrupt or prevent goal achievement. Also consistent with the model are findings that the presence of social structure, or rules governing conduct (which lessen interference) reduce the negative consequences of high density (Baum & Koman, 1976; Schopler & Walton, 1974). Finally, studies have directly linked the type of interference which occurs and the importance of blocked goals to the intensity of stress (McCallum et al., 1979; Morasch, Groner, & Keating, 1979; Schopler, McCallum, & Rusbult, 1978).

Related in some ways is Altman's (1975) **privacy regulation model**. According to Altman, high density has negative effects when breakdowns occur in the achievement of desired levels of privacy. As we stated

in Chapter 8, privacy is an interpersonal boundary process by which a person or group regulates interactions with others (Altman, 1975, p. 67). When achieved privacy is less than desired, control of social interaction is inadequate, and the person cannot regulate his or her level of interaction with others. Under these conditions, there may be negative consequences of high density. According to Altman, people cope with the inadequate privacy characteristic of high density by using stronger, or additional, privacy control mechanisms.

So, we now have a number of different views concerning what the critical determinants are of when high density will lead to negative effects (see Table 9–4). Without doubt, all of them are relevant, and there are probably other ways of conceptualizing the negative effects of high density as well. How can we resolve these competing explanations? Or, do we actually need to resolve them as much as to combine them into a more unified perspective? Despite the fact that the different formulations are presented as competing with one another, it is probably true that too much stimulation, overarousal, too many constraints on behavior, inadequate privacy, excessive unwanted social contact, interference, and resource inadequacy *each* account for some negative effects of high density (Baum & Fisher, 1977).

More recent conceptual efforts have focused on more parsimonious explanations for why high density has the effects that it does. One of these, the *control perspective*, has been used in this regard because it crosses the lines of the models in Table 9–4 and unifies diverse theoretical currents. We will discuss the control formulation in some detail here.

The Control Perspective

As you recall from Chapter 4, *perceived control* is a potent mediator of stress. When we believe that we can control a stressor or other aspects of a situation, the aversiveness

Table 9–4 Summary of Theoretical Perspectives on Crowding*

Conceptual Approach	Critical Cause(s) of Crowding	Primary Coping Mechanisms	Reference
Social overload	Excessive social contact; too much social stimulation	Escape stimulation; prioritize input and disregard low priorities; withdrawal	Milgram, 1970; Saegert, 1978
Behavior constraint	Reduced behavioral freedom	Aggressive behavior; leave situation; coordinate actions with others	Stokols, 1972; Sundstrom, 1978
Ecological	Scarcity of resources	Defense of group boundaries; exclusion of outsiders	Barker, 1968; Wicker, 1980
Arousal	Personal space violations plus appropriate attributions	Lower arousal to more optimal level	Evans, 1978; Paulus & Matthews, 1980
Unwanted interaction	Excessive unregulable or unwanted contact with others	Withdrawal; organization of small primary groups	Baum & Valins, 1977; Calhoun, 1970
Interference	Disruption or blocking of goal-directed behavior	Create structure; aggression; escape	Schopler & Stockdale, 1977; Sundstrom, 1978
Privacy regulation	Inability to maintain desired privacy	Privacy control mechanisms	Altman, 1975

Adapted from Stokols (1976).

of stress appears to be reduced. On the other hand, even if no other problems are apparent, losing or not having control can be stressful. Several researchers have proposed that high density can cause a loss of control (or prevent someone from ever having control), and that this loss of control is the primary mechanism by which density causes stress (Baum & Valins, 1979; Evans & Lepore, 1992; Lepore, Evans, & Schneider, 1992; Sherrod & Cohen, 1979).

Can we really explain many of the negative effects of high density as a loss of control? All of the theories outlined above—with the exception of the arousal theory—can be readily subsumed by the concept of control. *Overload models* assume that under conditions of high density we are bombarded by more stimuli than we can process—a situation

where a loss of control is likely. And Baum and Valins' notion of *unwanted interaction* is a control-based perspective. Negative effects are the result of contact that is too frequent, which makes control over when, where, and with whom people interact difficult to maintain. As a result, interactions become unpredictable and frequently unwanted. The *behavior constraint* notion is also control based, viewing high density as eliminating behavioral options and reducing freedom to behave as one might like. For example, having inadequate space can constrain our behavior by making it impossible to control the nature of interaction with others (Figure 9–11).

In addition, *privacy regulation models* are related to the concept of control. We can typically control the degree of intimacy in one-on-one interactions by adjusting the dis-

Figure 9–11   Although some members of this crowd are displaying signs of discomfort due to loss of individual control, many members of this crowd are enjoying this rock'n roll festival near Paris, France—but imagine being confined under such conditions for a week!

tance we stand from people, but in a very high-density room, we may find ourselves with no choice—we must stand close to people whether we know them well or not. In this manner, we can lose control over intimacy regulation. *Interference* can also be viewed as a threat to control, because our attempts to achieve one goal or another are repeatedly blocked or disrupted. And resource problems, the focus of *ecological* models, can limit our choices and restrict our ability to exercise control. Thus, to some extent, many of the "consequences" of high density that have been related to negative effects do cause a reduction in control. But, is there any direct research evidence for the relation between density and a loss of control (see Figure 9–12)?

Research examining the links between high density and loss of control has taken two different tacks. The first has been to manipulate personal control (i.e., provide some subjects, but not others, with perceived control), and to see if this has any effect on experience in high-density settings. Rodin, Solomon, and Metcalf (1978) attempted to manipulate whether or not people riding in a crowded elevator had control. First, they observed people's response to riding in crowded elevators, and found a tendency for them to gravitate toward the floor selection panel (a control panel, if you will). In effect, people attempted to "take control" in a high-density elevator by standing near the panel which regulates entry, exit, and floor selection. Next, Rodin and colleagues manipulated whether subjects were able to stand near the control panel (high-control condition) or not (low-control condition). The results indicated that subjects allowed to stand near the panel (i.e.,

Figure 9–12 As this Woodstock photo suggests, whether or not crowding leads to negative consequences depends in part on perceived control.

those who were given control) felt better, and thought the elevator was larger, than subjects not near the panel. Rodin and co-workers (1978) also examined the effects of control on the experience of high density in a laboratory context. Again, subjects were provided with varying degrees of control over the setting, and those with control felt better than those without.

A somewhat different approach to demonstrating the importance of control was taken by Sherrod (1974). Recall that in research on noise (see Chapter 5), Glass and Singer (1972) found that the negative aftereffects associated with exposure to noise were reduced if subjects had control over it. Sherrod conducted a similar study with density instead of noise as the environmental stressor. As in research on noise, negative aftereffects were associated with exposure to high density only when control was not available. Subjects who had perceived control did not exhibit negative aftereffects following exposure to high density.

Taken together, the above studies all demonstrate that high density associated with loss of control is more aversive than high density with control, and that introducing control can reduce the potential negative effects of high density. They do not, however, demonstrate that high density itself has consequences similar to those associated with loss of or lack of control.

Fortunately, that bit of evidence has been reported by other researchers. Rodin (1976) conducted two studies in field settings characterized by chronically high residential density. She attempted to ascertain whether living under high density was associated with helplessness-like behavior. **Learned help-**

CROWDING IN THE HOME AND IN THE SCHOOLS

Imagine yourself growing up in a small apartment with five other people who are continuously interacting with each other and with you. With so many people in so little space, you may grow up to feel the world is a complex place in which you have little power to influence events (cf. Altman, 1975; Baron & Rodin, 1978). What consequences does this have? Seligman (1975) has demonstrated that when we come to believe we cannot control our outcomes by responding appropriately (as may result from living in high-density conditions), we no longer perform effectively in a number of situations. This syndrome is called "learned helplessness."

Two interesting and provocative studies by Rodin (1976) demonstrated the relationship between residential density and susceptibility to "learned helplessness." In her first experiment, Rodin hypothesized and found that children who lived in high-density conditions were less likely than those in low-density conditions to try to control the administration of rewards they were to receive. In a second experiment, she exposed subjects from both groups to an initial frustrating task on which responses and outcomes were noncontingent. Rodin found that only children from high-density homes did significantly worse on a subsequent task for which outcomes were contingent. Thus, it appears that density in one's home is an important determinant of both the use of control and of performance after frustrating noncontingent reward situations.

A third study, by Saegert (1982), also focused on the consequences of residential density for children from low-income families, but this time on its effects for school performance. Children from high-density homes were more apt to be rated as behavior problems by teachers, and exhibited more evidence of distractibility and hyperactivity than children from low-density homes. In addition, reading scores were lower and vocabularies less developed for children from high-density homes. Though these effects could be due to various factors, evidence suggested that density played a role.

Besides the home environment, what other settings may be sources of "learned helplessness" training? As surprising as it may seem, one important culprit may be the schools. Baron and Rodin (1978) suggest that as class size increases, learned helplessness training begins to occur. They argue that larger classes lead to lower student expectations for control of reinforcement, because teacher feedback concerning student work becomes less discriminative. For example, as class size goes up, individualized student–teacher interactions decrease, and generalized (rather than individualized) praise and criticism increase. Clearly, such conditions could lead to a state of learned helplessness and its negative consequences for performance. If Baron and Rodin's hypothesis proves to be correct, it could have a profound impact on our educational system. What have your experiences been in small and large classes?

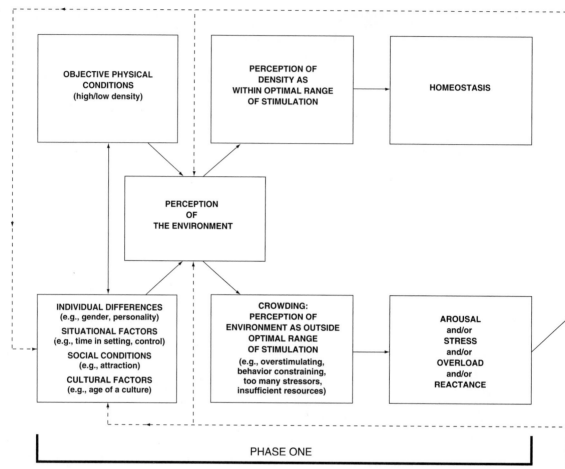

Figure 9–13 A conceptualization of the effects of high density on behavior based on our eclectic environment–behavior model

lessness is a syndrome in which people who are exposed to uncontrollable settings learn that they cannot control the setting, and hence stop trying to do so (Seligman, 1975). This manifests itself in reduced motivation and cognitive activity. Does chronic exposure to high density result in learned helplessness? It was found that Rodin's subjects, who were children and adolescents, showed symptoms of helplessness that were associated with the high density in their homes (see the box on page 351).

Baum and Valins (1977) also found symptoms of helplessness among people exposed to high density in a residential environment over a prolonged period of time. While neither Rodin (1976) nor Baum and Valins (1977) linked helplessness *directly* to loss of control in residential settings, this has been accomplished by Baum, Aiello, and Calesnick (1978) and Baum and Gatchel (1981). It was established in these studies that as people in high-density situations relinquished their beliefs that they could control their environ-

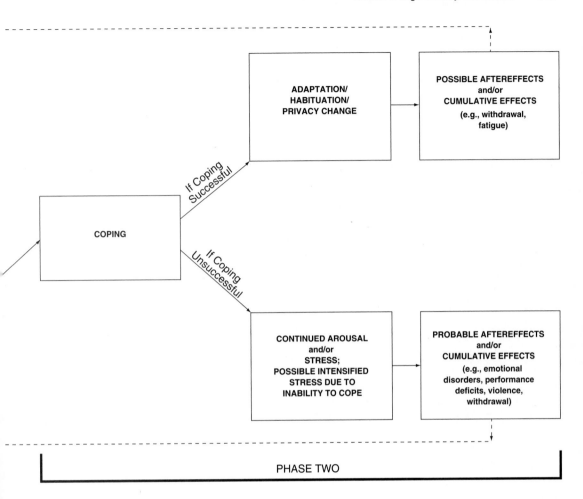

ment, their behavior became increasingly like that associated with helplessness.

Overall, there is compelling evidence that control is involved in the negative effects of high density. When control is available, high density has less impact on people than when it is not available. Further, chronic exposure to high density appears to be associated with learned helplessness. Additional evidence of the links posited by the control model is needed but it is fairly clear that the effect of high density is at least partly determined by people's perceptions of control.

A Summary Perspective on High-Density Effects

Given that high density involves an array of potentially disturbing elements (e.g., loss of control, overarousal, overstimulation), how can we explain the fact that it only *sometimes* influences our behavior? Many researchers (Desor 1972; Loo, 1973; Rapoport, 1975; Stokols, 1972) have addressed themselves to this issue. A conceptualization of the effects of density on humans is presented in Figure 9–13. As you will notice, the conceptual scheme is a special case of the general environment–behavior model presented in Chapter 4.

In Phase I of our conceptualization, an important distinction is made that explains why high density is sometimes stressful (leading to negative effects) and other times is not. In terms of this distinction (first proposed by Stokols, 1972), *high density* is viewed as a physical state involving potential inconveniences (e.g., loss of control, stimulus overload, lack of behavioral freedom, resources, or privacy), which may or may not be salient to a person in the situation. Whether or not these conditions are salient depends on: (1) individual differences between people (gender, personality, age); (2) situational conditions (what the person is doing; time in the setting; presence of other stressors); and (3) social conditions (relationships between people, intensity of interaction). If the negative aspects of high density are *not* salient, the environment is perceived as being within an optimal range, homeostasis is maintained, and no negative effects occur. If the potential negative aspects (e.g., overstimulation, behavior constraint) of high density *are* salient, crowding occurs. **Crowding** is conceptualized as a psychological state characterized by stress and having motivational properties (e.g., it elicits attempts to reduce discomfort).

Having incorporated the density–crowding distinction into our model, we turn now to Phase II, which specifies the consequences of the psychological state of crowding. As in other stressful situations (see Chapter 4), it is assumed that the stress associated with crowding involves coping responses that are directed toward reducing stress (e.g., withdrawal). Interestingly, the overload, behavior constraint, and ecological approaches, as well as the others, each predict qualitatively different types of coping responses (see Table 9–4 for a description of these varying responses). Regardless of these minor differences in the types of cop-

ing, the sequential links specified in Figure 9–13 between stress, coping, adaptation, and aftereffects conform to the general environment–behavior model found in Chapter 4. It is assumed that when coping is successful in handling stress, adaptation or adjustment occurs, and the individual is less likely to experience aftereffects or cumulative effects. If coping is unsuccessful, the stress continues, and the individual is extremely likely to experience aftereffects and cumulative effects (e.g., illness).

Coping is an important part of any model of crowding for two reasons. First, it is usually directed at reducing the causes or effects of crowding, and second, it is a continuous process. From the moment that crowding is first experienced or anticipated, people attempt to deal with it. These attempts are dynamic, continuously unfolding until adaptation is achieved, the crowding dissipates, or fatigue makes further coping impossible (e.g., Altman, 1975). The notion of dynamic coping underlying crowding suggests that responses to crowding change with the situation. Such a coping process has been addressed by research examining adjustments to high spatial and social density (Greenberg & Baum, 1979; Greenberg & Firestone, 1977). For example, Greenberg and Firestone observed adjustments in verbal and visual behavior in contexts where other forms of coping were blocked. Greenberg and Baum reported continuing adjustment and readjustment of social behaviors among subjects who anticipated changing degrees of crowding in their experimental session.

How well is our application of the general environment–behavior model to high-density situations supported by relevant data? Unfortunately, most of the studies of high density to date have had a practical rather than a conceptual focus, and few *explicit* attempts have been made to test the various relationships proposed in the model. While many of the studies we discussed in our literature review are implicitly supportive, they apply only to small parts of the "whole" encompassed by the model. However, a few experiments that have been done allow us to draw suggestive evidence about the sequential links we have posited. Such studies (e.g., Worchel & Teddlie, 1976) support many of the assertions, but we will have to await future research for a more precise test. At this point, we should view the model as a tentative but viable means of understanding the effects of high density on behavior. It can also serve as a source of hypotheses concerning the moderation and control of high-density effects (for an alternative model of high-density effects, see the box on pages 356–357).

ELIMINATING THE CAUSES AND EFFECTS OF CROWDING

At this point in our discussion, you might be wondering how we can eliminate the causes and the effects of crowding. We will explore the predictions derived from our general environment–behavior model, and apply them to address this issue.

Predictions From Our General Environment–Behavior Model Applied to High Density

One extremely valuable feature of our model is that it provides a framework for speculation and research about how to moderate the causes and effects of crowding. This can be of great conceptual and applied significance. As you recall, the model specifies that individual differences among people, situational conditions, and social conditions determine whether or not high density is perceived as "crowding." Research has supported the assertion that these three sets of factors can produce the experience of crowding, and is associated with negative consequences. We will briefly discuss representative individual differences, situational,

and social conditions found to affect our reactions to high density.

Identifying *individual difference* variables that determine whether high density is experienced as crowding is of practical value, since it allows us to select those individuals who will be most and least sensitive to the constraints of limited space. For example, we have found that in a variety of situations, males are more apt to experience crowding than females, and have suggested several explanations for this. There is some evidence, however, that this pattern of gender differences may be limited to laboratory settings, where there is no possibility of escape (Aiello, Thompson, & Brodzinsky, 1983). Under such conditions, women seem to handle stress better, perhaps because they are more apt than men to share their distress with others. In long-term high-density contexts, however, women may cope more *poorly* than men. For example, in dormitory crowding studies (e.g., Aiello, Baum, & Gormley, 1981) women sometimes report more crowding and negative effects. This may be because men cope with high density by leaving their rooms, whereas women are more involved with their roommates and spend more time in their room, which results in increased stress (Aiello, Thompson, & Baum, 1981).

In addition to gender, the amount of personal space people desire to maintain between themselves and others constitutes an individual difference variable which may affect the degree to which crowding is experienced. For example, Aiello et al. (1977) found that subjects with preferences for large interpersonal distances were more adversely affected in a high-density setting than those with smaller preferred distances. Individuals who liked to sit far away from others showed greater physiological arousal, discomfort, and poorer task performance than those who preferred to sit closer. Dooley (1974) has found evidence of similar effects.

Another important determinant of our

AN ALTERNATIVE APPROACH:
The Density–Intensity Model

We have summarized a model that distinguishes between density and crowding and that specifies a number of factors that may cause crowding and its attendant effects. Freedman (1975) takes another position, which has been a source of great debate among environmental psychologists. In general, his **density–intensity** model does not support the density-crowding distinction accepted by most researchers.

He also argues that density intensifies reactions that would occur in any case in a particular situation. High density heightens the importance of other people and *magnifies* our reactions to them. Thus, for Freedman, high density will intensify the pleasantness of positive situations and intensify the negativeness of aversive ones. From this viewpoint, any number of factors can cause a negative reaction in a high-density situation.

In research to support his notion, Freedman provided a link between density and the intensity of contagion, which occurs when the behaviors or emotions expressed by one person spread rapidly throughout a group of people. In a study using different room sizes and group sizes to vary density, Freedman, Birsky, and Cavoukian (1980) observed people's reactions to humorous films. After viewing the films, a confederate began to applaud, and the spread of this reaction throughout the group was noted. As one would expect from the density–intensity notion, contagion was more extensive in high-density groups. Freedman and Perlick (1979) similarly found intensification of contagion with high density; and Freedman (1975), Schiffenbauer and Schiavo (1975), and Aiello, Thompson, and Brodzinsky (1983)

reactions to high density is our level of social support. Lepore, Evans, and Schneider (1991) found that individuals who were experiencing high density and who had low social support had more negative psychological reactions than those with high social support. After very long exposure to high density, this buffering effect of social support on the negative consequences of high density disappeared, because long-term exposure to high density disrupted the very social networks that had protected people from its negative effects!

Research has focused on whether *personality characteristics* moderate our reactions to high density. Some of this work has focused on locus of control (i.e., whether people believe they, or outside forces, control their outcomes). It has typically but not always been found (cf. Walden, Nelson, & Smith, 1981) that internals (individuals who feel they control their fate) display a *higher* threshold of crowding than externals (individuals who feel events are controlled by outside forces; Schopler & Walton 1974; Schopler, McCallum, & Rusbult, 1978). One setting in which internals experienced crowding as *more* aversive than externals was in a dormitory setting where students were "tripled up" (Aiello, Vautier, & Bernstein, 1983). This may be because while externals "gave up" and stopped trying to control this difficult situation, internals persisted without success, experiencing stress along the

reported additional evidence consistent with the general model. On the other hand, several studies have found *reduced* appreciation of humor under high-density conditions (Prerost, 1982; Prerost & Brewer, 1980). In addition to the possible effects of high density on intensifying our appreciation (or lack of appreciation) of humor, other studies have found that high density may intensify our reactions to more negative stimuli (e.g., stressors). Lepore, Evans, and Palsane (1991) reported that social hassles in the home were associated with psychological symptoms *only* among people living under crowded conditions. In effect, crowding may intensify the effects of other stressors one may be experiencing. Lepore, Evans, and Schneider (1992) suggest that this may be due, in part, to lower perceived control, because crowding makes it impossible to avoid or escape social hassles.

There is no doubt that one of the effects of density *is* the magnification of responses to various situational variables. At baseball or football games, excitement is often intensified by larger crowds, while negativity may be amplified if the home team loses and the drive home is in bumper-to-bumper traffic. Yet, this is only one of the many effects of density. Freedman and co-workers (1980) are careful to point this out, and it remains clear that high density can exert independent effects as well as intensifying the affect that would otherwise be present. Identification of those cases in which intensification is the primary mechanism underlying individuals' response to high density and when it is not is an area for future research.

way. Not surprisingly, people who are highly affiliative are more tolerant of high density than those who are less affiliative (Miller & Nardini, 1977). In fact, high affiliative subjects experienced more stress in a low- than a high-density dormitory living situation (Miller, Rossbach, & Munson 1981).

When considering individual differences, it is important to note that the characteristics of a particular high-density setting may affect how an individual difference variable will impact on coping. For example, Baum et al. (1982) found that people who screen themselves from interaction and organize their surroundings were better able to cope with high *social* density than individuals who did not screen themselves. One

would expect that this "screening" variable would be less important under conditions of high *spatial* density.

We should also keep in mind that the individual differences we have discussed were found for North American subjects, and may not hold cross-culturally. Indeed, the personal space literature (see Chapter 8), correlational studies (Sundstrom, 1978), and work on privacy (Altman, 1975) suggest that we may expect cultural differences in reactions to high density. Research corroborates this assertion. For example, studies find that high density is related to social pathology in some places but not in others (e.g., Fuller et al., 1993; Galle & Gove, 1979). Similarly, Nasar and Min (1984) predicted and found that

Mediterraneans would respond more negatively than Asians when placed in a small, single dormitory room.

What differentiates the cultures where high density may be more, and less, associated with pathology? One factor could be the *age* of the culture. Young, as opposed to older cultures may have had less time to develop means of coping with high density. According to this logic, as cultures evolve, ways are developed to cope with density, and negative effects may decrease (Gifford, 1987). Some suggestive data support the above line of reasoning, although more research is clearly needed. One society which is very old, in which people may cope especially well with high density, is the Chinese culture. It has been suggested that the Chinese may have become so familiar and comfortable with high density that, when given the choice, people often opt for high- as opposed to low-density conditions (Aiello & Thompson, 1980b). Further, it has been suggested that the Chinese have developed an elaborate set of norms, rules, and coping strategies to support them in a "densely packed" existence. There are rules about access to space, a low level of emotional involvement is expected with others, and interaction between different groups (e.g., men and women; high- versus low-status individuals) is regulated. Further, sounds that others might view as noise are regarded as acceptable (Aiello & Thompson, 1980b; Anderson, 1972). Similar practices are found in other cultures that have adapted successfully to high density (Iwata, 1992; Munrowe & Munrowe, 1972).

However, other research casts doubt on the assumption that the Chinese have an affinity for high density. In a study of people living in Chinatown in San Francisco, Loo and Ong (1984) found that residents view crowding as undesirable and even harmful. The experience of crowding was also a major reason why they thought they might want to move. Overall, this research suggests that the Chinese like crowding no more than anyone else, and presents a forceful challenge to work implying that they bear up especially well under high density.

A final, related, individual difference variable that has been linked to reactions to high density is one's adaptation level from past experience under high-density conditions. Some investigators hypothesize that people with a history of high-density living are less likely to experience crowding in a novel situation than those with a history of isolation. In support of this hypothesis, it has been found that the Japanese, residents of Hong Kong, and the Logoli (all of whom live under extremely high density) have developed social mechanisms that may be viewed as adaptive for high-density living. Further, Booth (1976) reported that men who grew up in high-density situations were less apt to contract stress-related diseases if they lived in high density when they were adults. While several additional studies (e.g., Gove & Hughes, 1983; Sundstrom, 1978) support this "high-density experience-adaptation" hypothesis, Paulus and his colleagues (1975) found that the longer an inmate was imprisoned, the *lower* his or her tolerance for crowding. Inconsistent evidence is also reported by Lepore, Evans, and Palsane (1991), by Rohe (1982), and by Loo and Ong (1984). Other work by Webb and Worchel (1993) suggests that in addition to level of past experience under high density, expectations regarding present levels of density, and whether they have been confirmed or disconfirmed, may play a role in determining individuals' reactions to high-density confinement. This research may help to explain some of the inconsistencies in past research in this area.

In addition to being moderated by individual difference variables, reactions to high density are affected by *situational conditions*. An important situational condition is the degree of control we have. Complementing the studies we discussed earlier, additional research has found that allowing people in-

MORE THAN 57 VARIETIES OF CROWDING

The research we have reviewed thus far suggests that crowding has situational antecedents, an emotional component, and, of course, behavioral consequences. The theoretical notions introduced have pinpointed some of the situational factors associated with crowding, and the research we have reviewed has highlighted some of its affective and behavioral consequences. While we have "pieced the crowding story together" from a variety of sources, a study by Montano and Adamopoulous (1984) had subjects rate how they would feel and act in a variety of crowded situations, applied sophisticated statistical techniques, and yielded a picture of crowding quite consistent with the themes of this chapter—all in a single study.

The researchers specified four major situations in which people felt crowded, three major affective consequences, and five typical behavioral responses. The situations in which people became crowded were: (1) feeling that one's behavior was constrained; (2) being physically interfered with; (3) being uncomfortable due to the mere presence of many others; or (4) when high density caused expectations to be disappointed. What types of affective response did crowding elicit? It was associated with negative reactions to others and the situation, and under certain conditions, positive feelings. When is positive affect associated with crowding? According to Montano and Adamopoulous, this occurs only when people feel that they have coped successfully with it. Regarding the types of behaviors caused by crowding, the researchers identified five: (1) assertiveness; (2) rushing to complete activities so that one can flee to less dense environs; (3) physical withdrawal; (4) psychological withdrawal; and (5) adaptation—making the best of a bad situation! While this research did not involve people engaged in "real-world" experiences with high density, it is useful as corroborative evidence for earlier findings, and it suggests some new approaches. By crossing the four situations crowding was found to occur in and the three affective and five behavioral responses, it implies that crowding comes in at least 60 different varieties!

creased control over a situation leads to less perceived crowding (Langer & Saegert, 1977) and to fewer negative effects (Baum & Fisher, 1977; Langer & Saegert, 1977). The applied potential for introducing control into high-density situations is great. For example, providing individuals who live under high density with training that enhances control (e.g., giving pointers about how to share space and ensure privacy) may help alleviate crowding and its negative effects. Schmidt and Keating (1979) have identified

three types of control which might be introduced: cognitive control (accurate information), behavioral control (ability to work toward a goal), and decisional control (having choices available). They suggest that providing one or more of these to people in high density could ameliorate crowding stress.

Other situational conditions may affect reactions to high density as well. For example, at a constant level of density, men experience more negative effects when others are touching them, than when this is not the case (Nicosia et al., 1979). This supports Knowles' (1983) assertion that in addition to the more traditional measures of social and spatial density, the physical proximity of others is important to consider. All current measures of density assume that people are evenly distributed across space. However, it may not be only how many square feet per person there are in a room, but how close the others are to you that counts.

Does the amount of time we are confined to high-density conditions moderate our reaction? The relationship between time under high density and crowding is somewhat unclear, but it is probably fair to suggest that the longer the period of confinement, the more aversive the response (Aiello, Epstein, & Karlin, 1975b; Loo & Ong, 1984). Of course, as we noted earlier, very prolonged confinement under high density may affect one's adaptation level, and for such individuals, density may become less problematic. Whether we are in a primary environment (like a home) or a secondary environment (like a restaurant), and the extent to which other stressors (e.g., noise) are involved may also affect crowding. When we are in a primary environment (Stokols, 1976, 1978) and when other stressors are operating, we may be more likely to experience crowding. This will be especially true when we view others as responsible for our distress (Sundstrom, 1978). Finally, there is suggestive evidence that we are more likely to experience crowding when engaged in work than when engaged in recreation (Cohen, Sladen, & Bennett, 1975).

In addition to individual differences and situational conditions, *social conditions* can be manipulated to affect whether or not we are crowded. These variables make up the social "climate" of a high-density situation (e.g., the degree of friendship, and the level of social interaction and interference). For example, our relationship with the people we are with may determine how crowded we

feel: Less crowding is experienced with liked rather than disliked others (Fisher, 1974; Schaeffer & Patterson 1980), with others who engage in activities we approve rather than disapprove of (Gramann & Burdge, 1984; Womble & Studebaker, 1981), and with acquaintances rather than strangers (Cohen et al., 1975; Rotton, 1987b). To the extent that we experience social interference (interruptions) by others (especially if these are perceived as intentional; Stokols, 1978), or experience excessive proximity or immediacy (too direct eye contact or body orientation; Sundstrom, 1975), crowding is more likely. Finally, crowding is more often experienced in unstructured than in structured task situations (Baum & Koman, 1976).

High density within primary social groups (e.g., families) has repeatedly shown fewer negative effects than in other groups. For example, when density *within* apartment units is examined, it appears to be negligible as a factor associated with illness or behavior difficulties (e.g., Giel & Ormel, 1977). Degree of acquaintance with others and one's relative position in a group's dominance hierarchy also affect crowding: The presence of friends or the possession of high status tends to reduce the aversiveness of large numbers of people or cramped spaces (Arkkelin, 1978).

The dynamic way in which social conditions can affect crowding may be illustrated by considering, once again, studies on the effects of overassignment of student residents to dormitory rooms. You recall that this research assessed the consequences of having three students live in a room designed for only two. Initial study of this phenomenon (e.g., Aiello, 1983; Baron et al., 1976; Karlin, Epstein, & Aiello, 1978; Walden et al., 1981) revealed that the "tripling" of dormitory rooms was associated with negative mood, increased health complaints, and suppressed task performance. These findings made sense, given the increased difficulties of sharing resources, coordinating activities, and achieving privacy created by the addition of a third roommate. Yet the question remained—was this a problem of too many people or too little space? Baum et al. (1979) reasoned that it was neither. Going back to the social psychological literature on groups, they found confirmation of a notion that many of you already know: Three-person groups are very unstable and susceptible to coalition formation such that two people get together and exclude the third (e.g., Kelley & Arrowwood, 1960). Given this, it seemed possible that the primary problem in "tripling" was not that there were too many roommates or insufficient space. Instead, it was that there were three roommates, one of whom was likely to feel left out and, as a result, to have less control over the shared bedroom. This "isolate," when compared with the other two roommates, would have less input into how the room was arranged and used, feel generally more "left out," have greater difficulty achieving privacy, and feel more crowded.

Research examining the formation of coalitions in "tripled" dorm rooms provided support for this interpretation (e.g., Aiello et al., 1981a, 1983; Gormley & Aiello, 1982; Reddy et al., 1981). These studies indicated that students living in tripled rooms were especially likely to feel "left out" by roommates. Those who felt like isolates reported more problems related to using the room and more perceived crowding. Tripled residents who did not feel "left out" reported experiences and moods more like students living in doubled rooms (Baum et al., 1979).

An extension of this research examined the effects of tripled and quadrupled rooms (Reddy et al., 1981). If the instability of three-person groups was responsible for the effects of "tripling," one would expect residents of four-person rooms to feel less crowded than residents of three-person rooms. If, on the other hand, the primary problem was the absolute number of roommates, then quadru-

pled rooms would be associated with greater crowding. Results indicated that isolates were more likely in the tripled than in quadrupled rooms and that nonisolate residents of tripled rooms reported experiences similar to quadrupled residents. Isolates, on the other hand, reported more problems with crowding than either of the latter two groups. From this research, we can see the importance of considering social processes in attempting to understand crowding.

Architectural Mediators of Crowding

Now that we have tried to provide you with a feeling for some of the conditions that moderate the experience of crowding, it should be interesting to consider how we can modify existing environments or plan new ones so that crowding is less of a problem (for a complete discussion of the design process, see Chapter 11). What would you do if you were a planner charged with evaluating (and possibly modifying) some of the plans for a building which might affect the level of crowding residents are likely to experience? First, you would probably assess objective physical conditions (i.e., space allotted to each resident) in terms of its adequacy for the type of functions to be performed in that space. Next, you would estimate how spatial needs would be affected by anticipated situational conditions (e.g., how well the individuals occupying the space could be expected to get along) and individual differences (e.g., adaptation level). From your evaluation of objective physical space plus situational, social, and individual difference conditions, you would have an idea of how much of a crowding problem there would be. If you had anticipated that crowding would be a problem, you could institute some of the architectural modifications we will describe below.

How can environments be designed or modified to alleviate crowding and its consequences? A number of studies suggest alternatives that can be incorporated into existing structures or planned into new ones. For example, for males, greater ceiling height is associated with less crowding (Savinar, 1975), and it has been found that rooms with well-defined corners elicit less crowding than rooms with curved walls (Rotton, 1987b). In addition, rectangular rooms seem to elicit less crowding than square rooms of the same area (Desor, 1972), and rooms that contain visual escapes (e.g., windows and doors) are rated as less crowded than similar areas without such escapes. The latter findings suggest that in some cases, the *design* of a building affects how crowded people feel in a constant amount of objective space. Rapoport (1975) makes the important point that the level of density that people perceive, rather than the actual level of density, is apt to determine their behavior. Therefore, designs which lessen perceived density could be expected to be associated with less crowding and negative effects.

One type of design that seems to lessen perceived crowding is low- as opposed to high-rise buildings. High-rise buildings are associated with greater feelings of crowdedness, and less perceived control, safety, privacy, and satisfaction with relations with other residents, than low-rise buildings (McCarthy & Saegert, 1979). Some research suggests that residents of higher floors in high-rise buildings are less crowded than those on lower floors (Nasar & Min, 1984; Schiffenbauer, 1979), but other studies are equivocal on this point (e.g., Mandel, Baron, & Fisher, 1980).

Clearly, the above types of features would be fairly difficult to change in a structure that has already been built. In terms of more feasible modifications, placement of activities in the center of rooms rather than in a corner or along a wall elicits less crowding (Dabbs, Fuller, & Carr, 1973), and a number of studies (Baum, Reiss, & O'Hara, 1974; Desor, 1972; Evans, 1979b) provide evidence that adding flexible partitions to rooms

lessens feelings of crowding. In one study, "privacy cubicles" surrounded by high partitions and containing desk and storage space were placed in dormitory-style prison rooms. Inmates having the cubicles in their dormitories had more positive reactions to their environment and lower rates of noncontagious illnesses (McGuire & Gaes, 1982). Similarly, segmenting large dormitory rooms in prisons into smaller rooms by building a lounge area in the middle lowered illness complaints (Baum & Paulus, 1987). These studies suggest, incidentally, that at least in prisons, the number of people one must have contact with is a more important determinant of outcome than the amount of space one has. For a discussion of whether it is generally worse to experience high social or spatial density, see the box on page 363.

It has also been found that brightness (provided by wall and accent colors or appropriate light sources) leads to less perceived crowding (Mandel et al., 1980; Nasar & Min, 1984; Schiffenbauer, 1979), and that the presence of visual distractions (e.g., pictures on walls, advertisements on transportation vehicles) leads to more perceived space (Baum & Davis, 1976; Worchel & Teddlie, 1976). In addition, sociofugal seating arrangements (when people face away from each other) are associated with less crowding than sociopetal ones (when people face each other; Wener, 1977). However, this may not be the case when relations between interactants are good.

Interventions in High-Density Settings

While many intervention strategies can be derived from the various models of crowding, only a few have actually been implemented. Some have attempted to prevent crowding from occurring in the first place (e.g., by providing people with information on how to exert "control" over the situation, or by modifying high-density environments in ways that would help people to cope,

SOCIAL VERSUS SPATIAL DENSITY:
Which Is More Aversive?

Should a designer faced with the unenviable choice worry more about creating a design with high social density or high spatial density? Each type of density offers different problems to individuals experiencing it (Baum & Paulus, 1987). Increasing numbers of people bring with them more interaction, more need for social structure, more social interference, and greater threats to control. Too little space, on the other hand, may be associated with physical disruption, loss of intimacy regulation, spatial invasions, and physical constraints (Baum & Paulus, 1987).

Not surprisingly, then, research on high density suggests differences in the effects of high social and spatial density. And, based on a careful analysis, researchers have tentatively concluded that manipulations of social density are more aversive than manipulations of spatial density (cf. Baum & Valins, 1979; Paulus, 1977). Specifically, they have found that high social density will produce negative effects more consistently than high spatial density, and that while social density manipulations are generally aversive, spatial density manipulations are often problematic only to males in same-sex groups (Paulus, 1977). In natural settings, social density is clearly a more serious concern for people (Paulus, 1980). For example, Cox et al. (1984) report that while high social density led to very negative effects in prisoners, high spatial density had few negative effects. They conclude that the best way to house prisoners would be in small, single rooms. Others report consistent findings. For example, Ruback and Carr (1984) reported that prisoners who lived in single rooms liked their accommodations more, had higher perceived control, and experienced less stress than those in accommodations characterized by higher social density.

Why might an overabundance of others be more distressing than too little space? The answer is unclear, but there are some hypotheses. One explanation put forth by Baum and Valins suggests that people are more immediately aware of problems created by large numbers of others than by spatial limitations. Also, the loss of control that results when too many people are in a room is frequently more serious than that caused by being in too small a room. In addition, people may be threatened by the presence of many others. What are the theoretical consequences of the assertion that social and spatial density may affect us differently? While we should not draw the conclusion that the effects of spatial limitations are inconsequential, we should develop predictive frameworks that account for the differences in the two manipulations.

thereby reducing or preventing crowding). Others have focused on treating the consequences of crowding (e.g., dealing directly with the negative mood created by high density).

Preventing Crowding From Occurring

One form of intervention has involved providing what is often referred to as heightened *cognitive control* to people in high-density situations. Cognitive control is the increased sense of predictability or controllability that people gain when given prior warning or information about a situation. Much of the initial work in this area was done in medical settings; only later was it applied to high-density contexts. For example, providing patients with information about how they will feel, what will happen, or what they can do about their feelings *before* surgery can reduce distress and complications later on (e.g., Johnson & Leventhal, 1974). When behavioral control is limited, providing such information increases a person's sense of control and, as we noted in Chapters 4 and 5, perceived control can reduce the aversiveness of stress.

Some important work has found that increasing cognitive control is beneficial in high-density situations as well as in medical contexts. Langer and Saegert (1977) reported an experiment in which information about crowding was given to some subjects, but not others, before they entered grocery stores varying in actual levels of density. The information subjects were given focused on how they would feel if the store became crowded. All participants were given a task to perform that required them to move around the store to find a number of items. Not surprisingly, the results suggested that when density was higher, task performance was poorer. In addition, subjects who had been given prior information about crowding performed better and reported a more positive emotional experience than those who did not receive information. Having information about how they might feel allowed subjects to better select appropriate coping strategies and to behave more confidently (Langer & Saegert, 1977). This pattern of effects has been replicated both in laboratory and field settings (Baum, Fisher, & Solomon, 1981; Fisher & Baum, 1980; Paulus & Matthews, 1980). In one related study, Wener and Kaminoff (1983) introduced informational signs into the crowded lobby of a federal correctional

center. Visitors reported less perceived crowding, discomfort, anger and confusion.

Additional strategies for preventing crowding have involved architectural, as opposed to cognitive, interventions. Baum and Davis (1980), for example, reported a successful architectural intervention in high-density dormitories (see box on page 340). By altering the arrangement of interior dormitory space, they were able to prevent residents from experiencing crowding stress. Other strategies are sure to arise. It is important to understand that architectural interventions in high-density settings can be effective only if they consider the specific dynamics of the situation they are addressing.

Another thing to keep in mind in planning any intervention is that high density is not invariably negative, and one must consider the complexities of the situation before deciding whether it is even desirable to intervene. For example, a study by Szilagyi and Holland (1980) revealed that when an organization moved into a new building characterized by higher social density, employees reported less job autonomy, but greater feedback about their job performance from others, increased friendship opportunities, and work satisfaction. While it is not clear that higher social density is uniquely responsible for the reported effects, there may be situations in which, rather than decreasing social density, one might actually want to increase it!

Treating the Consequences of Crowding

In addition to interventions which determine whether or not crowding occurs, a second set of interventions focuses on moderating the effects of crowding when it does occur. Karlin, Rosen, and Epstein (1979) reported a study which sought to lower the anxiety and arousal associated with crowded transportation settings. Three therapeutic interventions were used to treat subjects in a laboratory analogue of a transportation context. Participants were given training in *muscle relaxation, cognitive reappraisal* (in-which they were told they could improve their mood by focusing on the positive aspects of the situation), or *imagery* (in which they were instructed to concentrate on a pleasant, distracting, pastoral image). A fourth group received initial instructions to relax, but was given no other training. Re-sponses to crowding among subjects in these four groups provided mixed support for the value of therapeutic intervention. Subjects given cognitive reappraisal instructions showed more positive responses to the setting than subjects in the other groups. The effectiveness of the muscle relaxation and imagery treatments in reducing the impact of high density was less marked.

CHAPTER SUMMARY

Considerations of global overpopulation make the study of the effects of high density particularly important. This area of investigation has become increasingly popular and has included research with both human and animal populations. Two types of density manipulations are commonly used: varying *spatial density* (in which space is manipulated and group size held constant), and varying *social density* (in which group size is manipulated and space is held constant). With animals, it appears that the physiological and behavioral effects of high density are almost uniformly negative. It has been found that animals experience changes in body organs and glandular malfunctions that affect birthrate and also experience severe disruptions of social and maternal behaviors. A number of conceptual schemes have been developed to account for animal reactions to density.

Human reactions to high density depend more on the particular situation. While density does not have a totally consistent negative effect on humans, it leads to aversive consequences on a variety of dimensions. Concerning its effect on feeling states, high density leads to negative affect (especially in males) and to higher physiological arousal. There is also some evidence that it is associated with illness.

In terms of effects on social behavior, high density has been found to result in less liking for others (especially in males), and it is associated with withdrawal from interaction. Also, there is suggestive evidence that high density leads to aggression and to lower incidence of prosocial behavior. Finally, for task performance, it leads to decrements for complex but not for simple tasks, and it may also be associated with aftereffects.

Overall, high density causes (1) immediate effects on behavior; (2) coping responses; and (3) aftereffects. A number of explanatory schemes (e.g., overload, behavior constraint, and ecological models) attempt to explain why high density is aversive, and each stresses a different element of density as critical. Why does high density not always lead to negative consequences? A model that differentiates between high density and crowding accounts for this finding. It is suggested that while high density contains negative aspects, it is individual differences and situational and social conditions that determine whether these are salient and whether "crowding" occurs. The model specifies a progression of effects that follow when crowding is experienced and also offers ways to eliminate the causes and effects of crowding.

SUGGESTED PROJECTS

1. In our discussion about eliminating the causes and effects of high density, we stated that individual differences, situational, and social conditions moderate perceived crowding. A simple procedure allows us to verify this relationship and many more that have been highlighted throughout the chapter. The procedure is the "model room technique." First, get a shoe box, or a somewhat larger size carton. Modify it a bit so that it looks something like a room. (You may be creative and include elaborate windows, draperies, and so on if you like, but be sure to leave the top off.) Next, take a large number of clothespins, small blocks, pieces of styrofoam, or the like, which can be modified to stand up and to look something like people. Now you are ready to start doing "model room" experiments.

How do you begin? First, decide what relationship you want to test. Let's assume you want to test the assertion that people will feel more crowded in primary environments than secondary ones. Have a willing subject imagine that the box is his or her living room (a primary environment). Tell the subject to place figures in the box up to the point at which he or she feels the room is crowded. Count the number of figures in the box, and then remove the figures. Next, tell the subject the box is a restaurant (a secondary environment) and ask him or her to place figures in the box until the space seems crowded. Determine how the number of figures placed in the box varies, depending on whether it is described as a primary or a secondary setting. You now have data concerning the "threshold" of crowding in primary and secondary environments. If you find a lower threshold of crowding in primary than in secondary environments, you may have supportive evidence for Stokols' (1976) assertion that we experience crowding more readily in a primary than in a secondary setting. Some other hypotheses to test using this procedure are listed below:

a. Test Baum and Valins' (1977) assertion that people who live in corridor-style dormitories avoid social contact situations more than people who live in suite-style dormitories. (To do this, you will need two groups of subjects, one living in corridor dormitories, the other living in suite dormitories.)

b. Test whether different personality types have different thresholds of crowding by first administering personality tests and then relating the test results to the number of figures the subjects place in the box.

2. By comparing other people's reactions in high- and low-density natural settings, you can get a feeling for how high density affects you. Select a "real-world" setting that varies over time in the number of people who are present. For example, a bus or train that becomes more crowded as it approaches the end of the line would be ideal. Your school cafeteria or library, which varies in terms of density over time, would also work. Then, pick a number of dimensions (e.g., friendliness of people toward one another, eye contact, defensive postures, object play) to observe for behavioral changes as population density increases. Compare how people respond on these dimensions in high- and low-density situations. By employing this procedure in a variety of settings, you can gain firsthand experience about how people react to high density.

3. We cited some evidence showing that people who like each other respond more favorably to high density than people who dislike each other. One reaction to high-density confinement with a disliked other should be a variety of coping strategies. Check whether high density with a disliked other leads to coping by making an informal study of residents on your dormitory floor. First, list five residents who like their roommates, and five who do not. Look into the rooms of both groups, and note the arrangement of furniture. If confinement with a disliked other leads to coping, furniture should

be arranged so as to block interaction and ensure privacy.

4. Make several comparisons concerning environmentally destructive behavior between high-rise and low-rise (i.e., high- and low-density) dormitories on your campus. Compare graffiti, damage to furniture and public telephones, and so on to assess whether aggressive behavior accompanies higher levels of density.

The City

INTRODUCTION

EFFECTS OF URBAN LIFE ON THE CITY DWELLER: CONCEPTUAL EFFORTS

Overload Notions

Adaptation Level

Environmental Stress

Behavior Constraint

The City as a Behavior Setting

Integrating the Various Formulations

EFFECTS OF URBAN LIFE ON THE CITY DWELLER: RESEARCH EVIDENCE

Stress

Affiliative Behavior

Prosocial Behavior

The Familiar Stranger

Crime

Environmental and Individual Difference Factors and Fear of Crime

Health

Homelessness

Summary

ENVIRONMENTAL SOLUTIONS TO URBAN PROBLEMS

A Little Piece of Nature: Parks and Urban Gardens

Designing Urban Playgrounds

Revitalizing Entire Urban Districts: Urban Renewal

Revitalizing Residential Areas

Defensible Space

Social Factors

Public Housing: Some Bad Examples

Low-Income Housing: More Favorable Alternatives

Gentrification

Revitalizing Commercial and Business Districts

Festival Marketplaces

Design Review

ESCAPING TO THE SUBURBS

CHAPTER SUMMARY

Suggested Projects

KEY TERMS

adaptive reuse
affiliative behavior
block organizations
City Beautiful Movement
defensible space
deindividuation
design review
diffusion of responsibility
edge cities
English Romantic style
environmental stress

familiar stranger
festival marketplaces
gentrification
homelessness
loose parts
placemaking
prosocial behavior
Pruitt-Igoe
urban homesteading
urban renewal
urban villages

INTRODUCTION

Cheryl anxiously rubbed her hands on her jeans as the big jet descended in its final approach to Boston's Logan Airport. It was not that the flight was responsible for her moist palms; the succession of miniature farms, villages, and waterways out the window had been far more entertaining than the slick magazine in the plane's seat pocket. What she feared was not the trip, but the destination—Boston. Of course Cheryl knew (and kept telling herself) that Boston was not a really big city compared to the packed towers of New York or the concrete sprawl of Los Angeles. And she would not be alone. Her cousin Jon would meet her near his office, just a short subway ride from the airport. But Boston was certainly too big for Cheryl. It was far too big for a person who had grown up in the pine ridges of northwestern Nebraska. "Cities should never grow larger than Scottsbluff, Nebraska, or Casper, Wyoming," she thought. "Certainly no larger than Rapid City, South Dakota. Why would anyone want to live with filth, crime, gangs, and noise? And how will I ever be able to handle traveling alone on the subway?"

A week later Cheryl was again at Logan, preparing to leave her favorite city. Boston had become a rich blend of new memories. Some

were centered on the suburbs—the home shared by her cousin and his family, trips to the town beach, and sight-seeing excursions to the historic towns of Lexington and Concord. Memories of the city itself were just as important, and just as fond. Her introduction had begun with a long walk down Commonwealth Avenue, the shady parkway between old brownstone apartments. She and Jon sat next to a statue and watched the city squirrels race among the trees. They strolled on through the Public Garden (and rode on one of the swan boats) and across the expanse of Boston Common. History was everywhere they walked. It colored the facades of the homes on stately Beacon Hill, added texture to the old headstones in a little graveyard tucked into the financial district, and creaked in the rigging of Old Ironsides down by the waterfront. She could almost feel the presence of John Hancock and Paul Revere. One morning was spent along the Charles River. They visited the science museum that perches across the water, then walked the banks of the Charles to a little playground. They walked on through the bustle of city traffic to the Faneuil Hall Marketplace. There they found food and music, and shops galore. Everything was so alive!

As the plane banked and began its climb

over the Charles, Cheryl strained to make out the waterfront aquarium, the Federal Center, and old Trinity Church sitting beneath a glassy city tower. She was already planning her return.

No environment more clearly shows the hand of humanity than cities. When some groups of humans gave up their nomadic life to settle permanently in groups, they began the trend toward concentration of people and services that eventually resulted in large cities in Mesopotamia, China, Egypt, and Europe. In the New World, Aztec, Inca, and Mayan cities were eventually replaced by huge urban centers like Mexico City and New York. In contrast with nature-dominated landscapes, cities are our creations—perhaps our delights, and perhaps our nightmares. Nowhere is there such diversity, novelty, intensity, and choice as in cities. They provide an immense variety of cultural and recreational facilities, such as concert halls, museums, sports stadiums, educational facilities, and all types of restaurants. Further, there is a much wider variety of services available to the average city dweller than to the resident of a small town. On the other hand, cities are, quite clearly, dangerous. They seem to attract crime, avarice, and noise. As Altman and Chemers (1980) observed, historical attitudes have changed, but at almost any given time it is possible to document both negative and positive attitudes toward urban life.

The city as a place is characterized by multiple and contrasting realities. Within the city both ends of almost any continuum (e.g., excitement and boredom; safety and danger) can and do exist simultaneously. Cities can pull people apart or bring them together; yield opportunities for us and in other ways constrain our behavior. There are good and bad, rich and poor, isolation and integration within the city's limits. Urban life is good for some people and bad for others, optimal for some activities but not for others (Krupat, 1985). And, of course, cities are not just one place, but a series of interconnecting, sometimes hierarchical districts (Bonnes et al., 1990).

However you choose to view cities, they are an environmental feature that you will probably have to contend with throughout your life. Cities and their suburban outgrowths are where most North Americans live. Today, nearly 80 percent of the population of the United States lives in small or large metropolitan areas (U.S. Bureau of the Census, 1990), compared with 6 percent in 1800 (Gottman, 1966). There were only seven metropolitan areas in the world in 1800 with a population of over 500,000, but 42 in 1900, and there are almost 500 today (*World Development Report,* 1987). A key feature of the next twenty-five years will be "mega cities" such as Mexico City, with populations in the dozens of millions (Figure 10–1). Simply saying that metropolitan areas are growing obscures important differences between the older central cities and their surrounding suburbs. As we shall see, the dramatic growth experienced by Canadian and United States metropolitan areas has occurred in the suburbs, not in the city cores (e.g., Garreau, 1991; Southworth & Owens, 1993). Growth and other changes present different opportunities and different challenges to the suburbs and their parent cities.

In this chapter we will discuss cities in some detail. It will become evident that cities are complex, large-scale environments that combine many of the environmental features already discussed in this book. As you read this chapter, keep in mind that there are important differences between cities in their desirability and livability which probably affect the consequences of residing in them. Too many studies on the effect of urban life have been done in New York City, which many would argue is hardly a representative city, and other cities may have received less attention than they deserve.

Our chapter will begin with a consideration of some conceptual perspectives that have been proposed for understanding and predicting the effects of urban life. We will then move on to a discussion of some of the consequences of city life. Finally, we will highlight various solutions that have been proposed to ameliorate some of

Figure 10–1 City living will probably be an inevitable fact of life for most of the world's population in the next century.

the city's problems. As we will see, some of these "solutions" create problems of their own. Nevertheless, as North America and the world become more and more urbanized, the need to "humanize" the city is a challenge we can hardly avoid.

EFFECTS OF URBAN LIFE ON THE CITY DWELLER: CONCEPTUAL EFFORTS

Before we attempt to broadly describe several of the major theoretical views of city life, we should reiterate a point that appears elsewhere in this text (see Chapter 6 and Chapter 11). As attractive as it is to perceive that we can exert control over our environments, it is usually an oversimplification to speak of any environment as *determining* behavior. For instance, although cities do have disproportionate rates of crime, many of their residents live fulfilled lives without being driven to vandalism, isolation, or despair. Instead of operating on people directly, as implied by deterministic theories, cities may actually be experienced as **urban villages** (Gans, 1962)—relatively homogenous, small social structures of neighborhoods or businesses. In other words, the day-to-day life of the average city dweller may not require him or her to deal with the monolithic city itself, but rather, a small part of it centered around his or her home or workplace. Perhaps one primary effect of the city is to provide the "critical mass" to allow various ethnic and social groups to establish enclaves. Thus, the size of the city is not irrelevant, but many of its effects may be indirect and may result in the positive richness of urban ethnic neighborhoods as well as crime and other negative effects (see Altman & Chemers, 1980; Fischer, 1976).

With this caution in mind, what types of

conceptual efforts are concerned with understanding and predicting some of the effects of urban life? Applying our eclectic model to cities, as depicted in Figure 10–2, should give you some ideas. As you read the descriptions of the various theoretical perspectives below, try to make predictions from them concerning how and when urban life can be expected to affect those who live in cities. Also think about the suggestions offered by each theory for preventing the negative aspects of city life and preserving the positive ones.

OVERLOAD NOTIONS

One of the most deterministic formulations is a form of overload theory (see Chapter 4). How do overload notions (cf. Milgram, 1970) apply to understanding and predicting urban behavior? Overload theorists hypothesize that an urban existence involves being exposed to a profusion of stimulation, including too much exposure to the actions and demands of others, confrontation with endless choices, and exposure to excessive visual and auditory stimulation. This plethora of stimuli is frequently more than we can deal with and requires us to employ coping strategies in order to lower stimulation to a more reasonable level. Coping strategies for dealing with urban life are many and varied and include setting priorities on inputs so that only important stimuli are attended to (which may result in ignoring those in need of certain types of help), erecting interpersonal barriers (e.g., behaving in an unfriendly fashion), establishing specialized institutions (e.g., welfare agencies) to absorb inputs, and shifting burdens to others (e.g., requiring exact change on buses). Even successful coping may be costly, leading to such aftereffects as exhaustion, fatigue, or disease. When successful coping does not occur, the individual will be subject to continued overload and is extremely likely to suffer serious physical or emotional damage.

ADAPTATION LEVEL

Contrasting with overload theory, which suggests that the high level of stimulation characteristic of the city will have negative effects, the adaptation level approach (cf. Geller, 1980) implies that this is not necessarily the case. Drawing on the concepts of optimal level of stimulation and adaptation level, which we have discussed in Chapter 4, Geller argues that stimuli (such as the urban setting) which are intense, complex, and/or novel may lead to *either* positive or negative effects. The effects will vary across persons (e.g., depending on their past experiences). For certain people the city may offer an optimal level of stimulation: It could also be argued that the city offers so much diversity (e.g., quiet parks, busy streets) that somewhere within its environs it could harbor an optimal level of stimulation for everyone. The effects of urban life will also vary over time. Those not used to the city often find it to be too noisy, too crowded, or too uncomfortable in general, but after they adapt, more complex stimuli are tolerated and may even be preferred. Also, we may find the city to be a perfect setting for some activities, but awful for others.

ENVIRONMENTAL STRESS

A number of researchers (cf. Glass & Singer, 1972) have applied the **environmental stress** approach to understanding and predicting reactions to urban life. In general, this approach views the presence of *particular* negative stimuli (e.g., noise, crowding) as critical for the negative effects of city life, as opposed to the overload assumption that too much stimulation per se is the critical element. The negative elements of city life may be experienced as threatening and may elicit stress reactions, which have emotional, behavioral, and physiological components. Stress reactions lead to a variety of coping strategies, which may be either constructive (e.g., using

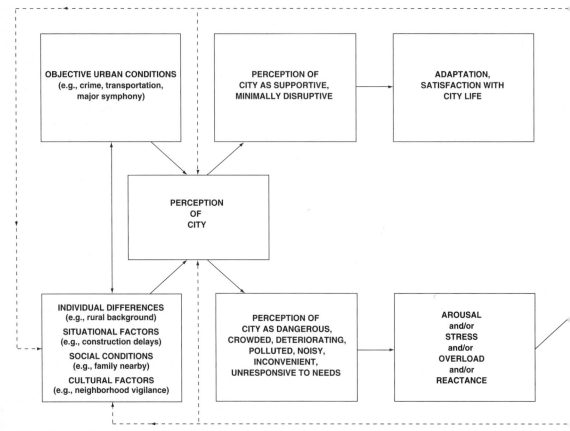

Figure 10–2   Our eclectic model applied to urban environments

reasonable means to control the stressor) or destructive (e.g., aggression). If coping is successful in eliminating threat, adaptation occurs, and long-term consequences of the stressor are often prevented. If coping is unsuccessful, long-term costs are likely to result.

BEHAVIOR CONSTRAINT

Besides overload and environmental stress notions, the behavior constraint formulation can be applied to the analysis of urban behavior. This formulation assumes that city dwellers experience constraints on their behavior (such as those caused by fear of crime, or getting "stuck" in traffic jams) that are not generally shared by people who live

in rural areas. Such constraints often determine whether or not they can achieve their goals in a setting (Stokols, 1978).

What kinds of consequences result from the feeling that one's behavior is constrained? Initially, behavior constraint notions predict that individuals experiencing this situation will evidence a negative feeling state and will make strong attempts to reassert their freedom. However, predictions of the consequences of long-term adaptation may be more pessimistic. If our efforts at reasserting control are repeatedly unsuccessful, or if we are overwhelmed by too many uncontrollable events, we may be less likely to attempt control of urban settings even when it is actually possible to control them. In effect, we

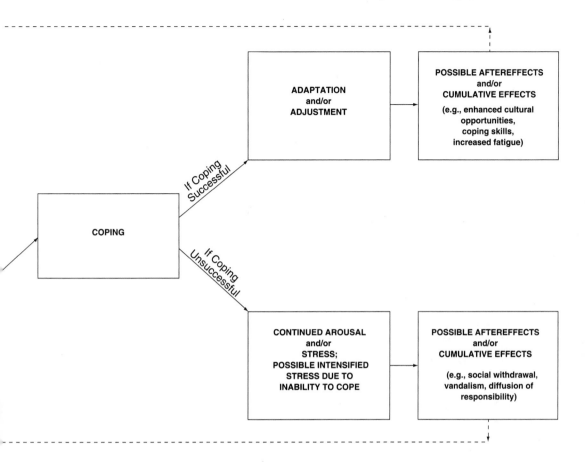

may experience learned helplessness. While city life does impose many constraints on behavior, it should be noted that in some ways it is less constraining than small town life. For example, urbanites probably have more control over the information others obtain about their activities than those living in small towns, and are less frequently constrained by unavailable resources.

THE CITY AS A BEHAVIOR SETTING

A final approach to understanding urban behavior seems to be gaining importance in environmental psychology. You may recall from Chapter 4 that Roger Barker emphasized the importance of behavior settings, a point of interaction between individuals, their physical setting, and standing patterns of behavior. Two different dimensions of Barker's theory have made it increasingly important in modern urban studies. First, the behavior setting approach takes a very molar or broad view of the interaction of humans and environments. Increasingly, researchers treat the city as a *place* or series of places (see Chapters 2 and 12). Places represent the nexus of setting and experience—a complex amalgam of memories, feelings, and more direct effects. This multi-variable, broad approach to understanding transactions between humans and their surroundings was anticipated and at least partly inspired by Barker's behavior setting analysis.

More directly, Barker's approach gave birth to staffing theory (Wicker, McGrath, & Armstrong, 1972). As you recall from Chapter 4, overstaffing occurs when the number of participants exceeds the capacity of the system. How does this concept apply to understanding behavior in urban settings? A brief look at any city is sufficient to convince us that we are looking at an overstaffed environment. In terms of overstaffing theory, city dwellers should respond to such conditions by experiencing feelings of competition and marginality, by establishing priorities for interaction, and by attempting to exclude others from their lives. If overstaffing is habitual, these behaviors may come to characterize everyday existence. However, it should be kept in mind that cities offer more diverse behavior settings and more behavior settings overall to choose from, and this could have positive effects.

INTEGRATING THE VARIOUS FORMULATIONS

Each of the views we have presented posits a different element of urban life as the critical factor in potential negative effects. Moreover, each suggests somewhat different reactions to urban life. How can we resolve the discrepancies in the various conceptual perspectives? Although the approaches are presented as competing with one another, it is probably the case that too much stimulation, too much stress, too many behavioral constraints, and overstaffing probably each account for some of the negative effects that may result from an urban existence. On the other hand, many of these same theoretical approaches account for the *desirable* stimulation and rich opportunities afforded by city life. Eventually, a "compromise" model may emerge, which subsumes the valid predictions of each approach by using a more parsimonious construct. The ways in which people are assumed to cope differ for the various models we have discussed. Nevertheless, when coping is successful in handling stress, adaptation or adjustment occurs, and the individual is less likely to experience aftereffects or cumulative effects. If coping is unsuccessful, the stress continues, and the individual is likely to experience aftereffects and cumulative effects (e.g., illness).

In the final section we will attend to research and designs aimed at capitalizing on the good aspects of urban life while minimizing its negative effects. First, however, we will examine a larger psychological literature which has aimed at documenting the negative effects of cities on residents and visitors.

EFFECTS OF URBAN LIFE ON THE CITY DWELLER: RESEARCH EVIDENCE

Research on the effects of urban life has relied on two methodological approaches. The *single variable approach* attempts to synthesize a picture of urban life from studies of how various individual stressors present in the city (e.g., noise, pollution) affect urbanites' behavior. These studies have often been done in "real-world" settings, where the stressor under study varies naturally, rather than at the will of an experimenter. For instance, to explore the effect of urban noise on psychiatric disorders, one might compare the mental health of the residents on two streets that differ only in their closeness to a noisy factory. This strategy may allow us to approximate a cause-and-effect relationship between a potential urban stressor and behavior, although the nonrandom assignment of subjects to conditions may lead to problems in causal inference.

While the single variable approach may allow us to synthesize a picture of urban life as the sum of the separate effects of various stressors, it does not allow us to understand the city as a place—the result of a multitude of individual elements. The city represents the simultaneous presence of a great many stressors, and the effects of cities on human behavior are determined in a very complex manner. A realistic view of the consequences of urban stressors may come from considering how they affect us collectively. Research using this approach generally compares cities (which obviously contain a full range of urban stressors) with nonurban areas on various dependent variable dimensions. One might attempt to assess how urban and rural life affect willingness to help others by comparing prosocial behavior in urban and rural settings. Such studies give us a feeling for how urban and rural conditions affect aspects of human behavior, but sacrifice the ability to identify a specific cause. Since cities and nonurban areas vary in many ways besides the presence or absence of environmental stressors, we must be aware that differences between urban and rural behaviors could be caused by different populations, social conditions, physical conditions, or a combination of these (cf. Korte, 1980). It should be noted, however, that urban versus rural comparisons are still one of our best opportunities to determine how city life affects behavior.

STRESS

Clearly, urban areas differ from each other and some are much better places to live than others. Nevertheless, comparisons of urban and rural areas generally suggest that cities contain more stressful environmental features. A number of stimuli identified as potential stressors are more prevalent in cities than in small towns. For example, noise levels have been found to increase with the size of a community (Dillman & Tremblay, 1977).

One study showed that the quietest times in inner city apartments were noisier than the noisiest moments in small town living areas (EPA, 1972). Pollution is common in cities. In fact, one breath of New York City air contains 70,000 dust and dirt particles, and just living in that city is equivalent to smoking 38 cigarettes a day (Rotton, 1978). In addition, both crowding and crime are much more frequent in urban than in rural areas (Fischer, 1976).

The pace of life seems faster in the city. "Pace" in this case, may include actual physical movement. For example, Table 10–1 shows that residents' walking speed varies as a function of the size of the local city population (Bornstein, 1979). The effect of population size is not always strong, however. In fact, there is greater variation in speed at different locations within the same city than between two cities (Sadalla et al., 1990), and speed may be influenced by sex, time of day, or even weather (Walmsley & Lewis, 1989). Sadalla et al. (1990) argue that more subjective, psychological measures of tempo are more representative of the perceived differences between cities than actual physical speed. That is, certain cities seem "fast paced" because of a complex mix of psychological factors, only some of which actually involve physical movement.

It is sad to note that the urbanites most intensely exposed to urban stressors are those

Table 10–1   Walking Speed in Cities of Various Sizes*

Country	Town/city	Population	Observed velocity (m/sec)
Ireland	Galway	29,375	1.25
	Limerick	57,161	1.27
	Dublin	679,748	1.56
Scotland	Inverness	53,179	1.43
	Edinburgh	470,085	1.51
United States	Seattle	503,000	1.46

*After M. H. Bornstein (1979). *The pace of life: revisited.* International Journal of Psychology, 14, *84.*

with other problems as well. People who are poor, poorly educated, and generally discriminated against by society live in those areas of the city with the greatest pollution (McCaull, 1977). The poor are probably exposed to more urban crowding, noise, and crime as well. Given the fact that these people are already vulnerable to stress, adding the environmental stressors characteristic of urban life can be especially problematic.

With all of the evidence indicating that living in the city is probably experienced as more stressful, do urban and rural dwellers really perceive different levels of stress? Although only a few studies directly compare urbanites and rural people, a study of individuals who had recently migrated to the city or to a rural area suggested that this may be the case (Franck, Unseld, & Wentworth, 1974). Investigators interviewed a sample of students who were newcomers to either a small town or a large city. It was observed that the urban newcomers reported experiencing significantly more tension when living in the city than in their previous residence; the reverse was observed for rural newcomers. When sources of stress were broken down into those associated with the physical environment and those associated with the social environment, some additional differences emerged. For physical stressors (e.g., pollution, noise, crowding), urbanites reported being affected far more adversely than rural dwellers. For social stressors, results depended on the particular stressor. Public social stressors (e.g., slums, aversive individuals one must deal with) were experienced more strongly by urban newcomers. However, some rural newcomers complained about the lack of cultural diversity in their environment. Personal social stressors (stressful personal relationships) did not differ significantly for the two groups. These findings are suggestive and should be interpreted with caution, as should all studies involving urban and rural comparisons.

Perhaps the most complete study of com-

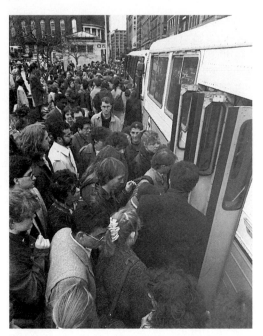

Figure 10–3 Commuting can be a source of urban stress.

muting as a source of stress (Figure 10–3) was done by faculty and students in the Social Ecology Program at the University of California-Irvine (Novaco et al., 1979; Stokols & Novaco, 1981). The research was a longitudinal field experiment, using urban commuters traveling varying distances to work. Subjects were tested twice in their work settings—18 months apart—to determine the effects of commuting stress. The data mostly corroborate earlier studies, but give a more complete picture of things. It was found that conditions that interfere with a commuter's movement (e.g., congestion) elicit stress reactions such as physiological arousal, negative mood, and performance deficits, and that the intensity of these responses depends on personality characteristics of the commuter. Also, when people view commuting in a negative light they attempt to change the situation (e.g., move closer to work, try other routes). Importantly, such coping often makes them feel better at the psychological level.

A study by Wohlwill and Kohn (1973) suggested that perception of stressors in urban and rural areas depends on one's adaptation level (measured by the size of the town one resided in previously). In their study, people from small, middle-size, and large communities who had migrated to Harrisburg, Pennsylvania, were asked to make judgments concerning extent of crowding, frequency of crime, and feelings of safety. Although the results were not totally consistent, it was found that individuals coming from relatively large communities assessed Harrisburg as safer, less crime-ridden, and less crowded than those coming from smaller communities. It is important to note that in addition to adaptation level, many other types of individual differences may affect the perception of stressors in cities. For example, variables such as one's length of residence, one's need for stimulation, and one's socioeconomic status might influence the way urban stressors are experienced. Unfortunately, little research has been done in this area, and what exists has been inconclusive. Further, although future research is clearly needed before we can draw such a conclusion, in addition to affecting people's experience of environmental stressors, individual difference variables will probably also be found to affect other responses to urban settings.

AFFILIATIVE BEHAVIOR

On a number of dimensions, city life seems to be associated with a decreased desire for **affiliative behavior**. This ties in well with several of the conceptual notions we have discussed as well as with conceptual formulations discussed elsewhere (e.g., Wirth, 1938), but can also be explained in terms of reinforcements derived from past experience with city life (e.g., more experiences with crime). In one study suggesting a lower degree of affiliation, Newman and McCauley (1977) found that subjects' eye contact with strangers who looked them in the eye was relatively rare in center city Philadelphia, more common in a Philadelphia suburb, and very common in a rural Pennsylvania town (Table 10–2). In a study extending these findings, McCauley, Coleman, and DeFusco (1977) showed that commuters were less willing to meet a stranger's eye when they arrived at a downtown terminal than when they were in a suburban train station. How did urbanites and ruralites respond facially to attempts by strangers to take candid photos of them? When the pictures were given to college students to rate, it was found that urbanites in the photos appeared to be less friendly, less easygoing, and more tense than ruralites (Krupat, 1982). Finally, Milgram (1977) reported that when undergraduate students approached strangers on the street and extended their hands in a friendly manner (as if to initiate a handshake), only 38.5 percent of city dwellers reciprocated, compared with 66 percent of small town dwellers.

While this pattern of effects suggests that city dwellers are apt to avoid contact with strangers, it is important to assess

Table 10–2   Percentage of Passersby Making Eye Contact With Male and Female Experimenters at Post Office and Store in Parkesburg, Bryn Mawr, and Philadelphia*

Sex of Experimenter	Parkesburg		Bryn Mawr		Philadelphia	
	Post Office	Store	Post Office	Store	Post Office	Store
Female	80	82	45	50	15	18
Male	75	73	40	45	12	10

*Reprinted from Joseph Newman and Clark McCauley. (1977, December). Eye contact with strangers in city, suburb, and small town. Environment and Behavior, 9, No. 4, 547–558.

whether this behavior extends to friends and acquaintances. In an experiment designed to test this hypothesis, McCauley and Taylor (1976) asked small-town and large-city residents about yesterday's telephone conversations with friends and acquaintances. Phone conversations in the city were just as likely to be with close friends and as intimate in subject matter as conversations in small towns. This pattern is corroborated by additional research (see Korte, 1980). Many other studies (e.g., Glenn & Hill, 1977; Key, 1968) show no urban–rural differences in contact with relatives.

PROSOCIAL BEHAVIOR

Overload notions suggest that the overstimulation of urban life leads us to filter out less important inputs—a needy stranger for instance. Does the urbanite's lack of desire to affiliate with strangers extend to a disregard for strangers who are in need? When a child claiming to be lost asked for aid in New York City and in several small towns, he or she was more likely to be the recipient of **prosocial** (helping) **behavior** in the smaller towns (Milgram, 1977). In a similar vein, Milgram found that willingness to allow a needy individual into one's house to use the telephone was higher in a small town than in a large city. Also, in Milgram's study 75 percent of all city respondents answered the person in need by shouting through a closed door, while 75 percent of all rural respondents opened the door, reinforcing our earlier conclusion about urbanite avoidance of affiliation with strangers. Additional studies (Gelfand et al., 1973; Korte & Kerr, 1975; Milgram, 1970) have also found that urbanites are less helpful than rural dwellers, and a meta-analysis (i.e., a statistical summary of all past research on the subject) by Steblay (1987) strongly supports the nonurban–urban difference in helping, though decreases in helping were found to begin at a higher threshold (i.e.,

communities with a population of 300,000 or more) than previously thought (cf. Amato, 1983). According to Levine et al. (1994), population *density* (the number of people in a restricted area) is more likely to be related to unhelpful behavior than population size (the total population of a city). In an ambitious study of 36 cities in different regions of the United States, Levine and his colleagues compared the correlation between population size and density and a group of six helping behaviors. Overall, population density was the strongest and most consistent predictor of helping, particularly in situations that required a fast, more spontaneous response.

Among a number of possible explanations for the lower helpfulness of urbanites, we first should examine overload theory. As that model would predict, the high levels of stimulation characteristic of the city make passersby less attentive to novel stimuli, such as someone needing help (Korte, 1980). Second, Fischer (1976) suggested that the diversity of appearance and behavior characteristic of others in urban areas may make people feel insecure and thus less likely to help, and third, Wirth (1938) has proposed that being brought up in an urban as opposed to a rural area elicits an "urban personality," which is simply not characterized by prosocial behavior. Overstaffing theory (detailed earlier) could offer a fourth explanation, and diffusion of responsibility notions (cf. Latané & Darley, 1970), a fifth. Work on diffusion of responsibility suggests that when there are many people around who could help (as would occur more in cities than in small towns), perceived responsibility to help lessens, which affects the likelihood of giving aid. Interestingly, meta-analytic work by Steblay (1987) suggests that it is the urban context rather than personality factors which is responsible for lower levels of urban helping. This discounts Wirth's "urban personality" theory, while lending a measure of support to several of the others.

Although much research suggests that there may often be less prosocial behavior in cities, other studies imply some important moderators of this pattern (Forbes & Gromoll, 1971; Korte, Ypma, & Toppen, 1975; Weiner, 1976). Korte and his colleagues suggested that urban and rural settings may lead to differences in helping only insofar as environmental input level (i.e., amount of incoming stimuli) is higher in cities. Their findings led them to conclude that input level may be the critical determinant of helping, rather than the urban-rural distinction per se. Similarly, others (e.g., Kammann, Thompson, & Irwin, 1979) suggest that pedestrian density in the area where help is to be given, rather than city size, is the major factor in whether or not aid will occur. And House and Wolf (1978) report intriguing evidence of lower urban helping only where crime rates make involvement inadvisable, suggesting that this may account for lack of prosocial action. Finally, Steblay (1987) reported that urban–nonurban differences were great only when the individual requesting help was male, and when the request for help was either very trivial or very serious.

Some studies have even found more helping in urban than in nonurban contexts. Weiner (1976) and Forbes and Gromoll (1971) found greater helping by individuals raised in cities than by those raised in small towns. Interpreting her findings, Weiner posited that different patterns of social-perceptual learning in the city and the country may cause urbanites to be more socially effective in certain circumstances. In effect, she suggests that the experience of growing up in the city allows one to learn skills that may be particularly adaptive in certain dependency situations. Also, it seems that deviants were more apt to receive aid in cities than in small towns (Hansson & Slade, 1977) and that the pattern of less helping in cities extends only to strangers and not friends (Korte, 1980). Given the above qualifications,

it is safe to conclude that additional variables may be operating.

THE FAMILIAR STRANGER

One thing our discussion has suggested is that urbanites are less likely to acknowledge strangers (e.g., by shaking hands and making eye contact) than rural dwellers. Some extremely interesting research by Milgram (1977) indicates that while city dwellers fail to display such amenities in everyday situations, they may show their feelings in other ways. Milgram and his students found that many city residents have a number of people in their lives who may be called familiar strangers. What is a **familiar stranger?** It is someone they observe repeatedly for a long period of time but never interact with, probably because of overload. Milgram found that commuters to New York City had an average of four individuals whom they recognized but never spoke to at their train station, and that 89.5 percent of the commuters had at least one "familiar stranger." How did the researchers find this out? They took pictures of groups waiting for a train at the station and had subjects tell them how many of those present met the definition of a "familiar stranger."

What is the difference in urbanites' behavior toward "familiar strangers" and other strangers? First, many passengers told the researchers they often think about their familiar strangers and try to figure out what kinds of lives they lead. According to evidence, urbanites are more likely to help a familiar stranger in need than an ordinary stranger. Finally, Milgram found that under some circumstances, familiar strangers do interact with each other, although it is rarely in the place where they usually meet. He suggests that the farther they are away from the scene of their routine encounter (a foreign country, for instance), the more likely they are to interact.

CRIME

Studies of victimization suggest that even what could be thought of as trivial crimes may have long-lasting consequences for victims' well-being (Greenberg & Ruback, 1984), and there is ample evidence that crime is more prevalent in urban than rural areas (Fischer, 1984). The rate of violent crimes per person is almost eight times greater in the largest cities than in extremely rural areas, and the rate of murders is three times as high (Fischer, 1984). When asked to list the top 10 problems facing their neighborhoods, residents of cities listed crime as the number one problem (Gallup Opinion Poll, April 4, 1981). An amusing anecdote related by Zimbardo (1969) suggests the intensity of crime in and around many cities. While repairing a flat tire alongside a highway in Queens, New York, a motorist was startled when he observed that his car hood was being raised, and a stranger was removing his battery. "Take it easy, buddy," said the thief to his assumed car-stripping colleague, "you can have the tires—all I want is the battery!"

Why is there more crime in cities than in small towns? Although these findings can be interpreted in terms of overload, stress, behavior constraint, or overstaffing notions, several other explanations have been offered. One is the theory of **deindividuation**. It was used by Zimbardo (1969) to explain why an "abandoned" car he left in New York City was stripped of all movable parts within 24 hours, while a similar car left in Palo Alto, California, was untouched. According to this theory, when we feel we are an anonymous member of a crowd (i.e., deindividuated), our inhibitions against antisocial behavior are released. This is partly because we feel it is very unlikely that we will be identified and punished. Under such conditions, criminal behavior is clearly less costly and is more likely to be engaged in. Other explanations for the higher levels of crime in urban areas include a lack of employment opportunities, the greater number of antisocial role models available, and the fact that there may be fewer prosocial models available than in nonurban areas. Another explanation is that there are simply more possible victims, more goods to steal, and more outlets for stolen goods in cities than elsewhere. Individuals who want to pursue crime may even migrate to the city.

Not surprisingly, feelings of being unsafe and concern about being a potential crime victim are greater for city residents (Fischer, 1984). Not only are crime rates higher in cities, but "urban incivilities" (e.g., physical deterioration) may make people feel more vulnerable. Feelings of vulnerability to crime can have several types of consequences. First, individuals residing in cities with populations over 50,000 trust others less than those living in areas with lower populations (NORC, 1987). Second, urbanites have greater fear of crime, which may lead to stress.

What are the effects of crime stress? Overall, there is little empirical evidence about its effects and the data are contradictory. Roberts (1977) found that crime stress was associated with emotional reactions of worry, fear of injury, fear of material loss, and feelings of loss of control. It would seem reasonable to assume that continued stress associated with crime (which is likely since the objective threat of crime does not dissipate) could have extremely negative effects (e.g., it may be associated with nervous disorders and learned helplessness). Also, fear about victimization through crime and associated stress could lead to a reduction in people's activities. In fact, compared to suburbanites, city dwellers report that they restrict their activities much more of the time due to fear of crime (Lavrakas, 1982). Far worse, fear of crime and crime stress has led a few, especially the elderly, to refrain entirely from leaving home (Ginsberg, 1975). Nevertheless, a number of studies have found few effects of fear of neighborhood crime on mental health and well-being (Kasl, 1976; Kasl & Harburg, 1972; Lawton, Nahemow, & Yeh, 1980). For example, one such study showed only scattered effects of crime on the well-being of adults and no effects on children (White et al., 1987).

Environmental and Individual Difference Factors and Fear of Crime

Imagine being afraid to go outside of your apartment to buy food or cash a check, or opening the door in terror when someone knocks, hoping he or she is not a criminal. Fear of crime and associated stress are major problems in urban areas. Interestingly, it has been found that fear of crime is increasing faster than actual crime rates (Taylor & Hale, 1986). In fact, in some cases, fear of crime in a subpopulation is not related to the true likelihood of being victimized (Maxfield, 1984).

Several rather complete conceptualizations have been offered of the various factors which affect fear of crime (for a review, see Taylor & Hale, 1986). However, our interest here is primarily to explore how fear is influenced by environmental factors. In the chapter on personal space and territoriality we discussed how territorial markers can moderate fear of victimization; here we will mention some other environmental determinants of crime stress.

Various aspects of the urban environment may impact on fear of crime, which varies from neighborhood to neighborhood (Maxfield, 1984). Teenage loitering, which can be facilitated or inhibited by environmental features, can elicit crime stress (Lavrakas, 1982; Lewis & Maxfield, 1980). It has also been suggested that physical decay of the environment and signs of urban "incivilities" (e.g., reports of crime; vandalism, graffiti, litter) can imply to people that the social order has broken down, and elicit fear of victimization (Lewis & Maxfield, 1980; White et al., 1987). This is especially likely when residents attribute the cause of the incivili-

ties to factors residing "within the neighborhood" (Taylor & Hale, 1986). Importantly, studies have shown that perceptions of incivilities are more strongly related to fear than the objective number of incivilities (Taylor & Hale, 1986). Finally, perceived loss of territorial control appears to be associated with fear of crime (Taylor & Hale, 1986).

While there is no evidence that street lighting affects actual levels of crime, it does decrease fear of crime (Tien et al., 1979). In addition, propinquity (discussed in detail in Chapter 12) affects how afraid people are of being victimized. The closer we live to a known crime victim, the more we fear that we could suffer the same fate (cf. Lavrakas, 1982). Finally, social interaction between neighbors may increase fear of crime to the extent that it increases knowledge of crime victims (Newman & Franck, 1981a).

In urban areas certain types of people seem to fear crime more than others. Those who are most concerned are those with lower incomes, females, blacks, the aged, and residents of the inner city (Clemente & Kleiman, 1977; Gordon et al., 1980). There are many possible reasons for this, ranging from greater victimization of some groups to a poorer ability of others (e.g., the aged, women) to defend themselves. Interestingly, in areas with the highest crime, age is not related to fear of crime. Where crime is a regular feature of daily life, the physical vulnerability associated with age may be a less important determinant of fear than other factors (Maxfield, 1984).

People with high fear of crime feel they must restrict their activities greatly to avoid being victimized (Lavrakas, 1982). Environmental designs which help promote social cohesion among residents (e.g., defensible space; Lavrakas, 1982, p. 343) may moderate fear and make people feel more comfortable "moving about." Also, having supportive neighbors who are accessible may act to quell fear of being victimized (Gubrium,

1974; Sundeen & Mathieu, 1976). For the aged, this seems to occur more often in socially homogeneous living situations (e.g., retirement communities) than in other settings.

HEALTH

We should be cautious in interpreting data relating health to urban and rural settings. Specialized medical care is generally more available in cities. Specialists, such as cardiologists and surgeons, are in especially short supply in rural areas (Dillman & Tremblay, 1977), and urban hospital facilities are superior. Individuals who are ill may migrate from the country (where they became sick) to the city (Srole, 1972). Because these factors make it difficult to interpret the findings of studies on urban–rural differences in health, the actual data are rather equivocal and depend on the particular disease.

Hay and Wantman (1969) studied the rate of hypertension and heart disease (both associated with stress) and found that hypertension rates were only slightly higher in New York City than in the nation overall. A study by Levine et al. (1988) found that in those cities where the "pace of life" was faster (which the authors termed "Type A cities"), death rates from coronary heart disease were greater. Interestingly, arthritis and rheumatism rates were found to be lower in New York City than in the country as a whole (Srole, 1972). On the other hand, tuberculosis, emphysema, bronchitis, lung cancer, and other respiratory diseases often associated with pollution occur more frequently in urban areas (Ford, 1976). Overall, it may be said that the effects of city life on health are not inherently pathological, and that the relationship between urban and rural environments and disease is complex.

Are there differences reflected in rates of mental illness? While it is clear that mental hospital admissions are higher in cities than in rural areas (Clinard, 1964; Mann, 1964), it is not certain that urbanites are actually less mentally healthy (Srole, 1972). For example, of 17 studies comparing paper-and-pencil measures of adjustment in areas of different size, three found more personality problems in larger cities, five found that such difficulties were more common in small communities, and nine found no differences (Fischer, 1976). Srole (1976) reports that inhabitants of large cities are less likely to show symptoms of imminent nervous breakdown than residents of small towns. On the other hand, Dohrenwend and Dohrenwend (1972) contend that some forms of mental illness (e.g., psychoses) are more prevalent in rural areas, while other forms (e.g., neuroses, personality disorders) predominate in urban areas.

While mental illness may not differ reliably in urban and rural areas, drug addiction is much more common in urban than in rural areas (Fischer, 1976). Obviously, this can be accounted for by the overload and stress notions we reviewed earlier. Some other explanations include: greater availability of drugs and liquor, better treatment of drug addicts and hence more reporting of these afflictions, and better record keeping in cities. Finally, and rather surprisingly, there is no consistent difference in the suicide rate between urban and rural areas (Gibbs, 1971).

HOMELESSNESS

Although **homelessness** occurs in rural areas, it is disproportionately an urban malady. Not surprisingly, most of the studies of homelessness have been done in cities, though it has been noted that the problems of the rural homeless differ somewhat from those of the urban homeless (Committee for Health Care for Homeless People, 1988). Although there have always been homeless people, their number has increased dramati-

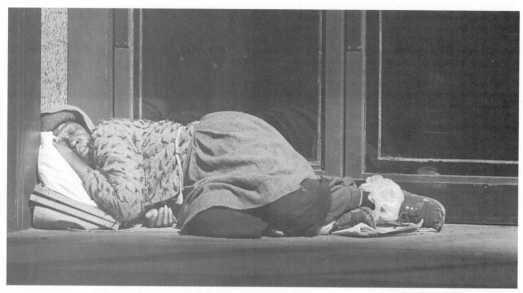

Figure 10–4 Homelessness is one of the saddest urban problems.

cally in the last few years, and their plight has become the focus of more and more public attention (Figure 10–4).

How is homelessness defined? The U.S. government defines it as occurring when a person is without a fixed, regular, and adequate nighttime residence, or when someone has a primary nighttime residence that is: (a) a shelter designed for temporary accommodations; (b) an institution that provides temporary residence for people intended to be institutionalized; or (c) a public or private place not designed for, or ordinarily used as, a regular sleeping accommodation for human beings.

Formal definitions for experiences like homelessness sometimes obscure insight. Rivlin (1990) provides a particularly dramatic description:

> Picture a day when you cannot be certain where you will sleep, how you will clean yourself, how you will find food, how you will hold on to your belongings (in settings where they can be stolen with ease), how you will be safe, how you will dress properly to go to work (for many homeless people do, indeed, work), and for some, how you will fill up the long hours of the day and do so in places that will tolerate your existence (p. 50).

Researchers emphasize that homelessness is not simply being "houseless." That is, homelessness is not just the lack of shelter, but the loss of security and social or economic support that is associated with unreliable shelter or the prospect of losing shelter as well (Bunston & Breton, 1992). As you might imagine, collecting reliable statistics about people without permanent residences is difficult, and estimates of the total homeless population and the proportion of different subgroups (e.g., women) varies (Bunston & Breton, 1992; Johnson, 1989; Rivlin, 1990). Some estimates suggest that on any given night in the United States, there are 735,000 homeless people, of whom many are children; that in a given year up to 3 million people will be homeless for one night or more; and that there are about 6 million Americans at risk of becoming homeless, primarily because of the high cost of housing relative to their income (Alliance Housing Council, 1988; Rivlin, 1990).

One adaptation to homelessness may be so-called "shelterization," characterized by low self-esteem and a dependency on the system (Grunberg & Eagle, 1990). From their study of homeless women in Toronto, Bunston and Breton (1992) concluded that the simple provision of shelter alone overlooks important needs for autonomy, programs to foster independent living, and education and job skills to break the cycle of homelessness.

The characteristics of the homeless differ dramatically from place to place, and estimates of the proportions of men, women, and children who are homeless vary. It does appear that the composition of the homeless is changing: Middle-aged men now make up a shrinking percentage of the homeless, and families with small children are the fastest growing segment of this population (U.S. Conference of Mayors, 1987) with families now accounting for about one-third of the homeless (Berck, 1992). As you can imagine, homelessness disrupts almost every facet of a family's life. Neighborhood friendships, privacy, and daily routines such as cooking or shopping are interrupted. For children, homelessness usually means changing schools, leaving teachers and friends behind. Not surprisingly, many children become restless, aggressive, or listless when they must move to a shelter (Neiman, 1988). Homeless adults are most likely never to have been married. In fact, a lack of support systems is one of the reasons for homelessness. In a study of single-parent homeless families, many women actually named their major

source of support as their children (McChesney, 1986). In the larger cities, minorities are overrepresented among the homeless. Interestingly, most homeless are long-term residents of particular cities, which negates some public officials' arguments that if they do more to help them, increased numbers of homeless will come to their city (Committee for Health Care for Homeless People, 1988).

Why are so many people homeless? Many individuals are homeless because their incomes have failed to keep up with sharply increased housing costs. Especially for those with few close family ties who have marginal incomes, the loss of even a few days' pay due to an injury, losing a job, or similar misfortune, can quickly result in homelessness. Another factor in the homelessness problem is society's failure to provide adequate community-based housing and care for people. Urban renewal and gentrification can also cause homelessness. **Gentrification** occurs when middle- and upper-income people move back to the city and occupy and improve areas formerly lived in by poor people. There are other reasons for homelessness as well. Many homeless families are "multi-problem families" (Bassuk, Rubin, & Lauriat, 1986) with fragmented social networks, and difficulty utilizing available public welfare services. In addition, certain health problems tend to cause homelessness (e.g., major mental illnesses like schizophrenia). In fact, some studies suggest that a very large percentage of the homeless have psychological or addictive disorders (Bassuk et al., 1986; Baum & Burnes, 1993), or diseases like AIDS, which may render one unable to pay rent and/or undesirable to landlords and even family due to stigma.

In addition to being a cause of homelessness, health and psychological problems can result from homelessness. Homelessness may increase the risk of developing many diseases, the likelihood of incurring trauma, and of being victimized (rape for women; violent assault for both sexes; Kelly, 1985). For those with medical problems, homelessness makes treatment extremely difficult. How can someone be on "bed rest" when they do not have a bed? How can they be on a restricted diet if they do not have food preparation facilities? The mortality rate for the homeless is three times that of the total American population, and the homeless die 20 years earlier than expected (Baum & Burnes, 1993). Homelessness is also associated with other risks (e.g., the fires used by street people to keep warm often cause burns). Mental illness was mentioned as a factor associated with becoming homeless, but it can also be a result of homelessness. The trauma of being homeless has negative psychological consequences and is associated with anxiety and depression. Homelessness can also contribute to alcoholism or drug addiction as an attempt to "medicate" the psychological pain of not having a place to live.

SUMMARY

Environmental stressors are more intensely present in urban than in rural settings. Stressors include noise, pollution, heat, crowding, "extra demand," crime, and homelessness. Studies suggest that individually and collectively these stressors have at least mildly negative effects on various dimensions of urban existence. Urban stressors are associated with less desire for affiliation with strangers, performance decrements, long-term behavioral effects, and differences in some health-related indices. These effects can be interpreted in terms of the urban stress model we have proposed. While urban problems abound, future research needs to focus more on the positive effects of city life.

Studies comparing life in urban and rural areas have focused primarily on the intensity of aversive environmental conditions (such as stress) across the two settings. We should encourage future research that allows us to make comparisons on positive as well as negative dimensions.

ENVIRONMENTAL SOLUTIONS TO URBAN PROBLEMS

Not surprisingly, many people and businesses have attempted to find true happiness by escaping from urban areas, a fact that has resulted in population declines for the urban cores of many North American cities even as the suburbs and metropolitan areas grow (e.g., Garreau, 1991; Southworth & Owens, 1993). Those who remain behind in the decaying city core are often individuals whose social or economic position makes them incapable of departing. This has left cities in deteriorating physical condition, with a dwindling tax base, and a population composed heavily of minority groups with high levels of unemployment and attendant social problems, such as crime. How can this situation be ameliorated? Many very significant social, economic, and physical changes are needed, but cities are an unwieldy aggregate of corporate and private interests only loosely controlled by overburdened governments. Perhaps the earliest and simplest approach was to add new amenities such as museums (see Chapter 13), parks, or playgrounds without attempting to change the basic structure of the city.

A LITTLE PIECE OF NATURE: PARKS AND URBAN GARDENS

One cure for what ails cities might be a little piece of the country. We saw in Chapter 2 that natural scenes have many psychological benefits, so perhaps going back to nature would help cities. Somewhat before medicine provided an explanation, citizens of Europe and North America began to suspect that outbreaks of diseases like cholera were tied to the unsanitary living conditions and close quarters of big cities. People needed to breathe, they said. In London, for example, the large open squares were believed to have positive health effects, and former royal parks across European cities were opened to the public in the new spirit of populism (Schuyler, 1986). Many American cities such as New York, however, lacked both the large squares and the history of royal parks. As their new nation became more urban, citizens of the United States began to seek out relief from urban noise, disease, and confusion. Initially many people went on outings to cemeteries, the first public or semi-public gardens in cities (Kostof, 1987). Just before

his death in 1852, the great American designer Andrew Downing was prominent in the ranks of those advocating the construction of city parks. Then, in 1857, 25-year-old Frederick Law Olmstead became the Superintendent of Construction for what was to become New York's Central Park (see Cranz, 1982; Hayward, 1989; Hiss, 1990; Kostof, 1987; and Schuyler, 1986, for reviews of urban park design in North America). With his associate Calvert Vaux (Downing's former partner), Olmstead created Central Park, North America's first great public park. Olmstead was inspired by the **English Romantic style**, a literary and artistic return to nature that was popularized by the European elite (see Chapter 2). Olmstead and Vaux sought to create an illusion of nature through careful manipulation of topography, water, and plant materials (see Figure 10–5). Parks were a form of landscape art meant to represent nature, not as it really was, but as

Figure 10–5   Illusion of nature created by Olmstead and Vaux in New York's Central Park

it ideally might be. In spite of modern intrusions and neglect, Central Park retains many of the romantic landscapes that first attracted visitors when the park opened in 1859. The ideas Olmstead and Vaux developed in Central Park were refined in Brooklyn's Prospect Park, and repeated by the Olmstead firm across North America (hundreds of Olmstead Parks remain: San Francisco's Golden Gate Park and Montreal's Mt. Royal are examples). In Boston Olmstead proposed and built an integrated necklace of interconnected parks along waterways, and his hand is also apparent in the design of a number of college campuses (see Chapter 11) across the continent.

The nineteenth-century park was a natural "pleasure ground," intended for the most part to provide quiet vistas and opportunities for reflection in the midst of expanding cities (Cranz, 1982). Open lawns in some cities supported herds of sheep, deer, or even reindeer, with the dual purpose of adding to the pastoral or picturesque landscape and keeping the lawns clipped. Parks were separated from the neighboring city with berms and barriers of vegetation, and although drives were provided for carriages and horses, pedestrian pathways were generally segregated. The park was also seen as a place where different ethnic groups could experience leisure and reflection together. Less charitably, Kostof (1987) suggests that one primary goal was to wean the working classes from their ethnic neighborhoods in order to make "good" Americans of them.

Even in the 1800s parks supported some organized group activities (ice skating became popular in Central Park, for instance), but at the turn of the century North Americans found themselves with more leisure, and a heightened desire to participate in organized activities. In many parks open pastures were replaced by ballfields and tennis courts. Some added private garden space, an approach that became even more common

with the onset of World War I. The special needs of children were also recognized, and playgrounds proliferated (Cranz, 1982). During this period of reform, parks were increasingly seen as sites for organized activities such as sports, and less as nature preserves to counter the stress of urban life.

Neglect, fences, crime, and conflict have left many parks at the end of the twentieth century with many of the problems of the surrounding city and anything but romantic reputations. Yet historic preservation efforts and the environmental movement have led to a park renaissance. Some efforts concentrate on the construction of new, specialized parks and cultural centers such as botanical gardens, zoos, and aquariums (see Chapter 13 for a discussion of some of these dual learning/leisure environments). Others seem aimed at refurbishing more traditional parks. In the latter case, it is unclear how well historic parks address the needs of modern city dwellers. Olmstead's vision may have been on the mark, but if not, to what degree should an old park evolve to meet the needs of a changing society? Part of this tension is between the need for environments to support both organized activities like sporting events and somewhat more passive pursuits. Simple contact with nature may be important; in fact, humans may have an automatic, biological thirst for it (Ulrich, 1993). On the other hand, Alexander et al. (1977) reported that people were unlikely to make regular use of parks that are more than three blocks from their homes. Despite variations in use levels, parks and playgrounds are amenities that are likely to enhance the quality of life for city residents.

Parks represent the desire of an urbanized society to maintain contact with nature. At a more personal level, private gardening may provide nature-based benefits for urban residents (Kaplan, 1984, 1985; Kaplan & Kaplan, 1987; Lewis, 1973). For example, Lewis (1973) researched the effects of providing recreational gardening environments for residents of run-down urban areas in New York City. The New York City Housing Authority sponsored recreational gardens. Groups of tenants wanting to garden could apply to the Authority, which gave them a garden site close to their project, turned over the ground for them, and also provided money for seeds or plants and a gardening manual.

Providing garden plots for residents has had many beneficial effects. Lewis (1973) reports that recreational gardening by inner-city residents led to pride in accomplishment, to increased self-esteem, and to reduced vandalism outside as well as inside the buildings. Social factors are important as well. In Kaplan's (1985) study cited above, residents who had adequate access to gardens found their neighbors to be more friendly and felt a stronger sense of community. Gardens add social cohesion in the community by providing a meeting place and a chance for people to work together toward a common end (Lewis, 1973). Gardening may also increase the proprietary sense of territoriality, and thus make nearby space more apt to be defended and defensible (see Chapter 8).

Why is recreational gardening beneficial? In addition to their natural beauty and potential as a food source, gardens may provide a restorative experience that allows people to recover from the stresses of day-to-day life (Kaplan & Kaplan, 1987). The chance to be outside, to labor, to see things grow, and to experience a diversion from the routine involves many of the same benefits observed in wilderness recreation (R. Kaplan, 1984; Talbot & Kaplan, 1986).

DESIGNING URBAN PLAYGROUNDS

One fact of nearly every childhood is play. Children play in all types of environmental contexts, including playgrounds, recreation rooms, museums, vacant lots, alleyways, street corners, and driveways. Most researchers believe that play activity has great significance for children, and serves as an important vehicle for learning about the world. The various types of recreational environments available or unavailable to a child could have a significant impact on the child's development. Also, the way in which available play spaces are designed can affect the experiences and benefits that children realize from their interaction with them. Can the design of play areas in our cities enrich the psychological growth of our children?

Much of the research on children's play environments has focused on playgrounds (Moore, 1989). Although this may overemphasize the importance of designed environments (neglecting back yards, streets, and vacant lots), it provides some of the standardization necessary for our discussion. Furthermore, because there is less space available for children to appropriate, playgrounds may be better used and more important in cities (Moore, 1989). The beginning of the playground movement in America can be traced to 1885 when a pile of sand was provided for a "sand garden," a play area for the children living near a mission in Boston (Dickason, 1983). This structured play experience was well supervised, and was apparently intended to "Americanize" the children of immigrants by enticing them to a site where they would be subject to instruction or propaganda. Although this goal may seem rather heavy handed, it represents an early recognition of the usefulness of formal play facilities in creating effective educational environments. Unfortunately, even today some teachers view time spent on the playground as "recess from the children time" (Brown & Burger, 1984), no doubt overlooking educational opportunities.

As early as 1935, researchers were able to demonstrate effects of different playground designs on children's behavior. According to Johnson (1935), when playground equipment was removed, children exercised less, played with dirt and sand more, played more games, but were also more likely to engage in undesirable behavior such as fighting. More recently, Weinstein and Pinciotti (1988) showed increases in active running, swinging, and balancing play and decreases in games and uninvolved behavior.

Modern researchers (e.g., Brown & Burger, 1984; Hayward et al., 1974) generally distinguish between three broad playground styles: *traditional, adventure,* and *contemporary playgrounds* (see Figures 10–6, A, B, and C). Perhaps you are most familiar with the traditional and contemporary playground types. Traditional playgrounds contain the standard apparatus (e.g., swings, monkey bars, jungle gyms). This is still the most widely spread playground type in the United States, and seems primarily geared toward exercise. Unfortunately, these playgrounds are often dangerous places with a variety of metal parts, chains, and (with a cu-

rious insensitivity to life and limb) concrete or asphalt paving. Aesthetics are not necessarily ignored. Sometimes pipes are fashioned into rocket ships or stagecoaches, and sometimes concrete is molded into animal shapes (Shaw, 1987).

Contemporary playgrounds include many of the same elements found in traditional designs, but with a flair for aesthetics and abstract shapes (e.g., the slide may extend from a multileveled wooden structure with a variety of ladders, balancing beams, ramps, bridges, and other delights). Note that in a contemporary playground a single apparatus often serves multiple rather than single play functions.

Hart (1987) remarks that highly manicured outdoor settings are usually controlled by adults, with the **loose parts** of scrap wood, dirt, and other materials systematically removed. These environments afford children

Figure 10–6 Playground styles (A) Traditional (B) Adventure (C) Contemporary

few opportunities for fantasy and spontaneous design. On the other hand, snow in the wintertime and the "odds and ends" that accumulate in untended lots or rural areas provide rich opportunities for children. Adventure playgrounds (at least the "official" versions) began in Denmark during World War II and encouraged youngsters to use scrap wood and other castoff materials to build their own world of fantasy and dirt. Instead of traditional play equipment, scraps of materials such as wood and tools like hammers, nails, and saws are supplied. Children are encouraged to build structures and to modify old ones as time goes on and interests evolve. Clearly these playgrounds require careful supervision, and the presence of adult supervisors makes possible activities such as cooking and gardening in addition to less structured digging and hammering. Some believe the adventure playground can expand the range of play opportunities available to children (Cooper, 1970; Hart, 1987; Moore, 1989; Nicholson, 1970). For instance, Moore (1989) concludes that adventure playgrounds support more fantasy and richer cognitive experiences. Of course some members of the community complain about their unplanned nature and unattractive appearance.

Different playgrounds attract different clientele. According to Moore's (1989) summary, girls are more often seen on traditional apparatus such as swings whereas boys seem more attracted to climbing apparatus and to ball games. On the other hand, Moore believes that settings dominated by nature attract a more equal mix of boys and girls and encourage more cooperative play. In a study that specifically compared the three primary playground designs, Hayward et al. (1974) found that each attracted a somewhat different clientele. Practically no preschool children attended the adventure playgrounds, while about one-third of the users in the other two settings fell into this age group. In contrast, older children were more likely to patronize the adventure playgrounds (Hayward et al., 1974). Finally fewer adults were present in adventure playgrounds than in the contemporary or traditional playgrounds. This latter finding is in all likelihood due to fewer young children being present, but it nevertheless has implications for the level of supervision in the three settings. The presence of adults may be one reason why fewer school-age children attended the traditional or contemporary playgrounds than the adventure playgrounds, since school-age children desire a degree of independence.

The activities engaged in at the three playgrounds differed as well, and the data imply that environmental features had a strong effect on behavior. In the traditional playground, swinging was the most common activity; but at the contemporary playground, children engaged in a continuous mode of activity which included playing on varied equipment. This result was probably due in part to the equipment at the contemporary playground (e.g., there was much more "multipurpose" equipment). At the adventure playground the most popular activity was playing in the "clubhouse," an option that did not exist in the other two settings.

The degree of novelty of an apparatus also seemed to affect its use: There were traditional slides at the traditional playground, but at the contemporary playground a slide was built on a cobblestone "mountain" with tunnels running through it. Whereas the novel slide was extremely popular, the traditional one was used relatively infrequently. Overall, for the three playgrounds, it may be seen that the opportunities and constraints provided by the environment predict the predominant activities engaged in by children. Such opportunities and constraints also affect how the children play (e.g., alone or in groups) and the focus of their interaction (e.g., on the "here and now" versus fantasy). For example, fantasy play was least common in the traditional playground.

Such pretend or imaginative play is of particular theoretical interest because it is thought to foster divergent, creative thinking. One recent study (Susa & Benedict, 1994) specifically examined the link between playground design, pretend play, and creativity. As expected, more pretend play occurred on a complex contemporary playground than on a somewhat more simple traditional playground. In addition, the researchers asked the children they had been observing on the playgrounds to try to think of different uses for a large wooden cable spool. At least for this measure, creativity was positively correlated with pretend play, leading to at least a tentative conclusion that playground design may foster creativity.

There seems to be general agreement among architects and educators that traditional playgrounds fall short of providing the desirable variety of educational, physical, and experiential challenges (Frost & Klein, 1979). On the other hand, not all empirical research demonstrates that contemporary playgrounds as a class are necessarily superior to more traditional designs. Brown and Burger (1984), for example, observed children at three contemporary and three traditional playgrounds. Although one of the three contemporary playgrounds was the most successful at promoting educationally desirable social, language, or motor behaviors, the overall levels of the measured behaviors were actually lowest at one of the other contemporary sites. The researchers concluded that although the poorly functioning playground appeared contemporary in design and was pleasing to the adult eye, these visual characteristics were not successful in promoting the desired play behaviors. In sum, children's play is affected by the success of each individual playground apparatus, the choice of sites for the playground, and the integration of the play spaces in addition to the particular design style (traditional or contemporary).

A number of researchers believe that environmental designers do not sufficiently weigh the preferences or concerns of children and parents (e.g., Bishop & Peterson, 1971; Moore, 1989). The reasoning that goes into play space design often involves untested assumptions about the nature of children and play (Brown & Burger, 1984; Hayward, Rothenberg, & Beasely, 1974). Consequently, we should ask how well the resultant play spaces actually meet the needs of the user population. Moore (1989) emphasizes the importance of community involvement. Especially in small and medium cities, new playground construction is increasingly a community project involving teachers, parents, public officials, and children themselves. The playground in Figure 10–7, for instance, was constructed as a community project under the supervision of a commercial design firm. During the course of the construction, hundreds of different individuals volunteered time and materials, and subsequent post-occupancy evaluation (see Chapter 11) resulted in the construction of two additions to ease congestion on the popular playground and to make it more accessible to physically challenged children.

Playground supervision is also important (Moore, 1989). Whereas the earliest city playgrounds were often supervised, those of this century have often either overlooked many safety concerns, or depended upon the design of apparatus to reduce injuries. With increasing concern about litigation, supervisors may become more common. An important opportunity will be overlooked if adults are merely monitors, however. The potential for well-trained playleaders or animators (playground leaders who are trained to elicit certain play behaviors, much as a play's director elicits different performances from his or her cast) to make playgrounds a richer, more effective learning environment is a particularly exciting challenge (Moore, 1989). In addition to the need for safety, we will paraphrase the playground design guidelines

Figure 10–7 A playground constructed as a community project

suggested by Shaw (1987) as a summary of desirable playground amenities. They should possess:

- *A Sense of Place.* Just as adults seem to prefer legible environments (those that can be easily understood or cognitively mapped), children will be most comfortable when spaces form a context that reflects an overall order.

- *Unity.* The environment's overall image should be unified. Individual parts should be connected physically and spatially; otherwise, most activity will center on the most complex pieces. Unity may also improve children's ability to develop and sustain workable cognitive maps.

- *A Variety of Spaces.* Playgrounds should include large spaces, small spaces, enclosed spaces, and open spaces. In particular, children may especially enjoy enclosed defensible spaces, a phenomenon Brown and Burger refer to as "encapsulation."

- *Key Places.* Key places are complex play structures that support a variety of activities.

- *A System of Pathways.* Key places need to be linked by a carefully chosen system of paths that provide children with choices and lead them to discover the variety of play options.

- *Three-Dimensional Layering.* The playground should not be thought of as a series of structures seated on a single plane, but as a three-dimensional arrangement of ramps, slides, tunnels, and ladders that allow children access to different elevations.

- *Loose Parts.* Loose parts are things to manipulate that are not part of the playground apparatus itself. Examples include balls, games, or building materials.

REVITALIZING ENTIRE URBAN DISTRICTS: URBAN RENEWAL

Urban renewal can be defined as an integrated series of steps taken to maintain and upgrade the environmental, economic, and social health of an urban area (Porteus, 1977). It is not really a new idea. More than a century ago at the Colombian Exposition in

Chicago (a world's fair), Daniel Burnham set out to create an entire city based on a coherent master plan that was to be free from the ills of unplanned urban disorder. The fair was a success. Although no new cities resulted, Burnham's plan led to what was called the **City Beautiful Movement**. These grand master plans featured classical architecture, arranged in an orderly fashion around public open spaces having plazas and pools. City Beautiful plans were adopted and at least partially executed in Chicago, Duluth, Cleveland, and San Francisco. For United States citizens, the most familiar of Burnham's projects may be his contribution to Washington D.C.'s Mall, with its flanking monuments and museums (Kostof, 1987).

A more modern initiative for urban renewal focused more clearly on the decaying residential and commercial sections of post-World War II cities. The assumption was that renewal would provide better housing, safer neighborhoods, and revitalized business districts. In effect, urban renewal was to be a panacea for many urban problems. For instance, there was assumed to be a causal relationship between poor housing and a "grab bag" of social ills. In fact, aside from studies relating poor housing to problems with physical and mental health (e.g., Duvall & Booth, 1978), there is little evidence to support this assumption.

The latter half of the twentieth century saw massive physical changes in the name of renewal: Houses and neighborhoods were razed and replaced by tall apartment complexes, and thousands of residents were relocated. Perhaps you can anticipate a natural conflict of interest between planners and those living in the slums that are torn down to make way for renewal. Planners hope to attract wealthy individuals and businesses back into the city, to destroy eyesores, and to keep the city sufficiently attractive so that people will make use of its cultural resources (Porteus, 1977). Especially in the early years of urban development, they tended to re-place slums with luxury apartments and office buildings, forcing residents to move elsewhere. Unfortunately, the people who are relocated often do not perceive their area as a slum at all but as a pleasant neighborhood (Fried & Gleicher, 1961).

What are the psychological consequences of demolishing neighborhoods and forcing people to relocate? Clearly, these depend on a large number of situational conditions, including attraction to the former neighborhood and family conditions, but relocation often has negative consequences. Destroying a neighborhood not only eliminates buildings, it can destroy a functioning social system and sense of identity for neighborhood residents. According to Gans (1962), slum areas provide not only cheap housing, but offer the types of social support people need to keep going in a crisis-ridden existence.

Boston's West End served as the location for an intensive study of the effect of renewal on a well-liked Italian working-class residential area. What were the consequences of relocation? Loss of home, neighborhood, and daily interactions with well-known neighbors caused an upheaval in people's lives and disrupted their routines, personal relationships, and expectations. This led to a grief reaction in many of those who were displaced, especially in those people who had been most satisfied with the status quo. Among women who reported liking their neighborhood very much, 73 percent displayed short-term reactions to extreme grief, including vomiting, intestinal disorders, crying spells, nausea, and depression. About 20 percent of the residents were depressed for as long as two years after moving. These types of reactions, and more severe health effects, may be most common in people who are already "vulnerable" (e.g., those with previous problems; Freeman, 1978). Interestingly, people's reactions were mediated by knowledge of their former neighborhoods. The greater the familiarity, the stronger the grief (Fried, 1963).

REVITALIZING RESIDENTIAL AREAS

If "wiping out" entire urban districts in an attempt to "save" them generates new problems, are there environmental steps we can take to target residential areas for revitalization? In this regard, let us examine defensible space, social networks, public housing, and gentrification.

Defensible Space

Newman and his colleagues (Newman, 1972, 1975; Newman & Franck, 1982) have focused on how physical aspects of a setting may affect resident-based control of the environment and ultimately lead to lower crime. Their ideas are captured in the concept of **defensible space**. Defensible spaces are clearly bounded, or semi-private, spaces that appear to belong to someone; that is, a visitor is likely to recognize them as someone's territory. Defensible spaces should also allow surveillance by providing visual accessibility. Newman argued that if we create such spaces through design, they will lead residents to feel ownership over them, foster informal surveillance, and promote social cohesion between neighbors. These behaviors should reduce certain types of crime and antisocial acts and elicit improved social relations among urbanites.

Defensible spaces could lead to lower crime for several reasons (Taylor, Gottfredson, & Brower, 1984). First, they could have a direct effect. It may be that spaces which look "defensible" lead potential offenders to assume that residents will actively respond to intruders, a notion which has been supported in work by Brower, Dockett, and Taylor (1983). Second, as suggested by Newman, defensible space may cause the formation of local ties among residents. This may occur because it makes people feel safer, which causes them to use the space more, to come into increased contact with neighbors, and ultimately, to develop more common ties.

Individuals with more ties are more apt to intervene to "defend" their neighborhood, are better able to discriminate neighbors from strangers, and, because shared norms develop, are more likely to know what types of activities should go on and what types should not (Taylor & Brower, 1985). The latter analysis was supported in research by Taylor et al. (1984). Finally, defensible space could lessen crime, since it may strengthen people's territorial functioning (i.e., because areas characterized by defensible space are well bounded and more defensible, they may elicit more proprietary attitudes).

Does the concept of defensible space have the predicted effects? There is definite support for at least part of the model. Newman (1972) compared two public housing projects in New York, one of which was high in defensible space, the other of which was low. The latter project had more crime and higher maintenance costs, and this could not be explained by tenant characteristics. However, while increased defensible space was associated with less crime, whether this was due to greater cohesion among neighbors and stronger territorial attitudes and behaviors, as suggested by defensible space theory, is unclear since this mediating link was not measured. Another study, a demonstration project in Hartford, Connecticut, implemented both physical and social changes designed to increase defensible space (Fowler, McCall, & Mangione, 1979). While the mediating variables posited by defensible space theory were again unmeasured, the changes which were implemented led to fewer burglaries, and residents perceived themselves to be less at risk. They reported walking in the neighborhood more, and believed it was easier to recognize strangers. The Five Oaks neighborhood of Dayton, Ohio, is the location of an even more recent application of Newman's approach (*Newsweek*, July 11, 1994). In order to create smaller, more defensible neighborhoods, streets and alleys were closed or blocked, and speed bumps were installed to slow traffic. Instead of one large residential neighborhood, Five Oaks was divided into smaller "mini-neighborhoods" by the modifications. At least according to preliminary results, traffic decreased by 67 percent, and crime was reduced by 26 percent since implementation of the modifications. We will report more examples of blocking off neighborhoods shortly.

In addition to physical changes to enhance defensible space, other interventions that will increase neighborhood cohesion or feelings of "ownership" should also lower crime. These could include increasing the extent of home ownership in an area, assisting neighborhoods in the development of local social ties, and similar initiatives. For example, block organizations can be sponsored and supported, and neighborhood clean-up and beautification contests can be run (Taylor et al., 1984). All of these may impact on some of the same types of social processes which the physical changes advocated by defensible space theorists are assumed to affect.

Some have criticized the way the defensible space theory was originally formulated (e.g., Taylor et al., 1980), including the supporting research literature (e.g., Patterson, 1977). One of the problems, as noted above, is that the social processes defensible space is assumed to affect were not measured in most studies. While the research suggests that factors associated with more defensible space may affect crime and other outcomes in a favorable way, there is little evidence that this occurs, as Newman believes, because defensible space creates feelings of ownership and affects the social fabric of a setting. Recent research (e.g., by Taylor and his associates and Newman and his) has tried to clarify and extend the model, and to measure the links between cognitions and behavior.

Other research suggests that the link between lower crime and the physical design

features advocated by the theory, while sometimes significant, is not terribly large and may be influenced by other factors (Taylor et al., 1984). In addition, not all research has found that defensible space works to lower crime, increase neighborhood cohesion, and so on (e.g., Mawby, 1977; Merry, 1981). Social and cultural factors (e.g., groups of residents from different ethnic groups who do not form cohesive bonds even when living in "defensible space") may sometimes cause defensible space to remain "undefended."

In addition to architectural features affecting defensible space, as suggested by Newman, Taylor and his associates (e.g., Taylor et al., 1980) believe defensible space research and application should draw more heavily on the concept of territoriality (see Chapter 8). They suggest that some critical environmental features for controlling crime are signs of defense, signs of appropriation, and signs of incivility (Hunter, 1978). Signs of defense are symbolic and real barriers directed toward strangers that keep unwanted outsiders away. Signs of appropriation are territorial markers suggesting that a space is used and cared for. Signs of incivility are physical and social cues (e.g., environmental deterioration) that indicate a decay in the social order. These territorial signs give information to other residents and to strangers which affects whether or not crime occurs. Taylor et al. believe that territorial signs which deter crime are more common in homogeneous neighborhoods, and where there are strong local social ties. As opposed to Newman's model, then, these authors suggest that sociocultural variables and social conditions, in addition to design, determine territorial cognitions and behaviors and ultimately the level of crime in a neighborhood. This model has been tested and has received support (e.g., Gottfredson, Brower, & Taylor, 1979; Newman & Franck, 1982; Taylor & Ferguson, 1978; Taylor et al., 1980, 1984).

A fairly recent means of promoting

territorial defense in cities is to barricade streets to keep nonresidents out (Crowe, 1991). A cul-de-sac design in a residential area serves a similar function: Traffic access is reduced so that residents may be more vigilant and criminals more conspicuous if they cruise through the area to scout out a target. With a gridlike street pattern, it is more difficult for neighbors to know who "belongs" in the area and who does not. By barricading strategic points in the neighborhood, residents hope to make cruising through the neighborhood by criminals more difficult. Barriers can be barrels filled with sand and linked by long boards, concrete construction barriers, or attractively designed brick walls with landscaping. Barricades are not without controversy; often, lower-income residents or those in mostly minority neighborhoods contend that barricades are designed to keep them out of well-to-do majority residential areas. Do barricades work? Atlas and LeBlanc (1994) report on one study of Miami Shores, a community in Florida that erected barriers over a period of years. Compared to other communities, some crime rates were lower after installation of the barricades. Part of the reduction, however, may have been due not to the barriers themselves, but to the need for neighbors to work together to implement the plan; in other words, social factors may have been at least as important as environmental ones, a topic we will explore next.

Social Factors

Neighborhood social networks could play a significant role in fostering the ability to cope with urban problems. Neighborhood social networks are people living nearby who care about and depend on each other. People with strong social networks enjoy better physical health and psychological well-being, are less fearful of victimization, and respond better to crisis events (e.g., Antonovsky, 1979; Holahan & Moos, 1981). Also, the presence of social networks helps regulate access to an area by strangers, leads to less reliance on police for dealing with disturbances, and can exert significant pressure to conform on social deviants living inside a neighborhood (e.g., Suttles, 1968; Wheeldon, 1969). When social cohesion is absent, urban decay can get a strong foothold. Under these conditions, **diffusion of responsibility** effects (Darley & Latané, 1968), in which people assume it is "someone else's" responsibility to deal with social problems, may occur. In addition, deindividuation (Zimbardo, 1969), in which people feel "lost in the crowd," unrecognizable, and therefore not responsible for their antisocial behavior, may occur.

Viable social networks are most likely to occur in certain situations. "Neighboring" in urban environments is greater when there is racial similarity, shared socioeconomic status, psychological "investment" in a neighborhood, satisfaction with conditions there, and a positive sense of well-being (Unger & Wandersman, 1983). Social networks can also be fostered or inhibited through environmental means. We will see later that they are very often strong in so-called "slums," and very weak in many urban renewal housing projects. Research by Newman (1972, 1975) and Newman and Franck (1982) has also shown that defensible space works to facilitate local social network formation (Figure 10–8).

One way in which social networks can function effectively for the good of an urban area is to form local organizations (often called "**block organizations**"). These work for improvements such as better lighting, police protection, street repairs, or other common goals. Residents' participation in block organizations may be predicted by several factors: how important the block environment is to the individual, whether a person believes he or she could perform the behaviors necessary to participate, the perceived existence of common needs among

Figure 10–8 Lack of defensible space inhibits local social network formation.

residents, and how much a person generally participates in activities with other residents (Wandersman & Florin, 1981).

Public Housing: Some Bad Examples

What happens when plans to revitalize the city displace the mostly poor residents of the decaying urban core? Forced relocation, such as through urban renewal, frequently results in one of two housing options. Although affected individuals are generally promised alternative housing, the promise is often unfulfilled, and many drift into other slums or even become homeless. There is a tremendous lack of affordable, alternative housing in the United States today, so the net result of urban renewal is often to lower the population of one slum neighborhood while increasing the population of another. Alternatively, people are relocated in public housing, which is low-rent housing built for those

with a relatively low income. Public housing often provides physical settings that are objectively much better than the residents' original homes, but such projects are often unsuccessful.

The classic example is the **Pruitt-Igoe** project in St. Louis, which was built in the inner city in 1954. In this project, 12,000 persons were relocated into 43 buildings 11 stories high, containing 2,762 apartments, and covering 57 acres. The buildings contained narrow hallways with no semiprivate areas for people to congregate—a design that was praised in *Architectural Forum* (April, 1951) for having no "wasted space." The project was expensive to build but very institutional in nature, containing such "features" as institutional wall tile (from which graffiti was easily removed), unattractive (but indestructible) light fixtures, and vandal-resistant radiators and elevators.

In spite of the construction expense, within a few years Pruitt-Igoe was a shambles. Take a walk with us through the project several years after it opened. First, there is a display of broken glass, tin cans, and abandoned cars covering the playgrounds and parking lots. Some of the building windows are broken; others have been boarded up with plywood. Inside, you smell the stench of urine, trash, and garbage. The elevator is in disrepair, and the presence of feces indicates it has been used as a toilet. Next, you notice that plumbing and electrical fixtures have been pulled out of apartment and hallway walls. When you come upon a resident and ask her about Pruitt-Igoe, she says she has no friends there; there is "nobody to help you." She also tells you that gangs have formed and that rape, vandalism, and robbery are common. Since crime frequently took place in elevators and stairwells, the upper floors have been abandoned (see Figure 10–9).

These conditions destroyed Pruitt-Igoe. By 1970, 27 of the 43 buildings were vacant; and the project has now been totally demol-ished. Why did Pruitt-Igoe fail so miserably? One explanation was proposed by Yancey (1972), who centered his argument around the lack of semiprivate, sociopetal spaces or other facilities that could promote social interaction and the formation of a social order. Typically "slums" are made up of low-rise tenements, narrow streets, and lots of doorways to businesses in which to stop and talk. The design of many urban renewal projects is far less successful in providing for such social interaction. This architectural failure may resist cohesion among residents, and promote conflict and crime.

Yancey also contended that the high-rise architectural design of the project was greatly to blame. It put children beyond their parents' sight and control whenever they were outside their house and gave them many hidden areas, such as stairwells and elevators, in which to cause mischief. Such areas also provided sanctuaries for teenagers and adults to engage in illicit activities almost anonymously. As one resident said, "All you have to do is knock out the lights on the landings above and below you. Then when someone

Figure 10–9 The demolition of Pruitt-Igoe in 1972

comes . . . they stumble around and you can hear them in time to get out" (Yancey, 1972, p. 133).

Other explanations have also been put forward for the demise of Pruitt-Igoe. One suggested by Rainwater (1966) is that such "features" as vandal-proof radiators and walls may convey a self-threatening message of inferiority to residents and may actually challenge them to destroy these objects. In another context, Sommer (1974) and Stainbrook (1966) proposed that the environment can convey negative information that may adversely affect behavior. In a sense, the stigma of poverty was highlighted by the design of Pruitt-Igoe. It, like many public housing developments, had a look that set it off from other types of housing, and it was easily identified as "housing for the poor." The lack of "defensible space" has also been suggested as an important explanation (Newman, 1972). Finally, it should be mentioned that Pruitt-Igoe was plagued by a poorly administered housing authority and by its isolation from the surrounding community.

Pruitt-Igoe is unfortunately not unique in its effects on residents, which has prompted other housing projects to be studied by social scientists. One study was conducted in Puerto Rico by Hollingshead and Rogler (1963). Their findings will give you a feeling for the obstacles a public housing project is up against, even if it incorporates the types of improvements we have suggested. The project in question was less crowded and had better facilities, lower rents, and a healthier atmosphere than the slums from which the residents had moved. However, while only 35 percent had disliked the slums, 86 percent of the men and 71 percent of the women disliked the project. When their reasons were examined, they reflected many complaints that could not easily be remedied by design changes. One problem was loneliness, since the designers had not made provisions for housing the extended family that

people had lived with in the slums. Residents also resented their unknown neighbors and felt bored because they had lost the companions and pastimes they were used to. Finally, some were unhappy because they could no longer engage in certain illegal activities they had practiced in the slums (e.g., selling stolen goods, prostitution) due to greater surveillance.

Low-Income Housing: More Favorable Alternatives

What factors are associated with satisfaction by residents of low-income housing? A study by Rent and Rent (1978) surveyed residents from many housing projects in South Carolina. Those who lived in single-family or "duplex" dwellings liked their residences much more than others. This satisfaction probably occurred, in part, because these residences were more often owned, which is another predictor of satisfaction in low-income housing. For other reasons, too (e.g., greater privacy), such dwellings produce more satisfaction. Not surprisingly, then, 75 percent of those surveyed said they would prefer to live in a single-family dwelling, and 83 percent wanted to own one. Another important predictor of housing satisfaction was having friends in the neighborhood (often these turn out to be neighbors). Generally, the more satisfied one was with his or her neighbors, the greater the attraction to the living situation. An interesting finding was that overall life satisfaction was associated with liking one's residence. The happier one was with his or her life, the more satisfied one was with living arrangements. Overall, then, social as well as physical factors may be important determinants of housing satisfaction among low-income individuals.

Fortunately, some of the recent trends in government housing assistance have more elements associated with residential satisfaction than earlier project housing. When government assistance is provided, the U.S.

government has more or less stopped building "high-rise" projects for low-income families. No "public housing" has been built for over a decade. Instead, people are placed more often in townhouses or small apartment buildings. There has also been increased government assistance with home ownership, direct housing subsidies for the poor (e.g., rent vouchers), and attempts to renovate or preserve current housing instead of demolition. This serves the admirable function of "fixing the building and leaving the people." Another recent innovation is "**urban homesteading**," where abandoned urban property is given to individuals who agree to rehabilitate it to meet existing housing codes and occupy it for a prescribed period of time. It has sometimes been quite successful, but in other instances the practical problems of having low-income families with limited resources play the role of "general contractor" have been overwhelming. There has, unfortunately, been one "backlash" from earlier fiascoes with public housing such as Pruitt-Igoe: Some municipalities refuse altogether to have any form of it within their boundaries.

When people must be moved due to urban renewal, are there some means of accomplishing this in a more humane way? One possibility would be to move people to a new setting in established social groups. This would maintain the social cohesion of the former neighborhood (Young & Willmott, 1957). It could also be maintained, to some extent, by moving people to redeveloped areas near their old neighborhood. Another important factor is citizen participation in planning the move and the new setting in which they will live (e.g., Arnstein, 1969). Designers and planners should encourage participation, and be especially sensitive to cultural or subcultural differences in housing preferences.

Gentrification

While urban renewal has had an effect on cities for many years, a more recent trend has been gentrification. Gentrification can be defined as the emergence of middle- and upper-class areas in parts of the inner city that were formerly deteriorated (London, Lee, & Lipton, 1986). Frequently, this follows renovations to buildings which were once attractive and desirable, but which have fallen into disrepair. After the renovation, wealthier tenants move in, and those who lived there before the renovation must find alternative housing. While gentrification is good for cities in many ways (e.g., it encourages "resettlement" by people with greater means, raises the tax base, and improves the environment), like urban renewal, it can be "bad news" for poor residents of the city. In addition, while gentrification and urban renewal continue to occur, we should keep in mind that a major threat to cities is still the disintegration and abandonment of urban housing (Henig, 1982).

Several conceptual perspectives have been proposed to explain the emerging trend of gentrification. Demographic explanations suggest that gentrification is due to population changes. For example, as increasing numbers of "baby boomers" reached adulthood in the seventies and eighties they put demands on the housing supply. Other factors include the declining birth rates in Canada and the United States, and the increasing number of women in the work force. Affluent, childless, working couples are not discouraged by the poor reputation of inner-city schools, and may want to live in the city, close to their jobs and recreational opportunities (London et al., 1986). In contrast, ecological approaches suggest that the ecology of the setting determines whether or not there will be gentrification (London et al., 1986). From this perspective, cities high in white-collar businesses, low in manufacturing, low in noxious land use, and which have long commuting distances should be most apt to experience gentrification (e.g., Lipton, 1977). A third approach, the sociocultural explanation, assumes that changing values, attitudes, and lifestyles are responsible for gentrification. Whereas the values of most Americans may have formerly been antiurban (Allen, 1980), this may be changing. In fact, it may even be becoming "in vogue" to live in the city among some population subgroups (e.g., yuppies).

Finally, political-economic explanations may take several forms. One implies that the decreasing availability of suburban land, rising transportation costs, inflation, the low cost of urban, inner-city dwellings, and antidiscrimination and school desegregation laws are all conspiring to encourage gentrification. Another perspective suggests that economic interests and political factors are responsible for gentrification, and that, in some sense, it has been willfully planned. The most cynical view is that powerful interest groups allow the city to deteriorate, mindful that gentrification could later yield major profits. They pursue gentrification for their own benefit, with little regard for individuals who would be displaced by it (London et al., 1986).

Do only the wealthy benefit from gentrification? While at first it may appear so, a closer analysis suggests that this may not be entirely correct. It has been found that while the owners of gentrified housing are "urban gentry" (e.g., young, highly educated professionals), the "renters" of such housing typically have much lower incomes, and pay a large proportion of them for rent. Thus, two types of people are moving into gentrified areas (DeGiovanni & Paulson, 1984).

There are various "costs" of gentrification. It has been found that gentrification often results in an increase in violent crimes (Taylor & Covington, 1988), as well as an increase in larceny and robbery (Covington & Taylor, 1989). This may occur, in part, from the close juxtaposition of the "haves" to the "have nots" in gentrifying areas. One of the major urban trends of the past decade, in fact, is an increasing gap between the very poor households and the other households in urban areas. This is the source of many current urban problems (e.g., violence and crime) and will probably play an even greater role in the future.

Another negative aspect of gentrification is that the poor who originally lived in the "slums" are often pressured to move out. Because they have few political advocates and little power, they are in a difficult situation. Henig (1982) argues that collective mobilization or other forms of protection for the victims of gentrification (e.g., those whose rents or property taxes are raised, or who are pressured or forced to relocate) is even more important than for victims of urban renewal. The federal government has not found effective means of monitoring gentrification for possible harm, and leaves much of the responsibility for dealing with those displaced to state and local officials. When these officials weigh their concerns over displacement of existing residents with their desire for an increased tax base, they often find it difficult to support the former (Henig, 1982). In addition, the private sector is resistant to policies to limit displacement due to gentrification. Not surprisingly, as with urban renewal, it has been found that being forced to relocate due to gentrification is associated with threats to health and well-being (Myers, 1978).

REVITALIZING COMMERCIAL AND BUSINESS DISTRICTS

North American cities are mere infants compared to many of their European counterparts, and North American cities (with the possible exception of Mexican archeological sites) have no opportunity to show the rich history of Paris or London, let alone the ancient cities of Athens or Rome. Moreover, until recently North Americans have shown a disregard for preserving the variety of different architectural styles, materials, and building sizes that once marked the core of cities (Day, 1992; Gratz, 1989; Kostof, 1987).

As Kostof (1987) complains, urban renewal often resulted in the indiscriminate destruction of the rich texture of old neighborhoods, replacing them with corporate towers. One part of what was lost was formal history— the architecture associated with important people and events. A different, but perhaps related loss is the sense of place created not by age per se, but by the sense of meaning created by architecture (see also Chapters 2 and 12 for other discussions of place). One current goal of many downtown revitalization projects is not to erase the past, but to preserve or even recapture it. For example, many cities have "rediscovered" their old farmer's markets (Sommer, 1989). Such **placemaking** may not be a simple task, because it relies not on a building's power to *determine* behavior, but on its ability to cue the memories that create the personal meaning and experience of place (Day, 1992). As we shall see, the results of these efforts are at least as varied as their goals, and projects that are successful on some counts may exacerbate other urban problems.

Festival Marketplaces

The proliferation of so-called **festival marketplaces** provides an example of both success and the potential dangers of urban revitalization projects. In the late 1960s a Boston architect, Benjamin Thompson, proposed a plan for restoring an historic area of Downtown Boston by creating a new retail marketplace. The proposed site lay midway between the waterfront and the Boston financial district. Its focus was three old market buildings adjacent to Faneuil Hall, a Colonial meetinghouse (Gratz, 1989). Thompson's plan for a revitalized marketplace ran counter to the conventional wisdom that downtown retail districts were destined to fail at the hands of suburban shopping malls. Unlike the parallel rediscovery of farmer's markets and flea markets (Sommer, 1989), Thompson's plan called for

a new retail emphasis to turn the old market into something not unlike a shopping mall, but with a sense of history. Funding was difficult, even when the project attracted the successful developer James Rouse. But funds were obtained, and the Faneuil Hall–Quincy Market district became the prototype for dozens of other festival marketplaces (see Figure 10–10). These marketplaces are busy retail and tourist centers that combine retail space, leisure, and a bit of theater. The so-called Rouseification of downtown Boston, Baltimore, and other American cities invokes what Hall (1988) calls the "city-as-stage." That is, the new city center, like theater, presents a wholesome, sanitized, and not quite real vision of urban life. Part of the mix includes a bow to history. In Boston the elements of history were Faneuil Hall, which was treated as an historic landmark, and the three old granite buildings of Quincy market which were renovated to serve as homes for retail outlets and food vendors. This rehabilitation and recycling of old structures for new uses is now known as **adaptive reuse** (Hall, 1988). In Baltimore's Inner Harbor, on the other hand, the old wharf and warehouse district was removed altogether and replaced by new retail pavilions, plazas, and a museum. Some connection to the historic waterfront was maintained (or recovered) by acquiring the three-masted frigate the SS Constellation and mooring it permanently near the pavilions (Kostof, 1987).

How can designers marry the architecture of the past with modern construction techniques and requirements? Much of the effect can be created by visually extending old facades through new edifices and by maintaining compatible size and mass (e.g., Hedman & Jaszewski, 1984). The new does not need to "pretend" to be old. Day's (1992) survey of public responses to a new 1.3 million square foot megastructure in St. Paul showed not only an appreciation for a carefully preserved and reconstructed facade, but

Figure 10–10 The festival marketplace in Baltimore's Inner Harbor

also for an adjoining glassy atrium that was apparently seen as linking the building to activity outside.

Such projects require massive funding. Baltimore's Inner Harbor area, for instance, attracted $180 million in federal funds, $58 million from the city, and only $28 million in private funds (Hall, 1988). At their best, such downtown attractions revitalize decaying older industrial cities. Rouse's Inner Harbor area of Baltimore, for instance, attracts 22 million visitors a year to its shops, a museum, and waterfront plazas (Hall, 1988). In Boston, the market area and a similar revitalization of the waterfront are part of a long pedestrian corridor through the heart of old Boston which stretches from the harbor, through the market, to the Boston Common and Public Garden area, and beyond to the gentrified brownstones of Commonwealth Avenue and Back Bay (this cohesive corridor is partly a result of Kevin Lynch's cognitive mapping studies reviewed in Chapter 3).

Despite these apparent successes, festival marketplaces and other so-called postmodern projects are not without their critics. As we said, they preserve not history, but an idealized presentation of urban life as it never was. At their worst, such developments (or their poor imitations) make little attempt to preserve real history, but instead treat historic structures as commodities and cater more to collective nostalgia than to a genuine understanding of the historic landscape (Kostof, 1987; Roberts & Schein, 1993). Their apparent spontaneous mix of sights and smells are, in fact, anything but accidental, and to some represents a publicly subsidized trendy superficiality. At their best, however, they may be delightful celebrations of the city.

Design Review

Both historic preservation and large-scale downtown revitalization projects operate on a massive scale. Most buildings are not part of such massive projects, of course. Unfortunately, when individual developers, landlords, and architects attempt to construct a new building, there may be a conflict between their individual goals or taste and those of the surrounding district (Devlin & Nasar, 1989; Nasar, 1994). Other projects are smaller still (a plan to refurbish an aging business facade, for instance) and may not even require the owner to hire an architect or other design professional. To ensure that building appearance is not discordant with the good of the community, cities may adopt **design review**, a case by case examination of proposed new projects that attempts to ensure that they will remain harmonious with both the architecture and the ongoing social fabric of a district. New York City's Times Square may provide examples of both the good of design review and the bad that can result from lack of oversight. When Times Square became

the target of revitalization plans in the middle 1980s, some observers reacted with mixed emotions. On the one hand, the plans signaled a return to health for the decaying theater district. On the other hand, some feared that huge new buildings would visually overwhelm the more modest historic district. According to Hiss (1990), an environmental simulation demonstrated the need for buildings to be set back at about the sixth floor to allow continued use of the traditional gaudy signs, and the New York City Planning Commission adopted both this suggestion and zoning regulations requiring developers to set aside space for businesses such as costume shops that serve the theater industry. Unfortunately (according to Hiss) the planning commission did not also require a second setback at approximately the twelfth floor to maintain historic levels of sunlight and sky.

ESCAPING TO THE SUBURBS

The great American dream appears to be to leave the city. Evidence of the dislike most city dwellers have for their environs is suggested by the finding that almost four in ten would like to move out of the city, though seven in ten say they could be induced to stay if conditions would improve (Gallup Poll, March, 1978, vol. 2). Only 15 percent of those living in communities with less than 50,000 residents express a desire to leave (Gallup Poll, April 19, 1981). In addition to crime, urbanites cite overcrowding, pollution, housing, traffic congestion, and noise as major reasons for leaving. Where would people rather live? A 1985 survey asked a representative American sample, "If you could live wherever you wanted, would you prefer a large city, a suburban area, a small town, or a rural area?" The results were: city, 9 percent; suburbs, 29 percent; small town, 37 per-

cent; rural area, 25 percent (ABC News/ Washington Post Survey, February 22, 1985). However, it does not appear that the city is being totally rejected: Many of those expressing a preference for suburban or rural areas still wanted to be near a medium-size or large city (Figure 10–11).

This explains the massive move to suburbia, but what exactly are suburbs? They are areas within a metropolis that are relatively distant from the historic city center. Suburban living has increased dramatically, especially since World War II, and at present more Americans live in the suburbs than in the center city or nonmetropolitan areas (Garreau, 1991). Why is this happening? Quite simply, because suburban living offers an answer to a number of urban problems. As one moves farther from the city, he or she is subjected to fewer crowds and to less

Figure 10–11 Many people preferring suburban or rural areas still want to be near a city.

dirt, noise, and pollution. In addition, although suburban crime rates are increasing, they are still much lower than in the city.

According to Garreau, suburbanization occurred in three phases. In the first phase, which began shortly after World War II, affluent city dwellers moved to new residential developments in the suburbs and governments built highways to allow them to travel to and from the central business district. In the 1960s, the second phase of suburban growth saw malls and other commercial establishments following the outflow of people. Finally, offices and corporate headquarters moved to the newly established **edge cities** that now ring the old urban core. Edge cities account not only for most metropolitan areas' population, but for most of its office and commercial space as well. Unlike the old city core, however, edge cities are largely the product of individual developers who try to make their particular developments spacious, attractive, and, of course, profitable. The results are mixed. Internally, each development can be well organized, but the fast pace of

building and the lack of a central political authority has also meant that adjacent neighborhoods, streets, and commercial zones are often not well integrated with each other (Southworth & Owens, 1993). The edge city consumes far more land for each unit of activity than did the old city core, and its vastness commits us to the automobile. Still, the edge city seems destined to remain the home of most North Americans well into the twenty-first century.

What are the individual consequences of the move to suburbia? There is some evidence that the move has a positive effect. Suburbanites are generally happier with their housing, their communities, and their lives than city dwellers, even when socioeconomic status and other differences between urban and rural populations are statistically controlled (Fischer, 1973; Marans & Rodgers, 1975). Also, people who move to the suburbs are much less afraid of crime victimization, and restrict their behavior less due to fear of crime (Lavrakas, 1982; Skogan & Maxfield, 1981). However, not all is well in suburbia.

The price of typical suburban houses is rising tremendously, and it appears that fewer and fewer people will be able to afford or to maintain a suburban lifestyle in the future. Further, as more and more people escape the city for the suburbs, crowding, pollution, and other urban problems are becoming suburban problems. As noted earlier, crime in the suburbs is increasing, and the use of drugs in suburban schools is cause for great concern. All this leaves one wondering if the suburban areas of today will be characterized by a full complement of "urban" problems in the future. But perhaps the worst problem created by the move to suburbia has its roots back in the cities. Cities are experiencing decreased populations, populations that are poorer, and that are more minority dominated than ever before. There is a declining tax base and an increasing demand for city services (e.g., police protection). This has occurred at a time when federal support has decreased. Unfortunately, the trend toward abandoning urban areas and moving to suburbia has jeopardized all that the city has to offer (Flynn, 1995; Garreau, 1991). We will have more to say about urban–suburban living in Chapter 12.

CHAPTER SUMMARY

The city is a salient environmental element in almost everyone's life. How does the urban setting affect individuals who live in it? A number of conceptual formulations have been derived to understand and predict the effects of the city on individuals; these include overload, environmental stress, behavior constraint, and overstaffing notions. Although they are often presented as competing concepts, it is probably true that overload, stress, constrained behavior, and insufficient resources each explains some of the consequences of an urban existence. Further, the predictions of each of the models can be integrated into the general environment–behavior formulation presented in Chapter 4. While this model has not been tested explicitly in research on cities, many of its assertions have been supported.

What are the results of experiments on the effects of city life? Two methodological perspectives (the "single variable" approach and the "urban versus rural" approach) have been used in past research. Each has its strengths and weaknesses. Overall, such urban stressors as noise, pollution, heat, crowding, and "extra demand," have at least moderately detrimental effects on city dwellers; the effects of homelessness and crime are much more severe. Further, when cities and nonurban areas are compared, there are urban–rural differences in terms of affiliative behavior, prosocial behavior, crime, stress, coping behavior, long-term aftereffects, and health. On most of these dimensions, urbanites come out on the short end. However, on dimensions not often studied by researchers (e.g., ability to adapt to diverse situations), urbanites may come out ahead.

Finally, a number of solutions have been tried to alleviate urban problems. One major attempt has been urban renewal. Unfortunately, this has often involved a conflict of interest between slum dwellers and city planners, with the former being forced to relocate. Forced relocation into public housing sometimes has disastrous consequences, which might be ameliorated by proper design of public housing. Gentrification is a more recent trend. Individuals return to the city and renovate housing that was formerly in bad condition. While this improves the urban area, it again causes relocation of original residents. The dream of most urbanites, however, is suburbia. This is attainable only for those whose socioeconomic level permits it. Research on suburban living shows that it offers a solution to some of the negative aspects of the city for those who can make the move.

SUGGESTED PROJECTS

1. One assumption we have made is that cities differ from small towns on a number of dimensions. To test this hypothesis, first buy copies of a few newspapers from large cities and small towns. Compare the following sections: entertainment, sports, and reports of local crime. Next, locate some telephone directories from large cities and small towns. Compare listings for the following: medical specialists, tradespeople, specialized restaurants of diverse nationalities, museums, religious institutions, educational facilities, and theaters. What pattern of urban–rural differences emerges on these various dimensions?

2. Think of three cities you have visited, and attempt to rate them in terms of "atmosphere." Can you identify specific physical or social aspects that led you to make these judgments? Do you think that historic districts are of much importance in determining your judgments?

3. What are your views of urban life? Has our assessment led you to become more positive or more negative toward cities than before? Write down your views and compare them with those of classmates.

4. Discuss this project with your instructor before you begin because many states have very strict rules regarding observation of children. Thus prepared, get permission from school officials to visit and observe a school playground (they may be eager to learn from you!). Would you classify the playground as traditional or contemporary? How do children use the playground? For instance, what playground equipment is most popular? Do children congregate in enclosed spaces? What are the functions of loose parts?

5. Try to replicate the studies Newman and McCauley did on reciprocation of eye contact (which signals accessibility for interactions). In a small town and then in a city, position yourself near a doorway. When people passing by are a few feet away, initiate eye contact. Record the number of reciprocal gestures you receive in both settings. Do your results replicate those of Newman and McCauley?

Architecture, Design, and Engineering for Human Behavior

INTRODUCTION

HISTORY, CULTURE, AND DESIGN PROCEDURES

THE PHYSICAL ENVIRONMENT: EXTENT OF INFLUENCE

    Architectural Determinism

    Environmental Possibilism

    Environmental Probabilism

THE DESIGNER'S PERSPECTIVE

THE PROCESS OF DESIGN: FOSTERING COMMUNICATION

    The Gaps

    Fostering Participation

SUBSTANTIVE CONTRIBUTIONS

    Privacy

    Materials and Color

    Illumination

    Windows

    Furnishings

    Architectural Aesthetics

SELECTING ALTERNATIVES: THE DESIGN CYCLE

    Stages in the Design Process

AMERICAN COLLEGE CAMPUSES: AN EXAMPLE OF DESIGN DYNAMICS

    Planning for the Future

HUMAN FACTORS: ENGINEERING FOR HUMAN DESIGN

    Communicating With Machines

CHAPTER SUMMARY

    Suggested Projects

KEY TERMS

applicability gap	human factors
commodity	mapping
congruence	normative theory
delight	pattern language
design alternatives	positive theory
design cycle	possibilism
determinism	post-occupancy evaluation (POE)
ergonomics	preindustrial vernacular design
firmness	primitive design
folk design tradition	probabilism
gaps	procedural theory
Gestalt theory	sociofugal
grand design tradition	sociopetal
habitability	substantive theory
Hawthorne effect	

INTRODUCTION

It's just an average day. You wake up slowly, glance at the clock, then realize that somehow you have overslept! "How could this happen?" you mutter, and then realize that the alarm did buzz, but you mistakenly turned it off completely instead of hitting the ten-minute "snooze" function. Your roommate smirks, but tosses the car keys. Starting the borrowed auto, you turn what you think is the headlight switch (you always drive with the headlights on—a news story you heard said it saves lives), only to be met with the thump-thump of the windshield wipers. Silly you. You turn off the wipers, find the lights, and motor to campus.

Twelve minutes twenty-seven seconds later you dash across a campus quadrangle. Across the lawn is an old brick building; one you've always found particularly attractive. In fact, you remember that it was the view of this building that first led you to apply for admission to your college. It is probably a good thing for those who value your tuition that instead you

did not notice the new classroom building on your first visit. You dash up the steps of the gray poured concrete box and slam into the door—it opens the other way. Unpredictable doors are just one inconvenience. It took you weeks your first year at college to learn your way through the labyrinth of corridors, at least one of which ends in a stairway that seems to go nowhere. "Who designed this place anyway?" you have often said. Sinking into your seat in class you notice your breath. Why doesn't the heat work? "It's too cold to lecture," the professor says, "class canceled."

In this chapter, our emphasis will be on the application of behavioral science to problems of design and engineering. Of course, in other chapters we have made references to applications of psychology that may assist in creating legible environments, that minimize the effects of stressors such as noise and air

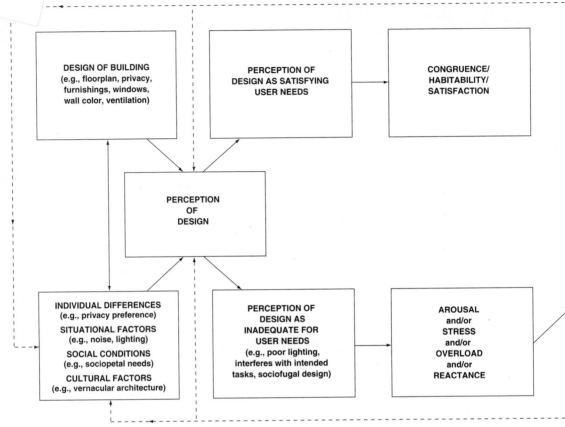

Figure 11–1   Our eclectic model applied to design

pollution, and that maximize spatial or social comfort. Nevertheless, we have not systematically investigated the relationship between the behavioral sciences and architects and other design professionals, or the smaller scale interactions between people and engineered machines and workspaces.

In Chapter 1 we defined environmental psychology as the "study of the interrelationship between behavior and experience and the built and natural environments." Much of this text is devoted to establishing an understanding of how humans are affected by different environmental experiences. However, our definition also recognizes that humans are part of the environment and that our behaviors often change it. Indeed, as we emphasized in Chapter 2, the

ability to manipulate or temper the environment is one characteristic of our species—a characteristic which has allowed us to inhabit most terrestrial environments and even outer space. As we proceed, you may find it worthwhile to examine how our eclectic model applies to our discussion of design in Figure 11–1. We may perceive specific design elements such as color, lighting, noise, or floorplan as facilitating or impairing our functioning in a specific setting. To the extent the design features impede our functioning (e.g., cause overload, constrain behavior) we cope through behavioral or cognitive changes. We can also use environment—behavior principles to modify the design so that we construct a setting more likely to yield a favorable outcome.

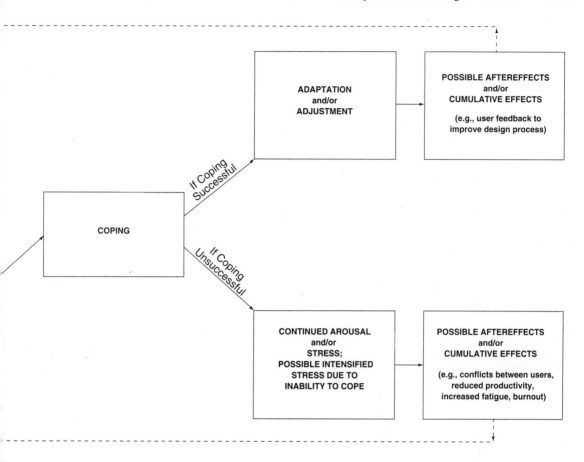

HISTORY, CULTURE, AND DESIGN PROCEDURES

If someone were to ask you to name five things you associate with ancient Egypt it is likely that among them you would name the Pyramids or the Sphinx. For ancient Greece a similar list might bring the Parthenon to mind, and symbols of modern Paris are likely to include Notre Dame, the Arch d'Triumph and the Eiffel Tower (see Figure 11–2).

Surely these are impressive (and relatively permanent) examples of design achievement, but are they really representative of the environments that most affect the average member of their societies? Rapoport (1969) notes that monuments and other "important" buildings represent a self-conscious attempt by the designer (or his or her patron), to impress—what Rapoport refers to as the **grand design tradition**. By intent, these constructions are unusual, specialized, and not representative of the variety of environments experienced by the common person. On the other hand, the **folk design tradition** (as expressed, for example, in the home of the common person) is a more direct expression of the day-to-day world of people as they live, shop, and work. Environmental psychology should concern itself with both the monumental architecture of public buildings and the more personal design of individual dwellings. Rapoport's

Figure 11–2   The Eiffel Tower is an example of high-style architecture.

summary of folk design across cultures will serve to highlight some of the broad issues confronting both designers and environmental psychologists in a variety of contexts.

Within the folk tradition Rapoport distinguishes between **primitive** and **preindustrial vernacular design.** In so-called "primitive" societies there is little specialization, and nearly everyone is capable of building his or her own shelter according to time-honored techniques which result in a standard style across all dwellings within the culture. The term "primitive" does not imply unsophisticated. Indeed, these shelters have evolved over time under the unforgiving challenges of survival, and they represent successful integrations of unique cultural and environmental demands. Given the resource and cultural constraints, a modern designer would be hard pressed to create a more durable and portable dwelling for a family than the Cheyenne teepee, or a more successful adaptation to Northern winters than the snow igloo (see Figure 11–3). Furthermore, these and other examples of primitive architecture are sensitive adaptations to climatic conditions such as temperature, wind direc-

Figure 11–3   Shelters in so-called primitive societies have evolved into very effective solutions to the challenges of this particular environment.

tion, and moisture rather than attempts at overcoming them with the huge energy expenditures needed to make the standard North American frame home habitable from Florida to Alaska.

As construction methods become more complex, a society may begin to rely on the knowledge and assistance of specialists or tradespersons. Rapoport refers to this as *preindustrial vernacular architecture*, characterized by slightly more individual variation in the design of individual buildings and by the addition of the tradesperson who has specific building knowledge. Again however, design in these societies is based on an evolved variation on an established and time-tested theme.

As Figure 11–4 illustrates, building design in industrial nations differs from design in traditional societies on a number of dimensions. For example, the designer is likely to be an architect or some other professional rather than a member of the family, the design is less constrained by climatic conditions, and the changes in building styles and construction techniques are likely to occur at a dramatically faster pace. Furthermore, shelter and survival are expectations rather than concerns among the middle-class or upper-class citizens who commission designs and purchase homes. Therefore, in addition to obvious structural concerns such as durability and safety, modern criteria for building design also include aesthetics, comfort, and efficiency of the people living and working within a construction. Particularly in the industrialized nations, a comfortable lifestyle has led to a high dependence on technology. We use energy to fuel our furnaces, power

Figure 11–4   Modern buildings (as with Canada's National Gallery of Art) emphasize aesthetics, individuality, and changing technology.

our air conditioners, and light our homes and factories. Unfortunately, the most common sources of energy are nonrenewable, and contribute to pollution problems (see Chapter 14). It is also easy to cite instances of technological mishaps as the price of our dependence. Later in the chapter we will discuss a few ways to avoid such mishaps, but in our technologically ambitious society, some errors are inevitable (see Chapter 7 for a discussion of human reactions to technological catastrophes such as nuclear power plant accidents).

THE PHYSICAL ENVIRONMENT: EXTENT OF INFLUENCE

An obvious assumption we have made in this textbook is that the environment is an important contributor to behavior. An underlying assumption of design is that we have at least moderate control over some of these environmental variables. Nevertheless, researchers as well as designers have had difficulty in agreeing on the extent of architecture's influence on behavior. First, let us revisit a discussion we began in Chapters 4 and 6 regarding the ability of the environment to cause or determine behavior. You will recall that we discussed three basic perspectives: determinism, possibilism, and probabilism.

ARCHITECTURAL DETERMINISM

One of the early conceptualizations of architectural influence on behavior was architectural **determinism**. Briefly, architectural determinism holds that the built environment directly shapes the behavior of the people within it. In its most extreme form, the physical environment is seen as the only, or at least the primary, cause of behavior. It has become clear, however, that such a view is too simplistic to adequately account for the effects of design. Franck (1984) criticizes this extreme determinism on several counts. First, this view exaggerates the importance of the physical environment by underestimating the importance of social and cultural factors. Second, determinism overlooks the importance of indirect environmental effects and interactions between several environmental variables acting in combination. Finally, determinism ignores the fact that people engage in transactions with the environment—that is, they are not passive, but influence and change the environment as it influences and changes them. A transactional view emphasizes the importance of choice and the dynamic nature of real-world design. Thus, design influences behavior, but our needs, ongoing activities, and relationships modify these effects.

ENVIRONMENTAL POSSIBILISM

Although we agree that "pure" architectural determinism is an overstatement, it would be unfortunate if the desire to avoid it becomes a barrier to the development of theory and research (Franck, 1984). Other perspectives on behavior in the built environment temper architectural determinism. One, called environmental **possibilism** (Porteus, 1977), views the environment as presenting us with opportunities as well as setting potential limits on behavior. The environment is unlikely to force or cause a particular behavior or decision to become inevitable; instead, the choices we make determine the degree to which opportunities are realized, or barriers surmounted. Rather than assuming that the environment completely determines behavior (as does determinism), environmental possibilism views the environment as a context in which behavior occurs. For instance, several very different designs might be almost equally successful in meeting your needs for shelter. Again, according to this conceptualization, our outcomes are jointly determined by the environment and the choices we make.

ENVIRONMENTAL PROBABILISM

Somewhere in between the determinist and the possibilist positions on architecture and behavior lies another orientation, environmental **probabilism** (Porteus, 1977). While determinism assumes that the environment determines behavior absolutely and possibilism ascribes such a large role to individual choice that it is hard to make predictions regarding environmental influence on behavior, probabilism is a compromise. It assumes that while an organism may choose a variety of responses in any environmental situation, there are probabilities associated with specific instances of design and behavior. These probabilities reflect the influence of both nonarchitectural factors and design variables on behavior. Thus, one can say that, given all we know about people and the particular environment they are in, some behaviors are more likely to occur than others.

A simple example will serve to illustrate environmental probabilism. Let us assume that you have a class with a small number of others in a very large room. Under these conditions, discussion is minimal. After studying everything you can find about classrooms, you decide to change the arrangement of the desks. You have learned that, in most cases, if you arrange seating in a circle, people will talk more. Thus the chances are good that if you rearrange your classroom in this way, you will help to create more discussion. However, if the class was scheduled late in the day, or if the instructor is dull you may not succeed. There are no "sure bets," according to probabilism.

THE DESIGNER'S PERSPECTIVE

For our discussion of architectural practice our framework will be Lang's (1987) outline of the relationship between behavioral science and design. Our primary focus will be on the potential to improve the process by which designers gather information and make design choices. As you will notice, much of the literature concerning procedure and collaboration consists of examples or recommendations rather than empirical facts. Nevertheless, we hope to outline some of the issues as they are perceived by designers, particularly those designers who are most eager to embrace environmental psychology.

According to Lang (1987, 1988) there is general agreement among architects that buildings and other designed environments must fulfill three basic purposes: commodity, firmness, and delight (see Figure 11–5). **Commodity** refers to the functional goal of a design (what is the building to be used for?), **firmness** to the structural integrity or permanence (will it last?), and **delight** encompasses aesthetic concerns. Different architects may place different emphasis on these interrelated dimensions, but in each case the designer must draw on his or her professional expertise in facing the challenges of a specific design. Of course, this need not be a lonely task. As we shall see, there are a number of reasons why it may be wise for designers to collaborate, both with other professionals and with the eventual occupants of a design. Design is a problem-solving process. In seeking solutions, designers must draw on an accumulation of organized data and ideas that are loosely organized as a system of theories or models.

Although this is a slightly different use of the term theory, it is consistent with our

Figure 11–5   The relationship between normative and substantive theories and design
After Lang, 1987. Creating architectural theory: The role of the behavioral sciences in environmental design. *New York: Van Nostrand Rinebold.*

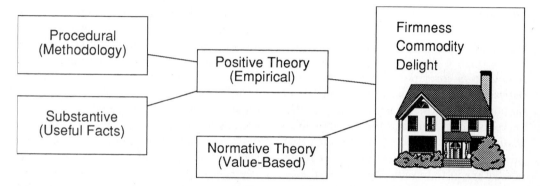

EARLY NORMATIVE ARCHITECTURAL INFLUENCE ON THE COLLEGE CAMPUS

Paul V. Turner's historical account of American campus planning (1984) offers an opportunity to ponder even broader normative influences, beginning with the establishment of the first colleges in eastern North America. According to Turner, the founders of the early English colonies placed considerable emphasis on higher education, and moved quickly to establish colleges in America. Harvard College was founded by 1636, only six years after the settlement of the Massachusetts Bay Colony. By 1640, it was occupying quarters in Cambridge (named for the English university that counted many of the Harvard founders among its alumni), and by the time of the American Revolution, there were nine degree granting institutions spread across the colonies. The importance of these institutions is reflected both in their number and their size. During most of the colonial period, the biggest buildings in America were built for higher education (Turner, 1984). The same American emphasis on education manifested itself more than a century later when the western migration of Americans and a new desire for practical education, led Congress to pass the Land Grant Act, establishing colleges in states across the new western frontier.

American colleges drew much of their architectural inspiration from the British colleges at Cambridge and Oxford. Unlike some of their counterparts on the European continent, these British institutions provided residences for their students. Throughout their early histories the individual colleges at Oxford and Cambridge enclosed inward-looking quadrangles modeled after their heritage from medieval monasteries. By the early seventeenth century, however, Cambridge had built several colleges following a more open style which was enclosed on only three sides. By then the British schools were also guided by an egalitarian desire to provide educational opportunities for those who could not have previously afforded them and a general increase in enthusiasm for higher education among aristocrats. Thus, enthusiasm for higher education was peaking in Britain just as the first settlers were

definition in Chapter 4. In this instance, theory provides a source of information and organization to which a designer can refer. Lang (1987, 1988) distinguishes between positive and normative theory. **Positive theory** attempts to discover predictable relationships between variables, in this instance, the effect of modifications of the physical environment on commodity, firmness, and delight. **Normative theory,** on the other hand, is based on value-laden descriptions and explanations of what ought to be done. Normative theory may express itself in design manifestos, iden-

tification with a particular design movement, or other differences in style. Our discussion will emphasize empirical or positive theory, but we would be foolish not to recognize the importance of the normative influence of history and culture on design (for a familiar example of the influence of cultural values on architecture, see box on pages 418–419). Of course, even the choice to emphasize positive theory represents the normative stance of our field.

Lang (1987, 1988) also differentiates between issues of **procedural** and **substantive**

establishing colonies in North America. The architectural style of American colleges reflected both the enthusiasm for higher education, and some of the values of Oxford and (particularly) Cambridge.

The British college template found a new expression in America, however. The three-sided quadrangles of Cambridge were opened up even more, and replaced by unattached individual buildings at Harvard and William and Mary. Eventually, many American colleges spread themselves across parklike settings like the one at Princeton (where the term "campus" was first used), establishing a unique pastoral setting that was quite different from their European counterparts. Some, built more or less symmetrically, created malls like the one at the University of Virginia (which still is true to the original design by founder Thomas Jefferson) that are found in some altered form on many modern campuses (Figure 11–6). In the nineteenth century, land grant colleges spread across the mid-continent. Frederick Law Olmstead, the founder of American landscape architecture, was responsible for many of their typically parklike designs. At about this time more and more women were admitted at some colleges and universities, athletic facilities became more important, and the curriculum broadened to embrace new disciplines. Some of these changes were echoed in an explosion of new buildings, or resisted by revivals of classical design, but, ultimately both the changes and the challenges became integrated into the architectural record still visible both at individual schools, and in college architecture generally.

Figure 11–6   The University of Virginia at Charlottesville still reflects Thomas Jefferson's early design.

theory (again refer to Figure 11–5). "Procedure" refers to the method of gathering data or making decisions, and "substance" to a series of useful facts about the relationship between environmental variables such as color, privacy, or furnishings and the ability of a design to provide commodity, firmness, and delight. We believe that psychology can make both procedural and substantive contributions to design.

THE PROCESS OF DESIGN: FOSTERING COMMUNICATION

The architect is faced with quite a challenge in attempting to design structures that address the needs of his or her clients. With hindsight it is probably an easy task for you to think of instances in your own home or campus environment in which building design is not congruent with the needs of you, the user. Ironically, the premium our society places on originality and the explosion of building technology make errors almost inevitable (e.g., Alexander et al., 1975; Rapoport, 1969).

One of psychology's most important contributions may be insights into the complex process of information gathering and decision making that occurs in the design process (Lang, 1987; Zeisel, 1981). We should think of design as an evolutionary process that involves selecting from a variety of alternatives in search of **congruence** or fit between buildings and their user (Michelson, 1977b). Designs that support or facilitate the desires and needs of the people using them are said to be congruent. However, arrangements of space inevitably restrict behavioral options (we cannot walk through a wall unless a door is there), and to the extent that these restrictions inhibit preferred ways of behaving, users will be dissatisfied and negative reactions will be manifested. Congruence

is also referred to as **habitability**, particularly in residential settings. Habitability refers to how well a particular environment fits the needs of those who live within it (Nelson, 1976).

In our discussion of behavior settings in Chapter 4, we emphasized that a particular physical setting might support a number of different behaviors depending on the specific program or occasion. One way to achieve greater congruence or habitability is to "design in" flexibility, thereby ensuring that the space can support a variety of behaviors (Zeisel, 1975). Flexibility might occur at several levels. At the most global, flexibility might include design provisions to allow an entire building to change its function—from administrative to classroom, for instance. Within a building, flexibility might be enhanced with flexible partitions, adjustable lighting and movable furniture (see Figure 11–7). At an even smaller scale, flexibility might in-

Figure 11–7   Flexible design allows buildings to change to meet a variety of functional needs.

clude provisions allowing individuals to adapt their own micro-environment. For example, O'Neil documented the importance of allowing workers to adjust their workplace furniture (O'Neil, 1994). Such personal adjustments not only allow the individual to "fine tune" his or her environment, but should increase perceived control (see Chapters 4 and 5).

The ability of a designer to adjust the physical environment to achieve congruence is determined in part by the number of potential **design alternatives** (or different ways we can think of to design or redesign a setting). Any given setting may offer a large number of design alternatives, but as different criteria are brought to bear, more and more alternatives will be ruled out. For example, some may be too expensive, others may be inappropriate due to their behavioral effects, and, of course, some may simply be out of style. The process of determining the proper design alternatives and weighing the importance of various criteria forms the heart of the design process. This is a complex un-

dertaking since there are many interrelationships among design alternatives as well as many different social, economic, artistic, and cultural pressures.

THE GAPS

In most introductory treatments of behavior-based design it has become common practice to speak of "the **gap**." In this instance, the term refers to a failure of communication (see Figure 11–8). In fact, there are several gaps, but the one most commonly discussed is based on the discontinuity between designers and those who will eventually live and work in their buildings (Thiel, 1994; Zeisel, 1975, 1981). Unlike primitive or preindustrial vernacular cultures, the eventual users of modern architecture (using clients) are seldom directly consulted in the design process. As several authors (e.g., Mitchell, 1974; Zeisel, 1975, 1981) have noted, often the architect only has direct contact with the paying client, perhaps a corporation or governmental agency. The problem is easy to

Figure 11–8 An illustration of the gaps between the paying and using client, between designers and clients, and between behavioral scientists and designers

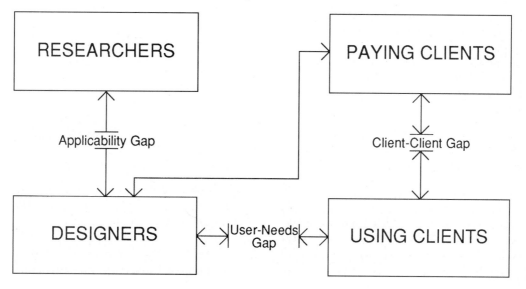

illustrate. Were you (or some other student before you) consulted by the architect responsible for the classrooms in which you learn or the residence halls in which you or your classmates dwell? Because most individuals buy either an older home or one designed and built by a developer, it is almost as unusual for a family to have an opportunity to participate directly in the design of their home.

Increasing communication between designers and their clients may seem to be an unremarkable suggestion, but successful communication is not accidental. The only reason to hire a designer in the first place is because the owner is incapable (or unwilling) to do the design alone. On the other hand, it may be that design education and training shapes and changes the expert's perceptions of the environment (Devlin, 1990; Groat, 1982; Kaplan & Kaplan, 1982; S. Kaplan, 1987). For example, Groat (1982) reported that accountants were more likely to classify buildings according to preference or building type, whereas architects were more likely to include judgments of building style, form, design quality, or historic significance. More recently, Devlin (1990) compared the content of published architectural reviews of two buildings with on-site interviews with nonarchitects. Architects apparently paid more attention to design ideas and concepts, whereas nonarchitects were more likely to make general affective (emotional) judgments or descriptions of the physical features of a building.

FOSTERING PARTICIPATION

There are several ways to improve the chances that the needs and wants of the using client are incorporated into a new design. One way to close the gap would be to train experts to be more sensitive to people's concerns (Kaplan & Kaplan, 1982). Even more straightforward, the users could be included in the actual design process (e.g., Kaplan & Kaplan, 1982; Kaplan & Kaplan, 1989; Theil, 1994). Kaplan and Kaplan (1982) lament that the single most striking aspect of participation as it is now practiced is how badly it works. Although design experts are likely to recognize the complexity and ambiguity of many design questions, they are asked to make quick, confident, and cost-effective decisions—a requirement that in the short term at least, is likely to conflict with the laborious process of gathering and assimilating data from the public (Dalholm & Rydberg-Mitchell, 1992; Kaplan & Kaplan, 1982).

Several themes that seem to characterize instances of successful participation were suggested by Kaplan and Kaplan (1982):

1. Involving the public at an early stage in design so that their suggestions can be fairly integrated into design alternatives. The public will rightfully feel offended if their participation is invited only when most of the decisions have already been made.
2. Availability of several concrete alternatives to react to. The designer's expertise can demonstrate the scope of design alternatives and present options that allow straightforward responses.
3. Presentation of possibilities in a format that is comprehensible. In particular, the use of visual or spatial material can make it possible for lay persons to visualize design alternatives.

To summarize, a concerted effort needs to be made to accurately communicate design alternatives to laypersons so that they may make substantive and informed decisions. Designers may have developed ways of visualizing design alternatives and communicating with other professionals that may not be comfortable for laypersons. Simulations such as models or drawings are frequently employed by designers in communicating with clients and other designers. Certainly new technology, especially new computer visualization programs and equipment, allow designers an unprecedented ability to model design alternatives (Decker, 1994; Theil, 1994), although the complexity of computer software makes it difficult for laypersons to use such programs to express their own ideas. Not all of what an architect reads in a drawing is necessarily perceived by laypersons, however. For instance, the symbols used by architects for windows, doors and other features may be unfamiliar to laypersons, and the scale may be distorted (Dalholm & Rydberg-Mitchell, 1992). The process can be reversed by asking laypersons to make drawings. Although users seem able to communicate relationships between the desired size and location of large spaces, bathrooms, doors, closets, and hallways are often drawn too small, leading Dalholm and Rydberg-Mitchell (1992) to advocate the use of small-scale or even full-scale models in addition to drawings. On the other hand, detail and exactness in simulation may actually be counterproductive. A model that pretends to be a perfect replica of an actual design is likely to be expensive, and may simply activate the human tendency to try to find all of the little discrepancies between the model and reality. Instead, the Kaplans (1982) propose very rough models, sometimes as simple as building blocks. These are inexpensive, adaptable, and enlist the viewer as a collaborator.

SUBSTANTIVE CONTRIBUTIONS

We have emphasized the importance of communication for gathering information about user needs and wants. Needs and wants form the basis of the program of a proposed construction. In order to support commodity, firmness, and delight, designers must match the program to materials, construction techniques, and spaces that support it. In other words, designers must consult a body of what Lang (1987, 1988) called substantive theory. Of course much of this body of knowledge is beyond the domain of behavioral science. Firmness is a very desirable characteristic of buildings, since it prevents the roof from falling on our heads, but structural materials are not the domain of psychology. On the other hand, most of this book might be seen as a source for designers who wish to gather information that will help them predict the aesthetic and behavioral effects of their design. Before beginning our review, we must acknowledge yet another gap in communication.

The **applicability gap** (Russell & Ward, 1982; Seidel, 1985) is a name given to the miscommunication between psychologists trying to understand the needs of architects, and designers who try to come to grips with the data and the implications of social and behavioral sciences (again, see Figure 11–8). Recognition of the applicability gap prompts questions regarding research methodology and philosophy of science, and represents an unresolved tension in the youthful field of environmental psychology. Altman (1973, 1975) emphasizes that the design process must reflect the different approaches of the various people involved in environmental design. In particular, he feels that practitioners, such as architects, are inclined to attend primarily to design criteria and to particular places or settings. Researchers, on the other hand, are more likely to stress ongoing behavioral processes, such as privacy, territoriality, or personal space. Academicians often value their independence, that is, their ability to choose to investigate almost any question that interests them. They are also typically (rightfully) committed to cautious interpretation of their data. Unfortunately, at least for those who wish to see the early application of behavioral design, these goals of science sometimes result in a situation that encourages psychologists to ask simple research questions that may show statistical elegance but that hold little promise for application. Furthermore, the implications of the research literature can be difficult for design professionals to extract from the jargon and statistical descriptions of research journals. If behavioral science is to offer designers useful data, it should be more responsive to practical questions of design. On the other hand, the whole point of statistics and careful research design is to ensure that conclusions are drawn carefully and objectively. Psychology will suffer painfully from sloppy or misinterpreted findings. This balance between caution in interpretation and relevance in research topics is likely to pose one of the thorniest problems for environmental psychology in the years to come.

On a different issue we might add that if a psychologist wishes to serve as a liaison between professionals and their clients, he or she would profit from a basic understanding of the graphics and technical references used by designers. In a sense, a successful liaison must be able to translate between the dialects spoken by both the professional and lay participants. The training of most psychologists is at least as inadequate in preparing them to understand design as a designer's training is in preparing her or him to interpret scientific research.

How eager are designers to integrate relevant behavioral information in their designs? "Cautious" would be the simplest answer. In fact, some (e.g., Sime, 1986) suggest that architecture in the late 1970s began to react against the idea of collaboration with social scientists, partly, no doubt, out of pure

frustration. More hopeful signs come from interdisciplinary design conferences. For example, each year the Environmental Design Research Association (EDRA) holds a conference that attracts behavioral scientists and designers who share an interest in behaviorally based design (Werner & Szigeti, 1987).

Again, behavioral research with promise for integration in design appears throughout this text. For instance, issues of perception, legibility, perceived control, ambient stress, and crowding are both theoretical and applied. The special challenges of particularly important environments have also led us to highlight behavioral settings such as schools, museums, the workplace, natural environments, and cities in Chapters 10, 12, and 13. Before we conclude our examination of architecture and design, however, we will inspect several additional dimensions of the physical environment that are particularly relevant to design.

PRIVACY

One of the most important aspects of the design of interior space is the amount of privacy it provides. Altman (1975) has defined privacy as the "selective control of access to the self or one's group." This definition has two important parts. The first is the notion of privacy as an ability to withdraw or separate ourselves from other people. In effect, this refers to the desire for seclusion. Both Altman, and Ittelson et al. (1974) recognize a second important aspect of privacy— the ability to personalize spaces in order to present information about ourselves. Thus, privacy represents a dynamic process of openness/closedness to others (Altman & Chemers, 1980). Personal space and territory are behavioral mechanisms that regulate privacy; crowding or the loss of perceived control represent failures to achieve it. Perhaps all humans have a desire both to communicate and to keep some aspects of our personalities or thoughts to ourselves. Architectural features or policies that encourage personalization will support the presentation of personal information, whereas other characteristics of the physical environment (the lack of walls in an office or school for instance; see Chapter 13) may prevent us from regulating what other people find out about us (see Figure 11–9A and 9B). Designs that optimize privacy have to consider both elements of Altman's definition, as well as the fact that privacy means different things to different people. For example, dormitories that house students one instead of two to a bedroom promote greater privacy. Likewise, the use of barriers around one's work area may increase the sense of privacy. Often, then, privacy adjustment is centered around the structures that partition interior space.

Figure 11–9A & 9B Privacy adjustment may be established with physical or even psychological barriers.

One way in which an environment can directly affect feelings of privacy is by increasing or decreasing the possibility of seeing and being seen by other people. This refers to visual intrusion—that sense of privacy that is more difficult to achieve when people can still be seen. If you lived in a glass house and could see people outside and vice versa, your sense of privacy would be less than if you could block them out. Consistent with this, research has indicated that barriers that block views of other people decrease the impact of these people, while barriers that do not obscure the view (e.g., clear panels) do not reduce their impact (e.g., Baum, Reiss, & O'Hara, 1974; Desor, 1972). Interestingly, some research suggests that the lack of auditory privacy may be even more troubling than losses of visual privacy. In particular, we are troubled by environments that make it likely that private conversations will be overheard (Sundstrom et al., 1994).

When an environment does not provide enough privacy for those using it, problems develop. Vinsel et al. (1980) found that students who dropped out of college for "nonacademic" reasons were less likely to have been able to achieve adequate privacy in their dormitories than those who stayed in school. Among the problems the "dropouts" mentioned were an inability to find a quiet place to be alone and a reluctance to invite people to their rooms. Studies have also shown that apartment building designs that do not promote privacy between apartment units are associated with resident dissatisfaction (Zeisel & Griffin, 1975).

MATERIALS AND COLOR

The old story of the Three Little Pigs suggests some simple differences in firmness as a function of materials. Of more interest to us are perceptual or evaluative differences between different types of building materials (see Figure 11–10).

Figure 11–10 This new bridge combines laminated wooden arches with metal hardware. The materials accentuate the bridge as a machine.

As Heimstra and McFarling (1978) noted some time ago, color is one of the most easily manipulated dimensions of environmental surfaces. In a business setting, for example, a coat of paint is far less costly than structural remodeling. Surprisingly, there is very little recent research directed specifically at the effectiveness of various manipulations of environmental color. Like Sanders and McCormick (1987), we are forced to conclude that the literature addressing the application of color is dominated by opinion rather than research.

A number of investigators have examined the possibility of a relationship between color and temperature. Early reports (e.g., Newhall, 1941; Ross, 1938; Wright & Rainwater, 1962) suggest that warm temperatures were most often associated with reds and oranges, whereas coolness was associated with blues and greens. But were these early investigations successful in delineating the psychological effects of color in a way that can be applied to design? That is, does the color of the walls in the room in which you are now reading affect your perception of the room's temperature? Many aspects of color are tangled in a web of symbolism. Simply asking subjects to report color-temperature associations may only tap an individual's ability to repeat these learned, perhaps wholly symbolic associations. The answer came from studies in which experimenters actually manipulated room color and temperature, while eliminating the demand on subjects to repeat learned color-temperature associations.

As a rule, investigators who have adequately controlled the tendency for subjects to try to respond "correctly" with the usual color-temperature symbolisms have failed to find useful effects (Bennett & Rey, 1972; Berry, 1961; Fanger, Breum, & Jerking, 1977; Greene & Bell, 1980). The study by Berry (1961) neatly makes our point. Berry chose to investigate the effects of color on the comfort of subjects seated in a heated room. Participants were ostensibly performing a task designed to determine the effects of colored light on performance in an automobile driving simulator. They were told that the lights generated a great deal of heat and that they should notify the experimenter when they became uncomfortably warm. Berry concluded that the color of the illumination (green, blue, yellow, amber) did not affect the level of tolerable heat. Subsequently, however, Berry asked the same subjects to rank samples of the experimental colors in terms of the amount of heat they transmitted. Thus cued, most ranked the colors in the conventional hue-heat order (again, warmth with amber, coolness with blue and green).

Some of the most useful design applications of color may come from studies showing that perception of spaciousness, or conversely, crowding, may be influenced by color. For instance, Acking and Kuller (1972) had subjects rate a series of slides depicting rooms which varied in color. Results indicated that lighter rooms were seen as more open and spacious. Similarly, Baum and Davis (1976) found that different intensities of the same color affected subjects' response to model rooms. Light-green rooms appeared larger and less crowded than identical rooms painted a darker green.

Our discussion of color introduced an important question about the effect of visible building materials. Are differences in the impressions of various materials based on direct differences in sensation, differences in utility (weather resistance, for instance), or are they symbolic? Sadalla and Sheets (1993) report that the materials covering the facades of houses may be perceived as indicators of the interpersonal style, creativity, and social class of the homeowner, especially if the homeowner was perceived as having a role in choosing the material. For example, wood coverings were associated with more "emotional," "weaker," "tender," and "feminine" owners.

ILLUMINATION

Different lighting conditions may also have subtle effects on social behavior and mood. Information regarding these effects of lighting on social relationships is scarce, and some of it seems contradictory. Two commonly held beliefs are that low levels of light lead to both greater intimacy and to quieter or reduced conversation (e.g., Feller, 1968; Saunders, Gustanski, & Lawton, 1974). Several studies support these common beliefs. For example, Gergen, Gergen, and Barton (1973) reported that when college students who were strangers to each other were placed in a dark room for several hours, considerable verbal and physical intimacy occurred between them. Darkness and anonymity had apparently removed some customary barriers to intimacy. More recently, Butler and Biner (1987) used a questionnaire format to determine the lighting preferences of a large sample of college students. Participants in the studies reported their preferred lighting levels, the importance of these lighting levels, and the degree to which they desired control over the lighting levels. Having the proper lighting level was rated as most important in instances in which individuals reported preferences for either a rather dark (e.g., during a romantic interlude) or very bright (cutting vegetables with a knife) lighting level. Predictably, control over the level of lighting was more important in some environments than others, and particularly important for those expressing strong lighting preferences.

In spite of these findings, the effects probably depend on the environmental context we are in. For example, dark spaces in the inner city may be depressing or frightening, while in other settings they can be quite romantic, facilitating intimacy. The importance of further investigation is highlighted by two recent studies which conflict with the two common beliefs about the social effects of illumination we cited above. With respect to the amount of intimate communication, Gifford (1988) reports a laboratory study of the effects of illumination levels on the amount and intimacy of written communication between female college students. As expected, a brightly lit room stimulated general communication, but brighter light actually encouraged more rather than less intimate communication. Furthermore, another study (Veitch & Kaye, 1988) found that sound levels were actually lower in the brighter of two experimental rooms for female students engaged in a discussion. Among several explanations for these results is the possibility that early studies may have tapped responses in situations in which people have learned to speak quietly (e.g., restaurants) because they have learned that it is appropriate, rather than because of some direct effect of low light levels on conversations.

WINDOWS

Perhaps the most persuasive support for the generous use of windows comes from a growing literature documenting therapeutic effects of hospital windows overlooking pleasant landscape views (e.g., Ulrich, 1984; Verderber, 1986). For example, Ulrich (1984) reports that patients with pleasant landscape views outside their hospital rooms had shorter postoperative hospital stays, required lower doses of painkillers, and had fewer negative evaluative comments from nurses. Other evidence of the importance of windows comes from studies of windowless schools. Originally designed to reduce distraction in the classroom, as well as to lower heating costs and vandalism, these school buildings typically contain few if any windows. Research has suggested that the absence of windows

in classrooms has no consistent effect on learning (some students improve, others show poorer performance), but that it does have a negative impact on mood (Karmel, 1965; see also Chapter 13).

Although we might conclude that windows are generally appreciated, preferences for the amount of window space vary across different types of spaces. For example, one survey found that large windows were preferred for family rooms, dorm rooms, and libraries. In these environments, factors such as a view, sunlight, and mood influenced window preferences. On the other hand, an absence of windows was desirable in public bathrooms where privacy seemed to be somewhat more important (Butler & Biner, 1989).

FURNISHINGS

Furniture, its arrangement, and other aspects of the interior environment are also important determinants of behavior. In classroom settings, for example, it appears that the use of nontraditional seating patterns can influence student performance; horseshoe arrangements, circular patterns, or other less formal departures from the standard "rows of desks facing the teacher" seem to generate more student interest and participation (Sommer, 1969). Some evidence even implies that within traditional classroom arrangements there are differences in performance according to where people sit. These findings are discussed in Chapter 8.

Many studies of furniture arrangements have been conducted in institutional settings. Reusch and Kees (1956) have noted that the way in which patients arrange their furniture expresses their feelings regarding interaction in their space. Some arrangements (called **sociopetal**) are open and welcome interaction, while others (called **sociofugal**) are closed and discourage social contact. Sommer and Ross (1958) described the relation between furniture arrangement and behavior in a geriatric hospital. When chairs were arranged in rows along the walls, patients did not interact very much. This arrangement was simply not conducive to talking; it did not suggest that interaction was appropriate. When Sommer and Ross changed the arrangement, clustering the chairs in small groups, people began to talk to each other. The new juxtaposition facilitated conversation while the old one seemed to inhibit it. Holahan (1972) found the same kind of effect in a psychiatric hospital—patients seated around the table talked to each other more than patients seated in rows against the walls (for a thorough discussion of design in selected institutional environments, see Chapter 12).

Furniture arrangements can be used to help structure the preexisting architectural layout of a setting. In most environmental contexts, the walls, the location of the doors, and so on are fixed—they are rather difficult to move. To some extent, these elements do structure the space inside a building. However, the placement of furniture often provides additional organization. For example, if you have a large living room, you may arrange the furniture to suggest two rooms. Or, you may arrange it to unify the room.

Arrangement is not the only aspect of furnishings that can affect mood and behavior. The quality of the furnishings is also important. Later, we will discuss studies of the effects of "pretty" and "ugly" rooms and discover that being in a pretty room can sometimes have beneficial psychological effects. Unfortunately, studies varying the quality of single pieces or sets of furniture have not been done systematically. However, research has also been done on the effects of large-scale improvements in furnishings. Holahan and Saegert (1973) reported on a large-scale refurbishing of a psychiatric hospital admissions ward, comparing it to another ward that was not redone. The refurbishing included bringing in new furniture, repainting, and creating different types of space. These improvements in the quality of the environment led to increases in social activity on the ward and demonstrated that the quality of an environment can influence mood and behavior. However, because the improvements were so extensive, it is difficult to know what was primarily responsible for the observed results.

Ultimately, any decision about furnishings will be based on several criteria, including cost, aesthetics, and the function of the setting. This latter criterion is often the most difficult to evaluate. Sometimes a given space is expected to facilitate communication between employees working near each other, to serve as a meeting room on occasion, and to impress clients who come for consultations. Some of these functions are at odds with each other, and the choice of arrangement of furnishings must be accomplished with these complex issues in mind.

ARCHITECTURAL AESTHETICS

One of the primary goals of a design is to evoke a pleasurable response from people viewing the finished setting. The study of aesthetics in architecture is an attempt to identify, understand and, eventually, to learn to create those features of an environment that lead to pleasurable responses. The problem is that aesthetic considerations in design may operate contrary to behavioral ones. Some of the most beautiful structures are also among the most impractical. However, one cannot simply dismiss aesthetic quality as less relevant than the behavioral effects of design. Indeed, there is evidence that aesthetics may be important in determining behavior (e.g., Nasar, 1994; Steinitz, 1968).

Some authors differentiate between two kinds of aesthetic design orientations (Lang, 1988; Nasar, 1994). *Formal aesthetics* include dimensions such as shape, proportion, scale, complexity, novelty, and illumination. On the other hand, *symbolic aesthetics* are affected by different sorts of meaning. Some meanings are denotative—for instance, a building's function (bank or prison) or style (postmodern, Gothic). Other symbolic meanings may be connotative. Is your campus library's architecture friendly? Imposing?

According to Nasar's review (1994, p. 384) the primary formal variables include: enclosure (openness, spaciousness, density, mystery), complexity (diversity, visual richness, ornamentation, information rate), and order (unity, order, clarity). Well-defined natural spaces that balance openness and enclosure are preferred to either wide-open or highly enclosed landscapes. Complexity reflects diversity and visual richness. According to Berlyne (1974), interest increases with complexity, whereas preference will peak at moderate complexity levels. Order, or the degree to which environments are legible (see Chapters 2 and 3) or coherent is also associated with increased preference.

Although not specifically discussed by Nasar, the Gestalt rules of perceptual organization (see Chapter 3) may also provide clues to the formal application. According to Lang (1987), formal aesthetics has traditionally been heavily dependent on the **Gestalt theory** of perception which views the organization of elements of visual form as units which can be perceived as either simple or complex. Although Gestalt theory is now considered to apply only to a rather limited number of situations, it appeals to the designer's need for an understanding of visual forms at a broad, holistic level. For many designers, the implication is that environments ordered according to these principles of "good form" will also be good environments, whereas other designers (e.g., Venturi, 1966) deliberately violate Gestalt principles as a means for obtaining visually richer environments.

Nasar (1994, p. 389) also outlines sources of symbolic aesthetics: naturalness, upkeep, intensity of use, and style. As we saw in Chapter 2, a number of authors have confirmed the importance of naturalness in aesthetic preference (e.g., Kaplan & Kaplan, 1989; Ulrich, 1992). Style, which incorporates meaning and normative dimensions has also been well documented as a source of aesthetic appreciation. Although style preferences may vary depending on the function of a particular building and even sociodemographic groups, vernacular architecture or architecture with an old and genuine "feel" may be appreciated more than modern styles.

Research has indicated that the aesthetic quality of a room, the extent to which it is pleasant or attractive for instance, may affect the sorts of evaluations we make while in that setting. In one classic study, Maslow and Mintz (1956) compared subjects' ratings of a series of photographs of individuals in a "beautiful" room (well-decorated, well-lit, etc.), an average room (a professor's office), and an "ugly" room (resembling a janitor's closet). Their results showed that subjects rated the persons in the photos most positively if they had been in the beautiful room, and most negatively if they had been in the ugly room.

Attractive environments also make people feel better. Research has shown that decorated spaces make people feel more comfortable than ones which have not been decorated (Campbell, 1979). Also, the good moods that are associated with pleasant environments seem to increase people's willingness to help each other (Sherrod et al., 1977). People feel more like talking to one another in pleasant settings (Russell & Mehrabian, 1978). Research has also suggested that decoration may be distracting (e.g., Baum & Davis, 1976), but whether this is necessarily a problem appears to depend on other factors (Worchel & Teddlie, 1976).

SELECTING ALTERNATIVES: THE DESIGN CYCLE

Whether the design criteria are behavioral or structural, normative or substantive, we see a need for a reliable model for integrating program, data, and design. Thus, design is seen as an example of problem solving. As a student of psychology, one thing you may have learned about problem solving is that it is not rational. We know that humans generally fall far short of the optimal solution to a problem, accepting instead solutions that "satisfice"—that is, solutions that are "good enough" (Kaplan & Kaplan, 1989; Simon, 1960). Because there is such a variety of apparently acceptable solutions for most projects, and because even poor designs may appear successful until after a great deal of effort has gone into developing them, one of the designer's most difficult problems may be in deciding when to stop design and begin construction. Instead of proceeding in a smooth, directed path, Zeisel (1981) suggests that a spiral metaphor is a better representation of the design process. In separate cycles, architects propose, test, and refine possible solutions to sets of related problems (see Figure 11–11). The result of each cycle will be a possible response to a particular design problem, but this decision may limit the alternative solutions to another set of problems. By testing ideas, finding conflicts, then retesting, the spiral will gradually narrow until it lies within the domain of acceptable solutions, at which point construction will begin.

STAGES IN THE DESIGN PROCESS

Each time we employ a design alternative to adjust our environment to make it more congruent (or habitable), we use the design process (again, see Figure 11–11 for one outline of the various stages involved in the design process). It begins with an awareness of both needs, and of potential design alternatives (environmental adjustments). Once a need and a possible design alternative have been specified, it is necessary to develop criteria for determining how effectively the proposed alternatives resolve the need. Although criteria may be physical in nature, as in quality specifications for building materials, as psychologists our interest is on behavioral criteria, such as ease of movement.

Frequently, some kind of research or evaluation must be performed in order to know whether specific design alternatives measure up to the criteria established for them. When such evaluation indicates the desirability of a particular alternative, additional steps must be taken to implement the design. Models of the design process that stress cooperation of environmental quality, and **post-occupancy evaluation (POE)** can be effective tools in going beyond this step and arriving at the goal of a habitable environment.

How can we be even more certain that improved design will follow awareness of environmental quality and environmental design alternatives? Ideally, a continuous cycle of design planning and evaluation should occur for every building project (Zeisel, 1975, 1981). We should note that other equally useful models, which we do not have the space to describe, also exist. (Interested readers might wish to consult Broadbent, 1973; Kaplan & Kaplan, 1982; and Weisman, 1983). Such a **design cycle** would permit information gained from an existing project to be applied immediately to the next project, which in turn should be evaluated for the planning phase of still another project. Zeisel's model of this process includes five distinct steps that would be repeated for every new design project (Figure 11–11).

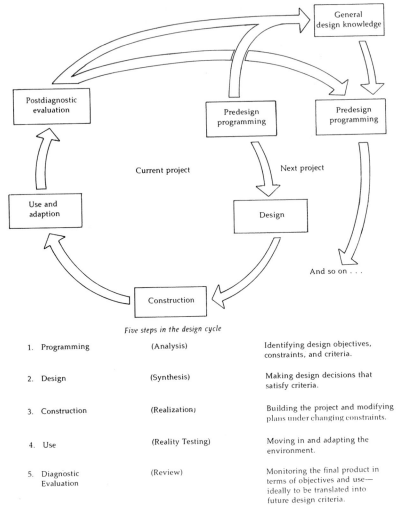

Five steps in the design cycle

1. Programming	(Analysis)	Identifying design objectives, constraints, and criteria.
2. Design	(Synthesis)	Making design decisions that satisfy criteria.
3. Construction	(Realization)	Building the project and modifying plans under changing constraints.
4. Use	(Reality Testing)	Moving in and adapting the environment.
5. Diagnostic Evaluation	(Review)	Monitoring the final product in terms of objectives and use— ideally to be translated into future design criteria.

Figure 11–11   Zeisel's design spiral

Adapted from Zeisel, 1975. Sociology and architectural design: Social science frontiers, No. 6. New York: Russell Sage Foundation.

AMERICAN COLLEGE CAMPUSES: AN EXAMPLE OF DESIGN DYNAMICS

Modern college campuses illustrate most of the issues outlined by Lang. What factors weighed most heavily in your decision to attend your college or university? Was your choice purely rational, or was it influenced by taste or even whimsy? According to one survey, 60 percent of college-bound students rank the visual environment as the most im-portant factor in choosing a college (Carnegie Foundation as reported by Gaines, 1991). The physical layouts of American colleges and universities reflect both their European heritage (particularly British) and the unique value Americans place on higher education. In spite of what seems to be a self-conscious desire to be perceived as unique or special, there are many common themes which can be identified on American college campuses. As Gaines (1991) notes, many have a core space or quadrangle such as:

- The Oval   Michigan State University
- The Heart   Earlham
- The Yard   Harvard
- Prexie's Pasture   University of Wyoming
- The Horseshoe   University of South Carolina
- The Lawn   University of Virginia
- The Meadow   Mills College
- The Plaza of the Americas   University of Florida

The buildings and grounds of campuses represent a rich physical record of changing design innovations and architectural norms. Architectural features are likely to become the symbol for the university or college, or even a state. Figure 11–12A shows The Old Well, a popular meeting spot at the University of North Carolina at Chapel Hill, and Figure 11–12B is the view of the Capitol of Wisconsin from Bascom Hill on the University of Wisconsin campus. As an aside, we cannot help but mention that the latter vista was threatened briefly in the late 1980s when a miscalculation nearly resulted in an addition to the main library which would have blocked part of Bascom Hill's view toward the State Capitol building. Plans were redrawn, the building was shortened by several stories, and the newly poured concrete stairwell (already visible in the distance in Figure 11–12B) was removed. We see this as an example of both the fallibility of design,

Figure 11–12A The Old Well, a popular meeting spot at the University of North Carolina, Chapel Hill

Figure 11–12B View from Bascom Hill at the University of Wisconsin, Madison

and the importance of landscapes and vistas to college campuses.

At many institutions the campus buildings and grounds reveal periods of stability and periods of growth, the establishment of new programs and the abandonment of those that have lost favor, and the effect of evolving architectural fashions from Georgian to post-modern (see box on page 418). For example, before the late 1960s most coeducational colleges and universities housed men and women in separate dormitories, or at the very least, on separate floors (also see Chapter 9 for an additional discussion of residence halls). As students began to demand less segregation between men and women, many residence halls mixed men and women's bathrooms, but often without investing in the expense of replacing the old sex-typed plumbing. The 1970s and 1980s introduced an era in which new regulations promoting safety, energy conservation, and accessibility for the physically challenged are now leaving their marks. A little detective work will probably reveal a variety of physical traces that reflect normative changes on a campus familiar to you.

Although some common campus design prototypes (the green parklike campus, for instance) dominate, there are clearly many exceptions and differences in expression of these prototypes. Unfortunately, one problem shared by campuses, urban and rural alike, is a fear of crime. Fear of sexual assault by women students, faculty, and staff results in both worry, and a restriction in freedom of movement, particularly at night (Day, 1994; Koss, Gudycz, & Wisiniewski, 1987). The degree to which sexual assault can be reduced by changes in grounds design is unclear. In fact, the actual number of cases of assault is often unknown. It may be that the frequency of sexual assault has been intentionally obscured on some campuses to preserve an image of safety. Furthermore, many assaults occur indoors and many assailants

are acquaintances. Nevertheless, some factors associated with fear on campus include the presence of features such as dense vegetation that provide an assailant a place to hide, low potential for escape, and poor lighting (Day, 1994; Fisher & Nasar, 1992; Kirk, 1988; Nasar & Fisher, 1992). Ironically, the same features that make a landscape attractive during the daylight hours (vegetation, enclosed space) make the same landscapes feared at night (Day, 1994; Shoen, 1991).

PLANNING FOR THE FUTURE

Most colleges and universities have a master plan, a map or series of maps with supporting documents which seek to coordinate future building projects. The goal of these plans is to prevent haphazard growth and isolated constructions that lack coordination with other campus facilities or design styles. (The box on pages 436–437 describes one example of the integration of psychology in the planning efforts of one small college.)

The layout of campus buildings sometimes resulted from immediate needs or a particular college administration's artistic sense. Some, such as Thomas Jefferson's University of Virginia, continue to reflect the cohesive vision of their past (Gaines, 1991; Turner, 1984). Our society has become more pluralistic ever since Jefferson's time, however, and to succeed aesthetically it may now be necessary for a campus to reflect the input of planners, social scientists, officials, and naturalists (Gaines, 1991). One of the best known proposals for user participation in college design was developed by Christopher Alexander and his colleagues (Alexander, 1979; Alexander, Ishikawa, & Silverstein, 1977; Alexander et al., 1975). Although this approach is quite normative, it does directly address the Kaplans' three themes (see page 422). Like Rapoport, Alexander believes that modern design has lost many of the advantages of participation and slow evolution that were characteristic of primitive and preindustrial cultures. In particular, Alexander attacks the modern approach in which roads are built by engineers, buildings by architects, and tract housing by developers. In Alexander's view, the average citizen has lost the ability to affect design, and designers have lost touch with the needs of those they serve. The Oregon Experience (Alexander et al., 1975) illustrates the participative process as Alexander would implement it on a college campus (in this case the University of Oregon).

Alexander advocates participative planning, but finds master plans themselves to be too rigid, too likely to constrain growth to

...g problems or situations that are designed to be understandable to both architects and laypersons.

HUMAN FACTORS: ENGINEERING FOR HUMAN DESIGN

Can careful design of the tools, machines, and workspaces in an office, kitchen, or factory increase productivity? Psychology's interest in facilitating human performance in different environments, especially our interactions with machines, has a long history that predates the establishment of the field of environmental psychology (see the box on page 439). For instance, there is considerable overlap between environmental psychology and the domain of **human factors** psychologists (human factors psychology is also sometimes referred to as engineering psychology, or, especially in Europe, as **ergonomics**). According to one popular textbook: "Human factors focuses on human beings and their interactions with products, equipment, facilities, procedures, and environments used in work and everyday living" (Sanders & McCormick, 1987, p. 4). In spite of their obvious similarity and common literature, the historical development and focus of human factors and environmental psy-

chology are somewhat different. First, although the definition makes it clear that human factors psychologists do not restrict themselves to work settings, many of them do and their field is often thought of as a subdiscipline of industrial/organizational psychology. Second, the dependent variable in human factors research is more likely to measure levels of performance on some task rather than emotional or cognitive responses.

Many of the early efforts of these investigators and practitioners focused not on the ambient environment, but on specific tools or procedures such as link analysis that might increase worker efficiency. For example, Taylor (1911) demonstrated dramatic improvements in efficiency when steel workers were issued the optimal-sized shovel for each shoveling task—smaller ones for heavy iron ore and larger ones for ashes. More recent human factors research emphasizes either the interactions between humans and machines (computers, aircraft, nuclear power

11-13 was mentioned in our discussion of cognitive maps in Chapter 3. ...u may recall that the map indicates the mean (average) ratings of pleasantness for a small college campus, and was obtained by electronically overlaying individual maps drawn by several hundred students. As you can see, the most pleasant area appears in the lower left corner of the map, which is the area depicted in the photograph in Figure 11-14. The map is actually just the most recent of a series of cognitive mapping exercises that have traced changing evaluations

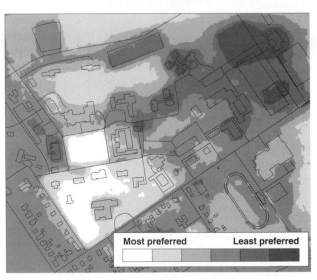

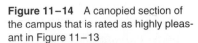

Most preferred   Least preferred

Figure 11-13 Pleasant and unpleasant areas of a college campus as rated by students

of the small campus (Greene & Connelly, 1988; Shoen, 1991). Could these data be useful for more than just academic purposes? As it happens, in the mid-1980s the university employed an architectural and planning firm to help create a new master plan to guide development for the next two decades. Architects for the project used some of the early results to determine preference zones for students and faculty. They also requested traffic pattern data (collected in a similar manner by asking students and faculty to draw their routes across campus on a typical day) summarized in Figure 11-15. Finally, they used their professional expertise and on-site observations to interpret the data and to create a new campus master plan (Figure

Figure 11-14 A canopied section of the campus that is rated as highly pleasant in Figure 11-13

11–16) that, among other things, removed parking lots and roads from the central campus. Subsequent studies (reported in Chapter 3) continue to be used for campus planning.

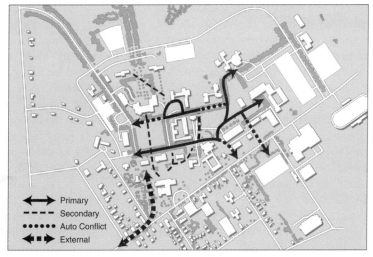

Figure 11–15   An architect's interpretation of traffic patterns on the college campus based on behavioral data.

Figure 11–16   Portions of the campus master plan that resulted partly from the analysis in Figures 11–13, 11–14, and 11–15

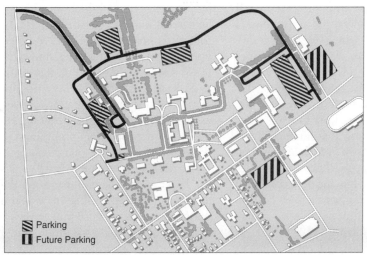

plants), the workstation, or the ambient environmental conditions such as noise, light, and temperature which we have discussed throughout much of this text.

One of the difficulties faced by human factors psychologists is having an opportunity to modify machine or systems engineering while the design process is underway. Often the human factors psychologist is brought into the design process either at the last minute before the system goes into production or in response to a failure in a pre-existing system. In these instances, human factors is likely to be "too little, too late" (Lim, Long, & Silcock, 1992).

Unfortunately, it is not difficult to find dramatic examples of instances in which human factors-related errors have catastrophic effects. A well-meaning safety check resulted in the Chernobyl nuclear power plant disaster, for instance. In Chapter 7 we discussed another dramatic nuclear incident. On March 29, 1979, an accident at Three Mile Island Unit 2 resulted in a crisis that lasted for several days, costing the plant owner over $1 billion and subjecting people living nearby to persistent stress. During the incident operators searched frantically to discover what was wrong with the reactor. Of the 1,600 windows and gauges in the control room (some 200 of which were flashing), several critical displays were in out-of-the-way locations, hidden by maintenance tags, or absent altogether. You may recognize this as a situation of information overload, discussed in Chapter 4. Resulting investigations revealed that many of the human errors that contributed to the accident resulted from grossly inadequate control room design (Smither, 1988). The incident sparked a flurry of interest in human factors, both in the nuclear power industry and more generally. Unfortunately, Chernobyl, airline accidents, and major power failures remind us that we are not yet truly the masters of our machines; many of us who interact with computers daily suspect the power in the relationship goes the other way.

COMMUNICATING WITH MACHINES

Perhaps you agree that features of a person's immediate work environment such as the displays and controls in an airplane's cockpit can greatly affect safety and health (see Figure 11–17). In general, human factors psychologists focus on the human–machine system, perhaps most easily understood as a communications cycle. The human being (pilot, driver, operator) makes decisions and communicates them to a machine through controls such as knobs, levers, steering wheels, or pedals. As it functions, the machine also communicates to the human operator through displays such as dials, gauges, or warning lights. No doubt, all of this seems simple enough, and it is unlikely that any engineer would knowingly design a machine that was impossible to control. The problem is making the human–machine system as efficient and error free as possible. Like human–human interactions, one important dimension of this communication process might be termed "trust." There are a number of instances in which an operation can be carried out by a person or left to the automatic control of a machine. When does an operator trust the machine, and when does he or she override the automatic functions (Lee & Moray, 1992)? The autopilot in an aircraft is one familiar example. Even more familiar might be the spell-checker in a computer word processing program. Does the flight officer trust the plane's autopilot? Do you trust your computer's spell-checker? In the latter example, a failure to use the spell-checking function is likely to reveal a number of instances in which you are less reliable than the machine. On the other hand, blindly trusting the software program may result in errors with homonyms, proper names, and other spelling nuances.

A HAWTHORNE IN THE SIDE OF ENVIRONMENTAL PSYCHOLOGY?

In the early 1900s Frederick Taylor proposed a management system based on the assumption that workers are primarily motivated by economic incentives. It was assumed that production would be greatest when pay was adequate and production techniques and the work environment were optimal. This approach was labeled scientific management and led to several investigations of environmental qualities such as heating and lighting. It also led to routine and standardized jobs and what some consider a rather unflattering picture of workers and their motivations.

One of the first real breaks with scientific management was promoted by a series of studies that took place beginning in the 1920s in the Hawthorne plant of the Western Electric Company near Chicago (Roethlisberger & Dickson, 1939). One of the early questions addressed by this project, which became known as the Hawthorne studies, was the effect of illumination on productivity. According to many reports, lighting levels were systematically varied for an experimental group, whereas a control group worked under constant illumination. Amazingly, both the experimental and control groups increased production. In follow-up observations, an experimental group was reported to have maintained their initial level of performance in spite of the fact that illumination had been reduced by 70 percent! Eventually the researchers only pretended to change the illumination level and yet workers continued to increase their production and to express pleasure with what they perceived to be better illumination. These bizarre results were interpreted at the time as suggesting that workers' performance increased as a result of novelty and the fact that workers knew they were being observed, rather than because of experimental changes. This interpretation came to be known as the **Hawthorne effect**.

In hindsight, the true meaning of the Hawthorne studies is open to discussion. A number of reviewers have pointed out methodological flaws that cast doubt on many of the conclusions drawn by the researchers (e.g., Franke & Kaul, 1978; Landesberger, 1958; Parsons, 1978). Indeed, the illumination studies which are so often recounted were never formally published and seem to have served mainly as an impetus for subsequent investigations of work schedules, supervision, and work group functions (Parsons, 1978).

Nevertheless, the illumination studies and the others that followed have had powerful effects, and in fact, probably led to a revolution in industrial/organizational psychology. In particular, the Hawthorne studies are often cited as the beginning of the human relations movement in American management (Landy, 1989; Saal & Knight, 1988). On the other hand, in focusing on the importance of the placebo-like "Hawthorne effect," these studies may have shifted research attention away from environmental variables such as illumination and delayed the development of what we now know as environmental psychology.

Figure 11-17　An aircraft cockpit

One of the most important principles in facilitating human–machine communication is what Norman (1988) calls **mapping**. Mapping refers to the relationship between the actions of an operator and those of a machine. Sometimes mapping is "natural," that is, consistent with physical or cultural analogies. For example, to move an object up, you should move the control up. Similarly, in order to unambiguously report an increase in altitude, perhaps an airplane's altimeter indicator should go up on a vertical scale (traditionally altimeters do not follow this advice, and the resulting errors in their use may account for at least some accidents; see Sanders & McCormick, 1987). In Chapter 3 we mentioned a powerful (but frequently violated) natural mapping known as forward-up equivalence (e.g., Levine, 1982)—what is up on a fixed information map in a mall or airport should be forward in the environment. Other mappings may at first seem just as obvious, but they may not be as clearly tied to natural events. To raise the volume of sound equipment, it is probably natural to raise a control lever, but most of us are also comfortable with a knob that requires a clockwise movement (Figure 11-18A). Does this seem unremarkable and natural? Now look at the knob in Figure 11-18B. What direction should you turn this knob to water the garden? In North America water faucets turn left to open (releasing more water) and right to close.

Consistent mapping relationships between human actions, controls, and displays

Figure 11–18A   A volume knob (turning right increases the volume)

Figure 11–18B   A water faucet (turning left increases the water flow)

are also sometimes referred to as "population stereotypes." These can become quite complex. Note the display–control pairs in Figures 11–19A through C. You might think of the display as a pressure gauge and the knob as the control that increases the pressure in some fictional machine. Which direction would you turn the knob in Figure 11–19A to increase the machine pressure? Which direction would you turn the knob in Figure 11–19B? Although most people would turn the knob clockwise in the first two instances, many would switch to counterclockwise for Figure 11–19C. In Figure

11–19C, one population stereotype conflicts with another. According to the clockwise-for-increase principle, people will turn a knob clockwise to increase the value on the display. On the other hand, Warrick's principle (see Sanders & McCormick, 1988) states that a pointer on a display will be expected to move in the same direction as the part of the control nearest it.

Figure 11–20 presents another example inspired by Norman's delightful book. The doors function in a simple manner; they are both opened by pressing a bar on a specific side. Unfortunately, the arrangement

Figure 11–19A, 19B, & 19C   Warrick's principle. If you turn the knob in A to increase pressure, in which direction should you turn the knob in B? In C?

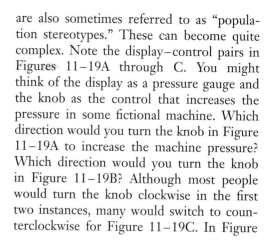

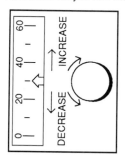

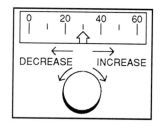

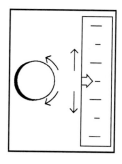

A   B   C

Figure 11–20 These doors fail to give users the information they need to know whether to press on the left or right side of the crash bars.

fails to make it clear which side should be pressed. Poor door design may be an inconvenience, but consider the implications of a mistaken control movement by a pilot traveling in a military jet at several times the speed of sound!

Another important consideration in human factors design is feedback. Have you ever borrowed a friend's car? In addition to facilitating design decisions and promoting communication between designers and their clients, environmental psychology ought also to serve as a source of substantive theory, that is, empirical data of use to designers. Indeed, this role as an archive of research findings is a more familiar one to many academic psychologists. Again, if the results of research are to be useful they must be:

1. Reliable and valid;
2. Responsive to the pragmatic needs of designers;
3. Communicated in a manner that is comprehensible to nonscientists.

CHAPTER SUMMARY

We began this chapter with a comparison between the design traditions of the industrialized nations and other less technological societies. We concluded that there is frequently a gap between modern designers and those who will eventually use or live in their constructions. We suggested that user participation may be one avenue to bridging this gap, and that a more responsive relationship between designers and researchers provided another.

The behavioral effects of several different individual features of built settings was another focus. We considered some effects of features such as privacy, materials,

aesthetics, and furnishings. We also examined formal models of the design process. For any given building there are several important criteria: cost, durability, aesthetic quality, and the like. Among these are behavioral considerations such as the congruence of fit between design and user needs. These criteria are used to decide between different design alternatives in a rather complex process. As an example of many of the issues of design we investigated the American college campus as both a product of culture, and a fertile environment for planning.

Finally, we considered human factors as an instance of communication. In this case, the focus was on increasing productivity and comfort by reducing errors between human users and the machines they try to control.

SUGGESTED PROJECTS

1. Ask several friends to list their most and least favorite buildings on your campus and to indicate the reasons for their choices. Is there any agreement between their likes and dislikes? Are these based on firmness? Commodity? Aesthetics? Does what you have learned about environmental psychology offer any insights into the reasons for their opinions, or ways to improve the least liked buildings to facilitate human behavior?

2. According to NASA, humans may soon establish a permanent settlement on the moon. What would be your goals in designing living and working quarters for these pioneers? Outline a proposal for acquiring the behavioral requirements for a successful design.

3. The design process is complicated and sometimes resistant to behavioral input. Assume that your college is building a new student center. How would you approach the possibility of providing information for the process? What design alternatives would you suggest?

4. Many college campuses have inspired someone (often a graduate) to write an account of their growth and development. Visit your college library to see if such a book has been written about a college campus familiar to you. With the book as a guide (if it is available) tour the campus. How does the architecture and use of campus buildings reflect the changes in cultural and educational values suggested by Turner's history of American college campuses?

5. Photocopy a map of your campus. Ask friends or classmates to draw lines indicating the paths they take during typical school days. Also ask them to indicate those areas of campus that they find most and least attractive. Collect and compare these maps. Do your friends agree about the most attractive and least attractive areas? Does this mapping technique identify commonly used travel corridors? Would this information be useful in considering the new location of a building, garden, or information kiosk?

6. In this chapter we discussed several population stereotypes regarding the human–machine system. Can you think of others? Make up a short survey to give to your friends to determine the relative strength of your proposed stereotypes. There will probably be some disagreements. What are the implications of ambiguous situations?

Design in Residential and Institutional Environments

INTRODUCTION

THE RESIDENTIAL SETTING

Attachment to Place

Homes

Preferences

Satisfaction With the Home Environment

Use of Space in the Home

Neighborhood and Community Environments

Propinquity: The Effect of Occupying Nearby Territories

Sense of Community

Summary of Residential Environments

INSTITUTIONAL ENVIRONMENTS

Hospital Settings

Designing for Hospital Visitors

Prison Design and Behavior

Designing for the Elderly

Noninstitutional Residences for the Elderly

Residential Care Facilities for the Elderly

Specialized Facilities for the Cognitively Impaired: Alzheimer Units

CHAPTER SUMMARY

Suggested Projects

KEY TERMS

age-segregated
Alzheimer's disease
assisted living
cohousing
continuum of care
custodial care
day–night reversal
dementia
double corridor design
environmental spoiling hypothesis
functional distance

intermediate care
objective physical distance
perceived control
person–environment congruence
place attachment
privacy gradient
propinquity
radial ward design
residential care
single corridor design
sundowning

INTRODUCTION

Your first breaths are taken in a sterile room with very institutional surroundings. Your parents take you "home," and place you in a strange container that looks like a cell with bars on two sides (which they call a "crib"), and when you look around, you see stuffed toys, a changing table, and a rocking chair. When you get a bit older you begin to explore your apartment, and continue to be affected greatly by its environment. After two years, your parents buy a house and are very proud of their "very own home." Soon it is time for you to attend school. On your first day you are amazed by the large number of desks, their arrangement, and the whole educational environment. In some ways the classroom setting is stimulating, but in other ways it constricts your behavior—you must get permission to move from your personal work station to another part of the setting. More time passes and you go to work. The work environment bears some similarity to the school setting, but in many ways it is different. You work in a large "open" office and, while you like the fact that you have easy access to your co-workers, you also feel you have insufficient privacy. You value your annual vacation, and enjoy

spending time in recreational environments, away from the work setting. As you move up the organizational ladder, you experience other work environments, and note their positive and negative effects on yourself and your co-workers. After you retire, you live in a large retirement community. Although you appreciate having other retired people as well as medical facilities nearby, you miss aspects of the more heterogeneous environment you lived in before. No matter what the nature of your home has been, you have generally been satisfied with it.

In previous chapters we have examined how specific aspects of the environment interact with our behavior. In Chapter 11 we saw how we can use knowledge of these environment–behavior relationships to design environments that will facilitate the behavior we want to occur. In this and the next chapter we will see how these principles can be brought together in specific environments. That is, we will select some settings that have been studied extensively by environmental psychologists and show how those particular environments influence

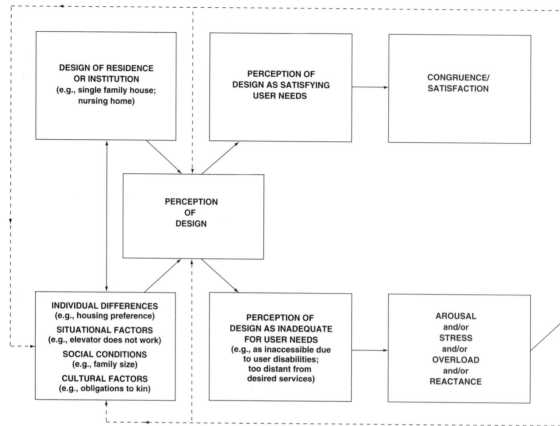

Figure 12–1   Application of our eclectic environment–behavior model to residential and institutional environments

behavior, and how the design of those environments can be modified to achieve desired effects. This chapter will examine environmental psychological research on residential settings, hospitals, prisons, and facilities for the elderly. The next chapter will continue the same theme by examining work environments, learning environments, and leisure settings. We should caution that numerous books and articles have been written on behavior in each of these environments, and that we have room to discuss only an outline of the relevant material on each of these topics. What we will emphasize is how some of the principles of environmental psychology can be applied to each setting.

Once again, we will find it useful to apply our eclectic model from Chapter 4 to our cur-

rent discussion, as depicted in Figure 12–1. Our perceptions of residential and institutional settings are influenced by individual differences (e.g., housing preference) as well as the physical setting itself, and these perceptions in turn influence our favorable or unfavorable interactions with the setting. Two concepts in particular will be common threads in this chapter. First, **person–environment congruence** is paramount: The setting facilitates the behaviors and goals appropriate to the setting—a major proposition in Barker's ecological psychology. To the extent congruence does not hold, arousal, overload, reactance, and other responses will occur and we will attempt to change the setting and/or change our behavior as we adapt to the conditions present. Aftereffects, in turn, may well

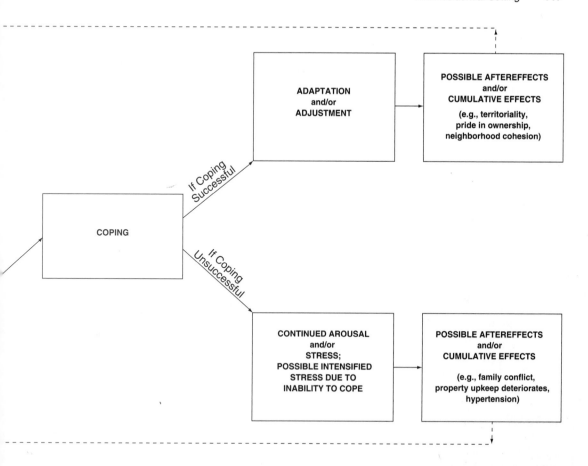

occur. A second common thread in this chapter is that **perceived control** (or lack thereof) is exceptionally important in the settings we will study: Our behavior in the setting is in part a function of the degree of perceived control the environment offers. Moreover, we will see that we can add design features to enhance personal control.

THE RESIDENTIAL SETTING

We have discussed elements of residential environments in early chapters—such as dormitories in Chapter 9—and will consider them in more detail in this one. It is no surprise that they have been mentioned so often—residential settings are so familiar and important to most of us that there has been a great deal of research interest in resi- dential design and improvement (for reviews and bibliographies, see Altman & Werner, 1985; Cooper Marcus & Sarkissian, 1985; Rullo, 1987; Tognoli, 1987). We will begin our discussion with the concept of attach- ment to place, then examine satisfaction, preference, and use of space in the home, and finally move to the larger neighborhood and community where we will discuss proximity and the sense of community.

ATTACHMENT TO PLACE

In Chapter 2 we observed how architectural and social factors contribute to a sense of place; such is certainly the case for our homes. Homes are important for reasons other than shelter. They also provide meaning and identity in our lives. For example, they signify status (e.g., Duncan, 1985), they structure our social relationships, they afford a location for major activities of daily living (e.g., eating, bathing), they are centers of regular and predictable events, and they trigger many of the memories central to our formative past, all of which contribute to a form of psychological bonding with this environment (Werner, Altman, & Oxley, 1985). These bonds can extend beyond the household to the neighborhood and larger regions. Environmental psychologists refer to this bonding as attachment to place or **place attachment** (Altman & Low, 1992; Giuliani & Feldman, 1993).

We noted in Chapter 10 on life in the city that attachment to home and neighborhood can be very strong, even for those who live in slum or near-slum areas. Fried (1963), for example, studied a group of families who were forced to move from the West End as part of a Boston urban renewal project. Although the new housing was a physical improvement, the loss of social bonds between friends in the neighborhood caused considerable grief. In fact, those with weaker attachment to the old place had an easier time adapting to the new one. Thus, social bonds can play a significant role in place attachment. In general, attachment to place includes an affective or emotional bond to the place (which bond may be mediated by social ties), memories and other cognitive interpretations that provide meaning to our experience with the place, and a sense of anxiety associated with potential removal from the place. The greater the attachment, the greater the distress can be if separation from the place is forced. For example, Holman and Silver (1994) found that residents of the Los Angeles area who lost homes to earthquakes and fires showed more distress the higher their attachment. If you attend a college or university away from home, the feeling of homesickness may in part be a result of your attachment to home (Burt, 1993). For a discussion of definitions of place attachment, see Giuliani and Feldman (1993).

The extent of residential place attachment can be influenced by bonds to more than just the home and associated social ties. Furnishings, antiques, heirlooms, and other objects can be part of the attachment (Belk, 1992) as can automobiles. In a study of two Bern, Switzerland, neighborhoods, Fuhrer, Kaiser, and Hartig (1993) found that home and neighborhood attachment was often associated with vehicles; moreover, lower transportation mobility was associated with higher attachment to place. If we live in a mobile society, then, does that mean that we are unlikely to form place attachment bonds? Perhaps the attachment to a specific place is weaker, but Feldman (1990) argues that attachment to a *type* of settlement (e.g., suburb versus city) remains strong even in the face of mobility (cf. Lalli, 1992). What happens when we do move from a place where we have become attached? Brown and Perkins (1992) describe three stages we go through in such disruptions: pre-disruption, disruption, and post-disruption. Adequate preparation in the pre-disruption phase (e.g., having previous experience with a move) and having a means of dealing with grief in the post-disruption phase can help reduce the stress of relocation. Since attachment to possessions can play a key role in attachment to the home, taking your possessions with you also helps adjust to the new place. If you lived in parts of Indonesia, a move would mean taking the whole house—wood structure and thatched roof—with you, much as mobile homes are transported in the Western world (Waterson, 1991). Other contributors to place attachment include institutions such as religion. Religious rituals in the home as well as in other sacred spaces can add to the bonding to place (Mazumdar & Mazumdar, 1993). Indeed, the variety of factors bearing on place attachment is such that even the homeless often show many of the characteristics of attachment to the place where they currently live (Bunston & Breton, 1992; Figure 12–2).

Attachment to place occurs over time. From our earliest childhood (Chawla, 1992) to our senior citizen years (Rubinstein & Parmelee, 1992), we form new attachments—and sometimes break old ones. Have you ever known someone who moved into your community and yet maintained strong attachment to an athletic team from the old community? As we form new bonds we use many mechanisms to maintain attachment to our former places. Baird and Bell (1995), for example, describe a case of a 26-year-old leukemia patient coping with treatment and

Figure 12–2 Even the homeless can show evidence of attachment to place. The White House is one place that tends to attract the homeless.

eventually death. Attachment to a hospital room became such that the patient requested it upon repeated admissions. Attachment to home—including family bonds—was such that the patient insisted on returning home to die. The hospital room had offered a view of a cemetery, and the patient became attached enough to it to choose a final gravesite within that view. Place attachment takes many forms, indeed.

HOMES

As you know, there are a number of different kinds of residential settings. The most common type, at least away from the core of the city, is the single-family detached house that many of us grew up in. In urban settings, row houses or two- or three-story apartment buildings may be the rule, while in many areas townhouses have become a predominant form. Also, of course, there are high-rise apartment buildings. Each of these kinds of environments is associated with a different style of living, and research has begun to address the similarities and differences among them. Much of the time, the differences have to do with density and the ability to screen out unwanted elements (e.g., noise, territorial intrusion). As a refresher, you might want to refer back to pages 340–341 where we discussed density and intrusion in another housing form, the campus residence hall.

Preferences

With all of these different forms of housing, it has become important to examine residential preferences. Research seems to suggest that people in North America and the British Commonwealth tend to describe the detached, single-family house as the "ideal" home (Cooper, 1972; Thorne, Hall, & Munro-Clark, 1982). This tendency does not appear to be a matter of socioeconomic class—people seem to reject apartment settings and prefer suburban homes regardless of ethnic or social background or the kind of housing environment they occupy (Dennis, 1966; Hancock, 1980; Ladd, 1972; Michelson, 1968).

Although you may have suspected that most people want a "nice little house in the suburbs," the reasons for this preference are not clear. Although very young and very old adults prefer living closer to the center of the city, most adults prefer to be farther away (Lindberg et al., 1992). The growth in popularity of the suburban detached house is attributable to many factors, including among others, pride in home ownership, government incentives (such as for tax deductible mortgage interest), and the growth of transportation systems leading into and out of large cities (e.g., Gans, 1967; Jackson, 1985; Warner, 1978). To environmental psychologists, however, the most compelling explanation is the way these settings structure space. We saw in Chapter 2 that legibility and cohesiveness are important dimensions determining preference for natural landscapes. The same applies to housing: People prefer well-structured space typical of the single-family house (Herzog, 1992)—space with clear boundaries that form a distinct whole. Michelson (1970) has argued that the ways in which space is distributed in areas dominated by single-family homes allows residents to avoid intense interaction with neighbors. Urban areas are sometimes characterized by close neighborhood ties, extended families, and extensive social interaction. The single-family house appears to permit residents to avoid or control these social factors to a greater degree. Michelson also reports some evidence that single-family housing is generally regarded as family oriented. Thus, people seem to want the family privacy afforded by these settings. Not all areas, of course, have close neighborhood ties and extensive social interaction (e.g., Altman & Wandersman, 1987; Wellman & Leighton, 1979). In these situations, as well, the single-family house

seems to offer a sense of security along with perceived control over relationships.

Choice of type of housing may be restricted by economic factors. Economic factors may make it difficult for young families to purchase single-family houses, in which case they may opt for townhouse or condominium settings, or apartment living (cf. van Vliet, 1983). A number of factors appear to determine the location that one lives in— where the house, townhouse, or the like is situated. Again, economic factors are important, since some areas of a city or its suburbs may be more expensive than others. Choices are often made between locations and types of housing. A family may be able to afford a single-family house in suburb A, but only a townhouse in suburb B. A number of things are ordinarily considered before making choices between locations and housing type (e.g., Shlay, 1985). The status communicated by housing types is very distinguishable, even for homes of 100 years ago (Cherulnik & Wilderman, 1986). Within housing types, building materials also convey status, with stone and brick having the highest status associations (Sadalla & Sheets, 1993).

Given the basic preference for the detached house, why might a family opt for a townhouse in a different suburb? Status may be an issue, if one of the two suburbs is very high or very low in prestige. Security and crime rates may be another—the detached home in suburb A may also be closer to high crime areas. Commuting time, closeness to and quality of schools, and availability of shopping and services may also be important. Clearly, preferences for and actual choice of housing is complex, with factors about the residential environment and its surrounding area being considered in each instance (see also Cook, 1988).

Satisfaction With the Home Environment

Despite the general preference for single-family houses in the suburbs, many people

LIFE IN THE SUBURBS:
Is it Really What You Think?

We have noted that living preferences fairly consistently show the majority of people want a single-family house, and that most envision the suburbs as the best location for such an arrangement. Schools, transportation, and recreational opportunities have some role in this vision. But just how ideal are suburbs? Jackson (1985) offers the history of the suburban movement in America, with a book appropriately titled *Crabgrass Frontier*. Although development on the outskirts of cities has been around since cities began, most of us think of "contemporary" suburbs as they have developed after World War II. The "prototype" planned development by William Levitt is alleged to have started the suburbanization boom. Said Levitt, reflecting the atmosphere of the times in 1948, "No man who owns his own house and lot can be a Communist. He has too much to do." Jackson observes that in seeking our private, suburban ownership, we also evolve along a sameness dimension—everyone has the same dreams, the same fence, the same yard, same cars, same commuting route, same "little boxes," and it still seems preferable to the city!

But is all well in paradise? Lublin (1985), among others, has summarized some of the ills befalling suburbia. Homeowners must worry about flight paths for new airports. Office buildings, commerce, and industry are retreating to suburbs to cut costs and eliminate commuting. Growth, traffic snarls, pollution, noise, strains on public services, and lack of workers to fill low-end jobs accompany these developments. Housing becomes more expensive. Developers buy houses to put in commercial projects. Restricting the heights of these buildings to preserve views means development spreads out and traffic congestion becomes worse. The 1980 census showed that 27 million Americans actually commute from one suburb to another (Lublin, 1985)! Ah, life in the suburbs!

live in other types of housing arrangements. Are they satisfied with their current housing, even though the ideal might be something else? As we will see, it appears that psychological factors are very important in determining satisfaction—factors that are often present no matter what the style or location of the home. As we become accustomed to a specific residential setting, we develop more and more satisfaction with our ability to perform basic tasks in it. The more easily and conveniently these functions can be performed, the more satisfied we usually become. The better we are able to adapt to the features of our residence (i.e., perform the de-

sired functions despite less than favorable design features), the more satisfied we are (Tognoli, 1987). Also recall that in the previous chapter we mentioned design alternatives as components of the design process. If an alternative dwelling is available for comparison that makes our own seem superior, we are more likely to be satisfied than if our own seems inferior (Tognoli, 1987). Thus, Wiesenfeld (1992) found that residents of public housing in Venezuela were satisfied with their housing compared to their previous quarters. Steidl (1972) found that the size and floor plan of rooms were often mentioned as problems that affect the performance of tasks. Not having enough room to work, having too many rooms to clean, and being too close to noisy areas of the house are among these problems. Galster and Hesser (1981) found that certain physical or environmental factors were associated with dissatisfaction. Poor plumbing, heating, or kitchen facilities were strongly related to dissatisfaction, as were neighborhood characteristics such as racial makeup, high density, or condition of the structures in the area (see also Michelson, 1977a). Similarly, Kaitilla (1993) found that small size of houses, small living/ dining areas, badly designed kitchen and bathroom facilities, and lack of storage space were associated with dissatisfaction in New Guinea public housing.

Physical and social factors are clearly interdependent in determining satisfaction (Anthony, Weidemann, & Chin, 1990; Weidemann & Anderson, 1982), but there are cross-cultural differences (e.g., Hourihan, 1984; Tognoli, 1987; Zube et al., 1985). Ross (1987) notes a particularly interesting problem in satisfaction among Australian aborigines who move into modern homes. Traditionally, aboriginal culture places high emphasis on taking care of relatives in need—bringing them into the home if necessary. Moreover, control over social pathology is handled by moving away—a relatively simple feat with a small, portable house and meager possessions. But a larger modern home is inviting to kin and makes moving difficult, such that residential satisfaction can be low; some aborigines even prefer smaller houses for this reason. Perceived control over social life is clearly related to residential satisfaction across cultures. Among residents of Canadian cooperatives, Cooper and Rodman (1994) found social control to be more important than control over physical aspects of the home in determining satisfaction. As another example, Pruchno et al. (1993) examined perceptions of space and satisfaction among American adults and children who were living in a house with a disabled elderly person. The more time the elderly person spent in space shared with the family, the more negative the perceptions.

Social ties also appear to be important in determining residential satisfaction. Fried and Gleicher (1961) found this to be more the case for residents of urban slums than for suburbanites. In urban areas, social ties appear to contribute to a sense of neighborhood and the sharing of outdoor space by residents. Greenbaum and Greenbaum (1981) found that group identity in a neighborhood is related to territorial personalization and social interaction. When people were able to establish social bonds with those around them, they took more care in decorating the exteriors of their residences and the neighborhood took on the aura of group-owned territory. Neighborhood ties are stronger on cul-de-sacs than on through streets. This effect is often reflected in more decorations at Christmas and Halloween on cul-de-sacs (Brown & Werner, 1985; Oxley et al., 1986; Figure 12–3).

Even teenagers show differences in neighborhood evaluations. Van Vliet (1981), for example, found that teenage Canadian residents of suburbs, relative to counterparts in a city, were more satisfied with neighborhood safety, "nice looks," friendliness, and quietness. City dwellers, however, rated their environment as having more things to do.

Other social factors can be significant sources of satisfaction or dissatisfaction for many people. We have already mentioned privacy regulation as an important consideration in the design of environments. How a residence is designed can affect the ease with which we achieve privacy. Individuals differ, however, in the amount of privacy they want. Privacy in the single-family home, as reported by the male members of the household, could take two forms (Altman, Nelson, & Lett, 1972). One type of family controls privacy without using physical features of the envi-

Figure 12–3 Neighborhood ties are often stronger on cul-de-sacs than on through streets, as sometimes reflected in holiday decorations.

ronment as a means of control. In these families, bedroom doors are rarely closed and few areas of the home are considered the domain of one family member. A second family type is more likely to use environmental controls over privacy. These families help to ensure privacy by designating rooms as specific territories for individual use. Clearly, one cannot use a single residential design and expect both types of families to be satisfied. Variety of interior design of homes helps to ensure that individual family styles can be accommodated (cf. Morris, 1987; Oseland & Donald, 1993; Shlay, 1987; see box on page 456).

Clearly, then, psychological and social factors are at least as important as physical factors in determining residential satisfaction. This point is especially evident in a study by Paulus, Nagar, and Camacho (1991) comparing U.S. army families of comparable socioeconomic status who rented either apartments or mobile homes. Table 12–1 details just how important nonphysical qual-

ities were for both types of housing in determining satisfaction; note the psychological reasons satisfaction was high for both types of housing.

Use of Space in the Home

Despite differences in the ways in which people arrange their homes, consistent space-use patterns emerge. Black (1968), for example, found that leisure reading was most common in the living room and least common in the kitchen and dining room. The kitchen is often the center of family activity (Mehrabian, 1976). Bedrooms are the most frequently occupied areas of the home (Parsons, 1972), and may become personalized or private areas for individual family members. Home interior designs clearly mediate social interactions (Bonnes et al., 1987; Werner, 1987; Figure 12–4).

The intended function of a room has important implications for its design and how it is used. Bedrooms are, for one thing,

Table 12–1 Comparison of Apartment and Mobile Home Living*

Apartments	Mobile Homes
Environmental Quality	
More Positive on	*More Positive on*
Attractiveness	Noise level
Other people in complex	Crime risk
Closeness of services	
Adequacy of recreation facilities	
Reason for Choosing Housing	
Fire safety	Distance between units
Weather safety	Lower noise levels
	Can have own place
	More space
	More privacy
	Better for raising children
Satisfaction High for Both Types of Housing Because of:	
High level of perceived choice in selection process	
Future expectation of housing quality improvement	
Current housing compares favorably to past housing or friends' housing	

Paulus et al., 1991.

intended to be private space, and thus are likely to be set off from less private areas. They may be located down a hallway from the living and kitchen areas, or on a different floor altogether. Bedrooms are also supposed to be for sleeping and therefore must be quiet. However, as Parsons (1972) notes, some sleepers prefer a noisier setting. Individual preferences are a problem for designers who wish to generalize designs across large numbers of residences (see box on page 459). The master bedroom and master suite have increased substantially in size in American homes over the past decade or so, accommodating more and more functions we are likely to perform there (Hasell & Peatross, 1990).

The bathroom is an especially interesting design problem. Consider the many functions or purposes of a bathroom. Kira (1976) identifies over 30 functions, including among others: brushing teeth, rinsing mouth, gargling, expectorating, cleaning and soaking dentures, vomiting, treating skin blemishes, cleaning ears, applying cosmetics, shaving, defecating, urinating, bathing, washing wounds, applying bandages, taking medicine, and inserting contact lenses. Each one of these functions can serve as the basis for bathroom design criteria. To the physical hygienic functions that we are all familiar with, we can also add some social functions. Many people use the bathroom as a "sanctum" for privacy. Social conventions frown on people interrupting one another while in the bathroom and, as a result, one can often escape there for a moment of peace and quiet. Thus, even though the bathroom can take on attributes of shared space, it can also serve as a place where privacy can be achieved on a transient basis. Of course, this is not the case with large bathrooms, such as those in a college dormitory. There, the small stalls within the bathroom may serve the same privacy function as the entire bathroom. The role of the bathroom in affording privacy should not be underestimated. Inman (cited in Meer, 1986) surveyed 200 households in Indiana. Regardless of how much space the rest of the house had, about half of all families with only one bathroom felt stressed because of a perceived lack of living space, compared to about 20 percent of those with more than one bathroom. She cautioned, however, that having more than three bathrooms increased stress because of problems related to cleaning and stocking!

Kira (1976) has examined the relationship between the design of bathrooms and their functions. Many of his suggestions are intended to increase convenience, including changes in sink and vanity design and placement of shower control knobs, electrical outlets, and so on. Other suggestions are more

Figure 12–4A & 4B Bedrooms are more likely to show signs of privatization and informality than are living rooms.

adventurous, and one goes completely against the notion of privacy in the bathroom. Kira (1976) proposes the creation of a living room bath which could be used for entertaining guests. He views such an unusual situation as a logical response to economic pressures. As residential settings become smaller because of energy and land costs, designers

PREFERENCES FOR MESSY AND NEAT ROOMS:
The Odd Couple

Residential satisfaction applies not only to entire neighborhoods but also to single rooms. Recall the Neil Simon play, movie, and television series about the "odd couple" who had to cope with each other's preference for a neat or messy apartment. A definite preference for a neat or messy room may be more than just a scriptwriter's whim. Personality and cultural background may influence whether a person will find satisfaction or annoyance with a room that is kept tidy or disorderly. Samuelson and Lindauer (1976) asked college students to describe rooms that were experimentally changed to look either messy or neat. The messy room had papers and pencils scattered about, an overflowing wastebasket, and a general look of disorder. In the neat room, objects were arranged in an orderly manner.

Students described the rooms differently and also showed different levels of preference for each room. Students who indicated they preferred more exciting or varied experiences were more satisfied with the messy room. Students less inclined toward experience-seeking (as measured by test scores) were more satisfied with the neat room. Just as each member of the odd couple found the apartment most satisfying when arranged his way, students differ in their preference for order or disorder in a setting. Those with adaptation levels closer to the "orderly" end of a "disorderly–orderly" dimension seem to find it easier to adapt to (and are more satisfied with) a neat room, whereas those whose adaptation levels lie closer to the "disorderly" end tend to be more comfortable in a messy room.

often include multipurpose space in homes. Because bathrooms are not used all of the time, they are prime candidates for new functions, and Kira argues that they can be used as living rooms as well as bath areas (Figure 12–5).

We noted above that master bedrooms have increased in size in recent years. Hasell and Peatross (1990) suggest that part of the motive behind this change is to accommodate the functions of two adults who work outside the home: As women more commonly enter the workforce, the master bedroom and bath need to allow both partners to get ready at the same time. Other design adjustments with the same root cause include larger and more open kitchens to allow more sharing of functions, and a separate private space for the woman of the house (comparable to the den that was stereotypically for the man of the house). Another trend today is that more and more people are working at home. Ahrentzen (1990) found that maintaining a separate workspace and restricting access to it, as well as rescheduling activities were mechanisms by which those who work at home accommodate work activities in the home.

So far, our discussion of space use has been for a typical middle-class American setting. Scheflen (1971) provides an alternative view of space use in the urban ghetto. Because many children share the same room, each can claim perhaps only one drawer and a quarter of a closet in the bedroom—if there is a separate bedroom at all. The kitchen is

Figure 12–5 Kira argues that bathrooms can be used for less privatized functions. Would you feel comfortable that way?

9 feet by 12 feet (2.7 m by 3.7 m), but a bed, cabinets, and closets take up much of this space. The refrigerator is across the room because the original space for it was designed in 1920 and is too small for any refrigerator available today. How does one adapt to such a kitchen where two adults cannot maneuver in it at the same time? Scheflen noted two options: (1) all dining occurs in the living room, or (2) an end table or child's play table is the kitchen table, so adults do not eat in the kitchen. There is one sofa and one chair in the living room, and a dominance hierarchy develops around their use, which varies from household to household. Territorial defense within the apartment is not achieved with physical partitions, but rather with behavior: Extending an elbow or leg keeps others a little farther away, and contours of posture help block visual access.

Noise and lack of privacy are such problems that studying is difficult at best and frequently nonexistent. Although many factors contribute to the social ills of the inner city, these adaptations to spatial restriction should be considered by anyone exploring solutions (cf. Merry, 1981, 1987; Oxman & Carmon, 1986).

We might note also that there are considerable cultural differences in the use of space at home. Kent (1991) classifies over 50 cultural groups worldwide based on their use of space. Some, such as the Mbuti Pygmy and the Navajo, rarely segment their living space for different tasks (e.g., eating, sleeping, entertaining). Others, such as Euramericans and Saudi Arabians, segment their space considerably. Interestingly, the congruence principle seems to hold, as design matches the culture: Those with little segmentation of functions tend to have homes with few barriers such as interior walls, and those with more segmentation of function have clearly defined, segmented spaces. What happens when a low-segmentation family is placed in a home with high physical segmentation and vice versa? Kent (1991) observes that under these circumstances remodeling occurs: Low-segmentation Navajos occupying a three-bedroom Western-style house were found to sleep and eat in the living room; high-segmentation Euramericans set up additional barriers in an otherwise low-segmentation house. Westernization in general tends to bring segmentation. Omata (1992), for example, observes how modern Japanese homes tend to have more private space than previously (Figure 12–6).

Figure 12–6A & 6B   These housing units have the same amount of floor space. The one at the top has relatively high segmentation, whereas the one below is much less segmented.

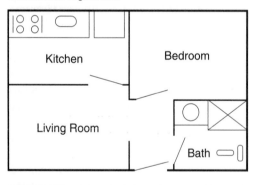

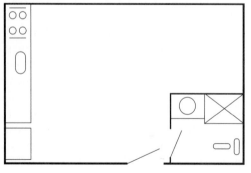

NEIGHBORHOOD AND COMMUNITY ENVIRONMENTS

Thus far, we have concentrated on environment–behavior properties of the individual household. Much of our residential life, however, centers around the neighborhood or community—our interactions with those proximal to us. But having multiple households in the same vicinity sets up a tension between desire for privacy and peace and quiet and the need to cooperate with others for mutual protection and social support. We conclude our section on residential environments by examining two important considerations: proximity and sense of community.

Propinquity: The Effect of Occupying Nearby Territories

Propinquity refers to "nearness" between places people occupy. How close you are to other residents in a housing development, an apartment building, or even a dormitory or an office building will affect your social outcomes with them (cf. Webber, 1963).

Two types of propinquity have been found to lead to favorable social outcomes. First, it has been observed that the closer the **objective physical distance** between two individuals, the more likely the individuals are to be friends. The classic study was conducted by Festinger, Schachter, and Back (1950), who investigated friendship patterns of apartment dwellers in Westgate West. When residents (who were randomly assigned to apartments) were asked, "Which three people do you see most often socially?" it was found that people were friendliest with those who lived near them. In fact, residents were more likely to be friendly with a neighbor one door away than with a neighbor two doors away and so on. Furthermore, this finding was replicated in a study by Ebbesen, Kjos, and Konecni (1976). Another study (Segal, 1974) provided corroborative

HOMES AND THE PRIVACY GRADIENT

Understanding people's social values and practices is extremely important for developing a home design that will provide desirable levels of privacy. In the United States, a number of modern designs are based on open architecture that includes the kitchen as part of the area for entertaining guests. In Peru, however, a **privacy gradient** exists that restricts certain areas in terms of entertaining (Zeisel, 1975). Formal friends and acquaintances are permitted only in the room intended for social activities. As guests become better known, they may be invited into other areas, but only those closest to the homeowner are ever permitted into the kitchen. Alexander (1969) suggested that a Peruvian house should be designed along a privacy gradient that places the sala (room for entertaining) at the front and the kitchen at the rear.

In French upper-middle-class homes, privacy is marked by distinct barriers. Carlisle (1982) observed that residents of these homes isolate intimate areas of the house with hallways, doors, grills, or curtains.

Why do we place so much emphasis on home ownership? Although there are many obvious economic and status reasons, Tognoli (1987) suggests that ownership implies less permeable boundaries (i.e., more control over privacy) than renting.

evidence for the data on objective distance–friendship choice. In this experiment, Segal noted the friendship choices among trainees at the Maryland Police Academy, where trainees were assigned to rooms and to seats in classrooms on the basis of the alphabetical order of their last names. In effect, alphabetical order served as a manipulation of propinquity, and it was found that individuals were most likely to become friendly with others whose last initials were close to theirs in the alphabet.

Objective physical distance is not the only predictor of attraction, however. It has been found that **functional distance**, defined as the likelihood of two individuals coming into contact, also predicts whether people will become friends or like each other (Ebbesen et al., 1976; Festinger et al., 1950). Functional distance becomes a more accurate predictor of friendship than objective physical distance

when architectural features of a building constrain individuals whose apartments or offices are physically distant from frequent interaction. For example, the concept of functional distance would best predict attraction between two individuals who live five floors apart in an apartment building (distant in an objective sense), but who have adjacent mailboxes in the lobby (Figure 12–7).

Why does propinquity lead to friendship? Sears et al. (1988) offer some fairly convincing explanations. First, it is impossible to find grounds for friendship with someone we have never met, and those who are close to us in terms of physical or functional distance are clearly more readily accessible to us and to each other than individuals who are more distant. Second, since we have to continue to interact in the future with others who live in close proximity to us, perhaps we try a bit harder to "see the good side" of

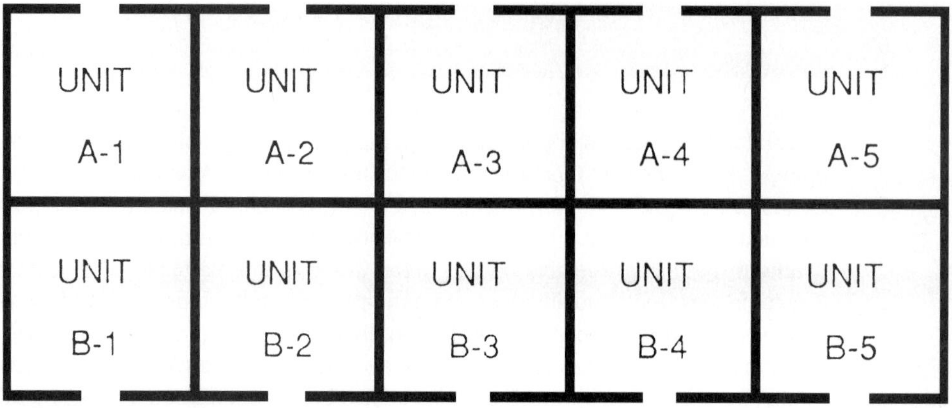

UNIT A-1	UNIT A-2	UNIT A-3	UNIT A-4	UNIT A-5
UNIT B-1	UNIT B-2	UNIT B-3	UNIT B-4	UNIT B-5

Figure 12–7   The distinction between functional distance and objective physical distance. The A and B units which share the same number are back-to-back and very close in objective physical distance. The functional distance for walking from Unit A-3 to B-3, however, is much greater. As a result, occupants of Unit B-3 are likely to be closer friends with occupants of any of the B units than with the occupants of any of the A units.

them and exert ourselves a bit harder to "make it work." Third, continued interaction with individuals obviously leads to a feeling of predictability and to a sense of security, which may make friendship more likely. Fourth, familiarity in and of itself may lead to attraction (Moreland & Zajonc, 1982; Saegert, Swap, & Zajonc, 1973; Zajonc, 1968).

However, it should be noted that propinquity is more likely to lead to attraction under cooperative conditions where there is equity between individuals than under competitive conditions where there is inequity. Familiar persons whom we see as rewarding are liked most (Swap, 1977). In addition, conditions of equality and cooperation promote enhanced attraction more effectively if prior attitudes toward another individual are neutral or mildly positive than if they are highly negative. Studies of functional and objective distance and friendship formation often examine homogeneous population groups— often newcomers needing help adjusting. Under these conditions, friendships are likely to form out of propinquity. On the other hand, propinquity can also create enemies. Ebbesen et al. (1976) found that more disliked

than liked others lived close to subjects. They interpreted their results in terms of an **environmental spoiling hypothesis**: Positive social relationships follow from frequent contacts (which may or may not stem from propinquity), but the activities of *some* can spoil the perceived quality of the living environment.

Satisfaction with one's neighborhood seems closely tied to this spoiling notion; spoiling, in turn, is a direct result of propinquity, since we would not object so much to what our neighbors do if their activity was far enough away that it did not disturb us. Merry (1987), for example, examined sources of neighborhood conflict. The most annoying complaints were social in nature— neighbors creating nuisances. Noise from neighbors, dogs making messes, vandalism, barking dogs, children playing in the street, children harassing adults, fights over street parking spaces, and trespassing were all sources of complaints—much more so than factors such as city services. As we indicated previously, greater ability to control these sources of aggravation is a major reason people prefer a single-family house in the suburbs; such homes typically have more distance between neighbors, fences to demarcate territory, private parking, and clearly defined areas for children to play such that they are less likely to be intrusive. This proximity/annoyance connection seems fairly universal. For example, lack of control over neighborhood noise was shown to be especially annoying in French neighborhoods (Levy-Leboyer & Naturel, 1991), and high neighborhood density was associated with low satisfaction in an Italian study (Bonnes, Bonaiuto, & Ercolani, 1991).

Sense of Community

Given that most of us must live within considerable proximity of our neighbors, what can we do to build a sense of community among our neighbors? A Dutch study suggests that neighborhood cohesion consists of two factors: neighboring (friendliness, looking out for each other's interests, providing social support) and sense of community. The relatively low cohesion found in higher-density multi-family housing was not due to lack of neighboring, but rather to lack of a sense of community (Weenig, Schmidt, & Midden, 1990; but cf. Keane, 1991).

One interesting design feature that may build a sense of community is a front porch on the dwelling. LaGanga (1994) describes how the small city of San Luis Obispo, California, struggled with a proposed city ordinance to require front porches on all new homes. The idea was to encourage more informal interaction with neighbors, learn who belongs and who does not, and build more sensitivity to annoyances.

Another factor in a sense of community is ownership. Signs of physical decay (litter, dilapidated housing, abandoned cars) are associated with fear of crime (Perkins, Meeks, & Taylor, 1992). Removing such signs of incivility may improve a sense of community, but the owner of the problem often does not live in the neighborhood.

Leavitt and Saegert (1989) describe how residents of Harlem reclaimed abandoned buildings and turned them into cooperatives; that is, the residents became owners of their buildings. Cooperation, caring, protection of common resources—all factors in a sense of community—were enhanced in this collaborative process.

Still another community-enhancing intervention is the community organization. Neighbors can begin with existing organizations or a facilitator can help build a new one, such as a Community Improvement Committee, a garden club, or a crimewatch program. Such organizations promote getting to know neighbors, improve communication, and give loosely connected neighbors a common purpose (Wandersman, 1981; Wandersman & Hess, 1985).

SUMMARY OF RESIDENTIAL ENVIRONMENTS

Homes provide more than shelter; they organize much of our individual and social life and provide bonding. Attachment to place includes a sense of bonding, memories about the place, and anxiety in the face of potential separation from the place; attachment occurs to both the home and community. People occupy many different styles of homes, although the preference tends to be for a single-family home in a quiet area away from city problems; privacy and control over annoyances seems to be behind this preference. Satisfaction with the home, on the other hand, seems related not so much to style or location but to whether or not the home facilitates desired functions and meets expectations. Space within the home can serve single or multiple functions; there are large cultural differences in how domestic and other functions are accomplished in the home, and the operation of the home has much to do with privacy expectations and accommodations for privacy. Propinquity can

COHOUSING:
Combining Privacy and Community

We have noted that apparently tension exists between privacy and community in housing design; the single-family home tends to maximize privacy but can minimize interactions with neighbors, whereas multi-family housing sacrifices privacy but can increase a sense of community. An alternative type of housing may be a good blend of the two. **Cohousing** communities, originally developed in Denmark, provide each family with their own detached unit, but have a common building for dining and larger scale entertaining. An example is EcoVillage planned in Ithaca, New York. The common building will house the large kitchen and dining hall, laundry facilities, and entertainment/recreation facilities. Much of the rationale is to share the larger, energy-consuming appliances. Adding solar and wind-generated power is an option, and the heating source for individual units will also be shared. Privacy will be afforded in the separate, detached family units which will contain bedrooms, baths, smaller living areas, and a small kitchen. Cohousing, then, attempts to offer privacy for private functions but to share facilities for functions where privacy is less of a concern.

lead to friendship formation or to perception of environmental spoiling; a sense of community promotes friendship and minimizes spoiling.

INSTITUTIONAL ENVIRONMENTS

Outside the home we can observe environment–behavior relationships in numerous settings. Some of these have received much attention by environmental psychologists, and we will look at a few of them in the rest of this and the following chapter. As with residences, congruence or person–environment fit is a theme in our descriptions. Perceived control and privacy issues are also paramount. Although some of the issues are the same, institutional environments differ somewhat from residential environments in several common ways. For one, they are shared with many more people than is typical of a home. That makes privacy more difficult to achieve, and territorial defense less likely—institutional settings tend to involve public territories (see Chapter 8). Second, many of the people who enter an institutional environment on a given day are there for the first time, so orientation and wayfinding aids become significant adaptive tools. Third, institutional settings usually serve multiple functions—learning, entertaining, shelter and so on—such that designs must accommodate multiple demands. Fourth, in part because of the multiple demands and in part because of sheer size and complexity, overstimulation is often a problem in these settings—too much noise, confusing paths of exploration, and/or distracting activities. Finally, all of the above can lead to loss of perceived control in such settings, so many of the design features promoting satisfaction involve restoration of control. Let us see, then, how design influences behavior in some of these settings. The remainder of this chapter will be dedicated to institutions where people also reside 24 hours per day—hospitals, prisons, nursing homes—so we will see some direct relevance to the section on residences. The following chapter will look at work, learning, and leisure environments—settings where people typically spend less time than in a residence.

HOSPITAL SETTINGS

Much of what we know about design in hospital settings is derived from research on acute care and psychiatric hospital environments (Reizenstein, 1982). Many data-based investigations have studied psychiatric patients, perhaps because of greater ease and accessibility in using these subjects. For several decades researchers have methodically studied advantages and disadvantages of various hospital design features. Two recent volumes summarize some of these findings and the methods used to assess innovations (Carpman & Grant, 1993; Moran, Anderson, & Paoli, 1990). We offer here a brief overview of some of the historic work.

One aspect of hospital settings that has received attention is the low control or "low choice" forced upon patients and visitors (Olsen, 1978; Taylor, 1979). Hospitals typically have a great number of rules and allow patients only minimal control over the small spaces that they use. Olsen has pointed out that hospital designs can communicate this message—that people are "sick and dependent and should behave in an accordingly passive manner" (Olsen, 1978, p. 7). Provision of greater spatial complexity or providing more options or variations in design can improve the situation and lead to more positive emotional responses (Olsen, 1978). Orig-

inally, hospitals for the mentally ill resembled prisons more than hospitals (Figure 12–8A and 8B). Today, the design of psychiatric facilities tends to resemble that of a dormitory or hotel built around a central nurses' station and lounge (Figure 12–9A and 9B).

Ronco (1972) observed that hospital settings are usually designed for staff rather than patient needs. For example, it is conceivable that a ward design that facilitates staff functioning might also cause a patient to sense an overwhelming loss of personal control and privacy. Such feelings in turn may contribute to the patient's becoming overly dependent on the hospital and withdrawing from normal activities. These and other considerations have led researchers to look for design alternatives that alleviate the negative effects of hospitalization and stimulate the healing process, as well as facilitate staff needs.

Do certain designs and locations of nurses' stations promote more efficient patient care (i.e., behavioral facilitation), as some suggest (cf. Lippert, 1971)? In order to answer this question, Trites et al. (1970) investigated nurse efficiency and staff satisfaction with three different hospital ward designs (Figure 12–10). In general, a **radial ward design** was found to be the most desirable (relative to **single** and **double corridor designs**), both in terms of saving unnecessary ward travel and of increasing time with patients. Moreover, members of the nursing staff indicated a preference for assignment to the radial ward. The fact that nursing staff in the radial unit had more free time was interpreted as an indication that more patients could be housed on the ward. In another ward study, however, Lippert (1971) found no one ward design particularly superior to another, using efficiency in patient care stops as the behavioral criterion. Nevertheless, it is clear that hospital design can have significant impact on the well-being of both patients and staff.

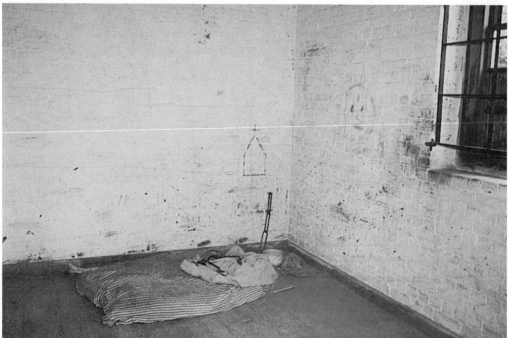

Figure 12–8A & 8B   Exterior and interior of the first hospital in the United States built specifically for the mentally ill. This facility was built in Williamsburg, Virginia in 1773.

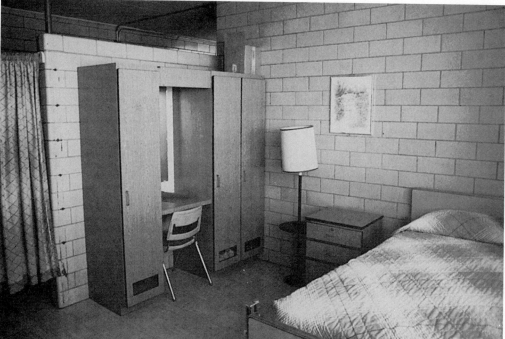

Figure 12–9A & 9B Exterior and interior of a contemporary mental health institute

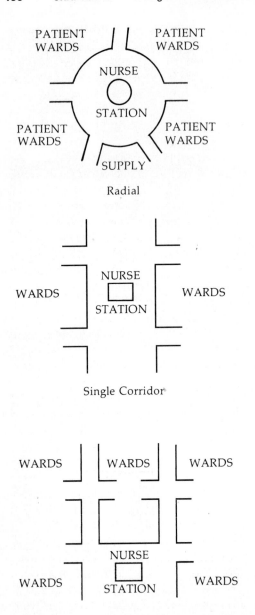

PATIENT WARDS
PATIENT WARDS
NURSE STATION
PATIENT WARDS
PATIENT WARDS
SUPPLY

Radial

WARDS
NURSE STATION
WARDS

Single Corridor

WARDS WARDS WARDS
NURSE STATION
WARDS WARDS

Double Corridor

Figure 12–10 These designs represent three types of hospital wards. The radial unit appeared to be the most desirable in terms of staff satisfaction and amount of time spent with patients.
Adapted from Trites, D., Galbraith, F. D., Sturdavant, M., & Leckwart, J. F., 1970. Influence of nursing unit design on the activities and subjective feelings of nursing personnel. Environment and Behavior, 2, 303–334.

Another issue that has received attention is the degree to which different designs affect social interaction among patients (see Devlin, 1992, for a review). Beckman (1974) suggests that an appropriate design is one which encourages patients to leave their rooms and seek out others, and which supports social interaction. Of course, for some types of patients (e.g., those in an intensive care unit), one might want to discourage some of this movement. This design goal reflects an understanding and concern for the same kinds of issues raised in studies of residential environments—the recognition that the arrangement of space can affect the frequency and quality of social contact.

We noted in previous chapters that some types of furniture arrangements (i.e., sociopetal versus sociofugal) facilitate patient interaction more than others. In addition, keeping down the number of beds on a ward promotes social interaction and reduces withdrawal (Ittelson, Proshansky, & Rivlin, 1970). Social interaction concerns extend to other relationships as well. Pill (1967), for example, discusses how designs that place nursing staff in close proximity to patients do not allow nurses to satisfy their privacy needs. Another important form of interaction, disclosure between patient and physician, is facilitated by pleasantly designed institutional settings (Reizenstein, 1976).

Several case studies of modifying psychiatric facilities are presented by Cherulnik (1993). In one, a corridor design and a suite design were compared with a control condition in which the previous institutional layout was unchanged. In the corridor design, one or two residents lived in each room with floor-to-ceiling walls and lockable doors. In the suite design, one to three residents were housed per room, with partitions used to separate sleeping areas and homelike furnishings supplied. Residents appeared most alert and purposive and interacted most with other residents (and less with staff) in the suite design; these desirable behaviors were least apparent in the traditional, unchanged control condition. In another case, dormitories were partitioned into two-room modules with added sound insulation and improved lighting; in addition, chairs were arranged in a semi-circle sociopetal configuration. Social interaction among the residents doubled after the design modification (see also Sommer & Ross, 1958).

Still other environmental features have been shown to have direct impact on well-being. A study of uncontrollable noise in the hospital showed that it increases experienced pain and is associated with greater use of painkillers by surgery patients (Minckley, 1968). One study has shown that windowless intensive care units have a higher incidence of postoperative problems, ranging from negative psychological outcomes to physiological complications (Wilson, 1972). Still another (reviewed in Chapter 11) compared surgery patients assigned to rooms looking out over a natural setting with patients in rooms whose windows faced a brick building. Patients in the rooms with a nice view had shorter postoperative stays in the hospital and used fewer pain-killing medications (Ulrich, 1984; see also Verderber, 1986). In describing attachment to place we mentioned a case study of a young leukemia patient coping with treatment and death (Baird & Bell, 1995). So powerful was the window effect for this patient that she preferred a hospital room with a view of a cemetery to a room with no view at all. As we described in Chapter 2, opportunities to view natural scenery seem to promote restorative experiences.

A series of studies by Wolfe and Rivlin (Rivlin & Wolfe, 1972; Wolfe, 1975) has examined a number of design variables and their effects on behavior in a children's psychiatric hospital. One important variable turned out to be bedroom size and occu-

pancy. Ittelson et al. (1970), for example, found that the more patients in a room, the fewer types of behavior were observed. Wolfe (1987) similarly reported that design elements which increased the number of children assigned to a hospital room decreased its use and had inhibiting effects on patients' behavior.

Design of play space in psychiatric facilities for children has also received attention (Rivlin, Wolfe, & Beyda, 1973). In general, little consideration is given to age level differences in planning play space in these facilities. Younger children, especially, seem to have difficulty in adapting to highly controlled hospital ward space. Rivlin and her colleagues suggested that the behaviors younger children display in handling their disorientation to ward space may be interpreted by staff members as part of their disorder. In reality, the younger child may be reacting as any child might to restrictions on play caused by inadequate space. Consequently, special care facilities should be designed not only for treating illnesses, but also for encouraging the normal activities of a particular age group.

Designing for Hospital Visitors

Thus far we have discussed some considerations for hospital residents and staff. Zimring, Carpman, and Michelson (1987) point out that hospitals should attend to design needs of visitors, as well. They note that in this day of cost-saving efforts, visitors can often perform basic caregiving tasks instead of the staff, such as adjusting pillows, feeding the patient, or providing psychosocial support. Yet, many visitors are themselves worried about the condition of the patient, and they are in an unfamiliar environment. Numerous design flaws—many of which are readily rectified—add more stress for the visitor.

For example, how easy is it to find your way through all the corridors? Most visitors have a difficult time with wayfinding (e.g., Carpman, Grant, & Simmons, 1983–1984). Good signs in everyday language instead of medical terminology would help, as would frequent "you-are-here" maps, or paper maps visitors could carry. As another example, visitors find hospital noise disturbing (Reizenstein et al., as cited in Zimring et al., 1987). Sound-absorbing materials (carpeting, furnishings) would help. Television sets are often positioned in patient rooms so that patients can see them from the bed, but visitors have to sit in uncomfortable positions for a good view (Carpman & Grant, 1984, as cited in Zimring et al., 1987). Privacy is also an issue: Visitors have no place to go for a private conversation. Conference rooms accessible to visitors, or screened portions of waiting areas could alleviate this design problem (Reizenstein et al., as cited in Zimring et al., 1987). The list of design concerns for visitors includes many other dimensions we have discussed previously in other contexts, such as lighting, segregation of smokers and nonsmokers, odors, and furniture arrangements in waiting areas and patient rooms. Indeed, all of these components communicate whether or not the visitor has been considered when the design was developed.

PRISON DESIGN AND BEHAVIOR

Even during economically difficult periods, one thing society seems to be able to fund is the building of more prisons. Given that prisoners are confined for long periods of time, it would seem that prison design could have important consequences. Recall from Chapter 9 that research by Paulus and his colleagues has led to some important conclusions regarding the behavioral effects of prison design. Among other things, they found that different architectural layouts of residence space in prisons affected behavior and health. Grouping prisoners together in large numbers was less healthy than grouping them together in small numbers (Cox et al., 1982; Cox, Paulus, & McCain, 1984; Schaeffer et al., 1988). Single- or double-occupancy cells were better (i.e., judged as less crowded) than were cells grouping small numbers of prisoners. Further, if large groups were "broken up" by partitions or segmentation of space (so that the large group became several smaller ones), psychological and physical health was improved.

These findings provide strong evidence that the design of prisons influences mood and behavior of prisoners. At one level, this is not surprising. Prisons are usually designed along functional criteria and are not built for aesthetic reasons. Space is designed to facilitate order and regimentation. Bars and walls are deliberate attempts to constrain behavior, and economy is usually an important factor in determining the use of space. However, it is also clear that prison designs can have unintended, demoralizing effects, and new prisons have been increasingly designed to avoid some of these consequences (Luxenberg, 1977). This has occurred in spite of objections based on differing penal philosophies and increased costs.

The ethic that guided traditional prison design evolved from nineteenth-century concepts of correctional activity. Treatment was seen as being best accomplished by isolation from society, both physically and symbolically. To some extent, prisons' clear separation from society may be traced to this ethic. Also, most people see prisoners as nonproductive elements of society, so we place a special emphasis on economy. As a result of these pressures, prisons are usually large, located in remote areas, and surrounded by high exterior walls that deny inmates visual access to the outside world.

"New" prison designs usually seek to do several things. First, they attempt to provide more "humane" environments, replacing gun towers with natural barriers, adding color and lighting to otherwise drab settings, and increasing opportunities for privacy by providing more single-occupancy cells and by designing windows so narrow they do not need bars (Figure 12–11A and 11B). There has also been an attempt to build more cells into exterior walls so that inmates can have a view of the outside world. Control over the environment has also been heightened in some prisons, with inmates gaining control over heating, lighting, and even privacy in their own cells. Rather than separate observational booths or rooms for guards, the guards are placed directly in the living quarters of the inmates to increase interaction. These improvements have been made in conjunction with changing philosophies in dealing with people who break the law. Wener, Frazier, and Farbstein (1985, 1987) have indicated that such designs help remove the fear of violence at the hands of other inmates, resulting in 30 to 90 percent reductions in violence, similar drops in vandalism (e.g., to mattresses and light fixtures) and graffiti, and the virtual disappearance of homosexual rape (Figure 12–12).

DESIGNING FOR THE ELDERLY

Those over age 65 are the fastest growing segment of the population in the industrialized world, and those over age 85 are the fastest growing subgroup of the elderly. In the United States, 12 percent of the population was over 65 in 1987, and that figure will rise to 20 percent by 2030. Japan is the most rapidly aging country in the world, where the elderly population will grow from 10 percent in 1987 to 23 percent by 2020 (Dickson, 1987). As a greater proportion of our population becomes aged, providing specialized short- and long-term residential care facilities for them becomes very important. Certain characteristics of the elderly should be kept in mind when designing such environments. Especially important to consider is that the elderly are a heterogeneous

Figure 12–11A & 11B   The top picture displays a traditional prison gun tower and security wall. The bottom picture is a more contemporary facility with windows so narrow they do not require bars.

lot. Too often, designers have assumed that the elderly are a homogeneous group, when actually they have only age and certain health problems in common. In fact, there is probably no other segment of the population with

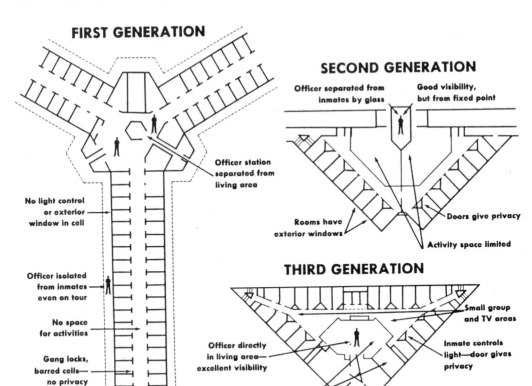

Figure 12–12 Floorplans of three generations of jails showing changes in surveillance and privacy. In third-generation jails, passive surveillance is replaced by active supervision; the officer becomes a service-providing professional rather than a turnkey, and must have skills in counseling, crisis intervention, and interpersonal communication. These changes can result in an increased sense of professionalism and the feeling that the job is challenging and desirable.

From Wener, Frazier, & Farbstein, 1987. Reprinted with permission from Psychology Today Magazine. *Copyright 1987, PT Partners, L.P.*

such a broad diversity of individual problems and needs. Some elderly citizens have trouble hearing, others have difficulty with vision, and still others have difficulty with locomotion. Many have no physical disabilities at all. Some elderly people suffer from psychological difficulties (e.g., withdrawal, distorted thought processes) while others do not. Another source of diversity in the elderly is the fact that individuals have established long-term behavior patterns, and these differ greatly among people. All of these considerations argue for "designing in" flexibility in any facility for the elderly. In gen-

eral, these facilities can be discussed as either institutional on noninstitutional, and together with in-home services such as Meals on Wheels they make up what is called a **continuum of care**. Institutional facilities are nursing homes and similar settings providing a relatively high level of care for residents, such as nursing care (e.g., administration of medications) and what is termed **custodial care**, or care for everyday needs such as meals and laundry. When the emphasis is on custodial care rather than medical care, the setting is often called **intermediate care** or **residential care** or **assisted living**. Despite our stereotypes, only 5 percent of those over age 65 live in nursing homes or similar facilities. Noninstitutional settings include retirement villages or similar housing where residents provide most of their own daily care. In Chapter 4 (box page 128), we described Lawton's model of environmental press and competence in the elderly, which holds that if the press of a specific environment is within the competence of the elderly to handle it, positive adaptation will occur. Design principles can be applied to institutional and noninstitutional facilities for the elderly to help them maintain competence (see also Altman, Lawton, & Wohlwill, 1984; Carp, 1987). If we use suitable designs to compensate for disabilities, we can enable the elderly to live as independently as possible in their own homes if feasible, and otherwise in suitable supportive settings. As their needs increase, accompanying design modifications along the continuum of care can help them maintain the highest degree of competence and control that their physical and cognitive condition will allow.

Noninstitutional Residences for the Elderly

In many ways, it is probably better if one can stay at home or in a relatively "homelike" setting without having to endure certain almost inevitable problems associated with institutional environments—certainly the elderly prefer it that way. Accordingly, special residential housing facilities for the elderly have been planned and built. Also, many services (e.g., "Meals on Wheels," home-based health care) are now made available to elderly citizens who are living "at home."

What type of residential housing for the aged seems to be best? Various elements (e.g., high and rising rents for people on fixed incomes, long-term residences being turned into condominiums) can make it difficult for the elderly to find a decent place to live at a reasonable price. Overall, studies suggest

that providing planned housing specifically for the elderly is superior to leaving them to find a residence on the "open market" (e.g., Carp, 1976; Lawton & Cohen, 1974). Is it best for the elderly to live in **age-segregated** or in heterogeneous environments? While arguments could be made citing costs and benefits of each environmental arrangement, the confluence of evidence suggests that the elderly prefer age-segregated housing. Living with others of one's own age is associated with housing satisfaction, neighborhood mobility, and positive morale (Grant, 1970; cf. Normoyle & Foley, 1988). Why is this the case? Perhaps it is because more similar others are in close proximity when the neighborhood is age-segregated, and both similarity and propinquity elicit attraction (Byrne, 1971). In addition, age segregation probably results in more activities that are appropriate to an elderly population. Also, specialized services (e.g., geriatric medical care) may be more easily targeted in an age-segregated setting, and annoyances, such as certain forms of noise, could be reduced.

What other factors should be taken into consideration when planning noninstitutional residences for the elderly? One important element in residential living for the aged population is adequate transportation. Too often, transportation is not sufficiently accessible for the elderly in the community. Planners should be certain there are bus routes running through areas with many senior citizens, and these should include stops at places where these individuals must go (i.e., medical complexes, shopping areas). Buses should also be accessible to elderly citizens (and others) with handicaps. In addition to making transportation systems physically available to the elderly, designers must explore means of making other aspects of the community accessible as well (e.g., Evans et al., 1984). Many elements in the environment (e.g., exterior stairways, nonautomatic doors) may be discouraging and dangerous to an elderly population.

Residential Care Facilities for the Elderly

How should designers approach the task of planning residential care facilities for this population? They should attempt to compensate as much as possible for the physical and psychological difficulties which some elderly individuals have, without unduly constraining the lives of people who have no particular problems (e.g., Baltes et al., 1987; Parmelee & Lawton, 1990). That is, designs should foster adaptation. A variety of environmental options should be provided, so that people can continue to engage in the same activities as they did prior to institutionalization. Also, it is important for designers to attempt to view things from the perspective of aged residents, which may differ from the ideas and needs of the staff of the facility or those of the designer. Too often facilities for the elderly are designed in accord with an architect's vision (which may not be sufficiently informed about the elderly), or are planned so that they make life easy for the nursing, cleaning, or maintenance staff of the institution. A study by Duffy et al. (1986), for example, found that designers and nursing home administrators were biased in favor of nursing home designs that emphasized social interaction, whereas residents who were not cognitively impaired actually preferred designs that fostered privacy.

A number of design features would seem to be useful to incorporate in a short- or long-term residential care facility for the elderly. First, it is important for the environment to provide for safety and convenience. To promote safety, a facility should permit sufficient staff surveillance to prevent accidents or to detect them when they do occur, while not eliciting the feeling that there is no privacy. In addition, specific design features should be included to prevent accidents (e.g., handrails in halls, "nonslip" surfaces), and aspects of the design certainly should not *cause*

accidents. For example, entrances should be protected from the elements: Many elderly are not steady on their feet, and snow, ice, rain, or wind around entrances can be extremely hazardous. Also, elements should be included that permit clients to notify staff if they have a problem in a private area (e.g., call buttons in bathrooms). The design should promote convenience by providing orientation aids (e.g., color-coded floors, cues to differentiate halls), as well as by affording comfort (e.g., chairs should be easy to get in and out of). Convenience is also fostered to the extent that the setting is "barrier free," and allows a large proportion of the population to move about independently. Finally, important facilities (e.g., bathrooms, communal areas) should be within easy access of rooms. In many ways, facilities conforming to the above criteria will promote feelings of personal control, prevent helplessness, and elicit positive outlooks in residents (for a review of the concepts of control and helplessness, see Chapter 4 and Rodin, 1986).

The design of a residential care facility for the elderly should also foster choice (and in doing so, feelings of control). The location of the facility should be sufficiently close to a community to allow residents to choose among a variety of available services (e.g., grocery stores, movie theaters; Smith, 1991). Choice is also facilitated when the design contains various types of spaces which can be used for special purposes (e.g., recreation, privacy, dyadic as opposed to large-group communication). Recreation areas should be designed to elicit communication (i.e., should be sociopetal), but some areas should afford privacy (i.e., should be sociofugal). It is very important that there be a range of social and recreational choices available to each resident (Lawton, 1979). Also, each resident should have access to both a bathtub and a shower, and it is preferable for each room to have individual heating controls. Bathrooms with "grab bars" and accessibility to wheelchairs improve safety and reduce dependence.

Without adequate degrees of choice being promoted by physical design, the environment can promote loss of perceived control and helplessness.

In addition to providing choices, objective physical conditions of the facility should be adequate and appropriate. Rooms should be of sufficient size, there should be enough recreational space for the resident population, and the construction should be of reasonable quality. Objective physical conditions affect patient behavior in many ways. When large sitting areas are occupied by relatively few residents, there seems to be a low level of physical interaction. Designs including long corridors appear to discourage resident mobility. When physical arrangements cause residents to be grouped in areas closely accessible to staff, some positive outcomes occur (e.g., the staff has more surveillance over accidents and danger, and interacts more with residents). However, some negative outcomes also occur under these circumstances (e.g., the staff may behave in ways that encourage patient dependency; Harris, Lipman, & Slater, 1977). It is also important for higher-functioning residents to have their own kitchen facility, or else residents tend to depend on staff members even to get a cup of coffee (Lipman & Slater, 1979). This situation encourages helplessness.

In addition to the physical environment, the social environment is extremely important to the well-being of the institutionalized elderly. A great deal of recent research has found that when the social environment fosters perceived choice and personal control, the well-being of the elderly is enhanced (cf. Rodin, 1986; Rowe & Kahn, 1987; Woodward & Wallston, 1987). Unfortunately, both the social conditions under which many people arrive at institutions and institutional life itself typically promote a loss of control (cf. Crozier & Burgess, 1992). The new resident is often stripped of his or her accustomed relationships and satisfactions, and must give up personal property which has served as a means of self-identification. Also, people frequently come to a residential care facility after having problems with illness, financial setbacks, and family difficulties, all of which foster a loss of control. Often, the family decides that the person cannot remain at home any longer and to which institution the person will go. The very character of institutional life (e.g., one must submit to rules and regulations, to authority, to "standardized" schedules and procedures) adds to one's loss of control (Wack & Rodin, 1978).

One's response to being relocated and entering a long-term residential care facility is more positive if he or she is afforded a degree of control over the process. Reactions are more favorable when the person has chosen to be institutionalized, has picked the particular facility that he or she will live in, and when the difference in control between the pre- and post-relocation environments is not great (Schulz & Brenner, 1977). In addition to providing control, one way to increase predictability (and hence resident well-being) is to give people preparatory information about their forthcoming move, which actually decreases mortality rates after relocation (Pastalan, 1976; Zweig & Csank, 1975). Another helpful procedure is to familiarize the resident with the building prior to the move by means of a three-dimensional model and slides of the various rooms and corridors (see Chapter 3). Among other things, this procedure aids wayfinding (and cognitive mapping) once the resident moves into the building (Hunt, 1984).

One problem for residents is that with subsequent declines (or improvements) in health, further relocation may be necessary. In order to minimize the negative effects of this movement, multilevel facilities—those that offer many levels of care and supervision in one place—are becoming popular. These are beneficial because they minimize the effects of relocation by making subsequent moves from one part of the facility to another, rather than from one facility to another. People can still have access to their friends and can be moved easily if their condition again improves or deteriorates. While this type of design offers benefits, it draws criticisms as well. Some say that the presence of people in deteriorated states of health can undermine the morale and create dependency (and even illness) in relatively more healthy residents (Gutman, 1978). The verdict still is not in on multilevel designs, and further research is necessary (Figure 12–13A and 13B).

Once one has relocated and is living in an institution for the elderly, aspects of the institutional environment (both physical and social) can foster a sense of loss of control. For example, a great deal more is done for residents of nursing homes than was the case in their former environments. What can we do to reverse this loss of control, which can eventually result in helplessness? One important element in solving the problem is for residents to be encouraged to do more things for themselves. In Chapter 4 we noted a study by Langer and Rodin (1976) in which one group of institutionalized elderly was treated in a way designed to increase feelings of control. In the group where control was fostered, residents were happier, their conditions had improved somewhat after several months, and they showed more activity (e.g., were more apt to attend a movie, and to participate in a contest) than in the condition where control was not encouraged.

Similar results were reported by Mercer and Kane (1979) and, in general, it seems that increasing control consistently leads to important psychosocial effects. Not only does it improve individual functioning, but it improves the overall atmosphere of the institution. Do the effects of control-increasing interventions persist? Here, the evidence is mixed: Some studies (e.g., Rodin & Langer, 1977) show long-term effects, while others (e.g., Schulz & Hanusa, 1978) do not. (We should note that Rodin and Langer instilled control by encouraging residents to make more decisions for themselves, whereas Schulz and Hanusa in part encouraged visitation and then discontinued it.)

Specialized Facilities for the Cognitively Impaired: Alzheimer Units

Although most elderly are not cognitively impaired, about 5 to 10 percent or so of those over 65 have **Alzheimer's disease**, which is characterized by loss of memory, confusion, impaired judgment, and progressive decline to more and more dependent states of existence. It is the fourth leading cause of death in the United States, afflicts at least four million Americans, and accounts for half of all nursing home admissions (e.g., Cook-Deegan, 1987). We have emphasized before the need to permit choice among nursing home residents. What happens when residents are so cognitively impaired that free choice can be dangerous? One answer is the creation of specialized Alzheimer units or dementia units within nursing homes or other suitable settings. (**Dementia** is a medical term meaning long-term loss of cognitive capabilities. Although Alzheimers' disease accounts for two-thirds of all dementias, there are many causes of dementia and the behavioral consequences of these diseases are such that the environmental interventions for them are essentially the same.)

Alzheimer units are designed with the idea that dementia patients display diminished judgment capabilities and progressive confusion. These residents are very prone to wandering off and can easily become lost. Traditionally, dementia victims have had to be physically or chemically restrained to prevent wandering and other potentially dangerous behavior. An Alzheimer unit attempts to minimize the need for these restraints: The setting is designed to make life safe and less restrictive by adjusting the environment to the behavior. For example, the units have locked access so that a key (or combination) is needed to leave the unit. Such an arrangement may sound cruel, but if it is carefully

Figure 12–13A & 13B   Providing several levels of care in a facility for the aged can minimze difficulties associated with relocation, but can also reduce the morale of healthier patients. An appropriate continuum of care provides an environment that supports the remaining capabilities of the residents.

designed, it permits minimal use of restraints: The residents can wander within the unit all they want without wandering off or otherwise endangering themselves. Most of the time the unit includes a secured outdoor area with open access for the residents, so they may wander in and out of the building but never away from the unit. A very important feature of these units is extra staffing and thorough training of the staff in behavioral management techniques, such as the use of reminiscence and diversion. Also, activities to keep the residents occupied are specially planned. Environmental considerations in-

clude nonglare floors (glare can increase confusion about orientation), extra orientation aids (such as pictures indicating locations of toilets; names of residents in large letters on the room door), pictures firmly affixed to walls (to prevent their inadvertent falling when touched out of curiosity), absence of "busy" interior decorations (which can add to confusion), and a lounge area with a Dutch door (i.e., a door with a bottom half that can be closed separately from the top half). The reason for this door is that at night, some residents will not be able to sleep, a phenomenon in Alzheimer's known as **day-night re-**

Figure 12–14 An example of a floor plan for a dementia unit. Note that the locked access still permits wandering through the facility, indoors and out.

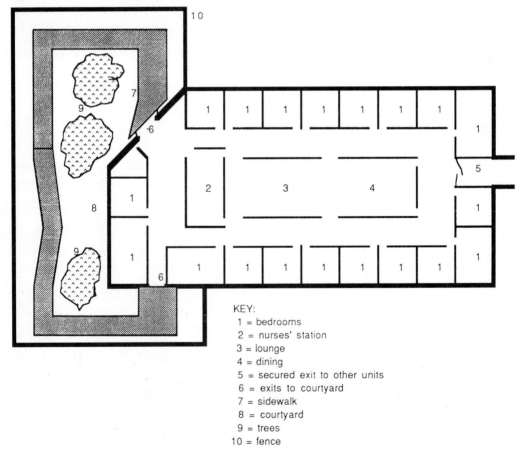

KEY:
1 = bedrooms
2 = nurses' station
3 = lounge
4 = dining
5 = secured exit to other units
6 = exits to courtyard
7 = sidewalk
8 = courtyard
9 = trees
10 = fence

versal or **sundowning**. If sleepless residents are forced to stay in their rooms, they will likely wake others. If permitted to roam in the lounge (with only the bottom half of the door closed to permit staff supervision), they typically do not disturb others. Although there are numerous variations of these dementia unit designs, a representative one is shown in Figure 12–14. How well do Alzheimer units work? Evidence suggests they have some merit (e.g., Ohta & Ohta, 1988). For example, Martichuski and Bell (1993)

explain how a well-designed facility with well-trained staff and a continuous activity program can reduce excess disability—the disability that occurs over and above the physiological cause of the dementia because of the environment in which the person lives. From a preliminary perspective, at least, the design of dementia units may have some desirable consequences (for additional reading on these units, see Calkins, 1987; Ohta & Ohta, 1988; Sloane et al., 1995; Sloane & Mathew, 1991).

CHAPTER SUMMARY

In American culture, strong preferences exist for single-family detached homes, apparently because such housing provides high control over social interaction. Economic and other factors, however, often lead to choices of other types of housing.

The more easily we can perform given tasks in a setting, the more satisfied we are with it. Other factors affecting residential satisfaction include noise, ease of cleaning, and adequate plumbing, heating, and kitchen facilities. For inner-city residents, satisfaction with a neighborhood is closely tied to social bonds.

Privacy is a significant mediator of activities in residences but is not a simple process. Whereas some families have a very open structure, others use design within the home to structure privacy for all family members. Another important issue is functional criteria in residential design. One current consideration is to combine several functions in one room, such as using a sunken bathtub as a conversation pit in a living room. Cultures differ greatly in segmentation of functions within the home.

Propinquity involves both objective physical distance and functional distance,

or the likelihood that two individuals will come into contact. Both types of propinquity facilitate the formation of friendships. Propinquity can also lead to annoyance and dissatisfaction; building a sense of community tends to maximize friendship and minimize annoyance.

Hospitals are often oriented toward a high-control, low-choice atmosphere to facilitate staff functioning. This tendency, however, reduces perceived control on the part of the patient, as well as privacy. Designs that restore control and foster social interaction can help in this regard, and can also facilitate patient recovery. A radial design of wards around a nursing station can improve staff efficiency and increase the amount of time staff spends with patients. Design features which could help hospital visitors include orientation maps, private areas, low-noise designs, and considerations for comfort.

Modern prison designs attempt to provide outdoor views and increased opportunities for privacy. Such designs are associated with reduced violence and vandalism.

Care facilities for the elderly need to consider the fact that characteristics and needs of the elderly vary widely, so designs should allow for flexibility. For those outside of institutions, planned housing in age-segregated areas seems to enhance satisfaction and morale; adequate transportation and shopping are also important (including for most of those in institutional settings). Whatever the setting, safety and convenience, choice and control, and physical conditions are important considerations. Large sitting areas may discourage social interaction. Long corridors may discourage mobility. Whereas proximity of residents to staff facilitates surveillance, it may also encourage dependence. Although providing several levels of care in one facility minimizes negative effects of relocation, morale of healthier residents can suffer from too much interaction with those in deteriorated states of health. Clearly, providing perceived control is one of the most effective interaction strategies for the institutionalized elderly. With dementia units, the idea is to adapt the environment to the special behavioral characteristics of the cognitively impaired.

SUGGESTED PROJECTS

1. Tour some model homes in the community. Compare the privacy available in the bedrooms, kitchens, and bathrooms. What behavioral adaptations do you anticipate once someone occupies the homes?

2. Observe the activities of an entire floor of a dormitory. In what ways do the behavioral adaptations resemble those of a private home? In what ways to they resemble those of a ghetto described by Scheflen?

3. Visit your local hospital and assess the following: (1) adequacy of orientation/wayfinding aids; (2) views from windows; (3) location of nurses' station relative to patient rooms. What improvements can you suggest?

4. Visit a nursing home or retirement home and note the location of lounge areas. Look for lounge areas that have a lot of interaction, and those with little interaction. What factors account for the differences? Can you identify design features intended to promote competence?

Work, Learning, and Leisure Environments

INTRODUCTION

WORK ENVIRONMENTS

A Brief History of Workplace Design

Ambient Work Environments

Noise

Music

Lighting

Windows

Furniture and Layout

Territoriality and Status in the Work Environment

Efficiency and Workflow

The Electronic Office

Designing the Office Landscape

Advantages of the Open-Plan Office

Disadvantages of the Open-Plan Office

Job Satisfaction and the Work Environment

Summary of Design in the Work Environment

LEARNING ENVIRONMENTS

Classroom Environments

Windowless Classrooms

The Open Classroom Concept

Environmental Complexity and Enrichment

Density

Day Care and Preschool Settings

Libraries

Multiple Functions

Orientation and Wayfinding

Visitor Behavior in Museum Environments

Wayfinding

Exploration

Fatigue in Museum Exploration

PEDESTRIAN ENVIRONMENTS: SHOPPING MALLS, PLAZAS, CROSSWALKS

MANAGEMENT OF NATURAL LANDS FOR LEISURE

Whose View?

Multiple Demands

Focusing on Needs and Outcomes

Congruence Between User and Setting

Prelude to Preservation

Summary: Leisure and Recreation Environments

CHAPTER SUMMARY

Suggested Projects

KEY TERMS

anthropocentric
assigned workspace
attraction gradient
carrying capacity
discontinuity
ecocentric
electronic cottage
exit gradient
extrinsic motivation
fixed workspace
friction–conformity model
intrinsic motivation
land ethic
landscaped office
link analysis

museum fatigue
open classrooms
open office
restorative environment
restorative experience
scientific management
solitude
space surround environment
video display terminal (VDT)
windowless classrooms
wind tunnel effect
workflow
workspace
you-are-here maps

INTRODUCTION

Harry and Sue were looking forward to the weekend. Harry's job at the factory was becoming more and more unpleasant. The machines were extremely loud and the company doctor had informed him last week he was losing his hearing in the sound frequencies most necessary for conversation. What was worse, relationships among his co-workers were deteriorating. Management was pressing for increased productivity, and the only way for him to produce more was to make faster trips between the supply room and his workstation. Other workers were doing the same thing, though, and they were all getting in each other's way. If his workstation could be closer to the supply room, at least one problem would be solved.

Sue was equally hassled. Her firm had just moved into a new office without interior walls. This change was supposed to reduce maintenance costs and increase ease of communication, with everyone in one large room. She could not stand it, though. She had to repri-

mand a secretary yesterday and there was no place to do it except at her desk where everyone else could hear the conversation. Her new workstation was attractive enough, and bristled with the latest in computer technology. Everything was efficient. The computer word processing program eliminated much of the time spent in rewriting. Company records were carefully filed in a database, and the computer could easily "talk" to those in various branch offices. Still, Sue seemed to be more tired lately. Her eyes hurt from staring at the computer screen, and she wondered if the pain in her back was not simply from spending too much time hunched over the keyboard. To make matters worse, her doctor had called today with unfavorable news on some lab tests, and it seemed as if everyone in the office heard at least her end of the conversation. Noise was a problem for her, too. She worked hard on a marketing report due today, but it took much longer than necessary because of all the distraction from phones ringing and everybody else talking.

The chatter of the copier ten feet from her desk did not help much either.

To get away from these headaches, Harry and Sue decided to go camping in the state park in the next county. After all, the convenience of the park was one reason they had chosen Rockport as a home. Arriving at the park entrance, the ranger informed them they were just in time to get one of the last two campsites available. They felt fortunate, though when they pulled into the campground it was discouraging to see that one of the remaining campsites was muddy and the other was next to a group of teenagers having a loud party. This was getting away from it all?

Have you had experiences similar to those described above? Unfortunately, they occur more often than we would like. Environmental psychologists have asked whether or not environmental design and management can make a difference in our lives of work, learning, and play. Are there ways of designing the factory, the classroom, the office, and the leisure setting so that undesired effects are minimized and desired results are maximized?

Admittedly, work, learning, and leisure seem worlds apart—unlikely companions in a chapter you might think. As we will see, however, the difference between work, learning, and leisure is often neither the activity we engage in nor the setting in which it takes place. The relative proportion of human time devoted to either work or leisure has varied from culture to culture (Csikszentmihalyi & Kleiber, 1991). Even in our time, it is hard to make an accurate estimate. Let's assume that most full-time job holders are required to work 8 hours a day, 5 days a week. If each worker gets 8 hours of sleep a night (56 hours a week), and works 40 hours, that should leave 72 hours per week for leisure or other activities. As Csikszentmihalyi and Kleiber (1991) point out, however, determining people's useful leisure time is not nearly so simple. Most people spend about 40 of the 72 "free" hours on nonwork, but not really discretionary activities like driving to and from work, shopping, household chores, and getting dressed. Many of the remaining 30 hours are likely to be committed to "getting ahead" at work (who really works just 40 hours, anyway?), or family responsibilities like coaching or watching athletic events. Both the large percentage of clearly allocated time devoted to work and learning and the scarcity (but importance) of leisure time argue for the importance of these environments in understanding the human condition.

WORK ENVIRONMENTS

In previous chapters we have discussed the effects of noise, temperature, and territorial identification on behavior, and in Chapter 11 we saw the importance of human factors engineering in facilitating the interaction of humans and machines. In the present section we will examine how these and other components of the environment can be incorporated into the process of designing the work environment, which is sometimes called the **workspace**. For those who wish to study the design of the work environment more thoroughly, detailed reviews of previous research exist elsewhere (Becker, 1981; Sundstrom, 1986b, 1987; Wineman, 1986). For our purposes, we will highlight some of the important findings of this research. As we begin, you might find it helpful to examine how our eclectic model applies to behavior in work settings (Figure 13–1). Briefly, we may perceive the work environment as fitting or not fitting our needs; the adaptive responses we employ and resulting potential aftereffects (e.g., fulfillment, exhaustion upon arriving "home") may be mediated by processes such as arousal, overload, or stress.

A BRIEF HISTORY OF WORKPLACE DESIGN

Before the Industrial Revolution, nonfarm work was typically done in small spaces, often in the craftsperson's or businessperson's home. Of course, even in early times, some specialized products required the labor of several persons, and the specialized work places sometimes took a shape dictated by their product. Ropewalks, for example, were buildings in which rope was woven. Before the introduction of modern coiling machines, the maximum length of a rope was dictated by the length of the building in which it was manufactured (Kostof, 1987). Hence, ropewalks were simple, but extremely long. One built in Charlestown, Massachusetts, in 1838 was a quarter of a mile long. Early factories were limited by their reliance on water for power and the sun for lighting. Because they required swiftly flowing streams, often they had to be constructed on remote sites far from the populated (but flat) coastal strip. Mill towns became self-contained communities, often wholly owned by one partnership (Kostof, 1987). The reliance on water to power these early mills and factories also dictated their shape. A water wheel outside the factory turned a long shaft that extended inside the building. Off this shaft ran a series of belts that powered the factory's machinery. Thus, the technology of the power source dictated a long building, and the need for sunlight limited building width to about 60 feet, or 18 meters (Sundstrom, 1986b; Figure 13–2).

Working conditions in early American factories were miserable, a situation which persisted through the early 1900s in North America. At that time several factors combined to cause rapid improvements (Sundstrom, 1986b). First, a tragic disregard for

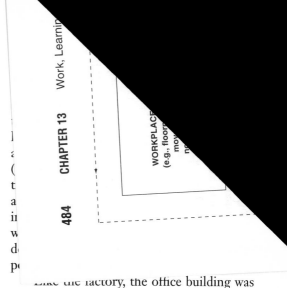

Like the factory, the office building was restricted by construction technology. Stone construction and the absence of elevators meant that buildings could not be more than six to ten stories high, and the need for adequate lighting through windows dictated a fairly narrow building. Two developments in technology changed both the factory and the office. First, iron and later structural steel, combined with concrete, made it possible to span larger spaces as well as to build higher and higher. (With stone construction, walls had to be so thick at the base for support of upper floors that tall buildings were impractical.) Second, commercially available electricity allowed for more extensive indoor lighting and elevators in tall buildings, as well as the ability to separate manufacturing machines from a central power shaft. It then became technologically possible to set up a factory or office in an almost infinite number of ways (Sundstrom, 1986b).

What will be the workplace of the future? The emergence of high technology, particularly the computer, has had a profound effect on the workplace. It may be that computers will take over tasks that were once routine, increasing both productivity and the quality of worklife. On the other hand, office automation may result in loss of employment, lowered skill requirements, and an inhumane workplace (Turnage, 1990). What

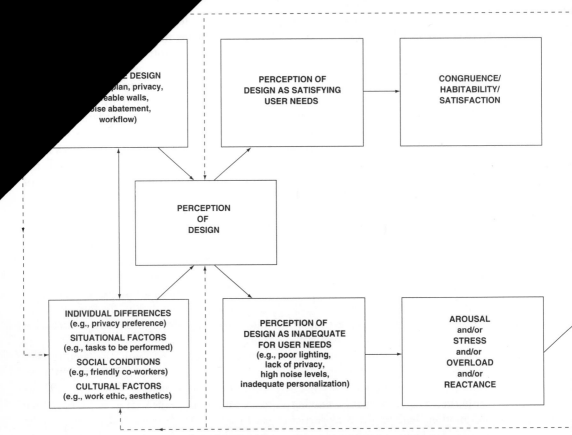

Figure 13-1 Our eclectic model applied to the workplace

will be the effects of the workplace in determining our quality of life as we reach toward a new century?

AMBIENT WORK ENVIRONMENTS

As a student of environmental psychology you will not be surprised to learn that the physical environment can affect productivity and satisfaction in work environments. Prior to the twentieth century, choking fumes and deafening noise, for example, were considered part of the normal manufacturing process. Concern for the safety and health of workers, along with studies showing that productivity and accident rates could be influenced by physical working conditions,

has led to standards for lighting, ventilation, noise, and so on which not only provide for greater safety, but also reduce threats to productivity and job satisfaction. In fact, the importance of the work environment is so obvious, modern workplace designers have been quite successful in manipulating many of the relevant dimensions; most of us expect to work in an environment that is well lit, not too warm, not too cold, and free from physically damaging noise levels. Of course for those in outdoor occupations, the environments cannot be as carefully controlled, and some other jobs typically require work in extreme conditions (for example, boiler tenders and airline ground crews). For these occupations, the ambient environment is the

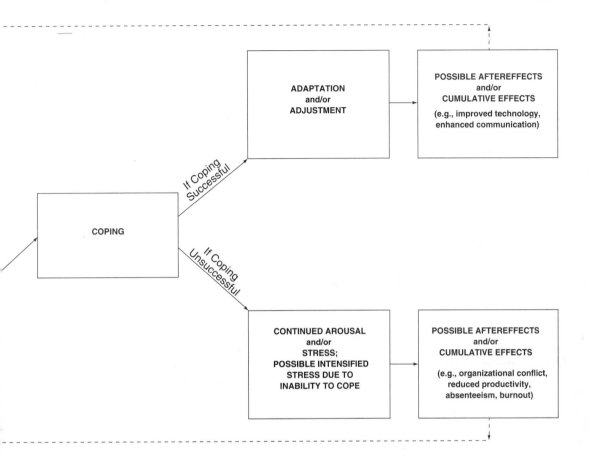

Figure 13–2 Early American factories were dependent on swift streams for power.

direct source of stress. We refer you to Chapters 4, 5, 6, and 7 for reviews of both theories and examples of individual stressor effects. In this chapter, however, we will restrict ourselves to what may be a more typical situation in which the heating, ventilating, and cooling system works, and the lights function.

Noise

Let us consider office noise as an example. You may recall that in Chapter 5 we defined noise as unwanted sound. Unlike visual distractions, noise cannot be easily avoided by turning one's head. From the perspective of the environmental load approach, workers in noisy offices are forced to process not only their particular tasks, but all ambient sound information as well (Loewen & Suedfeld, 1992). In one recent survey of more than two thousand workers, 54 percent said that they were bothered by noise. Researchers have concluded that one of the most distracting noises is overheard speech (presumably speech is meaningful, automatically attended to, and difficult to ignore; e.g., Boyce, 1974; Loewen & Suedfeld, 1993; Sundstrom, 1987, 1994). Preliminary evidence suggests that noise may act as a dissatisfier; that is, job satisfaction goes down in noisy conditions, but a corresponding increase in job satisfaction does not necessarily follow noise reduction efforts (Sundstrom et al., 1994).

Music

Music is another source of sound in the workplace—one that is technically considered noise only if someone does not like it. Do you like to read or study with music playing in the room? Does your answer depend on the *type* of music? Several of the theoretical models we discussed in Chapter 4 might be used to predict the effects of music (see also Figure 13–1). If it raises your arousal to some optimal level without either overarousing you or creating a distracting source of informa-

tion, we might expect your performance to improve. Sundstrom (1986b) reviewed the evidence on music in the workplace and reported that although much of the research is the private, inaccessible property of firms that sell music systems to businesses, published research may or may not support the idea that music enhances the work environment. At one time it was actually thought that singing and/or listening to music with a steady, somewhat upbeat rhythm improved productivity. Later it was felt that pleasant music made employees cheerful and the environment enjoyable. Research indicates that in factories, music may or may not slightly improve productivity, but employees like it anyway. In offices, music may facilitate vigilance tasks (e.g., where an employee must monitor a screen), although it can be distracting for some. At any rate, employees often report that music helps provide a pleasant atmosphere, which may ensure that it will always be found in some work settings.

Lighting

How does interior lighting affect our behavior? Investigations of performance effects of different lighting conditions date back to the beginning of this century (see the box on page 439). Lighting can affect how well we perform in many contexts, ranging from an examination to an experimental task in a laboratory, to a job on an automobile assembly line. At a very basic level, lighting affects performance by making it harder or easier to see what we are doing. At one extreme, the absence of light makes it impossible to take an exam because we cannot read the questions. On the other hand, we may not be able to see the questions on the exam if there is too much light.

As it turns out, illumination engineering is a rather complex task. Not only does one need to consider the amount, color, and location of a light source, but also reflectance from walls and ceilings, the contrast in luminance between a given area (the work table, for example) and the surroundings, and glare. Fortunately the Illumination Engineering Society has adopted recommendations for determining the appropriate levels of illumination for a variety of tasks and environments (Kaufman & Christensen, 1984). Generally, the data indicate that increasing illumination results in smaller and smaller improvements until performance levels off or drops because of glare or a reduction of the clarity of patterned visual stimuli (Logan & Berger, 1961; Sanders & McCormick, 1987). The disabling effects of glare can include light scattered by irregularities within the structure of the eye, and *transient adaptation* which occurs as the eyes are drawn to a bright light source and become adapted to it, thus reducing their sensitivity to less bright objects (Trotter, 1982). In particular, glare and other effects of poor lighting have become more important with increased proliferation of computer **video display terminals (VDTs)**. In general, greater performance improvements are achieved by improving the visual features of the task itself, such as the size and contrast of objects or messages, than by increasing illumination (Boyce, 1981). Nevertheless, Sanders and McCormick (1987) note that over the years the recommended levels of illumination have increased and are about five times greater than the levels recommended for the same tasks 30 years ago.

Windows

Perhaps the most pleasant light is natural. Windows figure prominently in the general ambience, as well as in the illumination of a setting. In factories, Pritchard (1964) has argued that the lack of windows does not reduce worker efficiency. On the other hand, research on underground factories in Sweden has suggested that workers in windowless environments tend to suffer more fatigue

and somatic distress (e.g., headaches) and to express more negative feelings about the setting (Hollister, 1968). To some extent, lack of windows can be compensated for by providing high levels of lighting and air conditioning, but the general conclusion to be drawn is that workers do not like windowless settings (Collins, 1975).

In office environments, the presence of windows also appears to be important. Research has indicated that regardless of whether occupants are satisfied with most aspects of their offices, not having windows leads to dissatisfaction (Ruys, 1970). The desire for windows in an office environment appears so strong that Ruys (1970) concluded that the problems created by windowless offices could not be corrected without installing windows. According to Collins (1975), windowlessness is particularly troublesome for those in sedentary jobs or restricted environments. Presumably, windows may provide these workers with stimulation and variety in an otherwise routine workday. Of course windows are important sources of information about the weather or time of day (Ruys, 1970; Sommer, 1983), but visual contact with the natural environment may be even more important (e.g., Heerwagen & Orians, 1986; Ulrich, 1984). For example, workers may attempt to compensate for a lack of windows by hanging landscape pictures, travel posters, and other decorations. In a study conducted in a university setting, Heerwagen and Orians (1986) found that decorations in windowless offices were dominated by nature scenes, such as landscape paintings. This finding would suggest that, consistent with our suggestion in Chapter 2, humans find **restorative experiences** in viewing nature, and this helps cope with stress in the office. On the other hand, a more recent summary of four studies (Biner et al., 1993) did not find evidence that window substitutes depicting nature, such as pictures or plants, could compensate for the absence of windows and concluded that space personalization was a more important reason that people used such substitutes in the office.

FURNITURE AND LAYOUT

The layout and design of the workplace may be an important determinant of people's impressions of the company or organization (for a closer look at furnishing and faculty offices, see the box on pages 494–495). The use of a desk as a "barrier" between the office occupant and a visitor can communicate a desire for physical and psychological distance, as well as status differences. Joiner (1971) observed that high-status office occupants were more likely to use a closed desk arrangement (the desk sits between the visitor and the office occupant) rather than an open placement (in which the desk is placed against the wall). Furthermore, desk arrangement can also have implications for the pleasantness of the interaction and the visitor's level of comfort (Morrow & McElroy, 1981). According to Zweigenhaft (1976), seating arranged at right angles is perceived as facilitating cooperation and affiliation. In one investigation of photos of reception areas, organizations judged by students and executives as the most considerate and likable had upholstered couches and chairs at right angles and prominently displayed floral arrangements. Firms rated as moderately considerate had four chairs surrounding a coffee table, contemporary artwork, and either one or three plants. Finally, the firms judged least considerate lacked artwork and had chairs placed directly facing one another across a coffee table (Ornstein, 1992).

Research has shown that decorated spaces make people feel more comfortable than do undecorated spaces (Campbell, 1979), and that good moods associated with pleasant environments seem to increase people's willingness to help each other (Sherrod et al.,

1977). Yet we can also guess that for some kinds of work, the positive feeling associated with decorated space may also be disruptive. People feel more like talking to one another in pleasant settings (Russell & Mehrabian, 1978), and to the extent that socializing in the office detracts from effective or efficient working, pleasantness can be a problem. Research has also suggested that room decorations may be distracting (e.g., Baum & Davis, 1976), but whether this is a problem depends on how a setting is perceived (Worchel & Teddlie, 1976).

TERRITORIALITY AND STATUS IN THE WORK ENVIRONMENT

We discussed territoriality in Chapter 8 as it relates to many of our relationships with the environment. Some researchers also believe that territories are important in work environments. Often the concept relates to assignment of a specific area or machine to a worker, and is termed **assigned workspace** (Sundstrom, 1986b). It is often believed, for example, that if a large machine in a factory is assigned to one worker, that worker will take better care of it than if all workers roam from machine to machine. The same concept is often called the **fixed workspace**. Sundstrom (1986b) suggests that the right to treat a workspace as a territory might lead to more personal attachment to it, more perceived control over it, and thus more of a sense of responsibility for it and more signs of personalization of the workspace. Whether workers in fact prefer clearly defined territories and whether territories improve job satisfaction or productivity is open to question. Most likely, territories become more important to workers the higher the rank they have in the organization. At higher ranks, territories may become symbols of status (Sundstrom, 1986b).

Status symbols in the office or factory may be important in several ways. For example, they communicate status and power to others, they compensate employees as a nonmonetary benefit, and they serve as props or tools (such as larger desks, filing cabinets, computer terminals), which the worker is privileged to use on the job (Sundstrom, 1986b). In addition to furnishings such as desks and size and comfort of chairs, typical status symbols include amount of floorspace, the capacity to regulate privacy and accessibility (e.g., through an enclosed office), and the right to personalize the workspace. One large firm, for example, provides carpeting, a bottle water dispenser, and plants as one moves up the corporate ladder. Apparently, the more one can attach status to the office space, the more satisfied one is with the job (Konar et al., 1982).

EFFICIENCY AND WORKFLOW

The principle of **workflow** (originally called straight-line flow of work) is based on the idea that the layout of a factory or office should provide for the shortest possible distance between workstations along which the work moves (e.g., Hicks, 1977). For example, an assembly line should be arranged so that workers do not have to spend long amounts of time walking from the point where they finish their assignment on a product back to the point where they start the assignment on the next item. Also, space for supplies should be provided as close to the assembly line as possible so that workers do not have to spend excessive time moving from the supply area to the assembly area. Similarly, an office should be arranged so that related departments are close to each other. If paperwork moves from Office A to Office B to Office C to Office D, in that order, the offices should not be arranged with A on the tenth floor, C next to it, B on the fifth floor, and D on the sixth floor. Rather, the offices should be located in the order that the paperwork actually flows.

On a smaller scale, similar considerations apply to the placement of the components of a workstation (the area of a factory or office assigned to an individual), such as tables, computer equipment, or even the knobs and dials on a control console. **Link analysis** is a term applied to the systematic investigation of the number of times a movement is made to adjust a control or read a display. Proper positioning of workspace elements will minimize the distances required for common or sensitive activities to reduce errors and fatigue (Sanders & McCormick, 1987).

THE ELECTRONIC OFFICE

Advances in computer technology (Figure 13–3) have made dramatic changes in the workplace (e.g., Carlopio & Gardner, 1992; Grandjean, Hunting, & Pidermann, 1983; Kleeman, 1988). At many colleges both faculty and students make extensive use of computer word processing programs for writing and revising memos, papers, and book chapters. The so-called "information highway" promises to revolutionize access to information (and the potential to generate an information glut). Soon trips to the business office, registrar, mailbox, or filing cabinet will be unnecessary, and we will have the "convenience" (some might say "misfortune") of never having to leave our desks. Whether this technology is a blessing or a curse may depend in part upon our ability to exploit the computer's strengths and adjust to its demands. With the proliferation of video display terminals (VDTs) workers began complaining of eyestrain, headaches, back pain, and fatigue (Carlopio & Gardner, 1992; Kleeman, 1988; Stellman et al., 1987; Turnage, 1990).

These concerns have sparked a number of investigations. Unfortunately, not all researchers have been able to control for task characteristics, office and workstation design, gender, pay, and benefits (Starr, Thompson, & Shute, 1982). In fact, several studies

Figure 13–3 Advancements in computer technology in the workplace have sometimes led to new problems for workers.

that have held these confounding variables constant have concluded that VDTs are not themselves responsible for most of the health complaints attributed to them. For example, in a comparison between directory assistance operators who used good quality VDTs and a similar group working from paper documents, Starr et al. (1982) found no evidence that the terminals were more likely to lead to eyestrain or decreases in comfort or morale. Although several studies have concluded that people read text from VDT screens more slowly (e.g., Gould & Grischowsky, 1984), Gould et al. (1987) found reading rates similar to those for good quality paper printing when displays were designed to combine dark letters on a light background, a high quality display terminal, and specially adjusted lettering.

This is not to say that VDTs are necessarily benign. Glare from lights and windows is likely to cause discomfort, so careful location of the display, adjustable workstation

furniture, and occasional breaks to rest the eyes and hands are recommended (Garcia & Wierwille, 1985; Kleeman, 1988; Rose, 1987). Unfortunately, it seems that many organizations focus on acquiring the newest technology without paying simultaneous attention to ergonomically designed (designed with human capabilities and needs in mind) furniture and input devices. In 1985, one survey found that only 5 to 10 percent of VDT workers had fully satisfactory ergonomic conditions (Westin et al., 1985). Furthermore, job-related stress may occur in part because of the indirect effects of VDTs on jobs (Turnage, 1990). Computers reduce the need for workers to move around the office to accomplish their jobs and this, combined with the possibility of computer monitoring of a worker's progress, may usher in an era of greater workloads, fewer breaks, and less autonomy (Sundstrom, 1986b; Turnage, 1990).

Overall, people with personal computers (PCs) report being more satisfied with their job and the work site than those without (Carlopio & Gardner, 1992). Some have speculated that this results from the possession of a status symbol (Davis, 1986) or it may simply be that a computer makes the worker more efficient. The same technology is capable of allowing exciting new freedoms to workers. For some, a trip to the "office" involves walking into a different room in the house. Communications networks now allow workers to perform many of their chores from home-based work stations, an **electronic cottage** (Toffler, 1980). As Sundstrom (1986b, 1987) notes, such an arrangement might eliminate much of the cost and inconvenience of commuting, but such a decentralized work force will put new demands on supervisors and weaken some of the organization's control. Indeed, the role of the employee may change to that of a contractor, and the office building may become essentially a conference center for those meetings that require face-to-face encounters rather than telephone or video conferences.

DESIGNING THE OFFICE LANDSCAPE

We have mentioned that the use of structural steel in buildings has allowed architects to design larger and larger open spaces. With previous construction methods, the need for support walls required a building to be separated into smaller rooms. Accordingly, a relatively small number of workers shared an office. Typically, a manager or executive would have a totally private office, and several clerical workers would share an adjoining space. Such office designs are still common today, but there is also an alternative permitted by a large open space. To facilitate workflow, for example, work stations for 100 or more clerks could be put in the same large room, with supervisors' offices along the sides of the large room. With the growth of the human relations movement in the 1950s, more open communication between workers and managers was encouraged, employees were allowed and even encouraged to participate in decision making, and barriers of status and authority became less prominent. These developments encouraged what is now known as the **landscaped office** or **open office** (Figure 13–4A and 4B). This concept probably originated in Germany with work by the Schnelle brothers and their Quickborner Team consulting firm (Sundstrom, 1986b). Basically, the idea involves arranging desks, filing cabinets, and other office furniture in such a manner as to make maximum use of the large open space but still provide for efficient workflow. The office landscape design typically places a

Figure 13–4A & 4B   Traditional (on left) versus open office design

supervisor very near workers and arranges work areas close together or far apart so that workflow and communication between related areas is unimpeded by myriad enclosed offices. In some schemes, portable screens are used to set areas off from others, or shelving and filing cabinets may accomplish the same purpose. As you might expect, such an office design has a number of advantages, but also carries with it a number of disadvantages (e.g., Becker et al., 1983; Brooks & Kaplan, 1972; Oldham, 1988; Oldham & Brass, 1979; Sundstrom, 1986b). Let us examine some of these separately.

Advantages of the Open-Plan Office

We have already mentioned one advantage of the open office: It provides for a more efficient flow of work and communication. In addition, it often costs less because there are no internal walls to construct, and lighting and ductwork can be shared by several workspaces. Maintenance costs may also be reduced due to less painting and faster cleaning of work areas, and more people can be accommodated in the same interior space without walls. Moreover, it is easier to make changes in the design of the office when new jobs are added or eliminated or the number of people working on a project changes, because there are no fixed walls to move or add to change spatial arrangements. Also, the open office permits easier supervision of workers. That is, a supervisor can see all workers from his or her desk without having to walk through several offices. Furthermore, there is evidence for social facilitation in nonprivate offices (Block & Stokes, 1989): A number of researchers have demonstrated that the mere presence of others improves performance, at least for simple tasks.

Disadvantages of the Open-Plan Office

Typically, changes in any environment cannot be made without trade-offs, and open offices are no exception. For all the potential advantages of the open office, it carries disadvantages that fall into two major categories: increased noise and distraction, and lack of adequate privacy. When offices are separated by walls, the noise from typewriters, phones, and duplicating machines in one area seldom penetrates into the next office. With the open office plan, however, the noises may be very distracting to those in neighboring workstations. Similarly, conversation travels, and as we saw in Chapter 5, noise that is interpretable as conversation is quite distracting. Indeed, although open offices may facilitate social conversations, there is little evidence that organizationally relevant communication improves (Wineman, 1982). Movement of people as they walk about doing assigned tasks is also more noticeable in the open office plan, and adds still another source of distraction. Solutions to the problem of noise and distraction include office machinery designed to be quieter, carpeting and other treatment to muffle sounds, and the use of portable barriers (partitions, shelving, cabinets) to help screen out the distraction. One less obvious solution to the distracting quality of overheard conversations is to actually *increase* the overall level of noise by adding a source of so-called "white noise." White noise is made up of all audible sound frequencies and might be described as a hissing or humming sound. Played at a constant level, it may mask the distracting character of conversations and other meaningful office sounds (Loewen & Suedfeld, 1992).

Loss of privacy is also very noticeable in open offices. Personal conversations are easily overheard and communication between supervisors and workers becomes more difficult to keep confidential. Just as open offices facilitate supervision, so they also reduce privacy for supervisors. Thus, supervisors seem to be more satisfied with traditional closed offices than nonsupervisors (Carlopio & Gardner, 1992). Every move a worker makes is open for public view. Phone calls with family members are overheard. Errors and embarrassing behavior are there for all to see, and personalizing the workspace with artwork or mementos may be discouraged. As with noise and distraction, use of portable barriers may help solve the privacy problem in the open office, but these barriers cannot provide the privacy of an enclosed, individual office (e.g., Hundert & Greenfield, 1969; Pile, 1978; Sundstrom, 1986b). Employees who move from a conventional office to an open arrangement may complain of loss of privacy and suffer from reduced job satisfaction (Oldham & Brass, 1979). Although recent evidence suggests that enclosure (open versus closed design) may not be as important as other factors such as the ability to adjust one's workspace (O'Neil, 1994), Oldham (1988) demonstrated the therapeutic effects of moving employees from an open office to either a partitioned office or a lower density open-plan office that allowed more space per employee.

In sum, open office plans provide both advantages and disadvantages. The increased opportunity for communication may facilitate some flow of work, but also increases distraction and reduces privacy. Depending on the functions to be accomplished in a given office, the disadvantages may outweigh the advantages (see also Becker et al., 1983; Block & Stokes, 1989; Goodrich, 1982; Marans & Spreckelmeyer, 1981; Sundstrom, Herbert, & Brown, 1982; Wineman, 1982).

JOB SATISFACTION AND THE WORK ENVIRONMENT

In addition to productivity, managers and others have become concerned that design of the work environment can influence job satisfaction. Although most research suggests that job satisfaction does not directly increase productivity (e.g., Landy, 1989), it is sometimes believed that the more satisfied

the worker, the better an employee he or she makes in terms of such factors as loyalty, absenteeism, and turnover. In general, employees do list physical conditions as important for job satisfaction, although the physical environment is not as important in this regard as such factors as job security, pay, and friendly co-workers (e.g., Crouch & Nimran, 1989; Herzberg, Mausner, & Syderman, 1959). One influential theory in industrial psychology and management suggests that an adequate work environment does not substantially enhance job satisfaction, but that a substandard environment definitely leads to dissatisfaction (Herzberg, 1966; Herzberg, Mausner, & Syderman, 1959). In Chapters 4 and 5 we emphasized the importance of perceived control in moderating the effects of environmental stressors. In that light, it may not be surprising than one recent postoccupancy evaluation of a successful office relocation emphasized the importance of targeting a limited number of small-scale (personally meaningful) improvements and enlisting employee participation in planning change (Spreckelmeyer, 1993).

SUMMARY OF DESIGN IN THE WORK ENVIRONMENT

Technological developments permit great flexibility in designing work environments. Central to workspace design are the issues of: (1) productivity, especially as it relates to workflow, safety, and health; and (2) job satisfaction. In general, work environments can be designed to maximize productivity through facilitating workflow and providing safe and healthy working conditions. Although job satisfaction is related to quality of the work environment, other factors such as the social environment are usually more important. The ability to treat a workspace as a territory and to adjust it and to personalize it serves as a form of status and may increase job satisfaction, especially at higher

THE FACULTY OFFICE

One environment ripe for investigation, and one with which you are probably familiar, is the university faculty office. Have you strolled down a hallway of professors' offices and speculated on the character of their occupants? Is a neat office the sign of a neat mind, or is it sterile and cold? Do decorations or living things make workplaces more hospitable? Does a particular office convey a sense of distance or welcome? Research on faculty offices has centered on three issues: the placement of the desk, aesthetics, and overall neatness.

Desk Placement Much of the interest in desk placement probably began with a survey of ten London firms conducted by Joiner (1971). He found that higher status individuals tended to place their desk between themselves and the door rather than against a side or back wall. This finding led Zweigenhaft (1976) to hypothesize that faculty who placed their desks between themselves and visiting students would be using the desk as a physical barrier (perhaps inadvertently) and would be perceived as more behaviorally distant than those who used a more barrier-free arrangement. Consistent with Joiner's observations regarding status, Zweigenhaft's survey found that senior faculty (full professors and associate professors) were more likely to use the closed desk (desk-between) arrangement. Furthermore, those faculty members who used an open desk arrangement, in which the desk did not separate the faculty person and his or her visitors, were more likely to be rated positively by students. Other researchers have also observed open desk placement to be associated with more positive student feelings (Morrow & McElroy, 1981) and also with positive evaluations by other faculty members (McElroy & Morrow, 1983). On the other hand, at least one attempt at replication failed to confirm the effect of desk placement (Campbell & Herren, 1978), and another found only a weak effect (Campbell, 1979). Perhaps a study by Hensley (1982) clarifies the situation. Hensley hypothesized that although there is a relationship between faculty desk placement and student evaluations, instead of the office arrangement causing more positive evaluations, both the evaluations of the teacher and the desk placement result from the influence of a

ranks in the organization. The nature of the workplace is changing. Fewer employees are exposed to extremes in temperature and noise. On the other hand, changes such as the mass introduction of desktop computers have the potential to become either new sources of work-related stress, or the source of a more involving and pleasant workplace.

LEARNING ENVIRONMENTS

Education is a central component of the socialization of youngsters and provides them with the tools for life. Accordingly, the effects of the design of learning environments on the activities within them has been of great interest to researchers. These envi-

third variable, the professor's formality or attitude toward education. Thus, a formal teacher is also likely to choose a more formal office, and an informal teacher is likely to have an open, informal desk arrangement. Hensley's results support his contention in that more traditional educational philosophies were more often associated with a closed desk arrangement. In addition, the desk arrangement was also affected by the number of advisees a professor had. Perhaps because a more open desk arrangement facilitates activities such as reviewing records or completing schedules, even traditional professors with a large number of advisees tended to adopt an open desk placement.

Aesthetics and Neatness at the Office   Campbell (1979) used slide photographs to investigate the effects of presence or absence of living things (four potted plants and two aquariums with fish) or art objects (four wall posters and a macramé hanging). Students associated these decorations with feelings of welcome and comfort, and expected the professor to be friendly and unhurried. Overall neatness may be even more important than decorations (see Figure 13–5). Very messy offices make the occupant appear to be busy and rushed, and to make visitors report that they would be less comfortable and welcome (Campbell, 1979; McElroy & Morrow, 1983; Morrow & McElroy, 1981). Morrow and McElroy also introduced an intermediate level of tidiness they refer to as "organized stacks." Interestingly, the organized stacks level of tidiness was evaluated as significantly more friendly, welcoming, and comfortable than either the messy or extremely neat office conditions (McElroy & Morrow, 1983; Morrow & McElroy, 1981).

Figure 13–5   What is the effect of a messy faculty office on students' perception of the occupant?

ronments may range from small dormitory study areas which we examined in Chapter 9, to a large formal library or museum settings which we study in this chapter, to even larger settings such as an entire university campus which we examined in Chapter 11. If design features are causing problems, they must be remedied in order to allow educational goals to be attained. If a design change can increase the effectiveness of education, so much the better. Let us now look at several design factors in a variety of educational settings.

CLASSROOM ENVIRONMENTS

Changes in classroom environments have been made more or less continuously since we abandoned the one-room schoolhouse. However, as we shall see, we are no longer bound to traditional designs for physical reasons, and research has indicated that changes in classroom design can result in more positive student attitudes and greater participation in class (Gump, 1984, 1987; Rivlin & Wolfe, 1985; Sommer & Olsen, 1980). Let us consider some of these innovations.

Windowless Classrooms

One innovation, the building of **windowless classrooms**, has not proven overwhelmingly successful. Originally designed to reduce distraction in the classroom, as well as to reduce heating costs, these new school buildings typically contain few if any windows. Research has suggested that the absence of windows in classrooms has no consistent effect on learning (some students improve, others show worse performance), but that it does reduce the pleasantness of students' moods (Ahrentzen et al., 1982; Karmel, 1965; Weinstein, 1979). A recent study in Sweden suggested that a windowless classroom may be associated with reduced growth

and lower concentration (Küller & Lindsten, 1992); because this study examined only two windowless and two windowed classrooms, the results must be interpreted with caution, although following the study, school authorities did add windows to the windowless rooms.

The Open Classroom Concept

The traditional design of classrooms, rectangularly shaped with straight rows of desks, dates back to medieval times, when the only source of light was natural light that came in through windows. Modern buildings, of course, do not rely solely on sunlight, so that new design alternatives are possible. **Open classrooms**, like open offices, are designed to free students from traditional barriers, such as restrictive seating. In such settings, students should have more opportunity to explore the learning environment (Figure 13–6).

Figure 13–6   A variation of an open classroom

Research evaluating these designs is confounded by the fact that the environment is typically not the only difference between open and traditional schools. That is, an "open education" philosophy implies freedom for students to move around and less structure in class activities. However, these could occur in a traditionally designed classroom and do not necessarily occur in open classrooms. Interestingly, Rivlin and Rothenberg (1976) found that behavior and performance in open-plan settings were not always consistent with the general philosophy of open education. In many open classrooms, students behave much as they do in traditional classrooms, and teachers often do not use all of the space provided. As is the case in traditional settings, students spend a great deal of time engaged in solitary tasks such as reading and writing. For example, Rothenberg and Rivlin (1975) found these percentages of total activities observed in one open classroom: writing 26 percent; arts and crafts 11.8 percent; talking 11.3 percent; reading 6.3 percent; working at projects 5.7 percent; and teaching 4.3 percent. However, Gump (1974) observed that students in open classrooms spend less time in directed activity than students in traditional settings, and that groups in open classrooms show greater variability in size. Such heightened flexibility in open-plan rooms is often accompanied by greater activity than in the traditional classroom.

Two serious problems with open-plan designs are that they provide inadequate privacy and foster too much noise (e.g., Ahrentzen et al., 1982; Brunetti, 1972; Rivlin & Rothenberg, 1976). These are the same problems we saw with open-plan offices. The flexibility provided by the open space can cause coordination problems, and frequently teachers do not know how to arrange furnishings so as to get the most use out of the space provided. Variable height partitions can reduce noise but still give the open

feeling (Evans & Lovell, 1979). It is conceivable that by combining aspects of traditional and open-design classrooms, better environments may be created. At present, however, reviews of this kind of physical design are mixed. Interestingly, Traub and Weiss (1974) found that suburban students' learning was not impaired in open classrooms, but city-dwelling students performed better in traditional than open classrooms. Moreover, the style of the teacher (e.g., lecture-oriented versus interactive), the age of the pupils, and whether they are learning disabled or have attention deficit disorders may be critical factors in the suitability of the open design. Overall, data-based studies indicate that open classroom designs are noisy, provide undesirable distractions, and do not foster adequate educational benefits to outweigh these problems (Bennett et al., 1980).

Environmental Complexity and Enrichment

What is the proper amount of environmental complexity in an educational setting? As we have seen elsewhere in this book, studies have indicated that the complexity of an environment can affect arousal and performance in that setting. Too many stimuli may distract students, create overload, or increase fatigue. However, extremely simple settings may be boring and equally detrimental to performance (cf. Sommer & Olsen, 1980).

Some researchers believe that classrooms should tend more toward the complex rather than the simple (Rosenzweig, 1966; Thompson & Heron, 1954). Having more stimuli and opportunities for environmental exploration present provides an enriched environment that facilitates learning. Others disagree, arguing that complex learning environments are distracting and make it difficult for the student to concentrate on school work (Vernon & McGill, 1957; Wohlwill, 1966). Comparative research is scant, but one study has examined the effects of variations in complexity of learning environments (Porteous, 1972). This study showed greater learning in less complex settings, supporting the position that overload and distraction are important problems in complex classrooms. Of course, classrooms serve more purposes than just learning content relevant to a specific topic. They also involve learning *how* to learn, learning social responsibility, and acquisition of cultural values. Different classroom environments may facilitate one of these purposes but not the others. How happy the pupil is in the setting may be the most important factor of all (Santrock, 1976), and working for the right fit between pupil and learning environment is probably worth the effort. Because things change with time, it is important to evaluate classroom design modifications continually. Wong, Sommer, and Cook (1992), for example, studied a University of California at Davis classroom that had been modified in the 1970s to provide a "softer" environment that would facilitate interaction among the students and instructor. Satisfaction had declined since 1974, but remained higher than in a prerenovation evaluation. Concerns were expressed about a 1970s color scheme and a faded carpet. Still, the design was perceived to enhance interaction.

Density

Whether the classroom is open or closed, windowless or windowed, or complex or simple, educators, parents, and students are concerned about the number of students in the class, or in the term more common to environmental psychologists, the *density* in the classroom (see also Chapter 9). In general, high density has minimal effects on learning of simple concepts appropriate to a lecture format, but interferes with learning of complex concepts and with activities that require students to interact (e.g., Smith & Connolly, 1980; Weinstein, 1979).

Day Care and Preschool Settings

As more and more families are characterized as single-parent with that parent working or as having dual-career parents, finding quality day care for children has become a paramount concern. Similarly, preschool programs are becoming fairly commonplace. A major goal of these settings is to teach scholastic skills (the alphabet, counting) as well as social skills (taking turns, sharing). Environment and behavior specialists have noted particular concerns with design features of these settings that impact the very youngest children—children whose age means they have very short attention spans and are easily distracted by visual movement and by noise. Design features that address these special concerns include carpeting to reduce noise and screens to reduce visual intrusion. Interestingly, Neill (1982) found that although carpeting increased teacher–pupil interaction, screens increased teacher time on paperwork and decreased their interaction with pupils. Also, activity areas that are separated from each other and traffic paths that reduce intrusion into these areas promote better learning behavior and may actually improve math and language skills and creativity (Nash, 1981; Weinstein, 1981).

LIBRARIES

Multiple Functions

Library designers have a number of unique problems with which they must deal. One familiar problem at university libraries is that patterns of use for study and reading areas move through periods of over- and underuse (e.g., Cziffra et al., 1975). Because underuse wastes space that could be used for books, a proposed design alternative for a university library would reserve the library for the storage and dispensation of materials. Reading and study areas would be eliminated from this setting and dispersed to other areas on the campus. For many students, such a separation of library and study functions would mean a major change in work style and would sometimes prove inconvenient. After all, the campus library often is the one place where students know they can get school work done (Figure 13–7)!

In another library use study, Lipetz (1970) observed how a sample of over 2,000 patrons used a library card catalog. Since a large proportion of users go to the catalog upon entering the building, the catalog is usually located near the entrance. As you might expect, the rate of library use varies across periods of the academic year, with some of the heaviest use occurring after vacations and semester breaks; designs for normal use may show signs of overstaffing during high-use periods. Now that most libraries are using a computerized catalog system, it is much easier to track catalog user patterns; even the computerized catalog is located near the entrance, but computeriza-

tion has allowed access to the catalog from stations throughout the library as well as from off-site locations.

Orientation and Wayfinding

Finding a book in a library is partly a problem of orientation to a large setting. Where do we start? Where do we go for help? Do we ask for information or try to find our way by reading signs? Pollet is one librarian who decades ago showed interest in helping libraries improve their orientation aids (e.g., Pollet, 1976; Pollet & Haskell, 1979). One of the most important observations she made is that library patrons must cope with information overload. Adding signs to help people find their way around contributes even more information to the environment. In particular, Pollet noted that clustering many signs together makes orientation information ineffective. People who are already receiving too much information are not apt to stop and look at a cluster of signs.

Figure 13–7 Libraries provide multiple functions—whether designed that way or not.

Libraries are learning to reduce the number of signs used and to experiment with critical locations of signs throughout the building. People need information at the point of making a decision about where to go next. One helpful technique is to use a specific color for orientation information. No matter where people are, they can look for that color and become oriented. However, Pollet concluded that using too many colors for different areas simply adds more information to be processed, and can cause disorientation (see also Chapter 3 on wayfinding).

As found in similar museum studies, many patrons will not ask for help in libraries. Pollet advocated a good sign system that would give patrons a sense of control over the environment instead of relying on attendants to answer questions. She also commented that it is hard to find attendants who can put up with answering the same questions all day. While library patrons may be experiencing stimulus overload, information attendants may experience understimulation, which can leave them bored and irritable.

VISITOR BEHAVIOR IN MUSEUM ENVIRONMENTS

If you visit a museum today, you probably go for a little entertainment, a little enlightenment, and a chance to get away from your normal routine and perhaps spend time with family or friends on an outing for the day—experiences consistent with those we will shortly discuss for participating in leisure activities. In a museum, you probably also think you have complete control over the decisions as to which exhibits to explore and how much time to spend viewing each one. Most assuredly, your visit to a modern museum is not a random event, but what happens during your visit is not as much under your complete control as you might think. Rather, a team of environmental psychologists and re-

lated professionals has probably designed each exhibit hall and each exhibit in order to influence your behavior in very specific ways. Today, museums, zoos, visitor centers at national parks, and similar facilities have functions that go beyond preservation and recreation. Indeed, a major purpose of these settings is to educate the visitor about history, nature, and culture. Together, environmental psychologists refer to this science as the study of *visitor behavior*, and to these settings as *informal learning environments*. These environments are a type of bridge between our previous look at traditional classrooms and the leisure settings we will explore at the end of this chapter. Indeed, museums can have the qualities of a **restorative environment** that we associate with leisure settings (Kaplan, Bardwell, & Slakter, 1993), as we mentioned in Chapter 4. Since we use museums less regularly than classrooms, the museum environment is somewhat more novel to us. Museums are also usually larger and do not provide a home base, such as a desk does in a classroom. In addition, the primary mode of activity in museums is exploration, as we make our way through halls and rooms, past endless cases of exhibits. In this section we will examine some of the design principles that apply to informal learning environments. To save space, we will concentrate on museums, but the principles apply to zoos and similar settings as well. The entire July 1988 issue of *Environment and Behavior* is devoted to this topic as it relates to zoological parks, and the November 1993 issue of the same journal is devoted to the environmental psychology of museums, if you would like to read more details about design and behavior in such settings.

Wayfinding

The ability to find things in a museum is related to wayfinding in any setting. Museums that are confusing or hard to explore may result in less satisfaction with the visit (Winkel et al., 1976). If you miss the exhibits you came to see because you could not find them, or if you find yourself constantly backtracking and going in circles, you probably have less fun than if everything were simpler. However, the complexity of museum environments is an almost inherent feature of their purpose—to display as many exhibits as possible.

One way of overcoming this inherent complexity is to provide aids for finding one's way through the museum. Winkel et al. (1976) suggest that people prefer to consult signs and maps and are uncomfortable if they have to ask museum employees for help, just as we saw for libraries. Maps that clearly depict a setting and identify the viewer's location on the map in relation to the setting seem to be particularly helpful. Such **you-are-here maps** show the position of the viewer and how to get from "here" to other parts of the setting (Levine, 1982; Levine, Marchon, & Hanley, 1984; see also Chapter 3). Not surprisingly, orientation aids such as maps and suggestions for what to see appear to increase satisfaction with the environment, and the simpler the map the better (Borun, 1977; Talbot et al., 1993).

Exploration

Research has also addressed the ways in which people explore museums. For example, people appear to have a right-handed bias; upon entering a gallery in a museum, they typically turn right and move around the room in that direction (Melton, 1933, 1936; Robinson, 1928). Once inside a museum, people usually stop at the first few exhibits and then become more selective, stopping at fewer the longer they explore (Melton, 1933). The more likely visitors are to explore a given exhibit, the higher its **attraction gradient**. Exits to other exhibit rooms are also important because people tend to use the first exit they see. Museum researchers refer to this "pull" of exits as the

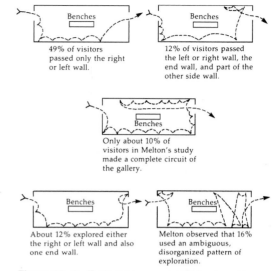

Figure 13–8 Typical movement patterns found in one study of visitors to an art museum

Adapted from A. W. Melton, 1933. Reprinted with permission from Museum News, January 15, 1933. Copyright © 1933, the American Association of Museums. All rights reserved.

exit gradient. Due in part to attraction gradients and exit gradients, most people see only a part of each exhibit room rather than seeing everything before moving on (Parsons & Loomis, 1973). These patterns are depicted in Figure 13–8.

Overload notions may help explain why orientation aids are so valuable in museums. It has been found that the most popular museum exhibits are those that are of moderate complexity (Lakota, 1975; Melton, 1972; O'Hare, 1974; Robinson, 1928). Fatigue in a museum is not only a simple matter of walking around, but is also affected by the stimulation provided by the exhibits (Robinson, 1928). It may be, then, that museums can create overload if they are too complex or if it is difficult to get around inside (see Figure 13–9A and 9B).

Fatigue in Museum Exploration

Predictable though it is, the pattern of physical movement within a museum shows some signs of being maladaptive. Walking in a

Figure 13–9A & 9B   Monotonous rows of display cases (top) can create overload. Modern museums (bottom) recognize the problem of environmental complexity and fatigue by creating exhibits that pace the amount of complexity so as to reduce fatigue and orient the visitor.

museum should facilitate exploration of the environment. Yet, as we have seen, visitors frequently move past much of the exhibit without stopping or looking at it, thereby missing many of the rewards to be gained from a museum visit. Why is exploratory movement not more complete? One explanation is that fatigue interferes with completing more thorough patterns of visual exploratory behavior.

Robinson (1928) first studied fatigue in museums many years ago. In spite of his work being old, many of his observatons on exploratory fatigue are still important. He concluded that fatigue was not due just to physical exertion but also to the visitor growing tired of maintaining a high level of attention. Borrowing from Gilman (1916), Robinson used the term **museum fatigue** to describe the phenomenon.

In a clever laboratory study, Robinson was able to demonstrate that museum fatigue was more than just physical exertion. He had persons seated at a table look at a series of copies of paintings from a gallery, presented in the same order as they hung in the gallery. Attention time for each painting was recorded and compared with the attention time observed in the gallery itself. It turned out that subjects seated at the table and looking through the stack of pictures began to show a drop in attention at about the same point in the sequence as visitors walking through the museum. Robinson concluded that museum fatigue was due to psychological satiation or boredom as well as to fatigue from physical activity. He did not mean that visitors were bored by the exhibits. Rather, he noted that after visitors concentrated on several stimulating exhibits for a long period, they became so satiated with the museum's environment that additional exhibits were relatively unstimulating. Recall from our discussion of information oveload in Chapter 4 that when we receive the massively complex stimulation typical of many museum environments, we tend to ignore less important cues in order to attend to more important ones. This is the sort of phenomenon that occurs with museum fatigue: We become so satiated with complex information that we spend less and less time looking at the details of various exhibits.

Museum fatigue can be alleviated somewhat by building what Robinson called **dis-continuity** into the design of an exhibit. Discontinuity refers to a change of pace in the stimuli presented. For example, a series of paintings might be broken up with a piece of sculpture or an arrangement of furniture. The number of paintings or objects displayed can also be reduced, since a single gallery may contain a collection large enough to tax the attention span of the most ardent art lover. Alleviating museum fatigue helps visitors gain more satisfaction from their exploration of the museum environment. It certainly helps to have labels with large print and interpretive explanations that are brief enough to avoid overload (Bitgood & Patterson, 1993). In addition, movement in an exhibit, such as a rotating wheel or a swinging pendulum, will boost the attraction gradient; however, movement in a previous exhibit may mean that lack of movement in a subsequent exhibit contributes to fatigue. An interactive exhibit is one solution: Encouraging the visitor to push a button to light up a section of the display case or lift a cover to see the answer to a question (called a "flip" by exhibit designers) helps maintain interest. Another solution is a **space surround environment**, in which the features of the exhibit entirely surround the visitor, as opposed to a series of separate display cases. In general, a space surround environment is superior in maintaining visitor interest (e.g., Thompson, 1993). As you can infer, there are an infinite number of possibilities for designing individual exhibits and sequencing them to maximize visitor attention and educational outcome. Evaluating the design before and after it is opened to the public is extremely important in assuring that the exhibit accomplishes its intended purpose (Bitgood & Loomis, 1993; Klein, 1993; Miles & Clarke, 1993). For further discussion of these museum exploration and exhibit design principles, see Bitgood, Roper, and Benefield (1988); Loomis (1987); Robillard (1984); and Thomson (1986).

PEDESTRIAN ENVIRONMENTS: SHOPPING MALLS, PLAZAS, CROSSWALKS

When we take a break from work or from the classroom, chances are we walk somewhere. Nearly every environment has characteristic patterns of pedestrian movement through it. People select paths and avoid obstacles in regular fashion. By understanding the development of these patterns, we can obtain important information about the design of several kinds of settings (e.g., Whyte, 1980). For example, designers sometimes construct pedestrian malls to eliminate some of the traffic congestion, noise, and clutter of an urban area (see box on page 505). Typically, these pedestrian malls contain trees and shrubs in planters, as well as fountains or waterfalls—one more example of using "natural" elements to restore a sense of peace to the stresses of the built environment. To the extent that we can make pedestrian movement easy and convenient, we also reduce the pollution associated with motorized travel.

Research has revealed a number of principles of pedestrian movement patterns. One basic rule of thumb is that people choose simple, direct routes, whether formalized as landscaped paths or freely chosen, as in walking across lawns (Preiser, 1972). The well-worn paths across lawns on most college campuses, despite the presence of nearby sidewalks, illustrate this principle. Another observation about movement patterns regards the speed with which people walk. Generally, people conform their speed to that of people around them (Preiser, 1973). Larger crowds appear to move more slowly, and people walk slower on carpeting than on bare floors. Moreover, pedestrians match their speed somewhat to the pace of background music. These and other basic movement patterns apply in several different settings (e.g., Bovy, 1975).

We mentioned that movement patterns must also consider the effects of obstacles, such as automobile traffic. Frequently, people must negotiate traffic while walking somewhere. They may have to cross a street in order to get to a classroom building, or pass through a crowded parking lot en route to a shopping mall. People walk slower in such situations and often experience uncertainty in deciding whether to cross the traffic or wait (Henderson & Jenkins, 1974). In addition to traffic, large crowds can inhibit our movement and change our patterns. The presence of people in one's way leads to frequent changes in speed and deviations from the most direct route one can take. For example, people will walk around a small group of persons who are standing and talking rather than following a direct route between or through a group (Cheyne & Efran, 1972; Knowles et al., 1976). Preiser (1973) has incorporated all of these influences on pedestrian movement into a **friction–conformity model**. That is, "frictions" such as those mentioned above impede pedestrian flow, and conformity pressures (e.g., the speed of others) exert additional influence on movement.

Knowles and Bassett (1976) have considered social cues that people use in deciding whether to stop or move in crowded settings. Their perception of whether a group is an interacting entity or a casual gathering of strangers appears to be important in determining behavior. When pedestrians encountered a group of people talking to one another, they moved on. When they encountered a casual group of people who were simply standing and looking up in the air, they were more likely to stop and join in the gazing.

Sometimes we like to watch others pass by us. "People watching" occurs when people seek out benches or seats where they can

PEDESTRIAN MALLS:
Progress or Eyesore?

A relatively new development in cities is the use of pedestrian malls to enhance city life. A street in a commercial downtown area is blocked off and turned into a plaza for pedestrians—no automobiles are allowed. The idea is to reduce traffic congestion, beautify the area, and encourage commerce in previously deteriorating areas. Whyte (e.g., 1974) has observed that pedestrian plaza areas can indeed liven up the environment. Food vendors, sunny areas, places to sit, and fountains promote the habitability of such spaces. Amato (1981) even observed that people were more likely to help another in need along an area converted to a pedestrian mall compared to when it was a "normal" street (Figure 13–10).

On the other hand, pedestrian malls can be a disappointment. Grossman (1987) summarizes some of the problems that can occur. A mall in Eugene, Oregon:

> . . . became a wasteland. Pedestrians stayed away, partly out of fear that the mall's many trees and fountains were hiding muggers. Motorists skirted the area, confused by the reconfigured street routes. With sales much slower than expected, merchants departed and storefronts were vacant. Downtown Eugene began to rebound two years ago when one block of the mall was reopened to traffic. Now the city is considering reopening two more of the mall's original eight blocks to vehicles. If it does, Eugene will have spent more than twice the mall's original $1 million development cost on revamping the mall (p. 27).

Grossman observes that Galveston, Burbank, Minneapolis, Grand Rapids, Chicago, and Little Rock faced similar decisions with pedestrian malls. What went wrong? For one thing, shoppers accustomed to suburban shopping malls did not have the convenience of free parking, a variety of stores, and short drives to shop in the evening. Derelicts, delinquents, drug dealers, and "boom boxes" could find their way to the malls and scare away customers. What can be done to change the situation? Solutions include allowing some motorized transportation along the malls, building hotels there to provide a ready shopping population, removing obstructions where muggers could hide, and sponsoring festivals along the mall to attract crowds.

Figure 13–10 Pedestrian malls such as this one block off motorized traffic to increase commerce and social opportunities. However, these areas can also involve elements that are opposite to the desired effects.

DESIGN RESEARCH FOR PEDESTRIAN WIND DISCOMFORT

No matter how efficient public transportation becomes, some pedestrian movement will be needed to get people to their final destination. Modern cities usually have high concentrations of pedestrian movement around business areas that consist of numerous high-rise buildings or skyscrapers. These buildings make it possible to locate many activities, such as work, shopping, entertainment, and living quarters, in a relatively small geographical area. However, there is increasing evidence that concentrated areas of high-rise buildings can alter ground level climate and pollution conditions because of the effects of building design on wind patterns (Hunt, 1975).

Engineers are now able to test the wind effects of proposed building designs in elaborate simulations that make use of wind tunnels (Peterka & Cermak, 1975). Such tests involve fitting models of proposed and existing buildings with pressure-sensitive recording devices. When the models are subjected to simulated wind levels typical of that city, researchers can examine structural stress effects as well as possible wind problems for pedestrians. Two common problems occur if a smokestack on a tall building is too short, or if a tall building is located too close upwind from a short one. Resulting wind patterns can force pollutants toward the ground and trap them there, causing a variety of discomforts for pedestrians. Another problem arises when high-speed winds 30 or more feet (9 m) off the ground strike a tall building. Typically,

Figure 13–11 Wind deflectors such as the V-shaped projection on this building can reduce the wind tunnel effect and increase comfort for pedestrians.

these winds are forced straight down. If the building has an open passageway at ground level, the winds rush through it causing a **wind tunnel effect**. Pedestrians, especially those carrying opened umbrellas, may be literally sucked through the passageway. Design alternatives that include wind deflectors are one means of solving this problem (Figure 13–11).

Such wind tunnel simulations enable researchers to test potential wind effects on entire city blocks (Peterka & Cermak, 1977). Design solutions to anticipated problems can also be tested. In one case, tests revealed that high winds in a plaza could be avoided by erecting partial walls at the entrance (Peterka & Cermak, 1973). The beauty of this type of research is that design alternatives can be tested before construction commitments are made.

watch others (Preiser, 1972). Snyder and Ostrander (1972) observed this phenomenon among residents of retirement homes, who often locate themselves in areas where they can watch staff and other residents. Similarly, Zeisel and Griffin (1975) reported that elderly residents of an apartment complex preferred to sit along sidewalk areas so that they could watch other people go by. People watching is certainly not restricted to the elderly. For example, teenagers who use an area shopping mall as a "hangout" may sit for hours watching people pass by, looking for friends and visiting with those they find.

Understanding pedestrian patterns is useful in several ways. Knowing how people move through shopping areas, for instance, may help in designing malls and arranging shops so that they are optimally patronized. In other settings, obstacles can be minimized and short, direct routes between places can be provided. By doing these things we can facilitate comfortable movement through a number of settings.

MANAGEMENT OF NATURAL LANDS FOR LEISURE

Most of us look forward to (or at least appreciate) the opportunity to take a break from hard work and intensive study. Often, our break lets us engage in leisure activity. Although we may choose from many types of leisure experiences, from reading a novel to watching a football game to relaxing on the beach, a more and more popular form of leisure is recreating in a natural setting— hiking in a wilderness, sightseeing in a national park, fishing in a favorite stream, and so on. Perhaps the popularity of such leisure in natural lands derives from the themes we introduced in Chapter 2—themes of biophilia, restorative experiences, and the like. We certainly believe these themes are important, and we have highlighted them throughout the book. However, we wish to use the last section of this chapter not just to expound on these themes again, but also to show yet another reason why natural leisure environments are important in the study of environmental psychology. Specifically, humans actively manage and design aspects of natural settings in much the same way as they design other environments, including work and learning environments. That is, many of the same principles we have discussed throughout the text—overload, perceived control, habitability/congruence, overstaffing, for example—apply to our management of natural settings for leisure; and certainly environmental quality is of paramount importance in these settings.

Before beginning our discussion, perhaps it would be useful for you to reflect on your personal understanding of the term "leisure." Of course all of us have an intuitive idea of what leisure is, but most researchers agree that leisure will be experienced when an individual is intrinsically motivated and perceives freedom of choice (Neulinger, 1981; Tinsley & Tinsley, 1986). **Intrinsic motivation** is a popular term that has resisted precise definition by psychologists; basically, it is the degree to which a behavior leads to personal satisfaction and enjoyment (Smither, 1988). Perhaps the term is best understood by contrasting it with the **extrinsic motivation** given to us by some external agent, such as pay, gifts, or praise. Several researchers have examined the importance of these dimensions. For example, Iso-Ahola (1986) found that students were more likely to perceive an activity as leisure if their participation had been voluntary, the rewards were intrinsic, and if the activity was not work-related.

WHOSE VIEW?

With some of our thoughts about nature from Chapter 2 in mind, let us begin our discussion of land management with two questions: What does it mean to "manage" land? and "For whom is land managed?" A person might respond to the first question with: "To take care of the land so that all of us can use it." To the second question one reply might be: "For all citizens of our nation, no matter what their religion, race, or social status." Although both answers are in some respects admirable, both reflect an **anthropocentric** or instrumental interpretation of management (Gee, 1994; Stokols, 1990; Thompsom & Barton, 1994). In both instances land is seen as a bounty *for humans*. In contrast, Thompson and Barton say an **ecocentric** view values nature for its own sake, not just its contribution to human welfare. Some (e.g., Gee, 1994) would like both psychology and natural resource management to give up the term "user" as a description of people in environments because it emphasizes the place of humans as superior to the earth, and treats land, vegetation, and animals as "resources" whose sole purpose is to serve humanity. Along these lines, the naturalist writer (and ex-forester) Aldo Leopold (1949) proposed that humans should think of themselves as part of a community that extends to soils, waters, plants, and animals. Thus, Leopold's **land ethic** removes *Homo sapiens* from the role of conqueror and makes us equal members of a natural community.

As psychologists our prejudice is in favor of humanity, although many psychologists certainly study other animals. Our science, and this book, aim to understand and improve the human condition. Nevertheless, we, too, grow uncomfortable with a purely anthropocentric position. The fields of resource management are not unaware, or even necessarily unsympathetic, to the demands implied by the land ethic as a fundamental principle of management. As the research literature catches up with the popularity of this land ethic, we may find that an ecocentric view will predominate over the more traditional utilitarian, economic focus.

As we began our discussion of natural environments we said that leisure requires that an individual is intrinsically motivated and perceives freedom of choice (Neulin-

ger, 1981; Tinsley & Tinsley, 1986). Simply stated, leisure means "being able to do what you want to do," but we must emphasize that leisure is an experience rather than an activity (e.g., Gunter, 1987; Tinsely & Tinsley, 1986). That is, different activities may lead to similar psychological experiences, or conversely, the same activity might yield different experiences (only some of which would be perceived as leisure) depending on the personality of the participant, the setting, or other factors. For example, the psychological experience of risk-taking might be met by mountain climbing or by downhill skiing. On the other hand, the experience of skiing for one person might focus on speed, for another the accomplishment of good form, and for a third individual, an opportunity to enjoy the company of a loved one. Furthermore, several very different environments might support quite similar kinds of leisure experiences. Thus, the leisure experience is jointly determined by environmental, social, and individual difference variables (see Figure 13–12). This observation is quite consistent with a transactional approach such as

Figure 13–12 Individual differences help determine leisure preferences.

Barker's (1987) studies of behavior settings discussed in Chapter 4.

MULTIPLE DEMANDS

Especially since World War II there has been a dramatic increase in the number of citizens who desire to maintain natural areas for recreation, aesthetic appreciation, or wildlife observation not associated with hunting or fishing. You might think that finding such a place should not be hard because vast areas of North America (in some states and provinces, more than 50 percent of the land) are publicly owned. However, more and more people are seeking to enjoy national parks, national forests, and other natural areas and now many facilities are stretched thin (e.g., Mitchell, 1994). As environmental psychologists would say, the popularity of natural areas has sometimes led to conditions of relatively high population density, crowding, and overstaffing. The most common complaint by hikers in the Grand Canyon is noise—noise from tourist aircraft that give visitors a popular aerial view of the spectacular scenery. During peak periods hikers looking to "get away from it all" have to listen to the drone of aircraft noise once every four minutes, and certainly the intermittent character of this noise makes adaptation to it very difficult.

How can parks, forests, and wilderness areas accommodate more visitors without changing the characteristics of the natural settings that attract people to them or interfering with complex natural ecosystems? What are the most important human benefits of leisure, and how can managers maximize them? How important are natural areas, and what are the trade-offs between recreation and other potential uses for the land? Recreational use often competes with other economically important resource capabilities (timber cutting or mining, for example), and may cause long-term damage to fragile natural environments (Pitt & Zube, 1987). In fact, the enjoyment of one recreational activity (particularly one involving advanced technology such as motorcycling or using a jet ski) may interfere with the enjoyment of other recreation activities. Environmental managers have historically been trained in professions such as forestry, wildlife and fisheries biology, or range management. Thus, managers trained in the natural sciences to support the sustained yield of commodities such as timber now find themselves managing for the enjoyment of recreationists (Pitt & Zube, 1987). Many of these questions have traditionally been the domain of economists; however, recreation is a resource use characterized by the behavior and experiences of people, so psychologists are increasingly involved in forest recreation research. The ability of an area to absorb use is termed **carrying capacity**. In the case of recreation, carrying capacity may include the resistance of an area to ecological damage, the availability of facilities such as campsites, and social carrying capacity, which refers to the desired level of social interaction (Pitt & Zube, 1987). As illustrated in Figure 13–13, the recreation production process can be seen as one of attempting to meet human recreational demands by managing the basic resources of a given site (Driver & Brown, 1983).

Perhaps an example will highlight some of these issues. Let's begin with a question: How much wilderness does our society require? Consider a hypothetical piece of land in Figure 13–14. It might be "developed" to provide water access for dozens of boaters, utility hook-ups could be installed for motor home owners, and the trail could be manicured to provide access for individuals who are unable to walk appreciable distances. Each of these modifications—which we can think of as *design alternatives*—would please some segment of the public. They would be *unlikely* to please a fit wilderness backpacker

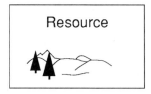

Resource

Activities

Experiences

Long-Term Benefits

Recreation Management Production Process

Figure 13–13 One version of the recreation production process

seeking solitude. For the backcountry traveler, any signs of human modification (and certainly boat docks and parking lots) may destroy the wilderness experience. What is a resource manager to do? On purely economic grounds the decision seems easy. More people can enjoy our hypothetical area (and spend more money at regional gas stations, restaurants, and convenience stores) if the area is "developed." On the other hand, every

Figure 13–14A A hypothetical piece of land relatively unmodified for human use

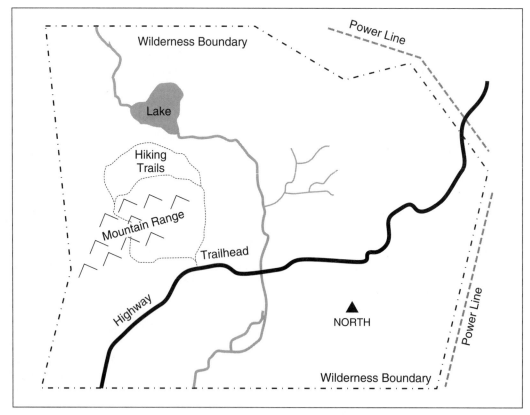

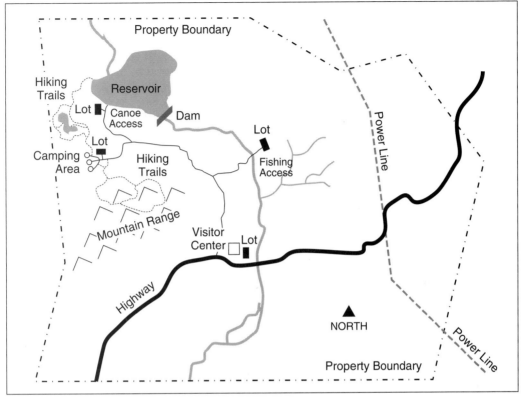

Figure 13–14B The same piece of land developed for extensive recreational use

instance of development creates long-term changes in the land that affect wildlife and plant habitats, watersheds, forests, and, of course, our hypothetical backpacker.

Many nations have created wilderness areas by legislative action and are considering establishing more. The acreage encompassed by national parks and monuments, national forests, and other generally natural areas far exceeds that which has been officially designated "wilderness." Should more land be reserved as "true" wilderness and be lost forever for lumbering, resort development, or even campgrounds? Returning to our hypothetical example, will as many different people enjoy a given parcel of land if it is declared wilderness as would use it if it were developed with an access road, sanitary facil-

ities, and picnic tables? The answer to the latter question is probably "no." If one measures the value of an area based only on the number of users, the wilderness seems to be an expensive luxury. On the other hand, it might be demonstrated that the wilderness provides unique experience opportunities that can be received nowhere else, and that, in the long run, the effects of recreation are beneficial not only to the individual, but to society in general.

Thus far we have only superimposed psychological variables on what remains basically an economic model of valuation and trade-offs. Some critics have expressed dismay at these present practices that treat landscapes and their animal inhabitants as commodities (e.g., Roberts, in press). What are the moral rights of wildlife to their particular habitat? What if providing for their requirements forces the withdrawal from use by humans? Western attitudes traditionally seem to accept humans' exploitative use of land, vegetation, and animals. But new voices have begun to demand that managers acknowledge the importance of spiritual and other difficult-to-measure values of natural environments for both members of the dominant culture, and minority groups such as American Indians. Although environmental psychology shares many of the views of science, the desire to measure concrete phenomena among them, adequate resource management will probably require a variety of methods—some of them quite phenomenological and foreign to experimental approaches.

FOCUSING ON NEEDS AND OUTCOMES

Even acknowledging spiritual needs, in order to evaluate the importance of natural leisure environments we should probably begin by outlining the rewards and benefits we receive from different activities. That is, as we saw in Chapter 11 on the design process, if we are going to be successful in our planning we should focus in part on user needs and wants, including desired outcomes. One classification of the psychological benefits of leisure participation (Tinsley & Johnson, 1984) names nine categories:

- Intellectual stimulation (e.g., working crossword puzzles)
- Catharsis (e.g., playing volleyball, jogging, or swimming)
- Expressive compensation (e.g., canoeing, camping, and hiking)
- Hedonistic companionship (e.g., drinking and socializing)
- Supportive companionship (e.g., picnicking or visiting friends and relatives)

- Secure solitude (e.g., collecting stamps or collecting autographs)
- Routine, temporary indulgence (e.g., shooting pool or playing cards)
- Moderate security (e.g., bowling or playing guitar)
- Expressive aestheticism (e.g., playing chess, woodworking, or painting)

The magnitude of the leisure experience probably varies from time to time and between individuals. For some, the feeling of freedom, increased sensitivity, and decreased awareness of the passage of time are profound. The result may be as concrete as cardiovascular and health benefits (Froelicher & Froelicher, 1991; Paffenbarger, Hyde, & Dow, 1991), more abstract benefits like the development of self-identity (Haggard & Williams, 1991) or spiritual development (McDonald & Schreyer, 1991; Roberts, in press). Indeed, several researchers suggest that the leisure state can be similar to mystic or peak experiences (Csikszentmihalyi & Kleiber, 1991; Tinsley & Tinsley, 1986).

Given the various types of recreational involvement at different points in the life cycle, and the fact that personality (e.g., Driver & Knopf, 1977) and socioeconomic status also affect one's type of recreational involvement (Marans, 1972), a very wide variety of environmental settings must be designed and made available to allow satisfaction of our needs. In addition to aspects of individuals (e.g., age, personality) affecting their use of recreation environments, the availability of recreational facilities in an area determines to some extent how we recreate (Marans, 1972). The presence of community swimming, tennis, and boating facilities increases the frequency of these recreational activities, and more people will probably spend their time skiing if there are ski slopes nearby. For some activities (e.g., water for swimming), an environmental setting is a necessary and sufficient condition to afford a particular recreational goal. For other recreational activities, the environmental setting may vary (e.g., we can jog the streets near our home, paths in a city park, or remote wilderness trails). In an overall sense, variation in recreational behavior may be viewed as an interaction between individual differences in people (e.g., their recreational wants and needs) and available recreation environments.

Why do people spend time in the "wilderness?" One answer may be derived from the environment–behavior models reviewed in Chapter 4. We may visit national parks to escape the overload or stress associated with daily life. This may partially explain why urbanites visit them more than those from rural areas. The behavior constraint approach would suggest that visits to the wilderness allow us to engage in many behaviors from which we are constrained in everyday life, although due to their primitive nature, wilderness settings probably also constrain our behavior in some ways. Overall, one way of viewing the wilderness experience is as a way of coping with stressful aspects of everyday life.

Other motivations for spending time in the wilderness may include the need to: develop, maintain, or project a particular type of self-image; retain or develop a new social identity; affiliate with certain other people; enhance our self-esteem; develop or display certain skills; exercise power; engage in self-fulfillment; or achieve mastery (Driver, 1972). In addition, one could add the aesthetic delight associated with many wilderness areas (e.g., breath-taking views) and the emotional experience such visits can generate (see Figure 13–15).

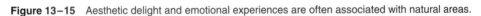

Figure 13–15 Aesthetic delight and emotional experiences are often associated with natural areas.

CONGRUENCE BETWEEN USER AND SETTING

We have noted in this and the previous two chapters that design of the built environment can be assessed in terms of its congruence or habitability—the fit of the environment to the user. Let us now see how this concept applies to leisure activity in natural settings. Who uses national parks and wilderness areas? Interestingly, some evidence suggests that while all types of people use them, users tend to be disproportionately higher income individuals, people with professional and technical occupations, those who live in urban areas, and people who have done college and postgraduate work (U.S. Department of the Interior, 1979).

What characteristics do we prefer in wilderness areas, and what do we find distasteful? The answers to these questions have important implications for resource planners. Several authors have remarked on the importance of **solitude**, for example (e.g., Hammitt, 1982). This probably refers to solitude from unknown others, since very few of those studied were traveling alone. In general, people in wilderness areas prefer to interact and to develop relationships with those in their own party, but not to meet others along the trail. Thus, although the absolute number of encounters with other people in wilderness areas is very low, recreation resource managers are regularly concerned with user complaints of overcrowding (Anderson & Brown, 1984; Manning, 1985). Of course, this is consistent with our discussion of crowding in Chapter 9, which emphasized that increasing density is perceived as crowding when it becomes inconvenient or restricts our freedom to engage in some desired behavior. Manning (1985) reviews some of the factors associated with perceived crowding in backcountry settings:

- *Characteristics of Visitors*   Several user characteristics are related to the likelihood of perceived crowding. For example, those who seek solitude are more likely to perceive crowding than those seeking excitement (e.g., Ditton, Fedler, & Graefe, 1982). In addition, more experienced users and those with "purist" attitudes toward the wilderness are likely to perceive more crowding (e.g., Schreyer & Roggenbuck, 1978).

- *Characteristics of Those Encountered*   The type of the other group encountered affects perceived crowding. Most groups object to loud, inconsiderate behavior (e.g., Owens, 1985; West 1982), but if others are perceived to be similar to one's group in behaviors and apparent values, the conflict and perceived crowding are minimized. In general, recreationists employing higher levels of technology are more likely to disrupt the experiences of their lower technology counterparts than the reverse. Canoeists tend to dislike meeting motorboats (Lucas, 1964); backpackers dislike encountering horses (Stankey, 1973). Thus, the low-technology recreationists are likely to be the first to be displaced.

- *Characteristics of the Situation*   Manning concludes his review by noting that characteristics of the situation can also affect tolerance for others. For example, people are usually more sensitive to others in nearby campsites than those met briefly on the trail, particularly if there is competition for facilities.

Of course there are strong individual differences in people's preferences in natural settings (e.g., how much solitude they desire, and which aesthetic features they prefer; Lucas, 1964). For example, while wilderness campers prefer solitude, others who could be called "general campers" (e.g., families who go camping) actually desire to meet and interact with people outside their immediate group. Part of what makes camping attractive to them is the expectation of meeting new people (Pitt & Zube, 1987). Also, more educated people, urbanites, males, and older people insist on an extremely pristine environment for their wilderness experience more than those with less education, ruralites, females, and younger people (Cicchetti, 1972). One's expectations for a setting also importantly affect his or her reactions to it (Westover, 1989). If we do not expect to meet other people and we do, this will be more disturbing than if we do expect to meet others and encounter them. Moreover, campers who expect good facilities and a particular level of comfort will be more disturbed if these conveniences are not present than will campers with lower expectations. In the same vein, whether or not we meet our objective in visiting a recreation area can affect our reactions to it (Driver & Knopf, 1976). Different recreational facilities carry with them different objectives. If we go fishing and fail to catch fish, we will be more dissatisfied than if we just came for the view.

What are the effects one actually experiences from spending time in wilderness settings? Presumably some of these benefits might be improvements in the health or well-being of individuals, regional or national economic development, or even useful changes in society as a whole (Driver & Rosenthal, 1982; Kaplan & Kaplan, 1989; Talbot & Kaplan, 1986). Many positive outcomes have been suggested (e.g., improved physical and mental health, realization of human potential, social benefits), but few have been documented through actual research. It is probably true that the outcomes one experiences from recreating in wilderness environments (and in other outdoor settings as well; Driver, 1975) depend jointly on physical elements (e.g., the scenery), facilities or equipment (e.g., having a good or a bad tent), characteristics of the user (e.g., the state of one's health), and managerial decisions (e.g., whether or not what we want to do is "al-

lowed"). What sorts of outcomes has research shown to be associated with spending time in wilderness settings? A number of studies suggest the potential for positive changes in self-concept or personality following a wilderness experience (e.g., Risk, 1976). For a group of psychiatric day-care patients, a five-day backpacking trip in the Sierras led to improvement in many areas (e.g., less obsessive thought patterns, fewer dependency needs, lower feelings of helplessness; Slotsky, 1973). Talbot and Kaplan (1986) reported the results from a long-term research program to determine the effects of the Outdoor Challenge program on teenage boys. Individuals began to notice more subtle details in their wilderness environment and developed an attitude of living with, rather than controlling, nature.

PRELUDE TO PRESERVATION

Our discussion of leisure experiences in natural areas highlights some of the concerns about preserving these lands for recreation and other uses, including nonhuman use. One of the factors that works against preservation is the multiple demands that people place on the resource in the first place. Often, the problem is not that people intentionally abuse the resource, but that collective demands from multiple users exceed the capacity of the resource to support all individual interests. In our next and final chapter we will see how environmental psychology can be used to address this issue and help preserve the environment for all.

SUMMARY: LEISURE AND RECREATION ENVIRONMENTS

Recreation and leisure opportunities are important for a growing number of people. Management and design considerations help to determine what opportunities are available in recreation and leisure environments.

We emphasized the importance of psychological experiences, rather than particular activities in motivating recreational behavior. For instance, wilderness hiking or camping may be viewed as ways of coping with stressful aspects of everyday life, but crowding, littering, and other problems associated with camping may work against the coping function, and desire for personal growth may be as important as escape.

CHAPTER SUMMARY

Work environments have developed flexibility because of technological innovations allowing removal of equipment from rigid power sources and construction of expansive and high-rise spaces. The quality of the work environment also affects job satisfaction, although job security, working relationships, and other factors are usually found to have more impact on job satisfaction than does quality of the environment.

A major innovation in office design is the open office plan, or office landscape. The advantages of the open office include reduced maintenance costs, easier communication, better workflow, and easier supervision. Disadvantages of open offices, which may in some circumstances outweigh advantages, include increased noise and other distractions, as well as reduced privacy.

The ability to treat one's workspace as a territory, as well as the right to personalize it, may serve as a form of status in the organization. Especially at high ranks in a firm, such territorial treatment and personalization may correlate with job satisfaction.

Research on classroom design has shown that windowless classrooms have no consistent effects on academic performance, but that presence of windows promotes pleasant moods. Open-plan classrooms also show mixed results, with some research showing an increase in activity associated with open classrooms, as well as increases in noise and decreases in privacy. Apparently, an optimal level of complexity in the classroom environment promotes learning.

Libraries have a problem of periodic overuse of facilities. One proposal would separate the "normal" library functions from the study function it often serves. In addition, evidence indicates that orientation aids would help many libraries. Orientation is also a problem in museums, with some evidence suggesting improved orientation enhances satisfaction. Exploration of a museum tends to be systematic and is heavily influenced by the attraction gradient of exhibits. Museum fatigue may be caused by overstimulation, and can be alleviated by designing discontinuity into exhibits.

Pedestrian movement also tends to be systematic, with people preferring the shortest route. Crowds slow down pedestrian movement, as does carpeting. People tend to match their walking speed to the flow of the crowd and to background music. A friction–conformity model helps explain these relationships.

Perhaps as a restorative counter to work and other life stresses, recreation and leisure opportunities are increasingly important. Design alternatives help determine which opportunities exist in a given recreation or leisure environment. Wilderness and camping experiences permit opportunities for personal growth and can help tame everyday stresses. However, crowded camping areas and other problems can defeat the stress-reducing aspects of camping. Among the most important expectations of wilderness campers are solitude and aesthetic appreciation. Solitude, aesthetic experiences, and other encounters during camping can improve our psychological outlook and benefit our health. Similarly, recreational exercise benefits our health and psychological outlook and can improve family and other social relationships.

SUGGESTED PROJECTS

1. Take a tour of various offices around your campus and note various types of personalization. Does personalization seem to vary with status, gender of the occupant, type of job, or academic specialization?

2. If your school has a large computer terminal room, conduct an informal observation of human factors in the student workplace. Are the terminals and furniture designed with an eye to human factors? Are there signs of fatigue among users? How do users adapt the workplace to their needs (keyboards in laps, books shading glare, etc.)? Can you offer suggestions for design improvements?

3. Try to visit open classrooms and conventional classrooms in your area. Which seem to have the most activity? Which seem to have more noise?

4. Visit your local museum or zoo and note exploration patterns of visitors. Can you identify attraction gradients and discontinuities? Do visitors tend to use the same route through displays?

5. Explore several types of recreation environments and note the concentration of ages in them, as well as the experiences or benefits people seem to be getting from them. Are there systematic differences? What design changes would be necessary to provide other recreational opportunities?

6. Recall that recreation managers distinguish between activity opportunities, experiences, and benefits. With a few friends, try to create a list of the *benefits* to yourself or to society that result from recreation in outdoor environments.

Changing Behavior to Save the Environment

INTRODUCTION

ENVIRONMENTAL PSYCHOLOGY AND SAVING THE ENVIRONMENT

THE COMMONS DILEMMA AS AN ENVIRONMENT–BEHAVIOR PROBLEM

ENCOURAGING ENVIRONMENTALLY RESPONSIBLE BEHAVIOR

CONSERVING ENERGY AND WATER

  Conserving Energy

    Antecedent Strategies

      Attitude Change and Education

      Commitment

      Modeling

      Prompts

    Contingent Strategies

      Rewards and Punishments

      Feedback

    Policy and Technological Innovations

  Conserving Water

SOURCE REDUCTION AND RECYCLING

  Antecedent Interventions

  Contingent Strategies

    Reinforcement

    Feedback

LITTERING

Antecedent Interventions

Consequent Strategies

VANDALISM

ENCOURAGING ENVIRONMENTALLY RESPONSIBLE BEHAVIOR: AN ASSESSMENT OF THE PRESENT AND THE FUTURE

CHAPTER SUMMARY

Suggested Projects

KEY TERMS

approach prompts
avoidance prompts
commons dilemma
consequent interventions
contingent interventions
dominant Western world view
environmental education
feedback
foot-in-the-door technique
free-rider
individual good–collective bad trap
missing hero situation
modeling

negative reinforcement
new ecological paradigm
nuts game
one-person trap
positive reinforcement
prompts
public goods problem
punishment
self-trap
social dilemmas
social traps
vandalism

INTRODUCTION

Imagine that you are a shepherd and that you share a pasture known as "the commons" with the other shepherds of your village. Further assume that the commons cannot be enlarged— it constitutes all the land you and the others have on which to graze your animals. Although you share the pasture land, the economic benefits you gain from your herd are yours, and from time to time you are confronted with the decision of whether to purchase another sheep for your flock. The commons is becoming depleted, but you feel that you would enjoy the economic advantage of owning another animal. After all, the commons could support one more sheep without too much further damage. You reason that the cost (to you) of one additional sheep grazing on the commons is quite low, and you conclude that you are acting rationally by deciding to make the purchase. However, force yourself to consider what would happen if all the shepherds added one extra animal. The eventual result would be complete depletion of the commons, and all would suffer. After you have ruminated on this for a while, you become uncertain about what to do.

This story is taken from Hardin's (1968) "The Tragedy of the Commons." As you have probably realized, it offers an excellent analogy with many aspects of contemporary life. Many resources are being consumed at too high a rate, which is endangering the future availability of the resource. At a personal level we often find ourselves faced with resource-related decisions that are modern-day equivalents of whether or not to add another sheep to our herd. Should we avoid buying paper plates in order to save trees? If we use paper plates can we avoid wasting water to wash dishes? In a sense, our needs are pitted against those of the larger community. We are faced with a choice between satisfying our immediate needs with the prospect of negative future consequences to society, and restricting our present consumption for the further good of the community. The way we resolve such dilemmas obviously has important implications. Hardin argues that if we want the commons to survive, each of us must give up some of our freedom. While the individual shepherd will benefit by adding to his or her flock, one must refrain for the greater good. But as logical as this seems, your experience may suggest to you that it will require more than reasoning to make people refrain from behaviors that are environmentally destructive, although personally satisfying. Unfortunately, people frequently fail to respond to reason alone.

John Platt (1973) considers situations such as the **commons dilemma**, in which short-term personal gains conflict with long-term societal needs, to be types of **social traps**. In general, Platt feels that social traps are hard to break out of, but claims it is essential for researchers to design strategies enabling us to do just that. Various methods have been suggested to help us break out of the commons dilemma (cf. Edney, 1980; Platt, 1973). For example, researchers have tried to increase short-term costs of environmentally destructive behaviors so that they become less attractive behavioral alternatives, and have attempted to decrease the costs of environmentally constructive acts. Environmental psychologists have also tried to educate people (e.g., by conducting environmental seminars) to make them realize their interdependence and to make the long-term societal costs of squandering resources more salient, and have advocated adding reinforcers to encourage behaviors incompatible with those that waste precious resources. Some have also supplied people with feedback about the extent to which they are depleting the commons and have assessed the effects on resource overconsumption of dividing up available resources (e.g., through rationing).

In this concluding chapter we will discuss a broad range of techniques that have been used by environmental psychologists in an attempt to study and change an array of human behaviors that are not in our best interests environmentally. Some environmentally destructive behaviors are easily amenable to conceptualization in terms of the "commons dilemma" and "social trap" analyses we have described, while others require a different type of conceptualization. Therefore, the approaches we will discuss for dealing with environmentally destructive behavior include the sorts of techniques mentioned as useful for attacking the "commons dilemma" type of problem, as well as other methods.

ENVIRONMENTAL PSYCHOLOGY AND SAVING THE ENVIRONMENT

Clearly, changing human behavior to save the environment is an extremely important topic. However, past research in environmental psychology has focused more on the effects of environmental variables (e.g., crowding, deteriorated environments) than on how to modify our behavior to save the environment. Environmental psychologists have documented that certain environments affect us adversely, but have done less research on how to change our behaviors so they do not have adverse effects on the environment. There is a big difference between knowing that people react negatively to filthy urban areas or to energy or other resource shortages, and getting them to do something about solving these problems. We need to devote more research attention to studying how we can have a positive effect on the environment, as opposed to focusing on how it affects us.

What unique contribution can environmental psychology make to help deal with the many environmental problems we face (e.g., insufficient and expensive fuels, air and water pollution, a generally deteriorating environment)? The approaches other disciplines have taken have emphasized physical technology. For example, a great deal of attention has been focused on developing

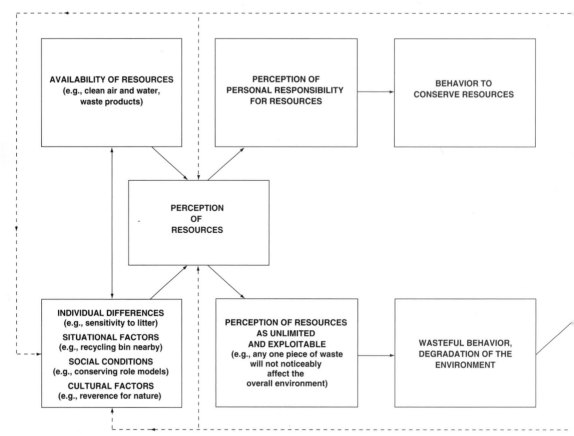

Figure 14–1 The eclectic model applied to behavior change to preserve the environment

nuclear and solar energy, and pollution abatement techniques. Many seem to think that solving our environmental problems only requires the right technologies. In contrast, relatively less attention has focused on strategies for preserving the environment which involve changes in people's behavior. Where these techniques have been used they are often regarded as "stopgap" measures, with the hope that technology will eventually bail us out of our current problems. We will argue that although physical technology certainly has a role, behavior change—sometimes involving substantial modifications in how we act on an "everyday" basis—will have to make a significant contribution if things are to improve. In

fact, sometimes behavior change will be more important than physical technology in effecting solutions.

Why do we (and many other environmental psychologists) feel this way? First, in some cases physical technologies have gotten us into this mess. Modern transportation has solved problems in locomotion, but has caused pollution, periodic energy shortages, and unsightly commercial "strips." Modern packaging allows us to preserve all types of food, but has created a tremendous litter problem. Most technologies have unfortunate "side effects," and in this chapter we will see that psychological techniques for behavior change could help eliminate them. Second, in cases (e.g., dealing with littering)

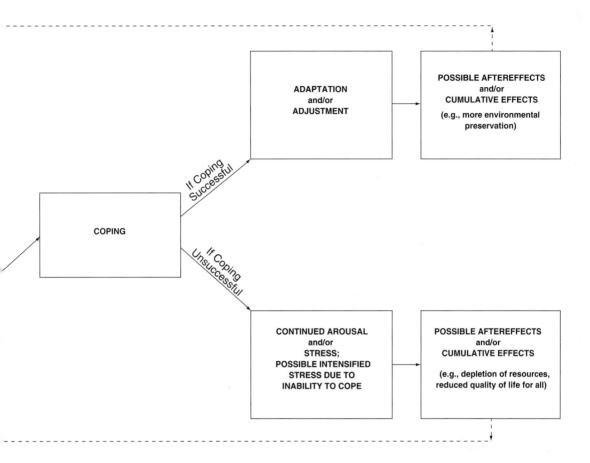

where physical technology cannot fix the problem, changing our behavior is the best means of coping. Even when certain efficient technologies promise cures for environmental problems (e.g., building smaller, more efficient homes, retrofitting existing ones), particular behaviors are often necessary to ensure that people use available technology. For example, motorists have disconnected catalytic converters in automobiles in order to increase gas mileage and eliminate attendant smells. By doing so, they subvert pollution control technology. More generally, we could say that the impact of any technology depends on people's behavior—how they *use* the technology. Finally, behavior does have strong effects on the environment: We would

not be exaggerating if we asserted that almost everything anyone of us does has either a positive or a negative impact on our environment.

The perspective we take in this chapter can be viewed within the framework of our eclectic model, as depicted in Figure 14–1. Experiencing the environment as outside our ideal—too much pollution or rapidly depleting resources, for example—motivates us to seek change. Additional inputs, such as feedback about our resource consumption or incentives to change our ways, motivate us to modify our own behavior, which in turn changes our perception of the situation.

Two questions remain: (1) Will changing our behavior to save the environment require a lower quality of life, and (2) can it be done? Generally, the answer to the first is "No." If we changed our behavior so fewer of us drove cars and more used public transportation, there would be less pollution, we would have significantly more money to spend, we could walk or ride bicycles anywhere, inflation would not be particularly linked to the price of foreign oil, and so on. In many ways, the quality of life would actually improve. We rephrase the second question: Do the behavior change techniques that we will be describing in this chapter work? We will leave that for you to decide after reading our presentation of the evidence in the coming pages. We will, however, suggest that there is lots of room for environmental psychologists to improve our environment-relevant behaviors. For example, energy consumption often varies by a factor of two or three for similar people living in identical homes (Socolow, 1978; Winnett et al., 1979). Their apparently different behavior seems to show up in energy use!

If we could influence environmentally relevant behaviors to improve the environment, what would we focus on? We would probably want to promote environmentally protective behaviors (e.g., picking up litter, recycling things), and discourage environmentally destructive ones (e.g., throwing litter on the ground, driving cars that are "gas hogs"; Cone & Hayes, 1980). It should be noted that both types of behaviors impact on the same problems. Encouraging environmentally protective acts (e.g., rewarding people for picking up litter) and discouraging environmentally destructive behavior (e.g., high fines for littering) will improve the litter situation. Unfortunately, programs that encourage protective behaviors do not necessarily inhibit destructive behaviors, and vice-versa (Cone & Hayes, 1980). Also, not all environmentally protective and destructive behaviors have the same impact on the environment. A program that stops people

from littering is sure to have direct environmental impact; one that encourages people to vote for conservation-oriented legislators will probably have a more diffuse impact. Finally, we should stress that the effects of any environmentally protective or destructive behavior are complex. Suppose we could get people to recycle all newspapers. This would save trees, but might cause water pollution from the ink removal process. It would save energy since we would not need to process virgin wood, but the recycling process itself uses a great deal of energy. Although most environmentally conscious people probably think that using paper cups causes less damage to the environment than using plastic ones, a case can actually be made that plastic is less harmful (Hocking, 1991)! Sometimes it is hard to figure out whether we are helping or hurting the environment (Figure 14–2).

Figure 14–2 Actions to "save" the environment often involve trade-offs. Actions with low impact on one segment of the environment often have high impact on another segment. For example, using paper plates to save water costs trees; using washable dishes saves trees but costs water. A (controversial) case can actually be made that plastic cups have less impact on the environment than paper cups.

As we proceed in this final chapter, we will have more to say about the reasons people are motivated to reduce environmentally destructive behavior, but at this point we would like to make a few comments about perceived risk, because people's perceptions of high or low risk influence their willingness to engage in destructive behavior (e.g., tampering with antipollution equipment on an automobile) as well as their willingness to engage in behavior that helps preserve the environment (e.g., reducing use of broadly toxic pesticides). Slovic (1987) points out that perception of risk is not the same as risk calculated by experts—the *perceived* risk may be higher or lower. Perceived risks tend to be higher if the activities associated with them are seen as uncontrollable, inequitable, catastrophic, unknown, dread, and likely to affect future generations; such is the case, for example, with people's perceived risks about nuclear power. Perceived risks tend to be lower if the activities associated with them are seen as voluntary, individual, not globally catastrophic, easily reduced, and of low risk to future generations; such is the case for swimming, power lawn mowers, and food preservatives. What is the risk to the individual and to the environment for one act of littering or for one person using an automobile instead of mass transit? People's perception is that the risk is minimal, in part because using the automobile and littering are seen as voluntary and controllable and any negative consequences will probably occur long after the specific act of littering or driving. In reality, the consequences of these activities build over time and increase as more and more people engage in them. We will see what we can do about these consequences in the remainder of the chapter.

What is the range of environmental problems that we would like to improve if we could? These may be categorized as (1) problems of environmental aesthetics (e.g., prevention and control of litter, protection of natural resources, preventing urban deterioration); (2) health-related problems (e.g., pollution, radiation, high levels of noise; and (3) resource problems (e.g., overconsumption of resources such as water or energy; Cone & Hayes, 1980). These categories are neither exhaustive nor mutually exclusive. Often, specific environmental problems, such as overdependence on the automobile, impact on all three categories. While we will not be able to deal with all of the environmental problems needing solutions, later in this chapter we will discuss specific approaches for coping with several of them in detail.

At this point, let us examine the commons dilemma in more detail to see how we can modify the situation to improve the outlook for the environment. We will then consider a range of environmental problems and the ameliorative techniques used by environmental psychologists to help solve them. Some of these techniques may hold great promise for solving the critical problems that now confront us.

THE COMMONS DILEMMA AS AN ENVIRONMENT–BEHAVIOR PROBLEM

Hardin's (1968) depiction of the tragedy of the commons has spawned numerous attempts to examine factors which might help us work out favorable solutions to the commons dilemma. To see how generalizable Hardin's propositions have become, it might be useful to enumerate examples of commons-like behavior beyond that of Hardin's shepherds. Hardin himself was interested in the problem of overpopulation: Seemingly self-serving motives for reproduction (e.g., having more labor to run the family farm) have a long-term negative consequence if the total population outstrips the food supply. Hardin himself borrowed the analogy of the commons from Lloyd (1833), who was also interested in how a selfish view could lead to disastrous overpopulation. Other examples of the commons dilemma are apparent when we consider some scenes typical on many college campuses. Parking lots are often jammed, with long lines of cars waiting for a space. The parking lot can be thought of as a commons: It is shared by all and owned by none of those who use it. Because parking spaces may be scarce, individuals acting in self-interest may arrive early to get a share of the valued resource. But as demand for parking spaces increases, you must arrive earlier and earlier to be assured of one. The result is that people who really need access early may be deprived of access because others have rushed in before them. Or consider space in campus dining areas around the noon hour. Space is limited, and many students use dining tables to socialize or to study for the next class. If they studied elsewhere, there would be room for all to eat. Libraries are not immune from commons-type behavior. Toward the end of each semester or quarter, demand for certain valued reference materials soars and access becomes constricted. In self-interest, someone may hold the material for an inordinate amount of time. If students (and faculty!) would use these materials throughout the term, the "crunch" disaster would not strike so badly at the end of the term. Scheduling of classes is also a type of commons. It appears that 10 A.M. is the most popular time for faculty to teach and for students to want to be in class. Accordingly, classroom space is scarcest at that hour, but is underutilized at other times of the day. Budgets also have the characteristics of a commons. If the members of a group allocate a fixed amount from which they all draw, such as for phone calls or photocopying, the tendency is for everyone to

spend more than their share from that part of the budget. If each participant decides, then, that it is in his or her best interest to spend a fair share before someone else uses it, the resource becomes depleted very quickly—to the detriment of all. Can you think of other examples of this type of dilemma (see Figure 14–3)?

Two other examples of a commons-type tragedy show how broadly applicable the analogy is to environmental problems. Pringle et al. (1993) document the tragic consequences of shared use of the Danube River. The Danube stretches 2,860 kilometers through nine different countries; about 12 percent of Europeans—86 million people—live within its basin. Through a canal, it links the North Sea to the Black Sea. It is a major transportation pathway but also provides drinking water, irrigation water, and hydroelectric power. However, it is also used to dispose of industrial and municipal waste. Any one nation's exploitation of the river has an environmental impact that is not terribly noticeable, but the sum of abuse by all nations is tragically detectable in the delta. Among other things, the fish harvest is down by as much as half, and some species show a 90 percent decline. Another interesting example of a commons tragedy comes from an attempt to use an environmentally friendly source of energy. Kerr (1991) describes how geothermal energy has been exploited at The Geysers, a natural steam-generating geological formation in Northern California. Production of electricity from this relatively clean energy bonanza began with one company in the 1960s, and today it provides 6 percent of California's electric power. But by 1988 the number of organizations tapping the energy source had increased to 11 users. Too many companies exploiting the limited resource will soon cut total electricity output by half, and a $3.5 billion investment may be lost. The problem once again is that whereas individual use of a resource can be

Figure 14–3A & 3B Some examples of a "commons" on a college campus. What other examples can you think of?

tolerated by the environment, the combined exploitation by a group often leads to overuse and tragic disaster.

We mentioned that Platt (1973) conceptualized the commons dilemma as a type of social trap. Platt described three such categories of social traps, each of which is relevant to environmentally destructive behavior. The *commons* type of trap, or **individual good–collective bad trap**, involves a group competing for a valued resource, such that destructive behavior by one participant has minor impact on the whole, but if all engage in the same individual behavior, the impact on the commons is disastrous. The **one-person trap**, or **self-trap**, involves a disastrous consequence to one person. Typical of these traps is addiction to drugs or food. The momentary pleasures of the present have disastrous consequences in the long run. The third type of trap is the **missing hero situation**. Whereas the commons trap and self-trap involve unfortunate actions which we take, the missing hero trap involves an action which we fail to take, such as refusing to help someone in need or failing to warn others of the toxicity of a substance with which they work.

Interestingly, Platt (1973) notes that all three of these traps can be analyzed in terms of the rewards and punishments (i.e., reinforcements) associated with them. There is a positive side to the situation which we seek, and a negative side which we want to avoid. The problem is that the positive and negative have become separated in time, or the negative has been diluted across the members of a group, so that the behavior leading to the short-term positive consequence is more likely to occur. For example, in the commons problem of overharvesting whales, the immediate reward of taking one whale seems more prominent than the long-term consequence of everyone else taking more whales. In a self-trap of overconsuming food, the short-term pleasure of an extra dessert seems overwhelming relative to the long-term consequence of damage to the body and to our appearance. In a missing-hero trap, there is an unpleasant component to the behavior we should be performing: The punishment is short term but the reward is long term, so we avoid the behavior. For example, we may fail to pick up litter because the inconvenience seems to outweigh the long-term benefit of an aesthetically pleasing environment.

How, then, do we resolve social traps? Platt argues that we simply rearrange the positive and negative consequences of our behavior. If we engage in a destructive behavior because it has immediate rewards, such as using an automobile rather than mass transit, we can impose a system of penalties for automobile use (such as heavy freeway tolls) and rewards for mass transit use (such as free rides on high-pollution days). Or, we could increase the unit cost of a resource, such as electricity, for those who use a large quantity, and reduce the unit cost for those who use little. For example, Oskamp et al. (1994) found that financial gain—that is, monetary reward—was a major motivator for businesses engaging in office paper recycling; similarly, Grasmick, Bursik, and Kinsey (1991) found that shame and embarrassment—that is, negative consequences—were significant motivators in an antilittering campaign. We will examine these ideas in more detail when we discuss specific use of rewards and punishments to prevent environmentally destructive behavior.

Edney (1980) points out that although this reinforcement interpretation of the commons dilemma is appealing in its simplicity, it ignores a number of human elements. For one, it ignores the long-established evidence that individuals are different from one another: They do not all respond in the same way to the same rearrangement of the circumstances for rewards and punishments. Reinforcement approaches also sidestep questions of conscience, altruism, ethics, and humanistic tendencies, and suggest that reason is dominated by questions of reward. Hopper and Nielsen (1991), for example, observed that altruistic motives influenced recycling behavior, and Axelrod and Lehman (1993) found that deeply held personal principles could guide environmentally conscious behavior. Similarly, Stern, Dietz, and Kalof (1993) observed that concern for consequences to others and to the environment, as well as concern for consequences to oneself, guide environmental consciousness.

We should mention that there are other

formulations of commons-type problems. To social psychologists, the problem is one of a class of **social dilemmas**, where individual interests are pitted against group interests (e.g., Messick et al., 1983). The entire September-October, 1990 issue of *Social Behaviour* is dedicated to social dilemmas, if you are interested in further reading. Economists refer to a variation of the issue as the **public goods problem** (e.g., Marwell & Ames, 1979). In this situation, individuals must all contribute to a common cause, such as paying taxes for mutual self-defense or contributing to a public television station. Any one person can fail to contribute, and the public cause will survive. However, if too many people get the idea of not contributing, the common good suffers. Those who do not contribute are termed **free-riders**, since they not only do not contribute, but also benefit from the public cause. For example, a person who sneaks onto a subway without paying or who poaches wildlife without a hunting license could be termed a free-rider.

In our discussion above we showed how Platt would rearrange rewards and punishments to solve the commons dilemma. Hardin (1968) suggests that some form of governance is necessary to manage the commons in a nondestructive manner. In his terms, we must have "mutual coercion mutually agreed upon" in order to regulate our tendencies toward overconsumption. Laboratory investigations using commons dilemma simulations (see box on page 530) have explored a number of factors, including forms of "governance," which might help us conserve the commons. It is instructive to review some of these laboratory findings.

Consistent with Platt's notions, laboratory studies do show that adding rewards for cooperative behavior and punishments for selfish behavior can help preserve the commons (e.g., Bell, Petersen, & Hautaluoma, 1989; Birjulin, Smith, & Bell 1993; Harvey, Bell, & Birjulin, 1993; Kline et al., 1984;

Komorita, 1987; Yamagishi, 1986). It has been found that cooperation among players is essential for pro-ecological (preservation) outcomes; consequently, there must be trust between participants (Edney, 1979; Moore et al., 1987; Mosler, 1993). Those who have a trusting and cooperative nature seem most able to manage the commons together (Parks, 1994). Also, if groups are allowed time to study the game and to communicate, they derive their own strategies, which frequently are pro-ecological; communication promotes commitments to cooperate in managing the commons (Brechner, 1977; Dawes, McTavish, & Shaklee, 1977; Edney & Harper, 1978a, 1978b; Kerr & Kaufman-Gilliland, 1994). Other research shows that giving groups immediate and detailed resource feedback about the effects of their behavior (Kline et al., 1984; Seligman & Darley, 1977; Stern, 1976) leads to maintaining the commons for a longer period of time. Groups who are afforded both feedback and communication are especially successful at maintaining the commons (Jorgenson & Papciak, 1981).

When one's individual behavior in a commons dilemma situation is subject to the scrutiny of others, he or she is less apt to overexploit the commons (Jerdee & Rosen, 1974). Other studies have explored the effects of knowing one is interdependent with others for a resource, rather than having his or her own supply (e.g., Edney & Bell, 1984). Generally, individually owned resources are handled more efficiently than common or "pooled" resources. In fact, obtaining knowledge of resource interdependence seems to increase the intensity of behaviors aimed at "getting as much as possible for oneself," which ends up depleting the commons (Brechner, 1977; Cass & Edney, 1978). This suggests that rationing resources could be a useful strategy.

Structural changes to the commons are usually more effective management strategies than trying to influence individuals (e.g., Messick et al., 1983; Samuelson et al.,

SIMULATING THE COMMONS DILEMMA:
How It's Done and What Is Found

To test different techniques for helping us break out of the commons dilemma, a number of simulations have been developed which incorporate the central elements that people face in such contexts. In these simulations, various interventions are attempted to determine those which would cause us to behave in a more constructive way. Thus far, the simulations have included computer analogs (e.g., Brechner, 1977; Cass & Edney, 1978; Fusco et al., 1991; Gifford & Wells, 1991), as well as noncomputerized methods involving portable (e.g., Edney, 1979) and nonportable apparatus (e.g., Edney & Harper, 1978b). In addition to being useful for exploring strategies for helping us to break out of the commons dilemma, simulations can be used as teaching devices to aid us in understanding the dynamics of our environmentally destructive behaviors.

To give you a feel for these simulation techniques, we will discuss Edney's (1979) "nuts game" simulation in some detail. Recall that commons dilemmas include: (1) a limited resource that may regenerate itself somewhat, but which can be endangered through overconsumption; and (2) people who have the choice between restricting current individual consumption for the good of society (and the future of the resource pool), and exploiting the resource for their own immediate good. A successful simulation would have to include these elements.

How can this be done? Edney's **nuts game** accomplishes it quite nicely. A small number of subjects enter the lab and sit around an open bowl that originally contains 10 hexagonal nuts, obtained from a hardware store. The bowl symbolizes the pool of resources (e.g., trees, whales, or oil), and the nuts symbolize the individual resources themselves. Participants are told that their goal is to obtain as many nuts as possible. (This simulates the fact that typically we try to maximize our outcomes in life.) Players can take as many nuts as they want at any time after a trial begins. The experimenter also states that the number of nuts remaining in the bowl after every 10-second interval will be doubled by him or her. This replenishment cycle simulates natural resource regeneration rates. The above events continue until the time limit for the game is exceeded, or until the players empty the bowl.

How do subjects behave during the "nuts game"? We would hope that they would take at most a few nuts out of the pool per 10-second period, which would allow the game to continue and maximize the long-term outcomes. However, in his research, Edney (1979) found that 65 percent of the groups depleted the pool completely before the first replenishment stage! They took out all 10 nuts (i.e., depleted the resource pool completely) during the first few seconds of the game. As in the "real world," people exploit the commons, with unfortunate results.

1984). For example, experiments have studied whether educating people about the optimal strategy for using resources in commons dilemma situations leads to pro-ecological action. As we will see later when we discuss environmental education, often it is quite ineffective (Edney & Harper, 1978b). Moral exhortation to be altruistic helps, but not much (Edney & Bell, 1983). On the other hand, when the structure of the situation is changed to promote communication, subjects arrive at an optimizing strategy themselves (Edney & Harper, 1978a, 1978b). Another structural change, that of breaking down the commons into individually owned territories, also improves conservation (e.g., Edney & Bell, 1983). This territorial or "privatization" solution actually eliminates the commons, and is not very practical for some resources, such as national parks or the air we breathe. It does, however eliminate the need to have an intricate system of rewards and punishments for harvesting behavior (Martichuski & Bell, 1991). Another structural solution, that of requiring that all members harvest in equal amounts, also has pro-ecological results (Edney & Bell, 1983). Freedom of choice and equality of harvesting outcomes also seem to improve harvesting efficiency (Edney & Bell, 1987).

The nature of the social relationship between participants can influence the fate of the commons. If those sharing the commons like each other, they seem to manage it more efficiently (Smith, Bell, & Fusco, 1988). If those sharing the commons identify with each other as a group, preservation is more likely (Brewer & Kramer, 1986; Kramer & Brewer, 1984). Also, different leadership and decision-making rules have been related to commons dilemma outcomes. A study by Shippee (1978) found that personal participation in choosing a group's leadership and in implementing decisions to limit resource use led to quite successful conservation results. This, coupled with the earlier findings on being involved in choosing an optimizing strategy, highlights the importance of individual participation.

What does all of the above mean? Clearly, commons dilemma analogs can give us useful hypotheses regarding how to deal with "real-life" situations. They might eventually provide important partial solutions to pressing contemporary problems. However, we must keep in mind that the external validity of these laboratory simulations has not been demonstrated, and thus it is still an open question as to whether or not the sorts of interventions which are successful in simulations would work in the real world. There is certainly some evidence that these laboratory studies have implications for the real world, although the linkage is not complete. Clearly, social—as opposed to technological—solutions must be considered. For example, we mentioned that numerous researchers (e.g., Edney & Bell, 1983) demonstrated the efficacy of dividing the commons into territories. Acheson (1975) observed that Maine lobstermen who were highly territorial in defending their ocean claims were more successful in maintaining productivity than those who were less territorial. In addition, Thompson and Stoutemyer (1991) found that focusing on long-term consequences improved water conservation, an issue they interpret as a commons dilemma. Such outcomes raise the question of whether some environmental policies might be better than others in achieving desired outcomes. We must also keep in mind that outcomes involve trade-offs. For example, if we divide a national park into privately owned territories as a strategy for preserving it, we would defeat the purpose of holding the park as a "common" good. Moreover, Edney and Bell (1983) found that a strategy of everyone sharing equally preserved the commons as well as did dividing it into territories. However, Edney (1981) observed that the sacrifices that must be made to preserve the commons are often unequally shared among the population (i.e., some harvest less than others; see Samuelson & Messick, 1986), and concluded that honesty and interpersonal trust are extremely important psychological qualities in any solution to the commons dilemma.

We conclude this section by noting that as individual action has more and more

THE WORLD AS A COMMONS:
New and Old Ecology

Aside from a number of examples of individual commons dilemmas, we might also consider the entire world as a commons. Environmental sociologist Riley Dunlap, drawing on the views of others, has suggested that a shift is occurring in how we view world resources (e.g., Dunlap, 1980; Dunlap & Van Liere, 1978, 1984). This shift takes the form of a contrast between a long-held **dominant Western world view** and a **new ecological paradigm** approach to the world's resources. We summarize these contrasting attitudes below.

The dominant Western world view holds that:

1. Humans are unique and have dominion over all other organisms.
2. We are masters of our own destiny—we have the intellectual and technological resources to solve any problem.
3. We have access to an infinite amount of resources.
4. Human history involves infinite progress for the better.

The new ecological paradigm holds that:

1. Humans are interdependent with other organisms, such that their preservation is to our advantage.
2. Many things we do have unintended negative consequences for the environment.
3. Some things, such as fossil fuels, are finite.
4. Ecological constraints, such as the carrying capacity of an environment, are placed upon us.

You may agree or disagree with some of the above contentions. The ones you endorse probably have much to do with how palatable you find the various strategies for managing the commons.

---

impact globally, the relevance of the commons dilemma becomes more and more apparent. As examples, (1) in connection with the greenhouse effect, individual use of fossil fuels seems harmless but collective use dangerously warms the entire planet (Kerr, 1988a); (2) the individual use of chlorofluorocarbons (e.g., for air-conditioning) seems harmless but collectively it creates an ozone hole over the planetary poles (Kerr, 1988b), which is why such refrigerants are being phased out; (3) the locally harmless use of fossil fuels creates acid rain when the collective output of the fuels precipitates over neighboring areas (Schindler, 1988); and (4) the singular launch of a space vehicle seems strictly an advancement of science, but the total output of waste products left in orbit from multiple launches endangers future launches (Marshall, 1985) and, along with night lighting from urbanization, interferes with astronomical studies of outer space (Waldrop, 1988). While it is easy to adopt a fatalistic attitude that we are hopelessly locked into one collective ecological disaster after another, there remains hope. Research has indeed shown that a variety of strategies can modify environmentally destructive behavior. We turn now to some strategies that have known outcomes in their applications, with the knowledge that the commons dilemma is a useful foundation for the implications of these strategies. Moreover, some of the same factors that influence outcomes in the commons are important for these strategies, such as rewards and punishments, communication, feedback, and social cohesion or attraction toward those who participate in the strategy.

ENCOURAGING ENVIRONMENTALLY RESPONSIBLE BEHAVIOR

How can psychologists use what they have learned to encourage environmentally appropriate behavior? Consider solid waste (garbage) as just one example that illustrates many of the characteristics of environmental problems in general. Estimates vary, but the typical American generates about 25 pounds of solid waste a week (Carless, 1992). All of this trash has to go somewhere, but landfills, which dispose of more than 70 percent of the waste stream, often leak toxic substances and fewer and fewer are being opened—at least in some geographic areas. Figure 14–4 shows one estimate of American municipal waste by weight. What should be apparent is that a large proportion of the waste stream could be eliminated, reused, recycled, or reclaimed. As a general principle, "preventing" environmental problems is usually more effective than "curing" them (Blumberg & Gottlieb, 1989). A joy ride avoided is energy saved; it requires less energy and fewer natural resources to reuse a bottle than to recycle it; and it costs far less to recycle an aluminum can than to manufacture one from virgin aluminum ore. Thus, in order of desirability, our behavioral goals should be to: (1) reduce our demands for energy, water, and other natural resources; (2) reuse rather than discard whenever possible; (3) reclaim or recycle what we cannot reuse; and (4) dispose of the remaining trash as safely as our knowledge will allow (Figure 14–5).

Figure 14–4 One estimate of municipal waste by weight
Adapted from Carless, 1992.

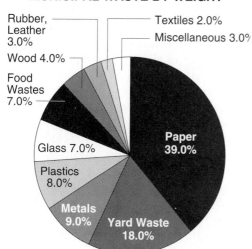

MUNICIPAL WASTE BY WEIGHT

Rubber, Leather 3.0%
Textiles 2.0%
Miscellaneous 3.0%
Wood 4.0%
Food Wastes 7.0%
Glass 7.0%
Plastics 8.0%
Metals 9.0%
Yard Waste 18.0%
Paper 39.0%

Figure 14–5 Reduction of the waste stream requires that we reduce the manufacture of unnecessary products, reuse what we can, and try to recycle the rest.

Of course, psychologists have not limited their investigations to solid waste management. The field can help encourage environmentally responsible behavior across the spectrum of human-created environmental problems with interventions aimed at individuals, groups, or even our whole society. However, we will limit our present discussion to selected topics that have attracted considerable psychological research: conservation, recycling, litter reduction, and vandalism. For further reading, we suggest you consult the March 1995 issue of *Environment and Behavior*, which is devoted entirely to psychologists' perspectives on litter control and recycling.

CONSERVING ENERGY AND WATER

Minerals, oil, water: these are part of an incomplete list of valuable natural resources. In the case of oil, known reserves fluctuate but the total resource is in increasingly short supply, at least in some parts of the world. Water, similarly, is abundant globally, but the supply of fresh water is inadequate in critical areas of human habitation and agriculture. In each case, the by-products of production and delivery create problems (some of catastrophic proportions) of their own. As we said, the most comprehensive strategy for avoiding the costs of production is to reduce our requirements for these resources.

CONSERVING ENERGY

In introducing Chapter 11 we remarked that one of the primary characteristics of humans as a species is our ability to modify the environment to meet our needs. For example, expending energy allows us to inhabit a variety of environments and increases our productivity and personal comfort. Unfortunately, overuse of energy may also be our undoing. Power plants contribute significantly to air pollution and global warming, and our dependence on fossil fuels for transportation and the generation of electricity makes us susceptible to the whims of the political climates in fuel-producing countries. At best, accidents in nuclear generation facilities like Chernobyl and Three Mile Island make us uneasy. Yet we are addicted. Consider the lowly lightbulb. Edison's invention allows us to push back the night, to remain productive after sunset and safer in our streets (Howard et al., 1993). We will not do without it, but can we do with less?

In the 1970s North Americans were faced with an oil shortage, and various forms of rationing were imposed. The new field of environmental psychology responded to the "energy crisis" with a flurry of research aimed at reducing energy consumption. During the 1980s, however, oil reserves increased, prices for oil decreased, and government funding for research into energy conservation was reduced. In addition to the reduction in both the sense of urgency and funding, some researchers felt ineffectual as they encountered deeply entrenched cultural practices and governmental policies. Sadly, research dwindled (Dwyer et al., 1993; Kempton, Darley, & Stern, 1992; Stern, 1992b). Of course a long-term concern about the availability of fossil fuels remains, but an additional new challenge in the 1990s is to reduce the side effects of energy production including air pollution, acid rain, and global warming. Unfortunately, it remains true that most methods for generating energy have negative consequences for the environment. In the case of carbon dioxide (the most important contributor to the "greenhouse effect"), the only feasible present method of reducing emissions is to burn lower quantities of fossil fuels like coal and oil. Consumption is the result of a number of individual behaviors, and it will become increasingly important for psychology to join the effort to reduce the consequences of our thirst for energy (Kempton et al., 1992).

Estimates vary, but households account for about one-fourth to one-third of direct energy use in the United States, with industry and commercial users accounting for the rest (Cone & Hayes, 1980; Stern, 1992b; Stern & Oskamp, 1987). Thus, private residences do not directly account for most of the energy used. Psychology is primarily a science of individual behavior, however, and the vast majority of published studies of psychological interventions are aimed at changing the use behaviors of individuals or households (Kempton et al., 1992; Stern, 1992b; Stern & Oskamp, 1987). Certainly there is ample reason to reduce residential consumption; according to one estimate, the energy consumption of the "typical" American home could be reduced by 50 percent by making some simple physical and behavioral changes (Socolow, 1978).

Antecedent Strategies

Antecedent strategies precede the behavior they are attempting to change. In many cases the primary targets are attitudes. These are the evaluative or affective (emotional) reactions of individuals to energy conservation. For instance, we might try to change attitudes through persuasive or informational messages. Simply stated, the goal of these strategies is to "make people care." Other approaches assume that people have a positive attitude, but aim to show them how to behave in ways consistent with what they already "care" about. For example, information about the energy efficiency of certain appliances can improve the success of individuals who are already trying to conserve. Of course, many types of information can serve both functions, and one recurring hope is that those who are well informed are more likely to adopt environmentally responsible views (Newhouse, 1990).

Attitude Change and Education

Environmental education involves making people aware of the scope and nature of environmental problems and of behavioral alternatives that might alleviate them. Even though people are frequently misinformed about energy use and its consequences (e.g., they believe that turning down thermostats in evenings during the winter will lead to increased "rebound" energy use when turned up in the morning), studies have suggested that simply educating them is not effective at changing energy-relevant behaviors (e.g., Dwyer et al., 1993; Heberlein, 1975; Kempton et al., 1985; Palmer, Lloyd, & Lloyd, 1978; Winnett et al., 1978). For example, Heberlein (1975) gave people either a booklet of energy-saving tips prepared by the electric company, an informational letter educating them about the personal and social costs of not conserving energy, or an informational pamphlet actually urging people to use more energy. What were the effects of the educational strategies? None of them had any appreciable effect on behavior. In a similar vein, Geller (1981) conducted educational workshops on energy use and found that they were very effective in changing reported attitudes and intentions regarding energy use, but follow-up audits of participants' homes revealed that the changes suggested in the workshops had not been implemented. Simple persuasion has been tried with some success. In two studies of college classrooms, a letter from a fellow professor (Luyben, 1980a) or from the college president (Luyben, 1980b) made it more likely that college professors would turn off classroom lights following their lectures. Somewhat less encouraging was a study of three Australian cities that evaluated the effect of two intensive persuasive television campaigns aimed at reducing gasoline consumption. One campaign emphasized the money-saving aspects of conservation, and the other presented gasoline conservation as a "civic duty." Despite some small reductions in gasoline consumption, the authors concluded that the television campaigns had not been cost effective. Of course, correct information is necessary if behavior is to be efficient and accurate, but information and even oral persuasion do not seem to be sufficient to ensure changes in behavior. Information also seems to affect attitudes, but it is not sufficient alone to promote behavior change (Syme et al., 1987).

Before we more carefully evaluate the success of attitude change and other educational strategies in promoting energy conservation, we should reconsider a question we posed earlier: Does an individual's attitude predict the likelihood that he or she will actually behave in ways that conserve energy? In the United States, general concern for the environment is high (Dunlap & Scarce, 1991), but the relationship between general pro-environmental attitudes and energy conserving behavior is uncertain. In fact, several researchers have concluded that general attitude toward energy use is not very predictive of eventual behavior (e.g., Geller, Winnett, & Everett, 1982; Newhouse, 1990; Olsen, 1981). Other researchers are more optimistic (e.g., Samuelson & Biek, 1991; Seligman, 1986; Stern & Oskamp, 1987). Whether or not general attitudes toward the environment predict specific behaviors, there is reason to believe that specific attitudes can be successful in predicting related energy consumption. One series of studies suggests that the primary attitudinal dimensions of specific energy concern are comfort and health, the trade-off between effort and savings, the perceived efficacy of individual conservation

efforts (i.e., can one person make a difference?), and the perceived legitimacy of the energy problem (Samuelson & Biek, 1991; Seligman, 1991). Our comfort and health seem to be particularly important. You will probably not be surprised to learn that messages that ask people to sacrifice comfort or health are often ineffective, even among people who express generally positive attitudes about the environment (cf. Kempton et al., 1992; Stern & Gardner, 1981).

Although the tie between general attitudes and behavior is often weak, interventions aimed at changing attitudes persist. Perhaps ironically, one attraction of attitude change is its potential for generalizability. That is, behavioral change would be efficient if we could change a few global attitudes which might then promote a variety of responsible behaviors across a number of settings. If they worked, such broad programs would be more efficient than those (based on consequent reinforcement strategies, perhaps) tailored to dozens of different situations. In particular, some theorists believe that it will ultimately be more important to teach consumers to recognize social traps (using the powerful metaphor of the commons dilemma) than to establish a number of consequent programs to promote conservation.

Under what conditions do educational programs on home energy conservation have the greatest potential for success? We think attitudes that are formed from direct behavioral experience are more predictive of later behavior than those that are more passive and abstract. For example, an educational program for high school students which included an energy audit and teaching students how to monitor home consumption positively affected student behaviors and those of parents (Stevens et al., 1979). This program may have been productive because it taught specific conservation behaviors, not general ones. An energy audit (especially a Type A audit in which an auditor comes to the home, makes specific suggestions, and discusses them with the owner or occupant) also shows special promise, though more evaluation is needed (Geller et al., 1982). Involving homeowners actively in an energy audit (e.g., having them go up to the attic with the auditor to examine it) also makes a difference (Stern & Aronson, 1984). In addition, one study (Gonzales, Aronson, & Costanzo, 1988) compared homeowners' reactions to auditors trained to utilize certain social psychological principles (e.g., to personalize their recommendations, to induce commitment, and to frame recommendations in terms of loss rather than gain). Auditors were also trained to use "vivid" language (e.g., telling people that the cracks under their doors were equivalent to having a hole the size of a basketball in their living room, or that their attic, which had little insulation, was "naked"). Unfortunately, although the trained auditors elicited greater compliance with their recommendations and generated more applications for finance programs to pay for home retrofitting, no differences were found in actual energy use.

Commitment

A theoretically different approach to energy savings in the home relies on the finding in social psychology that the greater one's degree of commitment to an issue (e.g., energy conservation), the more likely it is that his or her future behavior will follow (Lepper et al., 1973). In a series of studies, Pallak, Cook, and Sullivan (1980) manipulated the degree of commitment to energy conservation and measured subsequent energy use. One group of homeowners (high commitment) was told that the list of people participating in an energy conservation study would be made public along with the experiment's results; a second group (low commitment) was assured of anonymity. Subjects in the high commitment condition used less energy than those in the low commitment or a

third, control condition, and the effects persisted for as much as six months after the study had terminated.

Mass-transit systems typically consume far less fuel per passenger than private automobiles. One study (Bachman & Katzev, 1982) compared people who made a personal commitment to ride the bus, individuals who received free bus passes, and people who were both committed to riding the bus and who received free tickets. Although all three treatments increased bus use over a control group, those making a personal commitment seemed to show the most bus use, an effect that was still observed 12 weeks later. Thus, the more committed we can make people to conserve energy, the more likely they will be to engage in energy-saving behaviors.

Modeling

In addition to environmental education, the use of models has been used as an antecedent strategy to encourage residential energy conservation. Research tells us that **modeling** is most effective when the model is perceived positively, but is similar to the subject (cf. Bandura, 1977). Presumably, this similarity leads the subject to expect to receive rewards similar to the model if he or she performs the modeled behavior (Newhouse, 1990). In one modeling application, Winnett et al. (1981) produced a series of videotaped programs on how to adapt to cooler temperatures at home (e.g., change thermostats gradually, wear warmer clothing, use extra blankets). Models who enacted these behaviors were rewarded (i.e., the vignette ended with them being happy with each other); those who approached the situation inappropriately were punished (i.e., the vignette ended with them being angry with each other). Did the modeling intervention work? Yes, overall electricity use was down 14 percent and energy used for heating decreased 26 percent. Other studies (Winnett et al., 1984; Winnett et al., 1985) show that a videotaped presentation can result in energy savings for up to nine weeks.

Prompts

Prompts (cues that convey a message) have also been used to influence conservation. Modeling can be considered a type of prompt. Other types are **approach prompts**, which imply an incentive for engaging in a specific behavior (e.g., "Thank you for keeping the park clean"), and **avoidance prompts**, which imply a disincentive (e.g., "We frown on those who trample the grass"). Television announcers may prompt us to use energy wisely, or signs in university dormitories may remind us that "Empty rooms love darkness." These procedures are certainly cheaper than some other strategies we will discuss, but do they work? Sometimes—especially if they are specific, well timed, well placed, and the behavior they request is easily enacted (Geller et al., 1982; Stern & Oskamp, 1987). For example, the "Empty rooms love darkness" prompt would work best if placed on the back of the door you open to leave (well placed), and if it also said, "Turn off the lights when going out" (suggesting a specific behavioral response). An effective use of prompts to curtail unnecessary use of air conditioners was devised by Becker and Seligman (1978) who strategically placed a light in the kitchens of homes that would turn on when air conditioning was on and outside temperatures were below 68 °F (20 °C). The prompt indicated that air conditioning was unnecessary, and the light went off only when the air conditioner was turned off. This achieved an energy savings of 15 percent.

Contingent Strategies

So far, we have talked about antecedent strategies where the intervention occurs *before* the destructive or constructive behavior. **Contingent** or **consequent interventions**, on the other hand, occur *after* the target behaviors are observed. These strategies include reinforcement techniques and feedback; we will also include policy change and innovation here, since they are usually developed after the problem arises and seek to provide an incentive for change. **Positive reinforcement** uses reward—the person gains something valuable (e.g., money) for performing environmentally constructive acts (e.g., recycling). **Negative reinforcement** offers relief from a noxious situation (e.g., high energy bills) in exchange for desirable behavior (e.g., turning down the thermostat). **Punishment**, on the other hand, means an unpleasant consequence occurs (e.g., a fine) as a result of an undesirable behavior (e.g., bypassing a catalytic converter). **Feedback** simply provides information about whether one is attaining or failing to attain an environmental goal (e.g., lower fuel consumption). Often, a specific program implements several of these strategies at once. For example, high-occupancy vehicle lanes on freeways (lanes reserved for vehicles with several occupants) reward those who carpool, prompt those who do not carpool, and subject those who abuse them to fines. Let us see how successful these different types of interventions have been.

Rewards and Punishments

In the case of energy use, consumption carries built-in disincentives (the expense of natural gas, oil, or electricity). Large energy consumers such as companies and institutions have responded to incentives (rewards) and disincentives (fines) in predictable, rational ways (Dennis et al., 1990). For individuals the price incentive is not irrelevant, and at least some energy conservation measures may become common simply because they save money (Kempton et al., 1992). Unfortunately, individuals seem not to be as purely rational as companies, and this market approach does not seem to be very effective in reducing overall consumption. For instance, one study found that doubling the price of energy led to only a 10 percent decrease in use (Stern & Gardner, 1981). Individual consumers are more complex than institutions, reacting not only to economic changes, but to idiosyncratic personal factors as well (Dennis et al., 1990). Furthermore, market imperfections (for example, the landlord who buys a refrigerator may not be the person paying for the electricity it consumes if it is an inefficient model) and the low energy prices that have prevailed since the 1970s reduce the effectiveness of energy cost alone in changing consumer behavior. Finally, the costs of high utility rates fall disproportionately on the poor (e.g., Francis, 1983). In sum, relying on prices to guide behavior is ineffective and potentially unfair, so some researchers have examined the utility of adding additional consequent strategies.

Some of these reinforcement-based strategies (e.g., financial payments) have demonstrated consistent behavioral change. For example, Foxx and Hake (1977) offered subjects various rewards (e.g., cash, tours) to lower the number of miles they drove in private automobiles. The rewards led to a 20 percent reduction in miles driven, compared to a control group where mileage increased by about 5 percent. Other studies have found that competitions between teams enhance mileage reductions, and that giving lottery tickets (instead of cash payments) can be an effective motivator to drive less (Reichel & Geller, 1980). In housing, much of the research focuses on individually metered residences (e.g., private homes or apartments with separate meters). For example, some studies have simply paid residents of individually metered residences to lower their energy utilization. These techniques have proven quite effective in changing energy use both alone, and when combined with feedback (Cone & Hayes, 1980). Although paying people for lowering residential energy use is often effective in changing behavior, it

may be difficult to implement these consequent payments in a way that is cost effective. In addition, the effect is probably reduced if the rewards seem abstract or are not immediate. For example, in one study financial incentives in the form of tax credits were offered for home retrofitting, but were not sufficient to encourage a high level of this behavior (Stobaugh & Yergin, 1979).

In addition to adjusting utility rates, some studies have used reinforcers to change the pattern of our energy use. Utilities save money when they can rely on their least expensive sources of power, which is typically the case during hours of "nonpeak" demand. When demand "peaks," they must augment their supply with more expensive sources of power. Therefore, it is advantageous to utilities to shift the pattern of energy use from peak to nonpeak periods. To decrease peak demand in some places, financial incentives are provided (i.e., rates are lowered for consumers during nonpeak hours and raised during peak demand hours). These price incentives and disincentives may be effective in switching some discretionary energy-consuming activities (e.g., washing and drying clothes) from peak to nonpeak periods, with benefits to both the utility and the consumer.

Promoting energy conservation might seem to be more difficult in master-metered apartments where people do not get information about their energy use and frequently do not directly pay for it. One energy conservation method used in such master-metered apartments is rebating all or some part of the money saved by energy conscious residents. If $10,000 is saved through energy conservation in an apartment building, half might be divided among residents, the other half kept by management. This procedure becomes more effective for conservation as the proportion of savings given to residents increases, and when there is greater cohesion among residents (Slaven, Wodarski, &

Blackburn, 1981). Walker (1979) tried another reinforcement strategy with people living in master-metered apartments. It was publicized that people with thermostats set above 74 °F (23 °C) in summer who had their windows closed when air conditioning was on would receive a $5.00 payment. Apartments were selected randomly for inspection, and those meeting the criteria were reinforced. This technique led to a 4 to 8 percent savings in energy use throughout the apartment complex.

Feedback

Environmental feedback serves several consequent functions. Of course, it provides information about the relative effectiveness of different behaviors. It may also be reinforcing because it provides competency information; that is, it tells us when we are doing a good job. Of course feedback about energy consumption will be more effective if people know the relative importance of each of the components of total energy use (Dennis et al., 1990). For example, Costanzo et al. (1986) found that many consumers thought that turning off lights would save as much energy as using less hot water, but lighting accounts for less than 7 percent of most residential electric bills. Because this percentage is small it may be swamped by other energy expenditures. This may lead consumers to conclude incorrectly that their other conservation efforts are ineffective if their utility bills do not reflect savings from their efforts to turn out lights (Kempton & Montgomery, 1982; Seligman et al., 1979). Often, energy use feedback compares our consumption this year with the same period last year. Good feedback should correct for differences between current weather and weather during the corresponding period of the previous year so that doing better or worse is not an artifact of warmer or cooler temperatures. Although the focus should probably be on individual outcomes rather than on those received by a group, combining both individual and group-based feedback can be very effective (Winnett, Neal, & Grier, 1979).

In the 1970s, primarily in response to a crisis in the supply of oil, the United States imposed a reduced highway speed limit of 55 miles per hour. Compliance with these reduced speed limits should save gasoline, but compliance was spotty and speed limits have now increased on some highways. Feedback is also one approach to encouraging fuel conservation. For example, Van Houten and Nau (1981) posted signs reading NUMBER OF PEOPLE SPEEDING LAST WEEK: _____ BEST RECORD TO DATE: _____. According to these researchers, the signs were effective in reducing traffic speed—even more effective than increasing the number of tickets issued by police (Van Houten, Nau, & Marini, 1980). In another study, Rothstein (1980) arranged for a graph of gasoline consumption to be displayed during the evening news for seven successive nights. During the feedback period, local service stations reported a consumption decrease of 31.5 percent.

Studies have typically given energy consumption feedback in written form at agreed upon intervals, although in other experiments more sophisticated feedback devices (e.g., convenient mechanical energy meters) have been used. At present, we do not know which mode is most effective, or whether feedback on energy use is more effective if represented as a percentage change in use (compared to the previous year), the amount of money saved, absolute differences in kilowatt hours consumed, and so on (Cone & Hayes, 1980). The more frequent the energy consumption feedback, the more conservation occurs (Seligman & Darley, 1977), though relatively infrequent feedback can sometimes be surprisingly effective (Hayes & Cone, 1981). Feedback is more effective at decreasing energy use when the cost of energy relative to peoples' incomes is high (Winkler & Winnett, 1982), when people believe that the feedback accurately reflects their energy-consuming behavior, and when the household has made a commitment to save energy (Stern & Oskamp, 1987). Some studies suggest that feedback is especially effective during periods of high energy use (e.g., hot, humid days of summer; the coldest days of winter; Cone & Hayes, 1980), and giving customers energy reduction goals along with feedback enhances its effect (Becker, 1978). Conservation efforts due to feedback may be retained for as long as 12 weeks after the feedback program ends (Winnett et al., 1981).

While feedback is often effective in reducing energy use, giving it in some forms is not cost effective. Having someone read the meter and supply written feedback, at least on a frequent basis, can be quite expensive (Geller et al., 1982). Sometimes mechanical recording and/or signaling devices may be more cost effective, at least in the long run (cf. Becker & Seligman, 1978). But the least expensive form of feedback is self-monitoring—teaching people how to read their own power meters and encouraging them to do it regularly. Although much prompting may be necessary to get people to do this consistently, studies show that such procedures can result in conservation (Winnett, Neale, & Grier, 1979). Overall, research suggests that feedback is an effective technique for promoting residential energy conservation. Ellis and Gashell (1978) posit that to conserve energy in the home, people must be motivated to conserve and must learn how the home energy system works (i.e., what behaviors have what consequences for energy use). Thus, information and prompts do not motivate people, incentives motivate them but do not teach them the necessary relationships, and only feedback can (under ideal circumstances) provide both the necessary motivational and informational elements.

Policy and Technological Innovations

As desirable as changes in energy-using behavior are, direct consumptive behavior may not be the most effective target for intervention. Some social traps may be so potent that only some form of mutual coercion or managerial decision can achieve effective change. For instance, our use of private automobiles corresponds in many ways to the social trap analysis we described earlier. The short-term benefits of the private passenger car (e.g., convenience, privacy, and prestige) accrue to the driver, while some of its negative consequences (e.g., pollution, energy consumption) are longer range, and the costs are shared by the driver and others.

Some researchers believe that the greatest savings in energy use by individuals comes from changes in technology, regulations, or building codes (Kempton, Darley, & Stern, 1992; Stern, 1992a, 1992b; Stern & Gardner, 1981). In general, these require a one-time legislative or purchasing decision with savings that accrue automatically to each subsequent instance of energy-consuming behavior. For instance, more was probably accomplished by forcing automobile manufacturers to adopt more stringent fuel efficiency standards than could have been done by any conceivable effort to change the behavior of individual drivers (Stern, 1992b). In private residences, the 1980s saw the introduction of condensing pulse combustion furnaces that have efficiencies in excess of 90 percent compared to the 63 percent efficiency ratings of typical standard natural gas furnaces sold in the 1970s. Because space heating is the most important single energy expense in the home, the benefits of more efficient furnaces and better insulation can be substantial (Hirst et al., 1986). According to Stern and Gardner (1981), replacing six major home appliances with the most efficient substitute yields an energy savings of 33.2 percent, compared to a 12.5 percent savings from the most successful behavioral interventions aimed at encouraging consumers to use energy in the most efficient way. As Stern (1992b) reminds us, builders and manufacturers decide which consumer products to produce, but they do not themselves pay for the energy used by their products, so they may lack sufficient incentive to manufacture efficient products or to build efficient homes. Of course consumers can demand more efficient designs, but their ability to change the efficiency of buildings or appliances through their purchasing patterns is indirect. Legislated standards are also sometimes flawed. For example, because light trucks are not covered by the same fuel economy standards as cars, some manufacturers market certain light trucks as carlike recreational vehicles, lowering the fuel economy of United States vehicles overall (Kempton et al., 1992).

The value of even simple technological improvements was demonstrated by Howard et al. (1993), who devised a plan to replace incandescent bulbs in the University of Notre Dame dormitories with compact fluorescent bulbs that fit in the existing fixtures. Although the fluorescent bulbs are initially more expensive, they last longer and are more efficient, so over the lifetime of a fluorescent bulb the energy savings far exceed the initial higher cost. In spite of considerable resistance from university administrators and building supervisors, over 2,000 bulbs were initially placed in five experimental dormitories, each of which was paired with a similar untreated control condition dorm. According to the researchers, each fluorescent bulb saved an average of $2.30 in energy costs each month, quickly paying back its higher cost. Following this demonstration, Notre Dame instituted a plan to replace 8,000 incandescent bulbs, designed to save more than $190,000 between August 1994 and February 1997.

In spite of this apparent success, the Energy Star program to reduce the energy used by computers (discussed in the box on page 543) and the lighting efforts of Howard and his associates also illustrate some of the difficulties in establishing energy-saving technological innovations in homes and workplaces. A survey of potential computer purchasers, for example, showed enthusiasm for computers that are designed to use less electric-

ity, but only if they were no more expensive than standard models (Nadel, 1994). In extensions to the incandescent light replacement program at Notre Dame, Howard and his colleagues attempted to sell the new energy-saving fluorescent bulbs to private households. Despite an explanation of the environmental benefits and the promise of long-term savings, relatively few residential customers agreed to buy even one replacement bulb, and these purchases were primarily by individuals with higher incomes. Free-trial offers raised the participation by middle- and lower-income homes somewhat, but participation remained low (Howard et al., 1993). Individuals are cautious, often looking to their peers to separate genuine technological innovations from those that are scams or gimmicks (Dennis et al., 1990). Simply demonstrating technical superiority is not likely to be as successful as an approach that makes use of persuasive techniques from social psychology and marketing. Of course, persuasive communication may not have to be directed at all consumers. As we said, building supervisors and administrators were initially reluctant to install new energy-saving fluorescent bulbs, but once just a few individuals became convinced, large-scale changes were instituted. Thus, one effective approach seems to be a concentrated effort aimed at individuals who have the time and resources to evaluate new technologies and who make decisions resulting in high-volume purchases.

Although Stern and others (e.g., Kempton et al, 1992) may be correct in singling out technological innovations as an excellent source of energy savings, an approach that relies on improved technology also carries liabilities. Geller et al. (1982) suggest that we may underestimate the savings from behavioral interventions to promote conservation, and that some researchers have not considered all the energy waste involved in replacing old equipment with new (e.g., costs of disposal, energy used in the manufacturing

COMPUTERS:
A New Environmental Challenge

Few things have changed so much in the past two decades as the use of computers. Personal computers have gone from being rarities to common appliances in businesses, faculty offices, homes, and student rooms. The U.S. Environmental Protection Agency and the computer industry are cooperating in an energy conservation initiative with potential for both residential and commercial users. The Energy Star program aims to reduce computer power consumption by requiring the computer system unit and its monitor to switch to a power-down mode when turned on but not actually in use. In order to meet Energy Star compliance, neither the system unit nor the monitor can consume more than 30 watts in the power-down mode. System modifications are inexpensive and do not harm the performance for most computers, so manufacturers have been eager to offer Energy Star PCs. Some estimate that if everyone used only Energy Star compliant PCs, $2 billion could be saved annually (Nadel, 1994). In addition to becoming more common, personal computers have enjoyed dramatic increases in computing power. This (or even the Energy Star program) creates a tremendous incentive to replace yesterday's computer with something newer and more powerful. Of course almost all electric appliances eventually get replaced, but for computers this often happens long before they are worn out. In order to avoid burdening the waste stream, manufacturers are being encouraged to adopt a holistic program to minimize the generation of toxic chemicals during the manufacture of computers and to encourage recycling of computers and their accessories (PC Magazine, August, 1994).

process). More generally, we fear that misapplied programs focused on technological innovation might decrease the likelihood that individual consumers will accept personal responsibility for conserving energy, undermining other conservation efforts. Regardless of these points of contention, there is much to be said for developing psychological and other techniques for encouraging our purchase of the most energy-efficient equipment available.

CONSERVING WATER

Unlike fossil fuels, water is abundant. Nevertheless, the amount of available fresh water is a small fraction of the total in oceans or locked in polar ice. In many areas of North America water use exceeds the amount provided by rain and snow. In the West, the demands of agriculture, industry, and residential use require either expensive diversion of water or drilling to drain water from underground aquifers at a rate that greatly exceeds their natural recharge (Parfit, 1993; see Figure 14–6).

One study (Geller et al., 1983) investigated the effectiveness of water use feedback, an educational campaign encouraging conservation, and the installation of water conservation devices. Although the water conservation devices reduced subsequent consumption, neither feedback nor the educational intervention had an appreciable effect. In another

Figure 14–6 Particularly in the North American West, water use exceeds its replenishment.

second group received the same conservation suggestions, but these participants were actually given a water restrictor. Not surprisingly, those in the second group were more likely to install the water conservation devices than those who were only told about them. More interestingly, this group was more likely to adopt other conservation measures such as reducing their thermostats.

A California study examined a commons education group which received educational messages that focused on the long-term benefits of conservation and emphasized the effectiveness of individual action using Hardin's tragedy of the commons metaphor. A second group received information emphasizing the short-term economic advantage of water conservation. Participants in a third group received no educational messages, but were encouraged to conserve and were made aware that their water use was being monitored. For lower-middle-class residents, the appeal that focused on the long-term consequences of conservation and the necessity for individual action yielded less water consumption than did either the economic-based appeal to conserve or the control appeal (no educational message). For reasons that are unclear, the upper-middle-class residents did not show increased water conservation in response to any of the treatments (Thompson & Stoutemyer, 1991).

study consumers received information about measures to conserve water, including information about a shower water restrictor designed to reduce the use of hot water. A

SOURCE REDUCTION AND RECYCLING

Among the least positive effects of industrialization are the interrelated problems of material resource depletion and solid waste disposal. Some materials or goods are too rare to squander or lose, so we should promote their reuse to protect a dwindling resource. Others seem cheap and are regularly thrown away. When disposed of thoughtlessly these become litter; but even when disposed of

"properly" they contribute to a crisis in solid waste management (Figure 14–7).

In some instances materials are so valuable or durable that a high percentage are reused. The silverware and china you used as a child are probably good examples. Less familiar to younger generations are the refillable milk and soft drink bottles that were phased out in the 1960s and 1970s. Relatively

Figure 14–7   Even trash that is disposed of properly becomes part of the crisis of solid waste.

little psychological research has targeted reuse. In one Michigan study, however, volunteers from a small village received pamphlets advocating source reduction (for example, purchasing items in reusable containers, reusing aluminum foil, and avoiding overpackaged products). For some participants the arguments for source reduction were primarily economic, some were given environmental reasons, and some were provided with both economic and environmental reasons to source reduce. Subsequently, those in all three treatment groups reported more conservation behavior, and those receiving both economic and environmental rationales reported the most conservation (De Young et al., 1993).

Other items are not directly reused, but their material is recovered and remanufactured. Gold, for example, has been used and reused by humans for centuries. There is an

intriguing and real possibility that some of the gold in the jewelry you or your friends own was once part of a Spanish, Roman, or Egyptian treasure. There are two broad categories of resource recovery. In recycling a material is reused for its original purpose. For example, recycling aluminum cans instead of making them from raw aluminum ore saves money, energy (recycling aluminum cans uses 95 percent less energy than refining raw materials), and conserves the world's reserves of aluminum. Other materials are more difficult to recycle for their original use. For instance, the possibility that plastic food and beverage containers may accidentally become contaminated with pesticides or other harmful chemicals raises concerns about their reuse, but reclamation allows their material to be remanufactured into diverse products. Reclamation can be effective for less valuable materials as well. A bidding war broke out for used plastic soda bottles in the United States in 1995 and their price rose from $40 to $460 per ton (Miller, 1995). Polyethylene terephthalate (PET) soft drink bottles can be made into insulating fiberfill or yarns, and high-density polyethylene (HDPE) like that in plastic milk jugs can be reused as containers for products such as detergents and shampoo. Generally, the necessary consumer behavior is the same whether materials are separated for recycling or reclamation, so we will use the term "recycling" to refer to both.

Recycling of even seemingly mundane materials is not new. During World War II metal, newspaper, and glass were commonly collected for remanufacture (Burn, 1991; Oskamp et al., 1994). Unfortunately, recycling habits prompted by the war (or the depression that preceded it) began to fade in the postwar prosperity, and more and more products became disposable. Now many North American landfills are nearing their capacity, creating a "landfill crisis" (Oskamp et al., 1994). Presently three primary approaches to the management of solid waste are feasible. We could delay the confrontation by developing landfills, but new landfills can raise disposal costs, and old ones eventually leak. A second approach is to turn waste into energy through incineration. Although this remains attractive to some, opposition to incineration has grown with fears that incinerators expel toxic fumes or concentrate deadly pollutants in residual ash that has to be sent to landfills (see Blumberg & Gottlieb, 1989). The remaining approach, and the one now supported by many federal and state agencies, is to try to change the behavior of people (Porter, Leeming, & Dwyer, 1995; Vining & Ebreo, 1992).

Methods of recycling differ from place to place. Initially, many programs required individual households to transport their recyclables to a centralized drop-off facility. More recently, many municipalities have adopted recycling programs that only require households to separate their recyclables and leave them beside the street for curbside pickup. The specifics of collection and the materials that can be recycled vary from place to place. What nearly all approaches have in common, however, is a requirement for public participation (Howenstine, 1993).

ANTECEDENT INTERVENTIONS

How do those who recycle differ from those who do not? As you might expect, those who are better informed about recyclable materials and local recycling programs are probably more likely to be recyclers themselves (Vining & Ebreo, 1990). Although this suggests that at least some form of education might be important in facilitating recycling, there is little evidence that environmental education alone enhances recycling behavior.

As with energy conservation, several researchers have investigated the effects of commitment on recycling (e.g., Burn & Oskamp, 1986; Katzev & Pardini, 1987–1988; Pardini & Katzev, 1983–1984). In particular, the strength of commitment seems to be important to sustaining long-term recycling. In one study (Pardini & Katzev, 1983–1984), for example, those who made a strong (written) commitment to recycle newspapers and a group making only weaker verbal commitments both recycled more than a third group that received only information. Weeks later, however, only the strong-commitment group showed continued increases in paper recycling. In another study, Wang and Katzev (1990) asked residents of a retirement home to sign a group pledge to participate in a four-week recycling project. For the four weeks of the commitment, the weight of recycled material increased 47 percent over baseline measures. Additional observations indicated that recycling continued at a similar high rate for at least four weeks

ENCOURAGING RECYCLING VIA THE FOOT-IN-THE-DOOR TECHNIQUE

The above findings have some interesting implications. We might view responding to prompts, such as reminders to turn off lights, as analogous to initial requests in the foot-in-the-door technique. This would suggest that responding to the multiple "small requests" being made of us to improve the environment these days may in some way "prime" us to comply with the larger, more important environmental demands we will face in the years ahead. The phenomenon also suggests some potential problems with the use of reinforcement techniques for encouraging pro-ecological behavior. Self-perception theory in social psychology implies that often we infer our attitudes from observing our behavior and the circumstances under which it occurs (Bem, 1972). Arbuthnot et al. (1976–1977) proposed that people in their study agreed to the larger requests because after complying with the initial request, they inferred from their behavior that they had pro-environmental attitudes. They had no incentives for their initial compliance, thus they must really care about the environment. This pro-ecological self-perception may have been why long-term changes in recycling occurred in the foot-in-the-door study. On the other hand, what would people infer about themselves from their behavior after recycling because they were offered a financial reward or reinforcement? Bem would say that instead of inferring that they care about the environment—a conclusion which could be associated with continued recycling—they might conclude they merely did it for the money. Such a self-perception could lead them to stop recycling as soon as the rewards for it were removed.

following the group commitment. In a second study of college students, the same researchers compared two different commitment procedures and a reinforcement strategy. Some participants attended a five-minute talk about paper recycling, and were then asked to sign a group commitment to participate in the program. Individuals in a second treatment condition were approached individually, told of the recycling program, and were asked to sign a personal pledge to participate in the program. In addition, a third (incentive) treatment group was given a flyer explaining that everyone on their dorm hall would receive discount coupons for local businesses if 50 percent of the people on their hall recycled during a given week. All

three treatment groups recycled more often than a control group, but individuals who had committed to recycling showed greater recycling than those who had signed the group pledge. Perhaps the most interesting finding was that at least some of the students assigned to the individual-commitment group continued to recycle for some weeks after their commitment had expired, whereas more of both the reinforcement and the group commitment subjects reverted to near pre-treatment levels.

Goal setting is a related technique. Motivation theorists (e.g., Locke, 1968, 1970) tell us that specific and challenging goals are likely to result in more behavioral change than easy or general goals. Although goal setting is not a common variable in studies of conserving behavior (Dwyer et al., 1993), there is some evidence that both children (Hamad et al., 1980–1981) and college students (McCaul & Kopp, 1982) show higher compliance when they are assigned recycling goals. In fact, college students in the McCaul and Kopp study recycled 37 percent more.

One final related approach to encouraging recycling involves the **foot-in-the-door technique**, which has been used in some classic studies in social psychology on gaining compliance. Like the salesperson who stands a better chance of making the sale by initially getting a "foot in the door," environmental psychologists may be more apt to get people to recycle (or engage in other pro-ecological behavior) after eliciting a small commitment from them. The standard "foot-in-the-door" paradigm goes like this. The experimenter first makes a small request of the subject which very few are likely to refuse (e.g., sign a petition for a highly respectable pro-environmental cause). This is followed by progressively larger requests (e.g., recycle your soft drink containers). Because people who comply with the small initial request come to view themselves as interested in preserving the environment, they are more apt to agree to the second, larger request than are subjects who are never presented with the initial request. Arbuthnot et al. (1976–1977) used this strategy to increase recycling behavior. Their initial smaller requests were to have people answer survey items favoring environmental protection, to save aluminum cans for a week, and to send in a postcard urging officials to expand a local recycling program. Did being confronted with these initial requests affect long-term use of a recycling center? The answer is "yes." As long as 18 months after the initial request, subjects were more apt to use the center than those not exposed to the foot-in-the-door strategy.

CONTINGENT STRATEGIES

Reinforcement

Perhaps the most persuasive demonstrations of the usefulness of contingent rewards occur in those American states that have adopted "bottle bills." For instance, New York state began requiring a 5-cent returnable deposit on soft drink and beer containers in 1983. Before the law went into effect, recycling rates for the state were 5 percent for cans, 3 percent for glass, and 1 percent for plastics. During the first year after implementation, 59 percent of cans, 77 percent of glass, and 33 percent of plastic containers were recycled, accounting for about a 5 percent reduction in solid waste by weight (Wolf & Feldman, 1991). In addition to these widespread incentives, several researchers have demonstrated that monetary rewards or punishments can promote short-term recycling (e.g., Jacobs & Bailey, 1982; Luyben & Bailey, 1975). Unfortunately, behavior often quickly returns to baseline levels when the reinforcements are removed (e.g., DeYoung, 1986; Jacobs & Bailey, 1982).

Feedback

Katzev and Mishima (1992) investigated the effects of feedback on paper recycling on a small college campus. The mailroom's recycling containers labeled RECYCLABLE PAPER ONLY were located near both exits in the central mailroom. During the treatment period, a large sign reading: RECYCLABLE PAPER: _____ POUNDS COLLECTED YESTERDAY was placed between the two exits and updated each day during the treatment. During the week that feedback was posted, the weight of recycled paper increased 76.7 percent. Although records were maintained only for one week following the feedback treatment, the amount of recycled paper remained about 46 percent above baseline.

LITTERING

Part of the huge volume of trash generated by North Americans ends up as litter. It collects in public parks and forests, alongside highways and waterways, and in private land. In addition to being profoundly ugly, litter represents a hazard to our health and safety and may cause damage to plant and animal life (Geller et al., 1982). Who helps to create these unseemly conditions? Young people litter more than older ones; some studies suggest that males litter more than females; and people who are alone litter more than those in groups (Osborne & Powers, 1980). The whole range of strategies we have discussed (e.g., prompts, reinforcers) has been used in attempts to prevent people from littering, and to motivate them to clean up litter left by careless individuals. As we discuss the various techniques, we will see that some methods have been more effective than others (for detailed reviews, see Brasted, Mann, & Geller 1979; Cone & Hayes, 1980; Geller, 1987; Huffman et al., 1995; Osborne & Powers, 1980).

ANTECEDENT INTERVENTIONS

State bottle bill legislation has been effective in reducing roadside litter by 75 percent and in saving energy through recycling (Levitt & Leventhal, 1984; Osborne & Powers, 1980). Many studies have employed prompts and cues as antecedent strategies to prevent littering. For example, handbills with an antilitter prompt are less apt to be littered than those without a prompt (Geller et al., 1982). Generally, prompts that state the specific antilitter response desired (e.g., "Place this paper in a trash can") are more effective than less specific ones (e.g., "Keep the area clean"). Antilitter prompts are also more effective when given in close temporal proximity to

an opportunity to dispose of litter, when proper litter disposal is relatively convenient, and when the prompt is phrased in polite, nondemanding language (Geller et al., 1982; Stern & Oskamp, 1987). Even under optimal circumstances, the absolute magnitude of change effected by these sorts of prompts is often relatively small (though statistically significant), and to have a meaningful effect they may have to be experienced by many people over a long time frame. Other antecedent factors which may serve as prompts include the amount of litter already in a setting, the behavior of models, and the presence of trash receptacles. Generally, "litter begets litter"—the more littered an environment the more littered it becomes. In fact, studies have shown up to a five-fold increase in littering in "littered" as opposed to "clean" settings (e.g., Finnie, 1973; Geller, Witmer, & Tuso, 1977; Krauss, Freedman, & Whitcup, 1978).

In addition to the pattern noted in the box on page 550, an exception to the "litter begets litter" finding has been reported in some natural settings, where people are less apt to litter and more apt to pick up other people's trash when their picnic areas are littered than when clean. This may be because in such settings environmental cleanliness plays an especially important role for people, since they are there to appreciate natural beauty (cf. Geller et al., 1982). Directly observing the behavior of models can serve as a prompt that reduces or produces littering. Cialdini (1977) exposed subjects to a model who littered or did not litter in a clean or dirty environment. After seeing the model fail to litter in the clean setting, subjects littered the least; after seeing him litter in the dirty setting they littered the most. And Jason, Zolik, and Matese (1979) found that

IS A LITTLE LITTER A MORE EFFECTIVE PROMPT THAN NONE AT ALL?

We suggested that more environmentally destructive behavior typically occurs when there is evidence of previous misdeeds (litter on the ground) than when there is not. Whereas this is usually true, work by Cialdini, Reno, and Kallgren (1989) brought out an interesting caveat. While they found (like previous investigators) that a perfectly clean environment produces less littering than a dirty environment, they also observed that the least littering occurs in a setting that is clean except for one piece of litter. The studies were run as follows: Subjects were handed a public service-related circular as they walked down a path. Beforehand, the experimenter had positioned 0, 1, 2, 4, 8, or 16 pieces of litter in front of them. Surprisingly, 18 percent of the subjects littered in the "no litter" condition, but only 10 percent in the "one piece of litter" condition. Beyond that, littering by subjects increased proportionate to the amount of litter positioned by the experimenter. Why did Cialdini et al. observe such a "check mark" pattern for the relationship between the amount of litter in the environment and subsequent littering? They reasoned that while a perfectly clean environment makes the "no littering" norm salient, an environment clean except for one violation makes it even more salient. With increasing violations, however, the norm becomes undermined, and littering is facilitated. These findings are provocative, and if replicated in other contexts they could have practical implications for environmental education as well as environmental design. For example, do you think you would be more likely to return your shopping cart at the supermarket if all but one of the remaining carts were neatly stacked, or there were no violations of the "return your cart" norm?

observing a model who showed people how to pick up dog droppings with a "pooper scooper" led to a target area more free of feces. Unfortunately, other studies are less optimistic about the potential of models to prevent environmentally destructive behavior (cf. Geller et al., 1982).

A final antecedent strategy to prevent littering is the presence of waste receptacles. Finnie (1973) reported that compared to a condition in which no trash cans were in sight, their presence reduced littering by about 15 percent along city streets and by nearly 30 percent on highways. When a greater number of trash cans were present, littering decreased still more. The value of trash cans or similar objects as antilitter prompts may depend on their attractiveness or distinctiveness. Finnie (1973) observed that colorful garbage cans reduced littering by 14.9 percent over baseline levels, whereas ordinary cans led to a reduction of only 3.15 percent. Similarly, Miller et al. (1976) reported that brightly colored cans resembling birds were much more effective than plain cans in eliciting appropriate disposal. Finally, an ingenious garbage can in the shape of a hat worn by students to Clemson University football games greatly reduced trash in the area of the college football stadium (Miller et al., 1976; O'Neill, Blanck, & Joyner, 1980). Unfortunately, picking up someone else's litter and putting it in a receptacle is often a more costly behavior than depositing one's own litter, and it seems to be relatively unresponsive to prompts. For example, 10 experiments by Geller and associates (Geller, 1976; Geller, Mann, & Brasted, 1977) found that prompts have minimal effects on people's likelihood of picking up others' litter and disposing of it. The only exception may be in natural areas, such as campgrounds, where prompts may elicit such behavior (cf. Crump, Nunes, & Crossman, 1977). The ineffectiveness of prompts is especially unfortunate, since much money is spent on them by state litter control authorities and organizations such as Keep America Beautiful.

CONSEQUENT STRATEGIES

We turn now to consequence strategies for litter control (i.e., methods to encourage people to pick up existing litter), which (at least in the short run) have generally been more effective than antecedent techniques (Cone & Hayes, 1980). In the Clemson study just cited, for instance, the hat cans served both as prompts to prevent litter and as the sources of consequent reinforcement because the Clemson hat dispensed a mechanical "Thank you" to anyone who deposited litter (Miller et al., 1976; O'Neill, Blanck, & Joyner, 1980).

Reinforcement-based techniques are more successful than prompts in motivating people to clean up littered environments. In fact, when prompts are coupled with reinforcements for obeying them, they can be rather effective. Kohlenberg and Phillips (1973) positioned a prompt which said, "Depositing Litter May Be Rewarded," and

then proceeded to reward litter depositors on different reinforcement schedules. This technique precipitated a dramatic cleanup. Another study involved a combination of prompts, environmental education, and reinforcers (in this case feedback). Investigators organized local newspaper coverage about the littering problem (which served as a prompt and a form of education), along with daily feedback on littering in certain target areas. These methods accounted for a decrease in litter compared to baseline conditions (Schnelle et al., 1980). Other experiments have similarly coupled reinforcers with educational techniques and prompts. In these studies, the rewards generally account for much more of the resultant improvement in the litter situation than the other methods (Cone & Hayes, 1980). However, while reinforcement methods are useful, they sometimes require costly supervision to monitor behavior and dispense reinforcers. What alternatives are there for reinforcing litter depositors without supervision? Reinforcements can also be administered on the "honor system." A sign in a United States national forest area offered people either 25 cents (sent to them by mail) or a chance to win a larger reward if they filled a plastic trash bag with garbage and completed an information card stating their name and address. Compared to a prompt-only condition (which asked people to fill up a bag but offered no reward), the "honor system" reinforcement condition was much more successful (Powers, Osborne, & Anderson, 1973).

A clever and effective use of positive reinforcement that motivates people to pick up litter is the "litter lottery." A litter lottery offers people an opportunity to win valuable prizes just for depositing litter appropriately. In one version of the technique (Bacon-Prue et al., 1980; Hayes, Johnson, & Cone, 1975), experimenters distribute specially marked items on the ground amidst the litter that is habitually present. People are told some litter is marked in an undetectable fashion, and if an experimenter verifies that they have collected a marked item, they will be awarded a substantial prize. In another version (Kohlenberg & Phillips, 1973), the experimenter merely observes litter deposits and rewards ecologically minded people intermittently. Both techniques have achieved dramatic results toward cleaning up the environment, but both require costly human intervention. The "marked-item" strategy can, however, be "automated" and introduced widely. Imagine the following scenario for improving litter control throughout the world. Litter with invisible identifying marks could be distributed at random, as would special trash cans (indistinguishable from ordinary ones) that would deliver valuable reinforcers automatically if a marked item were deposited. Whenever you had some spare time, you might find yourself absentmindedly picking up garbage, throwing it in a trash can, and fantasizing about future wealth! Of course, the "novelty" of such a program might wear off after awhile, and it would be expensive to administer, which could detract from its overall usefulness. In conceiving of any technique for improving environmental conditions, one should be careful to think about ways in which it could be "subverted." One problem with the litter lottery is that it may not prevent people from throwing litter on the ground because the piece they throw away cannot possibly be "marked." Children participating in a litter lottery still disposed of litter inappropriately (La Hart & Bailey, 1975). On the other hand, the more garbage litter lottery participants deposit inappropriately, the more difficult it should be to find "marked" items. Adults may be aware of this contingency, and it may keep them from littering. Reinforcements based on the number of bags of litter collected may be problematic because people are encouraged to pick up large but not small pieces of litter. In fact, some individuals may not pick up litter from the target area at all, but may bring it from home. Even when rewards are based on some criterion for success such as a clean campsite, some people may "clean" the area by throwing trash somewhere else. However, even though these behavioral techniques can be subverted, they are still valuable tools for improving the environment for all.

VANDALISM

Vandalism can be defined as the "willful or malicious destruction, injury, disfigurement, or defacement of any public or private property" (Uniform Crime Reporting Handbook, 1978, p. 90). Thus, unlike failures to conserve resources or even thoughtless littering, vandalism is intentional. The results of a vandal's work may seem completely senseless, but their intent may reflect deep personal frustrations or even a calculated political expression (consider the Boston Tea Party). We might distinguish between several types of vandalism: acquisitive vandalism (looting, petty theft), tactical ideological vandalism (to draw attention to oneself or to an issue of concern), vindictive vandalism (aimed at revenge), play vandalism (to combat boredom), and malicious vandalism (due to diffuse frustration and rage, often occurring in public settings). Because the motives of vandals vary, so must society's response. How big a problem is vandalism? The challenges faced by the U.S. National Park Service provide an example. Most Civil War era battle fields in the United States continue to be sites of conflict—conflict between rangers and looters who dig through graves looking for buttons and other objects to sell on the black market. In the American Southwest, thousands of ancient Native American sites have been damaged or destroyed, and in Yellowstone National Park geysers and hot pools are destroyed by material people throw into them (Wilkinson, 1991). Overall, the cost in American schools, parks, recreation areas, public housing and transit systems is estimated at billions of dollars per year, and these costs are increasing rapidly. Unfortunately, the penalties for vandalizing sites of even national historic importance were, for many years, very low. It has been only recently that the U.S. Congress passed legislation making many acts of vandalism felonies.

In spite of its costs, relatively little empirical research has tried to address the problem, though it has been found that several physical and social conditions promote vandalism. As discussed in Chapter 10, when the design of a setting allows residents little territorial control, vandalism becomes more common (Ley & Cybriwsky, 1974a; Newman, 1972). Thus, preventative strategies could focus on increasing territorial control (e.g., designing areas to promote defensible space). Aesthetic factors associated with an object's appearance (e.g., physical beauty) and the extent to which a site is hardened (made difficult to vandalize), also affect the level of vandalism (Pablant & Baxter, 1975). Just as aesthetic variables affect how much we enjoy socially acceptable interactions with an object, they affect the pleasure we experience from vandalizing it. Objects that break in aesthetically interesting or pleasing ways may be more apt to be vandalized than those that break in dull, uninteresting ways (Allen & Greenberger, 1980; Greenberger & Allen,

Figure 14–8 Sturdy or protected objects may be less susceptible to damage.

1980). Designing objects (e.g., street lights) that will not break in a satisfying manner may be another way of decreasing vandalism (Figure 14–8).

As with our "litter begets littering" generalization, the presence of graffiti may encourage new "artists" (Samdahl & Christensen, 1985; Sharpe, 1976). Thus, one priority of both parks and cities is to clean up the signs of vandals as quickly as possible. Anaheim, California established an aggressive anti-graffiti campaign that included undercover police officers, rewards for information leading to the arrest and conviction of graffiti artists, a computerized database for tracking known graffiti "taggers" and their associates, and aggressive programs to remove graffiti (Molloy & Labahn, 1993). Other factors have been implicated as causes of vandalism. Allen and Greenberger (1980) suggest that low perceived control (see Chapter 4) will under certain conditions elicit vandalism. When we come to believe we cannot control our outcomes (e.g., college students may not feel that they have enough control over policies in the dormitories), we sometimes resort to vandalism as a way of showing ourselves and others that we can control at least certain things (Warzecha, Fisher, & Baron, 1988). This would suggest that the greater people's control over a setting, the less vandalism. Also, it has been suggested that vandalism results when there is a lack of fit between the person and the environment; for example, school vandalism may be due to poor congruence between personal characteristics of students and the social or physical environment of the school. Increasing the goodness of the fit through social and/or environmental means could help lower vandalism, according to this conceptualization. Work by Richards (1979) has identified peer relationships (i.e., associations with antisocial peers) and adult–child conflict as major causes of vandalism by middle-class adolescents. Vandalism may also occur due to financial need, in the pursuit of social causes, due to nonmalicious play, or due to poor achievement (cf. Cohen, 1973; Sabatino et al., 1978).

A rather complete model of vandalism has been proposed (Baron & Fisher, 1984; Fisher & Baron, 1982). This model encompasses many of the reasons suggested above for why vandalism occurs, under the concept of perceived inequity. What is perceived inequity? Equity theories in social psychology imply that we are socialized to believe we should treat others fairly (or equitably), and should be treated equitably by others. When this does not occur (i.e., when we perceive we are being inequitably or unfairly treated), we become upset and try to restore equity. This can be done in several ways, but it typically involves our attempting to get more out of the relationship for what we put into it, or trying to ensure that the other gets less out of the relationship for what he or she puts in. Fisher and Baron's model implies that vandalism may be one way of restoring equity in settings characterized by perceived inequity (or unfairness) between the parties. Vandalism can therefore be viewed as a way to restore equity by responding to one type of perceived rule-breaking unfairness in interpersonal relations with another type (i.e., disregard for another's property rights). In effect, some vandals seem to say, "If I don't get any respect, I won't give you any either." What kinds of inequity are apt to promote vandalism? It may occur as a product of ordinary economic exchange (e.g., between a shopkeeper and a customer), from discriminatory practices and inequitable rules and regulations (e.g., between employer and employee; housing authority and resident), and from aspects of the physical environment in and of itself (e.g., defective machines or facilities that cause an inequitable input/output ratio). Inflexible environmental settings such as windows that will not open, thermostats we cannot adjust, or dormitory furniture that will not move may also make it difficult for us to receive a fair level of outcomes relative to our inputs, and may promote vandalism. Will every instance of inequity result in vandalism? Obviously not. Fisher and Baron suggest that inequity will result in vandalism only when the person who feels inequitably treated has low perceived control—that is, little likelihood of influencing whether equity will be restored. When we have high perceived control we restore equity within the system (e.g., complain to the authorities), and when we have very low perceived control we become helpless, and simply accept our fate. But when we have moderate to low control, we are likely to opt for a way of restoring equity. For some, this method is vandalism—an immediate, low-effort, and certain means of paying society back. Fisher and Baron suggest that increasing perceptions of control, decreasing perceived inequity, or both, can be effective means of lowering vandalism (see Figure 14–9).

Figure 14–9 Intentional damage from vandalism is both unsightly and costly. Increasing perceptions of control, decreasing perceived inequity, or both, can be an effective means of lowering vandalism.

ENCOURAGING ENVIRONMENTALLY RESPONSIBLE BEHAVIOR: AN ASSESSMENT OF THE PRESENT AND THE FUTURE

How can we sum up the state of the art that deals with applying environmental psychology to moderate environmentally destructive behavior? The techniques discussed in this chapter give us a good start toward improving many adverse environmental conditions, but we still have a long way to go. Each of the methods we have presented has important strengths and weaknesses, and each needs to be refined and improved by researchers in the future. Presently, few studies directly compare the methods we have discussed for changing environmental behavior and attitudes (Dwyer et al., 1993). More complete comparisons and models remain as necessary first steps toward the creation of an overriding theory to help us conceptualize environmentally destruc-

tive behavior (e.g., Dwyer et al., 1993; Geller, 1990). Such a formulation would greatly enhance our efforts and could lead to a more focused approach by both researchers and practitioners. Current evidence suggests that the interventions we have reviewed differ substantially in their relative impact. Environmental education generally has the weakest impact, followed by prompts. Consequent or reinforcement strategies are much stronger, but the most impactful of all is probably policy and technological innovation. Yet often, the more effective the strategy, the more difficult and expensive it is to implement. In most cases, we find that combinations of strategies offer the most effective interventions in terms of both feasibility of outcome and favorability of results.

CHAPTER SUMMARY

Much environmentally destructive behavior can be conceptualized in terms of social traps. These are situations in which personal interests with a short-term focus conflict with societal needs with a long-term focus. For example, littering and purchasing non-returnable bottles are instances in which short-term individual convenience conflicts with the long-term needs of society. How can we escape from such traps? Research on the commons dilemma suggests dividing some common resources into territories helps, although this is not always practical. Increasing communication and trust and fostering attraction toward and group identification with those who share the commons also are valuable strategies. Altering reinforcements or consequences is also an exceptionally effective approach; adding positive consequences for conservation behavior or punishments for exploitative behavior helps preserve the commons for all. In this chapter, environmental education, use of environmentally relevant prompts, reinforcement-related techniques, and other methods are considered as potential means of altering environmentally destructive behavior. Each of these techniques has unique costs and benefits. Environmental education seems to be a relatively ineffective method, but may be less costly than some other methods. The use of environmentally related prompts is somewhat effective and relatively inexpensive. Finally, reinforcement techniques (positive reinforcement, negative reinforcement, punishment, and feedback) appear to be very effective in creating short-term change, but have several drawbacks. For example, reinforcement techniques may be quite expensive, and evidence shows that the effects often disappear when the reinforcement contin-

gency is withdrawn. In reviewing the major techniques for encouraging environmentally responsible behavior, we considered specific strategies used to cope with the overconsumption of resources, the waste stream crisis, litter, and vandalism. Behavioral solutions to some of these problems offer promise of significantly improving aspects of our environment.

SUGGESTED PROJECTS

1. Design an environmental education program that you feel would have an optimal chance of effectively changing behavior in an environmentally constructive direction. Use whatever media you like, focus on whatever population you desire, and choose a target behavior that corresponds to your area of major interest in environmental psychology.
2. Select an environmentally destructive target behavior and design a prompt that would help alleviate the problem. If you can get the necessary permission from authorities, attempt to test the effectiveness of your technique.
3. Test Cialdini et al.'s hypothesis that a setting with a single violation of a norm serves as a more effective prompt than one with no evidence of norm violation. Some possible subjects for your investigation are the appropriate return of shopping carts at a local supermarket, graffiti in a restroom, or vandalism in a university building.
4. If you have lived in a college dormitory, design a program (using the techniques described in this chapter) to help alleviate noise. Keep in mind the relative effectiveness of education, prompts, reinforcements, and policy changes and innovations.

acclimation – adaptation to one specific environmental stressor, such as temperature.

acclimatization – adaptation to multiple stresses in an environment, such as humidity, temperature, and wind.

accretion measures – unobtrusive indications of behavior, involving traces of additions to the environment, such as litter or fingerprints.

adaptation – weakening of a reaction (especially psychological) to a stimulus; becoming accustomed to a particular degree of a given type of stimulation; in Wohlwill's ideas, a shift in optimal stimulation.

adaptation level (AL) – an ideal level of stimulation that leads to maximum performance or satisfaction.

adaptive reuse – rehabilitation and recycling of old buildings for new uses, such as turning an old warehouse into apartments or a shopping center.

adequately staffed – in ecological psychology, a condition in which the number of applicants is between maintenance minimum and capacity.

adjustment – Sonnenfeld's idea of technological change of a stimulus, as opposed to adaptation, which refers to change in the response to the stimulus.

adrenal – of the adrenal glands, endocrine glands that sit on top of the kidneys; catecholamine secretions from the adrenal glands are characteristic of stress reactions.

affect – feelings or emotional states.

affective appraisals – emotions directed toward some component of the environment.

affiliative behavior – interactions with others; attachment.

affordances – in Gibson's theory of ecological perception, the properties of an object or place that give it constant and automatically detectable functions; the possibilities of use an environment provides.

aftereffects – consequences of a stimulus that occur after the stimulus has stopped; effects of a stressor on mood or behavior, often measured by task performance, that occur after termination of the stressor.

age-segregated – residential settings restricted to the elderly.

air ionization – condition in which molecules of air partially "split" into positively and negatively charged particles, or positive and negative ions.

air pollution syndrome (APS) – headache, fatigue, insomnia, depression, and the other symptoms occurring together and caused by combinations of air pollution.

alarm reaction – a startle response to a stressor; the first stage of Selye's GAS.

alveolar walls – portion of the lung where oxygen and carbon dioxide are exchanged between the blood and the atmosphere.

Alzheimer's disease – the most common progressive dementia, occurring primarily in the elderly, and accounting for half of all nursing home admissions.

ambient stressors – chronic, global stressors such as pollution, noise, or traffic congestion.

ambient temperature – surrounding or atmospheric temperature.

amplitude – the amount of energy in a sound, as represented by the height of the sound wave, perceived psychologically as loudness.

analog representation – the theoretical case in which a cognitive map is stored in memory in a picture form that corresponds point for point to the physical environment.

annoyance – in noise, the irritating or bothersome aspect.

antecedent behavioral change techniques – behavioral change techniques that occur before the target behavior and that are designed to increase the likelihood of favorable acts.

anthropocentric, anthropocentrism – viewing the natural environment from the perspective of how it meets human needs; *see also* homocentric, ecocentric.

anticipated crowding – when people expect to be crowded.

applicability gap – a two-way communications breakdown that occurs when scientists fail to ask questions with direct application to design problems or when designers neglect to employ those principles that have empirical support.

applicants – in ecological psychology, those who meet the membership requirements of a behavior setting and who are trying to become a part of it.

appraisal – cognitive assessment of a stressor along the dimensions of harm or loss, threat, and challenge.

approach prompts – prompts that supply an incentive for engaging in a particular behavior.

archival data – data that researchers may find in others' historical records, such as police crime reports, weather records, or hospital records.

arousal – a continuum of physiological or psychological activation ranging from sleep to excitement; crowding, personal space intrusions, or other stressors can lead to overarousal.

assigned workspace – designating a particular machine or area to a particular worker in order to create a feeling of ownership.

assisted living – a type of care for the elderly in which they can handle some daily functioning on their own but need assistance with other functions; also called residential care or intermediate care.

attitude – a relatively stable tendency to evaluate a person, object, or idea in a positive or negative way; many definitions stress the interrelationship of feelings, cognitions, and behaviors.

attraction gradient – the likelihood that the design of an exhibit will attract museum visitors to view it.

augmentation – the addition of nonexistent features to a cognitive map based on expectations of what "should" be there.

avoidance prompts – prompts that supply a disincentive for enacting a particular behavior.

background stressors – persistent, repetitive stressors whose impact is relatively gradual, including daily hassles.

barometric pressure – atmospheric pressure, as read by a barometer.

Beaufort Scale – a scale of wind force developed by Admiral Sir Francis Beaufort in 1806.

behavioral control – availability of a behavioral response that can change a threatening environmental event.

behavioral interference – the notion that under high density conditions, many negative effects are due to "getting in people's way" and similar mechanisms for blocking goals.

behavioral sink – area in which the negative effects of high density are intensified.

behavior constraint – a model that emphasizes how the environment (e.g., urban life, personal restrictions) may limit or interfere with activities, leading to loss of perceived control.

behavior mapping – a structured observational technique in which behaviors are observed, recorded, and located on a map of the setting being observed.

behavior setting – the basic unit of environment–behavior relationships; in Barker's ecological psychology, an entity that encompasses the location of a large volume of behavior; consists of the interdependency between the standing patterns of behavior and the physical milieu.

biophilia – the proposition that humans have evolved a biological affinity for natural environments.

biophobia – the proposition that humans have a genetic predisposition to learn to fear certain potentially dangerous elements of nature, such as spiders and snakes.

bivariate theory – a theory that relates only two variables, such as temperature and violence.

block organizations – neighborhood organizations formed to add social cohesiveness and overcome urban ills, which work for such improvements as better lighting, police protection, or street repairs.

capacity – in ecological psychology, the maximum number of inhabitants a behavior setting can hold; in overload notions, the limited capability for processing information.

carbon monoxide – a common pollutant caused by incomplete burning of substances containing carbon.

carrying capacity – the amount of use a resource can support; with respect to recreation, the carrying capacity could be variously defined as the number of people who can fit in a given area, the number who can be accommodated without resource damage, or the number who can receive a satisfactory experience such as solitude.

cataclysmic events – sudden, powerful events that require a great deal of adaptation in order for people to recover, avoid, or cope with their effects, such as natural disasters.

catecholamines – epinephrine (adrenaline), norepinephrine, and dopamine—secretions that energize various systems in the body.

challenge appraisal – a cognitive appraisal component of the stress model that focuses on the possibility of overcoming the stressor.

chill factor – *see* wind chill.

City Beautiful Movement – master planning of large city areas—such as the Mall in Washington, D.C.—deriving from the work of Daniel Burnham.

climate – average weather conditions or prevailing weather over a long period of time.

cognitive control – processing information about a threat in such a way as to appraise it as less threatening.

cognitive map – the brain's representation of the spatial environment.

coherence – in landscape evaluations, the degree to which the elements in a scene are organized and seem to fit together.

cohousing – a type of housing in which families have their own private residences but share larger facilities, such as a master kitchen and recreation area.

collative stimulus properties – characteristics of a stimulus that create perceptual conflict and cause us to compare it to other stimuli to resolve the conflict.

commodity – the functional goal (intended use) of a design.

commons dilemma – Hardin's notion that depletion of scarce resources can happen because people sharing a resource harvest it with short-term self-interest in mind rather than long-term group interest.

compensatory behaviors – in personal space, behaviors such as increased eye contact that make up for inappropriately far distances, such as leaning away from a person for inappropriately close distances.

complexity – with regard to landscape or architectural aesthetics, the variety and salience of elements in a scene.

complexity of spatial layout – the amount and difficulty of information that must be processed in order to move through the environment.

confounds – variables other than the ones being studied that also vary across different conditions, and thus that can account for systematic effects in the dependent variable.

congruence – the "fit" between user needs or preferences and the physical features of a setting.

consequent interventions – reinforcement, feedback, and other interventions that occur after the target behavior (e.g., littering, failure to recycle) occurs; *see also* contingent interventions.

conservation of resources (COR) theory – Hobfoll's proposal that the extent to which people lose important resources or are able to minimize this loss will determine how much stress is experienced from a natural disaster.

contingent interventions – reinforcement, feedback, and other interventions that occur contingent on the target behavior (e.g., littering, recycling) occurring or not occurring; *see also* consequent interventions.

continuum of care – a range of services to support the functioning level of the elderly (or others who need it) starting with in-home services and running through full-time nursing home care.

control – the perception that one's inputs and outcomes are linked; *see also* perceived control.

control models – environment–behavior models that emphasize consequences of loss of perceived control; the behavior constraint model is an example.

coping – handling stressors; efforts to restore equilibrium after stressful events.

core temperature – the temperature inside the body, also called deep body temperature.

correlational research – research that does not manipulate environmental occurrences or prescribe who should be involved as subjects; events occurring prior to the research and concurrent actions of other factors in the setting may interfere with the conclusions drawn.

corticosteroids – steroid compounds produced by the adrenal cortex; increased secretion is characteristic of alarm reactions.

crisis effect – the phenomenon wherein disaster events attract a great deal of attention while they are occurring (or shortly thereafter), but concern for future disasters decreases after that.

crowding – experiential state when the constraints of high density are salient to an individual.

cue utilization – the individual weights assigned by a person in making perceptual judgments based on past experiences, personality, or other characteristics.

curvilinear relationship – a relationship between two variables that is not a straight line, such as a U-shaped or inverted-U function.

custodial care – a level of care for the elderly in which someone else must provide assistance with everyday activities of daily living, such as laundry, bathing, and dressing.

daily hassles – stable, low-intensity problems encountered as part of one's routine, such as commuting.

day-night reversal – a condition in dementia in which the patient becomes very active at night; also called sundowning.

decibels (dB) – units of measure of loudness of sound, in the form of logarithmic representations of sound pressure.

decisional control – having a choice among several options.

decompression sickness – a condition caused by nitrogen bubbles forming in the blood when a person moves from high atmospheric pressure to low atmospheric pressure, as in "the bends."

deep body temperature – *see* core temperature.

deep ecology – a form of ecocentrism that is critical of modern technology, science, and political structures, believing that these endanger nature.

defensible space – clearly bounded or semi-private areas that appear to belong to someone.

degree of visual access – the extent to which different parts of a setting can be seen from a number of vantage points; access facilitates the learning of a new environment.

deindividuation – according to Zimbardo, loss of individual identity (i.e., feeling of anonymity) that releases otherwise inhibited antisocial behavior.

delight – the aesthetic goal of design.

dementia – a medical term meaning long-term loss of memory and confusion.

denial – ignoring or suppressing awareness of stressors and other problems.

density-intensity – Freedman's conceptualization that high density increases the intensity of behaviors and feelings that would have occurred anyway under lower density conditions.

dependent variable – in the experimental method, the behavior of the subject that is measured by the experimenter.

descriptive approach (to landscape assessment)–landscape assessment based on the judgments of professionals trained to detect patterns, primarily based on artistic judgment.

descriptive research – research that reports behavior, emotions, or other characteristics that occur in a given setting or in response to a specific event.

design alternatives – the list of potential solutions to a design problem.

design cycle – a continuous cycle of information gathering, planning, and evaluation; the cyclical nature allows information gathered from one project to add to the knowledge for subsequent designs.

design review – a case by case examination of proposed new building projects that attempts to ensure that they will remain harmonious with both the architecture and the ongoing social fabric of a district.

determinism – in a strict sense, a philosophical notion that circumstances have absolute causal relationships to events.

differentiation – distinctiveness; buildings or environments that are different or distinctive are more easily remembered.

diffusion of responsibility – an explanation for decreased helping behavior which posits that as the number of potential helpers increases each one assumes less individual responsibility for helping.

directed attention fatigue (DAF) – a state of mental exhaustion similar to overload; restorative experiences are thought to alleviate DAF.

disaster events – a powerful event that causes substantial disorganization, disruption, or destruction to an area, community, or series of communities.

discontinuity – the idea of changing a steady pattern in museum exhibits; breaking up the pattern helps relieve museum fatigue.

disruption – disturbance of individual, group, or organizational functioning and routine.

distortions – errors in cognitive maps based on inaccurate retrieval that leads us to put some things too close together, some too far apart, and misalign others.

districts – large geographical areas that are identified in cognitive maps; typically, the places within a district have a common character and often are given names such as the French Quarter, Chinatown, or the East End.

diversive exploration – arousal seeking in response to understimulation.

dominant Western world view – belief that human domination over infinite natural resources leads to inevitable progress.

double corridor design – hospital floorplan in which the nurses' station sits amid two (usually parallel) hallways.

ecocentric, ecocentrism – valuing nature for its own sake, instead of for how it supports humans.

ecological niche – according to Gibson's ecological perception, a set of affordances that are utilized.

ecological perception – the approach that emphasizes that

perception is holistic and direct; according to this view, patterns of stimulation give the perceiver immediate information about the environment—including its affordances—with little effort or cognitive activity.

ecological psychology – Barker's behavior setting approach to studying the interaction between humans and their environment.

ecological validity – the objective usefulness of various environmental stimuli in making accurate perceptual judgments.

edge cities – newer communities that now ring an older city and contain residential, commercial, and office buildings.

edges – elements in cognitive maps that limit or divide features, such as paths or districts; edges may be elements such as walls, rail yards, or water features.

effective temperature – an adjustment in perceived temperature to account for humidity, similar to the Temperature–Humidity Index.

electronic cottage – an in-the-home workplace connected to the parent organization by computers or other communication devices.

ELF-EMF – extremely low frequency electromagnetic fields associated with weather disturbances or power lines.

empirical – publicly observable.

empirical laws – statements of simple observable relationships between phenomena (often expressed in mathematical terms) that can be demonstrated time and time again.

empiricism – a position that holds that externally observable events are the only legitimate source of data.

English Romantic style – a literary and artistic return to the nature theme popular in the nineteenth century; it inspired Frederick Law Olmstead to design Central Park in New York.

en masse behavior pattern – in Barker's ecological psychology, the behavior of a group.

environment – one's surroundings; the word is frequently used to refer to a specific part of one's surroundings, as in social environment (referring to the people and groups among whom one lives), physical environment (all of the non-animal elements of one's surroundings, such as cities, wilderness, or farmland), or built environment (referring specifically to that part of the environment built by humans).

environmental assessment – describing and evaluating environments, such as through EQI or PEQI methods, or landscape preference methods.

environmental cognition – the ability or propensity to imagine and think about the spatial world.

environmental competence – *see* environmental press.

environmental education – making people aware of the scope and nature of environmental problems, and of behavioral alternatives to alleviate them.

Environmental Emotional Reaction Index (EERI) – an assessment of the emotional reactions of humans to some component of environmental quality.

environmental load – a theoretical position based on overload of information from the environment.

environmental press – a model which posits that the demands or press an environment places on its occupants as well as the competence of the occupants determine the consequences of interacting with the environment.

environmental psychology – the study of the interrelationship between behavior and experience and the built and natural environment.

Environmental Quality Index (EQI) – objective measures of environmental quality—the chemical or physical properties of water or air, for example.

environmental spoiling hypothesis – the notion that perceived quality of the living environment is determined largely by the number of unpleasant contacts with others.

environmental stress – *see* environmental stress model; stress.

environmental stress model – a theoretical perspective that emphasizes how the environment can elicit stress and coping reactions when it is evaluated to be threatening.

epinephrine – adrenaline, a catecholamine that energizes physiological systems in response to stress.

equilibrium – a state of balance; the steady state to which stress reactions try to restore the organism.

ergonomics – the discipline that concerns itself with the design and modification of equipment and workplaces to make them better adapted to the needs of humans; also called human factors.

erosion measures – trace measures that signify something taken away or worn down (e.g., wear patterns on carpet).

ethic – a system of morals or standards held by a person, culture, or religion, such as a land ethic.

ethological models – in personal space, formulations that assume that when space is inadequate, fear and discomfort are experienced due to feelings of aggression or threat.

event duration – how long an event lasts.

exit gradient – how much a gallery exit attracts a museum visitor to use it.

experiential realism – the extent to which the experimental manipulation has impact on the subject and is representative of events that occur in the real world.

experimental method – a way of conducting research that allows inferences about what might cause a given effect; by varying two factors and studying effects of these factors under controlled conditions one can observe specific causes for observed effects; *see also* random assignment.

external validity – the degree to which a research study's findings generalize to other contexts.

extra-individual behavior pattern – in Barker's ecological psychology, the behavior of large numbers of people.

extremely low frequency electromagnetic fields – *see* ELF-EMF.

extrinsic motivation – rewards that are administered by an outside agent and are satisfying, independent of the events that produced them.

familiar stranger – someone you observe repeatedly for a long period of time, but never interact with.

feedback – a technique that provides information about whether one is attaining or failing to attain an environmental goal; as such, it is a means for changing environmentally destructive behavior.

festival marketplaces – busy retail and tourist centers that combine retail space, leisure, and theater; the prototype is Boston's Quincy Market designed by James Rouse.

field experiments – experiments that are conducted in field settings as opposed to laboratory settings.

field methods – techniques for studying behavior outside the laboratory.

firmness – the design goal of permanence and structural integrity.

fixed workspace – assignment of a specific workspace or machine to a worker on a more or less permanent basis, as opposed to sharing the machine or space with others; also called assigned workspace.

folk design tradition – architecture based on the day-to-day needs of people as they live, shop, and work.

foot-in-the-door technique – a technique that increases compliance with a standard request by first asking for a small favor which the respondent is likely to agree to.

forward-up equivalence – in map design, having what is forward on the ground being at the top ("up") on the map.

free-rider – in the public goods problem, a person who fails to contribute to the common good but reaps the benefits of the contributions of the other participants.

frequency – the number of cycles per second in a sound wave, perceived psychologically as pitch.

friction-conformity model – Preiser's idea that pedestrians adjust their walking speed to barriers and to the flow of other pedestrian traffic.

frostbite – formation of ice crystals in the skin.

functional distance – a type of propinquity measured by the likelihood of two people coming into contact with each other, as in meeting at their mailboxes.

functionalism – a tradition within psychology that views behavior as a way of adapting or surviving the demands of the environment.

Gaia Hypothesis – the idea that heating and cooling of the earth (oceans, land, and atmosphere) as well as associated operations of living things are part of a self-regulating system.

galvanic skin response (GSR) – a way of measuring arousal from the electrical conductance of the skin as it changes with sweating.

gaps – lapses in communication between designers, users, behavioral scientists, or clients that result in design errors or oversights.

general adaptation syndrome (GAS) – Selye's stress model, which consists of the alarm reaction, the stage of resistance, and the stage of exhaustion.

generalizability – a measurement of how well a finding, relationship, or theory applies from one setting to another.

gentrification – the emergence of middle- and upper-class areas in parts of the inner city that were formerly deteriorated.

Gestalt perception or **Gestalt theory** – a perceptual perspective based on Gestalt principles.

Gestalt principles – perceptual principles developed by the Gestalt school of psychology that have heavily influenced architectural thinking; Gestalt principles are based on a holistic assumption that we read meaning—such as shape or melody—into perceptions beyond the mere sum of individual sensations.

grand design tradition – architecture, such as monuments or impressive facades, built to impress the populace, client, or other architects.

greenhouse effect – the excess heating of the earth due in part to carbon dioxide and other pollutants trapping too much heat close to the earth's surface.

habitability – the ability of a design to fit the needs of its inhabitants or users, especially in residential design.

habituation – the process (especially physiological) by which a person's responses to a particular stimulus become weaker over time.

harm or loss appraisal – a cognitive appraisal component of the stress model that focuses on damage already done.

Hawthorne effect – changes in behavior by virtue of observation alone rather than because of treatment effects.

hearing loss – permanent or temporary decrease in one's ability to hear caused by damage to the eardrum or to the tiny hair cells in the inner ear.

heat asthenia – fatigue and lethargy due to heat stress.

heat exhaustion – moderate condition of faintness, nausea, headache, and restlessness due to heat stress.

heat stroke – severe and life-threatening condition of heat stress in which the sweating mechanism breaks down.

hertz (Hz) – cycles per second of a sound wave.

heuristics – simple principles that facilitate decision making.

high density – situations characterized by high social or spatial density; a large number of people in an area.

hodometer – a device with sensors under a floor for measuring foot traffic.

homelessness – when a person does not have a fixed, regular, and adequate nighttime residence.

homeostatic – descriptive of automatic mechanisms that serve to maintain a state of balance, such as the sweating reaction to heat stress.

homocentric, homocentrism – viewing the natural environment from the perspective of how it meets human needs; *see also* anthropocentric, ecocentric.

human factors – the discipline that concerns itself with the design and modification of equipment and workplaces to make them better adapted to the needs of humans; also called ergonomics.

humidity – the concentration of water vapor in the atmosphere.

hypertension – a form of cardiovascular disease characterized by sustained elevation of blood pressure.

hypothalamus – a primitive part of the brain responsible in part for regulating temperature, hunger, thirst, aggression, and sex drive.

hypothermia – life-threatening decline in core temperature.

hypothesis – a scientific hunch or formal statement of an anticipated relationship between events.

hypoxia – reduced oxygen intake associated with low air pressure conditions, such as high altitudes.

independent variable – in the experimental method, the circumstances the experimenter manipulates in order to determine the impact on the dependent variable.

individual difference variables – variables that reflect differences in people in terms of background, personality, or other factors.

individual good–collective bad trap – a type of social trap in which a resource is depleted because short-term positive consequences of usage are experienced by the individual, but the long-term negative consequences are dispersed through the group.

individual personality traits – measurable personality factors such as internality–externality, authoritarianism, and so on.

informed consent – written permission from a subject agreeing to participate in a study after being informed of procedures, risks, and any circumstances which might alter the decision to participate.

inside density – population density indices using "inside" measures, such as number of people per residence or per room.

intermediate care – a level of care for the elderly in which custodial care is emphasized.

internal validity – the rigor with which a research study is constructed so that one knows whether observed effects are due to variables of interest as opposed to such methodological artifacts as confounds or failure to control extraneous variables.

internality–externality – personality variable that taps whether people believe they, or outside forces, control their outcomes.

interpersonal distance – the distance between people.

intervening construct – an inferred phenomenon that mediates the relationship between other events or concepts.

intrinsic motivation – the degree to which an activity provides personal satisfaction and enjoyment.

invasion of privacy – in research, access by the researcher into nonpublic activities of the research subject without the subject's permission.

laboratory methods – studying behavior (usually through systematic manipulation of variables) in a laboratory setting.

land ethic – Aldo Leopold's belief that humans share nature with a community of equal elements, including other species, soils, and water.

landmarks – structures or geographical entities that are distinctive; landmarks are usually visible from some distance, and include features such as tall buildings or monuments.

landscaped office – an open office; a large office area with few walls that is designed to be flexible and to facilitate the organizational processes that take place within it.

learned helplessness – Seligman's idea that once we believe we have lost control over the things that happen to us, we cease trying to change the situation; experienced state when people "learn" there is no contingency between their inputs and their outcomes.

legibility – the degree to which a scene is distinctive or memorable; in cognitive maps, the degree to which an area is easily learned or remembered.

lens model – the model of perception that emphasizes the active process by which humans make judgments based on probabilistic weighting of the variety of stimuli in the environment.

levee effect – the observation that once protective precautions are taken against a potential disaster, people tend to settle and live around these precautions, even though threats are still present.

linear perspective – the principle that parallel lines will appear to converge in the distance.

linear relationship – straight-line (monotonic or rectilinear) relationship between two variables.

link analysis – the systematic investigation of the movements an operator makes to adjust controls or to read displays.

long, hot summer effect – the belief that heat wave conditions precipitate violence.

loose parts – playground articles that can be manipulated, such as building materials or balls.

loudness – the physical perception of amplitude in a sound or noise.

low point – the point in a disaster at which victims perceive that the worst threat, harm, or adaptive demand has been reached; following this point, things gradually improve.

maintenance minimum – in ecological psychology, the minimum number of inhabitants needed to maintain a behavior setting.

mapping – in human factors, the relationship between the actions of an operator and those of a machine.

masking – covering up or eliminating the distinct perception of a sound or noise by adding another sound or noise of familiar frequency and similar or higher amplitude.

mediating variable – a variable that operates in a sequence between other variables, such as arousal mediating the relationship between noise and aggression.

missing hero situation – a type of social trap in which individuals fail to act for the benefit of the group because the penalty to the "hero" who does act seems inordinately large.

model – a relationship between concepts that is often based on analogies or metaphors.

modeling – an antecedent strategy in which others display or model the desired pro-environmental behavior.

modern design – the design tradition in industrialized societies; critics suggest that a premium is placed on originality and aesthetics at the expense of evolutionary development.

multidimensional scaling – a class of statistical procedures for displaying the relationships between concepts or places based on their similarity on several dimensions of interest.

museum fatigue – Robinson's notion that museum visitors tire because they must pay attention to so much information in exhibits.

mystery – in landscape assessment, the degree to which hidden information creates intrigue and leads a viewer to further investigate a scene.

narrow band – a sound or noise with relatively few frequencies in it.

nativism – the view that perceptual processes or other phenomena come to us automatically (i.e., are inborn) as opposed to having to be learned through experience.

natural disaster – a disaster that is caused by natural (nonhuman) factors; *see also* disaster events.

negative affect–escape model – the position that aggression increases with discomfort (such as from heat or pollution) up to a point, but then declines with further discomfort as escape motives become stronger than aggression motives.

negative ions – *see* air ionization.

negative reinforcement – removing a noxious stimulus; increases desirable environmental behavior because people are motivated to avoid unpleasant stimuli (e.g., fines) or to escape an ongoing noxious stimulus (e.g., high electric bills).

new ecological paradigm – belief that humans are interdependent with a fragile natural ecology that contains limited resources.

nodes – in cognitive maps, points where behavior is concentrated, such as at a place where major paths cross one another or intersect a landmark.

noise – sound that is undesirable or unwanted.

noise-induced permanent threshold shift (NIPTS) – hearing loss that is typically present a month or more after noise exposure ceases, characterized by increases in threshold below which sounds are inaudible.

nonperformers – in ecological psychology, those who carry out secondary roles in a behavior setting.

norepinephrine – a catecholamine related to epinephrine; high concentrations can be indicative of stress.

normative theory – approaches to design based on values and opinions rather than empirical facts.

nuts game – a simulation of the commons dilemma developed by Edney.

objective physical distance – propinquity measured in terms of actual distance, or "as the crow flies."

observation – watching people behave and recording what is seen.

olfactory membrane – a membrane at the top of the nasal passage that detects chemical substances that the brain interprets as odors.

one atmosphere – atmospheric pressure at sea level, or 14.7 pounds per square inch.

one-person trap – another term for self-trap.

open classrooms – schools designed with few interior walls so that students and teachers are free to move about.

open office – a large office area with few walls, which is designed to be flexible and to facilitate the organizational processes that take place within it.

outside density – population density indices using "outside" measures, such as number of persons, dwellings, or structures per acre.

overload – a condition in which stimulation from the environment exceeds the capacity of the person to process the inputs, resulting in ignoring of some information; *see also* environmental load.

overstaffed or **overstaffing** – in ecological psychology, a condition of having too many participants, where the number of "participants" exceeds the capacity of the system.

overstimulation – *see* overload.

oxides of nitrogen and sulfur – substances such as sulfur dioxide and nitrogen oxide that are especially caused by burning of fossil fuels and that can be major pollutants.

ozone – a form of oxygen in which three atoms are molecularly combined (O_3).

ozone hole – atmospheric reduction in ozone around the polar regions due in part to chlorofluorocarbons.

palliative – emotion-focused (as opposed to direct-action focused) coping processes, such as denial, using drugs, or appraising the situation as nonthreatening.

palmar sweat index – a measure of arousal that uses a chemical to react with sweat on the palms.

particulates – air pollutants that can "settle out" of the atmosphere, often containing mercury, lead, and other toxic substances.

passive smoking – exposure to secondary cigarette smoke, that is, smoke produced by other people's smoking.

paths – shared travel corridors identified in cognitive maps such as streets, walkways, or riverways.

pattern language – prescriptions for design problems presented in such a way that they can be utilized to allow user participation in design.

perceived control – belief that we can influence the things that are happening to us.

Perceived Environmental Quality Index (PEQI) – a subjective assessment of some characteristic of environmental quality as perceived by a human observer.

perception – the process of extracting meaning from the complex stimuli we encounter in everyday life.

performers – in ecological psychology, those who carry out the primary tasks in a behavior setting.

peripheral vasoconstriction – constriction (narrowing) of blood vessels in the arms and legs, as in response to cold stress.

peripheral vasodilation – dilation (widening) of blood vessels in the arms and legs, as in response to heat stress.

personal space – a body buffer zone that people maintain between themselves and others.

personal stressors – stressful events that affect one person or only a few people at a time, such as loss of a loved one or loss of a job.

person–environment congruence – the notion that the setting promotes the behavior and goals within it; the degree of "fit" between people and their environment.

phenomenology – a position that holds that subjective reports of personal experiences are the primary sources of valid data.

photochemical smog – air pollution resulting from sunlight combining a number of substances (including water vapor) that have been released into the atmosphere.

physical milieu – in Baker's ecological psychology, the physical component of the behavior setting.

physical-perceptual approach (to landscape assessment)– assessment strategies that emphasize the characteristics of the physical environment which can be statistically related to judgments of aesthetics.

piloerection – "goose bumps" or the stiffening of hairs on the skin.

pitch – the psychological perception of the frequency of a sound.

place attachment – psychological bonding to an environment.

placemaking – creating a sense of place by using architecture to cue the memories that create the personal meaning and sense of place, such as restoring or revitalizing a building or district.

policy capturing – a statistical procedure in which analysis shows the weights or relative importance an individual subject attaches to each of several predictor variables in making perceptual judgments.

positive ions – *see* air ionization.

positive reinforcement – when people are given positively valued stimuli for performing environmentally constructive acts.

positive theory – procedures or design components that are based on empirical observations rather than opinions or values.

possibilism – the notion that the environmental context makes possible some activities but does not force them to occur, as in climatological, geographical, or architectural probabilism.

post-disaster groups – development of cohesive groups following disasters.

post-occupancy evaluation (POE) – a retrospective evaluation used to suggest modifications of the present structure and to improve the available knowledge for future projects.

Post-Traumatic Stress Disorder (PTSD) – an anxiety disor-

video display terminal (VDT) – a computer display device; depending on the particular display, it may also be known as a Cathode Ray Tube (CRT).

wayfinding – the process of using stored spatial information to plan and carry out movement in the environment.

weather – relatively short-term changes in atmospheric conditions.

Weber-Fechner function – a psychophysical principle that says the higher the magnitude of a stimulus (e.g., loudness of a sound), the greater the difference in magnitude the next higher stimulus needs to be in order for it to be detected as different.

white noise – a very wide range of unpatterned sound frequencies, such as would be found when tuning a television to a channel with no station on it.

wide band – a sound or noise with many frequencies in it.

wind chill – the effect of wind intensifying consequences of cold temperature.

windowless classrooms – classroom learning environments without windows, designed to reduce distraction and conserve energy.

wind speed – straight-line velocity of wind, usually expressed in miles per hour or meters per second.

wind tunnel effect – a design phenomenon whereby building features, such as an open passageway below a structure, create high winds for pedestrians.

wind turbulence – gustiness and shifting directions of wind.

workflow – the movement of information or work materials between workstations.

workspace – the work environment.

Yerkes-Dodson Law – states that performance is maximal at intermediate levels of arousal and declines as arousal increases or decreases from this point.

you-are-here maps – maps displayed in public locations as orientation devices.

REFERENCES

Abelson, P. H. (1993). Power from wind turbines. *Science*, *261*, 1255.

Abey-Wickrama, I., A'Brook, M. F., Gattoni, F. E. G., & Herridge, C. F. (1969). Mental hospital admissions and aircraft noise. *Lancet*, *2*, 1275–1277.

Abramson, L. Y., Seligman, M. E. P., & Teasdale, J. D. (1978). Learned helplessness in humans: Critique and reformulation. *Journal of Abnormal Psychology*, *87*, 49–74.

Acheson, J. M. (1975). The lobster fiefs: Economic and ecological effects of territoriality in the Maine lobster industry. *Human Ecology*, *3*, 183–207.

Acking, D. A., & Kuller, R. (1972). The perception of an interior as a function of its color. *Ergonomics*, *15*, 645–654.

Acredolo, L. P. (1976). Frames of reference used by children for orientation in unfamiliar spaces. In G. Moore & R. Golledge (Eds.), *Environmental knowing*. Stroudsburg, PA: Dowden, Hutchinson, & Ross.

Acredolo, L. P. (1977). Developmental changes in the ability to coordinate perspectives of a large-scale environment. *Developmental Psychology*, *13*, 1–8.

Acton, W. I. (1970). Speech intelligibility in a background noise and noise-induced hearing loss. *Ergonomics*, *13*, 546–554.

Adam, J. M. (1967). Military problems of air transport and tropical service. In C. N. Davies, P. R. Davis, & F. H. Tyrer (Eds.), *The effects of abnormal physical conditions at work* (pp. 74–80). London: E & S Livingstone.

Adams, J. R. (1973). Review of *Defensible space*. *Man–Environment Systems*, 267–268.

Adams, L. & Zuckerman, D. (1991). The effect of lighting conditions on personal space requirements. *Journal of General Psychology*, *118*, 335–340.

Adams, P. R., & Adams, G. R. (1984). Mount Saint Helens's ashfall: Evidence for a disaster stress reaction. *American Psychologist*, *39*, 252–260.

Adler, A. (1943). Neuropsychiatric complications in victims of Boston's Coconut Grove disaster. *Journal of the American Medical Association*, *17*, 1098–1101.

Ahrentzen, S. B. (1990). Managing conflict by managing boundaries: How professional homeworkers cope with multiple roles at home. *Environment and Behavior*, *22*, 723–752.

Ahrentzen, S., & Evans, G. (1984). Distraction, privacy, and classroom design. *Environment and Behavior*, *16*, 437–454.

Ahrentzen, S., Jue, G. M., Skorpanich, M. A., & Evans, G. W. (1982). School environments and stress. In G. W. Evans (Ed.), *Environmental stress* (pp. 224–255). New York: Cambridge University Press.

Ahrentzen, S., Levine, D. W., & Michelson, W. (1989). Space, time, and activity in the home: A gender analysis. *Journal of Environmental Psychology*, *9*, 89–101.

Aiello, J. R. (1977). A further look at equilibrium theory: Visual interaction as a function of interpersonal distance. *Environmental Psychology and Nonverbal Behavior*, *1*, 122–140.

Aiello, J. R. (1987). Human spatial behavior. In D. Stokols & I. Altman (Eds.), *Handbook of environmental psychology* (Vol. 1, pp. 505–531). New York: Wiley-Interscience.

Aiello, J. R., Baum, A., & Gormley, F. B. (1981). Social determinants of residential crowding stress. *Personality and Social Psychology Bulletin*, *7*, 643–649.

Aiello, J. R., DeRisis, D., Epstein, Y., & Karlin, R. (1977). Crowding and the role of interpersonal distance preference. *Sociometry*, *40*, 271–282.

Aiello, J. R., Epstein, Y. M., & Karlin, R. A. (1975a). Effects of crowding on electrodermal activity. *Sociological Symposium*, *14*, 43–57.

Aiello, J. R., Epstein, Y. M., & Karlin, R. A. (1975b, April). *Field experimental research in human crowding*. Paper presented at the meeting of the Eastern Psychological Association.

Aiello, J. R., Nicosia, G. J., & Thompson, D. E. (1979). Physiological, social, and behavioral consequences of crowding on children and adolescents. *Child Development*, *50*, 195–202.

Aiello, J. R., & Thompson, D. E. (1980a). When compensation fails: Mediating effects of sex and locus of control at extended interaction distances. *Basic and Applied Social Psychology*, *1*, 65–82.

Aiello, J. R., & Thompson, D. E. (1980b). Personal space, crowding, and spatial behavior in a cultural context. In I. Altman, J. F. Wohlwill, & A. Rapoport (Eds.), *Human behavior and environment* (Vol. 4, pp. 107–178). New York: Plenum.

Aiello, J. R., Thompson, D. E., & Baum, A. (1981). The symbiotic relationship between social psychology and environmental psychology: Implications from crowding, personal space, and intimacy regulation research. In J. H. Harvey (Ed.), *Cognition and social behavior, and the environment* (pp. 423–438). Hillsdale, NJ: Erlbaum.

Aiello, J. R., Thompson, D. E., & Brodzinsky, D. M. (1983). How funny is crowding anyway? Effects of room size, group size, and the introduction of humor. *Basic and Applied Social Psychology*, *4*, 193–207.

Aiello, J. R., Vautier, J. S., & Bernstein, M. D. (1983, August). *Crowding stress: Impact of social support, group formation, and control*. Paper presented at the annual meeting of the American Psychological Association, Anaheim, CA.

Ajzen, I. (1985). From intentions to actions: A theory of planned behavior. In J. Kuhl & J. Beckman (Eds.), *Action-control: From cognition to behavior* (pp. 11–39). Heidelberg: Springer.

Ajzen, I., & Madden, T. J. (1986). Prediction of goal-directed behavior: The role of intention, perceived. *Journal of Experimental Social Psychology*, *22*, 453–474.

Albas, C. A. (1991). Proxemic behavior: A study of extrusion. *Journal of Social Psychology*, *131*, 697–702.

Albas, D. C., & Albas, C. A. (1989). Meaning in context: The impact of eye contact and perception of threat on proximity. *Journal of Social Psychology*, *129*, 525–531.

Albert, S., & Dabbs, J. M., Jr. (1970). Physical distance and persuasion. *Journal of Personality and Social Psychology*, *15*, 265–270.

Aldwin, C. A., & Revenson, T. A. (1987). Does coping help? A reexamination of the relation between coping and mental health. *Journal of Personality and Social Psychology*, *53*, 337–348.

Aldwin C., & Stokols, D. (1988). The effects of environmental change on individuals and groups: Some neglected issues in stress research. *Journal of Environmental Psychology*, *8*, 57–75.

Alexander, C. (1969). Major changes in environmental form required by social and psychological demands. *Ekistics*, *28*, 78–85.

Alexander, C. (1979). *The timeless way of building*. New York: Oxford University Press.

Alexander, C., Ishikawa, S., & Silverstein, M. (1977). *A pattern language*. New York: Oxford University Press.

Alexander, C., Silverstein, M., Angel, S., Ishikawa, S., & Abrams, D. (1975). *The Oregon experiment*. New York: Oxford University Press.

Allen, G. L. (1981). A developmental perspective on the effects of "subdividing" macrospatial experience. *Journal of Experimental Psychology: Human Learning and Memory, 7,* 120–132.

Allen, G. L., & Kirasic, K. C. (1985). Effects of the cognitive organization of knowledge on judgments of macrospatial distance. *Memory and Cognition, 13,* 218–227.

Allen, G. L., Siegel, A. W., & Rosinski, R. R. (1978). The role of perceptual context in structuring spatial knowledge. *Journal of Experimental Psychology: Human Learning and Memory, 4,* 617–630.

Allen, I. L. (1980). The ideology of dense neighborhood redevelopment: Cultural diversity and transcendent community experience. *Urban Affairs Quarterly, 15,* 409–428.

Allen, V. L., & Greenberger, D. B. (1980). Destruction and perceived control. In A. Baum & J. E. Singer (Eds.), *Advances in environmental psychology* (Vol. 2). Hillsdale, NJ: Erlbaum.

Allgeier, A. R., & Byrne, D. (1973). Attraction toward the opposite sex as a determinant of physical proximity. *Journal of Social Psychology, 90,* 213–219.

Alliance Housing Council. (1988). *Housing and homelessness.* Washington, DC: National Alliance to End Homelessness.

Alloy, L. B., Peterson, C., Abramson, L.Y., & Seligman, M. E. P. (1984). Attributional style and the generality of learned helplessness. *Journal of Personality and Social Psychology, 46,* 681–687.

Allport, F. H. (1955). *Theories of perception and the concept of structure.* New York: Wiley.

Allport, G., & Pettigrew, T. (1957). Cultural influence on the perception of movement: The trapezoidal illusion among the Zulus. *Journal of Abnormal and Social Psychology, 55,* 104–113.

Altman, I. (1973). Some perspectives on the study of man-environment phenomena. *Representative Research in Social Psychology, 4,* 109–126.

Altman, I. (1975). *The environment and social behavior.* Monterey, CA: Brooks/Cole.

Altman, I. (1976). Environmental psychology and social psychology. *Personality and Social Psychology Bulletin, 2,* 96–113.

Altman, I., & Chemers, M. (1980). *Culture and environment.* Monterey, CA: Brooks/Cole.

Altman, I., Lawton, M. P., & Wohlwill, J. F. (Eds.). (1984). *Elderly people and the environment.* New York: Plenum.

Altman, I., & Low, S. M. (Eds.). (1992). *Place attachment. Human Behavior and Environment: Advances in Theory and Research* (Vol. 12). New York: Plenum.

Altman, I., Nelson, P. A., & Lett, E. E. (1972, Spring). The ecology of home environments. *Catalog of Selected Documents in Psychology* (No. 150).

Altman, I., & Rogoff, B. (1987). World views in psychology: Trait, interactional, organismic, and transactional perspectives. In I. Altman & D. Stokols (Eds.), *Handbook of environmental psychology* (Vol. I, pp. 7–40). New York: Wiley-Interscience.

Altman, I., & Vinsel, A. M. (1977). Personal space: An analysis of E. T. Hall's proxemics framework. In I. Altman & J. F. Wohlwill (Eds.), *Human behavior and environment: Advances in theory and research* (Vol. 2, pp. 181–259). New York: Plenum.

Altman, I., & Wandersman, A. (Eds.). (1987). *Neighborhood and community environments.* New York: Plenum.

Altman, I., & Werner, C. M. (Eds.). (1985). *Home environments.* New York: Plenum.

Amato, P. R. (1981). The impact of the built environment on prosocial and affiliative behaviour: A field study of the Townsville city mall. *Australian Journal of Psychology, 33,* 297–303.

Amato, P. R. (1983). Helping behavior in urban and rural environments: Field studies based on taxonomic organization of helping episodes. *Journal of Personality and Social Psychology, 45,* 571–586.

Anderson, B., Erwin, N., Flynn, D., Lewis, L., & Erwin, J. (1977). Effects of short-term crowding on aggression in captive groups of pigtail monkeys. *Aggressive Behavior, 3,* 33–46.

Anderson, C. A. (1987). Temperature and aggression: Effects on quarterly, yearly, and city rates of violent and nonviolent crime. *Journal of Personality and Social Psychology, 52,* 1161–1173.

Anderson, C. A., (1989). Temperature and aggression: Ubiquitous effects of heat on occurrence of human violence. *Psychological Bulletin, 106,* 74–96.

Anderson, C. A., & Anderson, D. C. (1984). Ambient temperature and violent crime: Tests of the linear and curvilinear hypotheses. *Journal of Personality and Social Psychology, 46,* 91–97.

Anderson, C. A., & DeNeve, K. M. (1992). Temperature, aggression, and negative affect escape model. *Psychological Bulletin, 111,* 347–351.

Anderson, D. H., & Brown, P. J. (1984). The displacement process in recreation. *Journal of Leisure Research, 16,* 61–73.

Anderson, E. N., Jr. (1972). Some Chinese methods in dealing with crowding. *Urban Anthropology, 1,* 141–150.

Anderson, J. R., & Bower, G. H. (1973). *Human associative memory.* Washington, DC: Winston.

Ando, Y., & Hattori, H. (1973). Statistical studies in the effects of intense noise during human fetal life. *Journal of Sound and Vibration, 27,* 101–110.

Anthony, K. H., Weidemann, S., & Chin, Y. (1990). Housing perceptions of low-income single parents. *Environment and Behavior, 22,* 147–182.

Antonovsky, A. (1979). *Health, stress, and coping.* San Francisco: Jossey-Bass.

Appleton, J. (1975). *The experience of landscape.* London: Wiley.

Appleyard, D. (1969). Why buildings are known. *Environment and Behavior, 1,* 131–156.

Appleyard, D. (1970). Styles and methods of structuring a city. *Environment and Behavior, 2,* 101–117.

Appleyard, D. (1976). *Planning a pluralistic city.* Cambridge, MA: M.I.T. Press.

Appleyard, D., & Lintell, M. (1972). The environmental quality of city streets: The residents' viewpoint. *Journal of the American Institute of Planners, 38,* 84–101.

Aptekar, L., & Boore, J. A. (1990). The emotional effects of disaster on children: A review of the literature. *International Journal of Mental Health, 19,* 77–90.

Aragones, J. I., & Arredondo, J. M. (1985). Structure of urban cognitive maps. *Journal of Environmental Psychology, 5,* 197–212.

Arbuthnot, J., Tedeschi, R., Wayner, M., Turner, J., Kressel, S., & Rush, R. (1976–1977). The induction of sustained recycle behavior through the foot-in-the-door technique. *Journal of Environmental Systems, 6,* 355–358.

Archer, J. (1970). Effects of population density on behavior in rodents. In J. H. Crook (Ed.), *Social behavior in birds and mammals* (pp. 169–210). New York: Academic Press.

Ardrey, R. (1966). *The territorial imperative.* New York: Atheneum.

Argyle, M., & Dean, J. (1965). Eye-contact, distance and affiliation. *Sociometry, 28,* 289–304.

Arkkelin, D. (1978). *Effects of density, sex, and acquaintance level on reported pleasure, arousal, and dominance.* Doctoral dissertation, Bowling Green State University.

Arnstein, S. R. (1969). A ladder of citizen participation. *Journal of American Institute of Planners, 35,* 217.

Arreola, D. D. (1981). Fences as landscape taste: Tucson's barrios. *Journal of Cultural Geography, 2,* 96–105.

Arvey, R. D., Bouchard, T. J., Jr., Segal, N., & Abraham, L. M. (1989). Job satisfaction: Genetic and environmental components. *Journal of Applied Psychology, 74,* 187–192.

Assael, M., Pfeifer, Y., & Sulman, F. G. (1974). Influence of artificial air ionization on the human electroencephalogram. *International Journal of Biometeorology, 18,* 306–312.

Atlas, R. (1984). Violence in prison: Environmental influences. *Environment and Behavior, 16,* 275–306.

Atlas, R., & LeBlanc, W. G. (1994, October). Environmental barriers to crime. *Ergonomics in Design*, 9–16

Auble, D., & Britton, N. (1958). Anxiety as a factor influencing routine performance under auditory stimuli. *Journal of General Psychology*, *58*, 111–114.

Auliciems, A. (1972). Some observed relationships between the atmospheric environment and mental work. *Environmental Research*, *5*, 217–240.

Averill, J. R. (1973). Personal control over aversive stimuli and its relationship to stress. *Psychological Bulletin*, *80*, 286–303.

Axelrod, L. J., & Lehman, D. R. (1993). Responding to environmental concerns: What factors guide individual action? *Journal of Environmental Psychology*, *13*, 149–159.

Azuma, H. (1984). Secondary control as a heterogeneous category. *American Psychologist*, *39*, 970–971.

Bachman, W., & Katzev, R. (1982). The effects of non-contingent fee bus tickets and personal commitment on urban bus ridership. *Transportation Research*, *16A*, 103–108.

Bacon-Prue, A., Blount, R., Pickering, D., & Drabman, R. (1980). An evaluation of three litter control procedures—Trash receptacles, paid workers, and the marked item techinque. *Journal of Applied Behavior Analysis*, *13*, 165–170.

Bagley, C. (1989). Urban crowding and the murder rate in Bombay, India. *Perceptual and Motor Skills*, *69*, 1241–1242.

Baird, C. L., & Bell, P. A. (1995). Place attachment, isolation, and the power of a window in a hospital environment. *Psychological Reports*, *76*, 847–850.

Baird, J. C. (1979). Studies of the cognitive representation of spatial relations: I. Overview. *Journal of Experimental Psychology: General*, *108*, 90–91.

Baird, J. C., Merrill, A. A., & Tannenbaum, J. (1979). Studies of cognitive representations of spatial relations: II. A familiar environment. *Journal of Experimental Psychology: General*, *108*, 92–98.

Baird, L. L. (1969). Big school, small school: A critical examination of the hypothesis. *Journal of Educational Psychology*, *60*, 253–260.

Baker, G. W., & Chapman, D. W. (Eds.). (1962). *Man and society in disaster*. New York: Basic Books.

Baker, M. A., & Holding, D. H. (1993). The effects of noise and speech on cognitive task performance. *The Journal of General Psychology*, *120*, 339–355.

Balling, J. D., & Falk, J. H. (1982). Development of visual preference for natural environments. *Environment and Behavior*, *14*, 5–28.

Balogun, S. K. (1991). Personal space as affected by religions of the approaching and the approached people. *Indian Journal of Behaviour*, *15*, 45–50.

Baltes, M. M., Kindermann, T., Reisenzein, R., & Schmid, U. (1987). Further observational data on the behavioral and social world of institutions for the aged. *Psychology and Aging*, *2*, 390–403.

Bandura, A. (1973). *Aggression: A social learning analysis*. Englewood Cliffs, NJ: Prentice-Hall.

Bandura, A. (1977). *Social learning theory*. Englewood Cliffs, NJ: Prentice-Hall.

Banzinger, G., & Owens, K. (1978). Geophysical variables and behavior: II. Weather factors as predictors of local social indicators of maladaptation in two non-urban areas. *Psychological Reports*, *43*, 427–434.

Barabasz, A., & Barabasz, M. (1985). Effects of restricted environmental stimulation: Skin conductance, EEG alpha, and temperature responses. *Environment and Behavior*, *17*, 239–253.

Barabasz, A., & Barabasz, M. (1986). Antarctic isolation and inversion perception: Regression phenomena. *Environment and Behavior*, *18*, 285–292.

Barabasz, A. F., & Barabasz, M. (1993). *Clinical and experimental restricted environmental stimulation: New developments and perspectives*. New York: Springer.

Barash, D. P. (1973). Human ethology: Personal space reiterated. *Environment and Behavior*, *5*, 67–73.

Barber, N. (1990). Home color as a territorial marker. *Perceptual and Motor Skills*, *71*, 1107–1110.

Barefoot, J. C., Hoople, H., & McClay, D. (1972). Avoidance of an act which would violate personal space. *Psychonomic Science*, *28*, 205–206.

Barefoot, J., & Kleck, R. (1970). *The effects of race and physical proximity of a co-actor on the social facilitation of dominant responses*. Unpublished manuscript. Carleton University.

Barker, M. L. (1976). Planning for environmental indices: Observer appraisals of air quality. In K. H. Craik & E. H. Zube (Eds.), *Perceiving environmental quality: Research applications* (pp. 175–204). New York: Plenum.

Barker, R. G. (1960). Ecology and motivation. In M. R. Jones (Ed.), *Nebraska Symposium on Motivation* (Vol. 8, pp. 1–50). Lincoln: University of Nebraska Press.

Barker, R. G. (1968). *Ecological psychology: Concepts and methods for studying the environment of human behavior*. Stanford, CA: Stanford University Press.

Barker, R. G. (1979). Settings of a professional lifetime. *Journal of Personality and Social Psychology*, *37*, 2137–2157.

Barker, R. G. (1987). Prospecting in environmental psychology: Oskaloosa revisited. In D. Stokols & I. Altman (Eds.), *Handbook of environmental psychology* (Vol. II, pp. 1413–1432). New York: Wiley-Interscience.

Barker, R. G. (1990). Recollections of the Midwest Psychological Field Station. *Environment and Behavior*, *22*, 503–513.

Barker, R. G., & Gump, P. V. (1964). *Big school, small school*. Stanford, CA: Stanford University Press.

Barker, R. G., & Schoggen, P. (1973). *Qualities of community life*. San Francisco: Jossey-Bass.

Barker, R. G., & Wright, H. F. (1951). *One boy's day*. New York: Row, Peterson.

Barker, R. G., & Wright, H. F. (1955). *Midwest and its children*. New York: Row, Peterson.

Barnard, W. A., & Bell, P. A. (1982). An unobtrusive apparatus for measuring interpersonal distance. *Journal of General Psychology*, *107*, 85–90.

Baron, R. A. (1972). Aggression as a function of ambient temperature and prior anger arousal. *Journal of Personality and Social Psychology*, *21*, 183–189.

Baron, R. A. (1976). The reduction of human aggression: A field study of the influence of incompatible reactions. *Journal of Applied Social Psychology*, *6*, 260–274.

Baron, R. A. (1987a). Effects of negative ions on cognitive performance. *Journal of Applied Psychology*, *72*, 131–137.

Baron, R. A. (1987b). Effects of negative ions on interpersonal attraction: Evidence for intensification. *Journal of Personality and Social Psychology*, *52*, 547–553.

Baron, R. A., & Bell, P. A. (1975). Aggression and heat: Mediating effects of prior provocation and exposure to an aggressive model. *Journal of Personality and Social Psychology*, *31*, 825–832.

Baron, R. A., & Bell, P. A. (1976a). Aggression and heat: The influence of ambient temperature, negative affect, and a cooling drink on physical aggression. *Journal of Personality and Social Psychology*, *33*, 245–255.

Baron, R. A., & Bell, P. A. (1976b). Physical distance and helping: Some unexpected benefits of "crowding in" on others. *Journal of Applied Social Psychology*, *6*, 95–104.

Baron, R. A., & Byrne, D. (1994). *Social psychology: Understanding human interaction*. Needham Heights, MA: Allyn and Bacon.

Baron, R. A., Russell, G. W., & Arms, R. L. (1985). Negative ions and behavior: Impact on mood, memory, and aggression among Type A and Type B persons. *Journal of Personality and Social Psychology*, *48*, 746–754.

Baron, R. M., & Fisher, J. D. (1984). The equity-control model of vandalism: A refinement. In C. Levy-Leboyer (Ed.), *Vandalism: Behavior and motivations* (pp. 63–75). Amsterdam: North Holland.

Baron, R. M., & Kenny, D. A. (1986). The moderator-mediator variable distinction in social psychological research: Conceptual, strategic, and statistical considerations. *Journal of Personality and Social Psychology, 51,* 1173–1182.

Baron, R. M., Mandel, D. R., Adams, C. A., & Griffen, L. M. (1976). Effects of social density in university residential environments. *Journal of Personality and Social Psychology, 34,* 434–446.

Baron, R. M., & Rodin, J. (1978). Personal control as a mediator of crowding. In A. Baum, J. E. Singer, & S. Valins (Eds.), *Advances in environmental psychology* (Vol. 1, pp. 145–181). Hillsdale, NJ: Erlbaum.

Barrios, B. A., Corbitt, L. C., Estes, J. P., & Topping, J. S. (1976). Effects of social stigma on interpersonal distance. *The Psychological Record, 26,* 343–348.

Bartley, S. H. (1958). *Principles of perception.* New York: Harper.

Barton, A. (1969). *Communities in disaster.* Garden City, NY: Doubleday.

Barton, R. (1966). The patient's personal territory. *Hospital and Community Psychiatry, 17,* 336.

Bassuk, E., Rubin, L., & Lauriat, A. (1986). Characteristics of sheltered homeless families. *American Journal of Public Health, 76,* 1097–1101.

Bauer, R. M., Greve, K. W., Besch, E. L., Schramke, C. J., Crouch, J., Hicks, A., Ware, M. R., & Lyles, W. B. (1992). The role of psychological factors in the report of building-related symptoms in Sick Building Syndrome. *Journal of Consulting and Clinical Psychology, 60,* 213–219.

Baum, A. (1987). Toxins, technology, and natural disaster. In G. R. VandenBos & B. K. Bryant (Eds.), *Cataclysms, crises, and catastrophes: Psychology in action* (pp. 9–53). Washington, DC: American Psychological Association.

Baum, A., Aiello, J., & Calesnick, L. E. (1978). Crowding and personal control: Social density and the development of learned helplessness. *Journal of Personality and Social Psychology, 36,* 1000–1011.

Baum, A., Calesnick, L. E., Davis, G. E., & Gatchel, R. J. (1982). Individual differences in coping with crowding: Stimulus screening and social overload. *Journal of Personality and Social Psychology, 43,* 821–830.

Baum, A., Cohen, L., & Hall, M. (1993). Control and intrusive memories as possible determinants of chronic stress. *Psychosomatic Medicine, 55,* 274–286.

Baum, A., & Davis, G. E. (1976). Spatial and social aspects of crowding perception. *Environment and Behavior, 8,* 527–545.

Baum, A., & Davis, G. E. (1980). Reducing the stress of high-density living: An architectural intervention. *Journal of Personality and Social Psychology, 38,* 471–481.

Baum, A., & Fisher, J. D. (1977). *Situation-related information as a mediator of responses to crowding.* Unpublished manuscript, Trinity College.

Baum, A., Fisher, J. D., & Solomon, S. (1981). Type of information, familiarity, and the reduction of crowding stress. *Journal of Personality and Social Psychology, 40,* 11–23.

Baum, A., & Fleming, I. (1993). Implications of psychological research on stress and technological accidents. *American Psychologist, 48,* 665–672.

Baum, A., Fleming, I., Israel, A., & O'Keeffe, M. K. (1992). Symptoms of chronic stress following a natural disaster and discovery of a human-made hazard. *Environment and Behavior, 24,* 347–365.

Baum, A., Fleming, R., & Davidson, L. M. (1983). Natural disaster and technological catastrophe. *Environment and Behavior, 15,* 333–354.

Baum, A., & Gatchel, R. J. (1981). Cognitive determinants of response to uncontrollable events: Development of reactance and learned helplessness. *Journal of Personality and Social Psychology, 40,* 1078–1089.

Baum, A., Gatchel, R., Streufert, S., Baum, C. S., Fleming, R., & Singer, J. E. (1980). *Psychological stress for alternatives of de-*

contamination of TMI-2 reactor building atmosphere. U.S. Nuclear Regulatory Commission (NUREG/CR-1584).

Baum, A., & Greenberg, C. I. (1975). Waiting for a crowd: The behavioral and perceptual effects of anticipated crowding. *Journal of Personality and Social Psychology, 32,* 667–671.

Baum, A., Grunberg, N. E., & Singer, J. E. (1982). The use of physiological and neuroendocrinological measurements in the study of stress. *Health Psychology, 1,* 217–236.

Baum, A., & Koman, S. (1976). Differential response to anticipated crowding: Psychological effects of social and spatial density. *Journal of Personality and Social Psychology, 34,* 526–536.

Baum, A., & Paulus, P. B. (1987). Crowding. In D. Stokols & I. Altman (Eds.), *Handbook of environmental psychology* (Vol. I, pp. 533–570). New York: Wiley-Interscience.

Baum, A., Reiss, M., & O'Hara, J. (1974). Architectural variants of reaction to spatial invasion. *Environment and Behavior, 6,* 91–100.

Baum, A., Shapiro, A., Murray, D., & Wideman, M. (1979). Mediation of perceived crowding and control in residential dyads and triads. *Journal of Applied Social Psychology, 9,* 491–507.

Baum, A., Singer, J. E., & Baum, C. S. (1981). Stress and the environment. *Journal of Social Issues, 37,* 4–35.

Baum, A., & Valins, S. (1977). *Architecture and social behavior: Psychological studies of social density.* Hillsdale, NJ: Erlbaum.

Baum, A., & Valins, S. (1979). Architectural mediation of residential density and control: Crowding and the regulation of social contact. In L. Berkowitz (Ed.), *Advances in experimental social psychology* (Vol. 12, pp. 131–175). New York: Academic Press.

Baum, A. S., & Burnes, D. W. (1993, Spring). Facing the facts about homelessness. *Public Welfare,* 20–27, 46.

Baumeister, R. F. (1985). The championship choke. *Psychology Today, 19*(4), 48–52.

Baumeister, R. F., & Steinhilber, A. (1984). Paradoxical effects of supportive audiences on performance under pressure: The home field disadvantage in sports championships. *Journal of Personality and Social Psychology, 47,* 85–93.

Baxter, J. C., & Deanovich, B. S. (1970). Anxiety-arousing effects of inappropiate crowding. *Journal of Consulting and Clinical Psychology, 35,* 174–178.

Beal, J. B. (1974). Electrostatic fields, electromagnetic fields and ions—Mind/body/environment interrelationships. In J. G. Llaurado, A. Sances, & J. H. Battocletti (Eds.), *Biologic and clinical effects of low-frequency magnetic and electric fields* (pp. 5–20). Springfield, IL: Thomas.

Beard, R., & Grandstaff, N. (1970). Carbon monoxide exposure and cerebral function. *Annals of New York Academy of Sciences, 174,* 385–395.

Beard, R. R., & Wertheim, G.A. (1967). Behavioral impairment associated with small doses of carbon monoxide. *American Journal of Public Health, 57,* 2012–2022.

Bechtel, R. B. (1970). Human movement and architecture. In H. M. Proshansky, W. H. Ittelson, & L. G. Rivlin (Eds.), *Environmental psychology: Man and his physical setting* (pp. 642–645). New York: Holt, Rinehart and Winston.

Bechtel, R. B. (1977). *Enclosing behavior.* Stroudsberg, PA: Dowden, Hutchinson, & Ross.

Beck, R. J. (1971). *Out shopping in the urban crowd.* Paper presented at the meeting of the American Psychological Association, Washington, DC.

Beck, R. J., & Wood, D. (1976). Cognitive transformation of information from urban geographic fields to mental maps. *Environment and Behavior, 8,* 199–238.

Becker, F. D. (1973). Study of spatial markers. *Journal of Personality and Social Psychology, 26,* 439–445.

Becker, F. D. (1981). *Workspace: Creating environments in organizations.* New York: CBS Educational and Professional Publishing.

Becker, F. D., & Coniglio, C. (1975). Environmental messages: Personalization and territory. *Humanities, 11*, 55–74.

Becker, F. D., Gield, B., Gaylin, K., & Sayer, S. (1983). Office design in a community college: Effect of work and communication patterns. *Environment and Behavior, 15*, 699–726.

Becker, F. D., & Mayo, C. (1971). Delineating personal space and territoriality. *Environment and Behavior, 3*, 375–381.

Becker, F. D., Sommer, R., Bee, J., & Oxley, B. (1973). College classroom ecology. *Sociometry, 36*, 514–525.

Becker, L. J. (1978). The joint effect of feedback and goal setting on performance: A field study of residential energy conservation. *Journal of Applied Psychology, 63*, 228–233.

Becker, L., & Seligman, C. (1978). Reducing air-conditioning waste by signaling it is cool outside. *Personality and Social Psychology Bulletin, 4*, 412–415.

Beckman, R. (1974, November). Getting up and getting out: Progressive patient care. *Progressive Architecture*, p. 64.

Beighton, P. (1971). Fluid balance in the Saraha. *Nature, 233*, 275–277.

Belk, R. W. (1992). Attachment to possessions. In I. Altman & S. M. Low (Eds.), *Place Attachment* (pp. 37–62). New York: Plenum.

Bell, B., Kara, G., & Batterson, C. (1978). Service utilization and adjustment patterns of elderly tornado victims in an American disaster. *Mass Emergencies, 3*, 71–81.

Bell, C. R., Provins, K. A., & Hiorns, R. F. (1964). Visual and auditory vigilance during exposure to hot and humid conditions. *Ergonomics, 7*, 279–288.

Bell, P. A. (1978). Effects of heat and noise stress on primary and subsidiary task performance. *Human Factors, 20*, 749–752.

Bell, P. A. (1981). Physiological, comfort, performance, and social effects of heat stress. *Journal of Social Issues, 37*, 71–94.

Bell, P. A. (1982, August). *Theoretical interpretations of heat stress*. Paper presented at the meeting of the American Psychological Association, Washington, DC.

Bell, P. A. (1992). In defense of the negative affect escape model of heat and aggression. *Psychological Bulletin, 111*, 342–346.

Bell, P. A., & Barnard, S. W. (1977, May). *Sex differences in the effects of heat and noise stress on personal space permeability*. Paper presented at the meeting of the Rocky Mountain Psychological Association, Albuquerque, NM.

Bell, P. A., & Baron, R. A. (1974). Environmental influences on attraction: Effects of heat, attitude similarity, and personal evaluations. *Bulletin of the Psychonomic Society, 4*, 479–481.

Bell, P. A., & Baron, R. A. (1976). Aggression and heat: The mediating role of negative affect. *Journal of Applied Social Psychology, 6*, 18–30.

Bell, P. A., & Baron, R. A. (1977). Aggression and ambient temperature: The facilitating and inhibiting effects of hot and cold environments. *Bulletin of the Psychonomic Society, 9*, 443–445.

Bell, P. A., & Byrne, D. (1978). Repression-sensitization. In H. London & J. Exner (Eds.), *Dimensions of personality* (pp. 449–485). New York: Wiley.

Bell, P. A., & Doyle, D. P. (1983). Effects of heat and noise on helping behavior. *Psychological Reports, 53*, 955–959.

Bell, P. A., & Fusco, M. E. (1986). Linear and curvilinear relationships between temperature, affect, and violence: Reply to Cotton. *Journal of Applied Social Psychology, 16*, 802–807.

Bell, P. A., & Fusco, M. E. (1989). Heat and violence in the Dallas field data: Linearity, curvilinearity, and heteroscedasticity. *Journal of Applied Social Psychology, 19*, 1479–1482.

Bell, P. A., Garnard, D. B., & Heath, D. (1984). Effects of ambient temperature and seating arrangement on personal and evironmental evaluations. *Journal of General Psychology, 110*, 197–200.

Bell, P. A., & Greene, T. C. (1982). Thermal stress: Physiological, comfort, performance, and social effects of hot and cold environments. In G. W. Evans (Ed.), *Environmental stress* (pp. 75–105). London: Cambridge University Press.

Bell, P. A., Hess, S., Hill, E., Kukas, S., Richards, R. W., & Sargent, D. (1984). Noise and context-dependent memory. *Bulletin of the Psychonomic Society, 22*, 99–100.

Bell, P. A., Kline, L. M., & Barnard, W. A. (1988). Friendship and freedom of movement as moderators of sex differences in interpersonal distancing. *Journal of Social Psychology, 128*, 305–310.

Bell, P. A., Loomis, R. J., & Cervone, J. C. (1982). Effects of heat, social facilitation, sex differences, and task difficulty on reaction time. *Human Factors, 24*, 19–24.

Bell, P. A., Petersen, T. R., & Hautaluoma, J. E. (1989). The effect of punishment probability on overconsumption and stealing in a simulated commons. *Journal of Applied Social Psychology, 19*, 1483–1495.

Bell, R. W., Miller, C. E., Ordy, J. M., & Rolsten, C. (1971). Effects of population density and living space upon neuroanatomy, neurochemistry and behavior in the C57B1 10 mouse. *Journal of Comparative and Physiological Psychology, 75*, 258–263.

Belter, R. W., Foster, K. Y., Imm, P. S., & Finch, A. J., Jr. (1991, April). Parent vs. child reports of PTSD symptoms related to a catastrophic natural disaster. In J. M. Vogel (Chair) *Children's responses to natural disasters: The aftermath of Hurricane Hugo and the 1989 Bay Area earthquake*. Symposium conducted at the meeting of the Society for Research in Child Development, Seattle.

Bem, D. (1972). Self perception theory. In L. Berkowitz (Ed.), *Advances in experimental social psychology* (Vol. 6, pp. 1–62). New York: Academic Press.

Bem, D. J. (1971). *Beliefs, attitudes, and human affairs*. Belmont, CA: Brooks/Cole.

Benedak, T. (1952). *Psychosexual functions of women: Studies in psychosomatic medicine*. New York: Ronald Press.

Bennett, C. A., & Rey, P. (1972). What's so hot about red? *Human Factors, 14*, 149–154.

Bennett, N., Andreae, J., Hegarty, P., & Wade, B. (1980). *Open plan schools*. Atlantic Highlands, NJ: Humanities.

Bennett, R., Rafferty, J. M., Canivez, G. L., & Smith, J. M. (1983, May). *The effects of cold temperature on altruism and aggression*. Paper presented at the meeting of the Midwestern Psychological Association, Chicago, IL.

Bennett, W. R., Jr. (1994). *Health and low-frequency electromagnetic fields*. New Haven: Yale University Press.

Benson, G. P., & Zieman, G. L. (1981). *The relationship of weather to children's behavior problems*. Unpublished manuscript, Colorado State University, Fort Collins.

Beranek, L. L. (1956). Criteria for office quieting based on questionnaire rating studies. *Journal of the Acoustical Society of America, 28*, 833–850.

Beranek, L. L. (1957). Revised criteria for noise in buildings. *Noise Control, 3*, 19–26.

Berck, J. (1992). No place to be: Voices of homeless children. *Public Welfare*, 28–33.

Berglund, B., Berglund, U., & Lindvall, T. (1976). Psychological processing of odor mixtures. *Psychological Review, 83*, 432–441.

Bergman, B. A. (1971). *The effects of group size, personal space and success-failure on physiological arousal, test performance, and questionnaire responses*. Doctoral dissertation, Temple University.

Berk, L. E., & Goebel, B. L. (1987). High school size and extracurricular participation: A study of a small college environment. *Environment and Behavior, 19*, 53–76.

Berkowitz, L. (1970). The contagion of violence: An S-R mediational analysis of some effects of observed aggression. In W. J. Arnold & M. M. Page (Eds.), *Nebraska Symposium on Motivation* (Vol. 18, pp. 95–135). Lincoln: University of Nebraska Press.

Berlyne, D. E. (1960). *Conflict, arousal, and curiosity*. New York: McGraw-Hill.

Berlyne, D. E. (1974). *Studies in the new experimental aesthetics:*

Steps toward an objective psychology of aesthetic appreciation. New York: Halsted Press.

Bernaldez, F. G., Gallardo, D., & Abello, R. P. (1987). Children's landscape preferences: From rejection to attraction. *Journal of Environmental Psychology, 7,* 169–176.

Bernard, L. C., & Krupat, E. (1994). *Health psychology*. Orlando: Harcourt Brace.

Berry, P. C. (1961). Effects of colored illumination upon perceived temperature. *Journal of Applied Psychology, 45,* 248–250.

Best, J. B. (1986). *Cognitive psychology*. St. Paul, MN: West Publishing Company.

Bickman, L., Teger, A., Gabiele, T., McLaughin, C., Berger, M., & Sunaday, E. (1973). Dormitory density and helping behavior. *Environment and Behavior, 5,* 465–490.

Bih, H. (1992). The meaning of objects in environmental transitions: Experiences of Chinese students in the United States. *Journal of Environmental Psychology, 12,* 135–147.

Biner, P. M., Butler, D. L., Fischer, A. R., & Westergren, A. J. (1989). An arousal optimization model of lighting level preferences: An interaction of social situation and task demands. *Environment and Behavior, 21,* 3–16.

Biner, P. M., Butler, D. L., Lovegrove, T. E., & Burns, R. L. (1993). Windowlessness in the workplace: A reexamination of the compensation hypothesis. *Environment and Behavior, 25,* 205–227.

Birjulin, A. A., Smith, J. M., & Bell, P. A. (1993). Monetary reward, verbal reinforcement, and harvest strategy of others in the commons dilemma. *Journal of Social Psychology, 133,* 207–214.

Bishop, R. L., & Peterson, G. L. (1971). *A synthesis of environmental design recommendations from the visual preferences of children*. Chicago, IL: Northwestern University Department of Civil Engineering.

Bitgood, S. C., & Loomis, R. J. (1993). Introduction: Environmental design and evaluation in museums. *Environment and Behavior, 25,* 1993.

Bitgood, S. C., & Patterson, D. D. (1993). The effects of gallery changes on visitor reading and object viewing time. *Environment and Behavior, 25,* 761–781.

Bitgood, S., Roper, J. T., Jr., & Benefield, A. (Eds.). (1988). *Visitor studies-1988: Theory, research, and practice*. Jacksonville, AL: Center for Social Design.

Black, J. C. (1968). *Uses made of spaces in owner-occupied houses*. Unpublished doctoral dissertation, University of Utah, Salt Lake City.

Blackman, S., & Catalina, D. (1973). The moon and the emergency room. *Perceptual and Motor Skills, 37,* 624–626.

Blades, M. (1990). The reliability of data collected from sketch maps. *Journal of Environmental Psychology, 10,* 327–339.

Blades, M., & Spencer, C. (1987). Young children's strategies when using maps with landmarks. *Journal of Environmental Psychology, 7,* 201–217.

Blake, M. J. F. (1971). Temperament and time of day. In W. P. Colguhoun (Ed.), *Biological rhythms and human performance* (pp. 109–148). London: Academic Press.

Blaut, J. M., & Stea, D. (1974). Mapping at the age of three. *Journal of Geography, 73,* 5–9.

Bleda, P., & Bleda, S. (1978). Effects of sex and smoking on reactions to spatial invasion at a shopping mall. *Journal of Social Psychology, 104,* 311–312.

Bleda, P. R., & Sandman, P. H. (1977). In smoke's way: Socioemotional reactions to another's smoking. *Journal of Applied Psychology, 62,* 452–458.

Block, L. K., & Stokes, G. S. (1989). Performance and satisfaction in private versus nonprivate work settings. *Environment and Behavior, 21,* 277–297.

Blumberg, L., & Gottlieb, R. (1989). *War on waste: Can America win its battle with garbage?* Washington, DC: Island Press.

Boldero, J. (1995). The prediction of household recycling of newspapers: The role of attitudes, intentions, and situational factors. *Journal of Applied Social Psychology, 25,* 440–462.

Bolin, R. (1985). Disaster characteristics and psychosocial impacts. In B. J. Sowder (Ed.), *Disasters and mental health: Selected contemporary perspectives* (pp. 3–28). Rockville, MD: U.S. Department of Health and Human Services.

Bolin, R., & Klenow, J. D. (1982). Response of the elderly to disaster: An age-stratified analysis. *International Journal of Aging and Human Development, 16,* 283–296.

Bolt, Beranek, & Newman, Inc. (1982). Occupational noise: The subtle pollutant. In J. Ralof, *Science News, 121*(21), 347–350.

Bonio, S., Fonzi, A., & Saglione, G. (1978). Personal space and variations in the behavior of ten-year-olds. *Italian Journal of Psychology, 10,* 15–25.

Bonnes, M., Bonaiuto, M., & Ercolani, A. P. (1991). Crowding and residential satisfaction in the urban environment: A contextual approach. *Environment and Behavior, 23,* 531–552.

Bonnes, M., Giuliani, M.V., Amoni, F., & Bernard, Y. (1987). Cross-cultural rules for the optimization of the living room. *Environment and Behavior, 19,* 204–227.

Bonnes, M., Mannetti, L., Tanucci, G., & Secchiaroli, G. (1990). The city as a multi-place system: An analysis of people-urban environment transactions. *Journal of Environmental Psychology, 10,* 37–66.

Bonta, J. (1986). Prison crowding: Searching for the functional correlates. *American Psychologist, 41,* 99–101.

Booth, A. (1976). *Urban crowding and its consequences*. New York: Praeger.

Booth, W. (1988). Johnny Appleseed and the greenhouse. *Science, 242,* 19–20.

Borg, E. (1981). Noise, hearing, and hypertension (editorial). *Scandinavian Audiology, 10*(2), 125–126.

Bornstein, M. H. (1979). The pace of life revisited. *International Journal of Psychology, 14,* 83–90.

Borsky, P. N. (1969). Effects of noise on community behavior. In W. D. Ward & J. E. Fricke (Eds.), *Noise as a public health hazard*. Washington, DC: The American Speech and Hearing Association.

Borun, M. L. (1977). *Measuring the unmeasurable*. Washington, DC: Association for Science Technology Centers.

Bostrom, A., Fischhoff, B., & Morgan, M. G. (1992). Characterizing mental models of hazardous processes: A methodology and an application to radon. *Journal of Social Issues, 48,* 85–100.

Boucher, M. L. (1972). Effect of seating distance on interpersonal attraction in an interview situation. *Journal of Consulting and Clinical Psychology, 38,* 15–19.

Bouska, M. L., & Beatty, P. A. (1978). Clothing as a symbol of status: Its effect on control of interaction territory. *Bulletin of the Psychonomic Society, 4,* 235–238.

Bovy, P. (1975). *Pedestrian planning and design: A bibliography*. (No. 918). Council of Planning Librarians Exchange Bibliography.

Bowman, U. (1964). Alaska earthquake. *American Journal of Psychology, 121,* 313–317.

Boyanowsky, E. O., Calvert, J., Young, J., & Brideau, L. (1981–82). Toward a thermoregulatory model of violence. *Journal of Environmental Systems, 11,* 81–87.

Boyce, P. (1981). *Human factors in lighting*. New York: Macmillan.

Boyce, P. R. (1974). Users' assessments of a landscaped office. *Journal of Architectural Research, 3,* 44–62.

Bradley, J. S. (1992). Disturbance caused by residential air conditioner noise. *Journal of the Acoustical Society of America, 93,* 1978–1986.

Brantingham, P. A., & Brantingham, P. J. (1993). Nodes, paths, and edges: Consideration of the complexity of crime and the physical environment. *Journal of Environmental Psychology, 13,* 3–28.

Brasted, W., Mann, M., & Geller, E. S. (1979, Summer). Behavioral interventions for litter control: A critical review. *Cornell Journal of Social Relations, 14,* 75–90.

Brechner, K. C. (1977). An experimental analysis of social traps. *Journal of Experimental Social Psychology, 13,* 552–564.

Brehm, J. W. (1966). *A theory of psychological reactance.* New York: Academic Press.

Brehm, S. S., & Brehm, J. W. (1981). *Psychological reactance: A theory of freedom and control.* New York: Academic Press.

Breisacher, P. (1971). Neuropsychological effects of air pollution. *American Behavioral Scientist, 14,* 837–864.

Brewer, M. B., & Kramer, R. M. (1986). Choice behavior in social dilemmas: Effects of social density, group size, and decision framing. *Journal of Personality and Social Psychology, 50,* 543–549.

Briere, J., Downes, A., & Spensley, J. (1983). Summer in the city: Urban weather conditions and psychiatric emergency room visits. *Journal of Abnormal Psychology, 92,* 77–80.

Broadbent, D. E. (1954). Some effects of noise on visual performance. *Quarterly Journal of Experimental Psychology, 6,* 1–5.

Broadbent, D. E. (1958). *Perception and communication.* Oxford: Pergamon.

Broadbent, D. E. (1963). Differences and interactions between stresses. *Quarterly Journal of Experimental Psychology, 15,* 205–211.

Broadbent, D. E. (1971). *Decision and stress.* New York: Academic Press.

Broadbent, D. E., & Little, E. (1960). Effects of noise reduction in a work situation. *Occupational Psychology, 34,* 133–140.

Broadbent, G. B. (1973). *Design in architecture.* New York: Wiley.

Brodsky, C. M. (1983). "Allergic to everything": A medical subculture. *Psychosomatics, 24,* 731–742.

Brokemann, N. C., & Moller, A. T. (1973). Preferred seating position and distance in various situations. *Journal of Counseling Psychology, 20,* 504–508.

Bromet, E. (1980). *Preliminary report on the mental health of Three Mile Island residents.* Pittsburg, PA: Western Psychiatric Institute, University of Pittsburg.

Bromet, E., Hough, L., & Connell, M. (1984). Mental health of children near the Three Mile Island reactor. *Journal of Preventive Psychiatry, 2,* 275–301.

Bromet, E., Ryan, C., & Parkinson, D. (1986). Psychosocial correlates of occupational lead exposure. In A. H. Lebovits, A. Baum, & J. Singer (Eds.), *Advances in environmental psychology* (Vol. 6, pp. 19–31). Hillsdale, NJ: Erlbaum.

Bronzaft, A. L. (1981). The effect of a noise abatement program on reading ability. *Journal of Environmental Psychology, 1,* 215–222.

Bronzaft, A. L. (1985–86). Combating the unsilent enemy– Noise. *Prevention in Human Services, 4* (1–2), 179–192.

Bronzaft, A. L., & McCarthy, D. P. (1975). The effects of elevated train noise on reading ability. *Environment and Behavior, 7,* 517–527.

Brooks, M. J., & Kaplan, A. (1972). The office environment: Space planning and affective behavior. *Human Factors, 14,* 373–391.

Browder, A. A., Joselow, M. M., & Louria, D. B. (1973). The problem of lead poisoning. *Medicine, 52,* 121–139.

Brower, S., Dockett, K., & Taylor, R. (1983). Residents' perceptions of territorial features and perceived local threat. *Environment and Behavior, 15,* 419–437.

Brown, B. B. (1979, August). *Territoriality and residential burglary.* Paper presented at the meeting of the American Psychological Association, New York, NY.

Brown, B. B. (1987). Territoriality. In D. Stokols & I. Altman (Eds.), *Handbook of environmental psychology* (Vol. 1, pp. 505–531). New York: Wiley-Interscience.

Brown, B. B. (1992). The ecology of privacy and mood in a shared living group. *Journal of Environmental Psychology, 12,* 5–20.

Brown, B. B. & Bentley, D. L. (1993). Residential burglars judge risk: The role of territoriality. *Journal of Environmental Psychology, 13,* 51–61.

Brown, B. B., & Perkins, D. D. (1992). Disruptions in place attachment. In I. Altman & S. M. Low (Eds.), *Place attachment* (pp. 279–304). New York: Plenum.

Brown, B. B., & Werner, C. M. (1985). Social cohesiveness, territoriality, and holiday decorations: The influence of cul-de-sacs. *Environment and Behavior, 17,* 539–565.

Brown, C. E. (1981). Shared space invasion and race. *Personality and Social Psychology Bulletin, 7,* 103–108.

Brown, G. G., & Nixon, R. (1979). Exposure to polybrominated biphenyls: Some effects on personality and cognitive functioning. *Journal of the American Medical Association, 242,* 523–527.

Brown, G. I. (1964). The relationship between barometric pressure and relative humidity and classroom behavior. *Journal of Educational Research, 57,* 368–370.

Brown, I. D., & Poulton, E. C. (1961). Measuring the spare "mental capacity" of car drivers by a subsidiary task. *Ergonomics, 4,* 35–40.

Brown, J. G., & Burger, C. (1984). Playground design and preschool children's behaviors. *Environment and Behavior, 16,* 599–626.

Brown, P. (1992). Popular epidemiology and toxic waste contamination: Lay and professional ways of knowing. *Journal of Health and Social Behavior, 33,* 267–281.

Brunetti, F. A. (1972). Noise, distraction and privacy in conventional and open school environments. In W. J. Mitchell (Ed.), *Environmental design: Research and practice* (pp. 12–2–1–12–2–6). Los Angeles: University of California.

Brunswik, E. (1956). *Perception and the representative design of psychological experiments.* Berkeley: University of California Press.

Brunswik, E. (1959). The conceptual framework of psychology. In O. Neurath, R. Camp, & C. Morris (Eds.), *Foundation of the unity of science: Toward an international encyclopedia of unified science.* Chicago: University of Chicago Press.

Bryant, K. J. (1982). Personality correlates of sense of direction and geographical orientation. *Journal of Personality and Social Psychology, 43,* 1318–1324.

Budd, G. M. (1973). Australian physiological research in the Antarctic and Subarctic, with special reference to thermal stress and acclimatization. In O. E. Edholm & E. K. E. Gunderson (Eds.), *Polar human biology.* London: Heineman.

Bull, A. J., Burbage, S. E., Crandall, J. E., Fletcher, C. I., Lloyd, J. T., Ravenberg, R. L., & Rockett, S. L. (1972). Effects of noise and intolerance of ambiguity upon attraction for similar and dissimilar others. *Journal of Social Psychology, 88,* 151–152.

Bullen, R. B., Hede, A. J., & Kyriocos, C. (1986). Reactions to aircraft noise in residential areas around Australian airports. *Journal of Sound and Vibration, 108,* 199–228.

Bullinger, M. (1989). Psychological effects of air pollution on healthy residents: A time-series approach. *Journal of Environmental Psychology, 9,* 103–118.

Bunston, T., & Breton, M. (1992). Homes and homeless women. *Journal of Environmental Psychology, 12,* 149–162.

Burge, S., Hedge, A., Wilson, S., Bass, J. H., & Robertson, A. (1987). Sick building syndrome: A study of 4,373 office workers. *Annals of Occupational Hygiene, 31,* 493–504.

Burke, E. (1757). *Philosophical inquiry into the origin of our ideas of the sublime and beautiful.* Republished 1899 in *The Works of Edmund Burke* (Vol.1). Boston: Little, Brown, & Company.

Burn, S. M. (1991). Social psychology and the stimulation of recycling behaviors: The block leader approach. *Journal of Applied Social Psychology, 21,* 611–629.

Burn, S. M. & Oskamp, S. (1986). Increasing community recycling with persuasive communication and public commitment. *Journal of Applied Social Psychology, 16*, 9–41.

Burrows, A. A., & Zamarin, D. M. (1972). Aircraft noise and the community: Some recent survey findings. *Aerospace Medicine, 43*, 27–33.

Bursill, A. E. (1958). The restriction of peripheral vision during exposure to hot and humid conditions. *Quarterly Journal of Experimental Psychology, 10*, 113–129.

Burt, C. D. B. (1993). Concentration and academic ability following transition to university: An investigation of the effects of homesickness. *Journal of Environmental Psychology, 13*, 333–342.

Burton, I., & Kates, R. W. (1964). Perception of hazards in resource management. *Natural Resources Journal, 3*, 412–441.

Burton, I., Kates, R. W., & White, G. F. (1968). The human ecology of extreme geophysical events. *Natural hazard research working paper No. 1*, University of Toronto.

Butler, D. L., & Biner, P. M. (1987). Preferred lighting levels: Variability among settings, behaviors, and individuals. *Environment and Behavior, 19*, 695–721.

Butler, D. L., & Biner, P. M. (1989). Effects of setting on window preferences and factors associated with those preferences. *Environment and Behavior, 21*, 17–32.

Byers, R. K., & Lord, E. E. (1943). Late effects of lead poisoning on mental development. *American Journal of Diseases of Children, 66*, 471.

Byrne, D. (1971). *The attraction paradigm.* New York: Academic Press.

Byrne, D., Baskett, G. D., & Hodges, L. (1971). Behavioral indicators of interpersonal attraction. *Journal of Applied Social Psychology, 1*, 137–149.

Byrne, D., Ervin, C. R., & Lamberth, J. (1970). Continuity between the experimental study of attraction and real life computer dating. *Journal of Personality and Social Psychology, 16*, 157–165.

Byrne, R.W. (1979). Memory for urban geography. *Quarterly Journal of Experimental Psychology, 31*, 147–154.

Byrnes, G., & Kelly, I. W. (1992). Crisis calls and lunar cycles: A twenty-year review. *Psychological Reports, 71*, 779–785.

Caccioppo, J. T., & Petty, R. E. (1983). Foundations of social psychophysiology. In J. T. Cappioppo & R. E. Petty (Eds.), *Social psychophysiology: A sourcebook* (pp. 3–36). New York: Guilford.

Cadwallader, M. (1979). Problems in cognitive distance: Implications for cognitive mapping. *Environment and Behavior, 11*, 559–576.

Cahoon, R. L. (1972). Simple decision making at high altitude. *Ergonomics, 15*, 157–163.

Calhoun, J. B. (1962). Population density and social pathology. *Scientific American, 206*, 139–148.

Calhoun, J. B. (1964). The social use of space. In W. Mayer & R. Van Gelder (Eds.), *Physiological mammalogy* (pp. 2–187). New York: Academic Press.

Calhoun, J. B. (1967). Ecological factors in the development of behavioral anomalies. In J. Zubin & H. F. Hunt (Eds.), *Comparative psychopathology* (pp. 1–51). New York: Grune & Stratton.

Calhoun, J. B. (1970). Space and the strategy of life. *Ekistics, 29*, 425–437.

Calhoun, J. B. (1971). Space and the strategy of life. In A. H. Esser (Ed.), *Behavior and environment: The use of space by animals and men* (pp. 329–387). Bloomington: University of Indiana Press.

Calkins, M. P. (1987). *Designing for dementia.* Owings Mills, MD: National Health Publishing.

Cameron, P., Robertson, D., & Zaks, J. (1972). Sound pollution, noise pollution, and health: Community parameters. *Journal of Applied Psychology, 56*, 67–74.

Campbell, D. E. (1979). Interior office design and visitor response. *Journal of Applied Psychology, 64*, 648–653.

Campbell, D. E. (1982). Lunar-lunacy research: When enough is enough. *Environment and Behavior, 14*, 418–424.

Campbell, D. E., & Beets, J. L. (1977). Meteorological variables and behavior: An annotated bibliography. *JSAS Catalog of Selected Documents in Psychology, 7*, 1 (Ms. No. 1403).

Campbell, D. E., & Beets, J. L. (1978). Lunacy and the moon. *Psychological Bulletin, 85*, 1123–1129.

Campbell, D. E., & Beets, J. L. (1981). *Human response to naturally occurring weather phenomena: Effects of wind speed and direction.* Unpublished manuscript, Humboldt State University.

Campbell, D. E., & Herren, K. (1978). Interior arrangement of the faculty office. *Psychological Reports, 43*, 234.

Campbell, J. (1983). Ambient stressors. *Environment and Behavior, 15*, 355–380.

Campbell, J. B. (1992). Extraversion and noise sensitivity: A replication of Dornic and Ekehammar's study. *Personality and Individual Differences, 13*, 935–955.

Canino, G. J., Bravo, M., Rubio-Stipec, M., & Woodbury, M. (1990). The impact of disaster on mental health: Prospective and retrospective analyses. *International Journal of Mental Health, 19*, 51–69.

Cannon, W. B. (1929). *Bodily changes in pain, hunger, fear, and rage.* Boston: Branford.

Cannon, W. B. (1931). Studies on the conditions of activity in the endocrine organs, XXVII. Evidence that the medulliadrenal secretion is not continuous. *American Journal of Physiology, 98*, 447–452.

Canter, D. (1972, September). Royal Hospital for Sick Children: A psychological analysis. *Architect's Journal, 525–564.*

Canter, D., & Larkin, P. (1983). The environmental range of serial rapists. *Journal of Environmental Psychology, 13*, 63–69.

Cappella, J. N., & Greene, J. O. (1982). A discrepancy-arousal explanation of mutual influence in expressive behavior in adult and infant-adult interactions. *Communication Monographs, 49*, 89–114.

Carless (1992). *Taking out the trash.* Washington, DC: Island Press.

Carlisle, S. G. (1982). French homes and French character. *Landscape, 26*, 13–23.

Carlopio, J. R., & Gardner, D. (1992). Direct and interactive effects of the physical work environment on attitudes. *Environment and Behavior, 24*, 579–601.

Carp, F. (1987). Environment and aging. In D. Stokols & I. Altman (Eds.), *Handbook of environmental psychology* (Vol. 1, pp. 329–360). New York: Wiley-Interscience.

Carp, F. M. (1976). Housing and living environments of older people. In R. H. Binstock & E. Shanas (Eds.), *Handbook of aging and the social sciences* (pp. 244–271). New York: Van Nostrand.

Carpenter, C. R. (1958). Territoriality: A review of concepts and problems. In A. Roe & G. G. Simpson (Eds.), *Behavior and evolution.* New Haven, CT: Yale University Press.

Carpman, J. R., & Grant, M. A. (1993). *Design that cares: Planning health facilities for patients and visitors* (2nd ed.). Chicago: American Hospital Publishing, Inc.

Carpman, J. R., Grant, M. A., & Simmons, D. A. (1983–84). Wayfinding in the hospital environment: The impact of various floor numbering alternatives. *Journal of Environmental Systems, 13*, 353–364.

Cass, R., & Edney, J. J. (1978). The commons dilemma: A simulation testing the effects of resource visibility and territorial division. *Human Ecology, 6*, 371–386.

Caudill, B. D., & Aiello, J. R. (1979, April). *Interpersonal equilibrium: A study of convergent and predictive validity.* Paper presented at the meeting of the Eastern Psychological Association, Philadelphia.

Chaiken, S., & Stangor, C. (1987). Attitudes and attitude change. *Annual Review of Psychology, 38*, 575–630.

Chaouloff, F., & Zamfir, O. (1993). Psychoneuroendocrine outcomes of short-term crowding stress. *Physiology and Behavior*, *54*, 767–770.

Chapko, M. K., & Solomon, M. (1976). Air pollution and recreation behavior. *Journal of Social Psychology*, *100*, 149–150.

Charlson, R. J., Schwartz, S. E., Hales, J. M., Cess, R. D., Coakley, J. A., Jr., Hansen, J. E., & Hofmann, D. J. (1992). Climate forcing by anthropogenic aerosols. *Science*, *255*, 423–430.

Charry, J. M., & Hawkinshire, F. B. W. (1981). Effects of atmospheric electricity on some substrates of disordered social behavior. *Journal of Personality and Social Psychology*, *41*, 185–197.

Chawla, L. (1992). Childhood place attachments. In I. Altman & S. M. Low (Eds.), *Place attachment* (pp. 63–86). New York: Plenum.

Cherek, D. R. (1985). Effects of acute exposure to increased levels of background industrial noise on cigarette smoking behavior. *International Archives of Occupational and Environmental Health*, *56*, 23–30.

Cherulnik, P. D. (1993). *Applications of environment–behavior research: Case studies and analysis*. New York: Cambridge University Press.

Cherulnik, P. D., & Wilderman, S. K. (1986). Symbols of status in urban neighborhoods: Contemporary perceptions of nineteenth-century Boston. *Environment and Behavior*, *18*, 604–622.

Cheyne, J. A., & Efran, N. G. (1972). The effect of spatial and interpersonal variables on the invasion of group-controlled territories. *Sociometry*, *35*, 477–489.

Chowns, R. H. (1970). Mental hospital admissions and aircraft noise. *Lancet*, *I* (7644), 467.

Christensen, R. (1982). Alaskan winters: A mental health hazard? *Alaskan Medicine*, *24*, 89.

Christensen, R. (1984). Cabin fever: A folk belief and the misdiagnosis of complaints. *Journal of Mental Health Administration*, *11*, 2–3.

Christian, J. J. (1955). Effects of population size on the adrenal glands and reproductive organs of male mice in populations of fixed size. *The American Journal of Physiology*, *182*, 292–300.

Cialdini, R. (1977). *Littering as a function of extant litter*. Unpublished manuscript, Arizona State University.

Cialdini, R. B., & Kenrick, D. T. (1976). Altruism as hedonism: A social development perspective on the relationship of negative mood state and helping. *Journal of Personality and Social Psychology*, *54*, 907–914.

Cialdini, R. B., Reno, R. R., & Kallgren, C. A. (1989). *Using a focus theory of normative conduct to reduce littering in public places*. Unpublished manuscript, Arizona State University.

Cicchetti, C. (1972). A review of the empirical analyses that have been based upon the national survey. *Journal of Leisure Research*, *4*, 90–107.

Cini, M. A., Moreland, R. L., & Levine, J. M. (1993). Group staffing levels and responses to prospective and new group members. *Journal of Personality and Social Psychology*, *65*, 723–734.

Clark, R. E., & Flaherty, C. F. (1963). Contralateral effects of thermal stimuli on manual performance capability. *Journal of Applied Psychology*, *18*, 769–771.

Clemente, F., & Kleiman, M. B. (1977). Fear of crime in the United States. *Social Forces*, *51*, 176–531.

Clinard, M. B. (1964). Deviant behavior: Urban–rural contrasts. In L. E. Elias, Jr., J. Gillies, & S. Reimer (Eds.), *Metropolis: Values in conflict*. Belmont, CA: Wadsworth.

Cobb, S. (1976). Support as a moderator of life stress. *Psychosomatic Medicine*, *38*, 300–314.

Coffin, D., & Stokinger, H. (1977). Biological effects of air pollutants. In A. C. Stern (Ed.), *Air pollution* (3rd ed., Vol. 3). New York: Academic Press.

Cohen, H., Moss, S., & Zube, E. (1979). Pedestrians and wind in the urban environment. In A. D. Seidel & S. Danford (Eds.), *Environmental design: Research, theory, and application* (pp. 71–82). Washington, DC: Environmental Design Research Association.

Cohen, J. L., Sladen, B., & Bennett, B. (1975). The effects of situational variables on judgments of crowding. *Sociometry*, *38*, 273–281.

Cohen, M. R. (1973). Environmental information versus environmental attitudes. *Journal of Environmental Education*, *5*, 5–8.

Cohen, R., Goodnight, J. A., Poag, C. K., Cohen, S., Nichol, G. T., & Worley, P. (1986). Easing the transition of kindergarten: The affective and cognitive effects of different spatial familiarization experiences. *Environment and Behavior*, *18*, 330–345.

Cohen, S. (1978). Environmental load and the allocation of attention. In A. Baum, J. E. Singer, & S. Valins (Eds.), *Advances in environmental psychology* (Vol. 1, pp. 1–29). Hillsdale, NJ: Erlbaum.

Cohen, S. (1980). Aftereffects of stress on human performance and social behavior: A review of research and theory. *Psychological Bulletin*, *87*, 578–604.

Cohen, S., Evans, G. W., Krantz, D. S., & Stokols, D. (1980). Physiological, motivational, and cognitive effects of aircraft noise on children: Moving from the laboratory to the field. *American Psychologist*, *35*, 231–243.

Cohen, S., Evans, G. W., Krantz, D. S., Stokols, D., & Kelly, S. (1981). Aircraft noise and children: Longitudinal and cross-sectional evidence on adaptation to noise and the effectiveness of noise abatement. *Journal of Personality and Social Psychology*, *40*, 331–345.

Cohen, S., Evans, G. W., Stokols, D., & Krantz, D. S. (1986). *Behavior, health and environmental stress*. New York: Plenum.

Cohen, S., Glass, D. C., & Phillips, S. (1977). Environment and health. In H. E. Freeman, S. Levine, & L. G. Reeder (Eds.), *Handbook of medical sociology* (pp. 134–149). Englewood Cliffs, NJ: Prentice-Hall.

Cohen, S., Glass, D. C., & Singer, J. E. (1973). Apartment noise, auditory discrimination, and reading ability in children. *Journal of Experimental Social Psychology*, *9*, 407–422.

Cohen, S., & Hoberman, H. M. (1983). Positive events and social supports as buffers of life change stress. *Journal of Applied Social Psychology*, *13*, 99–125.

Cohen, S., Kamarck, T., & Mermelstein, R. (1983). A global measure of perceived stress. *Journal of Health and Social Behavior*, *24*, 385–396.

Cohen, S., & Lezak, A. (1977). Noise and inattentiveness to social cues. *Environment and Behavior*, *9*, 559–572.

Cohen, S., & Spacapan, S. (1978). The aftereffects of stress: An attentional interpretation. *Environmental Psychology and Nonverbal Behavior*, *3*, 43–57.

Cohen, S., & Spacapan, S. (1984). The social psychology of noise. In D. M. Jones & A. J. Chapman (Eds.), *Noise and society* (pp. 221–245). Chichester: Wiley.

Cohen, S., & Weinstein, N. D. (1982). Nonauditory effects of noise on behavior and health. In G.W. Evans (Ed.), *Environmental stress* (pp. 45–74). Cambridge: Cambridge University Press.

Cohen, S., & Wills, T. A. (1985). Stress, social support, and the buffering hypothesis. *Psychological Bulletin*, *8*, 310–357.

Cohn, E. G. (1990). Weather and violent crime: A reply to Perry and Simpson, 1987. *Environment and Behavior*, *22*, 280–294.

Cohn, E. G. (1993). The prediction of police calls for service: The influence of weather and temporal variables on rape and domestic violence. *Journal of Environmental Psychology*, *13*, 71–83.

Colligan, M. J., & Murphy, L. R. (1979). Mass psychogenic illness in organizations: An overview. *Journal of Occupational Psychology*, *52*, 77–90.

Colligan, M. J., & Murphy, L. R. (1982). A review of mass psychogenic illness in work settings. In M. J. Colligan, J. W. Pennebaker, & L. R. Murphy (Eds.), *Mass psychogenic illness*, (pp. 33–52). Hillsdale, NJ: Erlbaum.

Collins, A. M., & Loftus, E. F. (1975). A spreading activation theory of semantic processing. *Psychological Review, 82*, 407–428.

Collins, A. M., & Quillian, M. R. (1969). Retrieval time from semantic memory. *Journal of Verbal Learning and Verbal Behavior, 8*, 240–247.

Collins, B. L. (1975). Windows and people: A literature survey. *Psychological reaction to environments with and without windows.* NSB Building Science Series, 70, 88.

Collins, D. L., Baum, A., & Singer, J. (1983). Coping with chronic stress at Three Mile Island: Psychological and biochemical evidence. *Health Psychology, 2*, 149–166.

Committee for Health Care for Homeless People. (1988). *Homelessness, health and human needs.* Washington, DC: National Academy Press.

Commoner, B. (1963). *Science and survival.* New York: Viking.

Cone, J. D., & Hayes, S. C. (1980). *Environmental problems/behavioral solutions.* Monterey, CA: Brooks/Cole.

Conroy, J., III, & Sundstrom, E. (1977). Territorial dominance in a dyadic conversation as a function of similarity of opinion. *Journal of Personality and Social Psychology, 35*, 570–576.

Cook, C. C. (1988). Components of neighborhood satisfaction: Responses from urban and suburban single-parent women. *Environment and Behavior, 20*, 115–149.

Cook, M. (1970). Experiments on orientation and proxemics. *Human Relations, 23*, 61–76.

Cook, M., & Mineka, S. (1989). Observational conditioning of fear to fear-relevant versus fear-irrelevant stimuli in Rhesus monkeys. *Journal of Abnormal Psychology, 95*, 195–207.

Cook, M., & Mineka, S. (1990). Selective observations in the observational conditioning of fear in Rhesus monkeys. *Journal of Experimental Psychology: Animal Behavior Processes, 16*, 372–389.

Cook-Deegan, R. M. (1987). *Losing a million minds: Confronting the tragedy of Alzheimer's disease and other dementias.* Washington, DC: U.S. Government Printing Office.

Cooper, C. (1970). Adventure playground. *Landscape Architecture, 61*, 18–29, 88–91.

Cooper, C. (1972). The house as symbol. *Design and Environment, 14*, 178–182.

Cooper, M., & Rodman, M. C. (1994). Accessibility and quality of life in housing cooperatives. *Environment and Behavior, 26*, 49–70.

Cooper Marcus C., & Sarkissian, W. (1985). *Housing as if people mattered.* Berkeley, CA: University of California Press.

Corcoran, D. W. J. (1962). Noise and loss of sleep. *Quarterly Journal of Experimental Psychology, 14*, 178–182.

Cornell, E. H., & Hay, D. H. (1984). Children's acquisition of a route via different media. *Environment and Behavior, 16*, 627–642.

Cornoldi, C., & McDaniel, M. A. (1991). *Imagery and cognition.* New York: Springer.

Coss, R. G., & Moore, M. (1990). All that glistens: Water connotations in surface finishes. *Ecological Psychology, 2*, 367–380.

Costanzo, M., Archer, D., Aronson, E., & Pettgrew, T. (1986). Energy conservation behavior: The difficult path from information to action. *American Psychologist, 41*, 521–528.

Cotton, J. L. (1986). Ambient temperature and violent crime. *Journal of Applied Social Psychology, 16*, 786–801.

Couclelis, H., Golledge, R. G., Gale, N., & Tobler, W. (1987). Exploring the anchor-point hypothesis of spatial cognition. *Journal of Environmental Psychology, 7*, 99–122.

Coughlin, R. E. (1976). The perception and valuation of water quality: A review of research methods and findings. In K. H. Craik & E. H. Zube (Eds.), *Perceiving environmental quality: Research and applications* (pp. 205–228). New York: Plenum.

Cousins, J. H., Siegel, A. W., & Maxwell, S. E. (1983). Wayfinding and cognitive mapping in large-scale environments: A test of a developmental model. *Journal of Experimental Child Psychology, 35*, 120.

Covington, J., & Taylor, R. (1989). Gentrification and crime: Robbery and larceny changes in appreciating Baltimore neighborhoods during the 1970s. *Urban Affairs Quarterly, 25*, 140–170.

Cox, V. C., Paulus, P. B., & McCain, G. (1984). Prison crowding research: The relevance for prison housing standards and a general approach regarding crowding phenomena. *American Psychologist, 39*, 1148–1160.

Cox, V. C., Paulus, P. B., McCain, G., & Karlovac, M. (1982). The relationship between crowding and health. In A. Baum & J. E. Singer (Eds.), *Advances in environmental psychology* (Vol. 4, pp. 271–294). Hillsdale, NJ: Erlbaum.

Cozby, P. C. (1993). *Methods in behavioral research* (5th ed.). Mountain View, CA: Mayfield Publishing.

Craig, A. D., & Bushnell, M. C. (1994). The thermal grill illusion: Unmasking the burn of cold pain. *Science, 265*, 252–255.

Craig, K. J., Cruikshank, M., Gabelnick, D. A., & Baum, A. (1992, August). *Age, coping, and chronic stress following traumatic events.* Symposium at the annual meeting of the American Psychological Association, Washington, DC.

Craik, K. H. (1983). The psychology of the large-scale environment. In N. R. Feimer & E. S. Geller (Eds.), *Environmental psychology: directions and perspectives* (pp. 67–105). New York: Praeger.

Craik, K. H., & Appleyard, D. (1980). Streets of San Francisco: Brunswik's lens model applied to urban inference and assessment. *Journal of Social Issues, 36*, 72–85.

Craik, K. H., & Feimer, N. R. (1987). Environmental assessment. In D. Stokols & I. Altman (Eds.), *Handbook of environmental psychology*, (pp. 891–918). New York: Wiley.

Craik, K. H., & Zube, E. H. (1976). *Perceiving environmental quality: Research and applications.* New York: Plenum.

Cranz, G. (1982). *The politics of park design: A history of urban parks in America.* Cambridge, MA: M.I.T. Press.

Crawshaw, R. (1963). Reactions to a disaster. *Archives of General Psychiatry, 9*, 157–162.

Crockford, G. W. (1967). Heat problems and protective clothing in iron and steel works. In C. N. Davies, P. R. Davis, & F. H. Tyter (Eds.), *The effects of abnormal physical conditions at work* (pp. 144–156). London: E & S Livingstone.

Crook, M. A., & Langdon, F. J. (1974). The effects of aircraft noise on schools in the vicinity of the London Airport. *Journal of Sound and Vibration, 34*, 241–248.

Crouch, A., & Nimran, U. (1989). Perceived facilitators and inhibitors of work performance in an office environment. *Environment and Behavior, 21*, 206–226.

Crowe, M. J. (1968). Toward a "definitional model" of public perceptions of air pollution. *Journal of the Air Pollution Control Association, 18*, 154–157.

Crowe, T. (1991). *Crime prevention through environmental design: Applications of architectural design and space management concepts.* Boston: National Crime Prevention Institute/Butterworth-Heinemann.

Crozier, W. R., & Burgess, G. (1992). The influence of type of accommodation upon the spontaneous self-concept of the elderly. *Journal of Environmental Psychology, 12*, 129–133.

Crump, S. L., Nunes, D. L., & Crossman, E. K. (1977). The effects of litter on littering behavior in a forest environment. *Environment and Behavior, 9*, 137–146.

Csikszentmihalyi, M., & Kleiber, D. A. (1991). Leisure and self-actualization. In B. L. Driver, P. J. Brown, & G. L. Peterson (Eds.), *Benefits of leisure* (pp. 91–102). State College, PA: Venture Publishing, Inc.

Culver, R., Rotton, J., & Kelly, I. W. (1988). Geophysical variables and behavior: XLIX. Moon myths and mechanisms:

A critical examination of purported explanations of lunar-lunacy relations. *Psychological Reports, 62,* 683–710.

Cunningham, M. R. (1979). Weather, mood, and helping behavior: Quasi experiments with the sunshine Samaritan. *Journal of Personality and Social Psychology, 37,* 1947–1956.

Cunningham, M. R., Steinberg, J., & Grev, R. (1980). Wanting to and having to help: Separate motivations for positive mood and guilt-induced helping. *Journal of Personality and Social Psychology, 38,* 181–192.

Cuthbertson, B. H., & Nigg, J. M. (1987). Technological disaster and the nontherapeutic community: A question of true victimization. *Environment and Behavior, 19,* 462–483.

Cziffra, P., Graydon, E., Klath, N., & Wiggens, T. (1975). *Science and technology libraries space report.* Princeton, NJ: Princeton University Library.

Dabbs, J., Fuller, P., & Carr, S. (1973, August). *Personal space when cornered: College students and prison inmates.* Paper presented at the meeting of the American Psychological Association, Montreal, Canada.

Dabbs, J. M. (1971). Physical closeness and negative feelings. *Psychonomic Science, 23,* 141–143.

Dahlof, L., Hard, E., & Larsson, K. (1977). Influence of maternal stress on offspring sexual behavior. *Animal Behavior, 25,* 958–963.

Dalholm, E. H., & Rydberg-Mitchell, B. (1992). Communicating with lay people: Architecture & comportment/Architecture & behavior. *Architecture & Behavior, 8,* 241–262.

Damon, A. (1977). The residential environment, health, and behavior. Simple research opportunities, strategies, and some findings in the Solomon Islands and Boston, Massachusetts. In L. E. Hinckle, Jr., & W. C. Loring (Eds.), *The effect of the man-made environment on health and behavior.* Atlanta: Center for Disease Control, Public Health Service.

Daniel, T. C., & Boster, R. S. (1976). *Measuring landscape aesthetics: The scenic beauty estimation method* (Research Paper RM-167). Ft. Collins, CO: USDA Forest Service, Rocky Mountain Forest and Range Experiment Station.

Daniel, T. C., & Schroeder, H. (1979). Scenic beauty estimation model: Predicting scenic beauty of our national landscape. In G. H. Elsner & R. C. Smardon (Tech. Coords.), *Our national landscape* (pp. 524–531). General Technical Report No. PSW-35. Berkeley, CA: U.S. Department of Agriculture, Pacific Southwest Forest and Range Experiment Station.

Daniel, T. C., & Vining, J. (1983). Methodological issues in the assessment of landscape quality. In I. Altman & J. F. Wohlwill (Eds.), *Behavior and the natural environment* (pp. 39–84). New York: Plenum.

Darley, J. M., & Latané, B. (1968). Bystander intervention in emergencies: Diffusion of responsibility. *Journal of Personality and Social Psychology, 8,* 377–383.

Dart, F. E., & Pradham, P. L. (1967). The cross cultural teaching of science. *Science, 155,* 649–656.

Darwin, C. (1859). *On the origin of species.* London: Murray.

D'Atri, D. A., Fitzgerald, E. F., Kasl, S. V., & Ostfeld, A. M. (1981). Crowding in prison: The relationship between changes in housing mode and blood pressure. *Psychosomatic Medicine, 43,* 95–105.

Daves, W. F., & Swaffer, P. W. (1971). Effect of room size on critical interpersonal distance. *Perceptual and Motor Skills, 33,* 926.

Davidson, L. M., & Baum, A. (1986). Chronic stress and post traumatic stress disorders. *Journal of Consulting and Clinical Psychology, 54,* 303–308.

Davidson, L. M., Baum, A., & Collins, D. L. (1982). Stress and control-related problems at Three Mile Island. *Journal of Applied Social Psychology, 12,* 349–359.

Davidson, L. M., Fleming, I., & Baum, A. (1986). Post-traumatic stress as a function of chronic stress and toxic expo-

sures. In C. Figley (Ed.), *Trauma and its wake* (pp. 55–77). New York: Brunner Mazel.

Davidson, L. M., Fleming, R., & Baum, A. (1987). Chronic stress, catecholamines, and sleep disturbance at Three Mile Island. *Journal of Human Stress, 13,* 75–83.

Davies, D. R., & Hockey, G. R. J. (1966). The effects of noise and doubling the signal frequency on individual differences in visual vigilance performance. *British Journal of Psychology, 57,* 381–389.

Davis, B. (1989, January 5). Mars could become the place to live, but it needs work. *The Wall Street Journal,* pp. A1, A8.

Davis, D. D. (1986). *Managing technological innovation.* San Francisco, CA: Josey-Bass.

Davis, G., & Ayers, V. (1975). Photographic recording of environmental behavior. In W. Michelson (Ed.), *Behavioral research methods in environmental design* (pp. 235–279). Stroudsburg, PA: Dowden, Hutchinson & Ross.

Davis, G. E. (1977). *Crowding and helping: An empirical test of the social overload hypothesis.* Doctoral dissertion, State University of New York–Stony Brook.

Davis, K. A. (1972). *World urbanization 1950–1970* (Vol. 2). Berkeley: Institute of International Studies.

Davis, K. A. (1973). Introduction. In K. Davis (Ed.), *Cities.* San Francisco: Freeman.

Dawes, R. M., McTavish, J., & Shaklee, H. (1977). Behavior, communication and assumptions about other people's behaviors in a commons dilemma situation. *Journal of Personality and Social Psychology, 35,* 1–11.

Day, K. (1994). Conceptualizing women's fear of sexual assault on campus: A review of causes and recommendations for change. *Environment and Behavior, 26,* 742–765.

Day, L. L. (1992). Placemaking by design: Fitting a large new building into a historic district. *Environment and Behavior, 24,* 326–346.

Dean, L., Pugh, W., & Gunderson, E. (1975). Spatial and perceptual components of crowding: Effects on health and satisfaction. *Environment and Behavior, 7,* 225–236.

Dean, L., Pugh, W., & Gunderson, E. (1978). The behavioral effects of crowding. *Environment and Behavior, 10,* 419–431.

Dean, L. M., Willis, F. N., & Hewitt, J. (1975). Initial interaction distance among individuals equal and unequal in military rank. *Journal of Personality and Social Psychology, 32,* 294–299.

Decker, J. (1994). The validation of computer simulations for design guideline dispute resolution. *Environment and Behavior, 26,* 421–443.

DeFronzo, J. (1984). Climate and crime: Tests of an FBI assumption. *Environment and Behavior, 16,* 185–210.

DeGiovanni, F. F., & Paulson, N. A. (1984). Household diversity in revitalizing neighborhoods. *Urban Affairs Quarterly, 20*(2), 211–232.

DeGroot, I. (1967). Trends in public attitudes toward air pollution. *Journal of the Air Pollution Control Association, 17,* 679–681.

De Jonge, D. (1962). Images of urban areas. *Journal of American Institute of Planners, 28,* 266–276.

DeLoache, J. S. (1987). Rapid change in the functioning of very young children. *Science, 238,* 1556–1557.

DeLong, A. J. (1973). Kinesic signals at utterance boundaries in preschool children. *Dissertation Abstracts, 33.*

Denison, D. M., Ledwith, F., & Poulton, E. C. (1966). Complex reaction times at simulated cabin altitudes of 5,000 ft. and 8,000 ft. *Aerospace Medicine, 37,* 1010.

Dennis, M. L., Soderstrom, E. J., Koncinski, W. S., & Cavanaugh, B. (1990). Effective dissemination of energy-related information: Applying social psychology and evaluation research. *American Psychologist, 45,* 1109–1117.

Dennis, W. (1966). *Group values through children's drawings.* New York: McGraw-Hill.

Derogatis, L. R. (1977). *The SCL-90 Manual 1: Scoring, admin-*

istration, and procedures for the SCL-90. Baltimore: Johns Hopkins University School of Medicine, Clinical Psychometrics Unit.

DeSanctis, M., Halcomb, C. G., & Fedoravicius, A. S. (1981). *Meteorological determinants of human behavior: A holistic environmental perspective with special reference to air ionization and electrical field effects*. Unpublished manuscript, Texas Tech University, Lubbock, TX.

Desor, J. A. (1972). Toward a psychological theory of crowding. *Journal of Personality and Social Psychology, 21*, 79–83.

Devlin, A. S. (1976). The small-town cognitive map: Adjusting to a new environment. In G. T. Moore & R. G. Golledge (Eds.), *Environmental knowing* (pp. 58–66). Stroudsburg, PA: Dowden, Hutchinson, & Ross.

Devlin, A. S. (1992). Psychiatric ward renovation: Staff perception and patient behavior. *Environment and Behavior, 24*, 66–84.

Devlin, K. (1990). An examination of architectural interpretation: Architects versus non-architects. *Journal of Architectural and Planning Research, 7*, 235–244.

Devlin, K., & Nasar, J. L. (1989). The beauty and the beast: Some preliminary comparisons of "high" versus popular residential architecture and public versus architect judgements of same. *Journal of Environmental Psychology, 9*, 333–344.

Dew, M. A., Bromet, E. J., & Schulberg, H. C. (1987). Application of a temporal persistence model to community residents' long-term beliefs about the Three Mile Island nuclear accident. *Journal of Applied Social Psychology, 17*, 1071–1091.

Dexter, E. (1904). School deportment and weather. *Educational Review, 19*, 160–168.

DeYoung, R. (1986). Some psychological aspects of recycling: The structure of conservation satisfactions. *Environment and Behavior, 18*, 435–449.

DeYoung, R., Duncan, A., Frank, J., Gill, N., Rothman, S., Shenot, J., Shotkin, A., & Zweizig, M. (1993). Promoting source reduction behavior: The role of motivational behavior. *Environment and Behavior, 25*, 70–85.

Dickason, J. D. (1983). The origin of the playground: The role of the Boston women's clubs, 1885–1890. *Leisure Sciences, 6*, 83–98.

Dickson, D. (1987). Adjusting to an aging population. *Science, 236*, 772–773.

Dienstbier, R. A. (1989). Arousal and physiological toughness: Implications for mental and physical health. *Psychological Review, 96*, 84–100.

Dietrick, B. (1977, November). *The environment and burglary victimization in a metropolitan suburb*. Paper presented at the annual meeting of the American Society of Criminology, Atlanta, Georgia.

Dill, C. A., Gilden, E. R., Hill, P. C., & Hanselka, L. L. (1982). Federal human subjects regulations: A methodological artifact? *Personality and Social Psychology Bulletin, 8*, 417–425.

Dillman, D., & Tremblay, K., Jr. (1977). The quality of life in rural America. *Annals of the American Academy of Political and Social Sciences, 429*, 115–129.

Ditton, R. B., Fedler, A. J., & Graefe, A. R. (1982). Assessing recreational satisfaction among diverse participant groups. *Forest and river recreation: Research update*. St. Paul, MN: The University of Minnesota Agriculture Research Station.

Dohrenwend, B. S., & Dohrenwend, B. P. (1972). Psychiatric disorder in urban settings. In G. Caplan (Ed.), *American handbook of psychiatry* (Vol. 3, Rev. ed.). Warheit, NY: Basic Books.

Dohrenwend, B. P., Dohrenwend, B. S., Kasl, S. V., & Warheit, G. J. (1979). *Report of the Task Group on Behavioral Effects to the President's Commission on the Accident at Three Mile Island* (pp. 18–21). Washington, DC.

Dollinger, S. J., & Cramer, P. (1990). Children's defensive responses and emotional upset following a disaster: A projective assessment. *Journal of Personality Assessment, 541*, 116–127.

Donnerstein, E., & Wilson, D. W. (1976). Effects of noise and perceived control on ongoing and subsequent aggressive behavior. *Journal of Personality and Social Psychology, 34*, 774–781.

Dooley, B. B. (1974). *Crowding stress: The effects of social density on men with "close" or "far" personal space*. Unpublished doctoral dissertation, University of California at Los Angeles.

Dooley, D., Rook, K., & Catalano, R. (1987). Job and non-job stressors and their moderators. *Journal of Occupational Psychology, 60*, 115–132.

Doring, H. J., Hauf, G., & Seiberling, M. (1980). Effects of high intensity sound on the contractile function of the isolated ileum of guinea pigs and rabbits. In *Noise as a public health problem, Proceedings of the Third International Congress* (ASHA Report No. 10). Rockville, MD: American Speech and Hearing Association.

Dornic, S., & Ekehammar, B. (1990). Extraversion, neuroticism, and noise sensitivity. *Personality and Individual Differences, 11*, 989–992.

Downs, R. M., & Stea, D. (1977). *Maps in minds: Reflections on cognitive mapping*. New York: Harper & Row.

Drabek, T., & Quarantelli, E. (1967). Scapegoats, villains, and disasters. *Trans-Action, 4*, 12–17.

Drabek, T. E., & Stephenson, J. S. (1971). When disaster strikes. *Journal of Applied Social Psychology, 1*, 187–203.

Driver, B. L. (1972). Potential contributions of psychology to recreation resource management. In J. Wohlwill & D. H. Carson (Eds.), *Environment and the social sciences: Perspectives and applications* (pp. 233–244). Washington, DC: American Psychological Association.

Driver, B. L. (1975). Quantification of outdoor recreationists' preferences. In *Research camping and environmental education* (Pennsylvania State Series II). University Park, PA: Pennsylvania State University.

Driver, B. L., & Brown, P. J. (1983). Contributions of behavioral scientists to recreation resource management. In I. Altman & J. F. Wohlwill (Eds.), *Behavior and the environment* (pp. 307–339). New York: Plenum.

Driver, B. L., & Knopf, R. C. (1976). Temporary escape: One product of sport fisheries management. *Fisheries, 1*, 21–29.

Driver, B. L., & Knopf, R. C. (1977). Personality, outdoor recreation, and expected consequences. *Environment and Behavior, 9*, 169–193.

Driver, B. L., & Rosenthal, D. H. (1982). *Measuring and improving the effectiveness of public outdoor recreation programs*. Washington, DC: George Washington University Press.

Dubos, R. (1965). *Man adapting*. New Haven, CT: Yale University Press.

Duffy, M., Bailey, S., Beck, B., & Barker, D.G. (1986). Preferences in nursing home design: A comparison of residents, administrators, and designers. *Environment and Behavior, 18*, 246–257.

Duke, M. P., & Nowicki, S. (1972). A new measure and social learning model for interpersonal distance. *Journal of Experimental Research in Personality, 6*, 119–132.

Duke, M. P., & Wison, J. (1973). The measurement of interpersonal distance in pre-school children. *Journal of Genetic Psychology, 123*, 361–362.

Duncan, J., Jr. (1973). Landscape taste as a symbol of group identity: A Westchester County village. *The Geographical Review, 63*, 334–355.

Duncan, J. S. (1985). The house as a symbol of social structure: Notes on the language of objects among collectivistic groups. In I. Altman & C. M. Werner (Eds.), *Home environments* (pp. 133–151). New York: Plenum.

Dunlap, R. E. (Ed.). (1980, September/October). Ecology and the social sciences: An emerging paradigm. *American Behavioral Scientist, 24*, 1–149.

Dunlap, R. E., & Scarce, R. (1991). The polls-poll trends:

Environmental problems and protection. *Public Opinion Quarterly, 55,* 651–672.

Dunlap, R. E., & Van Liere, K. D. (1978, Summer). The "New Environmental Paradigm": A proposed measuring instrument and preliminary results. *Journal of Environmental Education, 9,* 10–19.

Dunlap, R. E., & Van Liere, K. D. (1984). Commitment to the dominant social paradigm and concern for environmental quality. *Social Science Quarterly, 65,* 1013–1028.

Duvall, D., & Booth, A. (1978). The housing environment and women's health. *Journal of Health and Social Behavior, 19,* 410–417.

Dwyer, W. O., Leeming, F. C., Cobern, M. K., Porter, B. E., & Jackson, J. M. (1993). Critical review of behavioral interventions to preserve the environment: Research since 1980. *Environment and Behavior, 25,* 275–321.

Dyson, M. L., & Passmore, N. I. (1992). Inter-male spacing and aggression in African painted reed frogs, *Hyperolius marmoratus. Ethology, 91,* 237–247.

Eagly, A. H., & Chaiken, S. (1993). *The psychology of attitudes.* Fort Worth, TX: Harcourt Brace Jovanovich.

Earls, R., Smith, E., Reich, W., & Jung, K. G. (1988). Investigating psychopathological consequences of a disaster in children: A pilot study incorporating a structured diagnostic interview. *Journal of the American Academy of Child and Adolescent Psychiatry, 27,* 90–95.

Easterbrook, J. A. (1959). The effects of emotion on cue-utilization and the organization of behavior. *Psychological Review, 66,* 183–201.

Ebbesen, E. B., Kjos, G. L., & Konecni, V. J. (1976). Spatial ecology: Its effects on the choice of friends and enemies. *Journal of Experimental Social Psychology, 12,* 505–518.

Eberts, E. H., & Lepper, M. R. (1975). Individual consistency in the proxemic behavior of pre-school children. *Journal of Personality and Social Psychology, 32,* 481–489.

Eckenrode, J., & Gore, S. (1981). Stressful events and social supports: The significance of context. In B. H. Gottlieb (Ed.), *Social networks and social support* (pp. 43–68). Beverly Hills, CA: Sage.

Edmonds, E. M., & Smith, L. R. (1985). Students' performance as a function of sex, noise, and intelligence. *Psychological Reports, 56,* 727–730.

Edney, J. J. (1972). Property, possession and permanence: A field study in human territoriality. *Journal of Applied Social Psychology, 2,* 275–282.

Edney, J. J. (1974). Human territoriality. *Psychological Bulletin, 81,* 959–975.

Edney, J. J. (1975). Territoriality and control: A field experiment. *Journal of Personality and Social Psychology, 31,* 1108–1115.

Edney, J. J. (1976). Human territories: Comment on functional properties. *Environment and Behavior, 8,* 31–48.

Edney, J. J. (1979). The nuts game: A concise commons dilemma analogue. *Environmental Psychology and Nonverbal Behavior, 3,* 252–254.

Edney, J. J. (1980). The commons problem: Alternative perspectives. *American Psychologist, 35,* 131–150.

Edney, J. J. (1981). Paradoxes on the commons: Scarcity and the problem of equality. *Journal of Community Psychology, 9,* 3–34.

Edney, J. J., & Bell, P. A. (1983). The commons dilemma: Comparing altruism, the Golden Rule, perfect equality of outcomes, and territoriality. *The Social Science Journal, 20,* 23–33.

Edney, J. J., & Bell, P. A. (1984). Sharing scarce resources: Group-outcome orientation, external disaster, and stealing in a simulated commons. *Small Group Behavior, 15,* 87–108.

Edney, J. J., & Bell, P. A. (1987). Freedom and equality in a simulated commons. *Political Psychology, 8,* 229–243.

Edney, J. J., & Harper, C. S. (1978a). Heroism in a resource crisis: A simulation study. *Environmental Management, 2,* 523–527.

Edney, J. J., & Harper, C. S. (1978b). The effects of information in a resource management problem: A social trap analog. *Human Ecology, 6,* 387–395.

Edney, J. J., & Uhlig, S. R. (1977). Individual and small group territories. *Small Group Behavior, 8,* 457–468.

Edwards, D. J. A. (1972). Approaching the unfamiliar: A study of human interaction distances. *Journal of Behavioral Sciences, 1,* 249–250.

Edwards, D. J. A. (1973). A cross-cultural study of social orientation and distance schemata by the method of doll placement. *Journal of Social Psychology, 89,* 165–173.

Efran, M. G., & Cheyne, J. A. (1973). Shared space: The cooperative control of spatial areas by two interacting individuals. *Canadian Journal of Behavioral Science, 5,* 201–210.

Efran, M. G., & Cheyne, J. A. (1974). Affective concomitants of the invasion of shared space: Behavioral, physiological, and verbal indicators. *Journal of Personality and Social Psychology, 29,* 219–226.

Eggertsen, R., Svensson, A., Magnusson, M., & Andren, L. (1987). Hemodynamic effects of loud noise before and after central sympathetic nervous stimulation. *Acta Medica Scandinavica, 221,* 159–164.

Ehrlich, P. (1968). *The population boom.* New York: Ballantine.

Eibl-Eibesfeldt, I. (1970). *Ethology: The biology of behavior.* New York: Holt, Rinehart and Winston.

Ellis, P., & Gashell, G. (1978). *A review of social research on the individual energy consumer.* Unpublished manuscript.

Ellsworth, P. C. (1977, August). *Some questions about the role of arousal in the interpretation of direct gaze.* Paper presented at the meeting of the American Psychological Association, San Francisco, CA.

Engen, T. (1982). *The perception of odor.* Reading, MA: Addison-Wesley.

EPA, Environmental Protection Agency (1972). *Report to the President and Congress on noise.* Washington, DC: U.S. Government Printing Office.

Epstein, Y. M., & Karlin, R. A. (1975). Effects of acute experimental crowding. *Journal of Applied Social Psychology, 5,* 34–53.

Erikson, K. T. (1976). Loss of communality at Buffalo Creek. *American Journal of Psychiatry, 133,* 302–305.

Ernsting, J. (1963). The ideal relationship between inspired oxygen concentration and cabin altitude. *Aerospace Medicine, 34,* 991–997.

Ernsting, J. (1967). Physiological hazards of low pressure. In C. N. Davies, P. R. Davis, & F. H. Tyrer (Eds.), *The effects of abnormal physical conditions at work* (pp. 90–100). London: E & S Livingstone.

Esser, A. H. (1976). Discussion of papers presented in the symposium "Theoretical and empirical issues with regard to privacy, territoriality, personal space, and crowding." *Environment and Behavior, 8,* 117–125.

Esser, A. H., Chamberlain, A. S., Chapple, E. P., & Kline, N. S. (1965). Territoriality of patients on a research ward. In J. Wortis (Ed.), *Recent advances in biological psychiatry.* New York: Plenum.

Evans, G. W. (1978). Human spatial behavior: The arousal model. In A. Baum & Y. Epstein (Eds.), *Human response to crowding* (pp. 283–302). Hillsdale, NJ: Erlbaum.

Evans, G. W. (1979a). Behavioral and physiological consequences of crowding in humans. *Journal of Applied Social Psychology, 9,* 27–46.

Evans, G. W. (1979b). Design implications of spatial research. In J. Aiello & A. Baum (Eds.), *Residential crowding and design* (pp. 197–215). New York: Plenum.

Evans, G. W. (1980). Environmental cognition. *Psychological Bulletin, 88,* 259–287.

Evans, G. W., Brennan, P. L., Skorpanich, M. A., & Held, D. (1984). Cognitive mapping and elderly adults: Verbal and location memory for urban landmarks. *Journal of Gerontology, 39*, 452–457.

Evans, G. W., & Cohen, S. (1987). Environmental stress. In D. Stokols & I. Altman (Eds.), *Handbook of environmental psychology* (Vol. 1, pp. 571–610). New York: Wiley-Interscience.

Evans, G. W., Fellows, J., Zorn, M., & Doty, K. (1980). Cognitive mapping and architecture. *Journal of Applied Psychology, 65*, 474–478.

Evans, G. W., & Howard, H. R. B. (1972). A methodological investigation of personal space. In W. J. Mitchell (Ed.), *Environmental design: Research and practice, Proceedings of EDRA3/AR8 Conference*. Los Angeles: University of California.

Evans, G. W., & Howard, R. B. (1973). Personal space. *Psychological Bulletin, 80*, 334–344.

Evans, G. W., Hygge, S., & Bullinger, M. (1993). *Psychology and the environment*. Unpublished manuscript, Cornell University.

Evans, G. W., & Jacobs, S. V. (1981). Air pollution and human behavior. *Journal of Social Issues, 37*, 95–125.

Evans, G. W., & Jacobs, S. V. (1982). Air pollution and human behavior. In G. W. Evans (Ed.), *Environmental stress* (pp. 105–132). Cambridge: Cambridge University Press.

Evans, G. W., Jacobs, S. V., Dooley, D., & Catalano, R. (1987). The interaction of stressful life events and chronic strains on community mental health. *American Journal of Community Psychology, 15*, 23–34.

Evans, G. W., Jacobs, S., & Frager, N. (1979, August). *Human adaptation to photochemical smog*. Paper presented at the meeting of the American Psychological Association, New York, NY.

Evans, G. W., Jacobs, S. V., & Frager, N. B. (1982). Behavioral responses to air pollution. In A. Baum & J. Singer (Eds.), *Advances in environmental psychology* (Vol. 4, pp. 237–270). Hillsdale, NJ: Erlbaum.

Evans, G. W., & Lepore, S. J. (1992). Conceptual and analytic issues in crowding research. *Journal of Environmental Psychology, 12*, 163–173.

Evans, G. W., & Lepore, S. J. (1993). Household crowding and social support: A quasi-experimental analysis. *Journal of Personality and Social Psychology, 65*, 308–316.

Evans, G. W., & Lovell, B. (1979). Design modification in an open-plan school. *Journal of Educational Psychology, 71*, 41–49.

Evans, G. W., Marrero, D. G., & Butler, P. A. (1981). Environmental learning and cognitive mapping. *Environment and Behavior, 13*, 83–104.

Evans, G. W., Palsane, M. N., Lepore, S. J., & Martin, J. (1989). Residential density and psychological health: The mediating effects of social support. *Journal of Personality and Social Psychology, 57*, 994–999.

Evans, G. W., & Pezdek, K. (1980). Cognitive mapping: Knowledge of real-world distance and location. *Journal of Experimental Psychology: Human Learning & Memory, 6*, 13–24.

Evans, G. W., Smith, C., & Pezdek, K. (1982). Cognitive maps and urban form. *American Planning Association Journal, 48*, 232–244.

Ewert, A. W. (1994). Playing the edge: Motivation and risk taking in a high-altitude wildernesslike environment. *Environment and Behavior, 26*, 3–24.

Eyles, J., Taylor, S. M., Johnson, N., & Baxter, J. (1993). Worrying about waste: Living close to solid waste disposal facilities in Southern Ontario. *Social Science and Medicine, 37*, 805–812.

Eysenck, M. W. (1975). Interactive effects of noise, activation level and dominance in memory latencies. *Journal of Experimental Psychology, 104*, 143–148.

Fagan, G., & Aiello, J. R. (1982). Development of personal space among Puerto Ricans. *Journal of Non-Verbal Behavior, 7*, 59–68.

Fanger, P. O., Breum, N. O., & Jerking, E. (1977). Can colour and noise influence man's thermal comfort? *Ergonomics, 20*, 11–18.

Faupel, C. E., & Styles, S. P. (1993). Disaster education, household preparedness, and stress responses following hurricane Hugo. *Environment and Behavior, 25*, 228–249.

Fazio, R. H. (1990). Multiple processes by which attitudes guide behavior: The MODE model as an integrative framework. In M. P. Zanna (Ed.), *Advances in experimental social psychology* (pp. 75–109). San Diego, CA: Academic Press.

Fazio, R. H., Chen, J., McDonel, E. C., Sherman, S. J. (1982). Attitude accessibility, and the strength of the object-evaluation association. *Journal of Experimental Social Psychology, 18*, 339–357.

Fazio, R. H., Sanbonmatsu, D. M., Powell, M. C., & Kardes, F. R. (1986). On the automatic activation of attitudes. *Journal of Personality and Social Psychology, 50*, 229–238.

Fazio, R. H., & Zanna, M. P. (1981). Direct experience and attitude–behavior consistency. *Advances in Experimental Social Psychology, 14*, 161–202.

Feather, N. T. (1961). The relationship of persistence at a task to expectation of success and achievement-related motives. *Journal of Abnormal and Social Psychology, 63*, 552–561.

Federal Bureau of Investigation (1981). *Uniform crime reports*. Washington, DC: U.S. Government Printing Office.

Fein, G. G., Schwartz, P. M., Jacobson, S. W., & Jacobson, J. L. (1983). Environmental toxins and behavioral development: A new role for psychological research. *American Psychologist, 38*, 118–119.

Feldman, R. M. (1990). Settlement-identity: Psychological bonds with home place in a mobile society. *Environment and Behavior, 22*, 183–229.

Felipe, N. J., & Sommer, R. (1966). Invasions of personal space. *Social Problems, 14*, 206–214.

Feller, R. A. (1968). Effect of varying corridor illumination on noise level in a residence hall. *The Journal of College Personnel, 9*, 150–152.

Festinger, L. A. (1954). A theory of social comparison processes. *Human Relations, 7*, 117–140.

Festinger, L. A. (1957). *A theory of cognitive dissonance*. Stanford, CA: Stanford University Press.

Festinger, L., Pepitone, A., & Newcomb, T. (1952). Some consequences of deindividuation in a group. *Journal of Abnormal and Social Psychology, 47*, 382–389.

Festinger, L. A., Schachter, S., & Back, K. (1950). *Social pressures in informal groups*. New York: Harper & Row.

Fidell, S., Barber, D., & Schultz, T. (1991). Revision of a dosage-effect relationship for the prevalence of annoyance due to general transportation noise. *Journal of the Acoustical Society of America, 89*, 221–233.

Fidell, S., & Silvati, L. (1991). An assessment of the effect of residential acoustic insulation on prevalence of annoyance in an airport community. *Journal of the Acoustical Society of America, 89*, 244–247.

Finckle, A. L., & Poppen, J. R. (1948). Clinical effects of noise and mechanical vibrations of a turbo-jet engine on man. *Journal of Applied Physiology, 1*, 183–204.

Fine, T. H., & Turner, J. W., Jr. (1982). The effect of brief restricted environmental stimulation therapy in the treatment of essential hypertension. *Behavior Research and Therapy, 20*, 567–570.

Fines, K. D. (1968). *Landscape evaluation: A research project in East Sussex*. Elmsford, NY: Pergamon.

Finnie, W. C. (1973). Field experiments in litter control. *Environment and Behavior, 5*, 123–144.

Fischer, C. S. (1973). Urban malaise. *Social Forces, 52*, 221–235.

Fischer, C. S. (1976). *The urban experience*. New York: Harcourt Brace Jovanovich.

Fischer, C. S. (1984). A phenomenological study of being criminally victimized: Contributions and constraints of qualitative research. *Journal of Social Issues, 40,* 161–178.

Fishbein, M., & Azjen, I. (1975). *Belief, attitude, intention, and behavior: An introduction to theory and research.* Reading, PA: Addison-Wesley.

Fisher, B., & Nasar, J. L. (1992). Fear of crime in relation to three exterior site features: Prospect, refuge, and escape. *Environment and Behavior, 24,* 35–56.

Fisher, D. L. (1993). Optimal performance engineering: Good, better, best. *Human Factors, 35,* 115–139.

Fisher, J. D. (1974). Situation-specific variables as determinants of perceived environmental aesthetic quality and perceived crowdedness. *Journal of Research in Personality, 8,* 177–188.

Fisher, J. D., & Baron, R. M. (1982). An equity-based model of vandalism. *Population and Environment, 5,* 182–200.

Fisher, J. D., & Baum, A. (1980). Situational and arousal-based messages and the reduction of crowding stress. *Journal of Applied Social Psychology, 10,* 191–201.

Fisher, J. D., & Byrne, D. (1975). Too close for comfort: Sex differences in response to invasions of personal space. *Journal of Personality and Social Psychology, 32,* 15–21.

Fleming, I. C. (1985). *The stress reducing functions of specific types of social support for victims of a technological catastrophe.* Unpublished doctoral dissertation, University of Maryland, College Park.

Fleming, I., Baum, A., & Weiss, L. (1987). Social density and perceived control as mediators of crowding stress in high-density residential neighborhoods. *Journal of Personality and Social Psychology, 52,* 899–906.

Fleming, R., Baum, A., Gisriel, M. M., & Gatchel, R. J. (1982). Mediation of stress at Three Mile Island by social support. *Journal of Human Stress, 8,* 14–22.

Florig, H. K. (1992). Containing the costs of the EMF problem. *Science, 257,* 468–469ff.

Flynn, C. B. (1979). Three Mile Island telephone survey. U.S. Nuclear Regulatory Commission (NUREF/CR-1093).

Flynn, R. (1995). America's cities: Centers of culture, commerce, and community—or collapsing hope? *Urban Affairs Review, 30,* 635–640.

Fogarty, S. J., & Hemsley, D. R. (1983, March). Depression and the accessibility of memories: A longitudinal study. *British Journal of Psychiatry, 142,* 232–237.

Foley, J. E., & Cohen, A. J. (1984). Working mental representations of the environment. *Environment and Behavior, 16,* 713–729.

Folkman, S. (1984). Personal control and stress and coping processes: A theoretical analysis. *Journal of Personality and Social Psychology, 46,* 839–852.

Forbes, G., & Gromoll, H. (1971). The lost letter technique as a measure of social variables: Some exploratory findings. *Social Forces, 50,* 113–115.

Ford, A. B. (1976). *Urban health in America.* New York: Oxford University Press.

Ford, J. G., & Graves, J. R. (1977). Differences between Mexican-American and white children in interpersonal distance and social touching. *Perceptual and Motor Skills, 45,* 779–785.

Forgays, D. G., & Forgays, D. K. (1992). Creativity enhancement through flotation isolation. *Journal of Environmental Psychology, 12,* 329–335.

Forgays, D. G., Forgays, D. K., Pudvah, M., & Wright, D. (1991). A direct comparison of the "wet" and "dry" flotation environments. *Journal of Environmental Psychology, 11,* 179–187.

Fortenberry, J. H., Maclean, J., Morris, P., & O'Connell, M. (1978). Mode of dress as a perceptual cue to deference. *Journal of Social Psychology, 104,* 139–140.

Fowler, F. J., McCall, M. E., & Mangione, T. W. (1979). *Reducing residential crime and fear: The Hartford neighborhood crime prevention program.* Washington, DC: U.S. Government Printing Office.

Fox, W. F. (1967). Human performance in the cold. *Human Factors, 9,* 203–220.

Foxx, R. M., & Hake, D. F. (1977). Gasoline conservation: A procedure for measuring and reducing the driving of college students. *Journal of Applied Behavior Analysis, 10,* 61–74.

Francis, R. S. (1983). Attitudes toward industrial pollution, strategies for protecting the environment, and environmental–economic trade-offs. *Journal of Applied Social Psychology, 13,* 310–327.

Franck, K. A. (1984). Exorcising the ghost of physical determinism. *Environment and Behavior, 16,* 441–435.

Franck, K. D., Unseld, C. T., & Wentworth, W. E. (1974). *Adaptation of the newcomer: A process of construction.* Unpublished manuscript, City University of New York.

Frank, R. H., & Kaul, J. D. (1978). The Hawthorne experiments: First statistical interpretation. *American Sociological Review, 43,* 623–643.

Franke, F. (1957). The causality of microtine cycles in Germany. *Journal of Wildlife Management, 21,* 113–121.

Frankel, A. S., & Barett, J. (1971). Variation in personal space as a function of authoritarianism, self-esteem, and racial characteristics of a stimulus situation. *Journal of Consulting and Clinical Psychology, 37,* 95–98.

Frankenhaeuser, M. (1971). Behavior and circulating catecholamines. *Brain Research, 31,* 241–262.

Frankenhaeuser, M. (1978). *Coping with stress: A psychobiological approach.* Reports from the Department of Psychology, University of Stockholm, 532.

Frankenhaeuser, M., Jarpe, G., & Mattel, G. (1961). Effects of intravenous infusions of adrenaline and noradrenaline on certain psychological and physiological functions. *Acta Physiologica Scandinavia, 51,* 175–186.

Frankenhaeuser, M., & Lundberg, U. (1977). The influence of cognitive set on performance and arousal under different noise loads. *Motivation and Emotion, 1,* 139–149.

Frazier, K. (1986). *People of Chaco: A canyon and its culture.* New York: Norton.

Freedman, J. L. (1975). *Crowding and behavior.* San Francisco: Freeman.

Freedman, J. L., Birsky, J., & Cavoukian, A. (1980). Environmental determinants of behavioral contagion: Density and number. *Basic and Applied Social Psychology, 1,* 155–161.

Freedman, J. L., Levy, A. S., Buchnan, R. W., & Price, J. (1972). Crowding and human aggressiveness. *Journal of Experimental Social Psychology, 8,* 528–548.

Freedman, J. L., & Perlick, D. (1979). Crowding, contagion, and laughter. *Journal of Experimental Social Psychology, 15,* 295–303.

Freedy, J. R., Shaw, D. L., Jarrell, M. P., & Masters, C. R. (1992). Towards an understanding of the psychological impact of natural disasters: An application of the conservation of resources stress model. *Journal of Traumatic Stress, 5,* 441–454.

Freeman, H. (1978). Mental health and the environment. *British Journal of Psychiatry, 132,* 113–124.

Frese, M. (1985). Stress at work and psychosomatic complaints: A causal interpretation. *Journal of Applied Psychology, 70,* 314–328.

Frey, J., Rotton, J., & Barry, T. (1979). The effects of the full moon on human behavior: Yet another failure to replicate. *Journal of Psychology, 103,* 159–162.

Fried, M. (1963). Grieving for a lost home. In L. J. Duhl (Ed.), *The urban condition* (pp. 151–171). New York: Basic Books.

Fried, M., & Gleicher, P. (1961). Some sources of residential satisfaction in an urban slum. *Journal of the American Institute of Planners, 27,* 305–315.

Frisancho, A. R. (1979). *Human adaptation*. St. Louis: Mosby.

Fritz, C. E., & Marks, E. S. (1954). The NORC studies of human behavior in disaster. *Journal of Social Issues, 10*, 26–41.

Froelicher, V. F., & Froelicher, E. S. (1991). Cardiovascular benefits of physical activity. In B. L. Driver, P. J. Brown, & G. L. Peterson (Eds.), *Benefits of leisure* (pp. 59–72). State College, PA: Venture Publishing.

Frost, J. L., & Klein, B. L. (1979). *Children's play and playgrounds*. Boston: Allyn & Bacon.

Fry, A. M., & Willis, F. N. (1971). Invasion of personal space as a function of the age of the invader. *Psychological Record, 2*, 385–389.

Fuhrer, U., Kaiser, F. G., & Hartig, T. (1993). Place attachment and mobility during leisure time. *Journal of Environmental Psychology, 13*, 309–321.

Fuller, T. D., Edwards, J. N., Sermsri, S., & Vorakitphokatorn, S. (1993). Housing, stress, and physical well-being: Evidence from Thailand. *Social Science and Medicine, 36*, 1417–1428.

Fuller, T. D., Edwards, J. N., Vorakitphokatorn, S., & Sermsri, S. (1993). Household crowding and family relations in Bangkok. *Social Problems, 40*, 410–430.

Fusco, M. E., Bell, P. A., Jorgensen, M. D., & Smith, J. M. (1991). Using a computer to study the commons dilemma. *Simulation & Gaming, 22*, 67–74.

Gaines, T. A. (1991). *The campus as a work of art*. New York: Praeger.

Gale, N., Golledge, R. G., Pelligrino, J. W., & Doherty, S. (1990). The aquisition and integration of route knowledge in an unfamiliar neighborhood. *Journal of Environmental Psychology, 10*, 3–26.

Gallagher, W. (1993). *The power of place: How our surroundings shape our thoughts, emotions, and actions*. New York: Poseidon Press/Simon & Schuster.

Gallant, S. J., Hamilton, J. A., Popiel, D. A., & Morokoff, P. J. (1991). Daily moods and symptoms: Effects of awareness of study focus, gender, menstrual cycle phase, and day of the week. *Health Psychology, 10*, 180–189.

Galle, O. R., & Gove, W. R. (1979). Crowding and behavior in Chicago, 1940–1970. In J. R. Aiello & A. Baum (Eds.), *Residential crowding and design* (pp. 23–39). New York: Plenum.

Galle, O. R., Gove, W. R., & McPherson, J. M. (1972). Population density and pathology: What are the relationships for man? *Science, 176*, 23–30.

Galloway, W. et al. (1974). Cited in J. Ralof (Ed.), Occupational noise—the subtle pollutant. *Science News, 121*(21), 347–350.

Galster, G., & Hesser, G. (1981). Residential satisfaction: Compositional and contextual correlates. *Environment and Behavior, 13*, 735–759.

Ganellen, R. J., & Blaney, P. H. (1984). Hardiness and social support as mediators of the effects of life stress. *Journal of Personality and Social Psychology, 47*, 156–163.

Gans, H. J. (1962). *The Organvillagers*. New York: Free Press.

Gans, H. J. (1967). *The Levittowners: Ways of life in a new suburban community*. New York: Random House.

Garber, J., & Seligman, M. E. P. (Eds.). (1981). *Human helplessness: Theory and applications*. New York: Academic Press.

Garcia, K. D., & Wierwille, W. W. (1985). Effects of glare on performance of VDT reading-comprehension task. *Human Factors, 27*, 163–173.

Gardner, G. T. (1978). Effects of federal human subjects regulations on data obtained in environmental stress research. *Journal of Personality and Social Psychology, 36*, 628–634.

Garland, H., & Pearce, J. (1967). Neurological complications of carbon monoxide poisoning. *Quarterly Journal of Medicine, 36*, 445–455.

Gärling, T., Böök, A., & Ergezen, N. (1982). Memory for the spatial layout of the everyday physical environment. *Scandinavian Journal of Psychology, 23*, 23–35.

Gärling, T., Böök, A., & Lindberg, E. (1984). Cognitive mapping of large-scale environments: The interrelationship between action plans, acquisition, and orientation. *Environment and Behavior, 16*, 3–34.

Gärling, T., Böök, A., & Lindberg, E. (1986). Spatial orientation and wayfinding in the designed environment: A conceptual analysis and some suggestions for postoccupany evaluation. *Journal of Architectural Planning Research, 3*, 55–64.

Gärling, T., & Evans, G. W. (1991). *Environment, cognition, and action*. New York: Oxford University Press.

Gärling, T., & Golledge, R., (Eds.). (1993). *Behaviour and environment: Psychological and geographical approaches*. Amsterdam: North Holland, Elsevier.

Gärling, T., Lindberg, E., Carreiras, M., & Böök, A. (1986). Reference systems in cognitive maps. *Journal of Environmental Psychology, 6*, 1–18.

Garmezy, N., & Rutter, M. (1985). Acute reactions to stress. In M. Rutter & L. Hersov (Eds.), *Child psychiatry: Modern approaches* (2nd ed., pp. 152–176). Oxford: Blackwell Scientific.

Garreau, J. (1991). *Edge city*. New York: Doubleday.

Garzino, S. J. (1982). Lunar effects on mental behavior: A defense of the empirical research. *Environment and Behavior, 4*, 395–417.

Gatchel, R. J., & Newberry, B. (1991). Psychophysiological effects of toxic chemical contamination exposure: A community field study. *Journal of Applied Social Psychology, 21*, 1961–1976.

Gatchel, R. J., Schaeffer, M. A., & Baum, A. (1985). A psychological field study of stress at Three Mile Island. *Psychophysiology, 22*, 175–181.

Gaydos, H. F. (1958). Effect on complex manual performance of cooling the body while maintaining the hands at normal temperatures. *Journal of Applied Physiology, 12*, 373–376.

Gaydos, H. F., & Dusek, E. R. (1958). Effects of localized hand cooling versus total body cooling on manual performance. *Journal of Applied Physiology, 12*, 377–380.

Gee, M. (1994). Questioning the concept of the "user." *Journal of Environmental Psychology, 14*, 113–124.

Geen, R. G. (1984). Preferred stimulation levels in introverts and extroverts: Effects on arousal and performance. *Journal of Personality and Social Psychology, 46*, 1303–1312.

Geen, R. G., & McCown, E. J. (1984). Effects of noise and attack on aggression and physiological arousal. *Motivation and Emotion, 8*, 231–241.

Geen, R. G., & O'Neal, E. C. (1969). Activation of cue-elicited aggression by general arousal. *Journal of Personality and Social Psychology, 11*, 289–292.

Geen, R. G., & O'Neal, E. C. (1976). *Perspectives on aggression*. New York: Academic Press.

Gelfand, D. M., Hartman, D. P., Walder, P., & Page, B. (1973). Who reports shoplifters? A field-experimental study. *Journal of Personality and Social Psychology, 25*, 276–285.

Geller, E. S. (1976). *Behavioral approaches to environmental problem solving: Littering and recycling*. Symposium presentation at the meeting of the Association for the Advancement of Behavior Therapy, New York.

Geller, E. S. (1980). Applications of behavioral analysis for litter control. In D. Glenwik & L. Jason (Eds.), *Behavioral community psychology: Progress and prospects*. New York: Praeger.

Geller, E. S. (1981). Evaluating energy conservation programs: Is verbal report enough? *Journal of Consumer Research, 8*, 331–335.

Geller, E. S. (1987). Environmental psychology and applied behavior analysis: From strange bedfellows to a productive marriage. In D. Stokols & I. Altman (Eds.), *Handbook of environmental psychology* (pp. 361–388). New York: Wiley-Interscience.

Geller, E. S. (1990). Where have all the flowers gone? *Journal of Applied Behavior Analysis, 23*, 269–273.

Geller, E. S., Erickson, J. B., & Buttram, B. A. (1983). Attempts to promote residential water conservation with educational, behavioral, and engineering strategies. *Population and Environment, 6*, 96–112.

Geller, E. S., Mann, M., & Brasted, W. (1977, August). *Trash can design: A determinant of litter-related behavior.* Paper presented at the meeting of the American Psychological Association, San Francisco, CA.

Geller, E. S., Winnett, R. A., & Everett, P. B. (1982). *Preserving the environment: New strategies for behavior change.* New York: Pergamon.

Geller, E. S., Witmer, J. F., & Orebaugh, A. L. (1976). Instructions as a determinant of paper disposal behaviors. *Environment and Behavior, 8*, 417–441.

Geller, E. S., Witmer, J. F., & Tuso, M. E. (1977). Environmental interventions for litter control. *Journal of Applied Psychology, 62*, 344–351.

Gergen, K. J., Gergen, M. K., & Barton, W. H. (1973). Deviance in the dark. *Psychology Today, 7*, 129–130.

Gibbs, J. P. (1971). Suicide. In R. K. Merton & R. A. Nisbet (Eds.), *Contemporary social problems* (3rd ed., pp. 281–321). New York: Harcourt Brace Jovanovich.

Gibbs, L. (1982). *Love Canal: My story.* Albany, NY: SUNY Press.

Gibbs, M. S. (1986). Psychopathological consequences of exposure to toxins in the water supply. In A. H. Lebovits, A. Baum, & J. Singer (Eds.), *Advances in environmental psychology* (pp. 47–70). Hillsdale, NJ: Erlbaum.

Gibson, B., Harris, P., & Werner, C. (1993). Intimacy and personal space: A classroom demonstration. *Teaching of Psychology, 20*, 180–181.

Gibson, B., & Werner, C. (1994). Airport waiting areas as behavior settings: The role of legibility cues in communicating the setting program. *Journal of Personality and Social Psychology, 66*, 1049–1060.

Gibson, J. J. (1950). *The perception of the visual world.* Boston: Houghton Mifflin.

Gibson, J. J. (1966). *The senses considered as perceptual systems.* Boston: Houghton Mifflin.

Gibson, J. J. (1979). *An ecological approach to visual perception.* Boston: Houghton Mifflin.

Giel, R., & Ormel, J. (1977). Crowding and subjective health in the Netherlands. *Social Psychiatry, 12*, 37–42.

Gifford, R. (1987). *Environmental psychology: Principles and practice.* Boston: Allyn & Bacon.

Gifford, R. (1988). Light, decor, arousal, comfort, and communication. *Journal of Environmental Psychology, 8*, 177–189.

Gifford, R., & Peacock, J. (1979). Crowding: More fearsome than crime-provoking? *Psychologia, 22*, 79–83.

Gifford, R., & Sacilotto, P. A. (1993). Social isolation and personal space: A field study. *Canadian Journal of Behavioural Science, 25*, 165–174.

Gifford, R., & Wells, J. (1991). FISH: A commons dilemma simulation. *Behavior Research Methods, Instrumentation, and Computers, 23*, 437–441.

Gilman, B. I. (1916). Museum fatigue. *Scientific Monthly, 12*, 62–64.

Gimblett, R. J., Itami, R. M., & Fitzgibbon, J. E. (1985). Mystery in an information processing model of landscape preference. *Landscape Journal, 4*, 87–95.

Ginsberg, Y. (1975). *Jews in a changing neighborhood.* New York: Free Press.

Ginsburg, H., Pollman, V., Wauson, W., & Hope, M. (1977). Variation of aggressive interaction among male elementary school children as a function of changes in social density. *Environmental Psychology and Nonverbal Behavior, 2*, 67–75.

Giuliani, M. V., & Feldman, R. (1993). Place attachment in a developmental and cultural context. *Journal of Environmental Psychology, 13*, 267–274.

Glacken, C. J. (1967). *Traces on the Rhodian shore.* Berkeley, CA: University of California Press.

Glass, D. C. (1976). *Behavior patterns, stress, and coronary disease.* Hillsdale, NJ: Erlbaum.

Glass, D. C., & Singer, J. E. (1972). *Urban stress.* New York: Academic Press.

Glass, D. C., Singer, J. E., & Friedman, L.W. (1969). Psychic cost of adaptation to an environmental stressor. *Journal of Personality and Social Psychology, 12*, 200–210.

Glass, D. C., Singer, J. E., Leonard, H. S., Krantz, D., Cohen, S., & Cummings, H. (1973). Perceived control of aversive stimulation and the reduction of stress responses. *Journal of Personality, 41*, 577–595.

Glenn, N., & Hill, L. (1977). Rural–urban differences in attitudes and behavior in the United States. *The Annals of the American Academy of Political and Social Science, 429*, 36–50.

Gleser, G., Green, B., & Winget, C. (1978). Quantifying interview data on psychic impairment of disaster survivors. *Journal of Nervous and Mental Disease, 166*, 209–216.

Gleser, G., Green, B., & Winget, C. (1981). *Prolonged psychosocial effects of disaster: A study of Buffalo Creek.* New York: Academic Press.

Glicksohn, J. (1994). Rotation, orientation, and cognitive mapping. *American Journal of Psychology, 107*, 39–51.

Gliner, J., Raven, P., Horvath, S., Drinkwater, B., & Sutton, J. (1975). Man's physiological response to long-term work during thermal and pollutant stress. *Journal of Applied Physiology, 39*, 628–632.

Glorig, A. (1971). Nonauditory effects of noise exposure. *Sound and Vibration, 5*, 28–29.

Goeckner, D., Greenough, W., & Maier, S. (1974). Escape learning deficit after overcrowded rearing in rats: Test of a helplessness hypothesis. *Bulletin of the Psychonomic Society, 3*, 54–57.

Gold, J. R. (1982). Territoriality and human spatial behavior. *Progress in Human Geography, 6*, 44–67.

Goldsmith, J. R. (1968). Effects of air pollution on human health. In A. C. Stern (Ed.), *Air pollution* (2nd ed., Vol. 1, pp. 335–386). New York: Academic Press.

Goldsmith, J., & Friberg, L. (1977). Effects of air pollution on human health. In A. C. Stern (Ed.), *Air pollution* (3rd ed., Vol. 3, pp. 457–610). New York: Academic Press.

Goldstein, E. B. (1989). *Sensation and perception.* Belmont, CA: Wadsworth.

Golledge, R. G. (1987). Environmental cognition. In D. Stokols & I. Altman (Eds.), *Handbook of environmental psychology* (pp. 131–174). New York: Wiley.

Golledge, R. G. (1993). Geographical perspectives on spatial cognition. In T. Gärling & R. G. Golledge (Eds.), *Behavior and environment: Psychological and geographical approaches* (pp. 16–46). Amsterdam: Elsevier Science Publishers B.V.

Golledge, R. G., Ruggles, A. J., Pellegrino, J. W., & Gale, N. (1993). Integrating route knowledge in an unfamiliar neighborhood: Along and across route experiments. *Journal of Environmental Psychology, 13*, 293–307.

Golledge, R. G., Smith, T. R., Pellegrino, J. W., Doherty, S., & Marshall, S. P. (1985). A conceptual model and empirical analysis of children's acquisition of spatial knowledge. *Journal of Environmental Psychology, 5*, 125–152.

Gonzales, M. H., Aronson, E., & Costanzo, M. A. (1988). Using social cognition to promote energy conservation: A quasi-experiment. *Journal of Applied Social Psychology, 18*, 1049–1066.

Goodrich, R. (1982). Seven office evaluations. *Environment and Behavior, 14*, 353–378.

Goranson, R. E., & King, D. (1970). *Rioting and daily temperature: Analysis of the U.S. riots in 1967.* York University, Toronto.

Gordon, M. S., Riger, S., Lebailly, R., & Heath, L. (1980).

Crime, women, and the quality of urban life. *Signs, 5,* 144–160.

Gormley, F. P., & Aiello, J. R. (1982). Social density, interpersonal relationships, and residential crowding stress. *Journal of Applied Social Psychology, 12,* 222–236.

Gottfredson, S. D., Brower, S., & Taylor, R. B. (1979, September). *Design, social networks, and human territoriality: Predicting crime-related and social control outcomes.* Paper presented at the meeting of the American Psychological Association, New York.

Gottman, J. (1966). The growing city as a social and political process. *Transactions of the Bartlett Society, 5,* 9–46.

Gould, J. D., Alfaro, L., Finn, R., Haupt, B., & Minuto, A. (1987). Reading from CRT displays can be as fast as reading from paper. *Human Factors, 29,* 497–517.

Gould, J. D., & Grischkowsky, N. (1984). Doing the same work with hard copy and with cathode-ray tube (CRT) computer terminals. *Human Factors, 26,* 323–337.

Gould, P., & White, R. (1982). *Mental maps* (2nd ed.). Boston: Allen & Unwin.

Gove, W. R., & Hughes, M. (1983). *Crowding in the household.* New York: Academic Press.

Gramann, J. H., & Burdge, R. J. (1984). Crowding perception determinants at intensively developed outdoor recreation sites. *Leisure Sciences, 6,* 167–186.

Grandjean, E., Graf, P., Lauber, A., Meier, H. P., & Muller, R. (1973). A survey on aircraft noise in Switzerland. In W. D. Ward (Ed.), *Proceedings of the International Congress on Noise as a Public Health Problem.* Washington, DC: U.S. Government Printing Office.

Grandjean, E., Hunting, W., & Piderman, M. (1983). VDT workstation design: Preferred settings and their effects. *Human Factors, 25,* 161–175.

Grandjean, P., Arnvig, E., & Beckmann, J. (1978). Psychological dysfunctions in lead-exposed workers. *Scandinavian Journal of Work, Environment and Health, 4,* 295–303.

Grant, D. P. (1970). Architect discovers the aged. *Gerontologist, 10,* 275–281.

Grasmick, H. G., Bursik, R. J., Jr., & Kinsey, K. A. (1991). Shame and embarrassment as deterents to noncompliance with the law: The case of an antilittering campaign. *Environment and Behavior, 23,* 233–251.

Gratz, R. B. (1989). *The living city.* New York: Simon & Schuster.

Green, B. L., Grace, M. C., Lindy, J. D., Gleser, G. C., Leonard, A. C., Korol, M., & Winget, C. (1990a). Buffalo Creek survivors in the second decade: Stability of stress symptoms. *American Journal of Orthopsychiatry, 60,* 43–54.

Green, B. L., Lindy, J. D., Grace, M. C., Gleser, G. C., & Leonard, A. C. (1990b). Buffalo Creek survivors in the second decade: Comparison with unexposed and non-litigant groups. *Journal of Applied Social Psychology, 20,* 1033–1050.

Green, B. L., Grace, M. C., Vary, M.G., Krammer, T. L., Gleser, G. C., & Leonard, A. C. (1994). Children of disaster in the second decade: A 17–year follow-up of Buffalo Creek survivors. *Journal of the American Academy of Child and Adolescent Psychiatry, 33,* 71–79.

Green, D. M., & Fidell, S. (1991). Variability in the criterion for reporting annoyance in community noise surveys. *Journal of the Acoustical Society of America, 89,* 234–243.

Greenbaum, P., & Rosenfeld, H. M. (1978). Patterns of avoidance in response to interpersonal staring and proximity: Effects of bystanders on drivers at a traffic intersection. *Journal of Personality and Social Psychology, 36,* 575–587.

Greenbaum, P. E., & Greenbaum, S. D. (1981). Territorial personalization: Group identity and social interaction in a Slavic-American neighborhood. *Environment and Behavior, 13,* 574–589.

Greenberg, C., & Firestone, I. (1977). Compensatory responses to crowding: Effects of personal space intrusion and privacy

reduction. *Journal of Personality and Social Psychology, 35,* 637–644.

Greenberg, C. I. (1979). Toward an integration of ecological psychology and industrial psychology: Undermanning theory, organization size, and job enrichment. *Environmental Psychology and Nonverbal Behavior, 3,* 228–242.

Greenberg, C. I., & Baum, A. (1979). Compensatory response to anticipated densities. *Journal of Applied Social Psychology, 9,* 1–12.

Greenberg, M. S., & Ruback, R. B. (1984). Criminal victimization: Introduction and overview. *Journal of Social Issues, 40,* 1–8.

Greenberger, D. B., & Allen, V. C. (1980). Destruction and complexity: An application of aesthetic theory. *Personality and Social Psychology Bulletin, 6,* 479–483.

Greenbie, B. B. (1982). The landscape of social symbols. *Landscape Research, 7,* 2–6.

Greene, L. R. (1977). Effects of verbal evaluation feedback and interpersonal distance on behavioral compliance. *Journal of Consulting Psychology, 24,* 10–14.

Greene, T. C., & Bell, P. A. (1980). Additional considerations concerning the effects of "warm" and "cool" wall colors on energy conservation. *Ergonomics, 23,* 949–954.

Greene, T. C., & Bell, P. A. (1986). Environmental stress. In M. A. Baker (Ed.), *Sex differences in human performance* (pp. 81–106). London: Wiley.

Greene, T. C., & Connelly, C. M. (1988). Computer analysis of aesthetic districts. In D. Lawrence, R. Habe, A. Hacker, & D. Sherrods (Eds.), *People's needs/planet management: Paths to co-existence,* (pp. 333–335). Washington, DC: Environmental Design Research Association.

Greene, W. A. (1966). The psychosocial setting of development of leukemia and hypomania. *Annals of the New York Academy of Science, 125,* 794–801.

Grieshop, J. I., & Stiles, M. C. (1989). Risk and home-pesticide users. *Environment and Behavior, 21,* 699–716.

Griffiths, I. D. (1975). The thermal environment. In D. C. Canter (Ed.), *Environmental interaction: Psychological approaches to our physical surroundings* (pp. 21–52). New York: International Universities Press.

Griffiths, I. D., & Boyce, P. R. (1971). Performance and thermal comfort. *Ergonomics, 14,* 457–468.

Griffiths, I. D., & Raw, G. J. (1987). Community and individual response to changes in traffic noise exposure. In H. S. Koelega (Ed.), *Environmental annoyance: Characterization, measurement, and control* (pp. 333–343). Amsterdam: Elsevier Science Publishers.

Griffitt, W. (1970). Environmental effects on interpersonal affective behavior: Ambient effective temperature and attraction. *Journal of Personality and Social Psychology, 15,* 240–244.

Griffitt, W., & Veitch, R. (1971). Hot and crowded: Influences of population density and temperature on interpersonal affective behavior. *Journal of Personality and Social Psychology, 17,* 92–98.

Groat, L. (1982). Meaning in post-modern architecture: An examination using the multiple sorting task. *Journal of Environmental Psychology, 2,* 3–22.

Grossman, L. M. (1987, June 17). City pedestrian malls fail to fulfill promise of revitalizing downtown. *The Wall Street Journal,* p. 27.

Grove, N. (1994, July). Recycling. *National Geographic, 186,* 92–115.

Grunberg, J., & Eagle, P. F. (1990). Shelterization: How the homeless adapt to shelter living. *Hospital and Community Psychiatry, 41,* 521–525.

Gubrium, J. F. (1974). Victimization in old age: Available evidence and three hypotheses. *Crime and Delinquency, 20,* 245–250.

Guenther, R. (1982, Aug. 4). Ways are found to minimize pollutants in airtight houses. *The Wall Street Journal,* p. 25.

Guilan, E., & Thomas, J. R. (1986). The effects of noise, cognitive set, and gender on mental arithmetic performance. *British Journal of Psychology, 77*, 503–511.

Gulliver, F. P. (1908). Orientation of maps. *Journal of Geography, 7*, 55–58.

Gump, P. V. (1974, August). Operating environments in schools of open and traditional design. *School Review, 84*, 574–593.

Gump, P. V. (1978). School environments. In I. Altman & J. F. Wohlwill (Eds.), *Children and the environment* (pp. 131–174). New York: Plenum.

Gump, P. V. (1987). School and classroom environments. In D. Stokols & I. Altman (Eds.), *Handbook of environmental psychology* (Vol. 1, pp. 691–732). New York: Wiley-Interscience.

Gunderson, E. K. E. (1968). Mental health problems in Antarctica. *Archives of Environmental Health, 17*, 558–564.

Gunter, B. G. (1987). The leisure experience: Selected properties. *Journal of Leisure Research, 19*, 115–130.

Guterbock, T. M. (1990). The effect of snow on urban density patterns in the United States. *Environment and Behavior, 22*, 358–386.

Gutman, G. M. (1978). Issues and findings relating to multilevel accommodation for seniors. *Journal of Gerontology, 33*, 592–600.

Haase, R. S., & Pepper, D. T. (1972). Nonverbal components of empathic communication. *Journal of Counseling Psychology, 19*, 417–424.

Haber, G. M. (1980). Territorial invasion in the classroom: Invadee response. *Environment and Behavior, 12*, 17–31.

Hackett, T. P., & Weisman, A. D. (1964). Reactions to the imminence of death. In G. H. Grosser, H. Weschler, & M. Greenblatt (Eds.), *The threat of impending disaster* (pp. 300–311). Cambridge, MA: M.I.T. Press.

Hackney, J., Linn, W., Karuza, S., Buckley, R., Law, D., Bates, D., Hazucha, M., Pengelly, L., & Silverman, F. (1977). Effects of ozone exposure in Canadians and Southern Californians. *Archives of Environmental Health, 32*, 110–116.

Haggard, L. M., & Werner, C. M. (1990). Situational support, privacy regulation, and stress. *Basic and Applied Social Psychology, 11*, 313–337.

Haggard, L. M., & Williams, D. R. (1991). Self-identity benefits of leisure activities. In B. L. Driver, P. J. Brown, & G. L. Peterson (Eds.), *Benefits of leisure* (pp. 103–119). State College, PA: Venture.

Hall, E. T. (1959). *The silent language.* New York: Doubleday.

Hall, E. T. (1963). A system for the notation of proxemic behavior. *American Anthropologist, 65*, 1003–1026.

Hall, E. T. (1966). *The hidden dimension.* New York: Doubleday.

Hall, E. T. (1968). Proxemics. *Current Anthropology, 9*, 83–107.

Hall, M., & Baum, A. (1995). Intrusive thoughts as determinants of distress in parents of children with cancer. *Journal of Applied Social Psychology*, in press.

Hall, P. (1988). *Cities of tomorrow: An intellectual history of urban planning and design.* Oxford: Basil Blackwell.

Hamad, C. D., Bettinger, R., Cooper, D., & Semb, G. (1980–1981). Using behavioral procedures to establish an elementary school paper recycling program. *Journal of Environmental Systems, 10*, 149–156.

Hambrick-Dixon, P. J. (1986). Effects of experimentally imposed noise on task performance of Black children attending day care centers near elevated subway trains. *Developmental Psychology, 22*, 259–264.

Hammitt, W. E. (1982). Cognitive dimensions of wilderness solitude. *Environment and Behavior, 14*, 478–493.

Hancock, J. (1980). The apartment house in urban America. In A. D. King (Ed.), *Building and society: Essays on the social development of the built environment* (pp. 151–189). London: Routledge & Kegan Paul.

Hancock, P. A. (1986). Sustained attention under thermal stress. *Psychological Bulletin, 99*, 263–281.

Handford, H. A., Dickerson Mayes, S., Mattison, R. E., Humphrey, J., Bagnato, S., Bixler, E., & Kales, J. (1986). Child and parent reaction to the Three Mile Island nuclear accident. *Journal of the American Academy of Child Psychiatry, 25*, 346–356.

Hansen, W. B., & Altman, I. (1976). Decorating personal places: A descriptive analysis. *Environment and Behavior, 8*, 491–505.

Hanson, S., Vitek, J. D., & Hanson, P. O. (1979). Natural disaster: Long-range impact on human response to future disaster threats. *Environment and Behavior, 11*, 268–284.

Hansson, R. O., Noulles, D., & Bellovich, S. J. (1982). Social comparison and urban-environmental stress. *Personality and Social Psychology Bulletin, 8*, 68–73.

Hansson, R. O., & Slade, K. M. (1977). Altruism toward a deviant in city and small town. *Journal of Applied Social Psychology, 7*, 272–279.

Harada, M. (1977). Cogenital alkyl mercury poisoning (congenital Minamata disease). *Pediatrician, 6*, 58–68.

Harburg, E., Erfrut, J. C., Chape, C., Hauenstein, L. S., Shull, W. J., & Schork, M. A. (1973). Socioecological stressor areas and black-white blood pressure. *Journal of Chronic Diseases, 26*, 595–611.

Hardin, G. (1968). The tragedy of the commons. *Science, 162*, 1243–1248.

Hargreaves, A. G. (1980, April). Coping with disaster. *American Journal of Nursing*, p. 683.

Harries, K. D., & Stadler, S. J. (1988). Heat and violence: New findings from Dallas field data, 1980–1981. *Journal of Applied Social Psychology, 18*, 129–138.

Harris, H., Lipman, A., & Slater, R. (1977). Architectural design: The spatial location and interactions of old people. *Gerontology, 23*, 390–400.

Harrison, A. A., Clearwater, Y. A., & McKay, C. P., (Eds.). (1991). *From Antarctica to outer space: Life in isolation and confinement.* New York: Springer.

Hart, R. A. (1987). Children's participation in planning and design. In C. Simon & T. G. David (Eds.), *Spaces for children* (pp. 217–239). New York: Plenum.

Hart, R. A., & Moore, G. T. (1973). The development of spatial cognition: A review. In R. M. Downes & D. Stea (Eds.), *Image and environment: Cognitive mapping and spatial behavior* (pp. 246–288). Chicago: Aldine.

Hart, R. H. (1970). The concept of APS: Air Pollution Syndrome(s). *Journal of South Carolina Medical Association, 66*, 71–73.

Hartig, T., Mang, M., & Evans, G. W. (1991). Restorative effects of natural environment experience. *Environment and Behavior, 23*, 3–26.

Hartsough, D. M., & Savitsky, J. C. (1984). Three Mile Island: Psychology and environmental policy at a crossroads. *American Psychologist, 39*, 1113–1122.

Harvey, M. L., Bell, P. A., & Birjulin, A. A. (1993). Punishment and type of feedback in a simulated commons dilemma. *Psychological Reports, 73*, 447–450.

Hasell, M. J., & Peatross, F. D. (1990). Exploring connections between women's changing roles and house forms. *Environment and Behavior, 22*, 3–26.

Hawkins, L. H., & Barker, T. (1978). Air ions and human performance. *Ergonomics, 21*, 273–278.

Hay, D. G., & Wantman, M. J. (1969). *Selected chronic diseases: Estimates of prevalence and of physician's service.* New York: Center for Social Research, Graduate Center, City University of New York.

Hayduk, L. A. (1978). Personal space: An evaluative and orienting overview. *Psychological Bulletin, 85*, 117–134.

Hayduk, L. A. (1981). The permeability of personal space. *Canadian Journal of Behavioral Science, 13*, 274–287.

Hayduk, L. A. (1983). Personal space: Where we now stand. *Psychological Bulletin, 94*, 293–335.

Hayduk, L. A. (1985). Personal space: The conceptual and measurement implications of structural equation models. *Canadian Journal of Behavior Science, 17*, 140–149.

Hayes, S. C., & Cone, J. D. (1981). Reduction of residential consumption of electricity through simple monthly feedback. *Journal of Applied Behavior Analysis, 14*, 81–88.

Hayes, S. C., Johnson, V. S., & Cone, J. D. (1975). The marked item technique: A practical procedure for litter control. *Journal of Applied Behavior Analysis, 8*, 381–386.

Hayward, D. G., Rothenberg, M., & Beasley, R. R. (1976). Children's play and urban playground environments: A comparison of traditional, contemporary, and adventure playground types. In H. M. Proshansky, W. H. Ittelson, & L. Rivlin (Eds.), *Environmental psychology* (2nd ed.). New York: Holt, Rinehart, and Winston.

Hayward, J. (1989). Urban parks: Research, planning, and social change. In I. Altman & E. H. Zube (Eds.), *Public places and spaces* (pp. 193–216). New York: Plenum.

Heath, D., & Williams, D. R. (1977). *Man at high altitude: The patho-physiology of acclimatization and adaptation.* Edinburgh: Churchill Livingstone.

Heaton, A. W., & Sigall, H. (1989). The "championship choke" revisited: The role of fear of acquiring a negative identity. *Journal of Applied Social Psychology, 19*, 1019–1033.

Hebb, D. O. (1972). *Textbook of psychology* (3rd ed.). Philadelphia: Saunders.

Heberlein, T. A. (1975). Conservation information: The energy crisis and electricity consumption in an apartment complex. *Energy Systems and Policy, 1*, 105–117.

Hecht, M. E. (1975). The decline of the grass lawn tradition in Tucson. *Landscape, 19*, 3–10.

Hedge, A. (1984). Evidence of a relationship between office design and self-reports of ill health among office workers in the United Kingdom. *Journal of Architectural and Planning Research, 1*, 163–174.

Hedge, A., Burge, P. S., Robertson, A. S., Wilson, S., & Harris-Bass, J. (1989). Work-related illness in offices: A proposed model of the sick building syndrome. *Environment International, 15*, 143–158.

Hedge, A., Erickson, W. A., & Rubin, G. (1994). The effects of alternative smoking policies on indoor air quality in 27 office buildings. *Annals of Occupational Hygiene, 38*, 265–278.

Hedge, A., Mitchell, G. E., & McCarthy, J. (1993). Effects of furniture integrated breathing zone filtration system indoor air quality, Sick Building Syndrome, productivity, and absenteeism. *Indoor Air 3*, 328–336.

Hediger, H. (1950). *Wild animals in captivity.* London: Butterworth.

Hedman, R., & Jaszewski, A. (1984). *Fundamentals of urban design.* Washington, DC: Planners Press.

Heerwagen, J. H., & Orians, G. H. (1986). Adaptions to windowlessness: A study of the use of visual decor in windowed and windowless offices. *Environment and Behavior, 18*, 623–639.

Heerwagen, J. H., & Orians, G. H. (1993). Humans, habitats, and aesthetics. In S. R. Kellert & E. O. Wilson, (Eds.), *The biophilia hypothesis* (pp. 138–172). Washington, DC: Island Press.

Heft, H. (1979a). The role of environmental features in route-learning: Two exploratory studies of wayfinding. *Environmental Psychology and Nonverbal Behavior, 3*, 172–185.

Heft, H. (1979b). Background and focal environmental conditions of the home and attention in young children. *Journal of Applied Social Psychology, 9*, 47–69.

Heft, H. (1981). An examination of constructivist and Gibsonian approaches to environmental psychology. *Population and Environment, 4*, 227–245.

Heft, H. (1983). Wayfinding as the perception of information over time. *Population and Environment, 6*, 133–150.

Heft, H. (1989). Affordances and the body: An intentional analysis of Gibson's ecological approach to visual perception. *Journal for the Theory of Social Behavior, 19*, 1–30.

Heft, H., & Wohlwill, J. F. (1987). Environmental cognition in children. In D. Stokols & I. Altman (Eds.), *Handbook of environmental psychology* (pp. 175–203). New York: Wiley.

Heimstra, N. W., & McFarling, L. H. (1978). *Environmental Psychology* (2nd ed.). Monterey, CA: Brooks/Cole.

Heller, J., Groff, B., & Solomon, S. (1977). Toward an understanding of crowding: The role of physical interaction. *Journal of Personality and Social Psychology, 35*, 183–190.

Helson, H. (1964). *Adaptation level theory.* New York: Harper & Row.

Henderson, L. F., & Jenkins, D. M. (1974). Response of pedestrians to traffic challenge. *Transportation Research, 8*, 71–74.

Henderson, S., & Bostock, T. (1977). Coping behavior after shipwreck. *British Journal of Psychiatry, 131*, 15–20.

Hendrick, C., Wells, K. S., & Faletti, M. V. (1982). Social and emotional effects of geographical relocation on elderly retirees. *Journal of Personality and Social Psychology, 42*, 951–962.

Henig, J. R. (1982). Neighborhood response to gentrification: Conditions to mobilization. *Urban Affairs Quarterly, 17*, 343–358.

Henry, D. O. (1994). Prehistoric cultural ecology in southern Jordan. *Science, 265*, 336–341.

Hensley, W. E. (1982). Professor proxemics: Personality and job demands as factors of faculty office arrangement. *Environment and Behavior, 14*, 581–591.

Hern, W. M. (1991). Proxemics: The application of theory to conflict arising from antiabortion demonstrations. *Population and Environment: A Journal of Interdisciplinary Studies, 12*, 379–388.

Herridge, C. F. (1974). Aircraft noise and mental health. *Journal of Psychosomatic Research, 18*, 239–243.

Herzberg, F. (1966). *Work and the nature of man.* Cleveland, OH: World Publishing.

Herzberg, F., Mausner, B., & Snyderman, B. (1959). *The motivation to work.* New York: Wiley.

Herzog, T. R. (1984). A cognitive analysis of preference for field-and-forest environments. *Landscape Research, 9*, 10–16.

Herzog, T. R. (1985). A cognitive analysis of preference for waterscapes. *Journal of Environmental Psychology, 5*, 225–241.

Herzog, T. R. (1987). A cognitive analysis of preference for natural environments: Mountains, canyons, deserts. *Landscape, 6*, 140–152.

Herzog, T. R. (1992). A cognitive analysis of preference for urban spaces. *Journal of Environmental Psychology, 12*, 237–248.

Herzog, T. R., & Smith, G. A. (1988). Danger, mystery, and environmental preference. *Enviroment and Behavior, 20*, 320–344.

Heshka, S., & Nelson, Y. (1972). Interpersonal speaking distance as a function of age, sex, and relationship. *Sociometry, 35*, 491–498.

Heshka, S., & Pylypuk, A. (1975, June). *Human crowding and adrenocortical activity.* Paper presented at the meeting of the Canadian Psychological Association, Quebec.

Hetherington, J., Daniel, T. C., & Brown, T. C. (1993). Is motion more important than it sounds?: The medium of presentation in environment perception research. *Journal of Environmental Psychology, 13*, 283–291.

Hicks, A. (1991). Sick building syndrome. *Southern Medical Journal, 84*, 65–72.

Hicks, P. E. (1977). *Introduction to industrial engineering and management science.* New York: McGraw-Hill.

Hill, J. W. (1967). Applied problems of hot work in the glass industry. In C. N. Davies, P. R. Davis, & F. H. Tyrer (Eds.), *The effects of abnormal physical conditions at work* (pp. 130–143). London: E & S Livingstone.

Hillmann, R. B., Brooks, C. I., & O'Brien, J. P. (1991). Differences in self-esteem of college freshmen as a function of classroom seating-row preference. *Psychological Record, 41,* 315–320.

Hiroto, D. S. (1974). Locus of control and learned helplessness. *Journal of Experimental Psychology, 102,* 187–193.

Hirst, E., Clinton, J., Geller, H., & Kroner, W. (1986). *Energy efficiency in buildings: Progress and promise.* Washington, DC: American Council for an Energy-Efficient Economy.

Hirtle, S. C., & Jonides, J. (1985). Evidence of hierarchies in cognitive maps. *Memory and Cognition, 13,* 208–217.

Hiss, T. (1990). *The experience of place.* New York: Alfred A. Knopf.

Hobfoll, S. E. (1989). Conservation of resources: A new attempt at conceptualizing stress. *American Psychologist, 44,* 513–524.

Hobfoll, S. E. (1991). Traumatic stress: A theory based on rapid loss of resources. *Anxiety Research, 4,* 187–197.

Hockey, G. R. J. (1979). Stress and the cognitive components of skilled performance. In V. Hamilton & D. M. Warburton (Eds.), *Human stress and cognition: An information processing approach* (pp. 141–179). New York: Wiley.

Hockey, G. R. J., & Hamilton, P. (1970). Arousal and information selection in short-term memory. *Nature, 226,* 866–867.

Hocking, M. B. (1991). Paper versus polystyrene: A complex choice. *Science, 251,* 504–505.

Hodgson, M. J., & Morey, P. R. (1989). Allergic and infectious agents in the outdoor air. *Immunology and Allergy Clinics of North America, 9,* 399–412.

Hoffman, M. (1991). Taking stock of Saddam's fiery legacy in Kuwait. *Science, 253,* 971.

Holahan, C. J. (1972). Seating patterns and patient behavior in an experimental dayroom. *Journal of Abnormal Psychology, 80,* 115–124.

Holahan, C. J. (1976). Environmental change in a psychiatric setting: A social systems analysis. *Human Relations, 29,* 153–166.

Holahan, C. J. (1978). *Environment and behavior.* New York: Plenum.

Holahan, C. J., & Moos, R. H. (1981). Social support and psychological distress: A longitudinal analysis. *Journal of Abnormal Psychology, 49,* 365–370.

Holahan, C. J., & Saegert, S. (1973). Behavioral and attitudinal effects of large-scale variation in the physical environment of psychiatric wards. *Journal of Abnormal Psychology, 83,* 454–462.

Holden, C. (1995). EMF good for trees? *Science, 267,* 451.

Holding, C. S. (1992). Clusters and reference points in cognitive representations of the environment. *Journal of Environmental Psychology, 12,* 45–56.

Hollander, J., & Yeostros, S. (1963). The effect of simultaneous variations of humidity and barometric pressure on arthritis. *Bulletin of the American Meteorological Society, 44,* 489–494.

Hollingshead, A. B., & Rogler, L. H. (1963). Attitudes toward slums and public housing in Puerto Rico. In L. J. Duhl (Ed.), *The urban condition* (pp. 229–245). New York: Simon & Schuster.

Hollister, F. D. (1968). *Greater London Council: A report on the problems of windowless environments.* London: Hobbs.

Holman, E. A., & Silver, R. C. (1994, August). *The relationship between place attachment and social relationships in coping with the southern California firestorms.* Paper presented at the meeting of the American Psychological Association, Los Angeles, CA.

Holmes, R. M. (1992). Children's artwork and nonverbal communication. *Child Study Journal, 22,* 157–166.

Hopper, J. R., & Nielsen, J. M. (1991). Recycling as altruistic behavior: Normative and behavioral strategies to expand participation in a community recycling program. *Environment and Behavior, 23,* 195–220.

Horowitz, M. J., Duff, D. F., & Stratton, L. O. (1964). Body-buffer zone. *Archives of General Psychiatry, 11,* 651–656.

Horvath, S. M., Dahms, T. E., & O'Hanlon, J. F. (1971). Carbon monoxide and human vigilance: A deleterious effect of present urban concentrations. *Archives of Environmental Health, 23,* 343–347.

Horvath, S. M., & Drechsler Parks, D. M. (1992). Air pollution and behavior. In D. M. Jones & A. P. Smith (Eds.), *Handbook of human performance* (Vol. 1, pp. 131–148). New York: Academic Press.

Hourihan, K. (1984). Context-dependent models of residential satisfaction: An analysis of housing groups in Cork, Ireland. *Environment and Behavior, 16,* 369–393.

House, J. S., & Wolf, S. (1978). Effects of urban residence on interpersonal trust and helping behavior. *Journal of Personality and Social Psychology, 36,* 1029–1043.

Houston, B. K., & Jones, T. M. (1967). Distractions and stroop color-word performance. *Journal of Experimental Psychology, 75,* 54–56.

Houts, P. S., Miller, R. W., Tokuhata, G. K., & Ham, K. S. (1980, April 8). *Health-related behavioral impact of the Three Mile Island nuclear incident.* Report submitted to the TMI Advisory Panel on Health Research Studies of the Pennsylvania Department of Health, Part I.

Howard, G. S., Delgado, E., Miller, D., & Gubbins, S. (1993). Transforming values into actions: Ecological preservation. *The Counseling Psychologist, 21,* 582–596.

Howenstine, E. (1993). Market segmentation for recycling. *Environment and Behavior, 25,* 86–102.

Hubel, D. H., & Wiesel, T. N. (1968). Receptive fields and functional architecture of monkey striate cortex. *Journal of Physiology* (London), *195,* 215–243.

Hubel, D. H., & Wiesel, T. N. (1979). Brain mechanisms of behavior. *Scientific American, 241,* 150–162.

Huerta, F., & Horton, R. (1978). Coping behavior of elderly flood victims. *The Gerontologist, 18,* 541–546.

Huffman, K. T., Grossnickle, W. F., Cope, J. G., & Huffman, K. P. (1995). Litter reduction: A review and integration of the literature. *Environment and Behavior, 27,* 153–183.

Hughes, J., & Goldman, M. (1978). Eye contact, facial expression, sex, and the violation of personal space. *Perceptual and Motor Skills, 46,* 579–584.

Hull, R. B., IV, & Revell, G. R. B. (1989). Cross-cultural comparison of landscape scenic beauty evaluations: A case study in Bali. *Journal of Environmental Psychology, 9,* 177–191.

Hummel, C. F. (1977). *Effects of induced cognitive sets in viewing air pollution scenes.* Unpublished doctoral dissertation, Colorado State University.

Hummel, C. F., Levitt, L., & Loomis, R. J. (1973). *Research strategies for measuring attitudes toward air pollution.* Unpublished manuscript, Colorado State University.

Hummel, C. F., Loomis, R. J., & Hebert, J. A. (1975). *Effects of city labels and cue utilization on air pollution judgments (Working Papers in Environmental-Social Psychology, No. 1).* Unpublished manuscript, Colorado State University.

Hundert, A. J., & Greenfield, N. (1969). Physical space and organizational behavior: A study of an office landscape. *Proceedings of the 77th Annual Convention of the American Psychological Association, 4,* 601–602.

Hunt, J. (1975). Fundamental studies of wind flow near buildings: Models and systems in architecture and buildings. *LUBFS Conference Proceedings (2).* Lancaster, England: Construction Press.

Hunt, M. E. (1984). Environmental learning without being there. *Environment and Behavior, 16,* 307–334.

Hunter, A. (1978). Persistence of local sentiments in mass society. In D. Street (Ed.), *Handbook of contemporary urban life* (pp. 133–162). San Francisco: Jossey-Bass.

Huntington, E. (1915). *Civilization and climate.* New Haven: Yale University Press.

Huntington, E. (1945). *Mainsprings of civilization.* New York: Wiley.

Hurt, H. (1975). The hottest place in the whole U.S.A. *Texas Monthly, 3*, 50–52, 84, 89–93.

Hygge, S. (1992). Heat and performance. In D. M. Jones & A. P. Smith (Eds.), *Handbook of human performance* (pp. 79–104). New York: Wiley.

Hygge, S. (1993). Classroom experiments on the effects of aircraft, traffic, train, and verbal noise on long-term recall and recognition and memory. In M. Vallet (Ed.), *Noise as a public health problem: Proceedings of the Sixth International Congress* (pp. 531–538). Paris: INGRETS.

Hynson, L. M. (1975). Rural–urban difference in satisfaction among the elderly. *Rural Sociology, 46*, 64–66.

Ickes, W., Patterson, M. L., Rajecki, D. W., & Tanford, S. (1982). Behavioral and cognitive consequences of reciprocal versus compensatory responses to preinteraction expectancies. *Social Cognition, 1*, 160–190.

Im, S. (1984). Visual preferences in enclosed urban spaces: An exploration of a scientific approach to environmental design. *Environment and Behavior, 16*, 235–262.

Isen, A. M. (1970). Success, failure, attention, and reaction to others: The warm glow of success. *Journal of Personality and Social Psychology, 15*, 294–301.

Isen, A. M., Shalker, T. E., Clark, M. & Karp, L. (1978). Affect, accessibility of material in memory, and behavior: A cognitive loop? *Journal of Personality and Social Psychology, 36*, 1–12.

Ising, H., & Melchert, H. U. (1980). Endocrine and cardiovascular effects of noise. In *Noise as a public health problem: Proceedings of the Third International Congress*. (ASHA Report No. 10). Rockville, MD: American Speech and Hearing Association.

Ising, H., Rebebtisch, E., Poustka, F., & Curio, I. (1990). Annoyance and health risk caused by military low-altitude flight noise. *International Archives of Occupational and Environmental Health, 62*, 357–363.

Iso-Ahola, S. E. (1986). A theory of substitutability of leisure behavior. *Leisure Science, 8*, 367–389.

Ittelson, W. H. (1970). Perception of the large-scale environment. *Transactions of the New York Academy of Sciences, 32*, 807–815.

Ittelson, W. H. (1973). Environmental perception and contemporary perceptual theory. In W. H. Ittelson (Ed.), *Environment and cognition* (pp. 1–19). New York: Seminar Press.

Ittelson, W. H. (1978). Environmental perception and urban experience. *Environment and Behavior, 10*, 193–213.

Ittelson, W. H., Proshansky, H. M., & Rivlin, L. G. (1970). A study of bedroom use on two psychiatric wards. *Hospital and Community Psychiatry, 21*, 25–28.

Ittelson, W. H., Proshansky, H. M., & Rivlin, L. G. (1972). Bedroom size and social interaction of the psychiatric ward. In J. Wohlwill & D. Carson (Eds.), *Environment and the social sciences* (pp. 95–104). Washington, DC: American Psychological Association.

Ittelson, W. H., Proshansky, H. M., Rivlin, L. G., & Winkel, G. H. (1974). *An introduction to environmental psychology*. New York: Holt, Rinehart and Winston.

Ittelson, W. H., Rivlin, L. G., & Proshansky, H. M. (1976). The use of behavioral maps in environmental psychology. In H. M. Proshansky, W. H. Ittelson, & L. G. Rivlin (Eds.), *Environmental psychology: People and their physical settings* (pp. 658–668). New York: Holt, Rinehart and Winston.

Iwata, O. (1984). The relationship of noise sensitivity to health and personality. *Japanese Psychological Research, 26*, 75–81.

Iwata, O. (1992). Crowding and behavior in Japanese public spaces: Some observations and speculations. 10th International Congress of the International Association for Cross-Cultural Psychology: Symposium on cross-cultural perspectives on crowding and behavior (1990, Nara, Japan). *Social Behavior and Personality, 20*, 57–70.

Jackson, E. L. (1981). Responses to earthquake hazard: The west coast of America. *Environment and Behavior, 3*, 387–416.

Jackson, K. (1985). *Crabgrass frontier*. London: Oxford University Press.

Jackson, S. W. (1986). *Melancholia and depression from Hippocratic times to modern times*. New Haven: Yale University Press.

Jacobs, H. E., & Bailey, J. S. (1982). Evaluating participation in a residential program. *Journal of Environmental Systems, 13*, 245–254.

Jacobs, S. V., Evans, G. W., Catalano, R., & Dooley, D. (1984). Air pollution and depressive symptomatology: Exploratory analyses of intervening psychosocial factors. *Population and Environment, 7*, 260–272.

Jain, U. (1993). Concomitants of population density in India. *Journal of Social Psychology, 133*, 331–336.

James, B. (1984). A few words about the home field advantage. In B. James (Ed.), *The Bill James baseball abstract 1984*. New York: Ballantine.

James, W. (1979). The dilemma of determinism. In F. H. Burkhardt, F. Bowers, & I. K. Skrupkelis (Eds.), *Will to believe* (pp. 114–140). Cambridge, MA: Harvard.

Janis, I. L. (1958). *Psychological stress: Psychoanalytic and behavioral studies of surgical patients*. New York: Wiley.

Janney, J., Minoru, M., & Holmes, T. (1977). Impact of natural catastrophe on life events. *Journal of Human Stress, 3*, 22–34.

Jansen, G. N. (1973). Non-auditory effects of noise—Physiological and psychological reactions in man. *Proceedings of the International Congress on Noise as a Public Health Problem*. Dubrovnik, Yugoslavia, May 13–18. Washington, DC: U.S. Environmental Protection Agency.

Jason, L. A., Zolik, E. S., & Matese, F. (1979). Prompting dog owners to pick up dog droppings. *American Journal of Community Psychology, 7*, 339–351.

Jenkins, L. M., Tarnopolsky, A., & Hand, D. G. (1979). Comparison of three studies of aircraft noise and psychiatric hospital admissions conducted on the same area. *Psychological Medicine, 9*, 681–693.

Jenkins, L. M., Tarnopolsky, A., & Hand, D. G. (1981). Psychiatric admissions and aircraft noise from London airport. Four-year three hospitals' study. *Psychological Medicine, 11*, 765–782.

Jerdee, T. H., & Rosen, B. (1974). The effects of opportunity to communicate and visibility of individual decisions on behavior in the common interest. *Journal of Applied Psychology, 59*, 712–716.

Job, R. F. S. (1988). Community response to noise: A review of factors influencing the relationship between noise exposure and reaction. *Journal of the Acoustical Society of America, 83*, 991–1001.

Johnson, A. K. (1989). Measurement and methodology: Problems and issues in research on homelessness. *Social Work Research and Abstracts, 25*, 12–20.

Johnson, J. E. (1973). Effects of accurate expectations about sensations on the sensory and distress components of pain. *Journal of Personality and Social Psychology, 27*, 261–275.

Johnson, J. E. (1976). Relations of divergent thinking and intelligence test scores with social and nonsocial make-believe play with preschool children. *Child Development, 47*, 1200–1203.

Johnson, J. E., & Leventhal, H. (1974). Effects of accurate expectations and behavioral instructions on reactions during a noxious medical examination. *Journal of Personality and Social Psychology, 29*, 710–718.

Johnson, M. W. (1935). The effect on behavior of variation in the amount of play equipment. *Child Development, 6*, 56–68.

Johnson, R., & Richards, B. (1988, November 2). The buyer of Sears Tower will face rather shattering problem: Windows. *The Wall Street Journal*, p. A8.

Joiner, D. (1971). Office territory. *New Society, 7*, 660–663.

Jones, C. J., Nesselroade, J. R., & Birkel, R. C. (1991). Examination of staffing level effects in the family household: An application of P-technique factor analysis. *Journal of Environmental Psychology, 11,* 59–73.

Jones, D. M., Smith, A. P., & Broadbent, D. E. (1979). Effects of moderate intensity noise on the Bakan Vigilance Task. *Journal of Applied Psychology, 64,* 627–634.

Jones, J. W. (1978). Adverse emotional reactions of nonsmokers to secondary cigarette smoke. *Environmental Psychology and Nonverbal Behavior, 3,* 125–127.

Jones, J. W., & Bogat, G. A. (1978). Air pollution and human aggression. *Psychological Reports, 43,* 721–722.

Jones, R. T., Ribbe, D. P., & Cunningham, P. (1994). Psychological correlates of fire disaster among children and adolescents. *Journal of Traumatic Stress, 7,* 117–122.

Jorgenson, D. O. (1981). Locus of control and preceived causal influence of the lunar cycle. *Perceptual and Motor Skills, 52,* 864.

Jorgenson, D. O., & Dukes, F. O. (1976). Deindividuation as a function of density and group membership. *Journal of Personality and Social Psychology, 34,* 24–29.

Jorgenson, D. O., & Papciak, A. S. (1981). The effects of communication, resource feedback and identifiability on behavior in a simulated commons. *Journal of Experimental Social Psychology, 17,* 373–385.

Joseph, S. A., Brewin, C. R., Yule, W., & Williams, R. (1993). Causal attributions and post-traumatic stress in adolescents. *Journal of Child Psychology and Psychiatry, 34,* 247–253.

Jourard, S. M., & Rubin, J. E. (1968). Self-disclosure and touching: A study of two modes of interpersonal encounter and their interrelation. *Journal of Humanistic Psychology, 8,* 39–48.

Joy, V. D., & Lehman, N. (1975). *The cost of crowding: Responses and adaptations.* Unpublished manuscript, New York State Department of Mental Hygiene.

Judge, P. G., & deWaal, F. B. (1993). Conflict avoidance among rhesus monkeys: Coping with short-term crowding. *Animal Behaviour, 46,* 221–232.

Jung, J. (1984). Social support and its relation to health: A critical examination. *Basic and Applied Social Psychology, 5,* 143–149.

Kahneman, D. (1973). *Attention and effort.* Englewood Cliffs, NJ: Prentice-Hall.

Kaitilla, S. (1993). Satisfaction with public housing in Papua New Guinea: The case of West Taraka housing scheme. *Environment and Behavior, 25,* 514–545.

Kalkstein, L. S., & Davis, R. E. (1989). Weather and human mortality: An evaluation of demographic and interregional responses in the United States. *Annals of the Association of American Geographers, 79,* 44–64.

Kalkstein, L. S., & Smoyer, K. E. (1993). The impact of climate change on human health: Some international implications. *Experientia, 49,* 969–979.

Kammann, R., Thompson, R., & Irwin, R. (1979). Unhelpful behavior in the street: City size or immediate pedestrian density? *Environment and Behavior, 11,* 245–250.

Kaniasty, K., & Norris, F. (1991, June). *In Search of "altruistic community": Social support following Hurricane Hugo.* Paper presented at the Third Biennial Conference on Community Research and Action, Tempe, AZ.

Kaniasty, K., & Norris, F. (1993). A test of the social support deterioration model in the context of natural disaster. *Journal of Personality and Social Psychology, 64,* 395–408.

Kaniasty, K., Norris, F., & Murrell, S. A. (1990). Received and perceived social support following natural disaster. *Journal of Applied Social Psychology, 20,* 85–144.

Kant, I. (1790). *The critique of pure reason* (republished in 1929). New York: Macmillan.

Kaplan, R. (1975). Some methods and strategies in the prediction of preference. In E. H. Zube, R. O. Brush, & J. G. Fabos (Eds.), *Landscape assessment* (pp. 118–129). Stroudsburg, PA: Dowden, Hutchinson, & Ross.

Kaplan, R. (1984). The impact of urban nature: A theoretical analysis. *Urban Ecology, 8,* 189–197.

Kaplan, R. (1985). Nature at the doorstep: Residential satisfaction and the nearby environment. *Journal of Architectural Planning Research, 2,* 115–127.

Kaplan, R. (1987). Validity in environment/behavior research. *Environment and Behavior, 19,* 495–500.

Kaplan, R., & Kaplan, S. (1987). The garden as a restorative experience. In M. Francis & R. T. Hester, Jr. (Eds.), *Meanings of the garden* (pp. 334–341). Davis, CA: University of California, Davis.

Kaplan, R., & Kaplan, S. (1989). *The experience of nature: A psychological perspective.* New York: Cambridge University Press.

Kaplan, S. (1975). An informal model for the prediction of preference. In E. H. Zube, R. O. Brush, & J. G. Fabos (Eds.), *Landscape assessment* (pp. 92–101). Stroudsburg, PA: Dowden, Hutchinson, & Ross.

Kaplan, S. (1976). Adaptation, structure, and knowledge. In G. Moore & R. Golledge (Eds.), *Environmental knowing* (pp. 32–45). Stroudsburg, PA: Dowden, Hutchinson, & Ross.

Kaplan, S. (1987). Aesthetics, affect, and cognition: Environmental preference from an evolutionary perspective. *Environment and Behavior, 19,* 3–32.

Kaplan, S., Bardwell, L. V., & Slakter, D. B. (1993). The museum as a restorative environment. *Environment and Behavior, 25,* 725–742.

Kaplan, S., & Kaplan, R. (1978). *Humanscape: Environments for people.* North Scituate, MA: Duxbury Press.

Kaplan, S., & Kaplan, R. (1982). *Cognition and the environment: Functioning in an uncertain world.* New York: Praeger.

Kaplan, S., & Kaplan, R. (1989). The visual environment: Public participation in design and planning. *Journal of Social Issues, 45,* 59–86.

Kaplan, S., Kaplan, R., & Wendt, J. S. (1972). Rated preference and complexity for natural and urban visual material. *Perception and Psychophysics, 12,* 354–356.

Karabenick, S., & Meisels, M. (1972). Effects of performance evaluation on interpersonal distance. *Journal of Personality, 40,* 257–286.

Kardiner, A., Linton, R., Du Bois, C., & West, J. (1945). *The psychological frontiers of society.* New York: Columbia University Press.

Karlin, R. A., Epstein, Y., & Aiello, J. (1978). Strategies for the investigation of crowding. In A. Esser & B. Greenbie (Eds.), *Design for communality and privacy* (pp. 71–88). New York: Plenum.

Karlin, R. A., McFarland, D., Aiello, J. R., & Epstein, Y. M. (1976). Normative mediation of reactions to crowding. *Environmental Psychology and Nonverbal Behavior, 1,* 30–40.

Karlin, R. A., Rosen, L., & Epstein, Y. (1979). Three into two doesn't go: A follow-up of the effects of over-crowded dormitory rooms. *Personality and Social Psychology Bulletin, 5,* 391–395.

Karmel, L. J. (1965). Effects of windowless classroom environment on high school students. *Perceptual and Motor Skills, 20,* 277–278.

Kasl, S. V. (1976). Effects of housing on mental and physical health. In *U.S. Department of Housing and Urban Development, Housing in the seventies* (working papers 1). Washington, DC: U.S. Government Printing Office.

Kasl, S. V., & Cobb, S. (1970). Blood pressure changes in men undergoing job stress: A preliminary report. *Psychosomatic Medicine, 32,* 19–38.

Kasl, S. V. & Harburg, E. (1972). Perceptions of the neighborhood and the desire to move out. *Journal of the American Institute of Planners, 38,* 318–324.

Kastka, J. (1980). *Noise annoyance reduction in residential areas by traffic control technics.* 10th International Congress on Acoustics, Sydney.

Kates, R. W. (1976). Experiencing the environment as hazard. In H. M. Proshansky, W. H. Ittelson, & L. G. Rivlin (Eds.),

Environmental psychology: People and their physical settings (2nd ed., pp. 401–418). New York: Holt, Rinehart and Winston.

Kates, R. W., Haas, J. E., Amaral, D. J., Olson, R. A., Ramos, R., & Olson, R. (1973). Human impact of the Managua earthquake: Transitional societies are peculiarly vulnerable to natural disasters. *Science, 182,* 981–989.

Katovich, M. (1986). Ceremonial openings in bureaucratic encounters: From shuffling feet to shuffling papers. In N. K. Denzin (Ed.), *Studies in symbolic interaction* (Vol. 6, pp. 307–333). Greenwich, CT: JAI Press.

Katz, P. (1937). *Animals and men.* New York: Longmans, Green.

Katzev, R., & Mishima, H. R. (1992). The use of posted feedback to promote recycling. *Psychological Reports, 71,* 259–264.

Katzev, R. D., & Pardini, A.U. (1987–1988). The comparative effectiveness of reward and commitment approaches in motivating community recycling. *Journal of Environmental Systems, 17,* 93–113.

Kaufman, J., & Christensen, J. (Eds.). (1984). *IES lighting handbook.* New York: Illuminating Engineering Society of North America.

Keane, C. (1991). Socioenvironmental determinants of community formation. *Environment and Behavior, 23,* 27–46.

Keating, J., & Snowball, H. (1977). Effects of crowding and depersonalization on perception of group atmosphere. *Perceptual and Motor Skills, 44,* 431–435.

Keller, L. M., Bouchard, T. J., Jr., Arvey, R. D., Segal, N. L., & Dawis, R. V. (1992). Work values: Genetic and environmental influences. *Journal of Applied Psychology, 77,* 79–88.

Kelley, H., & Arrowwood, A. (1960). Coalitions in the triad: Critique and experiment. *Sociometry, 23,* 231–244.

Kelly, I. W., Rotton, J., & Culver, R. (1985–86). The moon was full and nothing happened. *Skeptical Inquirer, 10,* 129–143.

Kelly, J. T. (1985). Trauma: With the example of San Francisco's shelter programs. In P. W. Brickner, L. K. Scharer, B. Conanan, A. Elvy, & M. Savarese (Eds.), *Health care of homeless people* (pp. 77–91). New York: Springer.

Kempton, W., Darley, J. M., & Stern, P. C. (1992). Psychological research for the new energy problems: Strategies and opportunities. *American Psychologist, 47,* 1213–1223.

Kempton, W., Harris, C. K., Keith, J. G., & Weil, J. S. (1985). Do consumers know what works in energy conservation? *Marriage and Family Review, 9,* 115–133.

Kempton, W., & Montgomery, L. (1982). Folk quantification of energy. *Energy—The International Journal, 7,* 817–827.

Kendler, K. S., Neale, M. C., Kessler, R. C., Heath, A. C., & Eaves, L. J. (1992). The genetic epidemiology of phobias in women. *Archives of General Psychiatry, 49,* 273–281.

Kenrick, D. T., & Johnson, G. A. (1979). Interpersonal attraction in aversive environments. A problem for the classical conditioning paradigm. *Journal of Personality and Social Psychology, 87,* 572–579.

Kenrick, D. T., & MacFarlane, S. W. (1986). Ambient temperature and horn honking: A field study of the heat/aggression relationship. *Environment and Behavior, 18,* 179–191.

Kent, S. (1991). Partitioning space: Cross-cultural factors influencing domestic spatial segmentation. *Environment and Behavior, 23,* 438–473.

Kent, S. J., von Gierke, H. E., & Tolan, G. D. (1986). Analysis of the potential association between noise-induced hearing loss and cardiovascular disease in USAF aircrew members. *Aviation Space Environmental Medicine, 4,* 348–361.

Kerr, N. L., & Kaufman-Gilliland, C. M. (1994). Communication, commitment, and cooperation in social dilemmas. *Journal of Personality and Social Psychology, 66,* 513–529.

Kerr, R. A. (1988a). Is the greenhouse here? *Science, 239,* 559–561.

Kerr, R. A. (1988b). Ozone hole bodes ill for the globe. *Science, 241,* 785–786.

Kerr, R. A. (1991). Geothermal tragedy of the commons. *Science, 253,* 134–135.

Kerr, R. A. (1992a). New assaults seen on Earth's ozone shield. *Science, 255,* 797–798.

Kerr, R. A. (1992b). When climate twitches, evolution takes great leaps. *Science, 257,* 1622–1624.

Kerr, R. A. (1993). Ozone takes a nosedive after the eruption of Mt. Pinatubo. *Science, 260,* 490–491.

Kessler, R. C., House, S. J., & Turner, J. B. (1987). Unemployment and health in a community sample. *Journal of Health and Social Behavior, 28,* 51–59.

Kevan, S. M. (1980). Perspectives on season of suicide: A review. *Social Science and Medicine, 14,* 369–378.

Key, W. (1968). Rural–urban social participation. In S. Fava (Ed.), *Urbanism in world perspective* (pp. 303–312). New York: Crowell.

Kilijanek, T. S., & Drabek, T. E. (1979). Assessing long-term impacts of a natural disaster: A focus on the elderly. *The Gerontologist, 19,* 555–566.

Kinarthy, E. L. (1975). *The effect of seating position on performance and personality in a college classroom.* Doctoral dissertation, University of Southern California.

Kira, A. (1976). *The bathroom.* New York: Viking.

Kirk, N. L. (1988, May). *Factors affecting perceptions of safety in a campus environment.* Paper presented at the annual conference of the Environmental Design Research Association, Pamona, CA.

Kirmeyer, S. L. (1978). Urban density and pathology. *Environment and Behavior, 10,* 247–270.

Kitchin, R. M. (1994). Cognitive maps: What are they and why study them? *Journal of Environmental Psychology, 14,* 1–19.

Kleeman, W. B. (1988). The politics of office design. *Environment and Behavior, 20,* 537–549.

Klein, H-J., (1993). Tracking visitor circulation in museum settings. *Environment and Behavior, 25,* 782–800.

Klein, K., & Beith, B. (1985). Re-examination of residual arousal as an explanation of aftereffects: Frustration tolerance versus response speed. *Journal of Applied Psychology, 70,* 642–650.

Klein, K., & Harris, B. (1979). Disruptive effects of disconfirmed expectancies about crowding. *Journal of Personality and Social Psychology, 37,* 769–777.

Kline, L. M., & Bell, P. A. (1983). Privacy preference and interpersonal distancing. *Psychological Reports, 53,* 1214.

Kline, L. M., Bell, P. A., & Babcock, A.M. (1984). Field dependence and interpersonal distance. *Bulletin of the Psychonomic Society, 22,* 421–422.

Kline, L. M., Harrison, A., Bell, P. A., Edney, J. J., & Hill, E. (1984). Verbal reinforcement and feedback as solutions to a simulated commons dilemma. *Psychological Documents, 14,* 24 (ms. No. 2648).

Kmiecik, C., Mausar, P., & Benziger, G. (1979). Attractiveness and interpersonal space. *Journal of Social Psychology, 108,* 227–278.

Knave, B. G., Wibom, R., Vas, M., Hedstrong, L. D., & Bergqvist, U. O. V. (1985). Work with video display terminals among office employees: I. Subjective symptoms and discomfort. *Scandinavian Journal of Work, Environment, & Health, 11,* 457–466.

Knowles, E. S. (1972). Boundaries around social space: Dyadic responses to an invader. *Environment and Behavior, 4,* 437–447.

Knowles, E. S. (1973). Boundaries around group interaction: The effect of group and member status on boundary permeability. *Journal of Personality and Social Psychology, 26,* 327–331.

Knowles, E. S. (1978). The gravity of crowding: Application of social physics to the effects of others. In A. Baum & Y. Epstein (Eds.), *Human response to crowding* (pp. 183–218). Hillsdale, NJ: Erlbaum.

Knowles, E. S. (1980a). An affiliative conflict theory of personal and group spatial behavior. In P. B. Paulus (Ed.), *Psychology of group influence* (pp. 133–188). Hillsdale, NJ: Erlbaum.

Knowles, E. S. (1980b). Convergent validity of personal space measures: Consistent results with low intercorrelations. *Journal of Nonverbal Behavior, 4*, 240–248.

Knowles, E. S. (1983). Social physics and the effects of others: Tests of the effects of audience size and distance on social judgments and behavior. *Journal of Personality and Social Psychology, 45*, 1263–1279.

Knowles, E. S., & Bassett, R. I. (1976). Groups and crowds as social entities: Effects of activity, size, and member similarity on nonmembers. *Journal of Personality and Social Psychology, 34*, 837–845.

Knowles, E. S., & Brickner, M. A. (1981). Social cohesion effects on spatial cohesion. *Personality and Social Psychology Bulletin, 7*, 309–313.

Knowles, E. S., & Johnson, P. K. (1974). Intrapersonal consistency and interpersonal distance. *JSAS Catalog of Selected Documents in Psychology, 4*, 124.

Knowles, E. S., Kreuser, B., Haas, S., Hyde, M., & Schuchart, G. E. (1976). Group size and the extension of social space boundaries. *Journal of Personality and Social Psychology, 33*, 647–654.

Koelega, H. S., & Brinkman, J. A. (1986). Noise and vigilance: An evaluative review. *Human Factors, 28*, 465–481.

Kohlenberg, R., & Phillips, T. (1973). Reinforcement and rate of litter depositing. *Journal of Applied Behavior Analysis, 6*, 391–396.

Kohler, W. (1970). *Gestalt psychology: An introduction to new concepts in modern psychology*. New York: Liveright.

Kojima, H. (1984). A significant stride toward the comparative study of control. *American Psychologist, 39*, 972–973.

Komorita, S. S. (1987). Cooperative choice in decomposed social dilemmas. *Personality and Social Psychology Bulletin, 13*, 53–63.

Konar, E., Sundstrom, E., Brady, C., Mandel, D., & Rice, R. (1982). Status markers in the office. *Environment and Behavior, 14*, 561–580.

Konecni, V. J., Libuser, L., Morton, H., & Ebbesen, E. B. (1975). Effects of a violation of personal space on escape and helping responses. *Journal of Experimental Social Psychology, 11*, 288–299.

Koneya, M. (1976). Location and interaction in row-and-column seating arrangements. *Environment and Behavior, 8*, 265–283.

Konzett, H. (1975). Jahre österreichische Pharmakologie. *Wien Med. Wochenscher, 125*(1–2 suppl.), 1–6.

Konzett, H., Hortnagel, H., Hortnagel, L., & Winkler, H. (1971). On the urinary output of vasopressin, epinephrine and norepinephrine during different stress situations. *Psychopharmacologia, 21*, 247–256.

Koocher, G. P. (1977). Bathroom behavior and human dignity. *Journal of Personality and Social Psychology, 35*, 120–121.

Koop, C. E. (1986). *The health consequences of involuntary smoking: A report of the Surgeon General*. Rockville, MD: U.S. Department of Health and Human Services, Public Health Service, Centers for Disease Control, Center for Health Promotion and Education, Office on Smoking and Health.

Korte, C. (1980). Urban–nonurban differences in social behavior and social psychological models of urban impact. *Journal of Social Issues, 36*, 29–51.

Korte, C., & Kerr, N. (1975). Responses to altruistic opportunities under urban and rural conditions. *Journal of Social Psychology, 95*, 183–184.

Korte, C., Ypma, I., & Toppen, A. (1975). Helpfulness in Dutch society as a function of urbanization and environmental input level. *Journal of Personality and Social Psychology, 32*, 996–1003.

Koscheyev, V. S., Martens, V. K., Kosenkov, A. A., Lartzev, M. A., & Leon, G. R. (1993). Psychological status of Chernobyl nuclear power plant operators after the natural disaster. *Journal of Traumatic Stress, 6*, 561–568.

Koss, M. P., Gudycz, C. A., & Wisiniewski, N. (1987). The scope of rape: Incidence and prevalence of sexual aggression and victimization in a national sample in higher education. *Journal of Counseling and Clinical Psychology, 55*, 162–170.

Kosslyn, S. M. (1975). Information representation in visual images. *Cognitive Psychology, 7*, 341–370.

Kosslyn, S. M. (1980). *Image and mind*. Cambridge, MA: Harvard University Press.

Kosslyn, S. M. (1983). *Ghosts in the mind's machine: Creating images in the brain*. New York: W. W. Norton.

Kosslyn, S. M., Ball, T. M., & Reiser, B. J. (1978). Visual images preserve metric spatial information: Evidence from studies of image scanning. *Journal of Experimental Psychology: Human Perception and Performance, 4*, 47–60.

Kostof, S. (1987). *America by design*. New York: Oxford University Press.

Kovach, E. J., Jr., Surrette, M. A., & Aamodt, M. G. (1988). Following informal street maps: Effects of map design. *Environment and Behavior, 20*, 683–699.

Kovrigin, S. D., & Mikheyev, A. P. (1965). *The effect of noise level on working efficiency*. Rept. N65–28297. Washington, DC: Joint Publications Research Service.

Kozlowski, L. T., & Bryant, K. (1977). Sense of direction, spatial orientation, and cognitive maps. *Journal of Experimental Psychology: Human Perception and Performance, 3*, 590–598.

Kramer, R. M., & Brewer, M. B. (1984). Effects of group identity on resource use in a simulated commons dilemma. *Journal of Personality and Social Psychology, 46*, 1044–1057.

Krauss, R. M., Freedman, J. L., & Whitcup, M. (1978). Field and laboratory studies of littering. *Journal of Experimental Social Psychology, 14*, 109–122.

Krebs, C. J. (1972). *Ecology: The experimental distribution and abundance*. New York: Harper & Row.

Kristeller, J. L., Schwartz, G. E., & Black, H. (1982). The use of restricted environmental stimulation therapy (REST) in the treatment of essential hypertension: Two case studies. *Behavior Research and Therapy, 20*, 561–566.

Kroling, P. (1985). Natural and artificial air ions—a biologically relevant climatic factor? *International Journal of Biometerology, 29*, 233–242.

Krupat, E. (1982). *People in cities*. Unpublished manuscript, Massachusetts College of Pharmacy and Allied Health Sciences.

Krupat, E. (1985). *People in cities: The urban environment and its effect*. New York: Cambridge University Press.

Kryter, K. D. (1970). *The effects of noise on man*. New York: Academic Press.

Kryter, K. D. (1990). Aircraft noise and social factors in psychiatric hospital admission rates: A re-examination of some data. *Psychological Medicine, 20*, 395–411.

Kuipers, B. (1982). The "map in the head" metaphor. *Environment and Behavior, 14*, 202–220.

Küller, R., & Lindsten, C. (1992). Health and behavior of children in classrooms with and without windows. *Journal of Environmental Psychology, 12*, 305–317.

Ladd, F. C. (1972). Black youths view their environments. *Journal of the American Institute of Planners, 38*, 108–115.

LaGanga, M. L. (1994, April 25). Can required porches prod people into neighborliness? *Los Angeles Times*, pp. A1, A12.

LaHart, D., & Bailey, J. S. (1975). Reducing children's littering on a nature trail. *Journal of Environmental Education, 7*, 37–45.

Lakota, R. A. (1975). *The National Museum of History as a behavioral environment. Part I: An environmental analysis of behavioral performance*. Washington, DC: Office of Museum Programs, The Smithsonian Institution.

Lalli, M. (1992). Urban-related identity: Theory, measurement, and empirical findings. *Journal of Environmental Psychology, 12*, 285–303.

Landesberger, H. A. (1958). *Hawthorne revisited*. Ithaca, NY: Cornell University Press.

Landy, F. J. (1989). *Psychology of work behavior*. Pacific Grove, CA: Brooks/Cole.

Lang, J. (1987). *Creating architectural theory: The role of the be-*

havioral sciences in environmental design. New York: Van Nostrand Reinhold.

Lang, J. (1988). Understanding normative theories of architecture. *Environment and Behavior, 20*, 601–632.

Langdon, P. (1984). The legacy of Kevin Lynch. *Planning*, 12–16.

Langer, E. J., & Rodin, J. (1976). The effects of choice and enhanced personal responsibility for the aged: A field experiment in an institutional setting. *Journal of Personality and Social Psychology, 34*, 191–198.

Langer, E., & Saegert, S. (1977). Crowding and cognitive cotol. *Journal of Personality and Social Psychology, 35*, 175–182.

Larson, J. H. & Lowe, W. (1990). Family cohesion and personal space in families with adolescents. *Journal of Family Issues, 11*, 101–108.

Laska, S. B. (1990). Homeowner adaptation to flooding: An application of the general hazards coping theory. *Environment and Behavior, 22*, 320–357.

Lassen, C. L. (1973). Effects of proximity on anxiety and communication in the initial psychiatric interview. *Journal of Abnormal Psychology, 81*, 226–232.

Latané, B., & Darley, J. M. (1970). *The unresponsive bystander: Why doesn't he help?* New York: Appleton-Century-Crofts.

Latta, R. M. (1978). Relation of status incongruence to personal space. *Personality and Social Psychology Bulletin, 4*, 143–146.

Lauman, E. O., & House, J. S. (1972). Living room styles and social attributes: The patterning of material artifacts in a modern urban community. In E. O. Lauman, P. M. Siegel, & R. W. Hodges (Eds.), *The logic of social hierachies* (pp. 189–203). Chicago: Markham.

Lave, L. B., & Seskin, E. P. (1973). *Air pollution and human health*. Baltimore: Johns Hopkins Press.

LaVerne, A. A. (1970). Nonspecific Air Pollution Syndrome (NAPS): Preliminary report. *Behavioral Neuropsychiatry, 2*, 19–21.

Laverty, W. H., Kelly, I. W., Flynn, M., & Rotton, J. (1992). Geophysical variables and behavior: LXVIII. Distal and lunar variables and traffic accidents in Saskatchewan 1984–1989. *Perceptual and Motor Skills, 74*, 483–488.

Lavrakas, P. J. (1982). Fear of crime and behavior restriction in urban and suburban neighborhoods. *Population and Environment, 5*, 242–264.

Lawson, B. R., & Walters, D. (1974). The effects of a new motorway on an established residential area. In D. Canter & T. Lee (Eds.), *Psychology and the built environment* (pp. 132–138). New York: Wiley.

Lawton, M. P. (1975). Competence, environmental press, and the adaptation of older people. In P. G. Windley & G. Ernst (Eds.), *Theory development in environment and aging* (pp. 13–83). Washington, DC: Gerontological Society.

Lawton, M. P. (1979). Therapeutic environments for the aged. In D. Canter & S. Canter (Eds.), *Designing for therapeutic environments: A review of research* (pp. 233–276). Chichester, England: Wiley.

Lawton, M. P., & Cohen, J. (1974). Environment and the well-being of elderly inner city residents. *Environment and Behavior, 6*, 194–211.

Lawton, M. P., & Nahemow, L. (1973). Ecology and the aging process. In C. Eisdorfer & M. P. Lawton (Eds.), *The psychology of adult development and aging* (pp. 619–674). Washington, DC: American Psychological Association.

Lawton, M. P., Nahemow, L., & Yeh, T. M. (1980). Neighborhood environment and the well-being of older tenants in planned housing. *Journal of Aging and Human Development, 11*, 211–227.

Lazarus, R. (1966). *Psychological stress and the coping process*. New York: McGraw-Hill.

Lazarus, R. S., & Cohen, J. B. (1977). Environmental stress. In I. Altman & J. F. Wohlwill (Eds.), *Human behavior and the environment: Current theory and research* (Vol. 2, pp. 89–127). New York: Plenum.

Lazarus, R. S., DeLongis, A., Folkman, S., & Gruen, R. (1985). Stress and adaptational outcomes: The problem of confounded measures. *American Psychologist, 40*, 770–779.

Lazarus, R. S., & Folkman, S. (1984). *Stress, appraisal, and coping*. New York: Springer.

Lazarus, R. S., & Launier, R. (1978). Stress-related transactions between person and environment. In L. A. Pervin & M. Lewis (Eds.), *Perspectives in interactional psychology* (pp. 287–327). New York: Plenum.

Leavitt, J., & Saegert, S. (1989). *From abandonment to hope: Community-households in Harlem*. New York: Columbia University Press.

LeBlanc, J. (1956). Impairment of manual dexterity in the cold. *Journal of Applied Physiology, 9*, 62–64.

LeBlanc, J. (1962). Local adaptation to cold of Gaspé fisherman. *Journal of Applied Physiology, 17*, 950–952.

LeBlanc, J. (1975). *Man in the cold*. Sprinfield, IL: Thomas.

Lebo, C. P., & Oliphant, K. P. (1968). Music as a source of acoustical trauma. *Laryngoscope, 78*, 1211–1218.

Lebovits, A., Bryne, M., & Strain, J. (1986). The case of asbestos-exposed workers: A psychological evaluation. In A. Lebovits, A. Baum, & J. Singer (Eds.), *Advances in environmental psychology* (Vol. 6, pp. 3–17). Hillsdale, NJ: Erlbaum.

Lee, D. H. K. (1964). Terrestrial animals in dry heat: Man in the desert. In D. B. Dill, E. G. Adolph, & C. G. Wilbur (Eds.), *Handbook of physiology* (pp. 551–582). Washington, DC: The American Physiological Society.

Lee, J., & Moray, N. (1992). Trust, control strategies and allocation of function in human-machine systems. *Ergonomics, 35*, 1243–1270.

Lee, T. R. (1970). Perceived distance as a function of direction in the city. *Environment and Behavior, 2*, 39–51.

Lehman, D. R., Wortman, C. B., & Williams, A. F. (1987). Long-term effects of losing a spouse or child in a motor vehicle crash. *Journal of Personality and Social Psychology, 52*, 218–231.

Leithead, C. S., & Lind, A. R. (1964). *Heat stress and heat disorders*. London: Cassell.

Lemke, S., & Moos, R. H. (1986). Quality of residential settings for elderly adults. *Journal of Gerontology, 41*, 268–276.

Leopold, A. (1949). *A Sand County almanac: And sketches here and there*. New York: Oxford University Press.

Leopold, R. L., & Dillon, H. (1963). Psychoanatomy of a disaster: A long term study of post-traumatic neurosis in survivors of a marine explosion. *American Journal of Psychiatry, 119*, 913–921.

Lepore, S. J., Evans, G. W., & Palsane, M. N. (1991). Social hassles and psychological health in the context of chronic crowding. *Journal of Health and Social Behavior, 32*, 357–367.

Lepore, S. J., Evans, G. W., & Schneider, M. L. (1991). Dynamic role of social support in the link between chronic stress and psychological distress. *Journal of Personality and Social Psychology, 61*, 899–909.

Lepore, S. J., Evans, G. W., & Schneider, M. L. (1992). Role of control and social support in explaining the stress of hassles and crowding. *Environment and Behavior, 24*, 795–811.

Lepper, M. R., Greene, D., & Nisbett, R. E. (1973). Undermining children's intrinsic interest with extrinsic reward: A test of the overjustification principle. *Journal of Personality and Social Psychology, 28*, 129–137.

Lerner, R. N., Iwawaki, S., & Chihara, T. (1976). Development of personal space schemata among Japanese children. *Developmental Psychology, 12*, 466–467.

Lester, D. (1979). Temporal variation in suicide and homicide. *American Journal of Epidemiology, 109*, 517–520.

Lester, D., Brockopp, G. W., & Priebe, K. (1969). Association between a full moon and completed suicide. *Psychological Reports, 25*, 598.

Levine, A., & Stone, R. (1986). Threats to people and what they value. Residents' perceptions of the hazards of Love Canal. In A. H. Lebovits, A. Baum, & J. Singer (Eds.), *Advances in environmental psychology* (Vol. 6, pp. 109–130). Hillsdale, NJ: Erlbaum.

Levine, A. G. (1982). *Love Canal: Science, politics and people*. Lexington, MA: Lexington Books, D.C. Heath.

Levine, D. W. (1994). True scores, error, reliability, and unit of analysis in environment and behavior research. *Environment and Behavior, 26,* 261–293.

Levine, M. (1982). You-are-here maps: Psychological considerations. *Environment and Behavior, 14,* 221–237.

Levine, M., Marchon, I., & Hanley, G. (1984). The placement and misplacement of you-are-here maps. *Environment and Behavior, 16,* 139–157.

Levine, R. (1988, November). City stress index: 25 best, 25 worst. *Psychology Today, 22,* 53–58.

Levine, R.V., Lynch, K., Miyake, K., & Lucia, M. (1988). *The Type A city: Coronary heart disease and the pace of life.* Unpublished manuscript, California State University, Fresno.

Levine, R. V., Martinez, T. S., Brase, G., & Sorenson, K. (1994). Helping in 36 U.S. cities. *Journal of Personality and Social Psychology, 67,* 69–82.

Levine, R. V., Miyake, K., & Lee, M. (1988). Places revisited: Psycho-social pathology in metropolitan areas. *Environment and Behavior, 21,* 531–553.

Levitt, L., & Leventhal, G. (1984, August). *Litter reduction: How effective is the New York State bottle bill?* Paper presented at the meeting of the American Psychological Association, Toronto, Canada.

Levy-Leboyer, C., & Naturel, V. (1991). Neighborhood noise annoyance. *Journal of Environmental Psychology, 11,* 75–86.

Lewin, K. (1951). Formalization and progress in psychology. In D. Cartwright (Ed.), *Field theory in social science.* New York: Harper.

Lewis, C. A. (1973). People–plant interaction: A new horticultural perspective. *American Horticulturist, 52,* 18–25.

Lewis, D. A., & Maxfield, M. G. (1980). Fear in the neighborhoods: An investigation of the impact of crime. *Journal of Research in Crime and Delinquency, 17,* 160–169.

Lewis, J., Baddeley, A. D., Bonham, K. G., & Lovett, D. (1970). Traffic pollution and mental efficiency. *Nature, 225,* 95–97.

Ley, D., & Cybriwsky, R. (1974a). The spatial ecology of stripped cars. *Environment and Behavior, 6,* 53–68.

Ley, D., & Cybriwsky, R. (1974b). Urban graffiti as territorial markers. *Annals of the Association of American Geographers, 64,* 491–505.

Lieber, A. L., & Sherin, C. R. (1972). Homicides and the lunar cycle: Toward a theory of lunar influence on human emotional disturbance. *American Journal of Psychiatry, 129,* 101–106.

Lifton, R. J., & Olson, E. (1976). The human meaning of total disaster. The Buffalo Creek experience. *Psychiatry, 39,* 1–18.

Lim, K. Y., Long, J. B., & Silcock, N. (1992). Integrating human factors with the Jackson system development method: An illustrated overview. *Ergonomics, 35,* 1135–1161.

Lima, B. R., Pai, S., Cavis, L., Haro, J. M., Lima, A. M., Toledo, V., Lozano, J., & Santacruz, H. (1991). Psychiatric disorders in primary health care clinics one year after a major Latin American disaster. *Stress Medicine, 7,* 25–32.

Lindberg, E., & Gärling, T. (1983). Acquisition of different types of locational information in cognitive maps: Automatic or effortful processing? *Psychological Research, 45,* 19–38.

Lindberg, E., Hartig, T., Garvill, J., & Gärling, T. (1992). Residential-location preferences across the lifespan. *Journal of Environmental Psychology, 12,* 187–198.

Link, J. M., & Pepler, R. D. (1970). Associated fluctuations in daily temperature, productivity and absenteeism. *ASHRAE Transactions, 76* (Pt. 2), 326–337.

Lipetz, B. (1970). *User requirements in identifying desired works in a large library.* New Haven: Yale University Library.

Lipman, A. (1967). Chairs as territory. *New Society, 20,* 564–566.

Lipman, A., & Slater, R. (1979). Homes for old people: Toward a positive environment. In D. Canter & S. Canter (Eds.), *Designing for therapeutic environments: A review of research* (pp. 277–308). Chichester, England: Wiley.

Lippert, S. (1971). Travel in nursing units. *Human Factors, 13,* 269–282.

Lipsey, M. W. (1977). Attitudes toward the environment and pollution. In S. Oskamp (Ed.), *Attitudes and opinions.* Englewood Cliffs, NJ: Prentice-Hall.

Lipton, S. G. (1977). Evidence of central city revival. *American Planning Association Journal, 45,* 136–147.

Little, K. B. (1965). Personal space. *Journal of Experimental Social Psychology, 1,* 237–247.

Little, K. B. (1968). Cultural variations in social schemata. *Journal of Personality and Social Psychology, 10,* 1–7.

Litton, R. B., Jr. (1972). Aesthetic dimensions of the landscape. In J. V. Krutilla (Ed.), *Natural environments: Studies in theoretical and applied analysis* (pp. 262–291). Baltimore, MD: Johns Hopkins University Press.

Lloyd, A. J., & Shurley, J. T. (1976). The effects of sensory perceptual isolation on single motor unit conditioning. *Psychophysiology, 13,* 340–361.

Lloyd, R., & Steinke, T. (1986). The identification of regional boundaries in cognitive maps. *Professional Geographer, 38,* 149–159.

Lloyd, W. F. (1833). *Two lectures on the checks to population.* New York: Augustus M. Kelley. (facsimilie edition, 1968).

Locke, E. A. (1968). Toward a theory of task motivation and incentives. *Organizational Behavior and Human Performance, 3,* 157–189.

Locke, E. A. (1970). Job satisfaction and job performance: A theoretical analysis. *Organizational Behavior and Human Performance, 5,* 484–500.

Lockhard, J. S., McVittie, R. I., & Isaac, L. M. (1977). Functional significance of the affiliative smile. *Bulletin of the Psychonomic Society, 9,* 367–370.

Loewen, L. J., Steel, G. D., & Suedfeld, P. (1993). Perceived safety from crime in the urban neighborhood. *Journal of Environmental Psychology, 13,* 321–331.

Loewen, L. J., & Suedfeld, P. (1992). Cognitive and arousal effects of masking office noise. *Environment and Behavior, 24,* 381–395.

Lofland, J. (1973). *Analyzing social settings.* New York: Belmont Books.

Logan, J., & Berger, E. (1961). Measurement of visual information cues. *Illuminating Engineering, 56,* 393–403.

Logue, J. N., Hansen, F., & Struening, E. (1979). Emotional and physical distress following Hurricane Agnes in the Wyoming Valley of Pennsylvania. *Public Health Reports, 94,* 495–502.

Lomranz, J., Shapira, A., Choresh, N., & Gilat, Y. (1975). Children's personal space as a function of age and sex. *Developmental Psychology, 1,* 541–545.

London, B., Lee, B., & Lipton, S. G. (1986). The determinants of gentrification in the United States: A city level analysis. *Urban Affairs Quarterly, 21,* 369–387.

Long, G. T., Selby, J. W., & Calhoun, L. G. (1980). Effects of situational stress and sex on interpersonal distance preference. *Journal of Psychology, 105,* 231–237.

Lonigan, C. J., Shannon, M. P., Taylor, C. M., Finch, A. J., & Sallee, F. R. (1994). Children exposed to disaster: II. Risk factors for the development of post-traumatic symptomatology. *Journal of the American Academy of Child and Adolescent Psychiatry, 33,* 94–105.

Loo, C. (1972). The effects of spatial density on the social behavior of children. *Journal of Applied Social Psychology, 4,* 372–381.

Loo, C. (1973). Important issues in researching the effects of crowding on humans. *Representative Research in Social Psychology, 4,* 219–226.

Loo, C. (1978). Density, crowding, and preschool children. In A. Baum & Y. Epstein (Eds.), *Human response to crowding* (pp. 371–388). Hillsdale, NJ: Erlbaum.

Loo, C., & Kennelly, D. (1979). Social density: Its effects on behaviors and perceptions of preschoolers. *Environmental Psychology and Nonverbal Behavior, 3,* 131–146.

Loo, C., & Smetana, J. (1978). The effects of crowding on the behavior and perception of 10-year-old boys. *Environmental Psychology and Nonverbal Behavior, 2,* 226–249.

Loo, C. M., & Ong, P. (1984). Crowding perceptions, attitudes, and consequences of crowding among the Chinese. *Environment and Behavior, 16,* 55–67.

Loomis, R. J. (1987). *Museum visitor evaluation: New tool for management.* Nashville, TN: American Association for State and Local History.

Lorenz, K. (1966). *On aggression.* New York: Harcourt Brace Jovanovich.

Lott, B. S., & Sommer, R. (1967). Seating arrangements and status. *Journal of Personality and Social Psychology, 7,* 90–95.

Love, K. D., & Aiello, J. R. (1980). Using projective techniques to measure interaction distance: A methodological note. *Personality and Social Psychology Bulletin, 6,* 102–104.

Lovelock, J. (1988). *The ages of Gaia.* New York: W. W. Norton.

Low, S. M., & Altman, I. (1992). Place attachment: A conceptual inquiry. In I. Altman & S. M. Low (Eds.), *Place attachment* (pp. 1–12). New York: Plenum.

Lozar, G. C. (1974). Methods and measures. In D. Carson, (Ed.), *Man–environment interactions: Evaluations and applications* (Part 2, pp. 171–202). Stroudsburg, PA: Dowden, Hutchinson & Ross.

Lublin, J. S. (1985, June 20). The suburban life: Trees, grass plus noise, traffic and pollution. *The Wall Street Journal,* p. 29.

Lucas, R. C. (1964). *The recreational capacity of the Quetico-Superior area* (Research Paper No. LS-15). St. Paul, MN: U.S. Department of Agriculture, Lake States Forest Experiment Station.

Lukas, J. S. (1975). Noise and sleep: A literature review and a proposed criterion for assessing effect. *Journal of the Acoustical Society of America, 58b,* 1232–1242.

Lundberg, U. (1976). Urban commuting: Crowdedness and catecholamine excretion. *Journal of Human Stress, 2,* 26–32.

Luquette, A. J., Landiss, C. W., & Merki, D. J. (1970). Some immediate effects of a smoking environment on children of elementary school age. *Journal of School Health, 40,* 533–536.

Lutz, W. (1994). The future of world population. *Population Bulletin, 49,* 2, 4, 26–27.

Luxenberg, S. (1977, July 17). Crime pays: A prison boom. *The New York Times,* pp. 1–5.

Luyben, P. D. (1980a). Effects of informational prompts on energy conservation in college classrooms. *Journal of Applied Behavior Analysis, 13,* 611–617.

Luyben, P. D. (1980b). Effects of a presidential prompt on energy conservation in college classrooms. *Journal of Environmental Systems, 10,* 17–25.

Luyben, P. D., & Bailey, J. S. (1975, March). *Newspaper recycling behaviors: The effects of reinforcement versus proximity of containers.* Paper presented at the meeting of the Midwestern Association for Behavior Analysis, Chicago, IL.

Lyles, W. B., Greve, K. W., Bauer, R. M., Ware, M. R., Schramke, C. J., Crouch, J., & Hicks, A. (1991). Sick building syndrome. *Southern Medical Journal, 84,* 65–72.

Lynch, K. (1960). *The image of the city.* Cambridge, MA: M.I.T. Press.

Lyons, E. (1983). Demographic correlates of landscape preference. *Environment and Behavior, 15,* 487–511.

Maccoby, E. (Ed.). (1966). *The development of sex differences.* Stanford, CA: Stanford University Press.

Maccoby, E., & Jacklin, C. (1974). *The psychology of sex.* Stanford, CA: Stanford University Press.

MacDonald, J. E., & Gifford, R. (1989). Territorial cues and defensible space theory: The burglar's point of view. *Journal of Environmental Psychology, 9,* 193–205.

MacDougall, J. M., Dembroski, T. M., Slaats, S., Herd, J.A., & Eliot, R. S. (1983, September). Selective cardiovascular effects of stress and cigarette smoking. *Journal of Human Stress, 9,* 13–21.

MacEachren, A. M. (1992). Learning spatial information from maps: Can orientation-specificity be overcome? *Professional Geographer, 44,* 431–443.

Mack, R. (1954). Ecological patterns in an industrial shop. *Social Forces, 32,* 118–138.

MacKenzie, S. T. (1975). *Noise and office work: Employee and employer concerns.* Ithaca, NY: New York State School of Industrial and Labor Relations, Cornell University.

Maida, C. A., Gordon, N. S., Steinberg, A., & Gordon, G. (1989). Psychological impact of disasters: Victims of the Baldwin Hills fire. *Journal of Traumatic Stress, 2,* 37–47.

Maier, S. F., Watkins, L. R., & Fleshner, M. (1994). Psychoneuroimmunology: The interface between behavior, brain, and immunity. *American Psychologist, 49,* 1004–1017.

Mandal, M. K., & Maitra, S. (1985). Perception of facial affect and physical proximity. *Perceptual and Motor Skills, 60,* 782.

Mandel, D. R., Baron, R. M., & Fisher, J. D. (1980). Room utilization and dimensions of density. *Environment and Behavior, 12,* 308–319.

Manfredo, M. J., Driver, B. L., & Brown, P. J. (1983). A test of concepts inherent in experience based setting management for outdoor recreation areas. *Journal of Leisure Research, 15,* 263–283.

Mann, P. H. (1964). *An approach to urban sociology.* London: Routledge & Kegan Paul.

Manning, R. E. (1985). Crowding norms in backcountry settings: A review and synthesis. *Journal of Leisure Research, 17,* 75–89.

Marans, R, W. (1972). Outdoor recreation behavior in residential environments. In J. F. Wohlwill & D. H. Carson (Eds.), *Environment and the social sciences: Perspectives and applications* (pp. 217–232). Washington, DC: American Psychological Association.

Marans, R. W., & Rodgers, W. (1975). Toward an understanding of community satisfaction. In A. Hawley & V. Rock (Eds.), *Metropolitan America in contemporary perspective* (pp. 229–352). New York: Halsted Press.

Marans, R. W., & Spreckelmeyer, K. F. (1981). *Evaluating built environments.* Ann Arbor: Institute for Social Research, The University of Michigan.

Marine, G. (1966). I've got nothing against the colored, understand. *Ramparts, 5,* 13–18.

Markham, S. (1947). *Climate and the energy of nations.* New York: Oxford.

Markowitz, J. S., & Gutterman, E. M. (1986). Predictors of psychological distress in the community following two toxic chemical incidents. In A. H. Lebovits, A. Baum, & J. E. Singer (Eds.), *Advances in environmental psychology* (Vol. 6, pp. 89–107). Hillsdale, NJ: Erlbaum.

Marshall, E. (1985). Space junk grows with weapons tests. *Science, 230,* 424–425.

Martichuski, D. K., & Bell, P. A. (1991). Reward, punishment, privatization, and moral suasion in a commons dilemma. *Journal of Applied Social Psychology, 21,* 1356–1369.

Martichuski, D. K., & Bell, P. A. (1993). Treating excess disabilities in special care units: A review of interventions. *American Journal of Alzheimer's Care & Research, 8(5),* 8–13.

Martin, R. A., Kuiper, N. A., Olinger, L. J., & Dobbin, J. (1987). Is stress always bad? Telic versus paratelic dominance as a stress-moderating variable. *Journal of Personality and Social Psychology, 53,* 970–982.

Martin, R. A., & Lefcourt, H. M. (1983). The sense of humor as a moderator of the relationship between stressors and moods. *Journal of Personality and Social Psychology, 45,* 1313– 1324.

Martindale, D. A. (1971). Territorial dominance behavior in dyadic verbal interactions. *Proceedings of the Annual Convention of the American Psychological Association, 6,* 305–306.

Marwell, G., & Ames, R. E. (1979). Experiments on the provisions of public goods. *American Journal of Sociology, 84,* 1335– 1360.

Maslow, A. H., & Mintz, N. C. (1956). Effects of esthetic surrounding: I. Initial effects of three esthetic conditions upon perceiving "energy" and "well-being" in faces. *Journal of Psychology, 41,* 247–254.

Mathews, K. E., & Canon, L. K. (1975). Environmental noise level as a determinant of helping behavior. *Journal of Personality and Social Psychology, 32,* 571–577.

Mathews, K. E., Canon, L. K., & Alexander, K. (1974). The influence of level of empathy and ambient noise on the body buffer zone. *Proceedings of the American Psychological Association Division of Personality and Social Psychology, 1,* 367–370.

Matus, V. (1988). *Design for northern climates: Cold-climate planning and environmental design.* New York: Van Nostrand Reinhold.

Mawby, R. I. (1977). Defensible space: A theoretical and empirical appraisal. *Urban Studies, 14,* 169–179.

Maxfield, M. G. (1984). The limits of vulnerability in explaining fear of crime: A comparative neighborhood analysis. *Research in Crime and Delinquency, 21,* 233–249.

Mazumdar, S., & Mazumdar, S. (1993). Sacred space and place attachment. *Journal of Environmental Psychology, 13,* 231–242.

McBride, G., King, M. G., & James, J. W. (1965). Social proximity effects on galvanic skin responses in human adults. *Journal of Psychology, 61,* 153–157.

McCain, G., Cox, V. C., & Paulus, P. B. (1976). The relationship between illness complaints and degree of crowding in a prison environment. *Environment and Behavior, 8,* 283–290.

McCallum, R., Rusbult, C., Hong, G., Walden, T., & Schopler, J. (1979). Effect of resource availability and importance of behavior on the experience of crowding. *Journal of Personality and Social Psychology, 37,* 1304–1313.

McCarthy, D. O., Ouimet, M. E., & Dunn, J. M. (1992). The effects of noise stress on leukocyte function in rats. *Research in Nursing and Health, 15,* 131–137.

McCarthy, D. P., & Saegert, S. (1979). Residential density, social overload, and social withdrawal. In J. R. Aiello & A. Baum (Eds.), *Residential crowding and design* (pp. 55–75). New York: Plenum.

McCaul, K. D., & Kopp, J. T. (1982). Effects of goal setting and commitment on increasing metal recycling. *Journal of Applied Psychology, 67,* 377–379.

McCauley, C., Coleman, G., & DeFusco, P. (1977). Commuters' eye contact with strangers in city and suburban train stations: Evidence of short-term adaptation to interpersonal overload in the city. *Environmental Psychology and Nonverbal Behavior, 2,* 215–225.

McCauley, C., & Taylor, J. (1976). Is there overload of acquaintances in the city? *Environmental Psychology and Nonverbal Behavior, 1,* 41–55.

McCaull, J. (1977). Discriminatory air pollution. If poor, don't breathe. *Environment, 18,* 26–31.

McChesney, K. Y. (1986). New findings on homeless families. *Family Professional, 1*(2).

McDonald, B. L., & Schreyer, R. (1991). Spiritual benefits of leisure participation and leisure settings. In B. L. Driver, P. J. Brown, & G. L. Peterson (Eds.), *Benefits of leisure* (pp. 179– 194). State College, PA: Venture.

McDonald, T. P., & Pellegrino, J. W. (1993). Psychological perspectives on spatial cognition. In T. Gärling & R. G. Golledge (Eds.), *Behavior and environment: Psychological and geographical approaches* (pp. 47–82). Amsterdam: Elsevier Science Publishers B.V.

McElroy, J. C., Morrow, P. C., & Wall, L. C. (1983). Generalizing impact of object language to other audiences: Peer response to office design. *Psychological Reports, 53,* 315–322.

McFarland, R. A. (1972). Psychophysiological implications of life at high altitude and including the role of oxygen in the process of aging. In M. K. Yousef, S. M. Horvath, & R. W. Bullard (Eds.), *Physiological adaptations: Desert and mountain* (pp. 157–181). New York: Academic Press.

McFarlane, A. (1987). Posttraumatic phenomena in a longitudinal study of children following a natural disaster. *Journal of the American Academy of Child and Adolescent Psychiatry, 26,* 764–769.

McFarlane, A. C., Policansky, S. K., & Irwin, C. (1987). A longitudinal study of the psychological morbidity in children due to a natural disaster. *Psychological Medicine, 17,* 727–738.

McGrath, J. E. (1970). *Social and psychological factors in stress.* New York: Holt, Rinehart and Winston.

McGuinness, D., & Sparks, J. (1979). Cognitive style and cognitive maps: Sex differences in representations. *Journal of Mental Imagery, 7,* 101–118.

McGuire, W. J. (1985). Attitudes and attitude change. In G. Lindsey & E. Aronson (Eds.), *The handbook of social psychology* (pp. 223–346). New York: Random House.

McGuire, W. J., & Gaes, G. G. (1982). *The effects of crowding versus age composition in aggregated prison assault rates.* Unpublished manuscript, Office of Research, Federal Prison System, Washington, DC.

McKechnie, G. E. (1977). Simulation techniques in environmental psychology. In D. Stokols (Ed.), *Perspectives on environment and behavior* (pp. 169–189). New York: Plenum.

McKinnon, W., Weisse, C. S., Reynolds, C. R., Bowles, C. A., & Baum, A. (1989). Chronic stress, leukocyte subpopulations, and humoral response to latent viruses. *Health Psychology, 8,* 389–402.

McLean, E. K., & Tarnopolsky, A. (1977). Noise, distress, and mental health. *Psychological Medicine, 7,* 19–62.

McLuhan, T. C. (1971). *Touch the earth: A self-portrait of Indian existence.* New York: Simon and Schuster.

McNally, R. J. (1987). Preparedness and phobias: A review. *Psychological Bulletin, 101,* 283–303.

McNamara, T. P. (1986). Mental representations of spatial relations. *Cognitive Psychology, 18,* 87–121.

McNamara, T. P., Hardey, J. K., & Hirtle, S. C. (1989). Subjective hierarchies in spatial memory. *Journal of Experimental Psychology: Learning, Memory, and Cognition, 15,* 211–227.

Medalia, N. Z. (1964). Air pollution as a socio-environmental health problem: A survey report. *Journal of Health and Human Behavior, 5,* 154–165.

Meer, J. (1986, May). The strife of bath. *Psychology Today, 20*(5), 6.

Mehrabian, A. (1968). Relationships of attitude to seated posture, orientation, and distance. *Journal of Personality and Social Psychology, 10,* 26–30.

Mehrabian, A. (1976). *Public places and private spaces.* New York: Basic Books.

Mehrabian, A. (1976–77). A questionnaire measure of individual differences in stimulus screening and associated differences in arousability. *Environmental Psychology and Nonverbal Behavior, 1,* 89–103.

Mehrabian, A., & Diamond, S. G. (1971a). Effects of furniture arrangement, props, and personality on social interaction. *Journal of Personality and Social Psychology, 20,* 18–30.

Mehrabian, A., & Diamond, S. G. (1971b). Seating arrangement and conversation. *Sociometry, 34,* 281–289.

Mehrabian, A., & Russell, J. A. (1974). *An approach to environmental psychology.* Cambridge, MA: M.I.T. Press.

Meisels, M., & Dosey, M. A. (1971). Personal space, anger arousal, and psychological defense. *Journal of Personality, 39,* 333–334.

Meisels, M., & Guardo, C. J. (1969). Development of personal space schemata. *Child Development, 49,* 1167–1178.

Melick, M. E. (1978). Life change and illness: Illness behavior of males in the recovery period of a natural disaster. *Journal of Health and Social Behavior, 19*, 335–342.

Melton, A. W. (1933). Studies of installation at the Pennsylvania Museum of Art. *Museum News, 10*, 5–8.

Melton, A. W. (1936). Distribution of attention in galleries in a museum of science and industry. *Museum News, 14*, 5–8.

Melton, A. W. (1972). Visitor behavior in museums: Some early research in environmental design. *Human Factors, 14*, 393–403.

Mendell, M. J., & Smith, A. H. (1990). Consistent patterns of elevated symptoms in air-conditioned office buildings: A reanalysis of epidemiologic studies. *American Journal of Public Health, 80*, 1193–1199.

Mendelsohn, R., & Orcutt, G. (1979). An empirical analysis of air pollution dose-response curves. *Journal of Environmental Economics and Management, 6*, 85–106.

Menninger, W. C. (1952). Psychological reactions in an emergency (flood). *American Journal of Psychiatry, 109*, 128–130.

Mercer, G. W., & Benjamin, M. L. (1980). Spatial behavior of university undergraduates in double-occupancy residence rooms: An inventory of effects. *Journal of Applied Social Psychology, 10*, 32–44.

Mercer, S., & Kane, R. A. (1979). Helplessness and hopelessness among the institutionalized aged: An experiment. *Health and Social Work, 4*, 90–116.

Merchant, C. (1992). *Radical ecology: The search for a livable world.* New York: Routledge.

Merrill, A., & Baird, J. C. (1979). Studies of the cognitive representation of spatial relations: III. Hypothetical environment. *Journal of Experimental Psychology: General, 108*, 99–106.

Merry, S. E. (1981). Defensible space undefended: Social factors in crime control through environmental design. *Urban Affairs Quarterly, 16*, 397–422.

Merry, S. E. (1987). Crowding, conflict, and neighborhood regulation. In I. Altman & A. Wandersman (Eds.), *Neighborhood and community environments* (pp. 35–68). New York: Plenum.

Messick, D. M., Wilke, H., Brewer, M. B., Kramer, R. M., Zemke, P. E., & Lui, L. (1983). Individual adaptations and structural change as solutions to social dilemmas. *Journal of Personality and Social Psychology, 44*, 294–309.

Michelini, R. L., Passalacqua, R., & Cusimano, J. (1976). Effects of seating arrangement on group participation. *Journal of Social Psychology, 99*, 179–186.

Michelson, W. (1968). Most people don't want what architects want. *Trans-Action, 5*, 37–43.

Michelson, W. (1970). *Man and his urban environment: A sociological approach.* Reading, MA: Addison-Wesley.

Michelson, W. (1977a). *Environmental choice, human behavior, and residential satisfaction.* New York: Oxford University Press.

Michelson, W. (1977b). From congruence to antecedent conditions: A search for the basis of environmental improvement. In D. Stokols (Ed.), *Perspectives in environment and behavior: Theory, research, and applications* (pp. 205–220). New York: Plenum.

Middlemist, R. D., Knowles, E. S., & Matter, C. F. (1976). Personal space invasions in the lavatory: Suggestive evidence for arousal. *Journal of Personality and Social Psychology, 33*, 541–546.

Middlemist, R. D., Knowles, E. S., & Matter, C. F. (1977). What to do and what to report: A reply to Koocher. *Journal of Personality and Social Psychology, 35*, 122–124.

Miles, R., & Clarke, G. (1993). Setting off on the right foot: Front-end evaluation. *Environment and Behavior, 25*, 698–709.

Miles, S. (1967). The medical hazards of diving. In C. N. Davies, P. R. Davis, & F. H. Tyrer (Eds.), *The effects of abnormal physical conditions at work* (pp. 111–120). London: E & S Livingstone.

Milgram, S. (1970). The experience of living in cities. *Science, 167*, 1461–1468.

Milgram, S. (1977). *The individual in a social world.* Reading, MA: Addison-Wesley.

Milgram, S., & Jodelet, D. (1976). Psychological maps of Paris. In H. Proshansky, W. Ittelson, & L. Rivlin (Eds.), *Environmental psychology* (pp. 104–124). New York: Holt, Rinehart and Winston.

Millar, K., & Steels, M. J. (1990). Sustained peripheral vasoconstriction while working in continuous intense noise. *Aviation, Space, and Environmental Medicine, 61*, 695–698.

Miller, G. A. (1956). The magical number seven, plus or minus two: Some limits on our capacity for processing information. *Psychological Review, 63*, 81–97.

Miller, G. T., Jr. (1995). *Environmental science: Working with the Earth* (5th ed.). Belmont, CA: Wadsworth.

Miller, I. W., III, & Norman, W. H. (1979). Learned helplessness in humans: A review and attribution theory model. *Psychological Bulletin, 86*, 93–118.

Miller, J. D. (1974). Effects of noise on people. *Journal of the Acoustical Society of America, 56*, 729–764.

Miller, J. F. (1978). *The effects of four proxemic zones on the performance of selected sixth- seventh- and eighth-grade students.* Doctoral dissertation, East Tennessee State University.

Miller, J. P. (1995, July 26). Bidding war breaks out for used plastic soda bottles. *The Wall Street Journal,* p. B4.

Miller, M. (1982). Cited in J. Raloff, Occupational noise—the subtle pollutant. *Science News, 121*, 347–350.

Miller, M., Albert, M., Bostick, D., & Geller, E. S. (1976, March). *Can the design of a trash can influence litter-related behavior?* Paper presented at the meeting of the Southeastern Psychological Association, New Orleans, LA.

Miller, S., & Nardini, R. M. (1977). Individual differences in the perception of crowding. *Environmental Psychology and Nonverbal Behavior, 2*, 3–13.

Miller, S., Rossbach, J., & Munson, R. (1981). Social density and affiliative tendency as determinants of dormitory residential outcomes. *Journal of Applied Social Psychology, 11*, 356–365.

Milne, G. (1977). Cyclone Tracey: 1. Some consequences of the evacuation for adult victims. *Australian Psychologist, 12*, 39–54.

Minckley, B. (1968). A study of noise and its relationship to patient discomfort in the recovery room. *Nursing Research, 17*, 247–250.

Miransky, J., & Langer, E. J. (1978). Burglary (non)prevention: An instance of relinquishing control. *Personality and Social Psychology Bulletin, 4*, 399–405.

Mitchell, H. (1974). Professional and client: An emerging collaborative relationship. In J. Lang (Ed.), *Designing for human behavior: Architecture and the behavioral sciences* (pp. 15–22). Stroudsburg, PA: Dowden, Hutchinson, & Ross.

Mitchell, J. G. (1994, October). Our national parks. *National Geographic, 186*, 2–55.

Mitchell, M. Y., Force, J. E., Carroll, M. S., & McLaughlin, W. J. (1991). Forest places of the heart: Incorporating special places into public management. *Journal of Forestry, 4*, 32–37.

Mocellin, J. S., Suedfeld, P., Bernadelz, J. P., & Barbarito, M. E. (1991). Levels of anxiety in polar environments. *Journal of Environmental Psychology, 11*, 265–275.

Mock, G. (1994). Atmosphere and climate. In A. L. Hammond (Ed.), *World resources, 1994–95* (pp. 197–212). New York: Oxford University Press.

Moeser, S. D. (1988). Cognitive Mapping in a complex building. *Environment and Behavior, 20*, 3–20.

Molloy, J. T., & Labahn, T. (1993). "Operation getup" targets taggers to curb gang-related graffiti. *The Police Chief,* 121–123.

Montagu, A. (1971). *Touching: The human significance of the skin.* New York: Columbia University Press.

Montano, D., & Adamopoulous, J. (1984). The perception of crowding in interpersonal situations: Affective and behavioral responses. *Environment and Behavior, 16*, 643–667.

Mooney, K. M., Cohn, E. S., & Swift, M. B. (1992). Physical

distance and AIDS: Too close for comfort? *Journal of Applied Social Psychology, 22,* 1442–1452.

Moore, G. (1987). Environment and behavior research in North America: History, developments, and unresolved issues. In D. Stokols & I. Altman (Eds.), *Handbook of environmental psychology* (Vol. 2, pp. 1359–1410).

Moore, G. T. (1979). Knowing about environmental knowing: The current state of theory and research about environmental cognition. *Environment and Behavior, 11,* 33–70.

Moore, H. E. (1958). Some emotional concomitants of disaster. *Mental Hygiene, 42,* 45–50.

Moore, R. C. (1989). Playgrounds at the crossroads: Policy and action research needed to ensure a viable future for public playgrounds in the United States. In I. Altman & E. H. Zube (Eds.), *Public places and spaces* (pp. 83–120). New York: Plenum.

Moore, S. F., Shaffer, L. S., Pollak, E. L., & Taylor-Lemke, P. (1987). The effects of interpersonal trust and prior common problem experience on commons management. *Journal of Social Psychology, 127,* 19–29.

Moos, R. H. (1976). *The human context: Environmental determinants of behavior.* New York: Wiley.

Moos, R. H., & Gerst, M. S. (1974). *University Residence Environment Scale.* Palo Alto, CA: Consulting Psychologists Press.

Moos, W. S. (1964). The effects of "Föhn" weather on accident rates in the city of Zurich (Switzerland). *Aerospace Medicine, 35,* 643–645.

Moran, R., Anderson, R., & Paoli, P. (Eds.). (1990). *Building for people in hospitals: Workers and consumers.* Shankill, Dublin: European Foundation for the Improvement of Living and Working Conditions.

Morasch, B., Groner, N., & Keating, J. (1979). Type of activity and failure as mediators of perceived crowding. *Personality and Social Psychology Bulletin, 5,* 223–226.

Moreland, R. L., & Zajonc, R. B. (1982). Exposure effects in person perception: Familiarity, similarity, and attraction. *Journal of Experimental Social Psychology, 18,* 395–415.

Morris, E. W. (1987). Comment on "Castles in the Sky." *Environment and Behavior, 19,* 115–119.

Morrow, P. C., & McElroy, J. C. (1981). Interior office design and visitor response. *Journal of Applied Psychology, 66,* 646–630.

Moser, G., & Levy-Leboyer, C. (1985). Inadequate environment and situation control: Is a malfunctioning phone always an occasion for aggression? *Environment and Behavior, 17,* 520–533.

Mosler, H. J. (1993). Self-dissemination of environmentally responsible behavior: The influence of trust in a commons dilemma game. *Journal of Environmental Psychology, 13,* 111–123.

Muecher, H., & Ungeheuer, H. (1961). Meteorological influences on reaction time, flicker fusion frequency, job accidents, and use of medical treatment. *Perceptual and Motor Skills, 12,* 163–168.

Munrowe, R. L., & Munrowe, R. H. (1972). Population density and affective relationships in three East African societies. *Journal of Social Psychology, 88,* 15–20.

Murphy-Berman, V., & Berman, J. (1978). The importance of choice and sex in invasions of interpersonal space. *Personality and Social Psychology Bulletin, 4,* 424–428.

Myers, K., Hale, C. S., Mykytowycz, R., & Hughes, R. L. (1971). Density, space, sociality and health. In A. H. Esser (Ed.), *Behavior and environment* (pp. 148–187). New York: Plenum.

Myers, P. (1978). Neighborhood conservation and the elderly. Washington, DC: Conservation Foundation.

Nadel, B. (1994, April). Energy star PCs: Power to the PC. *PC Magazine: The Independent Guide to Personal Computing, 13,* 114ff.

Nahemow, L., & Lawton, M. P. (1973). Toward an ecological theory of adaptation and aging. In W. F. E. Preisser (Ed.),

Environmental design research (Vol. 1, pp. 24–32). Stroudsberg, PA: Dowden, Hutchinson, & Ross.

Nasar, J. L. (1994). Urban design aesthetics: The evaluative qualities of building exteriors. *Environment and Behavior, 26,* 377–401.

Nasar, J. L., & Fisher, B. (1992). Design for vulnerability: Cues and reactions to fear of crime. *Sociology and Social Research, 76,* 48–58.

Nasar, J. L., & Min, M. S. (1984, August). *Modifiers of perceived spaciousness and crowding: A cross-cultural study.* Paper presented at the meeting of the American Psychological Association, Toronto, Canada.

Nash, B. C. (1981). The effects of classroom spatial organization on four- and five-year-old children's learning. *British Journal of Educational Psychology, 51,* 144–155.

Nash, R. (1982). *Wilderness and the American mind* (3rd ed.). New Haven: Yale University Press.

National Academy of Sciences. (1977). *Medical and biological effects of environmental pollutants.* Washington, DC: National Academy of Sciences.

National Academy of Sciences. (1981). *The effect on human health from long-term exposure to noise* (Report of Working Group 81). Washington, DC: National Academy Press.

Navarro, P. L., Simpson-Housley, P., & DeMan, A. F. (1987). Anxiety, locus of control, and appraisal of air pollution. *Perceptual and Motor Skills, 64,* 811–814.

Neal, A. (1969). *Help! For the small museum.* Boulder, CO: Pruett Press.

Needleman, H., Gunnoe, C., Leviton, A., Reed, R., Peresie, H., Maher, C., & Barrett, P. (1979). Deficits in psychologic and classroom performance of children with elevated dentine lead levels. *New England Journal of Medicine, 300,* 689–695.

Needleman, H. L., Leviton, A., & Bellinger, D. (1982). Lead-associated intellectual deficit. *New England Journal of Medicine, 306,* 367.

Neill, S. R. St. J. (1982). Experimental alterations in playroom layout and their effect on staff and child behavior. *Educational Psychology, 2,* 103–119.

Neiman, L. (1988). A critical review of resiliency literature and its relevance to homeless children. *Children's Environment Quarterly, 5,* 17–25.

Neisser, U. (1976). *Cognitive psychology.* New York: Appleton-Century-Crofts.

Nelson, P. D. (1976, September). *Psychologists in habitability research.* Paper presented at the meeting of the American Psychological Association, Washington, DC.

Nemecek, J., & Grandjean, E. (1973). Results of an ergometric investigation of large space offices. *Human Factors, 15,* 111–124.

Neulinger, J. (1981). *To leisure: An introduction.* Boston: Allyn & Bacon.

Newcombe, N. (1985). Method for the study of spatial cognition. In R. Cohen (Ed.), *The development of spatial cognition* (pp. 1–12). Hillsdale, NJ: Erlbaum.

Newhall, S. M. (1941). Warmth and coolness of colors. *The Psychological Record, 4,* 198–212.

Newhouse, N. (1990). Implications of attitude and behavior research for environmental conservation. *The Journal of Environmental Education, 22,* 1.

Newman, C. J. (1976). Children of disaster. Clinical observations at Buffalo Creek. *American Journal of Psychiatry, 133,* 306–309.

Newman, J., & McCauley, C. (1977). Eye contact with strangers in city, suburb, and small town. *Environment and Behavior, 9,* 547–558.

Newman, O. (1972). *Defensible space.* New York: Macmillan.

Newman, O. (1975). Reactions to the defensible space study and some further findings. *International Journal of Mental Health, 4,* 48–70.

Newman, O., & Franck, K. (1981a). *The effects of building size on personal crime and fear of crime.* Paper presented at the meeting of the American Sociological Association, Toronto, Ontario, Canada.

Newman, O., & Franck, K. (1981b). *Factors influencing crime and instability in urban housing developments. Draft Executive Summary.* New York: Institute for Community Analysis.

Newman, O., & Franck, K. (1982). The effects of building size on personal crime and fear of crime. *Population and Environment, 5,* 203–220.

Nicholson, M. (1970). *The environmental revolution.* London: Hodder & Stoughton.

Nicosia, G. J., Hyman, D., Karlin, R. A., Epstein, Y. M., & Aiello, J. R. (1979). Effects of bodily contact on reactions to crowding. *Journal of Applied Social Psychology, 9,* 508–523.

Nivison, M. E., & Endresen, I. M. (1993). An analysis of relationships among environmental noise, annoyance and sensitivity to noise, and the consequences for health and sleep. *Journal of Behavioral Medicine, 16,* 257–276.

Nolen-Hoeksema, S., & Morrow, J. (1991). A prospective study of depression and posttraumatic stress symptoms after a natural disaster: The 1989 Loma Prieta earthquake. *Journal of Personality and Social Psychology, 61,* 115–121.

Norman, D. A. (1988). *The psychology of everyday things.* New York: Basic Books.

Normoyle, J. B., & Foley, J. M. (1988). The defensible space model of fear and elderly public housing residents. *Environment and Behavior, 20,* 50–74.

Normoyle, J., & Lavrakas, P. J. (1984). Fear of crime in elderly women: Perceptions of control, predictability, and territoriality. *Personality and Social Psychology Bulletin, 10,* 191–202.

Norris, F., & Kaniasty, K. (1992). Reliability of delayed self-reports in research. *Journal of Traumatic Stress, 5,* 575–588.

Norris, F., & Murrell, S. (1984). Protective functions of resources related to life events, global stress, and depression in older adults. *Journal of Health and Social Behavior, 23,* 145–159.

Norris, F. H., & Uhl, G. A. (1993). Chronic stress as a mediator of acute stress: The case of Hurricane Hugo. *Journal of Applied Social Psychology, 23,* 1263–1284.

Norris-Baker, L., & Scheidt, R. J. (1990, August). *Impacts of understaffing on older residents of dying rural communities.* Paper presented at the meeting of the American Psychological Association, San Francisco, CA.

North, C. S., Smith, E. M., & Spitznagel, E. L. (1994). Posttraumatic stress disorder in survivors of a mass shooting. *American Journal of Psychiatry, 151,* 82–88.

Novaco, R. W., Stokols, D., Campbell, J., & Stokols, J. (1979). Transportation stress and community psychology. *American Journal of Community Psychology, 4,* 361–380.

Nowak, R. (1994). Chronobiologists out of sync over light therapy patients. *Science, 263,* 1217–1218.

Oak Ridge Associated Universities (1992, June). *Health effects of low-frequency electric and magnetic fields* (ORAU 92/F8). Oak Ridge, TN.

Oak Ridge Associated Universities Panel (1993). EMF and cancer. *Science, 260,* 13–14.

O'Donnel, R., Mikulka, P., Heining, P., & Theodore, J. (1971). Low-level carbon monoxide exposure and human psychomotor performance. *Journal of Applied Toxicology and Pharmacology, 18,* 593–602.

Oelschlaeger, M. (1991). *The idea of wilderness: From prehistory to the age of ecology.* New Haven, CT: Yale University Press.

O'Hare, M. (1974). The public's use of art: Visitor behavior in an art museum. *Curator, 17,* 309–320.

Ohta, R. J., & Ohta, B. M. (1988). Special units for Alzheimer's disease patients: A critical look. *The Gerontologist, 28,* 803–808.

Oldham, G. (1988). Effects of changes in workspace partitions and spatial density on employee reactions: A quasi-experiment. *Journal of Applied Psychology, 73,* 253–258.

Oldham, G. R., & Brass, D. J. (1979). Employee reactions to an open-plan office: A naturally occurring quasi-experiment. *Administrative Science Quarterly, 24,* 267–284.

Ollendick, D. G., & Hoffman, M. (1982). Assessment of psychological reactions in disaster victims. *Journal of Comparative Psychology, 10,* 157–167.

Olsen, M. E. (1981). Consumers' attitudes toward energy conservation. *Journal of Social Issues, 37,* 108–131.

Olsen, R. (1978). *The effect of the hospital environment.* Unpublished doctoral dissertation, City University of New York.

Olszewski, D. A., Rotton, J., & Soler, E. A. (1976, May). *Conversation, conglomerate noise, and behavioral aftereffects.* Paper presented at the meeting of the Midwestern Psychological Association, Chicago, IL.

Omata, K. (1992). Spatial organization of activities of Japanese families. *Journal of Environmental Psychology, 12,* 259–267.

O'Neal, E. C., Brunault, M. A., Carifio, M. S., Troutwine, R., & Epstein, J. (1980). Effects of insult upon personal space preferences. *Journal of Nonverbal Behavior, 5,* 56–62.

O'Neal, E. C., Brunault, M. A., Marquis, J. F., & Carifio, M. (1979). Anger and the body-buffer zone. *Journal of Social Psychology, 108,* 135–136.

O'Neal, E. C., Caldwell, C., & Gallup, G. (1975). *Territorial invasion and aggression in young children.* Unpublished manuscript, Tulane University.

O'Neal, E. C., & McDonald, P. J. (1976). The environmental psychology of aggression. In R. G. Geen & E. C. O'Neal (Eds.), *Prespectives on aggression* (pp. 169–192). New York: Academic Press.

O'Neil, M. J. (1994). Workspace adjustability, storage, and enclosure as predictors of employee reactions and performance. *Environment and Behavior, 26,* 504–526.

O'Neill, G. W., Blanck, L. S., & Joyner, M. A. (1980). The use of stimulus control over littering in a natural setting. *Journal of Applied Behavior Analysis, 13,* 379–381.

O'Neill, S. M., & Paluck, B. J. (1973). Altering territoriality through reinforcement. *Proceedings of the 81st Annual Convention of the American Psychological Association,* Montreal, Canada, *8,* 901–902.

O'Riordan, T. (1976). Attitudes, behavior, and environmental policy issues. In I. Altman & J. F. Wohlwill (Eds.), *Human behavior and environment: Advances in theory and research* (Vol. 1, pp. 1–36). New York: Plenum.

Orleans, P. (1973). Differential cognition of urban residents: Effects of social scale on mapping. In R. M. Downs & D. Stea (Eds.), *Image and environment: Cognitive mapping and spatial behavior* (pp. 115–130). Chicago: Aldine.

Orleans, P., & Schmidt, S. (1972). Mapping the city: Environmental cognition of urban residents. In W. Mitchell (Ed.), *EDRA 3* (pp. 1–4–1—1–4–9). Los Angeles: University of California.

Ornstein, S. (1992). First impressions of the symbolic meanings connoted by reception area design. *Environment and Behavior, 24,* 85–110.

Osborne, J. G., & Powers, R. B. (1980). Controlling the litter problem. In G. L. Martin & J. G. Osborne (Eds.), *Helping the community: Behavioral applications* (pp. 103–168). New York: Plenum.

Oseland, N., & Donald, I. (1993). The evaluation of space in homes: A facet study. *Journal of Environmental Psychology, 13,* 251–261.

OSHA (1981). Occupational noise exposure. "Hearing Conservation Amendment" (20 CFR Part 1910). *Federal Register, 45,* 11 (January 16).

Oskamp, S., Williams, R., Unipan, J., Steers, N., Mainieri, T., & Kurland, G. (1994). Psychological factors affecting paper recycling by businesses. *Environment and Behavior, 26,* 477–503.

Osmond, H. (1957). Function as the basis of psychiatric ward design. *Mental Hospitals* (Architectural Supplement), *8,* 23–29.

Ostfeld, R. S., Canham, C. D., & Pugh, S. R. (1993). Intrinsic density-dependent regulation of vole populations. *Nature, 366*, 259–261.

Owens, P. L. (1985). Conflict as a social interaction process in environment and behavior research: The example of leisure and recreation research. *Journal of Environmental Psychology, 5*, 243–259.

Oxley, D., & Barrera, M., Jr. (1984). Undermanning theory and the workplace: Implications of setting size for job satisfaction and social support. *Environment and Behavior, 16*, 211–234.

Oxley, D., Haggard, L. M., Werner, C. M., & Altman, I. (1986). Transactional qualities of neighborhood social networks: A case study of "Christmas Street." *Environment and Behavior, 18*, 640–677.

Oxman, R., & Carmon, N. (1986). Responsive public housing: An alternative for low-income families. *Environment and Behavior, 18*, 258–284.

Pablant, P., & Baxter, J. C. (1975, July). Environmental correlates of school vandalism. *Journal of the American Institute of Planners*, 270–279.

Paffenbarger, R.S., Jr., Hyde, R. T., & Dow, A. (1991). Health benefits of physical activity. In B. L. Driver, P. J. Brown, & G. L. Peterson (Eds.), *Benefits of leisure* (pp. 49–57). State College, PA: Venture.

Page, R. A. (1977). Noise and helping behavior. *Environment and Behavior, 9*, 559–572.

Page, R. A. (1978, May). *Environmental influences on prosocial behavior: The effect of temperature*. Paper presented at the meeting of the Midwestern Psychological Association, Chicago, IL.

Palamarek, D. L., & Rule, B. G. (1979). The effects of temperature and insult on the motivation to retaliate or escape. *Motivation and Emotion, 3*, 83–92.

Pallack, M. S., Cook, D. A., & Sullivan, J. J. (1980). Commitment and energy conservation. In L. Bickman (Ed.), *Applied Social Psychology Annual, 1*, 235–253.

Palmer, J. F., & Zube, E. H. (1976). Numerical and perceptual landscape classification. In E. H. Zube (Ed.), *Studies in landscape perception* (Publication No. R–76–1, pp. 43–57). Amherst Institute for Man and Environment: University of Massachusetts.

Palmer, M. H., Lloyd, M. E., & Lloyd, K. D. (1978). An experimental analysis of electricity conservation procedures. *Journal of Applied Behavior Analysis, 10*, 665–672.

Palmstierna, T., Huitfeldt, B., & Wistedt, B. (1991). The relationship of crowding and aggressive behavior on a psychiatric intensive care unit. *Hospital and Community Psychiatry, 42*, 1237–1240.

Pardini, A. U., & Katzev, R. D. (1983–1984). The effects of strength of commitment on newspaper recycling. *Journal of Environmental Systems, 13*, 245–254.

Parfit, M. (1993, November). Sharing the wealth of water. *National Geographic, 184(5a)*, 18–37.

Parker, G. (1977). Cyclone Tracy and Darwin evacuees. On the restoration of the species. *British Journal of Psychiatry, 130*, 548–555.

Parkes, C. M. (1972). *Bereavement: Studies of grief in adult life*. New York: International Universities Press.

Parks, C. D. (1994). The predictive ability of social values in resource dilemmas and public goods games. *Personality and Social Psychology Bulletin, 20*, 431–438.

Parmelee, P., & Lawton, M. P. (1990). The design of special environments for the aged. In J. Birren & K. W. Schaie (Eds.), *Handbook of the psychology of aging* (3rd ed., pp. 464–488). New York: Academic Press.

Parr, A. E. (1966). Psychological aspects of urbanology. *Journal of Social Issues, 22*, 39–45.

Parsons, H. M. (1972). The bedroom. *Human Factors, 14*, 421–450.

Parsons, H. M. (1978). What caused the Hawthorne effect? A scientific detective story. *Administration & Society, 10*, 259–283.

Parsons, P., & Loomis, R. J. (1973). *Patterns of museum visitor exploration: Then and now*. Washington, DC: The Smithsonian Institution.

Parsons, R. (1991). The potential influences of environmental perception on human health. *Journal of Environmental Psychology, 11*, 1–23.

Passini, R. (1984). Spatial representations, a wayfinding perspective. *Journal of Environmental Psychology, 4*, 153–164.

Pastalan, L. (1976). *Report on Pennsylvania nursing home relocation program: Interim research findings*. Ann Arbor: Institute of Gerontology, University of Michigan.

Patterson, A. H. (1977). Methodological developments in environment-behavioral research. In D. Stokols (Ed.), *Perspectives on environment and behavior* (pp. 325–344). New York: Plenum.

Patterson, A. H. (1978). Territorial behavior and fear of crime in the elderly. *Environmental Psychology and Nonverbal Behavior, 2*, 131–144.

Patterson, M. L. (1974, September). *Factors affecting interpersonal spatial proximity*. Paper presented at the meeting of the American Psychological Association, New Orleans, LA.

Patterson, M. L. (1976). An arousal model of interpersonal intimacy. *Psychological Review, 83*, 235–245.

Patterson, M. L. (1977). Interpersonal distance, affect, and equilibrium theory. *Journal of Social Psychology, 101*, 205–214.

Patterson, M. L. (1978). Arousal change and the cognitive labeling: Pursuing the mediators of intimacy exchange. *Environmental Psychology and Nonverbal Behavior, 3*, 17–22.

Patterson, M. L., & Holmes, D. S. (1966). Social interaction correlates of MMPI extraversion–introversion scale. *American Psychologist, 21*, 724–725.

Patterson, M. L., & Sechrest, L. B. (1970). Interpersonal distance and impression formation. *Journal of Personality, 38*, 161–166.

Patterson, M. L., Kelly, C. E., Kondracki, B. A., & Wulf, L. J. (1979). Effects of seating arrangement on small-group behavior. *Social Psychology Quarterly, 42*, 180–185.

Patterson, M. L., Mullens, S., & Romano, J. (1971). Compensatory reactions to spatial intrusion. *Sociometry, 34*, 114–121.

Paulhus, D. (1983). Sphere-specific measures of perceived control. *Journal of Personality and Social Psychology, 44*, 1253–1265.

Paulus, P. B. (1977, May). *Crowding in the laboratory and its relation to social facilitation*. Paper presented at the meeting of the Midwestern Psychological Association, Chicago, IL.

Paulus, P. B. (1980). Crowding. In P. B. Paulus (Ed.), *Psychology of group influence* (pp. 245–290). Hillsdale, NJ: Erlbaum.

Paulus, P. B. (1988). *Prison crowding: A psychological perspective*. NY: Springer.

Paulus, P. B., Annis, A. B., Seta, J. J., Schkade, J. K., & Matthews, R. W. (1976). Crowding does affect task performance. *Journal of Personality and Social Psychology, 34*, 248–253.

Paulus, P. B., Cox, V., McCain, G., & Chandler, J. (1975). Some effects of crowding in a prison environment. *Journal of Applied Social Psychology, 5*, 86–91.

Paulus, P. B., & Matthews, R. (1980). Crowding, attribution, and task performance. *Basic and Applied Social Psychology, 1*, 3–13.

Paulus, P. B., McCain, G., & Cox, V. (1981). Prison standards: Some pertinent data on crowding. *Federal Probation, 15*, 48–54.

Paulus, P. B., Nagar, D., & Camacho, L. M. (1991). Environmental and psychological factors in reactions to apartments and mobile homes. *Journal of Environmental Psychology, 11*, 143–161.

Pawson, I. G., & Jest, C. (1978). The high-altitude areas of the world and their cultures. In P. T. Baker (Ed.), *The biology of high-altitude peoples* (pp. 17–45). New York: Cambridge.

Pearce, G. P., & Patterson, A. M. (1993). The effect of space restriction and provision of toys during rearing on the behaviour, productivity and physiology of male pigs. *Applied Animal Behaviour Science, 36*, 11–28.

Pearce, P. L. (1977). Mental souvenirs: A study of tourists and their city maps. *Australian Journal of Psychology, 29*, 203–210.

Pearson, O. P. (1966). The prey of carnivores during one cycle of mouse abundance. *Journal of Animal Ecology, 35*, 217–233.

Pearson, O. P. (1971). Additional measurements of the impact of carnivores on California voles (Microtus Californicus). *Journal of Mammology, 52*, 41–49.

Pempus, E., Sawaya, C., & Cooper, R. E. (1975, August). *"Don't fence me in": Personal space depends on architectural enclosure*. Paper presented at the meeting of the American Psychological Association, Chicago, IL.

Penick, E. C., Powell, B. J., & Sieck, W. A. (1976). Mental health problems and natural disaster. Tornado victims. *Journal of Community Psychology, 4*, 64–67.

Pennebaker, J. W., & Newtson, D. (1983). Observation of a unique event: The psychological impact of the Mount Saint Helens volcano. In H. T. Reiss (Ed.), *Naturalistic approaches to studying social interaction. New directions for methodology of social and behavioral science* (No. 15, pp. 93–109). San Francisco: Jossey-Bass.

Penwarden, A. D. (1973). Acceptable wind speeds in towns. *Building Science, 8*, 259–267.

Pepler, R. D. (1963). Performance and well-being in heat. In J. Hardy (Ed.), *Temperature: Its measurement and control in science and industry* (Vol. 3, pp. 319–336). New York: Van Nostrand Reinhold.

Pepler, R. D. (1972). The thermal comfort of students in climate controlled and non-climate controlled schools. *ASHRAE Transactions, 78*, 97–109.

Perkins, D. D., Meeks, J. W., & Taylor, R. B. (1992). The physical environment of street blocks and resident perceptions of crime and disorder: Implications for theory and measurement. *Journal of Environmental Psychology, 12*, 21–34.

Perry, J. D., & Simpson, M. E. (1987). Violent crimes in a city: Environmental determinants. *Environment and Behavior, 19*, 77–90.

Persinger, M. A., Ludwig, H. W., & Ossenkopf, K. P. (1973). Psychophysiological effects of extremely low frequency electromagnetic fields: A review. *Perceptual and Motor Skills, 26*, 1131–1159.

Peterka, J. A., & Cermak, J. E. (1973). *Wind engineering study of Mountain Bell Denver Service Center* (Tech. Rep. CER73–74JAP–JEC14). Fort Collins, CO: Colorado State University Fluid Mechanics Program.

Peterka, J. A., & Cermak, J. E. (1975). *Wind engineering study of Merchant's Plaza, Indianapolis, IN* (Tech. Rep. CER74–75JAP–JEC47). Fort Collins, CO: Colorado State University Fluid Mechanics Program.

Peterka, J. A., & Cermak, J. E. (1977). *Wind tunnel study of phase I building, Block 141, Denver* (Tech. Rep. CER76–77JAP–JEC36). Fort Collins, CO: Colorado State University Fluid Mechanics Program.

Peterson, C., & Seligman, M. E. P. (1984). Causal explanations as a risk factor for depression: Theory and evidence. *Psychological Review, 91*, 347–374.

Peterson, G. L., Brown, T. C., McCollum, D. W., Bell, P. A., Birjulin, A. A., & Clarke, A. (1995). Estimation of willingness to accept compensation for public and private goods from the chooser reference point by the method of paired comparison. In R. Ready (Ed.), *Benefits and costs transfer in natural resource planning*. Lexington, KY: Seventh Interim Report of the W–133 Regional Reseach Project, University of Kentucky.

Peterson, R. L. (1975, August). *Air pollution and attendance in recreation behavior settings in the Los Angeles basin*. Paper presented at the meeting of the American Psychological Association, Chicago, IL.

Piaget, J., & Inhelder, B. (1967). *The child's conception of space*. New York: Norton.

Pile, J. F. (1978). *Open office planning*. New York: Whitney Library of Design.

Pill, R. (1967). Space and social structure in two children's wards. *Sociological Review, 15*, 179–192.

Pitelka, F. A. (1957). Some aspects of population structure in the short-term cycle of the brown lemming in northern Alaska. *Cold Spring Harbor Symposia on Quantitative Biology, 22*, 237–251.

Pitt, D. G. (1976). Physical dimensions of scenic quality in streams. In E. H. Zube (Ed.), *Studies in landscape perception* (Publication No. R–76–1, pp. 143–161). Amherst: Institute for Man and Environment, University of Massachusetts.

Pitt, D. G., & Zube, E. H. (1979). The Q-sort method: Use in landscape assessment research and in resource planning. *Proceedings of our national landscape: A conference on applied techniques for analysis and management of the visual resource*, USDA Forest Service General Technical Report PSW–35. Berkeley, CA: Pacific Southwest Forest and Range Experiment Station.

Pitt, D., & Zube, E. (1987). Management of natural environments. In D. Stokols & I. Altman (Eds.), *Handbook of environmental psychology* (pp. 1009–1042). New York: Wiley-Interscience.

Platt, J. (1973). Social traps. *American Psychologist, 28*, 641–651.

Ploeger, A. (1972). A 10–year follow-up of miners trapped for 2 weeks under threatening circumstances. In C. D. Spielberger & I. G. Sarson (Eds.), *Stress and anxiety* (Vol. 4, pp. 23–28). Washington, DC: Hemisphere.

Plotkin, W. B. (1978). Long-term eyes-closed alpha-enhancement training: Effects on alpha amplitudes and on experimental state. *Psychophysiology, 15*, 40–52.

Pollack, L. M., & Patterson, A. H. (1980). Territoriality and fear of crime in elderly and nonelderly homeowners. *Journal of Social Psychology, 111*, 119–129.

Pollet, D. (1976, February). You can get there from here. *Wilson Library Bulletin, 50*, 456–462.

Pollet, D., & Haskell, P. C. (1979). *Sign systems for libraries*. New York: Bowker.

Pontell, H. N., & Welsh, W. N. (1994). Incarceration as a deviant form of social control: Jail overcrowding in California. *Crime and Delinquency, 40*, 18–36.

Population Today, Population Update (1994, September). *22*, 6.

Porteous, C. W. (1972). *Learning as a function of molar environmental complexity*. Unpublished master's thesis, University of Victoria, British Columbia.

Porteous, J. D. (1985). Smellscape. *Progress in Human Geography, 9*, 358–378.

Porter, B. E., Leeming, F. C., & Dwyer, W. O. (1995). Solid waste recovery: A review of behavioral programs to increase recycling. *Environment and Behavior, 27*, 122–152.

Porteus, J. (1977). *Environment and behavior*. Reading, MA: Addison-Wesley.

Poulton, E. C. (1970). *The environment and human efficiency*. Springfield, IL: Thomas.

Poulton, E. C. (1976). Arousing environmental stress can improve performance, whatever people say. *Aviation Space and Environmental Medicine, 47*, 1193–1204.

Poulton, E. C. (1977). Continuous noise masks auditory feedback and inner speech. *Psychological Bulletin, 88*, 3–32.

Poulton, E. C., Hunt, J. C. R., Mumford, J. C., & Poulton, J. (1975). Mechanical disturbance produced by steady and gusty winds of moderate strength: Skilled performance and semantic assessments. *Ergonomics, 18*, 651–673.

Poulton, E. C., & Kerslake, D. McK. (1965). Initial stimulating effect of warmth upon perceptual efficiency. *Aerospace Medicine, 36*, 29–32.

Powers, R. B., Osborne, J. G., & Anderson, E. G. (1973). Positive reinforcement of litter removal in the natural environment. *Journal of Applied Behavior Analysis, 6*, 579–586.

Preiser, W. F. E. (1972). Application of unobtrusive observation techniques in building performance appraisal. In B. E. Foster (Ed.), *Performance concept in buildings*. (Special Publication No. 361, Vol. 1). Washington, DC: National Bureau of Standards.

Preiser, W. F. E. (1973). An analysis of unobtrusive observations of pedestrian movement and stationary behavior in a shopping mall. In R. Kuller (Ed.), *Architectural psychology* (pp. 287–300). Stroudsburg, PA: Dowden, Hutchinson, & Ross.

Prerost, F. J. (1982). The development of the mood inhibiting effects of crowding during adolescence. *Journal of Psychology*, *110*, 197–202.

Prerost, F. J., & Brewer, R. K. (1980). The appreciation of humor by males and females during conditions of crowding experimentally induced. *Psychology, A Journal of Human Behavior*, *17*, 15–17.

Price, J. (1978). Some age-related effects of the 1974 Brisbane floods. *Australia and New Zealand Journal of Psychiatry*, *12*, 55–58.

Price, J. L. (1971). *The effects of crowding on the social behavior of children*. Unpublished doctoral dissertation, Columbia University.

Pringle, C., Vellidis, G., Heliotis, F., Bandacu, D., & Cristofor, S. (1993). Environmental problems of the Danube delta. *American Scientist*, *81*, 350–361.

Pritchard, D. (1964). Industrial lighting in windowless factories. *Light and Lighting*, *57*, 265.

Proshansky, H. M. (1972). Methodology in environmental psychology: Problems and issues. *Human Factors*, *14*, 451–460.

Proshansky, H. M. (1973). Theoretical issues in "environmental psychology." *Representative Research in Social Psychology*, *4*, 93–107.

Proshansky, H. M. (1976a). Comment on environmental and social psychology. *Personality and Social Psychology Bulletin*, *2*, 359–363.

Proshansky, H. M. (1976b). Environmental psychology and the real world. *American Psychologist*, *31*, 303–310.

Proshansky, H. M., Ittelson, W. H., & Rivlin, L. G. (Eds.). (1970). *Environmental Psychology: Man and his physical setting*. New York: Holt, Rinehart and Winston.

Proulx, G. (1993). A stress model for people facing a fire. *Journal of Environmental Psychology*, *13*, 137–147.

Provins, K. A. (1958). Environmental conditions and driving efficiency: A review. *Ergonomics*, *2*, 63–88.

Provins, K. A. (1966). Environmental heat, body temperature, and behavior: An hypothesis. *Australian Journal of Psychology*, *18*, 118–129.

Provins, K. A., & Bell, C. R. (1970). Effects of heat stress on the performance of two tasks running concurrently. *Journal of Experimental Psychology*, *85*, 40–44.

Provins, K. A., & Clarke, R. S. J. (1960). The effect of cold on manual performance. *Journal of Occupational Medicine*, *2*, 169–176.

Pruchno, R. A., Dempsey, N. P., Carder, P., & Koropeckyj-Cox, T. (1993). Multigenerational households of caregiving families: Negotiating shared space. *Environment and Behavior*, *25*, 349–366.

Purcell, A. T., Lamb, R. J., Peron, E. M., & Falchero, S. (1994). Preference or preferences for landscape? *Journal of Environmental Psychology*, *14*, 195–209.

Putz, J., (1979). The effects of carbon monoxide on dual-task performance. *Human Factors*, *21*, 13–24.

Pylyshyn, Z. W. (1973). What the mind's eye tells the mind's brain: A critique of mental imagery. *Psychological Bulletin*, *80*, 1–24.

Pylyshyn, Z. W. (1981). The imagery debate: Analogue media versus tacit knowledge. *Psychological Review*, *88*, 16–45.

Quarantelli, E. L. (Ed.). (1978). *Disasters: Theory and research*. Beverly Hills, CA: Sage.

Quarantelli, E. L. (1985). Realities and mythologies in disaster films. *Communications*, *11*, 31–44.

Quarantelli, E. L., & Dynes, R. R. (1972). When disaster strikes. *Psychology Today*, *5*(9), 66–70.

Quick, A. D., & Crano, W. D. (1973, May). *Effects of sex, distance, and conversation in the invasion of personal space*. Paper presented at the meeting of the Midwestern Psychological Association.

Rainwater, L. (1966). Fear and the house as a haven in the lower class. *Journal of the American Institute of Planners*, *32*, 23–31.

Raloff, J. (1982). Occupational noise—The subtle pollutant. *Science News*, *121*, 347–350.

Ramsey, J. (1970). Oxygen reduction and reaction time in hypoxic and normal drivers. *Archives of Environmental Health*, *20*, 597–601.

Rangell, L. (1976). Discussion of the Buffalo Creek disaster: The course of psychic trauma. *American Journal of Psychiatry*, *133*, 313–316.

Rankin, R. E. (1969). Air pollution control and public apathy. *Journal of the Air Pollution Control Association*, *19*, 565–569.

Rapoport, A. (1969). *House form and culture*. Englewood Cliffs, NJ: Prentice-Hall.

Rapoport, A. (1975). Toward a redefinition of density. *Environment and Behavior*, *7*, 133–158.

Raw, G. J., & Griffiths, I. D. (1985). The effect of changes in aircraft noise exposure (letter to the editor). *Journal of Sound and Vibration*, *101*, 273–275.

Rawls, J. R., Trego, R. E., McGaffey, C. N., & Rawls, D. J. (1972). Personal space as a predictor of performance under close working conditions. *Journal of Social Psychology*, *86*, 261–267.

Reddy, D. M., Baum, A., Fleming, R., & Aiello, J. R. (1981). Mediation of social density by coalition formation. *Journal of Applied Social Psychology*, *11*, 529–537.

Regian, J. W., & Yadrick, R. M. (1994). Assessment of configurational knowledge of naturally- and artificially-acquired large-scale space. *Journal of Environmental Psychology*, *14*, 211–223.

Reichel, D. A., & Geller, E. S. (1980, March). *Group versus individual contingencies to conserve transportation energy*. Paper presented at the meeting of the Southeastern Psychological Association, Washington, DC.

Reichner, R. (1979). Differential responses to being ignored: The effects of architectural design and social density on interpersonal behavior. *Journal of Applied Social Psychology*, *9*, 13–26.

Reifman, A. S., Larrick, R. P., & Fein, S. (1991). Temper and temperature on the diamond: The heat-aggression relationship in major league baseball. *Personality and Social Psychology Bulletin*, *17*, 580–585.

Reisenzein, R. (1983). The Schachter theory of emotion: Two decades later. *Psychological Bulletin*, *94*, 239–264.

Reiter, R. (1985). Frequency distribution of positive and negative small ions, based on many years' recordings at two mountain stations located at 740 and 1780 m ASL. *International Journal of Biometeorology*, *29*, 223–231.

Reizenstein, J. E. (1976). *Social research and design: Cambridge hospital social service offices*. Springfield, VA: National Technical Information Service.

Reizenstein, J. E. (1982). Hospital design and human behavior: A review of the recent literature. In A. Baum & J. E. Singer (Eds.), *Advances in environmental psychology* (Vol. 4, pp. 137–170). Hillsdale, NJ: Erlbaum.

Relph, E. (1976). *Place and placeness*. London: Pion.

Remland, M. S., Jones, T. S., & Brinkman, H. (1991). Proxemic and haptic behavior in three European countries. *Journal of Nonverbal Behavior*, *15*, 215–232.

Rent, G. S., & Rent, C. S. (1978). Low income housing factors related to residential satisfaction. *Environment and Behavior*, *10*, 459–488.

Reusch, J., & Kees, W. (1956). *Nonverbal communication: Notes on the visual perception of human relations*. Berkeley, CA: University of California Press.

Richards, P. (1979). Middle class vandalism and the age–status conflict. *Social Problems*, *26*, 482–497.

Riley, R. B. (1992). Attachment to the ordinary landscape. In I. Altman & S. M. Low (Eds.), *Human behavior and environment: Advances in theory and research* (pp. 13–35). New York: Plenum.

Rim, Y. (1975). Psychological test performance during climatic heat stress from desert winds. *International Journal of Biometeorology, 19*, 37–40.

Risk, P. H. (1976). *Effects of an experimental wilderness survival experience on self-concept, personality, and values.* Unpublished doctoral dissertation: Michigan State University.

Rivlin, L. G. (1990). The significance of home and homelessness. *Marriage and Family Review, 15*, 39–56.

Rivlin, L. G. & Rothenberg, M. (1976). The use of space in open classrooms. In H. M. Proshansky, W. H. Ittelson, & L. G. Rivlin (Eds.), *Environmental psychology: People and their physical settings* (pp. 479–489). New York: Holt, Rinehart and Winston.

Rivlin, L. G., & Wolfe, M. (1972). The early history of a psychiatric hospital for children: Expectations and reality. *Environment and Behavior, 4*, 33–72.

Rivlin, L. G., & Wolfe, M. (1985). *Institutional settings in children's lives.* New York: Wiley-Interscience.

Rivlin, L. G., Wolfe, M., & Beyda, M. (1973). Age-related differences in the use of space. In W. F. E. Preiser (Ed.), *Environmental design research* (Vol.1, pp. 191–203). Stroudsberg, PA: Dowden, Hutchinson, & Ross.

Robbins, L. N., Fischbach, R. L., Smith, E. M., Cottler, L. B., Solomon, S. D., & Goldring, E. (1986). Impact of disaster on previously assessed mental health. In J. H. Shore (Ed.), *Disaster stress studies: New methods and findings* (pp. 22–48). Washington, DC: American Psychiatric Association.

Roberts, C. (1977). Stressful experiences in urban places: Some implications for design. *EDRA 8 Conference Proceedings.*

Roberts, E. A. (1995). A sense of place. In D. Dustin & B. L. Driver (Eds.), *Nature and the human spirit: Toward an expanded land management ethic* (in press).

Roberts, L. (1988). Is there life after climate change? *Science, 242*, 1010–1012.

Roberts, S. M., & Schein, R. H. (1993). The entrepreneurial city: Fabricating urban development in Syracuse, New York. *Professional Geographer, 45*, 21–33.

Robillard, D. A. (1984). *Public space design in museums* (R84–7). Milwaukee, WI: School of Architecture & Urban Planning, University of Wisconsin at Milwaukee.

Robinson, E. S. (1928). *The behavior of the museum visitor.* (*No. 5 in Publications of the American Association of Museums New Series.*) Washington, DC: American Association of Museums.

Rochford, E. B., Jr., & Blocker, T. J. (1991). Coping with "natural" hazards as stressors: The predictors of activism in a flood disaster. *Environment and Behavior, 23*, 171–194.

Rock, I., & Palmer, S. (1990, December). The legacy of Gestalt Psychology. *Scientific American*, 84–90.

Rodin, J. (1976). Crowding, perceived choice and response to controllable and uncontrollable outcomes. *Journal of Experimental Social Psychology, 12*, 564–578.

Rodin, J. (1986). Aging and health: Effects of the sense of control. *Science, 233*, 1271–1276.

Rodin, J., & Baum, A. (1978). Crowding and helplessness: Potential consequences of density and loss of control. In A. Baum & Y. Epstein (Eds.), *Human response to crowding* (pp. 389–401). Hillsdale, NJ: Erlbaum.

Rodin, J., & Langer, E. J. (1977). Long-term effects of a control-relevant intervention with the institutionalized aged. *Journal of Personality and Social Psychology, 35*, 897–902.

Rodin, J., Solomon, S., & Metcalf, J. (1978). Role of control in mediating perceptions of density. *Journal of Personality and Social Psychology, 36*, 989–999.

Roethlisberger, F. J., & Dickson, W. J. (1939). *Management and the worker.* Cambridge, MA: Harvard University Press.

Rohe, W. M. (1982). The response to density in residential settings: The mediating effects of social and personal variables. *Journal of Applied Social Psychology, 12*, 292–303.

Rohe, W., & Patterson, A. H. (1974, May). *The effects of varied levels of resources and density on behavior in a day care center.*

Paper presented to the Environmental Design Research Association, Milwaukee, WI.

Rohles, F. H. (1974). The modal comfort envelope and its use in current standards. *Human Factors, 16*, 314–322.

Ronco, P. (1972). Human factors applied to hospital patient care. *Human Factors, 14*, 461–470.

Rook, K. S., & Dooley, D. (1985). Applying social support research: Theoretical problems and future directions. *Journal of Social Issues, 41*, 5–28.

Rose, E. F., & Rose, M. (1971). Carbon monoxide: A challenge to the physician. *Clinical Medicine, 78*, 12–18.

Rose, L. (1987). Workplace video display terminals and visual fatigue. *Journal of Occupational Medicine, 29*, 321–324.

Rosen, S., Bergman, M., Plestor, M., Plestor, D., El-Mofty, A., & Satti, M. (1962). Presbycosis study of a relatively noise-free population in the Sudan. *Annals of Otology, Rhinology, and Laryngology, 71*, 727–743.

Rosenfeld, H. M., Breck, R. E., Smith, S. E., & Kehoe, S. (1984). Intimacy-mediators of the proximity-gaze compensation effect: Movement, controversial role, acquaintance, and gender. *Journal of Nonverbal Behavior, 8*, 235–249.

Rosenthal, N. E. (1993). *Winter blues: Seasonal Affective Disorder: What it is and how to overcome it.* New York: The Guilford Press.

Rosenthal, N. E., Sack, D. A., Gillen, J. C., Lewy, A. J., Goodwin, F. K., Davenport, Y., Mueller, P.S., Newssome, D.A., & Wehr, T.A. (1984). Seasonal Affective Disorder: A description of the syndrome and preliminary findings with light therapy. *Archives of General Psychiatry, 41*, 72–80.

Rosenzweig, M. R. (1966). Environmental complexity, cerebral change and behavior. *American Psychologist, 21*, 321–322.

Ross, H. (1987). *Just for living: Aboriginal perceptions of housing in northwest Australia.* Canberra: Aboriginal Studies Press.

Ross, P., Bluestone, H., & Hines, F. (1979). *Indicators of social well-being in U.S. counties.* Washington, DC: U.S. Department of Agriculture.

Ross, R. T. (1938). Studies in the psychology of the theater. *Psychological Record, 2*, 127–190.

Roth, S., & Cohen, L. J. (1986). Approach, avoidance, and coping with stress. *American Psychologist, 41*, 813–819.

Rothbaum, F., Weisz, J. R., & Snyder, S. S. (1982). Changing the world and changing the self: A two-process model of perceived control. *Journal of Personality and Social Psychology, 42*, 5–37.

Rothenberg, M., & Rivlin, L. (1975). *An ecological approach to the study of open classrooms.* Paper presented at a conference on Ecological Factors in Human Development, University of Surrey, England.

Rothstein, R. N. (1980). Television feedback used to modify gasoline consumption. *Behavior Therapy, 11*, 683–688.

Rotter, J. (1966). Generalized expectancies for internal versus external control of reinforcement. *Psychological Monographs, 80*, (Whole No. 609).

Rotton, J. (1978). *Air pollution is no choke.* Unpublished manuscript. University of Dayton.

Rotton, J. (1983). Affective and cognitive consequences of malodorous pollution. *Basic and Applied Social Psychology, 4*, 171–191.

Rotton, J. (1986). Determinism redux: Climate and cultural correlates of violence. *Environment and Behavior, 18*, 346–368.

Rotton, J. (1987a). Clearing the air about ions. *Skeptical Inquirer, 11*, 305–306.

Rotton, J. (1987b). Hemmed in and hating it: Effects of shape of room on tolerance for crowding. *Perceptual and Motor Skills, 64*, 285–286.

Rotton, J. (1990). Individuals under stress. In C. E. Kimble (Ed.), *Social psychology: Living with people.* New York: W. C. Brown.

Rotton, J. (1993a). Atmospheric and temporal correlates of sex crimes: Endogenous factors do not explain seasonal differences in rape. *Environment and Behavior, 25*, 625–642.

Rotton, J. (1993b). Geophysical variables and behavior: LXXIII. Ubiquitous errors: A reanalysis of Anderson's (1987) "temperature and aggression." *Psychological Reports, 73*, 259–271.

Rotton, J., Barry, T., Frey, J., & Soler, E. (1978). Air pollution and interpersonal attraction. *Journal of Applied Social Psychology, 8*, 57–71.

Rotton, J., Barry, T., & Kimble, C. A. (1985, August). *Climate and crime: Coping with multicolinearity*. Paper presented at the meeting of the American Psychological Association, Los Angeles, CA.

Rotton, J., & Frey, J. (1984). Psychological costs of air pollution: Atmospheric conditions, seasonal trends, and psychiatric emergencies. *Population and Environment, 7*, 3–16.

Rotton, J., & Frey, J. (1985). Air pollution, weather, and violent crimes: Concomitant time-series analysis of archival data. *Journal of Personality and Social Psychology, 49*, 1207–1220.

Rotton, J., Frey, J., Barry, T., Milligan, M., & Fitzpatrick, M. (1979). The air pollution experience and interpersonal aggression. *Journal of Applied Social Psychology, 9*, 397–412.

Rotton, J., & Kelly, I. W. (1985a). A scale for assessing belief in lunar effects: Reliability and concurrent validity. *Psychological Reports, 57*, 239–245.

Rotton, J., & Kelly, I. W. (1985b). Much ado about the full moon: A meta-analysis of lunar-lunacy research. *Psychological Bulletin, 97*, 286–306.

Rotton, J., & Kelly, I. W. (1987). Comment on "The lunar-lunacy relationship": More ado about the full moon. *Psychological Reports, 61*, 733–734.

Rotton, J., Kelly, I. W., & Elortegui, P. (1986). Assessing belief in lunar effects: Known-groups validation. *Psychological Reports, 59*, 171–174.

Rotton, J., Oszewski, D., Charleston, M., & Soler, E. (1978). Loud speech, conglomerate noise, and behavior aftereffects. *Journal of Applied Pscyhology, 63*, 360–365.

Rotton, J., Shats, M., & Standers, R. (1990). Temperature and pedestrian tempo: Walking without awareness. *Environment and Behavior, 22*, 650–674.

Rotton, J., & White, S. M. (1995). Air pollution, sick building syndrome, and social behavior. *Environment International, 6*, in press.

Rowe, J. W., & Kahn, R. L. (1987). Human aging: Usual and successful. *Science, 237*, 143–149.

Ruback, R. B., & Carr, T. S. (1984). Crowding in a women's prison: Attitudinal and behavioral effects. *Journal of Applied Social Psychology, 14*, 57–68.

Ruback, R. B., & Pandey, J. (1991). Crowding, perceived control, and relative power: An analysis of households in India. *Journal of Applied Social Psychology, 21*, 315–344.

Ruback, R. B., & Pandey, J. (1992). Very hot and really crowded: Quasi-experimental investigations of Indian "Tempos." *Environment and Behavior, 24*, 527–554.

Ruback, R. B., Pape, K. D., & Doriot, P. (1989). Waiting for a phone: Intrusion on callers leads to territorial defense. *Social Psychology Quarterly, 52*, 232–241.

Ruback, R. B., & Snow, J. N. (1993). Territoriality and nonconscious racism at waterfountains: Intruders and drinkers (Blacks and Whites) are affected by race. *Environment and Behavior, 25*, 250–267.

Rubin, A. I., & Elder, J. (1980). *Building for people*. Washington, DC: U.S. Government Printing Office Special Publication 474.

Rubin, E. S., Cooper, R. N., Frosch, R. A., Lee, T. H., Marland, G., Rosenfeld, A. H., & Stine, D. D. (1992). Realistic mitigation options for global warming. *Science, 257*, 148–266.

Rubinstein, R. L., & Parmelee, P. A. (1992). Attachment to place and the representation of the life course by the elderly. In I. Altman & S. M. Low (Eds.), *Place attachment* (pp. 139–163). New York: Plenum.

Rubonis, A. V., & Bickman, L. (1991). Psychological impairment in the wake of disaster: The disaster–psychopathology relationship. *Psychological Bulletin, 109*, 384–399.

Rullo, G. (1987). People and home interiors: A bibliography of recent psychological research. *Environment and Behavior, 19*, 250–259.

Rummo, N., & Sarlanis, K. (1974). The effect of carbon monoxide on several measures of vigilance in a simulated driving task. *Journal of Safety Research, 6*, 126–130.

Rumsey, N., Bull, R., & Gahagan, D. (1982). The effects of facial disfigurement on the proxemic behavior of the general public. *Journal of Applied Social Psychology, 12*, 137–150.

Russell, J. A., & Lanius, U. F. (1984). Adaptation level and the affective appraisal of environments. *Journal of Environmental Psychology, 4*, 119–135.

Russell, J. A., & Mehrabian, A. (1978). Environmental, task, and temperamental effects on work performance. *Humanitas, 14*, 75–95.

Russell, J. A., & Pratt, G. (1980). A description of the affective quality attributed to environments. *Journal of Personality and Social Psychology, 38*, 311–322.

Russell, J. A., & Snodgrass, J. (1987). Emotion and the environment. In D. Stokols & I. Altman (Eds.), *Handbook of environmental psychology* (Vol. 1, pp. 245–280). New York: Wiley-Interscience.

Russell, J. A., & Ward, L. M. (1982). Environmental psychology. *Annual Review of Psychology, 33*, 651–688.

Russell, J. A., Ward, L. M., & Pratt, G. (1981). Affective quality attributed to environments: A factor analytic study. *Environment and Behavior, 13*, 259–288.

Russell, M., Cole, P., & Brown, E. (1973). Absorption by nonsmokers of carbon monoxide from room air polluted by tobacco smoke. *Lancet, 1*, 576–579.

Russell, M. B., & Bernal, M. E. (1977). Temporal and climatic variables in naturalistic observation. *Journal of Applied Behavior Analysis, 10*, 399–405.

Rutland, A., Custance, D., & Campbell, R. N. (1993). The ability of three- to four-year-old children to use a map in a large-scale environment. *Journal of Environmental Psychology, 13*, 365–372.

Ruys, T. (1970). Windowless offices. *Man–Environment Systems, 1*, 49.

Ryden, M. B., Bossenmaier, M., & McLachlan, C. (1991). Aggressive behavior in cognitively impaired nursing home residents. *Research in Nursing and Health, 14*, 87–95.

Saal, F. E., & Knight, P. A. (1988). *Industrial/organizational psychology: Science and practice*. Pacific Grove, CA: Brooks/Cole.

Saarinen, T. F. (1969). *Perception of environment* (Resource Paper No. 5). Washington, DC: Association of American Geographers, Commission on College Geography.

Sabatino, D. A., Meald, J. E., Rothman, S. G., & Miller, T. L. (1978). Destructive norm-violating social behavior among adolescents. A review of protective efforts. *Adolescence, 13*, 675–680.

Sadalla, E. K., Burroughs, J., & Quaid, M. (1980). House form and social identity. In R. Stough (Ed.), *Proceedings of the 11th International Meeting of the Environmental Design Research Association, 11*, 201–206.

Sadalla, E. K., Burroughs, W. J., & Staplin, L. J. (1980). Reference points in spatial cognition. *Journal of Experimental Psychology: Human Learning and Memory, 6*, 516–528.

Sadalla, E. K., & Magel, S. G. (1980). The perception of traversed distance. *Environment and Behavior, 12*, 65–79.

Sadalla, E. K., Sheets, V., McMcreath, H. (1990). The cognition of urban tempo. *Environment and Behavior, 22*, 230–254.

Sadalla, E. K., & Sheets, V. S. (1993). Symbolism in building materials: Self-preservation and cognitive components. *Environment and Behavior, 25*, 155–180.

Sadalla, E. K., & Staplin, L. J. (1980a). An information storage model for distance cognition. *Environment and Behavior, 12,* 183–193.

Sadalla, E. K., & Staplin, L. J. (1980b). The perception of traversed distance: Intersections. *Environment and Behavior, 12,* 167–182.

Saegert, S. (1974). *Effects of spatial and social density on arousal, mood, and social orientation.* Unpublished doctoral dissertation, University of Michigan.

Saegert, S. (1982). Environment and children's mental health: Residential density and low income children. In A. Baum & J. E. Singer (Eds.), *Handbook of psychology and health* (Vol. 2, pp. 247–271). Hillsdale, NJ: Erlbaum.

Saegert, S., MacIntosh, E., & West, S. (1975). Two studies of crowding in urban public spaces. *Environment and Behavior, 1,* 159–184.

Saegert, S., Swap, W., & Zajonc, R. B. (1973). Exposure, context, and interpersonal attraction. *Journal of Personality and Social Psychology, 25,* 234–242.

Samdahl, D. M., & Christensen, H. H. (1985). Environmental cues and vandalism: An exploratory study of picnic table carving. *Environment and Behavior, 17,* 445–458.

Samuelson, C. D., & Biek, M. (1991). Attitudes toward energy conservation: A confirmatory factor analysis. *Journal of Applied Social Psychology, 21,* 549–568.

Samuelson, C. D., & Messick, D. M. (1986). Inequities in access to and use of shared resources in social dilemmas. *Journal of Personality and Social Psychology, 51,* 960–967.

Samuelson, C. D., Messick, D. M., Rutte, C. G., & Wilke, H. (1984). Individual and structural solutions to resource dilemmas in two cultures. *Journal of Personality and Social Psychology, 47,* 94–104.

Samuelson, D. J., & Lindauer, M. S. (1976). Perception, evaluation, and performance in a neat and messy room by high and low sensation seekers. *Environment and Behavior, 8,* 291–306.

Sanborn, D. E., Casey, T. M., & Niswander, G. D. (1970). Suicide: Seasonal patterns and related variables. *Diseases of the Nervous System, 31,* 702–704.

Sanders, G., Freilicher, J., & Lightman, S. L. (1990). Psychological stress of exposure to uncontrollable noise increases plasma oxytocin in high emotionality women. *Psychoneuroimmunology, 15,* 47–58.

Sanders, M. S., & McCormick, E. J. (1987). *Human factors in engineering and design* (6th ed.). New York: McGraw-Hill.

Sandman, P. M., Weinstein, N. D., & Klotz, M. L. (1987). Public response to the risk from geological radon. *Journal of Communication, 37,* 93–108.

Santrock, J. W. (1976). Affect and facilitative self-control: Influence of ecological setting, cognition, and social agent. *Journal of Educational Psychology, 68,* 529–535.

Saunders, M., Gustanski, J., & Lawton, M. (1974). Effect of ambient illumination on noise levels of groups. *Journal of Applied Psychology, 59,* 527–528.

Savinar, J. (1975). The effect of ceiling height on personal space. *Man–Environment Systems, 5,* 321–324.

Savitz, D. A., & Calle, E. E. (1987). Leukemia and occupational exposure to electromagnetic fields: Review of epidemiologic surveys. *Journal of Occupational Medicine, 29,* 47–51.

Savitz, D. A., Wachtel, H., Barnes, F. A., John, E. M., & Tvrdik, J. G. (1988). Case-control study of childhood cancer and exposure to 60–Hz magnetic fields. *American Journal of Epidemiology, 128,* 21–38.

Schachter, S. (1959). *The psychology of affiliation.* Stanford, CA: Stanford University Press.

Schachter, S., & Singer, J. E. (1962). Cognitive, social, and physiological determinants of emotional states. *Psychological Review, 69,* 379–399.

Schaeffer, G. H., & Patterson, M. L. (1980). Intimacy, arousal, and small group crowding. *Journal of Personality and Social Psychology, 38,* 283–290.

Schaeffer, M. A., Baum, A., Paulus, P. B., & Gaes, G. G. (1988). Architecturally mediated effects of social density in prison. *Environment and Behavior, 20,* 3–19.

Schavio, S. (1975, May). *Factors mediating responses of invasions of personal space.* Paper presented at the meeting of the Rocky Mountain Psychological Association, Salt Lake City, UT.

Scheflen, A. E. (1971). Living space in an urban ghetto. *Family Process, 10,* 429–450.

Scheflen, A. E. (1976). *Human territories: How we behave in space-time.* Englewood Cliffs, NJ: Prentice-Hall.

Scheier, M. F., Carver, C. S., & Gibbons, F. X. (1979). Self-directed attention, awareness of bodily states, and suggestibility. *Journal of Personality and Social Psychology, 37,* 1576–1588.

Scherer, S. E. (1974). Proxemic behavior of primary school children as a function of their socioeconomic class and subculture. *Journal of Personality and Social Psychology, 29,* 800–805.

Schettino, A. P., & Borden, R. J. (1976). Sex differences in response to naturalistic crowding: Affective reactions to group size and group density. *Personality and Social Psychology Bulletin, 2,* 67–70.

Schiffenbauer, A., & Schiavo, R. S. (1975). *Physical distance and attraction: An intensification effect.* Unpublished manuscript. Virginia Polytechnic Institute and State University.

Schiffenbauer, A. I. (1979). Designing for high-density living. In J. R. Aiello & A. Baum (Eds.), *Residential crowding and design* (pp. 229–240). New York: Plenum.

Schindler, D. W. (1988). Effects of acid rain on freshwater ecosystems. *Science, 239,* 149–157.

Schkade, J. (1977). *The effects of expectancy set and crowding on task performance.* Doctoral dissertation, University of Texas at Arlington.

Schmidt, D. E., & Keating, J. P. (1979). Human crowding and personality control: An integration of research. *Psychological Bulletin, 86,* 680–700.

Schmidt, J. R. (1976). *Territorial invasion and aggression.* Doctoral dissertation, Louisiana State University and Agricultural and Mechanical College.

Schneider, F. W., Lesko, W. A., & Garrett, W. A. (1980). Helping behavior in hot, comfortable, and cold temperatures. *Environment and Behavior, 12,* 231–240.

Schneiderman, N. (1982). Animal behavior models of coronary heart disease. In D. S. Krantz, A. Baum, & J. E. Singer (Eds.), *Handbook of psychology and health* (Vol. 3, pp. 19–56). Hillsdale, NJ: Erlbaum.

Schnelle, J. F., Gendrich, J. G., Beegle, G. P., Thomas, M. M., & McNess, M. P. (1980). Mass media techniques for prompting behavior change in the community. *Environment and Behavior, 12,* 157–166.

Schopler, J., McCallum, R., & Rusbult, C. (1978). *Behavioral interference and internality–externality as determinants of subject crowding.* Unpublished manuscript, University of North Carolina.

Schopler, J., & Stockdale, J. (1977). An interference analysis of crowding. *Environmental Psychology and Nonverbal Behavior, 1,* 81–88.

Schopler, J., & Walton, M. (1974). *The effects of structure, expected enjoyment, and participants's internality–externality upon feelings of being crowded.* Unpublished manuscript. University of North Carolina.

Schreyer, R., & Roggenbuck, J. W. (1978). The influence of experience expectations on crowding perceptions and psychological carrying capacities. *Leisure Science, 1,* 373–394.

Schulte, J. H. (1963). Effects of mild carbon monoxide intoxication. *Archives of Environmental Health, 7,* 524–530.

Schultz, D. B. (1965). *Sensory restriction.* New York: Academic Press.

Schulz, R. (1976). Effects of control and predictability on the physical and psychological well-being of the institutionalized aged. *Journal of Personality and Social Psychology, 33,* 563–573.

Schulz, R., & Brenner, G. (1977). Relocation of the aged: A review and theoretical analysis. *Journal of Gerontology*, *32*, 323–333.

Schulz, R., & Hanusa, B. H. (1978). Long-term effects of control and predictability-enhancing interventions: Findings and ethical issues. *Journal of Personality and Social Psychology*, *36*, 1194–1201.

Schussheim, M. J. (1974). *A modest commitment to cities*. Lexington, MA: Lexington Books.

Schutte, N., Malouff, J., Lawrence, E., Glazer, K., & Cabrales, E. (1992). Creation and validation of a scale measuring perceived control over the institutional environment. *Environment and Behavior*, *24*, 366–380.

Schuyler, D. (1986). *The new urban landscape: The redefinition of city form in nineteenth-century America*. Baltimore: Johns Hopkins University Press.

Schwartz, B., & Barsky, S.P. (1977). The home advantage. *Social Forces*, *55*, 641–661.

Schwartz, D. C. (1968, July–August). On the ecology of political violence: "The long hot summer" as a hypothesis. *American Behavioral Scientist*, 24–28.

Schwartz, H., & Werbik, H. (1971). Eine experimentelle Untersuchunguber den Einfluss der syntaktischen Information der Anordnung von Baukopern entlang einer Strasse auf Stimmungen des Betrachters. *Zeitschrift fur experimentelle und angewandte Psychologie*, *18*, 499–511.

Schwebel, A. I., & Cherlin, D. L. (1972). Physical and social distancing in teacher–pupil relationships. *Journal of Educational Psychology*, *63*, 543–550.

Scott, A. L. (1993). A beginning theory of personal space boundaries. *Perspectives in Psychiatric Care*, *29*, 12–21.

Searleman, A., & Herrmann, D. (1994). *Memory from a broader perspective*. New York: McGraw-Hill.

Sears, D. O., Peplau, L. A., Freedman, J. L., & Taylor, S. E. (1988). *Social Psychology* (6th ed.). Englewood Cliffs, NJ: Prentice-Hall.

Sebba, R., & Churchman, A (1983). Territories and territoriality in the home. *Environment and Behavior*, *15*, 191–210.

Segal, M. W. (1974). Alphabet and attraction: An unobtrusive measure of the effect of propinquity in a field setting. *Journal of Personality and Social Psychology*, *30*, 655–657.

Segall, M. H., Campbell, D. T., & Herskovits, M. J. (1966). *The influence of culture on visual perception*. Indianapolis: Bobbs-Merrill.

Seidel, A. D. (1985). What is success in E & B research utilization? *Environment and Behavior*, *17*, 47–70.

Seligman, C. (1986). Energy consumption, attitudes, and behavior. In M. J. Saks & L. Saxe (Eds.), *Advances in applied social psychology* (Vol. 3, pp. 153–180). Hillsdale, NJ: Erlbaum.

Seligman, C., & Darley, J. M. (1977). Feedback as a means of decreasing residential energy consumption. *Journal of Applied Psychology*, *62*, 363–368.

Seligman, C., Kriss, M., Darley, J. M., Fazio, R. H., Becker, L. J., & Pryor, J. B. (1979). Predicting summer energy consumption from homeowners' attitudes. *Journal of Applied Social Psychology*, *9*, 70–90.

Seligman, M. E. P. (1970). On the generality of the laws of learning. *Psychological Review*, *77*, 406–418.

Seligman, M. E. P. (1975). *Helplessness*. San Francisco: Freeman.

Seligman, M. E. P. (1991). *Learned optimism*. New York: Alfred A. Knopf.

Sell, R. (1976). *Cooperation and competition as a function of residential environment, consequences of game strategy choices, and perceived control*. Doctoral dissertation, State University of New York–Stony Brook.

Sells, S. B., & Will, D. P. (1971). *Accidents, police incidents, and weather: A further study of the city of Fort Worth, Texas, 1968*. Technical Report No. 15, Fort Worth Group Psychology Branch, Office of Naval Research and Institute of Behavioral Research, Texas Christian University, Fort Worth.

Selye, H. (1956). *The stress of life*. New York: McGraw-Hill.

Seta, J. J., Paulus, P. B., & Schkade, J. K. (1976). Effects of group size and proximity under cooperative conditions. *Journal of Personality and Social Psychology*, *34*, 47–53.

Shafer, E., Jr., Hamilton, J. F., & Schmidt, E. A. (1969). Natural landscape preferences: A predictive model. *Journal of Leisure Research*, *1*, 1–19.

Shaffer, D. R., & Sadowski, C. (1975). This table is mine: Respect for marked barroom tables as a function of gender of spatial marker and desirability of locale. *Sociometry*, *38*, 408–419.

Shannon, M. P., Lonigan, C. J., Finch, A. J., & Taylor, C. M. (1994). Children exposed to disaster: I. Epidemiology of post-traumatic symptoms and symptoms profiles. *Journal of the American Academy of Child and Adolescent Psychiatry*, *33*, 80–93.

Sharpe, G. W. (1976). *Interpreting the environment*. New York: Wiley.

Shaw, K. T., & Gifford, R. (1994). Residents' and burglars' assessment of burglary risk from defensible space cues. *Journal of Environmental Psychology*, *14*, 177–194.

Shaw, L. G. (1987). Designing playgrounds for able and disabled children. In C. S. Weinstein & T. G. David (Eds.), *Spaces for children* (pp. 187–213). New York: Plenum.

Sherrod, D. R. (1974). Crowding, perceived control and behavioral aftereffects. *Journal of Applied Social Psychology*, *4*, 171–186.

Sherrod, D. R., Armstrong, D., Hewitt, J., Madonia, B., Speno, S., & Fenyd, D. (1977). Environmental attention, affect and altruism. *Journal of Applied Social Psychology*, *7*, 359–371.

Sherrod, D. R., & Cohen, S. (1979). Density, personal control, and design. In J. Aiello & A. Baum (Eds.), *Residential crowding and design* (pp. 217–227). New York: Plenum.

Sherrod, D. R., & Downs, R. (1974). Environmental determinants of altruism: The effects of stimulus overload and perceived control on helping. *Journal of Experimental Social Psychology*, *10*, 468–479.

Shippee, G. E. (1978). *Leadership, group participation, and avoiding the tragedy of the commons*. Unpublished doctoral dissertation, Arizona State University, Tempe, AZ.

Shippee, G. E., Burroughs, J., & Wakefield, S. (1980). Dissonance theory revisited: Perception of environmental hazards in residential areas. *Environment and Behavior*, *12*, 35–51.

Shlay, A. B. (1985). Castles in the sky: Measuring housing and neighborhood ideology. *Environment and Behavior*, *17*, 593–626.

Shlay, A. B. (1987). Who governs housing preferences: Comment on Morris. *Environment and Behavior*, *19*, 121–136.

Shoen, K. (1991). *Districts of pleasantness and danger*. Unpublished manuscript, St. Lawrence University.

Shore, J. H., Tatum, E. L., & Volmer, W. M. (1986). Psychiatric reactions to disaster: The Mount St. Helens experience. *American Journal of Psychiatry*, *143*, 590–595.

Shusterman, D. (1992). Critical review: The health significance of environmental odor pollution. *Archives of Environmental Health*, *47*, 76–87.

Sieber, W. J., Rodin, J., Larson, L., Ortega, S., Cummings, N., Levy, S., Whiteside, T., & Herberman, R. (1992). Modulation of human natural killer cell activity by exposure to uncontrollable stress. *Brain, Behavior, and Immunity*, *6*, 141–156.

Siegel, A. W., & White, S. (1975). The development of spatial representations of large scale environments. In H. W. Reese (Ed.), *Advances in child development and behavior* (pp. 9–55). NY: Academic Press.

Siegel, J. M., & Steele, C. M. (1980). Environmental distraction and interpersonal judgements. *British Journal of Social and Clinical Psychology*, *19*, 23–32.

Sigelman, C. K., & Adams, R. M. (1990). Family interactions in public: Parent–child distance and touching. *Journal of Nonverbal Behavior*, *14*, 63–75.

Sime, J. D. (1986). Creating places or designing spaces? *Journal of Environmental Psychology, 6,* 49–63.

Simmel, G. (1957). The metropolis and mental life. In K. H. Wolff (Ed. & Trans.), *The sociology of Georg Simmel* (pp. 409–424). London: The Free Press of Glencoe.

Simon, H. A. (1960). *The new science of management decisions.* New York: Harper & Row.

Simpson, M., & Perry, J. D. (1990). Crime and climate: A reconsideration. *Environment and Behavior, 22,* 295–300.

Simpson-Housley, P., Moore, R. J., Larrain, P., & Blair, D. (1982). Repression–sensitization and flood hazard appraisal in Carman, Manitoba. *Psychological Reports, 50,* 839–842.

Sims, J. H., & Baumann, D. D. (1972). The tornado threat: Coping styles of the North and South. *Science, 176,* 1386–1391.

Singer, J. E., Lundberg, U., & Frankenhaeuser, M. (1978). Stress on the train: A study of urban commuting. In A. Baum, J. E. Singer, & S. Valins (Eds.), *Advances in environmental psychology* (Vol. 1, pp. 41–56). Hillsdale, NJ: Erlbaum.

Skeen, D. R. (1976). Influence of interpersonal distance in serial learning. *Psychological Reports, 39,* 579–582.

Skogan, W., & Maxfield, M. (1981). *Coping with crime.* Beverly Hills, CA: Sage.

Skolnick, P., Frasier, L., & Hadar, I. (1977). Do you speak to strangers? A study of invasions of personal space. *European Journal of Social Psychology, 7,* 375–381.

Skorjanc, A. D. (1991). Differences in interpersonal distance among nonoffenders as a function of perceived violence of offenders. *Perceptual and Motor Skills, 73,* 659–662.

Skotko, V. P., & Langmeyer, D. (1977). The effects of interaction distance and gender on self-disclosure in the dyad. *Sociometry, 40,* 178–182.

Skov, T., Cordtz, T., Jensen, L. K., Saugman, P., Schmidt, K., & Theilade, P. (1991). Modifications of health behavior in response to air pollution notifications in Copenhagen. *Social Science and Medicine, 33,* 621–626.

Slaven, R. E., Wodarksi, J. S., & Blackburn, B. L. (1981). A group contingency for electricity conservation in master-metered apartments. *Journal of Applied Behavior Analysis, 14,* 357–363.

Sloan, A. W. (1979). *Man in extreme environments.* Springfield, IL: Thomas.

Sloane, P. D., Lindeman, D. A., Phillips, C., Moritz, D. J., & Koch, G. (1995). Evaluating Alzheimer's special care units: Reviewing the evidence and identifying potential sources of study bias. *The Gerontologist, 35,* 103–111.

Sloane, P. D., & Mathew, L. J. (Eds.). (1991). *Dementia units in long-term care.* Baltimore, MD: Johns Hopkins University Press.

Slote, L. (1961). An experimental evaluation of man's reaction to an ionized air environment. *Proceedings of the International Conference on Ionization of the Air, 2,* 1–22.

Slotsky, R. J. (1973). *Wilderness experience: A therapeutic modality.* San Francisco, CA: California School of Professional Psychology.

Slovic, P. (1987). Perception of risk. *Science, 236,* 280–285.

Slovic, P., Fischhoff, B., & Lichtenstein, S. (1981). Preceived risk: Psychological factors and social implications. *Proceedings of the Royal Society of London, A 376,* 17–34.

Smith, A. P. (1982). The effects of noise and task priority on recall of order and location. *Acta Psychologica, 51,* 245–255.

Smith, A. P. (1988). Acute effects of noise exposure: An experimental investigation of the effects of noise and task parameters on cognitive vigilance tasks. *International Archives of Occupational and Environmental Health, 60,* 307–310.

Smith, A. P., & Jones, D. M. (1992). Noise and performance. In D. M. Jones & A. P. Smith (Eds.), *Handbook of human performance* (Vol. 1, pp. 1–18). San Diego, CA: Academic Press.

Smith, A. P., & Stansfield, S. (1986). Aircraft noise exposure, noise sensitivity, and everyday errors. *Environment and Behavior, 18,* 214–226.

Smith, E. E., Shoben, E. J., & Rips, L. J. (1974). Structure and process in semantic memory: A featural model for semantic decisions. *Psychological Review, 81,* 214–241.

Smith, E. M., North, C. S., McCool, R. E., & Shea, J. M. (1990). Acute postdisaster psychiatric disorders: Identification of persons at risk. *American Journal of Psychiatry, 147,* 202–206.

Smith, G. C. (1991). Grocery shopping patterns of the ambulatory elderly. *Environment and Behavior, 23,* 86–114.

Smith, J. M., Bell, P. A., & Fusco, M. E. (1988). The influence of attraction on a simulated commons dilemma. *Journal of General Psychology, 115,* 277–283.

Smith, M. J., Cohen, B. G. F., & Stammerjohn, L. W. (1981). An investigation of health complaints and job stress in video display operations. *Human Factors, 28,* 387–400.

Smith, P., & Connolly, K. (1977). Social and aggressive behavior in preschool children as a function of crowding. *Social Science Information, 16,* 601–620.

Smith, P., & Connolly, K. (1980). *The ecology of preschool behaviour.* New York: Cambridge University Press.

Smith, R. J., & Knowles, E. S. (1979). Affective and cognitive mediators of reactions to spatial invasions. *Journal of Experimental Social Psychology, 15,* 437–452.

Smither, R. D. (1988). *The psychology of work and human performance.* New York: Harper & Row.

Snyder, L. H., & Ostrander, E. R. (1972, June). *Spatial and physical considerations in the nursing home environment: An interim report of findings.* Paper presented at the Cornell University Conference on Nursing Homes, Ithaca, NY.

Snyder, R. L. (1966). Fertility and reproductive performance of grouped male mice. In K. Benirschke (Ed.), *Symposium on comparative aspects of reproductive behavior.* Berlin: Springer Press.

Socolow, R. H. (1978). *Saving energy in the home.* Cambridge, MA: Ballinger.

Solomon, S. D., & Canino, G. J. (1990). Appropriateness of DSM-III-R criteria for Posttraumatic Stress Disorder. *Comprehensive Psychiatry, 31,* 227–237.

Solso, R. L., & Johnson, H. H. (1994). *Experimental psychology: A case approach* (5th ed.). New York: HarperCollins.

Sommer, R. (1959). Studies in personal space. *Sociometry, 22,* 247–260.

Sommer, R. (1965). Further studies of small group ecology. *Sociometry, 28,* 337–348.

Sommer, R. (1969). *Personal space.* Englewood Cliffs, NJ: Prentice-Hall.

Sommer, R. (1972). *Design awareness.* San Francisco: Rinehart Press.

Sommer, R. (1974). *Tight spaces: Hard architecture and how to humanize it.* Englewood Cliffs, NJ: Prentice-Hall.

Sommer, R. (1983). *Social design: Creating buildings with people in mind.* Englewood Cliffs, NJ: Prentice-Hall.

Sommer, R. (1989). Farmers' markets as community events. In I. Altman & E. H. Zube (Eds.), *Public places and spaces* (pp. 57–82). New York: Plenum.

Sommer, R., & Olsen, H. (1980). The soft classroom. *Environment and Behavior, 12,* 3–16.

Sommer, R., & Ross, H. (1958). Social interaction on a geriatrics ward. *International Journal of Social Psychiatry, 4,* 128–133.

Sommer, R., & Wicker, A. W. (1991). Gas station psychology: The case for specialization in ecological psychology. *Environment and Behavior, 23,* 131–149.

Sommers, P., & Moos, R. (1976). The weather and human behavior. In R. H. Moos (Ed.), *The human context: Environmental determinants of behavior* (pp. 73–107). New York: Wiley.

Sonnenfeld, J. (1966). Variable values in space and landscape: An inquiry into the nature of environmental necessity. *Journal of Social Issues, 22,* 71–82.

Southwick, C. H. (1967). An experimental study of intragroup agonistic behavior in rhesus monkeys (Macaca mulatta). *Behavior, 28*, 182–209.

Southworth, M., & Owens, P. M. (1993). The evolving metropolis: Studies of community, neighborhood, and street form at the urban edge. *Journal of the American Planning Association, 59*, 271–287.

Spivey, G. H., Brown, C. P., Baloh, R. W., Campion, D. S., Valentine, J. L., Massey, F. J., Jr., Browdy, B. L., & Culver, B. D. (1979). Subclinical effects of chronic increased lead absorption—A prospective study. I. Study design and analysis of symptoms. *Journal of Occupational Medicine, 21*, 423–429.

Spreckelmeyer, K. F. (1993). Office relocation and environmental change: A case study. *Environment and Behavior, 25*, 181–204.

Spyker, J. M. (1975). Assessing the impact of low level chemicals on development: Behavioral and latent effects. *Federation Processings, 34*, 1835–1844.

Srivastava, P., & Mandal, M. K. (1990). Proximal spacing to facial affect expressions in schizophrenia. *Comprehensive Psychiatry, 31*, 119–124.

Srivastava, R. K. (1974). Undermanning theory in the context of mental health care environments. In D. H. Carson (Ed.), *Man—environment interactions* (Part 2, pp. 245–258). Stroudsberg, PA: Dowden, Hutchinson, & Ross.

Srole, L. (1972). Urbanization and mental health: Some reformulations. *American Scientist, 60*, 576–583.

Srole, L. (1976). The city vs. the country: New evidence on an ancient bias. In L. Srole & A. Fischer (Eds.), *Mental health in the metropolis* (2nd ed.). New York: Harper & Row.

Stahl, S. M., & Lebedun, M. (1974). Mystery gas: An analysis of mass hysteria. *Journal of Health and Social Behavior, 15*, 44–50.

Stainbrook, E. (1966). Architects not only design hospitals: They also design patient behavior. *Modern Hospital, 106*, 100.

Stankey, G. H. (1973). Visitor perception of wilderness recreation carrying capacity (Research Paper NO. INT–142, p. 62). Ogden, UT: U.S. Department of Agriculture, Intermountain Forest and Range Experiment Station.

Stansfield, S. A. (1992). Noise, noise sensitivity and psychiatric disorder: Epidemiological and psychophysiological studies. *Psychological Medicine, Monograph Supplement 22*. Cambridge University Press: Cambridge.

Stansfield, S. A., Sharp, D. S., Gallacher, J., & Babisch, W. (1993). Road traffic noise, noise sensitivity, and psychological disorder. *Psychological Medicine, 23*, 977–985.

Starr, S. J., Thompson, C. R., & Shute, S. J. (1982). Effects of video display terminals on telephone operators. *Human Factors, 24*, 699–711.

Stea, D., & Blaut, J. M. (1973). Some preliminary observations on spatial learning in school children. In R. Downs & D. Stea (Eds.), *Image and the environment* (pp. 226–234). Chicago: Aldine.

Steblay, N. M. (1987). Helping behavior in rural and urban environments: A meta analysis. *Psychological Bulletin, 102*, 346–356.

Steele, F. (1981). *The sense of place*. Boston: CBI.

Steidl, R. E. (1972). Difficulty factors in homemaking tasks: Implications for environmental design. *Human Factors, 14*, 471–482.

Steinglass, P., & Gerrity, E. (1990). Natural disasters and Post-Traumatic Stress Disorder: Short-term versus long-term recovery in two disaster-affected communities. *Journal of Applied Social Psychology, 20*, 1746–1765.

Steinitz, C. (1968). Meaning and congruence of urban form and activity. *Journal of the American Institute of Plannners, 34*, 233–248.

Stellman, J. M., Klitzman, S., Gordon, G. C., & Snow, B. R. (1987). Work environments and the well-being of clerical and VDT workers. *Journal of Occupational Behaviour, 8*, 95–114.

Stern, P. C. (1976). Effect of incentives and education on resource conservation decisions in a simulated commons dilemma. *Journal of Personality and Social Psychology, 25*, 1285–1292.

Stern, P. C. (1992a). Psychological dimensions of global environmental change. *Annual Review of Psychology, 43*, 269–302.

Stern, P. C. (1992b). What psychology knows about energy conservation. *American Psychologist, 47*, 1224–1232.

Stern, P. C., & Aronson, E. (Eds.). (1984). *Energy use: The human dimension*. New York: Freeman.

Stern, P. C., Dietz, T., & Kalof, L. (1993). Value orientations, gender, and environmental concern. *Environment and Behavior, 25*, 322–348.

Stern, P. C., & Gardner, G. T. (1981). Psychological research and energy policy. *American Psychologist, 4*, 329–342.

Stern, P. C., & Oskamp, S. (1987). Managing scarce environmental resources. In D. Stokols & I. Altman (Eds.), *Handbook of environmental psychology* (Vol. 2, pp. 1043–1088). New York: Wiley-Interscience.

Stevens, A., & Coupe, P. (1978). Distortions in judged spatial relations. *Cognitive Psychology, 10*, 422–437.

Stevens, S. S. (1955). The measurement of loudness. *Journal of the Acoustical Society of America, 27*, 815–829.

Stevens, W., Kushler, M., Jeppesen, J., & Leedom, N. (1979). *Youth energy education strategies: A statistical evaluation*. Lansing, MI: Energy Extension Service, Department of Commerce.

Stewart, T. R. (1987). Developing an observer-based measure of environmental annoyance. In H. S. Koelega (Ed.), *Environmental annoyance: Characterization, measurement, and control* (pp. 213–222). New York: Elsevier.

Stewart, T. R., Middleton, P., & Ely, D. (1983). Urban visual air quality judgments: Reliability and validity. *Journal of Environmental Psychology, 3*, 129–145.

Stires, L. (1980). Classroom seating location, student grades and attitudes: Environment or selection? *Environment and Behavior, 12*, 241–254.

Stobaugh, R., & Yergin, D. (1979). *Energy future: Report of the energy project of the Harvard Business School*. New York: Random House.

Stokols, D. (1972). On the distinction between density and crowding: Some implications for future research. *Psychological Review, 79*, 275–278.

Stokols, D. (1976). The experience of crowding in primary and secondary environments. *Environment and Behavior, 8*, 49–86.

Stokols, D. (1978). A typology of crowding experiences. In A. Baum & Y. Epstein (Eds.), *Human response to crowding* (pp. 219–255). Hillsdale, NJ: Erlbaum.

Stokols, D. (1979). A congruence analysis of human stress. In I. G. Sarason & C. D. Spielberger (Eds.), *Stress and anxiety* (Vol. 6, pp. 27–53). New York: Wiley.

Stokols, D. (1983). Editor's introduction: Theoretical directions of environment and behavior research. *Environment and Behavior, 15*, 259–272.

Stokols, D. (1990). Instrumental and spiritual views of people–environment relations. *American Psychologist, 45*, 641–646.

Stokols, D., & Altman, I. (Eds.). (1987). *Handbook of environmental psychology* (Vol. 1, pp. xi–xii). New York: Wiley.

Stokols, D. & Novaco, R. W. (1981). Transportation and well-being: An ecological perspective. In I. Altman, J. F. Wohlwill, & P. B. Everett (Eds.), *Transportation and behavior* (pp. 85–130). New York: Plenum.

Stokols, D., & Ohlig, W. (1975, August). *The experience of crowding under different social climates*. Paper presented at the meeting of the American Psychological Association, Chicago, IL.

Stokols, D., Rall, M., Pinner, B., & Schopler, J. (1973). Physical, social and personal determinants of the perception of crowding. *Environment and Behavior, 5*, 87–117.

Stone, G. L., & Morden, C. J. (1976). Effect of distance on verbal productivity. *Journal of Counseling Psychology, 23*, 486–488.

Stone, J., Breidenbach, S., & Heimstra, N. (1979). Annoyance response of nonsmokers to cigarette smoke. *Perceptual and Motor Skills, 49,* 907–916.

Stone, R. (1992). Polarized debate: EMFs and cancer. *Science, 258,* 1724–1725.

Stone, R. (1995). If the mercury soars, so may health hazards. *Science, 267,* 957–958.

Storms, M. D., & Thomas, G. C. (1977). Reactions to physical closeness. *Journal of Personality and Social Psychology, 35,* 412–418.

Strahilevitz, N., Strahilevitz, A., & Miller, J. E. (1979). Air pollution and the admission rate of psychiatric patients. *American Journal of Psychiatry, 136,* 206–207.

Strakhov, A. B. (1966). *Some questions of the mechanism of the action of noise on an organism* (Report N67–11646). Washington, DC: Joint Publication Research Service.

Strodtbeck, F., & Hook, H. (1961). The social dimension of a 12-man jury table. *Sociometry, 24,* 397–415.

Strube, M. J., & Werner, C. (1984). Psychological reactance and the relinquishment of control. *Personality and Social Psychology Bulletin, 10,* 225–234.

Suedfeld, P. (1975). The benefits of boredom: Sensory deprivation reconsidered. *American Scientist, 63,* 60–69.

Suedfeld, P. (1980). *Restricted environmental stimulation: Research and clinical applications.* New York: Wiley.

Suedfeld, P. (1991). Polar psychology: An overview. *Environment and Behavior, 23,* 653–665.

Suedfeld, P., & Baker-Brown, G. (1986). Restricted environmental therapy and aversive conditioning in smoking cessation: Active and placebo effects. *Behavior Research and Therapy, 24,* 421–428.

Suedfeld, P., & Mocellin, J. S. P. (1987). The "sensed presence" in unusual environments. *Environment and Behavior, 19,* 33–52.

Suedfeld, P., Roy, C., & Landon, P. B. (1982). Restricted environmental stimulation therapy in the treatment of essential hypertension. *Behavior Research and Therapy, 20,* 553–559.

Suedfeld, P., Schwartz, G., & Arnold, W. (1980). Study of restricted environmental stimulation therapy (REST) as a treatment for autistic children. *Journal of Autism and Developmental Disorders, 10,* 337–378.

Suedfeld, P., Turner, J. W., Jr., & Fine, T. H., (Eds.). (1990). *Restricted environmental stimulation: Theoretical and empirical developments in flotation REST.* New York: Springer.

Sullivan, M. A., Saylor, C., & Foster, S. C. (1991). Post-hurricane adjustment of preschoolers and their families. *Advances in Behavior, Research, and Therapy, 13,* 163–172.

Sulman, F. G., Danon, A., Pfeifer, Y., Tal, E., & Weller, C. P. (1970). Urinalysis of patients suffering from climatic heat stress (Sharav). *International Journal of Biometeorology, 14,* 45–53.

Sundeen, R. A., & Mathieu, J. T. (1976). Fear of crime and its consequences among elderly in three urban communities. *The Gerontologist, 16,* 211–219.

Sundstrom, E. (1975). An experimental study of crowding: Effects of room size, intrusion, and global-blocking on nonverbal behaviors, self-disclosure, and self-reported stress. *Journal of Personality and Social Psychology, 32,* 645–654.

Sundstrom, E. (1976). Interpersonal behavior and the physical environment. In L. S. Wrightsman (Ed.), *Social psychology* (2nd ed). Monterey, CA: Brooks/Cole.

Sundstrom, E. (1978). Crowding as a sequential process: Review of research of the effects of population density on humans. In A. Baum & Y. M. Epstein (Eds.), *Human response to crowding* (pp. 31–116). Hillsdale, NJ: Erlbaum.

Sundstrom, E. (1986a). Jobs in the eighties: Three views of work-redesign. *Journal of Environmental Psychology, 6,* 155–162.

Sundstrom, E. (1986b). *Work places: The psychology of the physical environment in offices and factories.* New York: Cambridge.

Sundstrom, E. (1987). Work environments: Offices and factories.

In D. Stokols & I. Altman (Eds.), *Handbook of environmental psychology* (pp. 733–782). New York: Wiley-Interscience.

Sundstrom, E., & Altman, I. (1976). Personal space and interpersonal relationships: Research review and theoretical model. *Human Ecology, 4,* 47–67.

Sundstrom, E., Herbert, R. K., & Brown, D. W. (1982). Privacy and communication in an open plan office. *Environment and Behavior, 14,* 379–392.

Sundstrom, E., & Sundstrom, M. G. (1977). Personal space invasions: What happens when the invader asks permission? *Environmental Psychology and Nonverbal Behavior, 2,* 76–82.

Sundstrom, E., Town, J. P., Rice, R. W., Osborn, D. P., & Brill, M. (1994). Office noise, satisfaction, and performance. *Environment and Behavior, 26,* 195–222.

Susa, A. M., & Benedict, J. O. (1994). The effects of playground design on pretend play and divergent thinking. *Environment and Behavior, 26,* 560–579.

Suter, T. W., Buzzi, R., Woodson, P. P., & Battig, K. (1983, December). Psychophysiological correlates of conflict solving and cigarette smoking. *Activitas Nervosa Superior, 25,* 261–272.

Suttles, G. D. (1968). *The social order of the slum: Ethnicity and territory in the inner city.* Chicago: University of Chicago Press.

Swan, J. A. (1970). Response to air pollution: A study of attitudes and coping strategies of high school youths. *Environment and Behavior, 2,* 127–152.

Swanson, C. P. (1973). *The natural history of man.* Englewood Cliffs, NJ: Prentice-Hall.

Swap, W. C. (1977). Interpersonal attraction and repeated exposure to rewarders and punishers. *Personality and Social Psychology Bulletin, 3,* 248–251.

Swartz, E. D., & Kowalski, J. M. (1992). Malignant memories: Reluctance to utilize mental health services after a disaster. *Journal of Nervous and Mental Disease, 180,* 767–771.

Sweeney, P. D., Anderson, K., & Bailey, S. (1986). Attributional style in depression: A meta-analytic review. *Journal of Personality and Social Psychology, 50,* 974–991.

Syme, G. L., Seligman, C., Kantola, S. J., & MacPherson, D. K. (1987). Evaluating a television campaign to promote petrol conservation. *Environment and Behavior, 19,* 444–461.

Szilagyi, A. D., & Holland, W. E. (1980). Changes in social density: Relationships with functional interaction and perceptions of job characteristics, role stress, and work satisfaction. *Journal of Applied Psychology, 65,* 28–33.

Talbot, J. F., & Kaplan, S. (1986). Perspectives on wilderness: Re-examining the value of extended wilderness experiences. *Journal of Environmental Psychology, 6,* 177–188.

Talbot, J. F., Kaplan, R., Kuo, F. E., & Kaplan, S. (1993). Factors that enhance effectiveness of visitor maps. *Environment and Behavior, 25,* 743–760.

Tasso, J., & Miller, E. (1976). The effects of the full moon on human behavior. *Journal of Psychology, 93,* 81–83.

Taubes, G. (1993). The ozone backlash. *Science, 260,* 1580–1583.

Taylor, F. W. (1911). *The principles of scientific management.* New York: Harper and Brothers.

Taylor, H. R., West, S. K., Rosenthal, F. S., Munoz, B., Newland, H. S., Abbey, H., & Emmett, E. A. (1988). Effect of ultraviolet radiation on cataract formation. *New England Journal of Medicine, 319,* 1429–1433.

Taylor, R. B. (1978). Human territoriality: A review and a model for future research. *Cornell Journal of Social Relations, 13,* 125–151.

Taylor, R. B. (1988). *Human territorial functioning.* Cambridge: Cambridge University Press.

Taylor, R. B., & Brooks, D. K. (1980). Temporary territories: Responses to intrusions in a public setting. *Population and Environment, 3,* 135–145.

Taylor, R. B., & Brower, S. (1985). Home and near-home territories. In I. Altman & C. Werner (Eds.), *Human behavior and* environment: *Current theory and research, Vol. 8: Home environments* (pp. 183–212). New York: Plenum.

Taylor, R. B., & Covington, J. (1988). Neighborhood changes. *Ecology and Violent Criminology, 26,* 553–591.

Taylor, R. B., & Ferguson, G. (1978, August). *Solitude and intimacy: Privacy experiences and the role of territoriality.* Paper presented at the meeting of the American Psychological Association, Toronto, Canada.

Taylor, R. B., Gottfredson, S. D., & Brower, S. (1981). Territorial cognitions and social climate in urban neighborhoods. *Basic and Applied Social Psychology, 2,* 289–303.

Taylor, R. B., Gottfredson, S., & Brower, S. (1984). Understanding block crime and fear. *Journal of Research in Crime and Delinquency, 21,* 303–331.

Taylor, R. B., & Hale, M. (1986). Testing alternative models of fear of crime. *Journal of Law and Criminology, 77,* 151–189.

Taylor, R. B., & Lanni, J. C. (1981). Territorial dominance: The influence of the resident advantage in triadic decision making. *Journal of Personality and Social Psychology, 41,* 909–915.

Taylor, R. B., & Stough, R. R. (1978). Territorial cognition: Assessing Altman's typology. *Journal of Personality and Social Psychology, 36,* 418–423.

Taylor, S. (1979). Hospital patient behavior: Reactance, helplessness, or control? *Journal of Social Issues, 35,* 156–184.

Taylor, V., & Quarantelli, E. (1976). *Some needed cross-cultural studies of disaster behavior.* Columbus, OH: Disaster Research Center.

Tennen, H., & Eller, S. J. (1977). Attributional components of learned helplessness and facilitation. *Journal of Personality and Social Psychology, 35,* 265–271.

Tennis, G. H., & Dabbs, J. M. (1975). Sex, setting and personal space: First grade through college. *Sociometry, 38,* 385–394.

Terr, L. C. (1979). Children of Chowchilla. *Psychoanalytical Study of Child, 34,* 547–643.

Terr, L. C. (1983). Chowchilla revisited: The effects of psychic trauma four years after a school-bus kidnapping. *American Journal of Psychiatry, 140,* 1543–1550.

Terry, R. L., & Lower, M. (1979). Perceptual withdrawal from an invasion of personal space. *Personality and Social Psychology Bulletin, 5,* 396–397.

Thalhofer, N. N. (1980). Violation of a spacing norm in high social density. *Journal of Applied Social Psychology, 10,* 175–183.

Theil, P. (1994). Beyond design review: Implications for design practice, education, and research. *Environment and Behavior, 26,* 363–376.

Theorell, T. (1990). Family history of hypertension—an individual trait interacting with spontaneously occurring job stressors. *Scandinavian Journal of Work and Environmental Health, 16(Suppl. 1),* 74–79.

Thoits, P. A. (1982). Conceptual, methodological, and theoretical problems in studying social support as a buffer against life stress. *Journal of Health and Social Behavior, 23,* 145–159.

Thompson, D. R. (1993). *Considering the museum visitor: An interactional approach to environmental design.* Unpublished doctoral dissertation, University of Wisconsin–Milwaukee.

Thompson, J., Chung, M. C., & Rosser, R. (1994). The Marchioness disaster: Preliminary report on psychological effects. *British Journal of Clinical Psychology, 33,* 75–77.

Thompson, M. P., Norris, F. H., & Hanacek, B. (1993). Age differences in the psychological consequences of Hurricane Hugo. *Psychology and Aging, 8,* 606–616.

Thompson, S. C. (1981). Will it hurt less if I can control it? A complex answer to a simple question. *Psychological Bulletin, 90,* 89–101.

Thompson, S. C., & Stoutemyer, K. (1991). Water use as a commons dilemma: The effects of education that focuses on long-term consequences and individual action. *Environment and Behavior, 23,* 314–333.

Thompson, S. C. G., & Barton, M. (1994). Ecocentric and anthropocentric attitudes toward the environment. *Journal of Environmental Psychology, 14,* 149–157.

Thompson, W. R., & Heron, W. (1954). The effects of restricting early experience on the problem-solving capacity of dogs. *Canadian Journal of Psychology, 8,* 17–31.

Thomson, G. (1986). *The museum environment* (2nd ed.). Stoneham, MA: Butterworth.

Thorndyke, P. W., & Hayes-Roth, B. (1982). Differences in spatial knowledge acquired from maps and navigation. *Cognitive psychology, 14,* 560–589.

Thorne, R., Hall, R., & Munro-Clark, M. (1982). Attitudes toward detached houses, terraces and apartments: Some current pressures towards less preferred but more accessible alternatives. In P. Bart, A. Chen, & G. Francescato (Eds.), *Knowledge for design: Proceedings of the 13th Environmental Design Research Association Conference* (pp. 435–448). Washington, DC: Environmental Design Research Association.

Thorson, J. A., & Powell, F. C. (1992). Rural and urban elderly construe health differently. *Journal of Psychology, 126,* 251–260.

Tichener, J., & Kapp, F. I. (1976). Family and character change at Buffalo Creek. *American Journal of Psychiatry, 133,* 295–299.

Tien, J. M., O'Donnell, V. F., Barnett, A., & Mirchandini, P. B. (1979). *Street lighting projects.* Washington, DC: Department of Justice.

Timasheff, N. S. (1967). *Sociological theory: Its nature and growth* (3rd ed.). New York: Random House.

Tinsley, H. E., & Johnson, T. L. (1984). A preliminary taxonomy of leisure activities. *Journal of Leisure Research, 16,* 234–244.

Tinsley, H. E., & Tinsley, D. J. (1986). A theory of the attributes, benefits, and causes of leisure experience. *Leisure Sciences, 8,* 1–45.

Toffler, A. (1980). *The third wave.* New York: Bantam Books.

Tognoli, J. (1980). Differences in women's and men's responses to domestic space. *Sex Roles, 6,* 833–842.

Tognoli, J. (1987). Residential environments. In D. Stokols & I. Altman (Eds.), *Handbook of environmental psychology* (Vol. 1, pp. 655–690). New York: Wiley-Interscience.

Tolman, E. C. (1948). Cognitive maps in rats and men. *Psychological Review, 55,* 189–208.

Tolman, E. C., Ritchie, B. F., & Kalish, D. (1946). Studies in spatial learning I. Orientation and the short-cut. *Journal of Experimental Psychology, 36,* 13–24.

Topf, M. (1992a). Stress effects of personal control over hospital noise. *Behavioral Medicine, 18,* 84–94.

Topf, M. (1992b). Stress effects of personal control over hospital noise on sleep. *Research in Nursing and Health, 15,* 19–28.

Traub, R. E., & Weiss, J. (1974). Studying openness in education: An Ontario example. *Journal of Research and Development in Education, 8,* 47–59.

Trice, H. M. (1966). *Alcoholism in America.* New York: McGraw-Hill.

Trites, D., Galbraith, F. D., Sturdavent, M., & Leckwart, J. F. (1970). Influence of nursing unit design on the activities and subjective feelings of nursing personnel. *Environment and Behavior, 2,* 303–334.

Tromp, S. W. (1980). *Biometeorology: The impact of weather and climate on humans and their environment.* Philadelphia: Heyden.

Trotter, D. (1982). *The lighting of underground mines.* Clausthal-Zellerfeld, Germany: Trans Tech Publications.

Trowbridge, C. C. (1913). On fundamental methods of orientation and "imaginary maps." *Science, 88,* 888–896.

Truscott, J. C., Parmelee, P., & Werner, C. (1977). Plate touching in restaurants—Preliminary observations of a food-related marking behavior in humans. *Journal of Personality and Social Psychology, 35,* 425–428.

Tuan, Y. (1974). *Topophilia: A study of environmental perception, attitude, and values.* Englewood Cliffs, NJ: Prentice-Hall.

Turk, A., Johnston, J. W., & Moulton, D. G. (Eds.). (1974). *Human responses to environmental odors*. New York: Academic Press.

Turk, A., Turk, J., Wittes, J. T., & Wittes, R. (1974). *Environmental science*. Philadelphia: Saunders.

Turnage, J. J. (1990). The challenge of new workplace technology for psychology. *American Psychologist, 45,* 171–178.

Turner, J. A., & Karasek, R. A., Jr. (1984). Software ergonomics: Effects of computer application design parameters on operator task performance and health. *Ergonomics, 27,* 663–690.

Turner, P. V. (1984). *Campus: An American planning tradition.* Cambridge, MA: M.I.T. Press.

Tversky, B. (1981). Distortions in memory for maps. *Cognitive Psychology, 13,* 407–433.

Tye, M. (1991). *The imagery debate.* Cambridge, MA: M.I.T. Press.

Tyler, T. R. (1981). Perceived control and behavioral reactions to crime. *Personality and Social Psychology Bulletin, 7,* 212–217.

Ugwuegbu, D. C., & Anusiem, A. U. (1982). Effects of stress on interpersonal distance in a simulated interview situation. *Journal of Social Psychology, 116,* 3–7.

Ulrich, R. S. (1977). Visual landscape preference: A model and applications. *Man–Environment Systems, 7,* 279–292.

Ulrich, R. S. (1979). Visual landscapes and psychological well-being. *Landscape Research, 4,* 17–23.

Ulrich, R. S. (1981). Natural versus urban scenes: Some psychophysiological effects. *Environment and Behavior, 13,* 523–556.

Ulrich, R. S. (1983). Aesthetic and affective responses to the natural environment. In I. Altman & J. Wohlwill (Eds.), *Human behavior and environment, Vol. 6: Behavior and the natural environment* (pp. 51–84). New York: Plenum.

Ulrich, R. S. (1984). View through a window may influence recovery from surgery. *Science, 224,* 420–421.

Ulrich, R. S. (1986). Human responses to vegetation and landscapes. *Landscape and Urban Planning, 13,* 29–44.

Ulrich, R. S. (1993). Biophilia and the conservation ethic. In S. R. Kellert & E. O. Wilson (Eds.), *The biophilia hypothesis* (pp. 73–137). Washington, DC: Island Press.

Ulrich, R. S., Simmons, R. F., Losito, B. D., Fiorito, E., Miles, M. A., & Zelson, M. (1991). Stress recovery during exposure to natural and urban environments. *Journal of Environmental Psychology, 11,* 201–230.

Unger, D., & Wandersman, A. (1983). Neighboring and its role in block organizations: An exploratory report. *American Journal of Community Psychology, 11,* 291–300.

Ury, H. K., Perkins, N. M., & Goldsmith, J. R. (1972). Motor vehicle accidents and vehicular pollution in Los Angeles. *Archives of Environmental Health, 25,* 314–322.

U.S. Bureau of the Census. (1990). *Statistical abstracts of the United States: 1990.* Washington, DC: U.S. Government Printing Office.

U.S. Conference of Mayors. (1987). *Status report on homeless families in America's cities: A 29–city survey.* Washington, DC: U.S. Conference of Mayors.

U.S. Riot Commission (1968). *Report of the National Advisory Commission on Civil Disorders.* New York: Bantam Books.

Vallet, M. (1987). The effects of non-acoustic factors on annoyance due to traffic noise. In H. S. Koelega (Ed.), *Environmental annoyance: Characterization, measurement, and control* (pp. 371–382). Amsterdam: Elsevier Science Publishers.

van der Pligt, J. (1985). Public attitudes to nuclear energy: Salience and anxiety. *Journal of Environmental Psychology, 5,* 87–97.

Vanetti, E. J., & Allen, G. L. (1988). Communicating environmental knowledge: The impact of verbal and spatial abilities on the production and comprehension of route directions. *Environment and Behavior, 20,* 667–682.

Van Houten, R., & Nau, P. A. (1981). A comparison of the ef-

fects of posted feedback and increased police surveilance on highway speeding. *Journal of Applied Behavior Analysis, 14,* 261–271.

Van Houten, R., Nau, P. A., & Marini, Z. (1980). An analysis of public posting in reducing speeding behavior on an urban highway. *Journal of Applied Behavioral Analysis, 13,* 283–295.

van Vliet, W. (1981). Neighborhood evaluations by city and suburban children. *Journal of the American Planning Association, 47,* 458–466.

van Vliet, W. (1983). Families in apartment buildings: Sad stories for children? *Environment and Behavior, 156,* 211–234.

Van Vugt, M., Meertens, R. M., & Van Lange, P. A. M. (1995). Car versus public transportation? The role of social value orientations in a real-life social dilemma. *Journal of Applied Social Psychology, 25,* 258–278.

Vaughan, E. (1993). Individual and cultural differences in adaptation to environmental risks. *American Psychologist, 48,* 673–680.

Veitch, J. A., & Kaye, S. M. (1988). Illumination effects on conversational sound levels and job candidate evaluations. *Journal of Environmental Psychology, 8,* 223–233.

Venturi, R. (1966). *Complexity and contradiction in architecture.* New York: Museum of Modern Art.

Verderber, S. (1986). Dimensions of person–window transactions in the hospital environment. *Environment and Behavior, 18,* 450–466.

Vernon, J., & McGill, T. E. (1957). The effect of sensory deprivation upon rote learning. *American Journal of Psychology, 70,* 637–639.

Vining, J., Daniel, T. C., & Schroeder, H. W. (1984). Predicting scenic values in forested residential landscapes. *Journal of Leisure Research, 16,* 124–135.

Vining, J., & Ebreo, A. (1990). What makes a recycler? A comparison of recyclers and nonrecyclers. *Environment and Behavior, 22,* 55–73.

Vining, J., & Ebreo, A. (1992). Predicting recycling behavior from global and specific environmental attitudes and changes in recycling behavior. *Journal of Applied Social Psychology, 22,* 1580–1607.

Vinsel, A., Brown, B., Altman, I., & Foss, C. (1980). Privacy regulation, territorial displays, and effectiveness of individual functioning. *Journal of Personality and Social Psychology, 39,* 1104–1115.

Vogel, J. M., & Vernberg, E. M. (1993). Part 1: Children's psychological responses to disasters. *Journal of Clinical Child Psychology, 22,* 464–484.

Von Wright, J., & Nuimi, L. (1979). Effects of white noise and irrelevant information on speeded classification: Developmental study. *Acta Psychologica, 43,* 157–166.

Wack, J., & Rodin, J. (1978). Nursing homes for the aged: The human consequences of legislation-shaped environments. *Journal of Social Issues, 34,* 6–21.

Walden, T. A., Nelson, P. A., & Smith, D. E. (1981). Crowding, privacy, and coping. *Environment and Behavior, 13,* 205–224.

Walder, D. N. (1967). Decompression sickness in tunnel workers. In C. N. Davies, P. R. Davis, & F. H. Tyrer (Eds.), *The effects of abnormal physical conditions at work* (pp. 101–110). London: E & S Livingstone.

Waldrop, M. M. (1988). Taking back the night. *Science, 241,* 1288–1289.

Walker, J. M. (1979). Energy demand behavior in a master-meter apartment complex: An experimental analysis. *Journal of Applied Psychology, 64,* 190–196.

Walmsley, D. J., & Lewis, G. J. (1989). The pace of pedestrian flows in cities. *Environment and Behavior, 21,* 123–150.

Wandersman, A. (1981). A framework of participation in community organizations. *Journal of Applied Behavioral Science, 17,* 27–58.

Wandersman, A., & Florin, P. (1981). A cognitive social learning approach to the crossroads of cognitive social behavior and the environment. In J. Harvey (Ed.), *Cognitive social behavior and environment*. Hillsdale, NJ: Erlbaum.

Wandersman, A., & Hess, R. (Eds.) (1985). *Beyond the individual: Environmental approaches and prevention*. New York: Haworth.

Wang, T. H., & Katzev, R. D. (1990). Group commitment and resource conservation: Two field experiments on promoting recycling. *Journal of Applied Social Psychology, 20*, 265–275.

Wann, D. L., & Weaver, K. A. (1993). The relationship between interaction levels and impression formation. *Bulletin of the Psychonomic Society, 31*, 548–550.

Ward, L. M., & Russell, J. A. (1981). Cognitive set and the perception of place. *Environment and Behavior, 13*, 610–632.

Ward, L. M., & Suedfeld, P. (1973). Human responses to highway noise. *Environmental Research, 6*, 306–326.

Ward, S. L., Newcombe, N., & Overton, W. F. (1986). Turn left at the church or three miles north: A study of direction giving and sex differences. *Environment and Behavior, 18*, 192–213.

Warner, S. B., Jr. (1978). *Streetcar suburbs: The process of growth in Boston, 1870–1900* (2nd ed.). Cambridge, MA: Harvard University Press.

Warren, D. H. (1994). Self-localization on plan and oblique maps. *Environment and Behavior, 26*, 71–98.

Warren, D. H., & Scott, T. E. (1993). Map alignment in traveling multisegment routes. *Environment and Behavior, 25*, 643–666.

Warzecha, S., Fisher, J. D., & Baron, R. M.(1988). The equity-control model as a predictor of vandalism among college students. *Journal of Applied Social Psychology, 18*, 80–91.

Waterson, R. (1991). *The living house: An anthropology of architecture in South East Asia*. Singapore: Oxford University Press.

Watson, O. M., & Graves, T. D. (1966). Quantitative research in proxemic behavior. *American Anthropologist, 68*, 971–985.

Webb, E. J., Campbell, D. T., Schwartz, R. D., Sechrest, L., & Grove, J. B. (1981). *Nonreactive measures in social sciences* (2nd ed.). Dallas: Houghton Mifflin.

Webb, W. M., & Worchel, S. (1993). Prior experience and expectation in the context of crowding. *Journal of Personality and Social Psychology, 65*, 512–521.

Webber, M. M. (1963). Order in diversity: Community without propinquity. In L. Wingo, Jr. (Ed.), *Cities and space: The future use of urban land* (pp. 23–54). Baltimore: The Johns Hopkins Press.

Weenig, M. W. H., Schmidt, T., & Midden, C. J. H. (1990). Social dimensions of neighborhoods and the effectiveness of information programs. *Environment and Behavior, 22*, 27–54.

Wehr, T. A., Jacobsen, F. M., Sack, D. A., Arendt, J., Tamarkin, L., & Rosenthal, N. E. (1986). Phototherapy of seasonal affective disorder. *Archives of General Psychiatry, 43*, 870–875.

Wehr, T. A., Sack, D. A., & Rosenthal, N. E. (1987). Seasonal affective disorder with summer depression and winter hypomania. *American Journal of Psychiatry, 144*, 1602–1603.

Weidemann, S., & Anderson, J. R. (1982). Residents' perceptions of satisfaction and safety: A basis for change in multi-family housing. *Environment and Behavior, 14*, 695–724.

Weil, R. J., & Dunsworth, F. A. (1958). Psychiatric aspects of disaster—a case history. Some experiences during the Springhill, Nova Scotia, mining disaster. *Canadian Psychiatric Association Journal, 3*, 11–17.

Weiner, F. H. (1976). Altruism, ambiance, and action: The effects of rural and urban rearing on helping behavior. *Journal of Personality and Social Psychology, 76*, 457–461.

Weinstein, C. S. (1979). The physical environment of the school: A review of the research. *Review of Educational Research, 49*, 577–610.

Weinstein, C. S. (1981). Classroom design as an external condition for learning. *Educational Technology, 21*, 12–19.

Weinstein, C. S., & Pinciotti, P. (1988). Changing a schoolyard: Intentions, design decisions, and behavioral outcomes. *Environment and Behavior, 20*, 345–371.

Weinstein, L. (1965). Social schemata of emotionally disturbed boys. *Journal of Abnormal Psychology, 76*, 457–461.

Weinstein, M. S. (1980). *Health in the city: Environmental and behavioral influences*. New York: Pergamon.

Weinstein, N. D. (1974). Effect of noise on intellectual performance. *Journal of Applied Psychology, 59*, 548–554.

Weinstein, N. D. (1976). The statistical prediction of environmental preferences. *Environment and Behavior, 8*, 611–626.

Weisman, G. D. (1983). Environmental programming and action research. *Environment and Behavior, 15*, 381–408.

Weisman, J. (1981). Wayfinding and the built environment. *Environment and Behavior, 13*, 189–204.

Weisner, T., & Weibel, J. (1981). Home environments and family lifestyles in California. *Environment and Behavior, 13*, 417–460.

Weiss, B. (1983). Behavioral toxicology and environmental health science. *American Psychologist, 38*, 1174–1187.

Weisse, C. S., Pato, C. N., McAllister, C. G., Littman, R., Breier, A., Paul, S. M., & Baum, A. (1990). Differential effects of controllable and uncontrollable acute stress on lymphocyte proliferation and leukocyte percentages in humans. *Brain, Behavior, and Immunity, 4*, 339–351.

Weisz, J. R., Rothbaum, F. M., & Blackburn, T. C. (1984). Standing out and standing in: The psychology of control in America and Japan. *American Psychologist, 39*, 955–969.

Wellens, A. R., & Goldberg, M. L. (1978). The effects of interpersonal distance and orientation upon the perception of social relationships. *Journal of Psychology, 99*, 39–47.

Wellman, B., & Leighton, B. (1979). Networks, neighborhoods, and communities: Approaches to the study of the community question. *Urban Affairs Quarterly, 14*, 363–390.

Wellman, J. D., & Buhyoff, G. J. (1980). Effects of regional familiarity on landscape preferences. *Journal of Environmental Management, 11*, 105–110.

Wener, R. (1977). Non-density factors in the perception of crowding. *Dissertation Abstracts International, 37D*, 3569–3570.

Wener, R., Frazier, F. W., & Farbstein, J. (1985). Three generations of evaluation and design of correctional facilities. *Environment and Behavior, 17*, 71–95.

Wener, R., Frazier, F. W., & Farbstein, J. (1987, June). Building better jails. *Psychology Today, 21*, 40–44, 48–49.

Wener, R., & Kaminoff, R. D. (1983). Improving environmental information: Effects of signs on perceived crowding and behavior. *Environment and Behavior, 15*, 3–20.

Wener, R., & Keys, C. (1988). The effects of changes in jail population densities on crowding, sick call, and spatial behavior. *Journal of Applied Social Psychology, 18*, 852–866.

Werner, C. M. (1987). Home interiors: A time and place for interpersonal relationships. *Environment and Behavior, 19*, 169–179.

Werner, C. M., Altman, I., & Oxley, D. (1985). Temporal aspects of homes: A transactional perspective. In I. Altman & C. M. Werner (Eds.), *Home environments* (pp. 1–32). New York: Plenum.

Werner, C. M., Brown, B. B., & Damron, G. (1981). Territorial marking in the game arcade. *Journal of Personality and Social Psychology, 41*, 1094–1104.

Werner, C. M., Peterson-Lewis, S., & Brown, B. B. (1989). Inferences about homeowners' sociability: Impact of Christmas decorations and other cues. *Journal of Environmental Psychology, 9*, 279–296.

Werner, R., & Szigeti, F. (Eds.). (1987). *Cumulative index to the ERDA proceedings: Volumes 1–18*. Washington, DC: Environmental Design Research Association.

West, P. C. (1982). Effects of user behavior on the perception of crowding in backcountry forest recreation. *Forest Science*, *28*, 95–105.

Westin, A. F., Schweder, H. A., Baker, M. A., & Lehman, J. (1985). *The changing workplace*. White Plains, NY: Knowledge Industry Publications.

Westover, T. N. (1989). Perceived crowding in recreational settings: An environment–behavior model. *Environment and Behavior*, *21*, 1169–1176.

Weyant, J. M. (1978). Effects of mood states, costs, and benefits on helping. *Journal of Personality and Social Psychology, 36*, 1169–1176.

Wheeldon, P. D. (1969). The operation of voluntary associations and personal networks in the political processes of an interethnic community. In J. C. Mitchell (Ed.), *Social networks in urban situations*. Manchester, NH: University of Manchester Press.

White, L. (1967). The historical roots of our ecologic crisis. *Science, 155*, 1203–1207.

White, M. (1975). Interpersonal distance as affected by room size, status, and sex. *Journal of Social Psychology, 95*, 241–249.

White, M., Kasl, S. V., Zahner, G. E. P., & Will, J. C. (1987). Perceived crime in the neighborhood and mental health of women and children. *Environment and Behavior, 19*, 588–613.

Whyte, W. H. (1974). The best street life in the world. *New York Magazine, 15*, 26–33.

Whyte, W. H. (1980). *The social life of small urban spaces*. New York: The Conservation Foundation.

Wicker, A. W. (1969). Size of church membership and members' support of church behavior settings. *Journal of Personality and Social Psychology, 13*, 278–288.

Wicker, A. W. (1973). Undermanning theory and research: Implications for the study of psychological and behavorial effects of excess populations. *Representative Research in Social Psychology, 4*, 185–206.

Wicker, A. W. (1979). *An introduction to ecological psychology*. Monterey, CA: Brooks/Cole.

Wicker, A. W. (1987). Behavior settings reconsidered: Temporal stages, resources, internal dynamics, context. In D. Stokols & I. Altman (Eds.), *Handbook of environmental psychology* (Vol. II, pp. 613–653). New York: Wiley-Interscience.

Wicker, A. W., & Kauma, C. (1974). Effects of a merger of a small and a large organization on members' behaviors and experiences. *Journal of Applied Psychology, 59*, 24–30.

Wicker, A. W., & Kirmeyer, S. (1976). From church to laboratory to national park: A program of research on excess and insufficient populations in behavior settings. In S. Wapner, S. B. Cohen, & B. Kaplan (Eds.), *Experiencing the environment* (pp. 157–185). New York: Plenum.

Wicker, A. W., Kirmeyer, S. L., Hanson, L., & Alexander, D. (1976). Effects of manning levels on subjective experiences, performance, and verbal interaction in groups. *Organizational Behavior and Human Performance, 17*, 251–274.

Wicker, A. W., McGrath, J. E., & Armstrong, G. E. (1972). Organization size and behavior setting capacity as determinants of member participation. *Behavioral Science, 17*, 499–513.

Wicker, A. W., & Mehler, A. (1971). Assimilation of new members in a large and a small church. *Journal of Applied Psychology, 55*, 151–156.

Wiesenfeld, E. (1992). Public housing evaluation in Venezuela: A case study. *Journal of Environmental Psychology, 12*, 213–223.

Wilding, J., & Mohindra, N. (1980). Effects of subvocal suppression, articulating aloud and noise on sequence recall. *British Journal of Psychology, 71*, 247–261.

Wilkinson, R. T. (1974). Individual differences in response to the environment. *Ergonomics, 17*, 745–756.

Wilkinson, R. T., Fox, R. H., Goldsmith, R., Hampton, I. F. G., & Lewis, H. E. (1964). Psychological and physiological responses to raised body temperature. *Journal of Applied Physiology, 19*, 287–291.

Wilkinson, T. (1991). Raiders of the parks. *National Parks*, *65*(September/October), 30–35.

Will, D. P., & Sells, S. B. (1969). *Prediction of police incidents and accidents by meteorological variables*. Technical Report No. 14, Group Psychology Branch, Office of Naval Research, Texas Christian University, Fort Worth.

Willems, E. P. (1990). Inside Midwest and its field station: The Barker effect. *Environment and Behavior, 22*, 468–491.

Williams, D. R., & Roggenbuck, J. W. (1984). *Measuring place attachment: Some preliminary results*. NRPA Symposium of Leisure Research, San Antonio, TX.

Williams, G. W., McGinnis, M. Y., & Lumia, A. R. (1992). The effects of olfactory bulbectomy and chronic psychosocial stress on serum glucocorticoids and sexual behavior in female rats. *Physiology and Behavior, 52*, 755–760.

Willis, F. N. (1966). Initial speaking distance as a function of the speakers' relationship. *Psychonomic Science, 5*, 221–222.

Willner, P., & Neiva, J. (1986). Brief exposure to uncontrollable but not to controllable noise biases the retrieval of information from memory. *British Journal of Clinical Psychology, 25*, 93–100.

Wills, T. A. (1981). Downward comparison principles in social psychology. *Psychological Bulletin, 90*, 245–271.

Wilson, E. O. (1975). *Sociobiology*. Cambridge, MA: Harvard University Press.

Wilson, E. O. (1984). *Biophilia: The human bond with other species*. Cambridge, MA: Harvard University Press.

Wilson, E. O. (1993). Biophilia and the conservation ethic. In S. R. Kellert & E. O. Wilson (Eds.), *The biophilia hypothesis* (pp. 31–41). Washington, DC: Island Press.

Wilson, S. (1972). Intensive care delirium. *Archives of Internal Medicine, 130*, 225.

Wineman, J. D. (1982). Office design and evaluation: An overview. *Environment and Behavior, 14*, 271–298.

Wineman, J. D. (1986). *Behavioral issues in office design*. New York: Van Nostrand Reinhold.

Winkel, G. H. (1987). Implications of environmental context for validity assessments. In D. Stokols & I. Altman (Eds.), *Handbook of environmental psychology* (Vol. I, pp. 71–98). New York: Wiley-Interscience.

Winkel, G., Olsen, R., Wheeler, F., & Cohen, M. (1976). *The museum visitor and orientational media: An experimental comparison of different approaches in the Smithsonian Institution and National Museum of History and Technology*. New York: City University of New York Center for Environment and Behavior.

Winkler, R. C., & Winnett, R. A. (1982). Behavioral interventions in resource management. *American Psychologist, 37*, 421–435.

Winneke, G., & Kastka, J. (1987). Comparison of odour-annoyance data from different industrial sources: Problems and implications. In H. S. Koelega (Ed.), *Environmental annoyance: Characterization, measurement, and control* (pp. 129–138). Amsterdam: Elsevier Science Publishers.

Winnett, R. A., Hatcher, J., Leckliter, I., Ford, T. R., Fishback, J. F., Riley, A. W., & Love, S. (1981). *The effects of videotape modeling and feedback on residential comfort, the thermal environment and electricity consumption: Winter and summer studies*. Unpublished manuscript. Department of Psychology, Virginia Polytechnic Institute and State University.

Winnett, R. A., Kagel, J. H., Battalio, R. C., & Winkler, R. C. (1978). Effects of monetary rebates, feedback and information on residential energy conservation. *Journal of Applied Psychology, 63*, 73–78.

Winnett, R. A., Leckliter, I. N., Chinn, D. E., & Stahl, B. (1984). Reducing energy consumption: The long-term effects of a single TV program. *Journal of Communication, 34*, 37–51.

Winnett, R. A., Leckliter, I. N., Chinn, D. E., Stall, B., & Love, S. Q. (1985). Effects of monetary rebates, feedback, and information on residential energy use. *Journal of Applied Behavior Analysis, 18*, 33–44.

Winnett, R. A., Neale, M. S., & Grier, H. C. (1979). The effects of self-monitoring and feedback on residential electricity consumption. *Journal of Applied Behavior Analysis, 12,* 173–184.

Winnett, R. A., Neale, M. S., Williams, K. R., Yokley, J., & Kauder, H. (1979). The effects of individual and group feedback on residential electricity consumption: Three replications. *Journal of Environmental Systems, 8,* 217–233.

Wirth, I. (1938). Urbanism as a way of life. *American Journal of Sociology, 44,* 1–24.

Wofford, J. C. (1966). Negative ionization: An investigation of behavioral effects. *Journal of Experimental Psychology, 71,* 608–611.

Wohlwill, J. F. (1966). The physical environment: A problem for a psychology of stimulation. *Journal of Social Issues, 22,* 29–38.

Wohlwill, J. F. (1970). The emerging discipline of environmental psychology. *American Psychologist, 25,* 303–312.

Wohlwill, J. F. (1973). The environment is not in the head. In W. F. E. Prieser (Ed.), *Environmental design research: Vol 2. Symposia and workshops. Proceedings of the Fourth International Environmental Design Research Association Conference* (pp. 166–181). Stroudsburg, PA: Dowden, Hutchinson, & Ross.

Wohlwill, J. F. (1974). Human response to levels of environmental stimulation. *Human Ecology, 2,* 127–147.

Wohlwill, J. F. (1976a). Environmental aesthetics: The environment as a source of affect. In I. Altman & J. F. Wohlwill (Eds.), *Human behavior and environment: Advances in theory and research* (Vol. 1, pp. 37–86). New York: Plenum.

Wohlwill, J. F. (1976b). Environmental aesthetics: The environment as a source of affect. In I. Altman & J. F. Wohlwill (Eds.), *Human behavior and environment: Advances in theory and research* (Vol. 1, pp. 37–86). New York: Plenum.

Wohlwill, J. F. (1976c). Searching for the environment in environmental cognition. In G. W. Moore & R. G. Golledge (Eds.), *Environmental knowing* (pp. 385–392). Stroudsburg, PA: Dowden, Hutchinson, & Ross.

Wohlwill, J. F. (1983). The concept of nature: A psychologist's view. In I. Altman & J. F. Wohlwill (Eds.), *Behavior and the natural environment* (pp. 5–37). New York: Plenum.

Wohlwill, J., & Kohn, I. (1973). The environment as experienced by the migrant: An adaptation level view. *Representative Research in Social Psychology, 4,* 135–164.

Wolf, N., & Feldman, E. (1991). *Plastics: America's packaging dilemma.* Washington, DC: Island Press.

Wolfe, M. (1975). Room size and density: Behavior patterns in a children's psychiatric facility. *Environment and Behavior, 7,* 199–225.

Womble, P., & Studebaker, S. (1981). Crowding in a national park campground: Katmai National Monument in Alaska. *Environment and Behavior, 13,* 557–573.

Wong, C. Y., Sommer, R., & Cook, E. J. (1992). The soft classroom 17 years later. *Journal of Environmental Psychology, 12,* 337–343.

Wood, J. M., Bootzin, R. R., Rosenham, D., & Nolen-Hoeksema, S. (1992). Effects of the 1989 San Francisco earthquake on frequency and content of nightmares. *Journal of Abnormal Psychology, 101,* 219–224.

Woodhead, M. M. (1964). Visual searching in intermittent noise. *Journal of Sound and Vibration, 1,* 157–161.

Woods, J. E. (1988). Recent developments for heating, cooling, and ventilating buildings. *State of the Art Reviews* (Stockholm, Sweden, Swedish Council for Building Research, Healthy Buildings), *1,* 99–197.

Woodson, P. P., Buzzi, R., Nil, R., & Battig, K. (1986). Effects of smoking on vegetative reactivity to noise in women. *Psychophysiology, 23,* 272–282.

Woodward, N. J., & Wallston, B. S. (1987). Age and health care beliefs: Self-efficacy as a mediator of low desire for control. *Psychology and Aging, 2,* 3–8.

Wooldredge, J. D., & Winfree, L. T. (1992). An aggregate-level study of inmate suicides and deaths due to natural causes in U.S. jails. *Journal of Research in Crime and Delinquency, 29,* 466–479.

Worchel, S., & Brown, E. H. (1984). The role of plausibility in influencing environmental attributions. *Journal of Experimental Social Psychology, 20,* 86–96.

Worchel, S., & Teddlie, C. (1976). The experience of crowding: A two-factor theory. *Journal of Personality and Social Psychology, 34,* 36–40.

World Development Report. (1987). Published for World Bank, Washington, DC (Table 33, 266–277). Oxford University Press.

Wortman, C. B., & Brehm, J. W. (1975). Responses to uncontrollable outcomes: An integration of reactance theory and the learned helplessness model. In L. Berkowitz (Ed.), *Advances in experimental social psychology* (Vol. 8, pp. 277–336). New York: Academic Press.

Wright, B., & Rainwater, L. (1962). The meaning of color. *Journal of General Psychology, 67,* 89–99.

Wright, K. M., Ursano, R. J., Bartone, P. T., & Ingraham, L. H. (1990). The shared experience of catastrophe: An expanded classification of the disaster community. *American Journal of Orthopsychiatry, 60,* 35–42.

Wright, R. A. (1984). Motivation, anxiety, and the difficulty of avoidant control. *Journal of Personality and Social Psychology, 46,* 1376–1388.

Wyndham, C. H. (1970). Adaptation to heat and cold. In D. H. K. Lee & D. Minard (Eds.), *Physiology, environment, and man* (pp. 177–204). New York: Academic Press.

Yamagishi, T. (1986). The provision of a sanctioning system as a public good. *Journal of Personality and Social Psychology, 51,* 110–116.

Yamamoto, T., Sawada, H., Minami, H., Ishii, S., & Inoue, W. (1992). Transition from the university to the workplace. *Environment and Behavior, 24,* 189–205.

Yancey, W. L. (1971). Architecture, interaction, and social control: The case of a large-scale public housing project. *Environment and Behavior, 3,* 3–21.

Yancey, W. L. (1972). Architecture, interaction, and social control: The case of a large scale housing project. In J. F. Wohlwill & D. H. Carson (Eds.), *Environment and the social sciences: Perspectives and applications* (pp. 126–136). Washington, DC: American Psychological Association.

Yinon, Y., & Bizman, A. (1980). Noise, success, and failure as determinants of helping behavior. *Personality and Social Psychology Bulletin, 6,* 125–130.

Young, M., & Willmott, P. (1957). *Family and kinship in East London.* Baltimore: Penguin.

Yule, W., & Williams, R. (1990). Post-traumatic stress reactions in children. *Journal of Traumatic Stress, 3,* 279–295.

Zajonc, R. B. (1968). Attitudinal effects of mere exposure. *Journal of Personality and Social Psychology, 8,* 1–29.

Zajonc, R. B. (1984). On the primacy of affect. *American Psychologist, 39,* 117–123.

Zajonc, R. B., Murphy, S. T., & Inglehart, M. (1989). Feeling and facial efference: Implications of the vascular theory of emotion. *Psychological Review, 96,* 395–416.

Zakay, D., Hayduk, L. A., & Tsal, Y. (1992). Personal space and distance misperception: Implications of a novel observation. *Bulletin of the Psychonomic Society, 30,* 33–35.

Zeisel, J. (1975). *Sociology and architectural design. Social science frontiers (6).* New York: Russell Sage Foundation.

Zeisel, J. (1981). *Inquiry by design: Tools for environment-behavior research.* Monterey, CA: Brooks/Cole.

Zeisel, J., & Griffin, M. (1975). *Charlesview housing: A diagnostic evaluation.* Cambridge, MA: Harvard University Graduate School of Design.

Zika, S., & Chamberlain, K. (1987). Relation of hassles and

personality to subjective well-being. *Journal of Personality and Social Psychology, 53,* 155–162.

Zillmann, D. (1979). *Hostility and aggression.* Hillsdale, NJ: Erlbaum.

Zillmann, D. (1983). Arousal and aggression. In R. G. Geen & E. Donnerstein (Eds.), *Aggression: Theoretical and empirical reviews* (Vol. 1, pp. 75–101). New York: Academic Press.

Zimbardo, P. G. (1969). The human choices: Individuation, reason, and order versus deindividuation, impulse, and chaos. In W. J. Arnold & D. Levine (Eds.), *Nebraska Symposium on Motivation* (pp. 237–307). Lincoln: University of Nebraska Press.

Zimring, C., Carpman, J. R., & Michelson, W. (1987). Design for special populations: Mentally retarded persons, children, hospital visitors. In D. Stokols & I. Altman (Eds.), *Handbook of environmental psychology* (Vol. 2, pp. 919–949). New York: Wiley-Interscience.

Zlutnick, S., & Altman, I. (1972). Crowding and human behavior. In J. Wohlwill & D. Carson (Eds.), *Environment and the social sciences: Perspectives and applications* (pp. 44–58). Washington, DC: American Psychological Association.

Zube, E. H. (1973). Rating everyday rural landscapes for the Northeastern U.S. *Landscape Architecture, 63,* 92–97.

Zube, E. H., & Mills, L. V., Jr. (1976). Cross-cultural explorations in landscape perception. In E. H. Zube (Ed.), *Studies in landscape perception* (Publication No. R–76–1). Amherst: Institute for Man and Environment, University of Massachusetts.

Zube, E. H., Pitt, D. G., & Anderson, T. W. (1974). *Perception and measurements of scenic resources in the southern Connecticut River Valley.* Amherst: Institute for Man and Environment, University of Massachusetts.

Zube, E. H., Pitt, D. G., & Evans, G. W. (1983). A lifespan developmental study of landscape assessment. *Journal of Environmental Psychology, 3,* 115–128.

Zube, E. H., Sell, J. L., & Taylor, J. G. (1982). Landscape perception: Research, application and theory. *Landscape Planning, 9,* 1–33.

Zube, E. H., Vining, J., Law, C. S., & Bechtel, R. B. (1985). Perceived urban residential quality: A cross-cultural bimodal study. *Environment and Behavior, 17,* 327–350.

Zubek, J. P. (Ed.). (1969). *Sensory deprivation: Fifteen years of research.* New York: Appleton-Century-Crofts.

Zuckerman, M. (1979). *Sensation seeking: Beyond the optimal level of arousal.* Hillsdale, NJ: Erlbaum.

Zweig, J., & Csank, J. (1975). Effects of relocation on chronically ill geriatric patients of a medical unit: Mortality rates. *Journal of the American Geriatrics Society, 23,* 132–136.

Zweigenhaft, R. (1976). Personal space in the faculty office: Desk placement and the student. *Journal of Applied Psychology, 61,* 529–532.

ACKNOWLEDGMENTS OF PERMISSION

Figure 2–10, p. 44, from Russell, J. A. and Lanius, U. F. (1984). Adaptation level and the affective appraisal of environments. *Journal of Environmental Psychology, 4.*

Table 2–1, p. 56, adapted from Kaplan, S. (1987). Aesthetics, affect, and cognition. *Environment and Behavior, 19, 3–32.*

Figure 3–6, p. 71, adapted from Brunswick, E. (1956). *Perception and the Representative Design of Psychological Experiments.* Berkeley: University of California Press.

Figure 3–10, p. 82, from Lynch, K. (1960). *The image of the city.* Cambridge, MA: M.I.T. Press.

Figure 3–12, p. 83, adapted from Appleyard, D. (1970). Styles and methods of structuring a city. *Environment and Behavior, 2,* 100–118. Reprinted by permission of Sage Publications, Inc.

Figure 3–17, p. 90, from Downs, R. M. and Stea, D. (1977). *Maps in Minds: Reflections on Cognitive Mapping.* Reprinted by permission of Harper and Row.

Figure 3–23, p. 104, adapted from Levine, M. (1982). You are here maps: Psychological considerations. *Environment and Behavior, 14,* 221–137. Reprinted by permission of Sage Publications.

Figure 3–24, p. 105, adapted from Levine, M. (1982). You are here maps: Psychological considerations. *Environment and Behavior, 14,* 221–137. Reprinted by permission of Sage Publications.

Table 4–1, p. 144, adapted from Wicker, A. W., and Kirmeyer, S. (1976). From church to laboratory to national park. In S. Wapner, B. Kaplan, and S. Cohen (Eds.), *Experiencing the Environment.* Used by permission of Plenum Publishing.

Figure 5–4A, p. 156, from Gardner, E. (1975). *Fundamentals of Neurology,* Sixth Edition, © 1975 by Saunders College Publishing, a division of Holt, Rinehart and Winston, Inc., reprinted by permission of the publisher.

Figure 5–4B, p. 157, from Gardner, E. (1975). *Fundamentals of Neurology,* Sixth Edition, © 1975 by Saunders College Publishing, a division of Holt, Rinehart and Winston, Inc., reprinted by permission of the publisher.

Figure 5–7, p. 165, adapted from Cherek, D. R. (1985). Effects of acute exposure to increased levels of background industrial noise on cigarette smoking behavior. *International Archives of Occupational and Environmental Health, 56,* 23–30. Reprinted by permission of Springer-Verlag.

Table 5–2, p. 168, from Weinstein, N. D. (1978). *Journal of Applied Psychology,* Table 1, p. 460.

Figure 5–9, p. 170, adapted from Glass, D. C. and Singer, J. F. (1972). *Urban Stress,* New York: Academic Press.

Figure 5–10, p. 173, from Sundstrom, E., Town, J. P., Rice, R. W., Osborn, D. P., & Brill, M. (1994). Office noise, satisfaction, and performance. *Environment and Behavior, 26,* 195–222. Reprinted by permission of Sage Publications, Inc.

Figure 5–11, p. 174, adapted from Miller, J. D. (1974). Effects of noise on people. *Journal of the Acoustical Society of America, 56,* 729–764.

Figure 5–12, p. 175, from Turk, A., Turk, J., and Wittes, J. T. (1978). *Environmental Science,* Third Edition, © 1978 by Saunders College Publishing, a division of Holt, Rinehart and Winston, Inc., reprinted by permission of the author.

Figure 5–13, p. 177, adapted from Geen, R. G. and O'Neal, E. C. (1969). Activation of cue elicited aggression by general arousal. *Journal of Personality and Social Psychology, 11,* 289–292. Copyright © 1969 by the

American Psychological Association. Reprinted by permission of the author and publisher.

Figure 5–14, p. 178, adapted from Donnerstein, E. and Wilson, D. W. (1976). Effects of noise and perceived control on ongoing and subsequent aggressive behavior. *Journal of Personality and Social Psychology*, vol. 34, pp. 774–781. Copyright © 1976 by the American Psychological Association. Reprinted by permission of the author and publisher.

Figure 5–15, p. 179, adapted from Mathews, K. E. and Cannon, I. K. (1975). Environmental noise level as a determinant of helping behavior. *Journal of Personality and Social Psychology*, vol. 32, pp. 571–577. Copyright (1975 by the American Psychological Association. Reprinted by permission of the author and publisher.

Figure 6–6, p. 203, from Goranson, R. E. and King, D. *Rioting and daily temperature: Analysis of the U.S. Riots in 1967*. Unpublished manuscript, York University, 1970. Reprinted by permission of the authors.

Table 6–3, p. 212, from Penwarden, A. D. (1973). Acceptable wind speeds in towns. *Building Science*, 8, 259–267.

Figure 7–6, p. 242, from Thompson, M. P., Norris, F. H., & Hanacek, B. (1993). Age differences in the psychological consequences of Hurricane Hugo. *Psychology and Aging*, 8, 606–616.

Figure 7–10, p. 256, courtesy of United States Environmental Protection Agency.

Table 7–4, p. 259, from Spyker, J. M. (1975). Assessing the impact of low level chemicals on development: Behavioral and latent effects. *Federation Processings*, 34, 1835–1844.

Table 7–6, p. 265, from *Newsweek*, Aug. 29, 1988. Copyright © 1988, *Newsweek, Inc.* All rights reserved. Reprinted by permission.

Figure 7–14, p. 267, from Evans, G.W., Jacobs, S.V., Dooley, D., & Catalano, R. (1987). The interaction of stressful life events and chronic strains on community mental health. *American Journal of Community Psychology*, 15, 23–34.

Table 8–1, p. 279, from Hall, E. T. (1963). A system for the notation of proxemic behavior. *American Anthropologist*, 65, 1003–1026. Reproduced by permission of the American Anthropological Association.

Figure 8–3, p. 285, from Aiello, J. R., and Aiello, T. 1974. The development of personal space: Proxemic behavior of children 6–16. *Human ecology*, 2, 177–189. Reprinted by permission of Plenum Publishing.

Figure 8–5, p. 289, from Sommer, R. (1976). Classroom ecology. *Journal of Applied Behavioral Science*, 3, 489–503. Copyright 1967 by NTL Publications.

Figure 8–7, p. 296, from Felipe, N. J. and Sommer, R. 1966. Invasions of personal space. *Social Problems, 14,* 206–214.

Table 8–2, p. 296, from Knoecni, V. J., Libuser, L., Morton, H., and Ebbesen, E. B. (1975). Effects of a violation of personal space and helping responses. *Journal of Experimental Social Psychology, 11,* 288–299.

Figure 8–9. p. 297, from Middlemist, R. D., Knowles, E. S. and Matter, C. F. (1976). Personal space invasions in the lavatory. Suggestive evidence from arousal. *Journal of Personality and Social Psychology, 33,* 541–546. Copyright 1976 by the American Psychological Association. Reprinted by permission of the author and publisher.

Table 8–3, p. 305, based on Altman, I. (1975). *The Environment and Social Behavior.* Monterey, CA: Brooks/Cole.

Table 8–4, p. 307, based on Taylor, R. B. (1978). Human territoriality: A review and a model for future research. *Cornell Journal of Social Relations, 13,* 125–151.

Table 8–5, p. 316, reprinted from Schwartz, B., and Barsky, S. P. (1977). The home advantage. *Social Forces, 55,* 1975. Copyright © the University of North Carolina Press.

Figure 8–12A & B, p. 318, from Brown and Altman, 1983; Brown, B. B., (1985). Residential territories cues to burglary. *Journal of Architectural Planning Research, 2,* 231–243.

Figure 8–13, p. 319, from Patterson, A. H. (1978). Territorial behavior and fear of crime in the elderly. *Environmental Psychology and Nonverbal Behavior, 3,* 131–144.

Figure 8–14, p. 321, from Duke, M. P. and Nowicki, S. (1972). A new measure and social learning model for interpersonal distance. *Journal of Experimental Research in Personality, 6,* 119–132. Used by permission of Academic Press.

Figure 9–2, p. 328, from "Population Density and Social Pathology" by John B. Calhoun. Copyright © 1962 by Scientific American Inc. All rights reserved.

Figure 9–7, p. 336, from Ross, M., Layton, B., Erickson, B., and Schloper, J. (1973). Affect, racial regard, and reactions to crowding. *Journal of Personality and Social Psychology, 28,* 69–76.

Figure 9–8, p. 338, based on Paulua, P. B., McCain, T., and Cox, V. (1978). Death rates, psychiatric commitments, blood pressure and perceived crowding as a function of institutional crowding. *Environmental Psychology and Nonverbal Behavior, 36,* 997–999.

Table 9–1, p. 339, based on Baron, R., Mandel, D., Adams, C., and Griffin, L. (1976). Effects of social density in university residential environments. *Journal of Personality and Social Psychology, 34,* 434–446.

Table 9–2, p. 339, based on Epstein, Y., and Karlin, R. (1975). Effects of acute experimental crowding. *Journal of Applied Social Psychology, 5,* 34–53.

Figures 9–9A & 9B, p. 340, from Baum, A. and Valins, S. (1977). *Architecture and Social Behavior: Psychological Studies of Social Density.* Hillsdale, NJ: Erlbaum. Published with permission of Lawrence Erlbaum Associates.

Table 9–3, p. 344, based on Paulus, P., Annis, A., Setta, M., Schade, J., and Matthews, R. (1976). Crowding does affect task performance. *Journal of Personality and Social Psychology, 34,* 248–253.

Figure 9–10, p. 345, based on Heller, J., Groff, B., and Solomon, S. (1977). Toward an understanding of crowding: The role of physical interaction. *Journal of Personality and Social Psychology,* vol. 35, pp. 83–190.

Table 9–4, p. 348, from Stokols, D. (1976). The experience of crowding in primary and secondary environments. *Environment and Behavior, 8,* 49–86.

Table 10–1, p. 377, from Bornstein, M. H. (1979). The pace of life: revisited. *International Journal of Psychology, 14,* 84.

Table 10–2, p. 379, from Newman, J., and McCauley, C. (1977). Eye contact with strangers in city, suburb, and small town. *Environment and Behavior, 9,* 547–558. Reprinted by permission of Sage Publications, Inc.

Figure 11–5, p. 417, adapted from Lang, J. (1987). *Creating Architectural Theory: The Role of the Behavioral Sciences in Environmental Design.* New York: Van Nostrand Reinhold Co.

Figure 11–8, p. 421, adapted from Zeisel, J. (1981). *Inquiry by Design.* Pacific Grove, A: Brooks/Cole.

Figure 11–11, p. 432, from Zeisel, J. (1975). The design cycle. *Sociology and Architectural Design.* Social Science Frontiers, No. 6. New York: Russell Sage Foundation. © 1975 Russell Sage Foundation. Used by permission.

Figures 11–19A, 11–19B & 11–19C, p. 441, adapted from Saunders, M. D., & McCormick, E. J., (1987). *Human Factors in Engineering and Design.* New York: McGraw- Hill Book Company.

Figure 12–10, p. 466, from Trites et al. (1970). *Environment and Behavior, 2,* 303–334. Reprinted by permission of Sage Publications, Inc.

Figure 12–12, p. 470, from Wener, R., Frazier, F. W., & Farbstein, J. (1987), June. Building better jails. *Psychology Today, 21,* 40–44, 48–49. Reprinted with permission from *Psychology Today Magazine.* Copyright 1987, PT Partners, L.P.

Figure 13–8, p. 501, reprinted with permission, from *Museum News,* January 15, 1993, the American Association of Museums. All rights reserved.

Figure 13–13, p. 510, adapted from Driver, B., and Brown, P. (1983). Contributions of behavioral scientists to recreation resource management. In I. Altman and J. F. Wohwill, (Eds.), *Behavior in the Natural Environment.* New York: Plenum Press.

Figure 14–4, p. 533, from Carless (1992). *Taking Out the Trash.* Washington, DC: Island Press.

AUTHOR INDEX

A

Aamodt, M. G., 106
Abbey, H., 220
Abey-Wickrama, I., 166
Abraham, L. M., 31
Abrams, D., 420, 434, 435
Abramson, L. Y., 130
Abello, R. P., 53, 55
A'Brook, M. F., 166
Acheson, J. M., 531
Acking, D. A., 427
Acredolo, L. P., 94
Acton, W. I., 174
Adamopoulous, J., 355
Adams, C. A., 338, 339, 360
Adams, G. R., 132
Adams, J. R., 317
Adams, L., 286
Adams, P. R., 132
Adams, R. M., 285
Adler, A., 248
Ahrentzen, S. B., 119, 309, 456, 496, 497
Aiello, J. R., 18, 276, 277, 278, 279, 280, 281, 282, 283, 284, 285, 286, 293, 295, 300, 301, 336, 337, 339, 342, 343, 344, 346, 352, 356, 357, 358, 359, 360, 361
Ajzen, I., 32
Albas, C. A., 282, 295
Albas, D. C., 282
Albert, M., 549
Albert, S., 292
Aldwin, C. A., 136, 138
Alexander, C., 176, 389, 420, 434, 435, 459
Alexander, D., 144
Alfaro, L., 490
Allen, G. L., 97, 100, 106, 403, 553
Allgeier, A. R., 280
Alloy, L. B., 130

Allport, F. H., 75
Altman, I., 6, 7, 19, 29, 34, 39, 58, 59, 112, 115, 122, 126, 274, 276, 278, 286, 291, 295, 304, 306, 307, 308, 309, 310, 313, 315, 317, 347, 351, 354, 358, 371, 372, 423, 424, 425, 447, 448, 450, 452, 471
Amaral, D. J., 236
Amato, P. R., 380, 505
Ames, R. E., 529
Amoni, F., 453
Anderson, B., 331
Anderson, C. A., 195, 203, 204, 205, 206, 294
Anderson, D. C., 203, 294
Anderson, D. H., 514
Anderson, E. G., 551
Anderson, E. N., 359
Anderson, J. R., 96, 452
Anderson, K., 130
Anderson, R., 463
Anderson, T. W., 49, 55
Anderson et al., 1977, 331
Ando, Y., 162
Andren, L., 164
Andreae, J., 497
Angel, S., 420, 434, 435
Annis, A. B., 344
Anthony, K. H., 452
Antonovsky, A., 398
Anusiem, A. U., 282
Appleton, J., 53
Appleyard, D., 72, 82, 88, 89, 90, 91, 92, 93, 102, 176
Aptekar, L., 241
Aragones, J. I., 81
Arbuthnot, J., 547, 548
Archer, J., 331
Ardrey, R., 305, 332
Arendt, J., 222
Argyle, M., 276, 295

Arkkelin, D., 360
Arms, R. L., 214
Armstrong, D., 129, 138, 170, 430, 488
Armstrong, G. E., 141, 144, 376
Arnold, W., 123
Arnstein, S. R., 402
Arnvig, E., 256
Aronson, E., 537
Arredondo, J. M., 81
Arreola, D. D., 312
Arrowood, A., 361
Arvey, R. D., 31
Assael, M., 214
Atlas, R., 219, 398
Auble, D., 167
Auliciems, A., 220
Averill, J. R., 128, 130
Axelrod, L. J., 528
Ayers, V., 19, 23
Azuma, H., 129

B

Babcock, A. M., 286
Babisch, W., 166, 167
Bachman, W., 537
Back, K., 458, 459
Bacon-Prue, A., 551
Baddeley, A. D., 267
Bagley, C., 343
Bailey, J. S., 548, 552
Bailey, S., 130, 472
Baird, C. L., 449, 467
Baird, L. L., 144
Baker, G. W., 132, 167
Baker, M. A., 167, 490
Baker-Brown, G., 123
Ball, T. M., 97
Balling, J. D., 53, 55
Balogun, S. K., 281
Baloh, R. W., 256
Baltes, M. M., 472

619

Bandacu, D., 526
Bandura, A., 176, 537
Banzinger, G., 213
Barabasz, A., 121, 123
Barabasz, M., 121, 123
Barash, D. P., 300
Barber, N., 159, 310
Bardwell, L. V., 120, 121, 500
Barefoot, J. C., 297, 301
Barker, D. G., 472
Barker, M. L., 262, 264
Barker, R. G., 10, 11, 16, 69, 108,
    139, 141, 142, 144, 145, 149,
    375, 376, 509
Barker, T., 214
Barnard, W. A., 19, 176, 281, 284,
    301, 331
Barnes, F. A., 215
Barnett, A., 383
Baron, R. A., 17, 31, 32, 33, 114,
    202, 203, 204, 205, 210, 214,
    299, 338, 339, 351, 362, 553,
    554
Baron, R. M., 362
Barrera, M., 145
Barrett, J., 286
Barrett, P., 259
Barrios, B. A., 281
Barry, T., 195, 205, 218, 219, 269
Barsky, S. P., 316
Bartley, S. H., 75
Barton, A., 247
Barton, M., 508
Barton, R., 317
Barton, W. H., 286, 427
Bartone, P. T., 237
Baskett, G. D., 287, 298
Bass, J. H., 257
Bassett, R. I., 301, 504
Bassuk, E., 386
Bates, D., 267
Battalio, R. C., 535
Batterson, C., 241
Battig, K., 164, 165
Bauer, R. M., 257
Baum, A., 22, 126, 131, 132, 133,
    134, 135, 136, 138, 162, 230,
    234, 236, 239, 241, 246, 248,
    249, 252, 253, 255, 260, 286,
    333, 335, 336, 337, 339, 340,
    341, 343, 346, 347, 348, 352,
    354, 357, 358, 359, 360, 361,
    362, 363, 364, 366, 386, 387,
    425, 427, 430, 468, 488
Baum, C. S., 132, 136
Baumann, D. D., 132, 233
Baumeister, R. F., 316
Baxter, J. C., 260, 552
Beal, J. B., 214
Beard, R. R., 267
Beasely, R. R., 391, 392, 393

Beck, B., 472
Beatty, P. A., 302
Bechtel, R. B., 19, 141, 452
Beck, R. J., 78, 86, 90, 91, 100
Becker, F. D., 288, 311, 312, 314,
    482, 492, 493
Becker, L., 538
Becker, L. J., 540, 541
Beckman, R., 466
Beckmann, J., 256
Bee, J., 288
Beegle, G. P., 551
Beets, J. L., 214, 218, 219
Beighton, P., 198
Beith, B., 116
Belk, R. W., 448
Bell, B., 241
Bell, C. R., 199
Bell, P. A., 19, 116, 135, 169, 176,
    180, 199, 201, 202, 204, 205,
    207, 208, 210, 281, 284, 286,
    299, 301, 331, 426, 449, 467,
    477, 529, 530, 531
Bell, R. W., 331
Bellinger, D., 259
Barrett, P., 259
Bellovich, S. J., 117
Belter, R. W., 241
Bem, D. J., 33, 547
Benedak, T., 284
Benedict, J. D., 393
Benefield, A., 503
Benjamin, M. L., 309
Bennett, B., 360
Bennett, C. A., 426
Bennett, N., 497
Bennett, R., 211
Bennett, W. R., 215
Benson, G. P., 200
Bentley, D. L., 320
Benziger, G., 300
Beranek, L. L., 159, 174
Berck, J., 386
Berger, E., 487
Berger, M., 22, 342
Berglund, B., 262
Bergman, B. A., 293, 344
Bergman, M., 161, 264, 529
Bergqvist, U. O. V., 257
Berk, L. E., 144
Berkowitz, L., 117, 176
Berlyne, D. E., 27, 50, 51, 54, 56,
    116, 117, 430
Berman, J., 300
Berman, V., 200
Bernal, M. E., 220
Bernaldez, F. G., 53, 55
Bernard, L. C., 139
Bernard, Y., 453
Bernstein, M. D., 346, 358
Berry, P. C., 426, 427
Besch, E. L., 257

Best, J. B., 99
Bettinger, R., 547
Beyda, M., 467
Bickman, L., 22, 234, 239, 342
Biek, M., 536
Bih, H., 124
Biner, P. M., 427, 428, 487
Birjulin, A. A., 529
Birkel, R. C., 145
Birsky, J., 356, 357
Bishop, R. L., 393
Bitgood, S. C., 503
Bizman, A., 180
Black, J. C., 123, 453
Blackburn, B. L., 540
Blackburn, T. C., 129
Blackman, S., 218
Blades, M., 86, 94
Blair, D., 234, 264
Blake, M. J. F., 168
Blanck, L. S., 550, 551
Blaney, P. H., 135
Blaut, J. M., 86, 94
Bleda, P. R., 268, 300
Bleda, S., 268, 300
Block, L. K., 492, 493
Blocker, T. J., 127
Blount, R., 551
Blumberg, L., 533, 546
Bogat, G. A., 265, 268
Bolin, R., 230, 241, 242
Bolt, 159
Bonaiuto, M., 461
Bonham, K. G., 267
Bonio, S., 296
Bonnes, M., 371, 453, 461
Bonta, J., 344
Böök, A., 79, 90, 96, 100, 102
Boore, J. A., 241
Booth, A., 359, 395
Booth, W., 191
Bootzin, R. R., 78, 86, 90, 91, 100,
    238
Borden, R. J., 343
Borg, E., 164
Bornstein, M. H., 377
Borsky, P. N., 159
Borun, M. L., 501
Bossenmaier, M., 298
Boster, R. S., 29, 49
Bostick, D., 549
Bostock, T., 249
Bostrom, A., 260
Bouchard, T. J., 31
Boucher, M. L., 292
Bouska, M. L., 302
Bovy, P., 504
Bower, G. H., 96
Bowles, C. A., 252
Bowman, U., 236
Boyanowsky, E. L., 206, 211

Boyce, P. R., 199, 486, 487
Brady, C., 489
Bradley, J. S., 160
Brantingham, P. A., 78
Brantingham, P. J., 78
Brase, G., 380
Brass, D. J., 141, 492, 493
Brasted, W., 549, 550
Bravo, M., 238
Brechner, K. C., 529, 530
Breck, R. E., 18, 295
Brehm, J. W., 126
Brehm, S. S., 126
Breidenbach, S., 268
Breier, A., 162
Breisacher, P., 267
Brennan, P. L., 471
Brenner, G., 473
Breton, M., 385, 386, 449
Breum, N. O., 426
Brewer, M. B., 357, 529, 531
Brickner, M. A., 302
Brideau, L., 206, 211
Briere, J., 266
Brill, M., 425, 486
Brinkman, J. A., 167
Brinkman, H., 283
Britton, N., 167
Broadbent, D. E., 116, 117, 118,
    167, 171, 172, 174
Broadbent, G. B., 431
Brockopp, G. W., 219
Brodsky, C. M., 257
Brodzinsky, D. M., 356, 357, 361
Brokemann, N. C., 289
Bromet, E., 241, 251, 252, 256
Bronzaft, A. L., 163, 182
Brooks, D. K., 397
Brooks, M. J., 288, 304, 309, 314,
    492
Browder, A. A., 256
Browdy, B. L., 256
Brower, S., 312, 396, 397
Brown, B. B., 254, 278, 286, 304,
    305, 306, 307, 308, 310, 312,
    313, 314, 317, 320, 425, 448,
    452
Brown, C. E., 302
Brown, C. P., 256
Brown, D. W., 493
Brown, E., 268
Brown, E. H., 345
Brown, G. G., 259
Brown, G. I., 220
Brown, I. D., 119
Brown, J. G., 390, 391, 393, 394
Brown, P. J., 509, 514
Brunault, M. A., 282
Brunetti, F. A., 497
Brunswik, E., 61, 71, 72, 75
Bryant, K. J., 92

Buckley, R., 267
Budd, G. M., 208
Bull, A. J., 176, 281
Bullen, R. B., 167
Bullinger, M., 171, 264
Bunston, T., 385, 386, 449
Burbage, S. E., 176
Burdge, R. J., 360
Burge, P. S., 258
Burge, S., 257
Burger, G., 390, 391, 393, 394
Burgess, G., 473
Burke, E., 35
Burn, S. M., 545, 546
Burnes, D. W., 386, 387
Burns, R. L., 487
Burroughs, J., 234
Burroughs, W. J., 98, 312
Burrows, A. A., 159
Bursik, R. J., 528
Bursill, A. E., 201
Burt, C. D. B., 448
Burton, I., 232
Bushnell, M. C., 196
Butler, D. L., 91, 427, 428, 487
Buttram, B. A., 543
Buzzi, R., 164, 165
Byers, R. K., 259
Byrne, D., 31, 32, 33, 135, 202, 280,
    281, 282, 287, 298, 299, 309,
    471
Byrne, M., 255, 256
Byrne, R. W., 88, 99, 100, 102
Byrnes, G., 219

C

Cabrales, E., 128
Cacioppo, J. T., 118
Cadwallader, M., 97
Cahoon, R. L., 217
Caldwell, C., 314
Calesnick, L. E., 352
Calhoun, J. B., 11, 138, 301, 325,
    328, 329, 330, 331, 333, 335
Calkins, M. P., 477
Calle, E. E., 214
Calvert, J., 206, 211
Camacho, L. M., 453
Cameron, P., 163
Campbell, D. E., 214, 218, 219, 430,
    488, 494, 495
Campbell, D. T., 22, 75
Campbell, J., 133, 378
Campbell, J. B., 168
Campbell, R. N., 94
Campion, D. S., 256
Canham, C. D., 327, 328
Canino, G. J., 238, 239
Canivez, G. L., 211
Cannon, W. B., 136
Canon, L. K., 176, 179

Canter, D., 78
Cappella, J. N., 277
Carder, P., 452
Carifio, M. S., 282
Carless, 533
Carlisle, S. G., 459
Carlopio, J. R., 489, 491, 492
Carmon, N., 457
Carp, F., 471
Carpenter, C. R., 304, 306
Carpman, J. R., 463, 467, 468
Carr, S., 286, 362
Carr, T. S., 344, 363
Carroll, M. S., 59
Carver, C. S., 117
Casey, T. M., 219
Cass, R., 529, 530
Catalano, R., 132, 264, 266, 269
Catalina, D., 218
Caudill, B. D., 18
Cavanaugh, B., 538, 539, 540, 542
Cavis, L., 238
Cavoukian, A., 356, 357
Cermak, J. E., 506
Cervone, J. C., 201
Cess, R. D., 190
Chaiken, S., 31, 32, 33
Chamberlain, A. S., 310
Chamberlain, K., 132
Chandler, J., 359
Chaouloff, F., 327
Chape, C., 133
Chapko, M. K., 269
Chapman, D. W., 132
Chapple, E. P., 310
Charleston, M., 138
Charlson, R. J., 190
Charry, J. M., 214
Chawla, L., 449
Chemers, M., 29, 34, 39, 59, 304,
    306, 371, 372, 424
Chen, J., 31
Cherek, D. R., 165
Cherlin, D. L., 288
Cherulnik, P. D., 450, 466
Cheyne, J. A., 302, 504
Chihara, T., 285
Chin, Y., 452
Chinn, D. E., 537, 538
Choresh, N., 285
Chowns, R. H., 166
Christensen, R., 211, 487, 553
Christian, J. J., 327, 332
Chung, M. C., 249
Churchman, A., 309, 312
Cialdini, R. B., 22, 206, 221, 549,
    550, 556
Cicchetti, C., 515
Cini, M. A., 144
Clark, M., 169
Clark, R. E., 210

Clarke, G., 503
Clarke, R. S. J., 210
Clearwater, 125
Clemente, F., 383
Clinard, M. B., 384
Clinton, J., 541
Coakley, J. A., 190
Cobb, S., 132, 135, 236
Cobern, M. K., 534, 535, 547, 555
Coffin, D., 264
Cohen, A. J., 97
Cohen, B. G. F., 257
Cohen, H., 213
Cohen, J., 471
Cohen, J. B., 131, 225
Cohen, J. L., 360
Cohen, L., 234, 239, 249, 252
Cohen, L. J., 136
Cohen, M. R., 164, 500, 501, 553
Cohen, R., 100, 104, 105
Cohen, S., 17, 100, 104, 105, 118,
    120, 130, 131, 133, 135, 138,
    161, 162, 163, 165, 166, 167,
    170, 178, 213, 236, 348
Cohn, E. G., 203, 206, 214, 281
Cole, P., 268
Coleman, G., 379
Colligan, M. J., 162, 257
Collins, A. M., 99
Collins, B. L., 487
Collins, D. L., 135, 246, 253
Commoner, B., 326
Cone, J. D., 524, 525, 535, 539, 540,
    541, 549, 550, 551
Coniglio, C., 312
Connell, M., 241
Connelly, C. M., 436
Connolly, K., 342, 498
Conroy, J., 315
Cook, C. C., 450
Cook, D. A., 537
Cook, E. J., 498
Cook, M., 39, 285
Cook-Deegan, R. M., 474
Cooper, C., 286, 452
Cooper, D., 547
Cooper, M., 452
Cooper, R. E., 286
Cooper, R. N., 191
Cooper Marcus, C., 447
Cope, J. G., 549
Corcoran, D. W. J., 169
Corbitt, L. C., 281
Cornell, E. H., 95, 100, 104
Cornodoli, C., 96
Coss, R. G., 57
Costanzo, M., 537, 540
Cottler, L. B., 240
Cotton, J. L., 203
Couclelis, H., 98
Coupe, P., 99, 107

Cousins, J. H., 95
Covington, J., 403
Cox, V. C., 338, 344, 359, 363, 468
Cozby, P. C., 22
Craig, A. D., 196
Craig, K. J., 241
Craik, K. H., 42, 43, 72
Cramer, P., 241
Crandaall, J. E., 176
Crano, W. D., 301
Cranz, G., 388, 389
Crawshaw, R., 240
Cristofor, S., 526
Crockford, G. W., 200
Crook, M. A., 163
Crossman, E. K., 550
Crouch, A., 493
Crouch, J., 257
Crowe, M. J., 263
Crowe, T., 398
Crozier, W. R., 473
Cruikshank, M., 241
Crump, S. L., 550
Csank, J., 473
Csikszentmihalyi, M., 482, 512
Culver, B. D., 256
Culver, R., 215, 218, 219
Cummings, H., 138
Cummings, N., 162
Cunningham, M. R., 206, 207, 211,
    214, 221, 241, 265
Curio, I., 159
Cusimano, J., 290
Custance, D., 94
Cuthbertson, B. H., 247, 248
Cybriwsky, R., 308, 311, 312, 317,
    552
Cziffra, P., 498

D

D'Atri, D. A., 337
Dabbs, J. M., 286, 292, 293, 362
Dahlof, L., 331
Dahms, T. E., 267
Dalholm, E. H., 422, 423
Damon, A., 163
Damron, G., 312, 314
Daniel, T. C., 29, 45, 47, 49, 56, 57
Dannon, A., 214
Darley, J. M., 380, 398, 529, 534,
    535, 536, 538, 540, 541, 542
Dart, F. E., 86
Darwin, C., 37
Davenport, Y., 222
Daves, W. F., 286
Davidson, L. M., 132, 230, 246,
    248, 252, 253, 260
Davies, D. R., 168
Davis, B., 191
Davis, D. D., 491
Davis, G., 19, 23

Davis, G. E., 341, 362, 364, 427,
    430, 488
Davis, R. E., 197
Dawes, R. M., 529
Dawis, R. V., 31
Day, K., 434
Day, L. L., 403, 404
Dean, L., 276, 281, 295, 338
Decker, J., 423
DeFronzo, J., 195, 203
DeFusco, P., 379
DeGiovanni, F. F., 403
DeGroot, I., 264
DeJonge, D., 88
Delgado, E., 534, 542
DeLoache, J. S., 94
DeLong, A. J., 310
DeLongis, A., 132, 139
DeMan, A. F., 264
Dembroski, T. M., 165
Dempsey, N. P., 452
DeNeve, K. M., 205, 206
Denison, D. M., 217
Dennis, M. L., 538, 539, 540, 542
Dennis, W., 450
DeRisis, D., 357
Derogatis, L. R., 17
DeSanctis, M., 214
Desor, J. A., 353, 362, 425
Devlin, A. S., 91, 466
Devlin, K., 406, 422
Dew, M. A., 252
DeWaal, F. B., 325, 328
Dexter, E., 213, 220
DeYoung, R., 545, 548
Diamond, S. G., 286, 290
Dickason, J. D., 390
Dickson, D., 439, 469
Dickerson Mayes, S., 241
Dienstbier, R. A., 118, 134
Dietz, T., 528
Dill, C. A., 129
Dillman, D., 377, 384
Dillon, H., 249
Ditton, R. B., 514
Dockett, K., 396
Doherty, S., 86
Dohrenwend, B. P., 251, 384
Dohrenwend, B. S., 251, 384
Dohrenwend et al., 1979, 251
Dollinger, S. J., 241
Donald, I., 453
Donnerstein, E., 127, 177, 178
Dooley, B. B., 342, 344, 357
Dooley, D., 132, 236, 264, 266, 269
Doring, H. J., 162
Doriot, P., 314
Dornic, S., 168
Dosey, M. A., 282
Doty, K., 012
Dow, A., 512

Downes, A., 266
Downs, R. M., 79, 127, 138, 180
Doyle, D. P., 180, 207
Drabek, T., 231, 250, 254
Drabman, R., 551
Drinkwater, B., 267
Driver, B. L., 509, 512, 513, 515
DuBois, C., 234
Dubos, R., 267, 327
Duff, D. F., 285
Duffy, M., 472
Duke, M. P., 279, 284, 285, 320
Dukes, F. O., 342
Duncan, A., 545
Duncan, J., 36, 448
Dunlap, R. E., 532, 536
Dunn, J. M., 162
Dunsworth, F. A., 248
Dusek, E. R., 210
Duvall, D., 395
Dwyer, W. O., 534, 535, 546, 547, 555
Dynes, R. R., 234
Dyson, M. L., 325, 328, 331

E

Eagle, P. F., 386
Eagly, A. H., 31
Earls, R., 240
Easterbrook, J. A., 118, 158
Eaves, L. J., 39
Ebbesen, E. B., 178, 296, 298, 458, 458, 460
Eberts, E. H., 284
Ebreo, A., 546
Eckenrode, J., 236
Edmonds, E. M., 169
Edney, J. J., 13, 306, 307, 309, 310, 313, 315, 521, 528, 529, 530, 531
Edwards, D. J. A., 280, 283
Edwards, J. N., 286, 338, 358, 362
Efran, M. G., 302, 504
Eggertsen, R., 164
Ehrlich, P., 326
Eibl-Eibesfeldt, I., 313
Ekehammar, B., 168
Elder, J., 20
Eliot, R. S., 165
Eller, S. J., 130
Ellis, P., 541
Ellsworth, P. C., 294
El-Mofty, A., 161, 264, 529
Elortegui, P., 219
Ely, D., 43
Emmett, E. A., 220
Endresen, I. M., 172
Engen, T., 64
Epstein, J., 282
Epstein, Y. M., 336, 337, 339, 344, 357, 360, 364

Ercolani, A. P., 461
Erfrut, J. C., 133
Ergezen, N., 90
Erickson, J. B., 543
Erickson, W. A., 257
Erikson, K. T., 240, 250
Ernsting, J., 216
Ervin, C. R., 280, 281
Erwin, J., 331
Erwin, N., 331
Esser, A. H., 306, 310
Estes, J. P., 281
Evans, G. W., 76, 78, 79, 81, 83, 84, 88, 90, 91, 92, 93, 95, 96, 97, 102, 116, 119, 121, 127, 130, 131, 133, 135, 136, 138, 161, 162, 163, 167, 170, 171, 262, 264, 265, 266, 267, 269, 276, 291, 296, 297, 335, 336, 337, 341, 345, 346, 348, 357, 358, 359, 362, 496, 497
Everett, P. B., 536, 537, 538, 541, 542, 548, 549
Ewert, A. W., 217
Eyles, J., 260
Eysenk, M. W., 257

F

Fagan, G., 18
Faletti, M. V., 135
Falk, J. H., 53, 55
Fanger, P. O., 426
Farbstein, J., 469
Faupel, C. E., 136
Fazio, R. H., 31, 33, 540
Feather, N. T., 21
Fedler, A. J., 514
Fedoravicius, A. S., 214
Feimer, N. R., 42
Fein, G. G., 203, 259
Feldman, R. M., 448, 548
Felipe, N. J., 295
Feller, R. A., 427
Fellows, J., 102
Fenyd, D., 129, 138, 170, 430, 488
Ferguson, G., 305, 397
Festinger, L. A., 33, 117, 458, 459
Fidell, S., 159, 160, 240
Finch, A. J., 241
Finckle, A. L., 164
Fine, T. H., 123
Finn, R., 490
Finnie, W. C., 549
Fiorito, E., 138
Firestone, I., 354
Fischbach, R. L., 240
Fischer, C. S., 372, 377, 380, 382, 384, 407
Fischhoff, B., 254, 260
Fishback, J. F., 537, 541
Fishbein, M., 32

Fisher, B., 434
Fisher, J. D., 17, 134, 295, 298, 299, 309, 347, 359, 360, 362, 364, 553, 554
Fitzgerald, E. F., 337
Fitzgibbon, J. E., 52
Fitzpatrick, M., 205, 269
Flaherty, C. F., 210
Fleming, I., 22, 132, 134, 230, 248, 252, 260
Fleming, R., 132, 136, 236, 361
Fleshner, M., 138
Fletcher, C. I., 176
Florig, H. J., 215
Florin, P., 399
Flynn, C. B., 251
Flynn, D., 331
Flynn, M., 219
Flynn, R., 408
Fogarty, S. J., 169
Foley, J. E., 97, 471
Folkman, S., 130, 131, 132, 134, 139
Fonzi, A., 296
Forbes, G., 381
Force, J. E., 59
Ford, A. B., 384
Ford, J. G., 284
Ford, T. R., 537, 541
Forgays, D. G., 121
Forgays, D. K., 121
Fortenberry, J. H., 302
Foss, C., 278, 286, 308, 425
Foster, K. Y., 241
Foster, S. C., 241, 537
Fowler, F. J., 396
Fox, R. H., 199
Fox, W. F., 210
Foxx, R. M., 539
Frager, N., 264, 265, 267
Francis, R. S., 539
Franck, K., 383, 396, 397, 398
Franck, K. A., 112, 416
Franck, K. D., 378
Frank, F., 332
Frank, J., 545
Franke, R. H., 439
Frankel, A. S., 286
Frankenhaeuser, M., 133, 135, 136, 337
Frasier, L., 300
Frazier, K., 194, 469
Freedman, J. L., 336, 343, 344, 356, 357, 459, 549
Freedy, J. R., 243
Freeman, H., 395
Freilicher, J., 166
Frese, M., 257
Frey, J., 203, 205, 211, 218, 219, 223, 266, 269
Friberg, L., 264

Fried, M., 395, 448, 452
Friedman, L. W., 170
Frisancho, A. R., 195, 197, 198, 215, 216, 220
Fritz, C. E., 231, 248
Froelicher, E. S., 512
Froelicher, V. F., 512
Frosch, R. A., 191
Frost, J. L., 393
Fry, A. M., 300
Fuhrer, U., 448
Fuller, T. D., 286, 338, 358, 362
Fusco, M. E., 30, 531

G

Gabelnick, D. A., 241
Gabiele, T., 22, 342
Gaes, G. G., 362, 468
Gahagan, D., 281
Gaines, T. A., 432, 433, 434
Galbraith, F. D., 463
Gallardo, D., 53, 55
Gale, N., 86, 95, 98
Gallacher, J., 166, 167
Gallant, S. J., 284
Galle, O. R., 343, 358
Galloway, W., 159
Gallup, G., 314
Galster, G., 452
Ganellen, R. J., 135
Gans, H. J., 372, 395, 450
Garber, J., 127
Garcia, K. D., 490
Gardner, G. T., 129, 489, 491, 492, 536, 539, 541
Gärling, T., 78, 79, 80, 83, 90, 91, 96, 100, 101, 102, 192, 450
Garmezy, N., 240
Garnand, D. B., 202
Garreau, J., 371, 387, 406, 407, 408
Garrett, W. A., 207
Garvill, J., 450
Garzino, S. J., 218
Gashell, G., 541
Gatchel, R. J., 132, 136, 236, 252, 260, 352
Gattoni, F. E. G., 166
Gaydos, H. F., 210
Gaylin, K., 492, 493
Gee, M., 508
Geen, R. G., 117, 168, 177, 313
Gelfand, D. M., 380
Geller, E. S., 21, 373, 535, 536, 537, 538, 539, 541, 542, 543, 548, 549, 550, 555
Geller, H., 541
Gendrich, J. G., 551
Gergen, K. J., 286, 427
Gergen, M. K., 286, 427
Gerrity, E., 239
Gerst, M. S., 17
Gibbons, F. X., 117

Gibbs, J. P., 384
Gibbs, L., 260
Gibbs, M. S., 260
Gibson, B., 142, 276
Gibson, J. J., 70, 73, 74, 75
Giel, R., 360
Gield, B., 492, 493
Gifford, R., 285, 320, 343, 358, 428, 530
Gilat, Y., 285
Glazer, K., 128
Gilden, E. R., 129
Gill, N., 545
Gillen, J. C., 222
Gilman, B. I., 503
Gimblett, R. J., 52
Ginsberg, Y., 382
Ginsburg, H., 342
Gisriel, M. M., 236
Giuliani, M. V., 448, 453
Glacken, C. J., 192
Glass, D. C., 12, 21, 76, 127, 133, 135, 138, 158, 161, 162, 163, 164, 165, 166, 167, 170, 173, 177, 346, 350, 373
Gleicher, P., 395, 452
Glenn, N., 380
Gleser, G., 240, 241, 248, 250, 251
Glicksohn, J., 96
Gliner, J., 267
Glorig, A., 164
Goebel, B. L., 144
Goeckner, D., 331
Gold, J. R., 306
Goldberg, M. L., 281
Goldman, M., 301, 302
Goldring, E., 240
Goldsmith, J. R., 209, 264
Goldsmith, R., 199
Goldstein, E. B., 47, 64, 66, 69, 70
Golledge, R. G., 78, 83, 86, 95, 98, 192
Gonzales, M. H., 537
Goodnight, J. A., 100, 104, 105
Goodrich, R., 493
Goodwin, F. K., 222
Goranson, R. E., 203
Gordon, D., 241, 489
Gordon, M. S., 241, 383
Gore, S., 236
Gormley, F. P., 357, 361
Gottfredson, S. D., 312, 396, 397
Gottlieb, R., 533, 546
Gottman, J., 371
Gould, P., 86
Gould, J. D., 490
Gove, W. R., 334, 343, 358, 359
Grace, M. C., 240, 251
Graefe, A. R., 514
Graf, P., 163
Gramann, J. H., 360
Grandjean, E., 163, 173, 489

Grandjean, P., 256
Grandstaff, N., 267
Grant, D. P., 463, 468, 471
Grasmick, H. G., 528
Gratz, R. B., 403, 404
Graves, J. R., 284
Graves, T. D., 283
Graydon, E., 498
Green, B., 240, 241, 248, 250, 251
Green, D. M., 159, 240
Greenbaum, P. E., 18
Greenbaum, S. D., 452
Greenberg, C. I., 133, 145, 336, 339, 340, 354, 382
Greenberger, D. B., 553
Greenbie, B. B., 53
Greene, D., 284, 537
Greene, J. O., 132, 277
Greene, L. R., 339, 289
Greene, T. C., 201, 208, 233, 426, 436
Greenfield, N., 493
Greenough, W., 331
Grev, R., 207
Greve, K. W., 257
Grier, H. C., 524, 540, 541
Griffen, L. M., 338, 339, 360
Griffin, M., 425, 506
Griffiths, I. D., 181, 182, 199, 200
Griffitt, W., 202
Grischowsky, N., 490
Groat, L., 422
Groff, B., 345, 347
Gromoll, H., 381
Grossnickle, W. F., 549
Groner, N., 347
Grove, J. B., 22
Gruen, R., 132, 139
Grunberg, J., 386
Grunberg, N. E., 133, 135, 358
Guardo, C. J., 284
Gubbins, S., 534, 542
Gubrium, J. F., 383
Gudycc, C. A., 434
Guenther, R., 262
Gulian, E., 169
Gulliver, F. P., 10
Gump, P. V., 10, 141, 144, 496, 497
Gunderson, E. K. F., 210, 338
Gunnoe, C., 259
Gustanski, J., 427
Guterbock, T. M., 192
Gutman, G. M., 474
Gutterman, E. M., 260

H

Haas, J. E., 236
Haas, S., 504
Haase, R. S., 281
Haber, G. M., 309, 311
Hackett, T. P., 132
Hackney, J., 267

Hadar, I., 300
Haggard, L. M., 314, 452, 512
Hake, D. F., 539
Halcomb, C. G., 214
Hale, C. S., 327
Hale, M., 383
Hales, J. M., 190
Hall, E. T., 10, 11, 275, 276, 278, 279, 283, 287, 288, 289, 291, 302
Hall, M., 234, 239, 249, 252
Hall, P., 404, 405
Hall, R., 449
Ham, K. S., 135, 251
Hamad, C. D., 547
Hambrick-Dixon, P. J., 170
Hamilton, J. A., 284
Hamilton, J. F., 48
Hamilton, P., 172
Hammitt, W. E., 514
Hampton, I. F. G., 199
Hanacek, B., 241, 242
Hancock, P. A., 199, 450
Hand, D. G., 166, 504
Handford, H. A., 241
Hanley, G., 103, 104, 501
Hanselka, L. L., 129
Hansen, J. E., 190
Hansen, W. B., 19
Hanson, L., 144
Hanson, S., 234, 239
Hansson, R. O., 117, 381
Hanusa, B. H., 128, 474
Harada, M., 259
Harburg, E., 133, 383
Hard, E., 331
Hardey, J. R., 98
Hardin, G., 520, 525, 529, 544
Hargreaves, A. G., 250
Haro, J. M., 238
Harper, C. S., 529, 530
Harries, K. D., 203
Harris, H., 276, 345, 473
Harris-Bass, J., 258
Harrison, A. A., 125, 529
Hart, R. A., 90, 391, 392
Hart, R. H., 265
Hartig, T., 121, 448, 4500
Hartman, D. P., 380
Hartsough, D. M., 132
Harvey, M. L., 529
Hasell, M. J., 454, 456
Haskell, P. C., 499
Hatcher, J., 537, 541
Hattori, H., 162
Hauenstein, L. S., 133
Hauf, G., 162
Hautaluoma, J. E., 529
Haupt, B., 490
Hawkins, L. H., 214
Hawkinshire, F. B. W., 214
Hay, D. G., 95, 100, 104, 384

Hayduk, L. A., 280, 283, 284, 285, 286, 291, 294
Hayes, S. C., 524, 525, 535, 539, 540, 541, 549, 550, 551
Hayes-Roth, B., 95, 96, 103
Hayward, D. G., 391, 392
Hayward, J., 388, 393
Hazucha, M., 267
Heath, A. C., 39
Heath, D., 202, 215
Heath, L., 383
Heaton, A. W., 316
Hebb, D. O., 116, 117
Heberlein, T. A., 535
Hebert, J. A., 263
Hecht, M. E., 37
Hede, A. J., 167
Hedge, A., 257, 258
Hediger, H., 275
Hedman, R., 404
Hedstrong, L. D., 257
Heerwagen, J. H., 47, 53, 56, 487
Heft, H., 47, 73, 91, 94, 122
Hegarty, P., 497
Heimstra, N. W., 6, 268, 426
Heining, P., 267
Held, D., 471
Heliotis, F., 526
Heller, J., 345, 347
Helson, H., 45
Hemsley, D. R., 169
Henderson, L. F., 504
Henderson, S., 249
Hendrick, C., 135
Henig, J. R., 402, 403
Henry, D. O., 192, 194
Hensley, W. E., 494, 495
Herbert, R. K., 493
Herberman, R., 162
Herd, J. A., 165
Hermann, D., 96
Hern, W. M., 298
Heron, W., 497
Herren, K., 94
Herridge, C. F., 166
Herskovits, M. J., 75
Herzberg, F., 493
Herzog, T. R., 13, 29, 52, 53, 57, 450
Heshka, S., 280, 337
Hess, R., 461
Hess, S., 169
Hesser, G., 452
Hewitt, J., 129, 138, 170, 281, 430, 488
Hicks, A., 257
Hicks, P. E., 489
Hill, E., 169, 529
Hill, J. W., 200, 370, 380
Hill, P. C., 129
Hillman, R. B., 288
Hiorns, R. F., 199
Hiroto, D. S., 130

Hirst, E., 541
Hirtle, S. C., 98
Hiss, T., 388, 406
Hoberman, H. M., 236
Hobfoll, S. E., 134, 243
Hockey, G. R. J., 168, 172
Hocking, M. B., 524
Hodges, L., 287, 298
Hodgson, M. J., 257
Hoffman, D. J., 190
Hoffman, M., 241
Holahan, C. J., 90, 317, 398, 429
Holding, C. S., 92, 98, 167
Holland, W. E., 364
Hollander, J., 218
Hollingshead, A. B., 401
Hollister, F. D., 487
Holman, E. A., 448
Holmes, R. M., 240, 281, 285
Hong, G., 347, 358
Hook, H., 90
Hoople, H., 301
Hope, M., 342
Hopper, J. R., 528
Horowitz, M. J., 285
Hortnagel, H., 135
Hortnagel, L., 135
Horton, R., 241
Horvath, S. M., 267
Hought, L., 241
Hourihan, K., 452
House, J. S., 132, 312, 381
Houston, B. K., 172
Houts, P. S., 136, 251
Howard, G. S., 276, 291, 296, 297, 534, 542
Howenstine, E., 546
Hubel, D. H., 47, 65
Huerta, F., 241
Huffman, K. P., 549
Huffman, K. T., 549
Hughes, J., 301, 302, 334, 359
Hughes, R. L., 327
Huitfeldt, B., 343
Hull, R. B., 57
Hummel, C. F., 263
Hundert, A. J., 493
Hunt, J., 506
Hunt, M. E., 100, 104, 105, 473
Hunter, A., 397
Hunting, W., 489
Huntington, E., 192, 194
Hurt, H., 195
Hyde, M., 504
Hyde, R. T., 512
Hygge, S., 171, 199
Hyman, D., 360

I

Ickes, W., 294
Im, S., 49
Imm, P. S., 241

Inglehart, M., 207
Ingraham, L. H., 237
Inhelder, B., 94
Inoue, W., 124
Irwin, R., 381
Isaac, L. M., 301
Isen, A. M., 169, 178
Ishii, S., 124
Ishikawa, S., 389, 420, 434, 435
Ising, H., 159, 163
Iso-Ahola, S. E., 507
Israel, A., 134
Itami, R. M., 52
Ittelson, W. H., 6, 7, 20, 66, 67, 126, 341, 424, 466, 467
Iwata, O., 167, 359
Iwawaki, S., 285

J

Jacklin, C., 91
Jackson, E. L., 234
Jackson, J. M., 534, 535, 547, 555
Jackson, K., 450, 451
Jackson, S. W., 222
Jacobs, H. E., 548
Jacobs, S. V., 127, 133, 262, 264, 265, 266, 267, 269
Jacobsen, F. M., 222
Jacobson, J. L., 259
Jacobson, S. W., 259
Jain, U., 287
James, B., 316
James, J. W., 296
James, W., 112
Janis, I. L., 135
Janney, J., 240
Jansen, G. N., 164
Jarpe, G., 136
Jarrell, M. P., 243
Jason, L. A., 549
Jaszewski, A., 404
Jeppesen, J., 536
Jenkins, L. M., 166, 504
Jensen, L. K., 264
Jerdee, T. H., 529
Jerking, E., 426
Jest, C., 215
Job, R. F. S., 167
Jodelet, D., 87, 88, 89
John, E. M., 215
Johnson, A. K., 385
Johnson, G. A., 176
Johnson, H. H., 22
Johnson, J. E., 134, 364
Johnson, M. W., 390
Johnson, N., 260
Johnson, P. K., 279
Johnson, R., 211
Johnson, T. L., 512
Johnson, V. S., 551
Johnston, J. W., 262

Joiner, D., 488, 494
Jones, C. J., 145
Jones, D. M., 167, 171
Jones, J. W., 265, 268
Jones, R. T., 241
Jones, T. M., 171, 172
Jones, T. S., 283
Jonides, J., 98
Jorgenson, D. O., 219, 529
Jorgenson, M. D., 205, 530, 531
Joselow, M. M., 256
Jourard, S. M., 281, 284
Joy, V. D., 342
Joyner, M. A., 550, 551
Judge, P. G., 325, 328
Jue, G. M., 496, 497
Jung, J., 135
Jung, K. G., 240

K

Kagel, J. H., 535
Kahn, R. L., 473
Kahneman, D., 117
Kaiser, F. G., 448
Kaitilla, S., 452
Kalish, D., 80
Kalkstein, L. S., 190, 197
Kallgren, C. A., 550, 556
Kalof, L., 528
Kamarck, T., 17
Kammann, R., 381
Kane, R. A., 474
Kaniasty, K., 236, 237, 240
Kant, I., 35
Kantola, S. J., 536
Kaplan, A., 492
Kaplan, R., 13, 29, 39, 45, 48, 51, 53, 57, 67, 72, 79, 83, 100, 113, 115, 120, 389, 390, 422, 423, 430, 431, 501, 515
Kaplan, S., 29, 39, 45, 48, 49, 51, 52, 54, 56, 57, 67, 72, 79, 83, 90, 100, 120, 121, 389, 390, 422, 423, 430, 431, 500, 501, 515
Kapp, F. I., 250
Kara, G., 241
Karabenick, S., 282, 285, 286
Kardes, F. R., 33
Kardiner, A., 234
Karlin, R. A., 336, 337, 339, 344, 357, 360, 364
Karlovac, M., 468
Karmel, L. J., 428, 496
Karp, L., 169
Karuza, J., 267
Kasl, S. V., 132, 133, 251, 337, 383
Kastka, J., 182, 262
Kates, R. W., 232, 233, 236
Katovich, M., 315
Katz, P., 275
Katzev, R. D., 537, 546, 548

Kaufman, J., 487
Kaufman-Gilliland, C. M., 529
Kaul, J. D., 439
Kauma, C., 144
Kaye, S. M., 428
Keane, C., 461
Keating, J., 339, 347, 359
Kees, W., 428
Kehoe, S., 18, 295
Keller, L. M., 31
Kelley, H., 361
Kelly, C. E., 290
Kelly, I. W., 215, 218, 219
Kelly, J. T., 387
Kelly, S., 130
Kempton, W., 534, 535, 536, 538, 540, 541, 542
Kendler, K. S., 39
Kennelly, D., 342
Kenny, D. A., 114
Kenrick, D. T., 176, 205, 206, 221
Kent, S. J., 164, 457, 458
Kerr, N., 380
Kerr, N. L., 529
Kerr, R. A., 190, 191, 194, 526, 532
Kerslake, D., 199, 201
Kessler, R. C., 39, 132
Kevan, S. M., 219, 221
Key, W., 370, 380, 394
Keys, C., 338
Kilijanek, T. S., 250
Kimble, C. A., 195
Kinarthy, E. L., 288
Kindermann, T., 472
King, D., 203
King, M. G., 296
Kinsey, K. A., 528
Kira, A., 454, 456
Kirasic, K. C., 97
Kirk, N. L., 434
Kirmeyer, S. L., 141, 144, 145, 338
Kitchin, R. M., 78, 79, 83
Kjos, G. L., 458, 459, 460
Klath, N., 498
Kleck, R., 297
Kleeman, W. B., 489, 490
Kleiber, D. A., 482, 512
Kleiman, M. B., 383
Klien, B. L., 393
Klein, H. J., 503
Klein, K., 116, 345
Klein, L. M., 331
Klenow, J. D., 241, 242
Kline, L. M., 19, 281, 286, 301, 529
Kline, N. S., 310
Klitzman, S., 489
Klotz, M. L., 260
Kmiecik, C., 300
Knave, B. G., 257
Knight, P. A., 439
Knopf, R. C., 512, 515

Knowles, E. S., 23, 114, 277, 279, 296, 298, 300, 301, 302, 345, 360, 504
Koch, G., 477
Koelega, H. S., 167
Kohlenberg, R., 551
Kohler, W., 4
Kohn, I., 379
Kojima, H., 129
Koman, S., 138, 340, 343, 347, 360
Komorita, S. S., 529
Koncinski, W. S., 538, 539, 540, 542
Konar, E., 489
Kondracki, B. A., 290
Konecni, V. J., 178, 296, 298, 458, 459, 460
Koneya, M., 288
Konzett, H., 135
Koocher, G. P., 23
Koop, C. E., 268
Kopp, J. T., 547
Kordtz, T., 264
Koropeckyj-Cox, T., 452
Korte, C., 377, 380, 381
Koscheyev, V. S., 253
Kosenkov, A. A., 253
Koss, M. P., 434
Kosslyn, S. M., 96, 97
Kostof, S., 388, 389, 395, 403, 404, 405, 483
Kovach, E. J., 106
Kovrigin, S. D., 174
Kowalski, L. T., 249
Kramer, R. M., 529, 531
Krammer, T. L., 240
Krantz, D. S., 130, 138, 161, 162, 163, 167, 170
Krauss, R. M., 549
Krebs, C. J., 332
Kressel, S., 547, 548
Kreuser, B., 504
Kriss, M., 540
Kristeller, J. L., 123
Kroling, P., 215
Kroner, W., 541
Krupat, E., 139, 371, 379
Kryter, K. D., 158, 161, 166, 174
Kuipers, B., 78
Kukas, S., 169
Küller, R., 427, 496
Kuo, F. E., 501
Kurland, G., 528, 535, 536, 538, 541, 545, 546, 549
Kushler, M., 536
Kyriocos, C., 167

L

La Hart, D., 552
Labahn, T., 553
Ladd, F. C., 450
LaGanga, M. L., 461

Lakota, R. A., 501
Lalli, M., 448
Lamberth, J., 280, 281
Landesberger, H. A., 439
Landiss, C. W., 268
Landon, P. B., 123
Landy, F. J., 439, 493
Lang, J., 70, 417, 418, 420, 423, 429, 430, 432
Langdon, P., 81, 163
Langer, E. J., 127, 128, 134, 359, 364, 474
Langmeyer, D., 289
Lanius, U. F., 42, 44, 45
Lanni, J. C., 315
Larkin, P., 78
Larrain, P., 234, 264
Larrick, R. P., 203
Larson, J. H., 285
Larson, L., 162
Larsson, K., 331
Lartzev, M. A., 253
Laska, S. B., 124
Lassen, C. L., 289
Latané, B., 380, 398
Latta, R. M., 281
Lauber, A., 163
Laumann, E. O., 312
Launier, R., 134
Lauriat, A., 386
LaVerne, A. A., 265
Laverty, W. H., 219
Lavrakas, P. J., 319, 382, 383, 407
Law, C. S., 452
Law, D., 267
Lawrence, E., 128
Lawson, B. R., 159
Lawton, M. P., 128, 383, 427, 471, 472
Lazarus, R. S., 131, 132, 133, 134, 136, 139, 225
Leavitt, J., 461
Lebailly, R., 383
Lebedun, M., 257
LeBlanc, J., 208, 398
Lebo, C. P., 161
Lebovits, A., 255, 256
Leckliter, I. N., 537, 538, 541
Leckwart, J. F., 463
Ledwith, F., 217
Lee, B., 388, 402, 403
Lee, D. H. K., 196
Lee, J., 438
Lee, J. R., 97
Lee, T. H., 191
Leedom, N., 536
Leeming, F. C., 534, 535, 546, 547, 555
Lefcourt, H. M., 136
Lehman, D. R., 132, 528
Lehman, J., 490

Lehmann, N., 342
Leighton, B., 450
Leithead, C. S., 198
Lemke, S., 128
Leon, G. R., 253
Leonard, A. C., 240, 251
Leonard, H. S., 138
Leopold, A., 38, 508
Leopold, R. L., 249
Lepore, S. J., 135, 163, 341, 348, 357, 358, 359
Lepper, M. R., 284, 537
Lerner, R. N., 285
Lesko, W. A., 207
Lester, D., 219
Lett, E. E., 309, 313, 452
Leventhal, G., 549
Leventhal, H., 134, 364
Levine, A. G., 260
Levine, D. W., 309
Levine, J. M., 144
Levine, M., 103, 104, 107, 440, 501
Levine, R., 139
Levine, R. V., 380, 384
Leviton, A., 259
Levitt, L., 263, 451, 549
Levy, A. S., 336, 343
Levy, S., 162
Levy-Leboyer, C., 127, 461
Lewin, K., 10
Lewis, C. A., 389, 390
Lewis, D. A., 383
Lewis, G. J., 377
Lewis, H. E., 199
Lewis, J., 267
Lewis, L., 331
Lewy, A. J., 222
Ley, D., 308, 311, 312, 317, 552
Lezak, A., 178
Libuser, L., 178, 296, 298
Lichtenstein, S., 254
Lieber, A. L., 218
Lifton, R. J., 250
Lightman, S. L., 166
Lim, K. Y., 438
Lima, A. M., 238
Lima, B. R., 238
Lind, A. R., 198
Lindauer, M. S., 456
Lindberg, E., 79, 96, 100, 102, 450
Lindeman, D. A., 477
Lindsten, C., 496
Lindvall, T., 262
Lindy, J. D., 251
Link, J. M., 200
Linn, W., 267
Lintell, M., 176
Linton, R., 234
Lipetz, B., 499
Lipman, A., 309, 473
Lippert, S., 463

Lipsey, M. W., 264
Lipton, S. G., 388, 402, 403
Little, K. B., 174, 272, 283, 286, 290
Littman, R., 162
Litton, R. B., 46
Lloyd, A. J., 123
Lloyd, J. T., 176
Lloyd, K. D., 535
Lloyd, M. E., 535
Lloyd, R., 86
Lloyd, W. F., 526
Locke, E. A., 547
Lockhard, J. S., 301
Loewen, L. J., 160, 486, 492
Lofland, J., 18
Logan, J., 487
Logue, J. N., 239
Lomranz, J., 285
London, B., 388, 402, 403
Long, G. T., 301, 438
Lonigan, C. J., 241
Loo, C. M., 76, 341, 342, 343, 353, 359, 360
Loomis, R. J., 201, 263, 501, 503
Lord, E. E., 259
Lorenz, K., 305, 313, 332
Losito, B. D., 138
Lott, B. S., 281
Louria, D. B., 256
Love, K. D., 280
Love, S. Q., 537, 538, 541
Lovegrove, T. E., 487
Lovell, B., 497
Lovelock, J., 190
Lovett, D., 267
Low, S. M., 58, 448, 458
Lowe, W., 285
Lower, M., 296
Lozar, G. C., 19
Lublin, J. S., 451
Lucia, M., 384
Lucas, R. C., 514
Ludwig, H. W., 214
Lui, L., 529, 531
Lukas, J. S., 169
Lumia, A. R., 331
Lundberg, U., 133, 337
Luquette, A. J., 268
Lutz, W., 326
Luxenberg, S., 468
Luyben, P. D., 535, 548
Lyles, W. B., 257
Lynch, K., 61, 81, 83, 84, 86, 87, 88, 98, 102, 107, 384
Lyons, E., 55

M

Maccoby, E., 91, 281, 284, 299, 336
Madonia, B., 129, 138, 170, 430, 488
MacDonald, J. E., 320
MacDougall, J. M., 165

MacEachren, A. M., 96
MacFarlane, S. W., 205
MacIntosh, E., 336, 344
Mack, R., 313
MacKenzie, S. T., 173, 174, 175
Maclean, J., 302
MacPherson, D. K., 536
Madden, T. J., 32
Magel, S. G., 97
Magnusson, M., 164
Maher, C., 259
Maida, C. A., 241
Maier, S. F., 138, 331
Mainieri, T., 528, 535, 536, 538, 541, 545, 546, 549
Maitra, S., 282
Malouff, J., 128
Mandal, M. K., 282, 285
Mandel, D. R., 17, 338, 339, 360, 362, 489
Mang, 121
Mangione, T. W., 396
Mann, P. H., 384, 549, 550
Mannetti, L., 371
Manning, R. E., 514
Marans, R. W., 407, 493, 512
Marchon, I., 103, 104, 501
Marerro, D. G., 91
Marine, G., 313
Marini, Z., 540
Markham, S., 194
Markowitz, J. S., 260
Marks, E. S., 231, 248
Marland, G., 191
Marquis, J. F., 282
Marshall, E., 532
Martens, V. K., 253
Martichuski, D. K., 477, 531
Martin, J., 341
Martin, R. A., 136, 138
Martindale, D. A., 315
Martinez, T. S., 380
Marwell, G., 529
Maslow, A. H., 430
Massey, F. J., 256
Masters, C. R., 243
Matese, F., 549
Mathew, L. J., 477
Mathews, K. E., 176, 179
Mathieu, J. T., 384
Mattell, G., 136
Matter, C. F., 23, 296
Matthews, R., 344, 346, 364
Mattison, R. E., 241
Matus, V., 210
Mausar, P., 300
Mausner, B., 493
Mawby, R. I., 397
Maxfield, M. G., 383, 407
Maxwell, S. E., 95
Mayo, C., 311, 314
Mazumdar, S., 58, 449

Mazumdar, S., 58, 449
McAllister, C. G., 162
McBride, G., 296
McCain, G., 338, 344, 363, 468
McCall, M. E., 396
McCallum, R., 347, 358
McCarthy, D. O., 163
McCarthy, D. P., 162, 182, 362
McCarthy, J., 257, 258
McCaul, K. D., 547
McCauley, C., 379, 380, 409
McCaull, J., 378
McChesney, K. Y., 386
McClain, G., 359
McClay, D., 301
McCool, R. E., 249
McCormick, E. J., 426, 435, 440, 441, 487, 489
McCown, E. J., 117
McDaniel, M. A., 96
McDonald, B. L., 512
McDonald, P. J., 313
McDonald, T. P., 78, 84, 95, 99
McDonel, E. C., 31
McElroy, J. C., 488, 494, 495
McFarland, D., 339
McFarland, R. A., 217
McFarlane, A., 240, 241
McFarling, L. H., 6, 426
McGaffey, C. N., 344
McGill, T. E., 497
McGinnis, M. Y., 331
McGrath, J. E., 132, 141, 144, 376
McGuinness, D., 92
McGuire, W. J., 31, 362
McKay, C. P., 125
McKechnie, G. E., 13
McKinnon, W., 252
McLachlan, C., 298
McLaughlin, C., 22, 342
McLaughlin, W. J., 59
McLean, E. K., 159
McLuhan, T. C., 34
McMreath, H., 377
McNally, R. J., 39
McNamara, T. P., 92, 96, 98, 100
McNess, M. P., 551
McPherson, J. M., 343
McTavish, J., 529
McVittie, R. I., 301
Meald, J. E., 553
Medalia, N. Z., 264
Meeks, J. W., 461
Meer, J., 454
Mehler, A., 144
Mehrabian, A., 50, 135, 281, 286, 290, 430, 453, 488
Meier, H. P., 163
Meisels, M., 282, 284, 285, 286
Melchert, H. U., 163
Melick, M. E., 240
Melton, A. W., 501

Mendell, M. J., 257
Mendelsohn, R., 264
Menninger, W. C., 234
Mercer, G. W., 309
Mercer, S., 474
Merchant, C., 35, 38
Merki, D. J., 268
Mermelstein, R., 17
Merry, S. E., 397, 457, 460
Messick, D. M., 529, 531
Metcalf, J., 349, 350
Michelini, R. L., 290
Michelson, W., 309, 420, 450, 452, 467, 468
Midden, C. J. H., 461
Middlemist, R. D., 23, 296
Middleton, P., 43
Mikheyev, A. P., 174
Mikulka, P., 267
Miler, R., 503
Miles, M. A., 138
Miles, S., 215, 217
Milgram, S., 87, 88, 89, 118, 119, 373, 379, 380, 381
Millar, K., 162
Miller, C. E., 331
Miller, D., 534, 542
Miller, E., 218
Miller, G. A., 97
Miller, I. W., 130
Miller, J. D., 166
Miller, J. E., 266
Miller, J. F., 287, 288
Miller, J. P., 545
Miller, M., 161, 549, 551
Miller, R. W., 135, 251
Miller, S., 358
Miller, T. L., 553
Milligan, M., 205, 269
Milne, G., 239
Min, M. S., 358, 362
Minami, H., 124
Minckley, B., 467
Mineka, S., 39
Minoru, M., 240
Mintz, N. C., 430
Minuto, A., 490
Miransky, J., 127
Mirchandini, P. B., 383
Mishima, H. R., 548
Mitchell, G. E., 257, 258
Mitchell, H., 421, 509
Mitchell, M. Y., 59
Miyake, K., 384
Mocellin, J. S., 122, 125
Moeser, S. D., 102, 103, 104
Mohindra, N., 171
Moller, A. T., 289
Molloy, J. T., 553
Montagu, A., 278
Montano, D., 355
Montgomery, L., 540

Mooney, K. M., 281
Moore, G., 10
Moore, G. T., 90
Moore, H. E., 132, 239
Moore, M., 57
Moore, R. C., 390, 392, 393
Moore, R. J., 234, 264
Moore, S. F., 529
Moos, R. H., 17, 128, 192, 194, 213, 218, 219, 220, 221, 398
Moran, R., 463
Morasch, B., 347
Moray, N., 438
Morden, C. J., 289
Moreland, R. L., 144, 460
Morey, P. R., 257
Morgan, M. G., 260
Moritz, D. J., 477
Morokoff, P. J., 284
Morris, E. W., 453
Morris, P., 302
Morton, H., 178, 296, 298
Morrow, J., 238
Morrow, P. C., 239, 488, 494, 495
Moser, G., 127
Mosler, H. J., 529
Moss, S., 213
Moulton, D. G, 262
Muecher, H., 195, 213, 218
Mueller, P. S., 222
Mullens, S., 296, 301
Muller, R., 163
Munoz, B., 220
Munro-Clark, M., 449
Munrowe, R. H., 359
Munrowe, R. L., 359
Munson, R., 358
Murphy, L. R., 162, 257
Murphy, S. T., 207
Murphy-Berman, V., 300
Murray, D.,
Murrell, S., 236, 237
Myers, P., 403
Myers, K., 327
Mykytowycz, R., 327

N

Nadel, B., 542, 543
Nagar, D., 453
Nahemow, L., 128, 383
Nardini, R. M., 358
Nasar, J. L., 358, 362, 406, 429, 430, 434
Nash, B. C., 498
Nash, R., 33, 34, 35, 36
Naturel, V., 461
Nau, P. A., 540
Navarro, P. L., 264
Neal, A., 540
Neale, M. C., 39
Neale, M. S., 524, 541
Needleman, H., 259

Neill, S. R., 498
Neiman, L., 386
Neisser, U., 66, 78
Neiva, J., 169
Nelson, P. A., 358, 360
Nelson, P. D., 280, 309, 313, 358, 420, 452
Nemecek, J., 173
Nesselroade, J. R., 145
Neulinger, J., 507, 508
Newberry, B., 260
Newcombe, N., 86, 92
Newhall, S. M., 426
Newhouse, N., 535, 536, 537
Newland, H. S., 220
Newman, 159
Newman, C. J., 240, 250
Newman, J., 379, 409
Newman, O., 317, 320, 383, 396, 397, 398, 401, 409, 552
Newssome, D. A., 222
Newtson, D., 132
Nichol, G. T., 100, 104, 105
Nicholson, M., 392
Nicosia, G. J., 342, 343, 360
Nielsen, J. M., 528
Nigg, J. M., 247, 248
Nil, R., 164
Nimran, U., 493
Niswander, G. D., 219
Nisbett, R. E., 284, 537
Nivison, M. E., 172
Nixon, R., 259
Nolen-Hoeksema, S., 78, 86, 90, 91, 100, 238, 239
Norman, D. A., 130, 440
Normoyle, J. B., 319, 471
Norris, F. H., 236, 237, 240, 241, 242
Norris-Baker, L., 145
North, C. S., 249
Noulles, D., 117
Novaco, R. W., 378
Nowak, R., 222
Nowicki, S., 279, 285, 320
Nuimi, L., 169
Nunes, D. L., 550

O

O'Brien, J. P., 288
O'Connell, M., 302
O'Donnel, R., 267
O'Donnell, V. F., 383
O'Hanlon, J. F., 267
O'Hara, J., 286, 362, 425
O'Hare, M., 501
O'Keefe, M. K., 134
O'Neal, E. C., 117, 177, 282, 313, 314
O'Neil, M. J., 421, 493
O'Neill, G. W., 550, 551
O'Neill, S. M., 313

O'Riordan, T., 33
Oelschlaeger, M., 33, 35, 37, 38
Ohlig, W., 338
Ohta, B. M., 477
Ohta, R. J., 477
Oldham, G. R., 141, 492, 493
Oliphant, K. P., 161
Ollendick, D. G., 241
Olsen, H., 496, 497
Olsen, M. E., 536
Olsen, R., 463, 500, 501
Olson, E., 250
Olson, R., 236
Olson, R. A., 236
Olszewski, D. A., 174
Omata, K., 458
Ong, P., 76, 359, 360
Orcutt, G., 264
Ordy, J. M., 331
Orebaugh, A. L., 21
Orians, G. H., 47, 53, 56, 487
Orleans, P., 91, 92
Ormel, J., 360
Ornstein, S., 488
Osborn, D. P., 425, 486
Osborne, J. G., 548, 549, 551
Oseland, N., 453
Oskamp, S., 528, 535, 536, 538, 541,
    545, 546, 549
Osmond, H., 10, 290
Ossenkopf, K. P., 214
Ostfeld, A. M., 337
Ostfeld, R. S., 327, 328
Ostrander, E. R., 506
Oszewski, D., 138
Ouimet, M. E., 162
Overton, W. F., 92
Owens, P. L., 213, 371, 387, 407, 514
Oxley, B., 288
Oxley, D., 145, 448, 52
Oxman, R., 457

P

Pablant, P., 552
Paffenbarger, R. S., 512
Page, B., 380
Page, R. A., 179, 180, 206
Pai, S., 238
Palamarek, D. L., 205
Pallak, M. S., 537
Palmer, J. F., 49
Palmer, M. H., 535
Palmer, S., 69, 70
Palmstierna, T., 343
Palsane, M. N., 341, 357, 359
Paluck, B. J., 313
Pandey, J., 201, 338
Paoli, P., 463
Papciak, A. S., 529
Pape, K. D., 314
Pardini, A. U., 546

Parfit, M., 543
Parker, G., 239
Parkes, C. M., 132
Parkinson, D., 256
Parks, C. D., 529
Parmelee, P., 312, 449, 472
Parr, A. E., 122
Parsons, H. M., 439, 453, 454
Parsons, P., 501
Parsons, R., 121
Passalacqua, R., 290
Passini, R., 87, 100, 101
Passmore, N. I., 325, 328, 331
Pastalan, L., 473
Pato, C. N., 162
Patterson, A. H., 10, 21, 319, 342
Patterson, A. M., 325, 328, 331
Patterson, D. D., 503
Patterson, M. L., 23, 284, 285, 286,
    290, 293, 294, 295, 296, 300,
    301, 360, 397
Paul, S. M., 162
Paulson, N. A., 403
Paulus, P. B., 116, 333, 335, 337,
    338, 343, 344, 345, 346, 259,
    362, 363, 364, 453, 454, 468
Pawson, I. G., 215
Peacock, J., 343
Pearce, G. P., 325, 328, 331
Pearce, P. L., 92
Peatross, F. D., 454, 456
Pellegrino, J. W., 78, 84, 86, 95, 99
Pezdek, K., 76, 102
Pempus, E., 286
Pengelly, L., 267
Penick, E. C., 239
Pennebaker, J. W., 132
Peplau, L. A., 459
Pepler, R. D., 199, 200, 201
Pepper, D. T., 281
Peresie, H., 259
Perkins, D. D., 209, 448, 461
Perlick, D., 356
Perry, J. D., 203, 206
Persinger, M. A., 214
Peterka, J. A., 506
Petersen, T. R., 529
Peterson, C., 130
Peterson, R. L., 269, 393
Peterson-Lewis, S., 312
Pettigrew, T., 75
Petty, R. E., 118
Pezdek, K., 97
Pfeifer, Y., 214
Philips, C., 477
Phillips, S., 162, 165, 166
Phillips, T., 166, 551
Piaget, J., 94, 95
Pickering, D., 551
Pidermann, M., 489
Pile, J. F., 493

Pill, R., 466
Pinciotti, P., 391
Pinner, B., 339
Pitelka, F. A., 332
Pitt, D. G., 49, 55, 509, 515
Platt, J., 521, 527, 528, 529
Plestor, D., 161, 264, 529
Plestor, M., 161, 264, 529
Ploeger, A., 249
Plotkin, W. B., 123
Poag, C. K., 100, 104, 105
Pollack, L. M., 319
Pollak, E. L., 529
Pollet, D., 499, 500
Pollman, V., 342
Pontell, H. N., 344
Popiel, D. A., 284
Poppen, J. R., 164
Porteous, C. W., 498
Porteous, J. D., 64
Porter, B. E., 534, 535, 546, 547, 555
Porteus, J., 394, 395, 416
Poulton, E. C., 119, 171, 199, 201,
    210, 213, 217
Poustka, F., 159
Powell, B. J., 239
Powell, M. C., 33
Powers, R. B., 548, 549, 551
Pradham, P. L., 86
Pratt, G., 42
Preiser, W. F. E., 19, 504, 506
Prerost, F. J., 357
Price, J., 241, 336, 343
Price, J. L., 342
Priebe, K., 219
Pringle, C., 526
Pritchard, D., 487
Proshansky, H. M., 6, 7, 10, 15, 20,
    66, 116, 126, 341, 424, 466, 467
Proulx, G., 131
Provins, K. A., 199, 201, 209, 210
Pryor, J. B., 540
Pruchno, R. A., 452
Pudvah, M., 121
Pugh, S. R., 327, 328
Pugh, W., 338
Putz, J., 267
Pylypuk, A., 337
Pylyshyn, Z. W., 96

Q

Quaid, M., 312
Quarantelli, E. L., 132, 227, 234,
    239, 254
Quick, A. D., 301
Quillian, M. R., 99

R

Rainwater, L., 401, 426
Rafferty, J. M., 211
Rajecki, D. W., 294

Rall, M., 339
Raloff, J., 159, 160, 161
Ramos, R., 236
Ramsey, J., 267
Rangell, L., 250
Rankin, R. E., 264
Rapoport, A., 353, 362, 413, 414, 415, 420, 434
Raven, P., 267
Ravenberg, R. L., 176
Raw, G. J., 181, 182
Rawels, D. J., 344
Rawls, J. R., 344
Rebebtisch, E., 159
Reddy, D. M., 361
Reed, R., 259
Reich, W., 240
Reichel, D. A., 539
Reichner, R., 341
Reifman, A. S., 203
Reisenzein, R., 117, 472
Reiser, B. J., 97
Reiss, M., 286, 362, 425
Reiter, R., 215
Reizenstein, J. E., 463, 466
Relph, E., 59
Remland, M. S., 283
Reno, R. R., 550, 556
Rent, C. S., 401
Rent, G. S., 401
Reusch, J., 428
Revell, G. R. B., 57
Revenson, T. A., 136
Rey, P., 426
Reynolds, C. R., 252
Ribbe, D. P., 241
Rice, R., 425, 486, 489
Richards, P., 211, 553
Richards, R. W., 169
Riger, S., 383
Riley, A. W., 537, 541
Riley, R. B., 59
Rim, Y., 213
Risk, P. H., 515
Ritchie, E. F., 80
Rivlin, L. G., 6, 7, 20, 66, 126, 312, 341, 385, 386, 424, 466, 467, 496, 497
Robbins, L. N., 240
Roberts, C., 382
Roberts, E. A., 58, 511, 512
Roberts, L., 190
Roberts, S. M., 405
Robertson, A., 257
Robertson, A. S., 258
Robertson, D., 163
Robillard, D. A., 503
Robinson, E. S., 501, 503
Rochford, E. B., 127
Rock, I., 69, 70
Rockett, S. L., 176

Rodgers, W., 407
Rodin, J., 126, 127, 128, 130, 162, 349, 350, 351, 352, 472, 473, 474
Rodman, M. C., 452
Roethlisberger, F. J., 439
Roggenbuck, J. W., 59, 514
Rogler, L. H., 401
Rogoff, B., 112, 115
Rohe, W. M., 342, 359
Rohles, F. H., 201
Rolsten, C., 331
Romano, J., 296, 301
Ronco, P., 463
Rook, K. S., 132, 236
Roper, J. T., 503
Rose, L., 490
Rose, E. F., 264
Rose, M., 264
Rosen, S., 364, 529
Rosenfeld, A. H., 191
Rosenfeld, H. M., 18, 295
Rosenham, D., 78, 86, 90, 91, 100, 238
Rosenthal, F. S., 220
Rosenthal, N. E., 222, 515
Rosenzweig, M. R., 497
Rosinski, R. R., 100
Ross, H., 290, 428, 429, 452, 467
Ross, R. T., 426
Rossbach, J., 358
Rosser, R., 249
Roth, S., 136
Rothbaum, F., 128, 129
Rothenberg, M., 391, 392, 393, 497
Rothman, S., 545, 553
Rothstein, R. N., 540
Rotter, J., 233
Rotton, J., 112, 132, 138, 174, 190, 195, 202, 203, 205, 206, 210, 211, 215, 218, 219, 223, 266, 269, 360, 362, 377
Rowe, J. W., 473
Roy, C., 123
Ruback, R. B., 201, 314, 338, 344, 363, 382
Rubin, A. I., 20, 257, 281, 284, 386
Rubin, E. S., 191
Rubinstein, R. L., 449
Rubio-Stipec, M., 238
Rubonis, A. V., 234, 239
Ruggles, A. J., 95
Rule, B. G., 205
Rullo, G., 447
Rummo, N., 267
Rumsey, N., 281
Rusbult, C., 347, 358
Rush, R., 547, 548
Russell, G. W., 214
Russell, J. A., 6, 42, 43, 44, 45, 50, 60, 80, 101, 116, 423, 430, 488
Russell, M., 268

Russell, M. B., 220
Rutland, A., 94
Rutte, C. G., 529
Rutter, M., 240
Ruys, T., 487
Ryan, C., 256
Rydberg-Mitchell, B., 422, 423
Ryden, M. B., 298

S

Saal, F. E., 439
Saarinen, T. F., 232
Sabatino, D. A., 553
Sacilotto, P. A., 285
Sack, D. A., 222
Sadalla, E. K., 97, 98, 312, 377, 427, 450
Sadowski, C., 311
Saegert, S., 127, 134, 317, 336, 337, 344, 351, 359, 362, 364, 429, 460, 461
Saglione, G., 296
Sallee, F. R., 241
Samdahl, D. M., 553
Samuelson, C. D., 529, 531, 536
Samuelson, D. J., 456
Sanbonmatsu, D. M., 33
Sanborn, D. E., 219
Sanders, G., 166
Sanders, M. S., 426, 435, 487, 489
Sandman, P. M., 260, 268
Santrock, J. W., 498
Sargent, D., 169
Sarkissian, W., 447
Sarlanis, K., 267
Satti, M., 161, 264, 529
Saugman, P., 264
Saunders, M., 427, 440, 441
Savinar, J., 286, 362
Savitsky, J. C., 132
Savitz, D. A., 214, 215
Sawada, H., 124
Sawaya, C., 286
Sayer, S., 492, 493
Saylor, C., 241, 537
Scare, R., 536
Schachter, S., 117, 132, 135, 458, 459
Schaeffer, G. H., 252, 360
Schaeffer, M. A., 468
Schavio, S., 301
Scheflen, A. E., 309, 456, 457, 478
Scheidt, R. J., 145
Scheier, M. F., 117
Schein, R. H., 405
Scherer, S. E., 284
Schettino, A. P., 343
Schiavo, R. S., 356
Schiffenbauer, A., 356, 362
Schindler, D. W., 532
Schkade, J. K., 116, 344, 345

Schmid, U., 472
Schmidt, D. E., 359
Schmidt, E. A., 48
Schmidt, J. R., 314
Schmidt, K., 264
Schmidt, S., 92
Schmidt, T., 461
Schneider, F. W., 207, 211, 341, 348, 357, 358
Schneiderman, N., 139
Schnelle, J. F., 551
Schoggen, P., 16, 141
Schopler, J., 339, 347, 358
Schork, W. J., 133
Schreyer, R., 512, 514
Schramke, C. J., 257
Schroeder, H., 49
Schuchart, G. E., 504
Schulberg, H. C., 252
Schultz, D. B., 121, 159
Schulz, R., 128, 473, 474
Schutte, N., 128
Schuyler, D., 388
Schwartz, B., 316
Schwartz, D. C., 205
Schwartz, H., 50
Schwartz, P., 123
Schwartz, P. M., 259
Schwartz, R. D., 22
Schwartz, S. E., 190
Schwebel, A. I., 288
Schweder, H. A., 490
Scott, S. L., 96, 276
Searleman, A., 96
Sears, D. O., 459
Sebba, R., 309, 312
Secchiaroli, G., 371
Sechrest, L. B., 22, 293
Segal, M. W., 458, 459
Segal, N., 31
Segall, M. H., 75
Seiberling, M., 162
Seidel, A. D., 423
Selby, J. W., 301
Seligman, C., 352, 529, 536, 538, 540, 541
Seligman, M. E. P., 39, 127, 130, 351
Sell, J. L., 45, 56
Sell, R., 45, 341
Sells, S. B., 220
Selye, H., 131, 135, 138, 327
Semb, G., 547
Sermsri, S., 286, 338, 358, 362
Seta, J. J., 116, 344
Shafer, E., 48
Shaffer, D. R., 311
Shaffer, L. S., 529
Shaklee, H., 529
Shalker, T. E., 169
Shannon, M. P., 241
Sharp, D. S., 166, 167

Sharpe, G. W., 553
Shapira, A., 285
Shapiro, A., 361
Shats, M., 205, 210
Shaw, D. L., 243
Shaw, L. G., 391, 394
Shea, J. M., 249
Sheets, K., 377
Sheets, V., 427, 450
Shenot, J., 545
Sherin, C. R., 218
Sherman, S. J., 31
Sherrod, D. R., 127, 129, 138, 170, 180, 346, 348, 350, 430, 488
Shippee, G. E., 234, 531
Shlay, A. B., 450, 453
Shoen, K., 434, 436
Shore, J. H., 238, 241
Shotkin, A., 545
Shull, W. J., 133
Shurley, J. T., 123
Shusterman, D., 265
Shute, S. J., 489
Sieber, W. J., 162
Sieck, W. A., 239
Siegel, A. W., 95, 100
Siegel, J. M., 176
Sigall, H., 316
Sigelman, C. K., 285
Silcock, N., 438
Silvati, L., 160
Silver, R. C., 448
Silverman, F., 267
Silverstein, M., 389, 420, 434, 435
Sime, J. D., 424
Simmel, G., 119
Simmons, D. A., 468
Simmons, R. F., 138
Simon, H. A., 431
Simpson, M., 203, 206
Simpson-Housley, P., 234, 264
Sims, J. H., 132, 233
Singer, J. E., 12, 21, 76, 117, 127, 131, 132, 133, 135, 136, 138, 158, 161, 162, 163, 164, 166, 167, 170, 173, 177, 253, 337, 346, 350, 358, 373
Skeen, D. R., 287
Skogan, W., 407
Skolnick, P., 300
Skorjanc, A. D., 282
Skorpanich, M. A., 471, 496, 497
Skotko, V. P., 289
Skov, T., 264
Slaats, S., 165
Slade, K. M., 381
Sladen, B., 360
Slakter, D. B., 120, 121, 500
Slater, R., 473
Slaven, R. E., 539
Sloan, A. W., 198

Sloane, P. D., 477
Slote, L., 214
Slovic, P., 254, 525
Smetana, J., 343
Smith, A. H., 257
Smith, A. P., 167, 171, 172
Smith, C., 76, 102
Smith, D. E., 358, 360
Smith, E., 240
Smith, E. M., 240, 249
Smith, G. A., 13, 53
Smith, G. C., 472
Smith, J. M., 205, 211, 529, 530, 531
Smith, L. R., 169
Smith, P., 342, 498
Smith, R. J., 296, 298, 300, 301
Smith, S. E., 18, 295
Smither, R. D., 438, 507
Smoyer, K. E., 190
Snodgrass, J., 6, 43, 45, 116
Snow, B. R., 489
Snow, J. N., 314
Snowball, H., 339
Snyder, L. H., 506
Snyder, R. L., 327, 328
Snyder, S. S., 128
Socolow, R. H., 524, 535
Soderstrom, E. J., 538, 539, 540, 542
Soler, E. A., 138, 174, 269
Solomon, S. D., 134, 239, 240, 269, 345, 347, 349, 350, 364
Solso, R. L., 22
Sommer, R., 77, 146, 275, 281, 283, 287, 288, 290, 295, 303, 310, 401, 404, 428, 429, 467, 487, 496, 497, 498
Sommers, P., 192, 194, 213, 219, 220, 221
Sonnenfeld, J., 125
Sorenson, K., 380
Southwick, C. H., 331
Southworth, M., 371, 387, 407
Spacapan, S., 120, 178
Sparks, J., 92
Spencer, C., 94
Speno, S., 129, 138, 170, 430, 488
Spensley, J., 266
Spivey, G. H., 256
Spreckelmeyer, K. F., 137, 493
Spyker, J. M., 258
Srivastava, P., 285
Srivastava, R. K., 145
Srole, L., 384
Stadler, S. J., 203
Stahl, B., 537, 538
Stahl, S. M., 257
Stainbrook, E., 401
Stammerjohn, L. W., 257
Standers, R., 205, 210
Stangor, C., 32, 33
Stankey, G. H., 514

Stansfield, S. A., 166, 167, 172
Staplin, L. J., 97, 98
Starr, S. J., 489
Stea, D., 79, 86, 94
Steblay, N. M., 380, 381
Steele, F., 57, 58, 59, 176
Steels, M. J., 162
Steerd, N., 528, 535, 536, 538, 541, 545, 546, 549
Steidl, R. E., 451
Steinberg, A., 241
Steinberg, J., 207
Steinglass, P., 239
Steinhilber, A., 316
Steinitz, C., 429
Steinke, T., 86
Stellman, J. M., 489
Stephenson, J. S., 231
Stern, P. C., 528, 529, 534, 535, 536, 537, 538, 539, 541, 542, 549
Stevens, A., 99, 107
Stevens, W., 536
Stewart, T. R., 43, 72
Stires, L., 289
Stobaugh, R., 539
Stockdale, J., 347
Stokes, G. S., 492, 493
Stokinger, H., 264
Stokols, D., 6, 57, 116, 126, 130, 131, 138, 161, 162, 163, 167, 170, 338, 339, 343, 346, 353, 354, 360, 366, 374, 378, 508
Stokols, J., 370
Stone, G. L., 289
Stone, J., 268
Stone, R., 190, 215, 260
Storms, M. D., 294
Stough, R. R., 304, 309, 315
Stoutemyer, K., 531, 544
Strahilevitz, N., 266
Strain, J., 255, 256
Strakhov, A. B., 166
Stratton, L. D., 285
Streufert, S., 132, 136
Stine, D. D., 191
Strodtbeck, F., 290
Strube, M. J., 126
Struening, E., 239
Studebaker, S., 360
Sturdavent, M., 463
Styles, S. P., 136
Suedfeld, P., 122, 123, 160, 163, 166, 223, 486, 492
Sullivan, M. A., 241, 537
Sulman, F. G., 214
Sunaday, E., 22, 342
Sundeen, R. A., 384
Sundstrom, E., 199, 200, 201, 295, 301, 310, 315, 336, 341, 347, 358, 359, 360, 425, 482, 483, 486, 488, 489, 490, 491, 492, 493

Sundstrom, M. G., 295, 301
Surrette, M. A., 106
Susa, A. M., 393
Suter, T. W., 165
Suttles, G. D., 308, 398
Sutton, J., 267
Svensson, A., 164
Swaffer, P. W., 286
Swan, J. A., 264
Swanson, C. P., 335
Swap, W. C., 460
Sweeney, P. D., 130
Swift, M. B., 281
Syderman, B., 493
Syme, G. L., 536
Szigeti, F., 424
Szilagyi, A. D., 364

T

Tal, E., 214
Talbot, J. F., 390, 501, 515
Tamarkin, L., 222
Tanford, S., 294
Tanucci, G., 371
Tarnopolsky, A., 159, 166, 504
Tasso, J., 218
Tatum, E. L., 238, 241
Taubes, G., 191
Taylor, C. M., 241
Taylor, F. W., 435, 439, 483
Taylor, H. R., 220
Taylor, J., 380
Taylor, J. G., 45, 56
Taylor, R. B., 304, 305, 309, 310, 311, 312, 314, 315, 336, 383, 396, 397, 403, 461
Taylor, S., 463
Taylor, S. E., 459
Taylor, S. M., 260
Taylor, V., 239
Taylor-Lemke, P., 529
Teasdale, J. D., 130
Teddlie, C., 339, 346, 355, 362, 430, 488
Tedeschi, R., 547, 548
Teger, A., 22, 342
Tennen, H., 130
Tennis, G. H., 286
Terr, L. C., 241
Terry, R. L., 296
Thalhofer, N. N., 301
Theil, P., 421, 422, 423
Theilade, P., 264
Theodore, J., 267
Theorell, T., 166
Thoits, P. A., 236
Thomas, G. C., 169
Thomas, J. R., 294
Thomas, M. M., 551
Thompson, C. R., 489
Thompson, J., 249

Thompson, M. P., 241, 242, 503
Thompson, D. E., 278, 283, 293, 295, 356, 357, 358, 359, 361
Thompson, R., 381
Thompson, S. C., 129, 130, 531, 544
Thompson, S. C. G., 508
Thompson, W. R., 497
Thomson, G., 503
Thorndyke, P. W., 95, 96, 103
Thorne, R., 449
Tien, J. M., 383
Timasheff, N. A., 194
Tinsley, D. J., 507, 508
Tinsley, H. E., 507, 508, 512
Titchener, J., 250
Tobler, W., 98
Toffler, A., 491
Tognoli, J., 57, 312, 447, 451, 452, 459
Tokuhata, G. K., 136, 251
Tolan, G. D., 164
Toledo, V., 238
Tolman, E. C., 80, 81, 93
Topf, M., 172
Toppen, A., 381
Topping, J. S., 281
Town, J. P., 425, 486
Traub, R. E., 497
Trego, R. E., 344
Tremblay, K., 377, 384
Trites, D., 463
Tromp, S. W., 195, 197, 199
Trotter, D., 487
Troutwine, R., 282
Trowbridge, C. C., 10, 80
Truscott, J. C., 312
Tsal, Y., 291
Tuan, Y., 34, 57
Turk, A., 175, 262
Turk, J., 175
Turnage, J. J., 483, 489, 490
Turner, J., 547, 548
Turner, J. B., 132
Turner, J. W., 123
Turner, P. V., 418, 434, 443
Tuso, M. E., 549
Tversky, B., 99
Tvrdik, J. G., 215
Tye, M., 96
Tyler, T. R., 127

U

Ugwuegbu, D. C., 282
Uhl, G. A., 240
Uhlig, S. R., 310, 315
Ulrich, R. S., 29, 39, 40, 41, 45, 47, 48, 49, 52, 53, 56, 57, 138, 389, 428, 430, 467, 487
Ungeheuer, H., 195, 213, 218
Unger, D., 398

Unipan, J., 528, 535, 536, 538, 541, 545, 546, 549
Unseld, C. T., 378
Ursano, R. J., 237
Ury, H. K., 209

V

Valentine, J. L., 256
Valins, S., 335, 340, 341, 346, 347, 348, 352, 363, 366
Vallet, M., 167, 182
van der Pligt, J., 115
Van Houten, R., 540
Van Liere, K. D., 532
van Vliet, W., 450, 452
Vanetti, E. J., 106
Vary, M. G., 240
Vas, M., 257
Vaughan, E., 125
Vautier, J. S., 346, 358
Veitch, J. A., 202, 428
Vellidis, G., 526
Venturi, R., 430
Verderber, S., 428, 467
Vernberg, E. M., 241
Vernon, J., 497
Vining, J., 45, 47, 49, 56, 57, 452, 546
Vinsel, A., 278, 286, 308, 425
Vitek, J. D., 234
Vogel, J. M., 241
Vollmer, W. M., 238, 241
von Gierke, H. E., 164
von Wright, J., 169
Vorakitphokatorn, S., 286, 338, 358, 362

W

Wachtel, H., 215
Wack, J., 473
Wade, B., 497
Wakefield, S., 234
Walden, T., 347
Walden, T. A., 358, 360
Walder, D. N., 215, 217
Walder, P., 380
Waldrop, M. M., 532
Walker, J. M., 540
Wallston, B. S., 130, 473
Walmsley, D. J., 377
Walters, D., 159
Walton, M., 347, 358
Wandersman, A., 398, 399, 450, 461
Wang, T. H., 546
Wann, D, L., 279
Wantman, M. J., 384
Ward, L. M., 42, 80, 101, 163, 166, 423
Ward, S. L., 92
Ware, M. R., 257
Warheit, G. J., 251
Warner, S. B., 450

Warren, D. H., 96
Warzecha, S., 553
Waterson, R., 449
Watkins, L. R., 138
Watson, O. M., 283
Wauson, W., 342
Wayner, M., 547, 548
Weaver, K. A., 279
Webb, E. J., 22
Webb, W. M., 359
Webber, M. M., 458
Weenig, M. W. H., 461
Wehr, T. A., 222
Weibel, J., 312
Weidemann, S., 452
Weiner, F. H., 381
Weinstein, C. S., 391, 496, 498
Weinstein, M. S., 20
Weinstein, N. D., 167, 260
Weisman, A. P., 132
Weisman, G. D., 431
Weisman, J., 102
Weisner, T., 312
Weiss, B., 266
Weiss, C. S., 252
Weiss, J., 22
Weiss, L., 497
Weisse, C. S., 162
Weisz, J. R., 128, 129
Wellens, A. R., 281
Weller, C. P., 214
Wellman, B., 450
Wells, J., 530
Wells, K. S., 135
Welsh, W. N., 344
Wendt, J. S., 51
Wener, R., 338, 362, 364, 469
Wentworth, W. E., 378
Werbik, H., 50
Werner, C. M., 126, 142, 276, 312, 314, 447, 448, 452, 453
Werner, R., 424
Wertheim, G. A., 267
West, J., 234
West, P. C., 336, 344, 514
West, S. K., 220
Westin, A. F., 490
Westover, T. N., 515
Weyant, J. M., 206, 221
Wheeldon, P. D., 398
Wheeler, F., 500, 501
Whitcup, M., 549
White, G. F., 232
White, L., 33, 35
White, M., 133, 286, 383
White, R., 86
White, S., 95
White, S. M., 269
Whiteside, T., 162
Whyte, W. H., 504, 505
Wibom, R., 257

Wicker, A. W., 139, 141, 143, 144, 145, 146, 376
Wideman, M., 361
Wierwille, W. W., 490
Wiesel, T. N., 47, 65
Wiesenfeld, E., 451
Wiggens, T., 498
Wilderman, S. K., 450
Wilding, J., 171
Wilke, H., 529, 531
Wilkinson, R. T., 199, 201, 552
Wilkinson, T., 552
Will, D. P., 220
Will, J. C., 133, 383
Williams, A. F., 132
Williams, D. R., 59, 215, 512
Williams, G. W., 331
Williams, R., 241, 528, 535, 536, 538, 541, 545, 546, 549
Willis, F. N., 281, 284, 300
Willmott, P., 402
Willner, P., 169
Wills, T. A., 117, 135, 236
Wilson, D. W., 127, 177, 178
Wilson, E. O., 39, 332, 333
Wilson, J., 284
Wilson, S., 257, 258, 467
Wineman, J. D., 482, 492, 493
Winfree, L. T., 338
Winget, C., 241, 248, 250
Winkel, G. H., 7, 10, 115, 424, 500, 501
Winkler, H., 135
Winkler, R. C., 535, 540
Winneke, G., 262
Winner, R. A., 549
Winnett, R. A., 524, 535, 536, 537, 538, 540, 541, 542, 548, 549
Wirth, I., 379, 380
Wisniewski, N., 434
Wistedt, B., 343
Witmer, J. F., 21
Wittes, J. J., 175
Wittes, R., 175
Wodarski, J. S., 539
Wofford, J. C., 214
Wohlwill, J. F., 7, 13, 29, 30, 45, 50, 51, 57, 83, 94, 122, 124, 149, 264, 379, 471, 497
Wolf, N., 381, 548
Wolfe, M., 467, 496
Womble, P., 360
Wong, C. Y., 498
Wood, 78, 86, 90, 91, 100, 238
Woodbury, M., 238
Woods, J. E., 257
Woodson, P. P., 164, 165
Woodward, N. J., 130, 473
Wooldredge, J. D., 338
Worchel, S., 339, 345, 346, 355, 359, 362, 430, 488

Worley, P., 100, 104, 105
Wortman, C. B., 126, 132
Wright, B., 426
Wright, D., 121
Wright, H. E., 10, 141
Wright, R. A., 147
Wright, K. M., 237
Wulf, L. J., 290
Wyndham, C. H., 201

Y

Yamagishi, T., 529
Yamamoto, T., 124
Yancey, W. L., 400, 401
Yeh, T. M., 383
Yeostros, S., 218
Yergin, D., 539

Yinon, Y., 180
Young, J., 206, 211
Young, M., 402
Ypma, I., 381
Yule, W., 241

Z

Zahner, G. E. P., 133, 383
Zajonc, R. B., 31, 207, 460
Zakay, D., 291
Zaks, J., 163
Zamarin, D. M., 159
Zamfir, O., 327
Zanna, M. P., 33
Zeisel, J., 420, 421, 425, 431, 459, 506
Zelson, M., 138

Zemke, P. E., 529, 531
Zieman, G. L., 200
Zika, S., 132
Zillmann, D., 117, 177
Zimbardo, P. G., 382, 398
Zimring, C., 467, 468
Zlutnick, S., 126
Zolik, E. S., 549
Zorn, M., 102
Zube, E. H., 42, 45, 49, 55, 56, 213, 452, 509, 515
Zubek, J. P., 121
Zuckerman, M., 122, 286
Zweig, J., 473
Zweigenhaft, R., 488, 494
Zweizig, M., 545

A

Acclimation, 197–198
Acclimatization
  barometric pressure and altitude, 216
  definition, 196
Accretion measures, 21
Action plans, in wayfinding, 100–102, *101*
Adaptation
  air pollution and, 267–268
  defined, 124
  informal definition, 45
  natural hazards and, 233
Adaptation level
  cities and, 373
  definition of, 45
  theory, 122–126
Adaptation level (AL), 122
Adaptation to stress, 136–138
Adaptation versus adjustment, 125
Adaptive reuse, 404
Adequately staffed, and staffing theory, 143
Adjustment, 125
Adrenal activity, and stress, 135
Adventure playgrounds, 391
Aesthetics
  architectural, 429–430
  environmental, 45–57
  formal, 50–51
Affect, population density and, 336
Affective appraisals, 43–45
Affiliative behavior, cities and, 379–380
Affordances
  definition, 4
  environmental perception and, 74–75
Aftereffects
  of noise, 170
  of overload, 120
  stress, 138–139

Age differences, personal space and, 284–285
Aggression
  heat and, 202–211
  noise and, 176–178
  population density and, 342–344
  territoriality and, 312–315
Air ionization, 214
Air pollution
  adaptation and, 267–269
  assessment, 43
  behavioral effects, 261–262
  health effects, 264–267, *265, 266*
  perception of, 262–264
  perception through smell, 262
  perception through vision, 262–263, *263*
  performance and, 267–269
  social behavior and, 269
Aircraft and human factors, 438–440, *440*
Alarm reaction, to stress, 135
Altitude, 215–221
Altruism
  cities and, 380–381
  heat and, 206
  noise and, 178–181
  population density and, 342
Alveolar walls, 216
Alzheimer's units, specialized facilities, 474–477
Ambient stressors, 132–133
Ambient temperature, 195
Amplitude of sound, 156
Analog representation, in cognitive maps, 96
Animal research applied to humans, 335
Animals
  behavioral consequences of high density, 328–331
  consequences of high density, 326–333

physiological consequences of high density, 327–338
Antecedent interventions
  behavioral strategies, 535
  litter reduction and, 549–550
  source reduction and recycling, 546
Anthropocentrism, as an attitude, 37, 508
Anticipated crowding, 343
Anxiety as a response to disasters, 250
Applicability gap, 423
Applicants, and staffing theory, 141
Appraisal, of stressors, 133–135
Architectural determinism, design and, 416
Archival data, 15
Arousal
  personal space and, 276
  personal space invasions and, 291, 296
  physiological, 116
  population density and, 337
  territoriality and, 307
Arousal theory
  definition, 116–118
  population density and, 346
Assigned workspace, 488
Assisted living for the elderly, 470
Attitude accessibility, 33
Attitude specificity, 32
Attitudes
  definition of, 31
  sources of, 29–41, *29*
Attitudes toward nature
  as predictors of behavior, 31–33, *32*
  biological influences on, 39–42
  contemporary, 36–38, *37*
  history of, 33–36, *35, 36*
  human nature and, *30*
  sources of, 31–42

Attraction
  heat and, 201–202, *202*
  personal space and, 280–281
  population density and, 339
Attraction gradient, museums and,
  501
Auditory system, structure of,
  154–158, *157*
Augmentation, in cognitive maps,
  89

B

Background stressors, 132–133
Barometric pressure and altitude
  acclimatization to high altitudes,
    216
  behavioral effects of high alti-
    tudes, 217
  high air pressure effects, 217
  medical, emotional, and behav-
    ioral effects of air-pressure
    changes, 217–221
  physiological effects of, 216
Bathrooms in residential settings,
  454–456
Beaufort Scale, 212
Bedrooms in residential settings,
  456–458
Behavior constraint
  natural disasters and, 242–243
  cities and, 374–375
  personal space and, 276
  personal space invasions and, 291
  population density and, 346, 348
  theory, 126–131
Behavior mapping, 20
Behavior settings
  characteristics, 139
  characteristics of, 140–141, *140*
  cities and, 375–376
  ecological psychology and,
    139–146
  historic development, 16
  physical milieu, 140
  staffing theory, 141–146, *145*
  standing patterns of behavior
    and, 140
Behavioral control, 128
Behavioral interference, population
  density and, 347
Behavioral sink, 329–331
Biophilia, 39–41
Biophobia, 39
Bivariate theory, 114
Block organizations, 398–399
Breathing difficulty, 217
Bubble, personal space, 277
Buffalo Creek Flood, 249–251

C

Capacity, and staffing theory, 141
Carbon monoxide (CO), 264

Carrying capacity of natural lands,
  509
Cataclysmic events, 131–132, 226
Catecholamines, and stress, 135
Central Park, New York, 388–389
Challenge appraisals, 134
Chernobyl, 253, 438
Children
  learned helplessness and, 351
  natural disasters and, 240–242
Chill factor, 207
Cigarette smoking, 268
Cigarette smoking and noise, *165*
Cities
  adaptation and, 373
  adaptation level and, 379
  affiliative behavior and,
    379–380, *379*
  altruism and, 380–381
  ancient, 371
  behavior constraint and,
    374–375
  behavior settings and, 375–376
  block organizations and social
    networks, 398–399
  City Beautiful Movement and,
    395
  commercial district revitalization
    and, 403–404
  commuting and, 378
  crime and, 382–384
  defensible space and, 396–398
  diffusion of responsibility and,
    398
  eclectic model of environment-
    behavior, 374–375
  effects of urban life, 372–376,
    372
  environmental stress and,
    373–374
  familiar strangers and, 381
  fear of crime and, 383–384
  festival marketplaces, 404–406
  health and, 384
  history of urban parks, 387–390
  homelessness and, 384–387, *385*
  mental health and, 384
  overload and, 373
  pace of life and, *377*
  parks and, 387–390
  playgrounds and, 390–394
  public housing and, 399–402
  responses to urban problems,
    387–406
  revitalizing residential areas,
    396–403
  single variable approach to re-
    search, 376
  social factors and revitalization,
    398–399
  stress and, 377–379
  suburbia and, 406–408, *407*

  urban and rural dwellers com-
    pared, 378
  urban gardens and, 390
  urban renewal and, 394–395
City Beautiful Movement, 395
Classroom environments. *See*
  Learning environments
Clean Air Act of 1977, 43
Climate
  acclimatization and, *198*
  biological adaptations to, 195
  definition of, 188
  determinism and, 185–192
  geographical and climatological
    determinism, 185–192, *193*
  possibilism and, 190
  probabilism and, 190
Cognitive control, 128
Cognitive control of crowding effects, 363–364
Cognitive maps
  access to cartographic maps, 95
  acquisition of, 93–96
  animals, 80
  behavioral measure, 18
  children and, 94–95
  college campuses and, 436–437
  current perspectives, 83–84
  definition of, 78–79
  distance estimates and, 87–91, 97
  distortions in, 88–91 *89, 90*
  districts, 81
  edges, 81
  egocentrism, 94–95
  elements of, 81, *82, 83*
  errors in, 88–93
  familiarity, 90–91
  gender differences and, 91–93
  geographical preferences and,
    86, *87*
  history of, 80–84
  landmarks, 81
  legibility and, 83–84, *84*
  memory and, 96–100
  methods of studying, 84–88
  networked storage and retrieval,
    99
  nodes, 81
  overview, 80
  paths, 81
  recognition tasks, 87
  reference points and, 98
  representation and, 96–97
  sequential, 82, *83*
  sketch maps, 84–86, *85*
  spatial and sequential styles, 82,
    83
  spatial cognition, 78
  structure in memory and,
    97–100
  survey knowledge, 82
Coherence, 54, *56*

Cohousing and residential settings, 462
Cold
    acclimatization to, 208
    and driving accidents, 209
    behavior and, 207–211
    health effects, 209–210
    performance and, 210
    physiological disorders resulting from, 208
    physiology of cold stress, 207–209
    social behavior and, 210–211
Collative stimulus properties, 50
College campuses
    cognitive mapping and, 436
    design and, 432–435
    planning and, 436–437
Color and design, 425–427
Comfortable Interpersonal Distance Scale (CIDS), 320
Commercial district revitalization, 403–404
Commitment and environmental education, 537
Commodity, 417
Commons dilemma
    environmental preservation and, 525–533
    simulations, 530
Communication
    design and, 419–423
    personal space invasion and, 291
Commuting, city dwellers and, 378
Compensatory behaviors and personal space, 276
Compensatory reactions, personal space and, 294
Complexity, 50, 54, 56
Complexity of the spatial layout, in wayfinding, 102
Congruence, design process and, 420
Consequent interventions, 538–541
Consequent strategies for litter reduction, 550–552
Conservation of resources (COR) and disaster impact, 243
Contemporary playgrounds, 391
Contingent strategies, source reduction and recycling, 548
Continuum of care for the elderly, 470
Contrast, 47
Control model
    behavior constraint and, 126–131
    population density and, 347–353
    territoriality and, 307–308
Coping strategies, and stress, 136
Core temperature, 196
Correlational research, 14–15

Correlational research, and population density, 334
Corridor-style dormitories, 340–341
Corticosteroids, and stress, 135
Crime
    cities and, 382–384
    territoriality and fear of crime, 319
Crisis effect, of natural disasters, 232
Crowding. see Population density
    architectural mediators of, 361–362
    crowding versus high density, 354
    density-intensity model and, 356
    eliminating the effects of, 355–365
    gender and, 357
    psychological state of, 354
Cultural differences, in environmental perception, 75
Culture and personal space, 283–284
Culture, as a source of attitudes, 31
Curvilinear relationship, 204
Custodial care for the elderly, 470

D

Daily hassles, 132–133, 225
Data collection methods, 15–22
Daycare and preschool environments, 498
Day-night reversal, 476
Decibels (dB), 157–158
Decompression sickness, 217
Deep body temperature, 196
Deep ecology, 38
Defensible space, city revitalization and, 396–398, 399
Degree of visual access, in wayfinding, 102
Delight, 417
Dementia, design for, 474–477, 474
Denial, of stress, 134
Dependent variable, 12
Depression as a response to disasters, 250
Descriptive landscape assessment, 46–48, 46
Descriptive research, 15
Design
    Alzheimer units, 474–477
    architectural aesthetics and, 429–430
    architectural determinism and, 416
    architectural practice and, 417–419
    campus history and, 418–419, 419
    college campuses and, 432–436, 433, 437
    color, 425–427

communication in the design process, 419–423
design alternatives, 421
design cycle, 431, 432
designing for the elderly, 469–477
eclectic model of environment-behavior, 412–413
environmental possibilism, 416
environmental probabilism and, 416–417
flexibility and, 420–421
folk design tradition, 413
fostering participation, 422–423
furniture and, 428–429
gaps in the design process, 421–423
Gestalt theory and, 430
grand design tradition, 413, 414
historic and cultural perspectives, 413–415
hospital settings and, 463–466
hospital visitors and, 467–468
human factors and, 435–442
illumination and, 427–428
libraries and, 498–500
materials and color, 425–427, 426
modern architecture, 415
museums and, 500–503
normative theory and, 416, 418
population density and, 361–363
positive theory and, 418
post-occupancy evaluation (POE), 431
preindustrial vernacular, 414
primitive, 414
prisons and, 468–469
privacy and, 424–425, 425
stages in design process, 431
substantive contributions, 423–430
territoriality and, 317–320
windows and, 428
Design alternatives, 421
Design cycle, 431, 432
Design for dementia, 474
Design review and urban revitalization, 405
Desk placement in faculty offices, 494
Determinism
    architectural, 416
    climate and, 190–192
    geographical and climatological, 187–194
    philosophical notion of, 112
Differentiation, in wayfinding, 102
Diffusion of responsibility, 398
Direct action coping strategies, 136

Directed attention fatigue (DAF), 120–121

Disaster events, 227

Disasters, eclectic model of environment-behavior and, 244–245

Discontinuity in museum design, 503

Disruption, and natural disasters, 228–229

Distance estimates, in cognitive maps, 87–88, 97

Distortions, in cognitive maps, 86, 88–91

Districts, in cognitive maps, 81

Diversity, and adaptation level, 124

Diversive exploration, 50

Dominant Western world view and environmental preservation, 532

Dormitories, population density and, 338, 340–341

Dormitory rooms, 456

Double corridor design, 463

E

Ear, structure of, *156*

Eclectic model of environment-behavior

  cities, *374–375*

  design, *412–413*

  disasters and, *244–245*

  high density, *352–353*

  introduction, *146–147*

  noise effects, *154–155*

  personal space, *292–293*

  preserving the environment, *522–523*

  residential settings, *446–447*

  weather, *188–189*

  work environments, *484–485*

Ecocentrism, 38, 508

Ecological model

  natural disasters and, 243

  population density and, 346, 349

Ecological niche, and affordances, 75

Ecological perception, 72–75

Ecological psychology, 139–146

Edge cities, suburbia and, 407

Edges, in cognitive maps, 81

Effective temperature, 199

Efficacy and natural disasters, 242

Egocentrism, in cognitive maps, 94–95

Elderly

  institutional environments for, 469–477

  noninstitutional residences for, 471–472

  residential care facilities for, 472–474

Electromagnetic fields (ELF-EMF), 214

Electronic cottage, 491

Electronic office, 489–491, *490*

Empirical laws, 113

Empiricism, 30, 65

Energy Star compliance, 543

Environmental assessment

  affective appraisals, 43–45

  definition, 42

  indices, 42–43

Environmental cognition. *See* Cognitive maps

Environmental competence, 128

Environmental content and landscape preference, 51

Environmental education

  environmental preservation and, 535–537

  positive reinforcement, 538

Environmental Emotional Reaction Index (EERI), 42–43

Environmental load theory, 118–121

Environmental perception

  affordances and, 74–75

  characteristics of, 64–67, *65*

  cue utilization and, 72

  cultural differences, 75

  ecological perception, 72–75

  ecological validity and, 72

  empiricism and, 65

  forced perspective and, 67–68, *68*

  functionalism and, 72–75

  Gestalt psychology, 69–70

  habituation, 76–77

  holistic analysis and, 68–70

  implications, 75

  information processing and, 66–67

  internal validity and, 68

  lens model and, 71–72

  linear perspective and, 67

  nativism versus learning, 70–75

  object perception and, 67–68

  perception of change, 77–78

  phenomenology and, 65

  policy capturing and, 72

  probabilistic, 71–72

  transactional approach, 69

Environmental possibilism, design and, 416

Environmental preservation

  antecedent strategies, 535, 549

  commons dilemma and, 525–533, *527*

  consequent strategies, 550–552

  contingent strategies and, 538–541

  contributions of psychology, 521–533, *524*

  eclectic model of environment-behavior, 522–523

  energy conservation, 534–543

environmental education, 535–538

  feedback and, 538, 540–541

  littering and, 548–552

  municipal waste, 533

  negative reinforcement and, 538

  policy and technological innovations, 541–543

  preventing versus curing problems, 533

  prompts and, 538

  punishment and, 538–540

  rewards and punishments, 538–540

  social traps and, 525–533

  source reduction and recycling, 544–548, *545*

  vandalism and, 552–555, *553*, *554*

  water conservation, 543–544, *544*

Environmental press, 128

Environmental probabilism, design and, 416–417

Environmental psychology

  characteristics of, 7–10, *8*, *9*

  content areas of, 24–25

  data collection and, 15–22, *19*

  definitions of, 6

  ethical considerations, 22–24

  historical development, 10–11

  rationale for, 2–5, *3*, *4*

  research methods, 10–15

Environmental Quality Index (EQI), 42

Environmental spoiling hypothesis, 460

Environmental stress, cities and, 373–374

Environment-behavior theories, 115–146

  adaptation level theory, 122–126

  arousal approach, 116–118

  behavior constraint approach, 126–131

  ecological psychology, 139–146

  environmental load approach, 118–121

  environmental stress theory, 131–139

  understimulation approach, 121–122

Equilibrium and personal space, 276, 291

Equilibrium, and stressors, 135

Ergonomics. *See* Human factors

Erosion measures, 21

Ethic, definition of, 31

Ethics, in environmental research, 22–24

Ethological model
personal space invasions and, 276, 291
territoriality and, 307
Event duration, and natural disasters, 230
Exit gradient, museums and, 501
Experiential realism, 13
Experimental method, 12–14
External validity, 12
Extra-individual behavior pattern, 139
Extrinsic motivation and leisure, 507

F

Familiar stranger, cities and, 381
Fear of crime, individual differences and, 383–384
Feedback, 538
Festival marketplaces and urban revitalization, 404–406, *405*
Field experiments, 12–13
Field experiments, and population density, 334
Field methods, 279
Firmness, 417
Fixed workspace, 488
Flight behavior and personal space, 295–296
Folk design tradition, 413
Foot-in-the-door, 547
Forced perspective, 67–68, *68*
Forward-up equivalence, in you-are-here maps, 104
Fostering participation in design, 422–423
Free riders, 529
Frequency of sound, 155–156
Friction conformity in pedestrian environments, 504–505
Frostbite, 208
Functional distance, 459–460, *460*
Functionalism, and environmental perception, 72–75
Furnishings and interior design, 428–429
Furniture, work environments and, 488

G

Gaia hypothesis, 190
Galvanic skin response (GSR), 118
Gaps in the design process, 421–423
Gardens, cities and, 390
Gender differences
anticipated crowding and, 343
cognitive maps and, 91–93
crowding and, 357
personal space and, 284
population density and, 357

response to invasion of personal space and, 298
General adaptation syndrome (GAS), 135
Generalizability, 115
Gentrification, 386, 402–403
Gestalt theory, 69–70, 430, *69, 70*
Gestalt theory and design, 430
Goal setting , source reduction and recycling, 547
Grand design tradition, 413
Green justice, 38
Greenhouse effect, 190
Groups
personal space and, 289–290, 302
territoriality and, 309–310

H

Habitability, design process and, 420
Habituation, in environmental perception, 76–77
Harm or loss appraisals, 133–134
Hawthorn effect, 439
Health
air pollution and, 264–267
cities and, 384
Hearing loss, 161
Heart attack, 197
Heat
aggression and, 202–206, *203, 206*
attraction and, 201–202, *202*
behavior and, 195–211
classroom settings and, 200
helping behavior and, 206
industrial settings and, 200
military settings and, 201
negative affect-escape model, 204
performance and, 199–201
physiological consequences of, 196–199
social behavior and, 201–208
Heat asthenia, 197
Heat exhaustion, 197
Heat stroke, 197
Hedonic tone, 50
Hertz (Hz), 156
Heuristics, 114
High density. See Population density
Hodometer, 19
Holistic analysis, in perception, 68–70
Home court advantage, 315
Homelessness
characteristics of, 385–386
cities and, 384–387
shelterization and, 386
Homeostasis, 148
Homes. See Residential settings
Homocentrism, as an attitude, 37
Hospital settings, 463–466

Hospital visitors, design and, 467–468
Human environments, characteristics of, 29–30
Human factors, 435–442
Human nature, characteristics of, 30
Humidity, 198–199
Hypertension, noise effects on, 161, 164
Hypothalamus, heat and, 196
Hypothermia, 208
Hypothesis, 113
Hypoxia, 215

I

Illumination
design and, 427–428
work environments and, 486–487
Immune system, noise effects on, 162–163
Incongruity, 50
Independent variable, 12
Individual differences
personal space and, 278, 282–286
population density and, 356–368
Individual good-collective bad trap, 527
individual personality traits, 285–286
Inferential structuring, in cognitive maps, 89
Information processing, 66–67
Informed consent, in research, 22–23
Inside density, 334
Institutional settings
Alzheimer units, 474–477
dementia, design for, 474–477
designing for the elderly, 469–475
hospital settings, 463–466, *464, 465, 466*
hospital visitors and, 467–468
prison design and behavior, 468–469, *469, 470*
Intensity, and adaptation level, 123–124
Intermediate care for the elderly, 470
Internal locus of control, 265
Internal validity, 12, 68
Internality-externality, 285
Interpersonal distance, 280–282
Interpersonal positioning effects, 287
Intervening constructs, 114
Intervention strategies for population density, 362–363
Interviews, 17
Intrinsic motivation, leisure and, 507
Invasion of privacy, in research, 23–24

J

Job satisfaction, 493

K

Kaplan model of environmental preference, 51–55, *56*

L

Laboratory methods, 279
Land ethic and natural lands, 38, 508
Landmarks, in cognitive maps, 81
Landscape assessment
    descriptive approach, 46–48
    individual differences, 55–56
    physical perceptual approach, 48–49
    psychological approach, 49–57
    theoretical approaches, 45–57
Landscaped office, 491–493
Learned helplessness
    behavior constraint and, 127
    children and, 351
    population density and, 352–353
    research results, 130
Learning environments
    classrooms and, 200, 495–498
    daycare and preschool environments, 498
    density and, 498
    environmental complexity and, 497–498
    heat and performance in schools, 200
    libraries, 498–500, *499*
    museums and, 500–503
    open classrooms and, 496–497
    personal space and, 286–289, *289*
    schools, population density and, 351
    windows and, 496
Legibility, 54, *56*
Legibility, in cognitive maps, 83–84
Leisure
    extrinsic motivation and, 507
    intrinsic motivation and, 507
Lens model, of environmental perception, 71–72, *71*
Levee effect, and natural disasters, 233
Libraries and wayfinding, 499–500
Lighting. *See* Illumination
Linear perspective, 67
Long hot summer effect, 187
Loose parts and playgrounds, 391
Loudness of sound, 156
Love Canal, 259–260
Low point, of disasters, 230, 245

M

Maintenance minimum, and staffing theory, 141

Mapping and human factors, 440
Maps, in wayfinding, 103–104
Masking noise, 173
Measures, choosing, 21–22
Mediating variables, 114
Memory, in cognitive maps, 96–100
Mental health, cities and, 384
Military settings, heat and, 201
Missing hero situation, 528
Modeling and environmental education, 537
Models versus theories, 113–114
Moon phases, 218–219
Müller-Lyer illusion, 75
Multidimensional scaling, in cognitive maps, 88
Museums
    discontinuity and, 503
    exploration and, *501*
    fatigue and, 501–503
    movement patterns, *501*
    museum environments, 500–503, *502*
    space surround environment, 503
    wayfinding and, 500–501
Music, work environments and, 486
Mystery, 52–54, *53, 56*

N

Narrow band sound, 156
National Environmental Policy Act of 1969 (NEPA), 42
Nativism, 30, 70
Natural disasters
    age and disaster effects, 238–242, *242*
    behavioral constraint, 242–243
    behavioral effects of, 234–242, *232, 235*
    characteristics of, 229–231, *231*
    children and, 240–241
    compared with technological catastrophes, 245
    consequences, 232–240
    definition of, 227, 229
    disruption and, *228*
    ecological model, 243
    examples of, *227*
    perception of natural hazards, 231–234
    post-traumatic stress-disorder (PTSD), 239
    stress and, 238
Natural lands
    anthropocentrism and, 508
    carrying capacity and, 509
    congruence between users and settings, 514–515
    contemporary attitudes toward, 36–38, *36*
    ecocentrism and, 508

historic attitudes toward, 33–36, *33*
    land ethic and, 508
    multiple management demands, *508*, 509–512, *510, 511*
    psychological benefits of leisure, 512–513, *513*
    recreation management and, 507–514, *510*
    solitude and, 514
Negative affect-escape model, 204
Negative ions, 214
Negative reinforcement, 538, 555
Neighborhood social networks, 398–399
Neighborhoods and residential settings, 458–461
New ecological paradigm, 532
Nightmare as a response to disasters, 250
Nitrogen oxide, 265
Nitrogen poisoning, 217
Nodes, in cognitive maps, 81
Noise
    aftereffects of, 170–172
    aggression and, 176–178
    altruism and, 178–181
    annoyance associated with, 158–159
    attraction and, 176
    costs to learning, 162–163
    damage from loud music, 161
    definition of, 153–154
    eclectic model of environment-behavior, 154–155
    effects of, 160–161
    health effects, 161–166, *165*
    hearing loss and, 161
    in work environments, 172–176
    interpersonal distance and, *174*
    job satisfaction and, 173, *173*
    mental health and, 166–167, *167*
    noise-sensitivity scale, 169
    occupational, 160, 486
    perception of, *153*, 154–156
    performance effects on children, 170–171
    performance-related effects and, 167
    permanent threshold shifts (NIPTS), 161
    sensitivity to, 168–169, *169*
    social behavior and, 176–181
    sources of, 159–160
    speech interference levels and, 174
    temporary threshold shifts (TTS), 161
    transportation noise, 159–160, *181*

urban, *152*, 162
work environments and, 486
Noise-induced permanent threshold
shifts (NIPTS), 161
Noise-Sensitivity Scale, *169*
Nonperformers, and staffing theory,
141
Nonverbal communication and per-
sonal space, 276
Normative influences, on attitudes,
32–33
Normative theory, 418
Novelty, 50

O

Object perception, 67
Objective physical distance and
propinquity, 458–459
Observational techniques, 18–20
Occupational noise, 160
Office environment. *See* Work envi-
ronment
Office landscape, 491–493
Olfactory membrane, 262
One person trap, 528
Open classrooms, 496–497
Open office, 491–493
Orientation, in you-are-here maps,
103–104
Outside density, 334
Overload
cities and, 373
information, 118–121
museum fatigue and, 501–503
personal space and, 275–276
personal space invasions and, 291
population density and, 346, 348
territoriality and, 307
Overstaffed, and staffing theory, 143
Oxygen poisoning, 217
Ozone, 220
Ozone exposure, *267*
Ozone hole, 190

P

Palliative coping strategies, 136
Palmar sweat index, 118
Parks
cities and, 387–390
English Romantic style and,
388–389
New York's Central Park,
388–389, *388*
Particulates in air pollution, 265
Passive smoking, 268
Paths, in cognitive maps, 81
Pattern language and design, 435
Patterning, and adaptation level, 124
Pedestrian environments
friction-conformity and, 504
pedestrian plazas, 505
wind and, 506

Perceived control
behavior, 32–33, 128–130
ethical implications, 129
noise and, 158
population density and, 347–348
Perceived Environmental Quality
Index (PEQI), 42
Perception
air pollution and, 262–264
conventional approaches to, 67–
68
ecological model, 72–75
Gestalt theory, 69–70
holistic, 68–70
sound and, 154–158
versus sensation, 64–65
Performance
air pollution and, 267–269
cold and, 210
heat and, 199–201
Performers, and staffing theory, 141
Peripheral vasoconstriction, 207
Peripheral vasodilation, 196
Personal space
age differences and, 284–285
arousal and, 276, 297
arousal and personal space invasions, 291, 296
attraction and, 280–281
behavior constraint and, 276
behavior constraint and personal
space invasions, 291
Comfortable Interpersonal Distance Scale (CIDS), *320*
communication and, 282, *283*
communication and personal
space invasion, 291
compensation versus reciprocation theory, 294
consequences of inappropriate
spacing, 290–295
consequences of invasion,
295–303, *297*
consequences of too much or too
little, 290–295
culture and race, 283–284
definition of, *275*
eclectic model of environment-
behavior, 292–293
effects of invading another's personal space, 301–303
equilibrium and personal space
invasions, 291
ethological model and, 276–278
flight behavior and, 295–296, *296*
functions of, 275–303
gender differences and, 284, *285*
gender differences in responses
to invasion, 298–299
group processes and, 289–290
individual difference variables
and, 282–286

interaction type and, 282
interpersonal positioning effects,
287
learning environments and,
287–289, *289*
methods of studying, 279–280
overload and, 275–276
personality and, 285–286
physical determinants, 286–287
privacy regulation and personal
space invasions, 291
professional interactions and,
289
schools and, 287
similarity and, 281–282
situational conditions and, 278
situational determinants of,
280–282
size of, 278
spatial zones that facilitate goal
fulfillment, 287–290
stress and, 276
zones, 276–277, *279*
Personal stressors, 132, 225
Personality
personal space and, 285–286
population density and, 358
Personalizing territories, 312
Person-environment congruence,
446
Phenomenology, in perception, 65
Photochemical smog, 265
Photographic measurement, 19
Physical determinants of personal
space, 286–287
Physical-perceptual landscape assessment, 48–49, *48*
Physiological effects, Barometric
pressure and altitude,
216–221
Piloerection, 207
Pitch, of sound, 155
Place
affective quality, 43–45
natural landscapes and, 57–59
Place attachment
natural landscapes and, 57–59, *58*
residential settings, 447–449
Placemaking in urban revitalization,
404
Playgrounds
adventure design, *391*
cities and, 390–394
contemporary design, *391*
design amenities, 394
desirable characteristics, 394
history of, 390–392
traditional design, *391*
Poorly staffed, 143
Population density
affect and, 336–337
aggression and, 342–344

aggression in children and, 343
architectural mediators of
    crowding, 361–362
attraction and, *339*
behavioral consequences in ani-
    mals, 328–331, *328, 329*
cognitive control and, 363–364
college dormitories and, 340–
    341, *340*
crowding, *326*
culture and, 358–359
eclectic model of environment-
    behavior, *352–353*
effects on animals, 326–333,
    331, 333
effects on humans, 333–365, *334*
gender differences and, 357
illness and, 337–338, *338*
individual differences and, 356
intervention strategies and,
    362–363
loss of control and, 349–353, *350*
methods for studying, 334–336
personality characteristics and,
    358
physiological arousal and, 337–
    338
physiological consequences for
    animals, 327–338
prevention of crowding effects,
    363–364
prosocial behavior and, 342
situational conditions and, 359–
    360
social behavior and, 339–344
social conditions and, 360
social density, 326
social versus spatial density,
    326–327, 363
spatial density, 327
task performance and, 342–346,
    344, 345
theoretical perspectives, 346, *348*
treating the consequences of
    crowding, 364–365
withdrawal and, 340–342
Population stereotypes and human
    factors, 441, *442*
Positive ions, 214
Positive reinforcement, 538
Positive theory, 418
Possibilism, and climate, 190
Post-occupancy evaluation (POE),
    431
Post-disaster groups, 247
Post-traumatic stress disorder
    (PTSD), 239
Preindustrial-vernacular design, 414
Preservationism, as an attitude, 38
Primary appraisal, of stress, 135
Primary control, 129
Primary territory, *304*

Primitive design, 414
Prison design and behavior, 468–
    469
Privacy
    interior design and, 424–425
    open-plan offices and, 492–493
    personal space and, 276
    personal space invasions and, 291
    population density, 347–348
    population density and, 348
    residential settings and, 462, 469
    territoriality and, 307
Privacy gradient, 459
Privacy versus community in resi-
    dential settings, 462
Probabilism, climate and, 190
Procedural theory, 418–419
Professional interactions, personal
    space and, 289
Prompts and environmental educa-
    tion, 538
Propinquity in residential settings,
    458–461
Propositional storage, in cognitive
    maps, 96
Prosocial behavior. *See* Altruism
Prospect, 53
Proximics, 11
Pruitt-Igoe, 399–401, *400*
Psychological landscape assessment,
    49–57
Psychological stress, 131
Public goods problem, 529
Public housing
    favorable alternatives, 401–402
    Pruitt-Igoe housing project,
        399–401
Public territory, 304
Punishment, 538–540

Q

Quasi-experimentation, and popula-
    tion density, 334
Questionnaires, 17

R

Radial ward hospital design, 463
Radon exposure, *256*, 260
Reactance, 126–127
Reciprocal response, personal space
    and, 294
Recognition tasks, in cognitive
    maps, 87
Recycling and source reduction,
    544–548
Reference points, in cognitive maps,
    98
Refractory periods, and stress, 138
Refuge, 53
Regression as a response to disasters,
    250
Reliability, in research, 15

Repression-sensitization, of stress,
    134
Residential care facilities for the el-
    derly, 469–475
Residential settings
    attachment to place, 447–449,
        449
    bathrooms, 454–456, *457*
    bedrooms, 454, *455*, 456–458
    cohousing, 462
    culture and, 457–458
    dormitory rooms, 456
    eclectic model of environment-
        behavior, 446–447
    homes, 449–458, *454*
    housing preferences, 449–450
    kitchens, 453
    living rooms, 453
    neighborhoods and, *453*, 458–461
    privacy and, 459, 462
    privacy gradients in, 459
    propinquity and, 458–461
    satisfaction, 450–453
    segmentation of function, *457*
    sense of community and, 461
    space-use, 453–456
Resourcism, as an attitude toward
    land, 37–38
Restorative environments, 40–41,
    41, 120, 500
Restorative experiences, 487–488
Restricted Environmental Stimula-
    tion Technique (REST), 123
Reticular formation, 116
Retrospective control, 129
Revitalizing cities, 396–404
Richly staffed environment, 143
Romanticism, influences on atti-
    tudes, 34–36

S

Scapegoats and disasters, 254
Scenic value, 45–57
Scientific management, 483
Screening, of stress, 134
Seasonal affective disorder (SAD),
    222
Seating positions and personal
    space, 287–289, *287*
Secondary appraisal, of stress, 135
Secondary control, 129
Secondary territory, 304
Segmentation of function in resi-
    dences, 457
Self-report measures, 15–18
Semantic networks, in cognitive
    maps, 99
Sensation, and sound, 155
Sensation, versus perception, 64–65
Sense of community, 461
Sensory deprivation, 121, 123
Sequential cognitive maps, 82

Shelterization, 386

Sick building syndrome, 254–257, *258*

Similarity, personal space and, 281, 282

Simulation methods, 13–14

single corridor design, 463

Single variable approach, cities and, 376

Situational conditions, personal space and, 278

Sketch maps, 84–86

Smoking, managing, 142

Social behavior
  air pollution and, 269
  cold and, 210–211
  heat and, 201–208

Social comparison, 117

Social density, 326

Social dilemmas, 529

Social support
  cataclysmic events and, 132
  natural disasters and, 236
  stress and, 135

Social versus spatial density, 363

Sociofugal space, 289, 428

Sociopetal space, 289, 428

Solitude and natural lands, 514

Sound waves, examples of, *156*

Sound, perception of, 154–158

Space surround environments in museums, 503

Spatial cognition. *See* Cognitive maps

Spatial configuration and landscape preference, 51

Spatial maps, 82

Spatial zones and goal fulfillment, 287

Specific exploration, 50

Staffing theory, 141–146

Staffing theory, and behavior settings, 141–146

Stage of exhaustion, and stress, 135

Stage of resistance, to stress, 135

Stages in design process, 431

Standing patterns of behavior, 140

Stress
  adaptation, 136–138
  aftereffects, 138–139
  air pollution and, 266
  alarm reaction to, 135
  ambient stressors, 132–133
  appraisal, 133–134
  background, 132–133
  cataclysmic events, 131–132
  city life and, 377–379
  coping strategies, 136
  daily hassles, 132–133, 225
  general adaptation syndrome, 135

personal space and, 276
personal stressors, 132
psychological, 131
refractory periods after, 138
responses to, 135–139
stage of exhaustion and, 135
stage of resistance, 135
systemic, 131

Stress approach, 131–139, *137*

Stress-related physical symptoms as a response to disasters, 250

Structure matching, in you-are-here maps, 103, *104*

Substantive contributions to design, 423–430

Substantive theory, 418–419

Suburbia, 406–408, 451

Suite-style dormitories, 340

Sulfur oxide, 265

Sundowning, 477

Sunlight, 220–221

Supersonic transport (SST), and noise, 175

Surprisingness, 50

Survey knowledge, in cognitive maps, 82

Symbolic barriers and territoriality, 318

Symptom checklists, for measurement, 17

Synomorphic, 140–141

Systemic stress, 131

T

Task performance
  measuring, 20–21
  population density and, 344–346

Technological catastrophes
  causes of, 244
  characteristics of, 245–248, *247, 251*
  compared with natural disasters, 243–246
  definition of, 229
  effects of, 248–254
  Three Mile Island, 250–251
  toxic exposure, 254–261

Technological innovation for energy conservation, 541–543

Temperature humidity index (THI), 199

Temporary threshold shifts (TTS), 161

Terraforming, 191

Territoriality
  aggression and, 312–315
  arousal and, 307
  between groups, 308–309
  communicating claims, 310–212, *311*
  control models and, 307–308

crime and, 317–320, *318, 319*
definition of, 303–305
design implications, 317–320
ethological models and, 307
fear of crime and, 319
functions of, 306–308
home court advantage, 316, *317*
home territory, 315–317
methods of studying, 308
organizing functions of, *307*
origins of, 305–306
overload and, 307
personalizing territories, 312
primary territory, 304, *304*
privacy regulation model and, 307
public territory, 304
secondary territory, 304
signals of, 310–312
symbolic barriers, 318
types of territories, 304–305
within groups, 309–310
work environments and, 488–489

Territory
  definition of, 275

Theory
  bivariate, 114
  definition of, 114
  eclectic model of environment-behavior, *146–147*
  environment-behavior theories, 115–146
  functions of, 114–115
  nature and functions of, 112–115
  population density and, 346–354

Thermoreceptors, 196

Threat appraisals, 134

Three Mile Island, 251, *252*, 438

Timbre of sound, 156

Tonal quality of sound, 155–156, *156*

Toxic exposure
  characteristics of, 254–255
  nonoccupational, 259–261
  work environment and, 255–259, *259*

Trace measures, 21

Traditional playgrounds, 391

Transactional approach, in perception, 69

Transactional approach, philosophical notion of, 112–113

Transition, in wayfinding, 102

Transportation noise, 159–160

U

Uncertainty-arousal, 50

Understaffing, and staffing theory, 143–146

Understaffing, consequences, *144*

Understimulation approach, 121–122

Unfocused anger as a response to disasters, 250
Unwanted interactions
density and, 347
dormitories and, 341
Urban areas. *See* Cities
Urban homesteading, 402
Urban renewal, cities and, 394–395
Urban villages, 372

V

Validity, in research, 15
Vandalism, 552–555
Video display terminals (VDTs), 487, 489–491

W

Warrick's principle, 441–442
Water conservation, 543–544
Wayfinding
action plans and, 100–102, *101*
characteristics that facilitate, 102
complexity of the spatial layout and, 102
definition of, 79–80
degree of visual access and, 102
differentiation and, 102
libraries and, 499–500
maps and, 103–104

models and photographs and, 104–106
museums and, 500–501
overview, 100
transition and, 102
you-are-here maps, 103–106
Weather
definition of, 188
eclectic model of environment-behavior, *188–189*
Weber-Fechner function, 77
White noise, 156
Wide band sound, 156
Wilderness. *See* Natural lands
Wind
behavior and, 211–214
behavioral effects, 213–214
pedestrian movement and, 506
perception and, 212–213
Wind tunnel effect, 506
Wind turbulence, 212
Windchill index, 207
Windows
classrooms and, 496
design and, 428
work environments and, 487–488
Withdrawal
population density and, 340–342
response to disasters, 250

Work environment
heat and, 200
toxic exposure and, 255–259
Work environments
ambient conditions and, 484–486, *485*
computer technology and, 489–491
eclectic model of environment-behavior, *484–485*
faculty office and, 494–495
history of workplace design, 483–484
job satisfaction and, 493
music and, 486
noise and, 486
office landscape and, 491–493
territoriality in, 488–489
windows and, 487–488
workflow and, 489

Y

Yerkes-Dodson Law, 117–118, *118*
You-are-here maps
forward-up equivalence and, 104
museums, 501
orientation and, 103–104
structure matching and, 103, *103*
wayfinding and, 103–106